List of Statutory Publications

(incorporating the lists of Statutory Instruments, Scottish Statutory Instruments and Statutory Rules of Northern Ireland)

2002

Published by the Stationery Office and available from:

The Stationery Office Ltd

(mail, telephone and fax orders only)

PO Box 29, Norwich NR3 1GN
Telephone orders/General enquiries 0870 600 5522
Text telephone for the hard of hearing 0870 240 3701

Fax orders 0870 6005533

You can now order books online at www.tso.co.uk

Stationery Office Bookshops

123 Kingsway, London WC2B 6PQ
020 7242 6393 Fax 020 7242 6394
68/69 Bull Street, Birmingham B4 6AD
0121 236 9696 Fax 0121 236 9699
9-21 Princess Street, Manchester M60 8AS
0161 834 7201 Fax 0161 833 0634
16 Arthur Street, Belfast BT1 4GD
028 9023 8451 Fax 028 9023 5401
The Stationery Office Oriel Bookshop,
18-19 High Street, Cardiff CF1 2BZ
029 2039 5548 Fax 029 2038 4347
71 Lothian Road, Edinburgh EH3 9AZ
0870 606 5566 Fax 0870 606 5588

The Stationery Office Accredited Agents
(see Yellow Pages)

and through good booksellers.

ISBN 0 11 500737 7

ISSN 1472-1058

London: The Stationery Office

© Crown Copyright 2004
Applications for reproduction should be made to The Copyright Unit, Her Majesty's Stationery Office, St Clement's House, 2-16 Colegate, Norwich NR3 1BQ

Printed in the United Kingdom for The Stationery Office Limited under the authority and superintendence of Carol Tullo, Controller of Her Majesty's Stationery Office, Queen's Printer of Acts of Parliament, Queen's Printer for Scotland and Government Printer of Northern Ireland

Contents

Preface	v
Copyright	vi
Standing orders	vi
List of abbreviations	vii
UK Legislation	1
Public general acts	1
Public general acts - explanatory notes	4
Local acts	6
Measures of the General Synod	None listed
Other statutory publications	6
Statutory Instruments arranged by subject headings	7
Statutory Instruments arranged by number	249
Subsidiary Numbers	296
Scottish Legislation	304
Acts of the Scottish Parliament	304
Acts of the Scottish Parliament - Explanatory notes	305
Scottish Statutory Instruments arranged by subject headings	306
Scottish Statutory Instruments arranged by number	349
Northern Ireland Legislation	358
Acts of the Northern Ireland Assembly	358
Acts of the Northern Ireland Assembly explanatory notes	359
Statutory Rules of Northern Ireland arranged by subject headings	359
Statutory Rules of Northern Ireland arranged by number	388
Alphabetical Index	395
Stationery Office Services	503
Terms and Conditions of Sale	504
Customer service	506

Preface

This Publication

This list contains details of all statutory publications. It is arranged in three main sections so that the primary and delegated legislation of the United Kingdom, Scotland and Northern Ireland are grouped together. Statutory Instruments made by the National Assembly for Wales are included within the UK section.

Each section has the same order of publications published during the year:

- Acts and Explanatory Notes, (although Explanatory Notes are not statutory publications, it is useful to have them listed alongside the Acts).
- Statutory Instruments or Statutory Rules, arranged under subject headings. Each entry includes, where available or appropriate: the enabling power; the date when the instrument was issued, made and laid and comes into force; a short note of any effect; territorial extent and classification; a note of the relevant EU legislation; pagination; ISBN and price;
- A numerical listing of the instruments, with their subject heading with a list of instruments which have subsidiary numbers (C for commencement orders; L for instruments relating to court fees or procedure in England and Wales; NI for Orders in Council relating only to Northern Ireland; W for instruments made by the National Assembly for Wales)

There is a single alphabetical, subject index.

Other Information

Details of later acts or statutory instruments may be found in the *TSO Daily List* which lists them on the day of publication. Previous years' statutory instruments were listed in the annual lists.

The full text of the general statutory instruments and statutory rules appear in the respective annual editions of *Statutory Instruments, Scottish Statutory Instruments, Statutory Instruments made by the National Assembly for Wales* and *Statutory Rules of Northern Ireland)*. They are also published on the Internet:

UK Acts and Statutory Instruments www.legislation.hmso.gov.uk
Scottish Acts and Statutory Instruments www.scotland-legislation.gov.uk
Northern Ireland Acts and Statutory Rules www.northernireland-legislation.gov.uk
Welsh Statutory Instruments www.wales-legislation.hmso.gov.uk

Copies of local instruments issued recently by The Stationery Office Limited may be obtained from the addresses on the back cover. Copies of local instruments unobtainable from The Stationery Office may be obtained at prevailing prices from

- Her Majesty's Stationery Office, Statutory Publications Unit, Admiralty Arch, North Entrance, the Mall, London, SW1A 2WH (from 1922 onwards – except for the years 1942, 1950, 1951 and up to SI no. 940 of 1952)
- Reader Information Services Department, Public Record Office, Kew, Richmond, Surrey TW9 4DU (as before, up to 1960)
- British Library, Official Publications and Social Sciences Service, Great Russell Street, London WC1B 3DG (as before, up to 1980)

The publications referred to in this catalogue shall be supplied to the customer only on the Stationery Office Ltd.'s terms and conditions of sale and not on any additional terms which may be included with the customer's order. Prices are subject to change without notice.

Copyright

Most Stationery Office publications are Crown or Parliamentary copyright. Information about the licensing arrangements for Crown and Parliamentary copyright can be found on HMSO's website at www.hmso.gov.uk Alternatively, you can apply for a licence by contacting HMSO at the following address:

HMSO
Licensing Division
St Clements House
2-16 Colegate
Norwich NR3 1BQ

Telephone: 01603 621000 Fax 01603 723000
e-mail : hmsolicensing@cabinet-office.x.gsi.gov.uk

Out-of-print publications

Photocopies of out-of-print Parliamentary, statutory and regulatory publications can be obtained by The Stationery Office from the British Library Document Supply Centre. Customers requiring this service should order through

The Stationery Office Ltd. (Photocopies Department)
51 Nine Elms Lane
London SW8 5DR

The department will advise the current cost for this service (tel. 0207 873 8455; fax 020 7873 8247). Please allow 28 days for delivery.

Standing Orders

Standing orders can be set up to ensure the receipt of all statutory publications in a particular subject area, without the need and trouble of placing individual orders. The subject categories used can be either broad or very specific.

For more information please contact our Standing Orders department on 0870 600 5522, or fax us on 0870 600 5533.

List of abbreviations

accord.	accordance
art(s).	article(s)
c.	chapter
C.	Commencement
CI.	Channel Islands
E.	England
EC	European Commission
EU.	European Union
G.	Guernsey
GB.	Great Britain
GLA	Greater London Authority
IOM.	Isle of Man
J.	Jersey
L.	Legal: fees or procedure in courts in E. & W.
NI.	Northern Ireland
para(s).	paragraph(s)
reg(s).	regulation(s)
s(s).	section(s)
S.	Scotland
sch(s).	schedule(s)
SI.	Statutory instrument(s)
SR.	Statutory rule(s) of Northern Ireland
SR & O.	Statutory rules and orders
SSI	Scottish Statutory Instrument
UK.	United Kingdom
W.	Wales

KINGSTON UPON HULL
CITY LIBRARIES

UK Legislation

Acts

Public General Acts 2002

Adoption and Children Act 2002: Elizabeth II. Chapter 38. – viii, 126p.: 30 cm. – An Act to restate and amend the law relating to adoption; to make further amendments of the law relating to children; to amend section 93 of the Local Government Act 2000. – Royal assent, 7th November 2002. – Explanatory notes to assist in the understanding of this Act are available separately (ISBN 0105638021). – 0 10 543802 2   £12.00

Animal Health Act 2002: Elizabeth II. Chapter 42. – iv, 25p.: 30 cm. – Royal assent, 7th November 2002. – An Act to amend the Animal Health Act 1981. Explanatory notes have been produced to assist in the understanding of this Act and are available separately (ISBN 0105642029). – 0 10 544202 X   £5.50

Appropriation Act 2002: Elizabeth II. Chapter 18. – 95p.: 30 cm. – Royal assent, 8th July 2002. – 0 10 541802 1   £9.00

Appropriation (No. 2) Act 2002: Elizabeth II. Chapter 44. – [8]p.: 30 cm. – Royal assent, 17th December 2002. – 0 10 544402 2   £1.75

British Overseas Territories Act 2002: Elizabeth II. Chapter 8. – [12]p.: 30 cm. – Royal assent, 26th February 2002. – Explanatory notes have been produced to assist in the understanding of this Act and are available separately (PGA 2002 8-EN, ISBN 0105608025). – 0 10 540802 6   £2.50

Civil Defence (Grant) Act 2002: Elizabeth II. Chapter 5. – [8]p.: 30 cm. – Royal assent, 26th February 2002. – Explanatory notes have been produced to assist in the understanding of this Act and are available separately (PGA 2002 5-EN, ISBN 0105605026). – 0 10 540502 7   £1.75

Commonhold and Leasehold Reform Act 2002: Elizabeth II. Chapter 15. – viii, 140p.: 30 cm. – Royal assent, 1st May 2002. – Explanatory notes have been produced to assist in the understanding of this Act and are available separately (ISBN 0105615021). – 0 10 541502 2   £13.50

Commonwealth Act 2002: Elizabeth II. Chapter 39. – [12]p.: 30 cm. – Royal assent, 7th November 2002. – An Act to amend the law with respect to the Commonwealth Institute; to make provision in connection with the admission of Cameroon and Mozambique to the Commonwealth. – 0 10 543902 9   £2.50

Consolidated Fund Act 2002: Elizabeth II. Chapter 10. – [8]p.: 30 cm. – Royal assent, 19th March 2002. – 0 10 541002 0   £1.75

Consolidated Fund (No. 2) Act 2002: Elizabeth II. Chapter 43. – [8]p.: 30 cm. – Royal assent, 17th December 2002. – 0 10 544302 6   £1.75

Copyright, etc. and Trade Marks (Offences and Enforcement) Act 2002: Elizabeth II. Chapter 25. – [2], 12, [1]p.: 30 cm. – Royal assent, 24th July 2002. – Explanatory notes have been produced to assist in the understanding of this Act and are available separately (ISBN 0105625027). – 0 10 542502 8   £3.50

Copyright (Visually Impaired Persons) Act 2002: Elizabeth II. Chapter 33. – [2], 8p.: 30 cm. – Royal assent, 7th November 2002. – An Act to permit, without infringement of copyright, the transfer of copyright works to formats accessible to visually impaired persons. – 0 10 543302 0   £2.50

Divorce (Religious Marriages) Act 2002: Elizabeth II. Chapter 27. – [4]p.: 30 cm. – Royal assent, 24th July 2002. – This Act is mainly concerned with the dissolution of Jewish religious marriages. – 0 10 542702 0   £1.75

Education Act 2002: Elizabeth II. Chapter 32. – xii, 221p.: 30 cm. – Royal assent, 24th July 2002. - Explanatory notes to assist in the understanding of this Act are available separately (ISBN 0105632023). – An Act to make provision about education, training and childcare. – 0 10 543202 4   £18.00

Electoral Fraud (Northern Ireland) Act 2002: Elizabeth II. Chapter 13. – [2], 9p.: 30 cm. – Royal assent, 1st May 2002. – Explanatory notes have been produced to assist in the understanding of this Act and are available separately (ISBN 0105613029). – 0 10 541302 X *£2.50*

Employee Share Schemes Act 2002: Elizabeth II. Chapter 34. – [8]p.: 30 cm. – Royal assent, 7th November 2002. – An Act to make provision relating to employee share schemes. – 0 10 543402 7 *£2.00*

Employment Act 2002: Elizabeth II. Chapter 22. – iii, 82p.: 30 cm. – Royal assent, 8th July 2002. - An Act to make provision for statutory rights to paternity and adoption leave and pay; to amend the law relating to statutory maternity leave and pay; to amend the Employment Tribunals Act 1996; to make provision for the use of statutory procedures in relation to employment disputes; to amend the law relating to particulars of employment; to make provision about compromise agreements; to make provision for questionnaires in relation to equal pay; to make provision in connection with trade union learning representatives; to amend section 110 of the Employment Rights Act 1996; to make provision about fixed-term work; to make provision about flexible working; to amend the law relating to maternity allowance; to make provision for work-focused interviews for partners of benefit claimants; to make provision about the use of information for, or relating to, employment and training. – Explanatory notes to assist in the understanding of this Act are available separately (ISBN 0105622028). – Issued with a correction slip, dated December 2002. – 0 10 542202 9 *£9.00*

Enterprise Act 2002: Elizabeth II. Chapter 40. – xiv, 439p.: 30 cm. – Royal assent, 7 November 2002. – Explanatory notes have been produced to assist in the understanding of this Act and are available separately (ISBN 0105640026). – With correction slips dated November 2002 (inserting the date of Royal Assent), June 2003, and September 2003. – 0 10 544002 7 *£31.00*

European Communities (Amendment) Act 2002: Elizabeth II. Chapter 3. – [8]p.: 30 cm. – Royal assent, 26th February 2002. – Explanatory notes have been produced to assist in the understanding of this Act and are available separately (ISBN 0105603023). – 0 10 540302 4 *£1.75*

European Parliamentary Elections Act 2002: Elizabeth II. Chapter 24. – [1], ii, 19, [1]p.: 30 cm. – Royal assent, 24th July 2002. – 0 10 542402 1 *£4.50*

Export Control Act 2002: Elizabeth II. Chapter 28. – [2], 12p.: 30 cm. – Royal assent, 24th July 2002. - Explanatory notes to assist in the understanding of this Act are available separately (ISBN 0105628026). – An Act to make provision enabling controls to be imposed on the exportation of goods, the transfer of technology, the provision of technical assistance overseas and activities connected with trade in controlled goods. – 0 10 542802 7 *£3.00*

Finance Act 2002: Elizabeth II. Chapter 23. – ix, 494p.: 30 cm. – Royal assent, 24th July 2002. – 0 10 542302 5 *£34.00*

Football (Disorder) (Amendment) Act 2002: Elizabeth II. Chapter 12. – [8]p.: 30 cm. – Royal assent, 1st May 2002. – Explanatory notes have been produced to assist in the understanding of this Act and are available separately (ISBN 0105612022). – 0 10 541202 3 *£2.00*

Homelessness Act 2002: Elizabeth II. Chapter 7. – [1], ii, 20p.: 30 cm. – Royal assent, 26th February 2002. – Explanatory notes have been produced to assist in the understanding of this Act and are available separately (ISBN 0105607029). – 0 10 540702 X *£4.00*

Industrial and Provident Societies Act 2002: Elizabeth II. Chapter 20. – [8]p.: 30 cm. – Royal assent, 8th July 2002. - An Act to enable the law relating to societies registered under the Industrial and Provident Societies Act 1965 to be amended so as to bring it into conformity with certain aspects of the law relating to companies; to amend the procedure whereby such a society may convert itself into, or amalgamate with or transfer its engagements to, a company. – 0 10 542002 6 *£2.00*

International Development Act 2002: Elizabeth II. Chapter 1. – [1], ii, 16p.: 30 cm. – Royal assent, 26th February 2002. – Explanatory notes have been produced to assist in the understanding of this Act and are available separately (ISBN 0105601020). – 0 10 540102 1 *£3.50*

Justice (Northern Ireland) Act 2002: Elizabeth II. Chapter 26. – vi, 130p.: 30 cm. – Royal assent, 24th July 2002. – Explanatory notes have been produced to assist in the understanding of this Act and are available separately (ISBN 0105626023). – 0 10 542602 4 *£12.00*

Land Registration Act 2002: Elizabeth II. Chapter 9. – vii, 86p.: 30 cm. – Royal assent, 26th February 2002. – Explanatory notes to assist in the understanding of this Act are available separately (ISBN 0105609021). – 0 10 540902 2 *£8.50*

Mobile Telephones (Re-programming) Act 2002: Elizabeth II. Chapter 31. – [4]p.: 30 cm. – Royal assent, 24th July 2002. – Explanatory notes to assist in the understanding of this Act are available separately (ISBN 0105631027). – 0 10 543102 8 *£1.75*

National Health Service Reform and Health Care Professions Act 2002: Elizabeth II. Chapter 17. – v, 101p.: 30 cm. – Royal assent, 25th June 2002. – Explanatory notes have been produced to assist in the understanding of this Act and are available separately (ISBN 0105617024). – 0 10 541702 5 *£10.50*

National Heritage Act 2002: Elizabeth II. Chapter 14. – [12]p.: 30 cm. – Royal assent, 1st May 2002. – With correction slip dated January 2003. – 0 10 541402 6 *£2.50*

National Insurance Contributions Act 2002: Elizabeth II. Chapter 19. – [2], 14p.: 30 cm. – Royal assent, 8th July 2002. - An Act to make provision for, and in connection with, increasing national insurance contributions and for applying the increases towards the cost of the National Health Service. – Explanatory notes to assist in the understanding of this Act will be available separately. – 0 10 541902 8 *£3.50*

Nationality, Immigration and Asylum Act 2002: Elizabeth II. Chapter 41. – viii, 126p.: 30 cm. – Royal assent, 7th November 2002. – Explanatory notes have been produced to assist in the understanding of this Act and are available separately (ISBN 0105611022). – 0 10 544102 3 *£12.00*

Northern Ireland Arms Decommissioning (Amendment) Act 2002: Elizabeth II. Chapter 6. – [4]p.: 30 cm. – Royal assent, 26th February 2002. – Explanatory notes have been produced to assist in the understanding of this Act and are available separately (ISBN 0105606022). 0 10 540602 3 *£1.50*

Office of Communications Act 2002: Elizabeth II. Chapter 11. – [2], 16p.: 30 cm. – Royal assent, 19th March 2002. – Explanatory notes to assist in the understanding of this Act are available separately (ISBN 0105611026). – 0 10 541102 7 *£3.50*

Police Reform Act 2002: Elizabeth II. Chapter 30. – vii, 177p.: 30 cm. – Royal assent, 24th July 2002. - Explanatory notes to assist in the understanding of this Act are available separately (ISBN 0105630020). – An Act to make new provision about the supervision, administration, functions and conduct of police forces, police officers and other persons serving with, or carrying out functions in relation to, the police; to amend police powers and to provide for the exercise of police powers by persons who are not police officers; to amend the law relating to anti-social behaviour orders; to amend the law relating to sex offender orders. – With correction slip dated January 2003. – 0 10 543002 1 *£16.50*

Private Hire Vehicles (Carriage of Guide Dogs etc.) Act 2002: Elizabeth II. Chapter 37. – [8]p.: 30 cm. – Royal assent, 7th November 2002. – An Act to make provision for the carriage of disabled persons accompanied by guide dogs, hearing dogs or other assistance dogs by drivers and operators of private hire vehicles. – Explanatory notes have been produced to assist in the understanding of the Act and are available separately (ISBN 0105637025). – 0 10 543702 6 *£2.00*

Proceeds of Crime Act 2002: Elizabeth II. Chapter 29. – xvii, 323p.: 30 cm. – Royal assent, 24th July 2002. - Explanatory notes to assist in the understanding of this Act are available separately (ISBN 0105629022). – An Act to establish the Assets Recovery Agency and make provision about the appointment of its Director and his functions (including Revenue functions), to provide for confiscation orders in relation to persons who benefit from criminal conduct and for restraint orders to prohibit dealing with property, to allow the recovery of property which is or represents property obtained through unlawful conduct or which is intended to be used in unlawful conduct, to make provision about money laundering, to make provision about investigations relating to benefit from criminal conduct or to property which is or represents property obtained through unlawful conduct or to money laundering, to make provision to give effect to overseas requests and orders made where property is found or believed to be obtained through criminal conduct. – 0 10 542902 3 *£23.60*

Public Trustee (Liability and Fees) Act 2002: Elizabeth II. Chapter 35. – [4]p.: 30 cm. – Royal assent, 7th November 2002. – An Act to amend the Public Trustee Act 1906 in respect of the liability and fees of the Public Trustee. – Explanatory notes to assist in the understanding of the Act are available separately (ISBN 0105635022). – 0 10 543502 3 *£1.50*

Sex Discrimination (Election Candidates) Act 2002: Elizabeth II. Chapter 2. – [8]p.: 30 cm. – Royal assent, 26th February 2002. – Explanatory notes have been produced to assist in the understanding of this Act and are available separately (PGA 2002 2-EN, ISBN 0105602027). – 0 10 540202 8 *£1.75*

State Pension Credit Act 2002: Elizabeth II. Chapter 16. – ii, 29p.: 30 cm. – Royal assent, 25th June 2002. – Explanatory notes to assist in the understanding of this Act are available separately (ISBN 0105616028). – 0 10 541602 9 *£6.00*

Tax Credits Act 2002: Elizabeth II. Chapter 21. – iii, 66p.: 30 cm. – Royal assent, 8th July 2002. - An Act to make provision for tax credits; to amend the law about child benefit and guardian's allowance. – Explanatory notes to assist in the understanding of this Act are available separately (ISBN 0105621021). – 0 10 542102 2 *£7.50*

Tobacco Advertising and Promotion Act 2002: Elizabeth II. Chapter 36. – [2], 11p.: 30 cm. – Royal assent, 7th November 2002. – An Act to control the advertising and promotion of tobacco products. – Explanatory notes to assist in the understanding of the Act are available separately (ISBN 0105636029). – 0 10 543602 X *£3.00*

Travel Concessions (Eligibility) Act 2002: Elizabeth II. Chapter 4. – [8]p.: 30 cm. – Royal assent, 26th February 2002. – Explanatory notes have been produced to assist in the understanding of this Act and are available separately (ISBN 010560402X). – 0 10 540402 0 *£1.75*

Public General Acts - Explanatory Notes 2002

Adoption and Children Act 2002: chapter 38: explanatory notes. – 82, [2]p.: 30 cm. – These notes refer to the Adoption and Children Act 2002 (c. 38) (ISBN 0105438022) which received Royal Assent on 7th November 2002. – 0 10 563802 1 *£9.00*

Anti-terrorism, Crime and Security Act 2001: chapter 24: explanatory notes. – 61p.: 30 cm. – These notes refer to the Anti-terrorism, Crime and Security Act 2001 (c. 24) (ISBN 0105424013) which received Royal Assent on 14 December 2001. – 0 10 562401 2 *£7.50*

British Overseas Territories Act 2002: chapter 8: explanatory notes. – [12]p.: 30 cm. – These notes refer to the British Overseas Territories Act 2002 (c. 8) (ISBN 0105408026) which received Royal Assent on 26 February 2002. – 0 10 560802 5 *£2.50*

Civil Defence (Grant) Act 2002: chapter 5: explanatory notes. – [8]p.: 30 cm. – These notes refer to the Civil Defence (Grant) Act 2002 (c. 5) (ISBN 0105405027) which received Royal Assent on 26 February 2002. – 0 10 560502 6 *£2.00*

Commonhold and Leasehold Reform Act 2002: chapter 15: explanatory notes. – 82, [1]p.: 30 cm. – These notes refer to the Commonhold and Leasehold Reform Act 2002 (c. 15) (ISBN 0105415022) which received Royal Assent on 1 May 2002. – 0 10 561502 1 *£9.00*

The Copyright, etc. and Trade Marks (Offences and Enforcement) Act 2002: chapter 25: explanatory notes. – [8]p.: 30 cm. – These notes refer to the Copyright, etc. and Trade Marks (Offences and Enforcement) Act 2002 (c. 25) (ISBN 0105425028) which received Royal Assent on 24 July 2002. – 0 10 562502 7 *£2.00*

Education Act 2002: chapter 32: explanatory notes. – 86p.: 30 cm. – These notes refer to the Education Act 2002 (c. 32) (ISBN 0105432024) which received Royal Assent on 24 July 2002. – 0 10 563202 3 *£9.00*

Electoral Fraud (Northern Ireland) Act 2002: chapter 13: explanatory notes. – [9]p.: 30 cm. – These notes refer to the Electoral Fraud (Northern Ireland) Act 2002 (c. 13) (ISBN 010541302X) which received Royal Assent on 9 May 2002. – 0 10 561302 9 *£2.50*

Employment Act 2002: chapter 22: explanatory notes. – 65p.: 30 cm. – These notes refer to the Employment Act 2002 (c. 22) (ISBN 0105422029) which received Royal Assent on 8 July 2002. – 0 10 562202 8 *£7.50*

Enterprise Act 2002: chapter 40: explanatory notes. – 154p., figs.: 30 cm. – These notes refer to the Enterprise Act 2002 (c. 40) (ISBN 0105440027) which received Royal Assent on 7th November 2002. – 0 10 564002 6 *£13.50*

European Communities (Amendment) Act 2002: chapter 3: explanatory notes. – [8]p.: 30 cm. – These notes refer to the European Communities (Amendment) Act 2002 (c. 3) (ISBN 0105403024) which received Royal Assent on 26 February 2002. – 0 10 560302 3 *£2.00*

European Communities (Finance) Act 2001: chapter 22: explanatory notes. – [8]p.: 30 cm. – These notes refer to the European Communities (Finance) Act 2001 (ISBN 0105422010) which received Royal Assent on 4 December 2001 (c. 22). – 0 10 562101 3 *£2.00*

Export Control Act 2002: chapter 28: explanatory notes. – 11p.: 30 cm. – These notes refer to the Export Control Act 2002 (c. 28) (ISBN 0105428027) which received Royal Assent on 24 July 2002. – 0 10 562802 6 *£3.00*

Football (Disorder) (Amendment) Act 2002: chapter 12: explanatory notes. – [8]p.: 30 cm. – These notes refer to the Football (Disorder) (Amendment) Act 2002 (c. 12) (ISBN 0105412023) which received Royal Assent on 1st May 2002. – 0 10 561202 2   £1.75

Homelessness Act 2002: chapter 7: explanatory notes. – [14]p.: 30 cm. – These notes refer to the Homelessness Act 2002 (c. 7) (ISBN 010540702X) which received Royal Assent on 26 February 2002. – 0 10 560702 9   £3.00

Human Reproductive Cloning Act 2001: chapter 23: explanatory notes. – [8]p.: 30 cm. – These notes refer to the Human Reproductive Cloning Act 2001 (c. 23) (ISBN 0105423017) which received Royal Assent on 4th December 2001. – 0 10 562201 X   £2.00

International Development Act 2002: chapter 1: explanatory notes. – [1], 8p.: 30 cm. – These notes refer to the International Development Act 2002 (c. 1) (ISBN 0105401021) which received Royal Assent on 26 February 2002. – 0 10 560102 0   £2.50

Justice (Northern Ireland) Act 2002: chapter 26: explanatory notes. – 50p.: 30 cm. – These notes refer to the Justice (Northern Ireland) Act 2002 (c. 26) (ISBN 0105426024) which received Royal Assent on 24th July 2002. – 0 10 562602 3   £7.50

Land Registration Act 2002: chapter 9: explanatory notes. – 82p.: 30 cm. – These notes refer to the Land Registration Act 2002 (c. 9) (ISBN 0105409022) which received Royal Assent on 26 February 2002. – 0 10 560902 1   £9.00

Mobile Telephones (Re-programming) Act 2002: chapter 31: explanatory notes. – [8]p.: 30 cm. – These notes refer to the Mobile Telephones (Re-programming) Act 2002 (c. 31) (ISBN 0105431028) which received Royal Assent on 24 July 2002. – 0 10 563102 7   £2.00

National Health Service Reform and Health Care Professions Act 2002: chapter 17: explanatory notes. – 56p.: 30 cm. – These notes refer to the National Health Service Reform and Health Care Professions Act 2002 (c. 17) (ISBN 0105417025) which received Royal Assent on 25 June 2002. – 0 10 561702 4   £7.50

Northern Ireland Arms Decommissioning (Amendment) Act 2002: chapter 6: explanatory notes. – [8]p.: 30 cm. – These notes refer to the Northern Ireland Arms Decommissioning (Amendment) Act 2002 (c. 6) (ISBN 0105406023) which received Royal Assent on 26 February 2002. – 0 10 560602 2   £2.00

Office of Communications Act 2002: chapter 11: explanatory notes. – [8]p.: 30 cm. – These notes refer to the Office of Communications Act 2002 (c. 11) (ISBN 0105411027) which received Royal Assent on 19 March 2002. – 0 10 561102 6   £2.50

Police Reform Act 2002: chapter 30: explanatory notes. – 96p.: 30 cm. – These notes refer to the Police Reform Act 2002 (c. 30) (ISBN 0105430021) which received Royal Assent on 24 July 2002. – 0 10 563002 0   £9.00

Private Hire Vehicles (Carriage of Guide Dogs etc.) Act 2002: chapter 37: explanatory notes. – [1], 4p.: 30 cm. – These notes refer to the Private Hire Vehicles (Carriage of Guide Dogs etc.) Act 2002 (c.37) (ISBN 0105437026) which received Royal Assent on 7th November 2002. – 0 10 563702 5   £2.00

Proceeds of Crime Act 2002: chapter 29: explanatory notes. – 130p.: 30 cm. – These notes refer to the Proceeds of Crime Act 2002 (c. 29) (ISBN 0105429023) which received Royal Assent on 24 July 2002. – 0 10 562902 2   £12.00

Public Trustee (Liability and Fees) Act 2002: chapter 35: explanatory notes. – 4, [1]p.: 30 cm. – These notes refer to the Public Trustee (Liability and Fees) Act 2002 (c. 35) (ISBN 0105435023) which received Royal Assent on 7th November 2002. – 0 10 563502 2   £2.00

Sex Discrimination (Election Candidates) Act 2002: chapter 2: explanatory notes. – [6]p.: 30 cm. – These notes refer to the Sex Discrimination (Election Candidates) Act 2002 (c. 2) (ISBN 0105402028) which received Royal Assent on 26 February 2002. – 0 10 560202 7   £2.00

State Pension Credit Act 2002: chapter 16: explanatory notes. – 44p.: 30 cm. – These notes refer to the State Pension Credit Act 2002 (c. 16) (ISBN 0105416029) which received Royal Assent on 25 June 2002. – 0 10 561602 8   £6.50

Tax Credits Act 2002: chapter 21: explanatory notes. – 41p.: 30 cm. – These notes refer to the Tax Credits Act 2002 (ISBN 0105421022) which received Royal Assent on 8 July 2002 (c. 21). – 0 10 562102 1   £6.50

Tobacco Advertising and Promotion Act 2002: chapter 36: explanatory notes. – 12, [1]p.: 30 cm. – These notes refer to the Tobacco Advertising and Promotion Act 2002 (c. 36) (ISBN 010543602X) which received Royal Assent on 7 November 2002. – 0 10 563602 9   £3.00

Travel Concessions (Eligibility) Act 2002: chapter 4: explanatory notes. – [8]p.: 30 cm. – These notes refer to the Travel Concessions (Eligibility) Act 2002 (c. 4) (ISBN 0105404020) which received Royal Assent on 26 February 2002. – 0 10 560402 X   £2.00

Local Acts 2002

Barclays Group Reorganisation Act 2002: Elizabeth II. Chapter iv. – [2], 17p.: 30 cm. – Royal assent, 7th November 2002. – An Act to provide for the reorganisation of the undertakings of Barclays Bank PLC and certain of its subsidiaries. – 0 10 510402 7 £4.00

City of London (Ward Elections) Act 2002: Elizabeth II. Chapter vi. – [2], 7p.: 30 cm. – Royal assent, 7th November 2002. – An Act to make further provision with respect to the qualification of voters at ward elections in the city of London. – 0 10 510602 X £2.50

Greenham and Cookham Commons Act 2002: Elizabeth II. Chapter i. – iii, 50p.: 30 cm. – Royal assent, 1st May 2002. – An Act to restore land at and in the vicinity of the Greenham and Cookham Commons as common land open to the public; to make provision for the conservation of the natural beauty of that land; to grant public access over that land in perpetuity and to make provision with respect to that public access ..– 0 10 510102 8 £7.50

HSBC Investment Banking Act 2002: Elizabeth II. Chapter iii. – 16p.: 30 cm. – Royal assent, 7th November 2002. - An Act to provide for the transfer of investment banking business of HSBC Investment Bank plc to HSBC Bank plc and the transfer of the private banking business of HSBC Investment Bank plc to HSBC Republic Bank (UK) Limited. – 0 10 510302 0 £3.50

Land at Palace Avenue, Kensington (Acquisition of Freehold) Act 2002: Elizabeth II. Chapter ii. – [8]p.: 30 cm. – Royal assent, 25th June 2002. - An Act to authorise the trustees of the Imperial Tobacco Pension Fund to acquire the freehold of land forming part of the Royal Garden Hotel, Kensington. – 0 10 510202 4 £2.00

Milford Haven Port Authority Act 2002: Elizabeth II. Chapter v. – [1], ii, 14p.: 30 cm. – Royal assent, 7th November 2002. – An Act to alter the constitution of and confer further powers upon the Milford Haven Port Authority. – 0 10 510502 3 £3.50

Other statutory publications

Board of Inland Revenue.

Tables of origins and destinations: Income Tax (Earnings and Pensions) Act 2003, chapter 1. – 211p.: 30 cm. – This is an accompanying document to the Income Tax (Earnings and Pensions) Act 2003, PGA 2003, chp. 1 (ISBN 010540103X). – 0 11 840498 9 £16.50

Her Majesty's Stationery Office.

Chronological table of local legislation 1797-1994 and Chronological table of private and personal acts 1539-1997. – 2000 supplement (including corrections to the first edition texts). – viii, 117p.: 30 cm. – Updates the first editions to December 31 2000. – This is the last Supplement to be published in print format but the original Tables and the cumulative Supplement will remain available from TSO. This data will be available (from March-April 2002) from http://www.legislation.hmso.gov.uk/chron-index.htm. – 0 11 043008 5 £45.00

Chronological table of the statutes [1235-2000]. – 2v. (xii, 2498p.): hdbk: 25 cm. – 2 vols. not sold separately. Part 1: Covering the period from 1235 to the end of 1969; Part 2: Covering the period from 1970 to the end of 2000. – 0 11 840396 6 £210.00 per set

The public general acts and General Synod measures 2000. – 4v. (a-l, 3865, ccclxvi, 80p.): hdbk: 30 cm. – 4 parts not sold separately. – Contents: Part 1 Chapters 1-16; Part 2 Chapters 17-27; Part 3 Chapters 28-45 and Measure 1; Part 4 Tables and index. – 0 11 840386 9 £465.00 per set

The public general acts and General Synod measures 2000: tables and index. – a-k, ccclxvi, 80p.: 30 cm. – 0 11 840388 5 £42.50

The public general acts and General Synod measures 2001. – 3v. (a-h, 1605, cdvii, 39p.): hdbk: 30 cm. – 3 parts not sold separately. – Contents: Part 1 Chapters 1-9; Part 2 Chapters 10-25, Measure 1; Part 3 Tables and index. – 0 11 840394 X £215.00 per set

The public general acts and General Synod measures 2001: tables and index. – a-h, cdvii, 39p.: 30 cm. – 0 11 840395 8 £42.50

Statutory instruments 1999

Part 3: Section 1 nos. 2395 to 2920; Section 2 nos. 2921 to 3323, Section 3 nos. 3324 to 3491. 1st September to 31st December 1999. – 3v. (p. i-xvii, A-T, 7731-10754, i-cdxl): hdbk: 31 cm. – 3 vols. not sold separately. – 0 11 840380 X *£465.00 per set*

Statutory instruments 2000

Part 1: Section 1 nos. 1 to 429; Section 2 nos. 430 to 790, Section 3 nos. 791 to 1168. 1st January to 31st March 2000. – 3v. (p. i-xxiii, 2898, xxv-xlv): hdbk: 30 cm. – 3 vols. not sold separately; boxed. – 0 11 840391 5 *£360.00 per set*

Part 2: Section 1 nos. 1173 to 1598; Section 2 nos. 1599 to 2004, Section 3 nos. 2008 to 2332. 1st May to 31st August 2000. – 3v. (p. i-xviii, 2899-6076, xix-lvi): hdbk: 30 cm. – 3 vols. not sold separately. – 0 11 840392 3 *£385.00 per set*

Part 3: Section 1 nos. 2333 to 2822; Section 2 nos. 2824 to 3208, Section 3 nos. 3209 to 3412. 1st September to 31st December 2000. – 3v. (xv, p. 6077 - 8771, ccclxiii): hdbk: 30 cm. – 3 vols. not sold separately. – 0 11 840393 1 *£340.00 per set*

H.M. Treasury.

Budget 2003: [pack of supporting documents]. – 7 v. (various pagings), figs., tables: 30 cm. – Not supplied on TSO Select or standing order services. – Contents: Index of documents ([4]p.; 30 cm); Budget 2003 press notices (ca. 60p.; 30 cm); Budget notes (ca. 100p.; 30 cm); Reviewing the residence and domicile rules as they affect the taxation of individuals: a background paper (H.M. Treasury/Inland Revenue) (April 2003) (ca. 40p.; 30 cm); Bridging the finance gap: a consultation on improving access to growth capital for small businesses (H.M. Treasury/Inland Revenue) (April 2003) (ca. 60p.; 30 cm); Public services: meeting the productivity challenge: a discussion document (April 2003); Budget 2003: building a Britain of economic strength and social justice (April 2003) (7p. (folded leaflet); 25 cm). – 0 11 049001 X *£30.00 per set*

Explanatory notes Finance Bill 2003. – 2v. (ca. 150; 150p.): 30 cm. – These notes refer to the Finance Bill published on 16th April 2003 (HC Bill 94-I & II, ISBN 0215702581). In 2 volumes not sold separately. With correction slip (dated May 2003). – 0 11 849025 7 *£36.50*

National Assembly for Wales.

Statutory instruments 1999. – xlii, 234p.: hdbk: 30 cm. – This is the first bound volume of Statutory Instruments made by the National Assembly for Wales. – Welsh title: Cynulliad Cenedlaethol Cymru 1999. – 0 11 840389 3 *£215.00*

Statutory Publications Office (Northern Ireland).

Northern Ireland statutes 2000: [binder]. – 1 binder: 31 cm. – 0 11 840385 0 *£20.00*

Statutory Instruments

Arranged by Subject Headings

Aggregates levy

The Aggregates Levy (General) Regulations 2002 No. 2002/761. – Enabling power: Finance Act 2001, ss. 17 (6), 23, 25 (1) (2), 30, 31 (3), 37, 38, 39, 45, sch. 6, para. 9 (2) (3), sch. 7, para. 2, sch. 8, paras 1, 9, 10, 11 & Finance Act 1997, s. 51 & Finance Act 1999, s. 132. – Issued: 27.03.2002. Made: 21.03.2002. Laid: 21.03.2002. Coming into force: 01.04.2002. Effect: S.I. 1997/1431 amended. Territorial extent & classification: E/W/S/NI. General. – 20p.: 30 cm. – 0 11 039588 3 *£3.50*

The Aggregates Levy (Northern Ireland Tax Credit) Regulations 2002 No. 2002/1927. – Enabling power: Finance Act 2001, ss. 17 (6), 30A, 45, sch. 7, para. 2. – Issued: 05.08.2002. Made: 25.07.2002. Laid: 25.07.2002. Coming into force: 15.08.2002. Effect: None. Territorial extent & classification: E/W/S/NI. General. – 4p.: 30 cm. – 0 11 042585 5 *£1.75*

The Aggregates Levy (Registration and Miscellaneous Provisions) (Amendment) Regulations 2002 No. 2002/1929. – Enabling power: Finance Act 2001, sch. 4, para. 6. – Issued: 05.08.2002. Made: 25.07.2002. Laid: 25.07.2002. Coming into force: 15.08.2002. Effect: S.I. 2001/4027 amended. Territorial extent & classification: E/W/S/NI. General. – 2p.: 30 cm. – 0 11 042587 1 *£1.50*

The Finance Act 2001, section 16, (Appointed Day) Order 2002 No. 2002/809 (C.20). – Enabling power: Finance Act 2001, s. 16 (6). Bringing into operation various provisions of the 2001 Act on 01.04.2002. – Issued: 05.04.2002. Made: 25.03.2002. Effect: None. Territorial extent & classification: E/W/S/NI. General. – 2p.: 30 cm. – 0 11 039651 0 *£1.50*

Agriculture

The Feedingstuffs (Zootechnical Products) (Amendment) (England, Scotland and Wales) Regulations 2002 No. 2002/696. – Enabling power: European Communities Act 1972, s. 2 (2). – Issued: 25.04.2002. Made: 14.03.2002. Laid: 15.03.2002. Coming into force: 31.03.2002. Effect: S.I. 1999/1871 amended in relation to England, Scotland and Wales. Territorial extent & classification: E/W/S. General. – 8p.: 30 cm. – 0 11 039827 0 *£2.00*

The Hemp (Third Country Imports) (Amendment) Regulations 2002 No. 2002/1924. – Enabling power: European Communities Act 1972, s. 2 (2). – Issued: 31.07.2002. Made: 22.07.2002. Laid: 23.07.2002. Coming into force: 01.09.2002. Effect: S.I. 2002/787 amended. Territorial extent & classification: E/W/S/NI. General– 2p.: 30 cm. – 0 11 042565 0 *£1.50*

The Hemp (Third Country Imports) Regulations 2002 No. 2002/787. – Enabling power: European Communities Act 1972, s. 2 (2). – Issued: 23.04.2002. Made: 25.03.2002. Laid: 25.03.2002. Coming into force: 01.05.2002. Effect: None. Territorial extent & classification: E/W/S/NI. General– 8p.: 30 cm. – EC note: Implement the requirements of art. 17a of EC REG 245/2001 concerning imported hemp and amended by REG 1093/2001, 52/2002 – 0 11 039785 1 *£2.00*

The Olive Oil (Marketing Standards) (Amendment) Regulations 2002 No. 2002/2761. – Enabling power: European Communities Act 1972, s. 2 (2). – Issued: 22.11.2002. Made: 06.11.2002. Laid: 07.11.2002. Coming into force: 30.11.2002. Effect: S.I. 1987/1783 amended. Territorial extent & classification: E/W/S. General. – 2p.: 30 cm. – EC note: These regs update the reference in S.I. 1987/1783 to Commission regulation 2568/91 so as to cover amendments of that Commission regulation up to and including those affected by Commission regulation 796/2002. Also updates reference to Council regulation 136/66 so as to cover amendments of that Council reg. up to and including those affected by Council reg.1513/2001 – 0 11 042994 X *£1.50*

Agriculture: Cereals marketing

The Home-Grown Cereals Authority (Rate of Levy) Order 2002 No. 2002/1461. – Enabling power: Cereals Marketing Act 1965, ss. 13 (3), 23 (1), 24 (1). – Issued: 14.06.2002. Made: 30.05.2002. Laid: 31.05.2002. Coming into force: 01.07.2002. Effect: None. Territorial extent & classification: E/W/S/NI. General. – 4p.: 30 cm. – 0 11 042334 8 *£1.75*

Agriculture: Pesticides, England and Wales

The Pesticides (Maximum Residue Levels in Crops, Food and Feeding Stuffs) (England and Wales) (Amendment) Regulations 2002 No. 2002/1767. – Enabling power: European Communities Act 1972, s. 2 (2).– Issued: 23.07.2002. Made: 10.07.2002. Laid: 11.07.2002. Coming into force: 01.09.2002. Effect: S.I. 1999/3483 amended. Territorial extent & classification: E/W. General. – 8p.: 30 cm. – EC note: Specifies maximum levels which crops, food and feeding stuffs may contain in implementation of DIR 2002/5/EC, 2002/23/EC – 0 11 042512 X *£2.00*

Agriculture, England

The Beef Labelling (Enforcement) (England) (Amendment) Regulations 2002 No. 2002/2315. – Enabling power: European Communities Act 1972, s. 2 (2). – Issued: 17.09.2002. Made: 05.09.2002. Laid: 10.09.2002. Coming into force: 01.10.2002. Effect: S.I. 2000/3047 amended. Territorial extent & classification: E. General. – 4p.: 30 cm. – 0 11 042753 X *£1.75*

The Bovines and Bovine Products (Trade) (Amendment) (England) Regulations 2002 No. 2002/2357. – Enabling power: European Communities Act 1972, s. 2 (2). – Issued: 07.10.2002. Made: 13.09.2002. Laid: 16.09.2002. Coming into force: 07.10.2002. Effect: S.I. 1999/1103 amended in relation to England. Territorial extent & classification: E. General. – EC note: Gives effect (for England) to DEC 98/692/EC and 98/564/EC which amended 98/256/EC. It also gives effect to 2002/670/EC (which amends 98/256/EC) concerning the despatch from England of bovine embryos and bone in veal carcasses from calves between 6 and 9 months exported under the Date Based Export Scheme (DBES). – 8p.: 30 cm. – 0 11 042835 8 *£2.00*

The Common Agricultural Policy Support Schemes (Appeals) Regulations 2002 No. 2002/646. – Enabling power: European Communities Act 1972, s. 2 (2). – Issued: 03.04.2002. Made: 11.03.2002. Laid: 14.03.2002. Coming into force: 08.04.2002. Effect: None. Territorial extent & classification: E. General. – 4p.: 30 cm. – EC note: Enables the Secretary of State for Environment, Food and Rural Affairs to establish a procedure for the further consideration of any application made under a Community scheme by way of appeal from the initial determination of that application by the Secretary of State – 0 11 039623 5 *£1.75*

The Feeding Stuffs (Amendment) Regulations 2002 No. 2002/892. – Enabling power: Agriculture Act 1970, ss. 66 (1), 68 (1) (1A), 69 (1), 74A, 75 (1), 76 (1), 77 (4), 78 (6), 79 (1), 84 & European Communities Act 1972, s. 2 (2). – Issued: 02.08.2002. Made: 23.05.2002. Laid: 24.05.2002. Coming into force: 01.07.2002. Effect: S.I. 1999/1663, 1872, 2325; 2000/2481 amended. Territorial extent & classification: E. General. – 12p.: 30 cm. – EC note: These Regs implement: Dir 2001/79/EC amending Dir 87/153/EEC, Dir 2001/102/EC amending Dir 1999/29/EEC, Dir 2002/1/EC amending Dir 94/39/EC. These Regs also provide for the enforcement of the following Commission Regs. Reg (EC) 2013/2001, Reg 2200/2001, Reg 256/2002. These regulations extend largely to England only but to the extent specified in reg.1 also apply to Wales and Northern Ireland – 0 11 042593 6 *£2.50*

The Food and Animal Feedingstuffs (Products of Animal Origin from China) (Control) (England) Regulations 2002 No. 2002/183. – Enabling power: European Communities Act 1972, s. 2 (2). – Issued: 26.02.2002. Made: 31.01.2002. Laid: 01.02.2002. Coming into force: 02.02.2002. Effect: None. Territorial extent & classification: E. General. – 4p.: 30 cm. – EC note: Implement EC DEC 2002/69/EC concerning certain protective measures with regard to the products of animal origin imported from China – Revoked by S.I. 2002/1614 (ISBN 0110424573) – 0 11 039365 1 *£1.75*

The Food and Animal Feedingstuffs (Products of Animal Origin from China) (Emergency Control) (England) Regulations 2002 No. 2002/1614. – Enabling power: European Communities Act 1972, s. 2 (2). – Issued: 15.07.2002. Made: 19.06.2002. Laid: 19.06.2002. Coming into force: 20.06.2002. Effect: S.I. 2002/183 revoked. Territorial extent & classification: E. General. – EC note: Implements, for England, Commission Decision 2002/69/EC as amended by Decision 2002/441/EC concerning certain protective measures with regard to the products of animal origin imported from China. – 8p.: 30 cm. – Revoked by S.I. 2002/2151 (ISBN 0110426827) – 0 11 042457 3   *£2.00*

The Hill Farm Allowance Regulations 2002 No. 2002/271. – Enabling power: European Communities Act 1972, s. 2 (2). – Issued: 07.03.2002. Made: 11.02.2002. Laid: 13.02.2002. Coming into force: 08.03.2002. Effect: S.I. 2000/3044 amended. Territorial extent & classification: E. General. – 12p.: 30 cm. – EC note: Implements EC REG 1750/1999, laying down detailed rules for the application of REG 1257/1999. Also implement chapter 9 of the England Rural Development Programme approved by the Commission, in particular arts. 13, 14, 15 – 0 11 039411 9   *£2.50*

The Nitrate Sensitive Areas (Amendment) Regulations 2002 No. 2002/744. – Enabling power: European Communities Act 1972, s. 2 (2). – Issued: 15.04.2002. Made: 18.03.2002. Laid: 19.03.2002. Coming into force: 10.04.2002. Effect: S.I. 1994/1729 amended. Territorial extent & classification: E. General. – 2p.: 30 cm. – 0 11 039744 4   *£1.50*

The Nitrate Vulnerable Zones (Additional Designations) (England) (No. 2) Regulations 2002 No. 2002/2614. – Enabling power: European Communities Act 1972, s. 2 (2). – Issued: 05.11.2002. Made: 15.10.2002. Laid: 17.10.2002. Coming into force: 19.12.2002 for reg. 18.10.2002 for remainder, in accord. with reg. 1(2). Effect: S.I. 1996/888; 1998/1202 amended in relation to England; S.I. 2000/2911 amended & S.I. 2002/2525 revoked. Territorial extent & classification: E. General. – EC note: These regs designate additional nitrate vulnerable zones and make provision for the purpose of implementing in England Council DIR 91/676, concerning the protection of waters against nitrate pollution caused by nitrates from agricultural sources. – 8p.: 30 cm. – 0 11 042932 X   *£2.00*

The Products of Animal Origin (Third Country Imports) (England) (Amendment) (No. 2) Regulations 2002 No. 2002/2570. – Enabling power: European Communities Act 1972, s. 2 (2). – Issued: 29.10.2002. Made: 10.10.2002. Laid: 10.10.2002. Coming into force: 11.10.2002. Effect: S.I. 2002/1227 amended. Territorial extent & classification: E. General. – 2p.: 30 cm. – EC note: These Regs, give effect to the following EC DECs: 2002/768, 770, 771 – Revoked by S.I. 2002/3206 (ISBN 011044616X) – 0 11 042897 8   *£1.50*

The Products of Animal Origin (Third Country Imports) (England) (Amendment) (No. 3) Regulations 2002 No. 2002/2639. – Enabling power: European Communities Act 1972, s. 2 (2). – Issued: 04.11.2002. Made: 21.10.2002. Laid: 21.10.2002. Coming into force: 23.10.2002. Effect: S.I. 2002/1227 amended. Territorial extent & classification: E. General. – 2p.: 30 cm. – EC note: These Regs. give effect in England to Commission decision 2002/794/EC. Revoked by S.I. 2002/3206 (ISBN 011044616X) – 0 11 042927 3   *£1.50*

The Products of Animal Origin (Third Country Imports) (England) (Amendment) (No. 4) Regulations 2002 No. 2002/3206. – Enabling power: European Communities Act 1972, s. 2 (2). – Issued: 23.01.2003. Made: 20.12.2002. Laid: 20.12.2002. Coming into force: 01.01.2003. Effect: S.I. 2002/1227 amended & 2002/2151, 2570, 2639 revoked. Territorial extent & classification: E. General. – 18p.: 30 cm. – EC note: These Regs implement EC DEC 2002/995/EC – 0 11 044616 X   *£3.50*

The Products of Animal Origin (Third Country Imports) (England) (Amendment) Regulations 2002 No. 2002/2151. – Enabling power: European Communities Act 1972, s. 2 (2). – Issued: 08.10.2002. Made: 19.08.2002. Laid: 19.08.2002. Coming into force: 20.08.2002. Effect: S.I. 2002/1227 amended & S.I. 2002/1614 revoked. Territorial extent & classification: E. General. – 2p.: 30 cm. – EC note: These Regs. update the reference to Commission Decision 2002/69/EC concerning certain protective measures with regard to products of animal origin imported from China by including references to Commission Decisions 2002/441/EC and 2002/573/EC – Revoked by S.I. 2002/3206 (ISBN 011044616X) – 0 11 042682 7   *£1.50*

The Products of Animal Origin (Third Country Imports) (England) Regulations 2002 No. 2002/1227. – Enabling power: European Communities Act 1972, s. 2 (2). – Issued: 19.06.2002. Made: 01.05.2002. Laid: 01.05.2002. Coming into force: 22.05.2002. Effect: S.I. 1995/1086; 1996/3125; 1997/2537 amended & disapplication of provisions for 1984/1918, 1996/3124, 3125; 1999/157. Territorial extent & classification: E. General. – 49p.: 30 cm. – EC note: These Regulations implement for England Council Directive 97/78/EC laying down the principles governing the organisation of veterinary checks on products entering the Community from third countries – 0 11 042350 X   *£7.50*

Agriculture, England: Livestock industries

The Artificial Insemination of Cattle (Animal Health) (Amendment) (England) Regulations 2002 No. 2002/824. – Enabling power: Animal Health and Welfare Act 1984, s. 10 (1) (2) (a). – Issued: 15.05.2002. Made: 26.03.2002. Laid: 26.03.2002. Coming into force: 18.04.2002. Effect: S.I. 1985/1861 amended in relation to England. Territorial extent & classification: E. General. – 4p.: 30 cm. – 0 11 039933 1   *£1.75*

Agriculture, England and Wales

The Milk Marketing Board (Dissolution) Order 2002 No. 2002/128. – Enabling power: Agriculture Act 1993, s. 14 (5). – Issued: 15.02.2002. Made: 29.01.2002. Coming into force: 31.01.2002. Effect: None. Territorial extent & classification: E/W. General. – 2p.: 30 cm. – 0 11 039305 8 *£1.50*

The Pesticides (Maximum Residue Levels in Crops, Food and Feeding Stuffs) (England and Wales) (Amendment) (No. 2) Regulations 2002 No. 2002/2723. – Enabling power: European Communities Act 1972, s. 2 (2). – Issued: 14.11.2002. Made: 31.10.2002. Laid: 01.11.2002. Coming into force: 30.11.2002. Effect: S.I. 1999/3483 amended. Territorial extent & classification: E/W. General. – 104p.: 30 cm. – EC note: These regulations add new residue levels that have been set by recent amendments to EC DIR/86/362; 86/363; and 90/642 by DIR 2002/42; 2002/66; 2002/71; and 2002/76 – 0 11 042953 2 *£10.50*

Agriculture, Wales

The Bovines and Bovine Products (Trade) (Amendment) (Wales) (No. 2) Regulations 2002 No. 2002/2325 (W.232). – Enabling power: European Communities Act 1972, s. 2 (2). – Issued: 01.10.2002. Made: 10.09.2002. Coming into force: 11.09.2002. Effect: S.I. 1999/1103 amended in relation to Wales. Territorial extent & classification: W. General. – EC note: Gives effect to DEC 2002/670/EC which amends 98/256/EC to enable the despatch from Wales of bovine embryos and bone in veal carcases from calves between 6 and 9 months exported from the Date Based Export Scheme (DBES). – 16p.: 30 cm. – 0 11 090574 1 *£3.00*

The Bovines and Bovine Products (Trade) (Amendment) (Wales) Regulations 2002 No. 2002/1174 (W.122). – Enabling power: European Communities Act 1972, s. 2 (2). – Issued: 22.05.2002. Made: 25.04.2002. Coming into force: 01.07.2002. Effect: S.I. 1999/1103 amended in relation to Wales. Territorial extent & classification: W. General. – In English and Welsh. Welsh title: Rheoliadau Bucholion a Chynhyrchion Buchol (Masnach) (Diwygio) (Cymru) 2002. – EC note: Gives effect (for Wales) to DEC 98/692/EC, 98/564/EC which amended DEC 98/256/EC. – 4p.: 30 cm. – 0 11 090489 3 *£1.75*

The Environmental Impact Assessment (Uncultivated Land and Semi-Natural Areas) (Wales) Regulations 2002 No. 2002/2127 (W.214). – Enabling power: European Communities Act 1972 s. 2 (2). – Issued: 29.08.2002. Made: 13.08.2002. Coming into force: 19.08.2002. Effect: None. Territorial extent & classification: W. General. – EC note: These Regs. implement, in relation to projects for the use of uncultivated land and semi-natural areas in Wales for intensive agricultural purposes, Council Dir. 85/337/EEC (as last amended by Council Dir. 97/11/EEC) and Council Dir. 1992/43/EEC (as last amended by Council Dir. 97/62/EEC). – 36p.: 30 cm. – 0 11 090560 1 *£6.50*

The Feeding Stuffs (Amendment) (Wales) Regulations 2002 No. 2002/1797 (W.172). – Enabling power: Agriculture Act 1970, ss. 66 (1), 68 (1) (1A), 69 (1), 74A, 75 (1), 76 (1), 77 (4), 78 (6), 79 (1), 84 & European Communities Act 1972, s. 2 (2). – Issued: 13.08.2002. Made: 09.07.2002. Coming into force: 05.08.2002. Effect: S.I. 1999/1663, 2325, 1872 amended in relation to Wales; 2001/343 (W.15) amended. Territorial extent & classification: W. General. – EC note: These Regs implement, for Wales: DIR 2001/79/EC amending 87/153/EEC, 2001/102/EC amending 1999/29/EEC, 2002/1/EC amending 94/39/EC. These Regs also provide for the enforcement of REGs (EC) 2013/2001, 2200/2001, 256/2002. – 16p.: 30 cm. – 0 11 090544 X *£3.00*

The Food and Animal Feedingstuffs (Products of Animal Origin from China) (Control) (Wales) Regulations 2002 No. 2002/203 (W.26). – Enabling power: European Communities Act 1972, s. 2 (2). – Issued: 15.03.2002. Made: 01.02.2002. Coming into force: 02.02.2002. Effect: None. Territorial extent & classification: W. General. – 8p.: 30 cm. – EC note: Implement DEC 2002/69/EC – Revoked by S.I. 2002/1798 (W.173) (ISBN 0110905245) – 0 11 090440 0 *£2.00*

The Food and Feedingstuffs (Products of Animal Origin from China) (Emergency Control) (Wales) Regulations 2002 No. 2002/1798 (W.173). – Enabling power: European Communities Act 1972, s. 2 (2). – Issued: 22.07.2002. Made: 11.07.2002. Coming into force: 12.07.2002. Effect: S.I. 2002/203 (W.26) revoked. Territorial extent & classification: W. General. – EC note: These Regs. implement DEC 2002/69/EC as amended by DEC 2002/441/EC. – 8p.: 30 cm. – 0 11 090524 5 *£2.00*

The Products of Animal Origin (Third Country Imports) (Wales) (Amendment) (No. 2) Regulations 2002 No. 2002/3230 (W.307). – Enabling power: European Communities Act 1972, s. 2 (2). – Issued: 05.02.2003. Made: 23.12.2002. Coming into force: 01.01.2003. Effect: S.I. 2002/1387 (W.136) amended. Territorial extent & classification: W. General. – Welsh title: Rheoliadau Cynhyrchion sy'n Deillio o Anifeiliaid (Mewnforion Trydydd Gwledydd) (Cymru) (Diwygio) (Rhif 2) 2002. – 20p.: 30 cm. – EC note: These Regs implement EC DEC of 09/12/02 (laying down interim safeguard measures with regard to imports of products of animal origin for personal consumption). This DEC is not yet published in the Official Journal – 0 11 090625 X *£3.50*

The Products of Animal Origin (Third Country Imports) (Wales) (Amendment) Regulations 2002 No. 2002/3011 (W.283). – Enabling power: European Communities Act 1972, s. 2 (2). – Issued: 27.12.2002. Made: 04.12.2002. Coming into force: 07.12.2002. Effect: S.I. 2002/1387 (W.136) amended. Territorial extent & classification: W. General. – 4p.: 30 cm. – EC note: These Regs. give effect in Wales to DEC 2002/794/EC concerning certain protective measures with regard to poultry meat, poultry meat products and poultry meat preparations intended for human consumption and imported from Brazil. They also correct a defect in S.I. 2002/1387 (W.136) by inserting a reference to DEC 2002/251/EC concerning certain protective measures with regard to poultry meat, and certain fishery and aquaculture products intended for human consumption and imported from Thailand. They also implement for Wales DIR 97/87/EC laying down the principles governing the organisation of veterinary checks on products entering the Community from third countries – 0 11 090603 9   £1.75

The Products of Animal Origin (Third Country Imports) (Wales) Regulations 2002 No. 2002/1387 (W.136). – Enabling power: European Communities Act 1972, s. 2 (2). – Issued: 27.06.2002. Made: 17.05.2002. Coming into force: 22.05.2002. Effect: S.I. 1995/1086; 1996/3125; 1997/2537 amended in relation to Wales & S.I. 1980/14; 1984/1918; 1996/3124, 3125; 1999/157 disapplied in relation to Wales. Territorial extent & classification: W. General. – 72p.: 30 cm. – EC note: Implements for Wales, Council directive 97/78/EC laying down principles governing the organisation of veterinary checks on products entering the Community from 3rd countries. When read with Annex I to the Agreement on the European Economic Area the Directive requires that products of animal origin entering the EEA, undergo specified veterinary checks at border inspection posts to ensure they comply with requirements laid down by Community legislation for the protection of animal and public health – 0 11 090510 5   £7.50

The Tir Mynydd (Wales) (Amendment) Regulations 2002 No. 2002/1806 (W.176). – Enabling power: European Communities Act 1972, s. 2 (2). – Issued: 02.08.2002. Made: 09.07.2002. Coming into force: 10.07.2002. Effect: S.I. 2001/496 (W.23), 1154 (W.61) amended. Territorial extent & classification: W. General. – 12p.: 30 cm. – In English & Welsh. Welsh title: Rheoliadau Tir Mynydd (Cymru) (Diwygio) 2002 – 0 11 090531 8   £2.50

Agriculture, Wales: Common agricultural policy

The Organic Products (Wales) Regulations 2002 No. 2002/3159 (W.294). – Enabling power: European Communities Act 1972, s. 2 (2). – Issued: 31.12.2002. Made: 17.12.2002. Coming into force: 31.12.2002. Effect: S.I. 1994/1721; 1996/3142 amended in relation to Wales & S.I. 2001/424 (W.18) amended & S.I. 1992/2111; 1993/405; 1994/2286; 1997/166 revoked in relation to Wales. Territorial extent & classification: W. General. – 20p.: 30 cm. – EC note: These regs provide for the continued administration, execution and enforcement of Council regulation (EEC) No. 2092/91 (amended by Council regulation 1804/1999) on organic production of agricultural products and indications referring thereto on agricultural products and foodstuffs and Commission regulation supplementing that regulation – 0 11 090607 1   £3.50

Agriculture, Wales: Livestock industries

The Artificial Insemination of Cattle (Animal Health) (Amendment) (Wales) Regulations 2002 No. 2002/1131 (W.118). – Enabling power: Animal Health and Welfare Act 1984, s. 10 (1) (2) (a). – Issued: 07.05.2002. Made: 17.04.2002. Coming into force: 18.04.2002. Effect: S.I. 1985/1861 amended in relation to Wales. Territorial extent & classification: W. General. – 8p.: 30 cm. – In English & Welsh. Welsh title: Rheoliadau Ffrwythloni Artiffisial Gwartheg (Iechyd Anifeiliaid) (Diwygio) (Cymru) 2002 – 0 11 090483 4   £2.00

Animals

The Animals (Scientific Procedures) Act 1986 (Fees) (Amendment) Order 2002 No. 2002/473. – Enabling power: Animals (Scientific Procedures) Act 1986, s. 8. – Issued: 11.03.2002. Made: 04.03.2002. Laid: 06.03.2002. Coming into force: 01.04.2002. Effect: S.I. 2000/480 amended. Territorial extent & classification: E/W/S. General. – 2p.: 30 cm. – 0 11 039435 6   £1.50

Animals, England

Fur Farming (Compensation Scheme) (England) Order 2002 No. 2002/221. – Enabling power: Fur Farming (Prohibition) Act 2000, s. 5. – Issued: 13.08.2002. Made: 05.02.2002. Laid: 07.02.2002. Coming into force: 01.03.2002. Effect: S.I. 2001/3853 revoked. Territorial extent & classification: E. General. – This S.I. supersedes S.I. 2001/3853, which was defective, and is being issued free of charge to all known recipients of that SI. – 20p.: 30 cm. – 0 11 042640 1   £3.50

Animals, England: Animal health

The Animal Gatherings (Interim Measures) (England) (Amendment) (No. 2) Order 2002 No. 2002/1765. – Enabling power: Animal Health Act 1981, ss. 1, 7, 8. – Issued: 30.07.2002. Made: 10.07.2002. Coming into force: 31.07.2002. Effect: S.I. 2002/202 amended. Territorial extent & classification: E. General. – 2p.: 30 cm. – Revoked by S.I. 2003/253 (ISBN 0110449797) – 0 11 042552 9 £1.50

The Animal Gatherings (Interim Measures) (England) (Amendment) Order 2002 No. 2002/1328. – Enabling power: Animal Health Act 1981, ss. 1, 7, 8. – Issued: 20.06.2002. Made: 13.05.2002. Coming into force: 15.05.2002. Effect: S.I. 2002/202 amended & S.I. 1925/1349 disapplied and replaced for a temporary period until 30.11.2002. Territorial extent & classification: E. General. – 4p.: 30 cm. – Revoked by S.I. 2003/253 (ISBN 0110449797) – 0 11 042371 2 £1.75

The Animal Gatherings (Interim Measures) (England) Order 2002 No. 2002/202. – Enabling power: Animal Health Act 1981, ss.1, 7, 8, 83. – Issued: 07.03.2002. Made: 05.02.2002 at 10.00 am. Coming into force: 11.02.2002. Effect: S.I. 1925/1349 amended. Territorial extent & classification: E. General. – 4p.: 30 cm. – Revoked by S.I. 2003/253 (ISBN 0110449797) – 0 11 039409 7 £1.75

The Animal Health Act 2002 (Commencement) Order 2002 No. 2002/3044 (C.101). – Enabling power: Animal Health Act 2002, s. 19 (1). Bringing into force various provisions of the 2002 Act on 13.01.2003, 14.01.2003, 24.03.2003 & 01.07.2003 in accord. with art. 2. – Issued: 22.01.2003. Made: 09.12.2002. Effect: None. Territorial extent & classification: E. General. – 2p.: 30 cm. – 0 11 044615 1 £1.50

The Animals and Animal Products (Import and Export) (England and Wales) (Amendment) (England) (No. 2) Regulations 2002 No. 2002/956. – Enabling power: European Communities Act 1972, s. 2 (2). – Issued: 26.04.2002. Made: 04.04.2002 at 2.30 pm. Laid: 04.04.2002. Coming into force: 04.04.2002 at 8.00 pm. Effect: S.I. 2000/1673 amended in relation to England. Territorial extent & classification: E. General. – EC note: Give effect to art. 1 of DEC 2002/242/EC amending for the 9th time DEC 2001/327/EC concerning restrictions to the movement of animals of susceptible species with regard to foot-and-mouth disease. – 2p.: 30 cm. – 0 11 039822 X £1.50

The Animals and Animal Products (Import and Export) (England and Wales) (Amendment) (England) Regulations 2002 No. 2002/467. – Enabling power: European Communities Act 1972, s. 2 (2). – Issued: 28.03.2002. Made: 04.03.2002. Laid: 04.03.2002. Coming into force: 06.03.2002. Effect: S.I. 2000/1673 amended in relation to England. Territorial extent & classification: E. General. – EC note: To make provision in relation to England to give effect to art. 4 of DEC 2002/153/EC concerning certain protection measures with regard to foot-and-mouth disease in the UK repealing DEC 2001/740/EC and amending for the 8th time DEC 2001/327/EC, and DEC 2001/327/EC concerning restrictions to the movement of animals of susceptible species with regard to foot-and-mouth disease. – 4p.: 30 cm. – 0 11 039606 5 £1.75

The Cattle Database (Amendment) (England) Regulations 2002 No. 2002/94. – Enabling power: European Communities Act 1972, s. 2 (2). – Issued: 27.02.2002. Made: 21.01.2002. Laid: 21.02.2002. Coming into force: 11.02.2002. Effect: S.I. 1998/1796 amended in relation to England. Territorial extent & classification: E. General. – 2p.: 30 cm. – 0 11 039379 1 £1.50

The Cattle (Identification of Older Animals) (Amendment) Regulations 2002 No. 2002/95. – Enabling power: European Communities Act 1972, s. 2 (2). – Issued: 18.02.2002. Made: 21.01.2002. Laid: 21.01.2002. Coming into force: 11.02.2002. Effect: S.I. 2000/2976 amended. Territorial extent & classification: E. General. – 2p.: 30 cm. – 0 11 039312 0 £1.50

The Disease Control (Interim Measures) (England) (Amendment No. 2) Order 2002 No. 2002/1348. – Enabling power: Animal Health Act 1981, ss. 1, 8 (1). – Issued: 14.06.2002. Made: 14.05.2002 at 5.20 pm. Coming into force: 15.05.2002. Effect: S.I. 2002/242 amended. Territorial extent & classification: E. General. – 8p.: 30 cm. – 0 11 042332 1 £2.00

The Disease Control (Interim Measures) (England) (Amendment No. 3) Order 2002 No. 2002/1764. – Enabling power: Animal Health Act 1981, ss. 1, 7, 8 (1), 87 (2). – Issued: 13.08.2002. Made: 10.07.2002. Coming into force: 31.07.2002. Effect: S.I. 2002/242 amended. Territorial extent & classification: E. General. – 4p.: 30 cm. – 0 11 042641 X £1.75

The Disease Control (Interim Measures) (England) (Amendment) Order 2002 No. 2002/907. – Enabling power: Animal Health Act 1981, ss. 1, 8 (1). – Issued: 24.04.2002. Made: 27.03.2002. Coming into force: 28.03.2002. Effect: S.I. 2002/242 amended. Territorial extent & classification: E. General. – 4p.: 30 cm. – 0 11 039810 6 £1.75

The Disease Control (Interim Measures) (England) (No. 2) (Amendment) Order 2002 No. 2002/2300. – Enabling power: Animal Health Act 1981, ss. 1, 8 (1). – Issued: 14.10.2002. Made: 05.09.2002. Coming into force: 30.09.2002. Effect: S.I. 2002/2152 amended. Territorial extent & classification: E. General. – 2p.: 30 cm. – Revoked by S.I. 2003/254 (ISBN 0110450159) – 0 11 042844 7 £1.50

The Disease Control (Interim Measures) (England) (No. 2) Order 2002 No. 2002/2152. – Enabling power: Animal Health Act 1981, ss. 1, 7, 8 (1), 83 (2), 87 (2). – Issued: 27.09.2002. Made: 16.08.2002 at 5 pm. Coming into force: 06.09.2002 (and shall cease to have effect on 01.02.2003). Effect: S.I. 2002/202 amended & S.I. 2002/242 revoked. Territorial extent & classification: E. General. – 21p.: 30 cm. – Revoked by S.I. 2003/254 (ISBN 0110450159) – 0 11 042803 X £4.00

The Disease Control (Interim Measures) (England) Order 2002 No. 2002/242. – Enabling power: Animal Health Act 1981, ss. 1, 7, 8 (1), 83 (2), 87 (2). – Issued: 02.04.2002. Made: 07.02.2002. Coming into force: 11.02.2002. Effect: 1981 c. 22 amended in relation to England. Territorial extent & classification: E. General. – 12p.: 30 cm. – Revoked by S.I. 2002/2152 (ISBN 011042803X) – 0 11 039611 1 £2.50

The Import and Export Restrictions (Foot-and-Mouth Disease) (No. 2) Regulations 2002 No. 2002/76. – Enabling power: European Communities Act 1972, s. 2 (2). – Issued: 18.04.2002. Made: 17.01.2002 at 4.45 pm. Laid: 17.01.2002. Coming into force: 17.01.2002 at 8.00 pm. Effect: S.I. 2002/2 revoked. Territorial extent & classification: E. General. – 26p.: 30 cm. – EC note: Implements, in England EC DEC 2002/37/EC amending for the sixth time DEC 2001/740/EC concerning certain protection measures with regard to foot-and-mouth disease in the UK – 0 11 039748 7 £4.50

The Import and Export Restrictions (Foot-and-Mouth Disease) (No. 3) Regulations 2002 No. 2002/119. – Enabling power: European Communities Act 1972, s. 2 (2). – Issued: 13.03.2002 Made: 25.01.2002 (2.00pm). Laid: 28.01.2002. Coming into force: 25.01.2002 at 8.00 pm, in accord. with art. 1. Effect: S.I. 2002/76 revoked in relation to England. Territorial extent & classification: E. General. – 16p.: 30 cm. – EC note: Implement, in England, EC DEC 2002/48/EC amending for the 7th time DEC 2001/740/EC concerning certain protection measures with regard to Foot-and-Mouth Disease in the UK – Revoked by S.I. 2002/468 (ISBN 0110396073) – 0 11 039437 2 £3.00

The Import and Export Restrictions (Foot-and-Mouth Disease) (No. 3) (Revocation) Regulations 2002 No. 2002/468. – Enabling power: European Communities Act 1972, s. 2 (2). – Issued: 28.03.2002 Made: 04.03.2002. Laid: 04.03.2002. Coming into force: 06.03.2002. Effect: S.I. 2002/119 revoked. Territorial extent & classification: E. General. – 2p.: 30 cm. – EC note: Implements, in England art. 3 of DEC 2002/153/EC which repealed DEC 2001/740/EC as amended concerning certain protection measures with regard to foot-and-mouth disease in the UK – 0 11 039607 3 £1.50

The Import and Export Restrictions (Foot-and-Mouth Disease) Regulations 2002 No. 2002/2. – Enabling power: European Communities Act 1972, s. 2 (2). – Issued: 18.04.2002. Made: 04.01.2002 at 3.45 pm. Laid: 04.01.2002. Coming into force: 04.01.2002 at 8.00 pm. Effect: S.I. 2001/4046 revoked. Territorial extent & classification: E. General. – 24p.: 30 cm. – EC note: Implements, in England EC DEC 2001/938/EC concerning certain protection measures with regard to foot-and-mouth disease in the UK and amending for the fifth time DEC 2001/740/EC – Revoked by S.I. 2002/76 (ISBN 0110397487) – 0 11 039747 9 £4.00

The Movement of Animals (Restrictions) (England) Order 2002 No. 2002/3229. – Enabling power: Animal Health Act 1981, ss. 1, 8 (1), 17 (1), 23, 83 (2), 87 (2) (5), 88 (2) (4). – Issued: 24.02.2003. Made: 23.12.2002. Coming into force: 20.01.2003. Effect: S.I. 1985/1765; 1990/760 revoked insofar as they apply to England. Territorial extent & classification: E. General. – 8p.: 30 cm. – This S.I. has been printed in consequence of a defect in the original print and is being issued free of charge to all known recipients – 0 11 044781 6 £2.00

The Pet Travel Scheme (Pilot Arrangements) (England) (Amendment) (No. 2) Order 2002 No. 2002/2850. – Enabling power: Animal Health Act 1981, s. 10. – Issued: 04.12.2002. Made: 18.11.2002. Laid: 20.11.2002. Coming into force: 11.12.2002. Effect: S.I. 1999/3443 amended. Territorial extent & classification: E. General. – [8]p.: 30 cm. – 0 11 044080 3 £2.00

The Pet Travel Scheme (Pilot Arrangements) (England) (Amendment) Order 2002 No. 2002/1011. – Enabling power: Animal Health Act 1981, s. 10. – Issued: 30.04.2002. Made: 08.04.2002. Laid: 08.04.2002. Coming into force: 01.05.2002. Effect: S.I. 1999/3443 amended. Territorial extent & classification: E. General. – 2p.: 30 cm. – 0 11 039835 1 £1.50

The Pigs (Records, Identification and Movement) (Interim Measures) (England) (No. 2) Order 2002 No. 2002/2154. – Enabling power: Animal Health Act 1981, ss.1, 8, 83 (2). – Issued: 23.09.2002. Made: 16.08.2002 at 5.15 pm. Coming into force: 06.09.2002 (and shall cease to have effect on 01.02.2003). Effect: S.I. 2002/241 revoked & S.I. 1995/11 will cease to have effect while this Order is in force. Territorial extent & classification: E. General. – 12p.: 30 cm. – 0 11 042781 5 £2.50

The Pigs (Records, Identification and Movement) (Interim Measures) (England) Order 2002 No. 2002/241. – Enabling power: Animal Health Act 1981, ss.1, 7 (1), 8 (1), 87 (2). – Issued: 07.03.2002. Made: 07.02.2002. Coming into force: 11.02.2002. Effect: S.I. 1995/11 amended in relation to England. Territorial extent & classification: E. General. – 12p.: 30 cm. – Revoked by S.I. 2002/2154 (0110427815) – 0 11 039410 0 £2.50

The Poultry Breeding Flocks, Hatcheries and Animal By-Products (Fees) (England) Order 2002 No. 2002/2875. – Enabling power: Animal Health Act 1981, s. 84 (1). – Issued: 03.12.2002. Made: 19.11.2002. Laid: 21.11.2002. Coming into force: 01.01.2003. Effect: S.I. 1993/1998 revoked in relation to England. Territorial extent & classification: E. General. – 4p.: 30 cm. – 0 11 044074 9 £1.75

The Sheep and Goat Identification and Movement (Interim Measures) (England) (Amendment) (No. 2) Order 2002 No. 2002/1349. – Enabling power: Animal Health Act 1981, ss. 1, 8 (1). – Issued: 14.06.2002. Made: 14.05.2002 at 5.25 pm. Coming into force: 15.05.2002. Effect: S.I. 2002/240 amended. Territorial extent & classification: E. General. – 4p.: 30 cm. – 0 11 042333 X £1.75

The Sheep and Goats Identification and Movement (Interim Measures) (England) (Amendment) Order 2002 No. 2002/764. – Enabling power: Animal Health Act 1981, ss.1, 8 (1). – Issued: 22.04.2002. Made: 20.03.2002. Coming into force: 21.03.2002 at 2.00 pm. Effect: S.I. 2002/240 amended. Territorial extent & classification: E. General. – 4p.: 30 cm. – 0 11 039776 2 £1.75

The Sheep and Goats Identification and Movement (Interim Measures) (England) (No. 2) Order 2002 No. 2002/2153. – Enabling power: Animal Health Act 1981, ss. 1, 8 (1). – Issued: 23.09.2002. Made: 16.08.2002 at 5.10 pm. Coming into force: 06.09.2002 (and shall cease to have effect on 01.02.2003). Effect: S.I. 2002/240 revoked. Territorial extent & classification: E. General. – 16p.: 30 cm. – 0 11 042780 7 £3.00

The Sheep and Goats Identification and Movement (Interim Measures) (England) Order 2002 No. 2002/240. – Enabling power: Animal Health Act 1981, ss.1, 8 (1). – Issued: 22.03.2002. Made: 07.02.2002. Coming into force: 11.02.2002. Effect: S.I. 2000/2027 revoked. Territorial extent & classification: E. General. – 12p.: 30 cm. – EC note: This Order revokes S.I. 2000/2027 which implemented directive 92/102/EEC. The implementation of those provisions is re-enacted in this Order – Revoked by S.I. 2002/2153 (0110427807) – 0 11 039528 X £2.50

The TSE (England) (Amendment) (No. 2) Regulations 2002 No. 2002/2860. – Enabling power: European Communities Act 1972, s. 2 (2). – Issued: 17.12.2002. Made: 18.11.2002. Laid: 20.11.2002. Coming into force: 11.12.2002. Effect: S.I. 2002/843 amended. Territorial extent & classification: E. General. – [8]p.: 30 cm. – 0 11 044180 X £2.00

The TSE (England) (Amendment) Regulations 2002 No. 2002/1253. – Enabling power: European Communities Act 1972, s. 2 (2). – Issued: 27.05.2002. Made: 03.05.2002. Laid: 03.05.2002. Coming into force: 27.05.2002. Effect: S.I. 2002/843 amended. Territorial extent & classification: E. General. – 2p.: 30 cm. – This S.I. has been made in consequence of errors in S.I. 2002/843 and is being issued free of charge to all known recipients of that S.I – 0 11 042246 5 £1.50

The TSE (England) Regulations 2002 No. 2002/843. – Enabling power: European Communities Act 1972, s. 2 (2). – Issued: 13.05.2002. Made: 27.03.2002. Laid: 27.03.2002. Coming into force: 19.04.2002. Effect: S.I. 1997/2964, 2965; 2001/2376 amended & S.I. 1996/3184; 1998/955, 1645, 1647, 3070 revoked, in relation to England & 1996/3183; 1998/954, 1646; 1999/882 revoked with savings, in relation to England & 2001/1644 revoked with savings. Territorial extent & classification: E. General. – 89p.: 30 cm. – EC note: These Regs. make provision in England, otherwise than in relation to trade, for the administration and enforcement of the following directly applicable Community REGs regarding the prevention, control and eradication of certain transmissible spongiform encephalopathies: 999/2001; 1248/2001 amending Annexes II, X and XI to 999/2001; 1326/2001 laying down transitional measures to permit the changeover to 999/2001 and amending Annexes VII and XI to that REG; 270/2002 amending 999/2001 and amending 1326/2001 – 0 11 039914 5 £9.00

Animals, England: Prevention of cruelty, England

The Protection of Animals (Anaesthetics) Amendment Order 2002 No. 2002/3215. – Enabling power: Protection of Animals (Anaesthetics) Act 1954, s. 1. – Issued: 28.01.2003. Made: 22.12.2002. Laid: 23.12.2002. Coming into force: 23.12.2002. Effect: Protection of Animals (Anaesthetics) Amendment Order 2003 revoked. [This S.I. has not been registered or published].Territorial extent & classification: E. General. – 2p.: 30 cm. – 0 11 044656 9 £1.50

The Welfare of Farmed Animals (England) (Amendment) Regulations 2002 No. 2002/1646. – Enabling power: Agriculture (Miscellaneous Provisions) Act 1968, s. 2. – Issued: 04.07.2002. Made: 24.06.2002. Laid: -.Coming into force: for all regs. except 2 (3), 3, 25.06.2002; for reg. 2 (3), 01.01.2003; for reg. 3, 01.01.2011. Effect: S.I. 1962/2557; 2000/1870 amended. Territorial extent & classification: E. General– Supersedes draft S.I. (ISBN 0110399633). – 8p.: 30 cm. – EC note: Gives effect to the provisions of DIR 99/74/EC laying down minimum standards for the protection of laying hens in establishments with 350 or more laying hens – 0 11 042417 4 £2.00

Animals, England and Wales: Animal health

The Foot-and-Mouth Disease Declaratory (Controlled Area) (England and Wales) (Revocation) Order 2002 No. 2002/277. – Enabling power: S.I. 1983/1950 art. 30 (1). – Made: 08.02.2002. Coming into force: 11.02.2002. Effect: S.I. 2001/1044 revoked. Territorial extent & classification: E/W. Local *Unpublished*

Animals, Wales

The Rabies (Importation of Dogs, Cats and Other Mammals) (Amendment) (Wales) Order 2002 No. 2002/882. – Enabling power: Animal Health Act 1981, ss. 1, 10, 24. – Issued: 20.05.2002. Made: 27.03.2002. Laid: 28.03.2002. Coming into force: 15.04.2002. Effect: S.I. 1974/2211 amended in relation to Wales. Territorial extent & classification: W. General. – With correction slip dated July 2002. – 4p.: 30 cm. – 0 11 039960 9 £1.75

Animals, Wales: Animal health

The Animal Gatherings (Interim Measures) (Wales) (Amendment) (No. 2) Order 2002 No. 2002/2060 (W.209). – Enabling power: Animal Health Act 1981, ss. 1, 7, 8. – Issued: 21.08.2002. Made: 31.07.2002. Coming into force: 01.08.2002. Effect: S.I. 2002/283 (W.34) amended. Territorial extent & classification: W. General. – In English and Welsh. Welsh title: Gorchymyn Crynoadau Anifeiliaid (Mesurau Dros Dro) (Cymru) (Diwygio) (Rhif 2) 2002. – 4p.: 30 cm. – Revoked by S.I. 2003/481 (W.67) (ISBN 0110906853) – 0 11 090555 5 £1.75

The Animal Gatherings (Interim Measures) (Wales) (Amendment) Order 2002 No. 2002/1358 (W.134). – Enabling power: Animal Health Act 1981, ss. 1, 7, 8. – Issued: 06.06.2002. Made: 14.05.2002. Coming into force: 15.05.2002. Effect: S.I. 2002/283 (W.34) amended. Territorial extent & classification: W. General. – In English and Welsh. Welsh title: Gorchymyn Crynoadau Anifeiliaid (Mesurau Dros Dro) (Cymru) (Diwygio) 2002. – 4p.: 30 cm. – Revoked by S.I. 2003/481 (W.67) (ISBN 0110906853) – 0 11 090499 0 *£1.75*

The Animal Gatherings (Interim Measures) (Wales) Order 2002 No. 2002/283 (W.34). – Enabling power: Animal Health Act 1981, ss. 1, 7, 8, 83. – Issued: 22.02.2002. Made: 08.02.2002. Coming into force: 11.02.2002. Effect: S.I. 1925/1349 temporarily disapplied & replaced in relation to Wales by this order (which will cease to have effect on 01.12.2002). Territorial extent & classification: W. General. – In English and Welsh. - Welsh title: Gorchymyn Crynoadau Anifeiliaid (Mesurau Dros Dro) (Cymru) 2002. – 8p.: 30 cm. – Revoked by S.I. 2003/481 (W.67) (ISBN 0110906853) – 0 11 090427 3 *£2.00*

The Animals and Animal Products (Import and Export) (England and Wales) (Amendment) (Wales) (No. 2) Regulations 2002 No. 2002/1039 (W.111). – Enabling power: European Communities Act 1972, s. 2 (2). – Issued: 29.04.2002. Made: 10.04.2002 at 10.20 am. Coming into force: 10.04.2002 at 12 noon. Effect: S.I. 2000/1673 amended in relation to Wales. Territorial extent & classification: W. General. – EC note: Give effect to DEC 2002/242/EC amending for the 9th time DEC 2001/327/EC concerning restrictions to the movement of animals of susceptible species with regard to foot-and-mouth disease. – In English and Welsh. Welsh title: Rheoliadau Anifeiliaid a Chynhyrchion Anifeiliaid (Mewnforio ac Allforio) (Lloegr a Chymru) (Diwygio) (Cymru) (Rhif 2) 2002. - 4p.: 30 cm. – 0 11 090474 5 *£1.75*

The Animals and Animal Products (Import and Export) (England and Wales) (Amendment) (Wales) Regulations 2002 No. 2002/430 (W.52). – Enabling power: European Communities Act 1972, s. 2 (2). – Issued: 15.03.2002. Made: 26.02.2002. Coming into force: 27.02.2002. Effect: S.I. 2000/1673 amended in relation to Wales. Territorial extent & classification: W. General. – EC note: Give effect to art. 4 of DEC 2002/153/EC, concerning certain protection measures with regard to foot-and-mouth disease in the UK, and DEC 2001/327/EC concerning restrictions to the movement of animals of susceptible species with regard to foot-and-mouth disease. – In English and Welsh. Welsh title: Rheoliadau Anifeiliaid a Chynhyrchion Anifeiliaid (Mewnforio ac Allforio) (Lloegr a Chymru) (Diwygio) (Cymru) 2002. – 4p.: 30 cm. – 0 11 090442 7 *£1.75*

The Cattle Database (Amendment) (Wales) Regulations 2002 No. 2002/304 (W.35). – Enabling power: European Communities Act 1972, s. 2 (2). – Issued: 22.02.2002. Made: 08.02.2002. Coming into force: 11.02.2002. Effect: S.I. 1998/1796 amended in relation to Wales. Territorial extent & classification: W. General. – In English and Welsh. - Welsh title: Rheoliadau'r Gronfa Ddata Gwartheg (Diwygio) (Cymru) 2002. - 4p.: 30 cm. – 0 11 090428 1 *£1.75*

The Cattle (Identification of Older Animals) (Wales) (Amendment) Regulations 2002 No. 2002/273 (W.29). – Enabling power: European Communities Act 1972, s. 2 (2). – Issued: 21.02.2002. Made: 08.02.2002. Coming into force: 11.02.2002. Effect: S.I. 2000/3339 (W.217) amended. Territorial extent & classification: W. General. – 4p.: 30 cm. – In English and Welsh. Welsh title: Rheoliadau Gwartheg (Adnabod Anifeiliaid Hyn) (Cymru) (Diwygio) 2002 – 0 11 090425 7 *£1.75*

The Disease Control (Interim Measures) (Wales) (Amendment) (No. 2) Order 2002 No. 2002/1356 (W.132). – Enabling power: Animal Health Act 1981, ss. 1, 8 (1). – Issued: 06.06.2002. Made: 14.05.2002. Coming into force: 15.05.2002. Effect: S.I. 2002/280 (W.32) amended. Territorial extent & classification: W. General. – In English and Welsh. Welsh title: Gorchymyn Rheoli Clefydau (Mesarau Dors Dro) (Cymru) (Diwygio) (Rhif 2) 2002. – 16p.: 30 cm. – 0 11 090498 2 *£3.00*

The Disease Control (Interim Measures) (Wales) (Amendment) (No. 3) Order 2002 No. 2002/2061 (W.210). – Enabling power: Animal Health Act 1981, ss. 1, 7, 8 (1), 87 (2). – Issued: 21.08.2002. Made: 31.07.2002. Coming into force: 01.08.2002. Effect: S.I. 2002/280 (W.32) amended. Territorial extent & classification: W. General. – In English and Welsh. Welsh title: Gorchymyn Rheoli Clefydau (Mesarau Dros Dro) (Cymru) (Diwygiad) (Rhif 3) 2002. – [8]p.: 30 cm. – 0 11 090556 3 *£2.00*

The Disease Control (Interim Measures) (Wales) (Amendment) Order 2002 No. 2002/1038 (W.110). – Enabling power: Animal Health Act 1981, ss. 1, 8 (1). – Issued: 29.04.2002. Made: 10.04.2002 at 10.20 am. Coming into force: 10.04.2002 at 12 noon. Effect: S.I. 2002/280 (W.32) amended. Territorial extent & classification: W. General. – In English and Welsh. Welsh title: Gorchymyn Rheoli Clefydau (Mesarau Dors Dro) (Cymru) (Diwygio) 2002. – 8p.: 30 cm. – 0 11 090473 7 *£2.00*

The Disease Control (Interim Measures) (Wales) (No. 2) (Amendment) Order 2002 No. 2002/2480 (W.243). – Enabling power: Animal Health Act 1981, ss. 1, 8 (1). – Issued: 15.10.2002. Made: 28.09.2002. Coming into force: 30.09.2002. Effect: S.I. 2002/2304 (W.229) amended. Territorial extent & classification: W. General. – 4p.: 30 cm. – Revoked by S.I. 2003/483 (W.69) (ISBN 0110906829) – 0 11 090575 X *£1.75*

The Disease Control (Interim Measures) (Wales) (No. 2) Order 2002 No. 2002/2304 (W.229). – Enabling power: Animal Health Act 1981, ss. 1, 7, 8 (1), 83 (2), 87 (2). Issued: 30.09.2002. Made: 05.09.2002 at 11.29 am. Coming into force: 06.09.2002 (and shall cease to have effect on 01.02.2003). Effect: S.I. 2002/283 (W.34) amended & S.I. 2002/280 (W.32) revoked. Territorial extent & classification: W. General. – 38p.: 30 cm. – Revoked by S.I. 2003/483 (W.69) (ISBN 0110906829) – 0 11 090573 3 *£6.50*

The Disease Control (Interim Measures) (Wales) Order 2002 No. 2002/280 (W.32). – Enabling power: Animal Health Act 1981, ss. 1, 7, 8 (1), 83 (2), 87 (2). – Issued: 26.02.2002. Made: 08.02.2002. Coming into force: 11.02.2002. Effect: None. Territorial extent & classification: W. General. – 12p.: 30 cm. – 0 11 090429 X *£2.50*

The Import and Export Restrictions (Foot-and-Mouth Disease) (Wales) (Amendment) Regulations 2002 No. 2002/85 (W.9). – Enabling power: European Communities Act 1972, s. 2 (2). – Issued: 01.02.2002. Made: 18.01.2002. Coming into force: 19.01.2002. Effect: S.I. 2002/8 (W.1) amended. Territorial extent & classification: W. General. – 12p.: 30 cm. – EC note: implement the Commission decision 2002/37/EC amending for the 6th time decision 2001/740/EC concerning certain protection measures with regard to foot and mouth disease in the UK – Revoked by S.I. 2002/130 (W.18) (ISBN 0110904249) – 0 11 090411 7 *£2.50*

The Import and Export Restrictions (Foot-and-Mouth Disease) (Wales) (No. 2) Regulations 2002 No. 2002/130 (W.18). – Enabling power: European Communities Act 1972, s. 2 (2). – Issued: 21.01.2002. Made: 25.01.2002. Coming into force: 26.01.2002. Effect: S.I. 2002/8 (W.1), 85 (W.9) revoked. Territorial extent & classification: W. General. – 20p.: 30 cm. – EC note: These Regs.implement (in relation to Wales) DEC 2002/48/EC (amending for the 7th time DEC 2001/740/EC concerning certain protection measures with regard to foot-and-mouth disease in the UK) – Revoked by S.I. 2002/431 (W.53) (ISBN 0110904435) – 0 11 090424 9 *£3.50*

The Import and Export Restrictions (Foot-and-Mouth Disease) (Wales) (No. 2) (Revocation) Regulations 2002 No. 2002/431 (W.53). – Enabling power: European Communities Act 1972, s. 2 (2). – Issued: 15.03.2002. Made: 26.02.2002. Coming into force: 27.02.2002. Effect: S.I. 2002/130 (W.18) revoked. Territorial extent & classification: W. General. – EC note: These Regs. give effect (in relation to Wales) to art. 3 of DEC 2002/153/EC (repealing DEC 2001/740/EC as amended) concerning certain protection measures with regard to foot-and-mouth disease in the UK. – In English and Welsh. Welsh title: Rheoliadau Cyfyngiadau Mewnforio ac Allforio (Clwy'r Traed a'r Genau) (Cymru) (Rhif 2) (Diddymu) 2002. – 4p.: 30 cm. – 0 11 090443 5 *£1.75*

The Import and Export Restrictions (Foot-and-Mouth Disease) (Wales) Regulations 2002 No. 2002/8 (W.1). – Enabling power: European Communities Act 1972, s. 2 (2). – Issued: 17.01.2002. Made: 04.01.2002. Coming into force: 05.01.2002. Effect: S.I. 1995/539 amended in relation to Wales & S.I. 2001/4047 (W.338) revoked. Territorial extent & classification: W. General. – 28p.: 30 cm. – EC note: implement the Commission decision 2001/938/EC, amending for the 5th time decision 2001/740/EC concerning certain protection measures with regard to foot and mouth disease in the UK – Revoked by S.I. 2002/130 (W.18) (ISBN 0110904249) – 0 11 090403 6 *£4.50*

The Pigs (Records, Identification and Movement) (Interim Measures) (Wales) (No. 2) Order 2002 No. 2002/2303 (W.228). – Enabling power: Animal Health Act 1981, ss. 1, 8, 83 (2). – Issued: 20.09.2002. Made: 05.09.2002 at 11.30 am. Coming into force: 06.09.2002. Effect: S.I. 2002/281 (W.33) revoked & S.I. 1995/11 shall cease to have effect whilst this order is in force. This Order shall cease to have effect on 01.02.2003. Territorial extent & classification: W. General. – 16p.: 30 cm. – In English and Welsh. Welsh title: Gorchymyn Moch (Cofnodion, Adnabod a Symud) (Mesurau Dros Dro) (Cymru) (Rhif 2) 2002 – 0 11 090571 7 *£3.00*

The Pigs (Records, Identification and Movement) (Interim Measures) (Wales) Order 2002 No. 2002/281 (W.33). – Enabling power: Animal Health Act 1981, ss. 1, 7 (1), 8 (1), 87 (2). – Issued: 26.02.2002. Made: 08.02.2002. Coming into force: 11.02.2002. Effect: None. Territorial extent & classification: W. General. – 16p.: 30 cm. – Revoked S.I. 2002/2303 (W.228) (ISBN 0110427750) – 0 11 090430 3 *£3.00*

The Sheep and Goats Identification and Movement (Interim Measures) (Revocation) (Wales) Regulations 2002 No. 2002/1354 (W.131). – Enabling power: European Communities Act 1972, s. 2 (2). – Issued: 18.06.2002. Made: 14.05.2002. Coming into force: 15.05.2002. Effect: S.I. 2002/274 (W.30); 2002/811 (W.91) revoked. Territorial extent & classification: W. General. – 4p.: 30 cm. – 0 11 090502 4 *£1.75*

The Sheep and Goats Identification and Movement (Interim Measures) (Wales) (Amendment) Order 2002 No. 2002/811 (W.91). – Enabling power: European Communities Act 1972, s. 2 (2). – Issued: 15.04.2002. Made: 21.03.2002 at 13.45 pm. Coming into force: 21.03.2002, at 2.00 pm. Effect: S.I. 2002/274 (W.30) amended. Territorial extent & classification: W. General. – In English and Welsh. Welsh title: Gorchymyn Adnabod a Symud Defaid a Geifr (Mesurau Dros Dro) (Cymru) (Diwygio) 2002. – 8p.: 30 cm. – Revoked by S.I. 2002/1354 (W.131) (ISBN 0110905024) – 0 11 090459 1 *£2.00*

The Sheep and Goats Identification and Movement (Interim Measures) (Wales) (No. 2) Order 2002 No. 2002/2302 (W.227). – Enabling power: Animal Health Act 1981, ss. 1, 8 (1). – Issued: 27.09.2002. Made: 05.09.2002 at 11.30 am. Coming into force: 06.09.2002 (and shall cease to have effect on 01.02.2003). Effect: S.I. 2002/1357 (W.133) revoked. Territorial extent & classification: W. General. – 20p.: 30 cm. – EC note: Implements the provisions relating to sheep and goats of the Council directive 92/102/EEC and provides interim disease control-related measures for the period from 06.09.2002 to 01.02.2003 – 0 11 090572 5 *£3.50*

The Sheep and Goats Identification and Movement (Interim Measures) (Wales) Order 2002 No. 2002/1357 (W.133). – Enabling power: Animal Health Act 1981, ss. 1, 8 (1). – Issued: 18.06.2002. Made: 14.05.2002. Coming into force: 15.05.2002. Effect: None. Territorial extent & classification: W. General. – 12p.: 30 cm. – EC note: Implements the provisions relating to sheep and goats of the Council directive 92/102/EEC and provides interim disease control-related measures for the period from 15.05.2002 to 30.11.2002 – Revoked by S.I. 2002/2302 (W.227) (ISBN 0110905725) – 0 11 090503 2 *£2.50*

The Sheep and Goats Identification and Movement (Interim Measures) (Wales) Regulations 2002 No. 2002/274 (W.30). – Enabling power: European Communities Act 1972, s. 2 (2). – Issued: 22.02.2002. Made: 08.02.2002. Coming into force: 11.02.2002. Effect: S.I. 2000/2335 (W.152) revoked. Territorial extent & classification: W. General. – EC note: Implement provisions of DIR 92/102/EEC on the identification and registration of animals, and provide interim disease control-related measures for the period 11.02.2002 to 30.11.2002. – 12p.: 30 cm. – Revoked by S.I. 2002/1354 (W.131) (ISBN 0110905024) – 0 11 090426 5 *£2.50*

The TSE (Wales) Regulations 2002 No. 2002/1416 (W.142). – Enabling power: European Communities Act 1972, s. 2 (2). – Issued: 30.07.2002. Made: 24.05.2002. Coming into force: 27.05.2002. Effect: S.I. 1997/2964, 2965; 2001/1303 (W.233), 2780 (W.33) amended in relation to Wales & S.I. 2001/2360 (W.197) revoked & S.I. 1996/3183, 3184; 1998/954, 955, 1645, 1646, 1647, 3070; 1999/882 revoked in relation to Wales. Territorial extent & classification: W. General. – EC note: These Regs. make provision in Wales, otherwise than in relation to trade, for the administration and enforcement of the following directly applicable Community REGs regarding certain transmissible spongiform cncephalopathies: 999/2001; 1248/2001 amending Annexes II, X and XI to 999/2001; 1326/2001 laying down transitional measures to permit the changeover to 999/2001 and amending Annexes VII and XI to that REG; 270/2002 amending 999/2001 and amending 1326/2001. – 112p.: 30 cm. – 0 11 090525 3 *£10.50*

Animals, Wales: Prevention of cruelty

The Welfare of Farmed Animals (Wales) (Amendment) Regulations 2002 No. 2002/1898 (W.199). – Enabling power: Agriculture (Miscellaneous Provisions) Act 1968, s. 2. – Issued: 13.08.2002. Made: 18.07.2002. Coming into force: 06.08.2002. Effect: S.I. 2001/2682 (W.223) amended. Territorial extent & classification: W. General– Welsh title: Rheoliadau Les Anifeiliaid a Ffermir (Cymru) (Diwygio) 2002. – EC note: Implements in relation to Wales DIR 1999/74/EC, laying down minimum standards for the protection of hens. – 12p.: 30 cm. – 0 11 090545 8 *£2.50*

Antarctica

The Antarctic (Amendment) Regulations 2002 No. 2002/2054. – Enabling power: Antarctic Act 1994, ss. 9 (1), 10 (1), 25 (1) (3), 32. – Issued: 12.08.2002. Made: 02.08.2002. Laid: 05.08.2002. Coming into force: 27.08.2002. Effect: S.I. 1995/490 amended. Territorial extent & classification: E/W/S/NI. General. – 12p., maps: 30 cm. – 0 11 042630 4 *£2.50*

Architects

The Architects' Qualifications (EC Recognition) Order 2002 No. 2002/2842. – Enabling power: European Communities Act 1972, s. 2 (2). – Issued: 02.12.2002. Made: 20.11.2002. Laid: 02.12.2002. Coming into force: 23.12.2002. Effect: 1997 c.22 amended. Territorial extent & classification: E/W/S/NI. General. – 4p.: 30 cm. – EC note: Implements Directive 2001/19/EC as regards architects. Directive 2001/19/EC amends Council directive 85/384/EEC on the mutual recognition of diplomas in architecture – 0 11 043322 X *£1.75*

Arms and ammunition

The Firearms (Amendment) Act 1988 (Firearms Consultative Committee) Order 2002 No. 2002/127. – Enabling power: Firearms (Amendment) Act 1988, s. 22 (8). – Issued: 08.02.2002. Made: 26.02.2002. Coming into force: 01.02.2002. Effect: S.I. 1996/3272; 2000/177 revoked. Territorial extent & classification: UK. General. – 2p.: 30 cm. – 0 11 039264 7 *£1.50*

Atomic energy and radioactive substances

The Atomic Energy (Americium) 2002 No. 2002/2533. – Enabling power: Atomic Energy Act 1946, s. 18 (1). – Issued: 15.10.2002. Made: 09.10.2002. Laid: 09.10.2002. Coming into force: 01.12.2002. Effect: None. Territorial extent and classification: E/W/S/NI. General. – 2p.: 30 cm. – 0 11 042849 8 *£1.50*

The Atomic Energy Authority (Special Constables) Order 2002 No. 2002/1151. – Enabling power: Anti-terrorism, Crime and Security Act 2001, s. 76 (2). – Issued: 29.04.2002. Made: 18.04.2002. Laid: 24.04.2002. Coming into force: 24.05.2002. Effect: None. Territorial extent and classification: E/W/S/NI General. – 2p.: 30 cm. – 0 11 039836 X *£1.50*

The Radioactive Material (Road Transport) (Definition of Radioactive Material) Order 2002 No. 2002/1092. – Enabling power: Radioactive Material (Road Transport) Act 1991, s. 1 (1) (h). – Issued: 27.05.2002. Made: 16.05.2002. Laid: 17.05.2002. Coming into force: 07.06.2002. Effect: None. Territorial extent & classification: E/W/S. General. – 2p.: 30 cm. – 0 11 042237 6 *£1.50*

The Radioactive Material (Road Transport) Regulations 2002 No. 2002/1093. – Enabling power: Radioactive Material (Road Transport) Act 1991, s. 2 (1) (2) (3). – Issued: 29.05.2002. Made: 16.05.2002. Laid: 17.05.2002. Coming into force: 07.06.2002. Effect: S.I. 1996/1350 revoked. Territorial extent & classification: E/W/S. General. – 96p., col. ill: 30 cm. – EC note: Implement regs made by the International Atomic Energy Agency in its safety standards series for the Safe Transport of Radioactive Material (1996 ed.No.TS-R-1) and additional requirements contained in the European Agreement concerning the international carriage of dangerous goods by road (ADR) as amended up to 1 July 2001. Also implement as respects GB provisions of Directive 96/29/EURATOM and Directive 2001/7/EC – 0 11 042248 1 *£9.50*

The Radioactive Substances (Natural Gas) Exemption Order 2002 No. 2002/1177. – Enabling power: Radioactive Substances Act 1993, s. 8 (6), 15 (2). – Issued: 03.05.2002. Made: 25.04.2002. Laid: 26.04.2002. Coming into force: 17.05.2002. Effect: None. Territorial extent & classification: GB. General. – 4p.: 30 cm. – 0 11 039872 6 *£1.75*

Banks and banking

The Electronic Money (Miscellaneous Amendments) Regulations 2002 No. 2002/765. – Enabling power: European Communities Act 1972, s. 2 (2) & Financial Services and Markets Act 2000, ss. 417 (1), 428 (3), sch. 3, para. 13 (1) (b) (iii). – Issued: 01.05.2002. Made: 21.03.2002. Laid: 21.03.2002. Coming into force: 27.04.2002. Effect: 1985 c. 6; 2000 c. 8; S.I. 1986/1032 (N.I. 6); 1995/1537; 1999/1876, 2979; 2000/262, 369; 2001/2511 amended. Territorial extent & classification: E/W/S/NI. General. – EC note: Make amendments to primary and secondary legislation in consequence of DIR 2000/46/EC on the taking up, pursuit of and prudential supervision of the business of electronic money institutions, and DIR 2000/28/EC amending DIR 2000/12/EC relating to the taking up and pursuit of the business of credit institutions. – 4p.: 30 cm. – 0 11 039855 6 *£1.75*

Betting, gaming and lotteries

The Betting, Gaming and Lotteries Act 1963 (Schedule 4) (Amendment) Order 2002 No. 2002/1930. – Enabling power: Betting, Gaming and Lotteries Act 1963, s. 10 (1C). – Issued: 29.07.2002. Made: 22.07.2002. Coming into force: 19.08.2002. Effect: 1963. c. 2 amended. Territorial extent & classification: E/W/S. General. – 2p.: 30 cm. – Supersedes draft S.I. (ISBN 0110423631) – 0 11 042546 4 *£1.50*

The Gaming Act (Variation of Fees) (England and Wales and Scotland) Order 2002 No. 2002/642. – Enabling power: Gaming Act 1968, ss. 48, 51 (4). – Issued: 15.03.2002. Made: 07.03.2002. Laid: 11.03.2002. Coming into force: 01.04.2002. Effect: S.I. 2000/1212; 2001/726 amended. Territorial extent & classification: E/W/S. General. – 4p.: 30 cm. – 0 11 039474 7 *£1.75*

The Gaming Act (Variation of Monetary Limits) Order 2002 No. 2002/1904. – Enabling power: Gaming Act 1968, ss. 20 (3) (8), 21 (8), 51 (4). – Issued: 29.07.2002. Made: 19.07.2002. Laid: 22.07.2002. Coming into force: 12.08.2002. Effect: 1968 c. 65; S.I. 2000/1213; 2001/757 amended. Territorial extent & classification: E/W/S. General. – 4p.: 30 cm. – 0 11 042537 5 *£1.75*

The Gaming (Bingo) Act (Fees) (Amendment) Order 2002 No. 2002/640. – Enabling power: Gaming (Bingo) Act 1985, sch., para. 5 (1). – Issued: 15.03.2002. Made: 07.03.2002. Laid: 11.03.2002. Coming into force: 01.04.2002. Effect: S.I. 1986/833 amended & S.I. 2001/727 revoked. Territorial extent & classification: E/W/S. General. – 2p.: 30 cm. – 0 11 039473 9 *£1.50*

The Gaming (Bingo) Act (Variation of Monetary Limit) Order 2002 No. 2002/1909. – Enabling power: Gaming (Bingo) Act 1985, ss. 2 (2) (b). – Issued: 29.07.2002. Made: 19.07.2002. Laid: 22.07.2002. Coming into force: 12.08.2002. Effect: S.I. 1998/2153 revoked. Territorial extent & classification: E/W/S. General. – 2p.: 30 cm. – 0 11 042538 3 *£1.50*

The Gaming Clubs (Bankers' Games) (Amendment) (No. 2) Regulations 2002 No. 2002/1407. – Enabling power: Gaming Act 1968, ss. 13 (2), 51. – Issued: 30.05.2002. Made: 22.05.2002. Laid: 23.05.2002. Coming into force: 17.06.2002. Effect: S.I. 1994/2899 amended. Territorial extent & classification: E/W/S. General. – 2p.: 30 cm. – This Statutory instrument has been made in consequence of a defect in S.I. 2002/1130 and is being issued free of charge to all known recipients of that S.I. – 0 11 042265 1 *£1.50*

The Gaming Clubs (Bankers' Games) (Amendment) Regulations 2002 No. 2002/1130. – Enabling power: Gaming Act 1968, ss. 13 (2), 15 (2), 51. – Issued: 24.04.2002. Made: 17.04.2002. Laid: 18.04.2002. Coming into force: 13.05.2002. Effect: S.I. 1994/2899 amended. Territorial extent & classification: E/W/S. General. – 8p.: 30 cm. – 0 11 039811 4 *£2.00*

The Gaming Clubs (Charges) (Amendment) Regulations 2002 No. 2002/1902. – Enabling power: Gaming Act 1968, s. 14 (2). – Issued: 29.07.2002. Made: 19.07.2002. Laid: 22.07.2002. Coming into force: 12.08.2002. Effect: S.I. 1984/248, 470 amended. Territorial extent & classification: E/W/S. General. – 2p.: 30 cm. – 0 11 042535 9 *£1.50*

The Gaming Clubs (Multiple Bingo) (Amendment) Regulations 2002 No. 2002/1901. – Enabling power: Gaming (Bingo) Act 1985, s. 3 (1). – Issued: 29.07.2002. Made: 19.07.2002. Laid: 22.07.2002. Coming into force: 12.08.2002. Effect: S.I. 1986/834 amended. Territorial extent & classification: E/W/S. General. – 2p.: 30 cm. – 0 11 042534 0 *£1.50*

The Lotteries (Gaming Board Fees) Order 2002 No. 2002/639. – Enabling power: Lotteries and Amusements Act 1976, ss. 18 (1) (e) (eee) (2), 24 (2), sch. 1A, paras. 6 (1) (a), sch. 2, para. 7 (1) (b). – Issued: 18.03.2002. Made: 07.03.2002. Laid: 11.03.2002. Coming into force: 01.04.2002. Effect: S.I. 2001/728 revoked. Territorial extent & classification: E/W/S. General. – 4p.: 30 cm. – 0 11 039472 0 *£1.75*

The Lotteries (Variation of Monetary Limits) Order 2002 No. 2002/1410. – Enabling power: Lotteries and Amusements Act 1976, ss. 18 (1) (b), 24 (2). – Issued: 30.05.2002. Made: 23.05.2002. Laid: 24.05.2002. Coming into force: 17.06.2002. Effect: 1976 c. 32 & S.I. 1989/1214, 1218 amended. Territorial extent & classification: E/W/S. General. – 2p.: 30 cm. – 0 11 042266 X   £1.50

Betting, gaming and lotteries, England and Wales

The Gaming Act (Variation of Fees) (England and Wales) Order 2002 No. 2002/637. – Enabling power: Gaming Act 1968, ss. 48, 51 (4). – Issued: 18.03.2002. Made: 07.03.2002. Laid: 11.03.2002. Coming into force: 01.04.2002. Effect: S.I. 2000/1212; 2001/725 amended. Territorial extent & classification: E/W. General. – 4p.: 30 cm. – Revoked by S.I. 2003/508 (ISBN 0110451082) – 0 11 039470 4   £1.75

The Gaming Clubs (Licensing) (Amendment) Regulations 2002 No. 2002/1910. – Enabling power: Gaming Act 1968, ss. 22 (3), 51. – Issued: 29.07.2002. Made: 19.07.2002. Laid: 22.07.2002. Coming into force: 12.08.2002. Effect: S.I. 1969/1110 amended in relation to England and Wales. Territorial extent & classification: E/W. General. – 2p.: 30 cm. – 0 11 042539 1   £1.50

British nationality

The British Overseas Territories Act 2002 (Commencement) Order 2002 No. 2002/1252 (C.34). – Enabling power: British Overseas Territories Act 2002, s. 8 (2). Bringing into operation various provisions of the 2002 Act on 21.05.2002. – Issued: 10.05.2002. Made: 01.05.2002. Effect: None. Territorial extent & classification: E/W/S/NI. General. – 2p.: 30 cm. – 0 11 039915 3   £1.50

British overseas territories

The British Overseas Territories Act 2002 (Commencement) Order 2002 No. 2002/1252 (C.34). – Enabling power: British Overseas Territories Act 2002, s. 8 (2). Bringing into operation various provisions of the 2002 Act on 21.05.2002. – Issued: 10.05.2002. Made: 01.05.2002. Effect: None. Territorial extent & classification: E/W/S/NI. General. – 2p.: 30 cm. – 0 11 039915 3   £1.50

Building and buildings, England and Wales

The Building (Amendment) (No. 2) Regulations 2002 No. 2002/2871. – Enabling power: Building Act 1984, ss. 1 (1), 47 (1), sch. 1, paras. 1, 2, 7, 8, 10. – Issued: 25.11.2002. Made: 16.11.2002. Laid: 25.11.2002. Coming into force: In accordance with reg. 1. Effect: S.I. 2000/2531 amended. Territorial extent & classification: E/W. General. – 8p.: 30 cm. – 0 11 043737 3   £2.00

The Building (Amendment) Regulations 2002 No. 2002/440. – Enabling power: Building Act 1984, s. 1 (1), sch. 1, paras. 2, 4, 10, 11. – Issued: 05.03.2002. Made: 28.02.2002. Laid: 05.03.2002. Coming into force: 01.04.2002. Effect: S.I. 2000/2531 amended & 1984 c. 55 modified. Territorial extent & classification: E/W. General. – 8p.: 30 cm. – With correction slip, dated March 2002, and correction slip dated October 2002 – 0 11 039413 5   £2.00

The Building (Approved Inspectors etc.) (Amendment) Regulations 2002 No. 2002/2872. – Enabling power: Building Act 1984, ss. 1 (1), 35, 47 (1), sch.1, paras. 1, 2, 10. – Issued: 25.11.2002. Made: 16.11.2002. Laid: 25.11.2002. Coming into force: In accord. with reg. 1. Effect: S.I. 2000/2532 amended. Territorial extent & classification: E/W. General. – 4p.: 30 cm. – 0 11 043738 1   £1.75

Canals and inland waterways, England and Wales

The Transport and Works (Applications and Objections Procedure) (England and Wales) (Amendment) Rules 2002 No. 2002/1965. – Enabling power: Transport and Works Act 1992, s. 6 (4) (5). – Issued: 07.08.2002. Made: 24.07.2002. Laid: 25.07.2002. Coming into force: 22.08.2002. Effect: S.I. 2000/2190 amended. Territorial extent & classification: E/W. General. – 4p.: 30 cm. – 0 11 042606 1   £1.75

The Wye Navigation Order 2002 No. 2002/1998. – Enabling power: Transport and Works Act 1992, ss. 3, 5, sch. 1, paras 1, 2, 4, 7, 8, 12, 13, 16. – Issued: 05.08.2002. Made: 25.07.2002. Coming into force: 15.08.2002. Effect: 1985 c. xlii amended & 1662 (13 & 14 Cha. 2) c. xiv; 1695 (7 & 8 Will. 3) c. 14; 1727 (13 Geo. 1) c. 34; 1809 (49 Geo. 3) c. lxxviii repealed (with savings). Territorial extent & classification: E/W. General. – 29p., map: 30 cm. – With correction slip, dated August 2002 – 0 11 042582 0   £6.50

Caribbean and North Atlantic territories

The Turks and Caicos Islands Constitution (Amendment) Order 2002 No. 2002/2637. – Enabling power: West Indies Act 1962, ss. 5, 7. – Issued: 04.11.2002. Made: 22.10.2002. Laid: 04.11.2002. Coming into force: In accordance with s. I (4). Effect: S.I. 1988/247 amended. Territorial extent & classification: E/W/S/NI. General. – 2p.: 30 cm. – 0 11 042904 4   £1.50

Channel Tunnel

The Channel Tunnel (Alcoholic Liquor and Tobacco Products) (Amendment) Order 2002 No. 2002/2693. – Enabling power: Channel Tunnel Act 1987, ss. 11, 13. – Issued: 11.11.2002. Made: 28.10.2002. Laid: 29.10.2002. Coming into force:01.12.2002. Effect: S.I. 2000/426 amended. Territorial extent & classification: E/W/S/NI. General. – 2p.: 30 cm. – 0 11 042945 1   £1.50

Charities, England and Wales

The Charities (Exception from Registration) (Amendment) Regulations 2002 No. 2002/1598. – Enabling power: Charities Act 1993, s. 3 (5) (13). – Issued: 28.06.2002. Made: 18.06.2002. Laid: 25.06.2002. Coming into force: 01.08.2002. Effect: S.I. 1996/180 amended & S.I. 2001/260 revoked. Territorial extent & classification: E/W. General. – 2p.: 30 cm. – 0 11 042393 3 *£1.50*

The Exempt Charities Order 2002 No. 2002/1626. – Enabling power: Charities Act 1993, sch. 2, para. (c). – Issued: 04.07.2002. Made: 26.06.2002. Coming into force: 27.06.2002. Effect: None. Territorial extent & classification: E/W. General. – 2p.: 30 cm. – 0 11 042412 3 *£1.50*

Children and young persons, England

The Care Standards Act 2000 (Commencement No. 13) (England) Order 2002 No. 2002/839 (C.22). – Enabling power: Care Standards Act 2000, ss. 118 (5) and (6), 122. Bringing into operation various provisions of the 2000 Act on 01.04.2002. – Issued: 19.04.2002. Made: 26.03.2002. Effect: None. Territorial extent & classification: E. General. – 8p.: 30 cm. – 0 11 039777 0 *£2.00*

The Care Standards Act 2000 (Commencement No. 14 (England) and Transitional, Savings and Amendment Provisions) Order 2002 No. 2002/1493 (C.43). – Enabling power: Care Standards Act 2000, ss. 118 (5) to (7), 122. Bringing into operation various provisions of the 2000 Act on 01.04.2002. – Issued: 14.06.2002. Made: 27.03.2002. Effect: S.I. 2001/3852, 4150 amended. Territorial extent & classification: E. General. – 12p.: 30 cm. – 0 11 042340 2 *£2.50*

The Care Standards Act 2000 (Commencement No. 15 (England) and Transitional Provisions) (Amendment) Order 2002 No. 2002/1790 (C.55). – Enabling power: Care Standards Act 2000, ss. 118 (5) to (7), 122. – Issued: 24.07.2002. Made: 31.05.2002. Effect: S.I. 2001/3852, 4150 amended. Territorial extent & classification: E. General. – The dates appointed for the coming into force of certain provisions of the Act are altered. – 8p.: 30 cm. – 0 11 042474 3 *£2.00*

The Care Standards Act 2000 (Commencement No. 16) (England) Order 2002 No. 2002/2215 (C.70). – Enabling power: Care Standards Act 2000, ss. 118 (1) (7), 122. Bringing into operation various provisions of the 2000 Act on 02.09.2002. – Issued: 10.09.2002. Made: 28.08.2002. Effect: None. Territorial extent & classification: E. General. – [8]p.: 30 cm. – 0 11 042735 1 *£2.00*

The Care Standards Act 2000 (Establishments and Agencies) (Miscellaneous Amendments) Regulations 2002 No. 2002/865. – Enabling power: Care Standards Act 2000, ss. 12 (2), 22 (1) (2) (a) to (d) (5) (c) (7) (c), 25 (1), 36 (3), 48 (1), 118 (5) to (7) & Children Act 1989, ss. 23 (2) (a) (9), 59 (2), sch. 2, para. 12. – Issued: 09.05.2002. Made: 27.03.2002. Laid:28.03.2002. Coming into force: 18.04.2002. Effect: S.I. 2001/3965, 3967, 3968, 3969; 2002/57 amended. Territorial extent & classification: E. General. – 8p.: 30 cm. – 0 11 039888 2 *£2.00*

Children Act (Miscellaneous Amendments) (England) Regulations 2002 No. 2002/546. – Enabling power: Children Act 1989, ss. 23 (2) (a) (f) (5) (9), 23A (3), 25 (2) (7), 26 (1) (2) (5) (6), 51 (4), 59 (2) to (5), 104 (4), sch. 2, paras. 12 to 14, sch. 4, para. 4 (1) (a), sch. 5, para. 7 (1) (a), sch. 6, paras. 10 (1) (a) (2) (1), & Care Standards Act 2000, s. 119 (1). – Issued: 30.04.2002. Made: 06.03.2002. Laid: 11.03.2002. Coming into force: 01.04.2002. Effect: S.I. 1991/890, 893, 894, 895, 1505, 1507, 2034; 2001/2874 amended. Territorial extent & classification: E. General. – 8p.: 30 cm. – 0 11 039843 2 *£2.00*

The Disqualification from Caring for Children (England) Regulations 2002 No. 2002/635. – Enabling power: Children Act 1989, s. 68 (1) (2). – Issued: 12.04.2002. Made: 07.03.2002. Laid: 11.03.2002. Coming into force: 01.04.2002. Effects: S.I 1999/2094 revoked. Territorial extent & classification: E. General. – 8p.: 30 cm. – 0 11 039721 5 *£2.00*

The Fostering Services Regulations 2002 No. 2002/57. – Enabling power: Care Standards Act 2000, ss. 22 (1) (2) (a) to (c) (e) to (j) (6) (7) (a) to (h) (j), 25 (1), 34 (1), 48 (1), 52 (1), 118 (5) to (7) & Children Act 1989 ss. 23 (2) (a) (9), 59 (2), 62 (3), sch. 2, para. 12. – Issued: 26.02.2002. Made: 14.01.2002. Laid: 15.01.2002. Coming into force: 01.04.2002. Effect: S.I. 1995/2015; 1997/2308; 1999/2768; 2001/2992 amended & S.I. 1991/910 revoked. Territorial extent & classification: E. General. – 35p.: 30 cm. – 0 11 039364 3 *£6.50*

The National Care Standards Commission (Children's Rights Director) Regulations 2002 No. 2002/1250. – Enabling power: Care Standards Act 2000, sch. 1, para. 10 (2). – Issued: 16.05.2002. Made: 01.05.2002. Laid: 03.05.2002. Coming into force: In accord. with reg. 1 (1). Effect: None. Territorial extent & classification: E. General. – 4p.: 30 cm. – 0 11 039934 X *£1.75*

The National Care Standards Commission (Inspection of Schools and Colleges) Regulations 2002 No. 2002/552. – Enabling power: Children Act 1989, ss. 87 (6), 104 (4). – Issued: 10.04.2002. Made: 07.03.2002. Laid: 11.03.2002. Coming into force: 01.04.2002. Effect: S.I. 1991/975 revoked. Territorial extent & classification: E. General. – 4p.: 30 cm. – 0 11 039686 3 *£1.75*

The Residential Family Centres Regulations 2002 No. 2002/3213. – Enabling power: Care Standards Act 2000, ss. 4 (6), 22 (1) (2) (a) to (d) (f) to (j) (5) (a) to (c) (7) (a) to (j), 25 (1), 34 (1), 35 (1), 118 (5) to (7). – Issued: 16.01.2003. Made: 21.12.2002. Laid: 23.12.2002. Coming into force: 01.04.2003. Effect: None. Territorial extent & classification: E. General. – 24p.: 30 cm. – 0 11 044588 0 *£4.00*

Children and young persons, England and Wales

The Care Standards Act 2000 (Commencement No. 11) Order 2002 No. 2002/629 (C.19). – Enabling power: Care Standards Act 2000, ss. 118 (7), 122. Bringing into operation various provisions of the 2000 Act on 18.03.2002, 01.04.2002, in accord. with art. 2 (2) (3). – Issued: 06.06.2002. Made: 15.03.2002. Effect: None. Territorial extent & classification: E/W. General. – 8p.: 30 cm. – 0 11 042304 6   £2.00

The Children and Family Court Advisory and Support Service (Miscellaneous Amendments) Order 2002 No. 2002/3220. – Enabling power: Criminal Justice and Court Services Act 2000, s. 77 (1) (2). – Issued: 03.01.2003. Made: 18.12.2002. Laid: 24.12.2002. Coming into force: 31.01.2003. Effect: S.I. 1983/1964; 1999/2784 (L.22); 2000/415 amended. Territorial extent & classification: E/W. General. – 2p.: 30 cm. – 0 11 044430 2   £1.50

The Local Authority Remands (Electronic Monitoring of Conditions) (Responsible Officer) Order 2002 No. 2002/845. – Enabling power: Children and Young Persons Act 1969, s. 23AA (6). – Issued: 05.04.2002. Made: 26.03.2002. Coming into force: 22.04.2002. Effect: None. Territorial extent & classification: E/W. General. – 8p.: 30 cm. – 0 11 039642 1   £2.00

The Protection of Children Act 1999 (Commencement No. 3) Order 2002 No. 2002/1436 (C. 40). – Enabling power: Protection of Children Act 1999, s. 14 (2). Bringing into operation various provisions of the Act on 12.03.2002 in accord. with art. 2. – Issued: 06.06.2002. Made: 11.03.2002. Effect: None. Territorial extent & classification: E/W. General. – 2p.: 30 cm. – 0 11 042308 9   £1.50

The Protection of Children and Vulnerable Adults and Care Standards Tribunal Regulations 2002 No. 2002/816. – Enabling power: Protection of Children Act 1999, s. 9 (2) to (4), sch. para. 2 (4). – Issued: 17.05.2002. Made: 25.03.2002. Laid: 25.03.2002. Coming into force: in accordance with reg. 1 (1). Effect: S.I. 2000/2619 revoked. Territorial extent & classification: E/W. General. – 36p.: 30 cm. – 0 11 039942 0   £6.50

Children and young persons, Wales

The Arrangements for Placement of Children (General) and the Review of Children's Cases (Amendment) (Wales) Regulations 2002 No. 2002/3013 (W.285). – Enabling power: Children Act 1989, ss. 23 (2) (a) (f), 26 (1) (2) (5) (6), 104 (4). – Issued: 16.12.2002. Made: 04.12.2002. Coming into force: 01.01.2003. Effect: S.I. 1991/890, 895 amended in relation to Wales. Territorial extent & classification: W. General. – In English & Welsh. Welsh title: Rheoliadau Trefniadau ar gyfer Lleoli Plant (Cyffredinol) ac Adolygu Achosion Plant (Diwygio) (Cymru) 2002. – 8p.: 30 cm. – 0 11 090595 4   £2.00

The Care Homes (Wales) Regulations 2002 No. 2002/324 (W.37). – Enabling power: Care Standards Act 2000, ss. 3 (3), 22 (1) (2) (a) to (d) (f) to (j) (5) (7) (a) to (j) (l), 25 (1), 33, 34 (1), 35, 118 (5) to (7). – Issued: 03.04.2002. Made: 12.02.2002. Coming into force: 01.04.2002. Effect: S.I. 1984/1345, 1578 revoked in relation to Wales. Territorial extent & classification: W. General. – In English & Welsh. Welsh title: Rheoliadau Cartrefi Gofal (Cymru) 2002. – 48p.: 30 cm. – 0 11 090452 4   £6.50

The Care Standards Act 2000 (Commencement No. 8 (Wales) and Transitional, Savings and Consequential Provisions) Order 2002 No. 2002/920 (W.108) (C.24). – Enabling power: Care Standards Act 2000, ss. 118 (5) to (7), 119, 122. Bringing into operation various provisions of the 2000 Act on 01.04.2002, in accord. with arts. 2, 3. – Issued: 24.06.2002. Made: 28.03.2002. Effect: S.I. 1996/708 amended. Territorial extent & classification: W. General. – 24p.: 30 cm. – 0 11 090509 1   £4.00

The Child Minding and Day Care (Wales) (Amendment) Regulations 2002 No. 2002/2171 (W.218). – Enabling power: Children Act 1989, ss. 79C, 79E, 104 (4). – Issued: 29.08.2002. Made: 22.07.2002 at 11.45 am. Coming into force: 22.07.2002 at 12 noon. Effect: S.I. 2002/812, 919 amended. Territorial extent & classification: W. General. – In English & Welsh. Welsh title: Rheoliadau Gwarchod Plant a Gofal Dydd (Cymru) (Diwygio) 2002. – [8]p.: 30 cm. – Revoked by S.I. 2002/2622 (W.254) (ISBN 0110905784) – 0 11 090561 X   £2.00

The Child Minding and Day Care (Wales) Regulations 2002 No. 2002/812 (W.92). – Enabling power: Children Act 1989, ss. 79C, 104 (4). – Issued: 01.05.2002. Made: 21.03.2002 at 1600 hours. Coming into force: 01.04.2002. Effect: None. Territorial extent & classification: W. General. – In English & Welsh. Welsh title: Rheoliadau Gwarchod Plant a Gofal Dydd (Cymru) 2002. – 28p.: 30 cm. – 0 11 090477 X   £4.50

The Children Act 1989 and the Care Standards Act 2000 (Miscellaneous Regulations) (Amendment) (Wales) (No. 2) Regulations 2002 No. 2002/2935 (W.277). – Enabling power: Children Act 1989, ss. 23 (2) (a) (f) (5) (9), 23A (3), 25 (2) (7), 26 (1) (2) (5) (6), 51 (4), 59 (2) to (5), 104 (4), sch. 2, paras. 13, 14, sch. 4, para. 4 (1) (a), sch. 5, para. 7 (1) (a), sch. 6, para. 10 (1) (a) (2) (l) & Care Standards Act 2000, ss. 3 (3), 12 (2) (a), 16 (1) (a) (3), 22 (1), 118 (6). – Issued: 20.12.2002. Made: 27.11.2002. Coming into force: 31.12.2002. Effect: S.I. 1991/890, 893, 894, 895, 1505, 1507, 2034; 2001/2189; 2002/324, 919, 921 amended. Territorial extent & classification: W. General. – 8p.: 30 cm. – In English and Welsh. Welsh title: Rheoliadau Deddf Plant 1989 a Deddf Safonau Gofal 2000 (Rheoliadau Amrywiol) (Diwygio) (Cymru) (Rhif 2) 2002 – 0 11 090601 2   £2.00

The Children Act 1989 and the Care Standards Act 2000 (Miscellaneous Regulations) (Amendment) (Wales) Regulations 2002 No. 2002/2622 (W.254). – Enabling power: Care Standards Act 2000, ss. 12 (2) (a), 16 (1) (a), 22 (1), (2) (a) (b), (7) (c), 118 (5) (6) & Children Act 1989, ss. 79C (2) (3) (b) (f) (g), 79E (2) (a), 104 (4). – Issued: 19.11.2002. Made: 17.10.2002. Coming into force: 18.10.2002. Effect: S.I. 2002/324 (W.37), 325 (W.38), 327 (W.40), 812 (W.192), 919 (W.107) amended & S.I. 2002/2171 (W.218) revoked. Territorial extent & classification: W. General. – 16p.: 30 cm. – In English and Welsh. - Welsh title: Rheoliadau Deddf Plant 1989 a Deddf Safonau Gofal 2000 (Rheoliadau Amrywiol) (Diwygio) (Cymru) 2002 –0 11 090578 4 *£3.00*

The Children (Leaving Care) (Amendment) (Wales) Regulations 2002 No. 2002/1855 (W.179). – Enabling power: Children Act 1989, ss. 23A (3), 104 (4), sch. 2, para. 19B (3). – Issued: 01.08.2002. Made: 16.07.2002. Coming into force: 01.08.2002. Effect: S.I. 2001/2189 (W.151) amended. Territorial extent & classification: W. General. – 4p.: 30 cm. – In English and Welsh. - Welsh title: Rheoliadau Plant (Ymadael â Gofal) (Diwygio) (Cymru) 2002 – 0 11 090529 6 *£1.75*

The Children's Homes (Wales) Regulations 2002 No. 2002/327 (W.40). – Enabling power: Care Standards Act 2000, ss. 1 (4), 22 (1) (2) (a) to (d) (f) to (j) (5) (a) (c) (7) (a) to (h) (j) (8) (c), 25 (1), 33, 34 (1), 35, 118 (5) to (7). – Issued: 28.03.2002. Made: 12.02.2002. Coming into force: 01.04.2002. Effect: S.I. 1993/3069; 1997/2308 amended & 1991/1506; 1994/1511 revoked in relation to Wales & S.I. 2001/140 revoked. Territorial extent & classification: W. General. – In English & Welsh. Welsh title: Rheoliadau Cartrefi Plant (Cymru) 2002. – 48p.: 30 cm. – 0 11 090448 6 *£6.50*

The Disqualification from Caring for Children (Wales) Regulations 2002 No. 2002/896 (W.102). – Enabling power: Children Act 1989, ss. 68 (1) (2), 104 (4), sch. 9A, para. 4. – Issued: 19.08.2002. Made: 26.03.2002. Coming into force: 01.04.2002. Effect: S.I. 1991/2094 revoked in relation to Wales. Territorial extent & classification: W. General. – 16p.: 30 cm. – In English and Welsh. - Welsh title: Rheoliadau Datgymhwyso rhag Gofalu am Blant (Cymru) 2002 – 0 11 090553 9 *£3.00*

The Inspection of Boarding Schools and Colleges (Powers and Fees) (Wales) Regulations 2002 No. 2002/3161 (W.296). – Enabling power: Children Act 1989, ss. 87 (6), 87D (2), 104 (4). – Issued: 15.01.2003. Made: 17.12.2002. Coming into force: 01.02.2003. Effect: S.I. 2002/921 (W.109) amended & S.I. 1991/975 revoked in relation to Wales. Territorial extent & classification: W. General. – 8p.: 30 cm. – In English and Welsh. Welsh title: Rheoliadau Arolygu Ysgolion a Cholegau Preswyl (Pwerau a Ffioedd) (Cymru) 2002 – 0 11 090616 0 *£2.00*

The Registration of Social Care and Independent Healthcare (Fees) (Wales) Regulations 2002 No. 2002/921 (W.109). – Enabling power: Care Standards Act 2000, ss. 12 (2), 15 (3), 16 (3), 118 (5) to (7) & Children Act 1989, ss. 79F, 104 (4), sch. 9A, para. 7. – Issued: 20.06.2002. Made: 28.03.2002. Coming into force: 01.04.2002. Effect: None. Territorial extent & classification: W. General. – 8p.: 30 cm. – 0 11 090507 5 *£2.00*

The Registration of Social Care and Independent Health Care (Wales) Regulations 2002 No. 2002/919 (W.107). – Enabling power: Care Standards Act 2000, ss. 12 (2), 14 (1) (d), 15 (3), 16 (1), 25 (1), 118 (5) to (7) & Children Act 1989, ss. 79E (2), 104 (4), sch. 9A, para. 6 (2). – Issued: 21.06.2002. Made: 28.03.2002. Coming into force: 01.04.2002. Effect: None. Territorial extent & classification: W. General. – 24p.: 30 cm. – 0 11 090506 7 *£4.00*

Chiropractors

The Chiropractors Act 1994 (Commencement No.6) Order 2002 No. 2002/312 (C.6). – Enabling power: Chiropractors Act 1994, s. 44 (3). Bringing into operation various provisions of the 1994 Act in accordance with art. 2. – Issued: 21.02.2002. Made: 31.01.2002. Effect: None. Territorial extent & classification: E/W/S/NI. General. – 4p.: 30 cm. – 0 11 039339 2 *£1.75*

The General Chiropractic Council (Election of Members and Chairman of Council) Rules Order 2002 No. 2002/1263. – Enabling power: Chiropractors Act 1994, s. 35 (2), sch. 1, paras. 10, 14 (5) (a). – Issued: 13.05.2002. Made: 20.03.2002. Coming into force: 28.03.2002. Effect: None. Territorial extent & classification: E/W/S/NI. General. – 12p.: 30 cm. – 0 11 039918 8 *£2.50*

The General Chiropractic Council (Registration of Chiropractors with Foreign Qualifications) Rules Order of Council 2002 No. 2002/2704. – Enabling power: Chiropractors Act 1994, ss. 3 (2) (6), 6 (2) to (4), 14 (4), 35 (2). – Issued: 05.11.2002. Made: 10.10.2002. Coming into force: 06.11.2002. Effect: None. Territorial extent & classification: E/W/S/NI. General. – 25, [1]p.: 30 cm. – 0 11 042928 1 *£4.50*

Chronically sick and disabled persons

The Health and Social Care Act 2001 (Commencement No. 9) Order 2002 No. 2002/1312 (C.36). – Enabling power: Health and Social Care Act 2001, s. 70 (2). Bringing into force various provisions of the 2001 Act on 15.04.2002 in accord. with arts. 2, 3. – Issued: 20.05.2002. Made: 14.04.2002. Effect: None. Territorial extent & classification: E/W/S. General. – 4p.: 30 cm. – 0 11 039943 9 *£1.75*

Cinemas and films

The European Convention on Cinematographic Co-production (Amendment) (No. 2) Order 2002 No. 2002/2635. – Enabling power: Films Act 1985, sch.1, para. 4 (7). – Issued: 28.10.2002. Made: 22.10.2002. Coming into force: 01.12.2002. Effect: S.I. 1994/1065 amended. Territorial extent & classification: E/W/S/NI. General. – 2p.: 30 cm. – 0 11 042899 4 *£1.50*

The European Convention on Cinematographic Co-production (Amendment) Order 2002 No. 2002/1398. – Enabling power: Films Act 1985, sch.1, para. 4 (7). – Issued: 28.05.2002. Made: 22.05.2002. Coming into force: 01.07.2002. Effect: S.I. 1994/1065 amended. Territorial extent & classification: E/W/S/NI. General. – 2p.: 30 cm. – 0 11 042245 7 *£1.50*

Cinemas and films, England and Wales

The Cinematograph (Safety) (Amendment) Regulations 2002 No. 2002/1903. – Enabling power: Cinemas Act 1985, s. 4 (1) (2) (a). – Issued: 29.07.2002. Made: 19.07.2002. Laid: 22.07.2002. Coming into force: 12.08.2002. Effect: S.I. 1955/1129 amended in relation to England and Wales. Territorial extent & classification: E/W. General. – 2p.: 30 cm. – 0 11 042536 7 *£1.50*

Civil aviation

The Aerodromes (Designation) (Facilities for Consultation) (Amendment) Order 2002 No. 2002/2421. – Enabling power: Civil Aviation Act 1982, s. 35 (1). – Issued: 04.10.2002. Made: 04.10.2002. Laid: 24.09.2002. Coming into force: 15.10.2002. Effect: S.I. 1996/1392 amended. Territorial extent & classification: E/W/S/NI. General. – 2p.: 30 cm. – 0 11 042828 5 *£1.50*

The Air Navigation (Amendment) (No. 2) Order 2002 No. 2002/1628. – Enabling power: Civil Aviation Act 1982, ss. 60 (other than (3) (r)), 61, 102, sch. 13. – Issued: 08.07.2002. Made: 26.06.2002. Laid: 08.07.2002. Coming into force: 30.07.2002. Effect: S.I. 2000/1562 amended. Territorial extent & classification: E/W/S/NI. General. – 4p.: 30 cm. – 0 11 042406 9 *£1.75*

The Air Navigation (Amendment) Order 2002 No. 2002/264. – Enabling power: Civil Aviation Act 1982, ss. 60 (other than sub-section (3) (r)), 61, 102, sch. 13– Issued: 22.02.2002. Made: 12.02.2002. Laid: 22.02.2002. Coming into force: 01.04.2002. Effect: S.I. 2000/1562 amended. Territorial extent & classification: E/W/S/NI. General. – 8p.: 30 cm. – 0 11 039333 3 *£2.00*

The Air Navigation (Dangerous Goods) Regulations 2002 No. 2002/2786. – Enabling power: S.I. 2000/1562, arts. 60 (1), 129 (5). – Issued: 19.11.2002. Made: 11.11.2002. Coming into force: 02.12.2002. Effect: S.I. 1994/3187; 1996/3100; 1997/2666; 1998/2536; 2001/918 revoked. Territorial extent & classification: E/W/S/NI. General. – 16p.: 30 cm. – 0 11 042971 0 *£3.00*

The Air Navigation (Environmental Standards) Order 2002 No. 2002/798. – Enabling power: Civil Aviation Act 1982, ss. 60 (1) (2) (a) (b) (3) (q) (r), 61 (1), 101 (1) (a), 102 (1) (2). – Issued: 04.04.2002. Made: 26.03.2002. Coming into force: 05.04.2002. Effect: S.I. 1986/599; 1988/1994; 1990/1514 revoked. Territorial extent & classification: E/W/S/NI. General. – Supersedes draft S.I. (ISBN 0110390865) issued 31 December 2001. – 20p.: 30 cm. – 0 11 039638 3 *£3.50*

The Air Navigation (General) (Amendment) Regulations 2002 No. 2002/733. – Enabling power: S.I. 2000/1562, art. 36 (1). – Issued: 25.03.2002. Made: 13.03.2002. Coming into force: 03.04.2002. Effect: S.I. 1993/1622 amended. Territorial extent & classification: E/W/S/NI. General. – 4p.: 30 cm. – 0 11 039521 2 *£1.75*

The Air Navigation (Jersey) (Amendment No, 2) Order 2002 No. 2002/1078. – Enabling power: Civil Aviation Act 1982, ss. 60 (3) (d) (h), 102, sch. 13. – Issued: 24.04.2002. Made: 17.04.2002. Coming into force: 24.04.2002. Effect: S.I. 2000/1346 amended. Territorial extent & classification: Jersey. General. – 2p.: 30 cm. – 0 11 039801 7 *£1.50*

The Air Navigation (Restriction of Flying) (Beating Retreat Ceremony) Regulations 2002 No. 2002/1469. – Enabling power: S.I. 2000/1562, art. 85. – Made: 29.05.2002. Coming into force: 11.06.2002. Effect: None. Territorial extent & classification: E. Local *Unpublished*

The Air Navigation (Restriction of Flying) (Biggin Hill) Regulations 2002 No. 2002/464. – Enabling power: S.I. 2000/1562, art. 85. – Made: 01.03.2002. Coming into force: 02.06.2002. Effect: None. Territorial extent & classification: E. Local *Unpublished*

The Air Navigation (Restriction of Flying) (Birmingham) Regulations 2002 No. 2002/24. – Enabling power: S.I. 2000/1562, art. 85. – Made: 04.01.2002. Coming into force: forthwith. Effect: None. Territorial extent & classification: E. Local – Revoked by S.I. 2002/25 (unpublished) *Unpublished*

The Air Navigation (Restriction of Flying) (Birmingham) (Revocation) Regulations 2002 No. 2002/25. – Enabling power: S.I. 2000/1562, art. 85. – Made: 07.01.2002. Coming into force: forthwith. Effect: S.I. 2002/24 revoked. Territorial extent & classification: E. Local *Unpublished*

The Air Navigation (Restriction of Flying) (Blackpool) Regulations 2002 No. 2002/1709. – Enabling power: S.I. 2000/1562, art. 85. – Made: 01.07.2002. Coming into force: 29.09.2002. Effect: None. Territorial extent & classification: E. Local *Unpublished*

The Air Navigation (Restriction of Flying) (Bournemouth) Regulations 2002 No. 2002/1996. – Enabling power: S.I. 2000/1562, art. 85. – Made: 19.07.2002. Coming into force: 06.10.2002. Effect: None. Territorial extent & classification: E. Local *Unpublished*

The Air Navigation (Restriction of Flying) (Brands Hatch) Regulations 2002 No. 2002/1707. – Enabling power: S.I. 2000/1562, art. 85. – Made: 01.07.2002. Coming into force: 28.07.2002. Effect: None. Territorial extent & classification: E. Local *Unpublished*

The Air Navigation (Restriction of Flying) (Buckingham Palace) Regulations 2002 No. 2002/1413. – Enabling power: S.I. 2000/1562, art. 85. – Made: 21.05.2002. Coming into force: 01.06.2002. Effect: None. Territorial extent & classification: E. Local *Unpublished*

The Air Navigation (Restriction of Flying) (Cardiff) (Amendment) Regulations 2002 No. 2002/290. – Enabling power: S.I. 2000/1562, art. 85. – Made: 01.02.2002. Coming into force: 02.02.2002. Effect: S.I. 2002/51 amended. Territorial extent & classification: E. Local *Unpublished*

The Air Navigation (Restriction of Flying) (Cardiff) Regulations 2002 No. 2002/51. – Enabling power: S.I. 2000/1562, art. 85. – Made: 11.01.2002. Coming into force: 31.01.2002. Effect: None. Territorial extent & classification: E. Local *Unpublished*

The Air Navigation (Restriction of Flying) (Central London) Regulations 2002 No. 2002/1024. – Enabling power: S.I. 2000/1562, art. 85. – Made: 08.04.2002. Coming into force: 09.04.2002. Effect: None. Territorial extent & classification: E. Local *Unpublished*

The Air Navigation (Restriction of Flying) (Cranfield) Regulations 2002 No. 2002/466. – Enabling power: S.I. 2000/1562, art. 85. – Made: 01.03.2002. Coming into force: 21.06.2002. Effect: None. Territorial extent & classification: E. Local *Unpublished*

The Air Navigation (Restriction of Flying) (Duxford) (No. 2) Regulations 2002 No. 2002/1228. – Enabling power: S.I. 2000/1562, art. 85. – Made: 29.04.2002. Coming into force: 13.07.2002. Effect: None. Territorial extent & classification: E. Local *Unpublished*

The Air Navigation (Restriction of Flying) (Duxford) (No. 3) Regulations 2002 No. 2002/1229. – Enabling power: S.I. 2000/1562, art. 85. – Made: 29.04.2002. Coming into force: 07.09.2002. Effect: None. Territorial extent & classification: E. Local *Unpublished*

The Air Navigation (Restriction of Flying) (Duxford) (No. 4) Regulations 2002 No. 2002/1230. – Enabling power: S.I. 2000/1562, art. 85. – Made: 29.04.2002. Coming into force: 13.10.2002. Effect: None. Territorial extent & classification: E. Local *Unpublished*

The Air Navigation (Restriction of Flying) (Duxford) Regulations 2002 No. 2002/1165. – Enabling power: S.I. 2000/1562, art. 85. – Made: 18.04.2002. Coming into force: 05.05.2002. Effect: None. Territorial extent & classification: E. Local *Unpublished*

The Air Navigation (Restriction of Flying) (Eastbourne) Regulations 2002 No. 2002/1704. – Enabling power: S.I. 2000/1562, art. 85. – Made: 17.06.2002. Coming into force: 15.08.2002. Effect: None. Territorial extent & classification: E. Local *Unpublished*

The Air Navigation (Restriction of Flying) (Fairford) Regulations 2002 No. 2002/1020. – Enabling power: S.I. 2000/1562, art. 85. – Made: 08.04.2002. Coming into force: 17.07.2002. Effect: None. Territorial extent & classification: E. Local *Unpublished*

The Air Navigation (Restriction of Flying) (Farnborough) Regulations 2002 No. 2002/734. – Enabling power: S.I. 2000/1562, art. 85. – Made: 15.03.2002. Coming into force: 15.07.2002. Effect: None. Territorial extent & classification: E. Local *Unpublished*

The Air Navigation (Restriction of Flying) (Foot and Mouth Disease) (Burial Sites) (Revocation) Regulations 2002 No. 2002/291. – Enabling power: S.I. 2000/1562, art. 85. – Made: 08.02.2002. Coming into force: Forthwith. Effect: S.I. 2001/2002 revoked. Territorial extent & classification: E. Local *Unpublished*

The Air Navigation (Restriction of Flying) (Foot and Mouth Disease) (Revocation) Regulations 2002 No. 2002/292. – Enabling power: S.I. 2000/1562, art. 85. – Made: 08.02.2002. Coming into force: Forthwith. Effect: S.I. 2001/1676 revoked. Territorial extent & classification: E. Local *Unpublished*

The Air Navigation (Restriction of Flying) (Glastonbury) Regulations 2002 No. 2002/1023. – Enabling power: S.I. 2000/1562, art. 85. – Made: 08.04.2002. Coming into force: 27.06.2002. Effect: None. Territorial extent & classification: E. Local *Unpublished*

The Air Navigation (Restriction of Flying) (Golden Jubilee) Regulations 2002 No. 2002/1412. – Enabling power: S.I. 2000/1562, art. 85. – Made: 21.05.2002. Coming into force: 04.06.2002. Effect: None. Territorial extent & classification: E. Local *Unpublished*

The Air Navigation (Restriction of Flying) (Haymarket) (Central London) Regulations 2002 No. 2002/1706. – Enabling power: S.I. 2000/1562, art. 85. – Made: 27.06.2002. Coming into force: forthwith. Effect: None. Territorial extent & classification: E. Local – Revoked by S.I. 2002/1705 (unpublished) *Unpublished*

The Air Navigation (Restriction of Flying) (Haymarket) (Central London) (Revocation) Regulations 2002 No. 2002/1705. – Enabling power: S.I. 2000/1562, art. 85. – Made: 27.06.2002. Coming into force: forthwith. Effect: S.I. 2002/1706 revoked. Territorial extent & classification: E. Local *Unpublished*

The Air Navigation (Restriction of Flying) (Henstridge) Regulations 2002 No. 2002/2218. – Enabling power: S.I. 2000/1562, art. 85. – Made: 27.08.2002. Coming into force: forthwith. Effect: None. Territorial extent & classification: E. Local – Revoked by S.I. 2002/2222 (unpublished) *Unpublished*

The Air Navigation (Restriction of Flying) (Henstridge) (Revocation) Regulations 2002 No. 2002/2222. – Enabling power: S.I. 2000/1562, art. 85. – Made: 28.08.2002. Coming into force: forthwith. Effect: S.I. 2002/2218 revoked. Territorial extent & classification: E. Local *Unpublished*

The Air Navigation (Restriction of Flying) (Hillsborough Castle) Regulations 2002 No. 2002/1725. – Enabling power: S.I. 2000/1562, art. 85. – Made: 03.07.2002. Coming into force: 04.07.2002. Effect: None. Territorial extent & classification: E. Local *Unpublished*

The Air Navigation (Restriction of Flying) (Jet Formation Display Teams) (No. 2) (Amendment) Regulations 2002 No. 2002/1075. – Enabling power: S.I. 2000/1562, art. 85. – Made: 10.04.2002. Coming into force: 25.05.2002. Effect: S.I. 2002/776 amended. Territorial extent & classification: E/W.S.NI. Local *Unpublished*

The Air Navigation (Restriction of Flying) (Jet Formation Display Teams) (No. 2) Regulations 2002 No. 2002/776. – Enabling power: S.I. 2000/1562, art. 85. – Made: 20.03.2002. Coming into force: 02.06.2002. Effect: None. Territorial extent & classification: E. Local *Unpublished*

The Air Navigation (Restriction of Flying) (Jet Formation Display Teams) (No. 2) (Second Amendment) Regulations 2002 No. 2002/1713. – Enabling power: S.I. 2000/1562, art. 85. – Made: 20.06.2002. Coming into force: 03.07.2002. Effect: S.I. 2002/776 amended. Territorial extent & classification: E. Local *Unpublished*

The Air Navigation (Restriction of Flying) (Jet Formation Display Teams) (No. 2) (Third Amendment) Regulations 2002 No. 2002/1839. – Enabling power: S.I. 2000/1562, art. 85. – Made: 11.07.2002. Coming into force: 19.07.2002. Effect: S.I. 2002/776 amended. Territorial extent & classification: E. Local *Unpublished*

The Air Navigation (Restriction of Flying) (Jet Formation Display Teams) (No. 3) Regulations 2002 No. 2002/2121. – Enabling power: S.I. 2000/1562, art. 85. – Made: 09.08.2002. Coming into force: 15.08.2002. Effect: None. Territorial extent & classification: E. Local *Unpublished*

The Air Navigation (Restriction of Flying) (Jet Formation Display Teams) Regulations 2002 No. 2002/463. – Enabling power: S.I. 2000/1562, art. 85. – Made: 01.03.2002. Coming into force: 20.03.2002. Effect: None. Territorial extent & classification: E. Local *Unpublished*

The Air Navigation (Restriction of Flying) (Lewknor) Regulations 2002 No. 2002/932. – Enabling power: S.I. 2000/1562, art. 85. – Made: 28.03.2002. Coming into force: forthwith. Effect: None. Territorial extent & classification: E. Local – Revoked by S.I. 2002/1026 (unpublished) *Unpublished*

The Air Navigation (Restriction of Flying) (Lewknor) (Revocation) Regulations 2002 No. 2002/1026. – Enabling power: S.I. 2000/1562, art. 85. – Made: 28.03.2002. Coming into force: forthwith. Effect: S.I. 2002/932 revoked. Territorial extent & classification: E. Local *Unpublished*

The Air Navigation (Restriction of Flying) (Manchester) Regulations 2002 No. 2002/1018. – Enabling power: S.I. 2000/1562, art. 85. Made: 08.04.2002. Coming into force: 22.07.2002. Effect: None. Territorial extent & classification: E. Local *Unpublished*

The Air Navigation (Restriction of Flying) (Millennium Dome) Regulations 2002 No. 2002/3073. – Enabling power: S.I. 2000/1562, art. 85. – Made: 11.12.2002. Coming into force: 31.12.2002. Effect: None. Territorial extent & classification: E. Local *Unpublished*

The Air Navigation (Restriction of Flying) (Newmarket) Regulations 2002 No. 2002/2138. – Enabling power: S.I. 2000/1562, art. 85. – Made: 13.08.2002. Coming into force: forthwith. Effect: None. Territorial extent & classification: E. Local – Revoked by S.I. 2002/2139 (unpublished) *Unpublished*

The Air Navigation (Restriction of Flying) (Newmarket) (Revocation) Regulations 2002 No. 2002/2139. – Enabling power: S.I. 2000/1562, art. 85. – Made: 14.08.2002. Coming into force: forthwith. Effect: S.I. 2002/2138 revoked. Territorial extent & classification: E. Local *Unpublished*

The Air Navigation (Restriction of Flying) (North Weald) Regulations 2002 No. 2002/294. – Enabling power: S.I. 2000/1562, art. 85. – Made: 08.02.2002. Coming into force: 17.05.2002. Effect: None. Territorial extent & classification: E. Local *Unpublished*

The Air Navigation (Restriction of Flying) (Nuclear Installations) (No. 2) (Second Amendment) Regulations 2002 No. 2002/1382. – Enabling power: S.I. 2000/1562, art. 85. – Made: 10.05.2002. Coming into force: forthwith. Effect: S.I. 2001/3768 amended. Territorial extent & classification: E. Local – Revoked by S.I. 2002/2254 (unpublished) *Unpublished*

The Air Navigation (Restriction of Flying) (Nuclear Installations) Regulations 2002 No. 2002/2254. – Enabling power: S.I. 2000/1562, art. 85. – Made: 02.09.2002. Coming into force: 05.09.2002. Effect: S.I. 2001/1607, 3600, 3768; 2002/1382 revoked. Territorial extent & classification: E. Local *Unpublished*

The Air Navigation (Restriction of Flying) (Pershore) Regulations 2002 No. 2002/3074. – Enabling power: S.I. 2000/1562, art. 85. – Made: 11.12.2002. Coming into force: 01.03.2003. Effect: None. Territorial extent & classification: E. Local – Revoked by S.I. 2003/1135 (unpublished) *Unpublished*

The Air Navigation (Restriction of Flying) (Perth) Regulations 2002 No. 2002/52. – Enabling power: S.I. 2000/1562, art. 85. – Made: 11.01.2002. Coming into force: 22.02.2002. Effect: None. Territorial extent & classification: E. Local *Unpublished*

The Air Navigation (Restriction of Flying) (Portadown) Regulations 2002 No. 2002/1022. – Enabling power: S.I. 2000/1562, art. 85. – Made: 08.04.2002. Coming into force: 27.06.2002. Effect: None. Territorial extent & classification: NI. Local *Unpublished*

The Air Navigation (Restriction of Flying) (Portsmouth and the English Channel) Regulations 2002 No. 2002/735. – Enabling power: S.I. 2000/1562, art. 85. – Made: 15.03.2002. Coming into force: 24.06.2002. Effect: None. Territorial extent & classification: E. Local *Unpublished*

The Air Navigation (Restriction of Flying) (Potter's Bar) Regulations 2002 No. 2002/1381. – Enabling power: S.I. 2000/1562, art. 85. – Made: 10.05.2002. Coming into force: forthwith. Effect: None. Territorial extent & classification: E. Local – Revoked by S.I. 2002/1380 (unpublished) *Unpublished*

The Air Navigation (Restriction of Flying) (Potter's Bar) (Revocation) Regulations 2002 No. 2002/1380. – Enabling power: S.I. 2000/1562, art. 85. – Made: 15.05.2002. Coming into force: forthwith. Effect: S.I. 2002/1381 revoked. Territorial extent & classification: E. Local *Unpublished*

The Air Navigation (Restriction of Flying) (Remembrance Sunday) Regulations 2002 No. 2002/2592. – Enabling power: S.I. 2000/1562, art. 85. – Made: 10.10.2002. Coming into force: 10.11.2002. Effect: None. Territorial extent & classification: E. Local *Unpublished*

The Air Navigation (Restriction of Flying) (Rivington) Regulations 2002 No. 2002/1017. – Enabling power: S.I. 2000/1562, art. 85. – Made: 08.04.2002. Coming into force: 22.07.2002. Effect: None. Territorial extent & classification: E. Local *Unpublished*

The Air Navigation (Restriction of Flying) (Royal Air Force Leuchars) Regulations 2002 No. 2002/1708. – Enabling power: S.I. 2000/1562, art. 85. – Made: 01.07.2002. Coming into force: 13.09.2002. Effect: None. Territorial extent & classification: E. Local *Unpublished*

The Air Navigation (Restriction of Flying) (Royal Air Force Waddington) Regulations 2002 No. 2002/1021. – Enabling power: S.I. 2000/1562, art. 85. – Made: 08.04.2002. Coming into force: 27.06.2002. Effect: None. Territorial extent & classification: E. Local *Unpublished*

The Air Navigation (Restriction of Flying) (Royal Albert Hall) Regulations 2002 No. 2002/2591. – Enabling power: S.I. 2000/1562, art. 85. – Made: 10.10.2002. Coming into force: 09.11.2002. Effect: None. Territorial extent & classification: E. Local *Unpublished*

The Air Navigation (Restriction of Flying) (Security Establishments in Northern Ireland) (Amendment) Regulations 2002 No. 2002/2747. – Enabling power: S.I. 2000/1562, art. 85. – Made: 31.10.2002. Coming into force: 01.01.2003. Effect: S.I. 1996/861 amended. Territorial extent & classification: NI. Local *Unpublished*

The Air Navigation (Restriction of Flying) (Silverstone and Turweston) Regulations 2002 No. 2002/1019. – Enabling power: S.I. 2000/1562, art. 85. – Made: 08.04.2002. Coming into force: 06.07.2002. Effect: None. Territorial extent & classification: E. Local *Unpublished*

The Air Navigation (Restriction of Flying) (Soham) Regulations 2002 No. 2002/2167. – Enabling power: S.I. 2000/1562, art. 85. – Made: 16.08.2002. Coming into force: forthwith. Effect: None. Territorial extent & classification: E. Local – Revoked by S.I. 2002/2168 (unpublished) *Unpublished*

The Air Navigation (Restriction of Flying) (Soham) (Revocation) Regulations 2002 No. 2002/2168. – Enabling power: S.I. 2000/1562, art. 85. – Made: 19.08.2002. Coming into force: forthwith. Effect: S.I. 2002/2167 revoked. Territorial extent & classification: E. Local *Unpublished*

The Air Navigation (Restriction of Flying) (Southend) Regulations 2002 No. 2002/465. – Enabling power: S.I. 2000/1562, art. 85. – Made: 01.03.2002. Coming into force: 02.06.2002. Effect: None. Territorial extent & classification: E. Local *Unpublished*

The Air Navigation (Restriction of Flying) (Southport) Regulations 2002 No. 2002/1712. – Enabling power: S.I. 2000/1562, art. 85. – Made: 17.06.2002. Coming into force: 31.08.2002. Effect: None. Territorial extent & classification: E. Local *Unpublished*

The Air Navigation (Restriction of Flying) (State Opening of Parliament) Regulations 2002 No. 2002/2746. – Enabling power: S.I. 2000/1562, art. 85. – Made: 31.10.2002. Coming into force: 13.11.2002. Effect: None. Territorial extent & classification: E. Local *Unpublished*

The Air Navigation (Restriction of Flying) (Stoke Newington) Regulations 2002 No. 2002/293. – Enabling power: S.I. 2000/1562, art. 85. – Made: 08.02.2002. Coming into force: 24.02.2002. Effect: None. Territorial extent & classification: E. Local *Unpublished*

The Air Navigation (Restriction of Flying) (St Paul's Cathedral) Regulations 2002 No. 2002/2255. – Enabling power: S.I. 2000/1562, art. 85. – Made: 02.09.2002. Coming into force: 11.09.2002. Effect: None. Territorial extent & classification: E. Local *Unpublished*

The Air Navigation (Restriction of Flying) (Sunbury) Regulations 2002 No. 2002/1232. – Enabling power: S.I. 2000/1562, art. 85. – Made: 23.04.2002. Coming into force: forthwith. Effect: None. Territorial extent & classification: E. Local – Revoked by S.I. 2002/1233 (unpublished) *Unpublished*

The Air Navigation (Restriction of Flying) (Sunbury) (Revocation) Regulations 2002 No. 2002/1233. – Enabling power: S.I. 2000/1562, art. 85. – Made: 25.04.2002. Coming into force: forthwith. Effect: S.I. 2002/1232 revoked. Territorial extent & classification: E. Local *Unpublished*

The Air Navigation (Restriction of Flying) (Sunderland) Regulations 2002 No. 2002/1231. – Enabling power: S.I. 2000/1562, art. 85. – Made: 29.04.2002. Coming into force: 27.07.2002. Effect: None. Territorial extent & classification: E. Local *Unpublished*

The Air Navigation (Restriction of Flying) (Swindon) Regulations 2002 No. 2002/1290. – Enabling power: S.I. 2000/1562, art. 85. – Made: 07.05.2002. Coming into force: forthwith. Effect: None. Territorial extent & classification: E. Local – Revoked by S.I. 2002/1292 (unpublished) *Unpublished*

The Air Navigation (Restriction of Flying) (Swindon) (Revocation) Regulations 2002 No. 2002/1292. – Enabling power: S.I. 2000/1562, art. 85. – Made: 08.03.2002. Coming into force: 08.05.2002. Effect: S.I. 2002/1290 revoked. Territorial extent & classification: E. Local *Unpublished*

The Air Navigation (Restriction of Flying) (Trooping the Colour Ceremony) Regulations 2002 No. 2002/1470. – Enabling power: S.I. 2000/1562, art. 85. – Made: 29.05.2002. Coming into force: 15.06.2002. Effect: None. Territorial extent & classification: E. Local *Unpublished*

The Air Navigation (Restriction of Flying) (Trowbridge) Regulations 2002 No. 2002/2056. – Enabling power: S.I. 2000/1562, art. 85. – Made: 01.08.2002. Coming into force: forthwith. Effect: None. Territorial extent & classification: E. Local – Revoked by S.I. 2002/2057 (unpublished) *Unpublished*

The Air Navigation (Restriction of Flying) (Trowbridge) (Revocation) Regulations 2002 No. 2002/2057. – Enabling power: S.I. 2000/1562, art. 85. – Made: 02.08.2002. Coming into force: forthwith. Effect: S.I. 2002/2056 revoked. Territorial extent & classification: E. Local *Unpublished*

The Air Navigation (Restriction of Flying) (Wagford) Regulations 2002 No. 2002/2208. – Enabling power: S.I. 2000/1562, art. 85. – Made: 17.08.2002. Coming into force: 17.08.2002. Effect: None. Territorial extent & classification: E. Local – Revoked by S.I. 2002/2293 (unpublished) *Unpublished*

The Air Navigation (Restriction of Flying) (Wagford) (Revocation) Regulations 2002 No. 2002/2293. – Enabling power: S.I. 2000/1562, art. 85. – Made: 03.09.2002. Coming into force: forthwith. Effect: S.I. 2002/2208 revoked. Territorial extent & classification: E. Local *Unpublished*

The Air Navigation (Restriction of Flying) (Westminster) (No. 2) (Amendment) Regulations 2002 No. 2002/1025. – Enabling power: S.I. 2000/1562, art. 85. – Made: 08.04.2002. Coming into force: forthwith. Effect: S.I. 2002/930 amended. Territorial extent & classification: E. Local *Unpublished*

The Air Navigation (Restriction of Flying) (Westminster) (No. 2) Regulations 2002 No. 2002/930. – Enabling power: S.I. 2000/1562, art. 85. – Made: 02.04.2002. Coming into force: 09.04.2002. Effect: None. Territorial extent & classification: E. Local *Unpublished*

The Air Navigation (Restriction of Flying) (Westminster) Regulations 2002 No. 2002/929. – Enabling power: S.I. 2000/1562, art. 85. – Made: 02.04.2002. Coming into force: 05.04.2002. Effect: None. Territorial extent & classification: E. Local *Unpublished*

The Air Navigation (Restriction of Flying) (Weston Park) (No. 2) Regulations 2002 No. 2002/1995. – Enabling power: S.I. 2000/1562, art. 85. – Made: 25.07.2002. Coming into force: 16.08.2002. Effect: None. Territorial extent & classification: E. Local *Unpublished*

The Air Navigation (Restriction of Flying) (Weston Park) Regulations 2002 No. 2002/1414. – Enabling power: S.I. 2000/1562, art. 85. – Made: 22.05.2002. Coming into force: 28.05.2002. Effect: None. Territorial extent & classification: E. Local *Unpublished*

The Air Navigation (Restriction of Flying) (Whitsand Bay) Regulations 2002 No. 2002/336. – Enabling power: S.I. 2000/1562, art. 85. – Made: 06.02.2002. Coming into force: forthwith. Effect: None. Territorial extent & classification: E. Local – Revoked by S.I. 2002/368 (unpublished) *Unpublished*

The Air Navigation (Restriction of Flying) (Whitsand Bay) (Revocation) Regulations 2002 No. 2002/368. – Enabling power: S.I. 2000/1562, art. 85. – Made: 18.02.2002. Coming into force: forthwith. Effect: S.I. 2002/336 revoked. Territorial extent & classification: E. Local *Unpublished*

The Air Navigation (Restriction of Flying) (Yarlswood) (Amendment) Regulations 2002 No. 2002/418. – Enabling power: S.I. 2000/1562, art. 85. Made: 25.02.2002. Coming into force: forthwith. Effect: S.I. 2002/417 amended. Territorial extent & classification: E. Local *Unpublished*

The Air Navigation (Restriction of Flying) (Yarlswood) Regulations 2002 No. 2002/417. – Enabling power: S.I. 2000/1562, art. 85. – Made: 24.02.2002. Coming into force: forthwith. Effect: None. Territorial extent & classification: E. Local – Revoked by S.I. 2002/1564 (unpublished) *Unpublished*

The Air Navigation (Restriction of Flying) (Yarlswood) (Revocation) Regulations 2002 No. 2002/1564. – Enabling power: S.I. 2000/1562, art. 85. – Made: 22.05.2002. Coming into force: forthwith. Effect: S.I. 2002/417 revoked. Territorial extent & classification: E. Local *Unpublished*

The Carriage by Air Acts (Implementation of the Montreal Convention 1999) Order 2002 No. 2002/263. – Enabling power: Carriage by Air Act 1961, s. 8A & Carriage by Air (Supplementary Provisions) Act 1962, s. 4A. – Issued: 21.02.2002. Made: 12.02.2002. Coming into force: In accord. with art. 1. Effect: 1961 c. 27; 1962 c. 43 amended. Territorial extent & classification: E/W/S/NI. General. – 28p.: 30 cm. – Schedule 2, part 2 in French. Supersedes draft S.I. (ISBN 0110388674) previously issued on 21.11.2001 – 0 11 039332 5 *£4.50*

Clean air, England

The Smoke Control Areas (Authorised Fuels) (England) (Amendment) Regulations 2002 No. 2002/3046. – Enabling power: Clean Air Act 1993, ss. 20 (6), 63 (1). – Issued: 23.12.2002. Made: 11.12.2002. Laid: 11.12.2002. Coming into force: 06.01.2003. Effect: S.I. 2001/3745 amended. Territorial extent & classification: E. General. – 4p.: 30 cm. – 0 11 044221 0 *£1.75*

Clean air, Wales

The Smoke Control Areas (Authorised Fuels) (Amendment) (Wales) Regulations 2002 No. 2002/3160 (W.295). – Enabling power: Clean Air Act 1993, ss. 20 (6), 63 (1). – Issued: 27.12.2002. Made: 17.12.2002. Coming into force: 31.12.2002. Effect: S.I. 2001/3762 (W.311) amended. Territorial extent & classification: W. General. – 4p.: 30 cm. – In English and Welsh. - Welsh title: Rheoliadau Ardaloedd Rheoli Mwg (Tanwyddau Awdurdodedig) (Diwygio) (Cymru) 2002 – 0 11 090608 X *£1.75*

Clerk of the Crown in Chancery

The Crown Office (Forms and Proclamations Rules) (Amendment) Order 2002 No. 2002/3131. – Enabling power: Crown Office Act 1877, s. 3. – Issued: 06.01.2003. Made: 17.12.2002. Laid: 06.01.2003. Coming into force: 27.01.2003. Effect: S.I. 1992/1730 amended. Territorial extent & classification: E/W/S/NI. General. – 2p.: 30 cm. – 0 11 044248 2 *£1.50*

Climate change levy

The Climate Change Levy (General) (Amendment) Regulations 2002 No. 2002/1152. – Enabling power: Finance Act 2000, s. 30, sch. 6, para. 41 (1). – Issued: 01.05.2002. Made: 24.04.2002. Laid: 25.04.2002. Coming into force: 01.06.2002. Effect: S.I. 2001/838 amended. Territorial extent & classification: E/W/S/NI. General. – 4p.: 30 cm. – 0 11 039852 1 *£1.75*

Coast protection, England

The Coast Protection (Notices) (England) Regulations 2002 No. 2002/1278. – Enabling power: Coast Protection Act 1949, ss. 5 (1) (2) (3), 44. – Issued: 20.05.2002. Made: 08.05.2002. Laid: 08.05.2002. Coming into force: 01.06.2002. Effect: S.I. 1950/124 revoked in relation to England. Territorial extent & classification: E. General. – 4p.: 30 cm. – 0 11 039961 7 *£1.75*

Companies

The Companies (Competent Authority) (Fees) Regulations 2002 No. 2002/502. – Enabling power: Companies Act 1985, s. 708 (1). – Issued: 19.04.2002. Made: 07.03.2002. Laid: 07.03.2002. Coming into force: 02.04.2002. Effect: None. Territorial extent & classification: E/W/S. General. – 4p.: 30 cm. – 0 11 039771 1 *£1.75*

The Companies (Disclosure of Information) (Designated Authorities) (No. 2) Order 2002 No. 2002/1889. – Enabling power: Companies Act 1985, s. 449 (1B) (1C) & Companies Act 1989, s. 87 (5). – Issued: 05.09.2002. Made: 19.07.2002. Laid: 22.07.2002. Coming into force: 14.08.2002. Effect: 1989 c. 40 amended. Territorial extent & classification: E/W/S/NI. General (article 2 does not apply to NI.). – 4p.: 30 cm. – 0 11 042714 9 *£1.75*

The Companies (Disqualification Orders) (Amendment No. 2) Regulations 2002 No. 2002/1834. – Enabling power: Company Directors Disqualification Act 1986, s. 18. – Issued: 23.07.2002. Made: 08.07.2002. Laid: 16.07.2002. Coming into force: 17.07.2002. Effect: S.I. 2001/967 amended & S.I. 2002/689 revoked. Territorial extent: E/W/S. General. – This S.I. has been made in consequence of a defect in S.I. 2002/689 and is being issued free of charge to all recipients of that SI. – 4p.: 30 cm. – 0 11 042520 0 *£1.75*

The Companies (Disqualification Orders) (Amendment) Regulations 2002 No. 2002/689. – Enabling power: Company Directors Disqualification Act 1986, s. 18. – Issued: 09.05.2002. Made: 07.03.2002. Coming into force: 02.04.2002. Effect: S.I. 2001/967 amended. Territorial extent: E/W/S. General. – 4p.: 30 cm. – Revoked by S.I. 2002/1834 (ISBN 0110425200) – 0 11 039907 2 *£1.75*

The Companies (Fees) (Amendment No. 2) Regulations 2002 No. 2002/2894. – Enabling power: Companies Act 1985, s. 708 (1) (2). – Issued: 29.11.2002. Made: 21.11.2002. Laid: 21.11.2002. Coming into force: 01.01.2003. Effect: S.I. 1991/1206 amended. Territorial extent & classification: E/W/S. General. – 2p.: 30 cm. – For approval by resolution of the House of Commons within 28 days, from 21.11.2002 – Superseded by S.I. of same number but different ISBN (ISBN 0110444531) issued on 07.01.2003 – 0 11 043983 X *£1.50*

The Companies (Fees) (Amendment No. 2) Regulations 2002 No. 2002/2894. – Enabling power: Companies Act 1985, s. 708 (1) (2). – Issued: 07.01.2003. Made: 21.11.2002. Laid: 21.11.2002. Coming into force: 01.01.2003. Effect: S.I. 1991/1206 amended. Territorial extent & classification: E/W/S. General. – With correction slip, dated March 2003. – 2p.: 30 cm. – Approved by both Houses of Parliament – Supersedes S.I. of the same number but different ISBN (ISBN 011043983X) issued on 29.11.2002 – 0 11 044453 1 *£1.50*

The Companies (Fees) (Amendment) Regulations 2002 No. 2002/317. – Enabling power: Companies Act 1985, s. 708 (1) (2). – Issued: 04.03.2002. Made: 13.02.2002. Laid: 14.02.2002. Coming into force: 01.04.2002. Effect: S.I. 1991/1206 amended. Territorial extent & classification: E/W/S. General. – 2p.: 30 cm. – For approval by resolution of each House of Parliament within 28 days from 13.02.2002 – Superseded by S.I. with same number (ISBN 0110395069) issued 20.03.2002 – 0 11 039400 3 *£1.50*

The Companies (Fees) (Amendment) Regulations 2002 No. 2002/317. – Enabling power: Companies Act 1985, s. 708 (1) (2). – Issued: 20.03.2002. Made: 13.02.2002. Laid: 14.02.2002. Coming into force: 01.04.2002. Effect: S.I. 1991/1206 amended. Territorial extent & classification: E/W/S. General. – 2p.: 30 cm. – Approved by resolution of each House of Parliament – Supersedes SI, issued 04.03.2002, with same number (ISBN 0110394003) – 0 11 039506 9 *£1.50*

The Companies (Forms) (Amendment) Regulations 2002 No. 2002/691. – Enabling power: Companies Act 1985, ss. 10 (2), 288 (2), 363 (2), 691 (1) (b), 692 (1), 744, sch. 21A, paras. 1, 4A (d), 7 (1), 9 (1) (b) (2) (4). – Issued: 17.06.2002. Made: 07.03.2002. Coming into force: 02.04.2002. Effect: None. Territorial extent & classification: E/W/S. General. – 60p.: 30 cm. – 0 11 039909 9 *£7.50*

The Companies (Particulars of Usual Residential Address) (Confidentiality Orders) Regulations 2002 No. 2002/912. – Enabling power: Companies Act 1985, s. 723B to E. – Issued: 19.04.2002. Made: 31.03.2002. Coming into force: 02.04.2002. Effect: None. Territorial extent & classification: E/W/S. General. – 16p.: 30 cm. – 0 11 039773 8 *£3.00*

The Companies (Principal Business Activities) (Amendment) Regulations 2002 No. 2002/3081. – Enabling power: Companies Act 1985, s. 364 (3). – Issued: 14.01.2003. Made: 13.12.2002. Laid: 16.12.2002. Coming into force: 01.01.2003. Effect: S.I. 1990/1766 amended. Territorial extent & classification: E/W/S. General. – 2p.: 30 cm. – 0 11 044549 X *£1.50*

The Companies (Summary Financial Statement) Amendment Regulations 2002 No. 2002/1780. – Enabling power: Companies Act 1985, s. 251 (3). – Issued: 01.08.2002. Made: 11.07.2002. Laid: 12.07.2002. Coming into force: In accord. with art 1(2). Effect: S.I. 1995/2092 amended. Territorial extent & classification: E/W/S. General. – 4p.: 30 cm. – 0 11 042579 0 *£1.75*

The Criminal Justice and Police Act 2001 (Commencement No.5) Order 2002 No. 2002/533 (C.15). – Enabling power: Criminal Justice and Police Act 2001, s. 138 (2). Bringing into force various provisions of the 2001 Act on 01.04.2002, 02.04.2002, in accord.with arts. 2, 3. – Issued: 25.03.2002. Made: 07.03.2002. Effect: None. Territorial extent & classification: UK. General. – 4p.: 30 cm. – 0 11 039580 8 *£1.75*

The Directors' Remuneration Report Regulations 2002 No. 2002/1986. – Enabling power: Companies Act 1985, s. 257. – Issued: 01.08.2002. Made: 25.07.2002. Laid -. Coming into force: 01.08.2002. Effect: 1985 c. 6 amended. Territorial extent & classification: E/W/S. General. – 16p.: 30 cm. – 0 11 042580 4 *£3.00*

The Insolvency Act 1986 (Amendment) (No. 2) Regulations 2002 No. 2002/1240. – Enabling power: European Communities Act 1972, s. 2 (2). – Issued: 29.05.2002. Made: 01.05.2002. Laid: 02.05.2002. Coming into force: 31.05.2002. Effect: 1986 c. 45 amended. Territorial extent & classification: E/W/S. General. – 4p.: 30 cm. – EC note: To make amendments to the Act as a result of the adoption by the Council of the EU of Regulation 1346/2000 on insolvency proceedings – 0 11 042249 X *£1.75*

Companies, Scotland

The Insolvency (Scotland) Amendment Rules 2002 No. 2002/2709 (S.10). – Enabling power: Insolvency Act 1986, s. 411. – Issued: 06.11.2002. Made: 29.10.2002. Laid: 29.10.2002. Coming into force: 01.01.2003. Effect: S.I. 1986/1915 (S.139) amended. Territorial extent & classification: S. General. – 32p.: 30 cm. – 0 11 042934 6 *£6.00*

Competition

The Merger Report (Interbrew SA and Bass PLC) (Interim Provision) (Revocation) Order 2002 No. 2002/108. – Enabling power: Fair Trading Act 1973, ss. 89 (2) (3) (a) (b) (bb), 90, 134. – Issued: 28.01.2002. Made: 22.01.2002. Laid: 23.01.2002. Coming into force: 28.01.2002. Effect: S.I. 2001/318 revoked. Territorial extent & classification: E/W/S/NI. General. – 2p.: 30 cm. – 0 11 039225 6 *£1.50*

The Supply of Beer (Tied Estate) (Revocation) Order 2002 No. 2002/3204. – Enabling power: Fair Trading Act 1973, ss. 56 (2), 90 (2) (3) (4), 134 (2), sch. 8, paras, 1, 2, 14. – Issued: 31.12.2002. Made: 20.12.2002. Coming into force: 17.01.2003. Effect: S.I. 1989/2390; 1997/1740 revoked. Territorial extent & classification: E/W/S/NI. General. – 2p.: 30 cm. – 0 11 044398 5 *£1.50*

Constitutional law

The Adjacent Waters Boundaries (Northern Ireland) Order 2002 No. 2002/791. – Enabling power: Northern Ireland Act 1998, s. 98 (8). – Issued: 09.04.2002. Made 26.03.2002. Coming into force: 28.03.2002. Effect: None. Territorial extent & classification: NI. general. – 12p., map, tables: 30 cm. – 0 11 039632 4 *£2.50*

The Housing (Scotland) Act 2001 (Housing Support Services Information) Order 2002 No. 2002/2264 (S.8). – Enabling power: Scotland Act 1988, ss. 104, 112 (1), 113. – Issued: 12.09.2002. Made: 03.09.2002. Laid: 06.09.2002. Coming into force: 01.10.2002. Effect: None. Territorial extent & classification: S. General. – 4p.: 30 cm. – 0 11 061611 1 *£1.75*

The National Assembly for Wales (Representation of the People) (Amendment) Order 2002 No. 2002/834. – Enabling power: Government of Wales Act 1998, s. 11. – Issued: 03.04.2002. Made: 25.03.2002. Coming into force: In accordance with art. 1. Effect: S.I. 1999/450 amended. Territorial extent & classification: W. General. – 24p.: 30 cm. – Revoked by S.I. 2003/284 (ISBN 0110456505) – 0 11 039625 1 *£4.00*

The Northern Ireland Act 2000 (Modification) Order 2002 No. 2002/2587. – Enabling power: Northern Ireland Act 2000, s. 6. – Issued: 25.10.2002. Made: 14.10.2002. Laid: 15.10.2002. Coming into force: 15.10.2002. Effect: 2000 c. 1 modified. Territorial extent & classification: NI. General. Laid for approval by resolution of each House of Parliament within 40 days beginning with the date on which the Order was made. – S.I. 2002/2587 previously published on 25.10.2002 is superseded by this ISBN with the same number, ISBN 0110429605. – 2p.: 30 cm. – 0 11 042886 2 *£1.50*

The Northern Ireland Act 2000 (Modification) Order 2002 No. 2002/2587. – Enabling power: Northern Ireland Act 2000, s. 6. – Issued: 13.11.2002. Made: 14.10.2002. Laid: 15.10.2002. Coming into force:15.10.2002. Effect: 2000 c.1 amended. Territorial extent & classification: NI. General. – 2p.: 30 cm. – Approved by both Houses of Parliament – S.I. 2002/2587 (ISBN 0110428862) issued 25.10.2002 is superseded by this S.I. with same number – 0 11 042960 5 *£1.50*

The Northern Ireland Act 2000 (Suspension of Devolved Government) Order 2002 No. 2002/2574. – Enabling power: Northern Ireland Act 2000, s. 2 (2). – Issued: 25.10.2002. Made: 14.10.2002. Laid: 15.10.2002. Coming into force: 15.10.2002. Effect: S.I. 2001/3231 revoked. Territorial extent & classification: NI. General. – Laid for approval by resolution of each House of Parliament within 40 days beginning with the date on which the Order was made. – This S.I. is superseded by ISBN 0110429591, which has the same number and is issued 13.11.2002. – 2p.: 30 cm. – 0 11 042885 4 *£1.50*

The Northern Ireland Act 2000 (Suspension of Devolved Government) Order 2002 No. 2002/2574. – Enabling power: Northern Ireland Act 2000, s. 2 (2). – Issued: 13.11.2002. Made: 14.10.2002. Laid: 15.10.2002. Coming into force: 15.10.2002. Effect: S.I. 2001/3231 revoked. Territorial extent & classification: NI. General. – Approved by both Houses of Parliament. – S.I. 2002/2574 (ISBN 0110428854) previously published 25.10.2002 is superseded by this SI, with the same number. – 2p.: 30 cm. – 0 11 042959 1 *£1.50*

The Scotland Act 1998 (Agency Arrangements) (Specification) (No. 2) Order 2002 No. 2002/800 (S.2). – Enabling power: Scotland Act 1998, ss. 93 (3), 113. – Issued: 05.04.2002. Made: 26.03.2002. Laid before Parliament: 09.04.2002. Laid before the Scottish Parliament: 28.03.2002. Coming into force: 03.05.2002. Effect: S.I. 2001/3917 revoked. Territorial extent & classification: S. General. – 4p.: 30 cm. – 0 11 061243 4 *£1.75*

The Scotland Act 1998 (Agency Arrangements) (Specification) Order 2002 No. 2002/261 (S.1). – Enabling power: Scotland Act 1998, ss. 93 (3), 113. – Issued: 04.03.2002. Made: 12.02.2002. Laid before Parliament: 22.02.2002. Laid before the Scottish Parliament: 15.02.2002. Coming into force: 15.03.2002. Effect: None. Territorial extent & classification: S. General. – 4p.: 30 cm. – 0 11 061071 7 *£1.75*

The Scotland Act 1998 (Cross-Border Public Authorities) (Adaptation of Functions etc.) (Amendment) Order 2002 No. 2002/2636. – Enabling power: Scotland Act 1998, ss. 89, 113. – Issued: 30.10.2002. Made: 22.10.2002. Laid before the Scottish Parliament: -. Coming into force: 23.10.2002. Effect: S.I. 1999/1747 amended. Territorial extent & classification: E/W/S/NI. General. – 4p.: 30 cm. – 0 11 061685 5 *£1.75*

The Scotland Act 1998 (Modifications of Schedule 5) Order 2002 No. 2002/1629 (S.5). – Enabling power: Scotland Act 1998, s. 30 (2). – Issued: 05.07.2002. Made: 26.06.2002. Coming into force: 27.06.2002. Effect: 1998 c. 46 amended. Territorial extent & classification: S. General. – 4p.: 30 cm. – 0 11 061498 4 *£1.75*

The Scotland Act 1998 (Transfer of Functions to the Scottish Ministers etc.) Order 2002 No. 2002/1630 (S.6). – Enabling power: Scotland Act 1998, ss. 63 (1) (b), 113, 124 (2). – Issued: 05.07.2002. Made: 26.06.2002. Coming into force: 27.06.2002. Effect: 1998 c. 46 modified. Territorial extent & classification: S. General. – 4p.: 30 cm. – 0 11 061504 2 *£1.75*

The Scottish Administration (Offices) Order 2002 No. 2002/801 (S.3). – Enabling power: Scotland Act 1998, s. 126 (8) (b). – Issued: 03.04.2002. Made: 26.03.2002. Laid before Parliament: 27.03.2002. Laid before the Scottish Parliament: 27.03.2002. Coming into force: In acc.with art. 1 (1). Effect: None. Territorial extent & classification: S. General. – 2p.: 30 cm. – 0 11 061249 3 *£1.50*

The Scottish Parliament (Elections etc.) Order 2002 No. 2002/2779 (S.11). – Enabling power: Scotland Act 1998, ss. 12 (1), 113. – Issued: 20.11.2002. Made: 06.11.2002. Coming into force: In accord. with art. 1. Effect: 1983 c. 2; 1998 c. 46 modified; S.I. 1994/1443; 2002/2779 amended & S.I. 1999/787 (with savings); 2001/1399, 1748, 1750 revoked. Territorial extent & classification: S. General. – 156p.: 30 cm. – 0 11 061714 2 *£13.50*

The Water Industry (Scotland) Act 2002 (Directions in the Interests of National Security) Order 2002 No. 2002/1264 (S.4). – Enabling power: Scotland Act 1998, ss. 104, 112 (1), 113. – Issued: 21.05.2002. Made: 01.05.2002 Laid: 08.05.2002. Coming into force: 31.05.2002. Effect: None. Territorial extent & classification: S. General. – 4p.: 30 cm. – 0 11 061412 7 *£1.75*

Welsh Administration Ombudsman (Jurisdiction) Order 2002 No. 2002/3146 (W. 292). – Enabling power: Government of Wales Act 1998, sch. 9, paras. 14 (3), 15 (2). – Issued: 24.12.2002. Made: 17.12.2002. Coming into force: 31.12.2002. Effect: 1998 c. 38 amended. Territorial extent & classification: W. General. – 4p.: 30 cm. – In English and Welsh. Welsh title: Gorchymyn Ombwdsmon Gweinyddiaeth Cymru (Awdurdodaeth) 2002 – 0 11 090605 5 *£1.75*

Consumer protection

The Dangerous Substances and Preparations (Safety) (Consolidation) (Amendment No. 2) Regulations 2002 No. 2002/2479. – Enabling power: Consumer Protection Act 1987, s. 11. – Issued: 07.10.2002. Made: 27.09.2002. Laid: 01.10.2002. Coming into force: 18.01.2003. Effect: S.I. 1994/2844 amended. Territorial extent & classification: E/W/S/NI. General. – 4p.: 30 cm. – EC note: These Regs. implement DIR 2001/41/EC which amended for the 21st time 76/769/EEC – Revoked by S.I. 2002/3010 (ISBN 0110441494) – 0 11 042836 6 *£1.75*

The Dangerous Substances and Preparations (Safety) (Consolidation) (Amendment No. 3) Regulations 2002 No. 2002/3010. – Enabling power: Consumer Protection Act 1987, s. 11. – Issued: 11.12.2002. Made: 04.12.2002. Laid: 05.12.2002. Coming into force: 18.01.2003. Effect: S.I. 1994/2844 amended & S.I. 2002/2479 revoked. Territorial extent & classification: E/W/S/NI. General. – EC note: These Regs. implement DIR 2001/41/EC which amended for the 21st time 76/769/EEC. – 4p.: 30 cm. – This statutory instrument has been made in consequence of a defect in S.I. 2002/2479 (ISBN 0110428366) and is being issued free of charge to all known recipients of that instrument – 0 11 044149 4 *£1.75*

The Dangerous Substances and Preparations (Safety) (Consolidation) (Amendment) Regulations 2002 No. 2002/1770. – Enabling power: European Communities Act 1972, s. 2 (2). – Issued: 17.07.2002. Made: 10.07.2002. Laid:11.07.2002. Coming into force: 01.08.2002. Effect: S.I. 1994/2844 amended. Territorial extent & classification: E/W/S/NI. General. – 2p.: 30 cm. – 0 11 042468 9 *£1.50*

The Medical Devices Regulations 2002 No. 2002/618. – Enabling power: European Communities Act 1972, s. 2 (2) & Finance Act 1973, s. 56 (1) (2) & Consumer Protection Act 1987, ss. 11, 27 (2). – Issued: 06.06.2002. Made: 20.05.2002. Laid: 21.05.2002. Coming into force: 13.06.2002. Effect: S.I. 2002/236 amended & S.I. 1992/3146; 1994/3017; 1995/1671, 2487; 1997/694; 2000/1315 revoked. Territorial extent & classification: E/W/S/NI. General. – EC note: Implements EC DIR 90/385; 93/42; 98/79. – 40p.: 30 cm. – 0 11 042317 8 £6.50

The Personal Protective Equipment Regulations 2002 No. 2002/1144. – Enabling power: European Communities Act 1972, s. 2 (2). – Issued: 26.04.2002. Made: 20.04.2002. Laid: 23.04.2002. Coming into force: 15.05.2002. Effect: S.I. 1992/3139; 1993/3074; 1994/2326; 1996/3039 revoked. Territorial extent & classification: E/W/S/NI. General. – 24p.: 30 cm. – EC note: These Regs maintain the implementation of Council directive 89/686/EEC as amended by Council directive 93/68/EEC, Council directive 93/05/EEC & Council directive 96/58/EC – 0 11 039830 0 £4.00

The Sale and Supply of Goods to Consumers Regulations 2002 No. 2002/3045. – Enabling power: European Communities Act 1972, s. 2 (2). – Issued: 03.01.2003. Made: 10.12.2002. Laid: 11.12.2002. Coming into force: 31.03.2003. Effect: 1973 c.13; 1977 c.50; 1979 c.54; 1982 c.29 amended. Territorial extent & classification: E/W/S/NI. General. – EC note: These Regs implement EC DIR 1999/44/EC on certain aspects of the sale of consumer goods and associated guarantees. – 12p.: 30 cm. – 0 11 044428 0 £2.50

The Tobacco Products (Manufacture, Presentation and Sale) (Safety) Regulations 2002 No. 2002/3041. – Enabling power: Consumer Protection Act 1987, s. 11 & European Communities Act 1972, s. 2 (2). – Issued: 13.12.2002. Made: 10.12.2002. Laid: 10.12.2002. Coming into force: In accord. with reg. 1. Effect: S.I. 1991/1530 revoked with saving (31.12.2002.) & S.I. 1992/2783 revoked (01.01.2004.); 1993/1947 revoked (31.12.2002.). Territorial extent & classification: E/W/S/NI. General. – 12p.: 30 cm. – EC note: Implements Directive 2001/37/EC. The Directive repeals Council Directive 89/622/EEC (as amended by Directive 92/41/EEC) concerning the labelling of tobacco products and Council Directive 90/239/EEC concerning the maximum tar yields of cigarettes – 0 11 044178 8 £2.50

Consumer protection, England and Wales

The Tobacco Advertising and Promotion Act 2002 (Commencement) Order 2002 No. 2002/2865 (C.90). – Enabling power: Tobacco Advertising and Promotion Act 2002, s. 22 (1) to (3). Bringing into operation various provisions of the 2002 Act on 20.11.2002, 14.02.2003 & 14.05.2003 in accordance with art. 2. – Issued: 21.11.2002. Made: 19.11.2002. Effect: None. Territorial extent & classification: E/W/NI. General. – With correction slip dated April 2003. – 4p.: 30 cm. – 0 11 042999 0 £1.75

Consumer protection, Northern Ireland

The Tobacco Advertising and Promotion Act 2002 (Commencement) Order 2002 No. 2002/2865 (C.90). – Enabling power: Tobacco Advertising and Promotion Act 2002, s. 22 (1) to (3). Bringing into operation various provisions of the 2002 Act on 20.11.2002, 14.02.2003 & 14.05.2003 in accordance with art. 2. – Issued: 21.11.2002. Made: 19.11.2002. Effect: None. Territorial extent & classification: E/W/NI. General. – With correction slip dated April 2003. – 4p.: 30 cm. – 0 11 042999 0 £1.75

Contracting out

The Contracting Out (Functions in Relation to Applications for Patents) Order 2002 No. 2002/3052. – Enabling power: Deregulation and Contracting Out Act 1994, ss. 69, 77 (1) (b), 79 (5). – Issued: 17.11.2002. Made: 11.12.2002. Laid: 05.11.2002. Coming into force: 12.12.2002. Effect: None. Territorial extent & classification: E/W/S/IoM. – 4p.: 30 cm. – Supersedes draft S.I. (ISBN 0110429672) issued 15 November 2002 – 0 11 044181 8 £1.75

The Contracting Out (Functions of Local Authorities: Income-related Benefits) Order 2002 No. 2002/1888. – Enabling power: Deregulation and Contracting Out Act 1994, ss. 69, 70 (2) (4), 77 (1). – Issued: 26.07.2002. Made: 18.07.2002. Coming into force: 25.07.2002. Effect: None. Territorial extent & classification: E/W/S. General. – Supersedes draft S.I. (ISBN 011042395X) issued 26 June 2002. – 4p.: 30 cm. – 0 11 042524 3 £1.75

Contracting out, England

The Contracting Out (Functions in relation to Apsley House) Order 2002 No. 2002/445. – Enabling power: Deregulation and Contracting Out Act 1994, s. 69. – Issued: 07.03.2002. Made: 28.02.2002. Coming into force: 01.03.2002. Effect: None. Territorial extent & classification: E. General. – 2p.: 30 cm. – Supersedes draft S.I. (ISBN 0110391578) – 0 11 039416 X £1.50

Contracting Out (Local Education Authority Functions) (England) Order 2002 No. 2002/928. – Enabling power: Deregulation and Contracting Out Act 1994, ss. 70 (2) (4), 77. – Issued: 12.04.2002. Made: 28.03.2002. Coming into force: 01.04.2002. Effect: None. Territorial extent & classification: E. General. – Supersedes draft S.I. (ISBN 011039304X) issued on 14.02.2002. – 8p.: 30 cm. – 0 11 039751 7 £2.00

Contracts, England and Wales

The Late Payment of Commercial Debts (Interest) Act 1998 (Commencement No.5) Order 2002 No. 2002/1673 (C.47). – Enabling power: Late Payment of Commercial Debts (Interest) Act 1998, s. 17 (2). Bringing into operation various provisions of the 1998 act on 07.08.2002. – Issued: 25.07.2002. Made: 22.06.2002. Effect: None. Territorial extent & classification: E/W/NI. General. – EC note: This Order partially implements DIR 2000/35/EC. – 2p.: 30 cm. – 0 11 042540 5 *£1.50*

The Late Payment of Commercial Debts (Rate of Interest) (No. 3) Order 2002 No. 2002/1675. – Enabling power: Late Payment of Commercial Debts (Interest) Act 1998, s. 6. – Issued: 25.07.2002. Made: 22.06.2002. Laid: 28.06.2002. Coming into force: 07.08.2002. Effect: S.I. 1998/2765 revoked in relation to England and Wales and Northern Ireland. Territorial extent & classification: E/W/NI. General. – EC note: This Order partially implements DIR 2000/35/EC. – 2p.: 30 cm. – 0 11 042542 1 *£1.50*

The Late Payment of Commercial Debts Regulations 2002 No. 2002/1674. – Enabling power: European Communities Act 1972, s. 2 (2). – Issued: 25.07.2002. Made: 22.06.2002. Laid: 28.06.2002. Coming into force: 07.08.2002. Effect: 1998 c. 20 amended & S.I. 1998/2482 revoked in relation to England, Wales and Northern Ireland. Territorial extent & classification: E/W/NI. General. – EC note: These Regs. implement DIR 2000/35/EC. – 4p.: 30 cm. – 0 11 042541 3 *£1.75*

Contracts, Northern Ireland

The Late Payment of Commercial Debts (Interest) Act 1998 (Commencement No.5) Order 2002 No. 2002/1673 (C.47). – Enabling power: Late Payment of Commercial Debts (Interest) Act 1998, s. 17 (2). Bringing into operation various provisions of the 1998 act on 07.08.2002. – Issued: 25.07.2002. Made: 22.06.2002. Effect: None. Territorial extent & classification: E/W/NI. General. – EC note: This Order partially implements DIR 2000/35/EC. – 2p.: 30 cm. – 0 11 042540 5 *£1.50*

The Late Payment of Commercial Debts (Rate of Interest) (No. 3) Order 2002 No. 2002/1675. – Enabling power: Late Payment of Commercial Debts (Interest) Act 1998, s. 6. – Issued: 25.07.2002. Made: 22.06.2002. Laid: 28.06.2002. Coming into force: 07.08.2002. Effect: S.I. 1998/2765 revoked in relation to England and Wales and Northern Ireland. Territorial extent & classification: E/W/NI. General. – EC note: This Order partially implements DIR 2000/35/EC. – 2p.: 30 cm. – 0 11 042542 1 *£1.50*

The Late Payment of Commercial Debts Regulations 2002 No. 2002/1674. – Enabling power: European Communities Act 1972, s. 2 (2). – Issued: 25.07.2002. Made: 22.06.2002. Laid: 28.06.2002. Coming into force: 07.08.2002. Effect: 1998 c. 20 amended & S.I. 1998/2482 revoked in relation to England, Wales and Northern Ireland. Territorial extent & classification: E/W/NI. General. – EC note: These Regs. implement DIR 2000/35/EC. – 4p.: 30 cm. – 0 11 042541 3 *£1.75*

Copyright

The Copyright, etc. and Trade Marks (Offences and Enforcement) Act 2002 (Commencement) Order 2002 No. 2002/2749 (C.84). – Enabling power: Copyright, etc. and Trade Marks (Offences and Enforcement) Act 2002, s. 7 (2). Bringing into operation various provisions of the 2002 Act on 20.11.2002. – Issued: 12.11.2002. Made: 05.11.2002. Effect: None. Territorial extent & classification:E/W/S/NI. General. – 2p.: 30 cm. – 0 11 042949 4 *£1.50*

Coroners

The Coroners' Records (Fees for Copies) Rules 2002 No. 2002/2401. – Enabling power: Coroners Act 1988, s. 24 (3). – Issued: 30.09.2002. Made: 18.09.2002. Coming into force: 01.11.2002. Effect: S.I. 1997/2544 revoked. Territorial extent & classification: E/W. General. – 2p.: 30 cm. – 0 11 042820 X *£1.50*

The Hertfordshire (Coroners' Districts) Order 2002 No. 2002/3084. – Enabling power: Coroners Act 1988, s. 4 (2). – Issued: 20.12.2002. Made: 16.12.2002. Laid: 17.12.2002. Coming into force: 01.01.2003. Effect: S.I. 1974/374; 1998/1799 revoked. Territorial extent & classification: E. General. – 2p.: 30 cm. – This S.I. has been reprinted in consequence of an error in the original print and is being issued free of charge to all known recipients of that Statutory instrument – 0 11 044229 6 *£1.50*

The Lancashire (Coroners' Districts) Order 2002 No. 2002/2257. – Enabling power: Coroners Act 1988, s. 4 (2). – Issued: 17.09.2002. Made: 02.09.2002. Laid: 04.09.2002. Coming into force: 16.09.2002. Effect: S.I. 1974/355 revoked. Territorial extent & classification: E. General. – 2p.: 30 cm. – 0 11 042771 8 *£1.50*

The Lincolnshire (Coroners' Districts) Order 2002 No. 2002/1588. – Enabling power: Coroners Act 1988, s. 4 (2). – Issued: 09.07.2002. Made: 13.06.2002. Laid: 17.06.2002. Coming into force: 01.08.2002. Effect: S.I. 1984/1795 revoked. Territorial extent & classification: E. General. – 4p.: 30 cm. – 0 11 042437 9 *£1.75*

Council tax, England

The Council Tax and Non-domestic Rating (Demand Notices) (England) (Amendment) Regulations 2002 No. 2002/180. – Enabling power: Local Government Finance Act 1988, s. 143 (1) (2), sch. 9, paras. 1, 2 (2) (ga) (h). – Issued: 07.02.2002. Made: 31.01.2002. Laid: 01.02.2002. Coming into force: 22.02.2002. Effect: S.I. 1993/191; 1995/121; 1997/394; 1998/47 amended & S.I. 2000/534 revoked with saving. Territorial extent & classification: E. General. – 8p.: 30 cm. – 0 11 039265 5 *£2.00*

Countryside, England

The Access to the Countryside (Provisional and Conclusive Maps) (England) Regulations 2002 No. 2002/1710. – Enabling power: Countryside and Rights of Way Act 2000, ss. 11 (1) (2) (3), 44 (2), 45 (1). – Issued: 09.07.2002. Made: 07.07.2002. Laid: 08.07.2002. Coming into force: 29.07.2002. Effect: None. Territorial extent & classification: E. General. – 29p.: 30 cm. – 0 11 042442 5 £6.00

The Local Access Forums (England) Regulations 2002 No. 2002/1836. – Enabling power: Countryside and Rights of Way Act 2000, ss. 94 (1) (3), 95 (1) (2) (5). – Issued: 25.07.2002. Made: 15.07.2002. Laid: 16.07.2002. Coming into force: 07.08.2002. Effect: None. Territorial extent & classification: E. General. – 8p.: 30 cm. – 0 11 042526 X £2.00

The Peak District National Park Authority (Restriction of Agricultural Operations) Order 2002 No. 2002/80. – Enabling power: Wildlife and Countryside Act 1981, ss. 42, 52 (1). – Issued: 28.03.2002. Made: 17.01.2002. Laid: 18.01.2002. Coming into force: 18.01.2002. Effect: None. Territorial extent & classification: E. Local. – 2p.: 30 cm. – 0 11 039605 7 £1.50

Vehicular Access Across Common and Other Land (England) Regulations 2002 No. 2002/1711. – Enabling power: Countryside and Rights of Way Act 2000, s. 68. – Issued: 12.07.2002. Made: 03.07.2002. Approved by both Houses of Parliament. Coming into force: 04.07.2002 in accord. with reg. 1 (1). Effect: None. Territorial extent & classification: E. General. – 8p.: 30 cm. – Supersedes draft S.I. issued on 05.06.2002 (ISBN 011042297X) – 0 11 042454 9 £2.00

Countryside, Wales

The Countryside Access (Appeals Procedures) (Wales) Regulations 2002 No. 2002/1794 (W.169). – Enabling power: Countryside and Rights of Way Act 2000, ss. 11, 32, 38 (6), 44. – Issued: 05.08.2002. Made: 09.07.2002. Coming into force: 01.08.2002. Effect: None. Territorial extent & classification: W. General. – 32p.: 30 cm. – In English & Welsh. Welsh title: Rheoliadau Mynediad i Gefn Gwlad (Gweithdrefnau Apelau) (Cymru) 2002 – 0 11 090533 4 £6.00

The Countryside Access (Provisional and Conclusive Maps) (Wales) Regulations 2002 No. 2002/1796 (W.171). – Enabling power: Countryside and Rights of Way Act 2000, ss. 11, 44. – Issued: 02.08.2002. Made: 09.07.2002. Coming into force: 01.08.2002. Effect: S.I. 2001/4001 (W.329) amended. Territorial extent & classification: W. General. – 20p.: 30 cm. – In English & Welsh. Welsh title: Rheoliadau Mynediad i Gefn Gwlad (Mapiau Dros Dro a Therfynol) (Cymru) 2002 – 0 11 090532 6 £3.50

The Countryside and Rights of Way Act 2000 (Commencement No. 3) (Wales) Order 2002 No. 2002/2615 (W.253) (C.82). – Enabling power: Countryside and Rights of Way Act 2000, s. 103 (3) (4). Bringing into operation various provisions of the 2000 Act on 01.11.2002. – Issued: 28.10.2002. Made: 15.10.2002. Effect: None. Territorial extent & classification: W. General. – In English and Welsh. Welsh title: Gorchymyn Deddf Cefn Gwlad a Hawliau Tramwy 2000 (Cychwyn Rhif 3) (Cymru) 2002. – 4p.: 30 cm. – 0 11 090577 6 £1.75

The Wildlife and Countryside (Sites of Special Scientific Interest, Appeals) (Wales) Regulations 2002 No. 2002/1772 (W.168). – Enabling power: Wildlife and Countryside Act 1981, ss. 28F (6), 28L (8) & Countryside and Rights of Way Act 2000, sch. 11, paras. 11 (2), 17 (3). – Issued: 13.08.2002. Made: 09.07.2002. Coming into force: 31.07.2002. Effect: None. Territorial extent & classification: W. General. – 16p.: 30 cm. – In English and Welsh. - Welsh title: Rheoliadau Bywyd Gwyllt a Chefn Gwlad (Safleoedd o Ddiddordeb Gwyddonol Arbennig, Apelau) (Cymru) 2002 – 0 11 090546 6 £3.00

County courts, England and Wales

The Civil Procedure (Amendment No. 2) Rules 2002 No. 2002/3219 (L.18). – Enabling power: Civil Procedure Act 1997, s. 2 (6) (a). – Issued: 03.01.2003. Made: 14.12.2002. Laid: 24.12.2002. Coming into force: 01.04.2003. in accord. with rule 1. Effect. S.I. 1998/3132 amended in relation to England and Wales. Territorial extent & classification: E/W. General. – 8p.: 30 cm. – 0 11 044429 9 £2.00

The Civil Procedure (Amendment) Rules 2002 No. 2002/2058 (L.10). – Enabling power: Civil Procedure Act 1997, s. 2. – Issued: 13.08.2002. Made: 23.07.2002. Laid: 06.08.2002. Coming into force: 01.10.2002, 02.12.2002, in accord., with rule 1. Effect: S.I. 1998/3132 amended in relation to England and Wales. Territorial extent & classification: E/W. General. – 36p.: 30 cm. – 0 11 042632 0 £6.50

The Civil Procedure (Modification of Enactments) Order 2002 No. 2002/439. – Enabling power: Civil Procedure Act 1997, s. 4 (1). Issued: 08.03.2002. Made: 28.02.2002. Laid: 01.03.2002. Coming into force: 25.03.2002. Effect: 1869 c. 62 (32 & 33 Vict); 1979 c. 53; 1981 c. 54; 1984 c. 28; S.I. 1991/1222; 1996/3215; 2000/1071 amended. Territorial extent & classification: E/W. General. – 4p.: 30 cm. – 0 11 039415 1 £1.75

The County Court Fees (Amendment) Order 2002 No. 2002/223 (L.3). – Enabling power: County Courts Act 1984. s. 128. – Issued: 13.02.2002. Made: 06.02.2002. Laid: 07.02.2002. Coming into force: 01.03.2002, 25.03.2002., in accord. with art. 1. Effect: S.I. 1999/689 amended. Territorial extent & classification: E/W. General. – 4p.: 30 cm. – 0 11 039296 5 £1.75

Criminal law

The Copyright, etc. and Trade Marks (Offences and Enforcement) Act 2002 (Commencement) Order 2002 No. 2002/2749 (C.84). – Enabling power: Copyright, etc. and Trade Marks (Offences and Enforcement) Act 2002, s. 7 (2). Bringing into operation various provisions of the 2002 Act on 20.11.2002. – Issued: 12.11.2002. Made: 05.11.2002. Effect: None. Territorial extent & classification:E/W/S/NI. General. – 2p.: 30 cm. – 0 11 042949 4   £1.50

The Criminal Justice and Police Act 2001 (Commencement No.4 and Transitional Provisions) Order 2002 No. 2002/344 (C.7). – Enabling power: Criminal Justice and Police Act 2001, ss. 109, 116 (7), 119 (7), 138 (2). Bringing into force various provisions of the 2001 Act on 01.03.2002, 01.04.2002, in accord.with arts. 2, 3. – Issued: 27.02.2002. Made: 16.02.2002. Effect: None. Territorial extent & classification: E/W/S. General. – 4p.: 30 cm. – 0 11 039390 2   £1.75

The Criminal Justice and Public Order Act 1994 (Commencement No. 13) Order 2002 No. 2002/447 (C.13). – Enabling power: Criminal Justice and Public Order Act 1994, s. 172 (2). Bringing into operation various provisions of the 1994 Act on 20.03.2002. – Issued: 07.03.2002. Made: 28.02.2002. Effect: None. Territorial extent & classification: UK. General. – 4p.: 30 cm. – 0 11 039418 6   £1.75

The Mobile Telephones (Re-programming) Act 2002 (Commencement) Order 2002 No. 2002/2294 (C.74). – Enabling power: Mobile Telephones (Re-progamming) Act 2002. s. 3 (2). Bringing into operation various provisions of the 2002 Act on 04.10.2002. – Issued: 16.09.2002. Made: 05.09.2002. Effect: None. Territorial extent & classification: UK. General. – 2p.: 30 cm. – 0 11 042751 3   £1.50

The Travel Restriction Order (Prescribed Removal Powers) Order 2002 No. 2002/313. – Enabling power: Criminal Justice and Police Act 2001, s. 37 (4). – Issued: 20.02.2002. Made: 13.02.2002. Laid: 20.02.2002. Coming into force: 01.04.2002. Effect: None. Territorial extent & classification: UK. General. – 2p.: 30 cm. – 0 11 039341 4   £1.50

The Zimbabwe (Freezing of Funds, other Financial Assets or Economic Resources) (Amendment) Regulations 2002 No. 2002/2530. – Enabling power: European Communities Act 1972, s. 2 (2). – Issued: 24.10.2002. Made: 07.10.2002. Laid: 08.10.2002. Coming into force: 31.10.2002. Effect: S.I. 2002/826 amended. Territorial extent & classification: E/W/S/NI. General. – EC note: These Regulations refer to Council Regulation 310/2002 as amended by Commission Regulations 1224/2002 & 1643/2002. – 2p.: 30 cm. – 0 11 042882 X   £1.50

The Zimbabwe (Freezing of Funds, other Financial Assets or Economic Resources) Regulations 2002 No. 2002/826. – Enabling power: European Communities Act 1972, s. 2 (2). – Issued: 19.06.2002. Made: 26.03.2002. Laid: 26.03.2002. Coming into force: 27.03.2002. Effect: None. Territorial extent & classification: E/W/S/NI. General. – EC note: These regulations provide that breaches of certain provisions of Council Reg (EC) No. 310/2002 are to be criminal offences. – 4p.: 30 cm. – 0 11 042352 6   £1.75

Criminal law, England and Wales

The Anti-Terrorism, Crime and Security Act 2001 (Commencement No. 3) Order 2002 No. 2002/228 (C.4). – Enabling power: Anti-Terrorism, Crime and Security Act 2001, s. 127 (1). Bringing into force various provisions of the 2001 Act on 14.02.2002. – Issued: 11.02.2002. Made: 04.02.2002. Effect: None. Territorial extent & classification: E/W/NI General. – 2p.: 30 cm. – 0 11 039288 4   £1.50

The Bail (Electronic Monitoring of Requirements) (Responsible Officer) Order 2002 No. 2002/844. – Enabling power: Bail Act 1976, s. 3AA (6). – Issued: 05.04.2002. Made: 26.03.2002. Coming into force: 22.04.2002. Effect: None. Territorial extent & classification: E/W. General. – 8p.: 30 cm. – 0 11 039645 6   £2.00

The Criminal Justice Act 1988 (Designated Countries and Territories) (Amendment) (No. 2) Order 2002 No. 2002/2844. – Enabling power: Criminal Justice Act 1988, s. 96. – Issued: 02.12.2002. Made: 20.11.2002. Laid: 02.12.2002. Coming into force: 23.12.2002. Effect: S.I. 1991/2873 amended. Territorial extent & classification: E/W. General. – 2p.: 30 cm. – 0 11 043336 X   £1.50

The Criminal Justice Act 1988 (Designated Countries and Territories) (Amendment) Order 2002 No. 2002/256. – Enabling power: Criminal Justice Act 1988, s. 96. – Issued: 22.02.2002. Made: 12.02.2002. Laid: 22.02.2002. Coming into force: 18.03.2002. Effect: S.I. 1991/2873 amended. Territorial extent & classification: E/W. General. – 2p.: 30 cm. – 0 11 039328 7   £1.50

The Criminal Justice Act 1988 (Offensive Weapons) Order 2002 No. 2002/1668. – Enabling power: Criminal Justice Act 1988, s. 141 (2). – Issued: 02.07.2002. Made: 22.06.2002. Coming into force: 23.06.2002. Effect: S.I. 1998/2019 amended. Territorial extent & classification: E/W/NI. General. – 2p.: 30 cm. – Supersedes draft S.I. issued 05.06.2002 (ISBN 0110423062) – 0 11 042407 7   £1.50

The Criminal Justice and Court Services Act 2000 (Commencement No. 9) Order 2002 No. 2002/1149 (C.28). – Enabling power: Criminal Justice and Court Services Act 2000, s. 80. Bringing into operation various provisions of the 2000 Act on 20.05.2002. – Issued: 14.05.2002. Made: 23.04.2002. Effect: None. Territorial extent & classification: E/W. General. – 2p.: 30 cm. – Printed with incorrect price – 0 11 039922 6   £1.50

The Criminal Justice and Court Services Act 2000 (Commencement No. 10) Order 2002 No. 2002/1862 (C.57). – Enabling power: Criminal Justice and Court Services Act 2000, s. 80. Bringing into operation various provisions of the 2000 Act on 02.09.2002. – Issued: 14.08.2002. Made: 18.07.2002. Effect: None. Territorial extent & classification: E/W. General. – 2p.: 30 cm. – 0 11 042647 9 £1.50

The Criminal Justice and Police Act 2001 (Amendment) Order 2003 No. 2002/1934. – Enabling power: Criminal Justice and Police Act 2001, s. 1 (2). – Issued: 29.07.2003. Made: 22.07.2002. Coming into force: 22.07.2002. Effect: 2001 c.16 amended. Territorial extent & classification: E/W. General. – 2p.: 30 cm. – Supersedes draft S.I. (ISBN 0110423194) issued 5th June 2002 – 0 11 042549 9 £1.50

The Criminal Justice and Police Act 2001 (Commencement No.6) Order 2002 No. 2002/1097 (C.27). – Enabling power: Criminal Justice and Police Act 2001, s. 138 (2). Bringing into force various provisions of the 2001 Act on 22.04.2001, 16.09.2002, in accord. with art. 2. – Issued: 26.04.2002. Made: 16.04.2002. Effect: None. Territorial extent & classification: E/W. General. – 4p.: 30 cm. – 0 11 039824 6 £1.75

The Criminal Justice and Police Act 2001 (Commencement No. 7) Order 2002 No. 2002/2050 (C.66). – Enabling power: Criminal Justice and Police Act 2001, s. 138 (2). Bringing into force various provisions of the 2001 Act on 12.08.2002 and 01.09.2002. – Issued: 09.08.2002. Made: 02.08.2002. Effect: None. Territorial extent & classification: UK [parts to E/W only and part to all UK]. General. – 4p.: 30 cm. – 0 11 042639 8 £1.75

The Criminal Justice and Police Act 2001 (Commencement No. 8) Order 2002 No. 2002/3032 (C.100). – Enabling power: Criminal Justice and Police Act 2001, s. 138 (2). Bringing into force various provisions of the 2001 Act on 01.01.2003, in accord. with art. 2. – Issued: 18.12.2002. Made: 06.12.2002. Effect: None. Territorial extent & classification: E/W. General. – 4p.: 30 cm. – 0 11 044197 4 £1.75

The Criminal Justice (International Co-operation) Act 1990 (Enforcement of Overseas Forfeiture Orders) (Amendment) (No. 2) Order 2002 No. 2002/2845. – Enabling power: Criminal Justice (International Co-operation) Act 1990, s. 9. – Issued: 02.12.2002. Made: 20.11.2002. Laid: 02.12.2002. Coming into force: 23.12.2002. Effect: S.I. 1991/1463, 1464 amended. Territorial extent & classification: E/W/NI. General. – 2p.: 30 cm. – 0 11 043349 1 £1.50

The Criminal Justice (International Co-operation) Act 1990 (Enforcement of Overseas Forfeiture Orders) (Amendment) Order 2002 No. 2002/255. – Enabling power: Criminal Justice (International Co-operation) Act 1990, s. 9. – Issued: 22.02.2002. Made: 12.02.2002. Laid: 22.02.2002. Coming into force: 18.03.2002. Effect: S.I. 1991/1463, 1464 amended. Territorial extent & classification: E/W/NI. General. – 4p.: 30 cm. – 0 11 039326 0 £1.75

The Drug Trafficking Act 1994 (Designated Countries and Territories) (Amendment) (No. 2) Order 2002 No. 2002/2846. – Enabling power: Drug Trafficking Act 1994, s. 39. – Issued: 02.12.2002. Made: 20.11.2002. Laid: 02.12.2002. Coming into force: 23.12.2002. Effect: S.I. 1996/2880 amended. Territorial extent & classification: E/W. General. – 2p.: 30 cm. – 0 11 043337 8 £1.50

The Drug Trafficking Act 1994 (Designated Countries and Territories) (Amendment) Order 2002 No. 2002/257. – Enabling power: Drug Trafficking Act 1994, s. 39. – Issued: 22.02.2002. Made: 12.02.2002. Laid: 22.02.2002. Coming into force: 18.03.2002. Effect: S.I. 1996/2880 amended. Territorial extent & classification: E/W. General. – 2p.: 30 cm. – 0 11 039329 5 £1.50

The Motor Salvage Operators (Specified Offences) Order 2002 No. 2002/1917. – Enabling power: Vehicles (Crime) Act 2001, s. 3 (4) (b). – Issued: 13.08.2002. Made: 17.07.2002. Laid: 24.07.2002. Coming into force: 21.10.2002. Effect: None. Territorial extent & classification: E/W. General. – 2p.: 30 cm. – 0 11 042633 9 £1.50

The Penalties for Disorderly Behaviour (Amount of Penalty) Order 2002 No. 2002/1837. – Enabling power: Criminal Justice and Police Act 2001, s. 3 (1). – Issued: 06.08.2002. Made: 16.07.2002. Laid: 17.07.2002. Coming into force: 08.08.2002. Effect: None. Territorial extent & classification: E/W. General. – 4p.: 30 cm. – 0 11 042603 7 £1.75

The Penalties for Disorderly Behaviour (Form of Penalty Notice) Regulations 2002 No. 2002/1838. – Enabling power: Criminal Justice and Police Act 2001, s. 3 (3) & Welsh Language Act 1993, s. 26 (3) (b). – Issued: 07.08.2002. Made: 16.07.2002. Laid: 17.07.2002. Coming into force: 08.08.2002. Effect: None. Territorial extent & classification: E/W. General. – 8p.: 30 cm. – 0 11 042605 3 £2.00

The Police and Criminal Evidence Act 1984 (Department of Trade and Industry Investigations) Order 2002 No. 2002/2326. – Enabling power: Police and Criminal Evidence Act 1984, s. 114A. – Issued: 18.09.2002. Made: 10.09.2002. Laid: 11.09.2002. Coming into force: 14.10.2002. Effect: 1984, c. 60 modified. Territorial extent & classification: E/W. General. – 4p.: 30 cm. – 0 11 042754 8 £1.75

The Police (Retention and Disposal of Items Seized) Regulations 2002 No. 2002/1372. – Enabling power: Criminal Justice and Public Order Act 1994, s. 60A. – Issued: 05.06.2002. Made: 15.05.2002. Laid: 17.05.2002. Coming into force: 10.06.2002. Effect: S.I. 1999/269 revoked in relation to England and Wales. Territorial extent & classification: E/W. General. – 4p.: 30 cm. – 0 11 042316 X £1.75

The Youth Justice and Criminal Evidence Act 1999 (Commencement No. 7) Order 2002 No. 2002/1739 (C.54). – Enabling power: Youth Justice and Criminal Evidence Act 1999, ss. 64 (4), 68 (3). Bringing into operation various provisions of the 1999 Act on 24.07.2002. – Issued: 23.07.2002. Made: 08.07.2002. Effect: None. Territorial extent & classification: E/W. General. – 4p.: 30 cm. – 0 11 042521 9 £1.75

Criminal law, Northern Ireland

The Anti-Terrorism, Crime and Security Act 2001 (Commencement No. 3) Order 2002 No. 2002/228 (C.4). – Enabling power: Anti-Terrorism, Crime and Security Act 2001, s. 127 (1). Bringing into force various provisions of the 2001 Act on 14.02.2002. – Issued: 11.02.2002. Made: 04.02.2002. Effect: None. Territorial extent & classification: E/W/NI General. – 2p.: 30 cm. – 0 11 039288 4   £1.50

The Criminal Justice Act 1988 (Offensive Weapons) Order 2002 No. 2002/1668. – Enabling power: Criminal Justice Act 1988, s. 141 (2). – Issued: 02.07.2002. Made: 22.06.2002. Coming into force: 23.06.2002. Effect: S.I. 1998/2019 amended. Territorial extent & classification: E/W/NI. General. – 2p.: 30 cm. – Supersedes draft S.I. issued 05.06.2002 (ISBN 0110423062) – 0 11 042407 7   £1.50

The Criminal Justice (International Co-operation) Act 1990 (Enforcement of Overseas Forfeiture Orders) (Amendment) (No. 2) Order 2002 No. 2002/2845. – Enabling power: Criminal Justice (International Co-operation) Act 1990, s. 9. – Issued: 02.12.2002. Made: 20.11.2002. Laid: 02.12.2002. Coming into force: 23.12.2002. Effect: S.I. 1991/1463, 1464 amended. Territorial extent & classification: E/W/NI. General. – 2p.: 30 cm. – 0 11 043349 1   £1.50

The Criminal Justice (International Co-operation) Act 1990 (Enforcement of Overseas Forfeiture Orders) (Amendment) Order 2002 No. 2002/255. – Enabling power: Criminal Justice (International Co-operation) Act 1990, s. 9. – Issued: 22.02.2002. Made: 12.02.2002. Laid: 22.02.2002. Coming into force: 18.03.2002. Effect: S.I. 1991/1463, 1464 amended. Territorial extent & classification: E/W/NI. General. – 4p.: 30 cm. – 0 11 039326 0   £1.75

Customs and excise

The Beer and Excise Warehousing (Amendment) Regulations 2002 No. 2002/1265. – Enabling power: Customs and Excise Management Act 1979, ss. 93 (2) (fa) (3), 118A (1) (2), & Alcoholic Liquor Duties Act 1979 s. 49 (1) (a) (b) (h) (j) (2). – Issued: 17.05.2002. Made: 07.05.2002. Laid: 09.05.2002. Coming into force: 01.06.2002. Effect: S.I. 1993/1228; 1988/809 amended. Territorial extent & classification: E/W/S/NI. General. – 4p.: 30 cm. – 0 11 039951 X   £1.75

The Biodiesel and Bioblend Regulations 2002 No. 2002/1928. – Enabling power: Hydrocarbon Oil Duties Act 1979, ss. 6AC (1) (a) (b) (2) (4), 21 (1) (a) (2), 24 (1), sch. 3, para. 11, sch. 4, para. 3 & Customs and Excise Management Act 1979, s. 118A (1) (2). – Issued: 06.08.2002. Made: 25.07.2002. Laid: 25.07.2002. Coming into force: 26.07.2002. Effect: S.I. 1995/2717 amended. Territorial extent & classification: E/W/S/NI. General. – 8p.: 30 cm. – 0 11 042608 8   £2.00

The Dual-use Items (Export Control) (Amendment) (No. 2) Regulations 2002 No. 2002/2033. – Enabling power: European Communities Act 1972, s. 2 (2). – Issued: 19.08.2002. Made: 29.07.2002. Laid: 01.08.2002. Coming into force: 21.08.2002. Effect: S.I. 2000/2620 amended. Territorial extent: E/W/S/NI. General. – 2p.: 30 cm. – EC note: Made in implementation of and pursuant to Council regulation (EC) 1334/2000 setting up a Community regime for the control of exports of dual-use items and technology – 0 11 042665 7   £1.50

The Dual-use Items (Export Control) (Amendment) Regulations 2002 No. 2002/50. – Enabling power: European Communities Act 1972, s. 2 (2). – Issued: 20.03.2002. Made: 14.01.2002. Laid: 15.01.2002. Coming into force: 05.02.2002. Effect: S.I. 2000/2620 amended. Territorial extent: E/W/S/NI. General. – 2p.: 30 cm. – EC note: Extends the definition of "the regulation" to include Council regulation 2432/2001 and creating a new schedule 1A to list amendments to regulation 1334/2000 – 0 11 039505 0   £1.50

The Excise Duties (Personal Reliefs) (Revocation) Order 2002 No. 2002/2691. – Enabling power: Customs and Excise Duties (General Reliefs) Act 1979, s. 13. – Issued: 11.11.2002. Made: 28.10.2002. Laid: 29.10.2002. Coming into force: 01.12.2002. Effect: S.I. 1992/3155; 1999/1617 revoked. Territorial extent & classification: E/W/S/NI. General. – 2p.: 30 cm. – For approval by resolution of the House of Commons within 28 days, from 28.10.2002 – Superseded by S.I. 2002/2691 (same number) (ISBN 0110440994) issued on 06.12.2002 – 0 11 042943 5   £1.50

The Excise Duties (Personal Reliefs) (Revocation) Order 2002 No. 2002/2691. – Enabling power: Customs and Excise Duties (General Reliefs) Act 1979, s. 13. – Issued: 06.12.2002. Made: 28.10.2002. Laid: 29.10.2002. Coming into force: 01.12.2002. Effect: S.I. 1992/3155; 1999/1617 revoked. Territorial extent & classification: E/W/S/NI. General. – 2p.: 30 cm. – Supersedes S.I. 2002/2691 (same number) (ISBN 0110429435) issued on 11.11.2002 – 0 11 044099 4   £1.50

The Excise Goods (Accompanying Documents) Regulations 2002 No. 2002/501. – Enabling power: Customs and Excise Management Act 1979, ss. 93 (1) (2) (a) (e) (fa) (fb) (g) (h) (j) (k) (3) (4) (5), 100G, 100H, 118A (1) (2) & Finance (No. 2) Act 1992, s. 1 & European Communities Act 1972, s. 2 (2). – Issued: 15.03.2002. Made: 06.03.2002. Laid: 08.03.2002. Coming into force: 01.04.2002. Effect: S.I. 1988/809; 1992/3135; 1993/1228; 1999/1278 amended. Territorial extent & classification: E/W/S/NI. General. – EC note: Implement requirements of DIR 92/12/EEC (as amended) in respect of the documentation required to accompany commercial movements of excise goods within the EU. – 24p.: 30 cm. – 0 11 039456 9   £4.00

The Excise Goods, Beer and Tobacco Products (Amendment) Regulations 2002 No. 2002/2692. – Enabling power: Finance (No. 2) Act 1992, s. 1. – Issued: 11.11.2002. Made: 28.10.2002. Laid: 29.10.2002. Coming into force: 01.12.2002. Effect: S.I. 1992/3135; 1993/1228; 2001/1712 amended. Territorial extent & classification: E/W/S/NI. General. – EC note: These Regs. implement the requirements of Council Directive 92/12/EEC. A transposition note setting out how these regs. implement the requirements of DIR 92/12/EEC is available at www.hmce.gov.uk. – 8p.: 30 cm. – 0 11 042944 3 *£2.00*

The Export of Goods (Control) (Amendment) Order 2002 No. 2002/2059. – Enabling power: Import, Export and Customs Powers (Defence) Act 1939, s. 1. – Issued: 12.09.2002. Made: 03.08.2002. Coming into force: 28.08.2002. Effect: S.I. 1994/1191 amended. Territorial extent & classification: E/W/S/NI. General. – 8p.: 30 cm. – With correction slip dated September 2002. – 0 11 042744 0 *£2.00*

The Export of Goods (Federal Republic of Yugoslavia) (Control) (Revocation) Order 2002 No. 2002/315. – Enabling power: Import, Export and Customs Powers (Defence) Act 1939, s. 1. – Issued: 21.02.2002. Made: 12.02.2002. Coming into force: 07.03.2002. Effect: S.I. 1998/1530 revoked. Territorial extent & classification: E/W/S/NI. General. – 2p.: 30 cm. – 0 11 039345 7 *£1.50*

The Federal Republic of Yugoslavia (Supply and Sale of Equipment) (Penalties and Licences) (Revocation) Regulations 2002 No. 2002/316. – Enabling power: European Communities Act 1972, s. 2 (2). – Issued: 26.02.2002. Made: 12.02.2002. Laid: 14.02.2002. Coming into force: 07.03.2002. Effect: S.I. 1998/1531; 1999/1775 revoked. Territorial extent & classification: E/W/S/NI. General. – 2p.: 30 cm. – 0 11 039382 1 *£1.50*

The Finance Act 2002, section 5 (6), (Appointed Date) Order 2002 No. 2002/1926 (C.61). – Enabling power: Finance Act 2002, s. 5 (6) (a). Bringing into force various provisions of the 2002 Act on 25.07.2002. – Issued: 05.08.2002. Made: 25.07.2002. Effect: None. Territorial extent & classification: E/W/S/NI. General. – 2p.: 30 cm. – 0 11 042586 3 *£1.50*

The Finance Act 2002, section 6, (Appointed Day) Order 2002 No. 2002/3056 (C.103). – Enabling power: Finance Act 2002, s. 6 (3). Bringing into force various provisions of the 2002 Act on 01.04.2003. – Issued: 17.01.2003. Made: 11.12.2002. Effect: None. Territorial extent & classification: E/W/S/NI. General. – 2p.: 30 cm. – 0 11 044584 8 *£1.50*

The Gaming Duty (Amendment) Regulations 2002 No. 2002/2310. – Enabling power: Finance Act 1997, ss. 12 (4), 14 (1). – Issued: 13.09.2002. Made: 06.09.2002. Laid: 09.09.2002. Coming into force: 01.10.2002. Effect: S.I. 1997/2196 amended & S.I. 2000/2408 revoked. Territorial extent & classification: E/W/S/NI. General. – 2p.: 30 cm. – 0 11 042746 7 *£1.50*

The Hydrocarbon Oil (Industrial Reliefs) Regulations 2002 No. 2002/1471. – Enabling power: Hydrocarbon Oil Duties Act 1979, s. 24 (1), sch. 4. – Issued: 28.06.2002. Made: 05.06.2002. Laid: 06.06.2002. Coming into force: for the purposes of regs. 5, 6: 01.07.2002; for all other purposes: 01.09.2002. Effect: S.I. 1973/1311 amended. Territorial extent & classification: E/W/S/NI. General. – 4p.: 30 cm. – 0 11 042394 1 *£1.75*

The Hydrocarbon Oil (Marking) Regulations 2002 No. 2002/1773. – Enabling power: Hydrocarbon Oil Duties Act 1979, s. 24 (1), 24A (3), sch. 4 & European Communities Act 1972, s. 2 (2). – Issued: 07.08.2002. Made: 16.07.2002. Laid: 16.07.2002. Coming into force: 01.08.2002. Effect: S.I. 1973/1311; 1996/1251 amended & S.I. 1985/1033; 1994/694 revoked. Territorial extent & classification: E/W/S/NI. General. – EC note: In part, the regulations implement Council Directive 95/60/EC on the fiscal marking of gas oils and kerosene. – 12p.: 30 cm. – 0 11 042616 9 *£2.50*

The Hydrocarbon Oil (Registered Dealers in Controlled Oil) Regulations 2002 No. 2002/3057. – Enabling power: Customs and Excise Management Act 1979, ss. 100G. 100H & Hydrocarbon Oil Duties Act 1979, ss. 23B, 24AA. – Issued: 17.01.2003. Made: 11.12.2002. Laid: 11.12.2002. Coming into force: 01.01.2003. Effect: None. Territorial extent & classification: E/W/S/NI. General. – 4p.: 30 cm. – 0 11 044583 X *£1.75*

The Lottery Duty (Amendment) Regulations 2002 No. 2002/2355. – Enabling power: Finance Act 1993, ss. 24 (2), 38. – Issued: 18.09.2002. Made: 11.09.2002. Laid: 13.09.2002. Coming into force: 17.10.2002. Effect: S.I. 1993/3212 amended. Territorial extent & classification: E/W/S/NI. General. – 2p.: 30 cm. – 0 11 042774 2 *£1.50*

The Lottery Duty (Instant Chances) (Amendment) Regulations 2002 No. 2002/2354. – Enabling power: Finance Act 1993, ss. 24 (2), 28 (2), 38. – Issued: 18.09.2002. Made: 11.09.2002. Laid: 13.09.2002. Coming into force: 17.10.2002. Effect: S.I. 1995/2815 amended. Territorial extent & classification: E/W/S/NI. General. – 2p.: 30 cm. – 0 11 042773 4 *£1.50*

The Origin of Goods (Petroleum Products) (Revocation) Regulations 2002 No. 2002/2266. – Enabling power: Customs and Excise Management Act 1979, s. 120 (1). – Issued: 11.09.2002. Made: 03.09.2002. Laid: 05.09.2002. Coming into force: 01.10.2002. Effect: S.I. 1988/1; 1992/3289 revoked. Territorial extent & classification: E/W/S/NI. General. – 2p.: 30 cm. – 0 11 042740 8 *£1.50*

The Other Fuel Substitutes (Rates of Excise Duty etc.) (Amendment) Order 2002 No. 2002/3042. – Enabling power: Hydrocarbon Oil Duties Act 1979, s. 6A. – Issued: 16.12.2002. Made: 10.12.2002. Laid: 10.12.2002. Coming into force: 01.01.2003. Effect: S.I. 1995/2716 amended. Territorial extent & classification: E/W/S/NI. General. – 2p.: 30 cm. – 0 11 044177 X *£1.50*

The Zimbabwe (Sale, Supply, Export and Shipment of Equipment) (Penalties and Licences) Regulations 2002 No. 2002/868. – Enabling power: European Communities Act 1972, s. 2 (2). – Issued: 24.04.2002. Made: 26.03.2002. Laid: 28.03.2002. Coming into force: 31.03.2002. Effect: None. Territorial extent & classification: E/W/S/NI. General. – EC note: These regulations provide that certain breaches of REG 310/2002 are to be criminal offences. – 4p.: 30 cm. – 0 11 039807 6   £1.75

Customs and excise, England

The Free Zone (Port of Tilbury) Designation Order 2002 No. 2002/1418. – Enabling power: Customs and Excise Management Act 1979, s. 100A. – Issued: 19.06.2002. Made: 24.05.2002. Coming into force: 02.06.2002. Effect: None. Territorial extent & classification: E. Local. – 2p.: 30 cm. – This Order shall have effect for a period of 10 years from the date of coming into force. It replaces the previous Order - S.I. 1992/1282 – 0 11 042360 7   £1.50

Damages, England and Wales

The Damages for Bereavement (Variation of Sum) (England and Wales) Order 2002 No. 2002/644. – Enabling power: Fatal Accidents Act 1976, s. 1A (5). – Issued: 20.03.2002. Made: 11.03.2002. Laid: 11.03.2002. Coming into force: 01.04.2002 Effect: 1976 c. 30 amended. Territorial extent & classification: E/W. General. – 2p.: 30 cm. – 0 11 039504 2   £1.50

Damages, Northern Ireland

The Damages for Bereavement (Variation of Sum) (Northern Ireland) Order 2002 No. 2002/645. – Enabling power: S.I. 1977/1251 (NI. 18), art. 3A (5). – Issued: 19.03.2002. Made: 11.03.2002. Laid: 11.03.2002. Coming into force: 01.04.2002. Effect: S.I. 1977/1251 (NI. 18) amended. Territorial extent & classification: NI. General. – 2p.: 30 cm. – 0 11 039476 3   £1.50

Data protection

The Data Protection (Processing of Sensitive Personal Data) (Elected Representatives) Order 2002 No. 2002/2905. – Enabling power: Data Protection Act 1998, s. 67 (2), sch. 3, para. 10. – Issued: 02.12.2002. Made: 19.11.2002. Laid:-. Coming into force: 17.12.2002 in accordance with art. 1. Effect: None. Territorial extent & classification: E/W/S/NI. General. – 8p.: 30 cm. – Supersedes draft S.I. (ISBN 011042851X) issued on 15.10.2002 – EC note: This Order contributes to the implementation of Directive 95/46/EC on the protection of individuals with regard to the processing of personal data and on the free movement of such data – 0 11 044030 7   £2.00

Data protection, England and Wales

The Information Tribunal (Enforcement Appeals) (Amendment) Rules 2002 No. 2002/2722. – Enabling power: Data Protection Act 1998, s. 67 (2), sch. 6, para. 7. – Issued: 07.11.2002. Made: 30.10.2002. Laid: 01.11.2002. Coming into force: 30.11.2002. Effect: S.I. 2000/189 amended. Territorial extent & classification: E/W. General. – 2p.: 30 cm. – 0 11 042940 0   £1.50

Defence

The Armed Forces Act 2001 (Commencement No. 2) Order 2002 No. 2002/345 (C.8). – Enabling power: Armed Forces Act 2001, s. 39 (2) (6). Bringing into operation various provisions of the 2001 Act on 28.02.2002. – Issued: 22.04.2002. Made: 18.02.2002. Effect: None. Territorial extent & classification: E/W/S/NI. General. – This Statutory Instrument has been reprinted in consequence of a defect in the original print and is being issued free of charge to all known recipients. – 2p.: 30 cm. – 0 11 039358 9   £1.50

The Army, Air Force and Naval Discipline Acts (Continuation) Order 2002 No. 2002/1820. – Enabling power: Armed Forces Act 2001, s. 1 (2). – Issued: 23.07.2002. Made: 16.07.2002. Coming into force: 01.09.2002. Effect: None. Territorial extent & classification: E/W/S/NI. General. – 2p.: 30 cm. – 0 11 042495 6   £1.50

The Courts-Martial (Army) (Amendment) Rules 2002 No. 2002/230. – Enabling power: Army Act 1955, ss. 92 (5), 103, 143 (1). – Issued: 12.02.2002. Made: 05.02.2002. Laid: 07.02.2002. Coming into force: 28.02.2002. Effect: S.I. 1997/169 amended. Territorial extent & classification: E/W/S/NI. General. – 2p.: 30 cm. – 0 11 039290 6   £1.50

The Courts-Martial (Royal Air Force) (Amendment) Rules 2002 No. 2002/229. – Enabling power: Air Force Act 1955, ss. 92 (5), 103, 143 (1). – Issued: 12.02.2002. Made: 05.02.2002. Laid: 07.02.2002. Coming into force: 28.02.2002. Effect: S.I. 1997/171 amended. Territorial extent & classification: E/W/S/NI. General. – 2p.: 30 cm. – 0 11 039289 2   £1.50

The Courts-Martial (Royal Navy) (Amendment) Rules 2002 No. 2002/231. – Enabling power: Naval Discipline Act 1957, s. 58. – Issued: 12.02.2002. Made: 05.02.2002. Laid: 07.02.2002. Coming into force: 28.02.2002. Effect: S.I. 1997/170 amended. Territorial extent & classification: E/W/S/NI. General. – 2p.: 30 cm. – 0 11 039291 4   £1.50

The Protection of Military Remains Act 1986 (Designation of Vessels and Controlled Sites) Order 2002 No. 2002/1761. – Enabling power: Protection of Military Remains Act 1986, s. 1 (2). – Issued: 16.07.2002. Made: 09.07.2002. Coming into force: 30.09.2002. Effect: None. Territorial extent & classification: E/W/S/NI. General. – 4p.: 30 cm. – 0 11 042460 3   £1.75

The Royal Marines Terms of Service (Amendment) Regulations 2002 No. 2002/201. – Enabling power: Armed Forces Act 1966, s. 2. – Issued: 11.02.2002. Made: 04.02.2002. Laid: 06.02.2002. Coming into force: 01.04.2002. Effect: S.I. 1988/1395 amended. Territorial extent & classification: E/W/S/NI. General. – 2p.: 30 cm. – 0 11 039275 2 *£1.50*

Dentists

The Dentists Act 1984 (Dental Auxiliaries) Order 2002 No. 2002/1399. – Enabling power: Dentists Act 1984, s. 46 (4) (a). – Issued: 31.05.2002. Made: 22.05.2002. Coming into force: 23.05.2002, in accord. with art. 1. Effect: None. Territorial extent & classification: E/W/S/NI. General. – Supersedes draft S.I. issued 5 May 2002 (ISBN 0110399110). – 2p.: 30 cm. – 0 11 042242 2 *£1.50*

The General Dental Council (Constitution) Amendment Order 2002 No. 2002/3134. – Enabling power: Dentists Act 1984, s. 1 (2A) (2B). – Issued: 06.01.2003. Made: 17.12.2002. Laid: 06.01.2003. Coming into force: 10.04.2003. Effect: S.I. 2002/1625 amended. Territorial extent & classification: E/W/S/NI. General. – 2p.: 30 cm. – 0 11 044252 0 *£1.50*

The General Dental Council (Constitution) Order 2002 No. 2002/1625. – Enabling power: Dentists Act 1984, s. 1 (2A) (2B). – Issued: 03.07.2002. Made: 26.06.2002. Laid: 27.06.2002. Coming into force: 18.07.2002. Effect: None. Territorial extent & classification: E/W/S/NI. General. – 2p.: 30 cm. – 0 11 042404 2 *£1.50*

The General Dental Council (Election of Members) Rules Order of Council 2002 No. 2002/2463. – Enabling power: Dentists Act 1984, sch. 1, para. 3 (2). – Issued: 02.10.2002. Made: 19.09.2002. Coming into force: 30.09.2002. Effect: None. Territorial extent & classification: E/W/S/NI. General. – 8p.: 30 cm. – 0 11 042823 4 *£2.00*

The General Dental Council (President of the Council) Rules Order of the Council 2002 No. 2002/2464. – Enabling power: Dentists Act 1984, sch. 1, para. 4 (2). – Issued: 02.10.2002. Made: 19.09.2002. Coming into force: 30.09.2002. Effect: None. Territorial extent & classification: E/W/S/NI. General. – 4p.: 30 cm. – 0 11 042824 2 *£1.75*

Dentists, England

The Dental Auxiliaries (Amendment) Regulations 2002 No. 2002/1671. – Enabling power: Dentists Act 1984, s. 45 (1) (2) (b). – Issued: 03.07.2002. Made: 14.06.2002. Laid: 25.04.2002. Coming into force: 01.07.2002. Effect: S.I. 1986/887 amended. Territorial extent & classification: E. General. – Supersedes draft S.I. (ISBN 0110398866). – 4p.: 30 cm. – 0 11 042409 3 *£1.75*

Deregulation

The Deregulation (Bingo and Other Gaming) Order 2002 No. 2002/460. – Enabling power: Deregulation and Contracting Out Act 1994, s. 1. – Issued: 08.03.2002. Made: 01.03.2002. Coming into force: 29.03.2002. Effect: 1968 c. 65; 1985 c. 35 amended. Territorial extent & classification: E/W/S. General. – Supersedes draft S.I. (ISBN 011039383X) issued 28.02.2002. – 4p.: 30 cm. – 0 11 039423 2 *£1.75*

The Deregulation (Correction of Birth and Death Entries in Registers or Other Records) Order 2002 No. 2002/1419. – Enabling power: Deregulation and Contracting Out Act 1994, s. 1. – Issued: 19.06.2002. Made: 23.05.2002. Coming into force: 24.07.2002. Effect: 1953 c. 20; 1957 c.58 amended. Territorial extent & classification: E/W/S/NI. General. – With correction dated July 2002. – 4p.: 30 cm. – 0 11 042367 4 *£1.75*

Deregulation, England and Wales

The Deregulation (Disposals of Dwelling-houses by Local Authorities) Order 2002 No. 2002/367. – Enabling power: Deregulation and Contracting Out Act 1994, s. 1. – Issued: 26.02.2002. Made: 19.02.2002. Coming into force: 20.02.2002. Effect: 1993 c.28 amended. Territorial extent & classification: E/W. General. – 4p.: 30 cm. – 0 11 039372 4 *£1.75*

The Deregulation (Restaurant Licensing Hours) Order 2002 No. 2002/493. – Enabling power: Deregulation and Contracting Out Act 1994, s. 1. – Issued: 13.03.2002. Made: 05.03.2002. Coming into force: 02.04.2002. Effect: 1964 c. 26 amended. Territorial extent & classification: E/W. General. – Supersedes draft S.I. issued 07.02.2002 (ISBN 0110392671). – 2p.: 30 cm. – 0 11 039439 9 *£1.50*

Derelict land, England

The Derelict Land Clearance Area (Combe Down Stone Mines, Bath) Order 2002 No. 2002/2053. – Enabling power: Derelict Land Act 1982, s. 1 (7) (8) (b). – Issued: 09.08.2002. Made: 31.07.2002. Laid: 09.08.2002. Coming into force: 30.08.2002. Effect: None. Territorial extent & classification: E. General. – 2p.: 30 cm. – 0 11 042623 1 *£1.50*

Devolution, Scotland

The Housing (Scotland) Act 2001 (Housing Support Services Information) Order 2002 No. 2002/2264 (S.8). – Enabling power: Scotland Act 1988, ss. 104, 112 (1), 113. – Issued: 12.09.2002. Made: 03.09.2002. Laid: 06.09.2002. Coming into force: 01.10.2002. Effect: None. Territorial extent & classification: S. General. – 4p.: 30 cm. – 0 11 061611 1 *£1.75*

The Scotland Act 1998 (Agency Arrangements) (Specification) (No. 2) Order 2002 No. 2002/800 (S.2). – Enabling power: Scotland Act 1998, ss. 93 (3), 113. – Issued: 05.04.2002. Made: 26.03.2002. Laid before Parliament: 09.04.2002. Laid before the Scottish Parliament: 28.03.2002. Coming into force: 03.05.2002. Effect: S.I. 2001/3917 revoked. Territorial extent & classification: S. General. – 4p.: 30 cm. – 0 11 061243 4 £1.75

The Scotland Act 1998 (Agency Arrangements) (Specification) Order 2002 No. 2002/261 (S.1). – Enabling power: Scotland Act 1998, ss. 93 (3), 113. – Issued: 04.03.2002. Made: 12.02.2002. Laid before Parliament: 22.02.2002. Laid before the Scottish Parliament: 15.02.2002. Coming into force: 15.03.2002. Effect: None. Territorial extent & classification: S. General. – 4p.: 30 cm. – 0 11 061071 7 £1.75

The Scotland Act 1998 (Modifications of Schedule 5) Order 2002 No. 2002/1629 (S.5). – Enabling power: Scotland Act 1998, s. 30 (2). – Issued: 05.07.2002. Made: 26.06.2002. Coming into force: 27.06.2002. Effect: 1998 c. 46 amended. Territorial extent & classification: S. General. – 4p.: 30 cm. – 0 11 061498 4 £1.75

The Scotland Act 1998 (Transfer of Functions to the Scottish Ministers etc.) Order 2002 No. 2002/1630 (S.6). – Enabling power: Scotland Act 1998, ss. 63 (1) (b), 113, 124 (2). – Issued: 05.07.2002. Made: 26.06.2002. Coming into force: 27.06.2002. Effect: 1998 c. 46 modified. Territorial extent & classification: S. General. – 4p.: 30 cm. – 0 11 061504 2 £1.75

The Scottish Administration (Offices) Order 2002 No. 2002/801 (S.3). – Enabling power: Scotland Act 1998, s. 126 (8) (b). – Issued: 03.04.2002. Made: 26.03.2002. Laid before Parliament: 27.03.2002. Laid before the Scottish Parliament: 27.03.2002. Coming into force: In acc.with art. 1 (1). Effect: None. Territorial extent & classification: S. General. – 2p.: 30 cm. – 0 11 061249 3 £1.50

The Scottish Parliament (Elections etc.) Order 2002 No. 2002/2779 (S.11). – Enabling power: Scotland Act 1998, ss. 12 (1), 113. – Issued: 20.11.2002. Made: 06.11.2002. Coming into force: In accord. with art. 1. Effect: 1983 c. 2; 1998 c. 46 modified; S.I. 1994/1443; 2002/2779 amended & S.I. 1999/787 (with savings); 2001/1399, 1748, 1750 revoked. Territorial extent & classification: S. General. – 156p.: 30 cm. – 0 11 061714 2 £13.50

The Water Industry (Scotland) Act 2002 (Directions in the Interests of National Security) Order 2002 No. 2002/1264 (S.4). – Enabling power: Scotland Act 1998, ss. 104, 112 (1), 113. – Issued: 21.05.2002. Made: 01.05.2002 Laid: 08.05.2002. Coming into force: 31.05.2002. Effect: None. Territorial extent & classification: S. General. – 4p.: 30 cm. – 0 11 061412 7 £1.75

Devolution, Wales

The National Assembly for Wales (Representation of the People) (Amendment) Order 2002 No. 2002/834. – Enabling power: Government of Wales Act 1998, s. 11. – Issued: 03.04.2002. Made: 25.03.2002. Coming into force: In accordance with art. 1. Effect: S.I. 1999/450 amended. Territorial extent & classification: W. General. – 24p.: 30 cm. – Revoked by S.I. 2003/284 (ISBN 0110456505) – 0 11 039625 1 £4.00

Diplomatic service

The Consular Fees (No. 2) Order 2002 No. 2002/2634. – Enabling power: Consular Fees Act 1980, s. 1 (1). – Issued: 30.10.2002. Made: 22.10.2002. Coming into force: 21.11.2002. Effect: S.I. 1999/3132 amended. Territorial extent & classification: E/W/S/NI. General. – 4p.: 30 cm. – 0 11 042903 6 £1.75

The Consular Fees Order 2002 No. 2002/1627. – Enabling power: Consular Fees Act 1980, s. 1 (1). – Issued: 02.07.2002. Made: 26.06.2002. Coming into force: 01.07.2002. Effect: S.I. 1999/3132 amended. Territorial extent & classification: E/W/S/NI. General. – 4p.: 30 cm. – 0 11 042405 0 £1.75

Disabled persons

The Disability Discrimination Code of Practice (Goods, Facilities, Services and Premises) (Appointed Day) Order 2002 No. 2002/720. – Enabling power: Disability Discrimination Act 1995, s. 53A (6) (a). – Issued: 22.03.2002. Made: 14.03.2002. Coming into force: 27.05.2002. Effect: None. Territorial extent & classification: E/W/S. General. – 2p.: 30 cm. – 0 11 039520 4 £1.50

The Disability Discrimination Code of Practice (Goods, Facilities, Services and Premises) Revocation Order 2002 No. 2002/721. – Enabling power: Disability Discrimination Act 1995, s. 52 (11). – Issued: 22.03.2002. Made: 14.03.2002. Laid: 22.03.2002. Coming into force: 27.05.2002. Effect: Disability Discrimination Act 1995 code of practice on the rights of access to goods, facilities, services and premises (ISBN 0112710557) revoked. Territorial extent & classification: E/W/S. General. – 2p.: 30 cm. – 0 11 039519 0 £1.50

The Disability Discrimination Codes of Practice (Education) (Appointed Day) Order 2002 No. 2002/2216. – Enabling power: Disability Discrimination Act 1995, ss. 53A (6) (a), 67 (1). – Issued: 10.09.2002. Made: 28.08.2002. Coming into force: 01.09.2002. Effect: None. Territorial extent & classification: E/W/S. General. – 4p.: 30 cm. – 0 11 042736 X £1.75

The Disability Discrimination (Designation of Educational Institutions) Order 2002 No. 2002/1459. – Enabling power: Disability Discrimination Act 1995, s. 28R (6) (c) (7) (e). – Issued: 20.06.2002. Made: 30.05.2002. Laid: 07.06.2002. Coming into force: 28.06.2002. Effect: None. Territorial extent & classification: E/W/S. General. – 4p.: 30 cm. – 0 11 042369 0 *£1.75*

The Disability Discrimination (Educational Institutions) (Alteration of Leasehold Premises) Regulations 2002 No. 2002/1458. – Enabling power: Disability Discrimination Act 1995, sch. 6, para. 13. – Issued: 20.06.2002. Made: 30.05.2002. Laid: 07.06.2002. Coming into force: 28.06.2002. Effect: 1995 c. 30 modified. Territorial extent & classification: E/W/S. General. – 4p.: 30 cm. – 0 11 042368 2 *£1.75*

Disability Discrimination (Services and Premises) (Amendment) Regulations 2002 No. 2002/1980. – Enabling power: Disability Discrimination Act 1995, ss. 19 (5) (c), 67 (1), 68 (1). – Issued: 27.08.2002. Made: 24.07.2002. Laid: 29.07.2002. Coming into force: 01.09.2002. Effect: S.I. 1996/1836 amended. Territorial extent & classification: E/W/S. General. – 2p.: 30 cm. – 0 11 042688 6 *£1.50*

The Public Service Vehicles Accessibility (Amendment) Regulations 2002 No. 2002/2981. – Enabling power: Disability Discrimination Act 1995, ss. 40 (1) (2) (6) (7), 67 (2). – Issued: 11.12.2002. Made: 03.12.2002. Laid: 05.12.2002. Coming into force: 31.12.2002. Effect: S.I. 2000/1970 amended. Territorial extent & classification: E/W/S. General. – 2p.: 30 cm. – 0 11 044132 X *£1.50*

The Rail Vehicle Accessibility (C2C Class 357/0 Vehicles) Exemption (Amendment) Order 2002 No. 2002/3002. – Enabling power: Disability Discrimination Act 1995, s. 47. – Issued: 12.12.2002. Made: 04.12.2002. Laid: 05.12.2002. Coming into force: 01.01.2003. Effect: S.I. 2001/3955 amended. Territorial extent & classification: E/W/S/NI. General. – 2p.: 30 cm. – 0 11 044136 2 *£1.50*

The Rail Vehicle Accessibility (Cairngorm Funicular Railway) Exemption Order 2002 No. 2002/657. – Enabling power: Disability Discrimination Act 1995, s. 47 (1) (3) (4). – Issued: 19.03.2002. Made: 08.03.2002. Laid: 13.03.2002. Coming into force: 03.04.2002. Effect: None. Territorial extent & classification: E/W/S/NI. General. – 4p.: 30 cm. – 0 11 039483 6 *£1.75*

The Rail Vehicle Accessibility (Croydon Tramlink Class CR4000 Vehicles) Exemption (Amendment) Order 2002 No. 2002/3001. – Enabling power: Disability Discrimination Act 1995, s. 47. – Issued: 12.12.2002. Made: 04.12.2002. Laid: 05.12.2002. Coming into force: 01.01.2003. Effect: S.I. 2001/3952 amended. Territorial extent & classification: E/W/S/NI. General. – 2p.: 30 cm. – 0 11 044166 4 *£1.50*

The Rail Vehicle Accessibility (East Hayling Light Railway Vehicles) Exemption Order 2002 No. 2002/285. – Enabling power: Disability Discrimination Act 1995, s. 47 (1). – Issued: 20.02.2002. Made: 11.02.2002. Laid: 13.02.2002. Coming into force: 07.03.2002. Effect: None. Territorial extent & classification: E/W/S. General. – 8p., ill.: 30 cm. – 0 11 039335 X *£2.00*

The Rail Vehicle Accessibility (Isle of Wight Railway LCDR No. 2515 Vehicle) Exemption Order 2002 No. 2002/1694. – Enabling power: Disability Discrimination Act 1995, s. 47 (1) (3) (4). – Issued: 09.07.2002. Made: 28.06.2002. Laid: 03.07.2002. Coming into force: 31.07.2002. Effect: None. Territorial extent & classification: E/W/S/NI. General. – 4p.: 30 cm. – 0 11 042433 6 *£1.75*

The Rail Vehicle Accessibility (Middleton Railway Drewry Car) Exemption Order 2002 No. 2002/1188. – Enabling power: Disability Discrimination Act 1995, s. 47 (1) (3) (4). – Issued: 07.05.2002. Made: 25.04.2002. Laid: 30.04.2002. Coming into force: 22.05.2002. Effect: None. Territorial extent & classification: E/W/S/NI. General. – 4p.: 30 cm. – 0 11 039894 7 *£1.75*

The Rail Vehicle Accessibility (South Central Class 375/3 Vehicles) Exemption Order 2002 No. 2002/1617. – Enabling power: Disability Discrimination Act 1995, s. 47 (1) (3) (4). – Issued: 11.07.2002. Made: 23.06.2002. Laid: 24.06.2002. Coming into force: 16.07.2002. Effect: None. Territorial extent & classification: E/W/S/NI. General. – 4p.: 30 cm. – 0 11 042450 6 *£1.75*

The Rail Vehicle Accessibility (South West Trains Class 458 Vehicles) Exemption (Amendment) Order 2002 No. 2002/1762. – Enabling power: Disability Discrimination Act 1995, s. 47. – Issued: 24.07.2002. Made: 10.07.2002. Laid: 10.07.2002. Coming into force: 31.07.2002. Effect: S.I. 2002/656 amended. Territorial extent & classification: E/W/S/NI. General. – 4p.: 30 cm. – 0 11 042518 9 *£1.75*

The Rail Vehicle Accessibility (South West Trains Class 458 Vehicles) Exemption Order 2002 No. 2002/656. – Enabling power: Disability Discrimination Act 1995, s. 47. – Issued: 19.03.2002. Made: 08.03.2002. Laid: 13.03.2002. Coming into force: 03.04.2002. Effect: S.I. 2001/848 revoked. Territorial extent & classification: E/W/S/NI. General. – 4p.: 30 cm. – 0 11 039482 8 *£1.75*

The Rail Vehicle Accessibility (Summerlee Tramcar No. 392) Exemption Order 2002 No. 2002/2873. – Enabling power: Disability Discrimination Act 1995, s. 47 (1) (3) (4). – Issued: 28.11.2002. Made: 20.11.2002. Laid: 21.11.2002. Coming into force: 15.12.2002. Effect: None. Territorial extent & classification: E/W/S/NI. General. – 4p.: 30 cm. – 0 11 043698 9 *£1.75*

The Rail Vehicle Accessibility (Virgin West Coast Class 390 Vehicles) Exemption Order 2002 No. 2002/1699. – Enabling power: Disability Discrimination Act 1995, s. 47 (1) (3) (4). – Issued: 18.07.2002. Made: 28.06.2002. Laid: 03.07.2002. Coming into force: 22.07.2002. Effect: None. Territorial extent & classification: E/W/S. General. – 4p.: 30 cm. – 0 11 042466 2 *£1.75*

Disabled persons, England

Disability Discrimination (Prescribed Periods for Accessibility Strategies and Plans for Schools) (England) Regulations 2002 No. 2002/1981. – Enabling power: Disability Discrimination Act 1995, ss. 28D (2) (9), 67 (1) (3) (a), 68 (1). – Issued: 28.08.2002. Made: 24.07.2002. Laid: 05.08.2002. Coming into force: 01.09.2002. Effect: None. Territorial extent & classification: E. General. – 2p.: 30 cm. – 0 11 042690 8 *£1.50*

Disabled persons, England and Wales

The Special Educational Needs and Disability Act 2001 (Commencement No. 3) Order 2002 No. 2002/1647 (C.49). – Enabling power: Special Educational Needs and Disability Act 2001, s. 43 (3) (7) (8). Bringing into operation various provisions of the 2001 Act on 30.05.2002. – Issued: 11.07.2002. Made: 29.05.2002. Effect: None. Territorial extent & classification: E/W. General. – 4p.: 30 cm. – 0 11 042448 4 *£1.75*

The Special Educational Needs and Disability Act 2001 (Commencement No. 4) Order 2002 No. 2002/1721 (C.50). – Enabling power: Special Educational Needs and Disability Act 2001, s. 43 (3) (7) (8). Bringing into operation various provisions of the 2001 Act on 01.07.2002. – Issued: 11.07.2002. Made: 24.06.2002. Effect: None. Territorial extent & classification: E/W. General. – 4p.: 30 cm. – 0 11 042449 2 *£1.75*

The Special Educational Needs and Disability Act 2001 (Commencement No. 5) Order 2002 No. 2002/2217 (C.71). – Enabling power: Special Educational Needs and Disability Act 2001, s. 43 (3) (7) (8) (9) (10). Bringing into operation various provisions on 01.09.2002. – Issued: 12.09.2002. Made: 28.08.2002. Effect: 1995 c.50 modified. Territorial extent & classification: E/W. General. – 8p.: 30 cm. – 0 11 042741 6 *£2.00*

The Special Educational Needs and Disability Tribunal (General Provisions and Disability Claims Procedure) Regulations 2002 No. 2002/1985. – Enabling power: Disability Discrimination Act 1995, ss. 28J (1) (2) (3) (8), 67 (1) (3), 68 (1) & Education Act 1996, ss. 333 (5), 334 (2), 336 (1), 569 (1), 579 (1). – Issued: 05.08.2002. Made: 24.07.2002. Laid: 05.08.2002. Coming into force: 01.09.2002. Effect: None. Territorial extent & classification: E/W. General. – 24p.: 30 cm. – 0 11 042598 7 *£4.00*

Ecclesiastical law, England

The Parochial Fees Order 2002 No. 2002/1894. – Enabling power: Ecclesiastical Fees Measure 1986, ss. 1, 2. – Issued: 01.08.2002. Laid before the General Synod in draft: 05.07.2002. Made (sealed by the Archbishops' Council): 17.07.2002. Laid: 24.07.2002. Coming into force: 01.01.2003. Effect: S.I. 2001/2666 revoked. Territorial extent & classification: E. General. – 8p.: 30 cm. – 0 11 042578 2 *£2.00*

Ecclesiastical law, England: Fees

The Ecclesiastical Judges, Legal Officers and Others (Fees) Order 2002 No. 2002/1892. – Enabling power: Ecclesiastical Fees Measure 1986, s. 6. – Issued: 01.08.2002. Made (approved by the General Synod): 05.07.2002. Laid: 24.07.2002. Coming into force: 01.01.2003. Effect: S.I. 2001/2671 revoked. Territorial extent & classification: E. General. – 8p.: 30 cm. – 0 11 042576 6 *£2.00*

The Legal Officers (Annual Fees) Order 2002 No. 2002/1893. – Enabling power: Ecclesiastical Fees Measure 1986, s. 5. – Issued: 01.08.2002. Made (approved by the General Synod): 06.07.2002. Laid: 24.07.2001. Coming into force: 01.01.2003. Effect: S.I. 2001/2665 revoked. Territorial extent & classification: E. General. – 8p.: 30 cm. – 0 11 042577 4 *£2.00*

Education

The Disability Discrimination (Designation of Educational Institutions) Order 2002 No. 2002/1459. – Enabling power: Disability Discrimination Act 1995, s. 28R (6) (c) (7) (e). – Issued: 20.06.2002. Made: 30.05.2002. Laid: 07.06.2002. Coming into force: 28.06.2002. Effect: None. Territorial extent & classification: E/W/S. General. – 4p.: 30 cm. – 0 11 042369 0 *£1.75*

The Disability Discrimination (Educational Institutions) (Alteration of Leasehold Premises) Regulations 2002 No. 2002/1458. – Enabling power: Disability Discrimination Act 1995, sch. 6, para. 13. – Issued: 20.06.2002. Made: 30.05.2002. Laid: 07.06.2002. Coming into force: 28.06.2002. Effect: 1995 c. 30 modified. Territorial extent & classification: E/W/S. General. – 4p.: 30 cm. – 0 11 042368 2 *£1.75*

The Education (Student Loans) (Repayment) (Amendment) (No. 2) Regulations 2002 No. 2002/2859. – Enabling power: Teaching and Higher Education Act 1998, ss. 22, 42 (6) & Education (Scotland) Act 1980, ss. 73(f), 73B. – Issued: 25.11.2002. Made: 10.11.2002. Laid: 25.11.2002. Coming into force: 16.12.2002. Effect: S.I. 2000/944 amended. Territorial extent & classification: E/W/S. General. – 2p.: 30 cm. – 0 11 043013 1 *£1.50*

Education, England

The Action for Learning Partnership, Bedford Education Action Zone (Extension) Order 2002 No. 2002/3104. – Enabling power: School Standards and Framework Act 1998, s. 10 (2). – Issued: 13.01.2003. Made: 16.12.2002. Laid: 20.12.2002. Coming into force: 10.01.2003. Effect: None. Territorial extent & classification: E. General. – 2p.: 30 cm. – 0 11 044537 6 *£1.50*

The Ashington Education Action Zone (Extension) Order 2002 No. 2002/3095. – Enabling power: School Standards and Framework Act 1998, s. 10 (2). – Issued: 13.01.2003. Made: 16.12.2002. Laid: 20.12.2002. Coming into force: 10.01.2003. Effect: None. Territorial extent & classification: E. General. – 2p.: 30 cm. – 0 11 044513 9 *£1.50*

The Bolton Education Action Zone (Extension) Order 2002 No. 2002/3098. – Enabling power: School Standards and Framework Act 1998, s. 10 (2). – Issued: 13.01.2003. Made: 16.12.2002. Laid: 20.12.2002. Coming into force: 10.01.2003. Effect: None. Territorial extent & classification: E. General. – 2p.: 30 cm. – 0 11 044522 8   *£1.50*

The Breaking the Cycle Bridgewater Education Action Zone (Extension) Order 2002 No. 2002/3096. – Enabling power: School Standards and Framework Act 1998, s. 10 (2). – Issued: 13.01.2003. Made: 16.12.2002. Laid: 20.12.2002. Coming into force: 10.01.2003. Effect: None. Territorial extent & classification: E. General. – 2p.: 30 cm. – 0 11 044514 7   *£1.50*

The Brinsbury College (Dissolution) Order 2002 No. 2002/1402. – Enabling power: Further and Higher Education Act 1992, s. 27. – Issued: 31.05.2002. Made: 21.05.2002. Laid: 23.05.2002. Coming into force: 01.08.2002. Effect: None. Territorial extent & classification: E. General. – 2p.: 30 cm. – 0 11 042278 3   *£1.50*

The Broomfield Agricultural College (Dissolution) Order 2002 No. 2002/243. – Enabling power: Further and Higher Education Act 1992, s. 27. – Issued: 25.02.2002. Made: 08.02.2002. Laid: 08.02.2002. Coming into force: 01.03.2002. Effect: None. Territorial extent & classification: E. General. – 2p.: 30 cm. – 0 11 039359 7   *£1.50*

The Camborne, Pool and Redruth Success Zone Education Action Zone (Extension) Order 2002 No. 2002/3085. – Enabling power: School Standards and Framework Act 1998, s. 10 (2). – Issued: 13.01.2003. Made: 16.12.2002. Laid: 20.12.2002. Coming into force: 10.01.2003. Effect: None. Territorial extent & classification: E. General. – 2p.: 30 cm. – 0 11 044470 1   *£1.50*

The Challenge for Corby Education Action Zone (Extension) Order 2002 No. 2002/3103. – Enabling power: School Standards and Framework Act 1998, s. 10 (2). – Issued: 13.01.2003. Made: 16.12.2002. Laid: 20.12.2002. Coming into force: 10.01.2003. Effect: None. Territorial extent & classification: E. General. – 2p.: 30 cm. – 0 11 044530 9   *£1.50*

The Clacton and Harwich Education Action Zone (Extension) Order 2002 No. 2002/3102. – Enabling power: School Standards and Framework Act 1998, s. 10 (2). – Issued: 13.01.2003. Made: 16.12.2002. Laid: 20.12.2002. Coming into force: 10.01.2003. Effect: None. Territorial extent & classification: E. General. – 2p.: 30 cm. – 0 11 044526 0   *£1.50*

The Community Learning Partnership Barrow-in-Furness Education Action Zone (Extension) Order 2002 No. 2002/3093. – Enabling power: School Standards and Framework Act 1998, s. 10 (2). – Issued: 13.01.2003. Made: 16.12.2002. Laid: 20.12.2002. Coming into force: 10.01.2003. Effect: None. Territorial extent & classification: E. General. – 2p.: 30 cm. – 0 11 044485 X   *£1.50*

The Coventry Millennium Education Action Zone (Extension) Order 2002 No. 2002/3099. – Enabling power: School Standards and Framework Act 1998, s. 10 (2). – Issued: 13.01.2003. Made: 16.12.2002. Laid: 20.12.2002. Coming into force: 10.01.2003. Effect: None. Territorial extent & classification: E. General. – 2p.: 30 cm. – 0 11 044523 6   *£1.50*

The Derby Tertiary College - Wilmorton (Dissolution) Order 2002 No. 2002/245. – Enabling power: Further and Higher Education Act 1992, s. 27. – Issued: 25.02.2002. Made: 08.02.2002. Laid: 08.02.2002. Coming into force: 01.03.2002. Effect: None. Territorial extent & classification: E. General. – 2p.: 30 cm. – 0 11 039361 9   *£1.50*

The Dingle Granby Toxteth Education Action Zone (Extension) Order 2002 No. 2002/3088. – Enabling power: School Standards and Framework Act 1998, s. 10 (2). – Issued: 13.01.2003. Made: 16.12.2002. Laid: 20.12.2002. Coming into force: 10.01.2003. Effect: None. Territorial extent & classification: E. General. – 2p.: 30 cm. – 0 11 044473 6   *£1.50*

The Diocese of Bradford (Educational Endowments) Order 2002 No. 2002/1477. – Enabling power: Education Act 1996, ss. 554, 556. – Made: 29.05.2002. Coming into force: 19.06.2002. Effect: None. Territorial extent & classification: E. Local *Unpublished*

The Diocese of Bristol (Educational Endowments) Order 2002 No. 2002/2049. – Enabling power: Education Act 1996, ss. 554, 556. – Made: 29.07.2002. Coming into force: 19.08.2002. Effect: None. Territorial extent & classification: E. Local *Unpublished*

The Diocese of Derby (Educational Endowments) Order 2002 No. 2002/772. – Enabling power: Education Act 1996, ss. 554, 556. – Made: 21.03.2002. Coming into force: 11.04.2002. Effect: None. Territorial extent & classification: E. Local *Unpublished*

The Diocese of Lichfield (Educational Endowments) Order 2002 No. 2002/1722. – Enabling power: Education Act 1996, ss. 554, 556. – Made: 02.07.2002. Coming into force: 23.07.2002. Effect: None. Territorial extent & classification: E. Local *Unpublished*

The Diocese of London (Educational Endowments) Order 2002 No. 2002/1254. – Enabling power: Education Act 1996, ss. 554, 556. – Made: 03.05.2002. Coming into force: 24.05.2002. Effect: None. Territorial extent & classification: E. Local *Unpublished*

The Diocese of Newcastle (Educational Endowments) (No. 2) Order 2002 No. 2002/2122. – Enabling power: Education Act 1996, ss. 554, 556. – Made: 13.08.2002. Coming into force: 03.09.2002. Effect: None. Territorial extent & classification: E. Local *Unpublished*

The Diocese of Newcastle (Educational Endowments) Order 2002 No. 2002/1994. – Enabling power: Education Act 1996, ss. 554, 556. – Made: 25.07.2002. Coming into force: 15.08.2002. Effect: None. Territorial extent & classification: E. Local *Unpublished*

The Diocese of York (Educational Endowments) Order 2002 No. 2002/1403. – Enabling power: Education Act 1996, ss. 554, 556 & Reverter of Sites Act 1987, s. 5. – Made: 21.05.2002. Coming into force: 11.06.2002. Effect: None. Territorial extent & classification: E. Local *Unpublished*

The Downham and Bellingham Education Action Zone (Extension) Order 2002 No. 2002/3100. – Enabling power: School Standards and Framework Act 1998, s. 10 (2). – Issued: 13.01.2003. Made: 16.12.2002. Laid: 20.12.2002. Coming into force: 10.01.2003. Effect: None. Territorial extent & classification: E. General. – 2p.: 30 cm. – 0 11 044524 4 *£1.50*

The Dudley Partnership for Achievement Education Action Zone (Extension) Order 2002 No. 2002/2768. – Enabling power: School Standards and Framework Act 1998, s. 10 (2). – Issued: 20.11.2002. Made: 07.11.2002. Laid: 08.11.2002. Coming into force: 01.12.2002. Effect: None. Territorial extent & classification: E. General. – 2p.: 30 cm. – 0 11 042979 6 *£1.50*

The Easington and Seaham Education Action Zone (Extension) Order 2002 No. 2002/3087. – Enabling power: School Standards and Framework Act 1998, s. 10 (2). – Issued: 13.01.2003. Made: 16.12.2002. Laid: 20.12.2002. Coming into force: 10.01.2003. Effect: None. Territorial extent & classification: E. General. – 2p.: 30 cm. – 0 11 044472 8 *£1.50*

The East Manchester Education Action Zone (Extension) Order 2002 No. 2002/2770. – Enabling power: School Standards and Framework Act 1998, s. 10 (2). – Issued: 20.11.2002. Made: 07.11.2002. Laid: 08.11.2002. Coming into force: 01.12.2002. Effect: None. Territorial extent & classification: E. General. – 2p.: 30 cm. – 0 11 042981 8 *£1.50*

The East Yorkshire College of Further Education, Bridlington (Dissolution) Order 2002 No. 2002/246. – Enabling power: Further and Higher Education Act 1992, s. 27. – Issued: 25.02.2002. Made: 08.02.2002. Laid: 08.02.2002. Coming into force: 01.03.2002. Effect: None. Territorial extent & classification: E. General. – 2p.: 30 cm. – 0 11 039362 7 *£1.50*

The Education Act 2002 (Commencement No. 1) (Amendment) Order 2002 No. 2002/2018 (C.64). – Enabling power: Education Act 2002, s. 216 (4). Bringing into operation various provisions of the 2002 Act on 02.09.2002. – Issued: 27.08.2002. Made: 29.07.2002. Effect: S.I. 2002/2002 amended. Territorial extent & classification: E. General. – This Statutory instrument has been made in consequence of an error in S.I. 2002/2002 and is being issued free of charge to all known recipients of that SI. – With correction slip dated September 2002. – 2p.: 30 cm. – 0 11 042686 X *£1.50*

The Education Act 2002 (Commencement No. 1) Order 2002 No. 2002/2002 (C.63). – Enabling power: Education Act 2002, s. 216 (2) (4). Bringing into operation various provisions of the 2002 Act on 26.07.2002. & 02.09.2002. – Issued: 27.08.2002. Made: 25.07.2002. Effect: None. Territorial extent & classification: E. General. – 2p.: 30 cm. – 0 11 042687 8 *£1.50*

The Education Act 2002 (Commencement No. 3 and Savings and Transitional Provisions) Order 2002 No. 2002/2952 (C.93). – Enabling power: Education Act 2002, s. 216 (4) (5). Bringing into operation various provisions of the 2002 Act on 20.01.2003. – Issued: 06.12.2002. Made: 26.11.2002. Effect: None. Territorial extent & classification: E. General. – 8p.: 30 cm. – This S.I. has been reprinted in consequence of printing errors in the original print and is being issued free of charge to all known recipients of that S.I. (23.12.2002.) – 0 11 044093 5 *£2.00*

The Education Act 2002 (Modification of Provisions) (England) Regulations 2002 No. 2002/2316. – Enabling power: Education Act 2002, s. 214. – Issued: 19.09.2002. Made: 09.09.2002. Laid 09.09.2002. Coming into force: 01.10.2002. Effect: 1998 c.31; S.I. 2002/2113 amended; 2002 c. 32 modified (some temporary). Territorial extent & classification: E. General. – 4p.: 30 cm. – 0 11 042772 6 *£1.75*

The Education Act 2002 (Modification of Provisions) (No. 2) (England) Regulations 2002 No. 2002/2953. – Enabling power: Education Act 2002, s. 214. – Issued: 05.12.2002. Made: 26.11.2002. Laid 02.12.2002. Coming into force: 23.12.2002. Effect: 1996 c. 56; 1997 c. 50; 1998 c. 31 modified & 2002 c. 32 temporarily modified. Territorial extent & classification: E. General. – 4p.: 30 cm. – 0 11 044097 8 *£1.75*

The Education Act 2002 (Transitional Provisions etc.) (England) Regulations 2002 No. 2002/2113. – Enabling power: School Standards and Framework Act 1998, s. 44 (5) (6) & Education Act 2002, s. 214. – Issued: 22.08.2002. Made: 08.08.2002. Laid 12.08.2002. Coming into force: 02.09.2002. Effect: 1998 c.31; 2002 c.32 modified (some temporary) & S.I. 1999/2163, 2262 modified. Territorial extent & classification: E. General. – 4p.: 30 cm. – 0 11 042673 8 *£1.75*

The Education Action Forum (Proceedings) (Amendment) Regulations 2002 No. 2002/2301. – Enabling power: School Standards and Framework Act 1998, s. 138 (7), sch. 1, para. 4. – Issued: 18.09.2002. Made: 05.09.2002. Laid: 06.09.2002. Coming into force: 01.10.2002. Effect: S.I. 1998/1964 amended in relation to England. Territorial extent & classification: E. General. – 2p.: 30 cm. – 0 11 042755 6 *£1.50*

The Education (Admission Forums) (England) Regulations 2002 No. 2002/2900. – Enabling power: School Standards and Framework Act 1998, ss. 85A (3), 85B (1), 138 (7). – Issued: 02.12.2002. Made: 18.11.2002. Laid: 02.12.2002. Coming into force: 20.01.2003. Effect: None. Territorial extent & classification: E. General. – 8p.: 30 cm. – 0 11 044036 6 *£2.00*

The Education (Admissions Appeals Arrangements) (England) Regulations 2002 No. 2002/2899. – Enabling power: School Standards and Framework Act 1998, ss. 94 (5) (5A) (5C), 95 (3) (3A) (3B), 138 (7). – Issued: 02.12.2002. Made: 18.11.2002. Laid: 02.12.2002. Coming into force: 20.01.2003. Effect: S.I. 1994/1303 are revoked in relation to England insofar as they relate to admission appeal panels. Territorial extent & classification: E. General. – 8p.: 30 cm. – 0 11 044035 8 *£2.00*

The Education (Assisted Places) (Amendment) (England) Regulations 2002 No. 2002/1979. – Enabling power: Education (Schools) Act 1997, s. 3 (1) (2) (5) (9). – Issued: 05.08.2002. Made: 24.07.2002. Laid: 05.08.2002. Coming into force: 01.09.2002. Effect: S.I. 1997/1968 amended in relation to England. Territorial extent & classification. E. General. – 4p.: 30 cm. – 0 11 042596 0 £1.75

The Education (Assisted Places) (Incidental Expenses) (Amendment) (England) Regulations 2002 No. 2002/1984. – Enabling power: Education (Schools) Act 1997, s. 3 (3) (9). – Issued: 05.08.2002. Made: 24.07.2002. Laid: 05.08.2002. Coming into force: 01.09.2002. Effect: S.I. 1997/1969 amended in relation to England. Territorial extent & classification. E. General. – 2p.: 30 cm. – 0 11 042595 2 £1.50

The Education (Budget Statements) (England) Regulations 2002 No. 2002/535. – Enabling power: School Standards and Framework Act 1998, ss. 52 (1) (3) (4), 138 (7). – Issued: 18.04.2002. Made: 07.03.2002. Laid: 08.03.2002. Coming into force: 29.03.2002. Effect: None. Territorial extent & classification: E. General. – 31p.: 30 cm. – With correction slip. – 0 11 039766 5 £6.00

The Education (Bursaries for School Teacher Training) (England) (Amendment) (No. 2) Regulations 2002 No. 2002/1137. – Enabling power: Education (No. 2) Act 1986, ss. 50, 63 (3). – Issued: 30.04.2002. Made: 19.04.2002. Laid: 19.04.2002. Coming into force: 13.05.2002. Effect: S.I. 2002/509 amended. Territorial extent & classification: E. General. – 2p.: 30 cm. – Revoked with savings by S.I. 2002/509 (ISBN 0110441389) – 0 11 039834 3 £1.50

The Education (Bursaries for School Teacher Training) (England) (Amendment) Regulations 2002 No. 2002/756. – Enabling power: Education (No. 2) Act 1986, ss. 50, 63 (3). – Issued: 05.04.2002. Made: 19.03.2002. Laid: 20.03.2002. Coming into force: 01.04.2002. Effect: S.I. 2002/509 amended. Territorial extent & classification: E. General. – 2p.: 30 cm. – This Statutory Instrument has been made to correct errors in S.I. 2002/509 and is being issued free of charge to all known recipients of that statutory instrument – Revoked with savings by S.I. 2002/3005 (ISBN 0110441389) – 0 11 039659 6 £1.50

The Education (Bursaries for School Teacher Training) (England) Regulations 2002 No. 2002/509. – Enabling power: Education (No. 2) Act 1986, ss. 50, 63 (3). – Issued: 28.03.2002. Made: 06.03.2002. Laid: 07.03.2002. Coming into force: 01.04.2002. Effect: None. Territorial extent & classification: E. General. – 8p.: 30 cm. – Revoked with savings by S.I. 2002/3005 (ISBN 0110441389) – 0 11 039602 2 £2.00

The Education (Bursaries for School Teacher Training) (England) (Revocation) Regulations 2002 No. 2002/3005. – Enabling power: Education (No. 2) Act 1986, ss. 50, 63 (3). – Issued: 12.12.2002. Made: 02.12.2002. Laid: 12.12.2002. Coming into force: 05.01.2003. Effect: S.I. 2002/509, 756, 1137 revoked with savings. Territorial extent & classification: E. General. – 4p.: 30 cm. – 0 11 044138 9 £1.75

The Education (Chief Inspector of Schools in England) Order 2002 No. 2002/252. – Enabling power: School Inspections Act 1996, s. 1 (1) (4). – Issued: 22.02.2002. Made: 12.02.2002. Laid 22.02.2002. Coming into force: 31.03.2002. Effect: S.I. 2000/3239; 2001/2556 revoked. Territorial extent & classification: E. General. – 2p.: 30 cm. – 0 11 039323 6 £1.50

The Education (Co-ordination of Admission Arrangements) (Primary Schools) (England) Regulations 2002 No. 2002/2903. – Enabling power: School Standards and Framework Act 1998, ss. 89B (1) (4) (5) (6), 89C (1) (2) (3) (4) (5), 138 (7). – Issued: 02.12.2002. Made: 18.11.2002. Laid: 02.12.2002. Coming into force: 20.01.2003. Effect: None. Territorial extent & classification: E. General. – 8p.: 30 cm. – 0 11 043981 3 £2.00

The Education (Co-ordination of Admission Arrangements) (Secondary Schools) (England) Regulations 2002 No. 2002/2904. – Enabling power: School Standards and Framework Act 1998, ss. 89B (1) (4) (5) (6), 89C (1) (2) (3) (4) (5), 138 (7) & Education Act 2002. s. 214 (1). – Issued: 02.12.2002. Made: 18.11.2002. Laid: 02.12.2002. Coming into force: 20.01.2003. Effect: None. Territorial extent & classification: E. General. – 8p.: 30 cm. – 0 11 043982 1 £2.00

The Education (Determination of Admission Arrangements) (Amendment) (England) Regulations 2002 No. 2002/2896. – Enabling power: School Standards and Framework Act 1998, ss. 89 (2) (2A) (8) (8A), 89A (3), 138 (7). – Issued: 02.12.2002. Made: 18.11.2002. Laid: 02.12.2002. Coming into force: 20.01.2003. Effect: S.I. 1999/126 amended. Territorial extent & classification: E. General. – 8p.: 30 cm. – 0 11 044032 3 £2.00

The Education Development Plans (England) (Amendment) Regulations 2002 No. 2002/423. – Enabling power: School Standards and Framework Act 1998, ss. 6 (4) (5), 7 (1), 138 (7) (8). – Issued: 27.03.2002. Made: 26.02.2002. Laid: 27.02.2002. Coming into force: 01.04.2002. Effect: S.I. 2001/3815 amended. Territorial extent & classification: E. General. – 4p.: 30 cm. – 0 11 039589 1 £1.75

The Education (Funding for Teacher Training) Designation (No. 2) Order 2002 No. 2002/2713. – Enabling power: Education Act 1994, s. 4 (2). – Issued: 11.11.2002. Made: 30.10.2002. Laid: 31.10.2002. Coming into force: 18.11.2002. Effect: None. Territorial extent & classification: E. General. – 4p.: 30 cm. – 0 11 042941 9 £1.75

The Education (Funding for Teacher Training) Designation (No. 3) Order 2002 No. 2002/3003. – Enabling power: Education Act 1994, s. 4 (2). – Issued: 11.12.2002. Made: 02.12.2002. Laid: 11.12.2002. Coming into force: 01.01.2003. Effect: None. Territorial extent & classification: E. General. – 2p.: 30 cm. – 0 11 044135 4 £1.50

The Education (Funding for Teacher Training) Designation Order 2002 No. 2002/479. – Enabling power: Education Act 1994, s. 4 (2). – Issued: 18.03.2002. Made: 04.03.2002. Laid: 05.03.2002. Coming into force: 26.03.2002. Effect: None. Territorial extent & classification: E. General. – 2p.: 30 cm. – 0 11 039466 6 £1.50

The Education (Governors' Annual Reports) (England) (Amendment) (No. 2) Regulations 2002 No. 2002/2214. – Enabling power: Education Act 2002, s. 30 (2). – Issued: 10.09.2002. Made: 28.08.2002. Laid: 29.08.2002. Coming into force: 02.10.2002. Effect: S.I. 1999/2157 amended. Territorial extent & classification: E. General. – 2p.: 30 cm. – 0 11 042734 3 *£1.50*

The Education (Governors' Annual Reports) (England) (Amendment) Regulations 2002 No. 2002/1171. – Enabling power: School Standards and Framework Act 1998, ss. 42 (1) (2), 138 (7) (8). – Issued: 07.05.2002. Made: 24.04.2002. Laid: 25.04.2002. Coming into force: 16.05.2002. Effect: S.I. 1999/2157 amended. Territorial extent & classification: E. General. – 8p.: 30 cm. – 0 11 039882 3 *£2.00*

The Education (Grants etc.) (Dance and Drama) (England) (Amendment) Regulations 2002 No. 2002/2064. – Enabling power: Education Act 1996, ss. 485, 489, 569 (4) (5). – Issued: 28.08.2002. Made: 31.07.2002. Laid: 09.08.2002. Coming into force: 01.09.2002. Effect: S.I. 2001/2857 amended. Territorial extent & classification: E. General. – 4p.: 30 cm. – 0 11 042692 4 *£1.75*

The Education (Grants in respect of Voluntary Aided Schools) (Amendment) (England) Regulations 2002 No. 2002/1720. – Enabling power: School Standards and Framework Act 1998, s. 138 (7), sch. , para. 5. – Issued: 22.07.2002. Made: 27.06.2002. Laid: 08.07.2002. Coming into force: 01.08.2002. Effect: S.I. 1999/2020 amended. Territorial extent & classification: E. General. – 2p.: 30 cm. – 0 11 042487 5 *£1.50*

The Education (Grants) (Music, Ballet and Choir Schools) (Amendment) (England) Regulations 2002 No. 2002/2004. – Enabling power: Education Act 1996, ss. 485, 489 (1), 569 (4). – Issued: 07.08.2002. Made: 29.07.2002. Laid: 07.08.2002. Coming into force: 01.09.2002. Effect: S.I. 2001/2743 amended. Territorial extent & classification: E. General. – 4p.: 30 cm. – 0 11 042607 X *£1.75*

The Education (Induction Arrangements for School Teachers) (Consolidation) (Amendment) (England) Regulations 2002 No. 2002/2063. – Enabling power: Teaching and Higher Education Act 1998, ss. 19, 42 (6) (7). – Issued: 27.08.2002. Made: 05.08.2002. Laid: 07.08.2002. Coming into force: 01.09.2002. Effect: S.I. 2001/2897 amended. Territorial extent & classification: E. General. – 2p.: 30 cm. – 0 11 042685 1 *£1.50*

Education (Information About Individual Pupils) (England) (Amendment) Regulations 2002 No. 2002/3112. – Enabling power: Education Act 1996, ss. 537A (1) (2), 569 (4). – Issued: 09.01.2003. Made: 10.12.2002. Laid: 18.12.2002. Coming into force: 16.01.2003. Effect: S.I. 2001/4020 amended. Territorial extent & classification: E. General. – 4p.: 30 cm. – 0 11 044458 2 *£1.75*

The Education (Inspectors of Schools in England) (No. 2) Order 2002 No. 2002/3156. – Enabling power: School Inspections Act 1996, s. 1 (2). – Issued: 27.12.2002. Made: 17.12.2002. Coming into force: 18.12.2002. Effect: None. Territorial extent & classification: E. General. – 4p.: 30 cm. – 0 11 044276 8 *£1.75*

The Education (Inspectors of Schools in England) Order 2002 No. 2002/1821. – Enabling power: School Inspections Act 1996, s. 1 (2). – Issued: 23.07.2002. Made: 16.07.2002. Coming into force: 17.07.2002. Effect: None. Territorial extent & classification: E. General. – 2p.: 30 cm. – 0 11 042496 4 *£1.50*

The Education (Listed Bodies) (England) Order 2002 No. 2002/1377. – Enabling power: Education Reform Act 1988, s. 216 (2). – Issued: 23.05.2002. Made: 10.05.2002. Coming into force: 23.05.2002. Effect: S.I. 2000/3332 revoked. Territorial extent & classification: E. General. – 16p.: 30 cm. – 0 11 039983 8 *£3.00*

Education (London Residuary Body) (Property Transfer) (Amendment No. 2) Order 2002 No. 2002/2760. – Enabling power: Education Reform Act 1988, ss. 187 (5) (6) (7), 231 (2), 232 (5). – Issued: 13.11.2002. Made: 05.11.2002. Laid: 08.11.2002. Coming into force: 29.11.2002. Effect: S.I. 1992/587 amended. Territorial extent & classification: E. General. – 2p.: 30 cm. – 0 11 042950 8 *£1.50*

Education (London Residuary Body) (Property Transfer) (Amendment) Order 2002 No. 2002/2003. – Enabling power: Education Reform Act 1988, ss. 187 (5) (6) (7), 231 (2), 232 (5). – Issued: 22.08.2002. Made: 29.07.2002. Laid: 07.08.2002. Coming into force: 01.09.2002. Effect: S.I. 1992/587 amended. Territorial extent & classification: E. General. – 2p.: 30 cm. – 0 11 042669 X *£1.50*

The Education Maintenance Allowance (Pilot Areas) (Amendment) Regulations 2002 No. 2002/1841. – Enabling power: Education Act 1996, ss. 518, 569 (4). – Issued: 23.07.2002. Made: 16.07.2002. Laid: 23.07.2002. Coming into force: 19.08.2002. Effect: S.I. 2001/2750 amended. Territorial extent & classification: E. General. – 4p.: 30 cm. – 0 11 042510 3 *£1.75*

The Education (Middle School) (England) Regulations 2002 No. 2002/1983. – Enabling power: Education Act 1996, s. 5 (4). – Issued: 05.08.2002. Made: 24.07.2002. Laid: 05.08.2002. Coming into force: 01.09.2002. Effect: S.I. 1980/918 amended in relation to England. Territorial extent & classification. E. General. – 4p.: 30 cm. – 0 11 042597 9 *£1.75*

The Education (National Curriculum) (Exceptions at Key Stage 4) (England) (Amendment) Regulations 2002 No. 2002/2048. – Enabling power: Education Act 1996, ss. 363, 368, 569. – Issued: 22.08.2002. Made: 01.08.2002. Laid: 09.08.2002. Coming into force: 01.09.2002. Effect: S.I. 2000/1140 amended & S.I. 1996/2083 revoked in relation to England. Territorial extent & classification: E. General. – 4p.: 30 cm. – Revoked by S.I. 2003/252 (ISBN 011044843X) – 0 11 042668 1 *£1.75*

Education (Non-maintained Special Schools) (England) (Amendment) Regulations 2002 No. 2002/1982. – Enabling power: Education Act 1996, ss. 342 (4) (a), 569 (1), 579 (1). – Issued: 28.08.2002. Made: 24.07.2002. Laid: 05.08.2002. Coming into force: 01.04.2003. Effect: S.I. 1999/2257 amended. Territorial extent & classification: E. General. – 2p.: 30 cm. – 0 11 042691 6 *£1.50*

The Education (Nursery Education and Early Years Development) (England) (Amendment) Regulations 2002 No. 2002/2466. – Enabling power: School Standards and Framework Act 1998, ss. 120 (1) (3), 121 (1) (9), 138 (8). – Issued: 04.10.2002. Made: 25.09.2002. Laid: 27.09.2002. Coming into force: 21.10.2002. Effect: S.I. 1999/1329 amended. Territorial extent & classification: E. General. – 2p.: 30 cm. – 0 11 042834 X £1.50

The Education (Objection to Admission Arrangements) (Amendment) (England) Regulations 2002 No. 2002/2901. – Enabling power: School Standards and Framework Act 1998, ss. 90 (1) (2) (3) (9) (10), 138 (7). – Issued: 02.12.2002. Made: 18.11.2002. Laid: 02.12.2002. Coming into force: 20.01.2003. Effect: S.I. 1999/125 amended. Territorial extent & classification: E. General. – 4p.: 30 cm. – 0 11 044051 X £1.75

The Education (Outturn Statements) (England) Regulations 2002 No. 2002/536. – Enabling power: School Standards and Framework Act 1998, ss. 52 (2) (3) (4), 138 (7) (8), 144 (1) (2) (g). – Issued: 05.04.2002. Made: 07.03.2002. Laid: 08.03.2002. Coming into force: 01.04.2002. Effect: S.I. 2001/570 revoked insofar as they apply to outturn statements as therein defined prepared by local education authorities in England. Territorial extent & classification: E. General. – 20p.: 30 cm. – Revoked by S.I. 2003/1153 (ISBN 0110459814) in relation to England and only in relation to the financial year beginning 1st April 2002 – 0 11 039658 8 £3.50

The Education (Pupil Exclusions and Appeals) (Maintained Schools) (England) Regulations 2002 No. 2002/3178. – Enabling power: Education Act 2002, ss. 52 (3) (4), 210 (7), 214. – Issued: 20.01.2003. Made: 17.12.2002. Laid: 19.12.2002. Coming into force: 20.01.2003. Effect: S.I. 1995/2089; 1999/2163; 2001/3446 amended in relation to England & S.I. 1994/1303; 1999/1868; 2000/294 revoked subject to reg. 9 (2) in relation to England. Territorial extent & classification: E. General. – 12p.: 30 cm. – 0 11 044594 5 £2.50

The Education (Pupil Exclusions and Appeals) (Pupil Referral Units) (England) Regulations 2002 No. 2002/3179. – Enabling power: Education Act 2002, ss. 52 (3) (4) (5), 210 (7), 214. – Issued: 20.01.2003. Made: 17.12.2002. Laid: 19.12.2002. Coming into force: 20.01.2003. Effect: S.I. 2002/2550 revoked subject to reg. 10 (2). Territorial extent & classification: E. General. – 8p.: 30 cm. – 0 11 044595 3 £2.00

The Education (Pupil Information) (England) (Amendment) Regulations 2002 No. 2002/1680. – Enabling power: Education Act 1996, ss. 408, 563, 569 (4). – Issued: 22.07.2002. Made: 28.06.2002. Laid: 28.06.2002. Coming into force: 19.07.2002. Effect: S.I. 2000/297 amended. Territorial extent & classification: E. General. – 8p.: 30 cm. – 0 11 042488 3 £2.00

The Education (Pupil Referral Units) (Appeals Against Permanent Exclusion) (England) Regulations 2002 No. 2002/2550. – Enabling power: Education Act 2002, ss. 52 (7) (8), 210 (7) & Education Act 1996, sch. 1, para. 3. – Issued: 21.10.2002. Made: 08.10.2002. Laid: 10.10.2002. Coming into force: 04.11.2002. Effect: 1998 c. 31 modified. Territorial extent & classification: E. General. – [8]p.: 30 cm. – Revoked by S.I. 2002/3179 (ISBN 0110445953) subject to reg. 10 (2) – 0 11 042863 3 £2.00

The Education (School Information) (England) (Amendment) Regulations 2002 No. 2002/1172. – Enabling power: Education Act 1996, ss. 537 (1) to (4), (6) to (8), 569 (4) & School Standards and Framework Act 1998, ss. 92 (3) (6), 138 (7) (8). – Issued: 07.05.2002. Made: 24.04.2002. Laid: 25.04.2002. Coming into force: 16.05.2002. Effect: S.I. 1998/2526 amended. Territorial extent & classification: E. General. – 4p.: 30 cm. – Revoked by S.I. 2002/2897 (ISBN 0110440331) with saving – 0 11 039883 1 £1.75

The Education (School Information) (England) Regulations 2002 No. 2002/2897. – Enabling power: Education Act 1996, ss. 29 (5), 408, 537, 569 (4) (5) & School Standards and Framework Act 1998, ss. 92, 138 (1). – Issued: 02.12.2002. Made: 18.11.2002. Laid: 02.12.2002. Coming into force: 20.01.2003. Effect: S.I. 1998/2526; 1999/251; 2002/1172 revoked with savings. Territorial extent & classification: E. General. – 20p.: 30 cm. – 0 11 044033 1 £3.50

The Education (School Performance Information) (England) (Amendment) Regulations 2002 No. 2002/2017. – Enabling power: Education Act 1996, ss. 29 (3), 408, 537, 537A (1) (2), 569 (4) (5). – Issued: 09.08.2002. Made: 30.07.2002. Laid: 01.08.2002. Coming into force: 22.08.2002. Effect: S.I. 2001/3446 amended. Territorial extent & classification: E. General. – 8p.: 30 cm. – 0 11 042627 4 £2.00

The Education (School Performance Targets) (England) (Amendment) (No. 2) Regulations 2002 No. 2002/2105. – Enabling power: Education Act 1997, ss. 19, 54 (3). – Issued: 23.08.2002. Made: 08.08.2002. Laid: 09.08.2002. Coming into force: 01.09.2002. Effect: S.I. 1998/1532 amended. Territorial extent & classification: E. General. – 2p.: 30 cm. – 0 11 042676 2 £1.50

The Education (School Performance Targets) (England) (Amendment) Regulations 2002 No. 2002/840. – Enabling power: Education Act 1997, ss. 19, 54 (3). – Issued: 19.04.2002. Made: 26.03.2002. Laid: 27.03.2002. Coming into force: 30.04.2002. Effect: S.I. 1998/1532 amended. Territorial extent & classification: E. General. – 2p.: 30 cm. – 0 11 039778 9 £1.50

Education (Special Educational Needs) (Approval of Independent Schools) (Amendment) (England) Regulations 2002 No. 2002/2072. – Enabling power: Education Act 1996, ss. 347 (2), 569 (4) (5). – Issued: 22.08.2002. Made: 06.08.2002. Laid: 07.08.2002. Coming into force: 28.08.2002. Effect: S.I. 1994/651 amended. Territorial extent & classification: E. General. – 2p.: 30 cm. – 0 11 042671 1 £1.50

Education (Special Educational Needs) (City Colleges) (England) Regulations 2002 No. 2002/2071. – Enabling power: Education Act 1996, ss. 483A (4), 569 (4). – Issued: 22.08.2002. Made: 06.08.2002. Laid: 07.08.2002. Coming into force: 28.08.2002. Effect: None. Territorial extent & classification: E. General. – 2p.: 30 cm. – 0 11 042670 3 *£1.50*

The Education Standards Fund (England) (Amendment) Regulations 2002 No. 2002/1738. – Enabling power: Education Act 1996, ss. 484, 489, 569 (4). – Issued: 05.08.2002. Made: 04.07.2002. Laid: 09.07.2002. Coming into force: 01.08.2002. Effect: S.I. 2002/510 amended. Territorial extent & classification: E. General. – 4p.: 30 cm. – 0 11 042594 4 *£1.75*

The Education Standards Fund (England) Regulations 2002 No. 2002/510. – Enabling power: Education Act 1996, ss. 484, 489, 569 (4). – Issued: 05.04.2002. Made: 06.03.2002. Laid: 07.03.2002. Coming into force: 01.04.2002. Effect: S.I. 2001/826, 3994 revoked. Territorial extent & classification: E. General. – 8p.: 30 cm. – 0 11 039657 X *£2.00*

The Education (Teachers' Qualifications and Health Standards) (England) (Amendment) Regulations 2002 No. 2002/1434. – Enabling power: Education Reform Act 1988, ss. 218 (1) (a) (2) (2A) (3), 232 (5). – Issued: 10.06.2002. Made: 24.05.2002. Laid: 29.05.2002. Coming into force: 01.09.2002. Effect: S.I. 1999/2166 amended. Territorial extent & classification: E. General. – 4p.: 30 cm. – Revoked by S.I. 2003/1662 (ISBN 0110467116) – 0 11 042325 9 *£1.75*

The Education (Teacher Training Bursaries) (England) Regulations 2002 No. 2002/508. – Enabling power: Education (No. 2) Act 1986, ss. 50, 63 (3). – Issued: 28.03.2002. Made: 06.03.2002. Laid: 07.03.2002. Coming into force: 01.04.2002. Effect: S.I. 2001/2622 revoked. Territorial extent & classification: E. General. – 4p.: 30 cm. – 0 11 039604 9 *£1.75*

The Education (Variation of Admission Arrangements) (England) Regulations 2002 No. 2002/2898. – Enabling power: School Standards and Framework Act 1998, ss. 89 (8) (e) (f), 138 (7). – Issued: 02.12.2002. Made: 18.11.2002. Laid: 02.12.2002. Coming into force: 20.01.2003. Effect: None. Territorial extent & classification: E. General. – 4p.: 30 cm. – 0 11 044034 X *£1.75*

The Epicentre LEAP Ellesmere Port Cheshire Education Action Zone (Extension) Order 2002 No. 2002/3101. – Enabling power: School Standards and Framework Act 1998, s. 10 (2). – Issued: 13.01.2003. Made: 16.12.2002. Laid: 20.12.2002. Coming into force: 10.01.2003. Effect: None. Territorial extent & classification: E. General. – 2p.: 30 cm. – 0 11 044525 2 *£1.50*

The Financing of Maintained Schools (England) (Amendment No. 2) Regulations 2002 No. 2002/2763. – Enabling power: School Standards and Framework Act 1998, s. 47. – Issued: 25.11.2002. Made: 07.11.2002. Laid: 08.11.2002. Coming into force: 01.12.2002. Effect: S.I. 2002/377 amended. Territorial extent & classification: E. General. – 4p.: 30 cm. – Revoked by S.I. 2002/2868 (ISBN 0110430115) – 0 11 042997 4 *£1.75*

The Financing of Maintained Schools (England) (Amendment No. 3) Regulations 2002 No. 2002/2868. – Enabling power: School Standards and Framework Act 1998, s. 47. – Issued: 26.11.2002. Made: 15.11.2002. Laid: 26.11.2002. Coming into force: 17.12.2002. Effect: S.I. 2002/377 amended & 2002/2763 revoked. Territorial extent & classification: E. General. – 4p.: 30 cm. – 0 11 043011 5 *£1.75*

The Financing of Maintained Schools (England) (Amendment) Regulations 2002 No. 2002/2062. – Enabling power: School Standards and Framework Act 1998, s. 48 (1). – Issued: 20.08.2002. Made: 05.08.2002. Laid: 06.08.2002. Coming into force: 02.09.2002. Effect: S.I. 2002/377 amended. Territorial extent & classification: E. General. – 2p.: 30 cm. – 0 11 042664 9 *£1.50*

The Financing of Maintained Schools (England) Regulations 2002 No. 2002/377. – Enabling power: School Standards and Framework Act 1998, ss. 46, 47, 48 (1) (2), 138 (7), sch. 14, para. 1 (7). – Issued: 19.03.2002. Made: 21.02.2002. Laid: 22.02.2002. Coming into force: 15.03.2002. Effect: S.I. 2000/478, 1090 revoked. Territorial extent & classification: E. General. – 32p.: 30 cm. – 0 11 039477 1 *£6.00*

The Gloucester Education Achievement Zone (Extension) Order 2002 No. 2002/3108. – Enabling power: School Standards and Framework Act 1998, s. 10 (2). – Issued: 13.01.2003. Made: 16.12.2002. Laid: 20.12.2002. Coming into force: 10.01.2003. Effect: None. Territorial extent & classification: E. General. – 2p.: 30 cm. – 0 11 044541 4 *£1.50*

The Government of Further Education Corporations (Revocation) (England) Regulations 2002 No. 2002/1094. – Enabling power: Further and Higher Education Act 1992, s. 21 (1). – Issued: 29.04.2002. Made: 15.04.2002. Laid: 16.04.2002. Coming into force: 13.05.2002. Effect: S.I. 1992/1957,1963 (in relation to England); S.I. 1992/2153; 1993/271; 1994/1435; 1995/1342, 1344, 1569, 3204; 1996/736, 1765; 1998/1332; 1999/707, 709, 1328; 2000/2173 revoked. Territorial extent & classification: E. General. – 2p.: 30 cm. – 0 11 039829 7 *£1.50*

The Greenwich-Time to Succeed Education Action Zone (Extension) Order 2002 No. 2002/2124. – Enabling power: School Standards and Framework Act 1998, s. 10 (2). – Issued: 27.08.2002. Made: 08.08.2002. Laid: 14.08.2002. Coming into force: 06.09.2002. Effect: None. Territorial extent & classification: E. General. – 2p.: 30 cm. – 0 11 042683 5 *£1.50*

The Hackney Education Action Zone (Extension) Order 2002 No. 2002/2764. – Enabling power: School Standards and Framework Act 1998, s. 10 (2). – Issued: 20.11.2002. Made: 07.11.2002. Laid: 08.11.2002. Coming into force: 01.12.2002. Effect: None. Territorial extent & classification: E. General. – 2p.: 30 cm. – 0 11 042975 3 *£1.50*

The Hamilton Oxford Schools Partnership Education Action Zone (Extension) Order 2002 No. 2002/2123. – Enabling power: School Standards and Framework Act 1998, s. 10 (2). – Issued: 27.08.2002. Made: 08.08.2002. Laid: 14.08.2002. Coming into force: 06.09.2002. Effect: None. Territorial extent & classification: E. General. – 2p.: 30 cm. – 0 11 042684 3 *£1.50*

The Hastings and St Leonards Education Action Zone (Extension) Order 2002 No. 2002/2774. – Enabling power: School Standards and Framework Act 1998, s. 10 (2). – Issued: 20.11.2002. Made: 07.11.2002. Laid: 08.11.2002. Coming into force: 01.12.2002. Effect: None. Territorial extent & classification: E. General. – 2p.: 30 cm. – 0 11 042985 0 *£1.50*

The Heart of Slough Education Action Zone (Extension) Order 2002 No. 2002/2775. – Enabling power: School Standards and Framework Act 1998, s. 10 (2). – Issued: 20.11.2002. Made: 07.11.2002. Laid: 08.11.2002. Coming into force: 01.12.2002. Effect: None. Territorial extent & classification: E. General. – 2p.: 30 cm. – 0 11 042986 9 *£1.50*

Langley Junior School (Change to School Session Times) Order 2002 No. 2002/3063. – Enabling power: Education Act 2002, s. 2 (1). – Issued: 06.01.2003. Made: 11.12.2002. Laid: 13.12.2002. Coming into force: 06.01.2003. Effect: None. Territorial extent & classification: E. General. – 2p.: 30 cm. – 0 11 044452 3 *£1.50*

The LEA Budget, Schools Budget and Individual Schools Budget (England) Regulations 2002 No. 2002/3199. – Enabling power: School Standards and Framework Act 1998, ss. 45A, 138 (7)– Issued: 22.01.2003. Made: 20.12.2002. Laid: 20.12.2002. Coming into force: 10.01.2003. Effect: None. Territorial extent & classification: E. General. – 12p.: 30 cm. – 0 11 044619 4 *£2.50*

The Learning Together East Cleveland Education Action Zone (Extension) Order 2002 No. 2002/3090. – Enabling power: School Standards and Framework Act 1998, s. 10 (2). – Issued: 13.01.2003. Made: 16.12.2002. Laid: 20.12.2002. Coming into force: 10.01.2003. Effect: None. Territorial extent & classification: E. General. – 2p.: 30 cm. – 0 11 044475 2 *£1.50*

The Leigh Park Education Action Zone (Extension) Order 2002 No. 2002/3094. – Enabling power: School Standards and Framework Act 1998, s. 10 (2). – Issued: 13.01.2003. Made: 16.12.2002. Laid: 20.12.2002. Coming into force: 10.01.2003. Effect: None. Territorial extent & classification: E. General. – 2p.: 30 cm. – 0 11 044512 0 *£1.50*

The Longley Park Sixth Form College (Government) Regulations 2002 No. 2002/2523. – Enabling power: Further and Higher Education Act 1992, ss. 20 (2), 21 (1) (2), 89 (4), sch. 4. – Issued: 23.10.2002. Made: 07.10.2002. Laid: 08.10.2002. Coming into force: 01.11.2002. Effect: None. Territorial extent & classification: E. General. – 16p.: 30 cm. – With correction slip, dated April 2003 – 0 11 042879 X *£3.00*

The Longley Park Sixth Form College (Incorporation) Order 2002 No. 2002/2522. – Enabling power: Further and Higher Education Act 1992, ss. 16 (1), 17. – Issued: 23.10.2002. Made: 07.10.2002. Laid: 08.10.2002. Coming into force: 01.11.2002. Effect: None. Territorial extent & classification: E. General. – 2p.: 30 cm. – 0 11 042878 1 *£1.50*

The Mackworth College (Dissolution) Order 2002 No. 2002/244. – Enabling power: Further and Higher Education Act 1992, s. 27. – Issued: 25.02.2002. Made: 08.02.2002. Laid: 08.02.2002. Coming into force: 01.03.2002. Effect: None. Territorial extent & classification: E. General. – 2p.: 30 cm. – 0 11 039360 0 *£1.50*

The New Horizons Kent-Somerset Virtual Education Action Zone (Extension) Order 2002 No. 2002/2772. – Enabling power: School Standards and Framework Act 1998, s. 10 (2). – Issued: 20.11.2002. Made: 07.11.2002. Laid: 08.11.2002. Coming into force: 01.12.2002. Effect: None. Territorial extent & classification: E. General. – 2p.: 30 cm. – 0 11 042983 4 *£1.50*

The North Derbyshire Tertiary College (Designated Staff) Order 2002 No. 2002/2996. – Enabling power: Further and Higher Education Act 1992, s. 26 (1) to (5). – Issued: 10.12.2002. Made: 02.12.2002. Laid: 10.12.2002. Coming into force: 31.12.2002. Effect: None. Territorial extent & classification: E. General. – 8p.: 30 cm. – 0 11 044133 8 *£2.00*

The North Derbyshire Tertiary College (Dissolution) Order 2002 No. 2002/1714. – Enabling power: Further and Higher Education Act 1992, s. 27. – Issued: 19.07.2002. Made: 03.07.2002. Laid: 04.07.2002. Coming into force: 01.12.2002. Effect: None. Territorial extent & classification: E. General. – 4p.: 30 cm. – 0 11 042477 8 *£1.75*

The North East Derbyshire Coalfields Education Action Zone (Extension) Order 2002 No. 2002/2765. – Enabling power: School Standards and Framework Act 1998, s. 10 (2). – Issued: 20.11.2002. Made: 07.11.2002. Laid: 08.11.2002. Coming into force: 01.12.2002. Effect: None. Territorial extent & classification: E. General. – 2p.: 30 cm. – 0 11 042976 1 *£1.50*

The North Gillingham Education Action Zone (Extension) Order 2002 No. 2002/3092. – Enabling power: School Standards and Framework Act 1998, s. 10 (2). – Issued: 13.01.2003. Made: 16.12.2002. Laid: 20.12.2002. Coming into force: 10.01.2003. Effect: None. Territorial extent & classification: E. General. – 2p.: 30 cm. – 0 11 044483 3 *£1.50*

The Peterlee Education Action Zone (Extension) Order 2002 No. 2002/3086. – Enabling power: School Standards and Framework Act 1998, s. 10 (2). – Issued: 13.01.2003. Made: 16.12.2002. Laid: 20.12.2002. Coming into force: 10.01.2003. Effect: None. Territorial extent & classification: E. General. – 2p.: 30 cm. – 0 11 044471 X *£1.50*

The Rainbow Education Action Zone in Stoke on Trent (Extension) Order 2002 No. 2002/3097. – Enabling power: School Standards and Framework Act 1998, s. 10 (2). – Issued: 13.01.2003. Made: 16.12.2002. Laid: 20.12.2002. Coming into force: 10.01.2003. Effect: None. Territorial extent & classification: E. General. – 2p.: 30 cm. – 0 11 044521 X *£1.50*

The Regulatory Reform (Voluntary Aided Schools Liabilities and Funding) (England) Order 2002 No. 2002/906. – Enabling power: Regulatory Reform Act 2001, s. 1. – Issued: 05.04.2002. Made: 27.03.2002. Coming into force: 01.04.2002. Effect: 1998 c. 31 amended. Territorial extent and classification: E. General. – 8p.: 30 cm. – Supersedes draft S.I. (ISBN 0110395867) previously published on 25.03.2002 – 0 11 039660 X *£2.00*

The School Companies (Private Finance Initiative Companies) Regulations 2002 No. 2002/3177. – Enabling power: Education Act 2002, ss. 12, 210 (7). – Issued: 16.01.2003. Made: 17.12.2002. Laid: 19.12.2002. Coming into force: 20.01.2003. Effect: None. Territorial extent & classification: E. General. – 8p.: 30 cm. – 0 11 044577 5 *£2.00*

The School Companies Regulations 2002 No. 2002/2978. – Enabling power: Education Act 2002, ss. 12, 210 (7). – Issued: 12.12.2002. Made: 26.11.2002. Laid: 12.12.2002. Coming into force: 20.01.2003. Effect: None. Territorial extent & classification: E. General. – 16p.: 30 cm. – 0 11 044113 3 *£3.00*

The Schools Forums (England) Regulations 2002 No. 2002/2114. – Enabling power: School Standards and Framework Act 1998, ss. 47 (1), 47A. – Issued: 23.08.2002. Made: 08.08.2002. Laid 12.08.2002. Coming into force: 02.09.2002. Effect: None. Territorial extent & classification: E. General. – With correction slip issued 2 September 2002. – 8p.: 30 cm. – 0 11 042680 0 *£2.00*

The South Bradford Community Learning Partnership Education Action Zone (Extension) Order 2002 No. 2002/3107. – Enabling power: School Standards and Framework Act 1998, s. 10 (2). – Issued: 13.01.2003. Made: 16.12.2002. Laid: 20.12.2002. Coming into force: 10.01.2003. Effect: None. Territorial extent & classification: E. General. – 2p.: 30 cm. – 0 11 044540 6 *£1.50*

The Southend Education Action Zone (Extension) Order 2002 No. 2002/2766. – Enabling power: School Standards and Framework Act 1998, s. 10 (2). – Issued: 20.11.2002. Made: 07.11.2002. Laid: 08.11.2002. Coming into force: 01.12.2002. Effect: None. Territorial extent & classification: E. General. – 2p.: 30 cm. – 0 11 042977 X *£1.50*

The Speke Garston Excellent Education Action Zone (Extension) Order 2002 No. 2002/3106. – Enabling power: School Standards and Framework Act 1998, s. 10 (2). – Issued: 13.01.2003. Made: 16.12.2002. Laid: 20.12.2002. Coming into force: 10.01.2003. Effect: None. Territorial extent & classification: E. General. – 2p.: 30 cm. – 0 11 044539 2 *£1.50*

The Sunderland Building Our Future Education Action Zone (Extension) Order 2002 No. 2002/3089. – Enabling power: School Standards and Framework Act 1998, s. 10 (2). – Issued: 13.01.2003. Made: 16.12.2002. Laid: 20.12.2002. Coming into force: 10.01.2003. Effect: None. Territorial extent & classification: E. General. – 2p.: 30 cm. – 0 11 044474 4 *£1.50*

The Teacher Training Agency (Additional Functions) (England) Order 2002 No. 2002/507. – Enabling power: Education Act 1994, s. 16 (1), 23 (2). – Issued: 28.03.2002. Made: 06.03.2002. Laid: 07.03.2002. Coming into force: 01.04.2002. Effect: S.I. 2001/2747 revoked. Territorial extent & classification: E. General. – 2p.: 30 cm. – 0 11 039603 0 *£1.50*

The Teeside Tertiary College (Dissolution) Order 2002 No. 2002/1695. – Enabling power: Further and Higher Education Act 1992, s. 27. – Issued: 19.07.2002. Made: 01.07.2002. Laid: 03.07.2002. Coming into force: 01.08.2002. Effect: None. Territorial extent & classification: E. General. – 2p.: 30 cm. – 0 11 042476 X *£1.50*

The Telford and Wrekin Education Action Zone (Extension) Order 2002 No. 2002/2767. – Enabling power: School Standards and Framework Act 1998, s. 10 (2). – Issued: 20.11.2002. Made: 07.11.2002. Laid: 08.11.2002. Coming into force: 01.12.2002. Effect: None. Territorial extent & classification: E. General. – 2p.: 30 cm. – 0 11 042978 8 *£1.50*

The Wakefield Community Learning Partnership Education Action Zone (Extension) Order 2002 No. 2002/3109. – Enabling power: School Standards and Framework Act 1998, s. 10 (2). – Issued: 13.01.2003. Made: 16.12.2002. Laid: 20.12.2002. Coming into force: 10.01.2003. Effect: None. Territorial extent & classification: E. General. – 2p.: 30 cm. – 0 11 044544 9 *£1.50*

The Wednesbury Education Action Zone (Extension) Order 2002 No. 2002/2773. – Enabling power: School Standards and Framework Act 1998, s. 10 (2). – Issued: 20.11.2002. Made: 07.11.2002. Laid: 08.11.2002. Coming into force: 01.12.2002. Effect: None. Territorial extent & classification: E. General. – 2p.: 30 cm. – 0 11 042984 2 *£1.50*

The Widening Horizons - North Islington Education Action Zone (Extension) Order 2002 No. 2002/2769. – Enabling power: School Standards and Framework Act 1998, s. 10 (2). – Issued: 20.11.2002. Made: 07.11.2002. Laid: 08.11.2002. Coming into force: 01.12.2002. Effect: None. Territorial extent & classification: E. General. – 2p.: 30 cm. – 0 11 042980 X *£1.50*

The Withernsea and Southern Holderness Rural Achievement Education Action Zone (Extension) Order 2002 No. 2002/3105. – Enabling power: School Standards and Framework Act 1998, s. 10 (2). – Issued: 13.01.2003. Made: 16.12.2002. Laid: 20.12.2002. Coming into force: 10.01.2003. Effect: None. Territorial extent & classification: E. General. – 2p.: 30 cm. – 0 11 044538 4 *£1.50*

The Wolverhampton Education Action Zone (Extension) Order 2002 No. 2002/3091. – Enabling power: School Standards and Framework Act 1998, s. 10 (2). – Issued: 13.01.2003. Made: 16.12.2002. Laid: 20.12.2002. Coming into force: 10.01.2003. Effect: None. Territorial extent & classification: E. General. – 2p.: 30 cm. – 0 11 044476 0 £1.50

The Wythenshawe Education Action Zone (Extension) Order 2002 No. 2002/2771. – Enabling power: School Standards and Framework Act 1998, s. 10 (2). – Issued: 20.11.2002. Made: 07.11.2002. Laid: 08.11.2002. Coming into force: 01.12.2002. Effect: None. Territorial extent & classification: E. General. – 2p.: 30 cm. – 0 11 042982 6 £1.50

Education, England and Wales

The Education Act 2002 (Commencement No. 2 and Savings and Transitional Provisions) Order 2002 No. 2002/2439 (C.79). – Enabling power: Education Act 2002, s. 216 (2) (4) (5). Bringing into operation various provisions of the 2002 Act on 01.10.2002. – Issued: 10.10.2002. Made: 22.09.2002. Effect: Measure of the General Synod 1991 no. 2; 1996 c. 56 amended. Territorial extent & classification: E/W. General. – 8p.: 30 cm. – 0 11 042840 4   £2.00

The Education (Birmingham College of Food, Tourism and Creative Studies) (Transfer to the Higher Education Sector) Order 2002 No. 2002/1136. – Enabling power: Education Reform Act 1988, s. 122A. – Issued: 25.04.2002. Made: 15.04.2002. Laid: 25.04.2002. Coming into force: 01.08.2002. Effect: None. Territorial extent & classification: E/W. General. – 2p.: 30 cm. – 0 11 039823 8   £1.50

The Education (Grants for Disabled Postgraduate Students) (Amendment) Regulations 2002 No. 2002/2104. – Enabling power: Teaching and Higher Education Act 1998, ss. 22 (1) (2), 42 (6), 43 (1). – Issued: 22.08.2002. Made: 08.08.2002. Laid: 09.08.2002. Coming into force: 01.09.2002. Effect: S.I. 2000/2330 amended. Territorial extent & classification: E/W. General. – 2p.: 30 cm. – 0 11 042672 X £1.50

The Education (Mandatory Awards) (Amendment) (No. 2) Regulations 2002 No. 2002/3060. – Enabling power: Education Act 1962, ss. 1, 4 (2), sch. 1, paras 3, 4 & Education Act 1973, s. 3 (1) (3). – Issued: 06.01.2003. Made: 11.12.2002. Laid: 13.12.2002. Coming into force: 03.01.2003. Effect: S.I. 2002/1330 amended. Territorial extent & classification: E/W. General. – 2p.: 30 cm. – Revoked by S.I. 2003/1994 (ISBN 0110472373) – 0 11 044451 5   £1.50

The Education (Mandatory Awards) (Amendment) Regulations 2002 No. 2002/2089. – Enabling power: Education Act 1962, ss. 1, 4 (2), sch. 1, paras 3, 4 & Education Act 1973, s. 3 (1) (3). – Issued: 23.08.2002. Made: 06.08.2002. Laid: 09.08.2002. Coming into force: 01.09.2002. Effect: S.I. 2002/1330 amended. Territorial extent & classification: E/W. General. – 2p.: 30 cm. – Revoked by S.I. 2003/1994 (ISBN 0110472373) – 0 11 042679 7   £1.50

The Education (Mandatory Awards) Regulations 2001 (Amendment) (No. 3) Regulations 2002 No. 2002/173. – Enabling power: Education Act 1962, ss. 1, 4 (2), sch. 1, paras. 3, 4 & Education Act 1973, s. 3 (1) (3). – Issued: 11.02.2002. Made: 31.01.2002. Laid: 31.01.2002. Coming into force: 21.02.2002. Effect: S.I. 2001/1734 amended. Territorial extent & classification: E/W. General. – 2p.: 30 cm. – Revoked by S.I 2002/232 (ISBN 0110393481) – 0 11 039286 8   £1.50

The Education (Mandatory Awards) Regulations 2001 (Amendment) (No. 4) Regulations 2002 No. 2002/232. – Enabling power: Education Act 1962, ss. 1, 4 (2), sch. 1, paras 3, 4 & Education Act 1973, s. 3 (1) (3). – Issued: 22.02.2002. Made: 06.02.2002. Laid: 07.02.2002. Coming into force: 20.02.2002. Effect: S.I. 2001/1734 amended & S.I. 2002/173 revoked. Territorial extent & classification: E/W. General. – This statutory instrument has been made in consequence of a defect in S.I. 2002/173 and is being issued free of charge to all known recipients of that instrument. – 2p.: 30 cm. – Revoked by S.I. 2002/1330 (ISBN 011042509X) – 0 11 039348 1   £1.50

The Education (Mandatory Awards) Regulations 2002 No. 2002/1330. – Enabling power: Education Act 1962, ss. 1, 4 (2), sch. 1, paras 3, 4 & Education Act 1973, s. 3 (1) (3). – Issued: 23.07.2002. Made: 13.05.2002. Laid: 14.05.2002. Coming into force: 01.09.2002. Effect: S.I. 2001/1734, 2613, 2800; 2002/232 revoked. Territorial extent & classification: E/W. General. – 36p.: 30 cm. – Revoked by S.I. 2003/1994 (ISBN 0110472373) – 0 11 042509 X   £6.50

The Education (QCA Levy) (Amendment) Regulations 2002 No. 2002/1331. – Enabling power: Education Act 1997, ss. 36, 54 (3). – Issued: 24.05.2002. Made: 10.05.2002. Laid: 14.05.2002. Coming into force: 01.07.2002. Effect: S.I. 2002/435 amended. Territorial extent & classification: E/W/NI. General. – QCA = Qualifications and Curriculum Authority. – 2p.: 30 cm. – This S.I. has been made in consequence of a defect in S.I. 2002/435 and is being issued free of charge to all known recipients of that S.I. – 0 11 039985 4   £1.50

The Education (QCA Levy) Regulations 2002 No. 2002/435. – Enabling power: Education Act 1997, ss. 36, 54 (3). – Issued: 10.03.2002. Made: 26.02.2002. Laid: 04.03.2002. Coming into force: 28.03.2002. Effect: None. Territorial extent & classification: E/W/NI. General. – QCA = Qualifications and Curriculum Authority. – 8p.: 30 cm. – 0 11 039465 8   £2.00

The Education (School Teachers' Pay and Conditions) (No. 2) Order 2002 No. 2002/2223. – Enabling power: School Teachers Pay and Conditions Act 1991, ss. 2 (1) (3) (4), 5 (4). – Issued: 20.09.2002. Made: 29.08.2002. Laid: 30.08.2002. Coming into force: 01.09.2002. Effect: S.I. 2001/3243, 3435; 2002/838 revoked. Territorial extent & classification: E/W. General. – 4p.: 30 cm. – Revoked by S.I. 2003/2169 (ISBN 0110473949) – 0 11 042775 0   £1.75

The Education (School Teachers' Pay and Conditions) Order 2002 No. 2002/838. – Enabling power: School Teachers' Pay and Conditions Act 1991, ss. 2 (1) (3) (4), 5 (4). – Issued: 26.04.2002. Made: 27.03.2002. Laid: 27.03.2002. Coming into force: 01.04.2002. Effect: School Teachers' Pay and Conditions Document 2001 (ISBN 0112711073) amended. Territorial extent & classification: E/W. General. – 8p.: 30 cm. – Revoked by S.I. 2002/2223 (ISBN 0110427750) – 0 11 039820 3 *£2.00*

The Education (Student Loans) (Amendment) (England and Wales) Regulations 2002 No. 2002/1329. – Enabling power: Education (Student Loans) Act 1990, s. 1 (2) (b) (7), sch. 2, para. 1 (1). – Issued: 31.05.2002. Made: 13.05.2002. Laid: 14.05.2002. Coming into force: 01.08.2002. Effect: S.I. 1998/211 amended. Territorial extent & classification: E/W. General. – 2p.: 30 cm. – 0 11 042277 5 *£1.50*

The Education (Student Loans) (Amendment) (No. 2) (England and Wales) Regulations 2002 No. 2002/1433. – Enabling power: Education (Student Loans) Act 1990, s. 1 (2) (b) (7), sch. 2, para. 1 (1). – Issued: 10.06.2002. Made: 27.05.2002. Laid: 29.05.2002. Coming into force: 01.08.2002. Effect: S.I. 1998/211 amended. Territorial extent & classification: E/W. General. – This S.I. has been made in consequence of a defect in S.I. 2002/1329 (ISBN 0110422775) and is being issued free of charge to all known recipients of that SI. – 2p.: 30 cm. – 0 11 042324 0 *£1.50*

Education (Student Loans) (Repayment) (Amendment) Regulations 2002 No. 2002/2087. – Enabling power: Teaching and Higher Education Act 1998, ss. 22, 42 (6) & Education Act 2002, ss. 186, 210. – Issued: 23.08.2002. Made: 06.08.2002. Laid: 09.08.2002. Coming into force: 01.09.2002. Effect: S.I. 2000/944 amended. Territorial extent & classification: E/W. General. – 4p.: 30 cm. – 0 11 042681 9 *£1.75*

The Education (Student Support) (Amendment) (No. 2) Regulations 2002 No. 2002/2088. – Enabling power: Teaching and Higher Education Act 1998, ss. 22, 42 (6), 43 (1). – Issued: 23.08.2002. Made: 06.08.2002. Laid: 09.08.2002. Coming into force: 01.09.2002. Effect: S.I. 2002/195 amended. Territorial extent & classification: E/W. General. – 2p.: 30 cm. – Revoked by S.I. 2002/3200 (ISBN 0110448677) – 0 11 042678 9 *£1.50*

The Education (Student Support) (Amendment) (No. 3) Regulations 2002 No. 2002/3059. – Enabling power: Teaching and Higher Education Act 1998, ss. 22, 42 (6), 43 (1). – Issued: 06.01.2003. Made: 11.12.2002. Laid: 13.12.2002. Coming into force: 03.01.2003. Effect: S.I. 2002/195 amended. Territorial extent & classification: E/W. General. – 2p.: 30 cm. – Revoked by S.I. 2003/1065 (ISBN 011045636X) – 0 11 044436 1 *£1.50*

The Education (Student Support) (Amendment) Regulations 2002 No. 2002/1318. – Enabling power: Teaching and Higher Education Act 1998, ss. 22, 42 (6), 43 (1). – Issued: 28.05.2002. Made: 09.05.2002. Laid: 13.05.2002. Coming into force: 03.06.2002. Effect: S.I. 2002/195 amended. Territorial extent & classification: E/W. General. – 4p.: 30 cm. – Revoked by S.I. 2002/3200 (ISBN 0110448677) – 0 11 042241 4 *£1.75*

The Education (Student Support) (No. 2) Regulations 2002 No. 2002/3200. – Enabling power: Teaching and Higher Education Act 1998, ss. 22, 42 (6), 43 (1). – Issued: 18.02.2003. Made: 19.12.2002. Laid: 20.12.2002. Coming into force: 10.01.2003. Effect: S.I. 2002/195, 1318, 2088 revoked. Territorial extent & classification: E/W. General. – 49, [1]p.: 30 cm. – 0 11 044867 7 *£7.50*

The Education (Student Support) Regulations 2001 (Amendment) (No. 3) Regulations 2002 No. 2002/174. – Enabling power: Teaching and Higher Education Act 1998, ss. 22, 42 (6), 43 (1). – Issued: 11.02.2002. Made: 31.01.2002. Laid: 31.01.2002. Coming into force: 21.02.2002. Effect: S.I. 2001/951 amended. Territorial extent & classification: E/W. General. – 2p.: 30 cm. – Revoked by S.I. 2002/195 (ISBN 0110394542) – 0 11 039287 6 *£1.50*

The Education (Student Support) Regulations 2002 No. 2002/195. – Enabling power: Teaching and Higher Education Act 1998, ss. 22, 42 (6), 43 (1). – Issued: 14.03.2002. Made: 04.02.2002. Laid: 04.02.2002. Coming into force: 25.02.2002. Effect: S.I. 2001/951, 1730, 2355; 2002/174 revoked (01.09.2002.). Territorial extent & classification: E/W. General. – 48p.: 30 cm. – Revoked by S.I. 2002/3200 (ISBN 0110448677) – 0 11 039454 2 *£6.50*

Education (Teacher Student Loans) (Repayment etc.) Regulations 2002 No. 2002/2086. – Enabling power: Education Act 2002, ss. 186, 210. – Issued: 29.08.2002. Made: 06.08.2002. Laid: 09.08.2002. Coming into force: 01.09.2002. Effect: None. Territorial extent & classification: E/W. General. – [12]p.: 30 cm. – 0 11 042698 3 *£2.50*

The Learning and Skills Act 2000 (Commencement No.4) and Transitional Provisions Order 2002 No. 2002/279 (C. 5). – Enabling power: Learning and Skills Act 2000, ss. 152 (6), 154 (1) (3). Bringing into operation various provisions of the 2000 Act on 01.03.2001, 01.04.2001, 01.09.2001, in accord. with art. 1 (1) (2) (3). – Issued: 19.02.2002. Made: 08.02.2002. Effect: None. Territorial extent & classification: E/W. General. – 2p.: 30 cm. – 0 11 039319 8 *£1.50*

The School Budget Shares (Prescribed Purposes) (England) Regulations 2002 No. 2002/378. – Enabling power: School Standards and Framework Act 1998, s. 50 (3) (b). – Issued: 18.03.2002. Made: 21.02.2002. Laid: 22.02.2002. Coming into force: 01.04.2002. Effect: None. Territorial extent & classification: E/W. General. – 2p.: 30 cm. – 0 11 039464 X *£1.50*

The School Teachers' Remuneration Order 2002 No. 2002/2103. – Enabling power: School Teachers' Pay and Conditions Act 1991, s. 5 (3). – Issued: 28.08.2002. Made: 08.08.2002. Laid: 09.08.2002. Coming into force: 01.09.2002. Effect: None. Territorial extent & classification: E/W. General. – 2p.: 30 cm. – 0 11 042694 0 *£1.50*

The Special Educational Needs and Disability Act 2001 (Commencement No. 3) Order 2002 No. 2002/1647 (C.49). – Enabling power: Special Educational Needs and Disability Act 2001, s. 43 (3) (7) (8). Bringing into operation various provisions of the 2001 Act on 30.05.2002. – Issued: 11.07.2002. Made: 29.05.2002. Effect: None. Territorial extent & classification: E/W. General. – 4p.: 30 cm. – 0 11 042448 4 *£1.75*

The Special Educational Needs and Disability Act 2001 (Commencement No. 4) Order 2002 No. 2002/1721 (C.50).
– Enabling power: Special Educational Needs and Disability Act 2001, s. 43 (3) (7) (8). Bringing into operation various provisions of the 2001 Act on 01.07.2002. – Issued: 11.07.2002. Made: 24.06.2002. Effect: None. Territorial extent & classification: E/W. General. – 4p.: 30 cm. – 0 11 042449 2 *£1.75*

The Special Educational Needs and Disability Act 2001 (Commencement No. 5) Order 2002 No. 2002/2217 (C.71).
– Enabling power: Special Educational Needs and Disability Act 2001, s. 43 (3) (7) (8) (9) (10). Bringing into operation various provisions on 01.09.2002. – Issued: 12.09.2002. Made: 28.08.2002. Effect: 1995 c.50 modified. Territorial extent & classification: E/W. General. – 8p.: 30 cm. – 0 11 042741 6 *£2.00*

The Special Educational Needs and Disability Tribunal (General Provisions and Disability Claims Procedure) Regulations 2002 No. 2002/1985. – Enabling power: Disability Discrimination Act 1995, ss. 28J (1) (2) (3) (8), 67 (1) (3), 68 (1) & Education Act 1996, ss. 333 (5), 334 (2), 336 (1), 569 (1), 579 (1). – Issued: 05.08.2002. Made: 24.07.2002. Laid: 05.08.2002. Coming into force: 01.09.2002. Effect: None. Territorial extent & classification: E/W. General. – 24p.: 30 cm. – 0 11 042598 7 *£4.00*

The Special Educational Needs Tribunal (Amendment) Regulations 2002 No. 2002/2787. – Enabling power: Education Act 1996, ss. 333 (5), 334 (2), 336 (1) (2) (2A), 569 (4). – Issued: 19.11.2002. Made: 11.11.2002. Laid: 19.11.2002. Coming into force: 10.12.2002. Effect: S.I. 2001/600 amended. Territorial extent & classification: E/W. General. – 8p.: 30 cm. – 0 11 042974 5 *£2.00*

The Teachers' Pensions (Amendment) Regulations 2002 No. 2002/3058. – Enabling power: Superannuation Act 1972, ss. 9, 12, sch. 3. – Issued: 19.12.2002. Made: 05.12.2002. Laid: 19.12.2002. Coming into force: 10.01.2003. Effect: S.I. 1997/3001 amended. Territorial extent & classification: E/W. General. – 4p.: 30 cm. – 0 11 044183 4 *£1.75*

Teacher Training Agency (Additional Functions) (No.2) (Amendment) Order 2002 No. 2002/2513. – Enabling power: Education Act 1994, ss. 16 (1), 23 (2). – Issued: 11.10.2002. Made: 03.10.2002. Laid: 04.10.2002. Coming into force: 25.10.2002. Effect: S.I. 2000/2174 amended. Territorial extent & classification: E/W. General. – 2p.: 30 cm. – Revoked by S.I. 2003/2038 (ISBN 011047273X) – 0 11 042842 0 *£1.50*

Education, Northern Ireland

The Education (QCA Levy) (Amendment) Regulations 2002 No. 2002/1331. – Enabling power: Education Act 1997, ss. 36, 54 (3). – Issued: 24.05.2002. Made: 10.05.2002. Laid: 14.05.2002. Coming into force: 01.07.2002. Effect: S.I. 2002/435 amended. Territorial extent & classification: E/W/NI. General. – QCA = Qualifications and Curriculum Authority. – 2p.: 30 cm. – This S.I. has been made in consequence of a defect in S.I. 2002/435 and is being issued free of charge to all known recipients of that S.I. – 0 11 039985 4 *£1.50*

The Education (QCA Levy) Regulations 2002 No. 2002/435.
– Enabling power: Education Act 1997, ss. 36, 54 (3). – Issued: 18.03.2002. Made: 26.02.2002. Laid: 04.03.2002. Coming into force: 28.03.2002. Effect: None. Territorial extent & classification: E/W/NI. General. – QCA = Qualifications and Curriculum Authority. – 8p.: 30 cm. – 0 11 039465 8 *£2.00*

Education, Wales

The Aberdare College (Dissolution) Order 2002 No. 2002/3121 (W.291). – Enabling power: Further and Higher Education 1992, s. 27. – Made: 15.12.2002. Coming into force: 01.01.2003. Effect: None. Territorial extent & classification: W. Local – In English and Welsh *Unpublished*

The Education Act 2002 (Commencement No. 1) (Wales) Order 2002 No. 2002/3185 (W.301) (C.107). – Enabling power: Education Act 2002, s. 216 (3) (4) (b) (5). Bringing into operation various provisions of the 2002 Act on 19.12.2002., 31.03.2003. & 01.09.2003. – Issued: 02.01.2003. Made: 18.12.2002. Effect: None. Territorial extent & classification: W. General. In English and Welsh. Welsh title: Gorchymyn Deddf Addysg 2002 (Cychwyn Rhif 1) (Cymru) 2002. – 20p.: 30 cm. – 0 11 090613 6 *£3.50*

The Education Act 2002 (Transitional Provisions) (Wales) Regulations 2002 No. 2002/3184 (W.300). – Enabling power: Education Act 2002, s. 214. – Issued: 31.12.2002. Made: 18.12.2002. Coming into force: 19.12.2002. Effect: 1996 c.57; 1997 c.50; 1998 c.31; 2000 c.32 modified in relation to Wales. Territorial extent & classification: W. General. In English and Welsh. Welsh title: Rheoliadau Deddf Addysg 2002 (Darpariaethau Trosiannol) (Cymru) 2002. – – 8p.: 30 cm. – 0 11 090612 8 *£2.00*

The Education (Amount to follow Permanently Excluded Pupil) (Amendment) (Wales) Regulations 2002 No. 2002/408. – Enabling power: Education Act 1996, ss. 494, 569 (4) (5). – Issued: 13.03.2002. Made: 06.03.2002. Laid: 07.03.2002. Coming into force: 01.04.2002. Effect: S.I. 1999/495 amended for Wales. Territorial extent & classification: W. General. – 2p.: 30 cm. – 0 11 039448 8 *£1.50*

The Education (Assembly Learning Grant Scheme) (Wales) (Amendment) Regulations 2002 No. 2002/2814 (W.271). – Enabling power: Education Act 1996, ss. 484, 489, 569 (4). – Issued: 26.11.2002. Made: 14.11.2002. Coming into force: 15.11.2002. Effect: S.I. 2002/1857 (W.181) amended. Territorial extent & classification: W. General. In English and Welsh. Welsh title: Rheoliadau Addysg (Cynllun Grant Dysgu'r Cynulliad) (Cymru) (Diwygio) 2002. – 4p.: 30 cm. – 0 11 090585 7 *£1.75*

The Education (Assembly Learning Grant Scheme) (Wales) Regulations 2002 No. 2002/1857 (W.181). – Enabling power: Education Act 1996, ss. 484, 489, 569 (4). – Issued: 06.08.2002. Made: 16.07.2002. Coming into force: 01.08.2002. Effect: None. Territorial extent & classification: W. General. – In English and Welsh. Welsh title: Rheoliadau Addysg (Cynllun Grant Dysgu'r Cynulliad) (Cymru) 2002. – The Assembly Learning Grant is an additional grant for Welsh students in further and higher education. – 8p.: 30 cm. – 0 11 090538 5 *£2.00*

The Education (Assisted Places) (Amendment) (Wales) Regulations 2002 No. 2002/1879 (W.188). – Enabling power: Education (Schools) Act 1997, s. 3 (1) (2) (5) (9). – Issued: 15.08.2002. Made: 18.07.2002. Coming into force: 01.09.2002. Effect: S.I. 1997/1968 amended in relation to Wales. Territorial extent & classification. W. General. – In English and Welsh. Welsh title: Rheoliadau Addysg (Lleoedd a Gynorthwyir) (Diwygio) (Cymru) 2002. – 8p.: 30 cm. – 0 11 090547 4 *£2.00*

The Education (Assisted Places) (Incidental Expenses) (Amendment) (Wales) Regulations 2002 No. 2002/1880 (W.189). – Enabling power: Education (Schools) Act 1997, s. 3 (3) (4) (5) (9). – Issued: 15.08.2002. Made: 18.07.2002. Coming into force: 01.09.2002. Effect: S.I. 1997/1969 amended in relation to Wales. Territorial extent & classification. W. General. – In English and Welsh. Welsh title: Rheoliadau Addysg (Lleoedd a Gynorthwyir) (Mân Dreuliau) (Diwygio) (Cymru) 2002. – 4p.: 30 cm. – 0 11 090548 2 *£1.75*

The Education (Budget Statements) (Wales) Regulations 2002 No. 2002/122 (W.16). – Enabling power: School Standards and Framework Act 1998, ss. 52 (1) (3) (4), 138 (7) (8) & Welsh Language Act 1993, s. 26. – Issued: 28.02.2002. Made: 25.01.2002. Coming into force: 01.02.2002. Effect: S.I. 1999/451 revoked in relation to Wales (However those regulations shall continue to apply in relation to the financial years beginning on 01.04.1999. & 01.04.2000. & 01.04.2001.). Territorial extent & classification: W. General. – 36p.: 30 cm. – In English and Welsh. Welsh title: Rheoliadau Addysg (Datganiadau Cyllideb) (Cymru) 2002 – 0 11 090433 8 *£6.50*

The Education (Capital Grants) (Wales) Regulations 2002 No. 2002/679 (W.76). – Enabling power: Education Act 1996, ss. 484, 489, 569 (4). – Issued: 25.03.2002. Made: 12.03.2002. Coming into force: 01.04.2002. Effect: None. Territorial extent & classification: W. General. – 8p.: 30 cm. – In English and Welsh. Welsh title: Rheoliadau Addysg (Grantiau Cyfalaf) (Cymru) 2002 – 0 11 090446 X *£2.00*

The Education (Chief Inspector of Education and Training in Wales) Order 2002 No. 2002/260. – Enabling power: School Inspections Act 1996, s. 4 (1) (4). – Issued: 26.02.2002. Made: 12.02.2002. Laid: 26.02.2002. Coming into force: 01.06.2002. Effect: S.I. 1997/288 revoked. Territorial extent & classification: W. General. – 2p.: 30 cm. – 0 11 039330 9 *£1.50*

The Education Development Plans (Wales) Regulations 2002 No. 2002/1187 (W.125). – Enabling power: School Standards and Framework Act 1998, ss. 6 (4) (5), 7 (1) (9), 138 (7) (8). – Issued: 10.05.2002. Made: 25.04.2002. Coming into force: 26.04.2002. Effect: S.I. 1999/1439 revoked. Territorial extent & classification: W. General. – 24p.: 30 cm. – In English & Welsh. Welsh title: Rheoliadau Cynlluniau Datblygu Addysg (Cymru) 2002. Known in Wales as an education strategic plan – W. series number misprinted on document as 135. – 0 11 090485 0 *£4.00*

The Education (Individual Pupils' Achievements) (Information) (Wales) (Amendment) Regulations 2002 No. 2002/46 (W.5). – Enabling power: Education Act 1996, ss. 408, 569 (4) (5). – Issued: 08.02.2002. Made: 14.01.2002. Coming into force: 04.02.2002. Effect: S.I. 1997/573 amended. Territorial extent & classification: W. General. – 4p.: 30 cm. – In English and Welsh. - Welsh title: Rheoliadau Addysg (Cyraeddiadau Disgyblion Unigol) (Gwybodaeth) (Cymru) (Diwygio) 2002 – 0 11 090415 X *£1.75*

The Education (Inspectors of Education and Training in Wales) (No. 2) Order 2002 No. 2002/2632. – Enabling power: School Inspections Act 1996, s. 4 (2). – Issued: 30.10.2002. Made: 22.10.2002. Coming into force: 20.11.2002. Effect: None. Territorial extent & classification: W. General. – 2p.: 30 cm. – 0 11 042902 8 *£1.50*

The Education (Inspectors of Education and Training in Wales) Order 2002 No. 2002/1079. – Enabling power: School Inspections Act 1996, s. 4 (2). – Issued: 23.04.2002. Made: 17.04.2002. Coming into force: 20.05.2002. Effect: None. Territorial extent & classification: W. General. – 2p.: 30 cm. – 0 11 039802 5 *£1.50*

The Education (Listed Bodies) (Wales) Order 2002 No. 2002/1667 (W.159). – Enabling power: Education Reform Act 1988, s. 216 (2). – Issued: 04.07.2002. Made: 25.06.2002. Coming into force: 09.07.2002. Effect: S.I. 1999/834 revoked in relation to Wales. Territorial extent & classification: W. General. – 20p.: 30 cm. – In English and Welsh. Welsh title: Gorchymyn Addysg (Cyrff sy'n Cael eu Rhestru) (Cymru) 2002 – 0 11 090515 6 *£3.50*

The Education (National Curriculum) (Assessment Arrangements for English, Welsh, Mathematics and Science) (Key Stage 1) (Wales) Order 2002 No. 2002/45 (W.4). – Enabling power: Education Act 1996, ss. 356 (2) (c) (5) to (8), 568 (5) (6). – Issued: 06.02.2002. Made: 14.01.2002. Coming into force: 04.02.2002. Effect: S.I. 1997/2011 revoked. Territorial extent & classification: W. General. – 8p.: 30 cm. – In English and Welsh – Welsh title reads: Gorchymyn Addysg (Y Cwricwlwm Cenedlaethol) (Y Trefniadau Asesu ar gyfer Cymraeg, Saesneg, Mathemateg a Gwyddoniaeth (Cyfnod Allweddol 1) (Cymru) 2002 – 0 11 090412 5 *£2.00*

The Education (Recognised Bodies) (Wales) Order 2002 No. 2002/1661 (W.157). – Enabling power: Education Reform Act 1988, s. 216 (1). – Issued: 03.07.2002. Made: 25.06.2002. Coming into force: 09.07.2002. Effect: S.I. 1999/833 revoked in relation to Wales. Territorial extent & classification: W. General. – 8p.: 30 cm. – In English and Welsh. Welsh title: Gorchymyn Addysg (Cyrff sy'n Cael eu Cydnabod) (Cymru) 2002 – 0 11 090513 X *£2.00*

The Education (School Day and School Year) (Amendment) (No. 2) (Wales) Regulations 2002 No. 2002/1556 (W.153). – Enabling power: Education Act 1996, ss. 551, 569 (4) (5). – Issued: 05.07.2002. Made: 11.06.2002. Coming into force: 30.07.2002. Effect: S.I. 2000/1323 (W.101) amended. Territorial extent & classification: W. General. – 4p.: 30 cm. – In English and Welsh. Welsh title: Rheoliadau Addysg (Y Diwrnod Ysgol a'r Flwyddyn Ysgol) (Diwygio) (Rhif 2) (Cymru) 2002 – 0 11 090517 2 *£1.75*

The Education (School Day and School Year) (Amendment) (Wales) Regulations 2002 No. 2002/107 (W.12). – Enabling power: Education Act 1996, ss. 551, 569 (4) (5). – Issued: 07.02.2002. Made: 22.01.2001. Coming into force: 18.02.2002. Effect: S.I. 2000/1323 (W.101) amended. Territorial extent & classification: W. General. – 4p.: 30 cm. – In English & Welsh. Welsh title: Rheoliadau Addysg (Y Diwrnod Ysgol a'r Flwyddyn Ysgol) (Cymru) (Diwygio) 2002 – 0 11 090416 8 *£1.75*

The Education (School Information) (Wales) (Amendment) Regulations 2002 No. 2002/1400 (W.139). – Enabling power: Education Act 1996, ss. 537, 569 (4) (5). – Issued: 05.06.2002. Made: 21.05.2002. Coming into force: 31.05.2002. Effect: S.I. 1999/1812 amended. Territorial extent & classification: W. General. – 4p.: 30 cm. – In English & Welsh. Welsh title: Rheoliadau Addysg (Gwybodaeth Ysgolion) (Cymru) (Diwygio) 2002 – 0 11 090496 6 *£1.75*

The Education (Special Educational Needs) (Wales) Regulations 2002 No. 2002/152 (W.20). – Enabling power: Education Act 1996, ss. 316A (2), 322 (4), 324 (2), 325 (2A) (2B), 328 (1) (3A) (3B) (6), 329 (2A), 329A (9), 569 (1) (2) (4), sch. 26, paras. 2, 3 (1) (3) (4), sch. 27, paras. 2 (3), 2B (3), 5 (3), 6 (3), 7 (1) (2), 8 (3A) (5), 11 (2A) (4). – Issued: 14.02.2002. Made: 29.01.2002. Coming into force: 01.04.2002. Effect: S.I. 1994/1047 revoked in relation to Wales. Territorial extent & classification. W. General. – In English and Welsh. Welsh title: Rheoliadau Addysg (Anghenion Addysgol Arbennig) (Cymru) 2002. – 48p.: 30 cm. – 0 11 090422 2 *£6.50*

The Education Standards Grants (Wales) Regulations 2002 No. 2002/438 (W.56). – Enabling power: Education Act 1996, ss. 484, 489, 569 (4). – Issued: 26.03.2002. Made: 28.02.2002. Coming into force: 01.04.2002. Effect: S.I. 2001/891 (W.42) revoked with saving. Territorial extent & classification: W. General. – 20p.: 30 cm. – In English and Welsh. Welsh title: Rheoliadau Grantiau Safonau Addysg (Cymru) 2002 – 0 11 090447 8 *£3.50*

The Education (Teachers' Qualifications and Health Standards) (Wales) (Amendment) Regulations 2002 No. 2002/2938 (W.279). – Enabling power: Education Reform Act 1988, ss. 218 (1) (a) (2), 232 (5) (6). – Issued: 13.12.2002. Made: 27.11.2002. Coming into force: 17.12.2002. Effect: S.I. 1999/2817 (W.18) amended. Territorial extent & classification: W. General. – 12p.: 30 cm. – In English and Welsh. Welsh title: Rheoliadau Addysg (Cymwysterau a Safonau Iechyd Athrawon) (Cymru) (Diwygio) 2002 – 0 11 090590 3 *£2.50*

The Financing of Maintained Schools (Amendment) (Wales) Regulations 2002 No. 2002/136 (W.19). – Enabling power: School Standards and Framework Act 1998, ss. 46 (2) (3), 138 (7) (8)– Issued: 07.02.2002. Made: 25.01.2002. Coming into force: 01.02.2002. Effect: S.I. 1999/101 amended. Territorial extent & classification: W. General. – In English and Welsh. Welsh title: Rheoliadau Ariannu Ysgolion a Gynhelir (Diwygio) (Cymru) 2002. – 8p.: 30 cm. – 0 11 090417 6 *£2.00*

The Further Education Teachers' Qualifications (Wales) Regulations 2002 No. 2002/1663 (W.158). – Enabling power: Education Reform Act 1988, ss. 218 (1) (b) (10) (aa), 232 (5) (6). – Issued: 03.07.2002. Made: 25.06.2002. Coming into force: 01.07.2002. Effect: S.I. 1999/2817 (W.18) amended. Territorial extent & classification: W. General. – 8p.: 30 cm. – In English and Welsh. - Welsh title: Rheoliadau Cymwysterau Athrawon Addysg Bellach (Cymru) 2002 – 0 11 090514 8 *£2.00*

The General Teaching Council for Wales (Amendment) Order 2002 No. 2002/2940 (W.281). – Enabling power: Teaching and Higher Education Act 1998, s. 8 (1) (2). – Issued: 13.12.2002. Made: 27.11.2002. Coming into force: 31.03.2003. Effect: S.I. 1998/2911 amended. Territorial extent & classification: W. General. – In English and Welsh. Welsh title: Gorchymyn Cyngor Addysgu Cyffredinol Cymru (Diwygio) 2002. – 4p.: 30 cm. – 0 11 090593 8 *£1.75*

The General Teaching Council for Wales (Fees) Regulations 2002 No. 2002/326 (W.39). – Enabling power: Teaching and Higher Education Act 1998, ss. 12, 42 (6) (7). – Issued: 07.03.2002. Made: 13.02.2002. Coming into force: 01.03.2002. Effect: None. Territorial extent & classification: W. General. – In English and Welsh. Welsh title: Rheoliadau Cyngor Addysgu Cyffredinol Cymru (Ffioedd) 2002. – 8p.: 30 cm. – 0 11 090439 7 *£2.00*

Local Education Authority (Post-compulsory Education Awards) (Wales) Regulations 2002 No. 2002/1856 (W.180). – Enabling power: Education Act 1996, ss. 518 (1) (b) (2), 569 (4). Issued: 06.08.2002. Made: 18.07.2002. Coming into force: 01.08.2002. Effect: S.I. 1999/229 revoked in relation to Wales (with saving). Territorial extent & classification: W. General. – In English and Welsh. Welsh title: Rheoliadau Awdurdodau Addysg Lleol (Dyfarndaliadau Addysg Ôl-orfodol) (Cymru) 2002. – 8p.: 30 cm. – 0 11 090540 7 *£2.00*

The School Government (Terms of Reference) (Amendment) (Wales) Regulations 2002 No. 2002/1396 (W.138). – Enabling power: School Standards and Framework Act 1998, ss. 38 (3), 138 (7) (8). – Issued: 05.06.2002. Made: 21.05.2002. Coming into force: 30.09.2002. Effect: S.I. 2000/3027 (W.195) amended. Territorial extent & classification: W. General. – 4p.: 30 cm. – In English and Welsh. Welsh title: Rheoliadau Llywodraethu Ysgolion (Cylch Gwaith) (Diwygio) (Cymru) 2002 – 0 11 090495 8 *£1.75*

The School Governors' Annual Reports (Wales) (Amendment) Regulations 2002 No. 2002/1401 (W.140). – Enabling power: School Standards and Framework Act 1998, ss. 42 (1) (2), 138 (7) (8). – Issued: 05.06.2002. Made: 21.05.2002. Coming into force: 31.05.2002. Effect: S.I. 2001/1110 (W.54) amended. Territorial extent & classification: W. General. – 4p.: 30 cm. – In English and Welsh. Welsh title: Rheoliadau Adroddiadau Blynyddol Llwyodraethwyr Ysgol (Cymru) (Diwygio) 2002 – 0 11 090497 4 *£1.75*

The School Organisation Proposals by the National Council for Education and Training for Wales Regulations 2002 No. 2002/432 (W.55). – Enabling power: School Standards and Framework Act 1998, s. 138 (7) (8), sch. 8, para. 5 & Learning and Skills Act 2000, s. 152 (5) (6), sch. 7, paras. 20 (2), 21, 22, 28 (2), 29, 30, 39 (2), 40, 41, 42 (4), 43 (4). – Issued: 19.03.2002. Made: 26.02.2002. Coming into force: 01.04.2002. Effect: None. Territorial extent & classification: W. General. – In English and Welsh. Welsh title: Rheoliadau Cynigion Trefniadaeth Ysgol gan Gyngor Cenedlaethol Cymru dros Addysg a Hyffordiant 2002. – 17p.: 30 cm. – 0 11 090441 9 *£3.50*

The School Teacher Appraisal (Wales) Regulations 2002 No. 2002/1394 (W.137). – Enabling power: Education (No. 2) Act 1986, ss. 49, 63 (3). – Issued: 05.06.2002. Made: 21.05.2002. Coming into force: 30.09.2002. Effect: S.I. 1999/2888 (W.25) revoked. Territorial extent & classification: W. General. – In English & Welsh. Welsh title: Rheoliadau Gwerthuso Athrawon Ysgol (Cymru) 2002. – 20p.: 30 cm. – 0 11 090494 X *£3.50*

The Special Educational Needs and Disability Act 2001 (Commencement) (Wales) Order 2002 No. 2002/74 (W.8) (C.1). – Enabling power: Special Educational Needs and Disability Act 2001, s. 43 (6) (7). Bringing into force various provisions of the 2001 Act on 21.01.2002, 01.04.2002, in accord. with arts, 4, 5. – Issued: 23.01.2002. Made: 17.01.2002. Effect: None. Territorial extent & classification: W. General. – 8p.: 30 cm. – In English and Welsh. Welsh title: Gorchymyn Deddf Anghenion Addysgol Arbennig ac Anabledd 2001(Cychwyn) (Cymru) 2002 – 0 11 090409 5 *£2.00*

The Special Educational Needs Code of Practice (Appointed Day) (Wales) Order 2002 No. 2002/156 (W.22). – Enabling power: Education Act 1996, s. 314 (4). – Issued: 11.02.2002. Made: 29.01.2002. Coming into force: 01.04.2002. Effect: None. Territorial extent & classification: W. General. – 4p.: 30 cm. – In English and Welsh. Welsh title: Gorchymyn Cod Ymarfer Anghenion Addysgol Arbennig (Diwrnod Penodedig) (Cymru) 2002 – 0 11 090419 2 *£1.75*

The Special Educational Needs (Provision of Information by Local Education Authorities) (Wales) Regulations 2002 No. 2002/157 (W.23). – Enabling power: Education Act 1996, ss. 29 (5), 569 (4) (5). – Issued: 11.02.2002. Made: 29.01.2002. Coming into force: 01.04.2002. Effect: None. Territorial extent & classification: W. General. – 8p.: 30 cm. – In English and Welsh. Welsh title: Rheoliadau Anghenion Addysgol Arbennig (Darparu Gwybodaeth gan Awdurdodau Addysg Lleol) (Cymru) 2002 – 0 11 090420 6 *£2.00*

Electoral Commission

The Electoral Commission (Limit on Public Awareness Expenditure) Order 2002 No. 2002/505. – Enabling power: Political Parties, Elections and Referendums Act 2000, s. 13 (6). – Issued: 11.03.2002. Made: 04.03.2002. Laid: 11.03.2002. Coming into force: 01.04.2002. Effect: S.I. 2001/1329 revoked. Territorial extent & classification: UK. General. – 2p.: 30 cm. – 0 11 039441 0 *£1.50*

Electricity

The Electricity and Gas (Determination of Turnover for Penalties) Order 2002 No. 2002/1111. – Enabling power: Electricity Act 1989, s. 27A (8) & Gas Act 1986, s. 30A (8). – Issued: 29.04.2002. Made: 12.04.2002. Coming into force: 13.04.2002. Effect: None. Territorial extent & classification: E/W/S. General. – 2p.: 30 cm. – Supersedes draft S.I. (0110394267) issued on 11.03.2002 – 0 11 039831 9 *£1.50*

The Electricity (Approval of Pattern or Construction and Installation and Certification) (Amendment) Regulations 2002 No. 2002/3129. – Enabling power: Electricity Act 1989, ss. 31, 60, sch. 7, paras. 2, 13. – Issued: 16.01.2003. Made: 12.12.2003. Coming into force: 01.02.2003. Effect: S.I. 1998/1565, 1566 amended. Territorial extent & classification: E/W/S. General. – 12p.: 30 cm. – 0 11 044579 1 *£2.50*

The Electricity (Connection Charges) (Amendment) Regulations 2002 No. 2002/3232. – Enabling power: Electricity Act 1989, ss. 19 (2) (3), 60, 64 (1). – Issued: 07.01.2003. Made: 20.12.2002. Laid: 31.12.2002. Coming into force: 01.06.2003. Effect: S.I. 2002/93 amended. Territorial extent and classification: E/W/S. General. – 4p.: 30 cm. – 0 11 044456 6 *£1.75*

The Electricity (Connection Charges) Regulations 2002 No. 2002/93. – Enabling power: Electricity Act 1989, ss. 19 (2) (3), 60, 64 (1). – Issued: 19.02.2002. Made: 17.01.2002. Laid: 21.01.2002. Coming into force: 11.02.2002. Effect: S.I. 1990/527 amended. Territorial extent and classification: E/W/S. General. – 4p.: 30 cm. – 0 11 039338 4 *£1.75*

The Electricity Safety, Quality and Continuity Regulations 2002 No. 2002/2665. – Enabling power: Electricity Act 1989, ss. 29, 30 (3), 60. – Issued: 30.10.2002. Made: 24.10.2002. Laid: 28.10.2002. Coming into force: 31.01.2003. Effect: S.I. 1988/1057; 1990/390; 1992/2961; 1994/533, 3021; 1998/2971 revoked. Territorial extent & classification: E/W/S. General. – 28p.: 30 cm. – 0 11 042920 6 *£4.50*

The Electricity (Standards of Performance) (Amendment No. 2) Regulations 2002 No. 2002/742. – Enabling power: Electricity Act 1989, ss. 39, 39A, 39B, 40B, 42A, 60. – Issued: 10.04.2002. Made: 11.03.2002. Coming into force: 31.03.2002 for regs. 1, 2 & 01.04.2002 for remainder. Effect: S.I. 2001/3265 amended & 2002/476 revoked (31.03.2002.). Territorial extent & classification: E/W/S. General. – 8p.: 30 cm. – 0 11 039669 3 *£2.00*

The Electricity (Standards of Performance) (Amendment) Regulations 2002 No. 2002/476. – Enabling power: Electricity Act 1989, ss. 39, 39A, 39B, 40B, 42A, 60. – Issued: 10.04.2002. Made: 17.01.2002. Coming into force: 01.04.2002. Effect: S.I. 2001/3265 amended. Territorial extent & classification: E/W/S. General. – 4p.: 30 cm. – Revoked by S.I. 2002/742 (ISBN 0110396693) – 0 11 039666 9 *£1.75*

The Measuring Instruments (EC Requirements) (Electrical Energy Meters) (Amendment) Regulations 2002 No. 2002/3082. – Enabling power: European Communities Act 1972, s. 2 (2). – Issued: 20.12.2002. Made: 12.12.2002. Laid: 16.12.2002. Coming into force: 01.02.2003. Effect: S.I. 1995/2607 amended. Territorial extent & classification: E/W/S/NI. General. – 8p.: 30 cm. – 0 11 044219 9 *£2.00*

Electricity, England and Wales

The Electricity (Exemption from the Requirement for a Generation Licence) (England and Wales) Order 2002 No. 2002/823. – Enabling power: Electricity Act 1989, s. 5. – Issued: 03.04.2002. Made: 26.03.2002. Laid: 26.03.2002. Coming into force: 22.04.2002. Effect: None. Territorial extent & classification: E/W. General. – 4p.: 30 cm. – 0 11 039622 7 *£1.75*

The Renewables Obligation Order 2002 No. 2002/914. – Enabling power: Electricity Act 1989, ss. 32 to 32C. – Issued: 10.04.2002. Made: 31.03.2002. Coming into force: 01.04.2002. Effect: None. Territorial extent and classification: E/W. General. – 16p.: 30 cm. – EC note: This Order includes provisions giving effect, for England and Wales, to art. 3.1 of the Directive on promotion of electricity produced from renewable energy sources in the internal market, DIR 2001/77/EC – Supersedes draft S.I. (ISBN 0110393376) previously published on 19.02.2002 – 0 11 039670 7 *£3.00*

Electronic communications

The Electronic Commerce Directive (Financial Services and Markets) (Amendment) Regulations 2002 No. 2002/2015. – Enabling power: European Communities Act 1972, s. 2 (2). – Issued: 20.09.2002. Made: 31.07.2002. Laid: 31.07.2002. Coming into force: 21.08.2002. Effect: S.I. 2002/1775 amended. Territorial extent & classification: E/W/S/NI. General. – EC note: These Regs. amend S.I. 2002/1755 ("the principal regulations") to take account of the enactment of S.I. 2002/2013 ("the general regulations"). The principal regs. give effect to DIR 2000/31/EC (the Electronic Commerce Directive) in respect of matters within the scope of regulation by the Financial Services Authority (FSA). The general regs. give effect to the Directive in other areas. The purpose of the amendment is to ensure that the two sets of regs. do not overlap. – 2p.: 30 cm. – 0 11 042778 5 *£1.50*

The Electronic Commerce Directive (Financial Services and Markets) Regulations 2002 No. 2002/1775. – Enabling power: Financial Services and Markets Act 2000, ss. 349 (1), 414, 428 (3). – Issued: 02.09.2002. Made: 12.07.2002. Laid: 12.07.2002. Coming into force: 18.07.2002, 21.08.2002, in accord. with art. 1. Effect: 2000 c.8; S.I. 2001/2188, 2256 amended. Territorial extent & classification: E/W/S/NI. General. – EC note: Implements DIR 2000/31/EC (the Electronic Commerce Directive). – 12p.: 30 cm. – 0 11 042699 1 *£2.50*

The Electronic Commerce (EC Directive) Regulations 2002 No. 2002/2013. – Enabling power: European Communities Act 1972, s. 2 (2). – Issued: 09.08.2002. Made: 30.07.2002. Laid: 31.07.2002. Coming into force: 23.10.2002. for reg.16 & 21.08.2002. for remainder. Effect: S.I. 2001/1422 amended. Territorial extent & classification: E/W/S/NI. General. – 12p.: 30 cm. – EC note: Implements arts. 3, 5, 6, 7 (1), 10 to 14, 18 (2), 20 of Directive 2000/31/EC on certain legal aspects of information society services in particular electronic commerce in the internal market. These Regs should be read with S.I. 2002/1775, 2002/1776, 2002/2015, and 2157. They make parallel provisions in those areas subject to regulation by the Financial Services Authority under the Financial Services and Markets Act 2000 – 0 11 042643 6 *£2.50*

The Electronic Signatures Regulations 2002 No. 2002/318. – Enabling power: European Communities Act 1972, s. 2 (2). – Issued: 04.03.2002. Made: 13.02.2002. Laid: 14.02.2002. Coming into force: 08.03.2002. Effect: None. Territorial extent & classification: E/W/S/NI. General. – 8p.: 30 cm. – EC note: These Regs. implement DIR 1999/93 – 0 11 039401 1 *£2.00*

The Financial Services and Markets Act 2000 (Financial Promotion) (Amendment) (Electronic Commerce Directive) Order 2002 No. 2002/2157. – Enabling power: Financial Services and Markets Act 2000, ss. 21 (5) (6), 238 (6) (7), 428 (3). – Issued: 02.09.2002. Made: 20.08.2002. Laid:-. Coming into force: 21.08.2002. Effect: S.I. 2001/1060, 1335 amended. Territorial extent & classification: E/W/S/NI. General. – EC note: This Order amends S.I. 2001/1335 to take account of DIR 2000/31/EC (the Electronic Communications Directive). – 8p.: 30 cm. – 0 11 042703 3 *£2.00*

The Financial Services and Markets Act 2000 (Regulated Activities) (Amendment) (No. 2) Order 2002 No. 2002/1776. – Enabling power: Financial Services and Markets Act 2000, ss. 22 (1) (5), 428 (3). – Issued: 02.09.2002. Made: 12.07.2002. Laid: 12.07.2002. Coming into force: 21.08.2002. Effect: S.I. 2001/544 amended. Territorial extent & classification: E/W/S/NI. General. – EC note: This Order amends S.I. 2001/544 to take account of DIR 2000/31/EC (the Electronic Communications Directive). – 4p.: 30 cm. – 0 11 042700 9 *£1.75*

The Office of Communications Act 2002 (Commencement No. 1) Order 2002 No. 2002/1483 (C.42). – Enabling power: Office of Communications Act 2002 , s. 7 (2). Bringing into force various provisions of the 2002 Act on 01.07.2002, in accord. with art. 2. – Issued: 17.06.2002. Made: 05.06.2002. Effect: None. Territorial extent & classification: E/W/S/NI. General. – 2p.: 30 cm. – 0 11 042351 8 *£1.50*

The Office of Communications Act 2002 (Commencement No. 2) Order 2002 No. 2002/2955 (C.94). – Enabling power: Office of Communications Act 2002 , s. 7 (2). Bringing into force various provisions of the 2002 Act on 29.11.2002. – Issued: 06.12.2002. Made: 29.11.2002. Effect: None. Territorial extent & classification: E/W/S/NI. General. – 2p.: 30 cm. – 0 11 044106 0 *£1.50*

The Office of Communications (Membership) Order 2002 No. 2002/2956. – Enabling power: Office of Communications Act 2002 , s. 1 (7). – Issued: 06.12.2002. Made: 29.11.2002. Laid: 02.12.2002. Coming into force: 24.12.2002. Effect: 2002 c.11 amended. Territorial extent & classification: E/W/S/NI. General. – 2p.: 30 cm. – 0 11 044107 9 *£1.50*

The Statutory Payment Schemes (Electronic Communications) Regulations 2002 No. 2002/3047. – Enabling power: Finance Act 1999, ss. 132, 133 (2). – Issued: 16.12.2002. Made: 11.12.2002. Laid: 11.12.2002. Coming into force: 01.01.2003. Effect: None. Territorial extent & classification: E/W/S/NI. General. – 4p.: 30 cm. – 0 11 044179 6 *£1.75*

Employment and training

The Industrial Training Levy (Construction Board) Order 2002 No. 2002/303. – Enabling power: Industrial Training Act 1982, ss. 11 (2), 12 (2) (3) (4). – Issued: 21.02.2002. Made: 11.02.2002. Coming into force: 18.02.2002. Effect: None. Territorial extent & classification: E/W/S. General. – 8p.: 30 cm. – Supersedes draft S.I. (ISBN 0110392191) issued on 25.01.2002 – 0 11 039344 9 *£2.00*

The Industrial Training Levy (Engineering Construction Board) Order 2002 No. 2002/302. – Enabling power: Industrial Training Act 1982, ss. 11 (2), 12 (2) (3) (4). – Issued: 21.02.2002. Made: 11.02.2002. Coming into force: 18.02.2002. Effect: None. Territorial extent & classification: E/W/S. General. – 8p.: 30 cm. – Supersedes draft S.I. (ISBN 0110392183) issued on 25.01.2002 – 0 11 039343 0 *£2.00*

Employment and training, England and Wales

The Learning and Skills Act 2000 (Commencement No.4) and Transitional Provisions Order 2002 No. 2002/279 (C. 5). – Enabling power: Learning and Skills Act 2000, ss. 152 (6), 154 (1) (3). Bringing into operation various provisions of the 2000 Act on 01.03.2001, 01.04.2001, 01.09.2001, in accord. with art. 1 (1) (2) (3). – Issued: 19.02.2002. Made: 08.02.2002. Effect: None. Territorial extent & classification: E/W. General. – 2p.: 30 cm. – 0 11 039319 8 *£1.50*

Employment tribunals, Scotland

The Employment Tribunals (Enforcement of Orders in Other Jurisdictions) (Scotland) Regulations 2002 No. 2002/2972 (S.12). – Enabling power: Civil Jurisdiction and Judgments Act 1982, s. 18 (1) (a), sch. 6, paras. 2 (2), 4 (1) & Employment Tribunals Act 1996, s.7 (1). – Issued: 24.12.2002. Made: 02.12.2002. Laid: 03.12.2002. Coming into force: 24.12.2002. Effect: S.I. 1995/1717 revoked. Territorial extent & classification: S. General. – 8p.: 30 cm. – 0 11 044241 5 *£2.00*

Energy conservation, England

The Home Energy Efficiency Scheme (England) (Amendment) Regulations 2002 No. 2002/115. – Enabling power: Social Security Act 1990, s. 15. – Issued: 31.01.2002. Made: 21.01.2002. Laid: 25.01.2002. Coming into force: 15.02.2002. Effect: S.I. 2000/1280 amended. Territorial extent & classification: E. General. – 4p.: 30 cm. – 0 11 039233 7 *£1.75*

Energy conservation, Wales

The Warm Homes and Energy Conservation Act 2000 (Commencement) (Wales) Order 2002 No. 2002/758 (W.81) (C.18). – Enabling power: Warm Homes and Energy Conservation Act 2000, s. 4 (3). Bringing into force various provisions of the 2000 Act on 01.04.2002. – Issued: 03.04.2002. Made: 19.03.2002. Effect: None. Territorial extent & classification: W. General. – 4p.: 30 cm. – In English and Welsh. Welsh title: Gorchymyn Deddf Cartrefi Cynnes ac Arbed Ynni 2000 (Cychwyn) (Cymru) 2002 – 0 11 090451 6 *£1.75*

Environmental protection

The Agricultural or Forestry Tractors and Tractor (Emission of Gaseous and Particulate Pollutants) Regulations 2002 No. 2002/1891. – Enabling power: European Communities Act 1972, s. 2 (2). – Issued: 30.07.2002. Made: 17.07.2002. Laid: 22.07.2002. Coming into force: 12.08.2002. Effect: None. Territorial extent & classification: E/W/S/NI. General. – 16p.: 30 cm. – EC note: These Regs. implement articles 4.3 to 4.5 of DIR 2000/25 – 0 11 042548 0 *£3.00*

The Environmental Protection (Controls on Ozone-depleting Substances) Regulations 2002 No. 2002/528. – Enabling power: European Communities Act 1972, s. 2 (2) & Environmental Protection Act 1990s. 140 (1) (2) (3) (b) (4) (9) & (as regards Scotland) Scotland Act 1998, s. 57 (2). – Issued: 02.04.2002. Made: 08.03.2002. Laid: 08.03.2002. Coming into force: 31.03.2002. Effect: S.I. 1994/199; 1996/506 revoked. Territorial extent & classification: E/W/S/NI. General. – 16p.: 30 cm. – EC note: These Regs. make provision in relation to REG (EC) 2037/2000, as amended by REG (EC) 2038/2000 amd 2039/2000 – 0 11 039613 8 *£3.00*

Genetically Modified Organisms (Deliberate Release) Regulations 2002 No. 2002/2443. – Enabling power: European Communities Act 1972, s. 2 (2) & Environmental Protection Act 1990, ss. 108 (7), 111 (1) (4) (5) (7) (11), 122 (1) (4), 123 (7), 156. – Issued: 21.10.2002. Made: 25.09.2002. Laid: 26.09.2002. Coming into force: 17.10.2002. Effect: 1990 c. 43; S.I. 1997/1900; 2000/2831 amended & S.I. 1992/3280; 1993/152; 1995/304 revoked in relation to England. Territorial extent & classification: E/W (save for provisions in respect of the UK continental shelf). General– 31p.: 30 cm. – EC note: Implement, in respect of England and the UK sector of the continental shelf, Council directive 2001/18/EC – 0 11 042858 7 *£6.00*

The National Emission Ceilings Regulations 2002 No. 2002/3118. – Enabling power: European Communities Act 1972, s. 2 (2). – Issued: 31.12.2002. Made: 16.12.2002. Laid: 17.12.2002. Coming into force: 10.01.2003. Effect: None. Territorial extent & classification: UK. General. – EC note: Implements in the UK European Parliament and Council Directive 2001/81/EC relating to national emission ceilings for certain atmospheric pollutants. – 8p.: 30 cm. – 0 11 044394 2 £2.00

The Non-Road Mobile Machinery (Emission of Gaseous and Particulate Pollutants) (Amendment) Regulations 2002 No. 2002/1649. – Enabling power: European Communities Act 1972, s. 2 (2). – Issued: 03.07.2002. Made: 24.06.2002. Laid: 26.06.2002. Coming into force: 17.07.2002. Effect: S.I. 1999/1053 amended. Territorial extent & classification: E/W/S/NI. General. – 2p.: 30 cm. – EC note: Implement EC DIR 2001/63/EC which amends Annex III & IV of DIR 97/68/EC – 0 11 042410 7 £1.50

The Offshore Chemicals Regulations 2002 No. 2002/1355. – Enabling power: Pollution Prevention and Control Act 1999, ss. 2, 7 (9). – Issued: 22.05.2002. Made: 14.05.2002. Coming into force: 15.05.2002. Effect: S.I. 1985/1699; S.R. 1995/234 amended. Territorial extent & classification: Territorial waters outside the UK. – Supersedes draft S.I. issued 2 April 2002 (ISBN 0110396219). – 16p.: 30 cm. – 0 11 039966 8 £3.00

The Offshore Installations (Emergency Pollution Control) Regulations 2002 No. 2002/1861. – Enabling power: Pollution, Prevention and Control Act 1999, ss. 3, 7 (9). – Issued: 25.07.2002. Made: 17.07.2002. Coming into force: 18.07.2002, in accord. with reg. 1. Effect: None. Territorial extent & classification: E/W/S/NI. General. – 4p.: 30 cm. – 0 11 042531 6 £1.75

Environmental protection, England

The Air Quality (England) (Amendment) Regulations 2002 No. 2002/3043. – Enabling power: Environment Act 1995, ss. 87 (1) (2), 91 (1). – Issued: 23.12.2002. Made: 10.12.2002. Coming into force: 11.12.2002. Effect: S.I. 2000/928 amended. Territorial extent & classification: E. General. – 4p.: 30 cm. – Supersedes draft S.I. (ISBN 0110429958) issued on 22.11.2002 – 0 11 044220 2 £1.75

The Air Quality Limit Values (Amendment) Regulations 2002 No. 2002/3117. – Enabling power: European Communities Act 1972, s. 2 (2). – Issued: 31.12.2002. Made: 16.12.2002. Laid: 17.12.2002. Coming into force: 10.01.2003. Effect: S.I. 2001/2315 amended in relation to England. Territorial extent & classification: E. General. – 8p.: 30 cm. – EC note: Implements in England, Directive 2000/69/EC relating to limit values for benzene and carbon monoxide in ambient air – Revoked by S.I. 2003/2121 (ISBN 0110474481) in relation to England – 0 11 044393 4 £2.00

The Dog Fouling (Fixed Penalty) (England) Order 2002 No. 2002/425. – Enabling power: Environmental Protection Act 1990, s. 88 ((7). – Issued: 19.03.2002. Made: 24.02.2002. Laid: 08.03.2002. Coming into force: 01.04.2002. Effect: S.I. 1996/2763 amended. Territorial extent & classification: E. General. – 2p.: 30 cm. – 0 11 039479 8 £1.50

The Environmental Protection (Restriction on Use of Lead Shot) (England) (Amendment) Regulations 2002 No. 2002/2102. – Enabling power: Environmental Protection Act 1990, s. 140. – Issued: 04.09.2002. Made: 08.08.2002. Laid: 09.08.2002. Coming into force: 01.09.2002. Effect: S.I. 1999/2170 amended. Territorial extent & classification: E. General. – 12p.: 30 cm. – 0 11 042713 0 £2.50

The Environmental Protection (Waste Recycling Payments) (Amendment) (England) Regulations 2002 No. 2002/531. – Enabling power: Environmental Protection Act 1990, s. 52 (8). – Issued: 02.04.2002. Made: 08.03.2002. Laid: 11.03.2002. Coming into force: 01.04.2002. Effect: S.I. 1992/462 amended & S.I. 2001/661 revoked. Territorial extent & classification: E. General. – 4p.: 30 cm. – Revoked by S.I. 2003/596 (ISBN 0110453204) – 0 11 039614 6 £1.75

The Litter (Fixed Penalty) (England) Order 2002 No. 2002/424. – Enabling power: Environmental Protection Act 1990, s. 88 (7). – Issued: 19.03.2002. Made: 24.02.2002. Laid: 08.03.2002. Coming into force: 01.04.2002. Effect: 1990 c. 43 amended & S.I. 1996/3055 revoked in relation to England. Territorial extent & classification: E. General. – 2p.: 30 cm. – 0 11 039478 X £1.50

The Producer Responsibility Obligations (Packaging Waste) (Amendment) (England) Regulations 2002 No. 2002/732. – Enabling power: Environment Act 1995, ss. 93, 94 (1) (c). – Issued: 18.04.2002. Made: 18.03.2002. Laid 20.03.2002. Coming into force: 21.03.2002. Effect: S.I. 1997/648 amended, in relation to England. Territorial extent & classification: E. General. – 2p.: 30 cm. – 0 11 039764 9 £1.50

The Waste Management Licensing (Amendment) (England) Regulations 2002 No. 2002/674. – Enabling power: Environmental Protection Act 1990, s. 29 (10). – Issued: 10.04.2002. Made: 12.03.2002. Laid: 13.03.2002. Coming into force: 14.03.2002. Effect: S.I. 1994/1056 amended. Territorial extent & classification: E. General. – 2p.: 30 cm. – 0 11 039676 6 £1.50

Environmental protection, England and Wales

The Financial Assistance for Environmental Purposes (No. 2) Order 2002 No. 2002/2021. – Enabling power: Environmental Protection Act 1990, s. 153 (4). – Issued: 09.08.2002. Made: 01.08.2002. Laid: 01.08.2002. Coming into force: 27.08.2002. Effect: 1990 c. 43 amended. Territorial extent & classification: E/W. General. – 2p.: 30 cm. – 0 11 042629 0 £1.50

The Financial Assistance for Environmental Purposes Order 2002 No. 2002/1686. – Enabling power: Environmental Protection Act 1990, s. 153 (4). – Issued: 12.07.2002. Made: 26.06.2002. Laid: 03.07.2002. Coming into force: 29.07.2002. Effect: 1990 c. 43 amended. Territorial extent & classification: E/W. General. – 2p.: 30 cm. – 0 11 042453 0 £1.50

The Landfill (England and Wales) Regulations 2002 No. 2002/1559. – Enabling power: Pollution Prevention and Control Act 1999, s. 2. – Issued: 17.06.2002. Made: 13.06.2002. Coming into force: 31.08.2002, for purposes of reg. 19 (1); 15.06.2002, for all other purposes. Effect: S.I. 1991/2839; 1994/1056; 2000/1973 amended. Territorial extent & classification: E/W. General. – EC note: These regs. set out a pollution control regime for landfills for the purpose of implementing EC DIR 99/31. – Supersedes draft S.I. (ISBN 0110395905). – 24p.: 30 cm. – 0 11 042370 4 *£4.00*

The Large Combustion Plants (England and Wales) Regulations 2002 No. 2002/2688. – Enabling power: Pollution Prevention and Control Act 1999, s. 2. – Issued: 13.11.2002. Made: 28.10.2002. Laid: 01.11.2002. Coming into force: 27.11.2002. Effect: S.I. 2000/1973 amended. Territorial extent & classification: E/W. General. – EC note: Partly implement in England and Wales the provisions of Council Directive 2001/80/EC on the limitations of emissions of certain pollutants into the air from large combustion plants. The remaining provisions of the Directive have been implemented in England & partly implemented in Wales by means of Directions issued to the Environment Agency. – 4p.: 30 cm. – 0 11 042952 4 *£1.75*

The Pollution Prevention and Control (Designation of Council Directives on Large Combustion Plants, Incineration of Waste and National Emission Ceilings) Order 2002 No. 2002/2528. – Enabling power: Pollution Prevention and Control Act 1999, sch. 1, para. 20 (2) (c). – Issued: 15.10.2002. Made: 07.10.2002. Coming into force: 09.10.2002. Effect: None. Territorial extent & classification: E/W. General. – EC note: This Order designates Council Directives 2000/76/EC, 2001/80/EC & 2001/81/EC as relevant directives for the purposes of the 1999 Act. – 2p.: 30 cm. – 0 11 042847 1 *£1.50*

The Pollution Prevention and Control (England and Wales) (Amendment) (No. 2) Regulations 2002 No. 2002/1702. – Enabling power: Pollution Prevention and Control Act 1999, s. 2. – Issued: 11.07.2002. Made: 03.07.2002. Laid: 03.07.2002. Coming into force: 25.07.2002. Effect: S.I. 2000/1973 amended. Territorial extent & classification: E/W. General. – 4p.: 30 cm. – 0 11 042441 7 *£1.75*

The Pollution Prevention and Control (England and Wales) (Amendment) Regulations 2002 No. 2002/275. – Enabling power: Pollution Prevention and Control Act 1999, s. 2. – Issued: 27.02.2002. Made: 11.02.2002. Laid: 15.02.2002. Coming into force: 01.04.2002. Effect: S.I. 2000/1973; 2001/503 amended. Territorial extent & classification: E/W. General. – 4p.: 30 cm. – 0 11 039380 5 *£1.75*

The Waste Incineration (England and Wales) Regulations 2002 No. 2002/2980. – Enabling power: Pollution Prevention and Control Act 1999, s. 2. – Issued: 16.12.2002. Made: 03.12.2002. Laid: 04.12.2002. Coming into force: 28.12.2002. Effect: S.I. 1994/1056; 2000/1973 amended. Territorial extent & classification: E/W. General. – EC note: Partly implement in England & Wales the provisions of Directive 2000/76/EC on the incineration of waste. – 8p.: 30 cm. – 0 11 044174 5 *£2.00*

Environmental protection, Wales

The Advisory Committee for Wales (Environment Agency) Abolition Order 2002 No. 2002/784 (W.85). – Enabling power: Government of Wales Act 1998, s. 28, sch. 4, pt. 1. – Issued: 18.04.2002. Made: 21.03.2002. Coming into force: 01.04.2002. Effect: 1995 c. 25 amended. Territorial extent & classification: W General. – 4p.: 30 cm. – In English & Welsh. Welsh title: Gorchymyn Diddymu Pwyllgor Ymgynghorol dros Gymru (Asiantaeth yr Amgylchedd) 2002 – 0 11 090464 8 *£1.75*

The Air Quality (Amendment) (Wales) Regulations 2002 No. 2002/3182 (W.298). – Enabling power: Environment Act 1995, s. 87 (1) (2). – Issued: 31.12.2002. Made: 17.12.2002. Coming into force: 31.12.2002. Effect: S.I. 2000/1940 (W.138) amended. Territorial extent & classification: W. General. – In English and Welsh. Welsh title: Rheoliadau Ansawdd Aer (Diwygio) (Cymru) 2002. – 8p.: 30 cm. – 0 11 090610 1 *£2.00*

The Air Quality Limit Values (Wales) Regulations 2002 No. 2002/3183 (W.299). – Enabling power: Government of Wales Act 1998, s. 29 & European Communities Act 1972, s. 2 (2). – Issued: 02.01.2003. Made: 17.12.2002. Coming into force: 31.12.2002. Effect: S.I. 1989/317 revoked with saving in relation to Wales & 2001/2683 (W.224) revoked. Territorial extent & classification: W. General. – 42p.: 30 cm. – In English and Welsh. Welsh title: Rheoliadau Gwerthoedd Terfyn Ansawdd Aer (Cymru) 2002 – EC note: Implements in Wales Council directive 96/62/EC on ambient air quality assessment and management, Council directive 99/30/EC relating to limit values for sulphur dioxide, nitrogen dioxide and oxides of nitrogen, particulate matter and lead in ambient air, and Council directive 2000/69/EC relating to limit values for benzene and carbon monoxide in ambient air – 0 11 090611 X *£6.50*

The Environmental Protection (Restriction on Use of Lead Shot) (Wales) Regulations 2002 No. 2002/1730 (W.164). – Enabling power: Environmental Protection Act 1990, s. 140. – Issued: 16.08.2002. Made: 04.07.2002. Coming into force: 01.09.2002. Effect: S.I. 2001/4003 (W.331) revoked. Territorial extent & classification: W. General. – In English and Welsh. Welsh title: Rheoliadau Diogelu'r Amgylchedd (Cyfyngu'r Defnydd ar Beledi Plwm) (Cymru) 2002. – 12p.: 30 cm. – 0 11 090550 4 *£2.50*

The Genetically Modified Organisms (Deliberate Release) (Wales) Regulations 2002 No. 2002/3188 (W.304). – Enabling power: European Communities Act 1972, s. 2 (2) & Environmental Protection Act 1990, ss. 106 (4) (5), 107 (8), 111 (1) (4) (5) (7) (11), 122 (1) (4), 123 (7), 126 (1). – Issued: 31.12.2002. Made: 18.12.2002. Coming into force: 31.12.2002. Effect: 1990 c. 43 & S.I. 1992/3280; 1993/152; 1995/304 revoked in relation to Wales & S.I. 1997/1900; 2000/2831 amended in relation to Wales. Territorial extent & classification: W. General– 53p.: 30 cm. – EC note: Implements in Wales only, Council directive 2001/18/EC on the deliberate release into the environment of genetically modified organisms and repealing Council directive 90/220/EEC – In English and Welsh. Welsh title: Rheoliadau Organeddau A Addaswyd Yn Enetig (Eu Gollwng Yn Fwriadol) (Cymru) 2002 0 11 090615 2 *£7.50*

The Producer Responsibility Obligations (Packaging Waste) (Amendment) (Wales) Regulations 2002 No. 2002/813 (W.93). – Enabling power: Environment Act 1995, ss. 93, 94 (1) (c). – Issued: 15.05.2002. Made: 21.03.2002. Coming into force: 22.03.2002. Effect: S.I. 1997/648 amended in relation to Wales. Territorial extent & classification: W. General. – In English and Welsh. Welsh title: Rheoliadau Rhwymedigaethau Cyfrifoldeb Cynhyrchwyr (Gwastraff Deunydd Pacio) (Diwygio) (Cymru) 2002. – 4p.: 30 cm. – 0 11 090486 9 £1.75

The Waste Management Licensing (Amendment) (Wales) Regulations 2002 No. 2002/1087 (W.114). – Enabling power: Environmental Protection Act 1990, s. 29 (10). – Issued: 15.05.2002. Made: 15.04.2002. Coming into force: 16.04.2002. Effect: S.I. 1994/1056 amended in relation to Wales. Territorial extent & classification: W. General. – In English and Welsh. Welsh title: Rheoliadau Trwyddedu Rheoli Gwastraff (Diwygio) (Cymru) 2002. – 4p.: 30 cm. – 0 11 090487 7 £1.75

European Communities

The EC Competition Law (Articles 84 and 85) Enforcement (Amendment) Regulations 2002 No. 2002/42. – Enabling power: European Communities Act 1972, s. 2 (2). – Issued: 28.01.2002. Made: 14.01.2002. Laid: 14.01.2002. Coming into force: 04.02.2002. Effect: S.I. 2001/2916 amended. Territorial extent & classification: E/W/S/NI. General. – 2p.: 30 cm. – 0 11 039196 9 £1.50

The European Communities (Definition of Treaties) (Agreement on Trade, Development and Co-operation between the European Community and its Member States, and the Republic of South Africa) Order 2002 No. 2002/3139. – Enabling power: European Communities Act 1972, s. 1 (3). – Issued: 27.12.2002. Made: 17.12.2002. Coming into force: In accord. with art. 1. Effect: None. Territorial extent & classification: E/W/S/NI. General. – 2p.: 30 cm. – 0 11 044273 3 £1.50

The European Communities (Definition of Treaties) (Stabilisation and Association Agreement between the European Communities and their Member States, and the Former Yugoslav Republic of Macedonia) Order 2002 No. 2002/2841. – Enabling power: European Communities Act 1972, s. 1 (3). – Issued: 27.11.2002. Made: 20.11.2002. Coming into force: In accord. with art. 1. Effect: None. Territorial extent & classification: E/W/S/NI. General. – 2p.: 30 cm. – 0 11 043214 2 £1.50

The European Communities (Designation) (No. 2) Order 2002 No. 2002/1080. – Enabling power: European Communities Act 1972, s. 2 (2) & Government of Wales Act 1998, s. 29 (1). – Issued: 29.04.2002. Made: 17.04.2002. Laid: 29.04.2002. Coming into force: 20.05.2002. Effect: None. Territorial extent & classification: W. General. – 4p.: 30 cm. – 0 11 039803 3 £1.75

The European Communities (Designation) (No. 3) Order 2002 No. 2002/1819. – Enabling power: European Communities Act 1972, s. 2 (2). – Issued: 26.07.2002. Made: 16.07.2002. Laid: 26.07.2002. Coming into force: 16.08.2002. Effect: S.I. 1993/1571; 1999/2788 amended. Territorial extent & classification: E/W/S/NI. General. – 4p.: 30 cm. – 0 11 042494 8 £1.75

The European Communities (Designation) (No. 4) Order 2002 No. 2002/2840. – Enabling power: European Communities Act 1972, s. 2 (2). – Issued: 02.12.2002. Made: 20.11.2002. Laid: 02.12.2002. Coming into force: 23.12.2002. Effect: S.I. 1981/1536; 1988/2240; 1992/1315; 1996/266 revoked in so far as they relate tp Ministers or government departments, or Northern Ireland departments, as specified in sch. 3. Territorial extent & classification: E/W/S/NI. General. – 4p.: 30 cm. – 0 11 043058 1 £1.75

The European Communities (Designation) Order 2002 No. 2002/248. – Enabling power: European Communities Act 1972, s. 2 (2) & Government of Wales Act 1998, s. 29 (1). – Issued: 19.02.2002. Made: 12.02.2002. Laid: 13.02.2002. Coming into force: 06.03.2002 Effect: S.I. 1989/1327; 2000/2812, 3919 amended. Territorial extent & classification: E/W/S/NI. General. – 4p.: 30 cm. – 0 11 039316 3 £1.75

Extradition

The European Convention on Extradition (Armenia and Georgia) (Amendment) Order 2002 No. 2002/1829. – Enabling power: Extradition Act 1989, s. 4 (1). – Issued: 26.07.2002. Made: 16.07.2002. Laid: 26.07.2002. Coming into force: 27.08.2002. Effect: S.I. 2001/962 amended. Territorial extent & classification: UK/CI/IoM. General. – 4p.: 30 cm. – 0 11 042504 9 £1.75

The European Convention on Extradition (Fiscal Offences) (Amendment) Order 2002 No. 2002/1830. – Enabling power: Extradition Act 1989, s. 4 (1). – Issued: 26.07.2002. Made: 16.07.2002. Laid: 26.07.2002. Coming into force: 27.08.2002. Effect: S.I. 2001/1453 amended. Territorial extent & classification: UK/CI/IoM. General. – 2p.: 30 cm. – 0 11 042505 7 £1.50

The European Union Extradition (Amendment) Regulations 2002 No. 2002/1662. – Enabling power: Anti-Terrorism, Crime and Security Act 2001, s. 111 (1) (3). – Issued: 01.07.2002. Made: 25.06.2002. Coming into force: 26.06.2002. Effect: 1989 c.33 amended. Territorial extent & classification: UK. General. – 2p.: 30 cm. – This Statutory instrument has been made in consequence of defects in S.I. 2002/419 and is being issued free of charge to all known recipients of that statutory instrument. Supersedes draft S.I. (ISBN 011039870X) published on 09.05.2002 – 0 11 042403 4 £1.50

The European Union Extradition Regulations 2002 No. 2002/419. – Enabling power: Anti-Terrorism, Crime and Security Act 2001, s. 111 (1) (3). – Issued: 05.03.2002. Made: 25.02.2002. Laid: -Coming into force: In accord. with art. 1 (1). Effect: 1989 c. 33 amended. Territorial extent & classification: UK. General. – Supersedes draft S.I. (ISBN 0110392205) issued 28.01.2002. – EC note: These regulations implement the provisions of the Convention drawn up on the basis of art. K.3 of the Treaty on European Union on simplified extradition procedures between the member states of the EU and the Convention drawn up on the basis of art. K.3 of the Treaty on European Union relating to extradition between member states of the EU. – 32p.: 30 cm. – 0 11 039399 6 *£6.50*

The Extradition (Overseas Territories) (Application to Hong Kong) Order 2002 No. 2002/1825. – Enabling power: Extradition Act 1989, s. 32 (2A). – Issued: 26.07.2002. Made: 16.07.2002. Laid: 26.07.2002. Coming into force: 16.08.2002. Effect: 1989 C.33 & S.I. 2002/1824 amended. Territorial extent & classification: E/W/S/NI. General. – 4p.: 30 cm. – 0 11 042500 6 *£1.75*

The Extradition (Overseas Territories) (Hong Kong) Order 2002 No. 2002/1824. – Enabling power: Hong Kong Act 1985, sch., para. 3 (2). – Issued: 26.07.2002. Made: 16.07.2002. Laid: 26.07.2002. Coming into force: 16.08.2002. Effect: 1989 c.33 amended. Territorial extent & classification: E/W/S/NI. General. – 2p.: 30 cm. – 0 11 042499 9 *£1.50*

The Extradition (Overseas Territories) Order 2002 No. 2002/1823. – Enabling power: Extradition Act 1989, ss. 32, 34 (3). – Issued: 26.07.2002. Made: 16.07.2002. Laid: 26.07.2002. Coming into force: 16.08.2002. Effect: 1989 c. 33 modified. Territorial extent & classification: E/W/S/NI. General. – 16p.: 30 cm. – 0 11 042498 0 *£3.00*

The Extradition (Terrorist Bombings) Order 2002 No. 2002/1831. – Enabling power: Extradition Act 1989, ss. 4 (1), 22 (3), 37 (3). – Issued: 26.07.2002. Made: 16.07.2002. Laid: 26.07.2002. Coming into force: 27.08.2002. Effect: None. Territorial extent & classification: UK/IoM/CI/Anguilla/Bermuda/British Antarctic Terr./British Indian Ocean Terr./British Virgin Is./Cayman Is./Falkland Is.& Dep./Gibraltar/Montserrat/Pitcairn, Henderson, Ducie & Oeno Is./St Helena & Dep./Sovereign Base Areas of Akrotiri & Dhelkelia/Turks & Caicos Is. General. – 12p.: 30 cm. – 0 11 042506 5 *£2.50*

Family law: Child support

The Child Support (Miscellaneous Amendments) Regulations 2002 No. 2002/1204. – Enabling power: Child Support Act 1991, ss. 14 (1), 16 (1) (4), 17 (5), 20 (4), 28B (2) (c), 28E (1), 28G, 46 (10), 51, 52 (4), 54, 57, sch. 1, paras. 5, 10, 11, sch. 4B, paras. 3, 4, 5 & Child Support, Pensions and Social Security Act 2000, s. 29. – Issued: 03.05.2002. Made: 29.04.2002. Laid: -. Coming into force: In accord. with reg. 1 (3). Effect: S.I. 1992/1812, 1815; 1996/2907; 1999/991; 2000/3173, 3186; 2001/155, 156, 157 amended. Territorial extent & classification: E/W/S. General. – 12p.: 30 cm. – Supersedes draft S.I. (ISBN 0110394518) – 0 11 039873 4 *£2.50*

The Child Support (Northern Ireland Reciprocal Arrangements) Amendment Regulations 2002 No. 2002/771. – Enabling power: Northern Ireland Act 1998, s. 87 (4) (9). – Issued: 26.03.2002. Made: 21.03.2002. Laid: 26.03.2002. Coming into force: 16.04.2002. Effect: S.I. 1993/584 amended. Territorial extent & classification: E/W/S. General. – 8p.: 30 cm. – 0 11 039594 8 *£2.00*

The Child Support (Temporary Compensation Payment Scheme) (Modification and Amendment) Regulations 2002 No. 2002/1854. – Enabling power: Child Support, Pensions and Social Security Act 2000, s. 27 (1) (9) (10). – Issued: 24.07.2002. Made: 16.07.2002. Coming into force: 17.07.2002. Effect: 2000 c. 19; S.I. 2000/3174 amended. Territorial extent & classification: E/W/S. General. – 2p.: 30 cm. – Supersedes draft S.I. (ISBN 0110423860) – 0 11 042513 8 *£1.50*

The Social Security and Child Support (Decisions and Appeals) (Miscellaneous Amendments) Regulations 2002 No. 2002/1379. – Enabling power: Vaccine Damage Payments Act 1979, s. 4 (2) (3) & Child Support Act 1991, s. 20 (4) (5) (6) & Jobseekers Act 1995, ss. 31, 35 (1), sch. 1, para. 4 & Social Security (Recovery of Benefits) Act 1997, s. 11 (5) (a) (b) & Social Security Act 1998, ss. 6 (3), 9 (1), 10A (1), 12 (2) (7), 14 (11), 16 (1), 24A (I), (2) (a), 28 (1), 79 (1) (3) (4) (6) (7), 84, sch. 1, para. 12 (1), sch. 2, para. 9, sch. 5, paras. 1 to 4, 6, 7 & Child Support, Pensions, and Social Security Act 2000, s. 68, sch. 7, paras. 3 (1), 6 (7) (8), 10 (1), 19 (1), 20 (1) (3), 23 (1). – Issued: 10.04.2002. Made: 15.05.2002Coming into force: 20.05.2002. Effect: S.I. 1999/991; 2001/1002 amended. Territorial extent & classification: E/W/S. General. – Supersedes draft S.I. (ISBN 0110397258) issued 10 April 2002. – 16p.: 30 cm. – 0 11 039975 7 *£3.00*

Family law, England and Wales

The Child Support Appeals (Jurisdiction of Courts) Order 2002 No. 2002/1915 (L.9). – Enabling power: Child Support Act 1991, s. 45 (1) (7). – Issued: 29.07.2002. Made: 20.07.2002. Coming into force: 21.07.2002 in accord. with art. 1 (2). Effect: S.I. 1993/961 revoked in relation to England and Wales. Territorial extent & classification: E/W. General. – 2p.: 30 cm. – 0 11 042562 6 *£1.50*

Fees and charges

The Community Design (Fees) Regulations 2002 No. 2002/2942. – Enabling power: Finance Act 1973, s. 56 (1) (2). – Issued: 30.12.2002. Made: 27.11.2002. Laid: 29.11.2002. Coming into force: 01.01.2003. Effect: None. Territorial extent & classification: E/W/S/NI. General. – 2p.: 30 cm. – 0 11 044396 9 *£1.50*

The Consular Fees Act 1980 (Fees) Order 2002 No. 2002/1618. – Enabling power: Finance Act 1987, s. 102. – Issued: 28.06.2002. Made: 20.06.2002. Coming into force: 21.06.2002. Effect: None. Territorial extent & classification: E/W/S/NI. General. – 2p.: 30 cm. – 0 11 042398 4 *£1.50*

The European Economic Interest Grouping (Fees) (Amendment No. 2) Regulations 2002 No. 2002/2928. – Enabling power: Finance Act 1973, s. 56 (1) (2). – Issued: 03.12.2002. Made: 25.11.2002. Laid: 27.11.2002. Coming into force: 01.01.2003. Effect: S.I. 1999/268 amended. Territorial extent & classification: E/W/S. General. – 2p.: 30 cm. – 0 11 044077 3 *£1.50*

The European Economic Interest Grouping (Fees) (Amendment) Regulations 2002 No. 2002/401. – Enabling power: Finance Act 1973, s. 56 (1) (2). – Issued: 15.03.2002. Made: 14.02.2002. Laid: 25.02.2002. Coming into force: 01.04.2002. Effect: S.I. 1999/268 amended. Territorial extent & classification: E/W/S. General. – 2p.: 30 cm. – 0 11 039468 2 *£1.50*

The Measuring Instruments (EEC Requirements) (Fees) (Amendment) Regulations 2002 No. 2002/511. – Enabling power: Finance Act 1973, s. 56 (1) (2). – Issued: 13.03.2002. Made: 06.03.2002. Laid: 07.03.2002. Coming into force: 01.04.2002. Effect: S.I. 1998/1177 amended. Territorial extent & classification:E/W/S. General. – 2p.: 30 cm. – 0 11 039453 4 *£1.50*

The Medicines for Human Use and Medical Devices (Fees and Miscellaneous Amendments) Regulations 2002 No. 2002/542. – Enabling power: European Communities Act 1972, s. 2 (2) & Finance Act 1973, s. 56 (1) (2) & Medicines Act 1971, s. 1 (1) (2). – Issued: 12.04.2002. Made: 11.03.2002. Laid: 11.03.2002. Coming into force: 01.04.2002. Effect: S.I. 1994/105, 3144; 1995/449, 1116 amended. Territorial extent & classification: E/W/S/NI. General. – 16p.: 30 cm. – 0 11 039673 1 *£3.00*

The Plant Protection Products (Fees) (Amendment) Regulations 2002 No. 2002/2733. – Enabling power: European Communities Act 1972, s. 2 (2). – Issued: 22.11.2002. Made: 03.11.2002. Laid: 04.11.2002. Coming into force: 30.11.2002. Effect: S.I. 2001/2477 amended. Territorial extent & classification: E/W/S. General.   4p.: 30 cm. – EC note: These regs cover fees to be paid in connection with product approval and related applications resulting from the implementation of Council directive 91/414/EEC – Revoked by S.I. 2003/660 (ISBN 0110455134) – 0 11 042993 1 *£1.75*

Financial services and markets

The Electronic Commerce Directive (Financial Services and Markets) (Amendment) Regulations 2002 No. 2002/2015. – Enabling power: European Communities Act 1972, s. 2 (2). – Issued: 20.09.2002. Made: 31.07.2002. Laid: 31.07.2002. Coming into force: 21.08.2002. Effect: S.I. 2002/1775 amended. Territorial extent & classification: E/W/S/NI. General. – EC note: These Regs. amend S.I. 2002/1755 ("the principal regulations") to take account of the enactment of S.I. 2002/2013 ("the general regulations"). The principal regs. give effect to DIR 2000/31/EC (the Electronic Commerce Directive) in respect of matters within the scope of regulation by the Financial Services Authority (FSA). The general regs. give effect to the Directive in other areas. The purpose of the amendment is to ensure that the two sets of regs. do not overlap. – 2p.: 30 cm. – 0 11 042778 5 *£1.50*

The Electronic Commerce Directive (Financial Services and Markets) Regulations 2002 No. 2002/1775. – Enabling power: Financial Services and Markets Act 2000, ss. 349 (1), 414, 428 (3). – Issued: 02.09.2002. Made: 12.07.2002. Laid: 12.07.2002. Coming into force: 18.07.2002, 21.08.2002, in accord. with art. 1. Effect: 2000 c.8; S.I. 2001/2188, 2256 amended. Territorial extent & classification: E/W/S/NI. General. – EC note: Implements DIR 2000/31/EC (the Electronic Commerce Directive). – 12p.: 30 cm. – 0 11 042699 1 *£2.50*

The Electronic Money (Miscellaneous Amendments) Regulations 2002 No. 2002/765. – Enabling power: European Communities Act 1972, s. 2 (2) & Financial Services and Markets Act 2000, ss. 417 (1), 428 (3), sch. 3, para. 13 (1) (b) (iii). – Issued: 01.05.2002. Made: 21.03.2002. Laid: 21.03.2002. Coming into force: 27.04.2002. Effect: 1985 c. 6; 2000 c. 8; S.I. 1986/1032 (N.I. 6); 1995/1537; 1999/1876, 2979; 2000/262, 369; 2001/2511 amended. Territorial extent & classification: E/W/S/NI. General. – EC note: Make amendments to primary and secondary legislation in consequence of DIR 2000/46/EC on the taking up, pursuit of and prudential supervision of the business of electronic money institutions, and DIR 2000/28/EC amending DIR 2000/12/EC relating to the taking up and pursuit of the business of credit institutions. – 4p.: 30 cm. – 0 11 039855 6 *£1.75*

The Financial Services and Markets Act 2000 (Administration Orders Relating to Insurers) Order 2002 No. 2002/1242. – Enabling power: Financial Services and Markets Act 2000, ss. 355 (2), 360, 426, 428 (3). – Issued: 19.06.2002. Made: 02.05.2002. Laid: 03.05.2002. Coming into force: 31.05.2002. Effect: 1986 c. 45 & S.I. 1986/1925 modified & S.I. 2001/2634 amended. Territorial extent & classification: E/W/S/NI. General. – 4p.: 30 cm. – 0 11 042354 2 *£1.75*

The Financial Services and Markets Act 2000 (Commencement of Mortgage Regulation) (Amendment) Order 2002 No. 2002/1777. – Enabling power: Financial Services and Markets Act 2000, ss. 21 (5) (9) (10), 22 (1) (5), 327 (6), 397 (9) (10) (14), 428 (3), sch. 2, para. 25. – Issued: 06.08.2002. Made: 12.07.2002. Laid: 12.07.2002. Coming into force: 30.08.2002 Effect: S.I. 2001/544, 1227, 1335, 3544, 3645, 3650 amended. Territorial extent & classification: E/W/S/NI. General. – 4p.: 30 cm. – 0 11 042600 2 *£1.75*

The Financial Services and Markets Act 2000 (Consequential Amendments and Transitional Provisions) (Credit Unions) Order 2002 No. 2002/1501. – Enabling power: Financial Services and Markets Act 2000, ss. 426 to 428. – Issued: 09.07.2002. Made: 10.06.2002. Laid: 10.06.2002. Coming into force: 02.07.2002. Effect: 1979 c. 34; 1985 c. 58; S.I. 2002/704 amended & Credit Unions (Insurance against Fraud) etc. Regulations 1980 (ISBN 0116003111); S.I. 1989/2423; 1993/3100; 2001/811 revoked. Territorial extent & classification: E/W/S/NI. General. – 16p.: 30 cm. – 0 11 042432 8 *£3.00*

The Financial Services and Markets Act 2000 (Consequential Amendments) Order 2002 No. 2002/1555. – Enabling power: Financial Services and Markets Act 2000, ss. 416 (4), 426, 427. – Issued: 06.08.2002. Made: 12.06.2002. Laid: 12.06.2002. Coming into force: 03.07.2002. Effect: 1923 c. 8; 1951 c. 65; 1969 c. 24 (N.I.); 1972 c. 70; 1975 c. 70; 1979 c. 34; 1980 c. 21; 1981 c. 28; 1985 c. 6; 1986 c. 45; 1992 c. 5, 8; 1993 c. 49; 1994 c. 21; 1998 c. 29, 41; 2000 c. 23, 27, 39; S.I. 1972/1703 (N.I. 10); 1979/1574 (N.I. 13); 1985/1205 (N.I. 12); 1987/1110; 1988/2238; 1989/1276, 2045 (N.I. 19); 1993/1933; 1994/2421; 1995/3213 (N.I. 22); 1996/2475; 1999/1549, 2979; 2000/1403, 2417, 2418; 2001/192, 853, 1389, 3352, 3364, 3647 & S.R. & O. (N.I.) 1953/43 & S.R. 1991/295 amended & 1981 c. 31; 1985 c. 46 repealed. Territorial extent & classification: E/W/S/NI. General. – 20p.: 30 cm. – 0 11 042602 9 *£3.50*

The Financial Services and Markets Act 2000 (Consequential Amendments) (Taxes) Order 2002 No. 2002/1409. – Enabling power: Financial Services and Markets Act 2000, s. 426. – Issued: 19.06.2002. Made: 23.05.2002. Laid: 24.05.2002. Coming into force: 02.07.2002. Effect: 1998 c. 8; 1989 c. 26 & S.I. 1995/1730; 1996/2991; 1997/473; 1998/1870 amended. Territorial extent & classification: E/W/S/NI. General. – 4p.: 30 cm. – 0 11 042359 3 *£1.75*

The Financial Services and Markets Act 2000 (Financial Promotion) (Amendment) (Electronic Commerce Directive) Order 2002 No. 2002/2157. – Enabling power: Financial Services and Markets Act 2000, ss. 21 (5) (6), 238 (6) (7), 428 (3). – Issued: 02.09.2002. Made: 20.08.2002. Laid:-. Coming into force: 21.08.2002. Effect: S.I. 2001/1060, 1335 amended. Territorial extent & classification: E/W/S/NI. General. – EC note: This Order amends S.I. 2001/1335 to take account of DIR 2000/31/EC (the Electronic Communications Directive). – 8p.: 30 cm. – 0 11 042703 3 *£2.00*

The Financial Services and Markets Act 2000 (Financial Promotion and Miscellaneous Amendments) Order 2002 No. 2002/1310. – Enabling power: Financial Services and Markets Act 2000, ss. 21 (5) (6), 22 (1) (5), 38, 238 (6) (7), 428 (3), sch. 2, para. 25. – Issued: 25.06.2002. Made: 09.05.2002. Laid: 10.05.2002. Coming into force: 05.06.2002. Effect: S.I. 2001/544, 1060, 1335 amended. Territorial extent & classification: E/W/S/NI. General. – 4p.: 30 cm. – 0 11 042387 9 *£1.75*

The Financial Services and Markets Act 2000 (Fourth Motor Insurance Directive) Regulations 2002 No. 2002/2706. – Enabling power: European Communities Act 1972, s. 2 (2) & Financial Services and Markets Act 2000, ss. 150 (3), 417 (1) (c). – Issued: 19.11.2002. Made: 28.10.2002. Laid: 29.10.2002. Coming into force: 20.11.2002. Effect: S.I. 2001/2256 amended. Territorial extent & classification: E/W/S/NI. General. – 4p.: 30 cm. – EC note: These Regs ensure that effect is given to one part of DIR 2000/26/EC .. relating to insurance against civil liability in respect of the use of motor vehicles – With correction slip dated December 2002 – 0 11 042968 0 *£1.75*

The Financial Services and Markets Act 2000 (Permission and Applications) (Credit Unions Etc.) Order 2002 No. 2002/704. – Enabling power: Financial Services and Markets Act 2000, ss. 426 to 428. – Issued: 15.05.2002. Made: 14.03.2002. Laid: 15.03.2002. Coming into force: 08.04.2002 for arts. 3, 4, 7 & 8; 02.07.2002 for all others. Effect: None. Territorial extent & classification: E/W/S/NI. General. – 8p.: 30 cm. – With correction slip, dated May 2002 – 0 11 039932 3 *£2.00*

The Financial Services and Markets Act 2000 (Regulated Activities) (Amendment) (No. 2) Order 2002 No. 2002/1776. – Enabling power: Financial Services and Markets Act 2000, ss. 22 (1) (5), 428 (3). – Issued: 02.09.2002. Made: 12.07.2002. Laid: 12.07.2002. Coming into force: 21.08.2002. Effect: S.I. 2001/544 amended. Territorial extent & classification: E/W/S/NI. General. – EC note: This Order amends S.I. 2001/544 to take account of DIR 2000/31/EC (the Electronic Communications Directive). – 4p.: 30 cm. – 0 11 042700 9 *£1.75*

The Financial Services and Markets Act 2000 (Regulated Activities) (Amendment) Order 2002 No. 2002/682. – Enabling power: Financial Services and Markets Act 2000, ss. 22 (1) (5), 428 (3), sch. 2, para. 25. – Issued: 07.05.2002. Made: 14.03.2002. Laid: 14.03.2002. Approved by both Houses of Parliament. Coming into force: 11.04.2002 & 27.04.2002 in accord. with art. 1 (2). Effect: S.I. 2001/544, 1227 amended. Territorial extent & classification: E/W/S/NI. General. – EC note: Gives effect to DIR 2000/46/EC on the taking up, pursuit of and prudential supervision of the business of electronic money institutions, and DIR 2000/28/EC amending DIR 2000/12/EC relating to the taking up and pursuit of the business of credit institutions. – Supersedes S.I. with same title and S.I. no. (ISBN 011039853X) issued 1 May 2002. – 12p.: 30 cm. – 0 11 039854 8 *£2.50*

The Financial Services and Markets Act 2000 (Regulated Activities) (Amendment) Order 2002 No. 2002/682. – Enabling power: Financial Services and Markets Act 2000, ss. 22 (1) (5), 428 (3), sch. 2, para. 25– Issued: 01.05.2002. Made: 14.03.2002. Laid: 14.03.2002. Coming into force: 11.04.2002 & 27.04.2002 in accord. with art. 1 (2). Effect: S.I. 2001/544, 1227 amended. Territorial extent & classification: E/W/S/NI. General. – EC note: Gives effect to DIR 2000/46/EC on the taking up, pursuit of and prudential supervision of the business of electronic money institutions, and DIR 2000/28/EC amending DIR 2000/12/EC relating to the taking up and pursuit of the business of credit institutions. – Superseded by reissue with same title and S.I. no. (ISBN 0110398548) issued 7 May 2002. – 12p.: 30 cm. – 0 11 039853 X *£2.50*

The Financial Services and Markets Act 2000 (Variation of Threshold Conditions) Order 2002 No. 2002/2707. – Enabling power: Financial Services and Markets Act 2000, sch. 6, para. 9, s. 428 (3). – Issued: 19.11.2002. Made: 28.10.2002. Laid: 29.10.2002. Coming into force: 19.01.2003. Effect: 2000 c.8 amended. Territorial extent & classification: E/W/S/NI. General. – 2p.: 30 cm. – EC note: This order includes provisions implementing the following EC legislation, DIR 2000/26/EC .. relating to insurance against civil liability in respect of the use of motor vehicles – With correction slip dated December 2002 – 0 11 042969 9 *£1.50*

Fish farming, Wales

The Fisheries and Aquaculture Structures (Grants) (Wales) Regulations 2002 No. 2002/675 (W.72). – Enabling power: European Communities Act 1972, s. 2 (2). – Issued: 19.04.2002. Made: 12.03.2002. Coming into force: 13.03.2002. Effect: None. Territorial extent & classification: W. General. – 20p.: 30 cm. – In English & Welsh. Welsh title: Rheoliadau Strwythurau Pysgodfeydd a Dyframaethu (Grantiau) (Cymru) 2002 – 0 11 090463 X *£3.50*

Food

The Dairy Produce Quotas (General Provisions) Regulations 2002 No. 2002/458. – Enabling power: European Communities Act 1972, s. 2 (2). – Issued: 02.04.2002. Made: 01.03.2002. Laid: 04.03.2002. Coming into force: 31.03.2002. Effect: None. Territorial extent & classification: UK. General. – 8p.: 30 cm. – 0 11 039612 X *£2.00*

The Dairy Produce Quotas Regulations 2002 No. 2002/457. – Enabling power: European Communities Act 1972, s. 2 (2). – Issued: 03.04.2002. Made: 01.03.2002. Laid: 04.03.2002. Coming into force: 31.03.2002. Effect: S.I. 1998/2880 amended & 1997/733, 1093; 2000/698, 2977 revoked in relation to England and with saving. Territorial extent & classification: UK. General. – EC note: Implement Reg 3950/92 establishing an additional levy in the milk and milk products sector, as last amended by Reg 603/2001 and Reg 1392/2001 laying down detailed rules for applying Reg 3950/92. – 32p.: 30 cm. – 0 11 039615 4 *£6.00*

The Welfare Food (Amendment) Regulations 2002 No. 2002/550. – Enabling power: Social Security Act 1988, s. 13 (3) (4) & Social Security Contributions and Benefits Act 1992, s. 175 (2) to (5). – Issued: 26.04.2002. Made: 05.03.2002. Laid: 11.03.2002. Coming into force: 01.04.2002. Effect: S.I. 1996/1434 amended & S.I. 1997/857; 1998/691; 1999/2561; 2001/758 revoked. Territorial extent & classification: E/W/S/NI. General. – 2p.: 30 cm. – 0 11 039816 5 *£1.50*

Food, England

The Animal By-products (Identification) (Amendment) (England) (No. 2) Regulations 2002 No. 2002/3231. – Enabling power: Food Safety Act 1990, ss. 16 (1) (c) (d) (f), 26 (3), 48 (1), sch. 1, para. 3. – Issued: 08.01.2003. Made: 22.12.2002. Laid: 30.12.2002. Coming into force: 01.04.2003. Effect: S.I. 1995/614 amended in relation to England. Territorial extent & classification: E. General. – 4p.: 30 cm. – 0 11 044457 4 *£1.75*

The Animal By-products (Identification) (Amendment) (England) Regulations 2002 No. 2002/1619. – Enabling power: Food Safety Act 1990, ss. 16 (1) (c) (d) (f), 26 (3), 48 (1), sch. 1, para. 3. – Issued: 02.07.2002. Made: 17.06.2002. Laid: 24.06.2002. Coming into force: 15.07.2002. Effect: S.I. 1995/614 amended in relation to England. Territorial extent & classification: E. General. – 8p.: 30 cm. – 0 11 042402 6 *£2.00*

The Contaminants in Food (England) (Amendment) Regulations 2002 No. 2002/1923. – Enabling power: Food Safety Act 1990, ss. 16 (1) (a) (f), 17 (2), 26 (1) (a) (3), 48 (1). – Issued: 06.08.2002. Made: 22.07.2002. Laid: 22.07.2002. Coming into force: 24.07.2002. Effect: S.I. 2002/890 amended in relation to England. Territorial extent & classification: E. General. – 4p.: 30 cm. – EC note: These regs. give effect to a correction to REG 563/2002. This statutory instrument, which has been made first in consequence of the correction of a defect in Commission Regulation (EC) 563/2002 which was reflected in S.I. 2002/890, and second to correct an error of the definition of "port health authority" in S.I. 2002/890, is being issued free of charge to all known recipients of that statutory instrument – Revoked by S.I. 2003/1478 (ISBN 0110463277) – 0 11 042619 3 *£1.75*

The Contaminants in Food (England) Regulations 2002 No. 2002/890. – Enabling power: Food Safety Act 1990, ss. 16 (1) (a) (f), 17 (2), 26 (1) (a) (3), 48 (1). – Issued: 25.06.2002. Made: 22.05.2002. Laid: 22.05.2002. Coming into force: 18.06.2002. Effect: 1990 c.16 modified & S.I. 1982/1727; 1985/67; 1990/2463, 2486; 1991/1476; 1992/1971; 1995/3124, 3267 amended & S.I. 1979/1254; 1997/1499 revoked. Territorial extent & classification: E. General. – 12p.: 30 cm. – EC note: Make provision for the enforcement and execution of Commission Reg.466/2001 and implement Commission directives, Dir.2001/22/EC, Dir.2002/26/EC and Dir. 2002/27/EC – Revoked by S.I. 2003/1478 (ISBN 0110463277) – 0 11 042382 8 *£2.50*

The Food and Animal Feedingstuffs (Products of Animal Origin from China) (Control) (England) Regulations 2002 No. 2002/183. – Enabling power: European Communities Act 1972, s. 2 (2). – Issued: 26.02.2002. Made: 31.01.2002. Laid: 01.02.2002. Coming into force: 02.02.2002. Effect: None. Territorial extent & classification: E. General. – 4p.: 30 cm. – EC note: Implement EC DEC 2002/69/EC concerning certain protective measures with regard to the products of animal origin imported from China – Revoked by S.I. 2002/1614 (ISBN 0110424573) – 0 11 039365 1 *£1.75*

The Food and Animal Feedingstuffs (Products of Animal Origin from China) (Emergency Control) (England) Regulations 2002 No. 2002/1614. – Enabling power: European Communities Act 1972, s. 2 (2). – Issued: 15.07.2002. Made: 19.06.2002. Laid: 19.06.2002. Coming into force: 20.06.2002. Effect: S.I. 2002/183 revoked. Territorial extent & classification: E. General. – EC note: Implements, for England, Commission Decision 2002/69/EC as amended by Decision 2002/441/EC concerning certain protective measures with regard to the products of animal origin imported from China. – 8p.: 30 cm. – Revoked by S.I. 2002/2151 (ISBN 0110426827) – 0 11 042457 3 *£2.00*

The Food (Control of Irradiation) (Amendment) (England) Regulations 2002 No. 2002/1922. – Enabling power: Food Safety Act 1990, ss. 16 (1) (3), 17 (1), 18 (1), 19 (1) (b), 26, 45, 48 (1), sch. 1, paras. 1, 4 (b). – Issued: 06.08.2002. Made: 23.07.2002. Laid: 24.07.2002. Coming into force: 14.08.2002. Effect: S.I. 1990/2490 amended in relation to England. Territorial extent & classification: E. General. – 4p.: 30 cm. – This statutory instrument has been made in consequence of defects in S.I. 1990/2490 caused by the amendments made to it by S.I. 2000/2254 and is being issued free of charge to all known recipients of S.I. 2000/2254 – 0 11 042610 X *£1.75*

The Food (Figs, Hazelnuts and Pistachios from Turkey) (Emergency Control) (England) (No. 2) Regulations 2002 No. 2002/2351. – Enabling power: European Communities Act 1972, s. 2 (2). – Issued: 24.09.2002. Made: 11.09.2002. Laid: 11.09.2002. Coming into force: 13.09.2002. Effect: S.I. 2002/773 revoked. Territorial extent & classification: E. General. – EC note: These Regs. revoke and re-enact S.I. 2002/773, implementing, for England, DEC 2002/80/EC as amended by 2002/233/EC and by 2002/679/EC. – 8p.: 30 cm. – 0 11 042797 1 *£2.00*

The Food (Figs, Hazelnuts and Pistachios from Turkey) (Emergency Control) (England) Regulations 2002 No. 2002/773. – Enabling power: European Communities Act 1972, s. 2 (2). – Issued: 07.05.2002. Made: 21.03.2002. Laid: 22.03.2002. Coming into force: 23.03.2002. Effect: None. Territorial extent & classification: E. General. – EC note: Implements, for England, DEC 2002/80/EC as amended by 2002/233/EC. – 8p.: 30 cm. – Revoked by S.I. 2002/2351 (0110427971) – 0 11 039876 9 *£2.00*

The Food for Particular Nutritional Uses (Addition of Substances for Specific Nutritional Purposes) (England) Regulations 2002 No. 2002/1817. – Enabling power: Food Safety Act 1990, ss. 16 (1) (f), 17 (1), 26 (3), 48 (1). – Issued: 12.08.2002. Made: 14.07.2002. Laid: 15.07.2002. Coming into force: 05.08.2002 and 01.04.2004 in accord. with reg. 1 (2) (3). Effect: S.I. 1990/1728 amended. Territorial extent & classification: E. General. – EC note: Implement DIR 2001/15/EC on substances that may be added for specific nutritional purposes in foods for particular nutritional uses. – 12p.: 30 cm. – 0 11 042631 2 *£2.50*

The Food (Jelly Confectionery) (Emergency Control) (England) Regulations 2002 No. 2002/931. – Enabling power: European Communities Act 1972, s. 2 (2). – Issued: 07.05.2002. Made: 03.04.2002. Laid: 03.04.2002. Coming into force: 04.04.2002. Effect: None. Territorial extent & classification: E. General. – EC note: Implements for England DEC 2002/247/EC suspending the placing on the market and import of jelly containing the food additive E425: Konjac. – 8p.: 30 cm. – 0 11 039875 0 *£2.00*

The Food (Peanuts from China) (Emergency Control) (England) (No. 2) Regulations 2002 No. 2002/2350. – Enabling power:European Communities Act 1972, s. 2 (2). – Issued: 24.09.2002. Made: 11.09.2002. Laid: 11.09.2002. Coming into force: 13.09.2002. Effect: S.I. 2002/774 revoked Territorial extent & classification: E. General. – EC note: These Regs. revoke and re-enact S.I. 2002/774, implementing, for England, DEC 2002/79/EC imposing special conditions on the import of peanuts and certain products derived from peanuts originating in, or consigned from China as amended by EC DEC 2002/233/EC and by 2002/678/EC. – 8p.: 30 cm. – 0 11 042794 7 *£2.00*

The Food (Peanuts from China) (Emergency Control) (England) Regulations 2002 No. 2002/774. – Enabling power:European Communities Act 1972, s. 2 (2). – Issued: 09.05.2002. Made: 21.03.2002. Laid: 22.03.2002. Coming into force: 23.03.2002. Effect: None. Territorial extent & classification: E. General. – EC note: Implements, for England, DEC 2002/79/EC imposing special conditions on the import of peanuts and certain products derived from peanuts originating in, or consigned from China as amended by EC DEC 2002/233/EC. – 8p.: 30 cm. – Revoked by S.I. 2002/2350 (ISBN 0110427947) – 0 11 039889 0 *£2.00*

The Food (Star Anise from Third Countries) (Emergency Control) (England) (Amendment) Order 2002 No. 2002/602. – Enabling power: Food Safety Act 1990, ss. 13 (1), 48 (1). – Issued: 07.05.2002. Made: 19.03.2002. Laid: 19.03.2002. Coming into force: 20.03.2002. Effect: S.I. 2002/334 amended. Territorial extent & classification: E. General. – This statutory instrument has been printed to correct errors in S.I. 2002/334 (ISBN 0110394291) and is being issued free of charge to all known recipients of that instrument. – 2p.: 30 cm. – 0 11 039877 7 *£1.50*

The Food (Star Anise from Third Countries) (Emergency Control) (England) Order 2002 No. 2002/334. – Enabling power: Food Safety Act 1990, ss. 13 (1), 48 (1). – Issued: 13.03.2002. Made: 14.02.2002. Laid: 15.02.2002. Coming into force: 16.02.2002. Effect: None. Territorial extent & classification: E. General. – 4p.: 30 cm. – Revoked by S.I. 2003/2338 (ISBN 0110475860). – EC note: Implements, for England, DEC 2002/75, laying down special conditions on the import form third countries of star anise – 0 11 039429 1 *£1.75*

The Foot-and-Mouth Disease (Marking of Meat, Meat Preparations and Meat Products) Regulations 2002 No. 2002/118. – Enabling power: European Communities Act 1972, s. 2 (2). – Issued: 27.02.2002. Made: 25.02.2002 at 2.00 p.m. Laid: 28.01.2002. Coming into force: 25.01.2002 at 8.00 p.m. Effect: S.I. 1994/3082; 1995/539, 3205 amended in relation to England. Territorial extent & classification: E. General. – 4p.: 30 cm. – EC note: These Regs. implement, for England, DEC 2002/49 amending for the second time 2001/304 concerning certain protection measures with regard to foot-and-mouth disease in the UK – 0 11 039381 3 *£1.75*

The Kava-kava in Food (England) Regulations 2002 No. 2002/3169. – Enabling power: Food Safety Act 1990, ss. 16 (1) (a) (e) (f), 18 (1) (c), 26 (1) (3), 48 (1). – Issued: 23.12.2002. Made: 18.12.2002. Laid: 23.12.2002. Coming into force: 13.01.2003. Effect: None. Territorial extent & classification: E. General. – 4p.: 30 cm. – 0 11 044247 4 *£1.75*

The Meat (Hazard Analysis and Critical Control Point) (England) Regulations 2002 No. 2002/889. – Enabling power: Food Safety Act 1990, ss. 16 (1) (b) (f), 17 (1). – Issued: 18.06.2002. Made: 16.05.2002. Laid: 16.05.2002. Coming into force: In accord. with reg. 2, 07.06.2002. & 07.01.2003. Effect: S.I. 1995/539, 540; 1996/3124 amended in relation to England. Territorial extent & classification: E. General. – EC note: These regs. give effect (for England) to DEC 2001/471/EC laying down rules for the regular checks on the general hygiene carried out by the operators in establishments according to DIR 64/433/EC on health conditions for the production and marketing of fresh meat and DIR 71/118/EC on health problems affecting the production and placing on the market of fresh poultry meat. – 16p.: 30 cm. – 0 11 042348 8 *£3.00*

The Plastic Materials and Articles in Contact with Food (Amendment) (England) (No. 2) Regulations 2002 No. 2002/3008. – Enabling power: Food Safety Act 1990, ss. 16 (2), 17 (1), 26 (1) (a) (3), 31, 48 (1). – Issued: 11.12.2002. Made: 04.12.2002. Laid: 11.12.2002. Coming into force: 28.02.2003. Effect: S.I. 1990/2463; 1998/1376 amended in relation to England. Territorial extent & Classification: E. General. – 8p.: 30 cm. – EC note: Implement Commission directive 2002/17/EC amending DIR 90/128/EEC – 0 11 044143 5 *£2.00*

The Plastic Materials and Articles in Contact with Food (Amendment) (England) Regulations 2002 No. 2002/2364. – Enabling power: Food Safety Act 1990, ss. 16 (2), 17 (1), 26 (1) (a) (3), 31, 48 (1). – Issued: 24.09.2002. Made: 16.09.2002. Laid: 16.09.2002. Coming into force: 30.11.2002. Effect: S.I. 1990/2463; 1998/1376 amended. Territorial extent & Classification: E. General. – 28p.: 30 cm. – EC note: These Regs. implement (for England) DIR 2001/62/EC amending 90/128/EEC; DIR 2002/16/EC; and (in minor respects) DIR 2002/17/EC amending 90/128/EEC. The Regs. also reflect the revocation with effect from 4th September 2002, of DIR 90/128/EEC as amended and its re-enactment in consolidated form by DIR 2002/72/EC – 0 11 042796 3 *£4.50*

The Products of Animal Origin (Third Country Imports) (England) (Amendment) Regulations 2002 No. 2002/2151. – Enabling power: European Communities Act 1972, s. 2 (2). – Issued: 08.10.2002. Made: 19.08.2002. Laid: 19.08.2002. Coming into force: 20.08.2002. Effect: S.I. 2002/1227 amended & S.I. 2002/1614 revoked. Territorial extent & classification: E. General. – 2p.: 30 cm. – EC note: These Regs. update the reference to Commission Decision 2002/69/EC concerning certain protective measures with regard to products of animal origin imported from China by including references to Commission Decisions 2002/441/EC and 2002/573/EC – Revoked by S.I. 2002/3206 (ISBN 011044616X) – 0 11 042682 7 *£1.50*

The Sweeteners in Food (Amendment) (England) Regulations 2002 No. 2002/379. – Enabling power: Food Safety Act 1990, ss. 16 (1) (a) (e), 17 (1), 26 (1) (3), 48 (1), sch. 1, para. 1. – Issued: 12.03.2002. Made: 21.02.2002. Laid: 22.02.2002. Coming into force: 15.03.2002. Effect: S.I. 1981/1063; 1984/1566; 1992/1978; 1995/3123, 3187; 1996/1499; 2001/2294 amended in relation to England. Territorial extent & classification: E. General. – EC note: These Regs bring up to date, in relation to England, the definition of Directive 95/31/EC on specific purity criteria to cover its amendment by DIR 2001/52 to substitute new purity criteria for mannitol and acesulfame K. – 8p.: 30 cm. – 0 11 039428 3 *£2.00*

Food, England and Wales

The Notification of Marketing of Food for Particular Nutritional Uses (England and Wales) Regulations 2002 No. 2002/333. – Enabling power: Food Safety Act 1990, ss.17 (1), 26 (1) (a) (3), 48 (1). – Issued: 28.02.2002. Made: 13.02.2002. Laid: 15.02.2002. Coming into force: 08.03.2002. Effect: None. Territorial extent & classification: E/W. General. – 4p.: 30 cm. – EC note: Implements for England and Wales art. 9 of Council directive 89/398/EEC, as amended by directive 1999/41/EC   0 11 039378 3 *£1.75*

Food, Wales

The Animal By-Products (Identification) (Amendment) (Wales) Regulations 2002 No. 2002/1472 (W.146). – Enabling power: Food Safety Act 1990, ss. 16 (1) (c) (d) (f), 26 (3), 48 (1), sch. 1, para. 3. – Issued: 11.07.2002. Made: 30.05.2002. Coming into force: 15.07.2002. Effect: S.I. 1995/614 amended in relation to Wales. Territorial extent & classification: W. General. – In English and Welsh. Welsh title: Rheoliadau Sgil-gynhyrchion Anifeiliaid (Adnabod) (Diwygio) (Cymru) 2002. – [12]p.: 30 cm. – 0 11 090520 2 *£2.50*

The Contaminants in Food (Wales) Regulations 2002 No. 2002/1886 (W.195). – Enabling power: Food Safety Act 1990, ss. 16 (1) (a) (f), 17 (2), 26 (1) (a) (3), 48 (1). – Issued: 15.08.2002. Made: 18.07.2002. Coming into force: 02.08.2002. Effect: S.I. 1982/1727; 1985/67; 1990/2463, 2486; 1991/1476; 1992/1971; 1995/3124, 3267 amended in relation to Wales & S.I. 1979/1254; 1997/1499 revoked in relation to Wales. Territorial extent & classification: W. General. – 20p.: 30 cm. – Revoked by S.I. 2003/1721 (W.188) (ISBN 0110907531). EC note: Makes provision for the enforcement and execution of Commission REG 466/2001 setting maximum levels for certain contaminants in foodstuffs and implements Commission directives 2001/22/EC, 2002/26/EC, 2002/27/EC – In English and Welsh. Welsh title: Rheoliadau Halogion mewn Bwyd (Cymru) 2002 – 0 11 090549 0 *£3.50*

The Dairy Produce Quotas (Wales) Regulations 2002 No. 2002/897 (W.103). – Enabling power: European Communities Act 1972, s. 2 (2). – Issued: 18.04.2002. Made: 27.03.2002. Laid: - Coming into force: 31.03.2002. Effect: S.I. 1997/733, 1093 revoked, insofar as they apply to Wales; S.I. 1998/2880 amended & S.I. 2000/972 (W.42), 3123 (W.201) revoked. Territorial extent & classification: W. General. – 32p.: 30 cm. – EC note: Implements EC REGS 3950/92, 1392/2001 – 0 11 090469 9 *£6.00*

The Food and Animal Feedingstuffs (Products of Animal Origin from China) (Control) (Wales) Regulations 2002 No. 2002/203 (W.26). – Enabling power: European Communities Act 1972, s. 2 (2). – Issued: 15.03.2002. Made: 01.02.2002. Coming into force: 02.02.2002. Effect: None. Territorial extent & classification: W. General. – 8p.: 30 cm. – EC note: Implement DEC 2002/69/EC – Revoked by S.I. 2002/1798 (W.173) (ISBN 0110905245) – 0 11 090440 0 *£2.00*

The Food and Feedingstuffs (Products of Animal Origin from China) (Emergency Control) (Wales) Regulations 2002 No. 2002/1798 (W.173). – Enabling power: European Communities Act 1972, s. 2 (2). – Issued: 22.07.2002. Made: 11.07.2002. Coming into force: 12.07.2002. Effect: S.I. 2002/203 (W.26) revoked. Territorial extent & classification: W. General. – EC note: These Regs. implement DEC 2002/69/EC as amended by DEC 2002/441/EC. – 8p.: 30 cm. – 0 11 090524 5 *£2.00*

The Food (Figs, Hazelnuts and Pistachios from Turkey) (Emergency Control) (Amendment) (Wales) Regulations 2002 No. 2002/1726 (W.161). – Enabling power: European Communities Act 1972, s. 2 (2). – Issued: 18.07.2002. Made: 04.07.2002. Coming into force: 05.07.2002. Effect: S.I. 2002/821 (W.97) amended. Territorial extent & classification: W. General. – 4p.: 30 cm. – 0 11 090522 9 *£1.75*

The Food (Figs, Hazelnuts and Pistachios from Turkey) (Emergency Control) (Wales) (No. 2) Regulations 2002 No. 2002/2296 (W.225). – Enabling power: European Communities Act 1972, s. 2 (2). – Issued: 16.09.2002. Made: 04.09.2002. Coming into force: 09.09.2002. Effect: S.I. 2002/821 (W.97) revoked. Territorial extent & classification: W. General. – 8p.: 30 cm. – EC note: Implement Commission decision 2002/80/EC imposing special conditions on the import of figs, hazelnuts & pistachios from Turkey, as amended by Decision 2002/233/EC and 2002/679/EC – 0 11 090570 9 *£2.00*

The Food (Figs, Hazelnuts and Pistachios from Turkey) (Emergency Control) (Wales) Regulations 2002 No. 2002/821 (W.97). – Enabling power: European Communities Act 1972, s. 2 (2). – Issued: 15.04.2002. Made: 25.03.2002. Coming into force: 26.03.2002. Effect: None. Territorial extent & classification: W. General. – EC note: Implements, for Wales, DEC 2002/80/EC as amended by 2002/233/EC. – 8p.: 30 cm. – Revoked by S.I. 2002/2296 (W.225) (ISBN 0110905709) – 0 11 090460 5 *£2.00*

The Food for Particular Nutritional Uses (Addition of Substances for Specific Nutritional Purposes) (Wales) Regulations 2002 No. 2002/2939 (W.280). – Enabling power: Food Safety Act 1990, ss. 16 (1) (f), 17 (1), 26 (3), 48 (1). – Issued: 16.12.2002. Made: 27.11.2002. Coming into force: 31.12.2002. & 01.04.2004 (reg. 1 (2) (3). Effect: S.I. 1990/1728 amended in relation to Wales. Territorial extent & classification: W. General. – EC note: Implements in Wales, Commission Directive 2001/15/EC on substances that may be added for specific nutritional purposes in foods for particular nutritional uses. – 16p.: 30 cm. – In English and Welsh. Welsh title: Rheoliadau Bwyd at Ddefnydd Maethol Neilltuol (Ychwanegu Sylweddau at Ddibenion Maethol Penodol) (Cymru) 2002 – 0 11 090591 1 *£3.00*

The Food (Jelly Confectionery) (Emergency Control) (Wales) Regulations 2002 No. 2002/1090 (W.115). – Enabling power: European Communities Act 1972, s. 2 (2). – Issued: 29.04.2002. Made: 15.04.2002. Coming into force: 16.04.2002. Effect: None. Territorial extent & classification: W. General. – EC note: Implement for Wales DEC 2002/247/EC suspending the placing on the market and import of jelly containing the food additive E425: Konjac. – 8p.: 30 cm. – 0 11 090475 3 *£2.00*

The Food (Peanuts from China) (Emergency Control) (Amendment) (Wales) Regulations 2002 No. 2002/1728 (W.162). – Enabling power: European Communities Act 1972, s. 2 (2). – Issued: 18.07.2002. Made: 04.07.2002. Coming into force: 05.07.2002. Effect: S.I. 2002/820 (W.96) amended. Territorial extent & classification: W. General. – 4p.: 30 cm. – 0 11 090523 7 *£1.75*

The Food (Peanuts from China) (Emergency Control) (No. 2) (Wales) Regulations 2002 No. 2002/2295 (W.224). – Enabling power: European Communities Act 1972, s. 2 (2). – Issued: 16.09.2002. Made: 04.09.2002. Coming into force: 09.09.2002. Effect: S.I. 2002/820 (W.96) revoked. Territorial extent & classification: W. General. – 8p.: 30 cm. – EC note: Implement Commission decision 2002/79/EC imposing special conditions on the import of peanuts from China, as amended by Decision 2002/233/EC and 2002/678/EC – 0 11 090569 5 *£2.00*

The Food (Peanuts from China) (Emergency Control) (Wales) Regulations 2002 No. 2002/820 (W.96). – Enabling power: European Communities Act 1972, s. 2 (2). – Issued: 16.04.2002. Made: 25.03.2002. Coming into force: 26.03.2002. Effect: None. Territorial extent & classification: W. General. – EC note: Implements, for Wales, DEC 2002/79/EC imposing special conditions on the import of peanuts and certain products derived from peanuts originating in, or consigned from China as amended by EC DEC 2002/233/EC. – 8p.: 30 cm. – Revoked by S.I. 2002/2295 (W.224) (ISBN 0110905695) – 0 11 090461 3 *£2.00*

The Food (Star Anise from Third Countries) (Emergency Control) (Wales) Order 2002 No. 2002/402 (W.50). – Enabling power: Food Safety Act 1990, ss. 13 (1), 48 (1). – Issued: 06.03.2002. Made: 22.02.2002. Coming into force: 23.02.2002. Effect: None. Territorial extent & classification: W. General. – EC note: Implements, for Wales, DEC 2002/75. – 8p.: 30 cm. – 0 11 090437 0 *£2.00*

The Foot-and-Mouth Disease (Marking of Meat, Meat Preparations and Meat Products) (Wales) Regulations 2002 No. 2002/129 (W.17). – Enabling power: European Communities Act 1972, s. 2 (2). – Issued: 21.02.2002. Made: 25.01.2002. Coming into force: 26.01.2002. Effect: S.I. 1994/3082; 1995/539, 3205 amended. Territorial extent & classification: W. General. – 4p.: 30 cm. – EC note: Implements (in relation to Wales) Commission DEC 2002/49/EC amending for the 2nd time DEC 2001/304/EC on marking and use of certain animal products in relation to DEC 2001/172/EC concerning certain protection measures with regard to foot-and-mouth disease in the UK – 0 11 090423 0 £1.75

The Kava-kava in Food (Wales) Regulations 2002 No. 2002/3157 (W.293). – Enabling power: Food Safety Act 1990, ss. 16 (1) (a) (e) (f), 18 (1) (c), 26 (1) (3), 48 (1). – Issued: 27.12.2002. Made: 17.12.2002. Coming into force: 09.01.2003. Effect: None. Territorial extent & classification: W. General. – Corrected reprint being issued free of charge to all known recipients of original (published 27.12.2002). – 4p.: 30 cm. – In English and Welsh. Welsh title Rheoliadau Cafa-cafa mewn Bwyd (Cymru) 2002. – 0 11 090606 3 £1.75

The Meat (Hazard Analysis and Critical Control Point) (Wales) Regulations 2002 No. 2002/1476 (W.148). – Enabling power: Food Safety Act 1990, ss. 16 (1) (b) (f), 17 (1) & European Communities Act 1972, s. 2 (2). – Issued: 03.07.2002. Made: 30.05.2002. Coming into force: 07.06.2002, except in relation to any small meat establishment; and 07.06.2003 in relation to any small meat establishment. Effect: S.I. 1995/539, 540; 1996/3124 amended in relation to Wales. Territorial extent & classification: W. General. – EC note: Give effect in Wales to EC DEC 2001/471/EC laying down rules for the regular checks on the general hygiene carried out by operators in establishments according to DIR 64/433/EEC on health conditions for the production and marketing of fresh meat and DIR 71/118/EEC. – 20p.: 30 cm. – In English and Welsh. Welsh title: Rheoliadau Cig (Dadansoddi Peryglon a Phwynt Rheoli Critigol) (Cymru) 2002 – 0 11 090512 1 £3.50

The Miscellaneous Food Additives (Amendment) (Wales) Regulations 2002 No. 2002/329 (W.42). – Enabling power: Food Safety Act 1990, ss. 16 (1) (a), 17 (1), 26 (1) (3), 48 (1), sch. 1, para. 1. – Issued: 27.02.2002. Made: 13.02.2002. Coming into force: 01.03.2002. Effect: S.I. 1995/3187 amended in relation to Wales & 2001/1787 (W.126) amended. Territorial extent & classification: W. General. – 8p.: 30 cm. – EC note: These Regs. implement, for Wales, DIR 2001/30 amending 96/77 regarding specific purity criteria, and 2001/5 amending 95/2 regarding additives. Subject to a transitional provision, the Regs. also implement provisions of the Annex to DIR 2001/30 – In English and Welsh. Welsh title: Rheoliadau Ychwanegion Bwyd Amrywiol (Diwygio) (Cymru) 2002. 0 0 11 090432 X £2.00

The Plastic Materials and Articles in Contact with Food (Amendment) (Wales) Regulations 2002 No. 2002/2834 (W.272). – Enabling power: Food Safety Act 1990, ss. 16 (2), 17 (1), 26 (1) (a), 31, 48 (1). – Issued: 29.11.2002. Made: 07.11.2002. Coming into force: 30.11.2002. Effect: S.I. 1998/1376; 1990/2463 amended in relation to Wales. Territorial extent & classification: W. General. – 40p.: 30 cm. – In English and Welsh. Welsh title: Rheoliadau Deunyddiau ac Eitemau Plastig mewn Cysylltiad â Bwyd (Diwygio) (Cymru) 2002 – EC note: Implement for Wales Commission directive 2001/62/EC (amending 90/128/EEC), DIR 2002/16/EC, DIR 2002/17/EC (amending 90/128/EEC) & reflect the revocation of 90/128/EC as amended & its re-enactment in consolidated form by 2002/72/EC – 0 11 090588 1 £6.50

The Poultry Meat, Farmed Game Bird Meat and Rabbit Meat (Hygiene and Inspection) (Amendment) (Wales) Regulations 2002 No. 2002/47 (W.6). – Enabling power: Food Safety Act 1990, ss. 16 (1) (b) (c) (d) (e) (f) (3), 17 (1), 19 (1) (b), 26, 48 (1), sch. 1, paras. 5 (1) (a) (2) (a), 6 (1) (a) & European Communities Act 1972, s. 2 (2). – Issued: 06.02.2002. Made: 14.01.2002. Coming into force: 01.02.2002, except 01.12.2002 for reg. 2, paras. (2) (3) (4) (5). Effect: S.I. 1995/540; 1996/3124 amended in relation to Wales. Territorial extent & classification: W. General. – EC note: Implement in part DIR 91/495/EEC and DIR 71/118/EEC. – 8p.: 30 cm. – In English and Welsh. Welsh title: Rheoliadau Cig Dofednod, Cig Adar Hela wedi'i Ffermio a Chig Cwningod (Hylendid ac Archwilio) (Diwygio) (Cymru) 2002 – 0 11 090413 3 £2.00

The Sweeteners in Food (Amendment) (Wales) Regulations 2002 No. 2002/330 (W.43). – Enabling power: Food Safety Act 1990, ss. 16 (1) (a) (e), 17 (1), 26 (1) (3), 48 (1), sch. 1, para. 1. – Issued: 06.03.2002. Made: 13.02.2002. Coming into force: 01.03.2002. Effect: S.I. 1995/3123; 1996/1499; 2001/2679 amended in relation to Wales. Territorial extent & classification: W. General. – EC note: These Regs. bring up to date the definition of "Directive 95/31/EC" so as to cover its amendment by DIR 2001/52. They also implement provisions of DIR 89/107 as regards the use as a sweetener of sucralose. – 12p.: 30 cm. – In English and Welsh. - Welsh title: Rheoliadau Melysyddion mewn Bwyd (Diwygio) (Cymru) 2002 – 0 11 090435 4 £2.50

Forestry, England and Wales

The Forestry (Felling of Trees) (England and Wales) (Amendment) Regulations 2002 No. 2002/226. – Enabling power: Forestry Act 1967, ss. 10 (1), 32 (1). – Issued: 15.02.2002. Made: 05.02.2002. Laid: 07.02.2002. Coming into force: 01.03.2002. Effect: S.I. 1979/791 amended. Territorial extent & classification: E/W. General. – 4p.: 30 cm. – 0 11 039306 6 £1.75

Freedom of information

The Freedom of Information (Additional Public Authorities) Order 2002 No. 2002/2623. – Enabling power: Freedom of Information Act 2000, ss. 4 (1) (6), 7 (2). – Issued: 25.10.2002. Made: 17.10.2002. Laid: 21.10.2002. Coming into force: 11.11.2002. Effect: 2000 c. 36 amended. Territorial extent & classification: GB/NI. General. – 4p.: 30 cm. – 0 11 042887 0 £1.75

The Freedom of Information (Excluded Welsh Authorities) Order 2002 No. 2002/2832. – Enabling power: Freedom of Information Act 2000, s. 83 (2). – Issued: 25.11.2002. Made: 11.11.2002. Coming into force: 30.11.2002. Effect: None. Territorial extent & classification: E/W/S/NI. General. – 4p.: 30 cm. – 0 11 043000 X £1.75

Freedom of information, England and Wales

The Freedom of Information Act 2000 (Commencement No. 2) Order 2002 No. 2002/2812 (C.86). – Enabling power: Freedom of Information Act 2000, s. 87 (3). Bringing into operation various provisions of the 2000 Act on 30.11.2002, 28.02.2003 & 30.06.2003 in accordance with arts. 2, 3, 4 & 5. – Issued: 21.11.2002. Made: 12.11.2002. Effect: None. Territorial extent & classification: E/W. General. – 12p.: 30 cm. – 0 11 042990 7 £2.50

The Information Tribunal (Enforcement Appeals) (Amendment) Rules 2002 No. 2002/2722. – Enabling power: Data Protection Act 1998, s. 67 (2), sch. 6, para. 7. – Issued: 07.11.2002. Made: 30.10.2002. Laid: 01.11.2002. Coming into force: 30.11.2002. Effect: S.I. 2000/189 amended. Territorial extent & classification: E/W. General. – 2p.: 30 cm. – 0 11 042940 0 £1.50

Gas

The Electricity and Gas (Determination of Turnover for Penalties) Order 2002 No. 2002/1111. – Enabling power: Electricity Act 1989, s. 27A (8) & Gas Act 1986, s. 30A (8). – Issued: 29.04.2002. Made: 12.04.2002. Coming into force: 13.04.2002. Effect: None. Territorial extent & classification: E/W/S. General. – 2p.: 30 cm. – Supersedes draft S.I. (0110394267) issued on 11.03.2002 – 0 11 039831 9 £1.50

The Gas (Calculation of Thermal Energy) (Amendment) Regulations 2002 No. 2002/3130. – Enabling power: Gas Act 1986, ss. 13 (2) (3), 47 (7). – Issued: 16.01.2003. Made: 12.12.2002. Coming into force: 01.02.2003. Effect: S.I. 1996/439 amended. Territorial extent & classification: E/W/S. General. – 2p.: 30 cm. – 0 11 044580 5 £1.50

The Gas (Connection Charges) (Amendment) Regulations 2002 No. 2002/1488. – Enabling power: Gas Act 1986, ss. 10 (7), 47 (3) (b). – Issued: 02.08.2002. Made: 09.06.2002. Coming into force: 01.07.2002. Effect: S.I. 2001/3267 amended. Territorial extent & classification: E/W/S/NI. General. – 2p.: 30 cm. – 0 11 042599 5 £1.50

The Gas (Standards of Performance) (Amendment) Regulations 2002 No. 2002/741. – Enabling power: Gas Act 1986, ss. 33A, 33AA, 33AB, 33D, 47. – Issued: 10.04.2002. Made: 11.03.2002. Laid:-. Coming into force: 01.04.2002. Effect: S.I. 2002/475 amended. Territorial extent & classification: E/W/S. General. – 8p.: 30 cm. – 0 11 039668 5 £2.00

The Gas (Standards of Performance) Regulations 2002 No. 2002/475. – Enabling power: Gas Act 1986, ss. 33A, 33AB, 33D, 47. – Issued: 10.04.2002. Made: 17.01.2002. Laid:-. Coming into force: 01.04.2002. Effect: None. Territorial extent & classification: E/W/S. General. – 12p.: 30 cm. – 0 11 039665 0 £2.50

Geneva conventions

The Geneva Conventions (Amendment) Act (Overseas Territories) Order 2002 No. 2002/1076. – Enabling power: Geneva Conventions Act 1957, s. 8 (2). – Issued: 23.04.2002. Made: 17.04.2002. Coming into force: 01.05.2002. Effect: 1995 c.27 amended. Territorial extent & classification: E/W/S/NI. General. – 4p.: 30 cm. – 0 11 039799 1 £1.75

Government resources and accounts

The Whole of Government Accounts (Designation of Bodies) Order 2002 No. 2002/454. – Enabling power: Government Resources and Accounts Act 2000, s. 10 (1). – Issued: 19.03.2002. Made: 01.03.2002. Laid: 04.03.2002. Coming into force: 01.04.2002. Effect: S.I. 2000/3357 amended. Territorial extent & classification: E/W/S/NI. General. – 8p.: 30 cm. – 0 11 039492 5 £2.00

Government trading funds

The ABRO Trading Fund Order 2002 No. 2002/719. – Enabling power: Government Trading Funds Act 1973, ss. 1, 2 (1) (7), 2AA (1), 2A (1), 2C (1), 6 (1). – Issued: 22.03.2002. Made: 14.03.2002. Coming into force: 01.04.2002. Effect: None. Territorial extent & classification: E/W/S/NI. General. – 4p.: 30 cm. – 0 11 039518 2 £1.75

The Queen Elizabeth II Conference Centre Trading Fund (Variation) Order 2002 No. 2002/1951. – Enabling power: Government Trading Funds Act 1973, ss. 1, 6. – Issued: 31.07.2002. Made: 23.07.2002. Coming into force: 24.07.2002. Effect: S.I. 1997/933 amended. Territorial extent & classification: E/W/S/NI. General. – 4p.: 30 cm. – 0 11 042553 7 £1.75

The Royal Mint Trading Fund (Extension and Variation) Order 2002 No. 2002/831. – Enabling power: Government Trading Funds Act 1973, ss. 1 (1), 2 (1), 6 (1). – Issued: 19.06.2002. Made: 26.03.2002. Coming into force: 01.04.2002. Effect: None. Territorial extent & classification: E/W/S/NI. General. – 4p.: 30 cm. – 0 11 042353 4 £1.75

Hallmark

The Hallmarking (International Convention) Order 2002 No. 2002/506. – Enabling power: Hallmarking Act 1973, ss. 2 (1) (c), 2 (3), 21 (1). – Issued: 13.03.2002. Made: 07.03.2002. Laid: 07.03.2002. Coming into force: 01.04.2002. Effect: S.I. 1976/730 revoked. Territorial extent & classification: E/W/S/NI. General. – 12p.: 30 cm. – 0 11 039452 6 *£2.50*

Harbours, docks, piers and ferries

The Brightlingsea Harbour Revision (Constitution) Order 2002 No. 2002/2476. – Enabling power: Harbours Act 1964, s. 14. – Issued: 04.10.2002. Made: 13.09.2002. Coming into force: 18.09.2002. Effect: S.I. 1981/1096 revoked. Territorial extent & classification: E/W/S. Local. – 8p.: 30 cm. – 0 11 042830 7 *£2.00*

The Dart Harbour and Navigation Harbour Revision (Constitution) Order 2002 No. 2002/2730. – Enabling power: Harbours Act 1964, s. 14. – Issued: 15.11.2002. Made: 01.11.2002. Coming into force: 04.11.2002. Effect: 1975 c. xxii amended. Territorial extent & classification: E/W/S. Local. – 12p.: 30 cm. – 0 11 042966 4 *£2.50*

The Felixstowe Dock and Railway Harbour Revision Order 2002 No. 2002/2618. – Enabling power: Harbours Act 1964, s. 14. – Issued: 04.11.2002. Made: 10.10.2002. Coming into force: 31.10.2002. Effect: 1974 c. i amended. Territorial extent & classification: E/W/S. Local. – 10, [1]p.: 30 cm. – 0 11 042926 5 *£2.50*

The Gloucester Harbour Revision (Constitution) Order 2002 No. 2002/3268. – Enabling power: Harbours Act 1964, s. 14. – Issued: 14.01.2003. Made: 12.12.2002. Coming into force: 16.12.2002. Effect: 13 & 14 Cha. 2 c. xiv (1662); 7 & 8 Will. 3 c. 14 (1695); 13 Geo 1 c. 34 (1727); 49 Geo. 3 c. lxxviii (1809); 1889 c.cvi; 1890 c.xcvii; S.I. 1988/1040; 1994/3162 amended. Territorial extent & classification: E/W/S. Local. – 12p.: 30 cm. – 0 11 044547 3 *£2.50*

The Lymington Harbour Revision (Constitution) Order 2002 No. 2002/2586. – Enabling power: Harbours Act 1964, s. 14. – Issued: 22.10.2002. Made: 11.10.2002. Coming into force: 15.10.2002. Effect: 1951 c. xxv amended. Territorial extent & classification: E/W/S. Local. – 8p.: 30 cm. – 0 11 042864 1 *£2.00*

The Mersey Docks and Harbour Company (Langton River Berth) Harbour Revision Order 2002 No. 2002/3127. – Enabling power: Harbours Act 1964, s. 14. – Issued: 30.12.2002. Made: 17.12.2002. Coming into force: 31.12.2002. Effect: None. Territorial extent & classification: E/W/S. Local. – 8p.: 30 cm. – 0 11 044245 8 *£2.00*

The Port of Ipswich (Transfer of Undertaking) Harbour Revision Order 2002 No. 2002/3269. – Enabling power: Harbours Act 1964, s. 14. – Issued: 14.01.2003. Made: 23.12.2002. Coming into force: 30.12.2002. Effect: 1949 c.xxix; 1950 c. xiv; 1961 c.xxxvi; 1964 c.xxxviii; 1971 c. xiv amended. Territorial extent & classification: E/W/S. Local. – 4p.: 30 cm. – 0 11 044548 1 *£1.75*

The Whitehaven Harbour Commissioners (Constitution) Harbour Revision Order 2002 No. 2002/306. – Enabling power: Harbours Act 1964, s. 15 (3). – Issued: 20.02.2002. Made: 11.02.2002. Coming into force: 04.03.2002. Effect: The Borough and Harbour of Whitehaven Scheme 1894 amended & S.I. 1991/238 revoked. Territorial extent & classification: E/W/S. Local. – 12p.: 30 cm. – 0 11 039336 8 *£2.50*

The Yarmouth (Isle of Wight) Harbour Revision Order 2002 No. 2002/311. – Enabling power: Harbours Act 1964, s. 14 (7). – Issued: 20.02.2002. Made: 11.02.2002. Coming into force: 04.03.2002. Effect: None. Territorial extent & classification: E/W/S. Local. – 4p.: 30 cm. – 0 11 039340 6 *£1.75*

Health and safety

The Chemicals (Hazard Information and Packaging for Supply) Regulations 2002 No. 2002/1689. – Enabling power: European Communities Act 1972, s. 2 (2) & Health and Safety at Work etc. Act 1974, ss. 15 (1) (2) (3) (c) (5) (b) (6) (b) (8) (9), 82 (3) (a), sch. 3, paras. 1 (1) (b) (c) (4) (5), 2 (1), 3 (2), 15 (1), 16. – Issued: 03.07.2002. Made: 28.06.2002. Laid: 03.07.2002. Coming into force: 24.07.2002. Effect: S.I. 1996/2092 amended & S.I. 1994/3247; 1996/1092; 1997/1460; 1998/3106; 1999/197; 1999/3165; 2000/2381 revoked. Territorial extent & classification: E/W/S. General. – 52p.: 30 cm. – EC note: Implements 1992/32/EEC; 1999/45/EC; 76/769/EC; 91/155/EEC; DIR 91/410/EEC; 92/37/EEC; 93/21/EEC, 72/EEC, 101/EEC, 112/EEC; 94/69/EC; 96/54/EC; 97/69/EC; 98/73/EC, 98/98/EC; 2000/32/EC, 33/EC; 2001/58/EC; 2001/59/EC; 2001/60/EC – 0 11 042419 0 *£7.50*

Control of Asbestos at Work Regulations 2002 No. 2002/2675. – Enabling power: Health and Safety at Work etc. Act 1974, ss. 15 (1) (2) (4) (5) (b) (6) (b) (9), 18 (2), 82 (3) (a), sch. 3, paras 1 (1) to (4), 3 (2), 6 (1), 8 to 11, 14, 15 (1), 16, 20. – Issued: 01.11.2002. Made: 24.10.2002. Laid: 31.10.2002. Coming into force: 21.11.2002 for all regs except 4 & 20; 21.05.2004 for reg. 4; 21.11.2004 for reg. 20. Effect: S.I. 1998/494 amended & S.I. 1987/2115; 1992/3068; 1990/3235 revoked (21.11.2002.). Territorial extent & classification: E/W/S/outside GB in relation to any activity to which sections 1 to 59 and 80 to 82 of the Health and Safety at Work etc. Act 1974 apply. General. – 17p.: 30 cm. – EC note: Implement for Great Britain: Council directive 76/769/EEC (as amended by DIR 83/478/EEC); DIR 83/477/EEC (as amended by DIR 91/382/EEC); DIR 90/394/EEC and DIR 98/34/EC – 0 11 042918 4 *£3.50*

The Control of Lead at Work Regulations 2002 No. 2002/2676. – Enabling power: Health and Safety at Work etc. Act 1974, ss. 15 (1) (2) (4) (a) (5) (b), 82 (3) (a), sch. 3, paras 1 (1) (b) (c) (2), 6 (1), 7, 8, 9, 11, 14, 15 (1), 16. – Issued: 01.11.2002. Made: 24.10.2002. Laid: 31.10.2002. Coming into force: 21.11.2002. Effect: S.I. 1998/543 revoked. Territorial extent & classification: E/W/S/outside GB in relation to any activity to which sections 1 to 59 and 80 to 82 of the Health and Safety at Work etc. Act 1974 apply. General. – EC note: Implement for Great Britain Council directive 98/24/EC on the protection of the health and safety of workers from risks related to chemical agents at work. – 13p.: 30 cm. – 0 11 042917 6 £3.00

The Control of Substances Hazardous to Health Regulations 2002 No. 2002/2677. – Enabling power: European Communities Act 1972, s. 2 (2) & Health and Safety at Work etc. Act 1974, ss. 15 (1) (2) (3) (b) (4) (5) (b) (6) (b) (9), 52 (2) (3), 82 (3) (a), sch. 3, paras 1 (1) to (4), 2, 6 (1), 8, 9, 11, 14, 15 (1), 16, 20. – Issued: 01.11.2002. Made: 24.10.2002. Laid: 31.10.2002. Coming into force: 21.11.2002. Effect: 1974 c. 37 modified & S.I. 1999/437 revoked. Territorial extent & classification:E/W/S/outside GB in relation to any activity to which sections 1 to 59 and 80 to 82 of the Health and Safety at Work etc. Act 1974 apply. General. – 28p.: 30 cm. – EC note: Implement for Great Britain: Council directive 78/610/EEC; point 3 of article 1 of DIR 89/677/EEC; DIR 90/394/EEC; that part of DIR 96/55/EC adapting to technical progress for the 2nd time Annex I to DIR 76/769/EEC; DIR 98/24/EC; DIR 2000/54/EC – 0 11 042919 2 £4.50

The Dangerous Substances and Explosive Atmospheres Regulations 2002 No. 2002/2776. – Enabling power: Health and Safety at Work etc Act 1974, ss. 15 (1) (2) (3) (a) (5), 80 (1), 82 (3) (a), sch. 3, paras. 1 (1) (2) (4), 6, 9, 11, 14, 16, 18 (b), 20. – Issued: 14.11.2002. Made: 07.11.2002. Laid: 14.11.2002. Coming into force: in accordance with regulation 1 (a) (b) (c). Effect: 1922 c.35; 1928 c.32; 1961 c.34 & S.I. 1929/952; 1957/859; 1976/2003; 1979/427; 1982/630; 1987/37; 1996/2095; 1997/1840 amended & S.I. 1960/1932; 1987/37; 1992/3004; 1996/2092, 2095 partially revoked (05.05.2003.) & S.R.& O. 1921/1825; 1928/82; 1929/992; 1930/34; 1939/571; 1946/2197; 1947/1442; & S.I. 1949/2224; 1952/1689; 1972/917; 1974/1587; 1983/977; 1983/979 revoked (05.05.2003.). Territorial extent & classification: E/W/S. General. – 20p.: 30 cm. – EC note: Implements EC DIR 98/24, so far as that directive relates to safety, and DIR 99/92 – 0 11 042957 5 £3.50

The Genetically Modified Organisms (Contained Use) (Amendment) Regulations 2002 No. 2002/63. – Enabling power: European Communities Act 1972, s. 2 (2) & Health and Safety At Work etc. Act 1974, ss. 15 (1) (2), 82 (3) (a), sch. 3, paras. 15 (1), 16. – Issued: 11.02.2002. Made: 16.01.2002. Laid: 17.01.2002. Coming into force: 08.02.2002. Effect: S.I. 2000/2831 amended. Territorial extent & classification: E/W/S. General. – 4p.: 30 cm. – 0 11 039273 6 £1.75

The Health and Safety at Work etc. Act 1974 (Application to Environmentally Hazardous Substances) Regulations 2002 No. 2002/282. – Enabling power: European Communities Act 1972, s. 2 (2). – Issued: 18.02.2002. Made: 11.02.2002. Laid: 18.02.2002. Coming into force: 11.03.2002. Effect: S.I. 1996/2075: 1999/40 revoked. Territorial extent & classification: E/W/S. General. – 4p.: 30 cm. – EC note: These Regs. enable regs. to be made under art. 15 of the 1974 Act to implement the following Directives: DIR 94/55; 96/49; 94/63; 96/35; 96/86; 96/87; 1999/47; 1999/48; 2000/61; 2000/62; 2001/6; 2001/7 – 0 11 039310 4 £1.75

The Health and Safety (Fees) Regulations 2002 No. 2002/655. – Enabling power: European Communities Act 1972, s. 2 (2) & Health and Safety at Work etc. Act 1974, ss. 43 (2) (4) (5) (6), 82 (3) (a). – Issued: 27.03.2002. Made: 12.03.2002 Laid: 12.03.2002. Coming into force: 02.04.2002. Effect: S.I. 2001/2626 revoked. Territorial extent & classification: E/W/S. General. – 36p.: 30 cm. – Revoked by S.I. 2003/547 (ISBN 0110451864) – 0 11 039596 4 £6.50

The Health and Safety (Miscellaneous Amendments) Regulations 2002 No. 2002/2174. – Enabling power: Health and Safety at Work etc. Act 1974, ss. 15 (1) (2) (3) (a), 82 (3) (a), sch. 3, paras. 1 (1) (2), 8 (1), 9, 10, 11, 14. – Issued: 27.08.2002. Made: 17.08.2002 Laid: 27.08.2002. Coming into force: 17.09.2002. Effect: S.I. 1981/917; 1992/2792, 2793, 2966, 3004; 1998/2306, 2307; 1999/2024 amended. Territorial extent & classification: E/W/S. General. – 8p.: 30 cm. – EC note: These regs., which apply to England, Wales and Scotland only, give effect to point 19.2 of Annex 2 to DIR 89/654/EEC (the Workplace Directive), and to arts. 4 & 5 of DIR 90/270/EEC. It gives effect to Annex II to DIR 90/269/EEC and full effect to arts. 4 (3) (4) (5) (8), to reg. 4 (4) and to art. 5 (1) of DIR 89/656/EEC. It gives complete or clearer effect to the following provisions of the Workplace Directive - arts. 2, 6 & Annex 1. point 2, points 7.3, point 16.2, 18.1.1., 20, and gives clearer effect to art. 4 of & point 2.8 of Annex 1 to DIR 95/63/EC – 0 11 042693 2 £2.00

The Notification of Installations Handling Hazardous Substances (Amendment) Regulations 2002 No. 2002/2979. – Enabling power: Health and Safety at Work etc. Act 1974, ss. 15 (1) (2) (3) (a), 82 (3) (a), sch. 3, paras. 1 (1), 15 (1). – Issued: 09.12.2002. Made: 02.12.2002. Laid: 09.12.2002. Coming into force: 30.12.2002. Effect: S.I. 1982/1357 amended. Territorial extent & classification: E/W/S. General. – 2p.: 30 cm. – 0 11 044115 X £1.50

The Notification of New Substances (Amendment) Regulations 2002 No. 2002/2176. – Enabling power: Health and Safety at Work etc. Act 1974, ss. 15 (1) (2), 82 (3) (a), sch. 3, para. 1 (1) (b) (5) & European Communities Act 1972, s. 2 (2). – Issued: 27.08.2002. Made: 17.08.2002. Laid: 27.08.2002. Coming into force: 17.09.2002. Effect: S.I. 1993/3050 amended. Territorial extent & classification: E/W/S. General. – 8p.: 30 cm. – EC note: Amends the principle regs. to incorporate a reduced test method for chemical intermediates thereby implementing paras. 7 & 8 of art. 1 of directive 2001/59/EC adapting to technical progress for the 28th time directive 67/548/EEC – 0 11 042696 7 £2.00

The Offshore Safety (Miscellaneous Amendments) Regulations 2002 No. 2002/2175. – Enabling power: Health and Safety at Work etc. Act 1974, ss. 15 (1) (3) (a), 82 (3) (a) & Offshore Safety Act 1992, s. 1 (2) (a). – Issued: 27.08.2002. Made: 17.08.2002. Laid: 27.08.2002. Coming into force: 17.09.2002. Effect: S.I. 1995/738 amended. Territorial extent & classification: E/W/S. General. – 2p.: 30 cm. – 0 11 042695 9 *£1.50*

The Packaging, Labelling and Carriage of Radioactive Material by Rail Regulations 2002 No. 2002/2099. – Enabling power: Health and Safety at Work etc. Act 1974, ss. 15 (1) (2) (4) (b) (5) (b) (6) (b), 82 (3) (a), sch. 3, paras. 1 (1) to (4), 3, 4 (1), 14, 15 (1), 16. – Issued: 12.08.2002. Made: 06.08.2002. Laid: 12.08.2002. Coming into force: 02.09.2002. Effect: S.I. 1999/303, 257, 2024, 3232; 2000/2688; 2001/2975 amended & S.I. 1996/2090 revoked. Territorial extent & classification:E/W/S. General. – 32p.: 30 cm. – EC note: Implement EC Directive 96/49/EC with regard to the transport of dangerous goods by rail (as amended by DIR 2000/62/EC and 2001/6/EC) insofar as it relates to radioactive material and make provision for the carriage of radioactive material by rail – 0 11 042651 7 *£6.00*

The Personal Protective Equipment Regulations 2002 No. 2002/1144. – Enabling power: European Communities Act 1972, s. 2 (2). – Issued: 26.04.2002. Made: 20.04.2002. Laid: 23.04.2002. Coming into force: 15.05.2002. Effect: S.I. 1992/3139; 1993/3074; 1994/2326; 1996/3039 revoked. Territorial extent & classification: E/W/S/NI. General. – 24p.: 30 cm. – EC note: These Regs maintain the implementation of Council directive 89/686/EEC as amended by Council directive 93/68/EEC, Council directive 93/05/EEC & Council directive 96/58/EC – 0 11 039830 0 *£4.00*

The Pressure Equipment (Amendment) Regulations 2002 No. 2002/1267. – Enabling power: European Communities Act 1972, s. 2 (2). – Issued: 15.05.2002. Made: 06.05.2002. Laid: 09.05.2002. Coming into force: 30.05.2002. Effect: S.I. 1999/2001 amended. Territorial extent & classification:E/W/S/NI. General. – EC note: These regs. amend S.I. 1999/2001 which implemented EC DIR 97/23/EC. – 2p.: 30 cm. – 0 11 039935 8 *£1.50*

Health care and associated professions

The Council for the Regulation of Health Care Professionals (Appointment etc.) Regulations 2002 No. 2002/2376. – Enabling power: National Health Service Reform and Health Care Professions Act 2002, s. 38 (5), sch. 7, para. 6. – Issued: 01.10.2002. Made: 17.09.2002. Laid: 18.09.2002. Coming into force: 10.10.2002. Effect: None. Territorial extent & classification: UK. General. – 8p.: 30 cm. – 0 11 042821 8 *£2.00*

The Health Act 1999 (Commencement No. 12) Order 2002 No. 2002/1167 (C.29). – Enabling power: Health Act 1999, s. 67 (1) (2). Bringing into operation certain provisions of the 1999 Act on 01.04.2002, in accord. with arts. 2 to 5. – Issued: 30.04.2002. Made: 27.03.2002. Effect: None. Territorial extent & classification: E/W/S/NI. General. – 8p.: 30 cm. – 0 11 039850 5 *£2.00*

The National Health Service Reform and Health Care Professions Act 2002 (Commencement No. 1) Order 2002 No. 2002/2202 (C.69). – Enabling power: National Health Service Reform and Health Care Professions Act 2002, ss. 38 (7), 42 (3). Bringing into force various provisions of the 2002 Act on 27.08.2002, 02.09.2002, 01.12.2002 & 01.04.2003 in accord. with arts. 2 & 3. – Issued: 08.10.2002. Made: 20.08.2002. Laid:-. Effect: 1968 c. 46 amended. Territorial extent & classification: UK. General. – 4p.: 30 cm. – 0 11 042838 2 *£1.75*

The National Health Service Reform and Health Care Professions Act 2002 (Commencement No. 2) Order 2002 No. 2002/2478 (C.80). – Enabling power: National Health Service Reform and Health Care Professions Act 2002, ss. 38 (7), 42 (3). Bringing into force various provisions of the 2002 Act on 01.10.2002. – Issued: 02.10.2002. Made: 27.09.2002. Effect: None. Territorial extent & classification: UK [parts to E/W only and parts to all UK]. General. – 4p.: 30 cm. – 0 11 042832 3 *£1.75*

Health care and associated professions: Doctors

The General Medical Council (Constitution) Order 2002 No. 2002/3136. – Enabling power: Medical Act 1983, s. 1 (2), sch. 1, paras. 3 (1) (3), 5, 7, 13. – Issued: 06.01.2003. Made: 17.12.2002. Laid: 06.01.2003. Coming into force: 27.01.2003. & 01.07.2003. Effect: S.I. 1979/112; 1987/157; 1989/496; 1996/1630 revoked. Territorial extent & classification: E/W/S/NI. General. – With correction slip dated March 2003. – 8p.: 30 cm. – 0 11 044264 4 *£2.00*

The Medical Act 1983 (Amendment) Order 2002 No. 2002/3135. – Enabling power: Health Act 1999, ss. 60, 62 (4). – Issued: 24.12.2002. Made: 17.12.2002. Coming into force: In accord.with art. 1 (2) (3). Effect: 1983 c. 54 amended; see schs. 1 and 2 for further consequential amendments. Territorial extent & classification: E/W/S/NI. General. – 57p.: 30 cm. – 0 11 044254 7 *£7.50*

Health care and associated professions: Health professions

The Council for Professions Supplementary to Medicine (Transfer of Staff and Property etc.) Order 2002 No. 2002/922. – Enabling power: S.I. 2002/254, art. 48 (2), sch. 2, para. 20. – Issued: 09.04.2002. Made: 22.03.2002. Coming into force: 01.04.2002. Effect: None. Territorial extent & classification:E/W/S/NI. General. – 4p.: 30 cm. – 0 11 039661 8 *£1.75*

The Health Professions Order 2001 No. 2002/254. – Enabling power: Health Act 1999, ss. 60, 62 (4). – Issued: 21.02.2002. Made: 12.02.2002. Coming into force: 12.02.2002.(for arts. 1, 48 (4)), the remainder in acc.with art. 1 (2). Effect: 1920 c. lxxxix; 1972 c.11; 1984 c.xxvii, c.39; 1991 c.xiii; 1994 c.23; 1998 c.29; 1999 c.8; 2000 c.37 amended. Territorial extent & classification: E/W/S/NI. General. – 48p.: 30 cm. – 0 11 039324 4 *£6.50*

The Health Professions Order 2001 (Consequential Amendments) Order 2002 No. 2002/880. – Enabling power: Health Act 1999, s. 63. – Issued: 30.04.2002. Made: 27.03.2002. Laid: 28.03.2002. Coming into force: 17.04.2002. Effect: S.I. 1964/939; 1974/494; 1978/41; 1980/1924; 1991/824; 1996/2374; 1999/2337, 2801; 2000/89; 2001/1042 amended. Territorial extent & classification: E/W/S/NI. General. – 4p.: 30 cm. – 0 11 039846 7 *£1.75*

The Health Professions Order 2001 (Transitional Provisions) Order 2002 No. 2002/1124. – Enabling power: S.I. 2002/254, art. 48 (2). – Issued: 23.04.2002. Made: 26.03.2002. Coming into force: for the purposes of art. 2 (a) (ii), the date of coming into force of art 27 (a) of the Health Professions Order 2001; for the purposes of art. 2 (c), the date of coming into force of art. 36 of the Health Professions Order 2001; for remainder 01.04.2002. Effect: None. Territorial extent & classification: E/W/S/NI. General. – 2p.: 30 cm. – 0 11 039804 1 *£1.50*

Highways, England and Wales

The A1 Trunk Road (Stannington Grade Separated Junction) Order 2002 No. 2002/2757. – Enabling power: Highways Act 1980, ss. 10, 41. – Issued: 18.11.2002. Made: 23.10.2002. Coming into force: 26.11.2002. Effect: None. Territorial extent & classification: E/W. Local. – 2p.: 30 cm. – With correction slip dated November 2002 – 0 11 042947 8 *£1.50*

The A5 London to Holyhead Trunk Road (Sketchley Meadow Junction Improvement) Order 2002 No. 2002/898. – Enabling power: Highways Act 1980, ss. 10, 41. – Issued: 03.04.2002. Made: 18.03.2002. Coming into force: 03.04.2002. Effect: None. Territorial extent & classification: E/W. Local. – 2p.: 30 cm. – 0 11 039656 1 *£1.50*

The A6 Trunk Road (Derby to Stockport) (Detrunking) Order 2002 No. 2002/1168. – Enabling power: Highways Act 1980, ss. 10, 12. – Issued: 03.05.2002. Made: 26.04.2002. Coming into force: 17.05.2002. Effect: None. Territorial extent & classification: E. Local. – 2p.: 30 cm. – 0 11 039858 0 *£1.50*

The A6 Trunk Road (Levens Slip Road) (Detrunking) Order 2002 No. 2002/2423. – Enabling power: Highways Act 1980, ss. 10, 12. – Issued: 30.09.2002. Made: 19.09.2002. Coming into force: 01.04.2003. Effect: None. Territorial extent & classification: E/W. Local. – [10]p., map (folded): 30 cm. – 0 11 042812 9 *£2.50*

The A15 Trunk Road (North of Lincoln to North Lincolnshire Border) (Detrunking) Order 2002 No. 2002/1208. – Enabling power: Highways Act 1980, ss. 10, 12. – Issued: 07.05.2002. Made: 26.04.2002. Coming into force: 17.05.2002. Effect: None. Territorial extent & classification: E. Local. – 2p.: 30 cm. – 0 11 039898 X *£1.50*

The A15 Trunk Road (South of M180) (Detrunking) Order 2002 No. 2002/1209. – Enabling power: Highways Act 1980, ss. 10, 12. – Issued: 07.05.2002. Made: 26.04.2002. Coming into force: 17.05.2002. Effect: None. Territorial extent & classification: E. Local. – 2p.: 30 cm. – 0 11 039899 8 *£1.50*

The A16 Trunk Road (Stamford to North East Lincolnshire) (Detrunking) Order 2002 No. 2002/1210. – Enabling power: Highways Act 1980, ss. 10, 12. – Issued: 07.05.2002. Made: 26.04.2002. Coming into force: 17.05.2002. Effect: None. Territorial extent & classification: E. Local. – 2p.: 30 cm. – 0 11 039900 5 *£1.50*

The A17 Trunk Road (Newark-on-Trent to Kings Lynn) (Detrunking) Order 2002 No. 2002/1211. – Enabling power: Highways Act 1980, ss. 10, 12. – Issued: 07.05.2002. Made: 26.04.2002. Coming into force: 17.05.2002. Effect: None. Territorial extent & classification: E. Local. – 2p.: 30 cm. – 0 11 039901 3 *£1.50*

The A21 Trunk Road (A2100 Junction Improvement John's Cross) (Detrunking) Order 2002 No. 2002/780. – Enabling power: Highways Act 1980, s. 10. – Issued: 28.03.2002. Made: 19.03.2002. Coming into force: 17.04.2002. Effect: None. Territorial extent & classification: E. Local. – 2p.: 30 cm. – 0 11 039601 4 *£1.50*

The A21 Trunk Road (A2100 Junction Improvement John's Cross) Order 2002 No. 2002/781. – Enabling power: Highways Act 1980, ss. 10, 41. – Issued: 28.03.2002. Made: 19.03.2002. Coming into force: 17.04.2002. Effect: None. Territorial extent & classification: E. Local. – 2p.: 30 cm. – 0 11 039600 6 *£1.50*

The A34 Trunk Road (Newtown, Great Wyrley, Staffordshire to the Southern Boundary of the A34/A500 Queensway Roundabout, Staffordshire) (Detrunking) Order 2002 No. 2002/1213. – Enabling power: Highways Act 1980, ss. 10,12. – Issued: 07.05.2002. Made: 26.04.2002. Coming into force: 16.05.2002. Effect: None. Territorial extent & classification: E/W. Local. – 2p.: 30 cm. – 0 11 039903 X *£1.50*

The A38 Trunk Road (Worcestershire/Gloucestershire) (Detrunking) Order 2002 No. 2002/1179. – Enabling power: Highways Act 1980, ss. 10, 12. – Issued: 03.05.2002. Made: 26.04.2002. Coming into force: 17.05.2002. Effect: None. Territorial extent & classification: E. Local. – 2p.: 30 cm. – 0 11 039860 2 *£1.50*

The A39 Trunk Road (Devon/Cornwall County Boundary to Indian Queens Cornwall) (Detrunking) Order 2002 No. 2002/1395. – Enabling power: Highways Act 1980, ss. 10, 12. – Issued: 24.05.2002. Made: 21.05.2002. Coming into force: 01.06.2002. Effect: None. Territorial extent & classification: E. Local. – 2p.: 30 cm. – 0 11 042243 0 *£1.50*

The A39 Trunk Road (Portmore Roundabout to the Devon/Cornwall County Boundary) (Detrunking) Order 2002 No. 2002/1679. – Enabling power: Highways Act 1980, ss. 10, 12. – Issued: 02.07.2002. Made: 26.06.2002. Coming into force: 01.07.2002. Effect: None. Territorial extent & classification: E/W. Local. – 2p.: 30 cm. – 0 11 042414 X *£1.50*

The A40 London to Fishguard Trunk Road (M40 Junction 8 to A44 Wolvercote Roundabout) (Detrunking) Order 2002 No. 2002/207. – Enabling power: Highways Act 1980, ss. 10, 12. – Issued: 08.02.2002. Made: 04.02.2002. Coming into force: 30.03.2002. Effect: None. Territorial extent & classification: E/W. Local. – 2p.: 30 cm. – 0 11 039278 7 *£1.50*

The A41 London to Birkenhead Trunk Road (Buckinghamshire) (Detrunking) Order 2001 No. 2002/215. – Enabling power: Highways Act 1980, ss. 10, 12. – Issued: 08.02.2002. Made: 04.02.2002. Coming into force: 30.03.2002. Effect: None. Territorial extent & classification: E/W. Local. – 2p., ill.: 30 cm. – 0 11 039279 5 *£1.50*

The A41 Trunk Road in Shropshire (A41/M54 Roundabout to the Telford & Wrekin Border) (Detrunking) Order 2002 No. 2002/342. – Enabling power: Highways Act 1980, ss. 10, 12. – Issued: 25.02.2002. Made: 11.02.2002. Coming into force: 01.04.2002. Effect: None. Territorial extent & classification: E/W. Local. – 2p.: 30 cm. – 0 11 039357 0 *£1.50*

The A41 Trunk Road Shropshire (Telford & Wrekin Border to the County of Cheshire Border) (Detrunking) Order 2002 No. 2002/341. – Enabling power: Highways Act 1980, ss. 10, 12. – Issued: 25.02.2002. Made: 11.02.2002. Coming into force: 01.04.2002. Effect: None. Territorial extent & classification: E/W. Local. – 2p.: 30 cm. – 0 11 039356 2 *£1.50*

The A41 Trunk Road (Staffordshire and Telford & Wrekin) (Detrunking) Order 2001 No. 2002/309. – Enabling power: Highways Act 1980, ss. 10, 12. – Issued: 19.02.2002. Made: 11.02.2002. Coming into force: 01.04.2002. Effect: None. Territorial extent & classification: E/W. Local. – 2p., ill.: 30 cm. – 0 11 039342 2 *£1.50*

The A41 Trunk Road (Staffordshire and Telford & Wrekin) (Detrunking) Order 2001 No. 2002/309. – Enabling power: Highways Act 1980, ss. 10, 12. – Issued: 19.02.2002. Made: 11.02.2002. Coming into force: 01.04.2002. Effect: None. Territorial extent & classification: E/W. Local. – 2p., ill.: 30 cm. – 0 11 039342 2 *£1.50*

The A44 London to Aberystwyth Trunk Road (A34 Peartree Roundabout to A40 Wolvercote Roundabout) (Detrunking) Order 2002 No. 2002/217. – Enabling power: Highways Act 1980, ss. 10, 12. – Issued: 08.02.2002. Made: 04.02.2002. Coming into force: 30.03.2002. Effect: None. Territorial extent & classification: E/W. Local. – 2p., ill.: 30 cm. – 0 11 039281 7 *£1.50*

The A44 London to Aberystwyth Trunk Road (A34 Peartree Roundabout to A40 Wolvercote Roundabout) (Detrunking) Order 2002 No. 2002/217. – Enabling power: Highways Act 1980, ss. 10, 12. – Issued: 08.02.2002. Made: 04.02.2002. Coming into force: 30.03.2002. Effect: None. Territorial extent & classification: E/W. Local. – 2p., ill.: 30 cm. – 0 11 039281 7 *£1.50*

The A45 Trunk Road (Weedon Road, Upton to the M45/A45 Roundabout, Dunchurch) (Detrunking) Order 2002 No. 2002/1178. – Enabling power: Highways Act 1980, ss. 10, 41. – Issued: 03.05.2002. Made: 26.04.2002. Coming into force: 16.05.2002. Effect: None. Territorial extent & classification: E. Local. – 2p.: 30 cm. – 0 11 039859 9 *£1.50*

The A46 Trunk Road (Ashchurch Station Bridge) (Detrunking) Order 2002 No. 2002/1595. – Enabling power: Highways Act 1980, ss. 10, 12. – Issued: 24.06.2002. Made: 06.06.2002. Coming into force: 01.07.2002. Effect: None. Territorial extent & classification: E/W. Local. – 8p., ill.: 30 cm. – 0 11 042385 2 *£2.75*

The A46 Trunk Road (Ashchurch Station Bridge) Order 2002 No. 2002/1594. – Enabling power: Highways Act 1980, ss. 10, 41. – Issued: 24.06.2002. Made: 06.06.2002. Coming into force: 01.07.2002. Effect: None. Territorial extent & classification: E/W. Local. – 8p., ill.: 30 cm. – 0 11 042384 4 *£2.75*

The A46 Trunk Road (North of Lincoln) (Detrunking) Order 2002 No. 2002/1212. – Enabling power: Highways Act 1980, ss. 10, 12. – Issued: 07.05.2002. Made: 26.04.2002. Coming into force: 17.05.2002. Effect: None. Territorial extent & classification: E. Local. – 2p.: 30 cm. – 0 11 039902 1 *£1.50*

The A49 Trunk Road in Shropshire (A49/A5 Preston Roundabout to A49/A41 Prees Heath Roundabout and A49/A41 Chester Road Roundabout to the County of Cheshire Border) (Detrunking) Order 2002 No. 2002/340. – Enabling power: Highways Act 1980, ss. 10, 12. – Issued: 25.02.2002. Made: 11.02.2002. Coming into force: 01.04.2002. Effect: None. Territorial extent & classification: E/W. Local. – 2p.: 30 cm. – 0 11 039354 6 *£1.50*

The A52 Trunk Road (Derby to Calton Moor) (Detrunking) Order 2002 No. 2002/1186. – Enabling power: Highways Act 1980, ss. 10, 12. – Issued: 03.05.2002. Made: 26.04.2002. Coming into force: 17.05.2002. Effect: None. Territorial extent & classification: E. Local. – 2p.: 30 cm. – 0 11 039867 X *£1.50*

The A57 Trunk Road (A57/M60/M67 Denton Roundabout to Manchester City Boundary) (Detrunking) Order 2002 No. 2002/1058. – Enabling power: Highways Act 1980, ss. 10, 12. – Issued: 19.04.2002. Made: 25.03.2002. Coming into force: 01.05.2002. Effect: None. Territorial extent & classification: E. Local. – 2p.: 30 cm. – 0 11 039767 3 *£1.50*

The A57 Trunk Road (M1 to A1) (Detrunking) Order 2002 No. 2002/1205. – Enabling power: Highways Act 1980, ss. 10, 12. – Issued: 07.05.2002. Made: 26.04.2002. Coming into force: 17.05.2002. Effect: None. Territorial extent & classification: E. Local. – 2p.: 30 cm. – 0 11 039895 5 *£1.50*

The A58 Trunk Road (Halifax to M62 Motorway, Chain Bar) (Detrunking) Order 2002 No. 2002/75. – Enabling power: Highways Act 1980, ss. 10, 12. Issued: 21.01.2002. Made: 14.01.2002. Coming into force: 28.01.2002. Effect: None. Territorial extent & classification: E. Local. – 4p.: 30 cm. – 0 11 039200 0 *£2.15*

The A61 Trunk Road (Alfreton to Sheffield) (Detrunking) Order 2002 No. 2002/1185. – Enabling power: Highways Act 1980, ss. 10, 12. – Issued: 03.05.2002. Made: 26.04.2002. Coming into force: 17.05.2002. Effect: None. Territorial extent & classification: E. Local. – 2p.: 30 cm. – 0 11 039866 1 *£1.50*

The A64 Trunk Road (Musham Bank Roundabout to Queen Margaret's Roundabout) (Detrunking) Order 2002 No. 2002/434. – Enabling power: Highways Act 1980, ss. 10, 12. – Issued: 06.03.2002. Made: 21.02.2002. Coming into force: 01.04.2002. Effect: None. Territorial extent & classification: E/W. Local. – 5p., map: 30 cm. – 0 11 039406 2 *£2.65*

The A65 Trunk Road (Thorlby Roundabout to North Yorkshire/City of Bradford Boundary) (Detrunking) Order 2002 No. 2002/2108. – Enabling power: Highways Act 1980, ss. 10, 12. – Issued: 22.08.2002. Made: 06.08.2002. Coming into force: 01.04.2003. Effect: None. Territorial extent & classification: E. Local. – 1 folded sheet (8p.): 30 cm. – 0 11 042662 2 *£2.00*

The A69 Trunk Road (M6 to Carlisle City Boundary) (Detrunking) Order 2002 No. 2002/2425. – Enabling power: Highways Act 1980, ss. 10, 12. – Issued: 30.09.2002. Made: 19.09.2002. Coming into force: 01.04.2003. Effect: None. Territorial extent & classification: E/W. Local. – [10]p., map (folded): 30 cm. – 0 11 042814 5 *£2.50*

The A282 Trunk Road (Dartford-Thurrock Crossing Charging Scheme) Order 2002 No. 2002/1040. – Enabling power: Transport Act 2000, ss. 167, 168, 171, 172 (2). – Issued: 12.04.2002. Made: 04.04.2002. Coming into force: 19.04.2002. Effect: None. Territorial extent & classification: E. Local. – 8p.: 30 cm. – 0 11 039761 4 *£2.00*

The A303 Trunk Road (Folly Bottom Junction) (Detrunking) Order 2002 No. 2002/1029. – Enabling power: Highways Act 1980, s. 10. – Issued: 18.04.2002. Made: 09.04.2002. Coming into force: 22.04.2002. Effect: None. Territorial extent & classification: E/W. Local. – 2p.: 30 cm. – 0 11 039759 2 *£1.50*

The A303 Trunk Road (Folly Bottom Junction Improvement Slip Roads) Order 2002 No. 2002/1030. – Enabling power: Highways Act 1980, ss. 10, 41. – Issued: 18.04.2002. Made: 09.04.2002. Coming into force: 22.04.2002. Effect: None. Territorial extent & classification: E/W. Local. – 2p.: 30 cm. – 0 11 039760 6 *£1.50*

The A361 Trunk Road (M5 Motorway Junction 27 to Portmore Roundabout Devon) (Detrunking) Order 2002 No. 2002/1678. – Enabling power: Highways Act 1980, ss. 10, 12. – Issued: 02.07.2002. Made: 26.06.2002. Coming into force: 01.07.2002. Effect: None. Territorial extent & classification: E/W. Local. – 2p.: 30 cm. – 0 11 042413 1 *£1.50*

The A423 Maidenhead to Oxford Trunk Road (A34 Hinksey Interchange to A4142 Heyford Hill Roundabout) (Detrunking) Order 2002 No. 2002/216. – Enabling power: Highways Act 1980, ss. 10, 12. – Issued: 08.02.2002. Made: 04.02.2002 Coming into force: 30.03.2002. Effect: None. Territorial extent & classification: E/W. Local. – 2p., ill.: 30 cm. – 0 11 039280 9 *£1.50*

The A449 Trunk Road (A5 Gailey Roundabout to the A34 Queensway, Stafford) (Detrunking) Order 2002 No. 2002/1215. – Enabling power: Highways Act 1980, ss. 10, 12. – Issued: 07.05.2002. Made: 26.04.2002. Coming into force: 17.05.2002. Effect: None. Territorial extent & classification: E. Local. – 2p.: 30 cm. – 0 11 039905 6 *£1.50*

The A452 Trunk Road (B5011 Ogley Road Junction to the A4041 Queslett Road East/B4138 Thornhill Road Roundabout) (Detrunking) Order 2002 No. 2002/1180. – Enabling power: Highways Act 1980, ss. 10, 12. – Issued: 03.05.2002. Made: 26.04.2002. Coming into force: 17.05.2002. Effect: None. Territorial extent & classification: E. Local. – 2p.: 30 cm. – 0 11 039861 0 *£1.50*

The A516 Trunk Road (West of Derby) (Detrunking) Order 2002 No. 2002/1182. – Enabling power: Highways Act 1980, ss. 10, 12. – Issued: 03.05.2002. Made: 26.04.2002. Coming into force: 17.05.2002. Effect: None. Territorial extent & classification: E. Local. – 2p.: 30 cm. – 0 11 039863 7 *£1.50*

The A523 Trunk Road (Calton Moor to Cheshire Border) (Detrunking) Order 2002 No. 2002/1181. – Enabling power: Highways Act 1980, ss. 10, 12. – Issued: 03.05.2002. Made: 26.04.2002. Coming into force: 17.05.2002. Effect: None. Territorial extent & classification: E. Local. – 2p.: 30 cm. – 0 11 039862 9 *£1.50*

The A523 Trunk Road (County of Cheshire) (Detrunking) Order 2002 No. 2002/1183. – Enabling power: Highways Act 1980, ss. 10, 12. – Issued: 03.05.2002. Made: 26.04.2002. Coming into force: 17.05.2002. Effect: None. Territorial extent & classification: E. Local. – 2p.: 30 cm. – 0 11 039864 5 *£1.50*

The A523 Trunk Road (Metropolitan Borough of Stockport) (Detrunking) Order 2002 No. 2002/1184. – Enabling power: Highways Act 1980, ss. 10, 12. – Issued: 03.05.2002. Made: 26.04.2002. Coming into force: 17.05.2002. Effect: None. Territorial extent & classification: E. Local. – 2p.: 30 cm. – 0 11 039865 3 *£1.50*

The A590 Trunk Road (Levens Slip Road) (Detrunking) Order 2002 No. 2002/2424. – Enabling power: Highways Act 1980, ss. 10, 12. – Issued: 30.09.2002. Made: 19.09.2002. Coming into force: 01.04.2003. Effect: None. Territorial extent & classification: E/W. Local. – [10]p., map (folded): 30 cm. – 0 11 042813 7 *£2.50*

The A595 Trunk Road (Lillyhall to A66 Chapel Brow) Order 2002 No. 2002/2422. – Enabling power: Highways Act 1980, s. 10. – Issued: 30.09.2002. Made: 19.09.2002. Coming into force: 01.04.2003. Effect: None. Territorial extent & classification: E/W. Local. – 8p., map (folded): 30 cm. – 0 11 042811 0 *£3.50*

The A596 Trunk Road (Calva Brow Junction, Workington) Order 2002 No. 2002/1315. – Enabling power: Highways Act 1980, s. 10. – Issued: 16.05.2002. Made: 08.05.2002. Coming into force: 24.05.2002. Effect: None. Territorial extent & classification: E. Local. – [6]p., ill.: 30 cm. – 0 11 039941 2 *£2.65*

The A606 Trunk Road (A52 to A46) (Detrunking) Order 2002 No. 2002/1206. – Enabling power: Highways Act 1980, ss. 10, 12. – Issued: 07.05.2002. Made: 26.04.2002. Coming into force: 17.05.2002. Effect: None. Territorial extent & classification: E. Local. – 2p.: 30 cm. – 0 11 039896 3 *£1.50*

The A614 Trunk Road (Leapool to Ollerton and Blyth to Bawtry) (Detrunking) Order 2002 No. 2002/1207. – Enabling power: Highways Act 1980, ss. 10, 12. – Issued: 07.05.2002. Made: 26.04.2002. Coming into force: 17.05.2002. Effect: None. Territorial extent & classification: E. Local. – 2p.: 30 cm. – 0 11 039897 1 *£1.50*

The A1041 Trunk Road (540m South of Abbotts Road to 240m Southwest of the Centre of Carlton New Bridge) (Detrunking) Order 2002 No. 2002/2107. – Enabling power: Highways Act 1980, ss. 10, 12. – Issued: 22.08.2002. Made: 06.08.2002. Coming into force: 01.04.2003. Effect: None. Territorial extent & classification: E. Local. – 4p.: 30 cm. – 0 11 042661 4 *£1.75*

The A5011 Trunk Road (Linley Road) (Detrunking) Order 2002 No. 2002/1214. – Enabling power: Highways Act 1980, ss. 10, 12. – Issued: 07.05.2002. Made: 26.04.2002. Coming into force: 17.05.2002. Effect: None. Territorial extent & classification: E. Local. – 2p.: 30 cm. – 0 11 039904 8 *£1.50*

The Devon County Council (Barnstaple Downstream Bridge) Scheme 2000 Confirmation Instrument 2002 No. 2002/1134. – Enabling power: Highways Act 1980, s. 106 (3). – Issued: 24.04.2002. Made: 17.04.2002. Coming into force: In accord. with art. 1. Effect: None. Territorial extent & classification: E. Local. – 4p., plan: 30 cm. – 0 11 039815 7 *£2.65*

The Dunham Bridge (Revision of Tolls) Order 2002 No. 2002/2246. – Enabling power: Transport Charges (Miscellaneous Provisions) Act 1954, s. 6. – Made: 02.09.2002. Coming into force: 09.09.2002. Effect: None. Territorial extent & classification: E. Local *Unpublished*

The Gloucestershire County Council (Castle Meads Bridge) Scheme 2001 Confirmation Instrument 2002 No. 2002/3239. – Enabling power: Highways Act 1980, s. 106 (3). – Issued: 13.01.2003. Made: 30.12.2002. Coming into force: In accord. with art. 1. Effect: None. Territorial extent & classification: E. Local. – 4p., plans: 30 cm. – 0 11 044466 3 *£2.25*

The Gloucestershire County Council (Two Mile Bend Bridge) Scheme 2001 Confirmation Instrument 2002 No. 2002/3238. – Enabling power: Highways Act 1980, s. 106 (3). – Issued: 13.01.2003. Made: 30.12.2002. Coming into force: In accord. with art. 1. Effect: None. Territorial extent & classification: E. Local. – 4p., plans: 30 cm. – 0 11 044465 5 *£2.25*

The Humber Bridge (Revision of Tolls) Order 2002 No. 2002/786. – Enabling power: Humber Bridge Act 1971, s. 10. – Made: 22.03.2002. Coming into force: 01.04.2002. Effect: S.I. 2000/264 revoked. Territorial extent & classification: E. Local *Unpublished*

The M25 Motorway (Heathrow Terminal 5 Access) (No. 1) Connecting Roads Scheme 2002 No. 2002/343. – Enabling power: Highways Act 1980, ss. 16, 17, 19. – Issued: 25.02.2002. Made: 13.02.2002. Coming into force: 05.03.2002. Effect: None. Territorial extent & classification: E/W. Local. – 8p., ill.: 30 cm. – 0 11 039355 4 *£2.00*

The New Roads and Street Works Act 1991 (Commencement No. 7) (England) Order 2002 No. 2002/3267 (C.110). – Enabling power: New Roads and Street Works Act 1991, s. 170. Bringing into operation various provisions of the 1991 Act on 01.05.2003. – Issued: 17.01.2003. Made: 20.12.2002. Effect: None. Territorial extent & classification: E. General. – 4p.: 30 cm. – 0 11 044578 3 *£1.75*

The Severn Bridges Tolls Order 2002 No. 2002/3004. – Enabling power: Severn Bridges Act 1992, s. 9 (2) (b). – Issued: 11.12.2002. Made: 02.12.2002. Coming into force: 01.01.2003. Effect: S.I. 2001/3886 revoked. Territorial extent & classification: E. Local. – 2p.: 30 cm. – 0 11 044147 8 *£1.50*

The Staffordshire County Council Trent and Mersey Canal Bridge Scheme 2001 Confirmation Instrument 2002 No. 2002/1809. – Enabling power: Highways Act 1980, s. 106 (3). – Issued: 23.07.2002. Made: -. Coming into force: In accord. with art. 1. Effect: None. Territorial extent & classification: E. Local. – 1 folded sheet, [2]p., map, plans: 30 cm. – 0 11 042489 1 *£4.50*

The Staffordshire County (Trent and Mersey Canal) Temporary Bridge Scheme 2001 Confirmation Instrument 2002 No. 2002/1810. – Enabling power: Highways Act 1980, s. 106 (3). – Issued: 23.07.2002. Made: 04.07.2002. Coming into force: In accord. with art. 1. Effect: None. Territorial extent & classification: E. Local. – 1 folded sheet, [2]p., map, plans: 30 cm. – 0 11 042490 5 *£4.50*

The Street Works (Charges for Occupation of the Highway) (England) (London Borough of Camden) Order 2002 No. 2002/124. – Enabling power: New Roads and Street Works Act 1991, s. 74A (2). – Made: 24.01.2002. Coming into force: 25.01.2002. Effect: None. Territorial extent & classification: E. Local *Unpublished*

The Street Works (Charges for Occupation of the Highway) (England) (Middlesbrough Borough Council) Order 2002 No. 2002/123. – Enabling power: New Roads and Street Works Act 1991, s. 74A (2). – Made: 24.01.2002. Coming into force: 25.01.2002. Effect: None. Territorial extent & classification: E. Local *Unpublished*

The Street Works (Charges for Occupation of the Highway) (England) (Transport for London) Order 2002 No. 2002/1664. – Enabling power: New Roads and Street Works Act 1991, s. 74A (2). – Made: 25.06.2002. Coming into force: 26.06.2002. Effect: None. Territorial extent & classification: E. Local *Unpublished*

The Street Works (Inspection Fees) (England) Regulations 2002 No. 2002/2092. – Enabling power: New Roads and Street Works Act 1991, ss. 75, 104 (1). – Issued: 14.08.2002. Made: 06.08.2002. Laid: 14.08.2002. Coming into force: 01.10.2002. Effect: S.I. 1992/1688 revoked in relation to England; S.I. 2001/788 revoked. Territorial extent & classification: E. General. – 4p.: 30 cm. – 0 11 042644 4 *£1.75*

The Street Works (Records) (England) Regulations 2002 No. 2002/3217. – Enabling power: New Roads and Street Works Act 1991, ss. 79, 104 (1). – Issued: 27.01.2003. Made: 20.12.2002. Laid: 24.12.2002. Coming into force: 01.05.2003. Effect: None. Territorial extent & classification: E. General. – 4p.: 30 cm. – 0 11 044626 7 *£1.75*

The Street Works (Recovery of Costs) (England) Regulations 2002 No. 2002/2091. – Enabling power: New Roads and Street Works Act 1991, ss. 96, 104 (1). – Issued: 16.08.2002. Made: 06.08.2002. Laid: 08.08.2002. Coming into force: 01.09.2002. Effect: None. Territorial extent & classification: E. General. – 4p.: 30 cm. – 0 11 042650 9
£1.75

The Street Works (Reinstatement) (Amendment) (England) Regulations 2002 No. 2002/1487. – Enabling power: New Roads and Street Works Act 1991, ss. 71, 104 (3). – Issued: 01.07.2002. Made: 08.06.2002. Laid: 10.06.2002. Coming into force: 01.07.2002. Effect: S.I. 1992/1689 amended in relation to England. Territorial extent & classification: E. General. – 4p.: 30 cm. – 0 11 042401 8 *£1.75*

The Wiltshire County Council (Semington Aqueduct) Scheme 2000 Confirmation Instrument 2002 No. 2002/1868. – Enabling power: Highways Act 1980, s. 106 (3), 108 (4). – Issued: 25.07.2002. Made: 17.07.2002. Coming into force: In accord. with art. 1. Effect: None. Territorial extent & classification: E. Local. – 1 folded sheet (4p.), maps, plans: 30 cm. – 0 11 042525 1 *£3.50*

Highways, Wales

The Street Works (Inspection Fees) (Amendment) (Wales) Regulations 2002 No. 2002/3181 (W.297). – Enabling power: New Roads and Street Works Act 1991, ss. 75, 104 (1). – Issued: 31.12.2002. Made: 17.12.2002. Coming into force: 01.01.2003. Effect: S.I. 1992/1688 amended in relation to Wales. Territorial extent & classification: W. General. – 4p.: 30 cm. – In English and Welsh. Welsh title: Rheoliadau Gweithfyedd Stryd (Ffioedd Archwilio) (Diwygio) (Cymru) 2002. – 0 11 090609 8 *£1.75*

Hong Kong

The Extradition (Overseas Territories) (Application to Hong Kong) Order 2002 No. 2002/1825. – Enabling power: Extradition Act 1989, s. 32 (2A). – Issued: 26.07.2002. Made: 16.07.2002. Laid: 26.07.2002. Coming into force: 16.08.2002. Effect: 1989 C.33 & S.I. 2002/1824 amended. Territorial extent & classification: E/W/S/NI. General. – 4p.: 30 cm. – 0 11 042500 6 *£1.75*

The Extradition (Overseas Territories) (Hong Kong) Order 2002 No. 2002/1824. – Enabling power: Hong Kong Act 1985, sch., para. 3 (2). – Issued: 26.07.2002. Made: 16.07.2002. Laid: 26.07.2002. Coming into force: 16.08.2002. Effect: 1989 c.33 amended. Territorial extent & classification: E/W/S/NI. General. – 2p.: 30 cm. – 0 11 042499 9 *£1.50*

Housing, England

The Allocation of Housing (England) Regulations 2002 No. 2002/3264. – Enabling power: Housing Act 1996, ss. 160 (4), 160A (3) (5), 172 (4). – Issued: 10.01.2003. Made: 18.12.2002. Laid: 10.01.2003. Coming into force: 31.01.2003. Effect: S.I. 2000/702 revoked. Territorial extent & classification: E. General. – 4p.: 30 cm. – 0 11 044464 7
£1.75

The Commonhold and Leasehold Reform Act 2002 (Commencement No. 1, Savings and Transitional Provisions) (England) Order 2002 No. 2002/1912 (C.58). – Enabling power: Commonhold and Leasehold Reform Act 2002, s. 181. Bringing into operation various provisions of the 2002 Act on 26.07.2002. – Issued: 26.07.2002. Made: 17.07.2002. Effect: None. Territorial extent & classification: E. General. – 8p.: 30 cm. – 0 11 042532 4 *£2.00*

The Homelessness Act 2002 (Commencement No. 1) (England) Order 2002 No. 2002/1799 (C.56). – Enabling power: Homelessness Act 2002, s. 20 (1). – Issued: 31.07.2002. Made:11.07.2002. Coming into force: 31.07.2002 & 01.10.2002 in accordance with art 2. Effect: None. Territorial extent & classification: E. General. – 2p.: 30 cm. – 0 11 042567 7 *£1.50*

The Homelessness Act 2002 (Commencement No. 2 and Transitional Provisions) (England) Order 2002 No. 2002/2324 (C.76). – Enabling power: Homelessness Act 2002, s. 20 (1) (2). Bringing into operation various provisions of the 2002 Act on 30.09.2002. – Issued: 16.09.2002. Made:10.09.2002. Effect: None. Territorial extent & classification: E. General. – 2p.: 30 cm. – 0 11 042752 1 *£1.50*

The Homelessness Act 2002 (Commencement No. 3) (England) Order 2002 No. 2002/3114 (C.104). – Enabling power: Homelessness Act 2002, s. 20 (1). Bringing into operation various provisions of the 2002 Act on 05.12.2002. & 31.01.2003. – Issued: 23.12.2002. Made: 04.12.2002. Effect: None. Territorial extent & classification: E. General. – 2p.: 30 cm. – 0 11 044224 5 *£1.50*

The Homelessness (Priority Need for Accommodation) (England) Order 2002 No. 2002/2051. – Enabling power: Housing Act 1996, s. 189 (2). – Issued: 09.08.2002. Made: 30.07.2002. Coming into force: 31.07.2002. Effect: None. Territorial extent & classification: E. General. – 4p.: 30 cm. – Supersedes draft S.I .(ISBN 011042378X) issued on 24.06.2002 – 0 11 042624 X *£1.75*

The Housing Renewal Grants (Amendment) (England) Regulations 2002 No. 2002/530. – Enabling power: Housing Grants, Construction and Regeneration Act 1996, ss. 30, 146 (1) (2)– Issued: 19.03.2002. Made: 06.03.2002. Laid: 11.03.2002. Coming into force: 01.04.2002. Effect: S.I. 1996/2890 amended in relation to England. Territorial extent & classification: E. General. – 12p.: 30 cm. – Corrected reprint. – 0 11 039502 6 *£2.50*

The Housing Renewal Grants (Prescribed Form and Particulars) (Amendment) (England) Regulations 2002 No. 2002/667. – Enabling power: Housing Grants, Construction and Regeneration Act 1996, ss. 2 (2) (4), 146 (1) (2). – Issued: 18.03.2002. Made: 11.03.2002. Coming into force: 01.04.2002. Effect: S.I. 1996/2891 amended. Territorial extent & classification: E. General. – 4p.: 30 cm. – 0 11 039489 5
£1.75

The Housing (Right to Acquire) (Discount) Order 2002 No. 2002/1091. – Enabling power: Housing Act 1996, s. 17 (1) (a) (5). – Issued: 19.04.2002. Made: 15.04.2002. Laid: 19.04.2002. Coming into force: 10.05.2002. Effect: S.I. 2001/1501 revoked. Territorial extent & classification: E. General. – 8p.: 30 cm. – 0 11 039779 7   *£2.00*

The Housing (Right to Buy) (Designated Rural Areas and Designated Regions) (England) Order 2002 No. 2002/1769. – Enabling power: Housing Act 1985, s. 157 (1) (c) (3) (a). – Issued: 16.07.2002. Made: 03.07.2002. Laid: 16.07.2002. Coming into force: 06.08.2002. Effect: None. Territorial extent & class: E. General. – 2p.: 30 cm. – 0 11 042469 7   *£1.50*

The Relocation Grants (Form of Application) (Amendment) (England) Regulations 2002 No. 2002/666. – Enabling power: Housing Grants, Construction and Regeneration Act 1996, ss. 132 (3) (4), 146 (1) (2). – Issued: 18.03.2002. Made: 11.03.2002. Coming into force: 01.04.2002. Effect: S.I. 1997/2847 amended. Territorial extent & classification: E. General. – 4p.: 30 cm. – 0 11 039488 7   *£1.75*

The Waltham Forest Housing Action Trust (Dissolution) Order 2002 No. 2002/86. – Enabling power: Housing Act 1988, s. 88. – Issued: 28.01.2002. Made: 18.01.2002. Laid: 28.01.2002. Coming into force: 31.03.2002. Effect: S.I. 1991/2773 revoked. Territorial extent & classification: E. Local. – 4p.: 30 cm. – 0 11 039221 3   *£1.75*

Housing, England and Wales

The Regulatory Reform (Housing Assistance) (England and Wales) Order 2002 No. 2002/1860. – Enabling power: Regulatory Reform Act 2001, s. 1. – Issued: 25.07.2002. Made: 18.07.2002. Laid: 17.04.2002. Coming into force: In accord. with art. 1 (2) (3). Effect: 1977 c. 42, 50; 1985 c. 68, 70; 1988 c. 9; 1989 c. 42; 1996 c. 53; 1998 c. 38; 2001 c. 16 amended. Territorial extent and classification: E/W. General. – 28p.: 30 cm. – 0 11 042523 5   *£4.50*

Housing, Scotland

The Housing (Scotland) Act 2001 (Accommodation for Asylum-seekers) Order 2002 No. 2002/2367 (S.9). – Enabling power: Scotland Act 1988, ss. 104, 112 (1). – Issued: 30.09.2002. Made: 16.09.2002. Laid: 17.09.2002. Coming into force: 30.09.2002. Effect: None. Territorial extent & classification: S. General. – 2p.: 30 cm. – 0 11 042826 9   *£1.50*

The Housing (Scotland) Act 2001 (Housing Support Services Information) Order 2002 No. 2002/2264 (S.8). – Enabling power: Scotland Act 1988, ss. 104, 112 (1), 113. – Issued: 12.09.2002. Made: 03.09.2002. Laid: 06.09.2002. Coming into force: 01.10.2002. Effect: None. Territorial extent & class: S. General. – 4p.: 30 cm. – 0 11 061611 1   *£1.75*

Housing, Wales

The Commonhold and Leasehold Reform Act 2002 (Commencement No. 1, Savings and Transitional Provisions) (Wales) Order 2002 No. 2002/3012 (W.284) (C.96). – Enabling power: Commonhold and Leasehold Reform Act 2002, s. 181. Bringing into operation various provisions of the 2002 Act on 01.01.2003, in accord. with art. 1 (2). – Issued: 24.12.2002. Made: 04.12.2002. Effect: None. Territorial extent & classification: W. General. – 12p.: 30 cm. – In English and Welsh. Welsh title: Gorchymyn Deddf Diwygio Deiliadaeth ar y Cyd a Lesddaliad 2002 (Cychwyn Rhif 1, Arbedion a Darpariaethau Trosiannol) 2002. – 0 11 090604 7   *£2.50*

The Disabled Facilities Grants and Home Repair Assistance (Maximum Amounts) (Amendment) (Wales) Order 2002 No. 2002/837 (W.99). – Enabling power: Housing Grants, Construction and Regeneration Act 1996, ss. 33, 146. – Issued: 18.04.2002. Made: 26.03.2002. Coming into force: 10.04.2002. Effect: S.I. 1996/2888 amended in relation to Wales. Territorial extent & classification: W. General. – 4p.: 30 cm. – In English and Welsh. Welsh title: Gorchymyn Grantiau Cyfleusterau i'r Anabl a Chymorth Trwsio Cartrefi (Uchafsymiau) (Diwygio) (Cymru) 2002 – 0 11 090466 4   *£1.75*

The Homelessness Act 2002 (Commencement) (Wales) Order 2002 No. 2002/1736 (W.166) (C.53). – Enabling power: Homelessness Act 2002, s. 20 (1) (3). Bringing into force various provisions of the 2000 Act on 30.09.2002 and 27.01.2003 in accord with art. 2. – Issued: 17.07.2002. Made: 04.07.2002. Effect: None. Territorial extent & classification: W. General. – [8]p.: 30 cm. – In English and Welsh. Welsh title: Gorchymyn Deddf Digartrefedd 2002 (Cychwyn) (Cymru) 2002 – 0 11 090521 0   *£2.00*

The Housing Renewal Grants (Amendment) (Wales) Regulations 2002 No. 2002/2798 (W.266). – Enabling power: Housing Grants, Construction and Regeneration Act 1996, ss. 30, 146 (1) (2). – Issued: 26.11.2002. Made: 12.11.2002. Coming into force: 13.11.2002. Effect: S.I. 1996/2890 amended in relation to Wales. Territorial extent & classification: W. General. – 16p.: 30 cm. – . – 0 11 090582 2   *£3.00*

The Housing Renewal Grants (Prescribed Forms and Particulars) (Amendment) (Wales) Regulations 2002 No. 2002/2799 (W.267). – Enabling power: Housing Grants, Construction and Regeneration Act 1996, ss. 2 (2) (4), 146 (1) (2) as extended by Welsh Language Act 1993, s. 26 (3). – Issued: 26.11.2002. Made: 12.11.2002. Coming into force: 13.11.2002. Effect: S.I. 1996/2891; 1998/1113 amended in relation to Wales. Territorial extent & classification: W. General. – 8p.: 30 cm. – In English and Welsh. Welsh title: Rheoliadau Grantiau Adnewyddu Tai (Ffurflenni a Manylion Rhagnodedig) (Diwygio) (Cymru) 2002.   0 11 090583 0   *£2.00*

The Housing (Right to Buy) (Priority of Charges) (Wales) Order 2002 No. 2002/763 (W.82). – Enabling power: Housing Act 1985, s. 156 (4). – Issued: 05.04.2002. Made: 19.03.2002. Coming into force: 08.04.2002. Effect: None. Territorial extent & classification: W. General. – In English and Welsh. Welsh title: Gorchymyn Tai (Hawl i Brynu) (Blaenoriaeth Arwystlon) (Cymru) 2002. – 4p.: 30 cm. – 0 11 090456 7   *£1.75*

The Relocation Grants (Forms of Application) (Amendment) (Wales) Regulations 2002 No. 2002/2800 (W.268). – Enabling power: Housing Grants, Construction and Regeneration Act 1996, ss. 132 (3) (4), 146 (1) (2) as extended by the Welsh Language Act 1993, s. 26 (3). – Issued: 26.11.2002. Made: 12.11.2002. Coming into force: 13.11.2002. Effect: S.I. 1997/2847; 1999/2315 amended in relation to Wales. Territorial extent & classification: W. General. – 8p.: 30 cm. – In English and Welsh. Welsh title: Rheoliadau Grantiau Adleoli (Ffurflen Gais) (Diwygio) (Cymru) 2002 – 0 11 090584 9 *£2.00*

Immigration

The Asylum Support (Amendment) (No. 2) Regulations 2002 No. 2002/2619. – Enabling power: Immigration and Asylum Act 1999, s. 166 (3), sch. 8, para. 3 (a). – Issued: 30.10.2002. Made: 16.10.2002. Laid: 21.10.2002. Coming into force: 11.11.2002. Effect: S.I. 2000/704 amended & S.I. 2000/3053 revoked. Territorial extent & classification: UK. General. – 2p.: 30 cm. – Revoked by S.I. 2003/755 (ISBN 0110454812) – 0 11 042911 7 *£1.50*

The Asylum Support (Amendment) (No. 3) Regulations 2002 No. 2002/3110. – Enabling power: Immigration and Asylum Act 1999, s. 95 (12), sch. 8, para. 12. – Issued: 31.12.2002. Made: 16.12.2002. Laid: 18.12.2002. Coming into force: 08.01.2003. Effect: S.I. 2000/704 amended. Territorial extent & classification: E/W/S/NI. General. – 4p.: 30 cm. – 0 11 044395 0 *£1.75*

The Asylum Support (Amendment) Regulations 2002 No. 2002/472. – Enabling power: Immigration and Asylum Act 1999, ss. 94 (3), 166 (3), sch. 8, paras. 3 (a), 4. – Issued: 20.03.2002. Made: 02.03.2002. Laid: 06.03.2002. Coming into force: 08.04.2002. Effect: S.I. 2000/704 amended. Territorial extent & classification: UK. General. – 4p.: 30 cm. – 0 11 039509 3 *£1.75*

The Asylum Support (Interim Provisions) (Amendment) Regulations 2002 No. 2002/471. – Enabling power: Immigration and Asylum Act 1999, ss. 94 (3), 166 (3), sch. 9, paras. 5, 6, 15. – Issued: 20.03.2002. Made: 02.03.2002. Laid: 06.03.2002. Coming into force: 01.04.2002. for regs. 1 to 3 & 08.04.2002. for regs. 4 & 5. Effect: S.I. 1999/3056 amended. Territorial extent & classification: UK. General. – 2p.: 30 cm. – 0 11 039510 7 *£1.50*

The Asylum Support (Repeal) Order 2002 No. 2002/782. – Enabling power: Immigration and Asylum Act 1999, s. 96 (5). – Issued: 27.03.2002. Made: 21.03.2002. Coming into force: 08.04.2002. Effect: 1999 c. 33 amended. Territorial extent & classification: UK. General. – Supersedes draft S.I. (ISBN 0110394216) issued 8 March 2002. – 2p.: 30 cm. – 0 11 039597 2 *£1.50*

The Immigration and Asylum Act 1999 (Commencement No. 11) Order 2002 No. 2002/2815 (C.88). – Enabling power: Immigration and Asylum Act 1999, ss. 166 (3), 170 (4). Bringing into force various provisions of the 1999 Act in accordance with art. 2. – Issued: 29.11.2002. Made: 15.11.2002. Effect: None. Territorial extent & classification: UK. General. – 12p.: 30 cm. – 0 11 044068 4 *£2.50*

The Immigration and Asylum Act 1999 (Part V Exemption: Relevant Employers) Order 2002 No. 2002/9. – Enabling power: Immigration and Asylum Act 1999, ss. 84 (4) (d), 166. – Issued: 15.01.2002. Made: 07.01.2002. Laid: 08.01.2002. Coming into force: 01.02.2002. Effect: None. Territorial extent & classification: UK. General. – 2p.: 30 cm. – 0 11 039137 3 *£1.50*

The Immigration and Asylum Act 1999 (Part V Exemption: Relevant Employers) Order 2002 No. 2002/3025. – Enabling power: Immigration and Asylum Act 1999, ss. 84 (4) (d), 166. – Issued: 19.12.2002. Made: 05.12.2002. Laid: 09.12.2002. Coming into force: 01.01.2003. Effect: None. Territorial extent & classification: E/W/S/NI. General. – 2p.: 30 cm. – 0 11 044217 2 *£1.50*

The Immigration and Asylum Appeals (One-Stop Procedure) (Amendment) Regulations 2002 No. 2002/2731. – Enabling power: Immigration and Asylum Act 1999, ss. 75, 166 (3). – Issued: 25.11.2002. Made: 06.11.2002. Laid: 07.11.2002. Coming into force: 08.11.2002. Effect: S.I. 2000/2244 amended. Territorial extent & classification: UK. General. – 2p.: 30 cm. – 0 11 043045 X *£1.50*

The Immigration Appeals (Family Visitor) Regulations 2002 No. 2002/1147. – Enabling power: Immigration and Asylum Act 1999, ss. 60 (6), 166 (3). – Issued: 09.05.2002. Made: 23.04.2002. Laid: 24.04.2002. Coming into force: 15.05.2002. Effect: S.I. 2000/2246 amended. Territorial extent & classification: UK. General. – 2p.: 30 cm. – 0 11 039917 X *£1.50*

The Immigration (Designation of Travel Bans) (Amendment No. 2) Order 2002 No. 2002/795. – Enabling power: Immigration Act 1971, s. 8B (5)– Issued: 11.04.2002. Made: 23.03.2002. Laid: 26.03.2002. Coming into force: 27.03.2002. Effect: S.I. 2000/2724 amended. Territorial extent & classification: UK. General. – 2p.: 30 cm. – 0 11 039675 8 *£1.50*

The Immigration (Designation of Travel Bans) (Amendment No. 3) Order 2002 No. 2002/3018. – Enabling power: Immigration Act 1971, s. 8B (5). – Issued: 19.12.2002. Made: 05.12.2002. Laid: 06.12.2002. Coming into force: 07.12.2002. Effect: S.I. 2000/2724 amended. Territorial extent & classification: E/W/S/NI. General. – 2p.: 30 cm. – 0 11 044198 2 *£1.50*

The Immigration (Designation of Travel Bans) (Amendment) Order 2002 No. 2002/192. – Enabling power: Immigration Act 1971, s. 8B (5)– Issued: 13.02.2002. Made: 01.02.2002. Laid: 05.02.2002. Coming into force: 06.02.2002. Effect: S.I. 2000/2724 amended. Territorial extent & classification: UK. General. – 2p.: 30 cm. – 0 11 039300 7 *£1.50*

The Immigration (Entry Otherwise than by Sea or Air) Order 2002 No. 2002/1832. – Enabling power: Immigration Act 1971, s. 10 (1). – Issued: 25.07.2002. Made: 16.07.2002. Coming into force: 17.07.2002. Effect: 1971 c. 77 modified. Territorial extent & classification: UK. General. – 4p.: 30 cm. – With correction slip, dated August 2002 – 0 11 042507 3 *£1.75*

The Immigration Services Commissioner (Registration Fee) Order 2002 No. 2002/2011. – Enabling power: Immigration and Asylum Act 1999, s. 166 (3), sch. 6, para. 5 (1). – Issued: 13.08.2002. Made: 30.07.2002. Laid: 06.08.2002. Coming into force: 01.09.2002. Effect: S.I. 2000/2735 revoked. Territorial extent & classification: E/W/S/NI. General. – 4p.: 30 cm. – 0 11 042645 2   £1.75

The Immigration (Short-term Holding Facilities) Regulations 2002 No. 2002/2538. – Enabling power: Immigration and Asylum Act 1999, s. 157 (1). – Issued: 11.10.2002. Made: 08.10.2002. Laid: 11.10.2002. Coming into force: 04.11.2002. Effect: Section 149 of 1999 c. 33 extended to short-term facilities. Territorial extent & classification: UK. General. – 2p.: 30 cm. – 0 11 042846 3   £1.50

The Immigration (Swiss Free Movement of Persons) (No. 3) Regulations 2002 No. 2002/1241. – Enabling power: European Communities Act 1972, s. 2 (2). – Issued: 10.05.2002. Made: 01.05.2002. Laid: 09.05.2002. Coming into force: 01.06.2002. Effect: S.I. 2000/2326 modified. Territorial extent & classification: UK. General. – 8p.: 30 cm. – Note: The Immigration (Swiss Movement of Persons) Regulations 2002 (S.I. 2002/1012) and the Immigration (Swiss Movement of Persons) (No. 2) Regulations 2002 (S.I. 2002/1013) have not been published – 0 11 039891 2   £2.00

The Immigration (Transit Visa) (Amendment No. 2) Order 2002 No. 2002/2758. – Enabling power: Immigration (Carrier's Liability) Act 1987, s. 1A (1) (2). – Issued: 25.11.2002. Made: 06.11.2002. Laid: 07.11.2002. Coming into force: 09.11.2002. Effect: S.I. 1993/1678 amended. Territorial extent & classification: UK. General. – 2p.: 30 cm. – Revoked by S.I. 2003/1185 (ISBN 0110459865) – 0 11 043046 8   £1.50

The Immigration (Transit Visa) (Amendment) Order 2002 No. 2002/825. – Enabling power: Immigration (Carriers' Liability) Act 1987, s. 1A (1) (2). – Issued: 05.04.2002. Made: 25.03.2002. Laid: 27.03.2002. Coming into force: 17.04.2002. Effect: S.I. 1993/1678 amended. Territorial extent & classification: UK. General. – 2p.: 30 cm. – Revoked by S.I. 2003/1185 (ISBN 0110459865) – 0 11 039643 X   £1.50

The Nationality, Immigration and Asylum Act 2002 (Commencement No. 1) Order 2002 No. 2002/2811 (C.87). – Enabling power: Nationality, Immigration and Asylum Act 2002, s. 162 (1) (6). Bringing into force various provisions of the 2002 Act in accordance with art. 2. – Issued: 29.11.2002. Made: 13.11.2002. Effect: None. Territorial extent & classification: UK. General. – 8p.: 30 cm. – 0 11 044052 8   £2.00

The Travel Documents (Fees) (Amendments) Regulations 2002 No. 2002/2155. – Enabling power: Immigration and Asylum Act 1999, ss. 27 (1), 166 (3). – Issued: 29.08.2002. Made: 19.08.2002. Laid: 20.08.2002. Coming into force: 10.09.2002. Effect: S.I. 1999/3339 amended. Territorial extent & classification: UK. General. – 2p.: 30 cm. – 0 11 042689 4   £1.50

The Withholding and Withdrawal of Support (Travel Assistance and Temporary Accommodation) Regulations 2002 No. 2002/3078. – Enabling power: Nationality, Immigration and Asylum Act 2002, s. 54, sch. 3, paras. 8, 9, 10, 11, 12, 16 (2), 17. – Issued: 24.12.2002. Made: 13.12.2002. Laid: 17.12.2002. Coming into force: 08.01.2003. Effect: None. Territorial extent & classification: E/W/S/NI. General. – 4p.: 30 cm. – 0 11 044277 6   £1.75

Immigration and asylum

The Carriers' Liability (Clandestine Entrants) (Level of Penalty: Code of Practice) Order 2002 No. 2002/2816. – Enabling power: Immigration and Asylum Act 1999, s. 32A (4). – Issued: 29.11.2002. Made: 15.11.2002. Laid: 15.11.2002. Coming into force: 08.12.2002. Effect: None. Territorial extent & classification: UK. General. – 2p.: 30 cm. – 0 11 044067 6   £1.50

The Carriers' Liability Regulations 2002 No. 2002/2817. – Enabling power: Immigration and Asylum Act 1999, ss. 32 (2A) (3) (10), 35 (5) (7) (9) (12) (13), 36 (2), 37 (5B) (7), 40A (4) (6), 166 (3), sch. 1, paras. 2, 5. – Issued: 29.11.2002. Made: 15.11.2002. Laid: 15.11.2002. Coming into force: 08.12.2002. Effect: S.I. 2000/685; 2001/311 revoked. Territorial extent & classification: UK. General. – 8p.: 30 cm. – 0 11 044066 8   £2.00

The Immigration Services Tribunal (Amendment) Rules 2002 No. 2002/1716. – Enabling power: Immigration and Asylum Act 1999, sch. 7, para. 7. – Issued: 16.07.2002. Made: 03.07.2002. Laid: 04.07.2002. Coming into force: 01.08.2002. Effect: S.I. 2000/2739 amended. Territorial extent & classification: E/W/S/NI. General. – 2p.: 30 cm. – 0 11 042464 6   £1.50

Income tax

The Capital Allowances (Energy-saving Plant and Machinery) (Amendment) Order 2002 No. 2002/1818. – Enabling power: Capital Allowances Act 2001, ss. 45A (3) (4), 45C (2) (b) (3) (b). – Issued: 06.08.2002. Made: 15.07.2002. Laid: 15.07.2002. Coming into force: 05.08.2002. Effect: S.I. 2001/2541 amended. Territorial extent & classification: E/W/S/NI. General. – 2p.: 30 cm. – 0 11 042601 0   £1.50

The Controlled Foreign Companies (Excluded Countries) (Amendment No. 2) Regulations 2002 No. 2002/2406. – Enabling power: Income and Corporation Taxes Act 1988, s. 748 (1) (e) (1A). – Issued: 01.10.2002. Made: 19.09.2002. Laid: 20.09.2002. Coming into force: 11.10.2002. Effect: S.I. 1998/3081 amended. Territorial extent & classification: E/W/S/NI. General. – 2p.: 25 cm. – 0 11 042822 6   £1.50

The Controlled Foreign Companies (Excluded Countries) (Amendment) Regulations 2002 No. 2002/1963. – Enabling power: Income and Corporation Taxes Act 1988, s. 748 (1) (e) (1A). – Issued: 09.08.2002. Made: 24.07.2002. Laid: 25.07.2002. Coming into force: 01.10.2002. Effect: S.I. 1998/3081 amended. Territorial extent & classification: E/W/S/NI. General. – 2p.: 25 cm. – 0 11 042621 5   £1.50

The Corporation Tax (Finance Leasing of Intangible Assets) Regulations 2002 No. 2002/1967. – Enabling power: Finance Act 2002, sch. 29, para. 104. – Issued: 02.09.2002. Made: 25.07.2002. Laid: 25.07.2002. Coming into force: 15.08.2002. Effect: None. Territorial extent & classification: E/W/S/NI. General. – 4p.: 30 cm. – 0 11 042702 5 *£1.75*

The Double Taxation Relief (Taxes on Income) (Lithuania) Order 2002 No. 2002/2847. – Enabling power: Income and Corporation Taxes Act 1988, s. 788. – Issued: 27.11.2002. Made: 20.11.2002. Coming into force: In accordance with article 2. Effect: None. Territorial extent & classification: E/W/S/NI. General. – 4p.: 30 cm. – Supersedes draft. S.I. (ISBN 0110426363) published on 13th August 2002 – 0 11 043361 0 *£1.75*

The Double Taxation Relief (Taxes on Income) (South Africa) Order 2002 No. 2002/3138. – Enabling power: Income and Corporation Taxes Act 1988, s. 788 (10). – Issued: 27.12.2002. Made: 17.12.2002. Coming into force: 17.12.2002. Effect: None. Territorial extent & classification: E/W/S/NI. General. – 18p.: 30 cm. – Supersedes draft S.I. (ISBN 0110429001) issued on 30.10.2002 – 0 11 044272 5 *£3.50*

The Double Taxation Relief (Taxes on Income) (Taiwan) Order 2002 No. 2002/3137. – Enabling power: Income and Corporation Taxes Act 1988, s. 788. – Issued: 27.12.2002. Made: 17.12.2002. Coming into force: 17.12.2002. Effect: None. Territorial extent & classification: E/W/S/NI. General. – 20p.: 30 cm. – Supersedes draft S.I. (ISBN 011042901X) issued on 30.10.2002 – 0 11 044267 9 *£3.50*

The Double Taxation Relief (Taxes on Income) (the United States of America) Order 2002 No. 2002/2848. – Enabling power: Income and Corporation Taxes Act 1988, s. 788. – Issued: 29.11.2002. Made: 20.11.2002. Coming into force: 20.11.2002. Effect: None. Territorial extent & classification: E/W/S/NI. General. – 37p.: 30 cm. – Supersedes draft S.I. (ISBN 0110425308) issued on 26.07.2002. - With correction slip dated February 2003 – 0 11 043591 5 *£6.50*

The Exchange Gains and Losses (Bringing into Account Gains or Losses) Regulations 2002 No. 2002/1970. – Enabling power: Finance Act 1996, s. 84A (8) to (10) & Finance Act 2002, sch. 23, para. 26 (5), sch. 26, para. 16 (8) to (10). – Issued: 16.08.2002. Made: 25.07.2002. Laid: 25.07.2002. Coming into force: 01.10.2002. Effect: None. Territorial extent & classification: E/W/S/NI. General. – 8p.: 30 cm. – 0 11 042657 6 *£2.00*

The Exchange Gains and Losses (Transitional Provisions and Savings) Regulations 2002 No. 2002/1969. – Enabling power: Finance Act 2002, s. 81. – Issued: 16.08.2002. Made: 25.07.2002. Laid: 25.07.2002. Coming into force: 01.10.2002. Effect: S.I. 1994/3226, 3227, 3231; 2000/3315 modified with savings. Territorial extent & classification: E/W/S/NI. General. – 8p.: 30 cm. – 0 11 042656 8 *£2.00*

The General Commissioners and Special Commissioners (Jurisdiction and Procedure) (Amendment) Regulations 2002 No. 2002/2976. – Enabling power: Taxes Management Act 1970, ss. 46A (1) (a) (1A) to (3), 56B & Social Security Contributions (Transfer of Functions etc.) Act 1999, s. 13 (3) & S.I.1999/671, art. 12 (3). – Issued: 10.12.2002. Made: 25.11.2002. Laid: 03.12.2002. Coming into force: 31.12.2002. Effect: S.I. 1994/1811, 1812 amended. Territorial extent & classification: E/W/S/NI. General. – 8p.: 30 cm. – This S.I. has been reprinted (23.12.2002.) to incorporate text omitted from the original and is being issued free of charge to all known recipients – 0 11 044116 8 *£2.00*

The Income and Corporation Taxes Act 1988, Section 349B (3), Order 2002 No. 2002/2931. – Enabling power: Income and Corporation Taxes Act 1988, s. 349B (8). – Issued: 06.12.2002. Made: 27.11.2002. Laid: 27.11.2002. Coming into force: 01.12.2002. Effect: 1988 c. 1 amended. Territorial extent & classification: E/W/S/NI. General. – 2p.: 30 cm. – 0 11 044111 7 *£1.50*

The Income Tax (Benefits in Kind) (Exemption for Employment Costs Resulting from Disability) Regulations 2002 No. 2002/1596. – Enabling power: Income and Corporation Taxes Act 1988, s. 155ZB. – Issued: 05.07.2002. Made: 18.06.2002. Laid: 18.06.2002. Coming into force: 09.07.2002. Effect: None. Territorial extent & classification: E/W/S/NI. General. – 2p.: 30 cm. – 0 11 042428 X *£1.50*

The Income Tax (Cash Equivalents of Car Fuel Benefits) Order 2002 No. 2002/706. – Enabling power: Income and Corporation Taxes Act 1988, s. 158 (4). – Issued: 03.05.2002. Made: 15.03.2002. Laid: 15.03.2002. Coming into force: 06.04.2002. Effect: 1988 c.1 amended. Territorial extent & classification: E/W/S/NI. General. – 2p.: 30 cm. – 0 11 039868 8 *£1.50*

The Income Tax (Employments and Electronic Communications) (Miscellaneous Provisions) Regulations 2002 No. 2002/680. – Enabling power: Income and Corporation Taxes Act 1988, s. 203 (10) & Finance Act 1999, s. 132. – Issued: 16.04.2002. Made: 13.03.2002. Laid: 13.03.2002. Coming into force: 08.04.2002. Effect: S.I. 1993/744 amended. Territorial extent & classification:E/W/S/NI. General. – 4p.: 30 cm. – 0 11 039746 0 *£1.75*

The Income Tax (Exemption of Minor Benefits) Regulations 2002 No. 2002/205. – Enabling power: Income and Corporation Taxes Act 1988, s. 155ZB. – Issued: 21.02.2002. Made: 04.02.2002. Laid: 05.02.2002. Coming into force: 06.04.2002. Effect: None. Territorial extent & classification: E/W/S/NI. General. – 4p.: 30 cm. – 0 11 039351 1 *£1.75*

The Income Tax (Indexation) (No. 2) Order 2002 No. 2002/2930. – Enabling power: Income and Corporation Taxes Act 1988, s. 257C (3). – Issued: 06.12.2002. Made: 27.11.2002. Coming into force: 27.11.2002. Effect: None. Territorial extent & classification: E/W/S/NI. General. – 2p.: 30 cm. – 0 11 044110 9 *£1.50*

The Income Tax (Indexation) Order 2002 No. 2002/707. – Enabling power: Income and Corporation Taxes Act 1988, ss. 1 (6), 257C (3). – Issued: 12.04.2002. Made: 15.03.2002. Coming into force: 06.04.2002. Effect: None. Territorial extent & classification: E/W/S/NI. General. – 2p.: 30 cm. – 0 11 039729 0 *£1.50*

The Income Tax (Prescribed Deposit-takers) Order 2002 No. 2002/1968. – Enabling power: Income and Corporation Taxes Act 1988, ss. 481 (2) (f), 482 (10). – Issued: 16.08.2002. Made: 25.07.2002. Laid: 25.07.2002. Coming into force: 01.10.2002. Effect: None. Territorial extent & classification: E/W/S/NI. General. – 2p.: 30 cm. – 0 11 042655 X *£1.50*

The Income Tax (Sub-contractors in the Construction Industry) (Amendment) Regulations 2002 No. 2002/2225. – Enabling power: Income and Corporation Taxes Act 1988, s. 566. – Issued: 19.09.2002. Made: 30.08.2002. Laid: 30.08.2002. Coming into force: 20.09.2002. Effect: S.I. 1993/743 amended. Territorial extent & classification: E/W/S/NI. General. – 2p.: 30 cm. – 0 11 042777 7 *£1.50*

The Individual Savings Account (Amendment No. 2) Regulations 2002 No. 2002/1974. – Enabling power: Income and Corporation Taxes Act 1988, s. 333 & Taxation of Chargeable Gains Act 1992, s. 151 & Finance Act 1998, s. 75. – Issued: 09.08.2002. Made: 25.07.2002. Laid: 25.07.2002. Coming into force: 01.10.2002. Effect: S.I. 1998/1870 amended. Territorial extent & classification: E/W/S/NI. General. – 2p.: 30 cm. – 0 11 042622 3 *£1.50*

The Individual Savings Account (Amendment No. 3) Regulations 2002 No. 2002/3158. – Enabling power: Income and Corporation Taxes Act 1988, s. 333 & Taxation of Chargeable Gains Act 1992, s. 151 & Finance Act 1998, s. 75. – Issued: 10.01.2003. Made: 18.12.2002. Laid: 18.12.2002. Coming into force: 08.01.2003. Effect: S.I. 1998/1870 amended. Territorial extent & classification: E/W/S/NI. General. – 8p.: 30 cm. – 0 11 044461 2 *£2.00*

The Individual Savings Account (Amendment) Regulations 2002 No. 2002/453. – Enabling power: Income and Corporation Taxes Act 1988, ss. 333, 333A, 333B. – Issued: 22.03.2002. Made: 28.02.2002. Laid: 04.03.2002. Coming into force: 06.04.2002. Effect: S.I. 1998/1870 amended. Territorial extent & classification: E/W/S/NI. General. – 4p.: 30 cm. – 0 11 039558 1 *£1.75*

The Open-ended Investment Companies (Tax) (Amendment) Regulations 2002 No. 2002/1973. – Enabling power: Finance Act 1995, s. 152. – Issued: 16.08.2002. Made: 25.07.2002. Laid: 25.07.2002. Coming into force: 01.10.2002. Effect: S.I. 1997/1154 amended. Territorial extent & classification: E/W/S/NI. General. – 2p.: 30 cm. – 0 11 042659 2 *£1.50*

The Retirement Benefits Schemes (Indexation of Earnings Cap) Order 2002 No. 2002/700. – Enabling power: Income and Corporation Taxes Act 1988, s. 590C (6). – Issued: 05.04.2002. Made: 15.03.2002. Coming into force: -. Effect: None. Territorial extent & classification: E/W/S/NI. General. – 2p.: 30 cm. – 0 11 039648 0 *£1.50*

The Retirement Benefits Schemes (Information Powers) (Amendment) Regulations 2002 No. 2002/3006. – Enabling power: Income and Corporation Taxes Act 1988, s. 605 (1A) (1B) (1D) (1E) and Finance Act 1999, s. 133 (1). – Issued: 11.12.2002. Made: 04.12.2002. Laid: 05.12.2002. Coming into force: 06.04.2003. Effect: S.I. 1995/3103 amended. Territorial extent & classification: E/W/S/NI. General. – 8p.: 30 cm. – 0 11 044145 1 *£2.00*

The Scottish Water (Transfer of Functions, etc.) (Tax Provisions) Order 2002 No. 2002/653. – Enabling power: Scotland Act 1998, ss. 104 (1), 112 (1) (5), 126 (1). – Issued: 12.04.2002. Made: 11.03.2002. Laid: 11.03.2002. Coming into force: 01.04.2002. Effect: None. Territorial extent & classification: S. General. – 4p.: 30 cm. – 0 11 039726 6 *£1.75*

The Venture Capital Trust (Exchange of Shares and Securities) Regulations 2002 No. 2002/2661. – Enabling power: Income and Corporation Taxes Act 1988, s. 842AA (5AD) & sch. 28B, para. 11B. – Issued: 14.11.2002. Made: 22.10.2002. Laid: 23.10.2002. Coming into force: 13.11.2002. Effect: None. Territorial extent & classification: E/W/S/NI. General. – 12p.: 30 cm. – 0 11 042961 3 *£2.50*

Industrial development

The Financial Assistance for Industry (Increase of Limit) Order 2002 No. 2002/151. Enabling power: Industrial Development Act 1982, s. 8 (5). – Issued: 06.02.2002. Made: 28.01.2002. Coming into force: 29.01.2002. Effect: 1982 c. 52 amended. Territorial extent & classification: E/W/S/NI. General. – 2p.: 30 cm. – Supersedes draft S.I. (ISBN 011039092X) – 0 11 039246 9 *£1.50*

Industrial organisation and development

The Horticultural Development Council (Amendment) Order 2002 No. 2002/1676. – Enabling power: Industrial Organisation and Development Act 1947, ss. 1, 4, 8, 14 (2). – Issued: 05.07.2002. Made: 28.06.2002. Coming into force: 01.10.2002. Effect: S.I. 1986/1110 amended. Territorial extent & classification: E/W/S. General. – 4p.: 30 cm. – Supersedes draft S.I. (ISBN 0110422791) issued on 28.05.2002 – 0 11 042421 2 *£1.75*

The Potato Industry Development Council (Amendment) Order 2002 No. 2002/3062. – Enabling power: Industrial Organisation and Development Act 1947, ss. 1, 3, 4, 8. – Issued: 20.12.2002. Made: 09.12.2002. Coming into force: 01.01.2003. Effect: S.I. 1997/266 amended. Territorial extent & classification: E/W/S. General. – 4p.: 30 cm. – Supersedes draft S.I. (ISBN 0110429656) issued 15 November 2002 – 0 11 044213 X *£1.75*

Inheritance tax

The General Commissioners and Special Commissioners (Jurisdiction and Procedure) (Amendment) Regulations 2002 No. 2002/2976. – Enabling power: Taxes Management Act 1970, ss. 46A (1) (a) (1A) to (3), 56B & Social Security Contributions (Transfer of Functions etc.) Act 1999, s. 13 (3) & S.I.1999/671, art. 12 (3). – Issued: 10.12.2002. Made: 25.11.2002. Laid: 03.12.2002. Coming into force: 31.12.2002. Effect: S.I. 1994/1811, 1812 amended. Territorial extent & classification: E/W/S/NI. General. – 8p.: 30 cm. – Corrected reprint. – 0 11 044116 8 *£2.00*

The Inheritance Tax (Delivery of Accounts) (Excepted Estates) Regulations 2002 No. 2002/1733. – Enabling power: Inheritance Tax Act 1984, s. 256 (1) (a). – Issued: 26.07.2002. Made: 05.07.2002. Laid: 08.07.2002. Coming into force: 01.08.2002. Effect: S.I. 1981/880, 881, 1441; 1983/1039, 1040, 1911; 1987/1127, 1128, 1129; 1989/1078, 1079, 1080; 1990/1110, 1111, 1112; 1991/1248, 1249, 1250; 1995/1459, 1460, 1461; 1996/1470, 1472, 1473; 1998/1429, 1430, 1431; 2000/965, 966, 967 revoked (in relation to deaths occurring on or after 06.04.2002). Territorial extent & classification: E/W/S/NI. General. – 8p.: 30 cm. – 0 11 042529 4 *£2.00*

The Inheritance Tax (Delivery of Accounts) (Excepted Settlements) Regulations 2002 No. 2002/1732. – Enabling power: Inheritance Tax Act 1984, s. 256 (1) (a). – Issued: 26.07.2002. Made: 05.07.2002. Laid: 08.07.2002. Coming into force: 01.08.2002. Effect: None. Territorial extent & classification: E/W/S/NI. General. – 4p.: 30 cm. – 0 11 042528 6 *£1.75*

The Inheritance Tax (Delivery of Accounts) (Excepted Transfers and Excepted Terminations) Regulations 2002 No. 2002/1731. – Enabling power: Inheritance Tax Act 1984, s. 256 (1) (a). – Issued: 19.07.2002. Made: 05.07.2002. Laid: 08.07.2002. Coming into force: 01.08.2002. Effect: S.I. 1981/1440 revoked. Territorial extent & classification: E/W/S/NI. General. – 4p.: 30 cm. – 0 11 042485 9 *£1.75*

The Inheritance Tax (Indexation) Order 2002 No. 2002/701. – Enabling power: Inheritance Tax Act 1984, s. 8 (4). – Issued: 12.04.2002. Made: 15.03.2002. Coming into force: 06.04.2002. Effect: None. Territorial extent & classification: E/W/S/NI. General. – 2p.: 30 cm. – 0 11 039727 4 *£1.50*

Insider dealing

The Insider Dealing (Securities and Regulated Markets) (Amendment) Order 2002 No. 2002/1874. – Enabling power: Criminal Justice Act 1993, ss. 60 (1), 62 (1), 64 (3). – Issued: 07.08.2002. Made: 18.07.2002. Coming into force: 19.07.2002. Effect: S.I. 1994/187 amended. Territorial extent & classification: E/W/S/NI. General. – Supersedes draft S.I. (ISBN 011042381X) issued 21 June 2002. – 2p.: 30 cm. – 0 11 042617 7 *£1.50*

Insolvency

The Insolvency Act 1986 (Amendment) (No. 2) Regulations 2002 No. 2002/1240. – Enabling power: European Communities Act 1972, s. 2 (2). – Issued: 29.05.2002. Made: 01.05.2002. Laid: 02.05.2002. Coming into force: 31.05.2002. Effect: 1986 c. 45 amended. Territorial extent & classification: E/W/S. General. – 4p.: 30 cm. – EC note: To make amendments to the Act as a result of the adoption by the Council of the EU of Regulation 1346/2000 on insolvency proceedings – 0 11 042249 X *£1.75*

The Insolvency Act 2000 (Commencement No. 3 and Transitional Provisions) Order 2002 No. 2002/2711 (C.83). – Enabling power: Insolvency Act 2000, s. 16 (1) (3). Bringing into operation various provisions of the 2000 Act on 01.01.2003, in accord. with arts. 3, 4, 5. – Issued: 12.11.2002. Made: 29.10.2002. Effect: None. Territorial extent & classification: E/W/S. General. – 4p.: 30 cm. – 0 11 042955 9 *£1.75*

The Insolvency Practitioners (Amendment) Regulations 2002 No. 2002/2710. – Enabling power: Insolvency Act 1986, ss. 390, 419. – Issued: 12.11.2002. Made: 29.10.2002. Laid: 29.10.2002. Coming into force: 01.01.2003. Effect: S.I. 1990/439 amended. Territorial extent & classification: E/W/S. General. – 2p.: 30 cm. – 0 11 042954 0 *£1.50*

The Occupational and Personal Pension Schemes (Bankruptcy) (No. 2) Regulations 2002 No. 2002/836. – Enabling power: Bankruptcy (Scotland) Act 1985, ss. 36C (4) (a) (7) (8), 36F (3) (a) and (6) to (8) & Insolvency Act 1986, ss. 342C (4) (a) (7) to (9), 342F (6) (a) (9) to (11) & Welfare Reform and Pensions Act 1999, ss. 11 (2) (h), 12 (1) to (3), 83 (1) (2) (4) (6). – Issued: 02.04.2002. Made: 26.03.2002. Laid: 02.04.2002. Coming into force: 06.04.2002. Effect: S.I. 2002/427 revoked. Territorial extent & classification: E/W/S. General– This S.I. supersedes S.I. 2002/427 published on 7th March 2002 and is being issued free of charge to all known recipients of that S.I. – 16p.: 30 cm. – 0 11 039626 X *£3.00*

The Occupational and Personal Pension Schemes (Bankruptcy) Regulations 2002 No. 2002/427. – Enabling power: Bankruptcy (Scotland) Act 1985, ss. 36C (4) (a) (7) (8), 36F (3) (a) and (6) to (8) & Insolvency Act 1986, ss. 342C (4) (a) (7) to (9), 342F (6) (a) (9) to (11) & Welfare Reform and Pensions Act 1999, ss. 11 (2) (h) (10), 12 (1) to (3), 83 (1) (2) (4) (6). – Issued: 07.03.2002. Made: 26.02.2002. Laid: 07.03.2002. Coming into force: 06.04.2002. Effect: None. Territorial extent & classification: E/W/S. General– 16p.: 30 cm. – Revoked by S.I. 2002/836 (ISBN 011039626X) – 0 11 039403 8 *£3.00*

Insolvency: Companies

The Insolvency Act 1986 (Amendment) (No. 3) Regulations 2002 No. 2002/1990. – Enabling power: Insolvency Act 1986, sch. A1, paras. 5, 45. – Issued: 01.08.2002. Made: 25.07.2002. Coming into force: In accord. with reg. 2. Effect: 1986 c. 45 amended. Territorial extent & classification: E/W/S. General. – 8p.: 30 cm. – 0 11 042588 X *£2.00*

The Insolvency Act 1986 (Amendment) Regulations 2002 No. 2002/1037. – Enabling power: European Communities Act 1972, s. 2 (2). – Issued: 01.05.2002. Made: 09.04.2002. Laid: 10.04.2002. Coming into force: 03.05.2002. Effect: 1986 c. 45 amended. Territorial extent & classification: E/W/S. General. – 4p.: 30 cm. – 0 11 039851 3 £1.75

Insolvency: Insolvency practitioners

The Insolvency Practitioners (Amendment) (No. 2) Regulations 2002 No. 2002/2748. – Enabling power: Insolvency Act 1986, ss. 390, 419. – Issued: 14.11.2002. Made: 05.11.2002. Laid: 06.11.2002. Coming into force: 01.01.2003. Effect: S.I. 2002/2710 amended. Territorial extent & classification: E/W/S. General. – This Statutory Instrument has been made to correct an error in S.I. 2002/2710 and is being issued free of charge to all known recipients of that Statutory Instrument. – 2p.: 30 cm. – 0 11 042948 6 £1.50

Insolvency, England and Wales

The Insolvent Partnerships (Amendment) (No. 2) Order 2002 No. 2002/2708. – Enabling power: Insolvency Act 1986, s. 420. – Issued: 06.11.2002. Made: 29.10.2002. Laid: 29.10.2002. Coming into force: 01.01.2003. Effect: 1986 c.45; S.I. 1994/2421 amended. Territorial extent & classification: E/W. General. – 24p.: 30 cm. – 0 11 042933 8 £4.00

The Insolvent Partnerships (Amendment) Order 2002 No. 2002/1308. – Enabling power: Insolvency Act 1986, s. 420 (1) (2). – Issued: 30.05.2002. Made: 09.05.2002. Laid: 10.05.2002. Coming into force: 31.05.2002. Effect: S.I. 1994/2421 amended. Territorial extent & classification: E/W. General. – 32p.: 30 cm. – EC note: Amends the 1994 Order (S.I. 1994/2421) in the light of Council regulation (EC) No. 1346/2000 on insolvency proceedings – 0 11 042280 5 £6.00

Insolvency, England and Wales: Companies

The Insolvency (Amendment) (No. 2) Rules 2002 No. 2002/2712. – Enabling power: Insolvency Act 1986, ss. 411, 412. – Issued: 13.11.2002. Made: 29.10.2002. Laid: 29.10.2002. Coming into force: 01.01.2003. Effect: S.I. 1986/1925 amended. Territorial extent & classification: E/W. General. – 48p.: 30 cm. – 0 11 042956 7 £6.50

The Insolvency (Amendment) Rules 2002 No. 2002/1307. – Enabling power: Insolvency Act 1986, ss. 411, 412. – Issued: 29.05.2002. Made: 09.05.2002. Laid: 10.05.2002. Coming into force: 31.05.2002. Effect: S.I. 1986/1925 amended. Territorial extent & classification: E/W. General. – 43p.: 30 cm. – 0 11 042264 3 £6.50

Insolvency, England and Wales: Individuals

The Administration of Insolvent Estates of Deceased Persons (Amendment) Order 2002 No. 2002/1309. – Enabling power: Insolvency Act 1986, s. 421 (1) (2). – Issued: 27.05.2002. Made: 09.05.2002. Laid: 10.05.2002. Coming into force: 31.05.2002. Effect: S.I. 1986/1999 amended. Territorial extent & classification: E/W. General. – EC note: This Order amends the 1986 Order in the light of REG (EC) no. 1346/2000 on insolvency proceedings which comes into force on 31 May 2002. – 16p.: 30 cm. – 0 11 039989 7 £3.00

Insolvency, Scotland

The Insolvency (Scotland) Amendment Rules 2002 No. 2002/2709 (S.10). – Enabling power: Insolvency Act 1986, s. 411. – Issued: 06.11.2002. Made: 29.10.2002. Laid: 29.10.2002. Coming into force: 01.01.2003. Effect: S.I. 1986/1915 (S.139) amended. Territorial extent & classification: S. General. – 32p.: 30 cm. – 0 11 042934 6 £6.00

International criminal court, England and Wales

The International Criminal Court Act 2001 (Enforcement of Fines, Forfeiture and Reparation Orders) (Amendment) Regulations 2002 No. 2002/822. – Enabling power: International Criminal Court Act 2001, s. 49. – Issued: 08.04.2002. Made: 25.03.2002. Laid: 08.04.2002. Coming into force: 01.05.2002. Effect: S.I. 2001/2379 amended. Territorial extent & classification: E/W/NI. General. – This S.I. has been made in consequence of defects in S.I. 2001/2379 and is being issued free of charge to all known recipients of that Statutory Instrument. – 2p.: 30 cm. – 0 11 039619 7 £1.50

International criminal court, Northern Ireland

The International Criminal Court Act 2001 (Enforcement of Fines, Forfeiture and Reparation Orders) (Amendment) Regulations 2002 No. 2002/822. – Enabling power: International Criminal Court Act 2001, s. 49. – Issued: 08.04.2002. Made: 25.03.2002. Laid: 08.04.2002. Coming into force: 01.05.2002. Effect: S.I. 2001/2379 amended. Territorial extent & classification: E/W/NI. General. – This S.I. has been made in consequence of defects in S.I. 2001/2379 and is being issued free of charge to all known recipients of that Statutory Instrument. – 2p.: 30 cm. – 0 11 039619 7 £1.50

International development

The African Development Fund (Additional Subscriptions) Order 2002 No. 2002/2404. – Enabling power: International Development Act 2002, s. 11. – Issued: 26.09.2002. Made: 16.09.2002. Laid:-. Coming into force: 16.09.2002. Effect: None. Territorial extent & classification: E/W/S/NI. General. – 2p.: 30 cm. – 0 11 042804 8 *£1.50*

The Caribbean Development Bank (Further Payments) Order 2002 No. 2002/2405. – Enabling power: International Development Act 2002, s. 11. – Issued: 26.09.2002. Made: 16.09.2002. Laid:-. Coming into force: 16.09.2002. Effect: None. Territorial extent & classification: E/W/S/NI. General. – 2p.: 30 cm. – 0 11 042805 6 *£1.50*

The International Development Act 2002 (Commencement) Order 2002 No. 2002/1408 (C.39). – Enabling power: International Development Act 2002, s. 20 (2). Bringing into operation certain sections of the 2002 Act on 17.06.2002. – Issued: 28.05.2002. Made: 22.05.2002. Effect: None. Territorial extent & classification: E/W/S/NI. General. – 2p.: 30 cm. – 0 11 042262 7 *£1.50*

International immunities and privileges

The International Criminal Court (Immunities and Privileges) Order 2002 No. 2002/793. – Enabling power: International Criminal Court Act 2001, sch. 1, para. 1. – Issued: 04.04.2002. Made: 26.03.2002. Coming into force: In accord. with art. 1. Effect: None. Territorial extent & classification: E/W/S/NI. General. – 2p.: 30 cm. – 0 11 039634 0 *£1.50*

The International Maritime Organisation (Immunities and Privileges) Order 2002 No. 2002/1826. – Enabling power: International Organisations Act 1968, ss. 1, 2, 10 (3). – Issued: 23.07.2002. Made: 16.07.2002. Coming into force: 17.07.2002. Effect: S.I. 1975/1209; 1999/2034 amended & 1968/1862; 1972/118; 1982/709 revoked. Territorial extent & classification: E/W/S/NI. General. – 8p.: 30 cm. – 0 11 042501 4 *£2.00*

The Specialized Agencies of the United Nations (Immunities and Privileges) (Amendment) Order 2002 No. 2002/1827. – Enabling power: International Organisations Act 1968, ss. 1, 10 (3). – Issued: 23.07.2002. Made: 16.07.2002. Coming into force: 17.07.2002. Effect: S.I. 1974/1260 amended. Territorial extent and classification: E/W/S/NI. General. – 2p.: 30 cm. – 0 11 042502 2 *£1.50*

The United Nations and International Court of Justice (Immunities and Privileges) (Amendment) Order 2002 No. 2002/1828. – Enabling power: International Organisations Act 1968, ss. 1, 10 (3). – Issued: 23.07.2002. Made: 16.07.2002. Coming into force: 17.07.2002. Effect: S.I. 1974/1261 amended. Territorial extent & classification: E/W/S/NI. General. – With correction slip dated August 2002. – 2p: 30 cm. – 0 11 042503 0 *£1.50*

Investigatory powers

The Regulation of Investigatory Powers (Covert Human Intelligence Sources: Code of Practice) Order 2002 No. 2002/1932. – Enabling power: Regulation of Investigatory Powers Act 2000, s. 71 (5). – Issued: 29.07.2002. Made: 22.07.2002. Coming into force: 01.08.2002. Effect: None. Territorial extent & classification: UK. General. – Supersedes draft. S.I. (ISBN 0110423801) issued 24th June 2002. This instrument brings into force on 01.08.2002 the code of practice "Covert human intelligence sources" (2002, TSO, ISBN 0113412851). – 2p.: 30 cm. – 0 11 042544 8 *£1.50*

The Regulation of Investigatory Powers (Covert Surveillance: Code of Practice) Order 2002 No. 2002/1933. – Enabling power: Regulation of Investigatory Powers Act 2000, s. 71 (5). – Issued: 29.07.2002. Made: 22.07.2002. Coming into force: 01.08.2002. Effect: None. Territorial extent & classification: UK. General. – Supersedes draft S.I. (ISBN 0110423798) issued 24th June 2002. This instrument brings into force on 01.08.2002 the code of practice "Covert surveillance" (2002, TSO, ISBN 0113412843). – 2p.: 30 cm. – 0 11 042545 6 *£1.50*

The Regulation of Investigatory Powers (Interception of Communications: Code of Practice) Order 2002 No. 2002/1693. – Enabling power: Regulation of Investigatory Powers Act 2000, s. 71 (5). – Issued: 05.07.2002. Made: 28.06.2002. Coming into force: 01.07.2002. Effect: None. Territorial extent & classification: UK. General. – 2p.: 30 cm. – Supersedes draft S.I. (ISBN 0110399501) issued on 17.05.2002 – 0 11 042425 5 *£1.50*

The Regulation of Investigatory Powers (Maintenance of Interception Capability) Order 2002 No. 2002/1931. – Enabling power: Regulation of Investigatory Powers Act 2000, ss. 12 (1) (2) (5), 78 (5). – Issued: 29.07.2002. Made: 22.07.2002. Coming into force: 01.08.2002. Effect: None. Territorial extent & classification: UK. General. – Supersedes draft S.I. (ISBN 0110423232). – 4p.: 30 cm. – 0 11 042543 X *£1.75*

The Regulation of Investigatory Powers (Prescription of Offices, Ranks, and Positions) (Amendment) Order 2002 No. 2002/1298. – Enabling power: Regulation of Investigatory Powers Act 2000, ss. 30 (1) (3), 78 (5). – Issued: 29.05.2002. Made: 07.05.2002. Laid: 10.05.2002. Coming into force: 17.06.2002. Effect: S.I. 2000/2417 amended. Territorial extent & classification: UK. General. – 2p.: 30 cm. – 0 11 042261 9 *£1.50*

Justices of the Peace, England and Wales

Commission Areas (West Mercia) Order 2002 No. 2002/1440. – Enabling power: Justices of the Peace Act 1997, s. 1 (2). – Issued: 13.06.2002. Made: 27.05.2002. Laid: 30.05.2002. Coming into force: 21.06.2002. Effect: S.I. 1999/3010 amended. Territorial extent & classification: E/W. General. – 2p.: 30 cm. – 0 11 042331 3 *£1.50*

The Justices of the Peace (Size and Chairmanship of Bench) Rules 2002 No. 2002/193. – Enabling power: Justices of the Peace Act 1997, s. 24. – Issued: 08.02.2002. Made: 31.01.2002. Laid: 04.02.2002. Coming into force: 01.03.2002. Effect: S.I. 1995/971; 1999/2396 revoked. Territorial extent & classification: E/W. General. – 12p.: 30 cm. – 0 11 039274 4 £2.50

The Petty Sessions Areas (Avon and Somerset) Order 2002 No. 2002/2662. – Enabling power: Justices of the Peace Act 1997, s. 4 (2). – Made: 23.10.2002. Coming into force: in accordance with art. 1. Effect: S.I. 1999/3009 amended. Territorial extent & classification: E/W Local. *Unpublished*

The Petty Sessions Areas (Nottinghamshire) Order 2002 No. 2002/2052. – Enabling power: Justices of the Peace Act 1997, s. 4 (2). – Made: 26.07.2002. Coming into force: in accordance with art. 1. Effect: S.I. 1999/3009 amended. Territorial extent & classification: E/W Local. *Unpublished*

The Petty Sessions Areas (Wigan and Leigh) Order 2002 No. 2002/2387. – Enabling power: Justices of the Peace Act 1997, s. 4 (2). – Made: 16.09.2002. Coming into force: in accordance with art. 1. Effect: S.I. 1999/3009 amended. Territorial extent & classification: E/W Local. *Unpublished*

Landfill tax

The Landfill Tax (Amendment) Regulations 2002 No. 2002/1. – Enabling power: Finance Act 1996, ss. 51 (1), 53 (1), 62 (1) (2). – Issued: 11.01.2002. Made: 03.01.2002. Laid: 07.01.2002. Coming into force: 01.02.2002. Effect: S.I. 1996/1527 amended. Territorial extent & classification: E/W/S/NI. General. – 4p.: 30 cm. – 0 11 039132 2 £1.75

Landlord and tenant, England

The Agricultural Holdings (Units of Production) (England) Order 2002 No. 2002/1925. – Enabling power: Agricultural Holdings Act 1986, sch. 6, para. 4. – Issued: 31.07.2002. Made: 22.07.2002. Laid: 23.07.2002. Coming into force: 12.09.2002. Effect: S.I. 2001/2751 revoked. Territorial extent & classification: E. General. – 8p.: 30 cm. – Revoked by S.I. 2003/2151 (ISBN 011047516X) – 0 11 042566 9 £2.00

The Assured Tenancies and Agricultural Occupancies (Forms) (Amendment) (England) Regulations 2002 No. 2002/337. – Enabling power: Housing Act 1988, ss. 13 (2), 45 (5). – Issued: 20.02.2002. Made: 18.02.2002. Coming into force: 20.02.2002. (for regs. 1, 2, 3) & 20.06.2002. (for reg.4). Effect: S.I. 1997/194 amended. Territorial extent & classification: E. General. – 8p.: 30 cm. – Revoked by S.I. 2003/260 (ISBN 0110448480) – 0 11 039349 X £2.00

The Leasehold Reform (Collective Enfranchisement) (Counter-notices) (England) Regulations 2002 No. 2002/3208. – Enabling power: Leasehold Reform, Housing and Urban Development Act 1993, s. 99 (6) (b). – Issued: 10.01.2003. Made: 20.12.2002. Coming into force: 10.04.2003. Effect: None. Territorial extent & classification: E. General. – 2p.: 30 cm. – 0 11 044400 0 £1.50

The Leasehold Reform (Notices) (Amendment) (England) Regulations 2002 No. 2002/1715. – Enabling power: Landlord and Tenant Act 1954, s. 66. – Issued: 12.07.2002. Made: 01.07.2002. Laid: 05.07.2002. Coming into force: 26.07.2002. Effect: S.I. 1997/640 amended. Territorial extent & classification: E. General. – 12p.: 30 cm. – 0 11 042446 8 £2.50

The Leasehold Reform (Notices) (Amendment) (No. 2) (England) Regulations 2002 No. 2002/3209. – Enabling power: Landlord and Tenant Act 1954, s. 66. – Issued: 10.01.2003. Made: 20.12.2002. Laid: 10.01.2003. Coming into force: 10.04.2003. Effect: S.I. 1997/640 amended. Territorial extent & classification: E. General. – 4p.: 30 cm. – 0 11 044401 9 £1.75

The Long Residential Tenancies (Principal Forms) (Amendment) (England) Regulations 2002 No. 2002/2227. – Enabling power: Local Government and Housing Act 1989, sch. 10, paras. 4 (1). – Issued: 05.09.2002. Made: 29.08.2002. Laid:-. Coming into force: 30.09.2002. Effect: S.I. 1997/3008 amended in relation to England. Territorial extent & classification: E. General. – 4p.: 30 cm. – 0 11 042716 5 £1.75

Landlord and tenant, Wales

The Leasehold Reform (Notices) (Amendment) (Wales) Regulations 2002 No. 2002/3187 (W.303). – Enabling power: Landlord and Tenant Act 1954, s. 66. – Issued: 31.12.2002. Made: 18.12.2002. Coming into force: 01.01.2003. Effect: S.I. 1997/640 amended in relation to Wales. Territorial extent & classification: W. General. – 16p.: 30 cm. – In English and Welsh. Welsh title: Rheoliadau Diwygio'r Drefn Brydlesol (Hysbysiadau) (Diwygio) (Cymru) 2002. – 0 11 090614 4 £3.00

Land registration, England and Wales

The Land Registration Rules 2002 No. 2002/2539 (L.11). – Enabling power: Land Registration Act 1925, ss. 54, 112, 144 & Land Registration and Land Charges Act 1971, s. 4. – Issued: 16.10.2002. Made: 01.10.2002. Laid: 09.10.2002. Coming into force: 02.12.2002. Effect: S.R. & O. 1925/1093; S.I. 1972/985; 1992/122 amended in relation to England and Wales. Territorial extent & classification: E/W. General. – 12p.: 30 cm. – 0 11 042848 X £2.50

Lands tribunal, England and Wales

The Lands Tribunal (Amendment) Rules 2002 No. 2002/770. – Enabling power: Lands Tribunal Act 1949, s. 3 & Finance Act 1990, s. 128. – Issued: 28.03.2002. Made: 21.03.2002. Coming into force: 01.05.2002. Effect: S.I. 1996/1021 amended. Territorial extent & classification: E/W. General. – 4p.: 30 cm. – 0 11 039598 0 £1.75

Legal aid and advice, England and Wales

The Civil Legal Aid (General) (Amendment No. 2) Regulations 2002 No. 2002/3033. – Enabling power: Legal Aid Act 1988, ss. 16, 34, 43. – Issued: 19.12.2002. Made: 05.12.2002. Laid: 09.12.2002. Coming into force: 31.12.2002. Effect: S.I. 1989/339 amended in relation to England and Wales. Territorial extent & classification: E/W. General. – 4p.: 30 cm. – 0 11 044208 3 £1.75

The Civil Legal Aid (General) (Amendment) Regulations 2002 No. 2002/711. – Enabling power: Legal Aid Act 1988, ss. 34, 43. – Issued: 22.03.2002. Made: 10.03.2002. Laid: 18.03.2002. Coming into force: 08.04.2002. Effect: S.I. 1989/339 amended. Territorial extent & classification: E/W. General. – 2p.: 30 cm. – 0 11 039560 3 £1.50

The Legal Aid in Family Proceedings (Remuneration) (Amendment) Regulations 2002 No. 2002/710. – Enabling power: Legal Aid Act 1988, ss. 34, 43. – Issued: 26.03.2002. Made: 18.03.2002. Laid: 18.03.2002. Coming into force: 08.04.2002. Effect: S.I. 1991/2038 amended. Territorial extent & classification: E/W. General. – 2p.: 30 cm. – 0 11 039582 4 £1.50

Legal Services Commission, England and Wales

The Community Legal Service (Financial) (Amendment No. 2) Regulations 2002 No. 2002/1766. – Enabling power: Access to Justice Act 1999, s. 7. – Issued: 17.07.2002. Made: 06.07.2002. Laid: 11.07.2002. Coming into force: 05.08.2002. Effect: S.I. 2000/516 amended. Territorial extent & classification: E/W. General. – 2p.: 30 cm. – 0 11 042467 0 £1.50

The Community Legal Service (Financial) (Amendment) Regulations 2002 No. 2002/709. – Enabling power: Access to Justice Act 1999, ss. 7, 10. – Issued: 26.03.2002. Made: 10.03.2002. Laid: 18.03.2002. Coming into force: 08.04.2002. Effect: S.I. 2000/516 amended. Territorial extent & classification: E/W. General. – 2p.: 30 cm. – 0 11 039581 6 £1.50

The Criminal Defence Service (Funding) (Amendment) Order 2002 No. 2002/714. – Enabling power: Access to Justice Act 1999, ss. 14 (3), 105, sch. 14, para. 9. – Issued: 26.03.2002. Made: 13.03.2002. Laid: 18.03.2002. Coming into force: 08.04.2002. Effect: S.I. 2001/855 amended. Territorial extent & classification: E/W. General. – 2p.: 30 cm. – 0 11 039585 9 £1.50

The Criminal Defence Service (General) (No. 2) (Amendment No. 2) Regulations 2002 No. 2002/2785. – Enabling power: Access to Justice Act 1999, ss. 12, 13. – Issued: 02.12.2002. Made: 11.11.2002. Laid: 11.11.2002. Coming into force: 02.12.2002. Effect: S.I. 2001/1437 amended. Territorial extent & classification: E/W. General. – 2p.: 30 cm. – 0 11 044028 5 £1.50

The Criminal Defence Service (General) (No. 2) (Amendment) Regulations 2002 No. 2002/712. – Enabling power: Access to Justice Act 1999, ss. 12, 13, 15, sch. 3. – Issued: 26.03.2002. Made: 13.03.2002. Laid: 18.03.2002. Coming into force: 08.04.2002. Effect: S.I. 2001/1437 amended. Territorial extent & classification: E/W. General. – 12p.: 30 cm. – 0 11 039583 2 £2.50

The Criminal Defence Service (Recovery of Defence Costs Orders) (Amendment) Regulations 2002 No. 2002/713. – Enabling power: Access to Justice Act 1999, s. 17 (3). – Issued: 26.03.2002. Made: 13.03.2002. Laid: 18.03.2002. Coming into force: 08.04.2002 Effect: S.I. 2001/856 amended. Territorial extent & classification: E/W. General. – 2p.: 30 cm. – 0 11 039584 0 £1.50

The Criminal Defence Service (Representation Order Appeals) (Amendment) Regulations 2002 No. 2002/1620. – Enabling power: Access to Justice Act 1999, s. 14, sch. 3, para. 4. – Issued: 28.06.2002. Made: 24.06.2002. Coming into force: 25.06.2002. Effect: S.I. 2001/1168 amended. Territorial extent & classification: E/W. General. – 2p.: 30 cm. – 0 11 042397 6 £1.50

Legal services, England and Wales

Access to Justice Act 1999 (Solicitors' Practising Certificates) Order 2002 No. 2002/3235. – Enabling power: Access to Justice Act 1999, s. 47 (1). – Issued: 09.01.2003. Made: 18.12.2002. Coming into force: 19.12.2002. Effect: 1974 c. 47 amended. Territorial extent & classification: E/W. General. – 2p.: 30 cm. – 0 11 044462 0 £1.50

The Appointment of Queen's Counsel Fees Order 2002 No. 2002/2037. – Enabling power: Access to Justice Act 1999, s. 45 (2). – Issued: 09.08.2002. Made: 27.07.2002. Laid: 02.08.2002. Coming into force: 27.08.2002. Effect: S.I. 1999/2138 revoked. Territorial extent & classification: E/W. General. – 2p.: 30 cm. – 0 11 042625 8 £1.50

Libraries

The Public Lending Right Scheme 1982 (Commencement of Variations) Order 2002 No. 2002/3123. – Enabling power: Public Lending Right Act 1979, s. 3 (7). – Issued: 20.12.2002. Made: 14.12.2002. Laid: 17.12.2002. Coming into force: 07.01.2002. Effect: Public Lending Right Scheme 1982 varied. Territorial extent & classification: E/W/S/NI. General. – 2p.: 30 cm. – 0 11 044714 X £1.50

Limited liability partnerships

The Limited Liability Partnerships (No. 2) Regulations 2002 No. 2002/913. – Enabling power: Limited Liability Partnerships Act 2000, ss. 15 to 17. – Issued: 19.04.2002. Made: 31.03.2002. Laid: 07.03.2002. Coming into force: 02.04.2002. Effect: 1985 c. 6 modified. Territorial extent and classification: E/W/S. General. – 4p.: 30 cm. – 0 11 039774 6 £1.75

The Limited Liability Partnerships (Particulars of Usual Residential Address) (Confidentiality Orders) Regulations 2002 No. 2002/915. – Enabling power: Companies Act 1985, s. 723B to F. – Issued: 19.04.2002. Made: 31.03.2002. Coming into force: 02.04.2002. Effect: 1985 c. 6; 2000 c. 12 amended. Territorial extent and classification: E/W/S. General. – 12p.: 30 cm. – 0 11 039775 4 £2.50

Local government, England

The Borough of Blackburn with Darwen and the City of Peterborough (Changes to Years of Elections) Order 2002 No. 2002/2876. – Enabling power: Local Government Act 2000, ss. 87, 105. – Issued: 27.11.2002. Made: 20.11.2002. Laid. 27.11.2002. Coming into force: 18.12.2002. Effect: S.I. 1997/777, 782 amended. Territorial extent & classification: E. Local. – 4p.: 30 cm. – 0 11 043699 7 £1.75

The Borough of Blackburn with Darwen (Electoral Changes) Order 2002 No. 2002/3223. – Enabling power: Local Government Act 1992, ss. 17, 26. – Issued: 06.01.2003. Made: 18.12.2002. Coming into force: 15.10.2003. & 06.05.2004. In accord. with art. 1 (2). Effect: S.I. 1997/782 amended (06.05.2004.). Territorial extent & classification: E. Local. – 8p.: 30 cm. – 0 11 044416 7 £2.00

The Borough of Blackpool (Electoral Changes) Order 2002 No. 2002/2240. – Enabling power: Local Government Act 1992, ss. 17, 26. – Issued: 06.09.2002. Made: 29.08.2002. Coming into force: In accord. with art. 1 (2). Effect: S.I. 1997/783 revoked (01.05.2003, with saving). Territorial extent & classification: E. Local. – 8p.: 30 cm. – 0 11 042723 8 £2.00

The Borough of Bournemouth (Electoral Changes) Order 2002 No. 2002/1783. – Enabling power: Local Government Act 1992, ss. 17, 26. – Issued: 18.07.2002. Made: 11.07.2002. Coming into force: In accord. with art. 1 (2) Effect: S.I. 1978/1813 amended (01.05.2003). Territorial extent & classification: E. Local. – 4p.: 30 cm. – 0 11 042479 4 £1.75

The Borough of Bracknell Forest (Electoral Changes) Order 2002 No. 2002/2371. – Enabling power: Local Government Act 1992, ss. 17, 26. – Issued: 20.09.2002. Made: 11.09.2002. Coming into force: In accord. with art. 1 (2). Effect: S.I. 1977/1273 amended. Territorial extent & classification: E. Local. – 8p.: 30 cm. – 0 11 042677 0 £2.00

The Borough of Burnley (Electoral Changes) (Amendment) Order 2002 No. 2002/2992. – Enabling power: Local Government Act 1992, ss. 17, 26. – Issued: 10.12.2002. Made: 02.12.2002. Coming into force: In accord. with art. 1 (2): 03.12.2002. Effect: S.I. 2001/2473 amended. Territorial extent & classification: E. Local. – 4p.: 30 cm. – 0 11 044131 1 £1.75

The Borough of Charnwood (Electoral Changes) Order 2002 No. 2002/2886. – Enabling power: Local Government Act 1992, ss. 17, 26. – Issued: 26.11.2002. Made: 19.11.2002. Coming into force: In accord. with art. 1 (2). Effect: S.I. 1980/777 revoked with saving (01.05.2003.). Territorial extent & classification: E. Local. – 8p.: 30 cm. – 0 11 043980 5 £2.00

The Borough of Christchurch (Electoral Changes) Order 2002 No. 2002/2241. – Enabling power: Local Government Act 1992, ss. 17, 26. – Issued: 06.09.2002. Made: 29.08.2002. Coming into force: In accord. with art. 1 (2). Effect: S.I. 1978/1841 revoked (01.05.2003, with saving). Territorial extent & classification: E. Local. – 8p.: 30 cm. – 0 11 042724 6 £2.00

The Borough of Crawley (Electoral Changes) Order 2002 No. 2002/2990. – Enabling power: Local Government Act 1992, ss. 17, 26. – Issued: 10.12.2002. Made: 02.12.2002. Coming into force: In accord. with art. 1 (2): 15.10.2003, 06.05.2004. Effect: S.I. 1977/1433 revoked with saving (06.05.2004.). Territorial extent & classification: E. Local. – 8p.: 30 cm. – 0 11 044128 1 £2.00

The Borough of Great Yarmouth (Electoral Changes) Order 2002 No. 2002/3228. – Enabling power: Local Government Act 1992, ss. 17, 26. – Issued: 06.01.2003. Made: 18.12.2002. Coming into force: 15.10.2003. & 06.05.2004. In accord. with art. 1 (2). Effect: S.I. 1979/710 revoked with saving (06.05.2004.). Territorial extent & classification: E. Local. – 8p.: 30 cm. – 0 11 044427 2 £2.00

The Borough of Halton (Electoral Changes) Order 2002 No. 2002/2242. – Enabling power: Local Government Act 1992, ss. 17, 26. – Issued: 06.09.2002. Made: 29.08.2002. Coming into force: In accord. with art. 1 (2). Effect: S.I. 1997/779 revoked (06.05.2004, with saving). Territorial extent & classification: E. Local. – 8p.: 30 cm. – 0 11 042725 4 £2.00

The Borough of Hinckley and Bosworth (Electoral Changes) Order 2002 No. 2002/2888. – Enabling power: Local Government Act 1992, ss. 17, 26. – Issued: 26.11.2002. Made: 19.11.2002. Coming into force: In accord. with art. 1 (2). Effect: S.I. 1980/138 revoked (01.05.2003). Territorial extent & classification: E. Local. – 8p.: 30 cm. – 0 11 043976 7 £2.00

The Borough of King's Lynn and West Norfolk (Electoral Changes) Order 2002 No. 2002/3227. – Enabling power: Local Government Act 1992, ss. 17, 26. – Issued: 06.01.2003. Made: 18.12.2002. Coming into force: 19.12.2002. & 01.05.2003. In accord. with art. 1 (2). Effect: S.I. 1979/1295 revoked with saving (01.05.2003.). Territorial extent & classification: E. Local. – 8p.: 30 cm. – 0 11 044426 4 £2.00

The Borough of Luton (Electoral Changes) Order 2002 No. 2002/1787. – Enabling power: Local Government Act 1992, ss. 17, 26. – Issued: 18.07.2002. Made: 11.07.2002. Coming into force: In accord. with art. 1 (2). Effect: S.I. 1975/1918 amended (01.05.2003). Territorial extent & classification: E. Local. – 4p.: 30 cm. – 0 11 042483 2 £1.75

The Borough of Medway (Electoral Changes) Order 2002 No. 2002/2235. – Enabling power: Local Government Act 1992, ss. 17, 26. – Issued: 06.09.2002. Made: 29.08.2002. Coming into force: In accord. with art. 1 (2). Effect: S.I. 1997/776 revoked (01.05.2003, with saving). Territorial extent & classification: E. Local. – 8p.: 30 cm. – 0 11 042718 1 £2.00

The Borough of Melton (Electoral Changes) Order 2002 No. 2002/2599. – Enabling power: Local Government Act 1992, ss. 17, 26. – Issued: 21.10.2002. Made: 12.10.2002. Coming into force: In accord. with art. 1 (2). Effect: S.I. 1977/731 revoked with saving (01.05.2003). Territorial extent & classification: E. Local. – [8]p.: 30 cm. – 0 11 042874 9 *£2.00*

The Borough of Milton Keynes (Electoral Changes) (Amendment) Order 2002 No. 2002/1034. – Enabling power: Local Government Act 1992, ss. 17, 26. – Issued: 17.04.2002. Made: 26.03.2002. Coming into force: 27.03.2002. Effect: S.I. 2001/4062 amended. Territorial extent & classification: E. Local. – 2p.: 30 cm. – 0 11 039752 5 *£1.50*

The Borough of Oadby and Wigston (Electoral Changes) Order 2002 No. 2002/2889. – Enabling power: Local Government Act 1992, ss. 17, 26. – Issued: 26.11.2002. Made: 19.11.2002. Coming into force: In accord. with art. 1 (2). Effect: S.I. 1977/723 revoked (01.05.2003). Territorial extent & classification: E. Local. – 8p.: 30 cm. – 0 11 043973 2 *£2.00*

The Borough of Poole (Electoral Changes) Order 2002 No. 2002/2887. – Enabling power: Local Government Act 1992, ss. 17, 26. – Issued: 26.11.2002. Made: 19.11.2002. Coming into force: In accord. with art. 1 (2). Effect: S.I. 1979/1347 revoked with saving (01.05.2003.). Territorial extent & classification: E. Local. – 8p.: 30 cm. – 0 11 043964 3 *£2.00*

The Borough of Reading (Electoral Changes) Order 2002 No. 2002/2892. – Enabling power: Local Government Act 1992, ss. 17, 26. – Issued: 27.11.2002. Made: 19.11.2002. Coming into force: In accord. with art. 1 (2). Effect: S.I. 1979/1346 revoked with savings (06.05.2004). Territorial extent & classification: E. Local. – 8p.: 30 cm. – 0 11 043974 0 *£2.00*

The Borough of Redditch (Electoral Changes) Order 2002 No. 2002/2986. – Enabling power: Local Government Act 1992, ss. 17, 26. – Issued: 10.12.2002. Made: 02.12.2002. Coming into force: In accord. with art. 1 (2): 15.10.2003, 06.05.2004. Effect: S.I. 1980/231 revoked with saving (06.05.2004.). Territorial extent & classification: E. Local. – 8p.: 30 cm. – 0 11 044119 2 *£2.00*

The Borough of Restormel (Electoral Changes) Order 2002 No. 2002/2601. – Enabling power: Local Government Act 1992, ss. 17, 26. – Issued: 21.10.2002. Made: 12.10.2002. Coming into force: In accord. with art. 1 (2). Effect: S.I. 1979/1670 revoked with saving (01.05.2003). Territorial extent & classification: E. Local. – [8]p.: 30 cm. – 0 11 042872 2 *£2.00*

The Borough of Slough (Electoral Changes) Order 2002 No. 2002/2600. – Enabling power: Local Government Act 1992, ss. 17, 26. – Issued: 21.10.2002. Made: 12.10.2002. Coming into force: In accord. with art. 1 (2). Effect: S.I. 1980/429 revoked with saving (06.05.2004). Territorial extent & classification: E. Local. – [8]p.: 30 cm. – 0 11 042873 0 *£2.00*

The Borough of South Ribble (Electoral Changes) (Amendment) Order 2002 No. 2002/1031. – Enabling power: Local Government Act 1992, ss. 17, 26. – Issued: 17.04.2002. Made: 26.03.2002. Coming into force: 27.03.2002. Effect: S.I. 2001/2431 amended. Territorial extent & classification: E. Local. – 2p.: 30 cm. – 0 11 039740 1 *£1.50*

The Borough of Telford and Wrekin (Electoral Changes) Order 2002 No. 2002/2373. – Enabling power: Local Government Act 1992, ss. 17, 26. – Issued: 20.09.2002. Made: 11.09.2002. Coming into force: In accord. with art. 1 (2). Effect: S.I. 1997/780 amended. Territorial extent & classification: E. Local. – 12p.: 30 cm. – 0 11 042783 1 *£2.50*

The Borough of Thurrock (Electoral Changes) Order 2002 No. 2002/2234. – Enabling power: Local Government Act 1992, ss. 17, 26. – Issued: 06.09.2002. Made: 29.08.2002. Coming into force: In accord. with art. 1 (2). Effect: S.I. 1997/775 revoked (06.05.2004, with saving). Territorial extent & classification: E. Local. – 8p.: 30 cm. – 0 11 042717 3 *£2.00*

The Borough of Torbay (Electoral Changes) Order 2002 No. 2002/1786. – Enabling power: Local Government Act 1992, ss. 17, 26. – Issued: 18.07.2002. Made: 11.07.2002. Coming into force: In accord. with art. 1 (2). Effect: S.I. 1979/1496 revoked (01.05.2003). Territorial extent & classification: E. Local. – 4p.: 30 cm. – 0 11 042478 6 *£1.75*

The Borough of Warrington (Electoral Changes) Order 2002 No. 2002/2237. – Enabling power: Local Government Act 1992, ss. 17, 26. – Issued: 06.09.2002. Made: 29.08.2002. Coming into force: In accord. with art. 1 (2). Effect: S.I. 1997/781 revoked (06.05.2004, with saving). Territorial extent & classification: E. Local. – 8p.: 30 cm. – 0 11 042720 3 *£2.00*

The Borough of Weymouth and Portland (Electoral Changes) Order 2002 No. 2002/2368. – Enabling power: Local Government Act 1992, ss. 17, 26. – Issued: 20.09.2002. Made: 11.09.2002. Coming into force: In accord. with art. 1 (2). Effect: S.I. 1978/1694 amended. Territorial extent & classification: E. Local. – 8p.: 30 cm. – 0 11 042785 8 *£2.00*

The Borough of Worthing (Electoral Changes) Order 2002 No. 2002/2884. – Enabling power: Local Government Act 1992, ss. 17, 26. – Issued: 26.11.2002. Made: 19.11.2002. Coming into force: In accord. with art. 1 (2). Effect: S.I. 1979/1266 revoked with savings (06.05.2004.). Territorial extent & classification: E. Local. – 8p.: 30 cm. – 0 11 043975 9 *£2.00*

The Boroughs of Halton, Thurrock and Warrington (Changes to Years of Elections) Order 2002 No. 2002/1670. – Enabling power: Local Government Act 2000, ss. 87, 105. – Issued: 03.07.2002. Made: 26.06.2002. Laid. 03.07.2002. Coming into force: 24.07.2002. Effect: S.I. 1997/775, 779, 781 amended. Territorial extent & classification: E. Local. – 4p.: 30 cm. – 0 11 042408 5 *£1.75*

The Bradford (Parishes) Order 2002 No. 2002/159. – Enabling power: Local Government and Rating Act 1997, ss. 14, 23. – Made: 28.01.2002. Coming into force: 29.01.2002 in accordance with art. 1 (1). Effect: None. Territorial extent & classification: E. Local *Unpublished*

The Brentwood (Parishes) (Amendment) Order 2002 No. 2002/375. – Enabling power: Local Government and Rating Act 1997, ss. 14, 23. – Made: 31.01.2002. Coming into force: In accordance with art. 2. Effect: S.I. 2002/81 amended. Territorial extent & classification: E. Local *Unpublished*

The Brentwood (Parishes) (No. 2) Order 2002 No. 2002/2877. – Enabling power: Local Government and Rating Act 1997, ss. 14, 23. – Made: 18.11.2002. Coming into force: 01.01.2003. Effect: None. Territorial extent & classification: E. Local *Unpublished*

The Brentwood (Parishes) Order 2002 No. 2002/81. – Enabling power: Local Government and Rating Act 1997, ss. 14, 23. – Made: 15.01.2002. Coming into force: 10.10.2002. Effect: None. Territorial extent & classification: E. Local *Unpublished*

The Broadland (Parishes) Order 2002 No. 2002/1774. – Enabling power: Local Government and Rating Act 1997, ss. 14, 23. Made: 09.07.2002. Coming into force: in accordance with art. 1 (1). Effect: None. Territorial extent & classification: E. Local *Unpublished*

The City of Cambridge (Electoral Changes) Order 2002 No. 2002/2369 – Enabling power: Local Government Act 1992, ss. 17, 26. – Issued: 20.09.2002. Made: 11.09.2002. Coming into force: In accord. with art. 1 (2). Effect: S.I. 1975/2143 amended. Territorial extent & classification: E. Local. – 8p.: 30 cm. – 0 11 042788 2 *£2.00*

The City of Leicester (Electoral Changes) Order 2002 No. 2002/2988. – Enabling power: Local Government Act 1992, ss. 17, 26. – Issued: 10.12.2002. Made: 02.12.2002. Coming into force: In accord. with art. 1 (2); 01.05.2003. Effect: S.I. 1979/1474 revoked (01.05.2003.). Territorial extent & classification: E. Local. – 4p.: 30 cm. – 0 11 044126 5 *£1.75*

The City of Norwich (Electoral Changes) Order 2002 No. 2002/3222. Enabling power: Local Government Act 1992, ss. 17, 26. – Issued: 06.01.2003. Made: 18.12.2002. Coming into force: 15.10.2003. & 06.05.2004. In accord. with art. 1 (2). Effect: S.I. 1977/1274 revoked with saving (06.05.2004.). Territorial extent & classification: E. Local. – 4p.: 30 cm. – With correction slip, dated February 2003 – 0 11 044415 9 *£1.75*

The City of Plymouth (Electoral Changes) Order 2002 No. 2002/2236. – Enabling power: Local Government Act 1992, ss. 17, 26. – Issued: 06.09.2002. Made: 28.08.2002. Coming into force: In accord. with art. 1 (2). Effect: S.I. 1978/1793 revoked (01.05.2003, with saving). Territorial extent & classification: E. Local. – 8p.: 30 cm. – 0 11 042719 X *£2.00*

The City of Plymouth (Scheme for Elections) Order 2002 No. 2002/2954. – Enabling power: Local Government Act 2000, ss. 86, 105. – Issued: 05.12.2002. Made: 28.11.2002. Laid. 05.12.2002. Coming into force: 31.12.2002. Effect: S.I. 1978/1793 revoked. Territorial extent & classification: E. Local. – 4p.: 30 cm. – 0 11 044098 6 *£1.75*

The City of Worcester (Electoral Changes) Order 2002 No. 2002/3225. – Enabling power: Local Government Act 1992, ss. 17, 26. – Issued: 06.01.2003. Made: 18.12.2002. Coming into force: 15.10.2003. & 06.05.2004. In accord. with art. 1 (2) (3). Effect: S.I. 1977/414 revoked with saving (06.05.2004.). Territorial extent & classification: E. Local. – 8p.: 30 cm. – 0 11 044425 6 *£2.00*

The County of Herefordshire District Council (Electoral Changes) Order 2002 No. 2002/187. – Enabling power: Local Government Act 1992, ss. 17, 26. – Issued: 07.02.2002. Made: 31.01.2002. Coming into force: In acc. with art. 1 (2). Effect: S.I. 1996/1867 amended & S.I. 1976/1757; 1977/413, 438; 1978/1843; 1991/816; 1997/1213 revoked (01.05.2003). Territorial extent & classification: E. Local. – 8p.: 30 cm. – 0 11 039269 8 *£2.00*

The District of Adur (Electoral Changes) Order 2002 No. 2002/2991. – Enabling power: Local Government Act 1992, ss. 17, 26. – Issued: 10.12.2002. Made: 02.12.2002. Coming into force: In accord. with art. 1(2): 15.10.2003, 06.05.2004. Effect: S.I. 1978/1434 revoked with saving (06.05.2004.). Territorial extent & classification: E. Local. – 8p.: 30 cm. – 0 11 044129 X *£2.00*

The District of Arun (Electoral Changes) Order 2002 No. 2002/2885. – Enabling power: Local Government Act 1992, ss. 17, 26. – Issued: 26.11.2002. Made: 19.11.2002. Coming into force: In accord. with art. 1 (2). Effect: S.I. 1980/652 revoked with saving (01.05.2003.). Territorial extent & classification: E. Local. – 8p.: 30 cm. – 0 11 043971 6 *£2.00*

The District of Aylesbury Vale (Electoral Changes) Order 2002 No. 2002/1788. – Enabling power: Local Government Act 1992, ss. 17, 26. – Issued: 18.07.2002. Made: 11.07.2002. Coming into force: In accord. with art. 1 (2). Effect: S.I. 1975/2083 amended (01.05.2003). Territorial extent & classification: E. Local. – 8p.: 30 cm. – 0 11 042480 8 *£2.00*

The District of Babergh (Electoral Changes) (Amendment) Order 2002 No. 2002/1036. – Enabling power: Local Government Act 1992, ss. 17, 26. – Issued: 17.04.2002. Made: 26.03.2002. Coming into force: 27.03.2002. Effect: S.I. 2001/3894 amended. Territorial extent & classification: E. Local. – 2p.: 30 cm. – 0 11 039755 X *£1.50*

The District of Blaby (Electoral Changes) Order 2002 No. 2002/2882. – Enabling power: Local Government Act 1992, ss. 17, 26. – Issued: 26.11.2002. Made: 19.11.2002. Coming into force: In accordance with art. 1 (2). Effect: S.I. 1980/1341 revoked with saving (01.05.2003.). Territorial extent & classification: E. Local. – 8p.: 30 cm. – 0 11 043972 4 *£2.00*

The District of Breckland (Electoral Changes) Order 2002 No. 2002/3221. – Enabling power: Local Government Act 1992, ss. 17, 26. – Issued: 06.01.2003. Made: 18.12.2002. Coming into force: 19.12.2002. & 01.05.2003. In accord. with art. 1 (2). Effect: S.I. 1978/1612 revoked with saving (01.05.2003.). Territorial extent & classification: E. Local. – 8p.: 30 cm. – 0 11 044407 8 *£2.00*

The District of Caradon (Electoral Changes) Order 2002 No. 2002/2602. – Enabling power: Local Government Act 1992, ss. 17, 26. – Issued: 21.10.2002. Made: 12.10.2002. Coming into force: In accord. with art. 1 (2). Effect: S.I. 1999/135 amended & 1980/757 revoked with saving (01.05.2003). Territorial extent & classification: E. Local. – [8]p.: 30 cm. – 0 11 042876 5 *£2.00*

The District of Carrick (Electoral Changes) Order 2002 No. 2002/2594. – Enabling power: Local Government Act 1992, ss. 17, 26. – Issued: 21.10.2002. Made: 12.10.2002. Coming into force: In accord. with art. 1 (2). Effect: S.I. 1978/1370 revoked with saving (01.05.2003). Territorial extent & classification: E. Local. – 8p.: 30 cm. – 0 11 042870 6 *£2.00*

The District of Chichester (Electoral Changes) Order 2002 No. 2002/2883. – Enabling power: Local Government Act 1992, ss. 17, 26. – Issued: 26.11.2002. Made: 19.11.2002. Coming into force: In accord. with art. 1 (2). Effect: S.I. 1977/865 revoked with saving (01.05.2003.). Territorial extent & classification: E. Local. – 8p.: 30 cm. – 0 11 043965 1 *£2.00*

The District of Chiltern (Electoral Changes) Order 2002 No. 2002/1784. – Enabling power: Local Government Act 1992, ss. 17, 26. – Issued: 18.07.2002. Made: 11.07.2002. Coming into force: In accord. with art. 1 (2). Effect: S.I. 1975/1990 amended (01.05.2003). Territorial extent & classification: E. Local. – 8p.: 30 cm. – 0 11 042481 6 *£2.00*

The District of Craven (Ribble Banks Parish Council) (Electoral Changes) Order 2002 No. 2002/1032. – Enabling power: Local Government Act 1992, ss. 17, 26. – Issued: 17.04.2002. Made: 26.03.2002. Coming into force: 27.03.2002. Effect: None. Territorial extent & classification: E. Local. – 2p.: 30 cm. – 0 11 039754 1 *£1.50*

The District of East Cambridgeshire (Electoral Changes) Order 2002 No. 2002/2596. – Enabling power: Local Government Act 1992, ss. 17, 26. – Issued: 21.10.2002. Made: 12.10.2002. Coming into force: In accord. with art. 1 (2). Effect: S.I. 1980/1340 revoked with saving (01.05.2003). Territorial extent & classification: E. Local. – 8p.: 30 cm. – 0 11 042869 2 *£2.00*

The District of East Dorset (Electoral Changes) Order 2002 No. 2002/2238. – Enabling power: Local Government Act 1992, ss. 17, 26. – Issued: 06.09.2002. Made: 29.08.2002. Coming into force: In accord. with art. 1 (2). Effect: S.I. 1980/1128 revoked (01.05.2003, with saving). Territorial extent & classification: E. Local. – 8p.: 30 cm. – 0 11 042721 1 *£2.00*

The District of East Riding (Electoral Changes) (Amendment) Order 2002 No. 2002/1033. – Enabling power: Local Government Act 1992, ss. 17, 26. – Issued: 17.04.2002. Made: 26.03.2002. Coming into force: 27.03.2002. Effect: S.I. 2001/3358 amended. Territorial extent and classification: E. Local. – 2p.: 30 cm. – 0 11 039753 3 *£1.50*

The District of Epping Forest (Electoral Changes) (Amendment) Order 2002 No. 2002/2982. – Enabling power: Local Government Act 1992, ss. 17, 26. – Issued: 10.12.2002. Made: 02.12.2002. Coming into force: In accord. with art. 1(2): 03.12.2002. Effect: S.I. 2001/2444 amended. Territorial extent & classification: E. Local. – 4p.: 30 cm. – 0 11 044118 4 *£1.75*

The District of Fenland (Electoral Changes) Order 2002 No. 2002/2595. – Enabling power: Local Government Act 1992, ss. 17, 26. – Issued: 21.10.2002. Made: 12.10.2002. Coming into force: In accord. with art. 1 (2). Effect: S.I. 1975/2088 revoked with saving (01.05.2003). Territorial extent & classification: E. Local. – 8p.: 30 cm. – 0 11 042871 4 *£2.00*

The District of Forest of Dean (Electoral Changes) (Amendment) Order 2002 No. 2002/1035. – Enabling power: Local Government Act 1992, ss. 17, 26. – Issued: 17.04.2002. Made: 26.03.2002. Coming into force: 27.03.2002. Effect: S.I. 2001/3880 amended. Territorial extent & classification: E. Local. – 2p.: 30 cm. – 0 11 039756 8 *£1.50*

The District of Harborough (Electoral Changes) Order 2002 No. 2002/2597. – Enabling power: Local Government Act 1992, ss. 17, 26. – Issued: 21.10.2002. Made: 12.10.2002. Coming into force: In accord. with art. 1 (2). Effect: S.I. 1979/1112 revoked with saving (01.05.2003). Territorial extent & classification: E. Local. – 8p.: 30 cm. – 0 11 042867 6 *£2.00*

The District of Horsham (Electoral Changes) Order 2002 No. 2002/2890. – Enabling power: Local Government Act 1992, ss. 17, 26. – Issued: 27.11.2002. Made: 19.11.2002. Coming into force: In accord. with art. 1 (2). Effect: S.I. 1978/1861 revoked with saving (01.05.2003). Territorial extent & classification: E. Local. – 8p.: 30 cm. – 0 11 043966 X *£2.00*

The District of Huntingdonshire (Electoral Changes) Order 2002 No. 2002/2984. – Enabling power: Local Government Act 1992, ss. 17, 26. – Issued: 12.02.2003. Made: 02.12.2002. Coming into force: In accord. with arts. 1 (2) (3) (4). Effect: S.I. 1976/401 revoked with saving (06.05.2004). Territorial extent & classification: E. Local. – Corrected reprint issued free of charge to all known recipients of the original print. – 12p.: 30 cm. – 0 11 044123 0 *£2.50*

The District of Kerrier (Electoral Changes) Order 2002 No. 2002/2604. – Enabling power: Local Government Act 1992, ss. 17, 26. – Issued: 21.10.2002. Made: 12.10.2002. Coming into force: In accord. with art. 1 (2). Effect: S.I. 1978/1356 revoked with saving (01.05.2003). Territorial extent & classification: E. Local. – [8]p.: 30 cm. – 0 11 042865 X *£2.00*

The District of Malvern Hills (Electoral Changes) Order 2002 No. 2002/3224. – Enabling power: Local Government Act 1992, ss. 17, 26. – Issued: 06.01.2003. Made: 18.12.2002. Coming into force: 19.12.2002. & 01.05.2003. In accord. with art. 1 (2). Effect: S.I. 1996/1867 amended (01.05.2003.). Territorial extent & classification: E. Local. – 8p.: 30 cm. – 0 11 044417 5   *£2.00*

The District of Mid Sussex (Electoral Changes) Order 2002 No. 2002/2891. – Enabling power: Local Government Act 1992, ss. 17, 26. – Issued: 26.11.2002. Made: 19.11.2002. Coming into force: In accord. with art. 1 (2). Effect: S.I. 1980/653 revoked (01.05.2003). Territorial extent & classification: E. Local. – 8p.: 30 cm. – 0 11 043967 8   *£2.00*

The District of North Cornwall (Electoral Changes) Order 2002 No. 2002/2603. – Enabling power: Local Government Act 1992, ss. 17, 26. – Issued: 21.10.2002. Made: 12.10.2002. Coming into force: In accord. with art. 1 (2). Effect: S.I. 1978/1806 revoked with saving (01.05.2003). Territorial extent & classification: E. Local. – [8]p.: 30 cm. – 0 11 042875 7   *£2.00*

The District of North Dorset (Electoral Changes) Order 2002 No. 2002/2239. – Enabling power: Local Government Act 1992, ss. 17, 26. – Issued: 06.09.2002. Made: 28.08.2002. Coming into force: In accord. with art. 1 (2). Effect: S.I. 1980/1487 revoked (01.05.2003, with saving). Territorial extent & classification: E. Local. – 8p.: 30 cm. – 0 11 042722 X   *£2.00*

The District of North West Leicestershire (Electoral Changes) Order 2002 No. 2002/2598. – Enabling power: Local Government Act 1992, ss. 17, 26. – Issued: 21.10.2002. Made: 12.10.2002. Coming into force: In accord. with art. 1 (2). Effect: S.I. 1980/778 revoked with saving (01.05.2003). Territorial extent & classification: E. Local. – 8p.: 30 cm. – 0 11 042866 8   *£2.00*

The District of Penwith (Electoral Changes) Order 2002 No. 2002/2593. – Enabling power: Local Government Act 1992, ss. 17, 26. – Issued: 21.10.2002. Made: 12.10.2002. Coming into force: In accord. with art. 1 (2). Effect: S.I. 1978/1505 revoked with saving (06.05.2004). Territorial extent & classification: E. Local. – 8p.: 30 cm. – 0 11 042868 4   *£2.00*

The District of South Bucks (Electoral Changes) Order 2002 No. 2002/1785. – Enabling power: Local Government Act 1992, ss. 17, 26. – Issued: 18.07.2002. Made: 11.07.2002. Coming into force: In accord. with art. 1 (2). Effect: S.I. 1980/428 amended (01.05.2003). Territorial extent & classification: E. Local. – 8p.: 30 cm. – 0 11 042482 4   *£2.00*

The District of South Cambridgeshire (Electoral Changes) Order 2002 No. 2002/2374. – Enabling power: Local Government Act 1992, ss. 17, 26. – Issued: 20.09.2002. Made: 11.09.2002. Coming into force: In accord. with art. 1 (2) (3). Effect: S.I. 1975/1991 amended. Territorial extent & classification: E. Local. – 8p.: 30 cm. – 0 11 042784 X   *£2.00*

The District of South Norfolk (Electoral Changes) Order 2002 No. 2002/3218. – Enabling power: Local Government Act 1992, ss. 17, 26. – Issued: 06.01.2003. Made: 18.12.2002. Coming into force: 19.12.2002. & 01.05.2003. In accord. with art. 1 (2). Effect: S.I. 1977/237 revoked with saving (01.05.2003.). Territorial extent & classification: E. Local. – 8p.: 30 cm. – 0 11 044406 X   *£2.00*

The District of South Oxfordshire (Electoral Changes) Order 2001 No. 2002/49. – Enabling power: Local Government Act 1992, ss. 17, 26. – Issued: 18.01.2002. Made: 20.12.2001. Coming into force: In acc. with art. 1 (2). Effect: S.I. 1980/1343 revoked (01.05.2003). Territorial extent & classification: E. Local. – 8p.: 30 cm. – 0 11 039194 2   *£2.00*

The District of Waveney (Electoral Changes) (Amendment) Order 2002 No. 2002/2983. – Enabling power: Local Government Act 1992, ss. 17, 26. – Issued: 10.12.2002. Made: 02.12.2002. Coming into force: In accord. with art. 1 (2): 03.12.2002. Effect: S.I. 2001/3889 amended. Territorial extent & classification: E. Local. – 4p.: 30 cm. – 0 11 044120 6   *£1.75*

The District of West Berkshire (Electoral Changes) Order 2002 No. 2002/2243. – Enabling power: Local Government Act 1992, ss. 17, 26. – Issued: 06.09.2002. Made: 29.08.2002. Coming into force: In accord. with art. 1 (2). Effect: S.I. 1996/1879 revoked (01.05.2003, with saving). Territorial extent & classification: E. Local. – 8p.: 30 cm. – 0 11 042726 2   *£2.00*

The District of West Dorset (Electoral Changes) Order 2002 No. 2002/2370. – Enabling power: Local Government Act 1992, ss. 17, 26. – Issued: 20.09.2002. Made: 11.09.2002. Coming into force: In accord. with art. 1 (2). Effect: S.I. 1980/643 revoked (01.05.2003). Territorial extent & classification: E. Local. – 8p.: 30 cm. – 0 11 042782 3   *£2.00*

The District of West Oxfordshire (Electoral Changes) Order 2001 No. 2002/48. – Enabling power: Local Government Act 1992, ss. 17, 26. – Issued: 18.01.2002. Made: 20.12.2001. Coming into force: In acc. with art. 1 (2) (3). Effect: S.I. 1977/681 revoked (01.05.2003). Territorial extent & classification: E. Local. – 8p.: 30 cm. – 0 11 039193 4   *£2.00*

The District of Wokingham (Electoral Changes) Order 2002 No. 2002/2989. – Enabling power: Local Government Act 1992, ss. 17, 26. – Issued: 10.02.2003. Made: 02.12.2002. Coming into force: In accord. with arts. 1 (2) (3) (4): 15.10.2003, 06.05.2004, 15.10.2005, 04.05.2006, 15.10.2006, 03.05.2007. Effect: S.I. 1978/1640 revoked with saving (06.05.2004.). Territorial extent & classification: E. Local. – Corrected reprint. – 12p.: 30 cm. – 0 11 044124 9   *£2.50*

The District of Wychavon (Electoral Changes) Order 2002 No. 2002/2987. – Enabling power: Local Government Act 1992, ss. 17, 26. – Issued: 10.12.2002. Made: 02.12.2002. Coming into force: In accord. with art. 1 (2): 01.05.2003. Effect: S.I. 1978/49 revoked with savings (01.05.2003.). Territorial extent & classification: E. Local. – 8p.: 30 cm. – 0 11 044127 3   *£2.00*

The District of Wycombe (Electoral Changes) Order 2002 No. 2002/1781. – Enabling power: Local Government Act 1992, ss. 17, 26. – Issued: 18.07.2002. Made: 11.07.2002. Coming into force: In accord. with art. 1 (2). Effect: S.I. 1980/842 amended (01.05.2003). Territorial extent & classification: E. Local. – 8p.: 30 cm. – 0 11 042484 0   £2.00

The District of Wyre Forest (Electoral Changes) Order 2002 No. 2002/2985. – Enabling power: Local Government Act 1992, ss. 17, 26. – Issued: 10.12.2002. Made: 02.12.2002. Coming into force: In accord. with art. 1 (2) (3): 15.10.2003, 06.05.2004, 15.10.2005, 04.05.2006. Effect: S.I. 1978/1495 revoked with saving (06.05.2004.). Territorial extent & classification: E. Local. – 8p.: 30 cm. – 0 11 044122 2   £2.00

The East Riding of Yorkshire (Parishes) Order 2002 No. 2002/3000. – Enabling power: Local Government and Rating Act 1997, ss. 14, 23. – Made: 02.12.2002. Coming into force: 03.12.2002 & 01.04.2003 in accordance with art. 1 (2). Effect: None. Territorial extent & classification: E. Local *Unpublished*

The East Staffordshire (Parishes and Electoral Changes) Order 2002 No. 2002/1060. – Enabling power: Local Government and Rating Act 1997, ss. 14, 23. – Made: 01.04.2002. Coming into force: in accordance with art. 1 (2). Effect: S.I. 2001/1443 amended. Territorial extent & classification: E. Local *Unpublished*

The Hambleton (Parishes) Order 2002 No. 2002/1068. – Enabling power: Local Government and Rating Act 1997, ss. 14, 23. – Made: 11.04.2002. Coming into force: in accordance with art. 1 (2). Effect: None. Territorial extent & classification: E. Local *Unpublished*

The Local Authorities (Access to Meetings and Documents) (Period of Notice) (England) Order 2002 No. 2002/715. – Enabling power: Local Government Act 1972, s. 100K (3). – Issued: 21.03.2002. Made: 14.03.2002. Laid: 21.03.2002. Coming into force: 01.10.2002. Effect: 1972 c. 70 amended. Territorial extent and classification: E. General. – 2p.: 30 cm. – 0 11 039515 8   £1.50

The Local Authorities (Capital Finance) (Amendment) (England) Regulations 2002 No. 2002/2299. – Enabling power: Local Government and Housing Act 1989, ss. 61 (4), 190 (1), sch. 3, paras. 11 (2), 15 (1). – Issued: 13.09.2002. Made: 05.09.2002. Laid: 09.09.2002. Coming into force: 30.09.2002. Effect: S.I. 1997/319 amended in relation to England. Territorial extent & classification: E. General. – 2p.: 30 cm. – 0 11 042748 3   £1.50

The Local Authorities (Capital Finance and Approved Investments) (Amendment) (England) Regulations 2002 No. 2002/451. – Enabling power: Local Government and Housing Act 1989, ss. 58 (9), 66 (1) (a), 190 (1). – Issued: 08.03.2002. Made: 01.03.2002. Laid: 08.03.2002. Coming into force: 01.04.2002. Effect: S.I. 1990/426; 1997/319 amended. Territorial extent & classification: E. General. – 4p.: 30 cm. – 0 11 039419 4   £1.75

The Local Authorities (Capital Finance) (Rate of Discount for 2002/03) (England) Regulations 2002 No. 2002/110. – Enabling power: Local Government and Housing Act 1989, s. 49 (2). – Issued: 30.01.2002. Made: 23.01.2002. Laid: 30.01.2002. Coming into force: 01.04.2002. Effect: None. Territorial extent & classification: E. General. – 2p.: 30 cm. – 0 11 039227 2   £1.50

The Local Authorities (Companies) (Amendment) (England) Order 2002 No. 2002/2298. – Enabling power: Local Government and Housing Act 1989, s. 39 (5) to (7). – Issued: 13.09.2002. Made: 05.09.2002. Laid: 09.09.2002. Coming into force: 30.09.2002. Effect: S.I. 1995/849 amended. Territorial extent & classification: E. General. – 4p.: 30 cm. – 0 11 042750 5   £1.75

The Local Authorities (Conduct of Referendums) (England) (Amendment) Regulations 2002 No. 2002/521. – Enabling power: Local Government Act 2000, ss. 45, 105. – Issued: 14.03.2002. Made: 07.03.2002. Coming into force: 08.03.2002. Effect: S.I. 2001/1298 amended. Territorial extent & classification: E. General. – 4p.: 30 cm. – Supersedes draft S.I. (ISBN 0110392949) previously issued on 12.02.2002 – 0 11 039455 0   £1.75

The Local Authorities (Discretionary Expenditure Limits) (England) Order 2002 No. 2002/2878. – Enabling power: Local Government Act 1972, s. 137 (4AA) (5). – Issued: 26.11.2002. Made: 19.11.2002. Laid: 26.11.2002. Coming into force: 31.03.2003. Effect: None. Territorial extent & classification: E. General. – 2p.: 30 cm. – 0 11 043934 1   £1.50

The Local Authorities (Elected Mayor and Mayor's Assistant) (England) Regulations 2002 No. 2002/975. – Enabling power: Local Government Act 2000, ss. 39 (5), 105, sch. 1, para. 6. – Issued: 10.04.2002. Made: 04.04.2002. Laid: 10.04.2002. Coming into force: 06.05.2002. Effect: None. Territorial extent & classification: E. General. – 4p.: 30 cm. – 0 11 039701 0   £1.75

The Local Authorities (Executive Arrangements) (Access to Information) (England) Amendment Regulations 2002 No. 2002/716. – Enabling power: Local Government Act 2000, ss. 22, 105. – Issued: 21.03.2002. Made: 14.03.2002. Laid: 21.03.2002. Coming into force: 15.04.2002. for regs. 1 to 13 & 01.10.2002. for reg. 14. Effect: S.I. 2000/3272 amended. Territorial extent and classification: E. General. – This S.I. has been made in consequence of defects in S.I. 2000/3272 and is being issued free of charge to all known recipients of that S.I. – 4p.: 30 cm. – 0 11 039514 X   £1.75

The Local Authorities (Executive Arrangements) (Modification of Enactments) (England) Order 2002 No. 2002/1057. – Enabling power: Local Government Act 2000, ss. 47, 105. – Issued: 18.04.2002. Made: 11.04.2002. Laid: 15.04.2002. Coming into force: 06.05.2002. Effect: 1903 c.20; 1915 c.83; 1972 c. 70; 1973 c.15; 1974 c.7; 1983 c.2; 1985 c.51; 1996 c.31; S.I. 1983/605; S.I. 1995/2061 modified & S.I. 2001/2237 amended. Territorial extent & classification: E. General. – 8p.: 30 cm. – 0 11 039770 3   £2.00

The Local Authorities (Goods and Services) (Public Bodies) (England) (No. 2) Order 2002 No. 2002/2244. – Enabling power: Local Authorities (Goods and Services) Act 1970, s. 1 (5) (6). – Issued: 09.09.2002. Made: 02.09.2002. Laid: 09.09.2002. Coming into force: 30.09.2002. Effect: None. Territorial extent & classification: E. General. – 2p.: 30 cm. – 0 11 042730 0 *£1.50*

The Local Authorities (Goods and Services) (Public Bodies) (England) (No. 3) Order 2002 No. 2002/2624. – Enabling power: Local Authorities (Goods and Services) Act 1970, s. 1 (5) (6). – Issued: 24.10.2002. Made: 17.10.2002. Laid: 24.10.2002. Coming into force: 14.11.2002. Effect: None. Territorial extent & classification: E. General. – 2p.: 30 cm. – 0 11 042884 6 *£1.50*

The Local Authorities (Goods and Services) (Public Bodies) (England) Order 2002 No. 2002/522. – Enabling power: Local Authorities (Goods and Services) Act 1970, s. 1 (5). – Issued: 15.03.2002. Made: 08.03.2002. Laid: 08.03.2002. Coming into force: 01.04.2002. Effect: None. Territorial extent & classification: E. General. – 2p.: 30 cm. – 0 11 039487 9 *£1.50*

The Local Authorities (Scheme for Elections of Specified Councils) (England) Order 2002 No. 2002/1962. – Enabling power: Local Government Act 2000, ss. 86, 87, 105. – Issued: 31.07.2002. Made: 24.07.2002. Laid: 29.07.2002. Coming into force: 19.08.2002. Effect: S.I. 2000/2058; 2001/1020, 1022, 3882, 4056, 4063 amended. Territorial extent & classification: E. Local. – 4p.: 30 cm. – 0 11 042572 3 *£1.75*

The Mid Sussex (Parishes) Order 2002 No. 2002/158. – Enabling power: Local Government and Rating Act 1997, ss. 14, 23. – Made: 28.01.2002. Coming into force: In accord.with art. 1 (2). Effect: None. Territorial extent & classification: E. Local *Unpublished*

The Newcastle upon Tyne (Parishes) Order 2002 No. 2002/2516. – Enabling power: Local Government and Rating Act 1997, ss. 14, 23. – Made: 02.10.2002. Coming into force: in accordance with art. 1 (2). Effect: None. Territorial extent & classification: E. Local *Unpublished*

The North East Lincolnshire (Parish) Order 2002 No. 2002/2999. – Enabling power: Local Government and Rating Act 1997, ss. 14, 23. – Made: 02.12.2002. Coming into force: 03.12.2002 & 01.04.2003 in accordance with art. 1 (2). Effect: None. Territorial extent & classification: E. Local *Unpublished*

The North Somerset (Parishes) Order 2002 No. 2002/2224. – Enabling power: Local Government and Rating Act 1997, ss. 14, 23. – Made: 27.08.2002. Coming into force: in accordance with art. 1 (2). Effect: None. Territorial extent & classification: E. Local *Unpublished*

The Oswestry (Parishes) Order 2002 No. 2002/1900. – Enabling power: Local Government and Rating Act 1997, ss. 14, 23. – Made: 19.07.2002. Coming into force: in accordance with art. 1 (2). Effect: None. Territorial extent & classification: E. Local *Unpublished*

The Preston (Parishes) Order 2002 No. 2002/3201. – Enabling power: Local Government and Rating Act 1997, ss. 14, 23. – Made: 17.12.2002. Coming into force: in accordance with art. 1 (2). Effect: None. Territorial extent & classification: E. Local *Unpublished*

The Richmondshire (Parishes) Order 2002 No. 2002/1059. – Enabling power: Local Government and Rating Act 1997, ss. 14, 23. – Made: 01.04.2002. Coming into force: in accordance with art. 1 (2). Effect: None. Territorial extent & classification: E. Local *Unpublished*

The Royal Borough of Windsor and Maidenhead (Electoral Changes) Order 2002 No. 2002/2372. – Enabling power: Local Government Act 1992, ss. 17, 26. – Issued: 20.09.2002. Made: 11.09.2002. Coming into force: In accord. with art. 1 (2). Effect: S.I. 1980/733 amended. Territorial extent & classification: E. Local. – 8p.: 30 cm. – 0 11 042786 6 *£2.00*

The Sedgefield (Parishes) Order 2002 No. 2002/1061. – Enabling power: Local Government and Rating Act 1997, ss. 14, 23. – Made: 01.04.2002. Coming into force: in accordance with art. 1 (2). Effect: None. Territorial extent & classification: E. Local *Unpublished*

The South Gloucestershire (Parishes) Order 2002 No. 2002/3022. – Enabling power: Local Government and Rating Act 1997, ss. 14, 23. – Made: 03.12.2002. Coming into force: in accordance with art. 1 (2). Effect: None. Territorial extent & classification: E. Local *Unpublished*

The St Albans (Parishes) Order 2002 No. 2002/3035. – Enabling power: Local Government and Rating Act 1997, ss. 14, 23. – Made: 06.12.2002. Coming into force: 07.12.2002 & 01.04.2003 in accordance with art. 1 (2). Effect: None. Territorial extent & classification: E. Local *Unpublished*

The St Edmundsbury (Parish) Order 2002 No. 2002/1216. – Enabling power: Local Government and Rating Act 1997, ss. 14, 23. – Made: 25.04.2002. Coming into force: in accordance with art. 1 (2). Effect: None. Territorial extent & classification: E. Local *Unpublished*

The Waverley (Parishes) Order 2002 No. 2002/2620. – Enabling power: Local Government and Rating Act 1997, ss. 14, 23. – Made: 14.10.2002. Coming into force: in accordance with art. 1 (2). Effect: None. Territorial extent & classification: E. Local *Unpublished*

The Wear Valley (Parish) Order 2002 No. 2002/3023. – Enabling power: Local Government and Rating Act 1997, ss. 14, 23. – Made: 04.12.2002. Coming into force: in accordance with art. 1 (2). Effect: None. Territorial extent & classification: E. Local *Unpublished*

Local government, England: Finance

The Local Authorities (Alteration of Requisite Calculations) (England) Regulations 2002 No. 2002/155. – Enabling power: Local Government Finance Act 1992, ss. 32 (9), 33 (4), 43 (7), 44 (4), 113 (2) & Greater London Authority Act 1999, ss. 86 (5), 88 (8), 89 (9), 420 (1). – Issued: 19.02.2002. Made: 30.01.2002. Laid: 31.01.2002. Coming into force: 01.02.2002. Effect: 1992 c. 14; 1999 c. 29 amended. Territorial extent & classification:E. General. – 4p.: 30 cm. – 0 11 039315 5 *£1.75*

Local government, England and Wales

The Audit Commission (Borrowing Limit) Order 2002 No. 2002/743. – Enabling power: Audit Commission Act 1998, sch. 1, para. 9 (2). – Issued: 25.03.2002. Made: 18.03.2002. Coming into force: 19.03.2002. Effect: None. Territorial extent & classification: E/W. General. – Supersedes draft S.I. (ISBN 0110393074) issued 14 February 2002. – 2p.: 30 cm. – 0 11 039530 1 *£1.50*

The Local Authorities (Mayoral Elections) (England and Wales) Regulations 2002 No. 2002/185. – Enabling power: Local Government Act 2000, ss. 44, 105. – Issued: 07.02.2002. Made: 31.01.2002. Coming into force: 01.02.2002. Effect: S.I. 1986/2214 amended & 1983 c. 2; 1985 c. 50; 2000 c. 2; S.I. 1986/1081, 2215; 1999/1214; 2000/427; 2001/341, 1298 modified. Territorial extent & classification: E/W. General. – Supersedes draft S.I. (ISBN 0110390946) issued on 03.01.2002. – 56p.: 30 cm. – 0 11 039266 3 *£7.50*

The Local Government Act 2000 (Commencement No. 8) Order 2002 No. 2002/1718 (C. 48). – Enabling power: Local Government Act 2000, ss. 105 (2), 108 (3) (7). Bringing into operation various provisions of the 2000 Act on 27.07.2002. – Issued: 12.07.2002. Made: 04.07.2002. Effect: None. Territorial extent and classification: E/W. General. – 4p.: 30 cm. – 0 11 042445 X *£1.75*

The Local Government Act 2000 (Model Code of Conduct) (Amendment) Order 2002 No. 2002/1719. – Enabling power: Local Government Act 2000, ss. 50 (1), 105 (2) (3) (4). – Issued: 12.07.2002. Made: 04.07.2002. Laid: 05.07.2002. Coming into force: 27.07.2002. Effect: S.I. 2001/3575, 3576, 3577, 3578 amended. Territorial extent & classification: E/W. General. – 2p.: 30 cm. – 0 11 042444 1 *£1.50*

The Local Government (Best Value) Performance Indicators and Performance Standards Order 2002 No. 2002/523. – Enabling power: Local Government Act 1999, ss. 4 (1) (2), 28 (1) (b). – Issued: 14.03.2002. Made: 08.03.2002. Laid: 08.03.2002. Coming into force: 01.04.2002. Effect: S.I. 2001/724 revoked. Territorial extent & classification: E./W. General. – 24p.: 30 cm. – Revoked by S.I. 2003/530 (ISBN 0110451724) – 0 11 039458 5 *£4.00*

The Local Government (Best Value) Performance Plans and Reviews Amendment and Specified Dates Order 2002 No. 2002/305. – Enabling power: Local Government Act 1999, ss. 5 (2), 6, 7 (6). – Issued: 27.02.2002. Made: 13.02.2002. Laid: 14.02.2002. Coming into force: 08.03.2002. Effect: S.I. 1999/3251 amended. Territorial extent & classification: E/W. General. – 2p.: 30 cm. – 0 11 039377 5 *£1.50*

The Local Government Commission for England (Winding-up) Order 2002 No. 2002/1723. – Enabling power: Political Parties, Elections and Referendums Act 2000, ss. 18 (6), 156 (5) (a). – Issued: 16.07.2002. Made: 01.07.2002. Laid: 10.07.2002. Coming into force: 01.08.2002. Effect: 1975 c. 24, 25, 70 amended. Territorial extent & classification: E/W. General. – 2p.: 30 cm. – 0 11 042465 4 *£1.50*

The Police Authorities (Best Value) Performance Indicators Order 2002 No. 2002/694. – Enabling power: Local Government Act 1999, s. 4 (1) (a). – Issued: 02.04.2002. Made: 13.03.2002. Laid: 15.03.2002. Coming into force: 01.04.2002. Effect: None. Territorial extent & classification: E/W. General. – 4p.: 30 cm. – Revoked by S.I. 2003/519 (ISBN 0110452763) – 0 11 039618 9 *£1.75*

The Relevant Authorities (Standards Committee) (Dispensations) Regulations 2002 No. 2002/339. – Enabling power: Local Government Act 2000, ss. 53 (6), 81 (5), 105 (2). – Issued: 25.02.2002. Made: 18.02.2002. Laid: 25.02.2002. Coming into force: 18.03.2002. Effect: None. Territorial extent & classification: E/W. General. – 4p.: 30 cm. – 0 11 039352 X *£1.75*

Local government, Wales

The Blaenau Gwent and Caerphilly (Tredegar and Rhymney) Order 2002 No. 2002/651 (W.68). – Enabling power: Local Government Act 1972, s. 58 (2). – Issued: 07.05.2002. Made: 05.03.2002. Coming into force: 06.04.2002 in accord. with art. 1 (2). Effect: None. Territorial extent & classification: W. General. – In English and Welsh. Welsh title: Gorchymyn Blaenau Gwent a Chaerffili (Tredegar a Rhymni) 2002. – 8p., maps: 30 cm. – 0 11 090478 8 *£2.00*

The Cardiff and Vale of Glamorgan (Michaelston and Grangetown) Order 2002 No. 2002/3273 (W.311). – Enabling power: Local Government Act 1972, s. 58 (2). – Issued: 05.02.2003. Made: 06.12.2002. Coming into force: in accord. with art. 1 (2). Effect: None. Territorial extent & classification: W. Local. – 8p., maps: 30 cm. – In English and Welsh. Welsh title: Gorchymyn Caerdydd a Bro Morgannwg (Llanfihangel-ynys-Afan a Grangetown) 2002 – 0 11 090628 4 *£3.00*

The Carmarthenshire and Pembrokeshire (Clynderwen, Cilymaenllwyd and Henllanfallteg) Order 2002 No. 2002/3270 (W.308). – Enabling power: Local Government Act 1972, s. 58 (2). – Issued: 18.02.2003. Made: 06.12.2002. Coming into force: In accord. with art. 1 (2). Effect: None. Territorial extent & classification: W. Local. – 16p., maps: 30 cm. – In English and Welsh. – Gorchymyn Sir Gaerfyrddin a Sir Benfro (Clynderwen, Cilymaenllwyd a Henllanfallteg) 2002. – 0 11 090642 X *£6.00*

The Ceredigion and Pembrokeshire (St Dogmaels) Order 2002 No. 2002/3272 (W.310). – Enabling power: Local Government Act 1972, s. 58 (2). – Issued: 05.02.2003. Made: 06.12.2002. Coming into force: in accord. with art. 1 (2). Effect: None. Territorial extent & classification: W. Local. – 8p., maps: 30 cm. – 0 11 090627 6 *£4.00*

The County Borough of Newport (Electoral Changes) Order 2002 No. 2002/3276 (W.314). – Enabling power: Local Government Act 1972, ss. 58 (2), 67 (4) (5). – Issued: 30.01.2003. Made: 06.12.2002. Coming into force: In acc. with art. 1 (2). Effect: None. Territorial extent & classification: W. Local. – 8p.: 30 cm. – 0 11 090623 3 *£2.00*

The County Borough of The Vale of Glamorgan (Electoral Changes) Order 2002 No. 2002/3277 (W.315). – Enabling power: Local Government Act 1972, ss. 58 (2), 67 (4) (5). – Issued: 12.02.2003. Made: 06.12.2002. Coming into force: 09.10.2003 & 06.05.2004 in accord. with art. 1 (2). Effect: None. Territorial extent & classification: W. Local. – 12p., maps: 30 cm. – 0 11 090638 1 *£3.00*

The County Borough of Torfaen (Electoral Changes) Order 2002 No. 2002/3279 (W.317). – Enabling power: Local Government Act 1972, ss. 58 (2), 67 (4) (5). – Issued: 18.02.2003. Made: 06.12.2002. Coming into force: In accord. with art. 1 (2). Effect: None. Territorial extent & classification: W. Local. – 8p.: 30 cm. – 0 11 090644 6 *£2.00*

The County of Ceredigion (Electoral Changes) Order 2002 No. 2002/3278 (W.316). – Enabling power: Local Government Act 1972, ss. 58 (2), 67 (4) (5). – Issued: 18.02.2003. Made: 03.12.2002. Coming into force: In accord. with art. 1 (2). Effect: None. Territorial extent & classification: W. Local. – 16p., maps: 30 cm. – 0 11 090643 8 *£5.00*

The County of Gwynedd (Electoral Changes) Order 2002 No. 2002/3274 (W.312). – Enabling power: Local Government Act 1972, ss. 58 (2), 67 (4) (5). – Issued: 30.01.2003. Made: 06.12.2002. Coming into force: In acc. with art. 1 (2). Effect: None. Territorial extent & classification: W. Local. – 12p.: 30 cm. – 0 11 090622 5 *£2.50*

The County of Monmouthshire (Electoral Changes) Order 2002 No. 2002/3275 (W.313). – Enabling power: Local Government Act 1972, ss. 58 (2), 67 (4) (5). – Issued: 05.02.2003. Made: 06.12.2002. Coming into force: In accord. with art. 1 (2). Effect: None. Territorial extent & classification: W. Local. – 12p., maps: 30 cm. – 0 11 090629 2 *£3.75*

The Local Authorities (Allowances for Members of County and County Borough Councils and National Park Authorities) (Wales) Regulations 2002 No. 2002/1895 (W.196). – Enabling power: Local Government and Housing Act 1989, ss. 18 (1) (2) (2A) (3) (3A) (4). – Issued: 27.08.2002. Made: 18.07.2002. Coming into force: 09.08.2002. Effect: S.I. 1991/351 revoked (with saving) in relation to Wales. Territorial extent & classification: W. General. – In English & Welsh. Welsh title: Rheoliadau Awdurdodau Lleol (Lwfansau i Aelodau Cynghorau Sir a Chynghorau Bwrdeistref Sirol ac Awdurdodau Parciau Cenedlaethol) (Cymru) 2002. – 16p.: 30 cm. – 0 11 090558 X *£3.00*

The Local Authorities (Alteration of Requisite Calculations) (Wales) Regulations 2002 No. 2002/328 (W.41). – Enabling power: Local Government Finance Act 1992, ss. 32 (9), 33 (4). – Issued: 06.03.2002. Made: 13.02.2002. Coming into force: 28.02.2002. Effect: 1992 c. 14 amended. Territorial extent & classification: W. General. – In English & Welsh. Welsh title: Rheoliadau Awdurdodau Lleol (Addasu Cyfrifiadau Angenrheidiol) (Cymru) 2002. – 4p.: 30 cm. – 0 11 090434 6 *£1.75*

The Local Authorities (Alternative Arrangements) (Amendment) (Wales) Regulations 2002 No. 2002/810 (W.90). – Enabling power: Local Government Act 2000, ss. 31 (1), 32, 106 (1). – Issued: 07.05.2002. Made: 21.03.2002. Coming into force: 01.04.2002. Effect: S.I. 2001/2284 (W.173) amended. Territorial extent & classification: W. General. – In English & Welsh. Welsh title: Rheoliadau Awdurdodau Lleol (Trefniadau Amgen) (Diwygio) (Cymru) 2002. – 8p.: 30 cm. – 0 11 090482 6 *£2.00*

The Local Authorities (Capital Finance and Approved Investments) (Amendment) (Wales) Regulations 2002 No. 2002/885 (W.100). – Enabling power: Local Government and Housing Act 1989, ss. 58 (9), 66 (1) (a). – Issued: 18.04.2002. Made: 26.03.2002. Coming into force: 01.04.2002. Effect: S.I. 1990/426; 1997/319 amended in relation to Wales. Territorial extent & classification: W. General. – 4p.: 30 cm. – In English and Welsh. Welsh title: Rheoliadau Awdurdodau Lleol (Cyllid Cyfalaf a Buddsoddiadau a Gymeradwywyd) (Diwygio) (Cymru) 2002 – 0 11 090467 2 *£1.75*

The Local Authorities (Capital Finance) (Approved Investments) (Amendment) (No. 2) (Wales) Regulations 2002 No. 2002/1884 (W.193). – Enabling power: Local Government and Housing Act 1989, s. 66 (1) (a). – Issued: 12.08.2002. Made: 18.07.2002. Coming into force: 01.09.2002. Effect: S.I. 1990/426 amended in relation to Wales. Territorial extent & classification: W. General. – 4p.: 30 cm. – In English and Welsh. Welsh title: Rheoliadau Awdurdodau Lleol (Cyllid Cyfalaf a Buddsoddiadau wedi'u Cymeradwyo) (Diwygio) (Rhif 2) (Cymru) 2002 – 0 11 090541 5 *£1.75*

The Local Authorities (Capital Finance) (Rate of Discount for 2002/2003) (Wales) Regulations 2002 No. 2002/785 (W.86). – Enabling power: Local Government and Housing Act 1989, s. 49 (2). – Issued: 19.04.2002. Made: 21.03.2002. Coming into force: 01.04.2002. Effect: None. Territorial extent & classification: W. General. – In English and Welsh. Welsh title: Rheoliadau Awdurdodau Lleol (Cyllid Cyfalaf) (Cyfradd y Disgownt ar gyfer 2002/2003) (Cymru) 2002. – 4p.: 30 cm. – 0 11 090465 6 *£1.75*

The Local Authorities (Companies) (Amendment) (Wales) Order 2002 No. 2002/2118 (W.213). – Enabling power: Local Government and Housing Act 1989, s. 39 (5) to (7). – Issued: 28.08.2002. Made: 18.07.2002. Coming into force: 01.09.2002. Effect: S.I. 1995/849 amended in relation to Wales. Territorial extent & classification: W. General. – 8p.: 30 cm. – In English & Welsh. Welsh title: Gorchymyn Awdurdodau Lleol (Cwmnïau) (Diwygio) (Cymru) 2002. – 0 11 090559 8 *£2.00*

The Local Authorities (Executive and Alternative Arrangements) (Modification of Enactments and Other Provisions) (Wales) Order 2002 No. 2002/808 (W.89). – Enabling power: Local Government Act 2000, ss. 47, 105, 106. – Issued: 24.05.2002. Made: 21.03.2002. Coming into force: 01.04.2002. Effect: 1972 c. 70; 1974 c. 7; 1976 c. 57; 1985 c. 67, c. 72; 1986 c. 10, c. 31; 1987 c. 21; 1988 c. 9, c. 41; 1989 c. 42; 1991 c. 56; 1992 c. 14; 1994 c. 40; 1996 c. 18, c. 31, c. 56; 1997 c. 25; 1998 c. 30; 2000 c. 6; S.I. 1983/1964; 1991/892, 1505; 1992/613; 1994/651 amended. Territorial extent & classification: W. General. – In English & Welsh. Welsh title: Gorchymyn Awdurdodau Lleol (Trefniadau Gweithrediaeth a Threfniadau Amgen) (Addasu Deddfiadau a Darpariaethau Eraill) (Cymru) 2002. – 32p.: 30 cm. – 0 11 090490 7 *£6.00*

The Local Authorities (Executive Arrangements) (Decisions, Documents and Meetings) (Wales) (Amendment) Regulations 2002 No. 2002/1385 (W.135). – Enabling power: Local Government Act 2000, ss. 22 (6) (7) (8) (9) (10) (11) (12), 105, 106. – Issued: 24.05.2002. Made: 16.05.2002. Coming into force: 17.05.2002. Effect: S.I. 2001/2290 (W.178) amended. Territorial extent & classification: W. General. – In English & Welsh. Welsh title: Rheoliadau Awdurdodau Lleol (Trefniadau Gweithrediaeth) (Penderfyniadau, Dogfennau a Chyfarfodydd) (Cymru) (Diwygio) 2002. – 4p.: 30 cm. – 0 11 090493 1 *£1.75*

The Local Authorities (Executive Arrangements) (Discharge of Functions) (Amendment) (Wales) Regulations 2002 No. 2002/2941 (W.282). – Enabling power: Local Government Act 2000, ss. 18 (1) (2), 19 (1) (2) (4) (5) (6), 20 (1) (2), 105 (2), 106 (1) (2). – Issued: 13.12.2002. Made: 27.11.2002. Coming into force: 20.12.2002. Effect: S.I. 2002/802 (W.87) amended. Territorial extent & classification: W. General. – 4p.: 30 cm. – Revoked by S.I. 2003/147 (W.17) (ISBN 0110906322) – In English & Welsh. Welsh title: Rheoliadau Awdurdodau Lleol (Trefniadau Gweithrediaeth) (Cyflawni Swyddogaethau) (Diwygio) (Cymru) 2002. – 0 11 090594 6 *£1.75*

The Local Authorities (Executive Arrangements) (Discharge of Functions) (Wales) Regulations 2002 No. 2002/802 (W.87). – Enabling power: Local Government Act 2000, ss. 18 (1) (2), 19 (1) (2) (4) (5) (6), 20 (1) (2), 105 (2), 106 (1) (2). – Issued: 07.05.2002. Made: 21.03.2002. Coming into force: 01.04.2002. Effect: S.I. 2001/2287 (W.175) revoked. Territorial extent & classification: W. General. – In English & Welsh. Welsh title: Rheoliadau Awdurdodau Lleol (Trefniadau Gweithrediaeth) (Cyflawni Swyddogaethau) (Cymru) 2002. – 12p.: 30 cm. – 0 11 090481 8 *£2.50*

The Local Authorities Executive Arrangements (Functions and Responsibilities) (Amendment) (Wales) Regulations 2002 No. 2002/783 (W.84). – Enabling power: Local Government Act 2000, ss. 13, 105, 106. – Issued: 23.04.2002. Made: 21.03.2002. Coming into force: 01.04.2002. Effect: S.I. 2001/2291 (W.179) amended. Territorial extent & classification: W. General. – In English & Welsh. Welsh title: Rheoliadau Trefniadau Gweithrediaeth Awdurdodau Lleol (Swyddogaethau a Chyfrifoldebau) (Diwygio) (Cymru) 2002. – 2p.: 30 cm. – 0 11 090470 2 *£1.75*

The Local Authorities (Executive Arrangements) (Modification of Enactments and Further Provisions) (Wales) Order 2002 No. 2002/803 (W.88). – Enabling power: Local Government Act 2000, ss. 47, 105, 106 (1). – Issued: 09.05.2002. Made: 21.03.2002. Coming into force: 01.04.2002. Effect: 1972 c.70; 1989 c.42; 2000 c.22 modified. Territorial extent & classification: W. General. – In English & Welsh. Welsh title: Gorchymyn Awdurdodau Lleol (Trefniadau Gweithrediaeth) (Addasu Deddfiadau a Darpariaethau Pellach) (Cymru) 2002. – 8p.: 30 cm. – 0 11 090484 2 *£2.00*

The Local Authorities (Goods and Services) (Public Bodies) (Wales) Order 2002 No. 2002/1729 (W.163). – Enabling power: Local Authorities (Goods and Services) Act 1970, s. 1 (5). – Issued: 01.08.2002. Made: 04.07.2002. Coming into force: 19.07.2002. Effect: None. Territorial extent & classification: W. General. – In English and Welsh. Welsh title: Gorchymyn Awdurdodau Lleol (Nwyddau a Gwasanaethau) (Cyrff Cyhoeddus) (Cymru) 2002. – 4p.: 30 cm. – 0 11 090528 8 *£1.75*

The Local Authorities (Operation of Different Executive or Alternative Arrangements) (Wales) Regulations 2002 No. 2002/2880 (W.276). – Enabling power: Local Government Act 2000, ss. 30 (1), 33 (7), 105 (2), 106 (1). – Issued: 29.11.2002. Made: 20.11.2002. Coming into force: 25.11.2002. Effect: None. Territorial extent & classification: W. General. – In English & Welsh. Welsh title: Rheoliadau Awdurdodau Lleol (Gweithredu Trefniadau Gweithredol neu Amgen Gwahanol) (Cymru) 2002. – [8]p.: 30 cm. – 0 11 090587 3 *£2.00*

The Local Government Act 2000 (Commencement No. 3) (Wales) Order 2002 No. 2002/1359 (C.37). – Enabling power: Local Government Act 2000, s. 108 (3) (7). Bringing into operation various provisions of the 2000 Act on 30.06.2002. – Issued: 29.05.2002. Made: 22.05.2002. Effect: None. Territorial extent & classification: W. General. – 8p.: 30 cm. – 0 11 042250 3 *£2.00*

The Local Government Best Value (Exclusion of Non-commercial Considerations) (Wales) Order 2002 No. 2002/678 (W.75). – Enabling power: Local Government Act 1999, ss. 19 (1) (2), 29. – Issued: 05.04.2002. Made: 12.03.2002. Coming into force: 31.03.2002. Effect: None. Territorial extent & classification: W. General. – 4p.: 30 cm. – In English and Welsh. Welsh title: Gorchymyn Gwerth Gorau Llywodraeth Leol (Hepgor Ystyriaethau Anfasnachol) (Cymru) 2002 – 0 11 090455 9 *£1.75*

The Local Government (Best Value Performance Indicators) (Wales) Order 2002 No. 2002/757 (W.80). – Enabling power: Local Government Act 1999, ss. 4 (1) (a) (2), 29 (1). – Issued: 03.04.2002. Made: 19.03.2002. Coming into force: 01.04.2002. Effect: S.I. 2001/1337 (W.83) revoked. Territorial extent & classification: W. General. – In English and Welsh. Welsh title: Gorchymyn Llywodraeth Leol (Dangosyddion Perfformiad Gwerth Gorau) (Cymru) 2002. – 24p.: 30 cm. – 0 11 090450 8 *£4.00*

The Local Government (Whole Authority Analyses and Improvement Plans) (Wales) Order 2002 No. 2002/886 (W.101). – Enabling power: Local Government Act 1999, ss. 5 (2), 6 (3), 7 (6), 29 (1). – Issued: 18.04.2002. Made: 27.03.2002. Coming into force: 01.04.2002. Effect: S.I. 2000/1271 (W.97) revoked. Territorial extent & classification: W. General. – 4p.: 30 cm. – In English and Welsh. Welsh title: Gorchymyn Llywodraeth Leol (Dadansoddiadau Awdurdodau Cyfan a Chynlluniau Gwella) (Cymru) 2002 – 0 11 090468 0 £1.75

The Neath Port Talbot and Swansea (Trebanos and Clydach) Order 2002 No. 2002/652 (W.69). – Enabling power: Local Government Act 1972, s. 58 (2). – Issued: 07.05.2002. Made: 05.03.2002. Coming into force: 06.04.2002. in accordance with art. 1 (2). Effect: None. Territorial extent & classification: W. General. – In English & Welsh. Welsh title: Gorchymyn Castell-nedd Port Talbot ac Abertawe (Trebannws a Chlydach) 2002. – 8p., maps: 30 cm. – 0 11 090479 6 £2.00

The Newport (Caerleon and Malpas) Order 2002 No. 2002/3271 (W.309). – Enabling power: Local Government Act 1972, s. 58 (2). – Issued: 05.02.2003. Made: 06.12.2002. Coming into force: In accord. with art. 1 (2). Effect: None. Territorial extent & classification: W. Local. – 8p., maps. 30 cm. – In English and Welsh. Welsh title: Gorchymyn Casnewydd (Caerllion a Malpas) 2002 – 0 11 090626 8 £3.00

The Rhondda Cynon Taff and Vale of Glamorgan (Llanharry, Pont-y-clun, Penllyn, Welsh St Donats and Pendoylan) Order 2002 No. 2002/654 (W.70). – Enabling power: Local Government Act 1972, s. 58 (2). – Issued: 07.05.2002. Made: 05.03.2002. Coming into force: 06.03.2002. in accordance with art. 1 (2). Effect: None. Territorial extent & classification: W. General. – In English & Welsh. Welsh title: Gorchymyn Rhondda Cynon Taf a Bro Morgannwg (Llanhari, Pont-y-clun, Penllyn, Llanddunwyd a Phendeulwyn) 2002. – 8p., maps: 30 cm. – 0 11 090480 X £2.00

Local government, Wales: Changes in local government areas

The Bridgend (Cynffig, Cornelly and Pyle Communities) (Electoral Changes) (Amendment) Order 2002 No. 2002/1432 (W.143). – Enabling power: Local Government Act 1992, ss. 58 (2), 67 (4) (5). – Issued: 14.06.2002. Made: 29.04.2002. Coming into force: 02.05.2002. Effect: S.I. 2002/1129 (W.117) amended. Territorial extent & classification: W. General. – 4p.: 30 cm. – 0 11 090501 6 £1.75

The Bridgend (Cynffig, Cornelly and Pyle Communities) (Electoral Changes) Order 2002 No. 2002/1129 (W.117). – Enabling power: Local Government Act 1972, ss. 58 (2), 67 (4) (5). – Issued: 14.06.2002. Made: 28.03.2002. Coming into force: 30.03.2002 for the purposes of art. 1 (2); 02.05.2002 for all other purposes. Effect: None. Territorial extent & classification: W. General. – [16]p., maps: 30 cm. – 0 11 090500 8 £3.40

London government

The Greater London Authority (Allocation of Grants for Precept Calculations) Regulations 2002 No. 2002/267. – Enabling power: Greater London Authority Act 1999, ss. 88 (3) (b), 89 (5) (b). – Issued: 23.04.2002. Made: 11.02.2002. Laid: 12.02.2002. Coming into force: 13.02.2002. Effect: None. Territorial extent & classification: E. General. – 2p.: 30 cm. – 0 11 039347 3 £1.50

The Greater London Authority (Declaration of Acceptance of Office) Order 2002 No. 2002/1044. – Enabling power: Greater London Authority Act 1999, ss. 28, 420 (1) & Local Government Act 2000, ss. 50 (1), 105 (2) (3) (4). – Issued: 21.02.2002. Made: 10.04.2002. Laid: 15.04.2002. Coming into force: 06.05.2002. Effect: S.I. 2001/3575 amended & S.I. 2000/308 revoked. Territorial extent & classification: E. General. – 4p.: 30 cm. – 0 11 039814 9 £1.75

London Service Permits (Appeals) Regulations 2002 No. 2002/614. – Enabling power: Greater London Authority Act 1999, s. 189 (5). – Issued: 18.03.2002. Made: 10.03.2002. Laid: 11.03.2002. Coming into force: 01.04.2002. Effect: None. Territorial extent & classification: E. General. – 2p.: 30 cm. 0 11 039460 7 £1.50

The Transport Act 2000 (Commencement No. 8 and Transitional Provisions) Order 2002 No. 2002/658 (C.16). – Enabling power: Transport Act 2000, ss. 275 (1) (2), 276. Bringing into operation various provisions of the 2000 Act on 01.04.2002. – Issued: 20.03.2002. Made: 10.03.2002. Effect: None. Territorial extent & classification: E/W/S. General. – 8p.: 30 cm. – 0 11 039499 2 £2.00

The Warrant Enforcement Staff Pensions Order 2002 No. 2002/1043. – Enabling power: Greater London Authority Act 1999, ss. 411 (1) (2) (c) (3) (g) (7), 420 (1) (b). – Issued: 18.04.2002. Made: 10.04.2002. Laid: 18.04.2002. Coming into force: 15.05.2002. Effect: None. Territorial extent & classification: E. General. – 2p.: 30 cm. – 0 11 039762 2 £1.50

Magistrates' courts, England and Wales

The Greater London Magistrates' Courts Authority (Pensions) Order 2002 No. 2002/2143. – Enabling power: Justices of the Peace Act 1997, s. 50 & Access to Justice Act 1999, sch. 14, para. 36. – Issued: 28.08.2002. Made: 16.08.2002. Laid: 19.08.2002. Coming into force: 13.09.2002. Effect: 1972 c. 11 amended. Territorial extent & classification: E/W. General. – 2p.: 30 cm. – 0 11 042697 5 £1.50

The Magistrates' Courts (Special Measures Directions) Rules 2002 No. 2002/1687 (L.4). – Enabling power: Magistrates' Courts Act 1980, s. 144 & Youth Justice and Criminal Evidence Act 1999, ss. 20 (6), 65 (1). – Issued: 05.07.2002. Made: 28.06.2002. Laid: 01.07.2002. Coming into force: 24.07.2002. Effect: S.I. 1992/2071 amended. Territorial extent & classification: E/W. General. – 12p.: 30 cm. – 0 11 042429 8 £2.50

Magistrates' courts, England and Wales: Procedure

The Magistrates' Courts (Anti-Social Behaviour Orders) Rules 2002 No. 2002/2784 (L.14). – Enabling power: Magistrates' Courts Act 1980, s. 144. – Issued: 21.11.2002. Made: 08.11.2002. Laid: 11.11.2002. Coming into force: 02.12.2002. Effect: S.I. 1998/2682 (L.10) revoked with savings. Territorial extent & classification: E/W. General. – 8p.: 30 cm. – 0 11 042989 3 *£2.00*

The Magistrates' Courts (Civil Jurisdiction and Judgments Act 1982) (Amendment) Rules 2002 No. 2002/194 (L.1). – Enabling power: Magistrates' Courts Act 1980, s. 144 & Civil Jurisdiction and Judgments Act 1982, s. 48. – Issued: 13.02.2002. Made: 31.01.2002. Laid: 05.02.2002. Coming into force: 01.03.2002. Effect: S.I. 1986/1962 amended. Territorial extent & classification: E/W. General. – EC note: These Rules implement provisions of Council Regulation (EC) no. 44/2001, which comes into force on 1st March 2002. – 4p.: 30 cm. – 0 11 039297 3 *£1.75*

The Magistrates' Courts (Detention and Forfeiture of Cash) Rules 2002 No. 2002/2998 (L.17). – Enabling power: Magistrates' Courts Act 1980, ss. 144, 145 (1) (a). – Issued: 19.12.2002. Made: 02.12.2002. Laid: 09.12.2002. Coming into force: 30.12.2002. Effect: None. Territorial extent & classification: E/W. General. – 16p.: 30 cm. – 0 11 044207 5 *£3.00*

The Magistrates' Courts (Extradition) (Amendment) Rules 2002 No. 2002/1135. – Enabling power: Magistrates' Courts Act 1980, s. 144. – Issued: 25.04.2002. Made: 18.04.2002. Laid: 19.04.2002. Coming into force: 13.05.2002. Effect: S.I. 1989/1597 amended. Territorial extent & classification: E/W. General. – 4p.: 30 cm. – 0 11 039819 X *£1.75*

The Magistrates' Courts (Reciprocal Enforcement of Maintenance Orders) (Amendment) Rules 2002 No. 2002/1734 (L.6). – Enabling power: Magistrates' Courts Act 1980, s. 144 (1). – Issued: 12.07.2002. Made: 07.07.2002. Laid: 08.07.2002. Coming into force: 20.08.2002. Effect: S.I. 1974/668 amended. Territorial extent & classification: E/W. General. – With correction slip dated August 2002. – 2p.: 30 cm. – 0 11 042455 7 *£1.50*

The Magistrates' Courts (Sex Offender Orders) Rules 2002 No. 2002/2782 (L.12). – Enabling power: Magistrates' Courts Act 1980, s. 144. – Issued: 21.11.2002. Made: 07.11.2002. Laid: 11.11.2002. Coming into force: 02.12.2002. Effect: S.I. 1998/2682 (L.10) revoked. Territorial extent & classification: E/W. General. – 8p.: 30 cm. – 0 11 042987 7 *£2.00*

Maintenance of dependants

The Maintenance Orders (Facilities for Enforcement) (Revocation) Order 2002 No. 2002/789. – Enabling power: Maintenance Orders Act 1958, s. 19. – Issued: 03.04.2002. Made: 26.03.2003. Coming into force: 28.05.2002. Effect: S.I. 1959/377 amended (revokes insofar as it extends the Maintenance Orders (Facilities for Enforcement) Act 1920 to Brunei and the territory of Newfoundland). Territorial extent and classification: E/W/S/NI. General. – 2p.: 30 cm. – 0 11 039630 8 *£1.50*

The Reciprocal Enforcement of Maintenance Orders (Designation of Reciprocating Countries) Order 2002 No. 2002/788. – Enabling power: Maintenance Orders (Reciprocal Enforcement) Act 1972, ss. 1, 24. – Issued: 09.04.2002. Made: 26.03.2002. Laid: 09.04.2002. Coming into force: 28.05.2002. Effect: None. Territorial extent & classification: E/W/S/NI. General. – 4p.: 30 cm. – 0 11 039629 4 *£1.75*

The Reciprocal Enforcement of Maintenance Orders (Hague Convention Countries) (Variation) Order 2002 No. 2002/2838. – Enabling power: Maintenance Orders (Reciprocal Enforcement) Act 1972, ss. 40, 45 (1). – Issued: 02.12.2002. Made: 20.11.2002. Laid: 02.12.2002. Coming into force: 15.01.2003. Effect: S.I. 1993/593 amended. Territorial extent & classification: E/W/S/NI. General. – 2p.: 30 cm. – 0 11 043056 5 *£1.50*

The Recovery Abroad of Maintenance (Convention Countries) Order 2002 No. 2002/2839. – Enabling power: Maintenance Orders (Reciprocal Enforcement) Asct 1972, ss. 25 (1), 45 (1). – Issued: 26.11.2002. Made: 20.11.2002. Coming into force: 15.01.2003. Effect: S.I. 1975/423 amended. Territorial extent & classification: E/W/S/NI. General. – 2p.: 30 cm. – 0 11 043057 3 *£1.50*

Medical profession

The European Specialist Medical Qualifications Amendment Regulations 2002 No. 2002/849. – Enabling power: European Communities Act 1972, s. 2 (2). – Issued: 26.04.2002. Made: 26.03.2002. Laid: 27.03.2002. Coming into force: 17.04.2002. Effect: S.I. 1995/3208 amended. Territorial extent & classification: E/W/S/NI. General. – 2p.: 30 cm. – 0 11 039818 1 *£1.50*

The General Medical Council (Fitness to Practise Committees) (Amendment) Rules Order of Council 2002 No. 2002/2572. – Enabling power: Medical Act 1983, sch. 1, paras. 19A, 20, 21, 21A, 21B, 22, sch. 4, paras. 1, 5, 5A 1) (2) (3). – Issued: 18.10.2002. Made: 10.10.2002. Laid: 11.10.2002. Coming into force: 01.11.2002. Effect: S.I. 1987/2174; 1988/2255; 1996/2125; 1997/1529: 2000/2052, 2053 amended. Territorial extent & classification: E/W/S/NI. General. – 8p.: 30 cm. – 0 11 042854 4 *£2.00*

Medical profession, England

The Abortion (Amendment) (England) Regulations 2002 No. 2002/887. – Enabling power: Abortion Act 1967, s. 2. – Issued: 12.04.2002. Made: 27.03.2002. Laid: 28.03.2002. Coming into force: 18.04.2002. Effect: S.I. 1991/499 amended. Territorial extent & classification: E. General. – 4p.: 30 cm. – 0 11 039719 3 *£1.75*

Medical profession, Wales

The Abortion (Amendment) (Wales) Regulations 2002 No. 2002/2879 (W.275). – Enabling power: Abortion Act 1967, s. 2. – Issued: 29.11.2002. Made: 20.11.2002. Coming into force: 17.12.2002. Effect: S.I. 1991/499 amended in relation to Wales. Territorial extent & classification: W. General. – 8p.: 30 cm. – 0 11 090586 5 *£2.00*

Medicines

The Health and Social Care Act 2001 (Commencement No. 8) Order 2002 No. 2002/1095 (C.26). – Enabling power: Health and Social Care Act 2001, ss. 64 (6) (8), 70 (2). Bringing into force various provisions of the 2001 Act on 06.03.2002, 08.03.2002, 01.04.2002, 31.05.2002 in accord. with art. 2. – Issued: 24.04.2002. Made: 05.03.2002. Effect: None. Territorial extent & classification: E/W/S/NI. General. – 4p.: 30 cm. – 0 11 039784 3 *£1.75*

The Marketing Authorisations for Veterinary Medicinal Products (Amendment) Regulations 2002 No. 2002/269. – Enabling power: European Communities Act 1972, s. 2 (2). – Issued: 18.04.2002. Made: 10.02.2002. Laid: 12.02.2002. Coming into force: 10.03.2002. Effect: S.I. 1994/3142 amended. Territorial extent & classification: E/W/S/NI. General. – EC note: Implement parts of EC DIR 2001/82/EC. – 8p: 30 cm. – 0 11 039763 0 *£2.00*

The Medicated Feedingstuffs (Amendment) (England, Scotland and Wales) Regulations 2002 No. 2002/697. – Enabling power: European Communities Act 1972, s. 2 (2). – Issued: 25.04.2002. Made: 14.03.2002. Laid: 15.03.2002. Coming into force: 31.03.2002. Effect: S.I. 1990/1046 amended in relation to England, Scotland and Wales. Territorial extent & classification: E/W/S. General. – 4p.: 30 cm. – 0 11 039828 9 *£1.75*

The Medicines (Codification Amendments Etc.) Regulations 2002 No. 2002/236. – Enabling power: European Communities Act 1972, s. 2 (2). – Issued: 26.02.2002. Made: 07.02.2002. Laid: 07.02.2002. Coming into force: 28.02.2002. Effect: 1968 c.67 & S.I. 1971/972, 974; 1976/1726; 1992/3146; 1993/2538; 1994/105, 1932, 1933, 2987, 3107, 3144; 1995/309, 449, 1116; 2000/123, 1763; 2001/1422, 3798 amended. Territorial extent & classification: E/W/S/NI. General. – 12p.: 30 cm. – EC note: Makes consequential amendments to the references in the Medicines Act 1968 & various statutory instruments relating to medicinal products and devices following the adoption of directive 2001/83/EC & implements Commission directive 2000/38/EC amending Chapter Va of Council directive 75/319/EEC – 0 11 039373 2 *£2.50*

The Medicines for Human Use and Medical Devices (Fees and Miscellaneous Amendments) Regulations 2002 No. 2002/542. – Enabling power: European Communities Act 1972, s. 2 (2) & Finance Act 1973, s. 56 (1) (2) & Medicines Act 1971, s. 1 (1) (2). – Issued: 12.04.2002. Made: 11.03.2002. Laid: 11.03.2002. Coming into force: 01.04.2002. Effect: S.I. 1994/105, 3144; 1995/449, 1116 amended. Territorial extent & classification: E/W/S/NI. General. – 16p.: 30 cm. – 0 11 039673 1 *£3.00*

Medicines (Products for Animal Use - Fees) (Amendment) Regulations 2002 No. 2002/2569. – Enabling power: Medicines Act 1971, s. 1 (1) (2) (3) (b) & European Communities Act 1972, s. 2 (2). – Issued: 04.11.2002. Made: 10.10.2002. Laid: 11.10.2002. Coming into force: 01.11.2002. Effect: S.I. 1998/2428 amended. Territorial extent & classification: UK. General. – 9, [1]p.: 30 cm. – 0 11 042929 X *£2.50*

The Medicines (Products Other Than Veterinary Drugs) (General Sale List) Amendment Order 2002 No. 2002/933. – Enabling power: Medicines Act 1968, ss. 51, 129 (4). – Issued: 12.04.2002. Made: 11.03.2002. Coming into force: 01.04.2002. Effect: S.I. 1984/769 amended. Territorial extent & classification: E/W/S/NI. General. – 4p.: 30 cm. – 0 11 039672 3 *£1.75*

The Prescription Only Medicines (Human Use) Amendment Order 2002 No. 2002/549. – Enabling power: Medicines Act 1968, ss. 58 (1) (4) (4A) (5), 59, 103 (2), 129 (4). – Issued: 12.04.2002. Made: 07.03.2002. Laid: 11.03.2002. Coming into force: 01.04.2002. Effect: S.I. 1997/1830 amended. Territorial extent & classification: E/W/S/NI. General. – 12p.: 30 cm. – 0 11 039674 X *£2.50*

Medicines, England

The Medicines for Human Use (Kava-kava) (Prohibition) Order 2002 No. 2002/3170. – Enabling power: Medicines Act 1968, s. 62 (1) (a) (2). – Issued: 23.12.2002. Made: 18.12.2002. Laid: 23.12.2002. Coming into force: 13.01.2003. Effect: None. Territorial extent & classification: E/NI. General. – 4p.: 30 cm. – 0 11 044246 6 *£1.75*

The Medicines (Pharmacies) (Applications for Registration and Fees) Amendment Regulations 2002 No. 2002/3024. – Enabling power: Medicines Act 1968, ss. 75 (1), 76 (1) (2) (6), 129 (5). – Issued: 10.12.2002. Made: 05.12.2002. Laid: 06.12.2002. Coming into force: 01.01.2003. Effect: S.I. 1973/1822 amended & S.I. 2001/3964 revoked. Territorial extent & classification: E/NI. General. – 4p.: 30 cm. – 0 11 044168 0 £1.75

Medicines, England and Wales

The Health and Social Care Act 2001 (Commencement No. 8) (Amendment) Order 2002 No. 2002/1170 (C.30). – Enabling power: Health and Social Care Act 2001, ss. 64 (6) (8), 70 (2). – Issued: 30.04.2002. Made: 26.03.2002. Effect: S.I. 2002/1095 (C.26) amended. Territorial extent & classification: E/W. General. – 2p.: 30 cm. – 0 11 039848 3 £1.50

Medicines, Northern Ireland

The Medicines for Human Use (Kava-kava) (Prohibition) Order 2002 No. 2002/3170. – Enabling power: Medicines Act 1968, s. 62 (1) (a) (2). – Issued: 23.12.2002. Made: 18.12.2002. Laid: 23.12.2002. Coming into force: 13.01.2003. Effect: None. Territorial extent & classification: E/NI. General. – 4p.: 30 cm. – 0 11 044246 6 £1.75

The Medicines (Pharmacies) (Applications for Registration and Fees) Amendment Regulations 2002 No. 2002/3024. – Enabling power: Medicines Act 1968, ss. 75 (1), 76 (1) (2) (6), 129 (5). – Issued: 10.12.2002. Made: 05.12.2002. Laid: 06.12.2002. Coming into force: 01.01.2003. Effect: S.I. 1973/1822 amended & S.I. 2001/3964 revoked. Territorial extent & classification: E/NI. General. – 4p.: 30 cm. – 0 11 044168 0 £1.75

Mental health, England and Wales

The Court of Protection (Amendment) Rules 2002 No. 2002/833. – Enabling power: Mental Health Act 1983, ss.106, 107, 108. – Issued: 12.04.2002. Made: 26.03.2002. Laid: 27.03.2002. Coming into force: 17.04.2002. Effect: S.I. 2001/824 amended. Territorial extent & classification: E/W. General. – 4p.: 30 cm. – 0 11 039731 2 £1.75

The Court of Protection (Enduring Powers of Attorney) (Amendment No. 2) Rules 2002 No. 2002/1944. – Enabling power: Mental Health Act 1983, ss. 106, 108. – Issued: 02.08.2002. Made: 23.07.2002. Laid: 26.07.2002. Coming into force: 31.08.2002. Effect: S.I. 2001/825 amended. Territorial extent & classification: E/W. General. – 12p.: 30 cm. – 0 11 042581 2 £2.50

The Court of Protection (Enduring Powers of Attorney) (Amendment) Rules 2002 No. 2002/832. – Enabling power: Mental Health Act 1983, ss. 106, 107, 108. – Issued: 12.04.2002. Made: 26.03.2002. Laid: 27.03.2002. Coming into force: 17.04.2002. Effect: S.I. 2001/825 amended. Territorial extent & classification: E/W. General. – 4p.: 30 cm. – 0 11 039730 4 £1.75

Merchant shipping

The Merchant Shipping (Confirmation of Legislation) (Bermuda) Order 2002 No. 2002/3132. – Enabling power: Merchant Shipping Act 1894, s. 735 (1). – Issued: 06.01.2003. Made: 17.12.2002. Laid: 06.01.2003. Coming into force: In accord.with art. 1. Effect: None. Territorial extent & classification: E/W/S/NI. General. – 2p.: 30 cm. – 0 11 044249 0 £1.50

The Merchant Shipping (Hours of Work) Regulations 2002 No. 2002/2125. – Enabling power: European Communities Act 1972, s. 2 (2) & Merchant Shipping Act 1995 ss. 85 (1) (a) (b) (3) (5) (7), 86 (1) (2). – Issued: 21.08.2002. Made: 13.08.2002. Laid: 14.08.2002. Coming into force: 07.09.2002. Effect: 1995 c. 21 & S.I. 1993/1213; 1997/1320; 1998/2411 amended. Territorial extent & classification: E/W/S/NI. General. – [12]p.: 30 cm. – EC note: These Regs. implement the majority of the provisions of Council Directive 1999/63/EC concerning the agreement on the organisation of working time of seafarers, and the European Parliament and Council Directive 1999/95/EC concerning the enforcement of provisions in respect of seafarers' hours of work on board ships calling at Community ports – 0 11 042666 5 £2.50

The Merchant Shipping (Light Dues) (Amendment) Regulations 2002 No. 2002/504. – Enabling power: Merchant Shipping Act 1995, s. 205 (5). – Issued: 15.03.2002. Made: 06.03.2002. Laid: 08.03.2002. Coming into force: 01.04.2002. Effect: S.I. 1997/562 amended. Territorial extent & classification: E/W/S/NI. General. – 2p.: 30 cm. – 0 11 039457 7 £1.50

The Merchant Shipping (Medical Examination) Regulations 2002 No. 2002/2055. – Enabling power: Merchant Shipping Act 1995, s. 85 (1) (a) (b) (3) (5) (7), 86 (1). – Issued: 13.08.2002. Made: 04.08.2002. Laid: 06.08.2002. Coming into force: 01.09.2002. Effect: S.I. 1983/808; 1985/512; 1990/1985 revoked. Territorial extent & classification: E/W/S/NI. General. – 8p.: 30 cm. – 0 11 042642 8 £2.00

The Merchant Shipping (Revocation) (Bermuda) Order 2002 No. 2002/3147. – Enabling power: Carriage of Goods by Sea Act 1971, s. 4 (1) (a) (3) & Merchant Shipping Act 1995, ss. 128 (1), 141 (1), 147 (3), 315 (2). – Issued: 27.12.2002. Made: 17.12.2002. Coming into force: In accord.with art. 1. Effect: S.I. 1973/1315, 1316; 1975/412; 1980/1510, 1520, 1521, 1522; 1982/1662, 1667; 1988/788; 1991/1703; 1992/2668; 1997/2581 revoked. Territorial extent & classification: E/W/S/NI. General. – 2p.: 30 cm. – 0 11 044274 1 £1.50

Merchant shipping: Safety

The Fishing Vessels (Safety of 15-24 Metre Vessels) Regulations 2002 No. 2002/2201. – Enabling power: Merchant Shipping Act 1995, ss. 43, 85 (1) (a) (3) (5) (7), 86 (1) (2), 307 & European Communities Act 1972, s. 2 (2). – Issued: 03.09.2002. Made: 21.08.2002. Laid: 23.08.2002. Coming into force: 23.11.2002. Effect: S.I. 1975/330, 2220; 1988/38; 1999/3210; 2001/9 amended. Territorial extent & classification: E/W/S/NI. General. – 12p.: 30 cm. – 0 11 042712 2 *£2.50*

The Merchant Shipping (Diving Safety) Regulations 2002 No. 2002/1587. – Enabling power: Merchant Shipping Act 1995, s. 88 (2), sch. 2. – Issued: 27.06.2002. Made: 13.06.2002. Laid: 17.06.2002. Coming into force: 01.09.2002. Effect: S.I. 1975/116, 2062 revoked. Territorial extent & classification: E/W/S/NI. General. – 12p.: 30 cm. – 0 11 042377 1 *£2.50*

The Merchant Shipping (Miscellaneous Amendments) Regulations 2002 No. 2002/1650. – Enabling power: Merchant Shipping Act 1995, ss. 85 (1) (a) (b) (3) (5) TO (7), 86 (1). – Issued: 08.07.2002. Made: 25.06.2002. Laid: 01.07.2002. Coming into force: 01.08.2002. Effect: S.I. 1998/2514, 2515 amended. Territorial extent & classification: E/W/S/NI. General. – 4p.: 30 cm. – This S.I. has been made in consequence of defects in S.I. 1998/2514 and S.I. 1998/2515 and is being issued free of charge to all known recipients of those SIs – 0 11 042422 0 *£1.75*

The Merchant Shipping (Safety of Navigation) Regulations 2002 No. 2002/1473. – Enabling power: Merchant Shipping Act 1995, ss. 77, 85 (1) (a) (b) (3) (5) to (7), 86 (1) (2) (a). – Issued: 18.06.2002. Made: 31.05.2002. Laid: 31.05.2002. Coming into force: 01.07.2002. Effect: 1995 c. 21; S.I. 1981/569, 570; 1995/1210; 1998/1691, 2771; 1999/2721; 2000/2687; 2002/1473 amended & S.I. 1981/571; 1992/2357; 1993/69; 1996/1749, 1815; 1997/1341, 2886; 1998/1419, 1692, 2647; 1999/17 revoked. Territorial extent & classification: E/W/S/NI. General. – 16p.: 30 cm. – 0 11 042349 6 *£3.00*

Ministers of the Crown

The Ministry of Agriculture, Fisheries and Food (Dissolution) Order 2002 No. 2002/794. – Enabling power: Ministers of the Crown Act 1975, s. 1. – Issued: 04.04.2002. Made: 26.03.2002. Coming into force: 27.03.02. Effect: 52 & 53 Vict. c. 30; 3 Edw. 7 c. 31; 9 Edw. 7 c. 15; 9 & 10 Geo. 5 c. 91; 12 & 13 Geo. 5 c. 16; 15 & 16 Geo. 5 c. 18; 9 & 10 Eliz. 2 c. 6; 1922 c. 16; 1925 c. 18, 21; 1949 c. 69; 1958 c. 51; 1964 c. 83; 1967 c. 10, 13; 1968 c. 67; 1970 c. 21; 1972 c. 66; 1974 c. 37; 1975 c. 24, 27; 1976 c. 70; 1979 c. 13; 1981 c. 22, 69; 1983 c. 30, 47; 1985 c. 12; 1986 c. 5, 49; 1988 c. 1, 16, 22; 1990 c. 8, 16; 1991 c. 54, 56; 1992 c. 51; 1995 c. 21; 1996 c. 18; 1999 c. 28; 2000 c. 23, 33, 37, 40; S.I. 1999/1820; 2000/181, 1081, 2417 amended. Territorial extent & classification: E/W/S. General. – Supersedes draft S.I. (ISBN 011039156X) issued 16 January 2002. – 16p.: 30 cm. – 0 11 039635 9 *£3.00*

The Secretaries of State for Education and Skills and for Work and Pensions Order 2002 No. 2002/1397. – Enabling power: Ministers of the Crown Act 1975, ss. 1, 2. – Issued: 28.05.2002. Made: 22.05.2002. Laid: 06.06.2002. Coming into force: 27.06.2002. Effect: 1958 ch. 16, 49; 1960 ch. 66; 1967 ch. 13; 1975 ch. xxx; 1988 ch. 1; 1992 ch. 4, 5; 1993 ch. 48; 1994 ch. 9, 23; 1995 ch. 18; 1996 ch. 50; 1998 ch. 31; 1999 ch. 10; 2000 ch. 23; S.I. 1981/1685; 1987/1968; 1987/1971; 1988/662; 1992/1814, 2182; 1993/494, 743, 744; 1996/207, 2570, 2891, 3195; 1997/2847; 1998/562, 3186; 1999/2277 amended. Territorial extent & classification: E/W/S/NI. General. – 16p.: 30 cm. – 0 11 042244 9 *£3.00*

The Transfer of Functions (Civil Defence) Order 2002 No. 2002/2633. – Enabling power: Ministers of the Crown Act 1975, s. 1. – Issued: 04.11.2002. Made: 22.10.2002. Laid: 04.11.2002. Coming into force: 25.11.2002. Effect: None. Territorial extent & classification: GB. General. – 2p.: 30 cm. – 0 11 042898 6 *£1.50*

Ministers of the Crown, England and Wales

The Transfer of Functions (Transport, Local Government and the Regions) Order 2002 No. 2002/2626. – Enabling power: Ministers of the Crown Act 1975, ss. 1, 2. – Issued: 04.11.2002. Made: 22.10.2002. Laid: 04.11.2002. Coming into force: 25.11.2002. Effect: 1949 c. 69; 1962 c. 46; 1964 c. 83; 1967 c. 13; 1968 c. 73; 1970 c. 69; 1971 c. 23; 1973 c. 41; 1980 c. 65; 1983 c. 2; 1984 c. 27; 1985 c. 50; 1986 c. 31, 56; 1990 c. 8, 9, 10; 1991 c. 57, 59; 1992 c. 42; 1996 c. 61; 1997 c. 8; 2000 c. 23, 41; 2001 c. 5; 2002 c. 24; S.I. 1999/672; 2001/2568 amended. Territorial extent & classification: E/W. General. – 16p.: 30 cm. – 0 11 042896 X *£3.00*

National assistance services, England

The National Assistance (Assessment of Resources) (Amendment) (England) Regulations 2002 No. 2002/410. – Enabling power: National Assistance Act 1948, s. 22 (5). – Issued: 15.03.2002. Made: 24.02.2002. Laid: 26.02.2002. Coming into force: 08.04.2002. Effect: S.I. 1992/2977; 2001/1066 amended. Territorial extent & classification: E. General. – 2p.: 30 cm. – 0 11 039449 6 *£1.50*

The National Assistance (Assessment of Resources) (Amendment) (No. 2) (England) Regulations 2002 No. 2002/2531. – Enabling power: National Assistance Act 1948, s. 22 (5). – Issued: 14.10.2002. Made: 08.10.2002. Laid: 08.10.2002. Coming into force: 14.10.02 & 28.10.02 in accord. with reg. 1. Effect: S.I. 1992/2977 amended. Territorial extent & classification: E. General. – 4p.: 30 cm. – 0 11 042852 8 *£1.75*

The National Assistance (Sums for Personal Requirements) (England) Regulations 2002 No. 2002/411. – Enabling power: National Assistance Act 1948, s. 22 (4). – Issued: 15.03.2002. Made: 24.02.2002. Laid: 26.02.2002. Coming into force: 08.04.2002. Effect: S.I. 2001/1005 revoked. Territorial extent & classification: E. General. – 2p.: 30 cm. – Revoked by S.I. 2003/628 (ISBN 0110455312) – 0 11 039450 X *£1.50*

National assistance services, Wales

The National Assistance (Assessment of Resources) (Amendment) (Wales) Regulations 2002 No. 2002/814 (W.94). – Enabling power: National Assistance Act 1948, s. 22 (5). – Issued: 26.04.2002. Made: 22.03.2002. Coming into force: 08.04.2002. Effect: S.I. 1992/2977 amended in relation to Wales. Territorial extent & classification: W. General. – 4p.: 30 cm. – In English & Welsh. Welsh title: Rheoliadau Cymorth Gwladol (Asesu Adnoddau) (Diwygio) (Cymru) 2002 – Revoked by S.I. 2003/897 (W.117) (ISBN 0110907116) – 0 11 090471 0 *£1.75*

The National Assistance (Sums for Personal Requirements) (Wales) Regulations 2002 No. 2002/815 (W.95). – Enabling power: National Assistance Act 1948, s. 22 (4). – Issued: 26.04.2002. Made: 22.03.2002. Coming into force: 08.04.2002. Effect: S.I. 2001/1408 (W.94) revoked. Territorial extent & classification: W. General. – 4p.: 30 cm. – In English & Welsh. Welsh title: Rheoliadau Cymorth Gwladol (Symiau at Anghenion Personol) (Cymru) 2002 – Revoked by S.I. 2003/892 (W.112) (ISBN 0110907108) – 0 11 090472 9 *£1.75*

National debt

The Irish Registers of Government Stock (Closure and Transfer) Order 2002 No. 2002/2521. – Enabling power: Finance Act 2002, s. 139. – Issued: 25.11.2002. Made: 14.10.2002. Laid: 14.10.2002. Coming into force: in accordance with art. 1. Effect: 1870 c.7; 1891 c,39; 1892 c.39; 1915 c.89; 1916 c.24; 1937 c.54; 1942 c.21; 1955 c.6; 1964 c.49; 1968 c.13; 1975 c.45; 1988 c.1 & S.I. 1965/1420, 1562, 2167; 1979/1678; 1998/1749 amended. Territorial extent and classification: E/W/S/NI. General. – 8p.: 30 cm. – With correction slip, dated January 2003 – 0 11 043010 7 *£2.00*

National Health Service

The Health and Social Care Act 2001 (Commencement No. 8) Order 2002 No. 2002/1095 (C.26). – Enabling power: Health and Social Care Act 2001, ss. 64 (6) (8), 70 (2). Bringing into force various provisions of the 2001 Act on 06.03.2002, 08.03.2002, 01.04.2002, 31.05.2002 in accord. with art. 2. – Issued: 24.04.2002. Made: 05.03.2002. Effect: None. Territorial extent & classification: E/W/S/NI. General. – 4p.: 30 cm. – 0 11 039784 3 *£1.75*

National Health Service, England

The Adur, Arun and Worthing Primary Care Trust (Establishment) Order 2002 No. 2002/989. – Enabling power: National Health Service Act 1977, ss. 16A (1) (2) (3), 126 (4), sch. 5A, para. 1. – Issued: 10.04.2002. Made: 25.03.2002. Coming into force: 01.04.2002. Effect: None. Territorial extent & classification: E. General. – 2p.: 30 cm. – 0 11 039704 5 *£1.50*

The Ashford Primary Care Trust (Establishment) Order 2002 No. 2002/992. – Enabling power: National Health Service Act 1977, ss. 16A (1) (2) (3), 126 (4), sch. 5A, para. 1. – Issued: 10.04.2002. Made: 25.03.2002. Coming into force: 01.04.2002. Effect: None. Territorial extent & classification: E. General. – 2p.: 30 cm. – 0 11 039709 6 *£1.50*

The Ashworth Hospital Authority (Abolition) Order 2002 No. 2002/559. – Enabling power: National Health Service Act 1977, ss. 11, 126 (4). – Issued: 09.05.2002. Made: 10.03.2002. Laid: 11.03.2002. Coming into force: 01.04.2002. Effect: S.I. 1996/488, 489 revoked. Territorial extent & classification: E. General. – 4p.: 30 cm. – 0 11 039887 4 *£1.75*

The Avon, Gloucestershire and Wiltshire Health Authority (Transfer of Trust Property) Order 2002 No. 2002/2281. – Enabling power: National Health Service Act 1977, ss. 92 (1), 126 (4). – Issued: 16.09.2002. Made: 04.09.2002. Laid: 05.09.2002. Coming into force: 30.09.2002. Effect: None. Territorial extent & classification: E. General. – 4p.: 30 cm. – 0 11 042761 0 *£1.75*

The Barnet, Enfield and Haringey Health Authority (Transfer of Trust Property) Order 2002 No. 2002/847. – Enabling power: National Health Service Act 1977, ss. 92 (1) (4), 126 (4). – Issued: 06.06.2002. Made: 26.03.2002. Laid: 28.03.2002. Coming into force: 01.04.2002. Effect: None. Territorial extent & classification: E. General. – 2p.: 30 cm. – 0 11 042302 X *£1.50*

The Barnsley Community and Priority Services National Health Service Trust (Dissolution) Order 2002 No. 2002/1294. – Enabling power: National Health Service Act 1977, s. 126 (3) & National Health Service and Community Care Act 1990, s. 5 (1), sch. 2, para. 29 (1). – Issued: 16.05.2002. Made: 21.03.2002. Coming into force: 01.04.2002. Effect: S.I. 1991/2323 revoked. Territorial extent & classification: E. General. – 2p.: 30 cm. – 0 11 039937 4 *£1.50*

The Barnsley Community and Priority Services National Health Service Trust (Transfer of Trust Property) Order 2002 No. 2002/631. – Enabling power: National Health Service Act 1977, ss. 92 (1), 126 (4). – Issued: 26.03.2002. Made: 08.03.2002. Laid: 11.03.2002. Coming into force: 01.04.2002. Effect: None. Territorial extent & classification: E. General. – 2p.: 30 cm. – 0 11 039579 4 *£1.50*

The Basildon and Thurrock General Hospitals National Health Service Trust (Change of Name) Order 2002 No. 2002/2617. – Enabling power: National Health Service Act 1977, s. 126 (3) & National Health Service and Community Care Act 1990, s. 5 (1), sch. 2, paras. 1, 3. – Issued: 18.10.2002. Made: 15.10.2002. Coming into force: 18.10.2002. Effect: S.I. 1991/2325 amended. Territorial extent & classification: E. General. – 2p.: 30 cm. – 0 11 042881 1 *£1.50*

The Birkenhead and Wallasey Primary Care Trust (Establishment) Order 2002 No. 2002/728. – Enabling power: National Health Service Act 1977, ss. 16A (1) (2) (3), 126 (4), sch. 5A, paras. 1, 2. – Issued: 25.03.2002. Made: 26.02.2002. Coming into force: 06.03.2002. Effect: None. Territorial extent & classification: E. General. – 4p.: 30 cm. – 0 11 039550 6 £1.75

The Birmingham and the Black Country Health Authority (Transfer of Trust Property) Order 2002 No. 2002/2269. – Enabling power: National Health Service Act 1977, ss. 92 (1), 126 (4). – Issued: 16.09.2002. Made: 04.09.2002. Laid: 05.09.2002. Coming into force: 30.09.2002. Effect: None. Territorial extent & classification: E. General. – 2p.: 30 cm. – 0 11 042766 1 £1.50

The Birmingham Health Authority (Transfer of Trust Property) Order 2002 No. 2002/600. – Enabling power: National Health Service Act 1977, ss. 92 (1), 126 (4). – Issued: 31.05.2002. Made: 08.03.2002. Laid: 11.03.2002. Coming into force: 01.04.2002. Effect: None. Territorial extent & classification: E. General. – 2p.: 30 cm. – 0 11 042272 4 £1.50

The Birmingham Specialist Community Health NHS Trust (Transfer of Trust Property) Order 2002 No. 2002/607. – Enabling power: National Health Service Act 1977, ss. 92 (1), 126 (4). – Issued: 26.03.2002. Made: 08.03.2002. Laid: 11.03.2002. Coming into force: 01.04.2002. Effect: None. Territorial extent & classification: E. General. – 2p.: 30 cm. – 0 11 039577 8 £1.50

The Blackpool, Fylde and Wyre Hospitals National Health Service Trust (Establishment) and the Blackpool, Wyre and Fylde Community Health Services National Health Service Trust and the Blackpool Victoria Hospital National Health Service Trust (Dissolution) Order 2002 No. 2002/1243. – Enabling power: National Health Service Act 1977, s. 126 (3) & National Health Service and Community Care Act 1990, s. 5 (1), sch. 2, paras. 1, 3, 4, 5, 29 (1). – Issued: 10.05.2002. Made: 24.03.2002. Coming into force: 01.04.2002. Effect: S.I. 1993/2597, 2598 revoked. Territorial extent & classification: E. General. – 4p.: 30 cm. – 0 11 039892 0 £1.75

The Bootle and Litherland Primary Care Trust (Establishment) Amendment Order 2002 No. 2002/1133. – Enabling power: National Health Service Act 1977, ss. 16A (1) (2) (3), 126 (3) (4), sch. 5A, para. 1. – Issued: 22.04.2002. Made: 24.03.2002. Coming into force: 01.04.2002. Effect: S.I. 2001/437 amended. Territorial extent & classification: E. General. – 2p.: 30 cm. – 0 11 039812 2 £1.50

The Bournewood Community and Mental Health National Health Service Trust Change of Name Order 2002 No. 2002/1338. – Enabling power: National Health Service Act 1977, s. 126 (3) (4) & National Health Service and Community Care Act 1990, s. 5 (1). – Issued: 21.05.2002. Made: 25.03.2002. Coming into force: 01.04.2002. Effect: S.I. 1994/3173 amended. Territorial extent & classification: E. General. – 2p.: 30 cm. – 0 11 039956 0 £1.50

The Bradford Community Health National Health Service Trust (Transfer of Trust Property) Order 2002 No. 2002/866. – Enabling power: National Health Service Act 1977, ss. 92 (1), 126 (4). – Issued: 27.05.2002. Made: 27.03.2002. Laid: 28.03.2002. Coming into force: 01.04.2002. Effect: None. Territorial extent & classification: E. General. – 2p.: 30 cm. – 0 11 042231 7 £1.50

The Bradford District Care Trust (Establishment) and the Bradford Community Health National Health Service Trust (Dissolution) Order 2002 No. 2002/1322. – Enabling power: National Health Service Act 1977, s. 126 (3) & National Health Service and Community Care Act 1990, s. 5 (1), sch. 2, paras. 3, 4, 29 (1) & Health and Social Care Act 2001, s. 45 (5). – Issued: 20.05.2002. Made: 19.03.2002. Coming into force: 01.04.2002. Effect: S.I. 1991/2330 revoked. Territorial extent & classification: E. General. – 4p.: 30 cm. – 0 11 039946 3 £1.75

The Brent & Harrow Health Authority (Transfer of Trust Property) Order 2002 No. 2002/573. – Enabling power: National Health Service Act 1977, ss. 92 (1), 126 (4). – Issued: 25.03.2002. Made: 08.03.2002. Laid: 11.03.2002. Coming into force: 01.04.2002. Effect: None. Territorial extent & classification: E. General. – 2p.: 30 cm. – 0 11 039533 6 £1.50

The Brent, Kensington, Chelsea and Westminster Mental Health National Health Service Trust Change of Name and (Establishment) Amendment Order 2002 No. 2002/1361. – Enabling power: National Health Service Act 1977, s. 126 (3) (4) & National Health Service and Community Care Act 1990, s. 5 (1). – Issued: 23.05.2002. Made: 22.03.2002. Coming into force: 01.04.2002. Effect: S.I. 1998/2966 amended. Territorial extent & classification: E. General. – 2p.: 30 cm. – 0 11 039969 2 £1.50

The Brent Primary Care Trust (Establishment) Order 2002 No. 2002/1005. – Enabling power: National Health Service Act 1977, ss. 16A (1) (2) (3), 126 (4), sch. 5A, para. 1. – Issued: 12.04.2002. Made: 20.03.2002. Coming into force: 01.04.2002. Effect: None. Territorial extent & classification: E. General. – 2p.: 30 cm. – 0 11 039734 7 £1.50

The Brighton and Hove City Primary Care Trust (Establishment) Order 2002 No. 2002/991. – Enabling power: National Health Service Act 1977, ss. 16A (1) (2) (3), 126 (4), sch. 5A, para. 1. – Issued: 10.04.2002. Made: 25.03.2002. Coming into force: 01.04.2002. Effect: None. Territorial extent & classification: E. General. – 2p.: 30 cm. – 0 11 039707 X £1.50

The Brighton and Sussex University Hospitals National Health Service Trust (Establishment) and the Mid Sussex National Health Service Trust (Dissolution) Order 2002 No. 2002/1363. – Enabling power: National Health Service Act 1977, s. 126 (3) & National Health Service and Community Care Act 1990, s. 5 (1), sch. 2, paras. 1, 3, 29 (1). – Issued: 23.05.2002. Made: 25.03.2002. Coming into force: 01.04.2002. Effect: S.I. 1994/165 revoked. Territorial extent & classification: E. General. – 4p.: 30 cm. – Revoked by S.I. 2003/868 (ISBN 0110454774) – 0 11 039965 X £1.75

The Buckinghamshire Health Authority (Transfer of Trust Property) No. 2 Order 2002 No. 2002/861. – Enabling power: National Health Service Act 1977, ss. 92 (1), 126 (4). – Issued: 06.06.2002. Made: 26.03.2002. Laid: 28.03.2002. Coming into force: 01.04.2002. Effect: None. Territorial extent & classification: E. General. – 2p.: 30 cm. – 0 11 042287 2
£1.50

The Buckinghamshire Health Authority (Transfer of Trust Property) No. 3 Order 2002 No. 2002/862. – Enabling power: National Health Service Act 1977, ss. 92 (1), 126 (4). – Issued: 06.06.2002. Made: 26.03.2002. Laid: 28.03.2002. Coming into force: 01.04.2002. Effect: None. Territorial extent & classification: E. General. – 2p.: 30 cm. – 0 11 042303 8
£1.50

The Buckinghamshire Health Authority (Transfer of Trust Property) No. 4 Order 2002 No. 2002/863. – Enabling power: National Health Service Act 1977, ss. 92 (1), 126 (4). – Issued: 30.05.2002. Made: 26.03.2002. Laid: 28.03.2002. Coming into force: 01.04.2002. Effect: None. Territorial extent & classification: E. General. – 2p.: 30 cm. – 0 11 042268 6
£1.50

The Buckinghamshire Hospitals National Health Service Trust (Establishment) and the South Buckinghamshire National Health Service Trust and Stoke Mandeville Hospital National Health Service Trust (Dissolution) Order 2002 No. 2002/2419. – Enabling power: National Health Service Act 1977, s. 126 (3) & National Health Service and Community Care Act 1990, s. 5 (1), sch. 2, paras. 1, 3, 4, 5, 29 (1). – Issued: 25.09.2002. Made: 20.09.2002. Coming into force: 01.10.2002. Effect: S.I. 1992/2575; 1993/2577 revoked. Territorial extent & classification: E. General. – 4p.: 30 cm. – 0 11 042809 9   *£1.75*

The Burntwood, Lichfield and Tamworth Primary Care Trust (Establishment) Amendment Order 2002 No. 2002/1114. – Enabling power: National Health Service Act 1977, ss. 16A (1) (2) (3), 126 (3) (4). – Issued: 19.04.2002. Made: 26.03.2002. Coming into force: 01.04.2002. Effect: S.I. 2001/67 amended. Territorial extent & classification: E. General. – 2p.: 30 cm. – 0 11 039780 0   *£1.50*

The Bury Health Care National Health Service Trust (Transfer of Trust Property) Order 2002 No. 2002/599. – Enabling power: National Health Service Act 1977, ss. 92 (1) (4), 126 (4). – Issued: 31.05.2002. Made: 08.03.2002. Laid: 11.03.2002. Coming into force: 01.04.2002. Effect: None. Territorial extent & classification: E. General. – 2p.: 30 cm. – 0 11 042273 2   *£1.50*

The Bury Primary Care Trust (Establishment) Order 2002 No. 2002/69. – Enabling power: National Health Service Act 1977, ss. 16A (1) (2) (3), 126 (4), sch. 5A, paras. 1, 2. – Issued: 24.01.2002. Made: 13.01.2002. Coming into force: 23.01.2002. Effect: None. Territorial extent & classification: E. General. – 4p.: 30 cm. – 0 11 039209 4   *£1.75*

The Calderdale Primary Care Trust (Establishment) Order 2002 No. 2002/144. – Enabling power: National Health Service Act 1977, ss. 16A (1) (2) (3), 126 (4), sch. 5A, paras. 1, 2. – Issued: 06.02.2002. Made: 19.01.2002. Coming into force: 25.01.2002. Effect: None. Territorial extent & classification: E. General. – 4p.: 30 cm. – 0 11 039260 4
£1.75

The Cambridgeshire and Peterborough Mental Health Partnership National Health Service Trust (Establishment) and the Lifespan Health Care Cambridge National Health Service Trust and the North West Anglia Health Care National Health Service Trust (Dissolution) Amendment Order 2002 No. 2002/1690. – Enabling power: National Health Service Act 1977, s. 126 (3) (4) & National Health Service and Community Care Act 1990, s. 5 (1), sch. 2, paras. 1, 3. – Issued: 04.07.2002. Made: 26.06.2002. Coming into force: 04.07.2002. Effect: S.I. 2002/647 amended. Territorial extent & classification: E. General. – This Statutory Instrument has been made in consequence of a defect in S.I. 2002/647 and is being issued free of charge to all known recipients of that S.I. – 4p.: 30 cm. – 0 11 042418 2   *£1.75*

The Cambridgeshire and Peterborough Mental Health Partnership National Health Service Trust (Establishment) and the Lifespan Health Care Cambridge National Health Service Trust and the North West Anglia Health Care National Health Service Trust (Dissolution) Order 2002 No. 2002/647. – Enabling power: National Health Service Act 1977, ss. 126 (3) & National Health Service and Community Care Act 1990, s. 5 (1), sch. 2, paras. 1, 3, 4, 5, 29 (1). – Issued: 25.03.2002. Made: 27.02.2002. Coming into force: 08.03.2002 except for art. 8; 01.04.2002 for art. 8. Effect: S.I. 1992/2570, 2571 revoked (01.04.2002). Territorial extent & classification: E. General. – 4p.: 30 cm. – 0 11 039532 8
£1.75

The Cambridgeshire Health Authority (Transfer of Trust Property) Order 2002 No. 2002/585. – Enabling power: National Health Service Act 1977, ss. 92 (1) (4), 126 (4). – Issued: 06.06.2002. Made: 08.03.2002. Laid: 11.03.2002. Coming into force: 01.04.2002. Effect: None. Territorial extent & classification: E. General. – 4p.: 30 cm. – 0 11 042281 3
£1.75

The Camden and Islington Mental Health National Health Service Trust (Establishment) Amendment Order 2002 No. 2002/1494. – Enabling power: National Health Service Act 1977, s. 126 (3) & National Health Service and Community Care Act 1990, s. 5 (1) & Health and Social Care Act 2001, s. 45 (5). – Issued: 14.06.2002. Made: 22.03.2002. Coming into force: 01.04.2002. Effect: S.I. 2001/1258 amended. Territorial extent & classification: E. General. – 2p.: 30 cm. – 0 11 042341 0   *£1.50*

The Camden Primary Care Trust (Establishment) Order 2002 No. 2002/1000. – Enabling power: National Health Service Act 1977, ss. 16A (1) (2) (3), 126 (4), sch. 5A, para. 1. – Issued: 10.04.2002. Made: 20.03.2002. Coming into force: 01.04.2002. Effect: None. Territorial extent & classification: E. General. – 2p.: 30 cm. – 0 11 039717 7
£1.50

The Cannock Chase Primary Care Trust (Establishment) Order 2002 No. 2002/946. – Enabling power: National Health Service Act 1977, ss. 16A (1) (2) (3), 126 (4), sch. 5A, paras. 1, 2. – Issued: 08.04.2002. Made: 10.03.2002. Coming into force: 20.03.2002. Effect: None. Territorial extent & classification: E. General. – 4p.: 30 cm. – 0 11 039682 0 *£1.75*

The Canterbury and Coastal Primary Care Trust (Establishment) Order 2002 No. 2002/983. – Enabling power: National Health Service Act 1977, ss. 16A (1) (2) (3), 126 (4), sch. 5A, para. 1. – Issued: 10.04.2002. Made: 25.03.2002. Coming into force: 01.04.2002. Effect: None. Territorial extent & classification: E. General. – 2p.: 30 cm. – 0 11 039720 7 *£1.50*

The Central Cheshire Primary Care Trust (Establishment) Order 2002 No. 2002/617. – Enabling power: National Health Service Act 1977, ss. 16A (1) (2) (3), 126 (4), sch. 5A, paras. 1, 2. – Issued: 25.03.2002. Made: 26.02.2002. Coming into force: 06.03.2002. Effect: None. Territorial extent & classification: E. General. – 4p.: 30 cm. – 0 11 039546 8 *£1.75*

The Central Derby Primary Care Trust (Establishment) Amendment Order 2002 No. 2002/1116. – Enabling power: National Health Service Act 1977, ss. 16A (1) (2) (3), 126 (3) (4), sch. 5A, paras. 1, 2. – Issued: 19.04.2002. Made: 21.03.2002. Coming into force: 01.04.2002. Effect: S.I. 2000/218 amended. Territorial extent & classification: E. General. – 2p.: 30 cm. – 0 11 039787 8 *£1.50*

The Cheshire and Wirral Partnership National Health Service Trust (Establishment) and the Wirral and West Cheshire Community National Health Service Trust (Dissolution) Order 2002 No. 2002/1244. – Enabling power: National Health Service Act 1977, s. 126 (3) & National Health Service and Community Care Act 1990, s. 5 (1), sch. 2, paras. 1, 3, 4, 5, 29 (1). – Issued: 10.05.2002. Made: 13.03.2002. Coming into force: 22.03.2002 except for art. 8; 01.04.2002 for art.8 only. Effect: S.I. 1997/833 revoked (01.04.2002). Territorial extent & classification: E. General. – 4p.: 30 cm. – 0 11 039893 9 *£1.75*

The Cheshire Community Healthcare National Health Service Trust (Dissolution) Order 2002 No. 2002/1496. – Enabling power: National Health Service Act 1977, s. 126 (3) & National Health Service and Community Care Act 1990, s. 5 (1), sch. 2, para. 29 (1). – Issued: 14.06.2002. Made: 24.03.2002. Coming into force: 01.04.2002. Effect: S.I. 1992/2462 revoked. Territorial extent & classification: E. General. – 2p.: 30 cm. – 0 11 042343 7 *£1.50*

The Cheshire Community Healthcare National Health Service Trust (Transfer of Trust Property) Order 2002 No. 2002/582. – Enabling power: National Health Service Act 1977, ss. 92 (1), 126 (4). – Issued: 06.06.2002. Made: 08.03.2002. Laid: 11.03.2002. Coming into force: 01.04.2002. Effect: None. Territorial extent & classification: E. General. – 2p.: 30 cm. – 0 11 042313 5 *£1.50*

The Cheshire West Primary Care Trust (Establishment) Order 2002 No. 2002/725. – Enabling power: National Health Service Act 1977, ss. 16A (1) (2) (3), 126 (4), sch. 5A, paras. 1, 2. – Issued: 25.03.2002. Made: 26.02.2002. Coming into force: 06.03.2002. Effect: None. Territorial extent & classification: E. General. – 4p.: 30 cm. – 0 11 039556 5 *£1.75*

The Chester and Halton Community National Health Service Trust (Dissolution) Order 2002 No. 2002/1499. – Enabling power: National Health Service Act 1977, s. 126 (3) & National Health Service and Community Care Act 1990, s. 5 (1), sch. 2, para. 29 (1). – Issued: 14.06.2002. Made: 24.03.2002. Coming into force: 01.04.2002. Effect: S.I. 1990/2406 revoked. Territorial extent & classification: E. General. – 2p.: 30 cm. – 0 11 042346 1 *£1.50*

The Commission for Patient and Public Involvement in Health (Functions) Regulations 2002 No. 2002/3007. – Enabling power: National Health Service Reform and Health Care Professions Act 2002, ss. 20 (2) (a) (b) (c) (g) (8) to (10), 38 (5) to (7). – Issued: 09.12.2002. Made: 05.12.2002. Laid: 05.12.2002. Coming into force: 01.01.2003. Effect: None. Territorial extent & classification: E. General. – 4p.: 30 cm. – 0 11 044148 6 *£1.75*

The Commission for Patient and Public Involvement in Health (Membership and Procedure) Regulations 2002 No. 2002/3038. – Enabling power: National Health Service Reform and Health Care Professions Act 2002, s. 38 (5) to (7), sch. 6, paras. 4, 5. – Issued: 19.12.2002. Made: 09.12.2002. Laid: 10.12.2002. Coming into force: 01.01.2003. Effect: None. Territorial extent & classification: E. General. – 12p.: 30 cm. – 0 11 044225 3 *£2.50*

The CommuniCare National Health Service Trust (Dissolution) Order 2002 No. 2002/1500. – Enabling power: National Health Service Act 1977, s. 126 (3) & National Health Service and Community Care Act 1990, s. 5 (1), sch. 2, para. 29 (1). – Issued: 14.06.2002. Made: 24.03.2002. Coming into force: 01.04.2002. Effect: S.I. 1993/2596 revoked. Territorial extent & classification: E. General. – 2p.: 30 cm. – 0 11 042347 X *£1.50*

The CommuniCare National Health Service Trust (Transfer of Trust Property) Order 2002 No. 2002/584. – Enabling power: National Health Service Act 1977, ss. 92 (1), 126 (4). – Issued: 28.05.2002. Made: 08.03.2002. Laid: 11.03.2002. Coming into force: 01.04.2002. Effect: None. Territorial extent & classification: E. General. – 2p.: 30 cm. – 0 11 042240 6 *£1.50*

The Community Healthcare Bolton National Health Service Trust (Dissolution) Order 2002 No. 2002/1492. – Enabling power: National Health Service Act 1977, s. 126 (3) & National Health Service and Community Care Act 1990, s. 5 (1), sch. 2, para. 29 (1). – Issued: 14.06.2002. Made: 24.03.2002. Coming into force: 01.04.2002. Effect: S.I. 1993/2595 revoked. Territorial extent & classification: E. General. – 2p.: 30 cm. – 0 11 042339 9 *£1.50*

The Community Health Care Service (North Derbyshire) National Health Service Trust (Transfer of Trust Property) Order 2002 No. 2002/583. – Enabling power: National Health Service Act 1977, ss. 92 (1), 126 (4). – Issued: 30.05.2002. Made: 08.03.2002. Laid: 11.03.2002. Coming into force: 01.04.2002. Effect: None. Territorial extent & classification: E. General. – 2p.: 30 cm. – 0 11 042271 6 *£1.50*

The Community Health Councils (Amendment) Regulations 2002 No. 2002/2106. – Enabling power: National Health Service Act 1977, s. 126 (4), sch. 7, para. 2 (a) (b). – Issued: 22.08.2002. Made: 07.08.2002. Laid: 09.08.2002. Coming into force: 31.08.2002. Effect: S.I. 1996/640 amended in relation to England. Territorial extent & classification: E. General. – 2p.: 30 cm. – With correction slip, dated September 2002 – 0 11 042653 3 *£1.50*

The Cornwall Healthcare National Health Service Trust Change of Name and (Establishment) Amendment Order 2002 No. 2002/1234. – Enabling power: National Health Service Act 1977, s. 126 (3) (4) & National Health Service and Community Care Act 1990, s. 5 (1). – Issued: 09.05.2002. Made: 25.03.2002. Coming into force: 01.04.2002. Effect: None. Territorial extent & classification: E. General. – 2p.: 30 cm. – 0 11 039884 X *£1.50*

The Counter Fraud and Security Management Service (Establishment and Constitution) Order 2002 No. 2002/3039. – Enabling power: National Health Service Act 1977, ss. 11 (1) (2) (4), sch. 5, para. 9 (7) (b). – Issued: 16.12.2002. Made: 10.12.2002. Laid: 10.12.2002. Coming into force: 01.01.2003. Effect: None. Territorial extent & classification: E. General. – 4p.: 30 cm. – 0 11 044184 2 *£1.75*

The Counter Fraud and Security Management Service Regulations 2002 No. 2002/3040. – Enabling power: National Health Service Act 1977, ss. 16, 126 (4), sch. 5, paras. 12, 16. – Issued: 13.01.2003. Made: 10.12.2002. Laid: 10.12.2002. Coming into force: 01.01.2003. Effect: None. Territorial extent & classification: E. General. – 12p.: 30 cm. – 0 11 044551 1 *£2.50*

The County Durham and Darlington Acute Hospitals National Health Service Trust (Establishment) and the North Durham Health Care National Health Service Trust and South Durham Health Care National Health Service (Dissolution) Order 2002 No. 2002/2420. – Enabling power: National Health Service Act 1977, s. 126 (3) & National Health Service and Community Care Act 1990, s. 5 (1), sch. 2, paras. 1, 3, 29 (1). – Issued: 25.09.2002. Made: 20.09.2002. Coming into force: 01.10.2002. Effect: S.I. 1998/832, 835 revoked. Territorial extent & classification: E. General. – 4p.: 30 cm. – 0 11 042808 0 *£1.75*

The County Durham and Tees Valley Health Authority (Transfer of Trust Property) Order 2002 No. 2002/2270. – Enabling power: National Health Service Act 1977, ss. 92 (1), 126 (4). – Issued: 16.09.2002. Made: 04.09.2002. Laid: 05.09.2002. Coming into force: 30.09.2002. Effect: None. Territorial extent & classification: E. General. – 2p.: 30 cm. – 0 11 042769 6 *£1.50*

The Coventry Primary Care Trust (Establishment) Order 2002 No. 2002/940. – Enabling power: National Health Service Act 1977, ss. 16A (1) (2) (3), 126 (4), sch. 5A, paras. 1, 2. – Issued: 08.04.2002. Made: 10.03.2002. Coming into force: 20.03.2002. Effect: None. Territorial extent & classification: E. General. – 4p.: 30 cm. – 0 11 039677 4 *£1.75*

The Coventry Primary Care Trust (Transfer of Trust Property) Order 2002 No. 2002/1692. – Enabling power: National Health Service Act 1977, ss. 92 (1), 126 (4). – Issued: 08.07.2002. Made: 01.07.2002. Laid: 02.07.2002. Coming into force: 23.07.2002. Effect: None. Territorial extent & classification: E. General. – 2p.: 30 cm. – 0 11 042431 X *£1.50*

The Craven, Harrogate and Rural District Primary Care Trust (Establishment) Order 2002 No. 2002/149. – Enabling power: National Health Service Act 1977, ss. 16A (1) (2) (3), 126 (4), sch. 5A, paras. 1, 2. – Issued: 06.02.2002. Made: 19.01.2002. Coming into force: 25.01.2002. Effect: None. Territorial extent & classification: E. General. – 4p.: 30 cm. – 0 11 039253 1 *£1.75*

The Crawley Primary Care Trust (Establishment) Order 2002 No. 2002/994. – Enabling power: National Health Service Act 1977, ss. 16A (1) (2) (3), 126 (4), sch. 5A, para. 1. – Issued: 10.04.2002. Made: 25.03.2002. Coming into force: 01.04.2002. Effect: None. Territorial extent & classification: E. General. – 2p.: 30 cm. – 0 11 039703 7 *£1.50*

The Croydon and Surrey Downs Community National Health Service Trust (Transfer of Trust Property) Order 2002 No. 2002/622. – Enabling power: National Health Service Act 1977, ss. 92 (1), 126 (4). – Issued: 26.03.2002. Made: 08.03.2002. Laid: 11.03.2002. Coming into force: 01.04.2002. Effect: None. Territorial extent & classification: E. General. – 2p.: 30 cm. – 0 11 039578 6 *£1.50*

The Croydon Health Authority (Transfer of Trust Property) Order 2002 No. 2002/571. – Enabling power: National Health Service Act 1977, ss. 92 (1), 126 (4). – Issued: 25.03.2002. Made: 08.03.2002. Laid: 11.03.2002. Coming into force: 01.04.2002. Effect: None. Territorial extent & classification: E. General. – 2p.: 30 cm. – 0 11 039555 7 *£1.50*

The Croydon Primary Care Trust (Establishment) Order 2002 No. 2002/1007. – Enabling power: National Health Service Act 1977, ss. 16A (1) (2) (3), 126 (4), sch. 5A, para. 1. – Issued: 12.04.2002. Made: 20.03.2002. Coming into force: 01.04.2002. Effect: None. Territorial extent & classification: E. General. – 2p.: 30 cm. – 0 11 039736 3 *£1.50*

The Cumbria and Lancashire Health Authority (Transfer of Trust Property) Order 2002 No. 2002/2282. – Enabling power: National Health Service Act 1977, ss. 92 (1), 126 (4). – Issued: 16.09.2002. Made: 04.09.2002. Laid: 05.09.2002. Coming into force: 30.09.2002. Effect: None. Territorial extent & classification: E. General. – 4p.: 30 cm. – 0 11 042767 X *£1.75*

The Darlington Primary Care Trust (Establishment) Order 2002 No. 2002/150. – Enabling power: National Health Service Act 1977, ss. 16A (1) (2) (3), 126 (4), sch. 5A, paras. 1, 2. – Issued: 06.02.2002. Made: 19.01.2002. Coming into force: 25.01.2002. Effect: None. Territorial extent & classification: E. General. – 4p.: 30 cm. – 0 11 039254 X *£1.75*

The Derwentside Primary Care Trust (Establishment) Order 2002 No. 2002/145. – Enabling power: National Health Service Act 1977, ss. 16A (1) (2) (3), 126 (4), sch. 5A, paras. 1, 2. – Issued: 06.02.2002. Made: 19.01.2002. Coming into force: 25.01.2002. Effect: None. Territorial extent & classification: E. General. – 4p.: 30 cm. – 0 11 039258 2 *£1.75*

The Doncaster Health Authority (Transfer of Trust Property) Order 2002 No. 2002/568. – Enabling power: National Health Service Act 1977, ss. 92 (1), 126 (4). – Issued: 26.03.2002. Made: 08.03.2002. Laid: 11.03.2002. Coming into force: 01.04.2002. Effect: None. Territorial extent & classification: E. General. – 2p.: 30 cm. – 0 11 039565 4 *£1.50*

The Doncaster Healthcare National Health Service Trust (Establishment) Amendment Order 2002 No. 2002/1295. – Enabling power: National Health Service Act 1977, s. 126 (3) (4) & National Health Service and Community Care Act 1990, s. 5 (1). – Issued: 16.05.2002. Made: 26.03.2002. Coming into force: 01.04.2002. Effect: S.I. 1991/2338 amended. Territorial extent & classification: E. General. – 2p.: 30 cm. – 0 11 039938 2 *£1.50*

The Durham and Chester-le-Street Primary Care Trust (Establishment) Order 2002 No. 2002/148. – Enabling power: National Health Service Act 1977, ss. 16A (1) (2) (3), 126 (4), sch. 5A, paras. 1, 2. – Issued: 06.02.2002. Made: 19.01.2002. Coming into force: 25.01.2002. Effect: None. Territorial extent & classification: E. General. – 4p.: 30 cm. – 0 11 039256 6 *£1.75*

The Durham Dales Primary Care Trust (Establishment) Order 2002 No. 2002/147. – Enabling power: National Health Service Act 1977, ss. 16A (1) (2) (3), 126 (4), sch. 5A, paras. 1, 2. – Issued: 06.02.2002. Made: 19.01.2002. Coming into force: 25.01.2002. Effect: None. Territorial extent & classification: E. General. – 4p.: 30 cm. – 0 11 039255 8 *£1.75*

The Ealing, Hammersmith & Hounslow Health Authority (Transfer of Trust Property) Order 2002 No. 2002/605. – Enabling power: National Health Service Act 1977, ss. 92 (1) (4), 126 (4). – Issued: 25.03.2002. Made: 08.03.2002. Laid: 11.03.2002. Coming into force: 01.04.2002. Effect: None. Territorial extent & classification: E. General. – 2p.: 30 cm. – 0 11 039541 7 *£1.50*

The Easington Primary Care Trust (Establishment) Order 2002 No. 2002/142. – Enabling power: National Health Service Act 1977, ss. 16A (1) (2) (3), 126 (4), sch. 5A, paras. 1, 2. – Issued: 06.02.2002. Made: 19.01.2002. Coming into force: 25.01.2002. Effect: None. Territorial extent & classification: E. General. – 4p.: 30 cm. – 0 11 039247 7 *£1.75*

The East Berkshire National Health Service Trust (Transfer of Trust Property) Order 2002 No. 2002/562. – Enabling power: National Health Service Act 1977, ss. 92 (1), 126 (4). – Issued: 25.03.2002. Made: 08.03.2002. Laid: 11.03.2002. Coming into force: 01.04.2002. Effect: None. Territorial extent & classification: E. General. – 2p.: 30 cm. – 0 11 039536 0 *£1.50*

The Eastbourne and County National Health Service Trust Change of Name and (Establishment) Amendment Order 2002 No. 2002/1495. – Enabling power: National Health Service Act 1977, s. 126 (3) (4) & National Health Service and Community Care Act 1990, s. 5 (1). – Issued: 14.06.2002. Made: 25.03.2002. Coming into force: 01.04.2002. Effect: S.I. 1992/2534 amended. Territorial extent & classification: E. General. – 2p.: 30 cm. – Revoked by S.I. 2002/2397 (ISBN 0110427955) – 0 11 042342 9 *£1.50*

The Eastbourne and County National Health Service Trust Change of Name and (Establishment) Amendment Order (No. 2) 2002 No. 2002/2397. – Enabling power: National Health Service Act 1977, s. 126 (3) & National Health Service and Community Care Act 1990, s. 5 (1), sch. 2, paras. 1, 3. – Issued: 24.09.2002. Made: 16.09.2002. Coming into force: 01.10.2002. Effect: S.I. 2002/1495 revoked. Territorial extent & classification: E. General. – 4p.: 30 cm. – 0 11 042795 5 *£1.75*

The Eastbourne Downs Primary Care Trust (Establishment) Order 2002 No. 2002/981. – Enabling power: National Health Service Act 1977, ss. 16A (1) (2) (3), 126 (4), sch. 5A, para. 1. – Issued: 10.04.2002. Made: 25.03.2002. Coming into force: 01.04.2002. Effect: None. Territorial extent & classification: E. General. – 2p.: 30 cm. – 0 11 039723 1 *£1.50*

The East Elmbridge and Mid Surrey Primary Care Trust (Establishment) Order 2002 No. 2002/982. – Enabling power: National Health Service Act 1977, ss. 16A (1) (2) (3), 126 (4), sch. 5A, para. 1. – Issued: 10.04.2002. Made: 25.03.2002. Coming into force: 01.04.2002. Effect: None. Territorial extent & classification: E. General. – 4p.: 30 cm. – 0 11 039718 5 *£1.75*

The Eastern Birmingham Primary Care Trust (Establishment) Order 2002 No. 2002/939. – Enabling power: National Health Service Act 1977, ss. 16A (1) (2) (3), 126 (4), sch. 5A, paras. 1, 2. – Issued: 08.04.2002. Made: 10.03.2002. Coming into force: 20.03.2002. Effect: None. Territorial extent & classification: E. General. – 4p.: 30 cm. – 0 11 039698 7 *£1.75*

The Eastern Cheshire Primary Care Trust (Establishment) Order 2002 No. 2002/726. – Enabling power: National Health Service Act 1977, ss. 16A (1) (2) (3), 126 (4), sch. 5A, paras. 1, 2. – Issued: 25.03.2002. Made: 26.02.2002. Coming into force: 06.03.2002. Effect: None. Territorial extent & classification: E. General. – 4p.: 30 cm. – 0 11 039548 4 *£1.75*

The East Gloucestershire National Health Service Trust (Transfer of Trust Property) No. 2 Order 2002 No. 2002/854. – Enabling power: National Health Service Act 1977, ss. 92 (1), 126 (4). – Issued: 06.06.2002. Made: 26.03.2002. Laid: 28.03.2002. Coming into force: 01.04.2002. Effect: None. Territorial extent & classification: E. General. – 2p.: 30 cm. – 0 11 042300 3 £1.50

The East Gloucestershire National Health Service Trust (Transfer of Trust Property) Order 2002 No. 2002/620. – Enabling power: National Health Service Act 1977, ss. 92 (1), 126 (4). – Issued: 06.06.2002. Made: 08.03.2002. Laid: 11.03.2002. Coming into force: 01.04.2002. Effect: None. Territorial extent & classification: E. General. – 2p.: 30 cm. – 0 11 042282 1 £1.50

The East Kent Coastal Primary Care Trust (Establishment) Order 2002 No. 2002/990. – Enabling power: National Health Service Act 1977, ss. 16A (1) (2) (3), 126 (4), sch. 5A, para. 1. – Issued: 10.04.2002. Made: 25.03.2002. Coming into force: 01.04.2002. Effect: None. Territorial extent & classification: E. General. – 2p.: 30 cm. – 0 11 039710 X £1.50

The East Kent Health Authority (Transfer of Trust Property) Order 2002 No. 2002/876. – Enabling power: National Health Service Act 1977, ss. 92 (1), 126 (4). – Issued: 06.06.2002. Made: 27.03.2002. Laid: 28.03.2002. Coming into force: 01.04.2002. Effect: None. Territorial extent & classification: E. General. – 2p.: 30 cm. – 0 11 042283 X £1.50

The East Lancashire Health Authority (Transfer of Trust Property) Order 2002 No. 2002/598. – Enabling power: National Health Service Act 1977, ss. 92 (1), 126 (4). – Issued: 06.06.2002. Made: 08.03.2002. Laid: 11.03.2002. Coming into force: 01.04.2002. Effect: None. Territorial extent & classification: E. General. – 2p.: 30 cm. – 0 11 042310 0 £1.50

The East Lancashire Hospitals National Health Service Trust (Establishment) and the Blackburn, Hyndburn and Ribble Valley Health Care National Health Service Trust and Burnley Health Care National Health Service Trust (Dissolution) Order 2002 No. 2002/2073. – Enabling power: National Health Service Act 1977, s. 126 (3) & National Health Service and Community Care Act 1990, s. 5 (1), sch. 2, paras. 1, 3, 4, 5, 29 (1). – Issued: 12.08.2002. Made: 05.08.2002. Coming into force: 01.09.2002. Effect: S.I. 1991/2331; 1993/2592 revoked. Territorial extent & classification: E. General. – 4p.: 30 cm. – 0 11 042637 1 £1.75

The Eastleigh and Test Valley South Primary Care Trust (Establishment) Order 2002 No. 2002/1119. – Enabling power: National Health Service Act 1977, ss. 16A (1) (2) (3), 126 (4), sch. 5A, para. 1. – Issued: 19.04.2002. Made: 25.03.2002. Coming into force: 01.04.2002. Effect: None. Territorial extent & classification: E. General. – 2p.: 30 cm. – 0 11 039790 8 £1.50

The East Staffordshire Primary Care Trust (Establishment) Order 2002 No. 2002/951. – Enabling power: National Health Service Act 1977, ss. 16A (1) (2) (3), 126 (4), sch. 5A, paras. 1, 2. – Issued: 08.04.2002. Made: 15.03.2002. Coming into force: 27.03.2002. Effect: None. Territorial extent & classification: E. General. – 4p.: 30 cm. – 0 11 039679 0 £1.75

The East Surrey Primary Care Trust (Establishment) Order 2002 No. 2002/988. – Enabling power: National Health Service Act 1977, ss. 16A (1) (2) (3), 126 (4), sch. 5A, para. 1. – Issued: 10.04.2002. Made: 25.03.2002. Coming into force: 01.04.2002. Effect: None. Territorial extent & classification: E. General. – 4p.: 30 cm. – 0 11 039715 0 £1.75

The Ellesmere Port and Neston Primary Care Trust (Establishment) Order 2002 No. 2002/724. – Enabling power: National Health Service Act 1977, ss. 16A (1) (2) (3), 126 (4), sch. 5A, paras. 1, 2. – Issued: 25.03.2002. Made: 26.02.2002. Coming into force: 06.03.2002. Effect: None. Territorial extent & classification: E. General. – 4p.: 30 cm. – 0 11 039545 X £1.75

The Essex Rivers Healthcare National Health Service Trust (Transfer of Trust Property) Order 2002 No. 2002/609. – Enabling power: National Health Service Act 1977, ss. 92 (1), 126 (4). – Issued: 26.03.2002. Made: 08.03.2002. Laid: 11.03.2002. Coming into force: 01.04.2002. Effect: None. Territorial extent & classification: E. General. – 2p.: 30 cm. – 0 11 039572 7 £1.50

The Fareham and Gosport Primary Care Trust (Establishment) Order 2002/1120. – Enabling power: National Health Service Act 1977, ss. 16A (1) (2) (3), 126 (4), sch. 5A, para. 1 Issued: 19.04.2002. Made: 25.03.2002. Coming into force: 01.04.2002. Effect: None. Territorial extent & classification: E. General . – 2p.: 30 cm. – 0 11 039792 4 £1.50

The Fenland Primary Care Trust (Establishment) Amendment Order 2002 No. 2002/1121. – Enabling power: National Health Service Act 1977, ss. 16A (1) (2) (3), 126 (3) (4), sch. 5A, para. 1. – Issued: 19.04.2002. Made: 24.03.2002. Coming into force: 01.04.2002. Effect: S.I. 2000/286 amended. Territorial extent & classification: E. General. – With correction slip dated June 2002. – 2p.: 30 cm. – 0 11 039794 0 £1.50

The Gateshead Primary Care Trust (Establishment) Order 2002 No. 2002/146. – Enabling power: National Health Service Act 1977, ss. 16A (1) (2) (3), 126 (4), sch. 5A, paras. 1, 2. – Issued: 06.02.2002. Made: 19.01.2002. Coming into force: 25.01.2002. Effect: None. Territorial extent & classification: E. General. – 4p.: 30 cm. – 0 11 039261 2 £1.75

The Gloucestershire Health Authority (Transfer of Trust Property) No. 2 Order 2002 No. 2002/864. – Enabling power: National Health Service Act 1977, ss. 92 (1), 126 (4). – Issued: 06.06.2002. Made: 26.03.2002. Laid: 28.03.2002. Coming into force: 01.04.2002. Effect: None. Territorial extent & classification: E. General. – 2p.: 30 cm. – 0 11 042285 6 £1.50

The Gloucestershire Health Authority (Transfer of Trust Property) Order 2002 No. 2002/621. – Enabling power: National Health Service Act 1977, ss. 92 (1) (4), 126 (4). – Issued: 25.03.2002. Made: 08.03.2002. Laid: 11.03.2002. Coming into force: 01.04.2002. Effect: None. Territorial extent & classification: E. General. – 2p.: 30 cm. – 0 11 039534 4 £1.50

The Gloucestershire Royal National Health Service Trust (Transfer of Trust Property) Order 2002 No. 2002/619. – Enabling power: National Health Service Act 1977, ss. 92 (1), 126 (4). – Issued: 06.06.2002. Made: 08.03.2002. Laid: 11.03.2002. Coming into force: 01.04.2002. Effect: None. Territorial extent & classification: E. General. – 2p.: 30 cm. – 0 11 042289 9 £1.50

The Greater Manchester Health Authority (Transfer of Trust Property) Order 2002 No. 2002/2271. – Enabling power: National Health Service Act 1977, ss. 92 (1), 126 (4). – Issued: 16.09.2002. Made: 04.09.2002. Laid: 05.09.2002. Coming into force: 30.09.2002. Effect: None. Territorial extent & classification: E. General. – 2p.: 30 cm. – 0 11 042758 0 £1.50

The Guildford and Waverley Primary Care Trust (Establishment) Order 2002 No. 2002/986. – Enabling power: National Health Service Act 1977, ss. 16A (1) (2) (3), 126 (4), sch. 5A, para. 1. – Issued: 10.04.2002. Made: 25.03.2002. Coming into force: 01.04.2002. Effect: None. Territorial extent & classification: E. General. – 2p.: 30 cm. – 0 11 039700 1 £1.50

The Halton Primary Care Trust (Establishment) Order 2002 No. 2002/66. – Enabling power: National Health Service Act 1977, ss. 16A (1) (2) (3), 126 (4), sch. 5A, paras. 1, 2. – Issued: 24.01.2002. Made: 13.01.2002. Coming into force: 23.01.2002. Effect: None. Territorial extent & classification: E. General. – 4p.: 30 cm. – 0 11 039207 8 £1.75

The Hambleton and Richmondshire Primary Care Trust (Establishment) Order 2002 No. 2002/357. – Enabling power: National Health Service Act 1977, ss. 16A (1) (2) (3), 126 (4), sch. 5A, paras. 1, 2. – Issued: 26.02.2002. Made: 29.01.2002. Coming into force: 08.02.2002. Effect: None. Territorial extent & classification: E. General. – 4p.: 30 cm. – 0 11 039376 7 £1.75

The Harrow and Hillingdon Healthcare National Health Service Trust (Transfer of Trust Property) Order 2002 No. 2002/623. – Enabling power: National Health Service Act 1977, ss. 92 (1), 126 (4). – Issued: 25.03.2002. Made: 08.03.2002. Laid: 11.03.2002. Coming into force: 01.04.2002. Effect: None. Territorial extent & classification: E. General. – 2p.: 30 cm. – 0 11 039540 9 £1.50

The Harrow Primary Care Trust (Establishment) Order 2002 No. 2002/1010. – Enabling power: National Health Service Act 1977, ss. 16A (1) (2) (3), 126 (4), sch. 5A, para. 1. – Issued: 12.04.2002. Made: 20.03.2002. Coming into force: 01.04.2002. Effect: None. Territorial extent & classification: E. General. – 2p.: 30 cm. – 0 11 039739 8 £1.50

The Health and Social Care Act 2001 (Commencement No. 10) (England) Order 2002 No. 2002/2363 (C.77). – Enabling power: Health and Social Care Act 2001, ss. 64 (6), 70 (2). Bringing into force various provisions of the 2001 Act on 12.09.2002, 30.09.2002, 31.03.2003, in accord. with arts. 2 (1) (2), 3. – Issued: 20.09.2002. Made: 11.09.2002. Effect: None. Territorial extent & classification: E. General. – 4p.: 30 cm. – 0 11 042776 9 £1.75

The Health Authorities (Establishment and Abolition) (England) Order 2002 No. 2002/553. – Enabling power: National Health Service Act 1977, ss. 8 (1) to (4) (6), 126 (3) (4) (5). – Issued: 26.04.2002. Made: 10.03.2002. Laid: 11.03.2002. Coming into force: 01.04.2002. Effect: S.I. 1996/624; 1999/616, 1024; 2000/1240, 1241; 2001/740 revoked. Territorial extent & classification: E. General. – 12p.: 30 cm. – 0 11 039825 4 £2.50

The Health Authorities (Membership and Procedure) Amendment (England) Regulations 2002 No. 2002/556. – Enabling power: National Health Service Act 1977, s. 126 (4) 128 (1), sch. 5, paras. 2, 3, 12. – Issued: 30.04.2002. Made: 11.03.2002. Laid: 11.03.2002. Coming into force: 01.04.2002. Effect: S.I. 1996/707 amended in relation to England. Territorial extent & classification: E. General. – 4p.: 30 cm. – 0 11 039849 1 £1.75

The Heart of Birmingham Teaching Primary Care Trust (Establishment) Order 2002 No. 2002/958. – Enabling power: National Health Service Act 1977, ss. 16A (1) (2) (3), 126 (4), sch. 5A, paras. 1, 2. – Issued: 10.04.2002. Made: 10.03.2002. Coming into force: 20.03.2002. Effect: None. Territorial extent & classification: E. General. – 4p.: 30 cm. – 0 11 039690 1 £1.75

The Hertfordshire Health Authority (Transfer of Trust Property) Order 2002 No. 2002/597. – Enabling power: National Health Service Act 1977, ss. 92 (1), 126 (4). – Issued: 29.05.2002. Made: 08.03.2002. Laid: 11.03.2002. Coming into force: 01.04.2002. Effect: None. Territorial extent & classification: E. General. – 2p.: 30 cm. – 0 11 042256 2 £1.50

The Hillingdon Health Authority (Transfer of Trust Property) Order 2002 No. 2002/570. – Enabling power: National Health Service Act 1977, ss. 92 (1), 126 (4). Issued: 25.03.2002. Made: 08.03.2002. Laid: 11.03.2002. Coming into force: 01.04.2002. Effect: None. Territorial extent & classification: E. General. – 2p.: 30 cm. – 0 11 039535 2 £1.50

The Horsham and Chanctonbury Primary Care Trust (Establishment) Order 2002 No. 2002/985. – Enabling power: National Health Service Act 1977, ss. 16A (1) (2) (3), 126 (4), sch. 5A, para. 1. – Issued: 10.04.2002. Made: 25.03.2002. Coming into force: 01.04.2002. Effect: None. Territorial extent & classification: E. General. – 2p.: 30 cm. – 0 11 039705 3 £1.50

The Huddersfield Central Primary Care Trust (Establishment) Order 2002 No. 2002/358. – Enabling power: National Health Service Act 1977, ss. 16A (1) (2) (3), 126 (4), sch. 5A, paras. 1, 2. – Issued: 26.02.2002. Made: 29.01.2002. Coming into force: 08.02.2002. Effect: None. Territorial extent & classification: E. General. – 4p.: 30 cm. – 0 11 039374 0 *£1.75*

The Invicta Community National Health Service Trust (Transfer of Trust Property) Order 2002 No. 2002/878. – Enabling power: National Health Service Act 1977, ss. 92 (1), 126 (4). – Issued: 06.06.2002. Made: 28.03.2002. Laid: 28.03.2002. Coming into force: 01.04.2002. Effect: None. Territorial extent & classification: E. General. – 2p.: 30 cm. – 0 11 042290 2 *£1.50*

The Islington Primary Care Trust (Establishment) Order 2002 No. 2002/1002. – Enabling power: National Health Service Act 1977, ss. 16A (1) (2) (3), 126 (4), sch. 5A, para. 1. – Issued: 12.04.2002. Made: 20.03.2002. Coming into force: 01.04.2002. Effect: None. Territorial extent & classification: E. General. – 2p.: 30 cm. – 0 11 039742 8 *£1.50*

The Kennet and North Wiltshire Primary Care Trust (Establishment) Order 2002 No. 2002/723. – Enabling power: National Health Service Act 1977, ss. 16A (1) (2) (3), 126 (4), sch. 5A, paras. 1, 2. – Issued: 25.03.2002. Made: 03.03.2002. Coming into force: 14.03.2002. Effect: None. Territorial extent & classification: E. General. – 4p.: 30 cm. – 0 11 039542 5 *£1.75*

The Kensington and Chelsea Primary Care Trust (Establishment) Order 2002 No. 2002/1004. – Enabling power: National Health Service Act 1977, ss. 16A (1) (2) (3), 126 (4), sch. 5A, para. 1. – Issued: 12.04.2002. Made: 20.03.2002. Coming into force: 01.04.2002. Effect: None. Territorial extent & classification: E. General. – 2p.: 30 cm. – 0 11 039735 5 *£1.50*

The Kensington & Chelsea and Westminster Health Authority (Transfer of Trust Property) Order 2002 No. 2002/572. – Enabling power: National Health Service Act 1977, ss. 92 (1), 126 (4). – Issued: 25.03.2002. Made: 08.03.2002. Laid: 11.03.2002. Coming into force: 01.04.2002. Effect: None. Territorial extent & classification: E. General. – 2p.: 30 cm. – 0 11 039538 7 *£1.50*

The Knowsley Primary Care Trust (Establishment) Order 2002 No. 2002/67. – Enabling power: National Health Service Act 1977, ss. 16A (1) (2) (3), 126 (4), sch. 5A, paras. 1, 2. – Issued: 24.01.2002. Made: 13.01.2002. Coming into force: 23.01.2002. Effect: None. Territorial extent & classification: E. General. – 4p.: 30 cm. – 0 11 039208 6 *£1.75*

The Lambeth Primary Care Trust (Establishment) Order 2002 No. 2002/999. – Enabling power: National Health Service Act 1977, ss. 16A (1) (2) (3), 126 (4), sch. 5A, para. 1. – Issued: 10.04.2002. Made: 20.03.2002. Coming into force: 01.04.2002. Effect: None. Territorial extent & classification: E. General. – 2p.: 30 cm. – 0 11 039722 3 *£1.50*

The Lambeth, Southwark and Lewisham Health Authority (Transfer of Trust Property) Order 2002 No. 2002/872. – Enabling power: National Health Service Act 1977, ss. 92 (1), 126 (4). – Issued: 28.05.2002. Made: 27.03.2002. Laid: 28.03.2002. Coming into force: 01.04.2002. Effect: None. Territorial extent & classification: E. General. – 2p.: 30 cm. – 0 11 042238 4 *£1.50*

The Lancashire Teaching Hospitals National Health Service Trust (Establishment) and the Chorley and South Ribble National Health Service Trust and Preston Acute Hospitals National Health Service Trust (Dissolution) Order 2002 No. 2002/2025. – Enabling power: National Health Service Act 1977, s. 126 (3) & National Health Service and Community Care Act 1990, s. 5 (1), sch. 2, paras. 1, 3, 29 (1). – Issued: 07.08.2002. Made: 29.07.2002. Coming into force: 01.08.2002. Effect: S.I. 1992/2470; 1993/2625 revoked. Territorial extent & classification: E. General. – 4p.: 30 cm. – 0 11 042618 5 *£1.75*

The Langbaurgh Primary Care Trust (Establishment) Order 2002 No. 2002/140. – Enabling power: National Health Service Act 1977, ss. 16A (1) (2) (3), 126 (4), sch. 5A, paras. 1, 2. – Issued: 06.02.2002. Made: 19.01.2002. Coming into force: 25.01.2002. Effect: None. Territorial extent & classification: E. General. – 4p.: 30 cm. – 0 11 039249 3 *£1.75*

The Leeds Community and Mental Health Services Teaching National Health Service Trust (Change of Name) Order 2002 No. 2002/1615. – Enabling power: National Health Service Act 1977, s. 126 (3) (4) & National Health Service and Community Care Act 1990, s. 5 (1). – Issued: 28.06.2002. Made: 19.06.2002. Coming into force: 01.07.2002. Effect: S.I. 1992/2497 amended. Territorial extent & classification: E. General. – 2p.: 30 cm. – 0 11 042389 5 *£1.50*

The Leicestershire and Rutland Healthcare National Health Service Trust Change of Name and (Establishment) Amendment Order 2002 No. 2002/1437. – Enabling power: National Health Service Act 1977, s 126 (3) & National Health Service and Community Care Act 1990, s. 5 (1). – Issued: 06.06.2002. Made: 26.03.2002. Coming into force: 01.04.2002. Effect: S.I. 1998/3069 amended. Territorial extent & classification: E. General. – 2p.: 30 cm. – 0 11 042318 6 *£1.50*

The Leicestershire Health Authority (Transfer of Trust Property) Order 2002 No. 2002/596. – Enabling power: National Health Service Act 1977, ss. 92 (1), 126 (4). – Issued: 06.06.2002. Made: 08.03.2002. Laid: 11.03.2002. Coming into force: 01.04.2002. Effect: None. Territorial extent & classification: E. General. – 2p.: 30 cm. – 0 11 042288 0 *£1.50*

The Leicestershire, Northamptonshire and Rutland Health Authority (Transfer of Trust Property) Order 2002 No. 2002/2272. – Enabling power: National Health Service Act 1977, ss. 92 (1), 126 (4). – Issued: 16.09.2002. Made: 04.09.2002. Laid: 05.09.2002. Coming into force: 30.09.2002. Effect: None. Territorial extent & classification: E. General. – 2p.: 30 cm. – 0 11 042759 9 *£1.50*

The Lewisham Primary Care Trust (Establishment) Order 2002 No. 2002/1001. – Enabling power: National Health Service Act 1977, ss. 16A (1) (2) (3), 126 (4), sch. 5A, para. 1. – Issued: 12.04.2002. Made: 20.03.2002. Coming into force: 01.04.2002. Effect: None. Territorial extent & classification: E. General. – 2p.: 30 cm. – 0 11 039741 X
£1.50

The Lifespan Healthcare Cambridge National Health Service Trust (Transfer of Trust Property) Order 2002 No. 2002/874. – Enabling power: National Health Service Act 1977, ss. 92 (1), 126 (4). – Issued: 27.05.2002. Made: 27.03.2002. Laid: 28.03.2002. Coming into force: 01.04.2002. Effect: None. Territorial extent & classification: E. General. – 2p.: 30 cm. – 0 11 042235 X   *£1.50*

The Lincolnshire Healthcare National Health Service Trust (Change of Name) Order 2002 No. 2002/891. – Enabling power: National Health Service Act 1977, s. 126 (3) (4) & National Health Service and Community Care Act 1990, s. 5 (1). – Issued: 31.05.2002. Made: 22.05.2002. Laid:-. Coming into force: 01.06.2002. Effect: S.I. 2001/221 amended. Territorial extent & classification: E. General. – 2p.: 30 cm. – 0 11 042274 0   *£1.50*

The Lincolnshire South West Primary Care Trust Change of Name Order 2002 No. 2002/1235. – Enabling power: National Health Service Act 1977, ss. 16A (1) (2), 126 (3) (4). – Issued: 09.05.2002. Made: 18.04.2002. Coming into force: 29.04.2002. Effect: S.I. 2001/273 amended. Territorial extent & classification: E. General. – 2p.: 30 cm. – 0 11 039885 8
£1.50

The Liverpool Health Authority (Transfer of Trust Property) Order 2002 No. 2002/595. – Enabling power: National Health Service Act 1977, ss. 92 (1), 126 (4). – Issued: 27.05.2002. Made: 08.03.2002. Laid: 11.03.2002. Coming into force: 01.04.2002. Effect: None. Territorial extent & classification: E. General. – 2p.: 30 cm. – 0 11 042229 5   *£1.50*

The Local Authority (Overview and Scrutiny Committees Health Scrutiny Functions) Regulations 2002 No. 2002/3048. – Enabling power: Health and Social Care Act 2001, ss. 7 (3) (4), 8 (2) (3) (4), 64 (6) to (8) & National Health Service Act 1977, ss. 17, 126 (4). – Issued: 19.12.2002. Made: 11.12.2002. Laid: 11.12.2002. Coming into force: 01.01.2003. Effect: None. Territorial extent & classification: E. General. – 8p.: 30 cm. – 0 11 044223 7
£2.00

The Maidstone and Malling Primary Care Trust Change of Name and (Establishment) Amendment Order 2002 No. 2002/1123. – Enabling power: National Health Service Act 1977, ss. 16A (1) (2) (3), 126 (3) (4), sch. 5A, para. 1. – Issued: 19.04.2002. Made: 25.03.2002. Coming into force: 01.04.2002. Effect: S.I. 2001/285 amended. Territorial extent & classification: E. General. – 2p.: 30 cm. – 0 11 039797 5
£1.50

The Manchester Mental Health and Social Care Trust (Establishment) Order 2002 No. 2002/1251. – Enabling power: National Health Service and Community Care Act 1990, s. 5 (1), sch. 2, paras. 3, 4 & Health and Social Care Act 2001, s. 45 (5). – Issued: 10.05.2002. Made: 22.03.2002. Coming into force: 01.04.2002. Effect: None. Territorial extent & classification: E. General. – 2p.: 30 cm. – 0 11 039912 9
£1.50

The Medway Primary Care Trust (Establishment) Order 2002 No. 2002/960. – Enabling power: National Health Service Act 1977, ss. 16A (1) (2) (3), 126 (4), sch. 5A, para. 1. – Issued: 10.04.2002. Made: 25.03.2002. Coming into force: 01.04.2002. Effect: None. Territorial extent & classification: E. General. – 4p.: 30 cm. – 0 11 039688 X
£1.75

The Merton, Sutton and Wandsworth Health Authority (Transfer of Trust Property) No. 2 Order 2002 No. 2002/871. – Enabling power: National Health Service Act 1977, ss. 92 (1), 126 (4). – Issued: 27.05.2002. Made: 27.03.2002. Laid: 28.03.2002. Coming into force: 01.04.2002. Effect: None. Territorial extent & classification: E. General. – 2p.: 30 cm. – 0 11 042232 5   *£1.50*

The Merton, Sutton and Wandsworth Health Authority (Transfer of Trust Property) Order 2002 No. 2002/870. – Enabling power: National Health Service Act 1977, ss. 92 (1), 126 (4). – Issued: 29.05.2002. Made: 27.03.2002. Laid: 28.03.2002. Coming into force: 01.04.2002. Effect: None. Territorial extent & classification: E. General. – 2p.: 30 cm. – 0 11 042254 6   *£1.50*

The Middlesbrough Primary Care Trust (Establishment) Order 2002 No. 2002/138. – Enabling power: National Health Service Act 1977, ss. 16A (1) (2) (3), 126 (4), sch. 5A, paras. 1, 2. – Issued: 06.02.2002. Made: 19.01.2002. Coming into force: 25.01.2002. Effect: None. Territorial extent & classification: E. General. – 4p.: 30 cm. – 0 11 039252 3
£1.75

The Mid-Sussex Health Authority (Transfer of Trust Property) Order 2002 No. 2002/851. – Enabling power: National Health Service Act 1977, ss. 92 (1), 126 (4). – Issued: 06.06.2002. Made: 27.03.2002. Laid: 20.03.2002. Coming into force: 01.04.2002. Effect: None. Territorial extent & classification: E. General. – 2p.: 30 cm. – 0 11 042299 6
£1.50

The Mid Yorkshire Hospitals National Health Service Trust (Establishment) and the Pinderfields and Pontefract Hospitals National Health Service Trust and the Dewsbury Health Care National Health Service Trust (Dissolution) Order 2002 No. 2002/1341. – Enabling power: National Health Service Act 1977, s. 126 (3) & National Health Service and Community Care Act 1990, s. 5 (1), sch. 2, paras. 1, 3, 29 (1). – Issued: 21.05.2002. Made: 19.03.2002. Coming into force: 01.04.2002. Effect: S.I. 1993/2548; 1997/582 revoked. Territorial extent & classification: E. General. – 4p.: 30 cm. – 0 11 039955 2   *£1.75*

The National Health Service (Charges for Drugs and Appliances) Amendment (No. 2) Regulations 2002 No. 2002/1386. – Enabling power: National Health Service Act 1977, ss. 77, 126 (4). – Issued: 13.06.2002. Made: 20.05.2002. Laid: 20.05.2002. Coming into force: 21.05.2002. Effect: S.I. 2000/620 amended. Territorial extent & classification: E. General. – 2p.: 30 cm. – 0 11 042330 5 *£1.50*

The National Health Service (Charges for Drugs and Appliances) Amendment (No. 3) Regulations 2002 No. 2002/2352. – Enabling power: National Health Service Act 1977, ss. 77, 83, 83A, 126 (4) & Health and Social Care Act 2001, s. 35. – Issued: 25.09.2002. Made: 11.09.2002. Laid: 11.09.2002. Coming into force: 01.10.2002. Effect: S.I. 2000/620 amended. Territorial extent & classification: E. General. – 4p.: 30 cm. – 0 11 042801 3 *£1.75*

The National Health Service (Charges for Drugs and Appliances) Amendment Regulations 2002 No. 2002/548. – Enabling power: National Health Service Act 1977, ss. 77, 83A, 126 (4). – Issued: 30.04.2002. Made: 07.03.2002. Laid: 11.03.2002. Coming into force: 01.04.2002. Effect: S.I. 2000/620 amended. Territorial extent & classification: E. General. – 4p.: 30 cm. – 0 11 039838 6 *£1.75*

The National Health Service (Clinical Negligence Scheme) Amendment Regulations 2002 No. 2002/1073. – Enabling power: National Health Service Act 1977, s. 126 (4) & National Health Service and Community Care Act 1990, s. 21. – Issued: 07.05.2002. Made: 11.04.2002. Laid: 15.04.2002. Coming into force: 06.05.2002. Effect: S.I. 1996/251 amended. Territorial extent & classification: E. General. – 4p.: 30 cm. – 0 11 039878 5 *£1.75*

The National Health Service (Dental Charges) Amendment Regulations 2002 No. 2002/544. – Enabling power: National Health Service Act 1977, s. 79A,, sch. 12, para. 3 (2) (3). – Issued: 05.06.2002. Made: 05.03.2002. Laid: 11.03.2002. Coming into force: 01.04.2002. Effect: S.I. 1989/394 amended & S.I. 2001/707 revoked. Territorial extent & classification: E. General. – 2p.: 30 cm. – Revoked by S.I. 2003/586 (ISBN 0110454294) – 0 11 042275 9 *£1.50*

The National Health Service (England) (Pilot Schemes: Miscellaneous Provisions and Consequential Amendments) Amendment Regulations 2002 No. 2002/543. – Enabling power: National Health Service (Primary Care) Act 1997, s. 11 (2) (c). – Issued: 26.04.2002. Made: 06.03.2002. Laid: 11.03.2002. Coming into force: 01.04.2002. Effect: S.I. 1998/646 amended. Territorial extent & classification: E. General. – 2p.: 30 cm. – 0 11 039817 3 *£1.50*

The National Health Service (Functions of Health Authorities) (England) (Support of Provision of Services and Appraisal) Regulations 2002 No. 2002/545. – Enabling power: National Health Service Act 1977, ss. 15 (1) (b) (1ZA), 126 (4). – Issued: 30.04.2002. Made: 08.03.2002. Laid: 11.03.2002. Coming into force: 01.04.2002. Effect: None. Territorial extent & classification: E. General. – 4p.: 30 cm. – 0 11 039845 9 *£1.75*

The National Health Service (Functions of Strategic Health Authorities and Primary Care Trusts and Administration Arrangements) (England) Regulations 2002 No. 2002/2375. – Enabling power: Health Service and Public Health Act 1968, s. 63 (5A) & National Health Service Act 1977, ss. 16, 16B, 16D, 17, 17A (4), 18, 51 (2), 126. – Issued: 25.09.2002. Made: 17.09.2002. Laid: 17.09.2002. Coming into force: 01.10.2002. Effect: S.I. 2000/89 amended & S.I. 1996/654; 2000/695; 2001/747 revoked. Territorial extent & classification: E. General. – 16p.: 30 cm. – With correction slip dated November 2002. – 0 11 042800 5 *£3.00*

The National Health Service (General Dental Services) Amendment Regulations 2002 No. 2002/558. – Enabling power: National Health Service Act 1977, ss. 15 (1), 35 (1), 36 (1) (4) to (8), 43ZA, 49O, 49Q, 49R, 126 (4). – Issued: 24.04.2002. Made: 11.03.2002. Laid: 11.03.2002. Coming into force: 01.04.2002. Effect: S.I. 1992/661 amended in relation to England. Territorial extent & classification: E. General. – 4p.: 30 cm. – 0 11 039781 9 *£1.75*

The National Health Service (General Medical Services) Amendment (No. 3) Regulations 2002 No. 2002/1768. – Enabling power: National Health Service Act 1977, ss. 29, 126 (4). – Issued: 18.07.2002. Made: 10.07.2002. Laid: 11.07.2002. Coming into force: 01.08.2002. Effect: S.I. 1992/635 amended. Territorial extent & classification: E. General. – 4p.: 30 cm. – 0 11 042473 5 *£1.75*

The National Health Service (General Medical Services) Amendment Regulations 2002 No. 2002/554. – Enabling power: National Health Service Act 1977, ss. 29, 29A, 29B, 43ZA, 49O, 49Q, 49R, 126 (4) & Health and Social Care Act 2001, s. 65. – Issued: 07.05.2002. Made: 08.03.2002. Laid: 11.03.2002. Coming into force: 01.04.2002. Effect: S.I. 1992/635 amended. Territorial extent & classification: E. General. – 16p.: 30 cm. – 0 11 039880 7 *£3.00*

The National Health Service (General Medical Services Supplementary List) (Amendment) Regulations 2002 No. 2002/848. – Enabling power: National Health Service Act 1977, s. 43D. – Issued: 24.04.2002. Made: 26.03.2002. Laid: 28.03.2002. Coming into force: 01.04.2002. Effect: S.I. 2001/3740 amended. Territorial extent & classification: E. General. – 2p.: 30 cm. – 0 11 039782 7 *£1.50*

The National Health Service (General Ophthalmic Services) Amendment Regulations 2002 No. 2002/601. – Enabling power: National Health Service Act 1977, ss. 38, 39, 43ZA, 49O, 49Q, 49R, 126 (4). – Issued: 27.05.2002. Made: 19.03.2002. Laid: 20.03.2002. Coming into force: 09.04.2002. Effect: S.I. 1986/975 amended in relation to England. Territorial extent & classification: E. General. – 8p.: 30 cm. – 0 11 039988 9 *£2.00*

The National Health Service Litigation Authority (Establishment and Constitution) Amendment Order 2002 No. 2002/2621. – Enabling power: National Health Service Act 1977, ss. 11 (1) (2) (4) (a), 126 (3) (4). – Issued: 25.10.2002. Made: 17.10.2002. Laid: 18.10.2002. Coming into force: 11.11.2002. Effect: S.I. 1995/2800 amended. Territorial extent & classification: E. General. – 2p.: 30 cm. – 0 11 042883 8 *£1.50*

The National Health Service (Local Pharmaceutical Services and Pharmaceutical Services) (No. 2) Regulations 2002 No. 2002/2016. – Enabling power: National Health Service Act 1977, ss. 41, 42, 43, 126 (4) & Health and Social Care Act 2001, ss. 33 (3) (a) (7) (9), 37 (b), 41, 65 (1). – Issued: 15.08.2002. Made: 31.07.2002. Laid: 31.07.2002. Coming into force: 20.08.2002. Effect: S.I. 1992/662 amended. Territorial extent & classification: E. General. – 8p.: 30 cm. – 0 11 042652 5 £2.00

The National Health Service (Local Pharmaceutical Services and Pharmaceutical Services) Regulations 2002 No. 2002/888. – Enabling power: National Health Service Act 1977, ss. 41, 42, 126 (4) & Health and Social Care Act 2001, ss. 28 (8), 30, 34, 65 (1), sch. 2, para. 1 (2) (b). – Issued: 31.05.2002. Made: 14.05.2002. Laid: 15.05.2002. Coming into force: 05.06.2002. Effect: S.I. 1992/662 amended. Territorial extent & classification: E. General. – 8p.: 30 cm. – 0 11 042276 7 £2.00

The National Health Service (Local Pharmaceutical Services etc.) Regulations 2002 No. 2002/2861. – Enabling power: National Health Service Act 1977, ss. 41, 42, 43, 45 (1ZA), 126 (4) & National Health Service (Primary Care) Act 1997, s. 39 (2) & Health and Social Care Act 2001, ss. 38, 41, 64 (8), 65 (1) (2) & National Health Service Reform and Health Care Professions Act 2002, ss. 38 (5) (7), 39. – Issued: 16.12.2002. Made: 19.11.2002. Laid: 19.11.2002. Coming into force: 12.12.2002. Effect: 1977 c.49 modified; 1993 c.46; 1999 c.8 & S.I. 1988/865; 1990/1718, 2024; 1992/635, 662; 1995/2801; 2000/89, 662, 1763; 2001/3798; 2002/888 amended in relation to England. Territorial extent & classification: E. General. – 16p.: 30 cm. – These regs apply to England only, except reg. 15 which applies to England and Wales – 0 11 044162 1 £3.00

The National Health Service (Miscellaneous Dental Charges Amendments) Regulations 2002 No. 2002/2353. – Enabling power: National Health Service Act 1977, ss. 37 (1C), 78 (1A), 79 (2) (A), 82, 83A, 126 (4), sch. 12, para. 2 (6) & National Health Service (Primary Care) Act 1997, ss. 17, 20. – Issued: 25.09.2002. Made: 11.09.2002. Laid: 11.09.2002. Coming into force: 01.10.2002. Effect: S.I. 1988/551; 1989/394 amended. Territorial extent & classification: E. General. – 8p.: 30 cm. – 0 11 042799 8 £2.00

The National Health Service (Optical Charges and Payments) Amendment (England) Regulations 2002 No. 2002/35. – Enabling power: National Health Service Act 1977, ss. 78 (1), 126 (4), sch. 12, para. 2A. – Issued: 24.01.2002. Made: 10.01.2002. Laid: 11.01.2002. Coming into force: 01.02.2002. Effect: S.I. 1997/818 amended. Territorial extent & classification: E. General. – 4p.: 30 cm. – 0 11 039203 5 £1.50

The National Health Service (Optical Charges and Payments) Amendment (No. 2) Regulations 2002 No. 2002/547. – Enabling power: National Health Service Act 1977, ss. 38, 78 (1), 126 (4), sch. 12, paras. 2, 2A. – Issued: 27.05.2002. Made: 11.03.2002. Laid: 11.03.2002. Coming into force: 01.04.2002, except for reg. 2; 09.04.2002, for reg. 2. Effect: S.I. 1997/818 amended in relation to England. Territorial extent & classification: E. General. – 4p.: 30 cm. – 0 11 039986 2 £1.75

The National Health Service (Optical Charges and Payments) Amendment (No. 3) (England) Regulations 2002 No. 2002/1326. – Enabling power: National Health Service Act 1977, sch. 12, para. 2A. – Issued: 30.05.2002. Made: 13.05.2002. Laid: 13.05.2002. Coming into force: 03.06.2002. Effect: S.I. 1997/818 amended in relation to England. Territorial extent & classification: E. General. – 2p.: 30 cm. – 0 11 042260 0 £1.50

The National Health Service (Out of Hours Medical Services) and National Health Service (General Medical Services) Amendment Regulations 2002 No. 2002/2548. – Enabling power: National Health Service Act 1977, ss. 15 (1) (1ZA), 17A (3), 29, 126 (4) & Health and Social Care Act 2001, ss. 18, 64 (6). – Issued: 05.11.2002. Made: 09.10.2002. Laid: 09.10.2002. Coming into force: 01.11.2002. Effect: S.I. 1992/635; 2002/2375 amended. Territorial extent & classification: E. General. – 12p.: 30 cm. – 0 11 042895 1 £2.50

The National Health Service (Pharmaceutical Services) and (General Medical Services) (No. 2) Amendment Regulations 2002 No. 2002/551. – Enabling power: National Health Service Act 1977, ss. 29, 41, 42, 43. – Issued: 07.05.2002. Made: 10.03.2002. Laid: 11.03.2002. Coming into force: 01.04.2002. Effect: S.I. 1992/635, 662 amended. Territorial extent & classification: E. General. – 4p.: 30 cm. – 0 11 039881 5 £1.75

The National Health Service (Primary Care) Act 1997 (Commencement No. 8) Order 2002 No. 2002/1616 (C.45). – Enabling power: National Health Service (Primary Care) Act 1997, s. 41 (3). Bringing into operation various provisions of the 1997 Act on 24.06.2002. – Issued: 28.06.2002. Made: 20.06.2002. Effect: None. Territorial extent & classification: E. General. – 4p.: 30 cm. – 0 11 042391 7 £1.75

The National Health Service Reform and Health Care Professions Act 2002 (Commencement No. 1) Order 2002 No. 2002/2202 (C.69). – Enabling power: National Health Service Reform and Health Care Professions Act 2002, ss. 38 (7), 42 (3). Bringing into force various provisions of the 2002 Act on 27.08.2002, 02.09.2002, 01.12.2002 & 01.04.2003 in accord. with arts. 2 & 3. – Issued: 08.10.2002. Made: 20.08.2002. Laid:-. Effect: 1968 c. 48 amended. Territorial extent & classification: UK. General. – 4p.: 30 cm. – 0 11 042830 2 £1.75

The National Health Service Reform and Health Care Professions Act 2002 (Supplementary, Consequential etc. Provisions) Regulations 2002 No. 2002/2469. – Enabling power: National Health Service Reform and Health Care Professions Act 2002, ss. 38 (5) (7), 39. – Issued: 18.10.2002. Made: 25.09.2002. Laid: 27.09.2002. Coming into force: 01.10.2002. Effect: approx. 100 Acts & S.Is amended, in accord. with schs. 1 to 12 & S.I 2000/595 revoked. Territorial extent & classification. E. General. – 52p.: 30 cm. – 0 11 042855 2 £7.50

The National Health Service (Travelling Expenses and Remission of Charges) Amendment Regulations 2002 No. 2002/580. – Enabling power: National Health Service Act 1977, ss. 83A, 126 (4), 128 (1). – Issued: 30.04.2002. Made: 18.03.2002. Laid: 18.03.2002. Coming into force: 08.04.2002. Effect: S.I. 1988/551 amended in relation to England. Territorial extent & classification: E. General. – 4p.: 30 cm. – Revoked by S.I. 2003/2382 (ISBN 0110475607) – 0 11 039839 4 *£1.75*

The National Health Service Trusts (Dissolution) Order 2002 No. 2002/1323. – Enabling power: National Health Service Act 1977, s. 126 (3) (4) & National Health Service and Community Care Act 1990, s. 5 (1), sch 2, para. 29 (1). – Issued: 17.05.2002. Made: 26.03.2002. Coming into force: 01.04.2002. Effect: S.I. 1990/2410; 1991/2384; 1992/2519, 2540, 2582, 2584; 1993/2569, 2570; 1994/848; 1999/794, 898 revoked. Territorial extent & classification: E. General. – 4p.: 30 cm. – 0 11 039947 1 *£1.75*

The National Health Service Trusts (Miscellaneous Dissolutions) Order 2002 No. 2002/2616. – Enabling power: National Health Service Act 1977, s. 126 (3) & National Health Service and Community Care Act 1990, s. 5 (1), sch 2, paras. 1, 29 (1), 30 (1). – Issued: 18.10.2002. Made: 14.10.2002. Coming into force: 18.10.2002. Effect: S.I. 1992/2552, 2553; 1994/162, 170; 1998/500, 517; 1999/3467 revoked. Territorial extent & classification: E. General. – 2p.: 30 cm. – 0 11 042880 3 *£1.50*

The National Health Service Trusts (Originating Capital) Order 2002 No. 2002/1336. – Enabling power: National Health Service and Community Care Act 1990, s. 9 (1). – Issued: 22.05.2002. Made: 25.03.2002. Coming into force: 01.04.2002. Effect: None. Territorial extent & classification: E. General. – 4p.: 30 cm. – 0 11 039959 5 *£1.75*

The Nelson and West Merton Primary Care Trust (Establishment) Amendment and Change of Name Order 2002 No. 2002/1009. – Enabling power: National Health Service Act 1977, ss. 16A (1) (2) (3), 126 (3) (4). – Issued: 12.04.2002. Made: 20.03.2002. Coming into force: 01.04.2002. Effect: S.I. 2000/254 amended. Territorial extent & classification: E. General. – 2p.: 30 cm. – 0 11 039733 9 *£1.50*

The Norfolk Health Authority (Transfer of Trust Property) Order 2002 No. 2002/594. – Enabling power: National Health Service Act 1977, ss. 92 (1), 126 (4). – Issued: 28.05.2002. Made: 08.03.2002. Laid: 11.03.2002. Coming into force: 01.04.2002. Effect: None. Territorial extent & classification: E. General. – 2p.: 30 cm. – 0 11 042239 2 *£1.50*

The Northallerton Health Services National Health Service Trust (Dissolution) Order 2002 No. 2002/1342. – Enabling power: National Health Service Act 1977, s. 126 (3) & National Health Service and Community Care Act 1990, s. 5 (1), sch. 2, para. 29 (1). – Issued: 21.05.2002. Made: 19.03.2002. Coming into force: 01.04.2002. Effect: S.I. 1991/2378 revoked. Territorial extent & classification: E. General. – 2p.: 30 cm. – 0 11 039957 9 *£1.50*

The Northampton Primary Care Trust (Establishment) Order 2002 No. 2002/980. – Enabling power: National Health Service Act 1977, ss. 16A (1) (2) (3), 126 (4), sch. 5A, paras. 1, 2. – Issued: 10.04.2002. Made: 18.03.2002. Coming into force: 27.03.2002. Effect: None. Territorial extent & classification: E. General. – 4p.: 30 cm. – 0 11 039702 9 *£1.75*

The Northamptonshire Heartlands Primary Care Trust (Establishment) Order 2002 No. 2002/997. – Enabling power: National Health Service Act 1977, ss. 16A (1) (2) (3), 126 (4), sch. 5A, paras. 1, 2. – Issued: 10.04.2002. Made: 18.03.2002. Coming into force: 27.03.2002. Effect: None. Territorial extent & classification: E. General. – 4p.: 30 cm. – 0 11 039712 6 *£1.75*

The North and East Devon Health Authority (Transfer of Trust Property) Order 2002 No. 2002/578. – Enabling power: National Health Service Act 1977, ss. 92 (1) (4), 126 (4). – Issued: 06.06.2002. Made: 08.03.2002. Laid: 11.03.2002. Coming into force: 01.04.2002. Effect: None. Territorial extent & classification: E. General. – 2p.: 30 cm. – 0 11 042312 7 *£1.50*

The North and East Devon Partnership National Health Service Trust Change of Name and (Establishment) Amendment Order 2002 No. 2002/731. – Enabling power: National Health Service Act 1977, s. 126 (3) (4) & National Health Service and Community Care Act 1990, s. 5 (1). – Issued: 25.03.2002. Made: 14.03.2002. Coming into force: 25.03.2002. Effect: S.I. 2001/1230 amended. Territorial extent & classification: E. General. – 2p.: 30 cm. – 0 11 039551 4 *£1.50*

The North Birmingham Primary Care Trust (Establishment) Order 2002 No. 2002/959. – Enabling power: National Health Service Act 1977, ss. 16A (1) (2) (3), 126 (4), sch. 5A, paras. 1, 2. – Issued: 10.04.2002. Made: 10.03.2002. Coming into force: 20.03.2002. Effect: None. Territorial extent & classification: E. General. – 4p.: 30 cm. – 0 11 039689 8 *£1.75*

The North Central London Health Authority (Transfer of Trust Property) Order 2002 No. 2002/2273. – Enabling power: National Health Service Act 1977, ss. 92 (1), 126 (4). – Issued: 16.09.2002. Made: 04.09.2002. Laid: 05.09.2002. Coming into force: 30.09.2002. Effect: None. Territorial extent & classification: E. General. – 2p.: 30 cm. – 0 11 042770 X *£1.50*

The North Cumbria Health Authority (Transfer of Trust Property) Order 2002 No. 2002/593. – Enabling power: National Health Service Act 1977, ss. 92 (1), 126 (4). – Issued: 27.05.2002. Made: 08.03.2002. Laid: 11.03.2002. Coming into force: 01.04.2002. Effect: None. Territorial extent & classification: E. General. – 2p.: 30 cm. – 0 11 042230 9 *£1.50*

The North Derbyshire Health Authority (Transfer of Trust Property) Order 2002 No. 2002/592. – Enabling power: National Health Service Act 1977, ss. 92 (1), 126 (4). – Issued: 29.05.2002. Made: 08.03.2002. Laid: 11.03.2002. Coming into force: 01.04.2002. Effect: None. Territorial extent & classification: E. General. – 2p.: 30 cm. – 0 11 042253 8 *£1.50*

The North Essex Health Authority (Transfer of Trust Property) Order 2002 No. 2002/586. – Enabling power: National Health Service Act 1977, ss. 92 (1) (4), 126 (4). – Issued: 06.06.2002. Made: 08.03.2002. Laid: 11.03.2002. Coming into force: 01.04.2002. Effect: None. Territorial extent & classification: E. General. – 2p.: 30 cm. – 0 11 042314 3 £1.50

The North Kirklees Primary Care Trust (Establishment) Order 2002 No. 2002/143. – Enabling power: National Health Service Act 1977, ss. 16A (1) (2) (3), 126 (4), sch. 5A, paras. 1, 2. – Issued: 06.02.2002. Made: 19.01.2002. Coming into force: 25.01.2002. Effect: None. Territorial extent & classification: E. General. – 4p.: 30 cm. – 0 11 039257 4 £1.75

The North Manchester Healthcare National Health Service Trust (Transfer of Trust Property) Order 2002 No. 2002/590. – Enabling power: National Health Service Act 1977, ss. 92 (1), 126 (4). – Issued: 06.06.2002. Made: 08.03.2002. Laid: 11.03.2002. Coming into force: 01.04.2002. Effect: None. Territorial extent & classification: E. General. – 2p.: 30 cm. – 0 11 042311 9 £1.50

The North Mersey Community National Health Service Trust (Dissolution) Order 2002 No. 2002/1497. – Enabling power: National Health Service Act 1977, s. 126 (3) & National Health Service and Community Care Act 1990, s. 5 (1), sch. 2, para. 29 (1). – Issued: 14.06.2002. Made: 24.03.2002. Coming into force: 01.04.2002. Effect: S.I. 1991/2376 revoked. Territorial extent & classification: E. General. – 2p.: 30 cm. – 0 11 042344 5 £1.50

The North Mersey Community National Health Service Trust (Transfer of Trust Property) Order 2002 No. 2002/577. – Enabling power: National Health Service Act 1977, ss. 92 (1) (4), 126 (4). – Issued: 30.05.2002. Made: 08.03.2002. Laid: 11.03.2002. Coming into force: 01.04.2002. Effect: None. Territorial extent & classification: E. General. – 2p.: 30 cm. – 0 11 042270 8 £1.50

The North Sefton and West Lancashire Community National Health Service Trust (Transfer of Trust Property) Order 2002 No. 2002/591. – Enabling power: National Health Service Act 1977, ss. 92 (1) (4), 126 (4). – Issued: 06.06.2002. Made: 08.03.2002. Laid: 11.03.2002. Coming into force: 01.04.2002. Effect: None. Territorial extent & classification: E. General. – 4p.: 30 cm. – 0 11 042309 7 £1.75

The North Somerset Primary Care Trust (Establishment) Order 2002 No. 2002/895. – Enabling power: National Health Service Act 1977, ss. 16A (1) (2) (3), 126 (4), sch. 5A, paras. 1, 2. – Issued: 19.04.2002. Made: 25.03.2002. Coming into force: 01.04.2002. Effect: None. Territorial extent & classification: E. General. – 2p.: 30 cm. – 0 11 039796 7 £1.50

The North Stoke Primary Care Trust (Establishment) Amendment (No. 2) Order 2002 No. 2002/1392. – Enabling power: National Health Service Act 1977, ss. 16A (1) (2) (3), 126 (3) (4). – Issued: 27.05.2002. Made: 12.05.2002. Laid: -Coming into force: 16.05.2002. Effect: S.I. 2000/2014 amended. Territorial extent & classification: E. General. – 2p.: 30 cm. – 0 11 042228 7 £1.50

The North Stoke Primary Care Trust (Establishment) Amendment Order 2002 No. 2002/1113. – Enabling power: National Health Service Act 1977, ss. 16A (1) (2) (3), 126 (3) (4). – Issued: 19.04.2002. Made: 26.03.2002. Coming into force: 01.04.2002. Effect: S.I. 2000/2014 amended. Territorial extent & classification: E. General. – 2p.: 30 cm. – 0 11 039795 9 £1.50

The North Surrey Primary Care Trust (Establishment) Order 2002 No. 2002/984. – Enabling power: National Health Service Act 1977, ss. 16A (1) (2) (3), 126 (4), sch. 5A, para. 1. – Issued: 10.04.2002. Made: 25.03.2002. Coming into force: 01.04.2002. Effect: None. Territorial extent & classification: E. General. – 2p.: 30 cm. – 0 11 039714 2 £1.50

The Northumberland Care Trust (Establishment) Order 2002 No. 2002/1122. – Enabling power: National Health Service Act 1977, ss. 16A (1) (2) (3), 126 (4) & Health and Social Care Act 2001, s. 45 (5). – Issued: 19.04.2002. Made: 22.03.2002. Coming into force: 01.04.2002. Effect: None. Territorial extent & classification: E. General. – 2p.: 30 cm. – 0 11 039791 6 £1.50

The Northumberland Health Authority (Transfer of Trust Property) Order 2002 No. 2002/850. – Enabling power: National Health Service Act 1977, ss. 92 (1), 126 (4). – Issued: 06.06.2002. Made: 27.03.2002. Laid: 28.03.2002. Coming into force: 01.04.2002. Effect: None. Territorial extent & classification: E. General. – 2p.: 30 cm. – 0 11 042315 1 £1.50

The Northumberland, Tyne & Wear Health Authority (Transfer of Trust Property) Order 2002 No. 2002/2275. – Enabling power: National Health Service Act 1977, ss. 92 (1), 126 (4). – Issued: 16.09.2002. Made: 04.09.2002. Laid: 05.09.2002. Coming into force: 30.09.2002. Effect: None. Territorial extent & classification: E. General. – 2p.: 30 cm. – 0 11 042762 9 £1.50

The North Warwickshire National Health Service Trust (Transfer of Trust Property) Order 2002 No. 2002/606. – Enabling power: National Health Service Act 1977, ss. 92 (1), 126 (4). – Issued: 26.03.2002. Made: 08.03.2002. Laid: 11.03.2002. Coming into force: 01.04.2002. Effect: None. Territorial extent & classification: E. General. – 2p.: 30 cm. – 0 11 039574 3 £1.50

The North Warwickshire Primary Care Trust (Establishment) Order 2002 No. 2002/634. – Enabling power: National Health Service Act 1977, ss. 16A (1) (2) (3), 126 (4), sch. 5A, paras. 1, 2. – Issued: 08.04.2002. Made: 10.03.2002. Coming into force: 20.03.2002. Effect: None. Territorial extent & classification: E. General. – 4p.: 30 cm. – 0 11 039681 2 £1.75

The North West Anglia Health Care National Health Service Trust (Transfer of Trust Property) Order 2002 No. 2002/560. – Enabling power: National Health Service Act 1977, ss. 92 (1), 126 (4). – Issued: 22.03.2002. Made: 08.03.2002. Laid: 11.03.2002. Coming into force: 01.04.2002. Effect: None. Territorial extent & classification: E. General. – 2p.: 30 cm. – 0 11 039513 1 £1.50

The North West London Health Authority (Transfer of Trust Property) Order 2002 No. 2002/2274. – Enabling power: National Health Service Act 1977, ss. 92 (1), 126 (4). – Issued: 16.09.2002. Made: 04.09.2002. Laid: 05.09.2002. Coming into force: 30.09.2002. Effect: None. Territorial extent & classification: E. General. – 2p.: 30 cm. – 0 11 042764 5 *£1.50*

The Oldbury and Smethwick Primary Care Trust (Establishment) Order 2002 No. 2002/949. – Enabling power: National Health Service Act 1977, ss. 16A (1) (2) (3), 126 (4), sch. 5A, paras. 1, 2. – Issued: 10.04.2002. Made: 10.03.2002. Coming into force: 20.03.2002. Effect: None. Territorial extent & classification: E. General. – 4p.: 30 cm. – 0 11 039685 5 *£1.75*

The Oldham National Health Service Trust (Transfer of Trust Property) Order 2002 No. 2002/579. – Enabling power: National Health Service Act 1977, ss. 92 (1) (4), 126 (4). – Issued: 27.05.2002. Made: 08.03.2002. Laid: 11.03.2002. Coming into force: 01.04.2002. Effect: None. Territorial extent & classification: E. General. – 2p.: 30 cm. – 0 11 042234 1 *£1.50*

The Oldham Primary Care Trust (Establishment) Order 2002 No. 2002/64. – Enabling power: National Health Service Act 1977, ss. 16A (1) (2) (3), 126 (4), sch. 5A, paras. 1, 2. – Issued: 24.01.2002. Made: 13.01.2002. Coming into force: 23.01.2002. Effect: None. Territorial extent & classification: E. General. – 4p.: 30 cm. – 0 11 039201 9 *£1.75*

The Oxfordshire Health Authority (Transfer of Trust Property) Order 2002 No. 2002/581. – Enabling power: National Health Service Act 1977, ss. 92 (1) (4), 126 (4). – Issued: 29.05.2002. Made: 08.03.2002. Laid: 11.03.2002. Coming into force: 01.04.2002. Effect: None. Territorial extent & classification: E. General. – 4p.: 30 cm. – 0 11 042251 1 *£1.75*

The Parkside National Health Service Trust (Transfer of Trust Property) No. 2 Order 2002 No. 2002/858. – Enabling power: National Health Service Act 1977, ss. 92 (1), 126 (4). – Issued: 06.06.2002. Made: 27.03.2002. Laid: 28.03.2002. Coming into force: 01.04.2002. Effect: None. Territorial extent & classification: E. General. – 4p.: 30 cm. – 0 11 042284 8 *£1.75*

The Parkside National Health Service Trust (Transfer of Trust Property) Order 2002 No. 2002/859. – Enabling power: National Health Service Act 1977, ss. 92 (1), 126 (4). – Issued: 30.05.2002. Made: 27.03.2002. Laid: 28.03.2002. Coming into force: 01.04.2002. Effect: None. Territorial extent & classification: E. General. – 2p.: 30 cm. – 0 11 042267 8 *£1.50*

The Pennine Acute Hospitals National Health Service Trust (Establishment) and the Bury Health Care National Health Service Trust, the Rochdale Healthcare National Health Service Trust, the Oldham National Health Service Trust and the North Manchester Healthcare National Health Service Trust (Dissolution) Order 2002 No. 2002/308. – Enabling power: National Health Service Act 1977, s. 126 (3) & National Health Service and Community Care Act 1990, s. 5 (1), sch. 2, paras 1, 3, 4, 5, 29 (1). – Issued: 20.02.2002. Made: 17.01.2002. Coming into force: 28.01.2002 except for art. 8 which comes into force on 01.04.2002. Effect: S.I. 1991/2382, 2926; 1993/2594, 2599 revoked (01.04.2002.). Territorial extent & classification: E. General. – 4p.: 30 cm. – 0 11 039321 X *£1.75*

The Poole Primary Care Trust (Establishment) Order 2002 No. 2002/727. – Enabling power: National Health Service Act 1977, ss. 16A (1) (2) (3), 126 (4), sch. 5A, paras. 1, 2. – Issued: 25.03.2002. Made: 03.03.2002. Coming into force: 14.03.2002. Effect: None. Territorial extent & classification: E. General. – 4p.: 30 cm. – 0 11 039531 X *£1.75*

The Portsmouth Healthcare National Health Service Trust (Transfer of Trust Property) Order 2002 No. 2002/628. – Enabling power: National Health Service Act 1977, ss. 92 (1) (4), 126 (4). – Issued: 26.03.2002. Made: 08.03.2002. Laid: 11.03.2002. Coming into force: 01.04.2002. Effect: None. Territorial extent & classification: E. General. – 2p.: 30 cm. – 0 11 039563 8 *£1.50*

The Primary Care Trusts (Dissolution) Order 2002 No. 2002/1325. – Enabling power: National Health Service Act 1977, ss. 16A (1) (2), 126 (3) (4). – Issued: 20.05.2002. Made: 26.03.2002. Coming into force: 01.04.2002. Effect: S.I. 2000/255, 256, 2042, 2158, 2338, 2339 revoked. Territorial extent & classification: E. General. – 2p.: 30 cm. – 0 11 039949 8 *£1.50*

The Primary Care Trusts (Establishment) Amendment Order 2002 No. 2002/1405. – Enabling power: National Health Service Act 1977, ss. 16A (1) (2), 126 (3) (4). – Issued: 30.05.2002. Made: 26.03.2002. Coming into force: 01.04.2002. Effect: Various amendments, see schedule. Territorial extent & classification: E. General. – 8p.: 30 cm. – 0 11 042259 7 *£2.00*

The Primary Care Trusts (Functions) (England) Amendment Regulations 2002 No. 2002/555. – Enabling power: National Health Service Act 1977, ss. 17, 17A (4), 18 (1) (1A), 126 (3) (4). – Issued: 30.04.2002. Made: 08.03.2002. Laid: 11.03.2002. Coming into force: 01.04.2002. Effect: S.I. 2000/695 amended. Territorial extent & classification: E. General. – 4p.: 30 cm. – 0 11 039837 8 *£1.75*

The Primary Care Trusts (Membership, Procedure and Administration Arrangements) Amendment (No. 2) (England) Regulations 2002 No. 2002/557. – Enabling power: National Health Service Act 1977, s. 126 (4), sch. 5A, para. 5 & Health and Social Care Act 2001, s. 45 (7). – Issued: 30.04.2002. Made: 08.03.2002. Laid: 11.03.2002. Coming into force: 01.04.2002. Effect: S.I. 2000/89; 2001/3787; 2002/38 amended. Territorial extent & classification: E. General. – 4p.: 30 cm. – 0 11 039840 8 *£1.75*

The Primary Care Trusts (Membership, Procedure and Administration Arrangements) (Amendment) (No. 3) (England) Regulations 2002 No. 2002/38. – Enabling power: National Health Service Act 1977, s. 126 (4), sch. 5A, para. 5. – Issued: 24.01.2002. Made: 13.01.2002. Laid: 14.01.2002. Coming into force: 04.02.2002. Effect: S.I. 2000/89 amended in relation to England & S.I. 2001/2631 revoked. Territorial extent & classification: E. General. – 2p.: 30 cm. – 0 11 039205 1 *£1.50*

The Redbridge and Waltham Forest Health Authority (Transfer of Trust Property) Order 2002 No. 2002/636. – Enabling power: National Health Service Act 1977, ss. 92 (1), 126 (4). – Issued: 26.03.2002. Made: 08.03.2002. Laid: 11.03.2002. Coming into force: 01.04.2002. Effect: None. Territorial extent & classification: E. General. – 2p.: 30 cm. – 0 11 039566 2 *£1.50*

The Redditch and Bromsgrove Primary Care Trust (Establishment) Order 2002 No. 2002/945. – Enabling power: National Health Service Act 1977, ss. 16A (1) (2) (3), 126 (4), sch. 5A, paras. 1, 2. – Issued: 08.04.2002. Made: 10.03.2002. Coming into force: 20.03.2002. Effect: None. Territorial extent & classification: E. General. – 4p.: 30 cm. – 0 11 039693 6 *£1.75*

The Retained Organs Commission (Amendment) Regulations 2002 No. 2002/34. – Enabling power: National Health Service Act 1977, ss. 11 (4), 126 (4), sch. 5, paras. 12. – Issued: 05.02.2002. Made: 10.01.2002. Laid: 11.01.2002. Coming into force: 01.02.2002. Effect: S.I. 2001/748 amended. Territorial extent & classification: E. General. – 2p.: 30 cm. – 0 11 039239 6 *£1.50*

The Riverside Community Health Care National Health Service Trust (Transfer of Trust Property) Order 2002 No. 2002/604. – Enabling power: National Health Service Act 1977, ss. 92 (1), (4), 126 (4). – Issued: 26.03.2002. Made: 08.03.2002. Laid: 11.03.2002. Coming into force: 01.04.2002. Effect: None. Territorial extent & classification: E. General. – 2p.: 30 cm. – 0 11 039568 9 *£1.50*

The Rochdale Healthcare National Health Service Trust (Transfer of Trust Property) Order 2002 No. 2002/564. – Enabling power: National Health Service Act 1977, ss. 92 (1) (4), 126 (4). – Issued: 26.03.2002. Made: 08.03.2002. Laid: 11.03.2002. Coming into force: 01.04.2002. Effect: None. Territorial extent & classification: E. General. – 2p.: 30 cm. – 0 11 039576 X *£1.50*

The Rochdale Primary Care Trust (Establishment) Order 2002 No. 2002/68. – Enabling power: National Health Service Act 1977, ss. 16A (1) (2) (3), 126 (4), sch. 5A, paras. 1, 2. – Issued: 24.01.2002. Made: 13.01.2002. Coming into force: 23.01.2002. Effect: None. Territorial extent & classification: E. General. – 4p.: 30 cm. – 0 11 039202 7 *£1.75*

The Rotherham Health Authority (Transfer of Trust Property) Order 2002 No. 2002/575. – Enabling power: National Health Service Act 1977, ss. 92 (1), 126 (4). – Issued: 26.03.2002. Made: 08.03.2002. Laid: 11.03.2002. Coming into force: 01.04.2002. Effect: None. Territorial extent & classification: E. General. – 2p.: 30 cm. – 0 11 039575 1 *£1.50*

The Rotherham Priority Health Services National Health Service Trust (Dissolution) Order 2002 No. 2002/1293. – Enabling power: National Health Service Act 1977, s. 126 (3) & National Health Service and Community Care Act 1990, s. 5 (1), sch. 2, para. 29 (1). – Issued: 16.05.2002. Made: 21.03.2002. Coming into force: 01.04.2002. Effect: S.I. 1992/2482 revoked. Territorial extent & classification: E. General. – 2p.: 30 cm. – 0 11 039936 6 *£1.50*

The Rotherham Priority Health Services National Health Service Trust (Transfer of Trust Property) Order 2002 No. 2002/627. – Enabling power: National Health Service Act 1977, ss. 92 (1) (4), 126 (4). – Issued: 26.03.2002. Made: 08.03.2002. Laid: 11.03.2002. Coming into force: 01.04.2002. Effect: None. Territorial extent & classification: E. General. – 2p.: 30 cm. – 0 11 039562 X *£1.50*

The Rowley Regis and Tipton Primary Care Trust (Establishment) Order 2002 No. 2002/938. – Enabling power: National Health Service Act 1977, ss. 16A (1) (2) (3), 126 (4), sch. 5A, paras. 1, 2. – Issued: 08.04.2002. Made: 10.03.2002. Coming into force: 20.03.2002. Effect: None. Territorial extent & classification: E. General. – 4p.: 30 cm. – 0 11 039697 9 *£1.75*

The Rugby Primary Care Trust (Establishment) Order 2002 No. 2002/944. – Enabling power: National Health Service Act 1977, ss. 16A (1) (2) (3), 126 (4), sch. 5A, paras. 1, 2. – Issued: 08.04.2002. Made: 10.03.2002. Coming into force: 20.03.2002. Effect: None. Territorial extent & classification: E. General. – 4p.: 30 cm. – 0 11 039694 1 *£1.75*

The Rushmoor and Hart Primary Care Trust (Change of Name) No. 2 Order 2002 No. 2002/1115. – Enabling power: National Health Service Act 1977, ss. 16A (1) (2) (3), 126 (3) (4). – Issued: 19.04.2002. Made: 25.03.2002. Coming into force: 01.04.2002. Effect: S.I. 2001/3297 amended. Territorial extent & classification: E. General. – 2p.: 30 cm. – 0 11 039793 2 *£1.50*

The Rushmoor and Hart Primary Care Trust (Change of Name) Order 2002 No. 2002/730. – Enabling power: National Health Service Act 1977, ss. 16A (1) (2) (3), 126 (3) (4). – Issued: 25.03.2002. Made: 26.02.2002. Coming into force: 08.03.2002. Effect: S.I. 2001/3297 amended. Territorial extent & classification: E. General. – 2p.: 30 cm. – 0 11 039553 0 *£1.50*

The Sandwell and West Birmingham Hospitals National Health Service Trust (Establishment) and the City Hospital National Health Service Trust and Sandwell Healthcare National Health Service Trust (Dissolution) Order 2002 No. 2002/1364. – Enabling power: National Health Service Act 1977, s. 126 (3) & National Health Service and Community Care Act 1990, s. 5 (1), sch. 2, paras. 1, 3, 29 (1). – Issued: 23.05.2002. Made: 26.03.2002. Coming into force: 01.04.2002. Effect: S.I. 1993/2545; 1994/172 revoked. Territorial extent & classification: E. General. – 4p.: 30 cm. – 0 11 039967 6 *£1.75*

The Sandwell Health Authority (Transfer of Trust Property) Order 2002 No. 2002/569. – Enabling power: National Health Service Act 1977, ss. 92 (1), 126 (4). – Issued: 25.03.2002. Made: 08.03.2002. Laid: 11.03.2002. Coming into force: 01.04.2002. Effect: None. Territorial extent & classification: E. General. – 2p.: 30 cm. – 0 11 039537 9 *£1.50*

The Scarborough, Whitby and Ryedale Primary Care Trust (Establishment) Order 2002 No. 2002/137. – Enabling power: National Health Service Act 1977, ss. 16A (1) (2) (3), 126 (4), sch. 5A, paras. 1, 2. – Issued: 06.02.2002. Made: 19.01.2002. Coming into force: 25.01.2002. Effect: None. Territorial extent & classification: E. General. – 4p.: 30 cm. – 0 11 039251 5 *£1.75*

The Sedgefield Primary Care Trust (Establishment) Order 2002 No. 2002/141. – Enabling power: National Health Service Act 1977, ss. 16A (1) (2) (3), 126 (4), sch. 5A, paras. 1, 2. – Issued: 06.02.2002. Made: 19.01.2002. Coming into force: 25.01.2002. Effect: None. Territorial extent & classification: E. General. – 4p.: 30 cm. – 0 11 039259 0 *£1.75*

The Sheffield Children's Hospital National Health Service Trust Change of Name and (Establishment) Amendment Order 2002 No. 2002/1297. – Enabling power: National Health Service Act 1977, s. 126 (3) (4) & National Health Service and Community Care Act 1990, s. 5 (1). – Issued: 16.05.2002. Made: 21.03.2002. Coming into force: 01.04.2002. Effect: S.I. 1991/2399 amended. Territorial extent & classification: E. General. – 2p.: 30 cm. – 0 11 039940 4 *£1.50*

The Shepway Primary Care Trust (Establishment) Order 2002 No. 2002/998. – Enabling power: National Health Service Act 1977, ss. 16A (1) (2) (3), 126 (4), sch. 5A, para. 1. – Issued: 10.04.2002. Made: 25.03.2002. Coming into force: 01.04.2002. Effect: None. Territorial extent & classification: E. General. – 2p.: 30 cm. – 0 11 039711 8 *£1.50*

The Shropshire County Primary Care Trust (Establishment) Order 2002 No. 2002/941. – Enabling power: National Health Service Act 1977, ss. 16A (1) (2) (3), 126 (4), sch. 5A, paras. 1, 2. – Issued: 08.04.2002. Made: 10.03.2002. Coming into force: 20.03.2002. Effect: None. Territorial extent & classification: E. General. – 4p.: 30 cm. – 0 11 039692 8 *£1.75*

The Shropshire Health Authority (Transfer of Trust Property) Order 2002 No. 2002/589. – Enabling power: National Health Service Act 1977, ss. 92 (1), 126 (4). – Issued: 06.06.2002. Made: 08.03.2002. Laid: 11.03.2002. Coming into force: 01.04.2002. Effect: None. Territorial extent & classification: E. General. – 2p.: 30 cm. – 0 11 042298 8 *£1.50*

The Shropshire's Community & Mental Health Services National Health Service Trust (Transfer of Trust Property) Order 2002 No. 2002/608. – Enabling power: National Health Service Act 1977, ss. 92 (1), 126 (4). – Issued: 26.03.2002. Made: 08.03.2002. Laid: 11.03.2002. Coming into force: 01.04.2002. Effect: None. Territorial extent & classification: E. General. – 2p.: 30 cm. – 0 11 039571 9 *£1.50*

The Somerset Health Authority (Transfer of Trust Property) Order 2002 No. 2002/625. – Enabling power: National Health Service Act 1977, ss. 92 (1) (4), 126 (4). – Issued: 26.03.2002. Made: 08.03.2002. Laid: 11.03.2002. Coming into force: 01.04.2002. Effect: None. Territorial extent & classification: E. General. – 2p.: 30 cm. – 0 11 039569 7 *£1.50*

The Southampton and South West Hampshire Health Authority (Transfer of Trust Property) Order 2002 No. 2002/587. – Enabling power: National Health Service Act 1977, ss. 92 (1) (4), 126 (4). – Issued: 06.06.2002. Made: 08.03.2002. Laid: 11.03.2002. Coming into force: 01.04.2002. Effect: None. Territorial extent & classification: E. General. – 2p.: 30 cm. – 0 11 042286 4 *£1.50*

The Southampton Community Health Services National Health Service Trust (Transfer of Trust Property) Order 2002 No. 2002/624. – Enabling power: National Health Service Act 1977, ss. 92 (1) (4), 126 (4). – Issued: 30.05.2002. Made: 08.03.2002. Laid: 11.03.2002. Coming into force: 01.04.2002. Effect: None. Territorial extent & classification: E. General. – 2p.: 30 cm. – 0 11 042258 9 *£1.50*

The Southampton East Healthcare Primary Care Trust (Establishment) (Amendment) Order 2002 No. 2002/729. – Enabling power: National Health Service Act 1977, ss. 16A (1) (2) (3), 126 (3) (4). – Issued: 25.03.2002. Made: 26.02.2002. Coming into force: 08.03.2002. Effect: S.I. 2000/257 amended. Territorial extent & classification: E. General. – 2p.: 30 cm. – 0 11 039552 2 *£1.50*

The South and West Devon Health Authority (Transfer of Trust Property) Order 2002 No. 2002/565. – Enabling power: National Health Service Act 1977, ss. 92 (1) (4), 126 (4). – Issued: 25.03.2002. Made: 08.03.2002. Laid: 11.03.2002. Coming into force: 01.04.2002. Effect: None. Territorial extent & classification: E. General. – 2p.: 30 cm. – 0 11 039549 2 *£1.50*

The South Birmingham Primary Care Trust (Establishment) Order 2002 No. 2002/616. – Enabling power: National Health Service Act 1977, ss. 16A (1) (2) (3), 126 (4), sch. 5A, paras. 1, 2. – Issued: 10.04.2002. Made: 10.03.2002. Coming into force: 20.03.2002. Effect: None. Territorial extent & classification: E. General. – 4p.: 30 cm. – 0 11 039687 1 *£1.75*

The South Buckinghamshire National Health Service Trust (Establishment) Amendment Order 2002 No. 2002/1490. – Enabling power: National Health Service Act 1977, s. 126 (3) (4) & National Health Service and Community Care Act 1990, s. 5 (1). – Issued: 14.06.2002. Made: 25.03.2002. Coming into force: 01.04.2002. Effect: S.I. 1992/2575 amended. Territorial extent & classification: E. General. – 2p.: 30 cm. – 0 11 042337 2 *£1.50*

The South Cambridgeshire Primary Care Trust (Establishment) Order 2002 No. 2002/71. – Enabling power: National Health Service Act 1977, ss. 16A (1) (2) (3), 126 (4), sch. 5A, paras. 1, 2. – Issued: 24.01.2002. Made: 13.01.2002. Coming into force: 23.01.2002. Effect: None. Territorial extent & classification: E. General. – 4p.: 30 cm. – 0 11 039210 8 *£1.75*

The South East London Health Authority (Transfer of Trust Property) Order 2002 No. 2002/2276. – Enabling power: National Health Service Act 1977, ss. 92 (1), 126 (4). – Issued: 16.09.2002. Made: 04.09.2002. Laid: 05.09.2002. Coming into force: 30.09.2002. Effect: None. Territorial extent & classification: E. General. – 2p.: 30 cm. – 0 11 042768 8 *£1.50*

The Southern Derbyshire Mental Health National Health Service Trust Change of Name and (Establishment) Amendment Order and the Community Health Care Service (North Derbyshire) National Health Service Trust (Dissolution) Order 2002 No. 2002/1296. – Enabling power: National Health Service Act 1977, s. 126 (3) (4) & National Health Service and Community Care Act 1990, s. 5 (1), sch. 2, paras. 1, 3, 29 (1). – Issued: 16.05.2002. Made: 26.03.2002. Coming into force: 01.04.2002. Effect: S.I. 1992/2473 amended & S.I. 1993/2602 revoked. Territorial extent & classification: E. General. – 4p.: 30 cm. – 0 11 039939 0 *£1.75*

The South Essex Health Authority (Transfer of Trust Property) Order 2002 No. 2002/574. – Enabling power: National Health Service Act 1977, ss. 92 (1), 126 (4). – Issued: 22.03.2002. Made: 08.03.2002. Laid: 11.03.2002. Coming into force: 01.04.2002. Effect: None. Territorial extent & classification: E. General. – 2p.: 30 cm. – 0 11 039516 6 *£1.50*

The South Essex Mental Health and Community Care National Health Service Trust Change of Name and (Establishment) Amendment Order 2002 No. 2002/1498. – Enabling power: National Health Service Act 1977, s. 126 (3) (4) & National Health Service and Community Care Act 1990, s. 5 (1). – Issued: 14.06.2002. Made: 24.03.2002. Coming into force: 01.04.2002. Effect: S.I. 2000/406 amended. Territorial extent & classification: E. General. – 2p.: 30 cm. – 0 11 042345 3 *£1.50*

The South Huddersfield Primary Care Trust (Establishment) Order 2002 No. 2002/356. – Enabling power: National Health Service Act 1977, ss. 16A (1) (2) (3), 126 (4), sch. 5A, paras. 1, 2. – Issued: 26.02.2002. Made: 29.01.2002. Coming into force: 08.02.2002. Effect: None. Territorial extent & classification: E. General. – 4p.: 30 cm. – 0 11 039375 9 *£1.75*

The South of Tyne and Wearside Mental Health National Health Service Trust (Establishment) and the Priority Healthcare Wearside National Health Service Trust (Dissolution) Order 2002 No. 2002/1324. – Enabling power: National Health Service Act 1977, s. 126 (3) & National Health Service and Community Care Act 1990, s. 5 (1), sch. 2, paras. 1, 3, 29 (1). – Issued: 20.05.2002. Made: 19.03.2002. Coming into force: 01.04.2002. Effect: S.I. 1993/2605 revoked. Territorial extent & classification: E. General. – 4p.: 30 cm. – 0 11 039948 X *£1.75*

The South Staffordshire Health Authority (Transfer of Trust Property) Order 2002 No. 2002/563. – Enabling power: National Health Service Act 1977, ss. 92 (1), 126 (4). – Issued: 25.03.2002. Made: 08.03.2002. Laid: 11.03.2002. Coming into force: 01.04.2002. Effect: None. Territorial extent & classification: E. General. – 2p.: 30 cm. – 0 11 039554 9 *£1.50*

The South Stoke Primary Care Trust (Establishment) Amendment (No. 2) Order 2002 No. 2002/1393. – Enabling power: National Health Service Act 1977, ss. 16A (1) (2) (3), 126 (3) (4). – Issued: 27.05.2002. Made: 09.05.2002. Coming into force: 16.05.2002. Effect: S.I. 2001/163 amended. Territorial extent & classification: E. General. – 2p.: 30 cm. – 0 11 042226 0 *£1.50*

The South Stoke Primary Care Trust (Establishment) Amendment Order 2002 No. 2002/1112. – Enabling power: National Health Service Act 1977, ss. 16A (1) (2) (3), 126 (3) (4). – Issued: 17.04.2002. Made: 26.03.2002. Coming into force: 01.04.2002. Effect: S.I. 2001/163 amended. Territorial extent & classification: E. General. – 2p.: 30 cm. – 0 11 039788 6 *£1.50*

The South Tees Acute Hospitals National Health Service Trust (Establishment) Amendment Order 2002 No. 2002/1491. – Enabling power: National Health Service Act 1977, s. 126 (3) (4) & National Health Service and Community Care Act 1990, s. 5 (1). – Issued: 14.06.2002. Made: 19.03.2002. Coming into force: 01.04.2002. Effect: S.I. 1991/2402 amended. Territorial extent & classification: E. General. – 2p.: 30 cm. – 0 11 042338 0 *£1.50*

The South Tyneside Primary Care Trust (Establishment) Order 2002 No. 2002/166. – Enabling power: National Health Service Act 1977, ss. 16A (1) (2) (3), 126 (4), sch. 5A, paras. 1, 2. – Issued: 12.02.2002. Made: 19.01.2002. Coming into force: 25.01.2002. Effect: None. Territorial extent & classification: E. General. – 4p.: 30 cm. – 0 11 039284 1 *£1.75*

The Southwark Primary Care Trust (Establishment) Order 2002 No. 2002/1003. – Enabling power: National Health Service Act 1977, ss. 16A (1) (2) (3), 126 (4), sch. 5A, para. 1. – Issued: 12.04.2002. Made: 20.03.2002. Coming into force: 01.04.2002. Effect: None. Territorial extent & classification: E. General. – 2p.: 30 cm. – 0 11 039738 X *£1.50*

The South Warwickshire Combined Care National Health Service Trust (Transfer of Trust Property) Order 2002 No. 2002/626. – Enabling power: National Health Service Act 1977, ss. 92 (1), 126 (4). – Issued: 26.03.2002. Made: 08.03.2002. Laid: 11.03.2002. Coming into force: 01.04.2002. Effect: None. Territorial extent & classification: E. General. – 2p.: 30 cm. – 0 11 039561 1 *£1.50*

The South Warwickshire Primary Care Trust (Establishment) Order 2002 No. 2002/942. – Enabling power: National Health Service Act 1977, ss. 16A (1) (2) (3), 126 (4), sch. 5A, paras. 1, 2. – Issued: 08.04.2002. Made: 10.03.2002. Coming into force: 20.03.2002. Effect: None. Territorial extent & classification: E. General. – 4p.: 30 cm. – 0 11 039696 0 *£1.75*

The South Western Staffordshire Primary Care Trust (Establishment) Order 2002 No. 2002/950. – Enabling power: National Health Service Act 1977, ss. 16A (1) (2) (3), 126 (4), sch. 5A, para. 1. – Issued: 08.04.2002. Made: 21.03.2002. Coming into force: 01.04.2002. Effect: None. Territorial extent & classification: E. General. – 2p.: 30 cm. – 0 11 039678 2 *£1.50*

The South West London Community National Health Service Trust (Transfer of Trust Property) No. 2 Order 2002 No. 2002/877. – Enabling power: National Health Service Act 1977, ss. 92 (1), 126 (4). – Issued: 06.06.2002. Made: 27.03.2002. Laid: 28.03.2002. Coming into force: 01.04.2002. Effect: None. Territorial extent & classification: E. General. – 4p.: 30 cm. – 0 11 042292 9 *£1.75*

The South West London Community National Health Service Trust (Transfer of Trust Property) Order 2002 No. 2002/873. – Enabling power: National Health Service Act 1977, ss. 92 (1), 126 (4). – Issued: 06.06.2002. Made: 27.03.2002. Laid: 28.03.2002. Coming into force: 01.04.2002. Effect: None. Territorial extent & classification: E. General. – 2p.: 30 cm. – 0 11 042295 3 *£1.50*

The South West Peninsula Health Authority (Transfer of Trust Property) Order 2002 No. 2002/2277. – Enabling power: National Health Service Act 1977, ss. 92 (1), 126 (4). – Issued: 16.09.2002. Made: 04.09.2002. Laid: 05.09.2002. Coming into force: 30.09.2002. Effect: None. Territorial extent & classification: E. General. – 2p.: 30 cm. – 0 11 042765 3 *£1.50*

The South West Yorkshire Mental Health National Health Service Trust (Establishment) and the Wakefield and Pontefract Community National Health Service Trust (Dissolution) Order 2002 No. 2002/1313. – Enabling power: National Health Service Act 1977, ss. 126 (3) & National Health Service and Community Care Act 1990, s. 5 (1), sch. 2, paras. 1, 3, 29 (1). – Issued: 20.05.2002. Made: 19.03.2002. Coming into force: 01.04.2002. Effect: S.I. 1992/2495 revoked. Territorial extent & classification: E. General. – 4p.: 30 cm. – 0 11 039944 7 *£1.75*

The South Worcestershire Primary Care Trust (Establishment) Order 2002 No. 2002/947. – Enabling power: National Health Service Act 1977, ss. 16A (1) (2) (3), 126 (4), sch. 5A, paras. 1, 2. – Issued: 08.04.2002. Made: 10.03.2002. Coming into force: 20.03.2002. Effect: None. Territorial extent & classification: E. General. – 4p.: 30 cm. – 0 11 039683 9 *£1.75*

The South Yorkshire Metropolitan Ambulance and Paramedic Service National Health Service Trust (Change of Name) Order 2002 No. 2002/1791. – Enabling power: National Health Service Act 1977, s. 126 (3) (4) & National Health Service and Community Care Act 1990, s. 5 (1). – Issued: 18.07.2002. Made: 09.07.2002. Coming into force: 19.07.2002. Effect: S.I. 1991/2404 amended. Territorial extent & classification: E. General. – 4p.: 30 cm. – 0 11 042472 7 *£1.75*

The St. Helens and Knowsley Community Health National Health Service Trust (Dissolution) Order 2002 No. 2002/1489. – Enabling power: National Health Service Act 1977, s. 126 (3) & National Health Service and Community Care Act 1990, s. 5 (1), sch. 2, para. 29 (1). – Issued: 14.06.2002. Made: 24.03.2002. Coming into force: 01.04.2002. Effect: S.I. 1991/2394 revoked. Territorial extent & classification: E. General. – 2p.: 30 cm. – 0 11 042336 4 *£1.50*

The St Helens and Knowsley Community Health National Health Service Trust (Transfer of Trust Property) Order 2002 No. 2002/566. – Enabling power: National Health Service Act 1977, ss. 92 (1), 126 (4). – Issued: 25.03.2002. Made: 08.03.2002. Laid: 11.03.2002. Coming into force: 01.04.2002. Effect: None. Territorial extent & classification: E. General. – 2p.: 30 cm. – 0 11 039543 3 *£1.50*

The St Helens Primary Care Trust (Establishment) Order 2002 No. 2002/70. – Enabling power: National Health Service Act 1977, ss. 16A (1) (2) (3), 126 (4), sch. 5A, paras. 1, 2. – Issued: 24.01.2002. Made: 13.04.2002. Coming into force: 23.01.2002. Effect: None. Territorial extent & classification: E. General. – 4p.: 30 cm. – 0 11 039204 3 *£1.75*

The Sunderland Health Authority (Transfer of Trust Property) Order 2002 No. 2002/869. – Enabling power: National Health Service Act 1977, ss. 92 (1), 126 (4). – Issued: 27.05.2002. Made: 27.03.2002. Laid: 28.03.2002. Coming into force: 01.04.2002. Effect: None. Territorial extent & classification: E. General. – 2p.: 30 cm. – 0 11 042236 8 *£1.50*

The Sunderland Teaching Primary Care Trust (Establishment) Order 2002 No. 2002/139. – Enabling power: National Health Service Act 1977, ss. 16A (1) (2) (3), 126 (4), sch. 5A, paras. 1, 2. – Issued: 06.02.2002. Made: 19.01.2002. Coming into force: 25.01.2002. Effect: None. Territorial extent & classification: E. General. – 4p.: 30 cm. – 0 11 039248 5 *£1.75*

The Surrey and Sussex Health Authority (Transfer of Trust Property) Order 2002 No. 2002/2283. – Enabling power: National Health Service Act 1977, ss. 92 (1), 126 (4). – Issued: 16.09.2002. Made: 04.09.2002. Laid: 05.09.2002. Coming into force: 30.09.2002. Effect: None. Territorial extent & classification: E. General. – 4p.: 30 cm. – 0 11 042757 2 *£1.75*

The Surrey and Sussex Healthcare National Health Service Trust (Transfer of Trust Property) Order 2002 No. 2002/856. – Enabling power: National Health Service Act 1977, ss. 92 (1), 126 (4). – Issued: 27.05.2002. Made: 26.03.2002. Laid: 28.03.2002. Coming into force: 01.04.2002. Effect: None. Territorial extent & classification: E. General. – 2p.: 30 cm. – 0 11 042233 3 *£1.50*

The Sussex Downs and Weald Primary Care Trust (Establishment) Order 2002 No. 2002/996. – Enabling power: National Health Service Act 1977, ss. 16A (1) (2) (3), 126 (4), sch. 5A, para. 1. – Issued: 10.04.2002. Made: 25.03.2002. Coming into force: 01.04.2002. Effect: None. Territorial extent & classification: E. General. – 2p.: 30 cm. – 0 11 039724 X *£1.50*

The Sussex Weald and Downs National Health Service Trust (Transfer of Trust Property) Order 2002 No. 2002/867. – Enabling power: National Health Service Act 1977, ss. 92 (1), 126 (4). – Issued: 29.05.2002. Made: 27.03.2002. Laid: 28.03.2002. Coming into force: 01.04.2002. Effect: None. Territorial extent & classification: E. General. – 2p.: 30 cm. – 0 11 042252 X *£1.50*

The Swale Primary Care Trust (Establishment) Order 2002 No. 2002/993. – Enabling power: National Health Service Act 1977, ss. 16A (1) (2) (3), 126 (4), sch. 5A, para. 1. – Issued: 10.04.2002. Made: 25.03.2002. Coming into force: 01.04.2002. Effect: None. Territorial extent & classification: E. General. – 2p.: 30 cm. – 0 11 039708 8 *£1.50*

The Swindon Primary Care Trust (Establishment) Order 2002 No. 2002/722. – Enabling power: National Health Service Act 1977, ss. 16A (1) (2) (3), 126 (4), sch. 5A, paras. 1, 2. – Issued: 25.03.2002. Made: 03.03.2002. Coming into force: 14.03.2002. Effect: None. Territorial extent & classification: E. General. – 4p.: 30 cm. – 0 11 039539 5 *£1.75*

The Tameside and Glossop Community and Priority Services National Health Service Trust (Transfer of Trust Property) No. 2 Order 2002 No. 2002/857. – Enabling power: National Health Service Act 1977, ss. 92 (1), 126 (4). – Issued: 30.05.2002. Made: 26.03.2002. Laid: 28.03.2002. Coming into force: 01.04.2002. Effect: None. Territorial extent & classification: E. General. – 2p.: 30 cm. – 0 11 042269 4 *£1.50*

The Tameside and Glossop Primary Care Trust (Establishment) Order 2002 No. 2002/1117. – Enabling power: National Health Service Act 1977, ss. 16A (1) (2) (3), 126 (4), sch. 5A, para. 1. – Issued: 19.04.2002. Made: 24.03.2002. Coming into force: 01.04.2002. Effect: None. Territorial extent & classification: E. General. – 2p.: 30 cm. – 0 11 039789 4 *£1.50*

The Tameside & Glossop Community and Priority Services National Health Service Trust (Transfer of Trust Property) Order 2002 No. 2002/630. – Enabling power: National Health Service Act 1977, ss. 92 (1), 126 (4). – Issued: 26.03.2002. Made: 08.03.2002. Laid: 11.03.2002. Coming into force: 01.04.2002. Effect: None. Territorial extent & classification: E. General. – 2p.: 30 cm. – 0 11 039570 0 *£1.50*

The Taunton and Somerset National Health Service Trust (Transfer of Trust Property) Order 2002 No. 2002/632. – Enabling power: National Health Service Act 1977, ss. 92 (1), 126 (4). – Issued: 25.03.2002. Made: 08.03.2002. Laid: 11.03.2002. Coming into force: 01.04.2002. Effect: None. Territorial extent & classification: E. General. – 2p.: 30 cm. – 0 11 039544 1 *£1.50*

The Teddington, Twickenham and Hamptons Primary Care Trust (Establishment) Amendment and Change of Name Order 2002 No. 2002/1008. – Enabling power: National Health Service Act 1977, ss. 16A (1) (2) (3), 126 (3) (4). – Issued: 12.04.2002. Made: 20.03.2002. Coming into force: 01.04.2002. Effect: S.I. 2001/278 amended. Territorial extent & classification: E. General. – 2p.: 30 cm. – 0 11 039743 6 *£1.50*

The Telford and Wrekin Primary Care Trust (Establishment) Order 2002 No. 2002/943. – Enabling power: National Health Service Act 1977, ss. 16A (1) (2) (3), 126 (4), sch. 5A, paras. 1, 2. – Issued: 08.04.2002. Made: 10.03.2002. Coming into force: 20.03.2002. Effect: None. Territorial extent & classification: E. General. – 4p.: 30 cm. – 0 11 039695 2 *£1.75*

The Thames Gateway National Health Service Trust (Transfer of Trust Property) Order 2002 No. 2002/879. – Enabling power: National Health Service Act 1977, ss. 92 (1), 126 (4). – Issued: 06.06.2002. Made: 27.03.2002. Laid: 28.03.2002. Coming into force: 01.04.2002. Effect: None. Territorial extent & classification: E. General. – 2p.: 30 cm. – 0 11 042291 0 *£1.50*

The Thames Valley Health Authority (Transfer of Trust Property) Order 2002 No. 2002/2278. – Enabling power: National Health Service Act 1977, ss. 92 (1), 126 (4). – Issued: 16.09.2002. Made: 04.09.2002. Laid: 05.09.2002. Coming into force: 30.09.2002. Effect: None. Territorial extent & classification: E. General. – 4p.: 30 cm. – 0 11 042756 4 *£1.75*

The Torbay Primary Care Trust and the Teignbridge Primary Care Trust (Establishment) Amendment Order 2002 No. 2002/1118. – Enabling power: National Health Service Act 1977, ss. 16A (1) (2), 126 (3) (4). – Issued: 19.04.2002. Made: 25.03.2002. Coming into force: 01.04.2002. Effect: S.I. 2000/2154; 2001/467 amended. Territorial extent & classification: E. General. – 2p.: 30 cm. – 0 11 039798 3 *£1.50*

The Trent Health Authority (Transfer of Trust Property) Order 2002 No. 2002/2279. – Enabling power: National Health Service Act 1977, ss. 92 (1), 126 (4). – Issued: 16.09.2002. Made: 04.09.2002. Laid: 05.09.2002. Coming into force: 30.09.2002. Effect: None. Territorial extent & classification: E. General. – 4p.: 30 cm. – 0 11 042760 2 *£1.75*

The Wakefield Health Authority (Transfer of Trust Property) Order 2002 No. 2002/852. – Enabling power: National Health Service Act 1977, ss. 92 (1), 126 (4). – Issued: 06.06.2002. Made: 26.03.2002. Laid: 28.03.2002. Coming into force: 01.04.2002. Effect: None. Territorial extent & classification: E. General. – 2p.: 30 cm. – 0 11 042301 1 *£1.50*

The Walsall Community Health National Health Service Trust (Transfer of Trust Property) Order 2002 No. 2002/855. – Enabling power: National Health Service Act 1977, ss. 92 (1), 126 (4). – Issued: 29.05.2002. Made: 26.03.2002. Laid: 28.03.2002. Coming into force: 01.04.2002. Effect: None. Territorial extent & classification: E. General. – 2p.: 30 cm. – 0 11 042255 4 *£1.50*

The Walsall Primary Care Trust (Establishment) Order 2002 No. 2002/894. – Enabling power: National Health Service Act 1977, ss. 16A (1) (2) (3), 126 (4), sch. 5A, paras. 1, 2. – Issued: 08.04.2002. Made: 10.03.2002. Coming into force: 20.03.2002. Effect: None. Territorial extent & classification: E. General. – 4p.: 30 cm. – 0 11 039680 4 *£1.75*

The Wandsworth Primary Care Trust (Establishment) Order 2002 No. 2002/893. – Enabling power: National Health Service Act 1977, ss. 16A (1) (2) (3), 126 (4), sch. 5A, para. 1. – Issued: 12.04.2002. Made: 20.03.2002. Coming into force: 01.04.2002. Effect: None. Territorial extent & classification: E. General. – 2p.: 30 cm. – 0 11 039737 1 *£1.50*

The Warrington Community Healthcare National Health Service Trust (Transfer of Trust Property) Order 2002 No. 2002/633. – Enabling power: National Health Service Act 1977, ss. 92 (1), 126 (4). – Issued: 26.03.2002. Made: 08.03.2002. Laid: 11.03.2002. Coming into force: 01.04.2002. Effect: None. Territorial extent & classification: E. General. – 2p.: 30 cm. – 0 11 039567 0 £1.50

The Warrington Primary Care Trust (Establishment) Order 2002 No. 2002/65. – Enabling power: National Health Service Act 1977, ss. 16A (1) (2) (3), 126 (4), sch. 5A, paras. 1, 2. – Issued: 24.01.2002. Made: 13.01.2002. Coming into force: 23.01.2002. Effect: None. Territorial extent & classification: E. General. – 4p.: 30 cm. – 0 11 039212 4 £1.75

The Warwickshire Health Authority (Transfer of Trust Property) Order 2002 No. 2002/588. – Enabling power: National Health Service Act 1977, ss. 92 (1), 126 (4). – Issued: 06.06.2002. Made: 08.03.2002. Laid: 11.03.2002. Coming into force: 01.04.2002. Effect: None. Territorial extent & classification: E. General. – 2p.: 30 cm. – 0 11 042305 4 £1.50

The Wednesbury and West Bromwich Primary Care Trust (Establishment) Order 2002 No. 2002/957. – Enabling power: National Health Service Act 1977, ss. 16A (1) (2) (3), 126 (4), sch. 5A, paras. 1, 2. – Issued: 08.04.2002. Made: 10.03.2002. Coming into force: 20.03.2002. Effect: None. Territorial extent & classification: E. General. – 4p.: 30 cm. – 0 11 039691 X £1.75

The Western Sussex Primary Care Trust (Establishment) Order 2002 No. 2002/987. – Enabling power: National Health Service Act 1977, ss. 16A (1) (2) (3), 126 (4), sch. 5A, para. 1. – Issued: 10.04.2002. Made: 25.03.2002. Coming into force: 01.04.2002. Effect: None. Territorial extent & classification: E. General. – 2p.: 30 cm. – 0 11 039713 4 £1.50

The West Kent Health Authority (Transfer of Trust Property) Order 2002 No. 2002/875. – Enabling power: National Health Service Act 1977, ss. 92 (1), 126 (4). – Issued: 06.06.2002. Made: 27.03.2002. Laid: 28.03.2002. Coming into force: 01.04.2002. Effect: None. Territorial extent & classification: E. General. – 2p.: 30 cm. – 0 11 042294 5 £1.50

The West Kent National Health Service and Social Care Trust (Establishment) and the Thames Gateway National Health Service Trust and Invicta Community Care National Health Service Trust (Dissolution) Order 2002 No. 2002/1337. – Enabling power: National Health Service Act 1977, s. 126 (3) & National Health Service and Community Care Act 1990, s. 5 (1), sch. 2, paras. 1, 3, 29 (1). – Issued: 21.05.2002. Made: 25.03.2002. Coming into force: 01.04.2002. Effect: S.I. 1997/419; 1998/805 revoked. Territorial extent & classification: E. General. – 4p.: 30 cm. – 0 11 039954 4 £1.75

The Westminster Primary Care Trust (Establishment) Order 2002 No. 2002/1006. – Enabling power: National Health Service Act 1977, ss. 16A (1) (2) (3), 126 (4), sch. 5A, para. 1. – Issued: 12.04.2002. Made: 20.03.2002. Coming into force: 01.04.2002. Effect: None. Territorial extent & classification: E. General. – 2p.: 30 cm. – 0 11 039732 0 £1.50

The West Sussex Health and Social Care National Health Service Trust (Establishment) and the Worthing Priority National Health Service Trust and Sussex Weald and Downs National Health Service Trust (Dissolution) Order 2002 No. 2002/1362. – Enabling power: National Health Service Act 1977, s. 126 (3) & National Health Service and Community Care Act 1990, s. 5 (1), sch. 2, paras. 1, 3, 29 (1). – Issued: 23.05.2002. Made: 25.03.2002. Coming into force: 01.04.2002. Effect: S.I. 1992/2520; 1993/2589 revoked. Territorial extent & classification: E. General. – 4p.: 30 cm. – 0 11 039968 4 £1.75

The West Sussex Health Authority (Transfer of Trust Property) Order 2002 No. 2002/853. – Enabling power: National Health Service Act 1977, ss. 92 (1), 126 (4). – Issued: 06.06.2002. Made: 26.03.2002. Laid: 28.03.2002. Coming into force: 01.04.2002. Effect: None. Territorial extent & classification: E. General. – 2p.: 30 cm. – 0 11 042293 7 £1.50

The West Yorkshire Health Authority (Transfer of Trust Property) Order 2002 No. 2002/2280. – Enabling power: National Health Service Act 1977, ss. 92 (1), 126 (4). – Issued: 16.09.2002. Made: 04.09.2002. Laid: 05.09.2002. Coming into force: 30.09.2002. Effect: None. Territorial extent & classification: E. General. – 4p.: 30 cm. – 0 11 042763 7 £1.75

The Wiltshire and Swindon Health Care National Health Service Trust (Dissolution) Order 2002 No. 2002/1335. – Enabling power: National Health Service Act 1977, s. 126 (3) & National Health Service and Community Care Act 1990, s. 5 (1), sch. 2, para. 29 (1). – Issued: 21.05.2002. Made: 25.03.2002. Coming into force: 01.04.2002. Effect: S.I. 1999/1770 revoked. Territorial extent & classification: E. General. – 2p.: 30 cm. – 0 11 039958 7 £1.50

The Wiltshire and Swindon Health Care National Health Service Trust (Transfer of Trust Property) Order 2002 No. 2002/567. – Enabling power: National Health Service Act 1977, ss. 92 (1), 126 (4). – Issued: 26.03.2002. Made: 08.03.2002. Laid: 11.03.2002. Coming into force: 01.04.2002. Effect: None. Territorial extent & classification: E. General. – 2p.: 30 cm. – 0 11 039564 6 £1.50

The Witham, Braintree and Halstead Care Trust (Establishment) Order 2002 No. 2002/2233. – Enabling power: National Health Service Act 1977, ss. 16A (1) (2) (3), 126 (4), sch. 5A, paras. 1, 2 & Health and Social Care Act 2001, s. 45 (5). – Issued: 06.09.2002. Made: 29.08.2002. Laid:-. Coming into force: 01.09.2002. Effect: None. Territorial extent & classification: E. General. – 4p.: 30 cm. – 0 11 042715 7 £1.75

The Woking Area Primary Care Trust (Establishment) Order 2002 No. 2002/995. – Enabling power: National Health Service Act 1977, ss. 16A (1) (2) (3), 126 (4), sch. 5A, para. 1. – Issued: 10.04.2002. Made: 25.03.2002. Coming into force: 01.04.2002. Effect: None. Territorial extent & classification: E. General. – 2p.: 30 cm. – 0 11 039716 9 *£1.50*

The Wolverhampton City Primary Care Trust (Establishment) Order 2002 No. 2002/948. – Enabling power: National Health Service Act 1977, ss. 16A (1) (2) (3), 126 (4), sch. 5A, para. 1. – Issued: 10.04.2002. Made: 21.03.2002. Coming into force: 01.04.2002. Effect: None. Territorial extent & classification: E. General. – 4p.: 30 cm. – 0 11 039684 7 *£1.75*

The Worcestershire Community and Mental Health National Health Service Trust Change of Name and (Establishment) Amendment Order 2002 No. 2002/1360. – Enabling power: National Health Service Act 1977, s. 126 (3) (4) & National Health Service and Community Care Act 1990, s. 5 (1). – Issued: 23.05.2002. Made: 26.03.2002. Coming into force: 01.04.2002. Effect: S.I. 1999/3472 amended. Territorial extent & classification: E. General. – 2p.: 30 cm. – 0 11 039964 1 *£1.50*

The Worcestershire Health Authority (Transfer of Trust Property) Order 2002 No. 2002/576. – Enabling power: National Health Service Act 1977, ss. 92 (1), 126 (4). – Issued: 25.03.2002. Made: 08.03.2002. Laid: 11.03.2002. Coming into force: 01.04.2002. Effect: None. Territorial extent & classification: E. General. – 2p.: 30 cm. – 0 11 039547 6 *£1.50*

National Health Service, England and Wales

The Abolition of the NHS Tribunal (Consequential Provisions) Regulations 2002 No. 2002/1920. – Enabling power: Health and Social Care Act 2001, s. 65 (1) (2). – Issued: 01.08.2002. Made: 24.07.2002. Laid: 01.08.2002. Coming into force: 26.08.2002. Effect: S.I. 1986/975; 1992/635, 661; 2001/3740 amended. Territorial extent & classification: E/W. General. – 8p.: 30 cm. – 0 11 042569 3 *£2.00*

The Family Health Services Appeal Authority (Procedure) (Amendment) Rules 2002 No. 2002/1921. – Enabling power: National Health Service Act 1977, s. 126 (4), sch. 9A. – Issued: 01.08.2002. Made: 23.07.2002. Laid: 01.08.2002. Coming into force: 26.08.2002. Effect: S.I. 2001/3750 amended. Territorial extent & classification: E/W. General. – 2p.: 30 cm. – 0 11 042568 5 *£1.50*

The Health and Social Care Act 2001 (Commencement No. 8) (Amendment) Order 2002 No. 2002/1170 (C.30). – Enabling power: Health and Social Care Act 2001, ss. 64 (6 (8)), 70 (2). – Issued: 30.04.2002. Made: 26.03.2002. Effect: S.I. 2002/1095 (C.26) amended. Territorial extent & classification: E/W. General. – 2p.: 30 cm. – 0 11 039848 3 *£1.50*

The Health Service (Control of Patient Information) Regulations 2002 No. 2002/1438. – Enabling power: Health and Social Care Act 2001, ss. 60 (1), 64 (6) (7) (8). – Issued: 08.06.2002. Made: 23.05.2002. Coming into force: 01.06.2002. Effect: None. Territorial extent & classification: E/W. General. – Supersedes draft SI, issued 7th May 2002 (ISBN 0110398904). – 8p.: 30 cm. – 0 11 042307 0 *£2.00*

The National Health Service Act 1977 and National Health Service and Community Care Act 1990 (Amendment) Amendment Regulations 2002 No. 2002/2932. – Enabling power: European Communities Act 1972, s. 2 (2). – Issued: 23.12.2002. Made: 27.11.2002. Laid: 27.11.2002. Coming into force: 28.11.2002. Effect: S.I. 2002/2759 amended in relation to England and Wales. Territorial extent & classification: E/W. General. – 2p.: 30 cm. – This S.I. has been printed to correct an error in S.I. 2002/2759 and is being issued free of charge to all known recipients of that S.I. – 0 11 044234 2 *£1.50*

The National Health Service Act 1977 and National Health Service and Community Care Act 1990 (Amendment) Regulations 2002 No. 2002/2759. – Enabling power: European Communities Act 1972, s. 2 (2). – Issued: 14.11.2002. Made: 07.11.2002. Laid: 07.11.2002. Coming into force: 29.11.2002. Effect: 1977 c.49; 1990 c.19 amended. Territorial extent & classification: E/W. General. – 2p.: 30 cm. – EC note: Amends the 1977 and 1990 act to implement European obligations arising from decisions of the European Court of Justice, in particular case C-157/99 and enable rights to be enjoyed relating to the freedom to provide services 0 11 042962 1 *£1.50*

The National Health Service (Compensation for Premature Retirement) Regulations 2002 No. 2002/1311. – Enabling power: Superannuation Act 1972, s. 24 (1) (3) (4), sch. 3, paras. 8, 9, 13. – Issued: 27.05.2002. Made: 10.05.2002. Laid: 10.05.2002. Coming into force: 31.05.2002. Effect: S.I. 1981/1263; 1991/584; 2000/605 amended & S.I. 1985/1659 revoked. Territorial extent & classification: E/W. General. – 12p.: 30 cm. – 0 11 039987 0 *£2.50*

The National Health Service Pension Scheme (Additional Voluntary Contributions) Amendment Regulations 2002 No. 2002/610. – Enabling power: Superannuation Act 1972, ss. 10 (1) (2) (2A) (3), sch. 3. – Issued: 30.04.2002. Made: 20.03.2002. Laid: 21.03.2002. Coming into force: 12.04.2002. Effect: S.I. 2000/619 amended. Territorial extent & classification: E/W. General. – 4p.: 30 cm. – 0 11 039844 0 *£1.75*

The National Health Service Pension Scheme (Amendment) Regulations 2002 No. 2002/561. – Enabling power: Superannuation Act 1972, ss. 10 (1) (2) (3), 12 (1) (2), sch. 3. – Issued: 30.04.2002. Made: 15.03.2002. Laid: 15.03.2002. Coming into force: 01.04.2001, 05.04.2002, in accord. with art. 1 (1) (2). Effect: S.I. 1995/300 amended (01.04.2001, 05.04.2002). Territorial extent & classification: E/W. General. – 8p.: 30 cm. – 0 11 039842 4 *£2.00*

The National Health Service Reform and Health Care Professions Act 2002 (Commencement No. 2) Order 2002 No. 2002/2478 (C.80). – Enabling power: National Health Service Reform and Health Care Professions Act 2002, ss. 38 (7), 42 (3). Bringing into force various provisions of the 2002 Act on 01.10.2002. – Issued: 02.10.2002. Made: 27.09.2002. Effect: None. Territorial extent & classification: UK [parts to E/W only and parts to all UK]. General. – 4p.: 30 cm. – 0 11 042832 3 *£1.75*

The National Health Service Reform and Health Care Professions Act 2002 (Commencement No. 3) Order 2002 No. 2002/3190 (C.108). – Enabling power: National Health Service Reform and Health Care Professions Act 2002, s. 42 (3). Bringing into force various provisions of the 2002 Act on 01.01.2003, in accord. with art. 2 (1). – Issued: 27.12.2002. Made: 18.12.2002. Laid:-. Effect: None. Territorial extent & classification: E/W. General. – 4p.: 30 cm. – 0 11 044387 X *£1.75*

The National Institute for Clinical Excellence (Amendment) Regulations 2002 No. 2002/1759. – Enabling power: National Health Service Act 1977, ss. 16 (2), 126 (4), sch. 5, para. 12. – Issued: 18.07.2002. Made: 09.07.2002. Laid: 09.07.2002. Coming into force: 01.08.2002. Effect: S.I. 1999/260 amended. Territorial extent & classification:E/W. General. – 4p.: 30 cm. – 0 11 042463 8 *£1.75*

The National Institute for Clinical Excellence (Establishment and Constitution) Amendment Order 2002 No. 2002/1760. – Enabling power: National Health Service Act 1977, ss. 11 (1) (2) (4), 126 (3) (4). – Issued: 18.07.2002. Made: 09.07.2002. Laid: 09.07.2002. Coming into force: 01.08.2002. Effect: S.I. 1999/220 amended. Territorial extent & classification: E/W. General. – 4p.: 30 cm. – 0 11 042462 X *£1.75*

The Road Traffic (NHS Charges) Amendment (No. 2) Regulations 2002 No. 2002/2995. – Enabling power: Road Traffic (NHS Charges) Act 1999, ss. 3 (2) (4), 16 (2), 17. – Issued: 11.12.2002. Made: 03.12.2002. Laid: 11.12.2002. Coming into force: 01.01.2003. Effect: S.I. 1999/785 amended. Territorial extent & classification: E/W. General. – 4p.: 30 cm. – 0 11 044121 4 *£1.75*

The Road Traffic (NHS Charges) Amendment Regulations 2002 No. 2002/237. – Enabling power: Road Traffic (NHS Charges) Act 1999, ss. 3 (2) (4), 16 (2), 17. – Issued: 13.03.2002. Made: 07.02.2002. Laid: 07.02.2002. Coming into force: 08.02.2002. Effect: S.I. 1999/785 amended & S.I. 2001/4030 revoked. Territorial extent & classification: E/W. General. – 2p.: 30 cm. – 0 11 039432 1 *£1.50*

National Health Service, Wales

The Health and Social Care Act 2001 (Commencement No. 2) (Wales) Order 2002 No. 2002/1475 (W.147) (C.41). – Enabling power: Health and Social Care Act 2001, ss 64 (6), 66, 70 (2). Bringing into operation various provisions of the 2001 Act on 01.07.2002. & 01.12.2002. – Issued: 05.07.2002. Made: 30.05.2002. Effect: None. Territorial extent & classification: W. General. – 12p.: 30 cm. – In English and Welsh. Welsh title: Gorchymyn Deddf Iechyd a Gofal Cymdeithasol 2001 (Cychwyn Rhif 2) (Cymru) 2002 – 0 11 090516 4 *£2.50*

The Health and Social Care Act 2001 (Commencement No. 3) (Wales) Order 2002 No. 2002/1919 (C.60). – Enabling power: Health and Social Care Act 2001, ss 64 (6) (8), 70 (2). Bringing into operation various provisions of the 2001 Act on 26.08.2002, in accord. with section 2. – Issued: 01.08.2002. Made: 22.07.2002. Effect: None. Territorial extent & classification: W. General. – 8p.: 30 cm. – 0 11 042570 7 *£2.00*

The National Health Service (General Dental Services) (Amendment) (Wales) (No. 2) Regulations 2002 No. 2002/1881 (W.190). – Enabling power: National Health Service Act 1977, ss. 15 (1), 35 (1), 36 (1) (1A) (4) to (8), 37 (1), 43ZA, 49F, 49I, 49L, 49M, 49N, 49O, 49P, 49R, 126 (4) & Health and Social Care Act 2001, s. 65. – Issued: 03.09.2002. Made: 18.07.2002. Coming into force: 26.08.2002. Effect: S.I. 1992/661 amended in relation to Wales. Territorial extent & classification: W. General. – 32p.: 30 cm. – In English and Welsh. Welsh title: Rheoliadau'r Gwasanaeth Iechyd Gwladol (Gwasanaethau Deintyddol Cyffredinol) (Diwygio) (Cymru) (Rhif 2) 2002 – 0 11 090562 8 *£6.00*

The National Health Service (General Dental Services) (Amendment) (Wales) Regulations 2002 No. 2002/918 (W.106). – Enabling power: National Health Service Act 1977, ss. 15 (1), 35 (1), 36 (1) (3), 126 (4). – Issued: 09.04.2002. Made: 28.03.2002. Coming into force: 01.04.2002. Effect: S.I. 1992/661 amended in relation to Wales. Territorial extent & classification: W. General. – 4p.: 30 cm. – In English and Welsh. Welsh title: Rheoliadau'r Gwasanaeth Iechyd Gwladol (Gwasanaethau Deintyddol Cyffredinol) (Diwygio) (Cymru) 2002 – 0 11 090458 3 *£1.75*

The National Health Service (General Medical Services) Amendment (No. 3) (Wales) Regulations 2002 No. 2002/1804 (W.174). – Enabling power: National Health Service Act 1977, ss. 29, 126 (4). – Issued: 01.08.2002. Made: 11.07.2002. Coming into force: 01.08.2002. Effect: S.I. 1992/635 amended in relation to Wales. Territorial extent & classification: W. General. – In English and Welsh. Welsh title: Rheoliadau'r Gwasanaeth Iechyd Gwladol (Gwasanaethau Meddygol Cyffredinol) (Diwygio) (Rhif 3) (Cymru) 2002. – 4p.: 30 cm. – 0 11 090530 X *£1.75*

The National Health Service (General Medical Services) (Amendment) (Wales) (No. 2) Regulations 2002 No. 2002/1896 (W.197). – Enabling power: National Health Service Act 1977, ss. 29, 29A, 29B, 43ZA, 49F, 49I, 49L, 49M, 49N, 49O, 49P, 49Q, 49R, 65, 126 (4). – Issued: 03.09.2002. Made: 18.07.2002. Coming into force: 26.08.2002. Effect: S.I. 1992/635 amended in relation to Wales. Territorial extent & classification: W. General. – In English and Welsh. Welsh title: Rheoliadau'r Gwasanaeth Iechyd Gwladol (Gwasanaethau Meddygol Cyffredinol) (Diwygio) (Cymru) (Rhif 2) 2002. – 40p.: 30 cm. – 0 11 090565 2 £6.50

The National Health Service (General Medical Services) (Amendment) (Wales) Regulations 2002 No. 2002/916 (W.104). – Enabling power: National Health Service Act 1977, ss. 29, 29A, 29B, 126 (4) & Health and Social Care Act 2001, s. 65. – Issued: 09.04.2002. Made: 28.03.2002. Coming into force: 01.04.2002. Effect: S.I. 1992/635 amended in relation to Wales. Territorial extent & classification: W. General. – 16p.: 30 cm. – In English and Welsh. Welsh title: Rheoliadau'r Gwasanaeth Iechyd Gwladol (Gwasanaethau Meddygol Cyffredinol) (Diwygio) (Cymru) 2002 – 0 11 090457 5 £3.00

The National Health Service (General Medical Services) (Supplementary List) (Wales) (Amendment), the National Health Service (General Medical Services) (Amendment) (Wales) (No. 3), the National Health Service (General Dental Services) (Amendment) (Wales) (No. 3) and the National Health Service (General Ophthalmic Services) (Amendment) (Wales) (No. 2) Regulations 2002 No. 2002/2802 (W.270). – Enabling power: National Health Service Act 1977, ss. 29, 29A, 29B, 38, 39, 43D, 43ZA, 49F, 49I, 49L, 49M, 49N, 49P, 49Q, 49R, 126 (4) & Health Social Care 2001, s. 65. – Issued: 10.12.2002. Made: 12.11.2002. Coming into force: 15.11.2002. Effect: S.I. 1986/975; 1992/635, 661 amended in relation to Wales & S.I. 2002/1882 (W.191) amended. Territorial extent & classification: W. General. – In English and Welsh. Welsh title: Rheoliadau'r Gwasanaeth Iechyd Gwladol (Rhestr Atodol Gwasanaethau Meddygol Cyffredinol) (Cymru) (Diwygio), y Gwasanaeth Iechyd Gwladol (Gwasanaethau Meddygol Cyffredinol) (Diwygio) (Cymru) (Rhif 3), y Gwasanaeth Iechyd Gwladol (Gwasanaethau Deintyddol Cyffredinol) (Diwygio) (Cymru) (Rhif 3) a'r Gwasanaeth Iechyd Gwladol (Gwasanaethau Offthalmig Cyffredinol) (Diwygio) (Cymru) (Rhif 2) 2002. – [12]p.: 30 cm. – 0 11 090589 X £2.00

The National Health Service (General Medical Services Supplementary List) (Wales) Regulations 2002 No. 2002/1882 (W.191). – Enabling power: National Health Service Act 1977, ss. 29, 43D, 126 (4) & Health and Social Care Act 2001, s. 65. – Issued: 03.09.2002. Made: 18.07.2002. Coming into force: 26.08.2002. Effect: None. Territorial extent & classification: W. General. – 36p.: 30 cm. – In English and Welsh. Welsh title: Rheoliadau'r Gwasanaeth Iechyd Gwladol (Rhestr Atodol Gwasanaethau Meddygol Cyffredinol) 2002 – 0 11 090563 6 £6.50

National Health Service (General Ophthalmic Services) Amendment (Wales) Regulations 2002 No. 2002/1883 (W.192). – Enabling power: National Health Service Act 1977, ss. 38, 39, 43ZA, 49F, 49I, 49L, 49M, 49N, 49O, 49P, 49Q, 49R, 126 (4) & Health and Social Care Act 2001, s. 65. – Issued: 03.09.2002. Made: 18.07.2002. Coming into force: 26.08.2002. Effect: S.I. 1986/975 amended in relation to Wales. Territorial extent & classification: W. General. – In English and Welsh. Welsh title: Rheoliadau'r Gwasanaeth Iechyd Gwladol (Gwasanaethau Offthalmig Cyffredinol) (Diwygio) (Cymru) 2002. – 40p.: 30 cm. – 0 11 090564 4 £6.50

The National Health Service (Optical Charges and Payments) (Amendment) (No. 2) (Wales) Regulations 2002 No. 2002/1506 (W.151). – Enabling power: National Health Service Act 1977, s. 126 (4), sch. 12, para. 2A. – Issued: 08.07.2002. Made: 10.06.2002. Coming into force: 11.06.2002. Effect: S.I. 1997/818 amended in relation to Wales. Territorial extent & classification: W. General. – In English and Welsh. Welsh title: Rheoliadau'r Gwasanaeth Iechyd Gwladol (Ffioedd a Thalidau Optegol) (Diwygio) (Rhif 2) (Cymru) 2002. – 4p.: 30 cm. – 0 11 090518 0 £1.75

The National Health Service (Optical Charges and Payments) (Amendment) (Wales) Regulations 2002 No. 2002/186 (W.25). – Enabling power: National Health Service Act 1977, s. 126 (4), sch. 12, para. 2A. – Issued: 13.02.2002. Made: 31.01.2002. Coming into force: 01.02.2002. Effect: S.I. 1997/818 amended in relation to Wales. Territorial extent & classification: W. General. – In English and Welsh. - Welsh title: Rheoliadau'r Gwasanaeth Iechyd Gwladol (Ffioedd a Thalidau Optegol) (Diwygio) (Cymru) 2002. – 4p.: 30 cm. – 0 11 090421 4 £1.75

The National Health Service (Optical Charges and Payments) and (General Ophthalmic Services) (Amendment) (Wales) Regulations 2002 No. 2002/917 (W.105). – Enabling power: National Health Service Act 1977, ss. 38, 39, 78, 126 (4), 127, sch. 12, paras. 2, 2A. – Issued: 17.05.2002. Made: 28.03.2002. Coming into force: 01.04.2002 & 09.04.2002 in accordance with art. 1 (2). Effect: S.I. 1986/975; 1997/818 amended in relation to Wales. Territorial extent & classification: W. General. – In English and Welsh. - Welsh title: Rheoliadau'r Gwasanaeth Iechyd Gwladol (Ffioedd a Thalidau Optegol) a (Gwasanaethau Offthalmig Cyffredinol) (Diwygio) (Cymru) 2002 – 8p.: 30 cm. – 0 11 090488 5 £2.00

The National Health Service (Pharmaceutical Services) and (General Medical Services) (Amendment) (Wales) Regulations 2002 No. 2002/3189 (W.305). – Enabling power: National Health Service Act 1977, ss. 29, 41, 42, 43, 126 (4). – Issued: 23.01.2003. Made: 18.12.2002. Coming into force: 01.01.2003. Effect: S.I. 1992/662, 635 amended in relation to Wales. Territorial extent & classification: W. General. – In English and Welsh. Welsh title: Rheoliadau'r Gwasanaeth Iechyd Gwladol (Gwasanaethau Fferyllol) a (Gwasanaethau Meddygol Cyffredinol) (Diwygio) (Cymru) 2002. – 8p.: 30 cm. – 0 11 090618 7 £2.00

The National Health Service Reform and Health Care Professions Act 2002 (Commencement) (Wales) Order 2002 No. 2002/2532 (W.248) (C.81). – Enabling power: National Health Service Reform and Health Care Professions Act 2000, ss. 38 (1), 42 (3) (4) (c) (d) (e) (iii) (iv). Bringing into operation for Wales various provisions of the 2002 Act on 10.10.2002. – Issued: 17.10.2002. Made: 07.10.2002. Effect: None. Territorial extent & classification: W. General. – 8p.: 30 cm. – 0 11 090576 8 £2.00

The Velindre National Health Service Trust (Establishment) Amendment (No. 2) Order 2002 No. 2002/2199 (W.219). – Enabling power: National Health Service Act 1977, s. 126 (3) & National Health Service and Community Care Act 1990, s. 5 (1) (6). – Issued: 09.09.2002. Made: 21.08.2002. Coming into force: 01.10.2002. Effect: S.I. 1993/2838 amended. Territorial extent & classification: W. General. – 4p.: 30 cm. – In English & Welsh. Welsh title: Gorchymyn Diwygio Ymddiriedolaeth Gwasanaeth Iechyd Gwladol Felindre (Sefydlu) (Rhif 2) 2002 – 0 11 090566 0 £1.75

The Velindre National Health Service Trust (Establishment) Amendment Order 2002 No. 2002/442 (W.57). – Enabling power: National Health Service Act 1977, s. 126 (3) & National Health Service and Community Care Act 1990, s. 5 (1) (6). – Issued: 22.03.2002. Made: 28.02.2002. Coming into force: 01.04.2002. Effect: S.I. 1993/2838 amended. Territorial extent & classification: W. General. – 4p.: 30 cm. – In English & Welsh. Welsh title: Gorchymyn Diwygio Ymddiriedolaeth Gwasanaeth Iechyd Gwladol Felindre (Sefydlu) 2002 – 0 11 090444 3 £1.75

National lottery, England

The Awards for All (England) Joint Scheme (Authorisation) Order 2002 No. 2002/638. – Enabling power: National Lottery etc. Act 1993, sch. 3A, paras. 2 (1), 3. – Issued: 18.03.2002. Made: 07.03.2002. Laid: 11.03.2002. Coming into force: 01.04.2002. Effect: None. Territorial extent & classification: E. General. – 2p.: 30 cm. – Revoked by S.I. 2003/664 (ISBN 0110452232) – 0 11 039471 2 £1.50

National lottery

The National Lottery (Licence Fees) (Amendment) Order 2002 No. 2002/3124. – Enabling power: National Lottery etc. Act 1993, ss. 7 (5), 60 (4). – Issued: 14.01.2003. Made: 16.12.2002. Laid: 17.12.2002. Coming into force: 13.01.2003. Effect: S.I. 2001/2506 amended. Territorial extent & classification: E/W/S/NI. General. – 2p.: 30 cm. – 0 11 044552 X £1.50

Northern Ireland

The Adjacent Waters Boundaries (Northern Ireland) Order 2002 No. 2002/791. – Enabling power: Northern Ireland Act 1998, s. 98 (8). – Issued: 09.04.2002. Made 26.03.2002. Coming into force: 28.03.2002. Effect: None. Territorial extent & classification: NI. General. – 12p., map, tables: 30 cm. – 0 11 039632 4 £2.50

The Company Directors Disqualification (Northern Ireland) Order 2002 No. 2002/3150 (N.I.4). – Enabling power: Northern Ireland Act 2000, sch. para. 1 (1). – Issued: 09.01.2003. Made: 17.12.2002. Coming into operation: On days to be appointed under art 1 (2). Effect: 1986 c.45; 1993 c.36; 1994 c.40; 1999 c.23 & S.I. 1981/226 (N.I. 6); 1986/1032 (N.I. 6); 1989/2404 (N.I. 18), 2405 (N.I. 19); 1990/593 (N.I. 5), 1504 (N.I. 10); 1992/231 (N.I. 1); 1994/426 (N.I. 1); 1995/3213 (N.I. 22); 1996/1632 (N.I. 11) amended. Territorial extent & classification: NI. General. – 22p.: 30 cm. – With correction slip dated July 2003 – 0 11 044282 2 £3.50

The Criminal Injuries Compensation (Northern Ireland) Order 2002 No. 2002/796 (N.I. 1). – Enabling power: Northern Ireland Act 1998, s. 85. – Issued: 09.04.2002. Made: 26.03.2002. Coming into force: In accord. with art. 1 (2). Effect: 1991 (N.I. 16) amended & 1988 (N.I. 4) repealed. Territorial extent & classification: NI. General. – With correction slip dated April 2002 adding the subsidiary number N.I. 1 to the instrument number. – Supersedes draft S.I. (ISBN 0110393708) previously published on 22.02.2002. – 12p.: 30 cm. – With correction slip. – 0 11 039636 7 £2.50

The Employment (Northern Ireland) Order 2002 No. 2002/2836 (N.I.2). – Enabling power: Northern Ireland Act 2000, sch., para. 1 (1). – Issued: 09.01.2003. Made: 20.11.2002. Coming into operation: On days to be appointed under art. 1 (2). Effect: 1992 c. 7, 8; S.I. 1992/807 (N.I.5); 1996/1919 (N.I.16), 1921 (N.I.18); 1999/671, 2790 (N.I.9) amended. Territorial extent & classification: NI. General. – 44p.: 30 cm. – 0 11 044280 6 £6.00

The Environment (Northern Ireland) Order 2002 No. 2002/3153 (N.I.7). – Enabling power: Northern Ireland Act 2000, sch., para. 1 (1). – Issued: 13.01.2003. Made: 17.12.2002. Coming into operation: In accord. with art. 1 (2) (3). Effect: 1878 c. 52; 1965 c. 23; 1990 c. 43; 1995 c. 21; 1996 c. 8; 1998 c. 47; S.I. 1978/1049 (N.I.19); 1981/158 (N.I.4); 1985/170 (N.I.1); 1989/492 (N.I.3); 1991/1220 (N.I.11); 1997/276 (N.I.2), 2778 (N.I.19); 1999/662 (N.I.6); 2002/3153 (N.I.7) amended & S.I. 1997/2777 (N.I.18) revoked. Territorial extent & classification: NI. General. – iii, 56p.: 30 cm. – EC note: Implement Council directive 96/61/EC and 96/62/EC – 0 11 044285 7 £7.00

The Fur Farming (Prohibition) (Northern Ireland) Order 2002 No. 2002/3151 (N.I.5). – Enabling power: Northern Ireland Act 2000, sch. para. 1 (1). – Issued: 09.01.2003. Made: 17.12.2002. Coming into operation: 01.01.2003. Effect: None. Territorial extent & classification: NI. General. – 8p.: 30 cm. – With correction slip dated July 2003), correcting the coming-into-force date to 01.01.2003 – 0 11 044283 0 £2.00

The Harbours (Northern Ireland) Order 2002 No. 2002/3155 (N.I.9). – Enabling power: Northern Ireland Act 2000, sch., para. 1 (1). – Issued: 09.01.2003. Made: 17.12.2002. Coming into force: 18.02.2002. Effect: None. Territorial extent & classification: NI. General. – [8]p.: 30 cm. – With correction slip dated July 2003, correcting the coming-into-force date to 18.02.2002 – 0 11 044287 3 £2.00

The Housing Support Services (Northern Ireland) Order 2002 No. 2002/3154 (N.I.8). – Enabling power: Northern Ireland Act 2000, sch., para. 1 (1). – Issued: 09.01.2003. Made: 17.12.2002. Laid: -. Coming into operation: On a day to be appointed under art. 1 (2). Effect: 1992 c.7 amended. Territorial extent & classification: NI. General. – [8]p.: 30 cm. – With correction slip dated July 2003 – 0 11 044286 5 *£1.75*

The Insolvency (Northern Ireland) Order 2002 No. 2002/3152 (N.I.6). – Enabling power: Northern Ireland Act 2000, sch., para. 1 (1). – Issued: 13.01.2003. Made: 17.12.2002. Coming into operation: In accord. with art. 1 (2) (3). Effect: S.I. 1989/2405 (N.I.19); 1990/1504 (N.I.10) amended. Territorial extent & classification: NI. General. – ii, 53p.: 30 cm. – 0 11 044284 9 *£7.00*

The Local Elections (Northern Ireland) (Amendment) Order 2002 No. 2002/2835. – Enabling power: Northern Ireland Act 1998, s. 84 (1) (3). – Issued: 29.11.2002. Made: 20.11.2002. Laid:-. Coming into force: In accord. with art. 2. Effect: S.I. 1985/454; 1990/595; 1991/1715 amended. Territorial extent & classification: NI. General. – 8p.: 30 cm. – Supersedes draft S.I. (ISBN 0110424581) issued on 11.07.2002 – 0 11 043048 4 *£2.00*

The Local Government (Miscellaneous Provisions) (Northern Ireland) Order 2002 No. 2002/3149 (N.I.3). – Enabling power: Northern Ireland Act 2000, sch. para. 1 (1). – Issued: 09.01.2003. Made: 17.12.2002. Coming into operation: In accord. with art. 1 (2) (3). Effect: S.I. 1972 (N.I. 22); 1977/2157 (N.I. 28); 1981/607 (N.I. 15); 1985/1208 (N.I. 15); 1992/810 (N.I. 6); 1994/1897 (N.I. 11) amended. Territorial extent & classification: NI. General. – 8p.: 30 cm. – 0 11 044281 4 *£2.00*

The Northern Ireland Act 1998 (Modification of Enactments) Order 2002 No. 2002/2843. – Enabling power: Northern Ireland Act 1998, s. 86 (1) (3) (a) (4). – Issued: 29.11.2002. Made: 20.11.2002. Coming into force: 21.11.2002. Effect: 1964 c.14 amended. Territorial extent & classification: NI. General. – 8p.: 30 cm. – Supersedes draft S.I. (ISBN 0110426045) issued on 06.08.2002 – 0 11 043334 3 *£2.00*

The Northern Ireland Act 1998 (Modification) Order 2002 No. 2002/265. – Enabling power: Northern Ireland Act 1998, s. 87 (7). – Issued: 22.02.2002. Made: 12.02.2002. Laid: 22.02.2002. Coming into force: 15.03.2002. Effect: 1998 c. 47 modified. Territorial extent & classification: E/W/S/NI. General. – 2p.: 30 cm. – 0 11 039334 1 *£1.50*

The Northern Ireland Act 2000 (Modification) Order 2002 No. 2002/2587. – Enabling power: Northern Ireland Act 2000, s. 6. – Issued: 25.10.2002. Made: 14.10.2002. Laid: 15.10.2002. Coming into force: 15.10.2002. Effect: 2000 c. 1 modified. Territorial extent & classification: NI. General. – Laid for approval by resolution of each House of Parliament within 40 days beginning with the date on which the Order was made. – S.I. 2002/2587 previously published on 25.10.2002 is superseded by this ISBN with the same number, ISBN 0110429605. – 2p.: 30 cm. – 0 11 042886 2 *£1.50*

The Northern Ireland Act 2000 (Modification) Order 2002 No. 2002/2587. – Enabling power: Northern Ireland Act 2000, s. 6. – Issued: 13.11.2002. Made: 14.10.2002. Laid: 15.10.2002. Coming into force:15.10.2002. Effect: 2000 c.1 amended. Territorial extent & classification: NI. General. – 2p.: 30 cm. – Approved by both Houses of Parliament – S.I. 2002/2587 (ISBN 0110428862) issued 25.10.2002 is superseded by this S.I. with same number – 0 11 042960 5 *£1.50*

The Northern Ireland Act 2000 (Prescribed Documents) Order 2002 No. 2002/3126. – Enabling power: Northern Ireland Act 2000, sch., para. 12 (4). – Issued: 29.01.2003. Made: 17.12.2002. Laid: 18.12.2002. Coming into force: 09.01.2003. Effect: None. Territorial extent & classification: NI. General. – 2p.: 30 cm. – 0 11 044654 2 *£1.50*

The Northern Ireland Act 2000 (Suspension of Devolved Government) Order 2002 No. 2002/2574. – Enabling power: Northern Ireland Act 2000, s. 2 (2). – Issued: 25.10.2002. Made: 14.10.2002. Laid: 15.10.2002. Coming into force: 15.10.2002. Effect: S.I. 2001/3231 revoked. Territorial extent & classification: NI. General. – Laid for approval by resolution of each House of Parliament within 40 days beginning with the date on which the Order was made. – This S.I. is superseded by ISBN 0110429591, which has the same number and is issued 13.11.2002. – 2p.: 30 cm. – 0 11 042885 4 *£1.50*

The Northern Ireland Act 2000 (Suspension of Devolved Government) Order 2002 No. 2002/2574. – Enabling power: Northern Ireland Act 2000, s. 2 (2). – Issued: 13.11.2002. Made: 14.10.2002. Laid: 15.10.2002. Coming into force: 15.10.2002. Effect: S.I. 2001/3231 revoked. Territorial extent & classification: NI. General. – Approved by both Houses of Parliament. – S.I. 2002/2574 (ISBN 0110428854) previously published 25.10.2002 is superseded by this SI, with the same number. – 2p.: 30 cm. – 0 11 042959 1 *£1.50*

The Northern Ireland Assembly (Elections) (Amendment) Order 2002 No. 2002/1964. – Enabling power: Northern Ireland Act 1998, s. 34 (4). – Issued: 01.08.2002. Made: 24.07.2002. Laid: -. Coming into force: 01.12.2002. Effect: S.I. 2001/2599 amended. Territorial extent & classification: NI. General. – Supersedes draft S.I. (ISBN 0110424239). – 2p.: 30 cm. – 0 11 042564 2 *£1.50*

The Sea Fisheries (Northern Ireland) Order 2002 No. 2002/790. – Enabling power: Northern Ireland Act 1998, ss. 6 (4), 86 (1) (3) (4) (5). – Issued: 09.04.2002. Made: 26.03.2002. Coming into force: 28.03.2002. Effect: 1962 c.31; 1966 c.17 (NI); 1968 c.77; 1976 c.86; 1981 c.29; S.I. 1981/227 (NI.); 1983 c. 8 modified. Territorial extent & classification: NI. General. – Supersedes draft S.I. (ISBN 0110392442) issued 07/02/2002. – 12p.: 30 cm. – 0 11 039631 6 *£2.50*

Nurses and midwives

The Nursing and Midwifery Order 2001 No. 2002/253. – Enabling power: Health Act 1999, ss. 60, 62 (4). – Issued: 21.02.2002. Made: 12.02.2002. Coming into force: 12.02.2002.(for arts. 1, 54 (4)), the remainder in acc.with art. 1 (2). Effect: 1967 c.13; 1968 c.67; 1973 c.41; 1975 c.24, 25; 1977 c.49; 1978 c.30; 1984 c.23, 39; 1989 c.41; 1994 c.23; 1996 c.18; 1998 c.29, 38; 1999 c.8; 2000 c.36 & S.I. 1992/3204 (NI. 20) amended. Territorial extent & classification: E/W/S/NI. General. – 52p.: 30 cm. – 0 11 039325 2 £7.50

The Nursing and Midwifery Order 2001 (Consequential Amendments) Order 2002 No. 2002/881. – Enabling power: Health Act 1999, s. 63. – Issued: 30.04.2002. Made: 27.03.2002. Laid: 28.03.2002. Coming into force: 17.04.2002. Effect: S.I. 1976/615; 1987/235, 481; 1990/1330, 1718, 2024, 1991/824; 1992/635; 1994/2889; 1995/201; 1996/2374; 1998/3186; 1999/450, 680, 787, 1379, 2801; 2000/89; 2001/341, 400, 497, 747, 1042 amended. Territorial extent & classification: E/W/S/NI. General. – 8p.: 30 cm. – 0 11 039841 6 £2.00

The Nursing and Midwifery Order 2001 (Transitional Provisions) Order 2002 No. 2002/1125. – Enabling power: S.I. 2002/253, art. 54 (2). – Issued: 23.04.2002. Made: 26.03.2002. Coming into force: for the purposes of art. 2 (a) (ii), the date of coming into force of art 27 (a) of the Nursing and Midwifery Order 2001; for the purposes of art. 2 (c), the date of coming into force of art. 36 of the Nursing and Midwifery Order 2001; remainder 01.04.2002. Effect: None. Territorial extent & classification: E/W/S/NI. General. – 2p.: 30 cm. – 0 11 039805 X £1.50

The Nursing and Midwifery (Transfer of Staff and Property etc.) Order 2002 No. 2002/923. – Enabling power: S.I. 2002/253, art. 54 (2), sch. 2, paras. 20. 21. 23, 25 (1). – Issued: 09.04.2002. Made: 22.03.2002. Coming into force: 01.04.2002. Effect: None. Territorial extent & classification: E/W/S/NI. General. – 4p.: 30 cm. – 0 11 039662 6 £1.75

Nurses, midwives and health visitors

The Nurses, Midwives and Health Visitors (Amendment) Rules Approval Order 2002 No. 2002/1169. – Enabling power: Nurses, Midwives and Health Visitors Act 1997, s. 19 (5). – Issued: 30.04.2002. Made: 12.03.2002. Coming into force: 31.03.2002. Effect: S.I. 1983/873 amended. Territorial extent & classification: E/W/S/NI. General. – 4p.: 30 cm. – 0 11 039847 5 £1.75

Nurses, midwives and health visitors, England

Nurses Agencies Regulations 2002 No. 2002/3212. – Enabling power: Care Standards Act 2000, ss. 4 (6), 22 (1) (2) (a) to (c) (f) to (j) (7) (a) to (h) (j), 25, 34 (1), 35, 118 (5) to (7). – Issued: 17.01.2003. Made: 21.12.2002. Laid: 23.12.2002. Coming into force: 01.04.2003. Effect: None. Territorial extent & classification: E. General. – 16p.: 30 cm. – 0 11 044602 X £3.00

Nurses, midwives and health visitors, England and Wales

The Nurses, Midwives and Health Visitors (Professional Conduct) (Amendment No. 2) Rules 2002 Approval Order 2002 No. 2002/708. – Enabling power: Nurses, Midwives and Health Visitors Act 1997, s. 19 (5). – Issued: 21.03.2002. Made: 11.03.2002. Coming into force: 31.03.2002. Effect: S.I. 1993/893 amended. Territorial extent & classification: E/W. General. – 8p.: 30 cm. – 0 11 039511 5 £2.00

The Nurses, Midwives and Health Visitors (Professional Conduct) (Amendment) Rules 2002 Approval Order 2002 No. 2002/82. – Enabling power: Nurses, Midwives and Health Visitors Act 1997, s. 19 (5). – Issued: 29.01.2002. Made: 18.01.2002. Coming into force: 18.02.2002. Effect: S.I. 1993/893 amended. Territorial extent & classification: E/W. General. – 4p.: 30 cm. – 0 11 039226 4 £1.75

Offshore installations

The Offshore Installations (Safety Zones) (No. 2) Order 2002 No. 2002/2467. – Enabling power: Petroleum Act 1987, s. 22 (1) (2). – Issued: 02.10.2002. Made: 24.09.2002. Coming into force: 21.10.2002. Effect: S.I. 1997/735 amended. Territorial extent & classification: E/W/S. General. – 4p.: 30 cm. – 0 11 042825 0 £1.75

The Offshore Installations (Safety Zones) Order 2002 No. 2002/1063. – Enabling power: Petroleum Act 1987, s. 22 (1) (2). – Issued: 19.04.2002. Made: 11.04.2002. Coming into force: 02.05.2002. Effect: None. Territorial extent & classification: E/W/S/NI. General. – 4p.: 30 cm. – 0 11 039769 X £1.75

Opticians

The General Optical Council (Registration and Enrolment (Amendment) Rules) Order of Council 2002 No. 2002/775. – Enabling power: Opticians Act 1989, s. 10. – Issued: 28.03.2002. Made: 13.03.2002. Coming into force: 01.04.2002. Effect: S.I. 1977/176 amended & S.I. 2001/1131 revoked. Territorial extent & classification: E/W/S/NI. General. – 4p.: 25 cm. – Revoked by S.I. 2003/1080 (ISBN 0110457056) – 0 11 039595 6 £1.75

Osteopaths

The General Osteopathic Council (Election of Members and Chairman of Council) Rules Order of Council 2002 No. 2002/827. – Enabling power: Osteopaths Act 1993, s. 36. – Issued: 05.04.2002. Made: 06.03.2002. Coming into force: 26.03.2002. Effect: S.I. 2001/15 revoked. Territorial extent & classification:E/W/S/NI. General. – 8p.: 30 cm. –
0 11 039640 5 £2.00

The Osteopaths Act 1993 (Commencement No. 7) Order 2002 No. 2002/500 (C.14). – Enabling power: Osteopaths Act 1993, s. 42 (2) (4). Bringing into operation various provisions of the 1993 Act on 03.03.2002. – Issued: 13.03.2002. Made: 26.02.2002. Laid:-. Effect: None. Territorial extent & classification: E/W/S/NI. General. – 4p.: 30 cm. – 0 11 039436 4 £1.75

Overseas territories

The Anti-terrorism (Financial and Other Measures) (Overseas Territories) Order 2002 No. 2002/1822. – Enabling power: Saint Helena Act 1833, s. 112 & British Settlements Acts 1887 & 1945. – Issued: 26.07.2002. Made: 16.07.2002. Laid: 26.07.2002. Coming into force: 01.08.2002. Effect: None. Territorial extent & classification: E/W/S/NI. General. – 28p.: 30 cm. – 0 11 042497 2 £4.50

The Overseas Territories (Zimbabwe) (Restricted Measures) Order 2002 No. 2002/1077. – Enabling power: Saint Helena Act 1833, s. 112 & British Settlements Acts 1887 & 1945. – Issued: 23.04.2002. Made: 17.14.2002. Laid: 18.04.2002. Coming into force: 19.04.2002. Effect: None. Territorial extent & classification: E/W/S/NI. General. – 16p.: 30 cm. – 0 11 039800 9 £3.00

The Overseas Territories (Zimbabwe) (Restrictive Measures) (Amendment) Order 2002 No. 2002/2627. – Enabling power: Saint Helena Act 1833, s. 112 & British Settlements Acts 1887 & 1945– Issued: 28.10.2002. Made: 22.10.2002. Laid: 23.10.2002. Coming into force: 24.10.2002. Effect: S.I. 2002/1077 amended. Territorial extent & classification: E/W/S/NI. General. – 4p.: 30 cm. –
0 11 042892 7 £1.75

Parliament

The Parliamentary Pensions (Amendment) (No. 2) Regulations 2002 No. 2002/1887. Enabling power: Parliamentary and other Pensions Act 1987, s. 2 (1) (4). – Issued: 25.10.2002. Made: 22.07.2002. Laid: 22.07.2002. Coming into force: 05.08.2002. Effect: S.I. 1993/3253 amended. Territorial extent & classification: E/W/S/NI. General. – This S.I. has been made in consequence of defects on S.I. 2002/1807 and is being issued free of charge to all known recipients of that statutory instrument. – 4p.: 30 cm. –
0 11 042527 8 £1.75

The Parliamentary Pensions (Amendment) Regulations 2002 No. 2002/1807. – Enabling power: Parliamentary and other Pensions Act 1987, s. 2 (1) (4). – Issued: 23.07.2002. Made: 15.07.2002. Laid: 15.07.2002. Coming into force: 05.08.2002. Effect: S.I. 1993/3253 amended. Territorial extent & classification: E/W/S/NI. General. – 8p.: 30 cm. –
0 11 042491 3 £2.00

Partnership

The Limited Liability Partnerships (No. 2) Regulations 2002 No. 2002/913. – Enabling power: Limited Liability Partnerships Act 2000, ss. 15 to 17. – Issued: 19.04.2002. Made: 31.03.2002. Laid: 07.03.2002. Coming into force: 02.04.2002. Effect: 1985 c. 6 modified. Territorial extent and classification: E/W/S. General. – 4p.: 30 cm. –
0 11 039774 6 £1.75

The Limited Liability Partnerships (Particulars of Usual Residential Address) (Confidentiality Orders) Regulations 2002 No. 2002/915. – Enabling power: Companies Act 1985, s. 723B to F. – Issued: 19.04.2002. Made: 31.03.2002. Coming into force: 02.04.2002. Effect: 1985 c. 6; 2000 c. 12 amended. Territorial extent and classification: E/W/S. General. – 12p.: 30 cm. – 0 11 039775 4 £2.50

The Limited Partnerships (Unrestricted Size) No. 4 Regulations 2002 No. 2002/376. – Enabling power: Companies Act 1985, ss. 717 (1) (d), 744. – Issued: 15.03.2002. Made: 13.02.2002. Coming into force. 22.03.2002. Effect: None. Territorial extent and classification: E/W/S. General. – 2p.: 30 cm. – 0 11 039467 4 £1.50

Partnership: Limited liability partnerships

The Limited Liability Partnerships (Competent Authority) (Fees) Regulations 2002 No. 2002/503. – Enabling power: Companies Act 1985, s. 708 (1) (2). – Issued: 19.04.2002. Made: 07.03.2002. Laid: 07.03.2002. Coming into force: 02.04.2002. Effect: None. Territorial extent & classification: E/W/S. General. – 4p.: 30 cm. – 0 11 039772 X £1.75

The Limited Liability Partnerships (Fees) (Amendment) Regulations 2002 No. 2002/2895. – Enabling power: Companies Act 1985, s. 708 (1) (2). – Issued: 28.11.2002. Made: 21.11.2002. Laid: 21.11.2002. Coming into force: 01.01.2003. Effect: S.I. 2001/969 amended. Territorial extent and classification: E/W/S. General. – 2p.: 30 cm. –
0 11 043985 6 £1.50

The Limited Liability Partnerships (Forms) Regulations 2002 No. 2002/690. – Enabling power: Companies Act 1985, ss. 363, 288A, 706. – Issued: 09.05.2002. Made: 07.03.2002. Coming into force: 02.04.2002. Effect: None. Territorial extent and classification: E/W/S. General. – 8p.: 30 cm. –
0 11 039908 0 £2.00

Patents

The Patents (Amendment) Rules 2002 No. 2002/529. – Enabling power: Patents Act 1977, s. 123. – Issued: 05.04.2002. Made: 07.03.2002. Laid: 08.03.2002. Coming into force: 01.04.2002. Effect: S.I. 1995/2093 amended. Territorial extent & classification: E/W/S/NI. General. – 4p.: 30 cm. – 0 11 039655 3 £1.75

The Patents and Plant Variety Rights (Compulsory Licensing) Regulations 2002 No. 2002/247. – Enabling power: European Communities Act 1972, s. 2 (2). – Issued: 01.03.2002. Made: 07.02.2002. Laid: 08.02.2002. Coming into force: 01.03.2002. Effect: None. Territorial extent & classification: E/W/S/NI. General. – EC note: Implement art. 12 of DIR 98/44 on the legal protection of biotechnological inventions. – 12p.: 30 cm. – 0 11 039398 8 £2.50

Pensions

The Child Support, Pensions and Social Security Act 2000 (Commencement No. 11) Order 2002 No. 2002/437 (C.12). – Enabling power: Child Support, Pensions and Social Security Act 2000, s. 86 (2) (3) (a). Bringing into operation various provisions of the 2000 Act on 01.03.2002, 01.04.2002, 06.04.2002, in accord. with art. 3 (1) (2) (3). – Issued: 06.03.2002. Made: 27.02.2002. Effect: S.I. 2001/2295 (C.76) amended. Territorial extent & classification: E/W/S. General. – 8p.: 30 cm. – 0 11 039412 7 £2.00

The Guaranteed Minimum Pensions Increase Order 2002 No. 2002/649. – Enabling power: Pension Schemes Act 1993, s. 109 (4). – Issued: 18.03.2002. Made: 11.03.2002. Coming into force: 06.04.2002. Effect: None. Territorial extent & classification: E/W/S. General. – 2p.: 30 cm. – Supersedes draft S.I. (ISBN 011039271X) previously issued on 06.02.2002 – 0 11 039462 3 £1.50

The Judicial Pensions (Pensions Appeal Tribunals) Order 2002 No. 2002/1347. – Enabling power: Judicial Pensions and Retirement Act 1993, s. 1 (8). – Issued: 22.05.2002. Made: 14.05.2002. Laid: 15.05.2002. Coming into force: 07.06.2002. Effect: 1993 c. 8 amended. Territorial extent & classification: E/W/S/NI. General. – 2p.: 30 cm. – 0 11 039977 3 £1.50

The National Ports Council Pension Scheme (Excess Statutory Surplus) Order 2002 No. 2002/346. – Enabling power: Pensions Act 1995, ss. 72, 174. – Issued: 26.01.2002. Made: 18.02.2002. Laid: 19.02.2002. Coming into force: 13.03.2002. Effect: None. Territorial extent & classification: E/W/S/NI. General. – 4p.: 25 cm. – 0 11 039369 4 £1.75

The Naval, Military and Air Forces Etc. (Disablement and Death) Service Pensions Amendment Order 2002 No. 2002/792. – Enabling power: Naval and Marine Pay and Pensions Act 1865, s. 3 & Pensions and Yeomanry Pay Act 1884, s. 2 (1) & Air Force (Constitution) Act 1917, s. 2 (1) & Social Security (Miscellaneous Provisions) Act 1977, ss. 12 (1), 24 (3). – Issued: 04.04.2002. Made: 26.03.2002. Laid: 04.04.2002. Coming into force: 08.04.2002. Effect: S.I. 1983/883 amended. Territorial extent & classification: E/W/S. General. – 16p.: 30 cm. – 0 11 039633 2 £3.00

The Occupational and Personal Pension Schemes (Bankruptcy) (No. 2) Regulations 2002 No. 2002/836. – Enabling power: Bankruptcy (Scotland) Act 1985, ss. 36C (4) (a) (7) (8), 36F (3) (a) and (6) to (8) & Insolvency Act 1986, ss. 342C (4) (a) (7) to (9), 342F (6) (a) (9) to (11) & Welfare Reform and Pensions Act 1999, ss. 11 (2) (h), 12 (1) to (3), 83 (1) (2) (4) (6). – Issued: 02.04.2002. Made: 26.03.2002. Laid: 02.04.2002. Coming into force: 06.04.2002. Effect: S.I. 2002/427 revoked. Territorial extent & classification: E/W/S. General– This S.I. supersedes S.I. 2002/427 published on 7th March 2002 and is being issued free of charge to all known recipients of that S.I. – 16p.: 30 cm. – 0 11 039626 X £3.00

The Occupational and Personal Pension Schemes (Bankruptcy) Regulations 2002 No. 2002/427. – Enabling power: Bankruptcy (Scotland) Act 1985, ss. 36C (4) (a) (7) (8), 36F (3) (a) and (6) to (8) & Insolvency Act 1986, ss. 342C (4) (a) (7) to (9), 342F (6) (a) (9) to (11) & Welfare Reform and Pensions Act 1999, ss. 11 (2) (h) (10), 12 (1) to (3), 83 (1) (2) (4) (6). – Issued: 07.03.2002. Made: 26.02.2002. Laid: 07.03.2002. Coming into force: 06.04.2002. Effect: None. Territorial extent & classification: E/W/S. General– 16p.: 30 cm. – Revoked by S.I. 2002/836 (ISBN 011039626X) – 0 11 039403 8 £3.00

The Occupational and Personal Pension Schemes (Contracting-out) (Miscellaneous Amendments) Regulations 2002 No. 2002/681. – Enabling power: Pension Schemes Act 1993, ss. 8 (3) (b), 9 (2B) (c) (3) (aa), 11 (5), 21, 28 (1A) (2) (4), 28A, 32, 32A (2), 34 (1), 55 (2) (2B) (2C), 56 (2), 57 (2), 156 (2), 181 (1), 182 (2) (3), 183 (1) & Pension Schemes (Northern Ireland) Act 1993, ss. 38A (2C) (2D), 51 (2) (2ZA) (2B) (2C), 52 (2) (7), 53 (2) (5), 177 (2) to (4) (7), 178 (1) & Pensions Act 1995, ss. 40 (1) (2), 67 (5) (b), 91 (5), 92 (6), 124 (1), 174 (2) (3). – Issued: 15.03.2002. Made: 13.03.2002. Laid: 15.03.2002. Coming into force: 06.04.2002. Effect: S.I. 1996/1172, 1461, 1537, 2517, 3127; 1997/470, 785; 2000/750 & S.R. 1996/493 amended. Territorial extent & classification: E/W/S/NI. General. – 16p.: 30 cm. – 0 11 039491 7 £3.00

The Occupational and Personal Pension Schemes (Disclosure of Information) Amendment Regulations 2002 No. 2002/1383. – Enabling power: Pension Schemes Act 1993, ss. 113, 181 (1), 182 (2) (3), 183 (1). – Issued: 20.05.2002. Made: 15.05.2002. Laid: 20.05.2002. Coming into force: 06.04.2003. Effect: S.I. 1987/1110; 1996/1655; 2000/1403 amended. Territorial extent & classification: E/W/S. General– 12p.: 30 cm. – 0 11 039976 5 £2.50

The Occupational Pension Schemes (Member-nominated Trustees and Directors) Amendment Regulations 2002 No. 2002/2327. – Enabling power: Pensions Act 1995, ss. 17 (1) (c), 19 (1) (c), 21 (5) (6), 124 (1). – Issued: 13.09.2002. Made: 09.09.2002. Laid: 13.09.2002. Coming into force: 06.10.2002. Effect: S.I. 1996/1216 amended. Territorial extent & classification: E/W/S. General. – With correction slip dated October 2002. – 4p.: 30 cm. – 0 11 042779 3 £1.75

The Occupational Pension Schemes (Minimum Funding Requirement and Miscellaneous Amendments) Regulations 2002 No. 2002/380. – Enabling power: Pensions Act 1995, ss. 56 (3), 57 (1) (b) (2) (5), 58 (2) (4) (b) (6) (a), 59 (3), 61, 73 (3), 75 (5), 120 (1), 124 (1), 125 (2), 174 (2) (3), 175 (1). – Issued: 26.02.2002. Made: 22.02.2002. Laid: 26.02.2002. Coming into force: 19.03.2002. Effect: 1995 c. 26 & S.I. 1996/1536, 3126, 3128 amended. Territorial extent & classification: E/W/S. General. – 8p.: 30 cm. – 0 11 039387 2 *£2.00*

The Occupational Pension Schemes (Winding Up Notices and Reports etc.) Regulations 2002 No. 2002/459. – Enabling power: Pensions Act 1993, ss. 113 (1) and Pensions Act 1995, ss. 10 (2) (b) (3), 23 (2), 26B (3) (b), 26C (2) (3), 49A (2) (b) (3), 71A (4), 72A (1) (b) (2) (7) (8) (a), 72B (2) (c) (iii) (3) (5) (c) (6) (c) (8) (b), 118 (2), 124 (3E), 174 (2) (3). – Issued: 07.03.2002. Made: 04.03.2002. Laid: 07.03.2002. Coming into force: 01.04.2002. Effect: S.I. 1996/1655 amended. Territorial extent & classification: E/W/S. General– 12p.: 30 cm. – 0 11 039422 4 *£2.50*

The Occupational Pensions (Revaluation) Order 2002 No. 2002/2951. – Enabling power: Pension Schemes Act 1993, sch. 3, para. 2 (1). – Issued: 05.12.2002. Made: 28.11.2002. Laid: 05.12.2002. Coming into force: 01.01.2003, 20.01.2003, in accord. with art. 1 (1). Effect: None. Territorial extent & classification: E/W/S. General. – 2p.: 30 cm. – 0 11 044091 9 *£1.50*

The Pensions Increase (Review) Order 2002 No. 2002/699. – Enabling power: Social Security Pensions Act 1975, s. 59 (1) (2) (5) (5ZA). – Issued: 27.03.2002. Made: 14.03.2002. Laid: 15.03.2002. Coming into force: 08.04.2002. Effect: None. Territorial extent & classification: E/W/S/NI. General. – 4p.: 30 cm. – 0 11 039587 5 *£1.75*

The Pensions (Polish Forces) Scheme (Extension) Order 2002 No. 2002/671. – Enabling power: Polish Resettlement Act 1947, s. 1. – Issued: 19.03.2002. Made: 11.03.2002. Coming into force: 27.03.2002. Effect: None. Territorial extent & classification: E/W/S. General. – 2p.: 30 cm. – 0 11 039480 1 *£1.50*

The Personal Injuries (Civilians) Amendment Scheme 2002 No. 2002/672. – Enabling power: Personal Injuries (Emergency Provisions) Act 1939, ss. 1, 2. – Issued: 19.03.2002. Made: 11.03.2002. Laid: 14.03.2002. Coming into force: 08.04.2002. Effect: S.I. 1983/686 amended. Territorial extent & classification: E/W/S. General. – 8p.: 30 cm. – 0 11 039481 X *£2.00*

The Stakeholder Pension Schemes (Amendment No. 2) Regulations 2002 No. 2002/2098. – Enabling power: Welfare Reform and Pensions Act 1999, ss. 1 (1) (b), 8 (1), 83 (4) (a) (b) (6) (a). – Issued: 14.08.2002. Made: 08.08.2002. Laid: 14.08.2002. Coming into force: 09.09.2002. Effect: S.I. 2000/1403 amended. Territorial extent & classification: E/W/S. General. – [8]p.: 30 cm. – 0 11 042648 7 *£2.00*

The Stakeholder Pension Schemes (Amendment) Regulations 2002 No. 2002/1480. – Enabling power: Welfare Reform and Pensions Act 1999, ss. 1 (1) (b), 8 (1), 83 (4) (6) (a). – Issued: 11.06.2002. Made: 06.06.2002. Laid: 11.06.2002. Coming into force: 04.07.2002. Effect: S.I. 2000/1403 amended. Territorial extent & classification: E/W/S. General. – 2p.: 30 cm. – 0 11 042328 3 *£1.50*

The Superannuation (Admission to Schedule 1 to the Superannuation Act 1972) Order 2002 No. 2002/1913. – Enabling power: Superannuation Act 1972, s. 1 (5) (8) (a). – Issued: 10.09.2002. Made: 22.07.2002. Laid: 22.07.2002. Coming into force: 12.08.2002. Effect: 1972 c. 11 amended. Territorial extent & classification: GB. General. – 2p.: 30 cm. – 0 11 042739 4 *£1.50*

The Welfare Reform and Pensions Act 1999 (Commencement No. 13) Order 2002 No. 2002/153 (C.3). – Enabling power: Welfare Reform and Pensions Act 1999, s. 89 (1). Bringing into force various provisions of the 1999 Act in accord. with art. 2. – Issued: 05.02.2002. Made: 30.01.2002. Effect: S.I. 2001/4049 (C.130) amended. Territorial extent & classification: E/W/S. General. – 8p.: 30 cm. – 0 11 039250 7 *£2.00*

The Welfare Reform and Pensions Act 1999 (Commencement No. 14) Order 2002 No. 2002/381 (C.9). – Enabling power: Welfare Reform and Pensions Act 1999, s. 89 (1). Bringing into force various provisions of the 1999 Act on 19.03.2002. – Issued: 26.02.2002. Made: 22.02.2002. Effect: None. Territorial extent & classification: E/W/S. General. – 8p.: 30 cm. – 0 11 039388 0 *£2.00*

The Welfare Reform and Pensions Act 1999 (Commencement No. 15) Order 2002 No. 2002/818 (C.21). – Enabling power: Welfare Reform and Pensions Act 1999, s. 89 (1). Bringing into force various provisions of the 1999 Act on 26.03.2002, 06.04.2002, in accord. with art. 3. – Issued: 02.04.2002. Made: 25.03.2002. Effect: S.I. 2002/153 (C.3) amended. Territorial extent & classification: E/W/S. General. – This Order has been made in consequence of a defect in S.I. 2002/153 (C.3) and is being issued free of charge to all known recipients of that S.I. – 8p.: 30 cm. – 0 11 039616 2 *£2.00*

Pensions, England

The Warrant Enforcement Staff Pensions Order 2002 No. 2002/1043. – Enabling power: Greater London Authority Act 1999, ss. 411 (1) (2) (c) (3) (g) (7), 420 (1) (b). – Issued: 18.04.2002. Made: 10.04.2002. Laid: 18.04.2002. Coming into force: 15.05.2002. Effect: None. Territorial extent & classification: E. General. – 2p.: 30 cm. – 0 11 039762 2 *£1.50*

Pensions, England and Wales

The Greater London Magistrates' Courts Authority (Pensions) Order 2002 No. 2002/2143. – Enabling power: Justices of the Peace Act 1997, s. 50 & Access to Justice Act 1999, sch. 14, para. 36. – Issued: 28.08.2002. Made: 16.08.2002. Laid: 19.08.2002. Coming into force: 13.09.2002. Effect: 1972 c. 11 amended. Territorial extent & classification: E/W. General. – 2p.: 30 cm. – 0 11 042697 5 *£1.50*

The Judicial Pensions and Retirement Act 1993 (Certain Qualifying Judicial Offices) (Amendment) Order 2002 No. 2002/3083. – Enabling power: Judicial Pensions and Retirement Act 1993, s. 1 (8). – Issued: 24.12.2002. Made: 16.12.2002. Laid: 16.12.2002. Coming into force: 15.01.2003. Effect: 1993 c. 8 amended in relation to England and Wales only. Territorial extent & classification: E/W. General. – 2p.: 30 cm. – 0 11 044243 1 *£1.50*

The Local Government (Early Termination of Employment) (Discretionary Compensation) (England and Wales) (Miscellaneous) Regulations 2002 No. 2002/769. – Enabling power: Superannuation Act 1972, s. 24. – Issued: 27.03.2002. Made: 21.03.2002. Laid: 27.03.2002. Coming into force: 17.04.2002. Effect: S.I. 2000/1410 amended. Territorial extent & classification: E/W. General. – 8p.: 30 cm. – 0 11 039593 X *£2.00*

The Local Government Pension Scheme (Amendment) Regulations 2002 No. 2002/206. – Enabling power: Superannuation Act 1972, ss. 7, 12. – Issued: 13.02.2002. Made: 05.02.2002. Laid: 13.02.2002. Coming into force: 01.04.1998, 01.04.2001, 02.04.2001, 06.03.2002, in accord. with art. 1 (2). Effect: S.I. 1997/1612 amended. Territorial extent & classification: E/W. General. – 4p.: 30 cm. – 0 11 039282 5 *£1.75*

The Local Government Pension Scheme (Management and Investment of Funds) (Amendment) Regulations 2002 No. 2002/1852. – Enabling power: Superannuation Act 1972, s. 7. – Issued: 19.07.2002. Made: 05.07.2002. Laid: 19.07.2002. Coming into force: 09.08.2002. Effect: S.I. 1998/1831 amended. Territorial extent & classification: E/W. General. – 4p.: 30 cm. – 0 11 042514 6 *£1.75*

The Local Government Pension Scheme (Miscellaneous) Regulations 2002 No. 2002/819. – Enabling power: Superannuation Act 1972, ss. 7, 12. – Issued: 04.04.2002. Made: 26.03.2002. Laid: 26.03.2002. Coming into force: 16.04.2002. Effect: S.I. 1997/1612; 2001/2866 amended. Territorial extent & classification: E/W. General. – 8p.: 30 cm. – 0 11 039624 3 *£2.00*

The Metropolitan Police Authority (Civil Staff Pensions) Order 2002 No. 2002/2468. – Enabling power: Greater London Authority Act 1999, s. 411. – Issued: 02.10.2002. Made: 24.09.2002. Laid: 30.09.2002. Coming into force: 31.10.2002 (but has effect from 01.09.2002). Effect: None. Territorial extent & classification: E/W. General. – 4p.: 30 cm. – 0 11 042831 5 *£1.75*

The Police Pensions (Pension Sharing) Regulations 2002 No. 2002/3202. – Enabling power: Police Pensions Act 1976, ss. 1 to 6, 7 (1). – Issued: 23.01.2003. Made: 20.12.2003. Laid: 08.01.2003. Coming into force: 01.02.2003. Effect: S.I. 1987/257, 2215; 19911304 amended. Territorial extent & classification: E/W. General. – 12p.: 30 cm. – 0 11 044620 8 *£2.50*

Pesticides

The Plant Protection Products (Fees) (Amendment) Regulations 2002 No. 2002/2733. – Enabling power: European Communities Act 1972, s. 2 (2). – Issued: 22.11.2002. Made: 03.11.2002. Laid: 04.11.2002. Coming into force: 30.11.2002. Effect: S.I. 2001/2477 amended. Territorial extent & classification: E/W/S. General. – 4p.: 30 cm. – EC note: These regs cover fees to be paid in connection with product approval and related applications resulting from the implementation of Council directive 91/414/EEC – Revoked by S.I. 2003/660 (ISBN 0110455134) – 0 11 042993 1 *£1.75*

Pesticides, England and Wales

The Pesticides (Maximum Residue Levels in Crops, Food and Feeding Stuffs) (England and Wales) (Amendment) (No. 2) Regulations 2002 No. 2002/2723. – Enabling power: European Communities Act 1972, s. 2 (2). – Issued: 14.11.2002. Made: 31.10.2002. Laid: 01.11.2002. Coming into force: 30.11.2002. Effect: S.I. 1999/3483 amended. Territorial extent & classification: E/W. General. – 104p.: 30 cm. – EC note: These regulations add new residue levels that have been set by recent amendments to EC DIR/86/362; 86/363; and 90/642 by DIR 2002/42; 2002/66; 2002/71; and 2002/76 – 0 11 042953 2 *£10.50*

The Plant Protection Products (Amendment) (No. 2) Regulations 2002 No. 2002/1460. – Enabling power: European Communities Act 1972, s. 2 (2). – Issued: 20.06.2002. Made: 30.05.2002. Laid: 31.05.2002. Coming into force: 01.07.2002. Effect: S.I. 1995/887 amended & 2002/526 revoked. Territorial extent & classification: E/W. General. – 4p.: 30 cm. – EC note: These Regs. amend the definition of "the Directive" in the 1995 Regs. so as to implement DIR 2001/414/EC, 2001/99/EC, 2001/103/EC and 2002/18/EC and makes transitional arrangements for the continuation of provisional approvals for substances in DIR 2001/87/EC and 2001/49/EC – Revoked by S.I. 2002/2874 (ISBN 0110440900) – 0 11 042372 0 *£1.75*

The Plant Protection Products (Amendment) (No. 3) Regulations 2002 No. 2002/2874. – Enabling power: European Communities Act 1972, s. 2 (2). – Issued: 04.12.2002. Made: 21.11.2002. Laid: 21.11.2002. Coming into force: 31.12.2002. Effect: S.I. 1995/887 amended in relation to England & Wales & 2002/1460 revoked. Territorial extent & classification: E/W. General. – EC note: These Regs. implement for the first time Commission Directives 2002/48/EC, 2002/64/EC and 2002/81/EC regarding the named substances listed in Annex 1 and will amend the definition further on 01/03/2003 when they implement Commission Directive 2002/37/EC. – [8]p.: 30 cm. – 0 11 044090 0 *£2.00*

The Plant Protection Products (Amendment) Regulations 2002 No. 2002/526. – Enabling power: European Communities Act 1972, s. 2 (2). – Issued: 18.03.2002. Made: 07.03.2002. Laid: 08.03.2002. Coming into force: 31.03.2002. Effect: S.I. 1995/887 amended & 2001/3814 revoked. Territorial extent & classification: E/W. General. – EC note: These Regs. amend the definition of "the Directive" in the 1995 Regs. so as to implement DIR 2001/87/EC, and make transitional arrangements for the continuation of provisional approvals for substances in DIR 2001/87/EC, 2001/49/EC and 2001/28/EC. – 4p.: 30 cm. – Revoked by S.I. 2002/1460 (ISBN 0110423720) – 0 11 039463 1 *£1.75*

Pilotage

The Port of Larne (Pilotage Functions) Order 2002 No. 2002/3037. – Enabling power: Pilotage Act 1987, s. 1 (4). – Issued: 17.12.2002. Made: 09.12.2002. Laid: 10.12.2002. Coming into force: 31.12.2002. Effect: None. Territorial extent & classification: E/W/S/NI. Local. – 2p.: 30 cm. – 0 11 044176 1 *£1.50*

Pitcairn Islands

The Pitcairn (Amendment) Order 2002 No. 2002/2638. – Enabling power: British Settlements Act 1887 & British Settlements Act 1945. – Issued: 04.11.2002. Made: 22.10.2002. Laid: 04.11.2002. Coming into force: 20.11.2002. Effect: S.I. 1970/1434 amended. Territorial extent & classification: E/W/S/NI. General. – 2p.: 30 cm. – 0 11 042905 2 *£1.50*

The Pitcairn Court of Appeal Order 2000 (Amendment) Order 2002 No. 2002/249. – Enabling power: British Settlements Acts 1887 & 1945. – Issued: 22.02.2002. Made: 12.02.2002. Laid: 22.02.2002. Coming into force: 04.03.2002. Effect: S.I. 2000/1341 amended. Territorial extent & classification: E/W/S/NI. General. – 2p.: 30 cm. – 0 11 039322 8 *£1.50*

Plant breeders' rights

The Patents and Plant Variety Rights (Compulsory Licensing) Regulations 2002 No. 2002/247. – Enabling power: European Communities Act 1972, s. 2 (2). – Issued: 01.03.2002. Made: 07.02.2002. Laid: 08.02.2002. Coming into force: 01.03.2002. Effect: None. Territorial extent & classification: E/W/S/NI. General. – EC note: Implement art. 12 of DIR 98/44 on the legal protection of biotechnological inventions. – 12p.: 30 cm. – 0 11 039398 8 *£2.50*

The Plant Breeders' Rights (Fees) (Amendment) Regulations 2002 No. 2002/1677. – Enabling power: Plant Varieties Act 1997, ss. 29 (1) (2), 48 (1). – Issued: 12.07.2002. Made: 27.06.2002. Laid: 02.07.2002. Coming into force: 23.007.2002. Effect: S.I. 1998/1021 amended. Territorial extent & classification:E/W/S/NI. General. – 8p.: 30 cm. – With correction slip, dated July 2002 – 0 11 042452 2 *£2.00*

Plant health

The Plant Health (Forestry) (Great Britain) (Amendment) (No. 2) Order 2002 No. 2002/927. – Enabling power: Plant Health Act 1967, ss. 2, 3 (1) to (4). – Issued: 26.04.2002. Made: 28.03.2002. Laid: 04.04.2002. Coming into force: 26.04.2002. Effect: S.I. 1993/1283 amended. Territorial extent & classification: E/W/S. General. – 4p.: 30 cm. – EC note: This Order implements certain elements of Commission directives 2002/29/EC & 2002/28/EC in Great Britain which are not implemented in other legislation – 0 11 039821 1 *£1.75*

The Plant Health (Forestry) (Great Britain) (Amendment) Order 2002 No. 2002/295. – Enabling power: Plant Health Act 1967, ss. 2, 3 (1) to (4). – Issued: 13.03.2002. Made: 12.02.2002. Laid: 12.02.2002. Coming into force: 05.03.2002. Effect: S.I. 1993/1283 amended. Territorial extent & classification: E/W/S. General. – 8p.: 30 cm. – EC note: This Order implements certain measures required by EC DIR 2001/32/EC & 2001/33/EC – 0 11 039442 9 *£2.00*

The Plant Health (Forestry) (Phytophthora ramorum) (Great Britain) (No. 2) Order 2002 No. 2002/2589. – Enabling power: Plant Health Act 1967, ss. 2, 3 (1) (2) (b) (3) (4). – Issued: 19.11.2002. Made: 15.10.2002. Laid: 15.10.2002. Coming into force: 05.11.2002. Effect: S.I. 2002/1478 revoked with saving. Territorial extent & classification: GB. General. – 8p.: 30 cm. – EC note: Implements Commission Decision 2002/757/EC in Great Britain insofar as it relates to forest trees, wood and bark – 0 11 042970 2 *£2.00*

The Plant Health (Forestry) (Phytophthora ramorum) (Great Britain) Order 2002 No. 2002/1478. – Enabling power: Plant Health Act 1967, ss. 2, 3 (1) (2) (b) (4). – Issued: 08.07.2002. Made: 08.06.2002. Laid: 06.06.2002. Coming into force: 27.06.2002. Effect: None. Territorial extent & classification: E/W/S. General. – 8p.: 30 cm. – Revoked by S.I. 2002/2589 (0110429702) – 0 11 042427 1 *£2.00*

Plant health, England

The Plant Health (England) (Amendment) Order 2002 No. 2002/1067. – Enabling power: Plant Health Act 1967, ss. 2, 3 (1) to (4), 4 (1). – Issued: 09.05.2002. Made: 15.04.2002. Laid: 15.04.2002. Coming into force: 06.05.2002. Effect: S.I. 1993/1320 amended in relation to England. Territorial extent & classification: E. General. – 4p.: 30 cm. – EC note: Implements certain elements of EC DIR 2002/28/EC, 2002/29/EC and 2002/32/EC in relation to England – 0 11 039906 4 £1.75

The Plant Health (Phytophthora ramorum) (England) (No. 2) Order 2002 No. 2002/2573. – Enabling power: Plant Health Act 1967, ss. 2, 3 (1) (2) (b) (3) (4), 4 (1) (b). – Issued: 13.11.2002. Made: 11.10.2002. Laid: 11.10.2002. Coming into force: 01.11.2002. Effect: S.I. 2002/1299 revoked with saving. Territorial extent & classification: E. General. – 8p.: 30 cm. – EC note: Implements Commission Decision 2002/757/EC in England insofar as it relates to plants other than forest trees – 0 11 042951 6 £2.00

The Plant Health (Phytophthora ramorum) (England) Order 2002 No. 2002/1299. – Enabling power: Plant Health Act 1967, ss. 2, 3 (1) (2) (b) (4), 4 (1) (b). – Issued: 23.05.2002. Made: 09.05.2002. Laid: 09.05.2002. Coming into force: 13.05.2002. Effect: None. Territorial extent & classification: E. General. – 8p.: 30 cm. – Revoked by S.I. 2002/2573 (ISBN 0110429516) – 0 11 039984 6 £2.00

The Potatoes Originating in Egypt (Amendment) (England) Regulations 2002 No. 2002/2902. – Enabling power: European Communities Act 1972, s. 2 (2). – Issued: 16.12.2002. Made: 21.11.2002. Laid: 22.11.2002. Coming into force: 13.12.2002. Effect: S.I. 1998/201 amended in relation to England. Territorial extent & classification: E. General. – EC note: Implements in England, Commission Decision 2002/903/EC amending Decision 96/301/EC. – 2p.: 30 cm. – 0 11 044175 3 £1.50

Plant health, England and Wales

The Treatment of Spruce Bark (Amendment) Order 2002 No. 2002/296. – Enabling power: Plant Health Act 1967, s. 3 (1) to (4). – Issued: 13.03.2002. Made: 12.02.2002. Laid: 12.02.2002. Coming into force: 05.03.2002. Effect: S.I. 1993/1282 amended & S.I. 1994/3093 revoked. Territorial extent & classification: E/W. General. – 4p.: 30 cm. – 0 11 039443 7 £1.75

Plant health, Wales

The Plant Health (Amendment) (Wales) Order 2002 No. 2002/1805 (W.175). – Enabling power: Plant Health Act 1967, ss. 2, 3 (1) to (4), 4 (1). – Issued: 29.07.2002. Made: 11.07.2002. Coming into force: 06.08.2002. Effect: S.I. 1993/1320 amended in relation to Wales. Territorial extent & classification: W. General. – EC note: Implements certain elements of DIR 2002/29/EC and 2002/28/EC in Wales. – In English & Welsh. Welsh title: Gorchymyn Iechyd Planhigion (Diwygio) (Cymru) 2002. – 8p.: 30 cm. – 0 11 090527 X £2.00

The Plant Health (Phytophthora ramorum) (Wales) (No. 2) Order 2002 No. 2002/2762 (W.263). – Enabling power: Plant Health Act 1967, ss. 2, 3 (1) (2) (b) (3) (4), 4 (1) (b). – Issued: 05.11.2002. Made: 05.11.2002. Coming into force: 08.11.2002. Effect: S.I. 2002/1350 (W.13) revoked with saving. Territorial extent & classification: W. General. – 8p.: 30 cm. – 0 11 090579 2 £2.00

The Plant Health (Phytophthora ramorum) (Wales) Order 2002 No. 2002/1350 (W.130). – Enabling power: Plant Health Act 1967, ss. 2, 3 (1) (2) (b) (4), 4 (1) (b). – Issued: 23.05.2002. Made: 14.05.2002. at 3.55 pm. Coming into force: 14.05.2002. at 4.30 pm. Effect: None. Territorial extent & classification: W. General. – 8p.: 30 cm. – Revoked with saving by S.I. 2002/2762 (W.263) (ISBN 0110905792) – 0 11 090491 5 £2.00

The Potatoes Originating in Egypt (Amendment) (Wales) (No. 2) Regulations 2002 No. 2002/3226 (W.306). – Enabling power: European Communities Act 1972, s. 2 (2). – Issued: 17.01.2003. Made: 23.12.2002. Coming into force: 24.12.2002. Effect: S.I. 1998/201 amended in relation to Wales. Territorial extent & classification: W. General. – EC note: Implements in Wales Commission decision 2002/903/EC amending decision 96/301/EC. – In English & Welsh. Welsh title: Rheoliadau Tatws sy'n Deillio o'r Aifft (Diwygio) (Cymru) (Rhif 2) 2002. – 4p.: 30 cm. – 0 11 090617 9 £1.75

The Potatoes Originating in Egypt (Amendment) (Wales) Regulations 2002 No. 2002/120 (W.14). – Enabling power: European Communities Act 1972, s. 2 (2). – Issued: 07.03.2002. Made: 25.01.2002. Coming into force: 18.02.2002. Effect: S.I. 1998/201 amended in relation to Wales. Territorial extent & classification: W. General. – EC note: Implement for Wales DEC 2000/664/EC amending 96/301/EC. – In English & Welsh. Welsh title: Rheoliadau Tatws sy'n Deillio o'r Aifft (Diwygio) (Cymru) 2002. – 4p.: 30 cm. – 0 11 090438 9 £1.75

Police

The Atomic Energy Authority (Special Constables) Order 2002 No. 2002/1151. – Enabling power: Anti-terrorism, Crime and Security Act 2001, s. 76 (2). – Issued: 29.04.2002. Made: 18.04.2002. Laid: 24.04.2002. Coming into force: 24.05.2002. Effect: None. Territorial extent and classification: E/W/S/NI General. – 2p.: 30 cm. – 0 11 039836 X £1.50

The Criminal Justice and Police Act 2001 (Central Police Training and Development Authority) (Transitional Provisions) Order 2002 No. 2002/534. – Enabling power: Criminal Justice and Police Act 2001, s. 103. – Issued: 25.03.2002. Made: 07.03.2002. Laid: 11.03.2002. Coming into force: 01.04.2002. Effect: None. Territorial extent & classification: UK. General. – 4p.: 30 cm. – 0 11 039573 5 £1.75

The Criminal Justice and Police Act 2001 (Commencement No.4 and Transitional Provisions) Order 2002 No. 2002/344 (C.7). – Enabling power: Criminal Justice and Police Act 2001, ss. 109, 116 (7), 119 (7), 138 (2). Bringing into force various provisions of the 2001 Act on 01.03.2002, 01.04.2002, in accord.with arts. 2, 3. – Issued: 27.02.2002. Made: 16.02.2002. Effect: None. Territorial extent & classification: E/W/S. General. – 4p.: 30 cm. – 0 11 039390 2 £1.75

The Criminal Justice and Police Act 2001 (Commencement No.5) Order 2002 No. 2002/533 (C.15). – Enabling power: Criminal Justice and Police Act 2001, s. 138 (2). Bringing into force various provisions of the 2001 Act on 01.04.2002, 02.04.2002, in accord.with arts. 2, 3. – Issued: 25.03.2002. Made: 07.03.2002. Effect: None. Territorial extent & classification: UK. General. – 4p.: 30 cm. – 0 11 039580 8 £1.75

The Criminal Justice and Police Act 2001 (Commencement No. 7) Order 2002 No. 2002/2050 (C.66). – Enabling power: Criminal Justice and Police Act 2001, s. 138 (2). Bringing into force various provisions of the 2001 Act on 12.08.2002 and 01.09.2002. – Issued: 09.08.2002. Made: 02.08.2002. Effect: None. Territorial extent & classification: UK [parts to E/W only and part to all UK]. General. – 4p.: 30 cm. – 0 11 042639 8 £1.75

The National Criminal Intelligence Service (Secretary of State's Objectives) Order 2002 No. 2002/778. – Enabling power: Police Act 1997, s. 26 (1). – Issued: 05.04.2002. Made: 21.03.2002. Laid: 26.03.2002. Coming into force: 01.04.2002. Effect: S.I. 1999/822 revoked. Territorial extent & classification: UK. General. – 2p.: 30 cm. – 0 11 039644 8 £1.50

The Police Reform Act 2002 (Commencement No. 1) Order 2002 No. 2002/2306 (C.75). – Enabling power: Police Reform Act 2002, s. 108 (2). Bringing into operation various provisions of the 2002 Act on 01.10.2002 & 01.11.2002, in accord. with arts. 2, 3, 4, 5. – Issued: 20.09.2002. Made: 05.09.2002. Effect: None. Territorial extent & classification: UK. General. – 4p.: 30 cm. – 0 11 042790 4 £1.75

The Police Reform Act 2002 (Commencement No. 3) Order 2002 No. 2002/2750 (C.85). – Enabling power: Police Reform Act 2002, s. 108 (2). Bringing into operation various provisions of the 2002 Act on 02.12.2002 & 01.01.2003. & 03.02.2003, in accord. with arts. 2, 3, 4, 5. – Issued: 25.11.2002. Made: 05.11.2002. Effect: None. Territorial extent & classification: UK. General. – 4p.: 30 cm. – 0 11 043047 6 £1.75

Police, England and Wales

The Attestation of Constables (Welsh Language) Order 2002 No. 2002/2312. – Enabling power: Welsh Language Act 1993, s. 26 (2). – Issued: 20.09.2002. Made: 05.09.2002. Laid: 10.09.2002. Coming into force: 01.10.2002. Effect: None. Territorial extent & classification: E/W. General. – 2p.: 30 cm. – 0 11 042787 4 £1.50

The Criminal Justice and Police Act 2001 (Commencement No. 8) Order 2002 No. 2002/3032 (C.100). – Enabling power: Criminal Justice and Police Act 2001, s. 138 (2). Bringing into force various provisions of the 2001 Act on 01.01.2003, in accord. with art. 2. – Issued: 18.12.2002. Made: 06.12.2002. Effect: None. Territorial extent & classification: E/W. General. – 4p.: 30 cm. – 0 11 044197 4 £1.75

The Functions of Traffic Wardens (Amendment) Order 2002 No. 2002/2975. – Enabling power: Road Traffic Regulation Act 1984, ss. 95 (5), 96. – Issued: 05.12.2002. Made: 29.11.2002. Coming into force: 02.12.2002. Effect: S.I. 1970/1958 amended. Territorial extent & classification: E/W. General. – 2p.: 30 cm. – Supersedes draft S.I. (ISBN 0110429362) issued on 05.11.2002 – 0 11 044112 5 £1.50

The Metropolitan Police Authority (Civil Staff Pensions) Order 2002 No. 2002/2468. – Enabling power: Greater London Authority Act 1999, s. 411. – Issued: 02.10.2002. Made: 24.09.2002. Laid: 30.09.2002. Coming into force: 31.10.2002 (but has effect from 01.09.2002). Effect: None. Territorial extent & classification: E/W. General. – 4p.: 30 cm. – 0 11 042831 5 £1.75

The National Crime Squad (Secretary of State's Objectives) Order 2002 No. 2002/779. – Enabling power: Police Act 1997, s. 71 (1). – Issued: 05.04.2002. Made: 21.03.2002. Laid: 26.03.2002. Coming into force: 01.04.2002. Effect: S.I. 1999/821 revoked. Territorial extent & classification: E/W. General. – 2p.: 30 cm. – 0 11 039647 2 £1.50

The Police Act 1997 (Commencement No. 9) Order 2002 No. 2002/413 (C.11). – Enabling power: Police Act 1997, s. 135. Bringing into operation various provisions of the 1997 Act on 01.03.2002. – Issued: 28.02.2002. Made: 22.02.2002. Effect: None. Territorial extent & classification: E/W. General. – 2p.: 30 cm. – 0 11 039395 3 £1.50

The Police Act 1997 (Criminal Records) Regulations 2002 No. 2002/233. – Enabling power: Police Act 1997, ss. 113 (1) (b), 114 (1) (b), 115 (1) (b) (10), 116 (1) (b), 118 (3), 125 (5). – Issued: 13.02.2002. Made: 07.02.2002. Laid: 07.02.2002. Coming into force: 01.03.2002. Effect: None. Territorial extent & classification: E/W. General. – With correction slip dated February 2002. – 12p.: 30 cm. – 0 11 039301 5 £2.50

The Police Act 1997 (Enhanced Criminal Record Certificates) (Protection of Vulnerable Adults) Regulations 2002 No. 2002/446. – Enabling power: Police Act 1997, s. 115 (4). – Issued: 07.03.2002. Made: 28.02.2002. Coming into force: 01.03.2002. Effect: None. Territorial extent & classification: E/W. General. – Supersedes draft S.I. laid before Parliament on 30th January 2002, which was not published– 2p.: 30 cm. – Supersedes draft S.I. (ISBN 0110393031) – 0 11 039417 8 *£1.50*

The Police (Amendment) (No. 2) Regulations 2002 No. 2002/2529. – Enabling power: Police Act 1996, s. 50 & Police Pensions Act 1976, s. 1. – Issued: 17.10.2002. Made: 04.10.2002. Laid: 11.10.2002. Coming into force: 01.11.2002. Effect: S.I. 1987/257; 1995/215 amended. Territorial extent & classification: E/W. General. – 2p.: 30 cm. – Revoked with saving by S.I. 2003/527 (ISBN 0110454499) – 0 11 042857 9 *£1.50*

The Police (Amendment) (No. 3) Regulations 2002 No. 2002/3162. – Enabling power: Police Act 1996, s. 50. – Issued: 16.01.2003. Made: 18.12.2002. Laid: 19.12.2002. Coming into force: 03.02.2003. Effect: S.I. 1995/215 amended. Territorial extent & classification: E/W. General. – 4p.: 30 cm. – Revoked with saving by S.I. 2003/527 (ISBN 0110454499) – 0 11 044585 6 *£1.75*

The Police (Amendment) Regulations 2002 No. 2002/1758. – Enabling power: Police Act 1996, s. 50. – Issued: 24.07.2002. Made: 09.07.2002. Laid: 10.07.2002. Coming into force: 01.08.2002. Effect: S.I. 1995/215 amended. Territorial extent & classification: E/W. General. – 4p.: 30 cm. – Revoked with saving by S.I. 2003/527 (ISBN 0110454499) – 0 11 042522 7 *£1.75*

The Police and Criminal Evidence Act 1984 (Codes of Practice) (Modifications to Code C and Code D) (Certain Police Areas) (Amendment) Order 2002 No. 2002/1863. – Enabling power: Police and Criminal Evidence Act 1984, s. 67 (7A). – Issued: 14.08.2002. Made: 18.07.2002. Laid: 22.07.2002. Coming into force: 02.09.2002. Effect: S.I. 2002/1150 amended. Territorial extent & classification: E/W. General. – 2p.: 30 cm. – Revoked by S.I. 2003/704 (ISBN 0110454510) – 0 11 042649 5 *£1.50*

The Police and Criminal Evidence Act 1984 (Codes of Practice) (Modifications to Code C and Code D) (Certain Police Areas) Order 2002 No. 2002/1150. – Enabling power: Police and Criminal Evidence Act 1984, s. 67 (7A). – Issued: 14.05.2002. Made: 23.04.2002. Laid: 29.04.2002. Coming into force: 20.05.2002. Effect: S.I. 2001/2254 revoked. Territorial extent & classification: E/W. General. – 4p.: 30 cm. – Revoked by S.I. 2003/704 (ISBN 0110454510) – 0 11 039921 8 *£1.75*

The Police and Criminal Evidence Act 1984 (Codes of Practice) (Statutory Powers of Stop and Search) Order 2002 No. 2002/Unnumbered. – Enabling power: Police and Criminal Evidence Act 1984, s. 67 (4). – Issued: 29.11.2002. Made: 11.11.2002. Laid: 13.11.2002. Coming into force: 01.04.2003. Effect: None. Territorial extent & classification: E/W. – 2p.: 30 cm. – Superseded by S.I. 2002/3075 (ISBN 0110441966) issued on 19.12.2002. For approval by resolution of each House of Parliament – 0 11 044069 2 *£1.50*

The Police and Criminal Evidence Act 1984 (Codes of Practice) (Statutory Powers of Stop and Search) Order 2002 No. 2002/3075. – Enabling power: Police and Criminal Evidence Act 1984, s. 67 (4). – Issued: 19.12.2002. Made: 11.11.2002. Laid: 13.11.2002. Coming into force: 01.04.2003. Effect: None. Territorial extent & classification: E/W. General. – 2p.: 30 cm. – Supersedes draft S.I. (ISBN 0110440692) issued on 29.11.2002 – 0 11 044196 6 *£1.50*

The Police and Criminal Evidence Act 1984 (Codes of Practice) (Temporary Modifications to Code D) Order 2002 No. 2002/615. – Enabling power: Police and Criminal Evidence Act 1984, s. 67 (7A). – Issued: 20.03.2002. Made: 03.03.2002. Laid: 11.03.2002. Coming into force: 01.04.2002. Effect: None. Territorial extent & classification: E/W. General. – 20p.: 30 cm. – Revoked by S.I. 2003/704 (ISBN 0110454510) – 0 11 039508 5 *£3.50*

The Police and Criminal Evidence Act 1984 (Codes of Practice) (Visual Recording of Interviews) Order 2002 No. 2002/Unnumbered. – Enabling power: Police and Criminal Evidence Act 1984, s. 67 (4). – Issued: 26.04.2002. Made:11.04.2002. Laid: 15.04.2002. Coming into force: 07.05.2002. Effect: None. Territorial extent & classification: E/W. General. – Superseded by S.I. 2002/1266 ISBN 0110399196. – 2p.: 30 cm. – 0 11 039826 2 *£1.50*

The Police and Criminal Evidence Act 1984 (Codes of Practice) (Visual Recording of Interviews) Order 2002 No. 2002/1266. – Enabling power: Police and Criminal Evidence Act 1984, s. 67 (4). – Issued: 14.05.2002. Made: 11.04.2002. Laid: 15.04.2002. Coming into force: 07.05.2002. Effect: None. Territorial extent & classification: E/W. General. – 2p.: 30 cm. – 0 11 039919 6 *£1.50*

The Police and Criminal Evidence Act 1984 (Visual Recording of Interviews) (Certain Police Areas) (No. 2) Order 2002 No. 2002/2527. – Enabling power: Police and Criminal Evidence Act 1984, s. 60A (1) (b) (2). – Issued: 16.10.2002. Made: 07.100.2002. Laid: 09.10.2002. Coming into force: 30.10.2002. Effect: None. Territorial extent & classification: E/W. General. – 2p.: 30 cm. – 0 11 042853 6 *£1.50*

The Police and Criminal Evidence Act 1984 (Visual Recording of Interviews) (Certain Police Areas) Order 2002 No. 2002/1069. – Enabling power: Police and Criminal Evidence Act 1984, s. 60A (1) (b) (2). – Issued: 14.05.2002. Made: 12.04.2002. Laid: 16.04.2002. Coming into force: 08.05.2002. Effect: None. Territorial extent & classification: E/W. General. – 2p.: 30 cm. – 0 11 039920 X *£1.50*

The Police Authorities (Best Value) Performance Indicators Order 2002 No. 2002/694. – Enabling power: Local Government Act 1999, s. 4 (1) (a). – Issued: 02.04.2002. Made: 13.03.2002. Laid: 15.03.2002. Coming into force: 01.04.2002. Effect: None. Territorial extent & classification: E/W. General. – 4p.: 30 cm. – Revoked by S.I. 2003/519 (ISBN 0110452763) – 0 11 039618 9 *£1.75*

The Police Authorities (Selection Panel) (Amendment) Regulations 2002 No. 2002/1282. – Enabling power: Police Act 1996, sch. 3, para. 11. – Issued: 20.05.2002. Made: 07.05.2002. Laid: 15.05.2002. Coming into force: 10.06.2002. Effect: S.I. 1994/2023 amended. Territorial extent & classification: E/W. General. – 2p.: 30 cm. – 0 11 039962 5 £1.50

The Police Authorities (Three-year Strategy Plans) Regulations 2002 No. 2002/2526. – Enabling power: Police Act 1996, s. 6A (14). – Issued: 17.10.2002. Made: 06.10.2002. Laid: 09.10.2002. Coming into force: 01.11.2002. Effect: None. Territorial extent & classification: E/W. General. – 2p.: 30 cm. – 0 11 042856 0 £1.50

The Police Pensions (Pension Sharing) Regulations 2002 No. 2002/3202. – Enabling power: Police Pensions Act 1976, ss. 1 to 6, 7 (1). – Issued: 23.01.2003. Made: 20.12.2003. Laid: 08.01.2003. Coming into force: 01.02.2003. Effect: S.I. 1987/257, 2215; 19911304 amended. Territorial extent & classification: E/W. General. – 12p.: 30 cm. – 0 11 044620 8 £2.50

The Police (Promotion) (Amendment) Regulations 2002 No. 2002/767. – Enabling power: Police Act 1996, s. 50. – Issued: 05.04.2002. Made: 20.03.2002. Laid: 21.03.2002. Coming into force: 12.04.2002. Effect: S.I. 1996/1685 amended. Territorial extent & classification: E/W. General. – 2p.: 30 cm. – 0 11 039646 4 £1.50

The Police (Property) (Amendment) Regulations 2002 No. 2002/2313. Enabling power: Police (Property) Act 1897, ss. 2, 2A (3). – Issued: 20.09.2002. Made: 05.09.2002. Laid: 10.09.2002. Coming into force: 01.10.2002. Effect: S.I. 1997/1908 amended. Territorial extent & classification: E/W. General. – 2p.: 30 cm. – 0 11 042789 0 £1.50

The Police (Retention and Disposal of Motor Vehicles) Regulations 2002 No. 2002/3049. – Enabling power: Police Reform Act 2002, ss. 60, 105 (4). – Issued: 19.12.2002. Made: 11.12.2002. Laid: 11.12.2002. Coming into force: 01.01.2003. Effect: None. Territorial extent & classification: E/W. General. – 4p.: 30 cm. – 0 11 044218 0 £1.75

The Police (Secretary of State's Objectives) Order 2002 No. 2002/695. – Enabling power: Police Act 1996, s. 37 (1). – Issued: 02.04.2002. Made: 13.03.2002. Laid: 15.03.2002. Coming into force: 01.04.2002. Effect: S.I. 1999/3424 revoked. Territorial extent & classification: E/W. General. – 2p.: 30 cm. – Revoked by S.I. 2003/830 (ISBN 0110454892) – 0 11 039620 0 £1.50

The Special Constables (Amendment) Regulations 2002 No. 2002/3180. – Enabling power: Police Act 1996, ss. 50 (7), 51. – Issued: 16.01.2003. Made: 18.12.2002. Laid: 19.12.2002. Coming into force: for reg. 2 (2) 03.02.2003; for the remainder 10.01.2003. Effect: S.I. 1965/536 amended & S.I. 1992/1526 revoked (10.01.2003). Territorial extent & classification: E/W. General. – 4p.: 30 cm. – 0 11 044586 4 £1.75

Port health authorities, England and Wales

The Falmouth & Truro Port Health Authority (Amendment) Order 2001 No. 2002/2000. – Enabling power: Public Health (Control of Disease) Act 1984, ss. 2, 4. – Issued: 05.08.2002. Made: 31.01.2002. Coming into force: 01.02.2001. Effect: S.I.1988/2075 amended. Territorial extent & classification: E/W. General. – 2p.: 30 cm. – 0 11 042592 8 £1.50

Postal services

The Postal Services Act 2000 (Determination of Turnover for Penalties) (Amendment) Order 2002 No. 2002/125. – Enabling power: Postal Services Act 2000, s. 30 (2). – Issued: 04.02.2002. Made: 25.01.2002. Coming into force: 26.01.2002. Effect: S.I. 2001/1135 amended. Territorial extent & classification: E/W/S/NI. General. – 2p.: 30 cm. – 0 11 039237 X £1.50

The Postal Services Act 2000 (Modification of Section 7) Order 2002 No. 2002/200. – Enabling power: Postal Services Act 2000, s. 8. – Issued: 11.02.2002. Made: 04.02.2002. Coming into force: 05.02.2002. Effect: 2000 c. 26 amended. Territorial extent & classification: E/W/S/NI. General. – Supersedes draft S.I. (ISBN 0110392140) issued 23.01.2002. – 2p.: 30 cm. – 0 11 039277 9 £1.50

The Postal Services (EC Directive) Regulations 2002 No. 2002/3050. – Enabling power: European Communities Act 1972, s. 2 (2). – Issued: 27.12.2002. Made: 11.12.2002. Laid: 11.12.2002. Coming into force: 01.01.2003 for all except Reg. 8; 01.01.2006. for Reg 8. Effect: 2000 ch. 26 amended. Territorial extent & classification: E/W/S/NI. General. – 8p.: 30 cm. – EC note: DIR 97/67/EC has been amended by DIR 2002/39/EC, and these Regs. implement these changes by amending the Postal Services Act 2000 – 0 11 044397 7 £2.00

Post office

The Telecommunication Services (Channel Islands) Order 2002 No. 2002/799. – Enabling power: Post Office Act 1969, s. 87 (1) (2). – Issued: 03.04.2002. Made: 26.03.2002. Coming into force: 29.03.2002. Effect: S.I. 1972/1814, 1815, 1816 revoked. Territorial extent & classification: CI/IoM . General [applies to the Bailiwick of Jersey for art. 3(a) (c); to the Bailiwick of Guernsey for art. 3(b) and (c); to the UK and to the Isle of Man for art. 3(c)]. – 2p.: 30 cm. – 0 11 039639 1 £1.50

Powers of attorney, England and Wales

The Court of Protection (Enduring Powers of Attorney) (Amendment No. 2) Rules 2002 No. 2002/1944. – Enabling power: Mental Health Act 1983, ss. 106, 108. – Issued: 02.08.2002. Made: 23.07.2002. Laid: 26.07.2002. Coming into force: 31.08.2002. Effect: S.I. 2001/825 amended. Territorial extent & classification: E/W. General. – 12p.: 30 cm. – 0 11 042581 2 £2.50

The Court of Protection (Enduring Powers of Attorney) (Amendment) Rules 2002 No. 2002/832. – Enabling power: Mental Health Act 1983, ss. 106, 107, 108. – Issued: 12.04.2002. Made: 26.03.2002. Laid: 27.03.2002. Coming into force: 17.04.2002. Effect: S.I. 2001/825 amended. Territorial extent & classification: E/W. General. – 4p.: 30 cm. – 0 11 039730 4 £1.75

Prevention and suppression of terrorism

The Anti-Terrorism, Crime and Security Act 2001 (Commencement No. 4) Order 2002 No. 2002/1279 (C.35). – Enabling power: Anti-Terrorism, Crime and Security Act 2001, s. 127 (1). Bringing into force various provisions of the 2001 Act on 31.05.2002. – Issued: 14.05.2002. Made: 04.05.2002. Effect: None. Territorial extent & classification: E/W/S/NI. General. – 2p.: 30 cm. – 0 11 039924 2 £1.50

The Anti-Terrorism, Crime and Security Act 2001 (Commencement No. 5) Order 2002 No. 2002/1558 (C.44). – Enabling power: Anti-Terrorism, Crime and Security Act 2001, s. 127 (1). Bringing into force various provisions of the 2001 Act on 07.07.2002. – Issued: 28.06.2002. Made: 10.06.2002. Effect: None. Territorial extent & classification: E/W/S/NI. General. – 2p.: 30 cm. – 0 11 042392 5 £1.50

The Pathogens Access Appeal Commission (Procedure) Rules 2002 No. 2002/1845. – Enabling power: Anti-Terrorism, Crime and Security Act 2001, sch. 6, para. 5. – Issued: 22.07.2002. Made: 16.07.2002. Coming into force: 23.07.2002. Effect: None. Territorial extent & classification: E/W/S/NI. General. – 12p.: 30 cm. – 0 11 042517 0 £2.50

Schedule 7 to the Terrorism Act 2000 (Information) Order 2002 No. 2002/1945. – Enabling power: Terrorism Act 2000, sch. 7, para. 17 (4). – Issued: 29.07.2002. Made: 22.07.2002. Coming into force: 22.08.2002. Effect: None. Territorial extent & classification: UK. General. – Supersedes draft S.I. (ISBN 011042459X) issued 15th July 2002. – 2p.: 30 cm. – 0 11 042550 2 £1.50

The Security of Pathogens and Toxins (Exceptions to Dangerous Substances) Regulations 2002 No. 2002/1281. – Enabling power: Anti-Terrorism, Crime and Security Act 2001, s. 74 (1). – Issued: 14.05.2002. Made: 04.05.2002. Laid: 10.05.2002. Coming into force: 31.05.2002. Effect: None. Territorial extent & classification: E/W/S. General. – 4p.: 30 cm. – 0 11 039923 4 £1.75

The Terrorism Act 2000 (Proscribed Organisations) (Amendment) Order 2002 No. 2002/2724. – Enabling power: Terrorism Act 2000, s. 3 (3) (a) (c). – Issued: 06.11.2002. Made: 31.10.2002. Coming into force: 01.11.2002. Effect: 2000 c. 11 amended. Territorial extent & classification: UK. General. – 2p.: 30 cm. – 0 11 042939 7 £1.50

Prisons, England and Wales

The Closure of Prisons (H.M. Prison Haslar) Order 2002 No. 2002/77. – Enabling power: Prison Act 1952, s. 37. – Issued: 25.01.2002. Made: 17.01.2002. Laid: 18.01.2002. Coming into force: 08.02.2002. Effect: None. Territorial extent & classification: E/W. Local. – 2p.: 30 cm. – 0 11 039216 7 £1.50

The Closure of Prisons (H.M. Young Offender Institution Dover) Order 2002 No. 2002/78. – Enabling power: Prison Act 1952, s. 37. – Issued: 25.01.2002. Made: 17.01.2002. Laid: 18.01.2002. Coming into force: 08.02.2002. Effect: None. Territorial extent & classification: E/W. Local. – 2p.: 30 cm. – 0 11 039217 5 £1.50

The Prison (Amendment) Rules 2002 No. 2002/2116. – Enabling power: Prison Act 1952, s. 47. – Issued: 09.09.2002. Made: 14.08.2002. Laid: 14.08.2002. Coming into force: 15.08.2002. Effect: S.I. 1999/728 amended. Territorial extent & classification: E/W. General. – 4p.: 30 cm. – 0 11 042737 8 £1.75

The Release of Short-term Prisoners on Licence (Amendment of Requisite Period) Order 2002 No. 2002/2933. – Enabling power: Criminal Justice Act 1991, s. 34A (5) (b). – Issued: 02.12.2002. Made: 26.11.2002. Coming into force: 16.12.2002. Effect: 1991 c. 53 amended. Territorial extent & classification: E/W. General. – 2p.: 30 cm. – Revoked by S.I. 2003/1602 (ISBN 0110466098). Supersedes draft S.I. (ISBN 0110429915) issued on 20.11.2002 – 0 11 044078 1 £1.50

Private security industry

The Private Security Industry Act 2001 (Commencement No. 1) Order 2002 No. 2002/3125 (C.105). – Enabling power: Private Security Industry Act 2001, s. 26 (2). Bringing into force various provisions of the 2001 Act in accord. with arts. 2, 3, 4, 01.01.2003, 01.04.2003. – Issued: 20.12.2002. Made: 13.12.2002. Effect: None. Territorial extent & classification: E/W/S/NI. General. – 2p.: 30 cm. – 0 11 044244 X £1.50

Proceeds of crime

The Proceeds of Crime Act 2002 (Cash Searches: Code of Practice) Order 2002 No. 2002/3115. – Enabling power: Proceeds of Crime Act 2002, s. 292 (4). – Issued: 20.12.2002. Made: 16.12.2002. Coming into force: In accord. with art. 1, 30.12.2002. Effect: None. Territorial extent & classification: E/W/S/NI. General. – 2p.: 30 cm. – Supersedes draft S.I. (ISBN 0110441141) issued on 06.12.2002 – 0 11 044238 5 £1.50

The Proceeds of Crime Act 2002 (Commencement No. 1 and Savings) Order 2002 No. 2002/3015 (C.98). – Enabling power: Proceeds of Crime Act 2002, ss. 458 (1), 459 (2). Bringing into operation various provisions of this act on 30.12.2002, in accord. with art. 2. – Issued: 19.12.2002. Made: 04.12.2002. Coming into force: .-. Effect: None. Territorial extent & classification: E/W/S/NI. General. – 4p.: 30 cm. – 0 11 044214 8   *£1.75*

The Proceeds of Crime Act 2002 (Commencement No. 2) Order 2002 No. 2002/3055 (C.102). – Enabling power: Proceeds of Crime Act 2002, s. 458 (1). Bringing into operation various provisions of this act on 13.01.2002, in accord. with art. 2. – Issued: 19.12.2002. Made: 11.12.2002. Effect: None. Territorial extent & classification: E/W/S/NI. General. – 2p.: 30 cm. – 0 11 044216 4   *£1.50*

The Proceeds of Crime Act 2002 (Commencement No. 3) Order 2002 No. 2002/3145 (C.106). – Enabling power: Proceeds of Crime Act 2002, s. 458 (1). Bringing into operation various provisions of the 2002 Act on 30.12.2002. – Issued: 10.01.2003. Made: 17.12.2002. Effect: None. Territorial extent & classification: E/W/S/NI. General. – 4p.: 30 cm. – 0 11 044469 8   *£1.75*

The Proceeds of Crime Act 2002 (Enforcement in different parts of the United Kingdom) Order 2002 No. 2002/3133. – Enabling power: Proceeds of Crime Act 2002, s. 443. – Issued: 06.01.2003. Made: 17.12.2002. Laid: 06.01.2003. Coming into force: 24.02.2003. Effect: None. Territorial extent & classification: E/W/S/NI. General. – 8p.: 30 cm. – 0 11 044250 4   *£2.00*

The Proceeds of Crime Act 2002 (Recovery of Cash in Summary Proceedings: Minimum Amount) Order 2002 No. 2002/3016. – Enabling power: Proceeds of Crime Act 2002, s. 303. – Issued: 19.12.2002. Made: 04.12.2002. Laid: 06.12.2002. Coming into force: 30.12.2002. Effect: None. Territorial extent & classification: E/W/S/NI. General. – 2p.: 30 cm. – 0 11 044215 6   *£1.50*

Professional qualifications

The European Communities (Recognition of Professional Qualifications) (Amendment) Regulations 2002 No. 2002/3051. – Enabling power: European Communities Act 1972, s. 2 (2). – Issued: 18.12.2002. Made: 11.12.2002. Laid: 11.12.2002. Coming into force: 01.01.2003. Effect: S.I. 1991/824 amended. Territorial extent & classification: E/W/S. General. – 4p.: 30 cm. – EC note: These Regs. give effect in the UK to those parts of DIR 2001/19/EO which amend DIR 89/48/EEC on a general system for the recognition of higher-education diplomas awarded on completion of a professional education and training of at least three years' duration. The Regs. also amend the 1991 Regs. to provide for their application in relation to the European Economic Area and Switzerland – 0 11 044182 6   *£1.75*

The European Communities (Recognition of Professional Qualifications) (Second General System) Regulations 2002 No. 2002/2934. – Enabling power: European Communities Act 1972, s. 2 (2). – Issued: 04.12.2002. Made: 26.11.2002. Laid: 04.12.2002. Coming into force: 01.01.2003. Effect: S.I. 1996/2374; 1999/67; 2001/200 revoked. Territorial extent & classification: UK. General. – 40p.: 30 cm. – EC note: These Regs. implement part of Directive 92/51/EEC supplementing DIR 89/48/EC, 94/38/EC, 95/43/EC, 2000/5/EC and article 2 of DIR 2001/19/EC. The Regs. extend to the states of the European Economic Area (EEA) and Switzerland – 0 11 044092 7   *£6.50*

The European Communities (Recognition of Qualifications and Experience) (Third General System) (Amendment) Regulations 2002 No. 2002/2036. – Enabling power: European Communities Act 1972, s. 2 (2). – Issued: 23.08.2002. Made: 01.08.2002. Laid: 02.08.2002. Coming into force: 08.08.2002. Effect: S.I. 2002/1597 amended. Territorial extent & classification: E/W/S/NI. General. – This Statutory Instrument has been made in consequence of a defect in S.I. 2002/1597 and is being issued free of charge to all known recipients of that Statutory Instrument. – 2p.: 30 cm. – 0 11 042675 4   *£1.50*

The European Communities (Recognition of Qualifications and Experience) (Third General System) Regulations 2002 No. 2002/1597. – Enabling power: European Communities Act 1972, s. 2 (2). – Issued: 02.07.2002. Made: 18.06.2002. Laid: 18.06.2002. Coming into force: 16.07.2002. Effect: 1975 c. 35 amended. Territorial extent & classification. E/W/S/NI. General. – EC note: These Regs. implement DIR 99/42. – 8p.: 30 cm. – 0 11 042399 2   *£2.00*

Protection of wrecks, England

The Protection of Wrecks (Designation) Order 2002 No. 2002/1858. – Enabling power: Protection of Wrecks Act 1973, s. 1 (1) (2) (4). – Issued: 05.08.2002. Made: 17.07.2002. Laid: 17.07.2002. Coming into force: 18.07.2002. Effect: None. Territorial extent & classification: E. General. – 2p.: 30 cm. – 0 11 042590 1   *£1.50*

Protection of wrecks, Wales

The Protection of Wrecks (Designation of "The Diamond") (Wales) Order 2002 No. 2002/1042 (W.113). – Enabling power: Protection of Wrecks Act 1973, s. 1 (1) (2) (4). – Made: 27.03.2002. Coming into force: 01.04.2002. Effect: None. Territorial extent & classification: W. Local – In English and Welsh *Unpublished*

Public health

The Regulatory Reform (Vaccine Damage Payments Act 1979) Order 2002 No. 2002/1592. – Enabling power: Regulatory Reform Act 2001, ss. 1, 4 (3), 15 (3). – Issued: 24.06.2002. Made: 15.06.2002. Coming into force: 16.06.2002. Effect: 1979 c. 17 amended. Territorial extent and classification: E/W/S. General. – Supersedes draft S.I. (ISBN 0110399528) issued 16 May 2002. – 4p.: 30 cm. – 0 11 042376 3 *£1.75*

Public health, England

The Care Standards Act 2000 (Commencement No. 14 (England) and Transitional, Savings and Amendment Provisions) Order 2002 No. 2002/1493 (C.43). – Enabling power: Care Standards Act 2000, ss. 118 (5) to (7), 122. Bringing into operation various provisions of the 2000 Act on 01.04.2002. – Issued: 14.06.2002. Made: 27.03.2002. Effect: S.I. 2001/3852, 4150 amended. Territorial extent & classification: E. General. – 12p.: 30 cm. – 0 11 042340 2 *£2.50*

The Care Standards Act 2000 (Commencement No. 15 (England) and Transitional Provisions) (Amendment) Order 2002 No. 2002/1790 (C.55). – Enabling power: Care Standards Act 2000, ss. 118 (5) to (7), 122. – Issued: 24.07.2002. Made: 31.05.2002. Effect: S.I. 2001/3852, 4150 amended. Territorial extent & classification: E. General. – The dates appointed for the coming into force of certain provisions of the Act are altered. – 8p.: 30 cm. – 0 11 042474 3 *£2.00*

The Care Standards Act 2000 (Establishments and Agencies) (Miscellaneous Amendments) Regulations 2002 No. 2002/865. – Enabling power: Care Standards Act 2000, ss. 12 (2), 22 (1) (2) (a) to (d) (5) (c) (7) (c), 25 (1), 36 (3), 48 (1), 118 (5) to (7) & Children Act 1989, ss. 23 (2) (a) (9), 59 (2), sch. 2, para. 12. – Issued: 09.05.2002. Made: 27.03.2002. Laid: 28.03.2002. Coming into force: 18.04.2002. Effect: S.I. 2001/3965, 3967, 3968, 3969; 2002/57 amended. Territorial extent & classification: E. General. – 8p.: 30 cm. – 0 11 039888 2 *£2.00*

The Control of Noise (Codes of Practice for Construction and Open Sites) (England) Order 2002 No. 2002/461. – Enabling power: Control of Pollution Act 1974, ss. 71, 104 (1). – Issued: 13.03.2002. Made: 04.03.2002. Laid: 04.03.2002. Coming into force: 25.03.2002. Effect: S.I. 1984/1992; 1987/1730 revoked with regard to England. Territorial extent & classification: E. General. – 4p.: 30 cm. – 0 11 039444 5 *£1.75*

The National Care Standards Commission (Director of Private and Voluntary Health Care) Regulations 2002 No. 2002/603. – Enabling power: Care Standards Act 2000, sch. 1, para. 11 (2). – Issued: 24.04.2002. Made: 18.03.2002. Laid: 19.03.2002. Coming into force: 15.04.2002. Effect: None. Territorial extent & classification: E. General. – 4p.: 30 cm. – 0 11 039783 5 *£1.75*

The National Care Standards Commission (Fees and Frequency of Inspections) (Amendment) (No. 2) Regulations 2002 No. 2002/2070. – Enabling power: Care Standards Act 2000, ss. 12 (2), 16 (3), 31 (7), 118 (5) to (7). – Issued: 12.08.2002. Made: 05.08.2002. Laid: 06.08.2002. Coming into force: 01.09.2002. Effect: S.I. 2001/3980 amended. Territorial extent & classification: E. General. – 2p.: 30 cm. – 0 11 042638 X *£1.50*

The National Care Standards Commission (Fees and Frequency of Inspections) Amendment (No. 3) Regulations 2002 No. 2002/3211. – Enabling power: Care Standards Act 2000, ss. 12 (2), 16 (3), 31 (7), 118 (5) to (7). – Issued: 17.01.2003. Made: 21.12.2002. Laid: 23.12.2002. Coming into force: 01.01.2003. Effect: S.I. 2001/3980 amended. Territorial extent & classification: E. General. – 4p.: 30 cm. – 0 11 044600 3 *£1.75*

The National Care Standards Commission (Fees and Frequency of Inspections) (Amendment) Regulations 2002 No. 2002/1505. – Enabling power: Care Standards Act 2000, ss. 12 (2), 16 (3), 31 (7), 118 (5) to (7). – Issued: 28.06.2002. Made: 10.06.2002. Laid: 10.06.2002. Coming into force: 01.07.2002. Effect: S.I. 2001/3980 amended. Territorial extent & classification: E. General. – 2p.: 30 cm. – 0 11 042390 9 *£1.50*

Public health, England and Wales

The Care Standards Act 2000 (Commencement No. 11) Order 2002 No. 2002/629 (C.19). – Enabling power: Care Standards Act 2000, ss. 118 (7), 122. Bringing into operation various provisions of the 2000 Act on 18.03.2002, 01.04.2002, in accord. with art. 2 (2) (3). – Issued: 06.06.2002. Made: 15.03.2002. Effect: None. Territorial extent & classification: E/W. General. – 8p.: 30 cm. – 0 11 042304 6 *£2.00*

The Protection of Children and Vulnerable Adults and Care Standards Tribunal Regulations 2002 No. 2002/816. – Enabling power: Protection of Children Act 1999, s. 9 (2) to (4), sch. para. 2 (4). – Issued: 17.05.2002. Made: 25.03.2002. Laid: 25.03.2002. Coming into force: in accordance with reg. 1 (1). Effect: S.I. 2000/2619 revoked. Territorial extent & classification: E/W. General. – 36p.: 30 cm. – 0 11 039942 0 *£6.50*

Public health, Wales

The Care Standards Act 2000 (Commencement No. 8 (Wales) and Transitional, Savings and Consequential Provisions) Order 2002 No. 2002/920 (W.108) (C.24). – Enabling power: Care Standards Act 2000, ss. 118 (5) to (7), 119, 122. Bringing into operation various provisions of the 2000 Act on 01.04.2002, in accord. with arts. 2, 3. – Issued: 24.06.2002. Made: 28.03.2002. Effect: S.I. 1996/708 amended. Territorial extent & classification: W. General. – 24p.: 30 cm. – 0 11 090509 1 *£4.00*

The Children Act 1989 and the Care Standards Act 2000 (Miscellaneous Regulations) (Amendment) (Wales) Regulations 2002 No. 2002/2622 (W.254). – Enabling power: Care Standards Act 2000, ss. 12 (2) (a), 16 (1) (a), 22 (1), (2) (a) (b), (7) (c), 118 (5) (6) & Children Act 1989, ss. 79C (2) (3) (b) (f) (g), 79E (2) (a), 104 (4). – Issued: 19.11.2002. Made: 17.10.2002. Coming into force: 18.10.2002. Effect: S.I. 2002/324 (W.37), 325 (W.38), 327 (W.40), 812 (W.192), 919 (W.107) amended & S.I. 2002/2171 (W.218) revoked. Territorial extent & classification: W. General. – 16p.: 30 cm. – 0 11 090578 4 *£3.00*

The Control of Noise (Codes of Practice for Construction and Open Sites) (Wales) Order 2002 No. 2002/1795 (W.170). – Enabling power: Control of Pollution Act 1974, ss. 71, 104 (1). – Issued: 29.07.2002. Made: 09.07.2002. Coming into force: 01.08.2002. Effect: S.I. 1984/1992; 1987/1730 revoked in relation to Wales. Territorial extent & classification: W. General. – 4p.: 30 cm. – In English and Welsh. Welsh title: Gorchymyn Rheoli Swn (Codau Ymarfer ar gyfer Safleoedd Adeiladu a Safleoedd Agored) (Cymru) 2001 – 0 11 090526 1 *£1.75*

Private and Voluntary Health Care (Wales) Regulations 2002 No. 2002/325 (W.38). – Enabling power: Care Standards Act 2000, ss. 2 (4) (7) (f) (8), 22 (1) (2) (a) to (d) (f) to (j) (5) (a) (7) (a) to (h) (j) (k), 25 (1), 34 (1), 35, 118 (5) to (7). – Issued: 03.04.2002. Made: 12.02.2002. Coming into force: 01.04.2002. Effect: None. Territorial extent & classification: W. General. – In English & Welsh. Welsh title: Rheoliadau Gofal Iechyd Preifat a Gwirfoddol (Cymru) 2002. – 48p.: 30 cm. – 0 11 090453 2 *£6.50*

The Registration of Social Care and Independent Healthcare (Fees) (Wales) Regulations 2002 No. 2002/921 (W.109). – Enabling power: Care Standards Act 2000, ss. 12 (2), 15 (3), 16 (3), 118 (5) to (7) & Children Act 1989, ss. 79F, 104 (4), sch. 9A, para. 7. – Issued: 20.06.2002. Made: 28.03.2002. Coming into force: 01.04.2002. Effect: None. Territorial extent & classification: W. General. – 8p.: 30 cm. – 0 11 090507 5 *£2.00*

The Registration of Social Care and Independent Health Care (Wales) Regulations 2002 No. 2002/919 (W.107). – Enabling power: Care Standards Act 2000, ss. 12 (2), 14 (1) (d), 15 (3), 16 (1), 25 (1), 118 (5) to (7) & Children Act 1989, ss. 79E (2), 104 (4), sch. 9A, para. 6 (2). – Issued: 21.06.2002. Made: 28.03.2002. Coming into force: 01.04.2002. Effect: None. Territorial extent & classification: W. General. – 24p.: 30 cm. – 0 11 090506 7 *£4.00*

Public passenger transport

The Community Bus (Amendment) Regulations 2002 No. 2002/2537. – Enabling power: Public Passenger Vehicles Act 1981, ss. 52 (1), 60 (1) (e). – Issued: 21.10.2002. Made: 06.10.2002. Laid: 10.10.2002. Coming into force: 01.11.2002. Effect: S.I. 1986/1245 amended. Territorial extent & classification: E/W/S. General. – 2p.: 30 cm. – 0 11 042862 5 *£1.50*

The Minibus and Other Section 19 Permit Buses (Amendment) Regulations 2002 No. 2002/2534. – Enabling power: Public Passenger Vehicles Act 1981, ss. 52 (1), 60 (1) (e) (1A). – Issued: 21.10.2002. Made: 06.10.2002. Laid: 10.10.2002. Coming into force: 01.11.2002. Effect: S.I. 1987/1230 amended. Territorial extent & classification: E/W/S. General. – 2p.: 30 cm. – 0 11 042859 5 *£1.50*

The Public Service Vehicles (Conduct of Drivers, Inspectors, Conductors and Passengers) (Amendment) Regulations 2002 No. 2002/1724. – Enabling power: Public Passenger Vehicles Act 1981, ss. 24 (1), 25 (1), 60 (1) (1A). – Issued: 12.07.2002. Made: 02.07.2002. Laid: 12.07.2002. Coming into force: 01.10.2002. Effect: S.I. 1990/1020 amended. Territorial extent & classification: E/W/S. General. – 8p.: 30 cm. – 0 11 042456 5 *£2.00*

The Public Service Vehicles (Operators' Licences) (Fees) (Amendment) Regulations 2002 No. 2002/2535. – Enabling power: Public Passenger Vehicles Act 1981, ss. 52 (1), 60 (1) (e) (1A). – Issued: 21.10.2002. Made: 06.10.2002. Laid: 10.10.2002. Coming into force: 01.11.2002. Effect: S.I. 1995/2909 amended. Territorial extent & classification: E/W/S. General. – [8]p.: 30 cm. – 0 11 042860 9 *£2.00*

Public passenger transport, England

The Bus Service Operators Grant (England) Regulations 2002 No. 2002/1015. – Enabling power: Transport Act 2000, s. 154 (5). – Issued: 17.04.2002. Made: 09.04.2002. Laid: 10.04.2002. Coming into force: 01.05.2002. Effect: None. Territorial extent & classification: E. General. – 4p.: 30 cm. – 0 11 039749 5 *£1.75*

London Service Permits (Appeals) Regulations 2002 No. 2002/614. – Enabling power: Greater London Authority Act 1999, s. 189 (5). – Issued: 18.03.2002. Made: 10.03.2002. Laid: 11.03.2002. Coming into force: 01.04.2002. Effect: None. Territorial extent & classification: E. General. – 2p.: 30 cm. – 0 11 039460 7 *£1.50*

The Transport Act 2000 (Commencement No. 9 and Transitional Provisions) Order 2002 No. 2002/1014 (C.25). – Enabling power: Transport Act 2000, ss. 275 (1) (2), 276. Bringing into operation various provisions of the 2000 Act on 01.05.2002. – Issued: 17.04.2002. Made: 09.04.2002. Effect: None. Territorial extent & classification: E/W/S [some parts apply only to England]. General. – 8p.: 30 cm. – 0 11 039758 4 *£2.00*

The Travel Concessions (Eligible Services) Order 2002 No. 2002/1016. – Enabling power: Transport Act 1985, s. 94 & Transport Act 2000, s. 146. – Issued: 17.04.2002. Made: 09.04.2002. Laid: 10.04.2002. Coming into force: 01.05.2002. Effect: None. Territorial extent & classification: E. General. – 2p.: 30 cm. – 0 11 039750 9 *£1.50*

Public passenger transport, England and Wales

The Public Service Vehicles (Registration of Local Services) (Amendment) (England and Wales) Regulations 2002 No. 2002/182. – Enabling power: Transport Act 1985, ss. 6 (3) (a) (8) (a) 9 (a). – Issued: 08.02.2002. Made: 31.01.2002. Laid: 01.02.2002. Coming into force: 01.03.2002. Effect: S.I. 1986/1671 amended. Territorial extent & classification: E/W. General. – 2p.: 30 cm. – 0 11 039268 X £1.50

The Public Service Vehicles (Registration of Local Services) (Amendment) (No. 2) (England and Wales) Regulations 2002 No. 2002/2536. – Enabling power: Public Passenger Vehicles Act 1981, ss. 52 (1), 60 (1) (e) (1A). – Issued: 21.10.2002. Made: 06.10.2002. Laid: 10.10.2002. Coming into force: 01.11.2002. Effect: S.I. 1986/1671 amended. Territorial extent & classification: E/W. General. – 2p.: 30 cm. – 0 11 042861 7 £1.50

Public passenger transport, Wales

The Bus Service Operators Grant (Wales) Regulations 2002 No. 2002/2022 (W.206). – Enabling power: Transport Act 2000, s. 154 (5). – Issued: 16.08.2002. Made: 31.07.2002. Coming into force: 14.08.2002. Effect: None. Territorial extent & classification: W. General. – 8p.: 30 cm. – 0 11 090551 2 £2.00

The Quality Partnership Schemes (Existing Facilities) (Wales) Regulations 2002 No. 2002/3017 (W.287). – Enabling power: Transport Act 2000, s. 119. – Issued: 16.12.2002. Made: 04.12.2002. Coming into force: 20.12.2002. Effect: None. Territorial extent & classification: W. General. – 4p.: 30 cm. – In English and Welsh. Welsh title: Rheoliadau Cynlluniau Partneriaethau Ansawdd (Cyfleusterau sy'n Bodoli Eisioes) (Cymru) 2002 – 0 11 090597 0 £1.75

The Travel Concessions (Eligible Services) (Wales) Order 2002 No. 2002/2023 (W.207). – Enabling power: Transport Act 1985, s. 94 (4) & Transport Act 2000, s. 146. – Issued: 19.08.2002. Made: 31.07.2002. Coming into force: 14.08.2002. Effect: None. Territorial extent & classification: W. General. – 8p.: 30 cm. – 0 11 090554 7 £2.00

Race relations

The Race Relations Act 1976 (General Statutory Duty: Code of Practice) Order 2002 No. 2002/1435. – Enabling power: Race Relations Act 1976, s. 71C (8). – Issued: 12.06.2002. Made: 28.05.2002. Laid: 29.05.2002. Coming into force: 30.05.2002. Effect: None. Territorial extent & classification: E/W/S/NI. General. – 2p.: 30 cm. – 0 11 042327 5 £1.50

Race relations, Scotland

The Race Relations Act 1976 (General Statutory Duty: Code of Practice) (Scotland) Order 2002 No. 2002/3111 (S.13). – Enabling power: Race Relations Act 1976, s. 71C (8). – Issued: 17.01.2003. Made: 16.12.2002. Laid: 17.12.2002. Coming into force: 18.12.2002. Effect: None. Territorial extent & classification: S. General. – 2p.: 30 cm. – 0 11 044587 2 £1.50

Rating and valuation, England

The Council Tax and Non-domestic Rating (Demand Notices) (England) (Amendment) Regulations 2002 No. 2002/180. – Enabling power: Local Government Finance Act 1988, s. 143 (1) (2), sch. 9, paras. 1, 2 (2) (ga) (h). – Issued: 07.02.2002. Made: 31.01.2002. Laid: 01.02.2002. Coming into force: 22.02.2002. Effect: S.I. 1993/191; 1995/121; 1997/394; 1998/47 amended & S.I. 2000/534 revoked with saving. Territorial extent & classification: E. General. – 8p.: 30 cm. – 0 11 039265 5 £2.00

The Non-Domestic Rating (Alteration of Lists and Appeals) (Amendment) (England) Regulations 2002 No. 2002/498. – Enabling power: Local Government Finance Act 1988, ss. 55 (2) (4) (6), 143 (1) (2), sch. 7A, paras. 10 to 12. – Issued: 15.04.2002. Made: 06.03.2002. Laid: 08.03.2002. Coming into force: 01.04.2002. Effect: S.I. 1993/291 amended in relation to England. Territorial extent & classification: E. General. – 4p.: 30 cm. – This Statutory Instrument has been made in consequence of defects to S.I. 2002/same number and is being issued free of charge to all known recipients of that statutory instrument – 0 11 039501 8 £1.75

The Non-Domestic Rating Contributions (England) (Amendment) Regulations 2002 No. 2002/3021. – Enabling power: Local Government Finance Act 1988, s. 143 (1) (2), sch. 8, paras. 4, 6. – Issued: 10.12.2002. Made: 05.12.2002. Laid: 10.12.2002. Coming into force: 31.12.2002. Effect: S.I. 1992/3082 amended. Territorial extent & classification: E. General. – 4p.: 30 cm. – 0 11 044165 6 £1.75

Rating and valuation, Wales

The Non-Domestic Rating (Alteration of Lists and Appeals) (Amendment) (Wales) Regulations 2002 No. 2002/1735 (W.165). – Enabling power: Local Government Finance Act 1988, ss. 55 (2) (4) (6), 143 (1) (2), sch. 7A, paras. 10 to 12. – Issued: 05.08.2002. Made: 04.07.2002. Coming into force: 23.07.2002. Effect: S.I. 1993/291 amended. Territorial extent & classification: W. General. – 8p.: 30 cm. – In English & Welsh. Welsh title: Rheoliadau Ardrethu Annomestig (Newid Rhestri ac Apelau) (Diwygio) (Cymru) 2002 – 0 11 090539 3 £2.00

The Non-domestic Rating Contributions (Wales) (Amendment) Regulations 2002 No. 2002/3054 (W.289). – Enabling power: Local Government Finance Act 1988, ss. 140 (4), 143 (1) (2), sch. 8, paras. 4, 5, 6. – Issued: 20.12.2002. Made: 10.12.2002. Coming into force: 31.12.2002. Effect: S.I. 1992/3238 amended. Territorial extent & classification: W. General. – [8]p.: 30 cm. – In English & Welsh. Welsh title: Rheoliadau Cyfraniadau Ardrethu Annomestig (Cymru) (Diwygio) 2002 – 0 11 090600 4 *£2.00*

The Non-domestic Rating (Rural Rate Relief) (Wales) Order 2002 No. 2002/331 (W.44). – Enabling power: Local Government Finance Act 1988, ss. 43 (6B) (b) (c) (ii), 47 (3A) (b). – Issued: 06.03.2002. Made: 13.02.2002. Coming into force: 01.04.2002. Effect: S.I. 1998/2963 amended. Territorial extent & classification: W. General. – 8p.: 30 cm. – In English & Welsh. Welsh title: Gorchymyn Ardrethu Annomestig (Rhyddhad Ardrethi Gwledig) (Cymru) 2002 – 0 11 090436 2 *£2.00*

The Rating Lists (Valuation Date) (Wales) Order 2002 No. 2002/3186 (W.302). – Enabling power: Local Government Finance Act 1988, sch. 6, para. 2 (3) (b). – Issued: 28.01.2003. Made: 18.12.2002. Coming into force: 01.03.2003. Effect: S.I. 1998/93 revoked in relation to Wales. Territorial extent & classification: W. General. – 4p.: 30 cm. – In English and Welsh. Welsh title: Gorchymyn y Rhestrau Ardrethu (Dyddiad Prisio) (Cymru) 2002 – 0 11 090621 7 *£1.75*

Registration of births, deaths, marriages, etc

The Service Departments Registers (Amendment) Order 2002 No. 2002/3122. – Enabling power: Registration of Births, Deaths and Marriages (Special Provisions) Act 1957, ss. 1, 2, 3, 5, 6. – Issued: 23.12.2002. Made: 17.12.2002. Coming into force: 18.12.2002. Effect: S.I. 1959/406 amended. Territorial extent & classification: E/W/S/NI. General. – 2p.: 30 cm. – 0 11 044240 7 *£1.50*

Registration of births, deaths, marriages, etc., England and Wales

The Registration of Births, Deaths and Marriages (Fees) Order 2002 No. 2002/3076. – Enabling power: Public Expenditure and Receipts Act 1968, s. 5 (1) (2), sch. 3, paras 1, 2. – Issued: 10.01.2003. Made: 11.12.2002. Laid: 13.12.2002. Coming into force: 01.04.2003. Effect: S.I. 1999/3311; 2000/3165 revoked. Territorial extent & classification: E/W. General. – 4p.: 30 cm. – 0 11 044460 4 *£1.75*

Registration of political parties

The Registered Parties (Non-constituent and Non-affiliated Organisations) (Amendment) Order 2002 No. 2002/414. – Enabling power: Political Parties, Elections and Referendums Act 2000, s. 26 (8) (c). – Issued: 04.03.2002. Made: 21.02.2002. Laid: 04.03.2002. Coming into force: 01.04.2002. Effect: S.I. 2000/3183 amended. Territorial extent & classification: UK [but relates to Irish organisations specifically]. General. – 2p.: 30 cm. – 0 11 039397 X *£1.50*

Regulatory reform

The Regulatory Reform (Carer's Allowance) Order 2002 No. 2002/1457. – Enabling power: Regulatory Reform Act 2001, s. 1. – Issued: 06.06.2002. Made: 29.05.02. Coming into force: 01.09.2002, 28.10.2002, 01.04.2002 in accord with arts. 1 & 2. Effect: 1992 c. 4 amended. Territorial extent and classification: E/W/S. General. – 4p.: 30 cm. – Supersedes draft S.I. (ISBN 0110399749) published on 22.05.02 – 0 11 042321 6 *£1.75*

The Regulatory Reform (Removal of 20 Member Limit in Partnerships etc.) Order 2002 No. 2002/3203. – Enabling power: Regulatory Reform Act 2001, s. 1. – Issued: 07.01.2003. Made: 20.12.2002. Coming into force: 21.12.2002. Effect: 7 Edw. 7 c. 24; 1985 c. 6; 1992 c. 52 amended. Territorial extent and classification: E/W/S. General. – 4p.: 30 cm. – 0 11 044454 X *£1.75*

The Regulatory Reform (Vaccine Damage Payments Act 1979) Order 2002 No. 2002/1592. – Enabling power: Regulatory Reform Act 2001, ss. 1, 4 (3), 15 (3). – Issued: 24.06.2002. Made: 15.06.2002. Coming into force: 16.06.2002. Effect: 1979 c. 17 amended. Territorial extent and classification: E/W/S. General. – Supersedes draft S.I. (ISBN 0110399528) issued 16 May 2002. – 4p.: 30 cm. – 0 11 042376 3 *£1.75*

Regulatory reform, England

The Regulatory Reform (Voluntary Aided Schools Liabilities and Funding) (England) Order 2002 No. 2002/906. – Enabling power: Regulatory Reform Act 2001, s. 1. – Issued: 05.04.2002. Made: 27.03.2002. Coming into force: 01.04.2002. Effect: 1998 c. 31 amended. Territorial extent and classification: E. General. – 8p.: 30 cm. – Supersedes draft S.I. (ISBN 0110395867) previously published on 25.03.2002 – 0 11 039660 X *£2.00*

Regulatory reform, England and Wales

The Regulatory Reform (Golden Jubilee Licensing) Order 2002 No. 2002/1062. – Enabling power: Regulatory Reform Act 2001, s. 1. – Issued: 18.04.2002. Made: 28.03.2002. Coming into force: 29.03.2002. Effect: S.I. 2001/3937 amended. Territorial extent and classification: E/W. General. – Supersedes draft S.I. (ISBN 0110396715) issued 10 April 2002. – 4p.: 30 cm. – 0 11 039765 7 *£1.75*

The Regulatory Reform (Housing Assistance) (England and Wales) Order 2002 No. 2002/1860. – Enabling power: Regulatory Reform Act 2001, s. 1. – Issued: 25.07.2002. Made: 18.07.2002. Laid: 17.04.2002. Coming into force: In accord. with art. 1 (2) (3). Effect: 1977 c. 42, 50; 1985 c. 68, 70; 1988 c. 9; 1989 c. 42; 1996 c. 53; 1998 c. 38; 2001 c. 16 amended. Territorial extent and classification: E/W. General. – 28p.: 30 cm. – 0 11 042523 5 *£4.50*

The Regulatory Reform (Special Occasions Licensing) Order 2002 No. 2002/3205. – Enabling power: Regulatory Reform Act 2001, s. 1. – Issued: 25.02.2003. Made: 20.12.2002. Coming into force: 21.12.2002. Effect: 1963 c. 33; 1982 c. 30; S.I. 2001/3937 amended. Territorial extent and classification: E/W. General. – 4p.: 30 cm. – 0 11 044392 6 *£1.75*

Rehabilitation of offenders, England and Wales

The Rehabilitation of Offenders Act 1974 (Exceptions) (Amendment) Order 2002 No. 2002/441. – Enabling power: Rehabilitation of Offenders Act 1974, s. 4 (4), 7(4), 10(1). – Issued: 06.03.2002 Made: 28.02.2002. Coming into force: In accord. with art. 1 (2). Effect: S.I. 1975/1023 amended. Territorial extent and classification: E/W. General. – Supersedes draft S.I. (ISBN 0110393023) issued on 12.02.2002. – 4p.: 30 cm. – 0 11 039414 3 *£1.75*

Representation of the people

The Elections (Policy Development Grants Scheme) Order 2002 No. 2002/224. – Enabling power: Political Parties, Elections and Referendums Act 2000, s. 12. – Issued: 13.02.2002. Made: 05.02.2002. Laid: 07.02.2002. Coming into force: 05.03.2002. Effect: None. Territorial extent & classification: E/W/S/NI. General. – 8p.: 30 cm. – 0 11 039292 2 *£2.00*

Representation of the people, England and Wales

The Representation of the People (England and Wales) (Amendment) Regulations 2002 No. 2002/1871. – Enabling power: Representation of the People Act 1983, ss. 53, 201 (1) (3) of Rule 24 of sch. 1, sch. 2, paras. 10 to 13. – Issued: 26.07.2002. Made: 18.07.2002. Coming into force: In accord.with reg. 2. Effect: S.I. 2001/341, 1700 amended & 2001/2720 revoked (16.10.2002.). Territorial extent & classification: E/W. General. – 24p.: 30 cm. – 0 11 042533 2 *£4.00*

Representation of the people, Northern Ireland

The Electoral Fraud (Northern Ireland) Act 2002 (Commencement) Order 2002 No. 2002/1648 (C.46). – Enabling power: Electoral Fraud (Northern Ireland) Act 2002, s. 8 (3). Bringing into force various provisions of the 2002 Act on dates set out in arts. 2 to 4. – Issued: 01.07.2002. Made: 21.06.2002. Effect: None. Territorial extent & classification: NI. General. – 2p.: 30 cm. – 0 11 042400 X *£1.50*

The Representation of the People (Northern Ireland) (Amendment) Regulations 2002 No. 2002/1873. – Enabling power: Political Parties, Elections and Referendums Act 2000, sch. 1. – Issued: 01.08.2002. Made: 24.07.2002. Coming into force: In accord. with reg. 2. Effect: 1983 c. 2; S.I. 2001/400, 1877 amended & S.I. 2001/2725 revoked. Territorial extent & classification: NI. General. – Supersedes draft S.I. (ISBN 0110424247). – 24p.: 30 cm. – 0 11 042563 4 *£4.00*

Representation of the people, Scotland

Representation of the People (Scotland) (Amendment) Regulations 2002 No. 2002/1872 (S.7). – Enabling power: Representation of the People Act 1983, ss. 53, 201 (1) (3), rule 24, sch. 1, sch. 2, paras. 10 to 13. – Issued: 05.08.2002. Made: 18.07.2002. Coming into force: In accord. with reg. 2. Effect: S.I. 2001/497, 1749 amended & S.I. 2001/2817 revoked (18.11.2002). Territorial extent & classification: S. General. – 24p.: 30 cm. – 0 11 061571 9 *£4.00*

Representation of the people, Wales

The National Assembly for Wales (Representation of the People) (Amendment) Order 2002 No. 2002/834. – Enabling power: Government of Wales Act 1998, s. 11. – Issued: 03.04.2002. Made: 25.03.2002. Coming into force: In accordance with art. 1. Effect: S.I. 1999/450 amended. Territorial extent & classification: W. General. – 24p.: 30 cm. – Revoked by S.I. 2003/284 (ISBN 0110456505) – 0 11 039625 1 *£4.00*

The National Assembly for Wales (Returning Officers' Charges) Order 2002 No. 2002/3053 (W.288). – Enabling power: S.I. 1999/450, art. 20 (1) (2). – Issued: 23.12.2002. Made: 10.12.2002. Coming into force: 01.01.2003. Effect: S.I. 1999/42 revoked. Territorial extent & classification: W. General. – 12p.: 30 cm. – In English and Welsh. Welsh title: Gorchymyn Cynulliad Cenedlaethol Cymru (Taliadau Swyddogion Canlyniadau) 2002 – 0 11 090602 0 *£2.50*

Rights of way, England

The Countryside and Rights of Way Act 2000 (Commencement No. 2) Order 2002 No. 2002/2833 (C.89). – Enabling power: Countryside and Rights of Way Act 2000, s. 103 (3) (4). Bringing into operation various provisions of the 2000 Act on 21.11.2002. – Issued: 22.11.2002. Made: 16.11.2002. Effect: None. Territorial extent & classification: E. General. – 4p.: 30 cm. – 0 11 042998 2 *£1.75*

River, England and Wales: Salmon and freshwater fisheries

The Diseases of Fish (Control) (Amendment) (England and Wales) Regulations 2002 No. 2002/284. – Enabling power: European Communities Act 1972, s. 2 (2). – Issued: 22.03.2002. Made: 11.02.2002. Laid: 12.02.2002. Coming into force: 10.03.2002. Effect: S.I. 1994/1447 amended. Territorial extent & classification: E/W. General. – 8p.: 30 cm. – EC note: Implement in relation to England and Wales amendments to "the directive" (Dir. 93/53/EEC) made by directive 2000/27/EC – 0 11 039529 8 *£2.00*

Road traffic

The Driving Licences (Designation of Relevant External Law) Order 2002 No. 2002/2690. – Enabling power: Road Traffic Act 1988, s. 89 (2) (c). – Issued: 21.10.2002. Made: 14.10.2002. Laid:-. Coming into force: 01.11.2002. Effect: None. Territorial extent & classification: E/W/S. General. – 2p.: 30 cm. – 0 11 042877 3 *£1.50*

The Driving Licences (Exchangeable Licences) (Amendment) Order 2002 No. 2002/1593. – Enabling power: Road Traffic Act 1988, s. 108 (2). – Issued: 25.06.2002. Made: 17.06.2002. Coming into force: 21.06.2002. Effect: 1988 c.52 & S.I. 1984/672 amended. Territorial extent & classification: E/W/S. General. – 2p.: 30 cm. – 0 11 042383 6 *£1.50*

The Driving Licences (Exchangeable Licences) Order 2002 No. 2002/2379. – Enabling power: Road Traffic Act 1988, s. 108 (2) (b) (2A) (2B). – Issued: 24.09.2002. Made: 14.09.2002. Coming into force: 20.09.2002. Effect: None. Territorial extent & classification: E/W/S. General. – 4p.: 30 cm. – 0 11 042791 2 *£1.75*

The European Communities (Rights against Insurers) Regulations 2002 No. 2002/3061. – Enabling power: European Communities Act 1972, s. 2 (2). – Issued: 24.12.2002. Made: 10.12.2002. Laid: 12.12.2002. Coming into force: 19.01.2003. Effect: None. Territorial extent & classification: E/W/S/NI. General. – 4p.: 30 cm. – EC note: These Regs. give effect in part to DIR 2000/26/EC which amends DIR 73/239/EEC and 88/357/EEC (Fourth Motor Insurance Directive). The Fourth Motor Insurance Directive supplements the arrangements established by DIRs 72/166/EEC, 84/5/EEC, and 90/232/EEC – 0 11 044242 3 *£1.75*

The Goods Vehicles (Community Authorisations) (Modification of the Road Traffic (Foreign Vehicles) Act 1972) Regulations 2002 No. 2002/1415. – Enabling power: European Communities Act 1972, s. 2 (2). – Issued: 07.06.2002. Made: 24.05.2002. Laid: 27.05.2002. Coming into force: 01.07.2002. Effect: 1972 c.27 amended. Territorial extent & classification: E/W/S/NI. General. – 2p.: 30 cm. – EC note: Provides powers for the implementation of S.I. 1992/3077 which gave effect in the UK to EC REG 881/92 – 0 11 042320 8 *£1.50*

The Goods Vehicles (Licensing of Operators) (Fees) (Amendment) Regulations 2002 No. 2002/2778. – Enabling power: Goods Vehicles (Licensing of Operators) Act 1995, ss. 45 (1), 57 (1), 58 (1). – Issued: 18.11.2002. Made: 08.11.2002 Laid: 08.11.2002. Coming into force: 01.12.2002. Effect: S.I. 1995/3000 amended. Territorial extent & classification: E/W/S. General. – 2p.: 30 cm. – 0 11 042964 8 *£1.50*

The Motor Cars (Driving Instruction) (Amendment) Regulations 2002 No. 2002/2640. – Enabling power: Road Traffic Act 1988, ss. 125 (3) (a), 132. – Issued: 29.10.2002. Made: 20.10.2002. Laid: 23.10.2002. Coming into force: 14.11.2002. Effect: S.I. 1989/2057 amended. Territorial extent & classification:E/W/S. General. – 4p.: 30 cm. – 0 11 042906 0 *£1.75*

The Motor Vehicles (Driving Licences) (Amendment) Regulations 2002 No. 2002/2641. – Enabling power: Road Traffic Act 1988, ss. 89 (3) (4) (5), 105 (1) (3). – Issued: 29.10.2002. Made: 21.10.2002. Laid: 23.10.2002. Coming into force: 14.11.2002. Effect: S.I. 1999/2864 amended. Territorial extent classification: E/W/S. General. – 4p.: 30 cm. – 0 11 042907 9 *£1.75*

The Motor Vehicles (EC Type Approval) (Amendment) (No. 2) Regulations 2002 No. 2002/2743. – Enabling power: European Communities Act 1972, s. 2 (2). – Issued: 12.11.2002. Made: 03.11.2002. Laid: 06.11.2002. Coming into force: 27.11.2002. Effect: S.I. 1998/2051 amended. Territorial extent & classification: E/W/S/NI. General. – 2p.: 30 cm. – EC note: Regulation 2 inserts a reference to EC DIR 2002/78/EC in Sch. 1 of the 1998 regulations, thereby implementing that Directive for the purposes of EC type approval procedures – 0 11 042946 X *£1.50*

The Motor Vehicles (EC Type Approval) (Amendment) Regulations 2002 No. 2002/1835. – Enabling power: European Communities Act 1972, s. 2 (2). – Issued: 23.07.2002. Made: 12.07.2002. Laid: 17.07.2002. Coming into force: 07.08.2002. Effect: S.I. 1998/2051 amended. Territorial extent & classification: E/W/S/NI. General. – 4p.: 30 cm. – EC note: In the 1998 Regulations (S.I. 1998/2051) amends the definition of the framework to include Directive 2001/116/EC which consolidates certain amendments to the framework directive Council directive 70/156/EEC and in particular provides new annexes for use by manufacturers and approval authorities in applying for and granting type approvals. Inserts references in the table in schedule 1 to recent EC directives, so implementing them for purposes of EC type approval procedures – 0 11 042508 1 *£1.75*

The Public Service Vehicles (Conditions of Fitness, Equipment, Use and Certification) (Amendment) Regulations 2002 No. 2002/335. – Enabling power: Public Passenger Vehicles Act 1981, ss. 6, 10, 60 & Road Traffic Act 1988, s. 41 (1) (5). – Issued: 27.02.2002. Made: 15.02.2002. Laid: 20.02.2002. Coming into force: 18.03.2002. Effect: S.I. 1981/257 amended. Territorial extent & classification: E/W/S/NI. General. – 12p.: 30 cm. – 0 11 039371 6 *£2.50*

The Road Vehicles (Construction and Use) (Amendment) (No. 2) Regulations 2002 No. 2002/1474. – Enabling power: Road Traffic Act 1988, s. 41 (1) (2) (5). – Issued: 21.06.2002. Made: 31.05.2002. Laid: 31.05.2002. Coming into force: for regs. 2, 3, 5: 01.07.2002; for reg. 4: 01.08.2002, in accord. with art. 1. Effect: S.I. 1986/1078 amended. Territorial extent & classification: E/W/S/NI. General. – 4p.: 30 cm. – EC note: These Regs. further amend the 1986 Regs.adding a reference to DIR 2001/27/EC in relation to smoke, gas and other similar emissions – 0 11 042374 7 *£1.75*

The Road Vehicles (Construction and Use) (Amendment) (No. 3) Regulations 2002 No. 2002/2126. – Enabling power: Road Traffic Act 1988, s. 41 (1) (2) (5). – Issued: 21.08.2002. Made: 13.08.2002. Laid: 14.08.2002. Coming into force: 04.09.2002. Effect: S.I. 1986/1078 amended. Territorial extent & classification: E/W/S. General. – 4p.: 30 cm. – EC note: These Regs. further amend the 1986 Regs. in line with Directive 95/54/EC – 0 11 042667 3 *£1.75*

The Road Vehicles (Construction and Use) (Amendment) Regulations 2002 No. 2002/227. – Enabling power: Road Traffic Act 1988, s. 41 (1) (2) (5). – Issued: 18.02.2002. Made: 01.02.2002. Laid: 08.02.2002. Coming into force: 01.03.2002. Effect: S.I. 1986/1078 amended. Territorial extent & classification: E/W/S. General. – 2p.: 30 cm. – EC note: Further amend the 1986 regs (S.I. 1986/1078) in relation to in-service exhaust emissions tests as a result of the requirement to implement Commission directive 2001/9/EC which amended Council directive 96/96/EC – 0 11 039311 2 *£1.50*

The Road Vehicles (Display of Registration Marks) (Amendment) Regulations 2002 No. 2002/2687. – Enabling power: Vehicle Excise and Registration Act 1994, ss. 23 (3) (4), 57– Issued: 04.11.2002. Made: 24.10.2002. Laid: 01.11.2002. Coming into force: 22.11.2002. Effect: S.I. 2001/561 amended. Territorial extent & classification: E/W/S/NI. General. – 4p.: 30 cm. – 0 11 042925 7 *£1.75*

The Road Vehicles (Registration and Licensing) (Amendment) Regulations 2002 No. 2002/2382. – Enabling power: Vehicle Excise and Registration Act 1994, ss. 22 (1) (a) (f) (h), 22A, 57 (1) (2) (3) (5). – Issued: 26.09.2002. Made: 18.09.2002. Laid: 18.09.2002. Coming into force: 09.10.2002, 07.04.2003, in accord. with reg. 1 (2). Effect: S.I. 1971/450 amended. Territorial extent & classification: E/W/S. General. – 4p.: 30 cm. – Revoked by S.I. 2002/2742 (ISBN 011042963X) – 0 11 042807 2 *£1.75*

The Road Vehicles (Registration and Licensing) Regulations 2002 No. 2002/2742. – Enabling power: Vehicle Excise and Registration Act 1994, ss. 7 (6), 10 (1), 11 (1) (1A), 12 (2) (3) (4), 14 (3) (b) (4), 21 (3), 22 (1) (1A) (1B) (1C) (1D) (1E) (1G) (2) (2A) (2B) (2C) (4), 22A, 23 (5), 25, 33 (1) (b) (1A) (c) (3) (a) (4) (5), 52 (1), 57 (1) (2) (3), 59 (2) (a), 61A, 61B, 62 (1), sch. 1, paras 1 (2B), 3 (5), 5 (3) (e) (4) (c), sch. 2, paras 2A, 24. – Issued: 18.11.2002. Made: 04.11.2002. Laid: 08.11.2002. Coming into force: 30.11.2002 except regs 15 (3), 20 (4) (5) which come into force on 07.04.2003. Effect: S.I. 1970/1997 amended & S.I. 1971/450; 1972/1865; 1973/870; 1975/1342; 1976/1680, 2088, 2089, 2180; 1977/230, 231; 1978/1536, 1541; 1981/366, 367, 931; 1982/1802; 1983/1248; 1986/607, 706, 1177, 1178, 1467, 2100, 2101, 2102; 1987/2085, 2086, 2122, 2123, 2124; 1988/847, 1130; 1989/1376, 1377; 1990/2185, 2186; 1993/1759, 1760; 1994/1364, 1911, 2735, 3296, 3297; 1995/1470, 1471; 1996/2800; 1997/401, 3025; 1998/572, 995, 3094; 1999/713; 2000/1369, 3274; 2002/2381, 2382; S.R. & O. (N.I.) 1973/352, 490 revoked. Territorial extent & classification: E/W/S/NI. General. – 40p.: 30 cm. – 0 11 042963 X *£6.50*

Road Vehicles (Testing) (Disclosure of Information) (Great Britain) Regulations 2002 No. 2002/2426. – Enabling power: European Communities Act 1972, s. 2 (2). – Issued: 30.09.2002. Made: 23.09.2002. Laid: 24.09.2002. Coming into force: 15.10.2002. Effect: None. Territorial extent & classification: E/W/S. General. – EC note: These regulations complete the transposition in Great Britain of Directive 2000/30. – 2p.: 30 cm. – 0 11 042819 6 *£1.50*

The Traffic Signs Regulations and General Directions 2002 No. 2002/3113. – Enabling power: Road Traffic Regulation Act 1984, ss. 64, 65, 85 (2) & Road Traffic Act 1988 s. 36 (5). – Issued: 10.01.2003. Made: 16.12.2002. Laid: 10.01.2003. Coming into force: 31.01.2003. Effect: S.I. 1994/1519; 1995/2769, 3107; 1999/1723 revoked. Territorial extent & classification: E/W/S. General. – 447p., col. ill.: 30 cm. – 0 11 042942 7 *£40.00*

The Transport Act 2000 (Commencement No. 9 and Transitional Provisions) Order 2002 No. 2002/1014 (C.25). – Enabling power: Transport Act 2000, ss. 275 (1) (2), 276. Bringing into operation various provisions of the 2000 Act on 01.05.2002. – Issued: 17.04.2002. Made: 09.04.2002. Effect: None. Territorial extent & classification: E/W/S [some parts apply only to England]. General. – 8p.: 30 cm. – 0 11 039758 4 *£2.00*

The Vehicle Excise Duty (Designation of Small Islands) (Amendment) Order 2002 No. 2002/1072. – Enabling power: Vehicle Excise and Registration Act 1994, sch. 1, para. 18 (4). – Issued: 24.04.2002. Made: 14.04.2002. Laid: 17.04.2002. Coming into force: 01.06.2002. Effect: S.I. 1995/1397 amended. Territorial extent & classification: E/W/S/NI. General. – 2p.: 30 cm. – 0 11 039786 X *£1.50*

The Vehicle Excise Duty (Immobilisation, Removal and Disposal of Vehicles) (Amendment) Regulations 2002 No. 2002/745. – Enabling power: Vehicle Excise and Registration Act 1994, s. 57 (1) (2) (a), sch. 2A, para. 3 (3) (4). – Issued: 02.04.2002. Made: 18.03.2002. Laid: 19.03.2002. Coming into force: 09.04.2002. Effect: S.I. 1997/2439 amended. Territorial extent & classification: E/W/S/NI. General. – 4p.: 30 cm. – 0 11 039599 9 £1.75

The Vehicles (Crime) Act 2001 (Commencement No. 4) Order 2002 No. 2002/2377 (C.78). – Enabling power: Vehicles (Crime) Act 2001, s. 44. Bringing into operation various provisions of the 2001 Act on 17.09.2002. – Issued: 24.09.2002. Made: 16.09.2002. Effect: None. Territorial extent & classification: E/W/S/NI. General. – 2p.: 30 cm. – 0 11 042792 0 £1.50

Road traffic: Speed limits

The A1 Trunk Road (Biggleswade North to Beeston, Bedfordshire) (60 Miles Per Hour Speed Limit) Order 2002 No. 2002/1532. – Enabling power: Road Traffic Regulation Act 1984, s. 84 (1) (a) (2), sch. 9, para. 27 (1). – Made: 31.05.2002. Coming into force: 17.06.2002. Effect: S.I. 1994/2938 varied. Territorial extent & classification: E. Local *Unpublished*

The A1 Trunk Road (North Brunton Interchange) (40 Miles Per Hour Speed Limit) Order 2002 No. 2002/2178. – Enabling power: Road Traffic Regulation Act 1984, s. 84 (1) (a) (2), sch. 9, para. 27 (1). – Made: 13.08.2002. Coming into force: 16.08.2002. Effect: None. Territorial extent & classification: E. Local *Unpublished*

The A1 Trunk Road (Rainton Crossroads) (Derestriction) Order 2002 No. 2002/1431. – Enabling power: Road Traffic Regulation Act 1984, ss. 82 (2), 83 (1). – Made: 23.05.2002. Coming into force: 31.05.2002. Effect: None. Territorial extent & classification: E. Local *Unpublished*

The A5 Trunk Road (Caddington Turn, Dunstable, Bedfordshire) (50 Miles Per Hour Speed Limit) Order 2002 No. 2002/2649. – Enabling power: Road Traffic Regulation Act 1984, s. 84 (1) (a) (2), sch. 9, para. 27 (1). – Made: 18.10.2002. Coming into force: 01.11.2002. Effect: S.I. 1984/2053 varied & S.I. 1992/1994 revoked. Territorial extent & classification: E. Local *Unpublished*

The A6 Trunk Road (Clapham Bypass and Bedford Road, Milton Ernest, Bedfordshire) (50 Miles Per Hour Speed Limit) Order 2002 No. 2002/2964. – Enabling power: Road Traffic Regulation Act 1984, s. 84 (1) (a) (2), sch. 9, para. 27 (1). – Made: 28.11.2002. Coming into force: 12.12.2002. Effect: S.I. 1984/2054; 1991/1275 varied. Territorial extent & classification: E. Local *Unpublished*

The A6 Trunk Road (Clapham Bypass, Bedfordshire) (Derestriction) Order 2002 No. 2002/2959. – Enabling power: Road Traffic Regulation Act 1984, ss. 82 (2), 83 (1). – Made: 28.11.2002. Coming into force: 12.12.2002. Effect: None. Territorial extent & classification: E. Local *Unpublished*

The A6 Trunk Road (Clapham Bypass, C46 Highfield Road Northbound Slip Road, Bedfordshire) (30 Miles Per Hour Speed Limit) Order 2002 No. 2002/2962. – Enabling power: Road Traffic Regulation Act 1984, s. 84 (1) (a) (2). – Made: 28.11.2002. Coming into force: 12.12.2002. Effect: None. Territorial extent & classification: E. Local *Unpublished*

The A6 Trunk Road (Hathern, Leicestershire) (40 Miles Per Hour Speed Limit) Order 2002 No. 2002/1196. – Enabling power: Road Traffic Regulation Act 1984, s. 84 (1) (a) (2), sch. 9, para. 27 (1). – Made: 08.04.2002. Coming into force: 22.04.2002. Effect: None. Territorial extent & classification: E. Local *Unpublished*

The A6 Trunk Road (Milton Road, Clapham, Bedfordshire) (40 Miles Per Hour Speed Limit) Order 2002 No. 2002/2963. – Enabling power: Road Traffic Regulation Act 1984, s. 84 (1) (a) (2), sch. 9, para. 27 (1). – Made: 28.11.2002. Coming into force: 12.12.2002. Effect: S.I. 1984/2054 varied. Territorial extent & classification: E. Local *Unpublished*

The A7 Trunk Road (Longtown) (30 Miles Per Hour Speed Limit) Order 2002 No. 2002/3034. – Enabling power: Road Traffic Regulation Act 1984, s. 84 (1) (a) (2). – Made: 05.12.2002. Coming into force: 12.12.2002. Effect: None. Territorial extent & classification: E. Local *Unpublished*

The A12 Trunk Road (Hatfield Peverel, Essex) (Derestriction) Order 2002 No. 2002/1104. – Enabling power: Road Traffic Regulation Act 1984, ss. 82 (2), 83 (1). – Made: 12.04.2002. Coming into force: 26.04.2002. Effect: None. Territorial extent & classification: E. Local *Unpublished*

The A16 Trunk Road (Burwell, Lincolnshire) (Derestriction) Order 2002 No. 2002/1530. – Enabling power: Road Traffic Regulation Act 1984, ss. 82 (2), 83 (1). – Made: 24.05.2002. Coming into force: 07.06.2002. Effect: None. Territorial extent & classification: E. Local *Unpublished*

The A17 Trunk Road (East Heckington to Swineshead, Lincolnshire) (40 Miles Per Hour and 50 Miles Per Hour Speed Limit) Order 2002 No. 2002/760. – Enabling power: Road Traffic Regulation Act 1984, s. 84 (1) (a) (2), sch. 9, para. 27 (1). – Made: 11.03.2002. Coming into force: 25.03.2002. Effect: None. Territorial extent & classification: E. Local *Unpublished*

The A17 Trunk Road (Saracens Head, Lincolnshire) (Derestriction) Order 2002 No. 2002/1548. – Enabling power: Road Traffic Regulation Act 1984, ss. 82 (2), 83 (1). – Made: 24.05.2002. Coming into force: 07.06.2002. Effect: None. Territorial extent & classification: E. Local *Unpublished*

The A19 Trunk Road (Sheraton Interchange to Crathorne Interchange) (Temporary 50 Miles Per Hour Speed Restriction) Order 2002 No. 2002/2394. – Enabling power: Road Traffic Regulation Act 1984, ss. 82 (2), 83 (1). – Made: 13.09.2002. Coming into force: 16.09.2002. Effect: None. Territorial extent & classification: E. Local *Unpublished*

The A19 Trunk Road (Sheraton Interchange to Dalton Piercy Junction) (Derestriction) Order 2002 No. 2002/2027. – Enabling power: Road Traffic Regulation Act 1984, ss. 82 (2), 83 (1). – Made: 09.07.2002. Coming into force: 12.07.2002. Effect: None. Territorial extent & classification: E. Local *Unpublished*

The A19 Trunk Road (Shipton Road, York) (Derestriction) Order 2002 No. 2002/1317. – Enabling power: Road Traffic Regulation Act 1984, ss. 82 (2), 83 (1), sch. 9, para. 27 (1). – Made: 08.05.2002. Coming into force: 13.05.2002. Effect: S.I. 1988/380 varied. Territorial extent & classification: E. Local *Unpublished*

The A36 Trunk Road (Churchill Way and Southampton Road, Salisbury) (40 MPH Speed Limit) Consolidation Order 2002 No. 2002/1319. – Enabling power: Road Traffic Regulation Act 1984, s. 84 (1) (a) (2), sch. 9, para. 27 (1). – Made: 07.05.2002. Coming into force: 16.05.2002. Effect: S.I. 1974/871 revoked. Territorial extent & classification: E. Local *Unpublished*

The A36 Trunk Road (Knook) (40 mph and 50 mph Speed Limit) (Amendment) Order 2002 No. 2002/1305. – Enabling power: Road Traffic Regulation Act 1984, s. 84 (1) (a) (2), sch. 9, para. 27 (1). – Made: 25.03.2002. Coming into force: 30.03.2002. Effect: S.I. 1996/902 varied. Territorial extent & classification: E. Local *Unpublished*

The A36 Trunk Road (Knook) (40 mph and 50 mph Speed Limit) Order 2002 No. 2002/884. – Enabling power: Road Traffic Regulation Act 1984, s. 84 (1) (2), sch. 9, para. 27 (1). – Made: 25.03.2002. Coming into force: 02.04.2002. Effect: S.I. 1996/902 varied. Territorial extent & classification: E. Local *Unpublished*

The A36 Trunk Road (Warminster Road, Bath) (40 mph Speed Limit) Order 2002 No. 2002/2967. – Enabling power: Road Traffic Regulation Act 1984, ss. 82 (2), 83 (1), 84 (1) (2), sch. 9, para. 27 (1). – Made: 06.11.2002. Coming into force: 14.11.2002. Effect: S.I. 1990/1006 revoked & any Order made under the Road Traffic Regulation Act 1984, or any enactment replaced by that Act, which imposes a speed limit on a length of the A36 Trunk Road, Warminster Road, Bath, from a point approx. 140 metres east of the junction of Bathampton Lane to a point 238 metres east of the junction of Down Lane, is revoked. Territorial extent & classification: E. Local *Unpublished*

The A36 Trunk Road (West Wellow) (40 mph Speed Limit) Order 2002 No. 2002/361. – Enabling power: Road Traffic Regulation Act 1984, s. 84 (1) (a) (2), sch. 9, para. 27 (1). – Made: 11.02.2002. Coming into force: 20.02.2002. Effect: S.I. 1996/1652 varied. Territorial extent & classification: E. Local *Unpublished*

The A40 Trunk Road (Churcham, Gloucestershire) (50 Miles Per Hour Speed Limit) Order 2002 No. 2002/1653. – Enabling power: Road Traffic Regulation Act 1984, s. 84 (1) (a) (2), sch. 9, para. 27 (1). – Made: 27.05.2002. Coming into force: 10.06.2002. Effect: None. Territorial extent & classification: E. Local *Unpublished*

The A43 Trunk Road (Towcester to M40 Dualling, Northamptonshire) (Derestriction) Order 2002 No. 2002/2606. – Enabling power: Road Traffic Regulation Act 1984, ss. 82 (2), 83 (1). – Made: 11.10.2002. Coming into force: 25.10.2002. Effect: None. Territorial extent & classification: E. Local *Unpublished*

The A45 Trunk Road (Daventry Road, Onley) (Derestriction) Order 2002 No. 2002/2045. – Enabling power: Road Traffic Regulation Act 1984, ss. 82 (2), 83 (1). – Made: 03.07.2002. Coming into force: 17.07.2002. Effect: None. Territorial extent & classification: E. Local *Unpublished*

The A46 Trunk Road (Upper Swainswick to Pennsylvania) (40 and 50MPH Speed Limits) Order 2002 No. 2002/1907. – Enabling power: Road Traffic Regulation Act 1984, s. 84 (1) (a) (2). – Made: 28.06.2002. Coming into force: 09.07.2002. Effect: S.I. 1995/1254 revoked. Territorial extent & classification: E. Local *Unpublished*

The A46 Trunk Road (Winthorpe, Newark, Nottinghamshire) (Derestriction) Order 2002 No. 2002/1195. – Enabling power: Road Traffic Regulation Act 1984, ss. 82 (2), 83 (1). – Made: 08.04.2002. Coming into force: 22.04.2002. Effect: None. Territorial extent & classification: E. Local *Unpublished*

The A49 Trunk Road (Beeston and Tiverton) (40 Miles Per Hour Speed Limit) Order 2002 No. 2002/1138. – Enabling power: Road Traffic Regulation Act 1984, s. 84 (1) (a) (2). – Made: 28.03.2002. Coming into force: 14.04.2002. Effect: None. Territorial extent & classification: E. Local *Unpublished*

The A49 Trunk Road (Prees Green) (50 Miles Per Hour Speed Limit) Order 2002 No. 2002/611. – Enabling power: Road Traffic Regulation Act 1984, s. 84 (1) (a) (2). – Made: 06.03.2002. Coming into force: 12.03.2002. Effect: None. Territorial extent & classification: E. Local *Unpublished*

The A50 Trunk Road (Uttoxeter, Staffordshire) (40 Miles Per Hour Speed Limit) Order 2002 No. 2002/1580. – Enabling power: Road Traffic Regulation Act 1984, s. 84 (1) (a) (2), sch. 9, para. 27 (1). – Made: 10.06.2002. Coming into force: 24.06.2002. Effect: S.I. 1986/671; 1998/2056 varied. Territorial extent & classification: E. Local *Unpublished*

The A52 Trunk Road (Grantham Road, Radcliffe on Trent, Nottinghamshire) (40 Miles Per Hour Speed Limit) Order 2002 No. 2002/347. – Enabling power: Road Traffic Regulation Act 1984, s. 84 (1) (a) (2), sch. 9, para. 27 (1). – Made: 11.01.2002. Coming into force: 25.01.2002. Effect: The Nottinghamshire County Council (40 M.P.H. Speed Limit) (No. 1) Order 1967 revoked. Territorial extent & classification: E. Local *Unpublished*

The A63 Trunk Road (Selby) (Restriction) Order 2002 No. 2002/2576. – Enabling power: Road Traffic Regulation Act 1984, ss. 82 (2), 83 (1), 84 (1) (a) (2), sch. 9, para 27 (1). – Made: 09.10.2002. Coming into force: 14.10.2002. Effect: None. Territorial extent & classification: E. Local *Unpublished*

The A63 Trunk Road (Thorpe Park Link Roads) (40 Miles Per Hour Speed Limit) Order 2002 No. 2002/1988. – Enabling power: Road Traffic Regulation Act 1984, ss. 84 (1) (a) (2), 122A. – Made: 09.07.2002. Coming into force: 12.07.2002. Effect: None. Territorial extent & classification: E. Local *Unpublished*

The A64 Trunk Road (Rillington) (Restriction) Order 2002 No. 2002/1126. – Enabling power: Road Traffic Regulation Act 1984, ss. 82 (2), 83 (1), 84 (1) (a) (2), sch. 9, para. 27 (1). – Made: 16.04.2002. Coming into force: 19.04.2002. Effect: S.I. 1964/1319; 1996/2741 varied. Territorial extent & classification: E. Local *Unpublished*

The A339 Trunk Road (Newtown Road and Sandleford Link) (50 Miles Per Hour Speed Limit) Order 2002 No. 2002/1642. – Enabling power: Road Traffic Regulation Act 1984, s. 84 (1) (a) (2). – Made: 17.06.2002. Coming into force: 01.07.2002. Effect: None. Territorial extent & classification: E. Local *Unpublished*

The A435 Trunk Road (Gorcott Hill to Studley, Warwickshire) (Restriction and 40 Miles per Hour Speed Limit) Order 2002 No. 2002/2906. – Enabling power: Road Traffic Regulation Act 1984, ss. 82 (2), 83 (1), 84 (1) (a) (2). – Made: 18.11.2002. Coming into force: 02.12.2002. Effect: None. Territorial extent & classification: E. Local *Unpublished*

The A523 Trunk Road (Bosley, Cheshire) (40 Miles Per Hour Speed Limit) Order 2002 No. 2002/1202. – Enabling power: Road Traffic Regulation Act 1984, s. 84 (1) (a) (2). – Made: 05.04.2002. Coming into force: 19.04.2002. Effect: None. Territorial extent & classification: E. Local *Unpublished*

The A523 Trunk Road (Fools Nook to Macclesfield (South), Cheshire) (40 Miles Per Hour and 50 Miles Per Hour Speed Limit) Order 2002 No. 2002/1197. – Enabling power: Road Traffic Regulation Act 1984, s. 84 (1) (a) (2), sch. 9, para. 27 (1). – Made: 05.04.2002. Coming into force: 19.04.2002. Effect: S.I. 1971/1887; 1994/2883 revoked. Territorial extent & classification: E. Local *Unpublished*

The A523 Trunk Road (Leek, Staffordshire) (40 Miles Per Hour Speed Limit) Order 2002 No. 2002/1203. – Enabling power: Road Traffic Regulation Act 1984, s. 84 (1) (a) (2). – Made: 05.04.2002. Coming into force: 19.04.2002. Effect: None. Territorial extent & classification: E. Local *Unpublished*

The A523 Trunk Road (Macclesfield Relief Road) (Derestriction) Order 1993 Variation Order 2002 No. 2002/1083. – Enabling power: Road Traffic Regulation Act 1984, ss. 82 (2), 83 (1), sch. 9, para. 27 (1). – Made: 05.04.2002. Coming into force: 19.04.2002. Effect: S.I. 1993/2502 varied. Territorial extent & classification: E. Local *Unpublished*

The A523 Trunk Road (Poynton (South), Cheshire) (40 Miles Per Hour Speed Limit) Order 2002 No. 2002/1082. – Enabling power: Road Traffic Regulation Act 1984, s. 84 (1) (a) (2), sch. 9, para. 27 (1). – Made: 05.04.2002. Coming into force: 19.04.2002. Effect: S.I. 1981/1724 revoked. Territorial extent & classification: E. Local *Unpublished*

The A523 Trunk Road (Poynton to Hazel Grove, Cheshire and Stockport) (40 Miles Per Hour Speed Limit) Order 2002 No. 2002/1085. – Enabling power: Road Traffic Regulation Act 1984, s. 84 (1) (a) (2), sch. 9, para. 27 (1). – Made: 05.04.2002. Coming into force: 19.04.2002. Effect: S.I. 1980/902 revoked. Territorial extent & classification: E. Local *Unpublished*

The A523 Trunk Road (Prestbury, Cheshire) (40 Miles Per Hour Speed Limit) Order 2002 No. 2002/1603. – Enabling power: Road Traffic Regulation Act 1984, s. 84 (1) (a) (2), sch. 9, para. 27 (1). – Made: 06.06.2002. Coming into force: 20.06.2002. Effect: S.I. 1993/2502 varied. Territorial extent & classification: E. Local *Unpublished*

The A523 Trunk Road (Prestbury to Poynton, Cheshire) (50 Miles Per Hour Speed Limit) Order 2002 No. 2002/1605. – Enabling power: Road Traffic Regulation Act 1984, s. 84 (1) (a) (2), sch. 9, para. 27 (1). – Made: 06.06.2002. Coming into force: 20.06.2002. Effect: None. Territorial extent & classification: E. Local *Unpublished*

The A523 Trunk Road (Rushton Spencer, Staffordshire) (40 Miles Per Hour Speed Limit) Order 2002 No. 2002/1198. – Enabling power: Road Traffic Regulation Act 1984, s. 84 (1) (a) (2), sch. 9, para. 27 (1). – Made: 05.04.2002. Coming into force: 19.04.2002. Effect: S.I. 1989/263 revoked. Territorial extent & classification: E. Local *Unpublished*

The A565 Trunk Road (Southport New Road, Mere Brow) (50 Miles Per Hour Speed Limit) Order 2002 No. 2002/404. – Enabling power: Road Traffic Regulation Act 1984, s. 84 (1) (a) (2). – Made: 21.02.2002. Coming into force: 25.02.2002. Effect: None. Territorial extent & classification: E. Local *Unpublished*

The A570 Trunk Road (Ormskirk Road, Bickerstaff) (40 Miles Per Hour Speed Limit) Order 2002 No. 2002/2204. – Enabling power: Road Traffic Regulation Act 1984, s. 84 (1) (a) (2), sch. 9, para. 27 (1). – Made: 21.08.2002. Coming into force: 26.08.2002. Effect: None. Territorial extent & classification: E. Local *Unpublished*

The A585 Trunk Road (Kirkham to Fleetwood) (50 Miles Per Hour Speed Limit) Order 2002 No. 2002/3064. – Enabling power: Road Traffic Regulation Act 1984, s. 84 (1) (a) (2), sch. 9, para. 27 (1). – Made: 10.12.2002. Coming into force: 16.12.2002. Effect: S.I. 1989/1510 amended. Territorial extent & classification: E. Local *Unpublished*

The A595 and A596 Trunk Roads (Lillyhall, Workington) (50 Miles Per Hour Speed Limit) Order 2002 No. 2002/1770. – Enabling power: Road Traffic Regulation Act 1984, s. 84 (1) (a) (2), sch. 9, para. 27 (1). – Made: 10.07.2002. Coming into force: 19.07.2002. Effect: None. Territorial extent & classification: E. Local *Unpublished*

The A614 Trunk Road (Howden) (Restriction) Order 2002 No. 2002/1246. – Enabling power: Road Traffic Regulation Act 1984, ss. 82 (2), 83 (1), 84(1) (a) (2), sch. 9, para. 27 (1). – Made: 01.05.2002. Coming into force: 03.05.2002. Effect: None. Territorial extent & classification: E. Local *Unpublished*

The A646 Trunk Road (Burnley Road, Hebden Bridge to Clog Works) (40 Miles Per Hour Speed Limit) Order 2002 No. 2002/2332. – Enabling power: Road Traffic Regulation Act 1984, s. 84 (1) (a) (2). – Made: 04.09.2002. Coming into force: 09.09.2002. Effect: None. Territorial extent & classification: E. Local *Unpublished*

The A696 Trunk Road (Otterburn) (Restriction) Order 2002 No. 2002/978. – Enabling power: Road Traffic Regulation Act 1984, ss. 82 (2), 83 (1), 84 (1) (a) (2). – Made: 03.04.2002. Coming into force: 08.04.2002. Effect: None. Territorial extent & classification: E. Local *Unpublished*

The A6120 Trunk Road (Moortown) (40 Miles Per Hour Speed Limit) Order 2002 No. 2002/804. – Enabling power: Road Traffic Regulation Act 1984, s. 84 (1) (a) (2), sch. 9, 27 (1). – Made: 20.03.2002. Coming into force: 24.03.2002. Effect: None. Territorial extent & classification: E. Local *Unpublished*

The A6120 Trunk Road (Wetherby Road to York Road) (40 Miles Per Hour Speed Limit) Order 2002 No. 2002/1321. – Enabling power: Road Traffic Regulation Act 1984, s. 84 (1) (a) (2), sch. 9, para. 27 (1). – Made: 08.05.2002. Coming into force: 10.05.2002. Effect: None. Territorial extent & classification: E. Local *Unpublished*

The M5 Motorway (Avonmouth Bridge, Separate Track and Footway) (15 mph Speed Limit) Order 2002 No. 2002/1905. – Enabling power: Road Traffic Regulation Act 1984, s. 84 (1) (a) (2), sch. 9, para. 27 (1). – Made: 18.07.2002. Coming into force: 29.07.2002. Effect: S.I. 1995/1254 revoked. Territorial extent & classification: E. Local *Unpublished*

Road traffic: Traffic regulation

The A1(M) Motorway (Alconbury - Sawtry, Cambridgeshire) (Temporary Prohibition of Traffic) Order 2002 No. 2002/2431. – Enabling power: Road Traffic Regulation Act 1984, s. 14 (1) (a). – Made: 20.09.2002. Coming into force: 27.09.2002. Effect: None. Territorial extent & classification: E. Local *Unpublished*

The A1(M) Motorway (Allerton Park Interchange) (Temporary Prohibition of Traffic) Order 2002 No. 2002/1955. – Enabling power: Road Traffic Regulation Act 1984, s. 14 (1) (a). – Made: 17.07.2002. Coming into force: 21.07.2002. Effect: None. Territorial extent & classification: E. Local *Unpublished*

The A1(M) Motorway and A1 Trunk Road (Stevenage, Hertfordshire - Langford, Bedfordshire) (Temporary Restriction and Prohibition of Traffic) Order 2002 No. 2002/2433. – Enabling power: Road Traffic Regulation Act 1984, s. 14 (1) (a) (7). – Made: 20.09.2002. Coming into force: 27.09.2002. Effect: None. Territorial extent & classification: E. Local *Unpublished*

The A1(M) Motorway and the A1001 Trunk Road (Junctions 2 - 4) (Temporary Prohibition of Traffic) Order 2002 No. 2002/2046. – Enabling power: Road Traffic Regulation Act 1984, s. 14 (1) (a). – Made: 29.07.2002. Coming into force: 01.08.2002. Effect: None. Territorial extent & classification: E. Local *Unpublished*

The A1(M) Motorway and the M18 Motorway (Wadworth Interchange) (Temporary Restriction and Prohibition of Traffic) Order 2002 No. 2002/1612. – Enabling power: Road Traffic Regulation Act 1984, s. 14 (1) (a) (7). – Made: 18.06.2002. Coming into force: 19.06.2002. Effect: None. Territorial extent & classification: E. Local *Unpublished*

The A1(M) Motorway (Blind Lane Interchange) (Temporary Prohibition of Traffic) Order 2002 No. 2002/362. – Enabling power: Road Traffic Regulation Act 1984, s. 14 (1) (a). – Made: 14.02.2002. Coming into force: 18.02.2002. Effect: None. Territorial extent & classification: E. Local *Unpublished*

The A1(M) Motorway (Cornforth and Junction 59) (Temporary Restriction and Prohibition of Traffic) Order 2002 No. 2002/2289. – Enabling power: Road Traffic Regulation Act 1984, s. 14 (1) (a) (7). – Made: 03.09.2002. Coming into force: 08.09.2002. Effect: None. Territorial extent & classification: E. Local *Unpublished*

The A1 (M) Motorway (Hatfield Tunnel) (Temporary Prohibition of Traffic) Order 2002 No. 2002/2739. – Enabling power: Road Traffic Regulation Act 1984, s. 14 (1) (a), sch. 9, para. 27 (1). – Made: 04.11.2002. Coming into force: 11.11.2002. Effect: S.I. 2001/3978 revoked. Territorial extent & classification: E. Local *Unpublished*

The A1 (M) Motorway (Junction 4, Link and Slip Roads) (Temporary Prohibition of Traffic) Order 2002 No. 2002/405. – Enabling power: Road Traffic Regulation Act 1984, s. 14 (1) (a). – Made: 25.02.2002. Coming into force: 02.03.2002. Effect: None. Territorial extent & classification: E. Local *Unpublished*

The A1(M) Motorway (Junction 34 to Junction 35) (Temporary Restriction and Prohibition of Traffic) Order 2002 No. 2002/1745. – Enabling power: Road Traffic Regulation Act 1984, s. 14 (1) (a) (7). – Made: 02.07.2002. Coming into force: 05.07.2002. Effect: None. Territorial extent & classification: E. Local *Unpublished*

The A1(M) Motorway (Junction 44 & Junction 45) (Temporary Restriction and Prohibition of Traffic) Order 2002 No. 2002/462. – Enabling power: Road Traffic Regulation Act 1984, s. 14 (1) (a) (7). – Made: 01.03.2002. Coming into force: 03.03.2002. Effect: None. Territorial extent & classification: E. Local *Unpublished*

The A1(M) Motorway (Junctions 6 - 5) (Temporary Restriction and Prohibition of Traffic) Order 2002 No. 2002/213. – Enabling power: Road Traffic Regulation Act 1984, s. 14 (1) (a) (7). – Made: 04.02.2002. Coming into force: 09.02.2002. Effect: None. Territorial extent & classification: E. Local *Unpublished*

The A1(M) Motorway (Junctions 6 - 7, Hertfordshire) (Temporary Restriction and Prohibition of Traffic) Order 2002 No. 2002/1748. – Enabling power: Road Traffic Regulation Act 1984, s. 14 (1) (a) (7). – Made: 01.07.2002. Coming into force: 08.07.2002. Effect: None. Territorial extent & classification: E. Local *Unpublished*

The A1(M) Motorway (Junctions 6-8) (Hertfordshire) (Temporary Restriction and Prohibition of Traffic) Order 2002 No. 2002/1285. – Enabling power: Road Traffic Regulation Act 1984, s. 14 (1) (a) (7). – Made: 07.05.2002. Coming into force: 14.05.2002. Effect: None. Territorial extent & classification: E. Local *Unpublished*

The A1(M) Motorway (Junctions 8 - 9) Hertfordshire (Temporary Restriction and Prohibition of Traffic) Order 2002 No. 2002/1565. – Enabling power: Road Traffic Regulation Act 1984, s. 14 (1) (a) (7). – Made: 05.06.2002. Coming into force: 12.06.2002. Effect: None. Territorial extent & classification: E. Local *Unpublished*

The A1(M) Motorway (Micklefield) (Temporary Restriction and Prohibition of Traffic) Order 2002 No. 2002/2290. – Enabling power: Road Traffic Regulation Act 1984, s. 14 (1) (a) (7). – Made: 02.09.2002. Coming into force: 03.09.2002. Effect: None. Territorial extent & classification: E. Local *Unpublished*

The A1(M) Motorway (River Don Viaduct) (Temporary Restriction and Prohibition of Traffic) Order 2002 No. 2002/759. – Enabling power: Road Traffic Regulation Act 1984, s. 14 (1) (a) (7). Made: 28.02.2002. Coming into force: 03.03.2002. Effect: None. Territorial extent & classification: E. Local *Unpublished*

The A1 Trunk Road and the A1(M) Motorway (Baldersby to Blind Lane) (Temporary 40 Miles Per Hour Speed Restriction) Order 2002 No. 2002/2436. – Enabling power: Road Traffic Regulation Act 1984, s. 14 (1) (a). – Made: 19.09.2002. Coming into force: 22.09.2002. Effect: None. Territorial extent & classification: E. Local *Unpublished*

The A1 Trunk Road (Baldersby Interchange) (Temporary Prohibition of Traffic) Order 2002 No. 2002/2039. – Enabling power: Road Traffic Regulation Act 1984, s. 14 (1) (a). – Made: 30.07.2002. Coming into force: 04.08.2002. Effect: None. Territorial extent & classification: E. Local *Unpublished*

The A1 Trunk Road (Barnsdale Bar to Darrington) (Temporary Restriction and Prohibition of Traffic) Order 2002 No. 2002/2796. – Enabling power: Road Traffic Regulation Act 1984, s. 14 (1) (a). – Made: 06.11.2002. Coming into force: 10.11.2002. Effect: None. Territorial extent & classification: E. Local *Unpublished*

The A1 Trunk Road (Beeston, Bedfordshire) (Prohibition of Entry, Right Turns and "U" Turns) Order 2002 No. 2002/58. – Enabling power: Road Traffic Regulation Act 1984, ss. 1 (1), 2 (1) (2). – Made: 11.01.2002. Coming into force: 25.01.2002. Effect: None. Territorial extent & classification: E. Local *Unpublished*

The A1 Trunk Road (Biggleswade - Sandy, Bedfordshire) (Temporary Prohibition of Traffic) Order 2002 No. 2002/1644. – Enabling power: Road Traffic Regulation Act 1984, s. 14 (1) (a). – Made: 14.06.2002. Coming into force: 21.06.2002. Effect: None. Territorial extent & classification: E. Local *Unpublished*

The A1 Trunk Road (Black Cat Roundabout, Bedfordshire) (Temporary 40 Miles Per Hour Speed Restriction) Order 2002 No. 2002/1848. – Enabling power: Road Traffic Regulation Act 1984, s. 14 (1) (a). – Made: 12.07.2002. Coming into force: 19.07.2002. Effect: None. Territorial extent & classification: E. Local *Unpublished*

The A1 Trunk Road (Buckden - Hail Bridge, Cambridgeshire) (Temporary Restriction and Prohibition of Traffic) Order 2002 No. 2002/1581. – Enabling power: Road Traffic Regulation Act 1984, s. 14 (1) (a). – Made: 10.06.2002. Coming into force: 17.06.2002. Effect: None. Territorial extent & classification: E. Local *Unpublished*

The A1 Trunk Road (Buckden - Hail Bridge, Cambridgeshire) (Temporary Restriction and Prohibition of Traffic) Order 2002 No. 2002/2462. – Enabling power: Road Traffic Regulation Act 1984, s. 14 (1) (a). – Made: 23.09.2002. Coming into force: 30.09.2002. Effect: None. Territorial extent & classification: E. Local *Unpublished*

The A1 Trunk Road (Catterick South to East Appleton) (Temporary Restriction and Prohibition of Traffic) Order 2002 No. 2002/1657. – Enabling power: Road Traffic Regulation Act 1984, s. 14 (1) (a). Made: 20.06.2002. Coming into force: 23.06.2002. Effect: None. Territorial extent & classification: E. Local *Unpublished*

The A1 Trunk Road (Consett Route Interchange) (Temporary Prohibition of Traffic) Order 2002 No. 2002/1641. – Enabling power: Road Traffic Regulation Act 1984, s. 14 (1) (a). – Made: 20.06.2002. Coming into force: 23.06.2002. Effect: None. Territorial extent & classification: E. Local *Unpublished*

The A1 Trunk Road (Dishforth Interchange) (Temporary Prohibition of Traffic) Order 2002 No. 2002/2145. – Enabling power: Road Traffic Regulation Act 1984, s. 14 (1) (a). – Made: 14.08.2002. Coming into force: 18.08.2002. Effect: None. Territorial extent & classification: E. Local *Unpublished*

The A1 Trunk Road (Eaton Socon Bypass, Cambridgeshire) (Temporary Restriction and Prohibition of Traffic) Order 2002 No. 2002/1534. – Enabling power: Road Traffic Regulation Act 1984, s. 14 (1) (a). – Made: 31.05.2002. Coming into force: 10.06.2002. Effect: None. Territorial extent & classification: E. Local *Unpublished*

The A1 Trunk Road (Gateshead/Newcastle Western Bypass) (Temporary Restriction and Prohibition of Traffic) Order 2002 No. 2002/2165. – Enabling power: Road Traffic Regulation Act 1984, s. 14 (1) (a). – Made: 16.08.2002. Coming into force: 18.08.2002. Effect: None. Territorial extent & classification: E. Local *Unpublished*

The A1 Trunk Road (Holtby Grange to Leeming) and the A66 Trunk Road (Temporary Restriction and Prohibition of Traffic) Order 2002 No. 2002/2361. – Enabling power: Road Traffic Regulation Act 1984, s. 14 (1) (a). – Made: 09.09.2002. Coming into force: 15.09.2002. Effect: None. Territorial extent & classification: E. Local *Unpublished*

The A1 Trunk Road (Junction with A6121, Stamford) (Southbound Entry and Exit Slip Road) (Temporary Prohibition of Traffic) Order 2002 No. 2002/1443. – Enabling power: Road Traffic Regulation Act 1984, s. 14 (1) (a). – Made: 24.05.2002. Coming into force: 02.06.2002. Effect: None. Territorial extent & classification: E. Local *Unpublished*

The A1 Trunk Road (Junction with the A606 at Stamford) (Slip Roads) (Temporary 40 Miles Per Hour Speed Restriction) (No. 2) Order 2002 No. 2002/3262. – Enabling power: Road Traffic Regulation Act 1984, s. 14 (1) (a). – Made: 30.12.2002. Coming into force: 06.01.2003. Effect: None. Territorial extent & classification: E. Local *Unpublished*

The A1 Trunk Road (Junction with the A606 at Stamford) (Slip Roads) (Temporary 40 Miles Per Hour Speed Restriction) Order 2002 No. 2002/2177. – Enabling power: Road Traffic Regulation Act 1984, s. 14 (1) (a). – Made: 02.09.2002. Coming into force: 09.09.2002. Effect: None. Territorial extent & classification: E. Local *Unpublished*

The A1 Trunk Road (Lobley Hill Interchange) (Temporary Restriction and Prohibition of Traffic) Order 2002 No. 2002/2605. – Enabling power: Road Traffic Regulation Act 1984, s. 14 (1) (a). – Made: 10.10.2002. Coming into force: 11.10.2002. Effect: None. Territorial extent & classification: E. Local *Unpublished*

The A1 Trunk Road (Long Bennington) (Temporary Restriction and Prohibition of Traffic) Order 2002 No. 2002/297. – Enabling power: Road Traffic Regulation Act 1984, s. 14 (1) (a). – Made: 11.02.2002. Coming into force: 18.02.2002. Effect: None. Territorial extent & classification: E. Local *Unpublished*

The A1 Trunk Road (Northbound Exit Slip Road, Ferrybridge Interchange) (Temporary Prohibition of Traffic) Order 2002 No. 2002/1261. – Enabling power: Road Traffic Regulation Act 1984, s. 14 (1) (a). – Made: 02.05.2002. Coming into force: 08.05.2002. Effect: None. Territorial extent & classification: E. Local *Unpublished*

The A1 Trunk Road (North Brunton Interchange) (Temporary Prohibition of Traffic) Order 2002 No. 2002/1427. – Enabling power: Road Traffic Regulation Act 1984, s. 14 (1) (a). – Made: 13.05.2002. Coming into force: 16.05.2002. Effect: None. Territorial extent & classification: E. Local *Unpublished*

The A1 Trunk Road (North Brunton Interchange) (Temporary Restriction of Traffic) Order 2002 No. 2002/1426. – Enabling power: Road Traffic Regulation Act 1984, s. 14 (1) (a). – Made: 23.05.2002. Coming into force: 26.05.2002. Effect: None. Territorial extent & classification: E. Local *Unpublished*

The A1 Trunk Road (Oaktree Filling Station, Burneston) (Temporary Restriction and Prohibition of Traffic) Order 2002 No. 2002/17. – Enabling power: Road Traffic Regulation Act 1984, s. 14 (1) (a). – Made: 04.01.2002. Coming into force: 06.01.2002. Effect: None. Territorial extent & classification: E. Local *Unpublished*

The A1 Trunk Road (Radwell, Hertfordshire) (Prohibition of Entry) Order 2002 No. 2002/348. – Enabling power:Road Traffic Regulation Act 1984, ss. 1 (1), 2 (1) (2). – Made: 15.02.2002. Coming into force: 01.03.2002. Effect: None. Territorial extent & classification: E. Local *Unpublished*

The A1 Trunk Road (Ranby to Markham Moor, Nottinghamshire) (Temporary Restriction and Prohibition of Traffic) Order 2002 No. 2002/1515. – Enabling power: Road Traffic Regulation Act 1984, s. 14 (1) (a) (5) (b). – Made: 31.05.2002. Coming into force: 07.06.2002. Effect: None. Territorial extent & classification: E. Local *Unpublished*

The A1 Trunk Road (River Coquet Bridge) (Temporary Restriction and Prohibition of Traffic) Order 2002 No. 2002/198. – Enabling power: Road Traffic Regulation Act 1984, s. 14 (1) (a). – Made: 01.02.2002. Coming into force: 03.02.2002. Effect: None. Territorial extent & classification: E. Local *Unpublished*

The A1 Trunk Road (Scotch Corner) (Temporary Restriction and Prohibition of Traffic) Order 2002 No. 2002/1683. – Enabling power: Road Traffic Regulation Act 1984, s. 14 (1) (a). – Made: 27.06.2002. Coming into force: 30.06.2002. Effect: None. Territorial extent & classification: E. Local *Unpublished*

The A1 Trunk Road (Smearfield and Haggerston) (Temporary Restriction and Prohibition of Traffic) Order 2002 No. 2002/1613. – Enabling power: Road Traffic Regulation Act 1984, s. 14 (1) (a). – Made: 18.06.2002. Coming into force: 23.06.2002. Effect: None. Territorial extent & classification: E. Local *Unpublished*

The A1 Trunk Road (Southbound Exit Slip Road, Balderton, Nottinghamshire) (Temporary 30 Miles Per Hour Speed Restriction) Order 2002 No. 2002/133. – Enabling power: Road Traffic Regulation Act 1984, s. 14 (1) (a). – Made: 25.01.2002. Coming into force: 01.02.2002. Effect: None. Territorial extent & classification: E. Local *Unpublished*

The A1 Trunk Road (Southbound Exit Slip Road, known as Great North Road, Balderton) (One Way Traffic) Order 2002 No. 2002/2044. – Enabling power: Road Traffic Regulation Act 1984, ss. 1 (1), 2 (1) (2). – Made: 22.07.2002. Coming into force: 05.08.2002. Effect: None. Territorial extent & classification: E. Local *Unpublished*

The A1 Trunk Road (Stibbington, Cambridgeshire) (Temporary Restriction and Prohibition of Traffic) Order 2002 No. 2002/3261. – Enabling power: Road Traffic Regulation Act 1984, s. 14 (1) (a). – Made: 27.12.2002. Coming into force: 03.01.2003. Effect: None. Territorial extent & classification: E. Local *Unpublished*

The A1 Trunk Road (Thorns Farm, Grantham Bypass, Lincolnshire) (Closure of Gap in the Central Reservation) Order 2002 No. 2002/963. – Enabling power: Road Traffic Regulation Act 1984, ss. 1 (1), 2 (1) (2). – Made: 28.03.2002. Coming into force: 11.04.2002. Effect: None. Territorial extent & classification: E. Local *Unpublished*

The A1 Trunk Road (Various Lengths, Bedfordshire-Cambridgeshire) (Temporary 40 Miles Per Hour Speed Restriction) Order 2002 No. 2002/1467. – Enabling power: Road Traffic Regulation Act 1984, s. 14 (1) (a). – Made: 24.05.2002. Coming into force: 31.05.2002. Effect: None. Territorial extent & classification: E. Local *Unpublished*

The A1 Trunk Road (Warreners to Tritlington and Burgham to Bockenfield) (Temporary Restriction and Prohibition of Traffic) Order 2002 No. 2002/2674. – Enabling power: Road Traffic Regulation Act 1984, s. 14 (1) (a). – Made: 23.10.2002. Coming into force: 26.10.2002. Effect: None. Territorial extent & classification: E. Local *Unpublished*

The A2 Trunk Road (Brenley Corner - Guston) (Temporary 40 Miles Per Hour Speed Restriction) Order 2002 No. 2002/1752. – Enabling power: Road Traffic Regulation Act 1984, s. 14 (1) (a). – Made: 01.07.2002. Coming into force: 08.07.2002. Effect: None. Territorial extent & classification: E. Local *Unpublished*

The A2 Trunk Road (Bridge, Slip Roads) (Temporary Prohibition of Traffic) Order 2002 No. 2002/2292. – Enabling power: Road Traffic Regulation Act 1984, s. 14 (1) (a). – Made: 02.09.2002. Coming into force: 07.09.2002. Effect: None. Territorial extent & classification: E. Local *Unpublished*

The A2 Trunk Road (Canterbury Bypass) (Temporary Restriction and Prohibition of Traffic) Order 2002 No. 2002/2081. – Enabling power: Road Traffic Regulation Act 1984, s. 14 (1) (a). – Made: 05.08.2002. Coming into force: 10.08.2002. Effect: None. Territorial extent & classification: E. Local *Unpublished*

The A2 Trunk Road (Cobham Junction, Slip Roads) (Temporary Prohibition of Traffic) Order 2002 No. 2002/483. – Enabling power: Road Traffic Regulation Act 1984, s. 14 (1) (a). – Made: 04.03.2002. Coming into force: 11.03.2002. Effect: None. Territorial extent & classification: E. Local *Unpublished*

The A2 Trunk Road (Gate Services, Slip Roads) (Temporary Prohibition of Traffic) Order 2002 No. 2002/2808. – Enabling power: Road Traffic Regulation Act 1984, s. 14 (1) (a). – Made: 11.11.2002. Coming into force: 16.11.2002. Effect: None. Territorial extent & classification: E. Local *Unpublished*

The A2 Trunk Road (Horselees Road Bridge) (Temporary 40 Miles Per Hour Speed Restriction) Order 2002 No. 2002/2342. – Enabling power: Road Traffic Regulation Act 1984, s. 14 (1) (a). – Made: 09.09.2002. Coming into force: 14.09.2002. Effect: None. Territorial extent & classification: E. Local *Unpublished*

The A2 Trunk Road (Jubilee Way, Coastguard Carriageway) (Temporary Prohibition of Traffic) Order 2002 No. 2002/2447. – Enabling power: Road Traffic Regulation Act 1984, s. 14 (1) (a). – Made: 23.09.2002. Coming into force: 01.10.2002. Effect: None. Territorial extent & classification: E. Local *Unpublished*

The A2 Trunk Road (M25 Junction 2 - A227 Junction) (Temporary Restriction and Prohibition of Traffic) Order 2002 No. 2002/1631. – Enabling power: Road Traffic Regulation Act 1984, ss. 14 (1) (a), 15 (2). – Made: 24.06.2002. Coming into force: 29.06.2002. Effect: None. Territorial extent & classification: E. Local *Unpublished*

The A2 Trunk Road (Pepper Hill, Londonbound Slip Road) (Temporary Prohibition of Traffic) Order 2002 No. 2002/1624. – Enabling power: Road Traffic Regulation Act 1984, s. 14 (1) (a). – Made: 24.06.2002. Coming into force: 29.06.2002. Effect: None. Territorial extent & classification: E. Local *Unpublished*

The A2 Trunk Road (Pepper Hill, Slip Roads) (Temporary Prohibition of Traffic) Order 2002 No. 2002/3167. – Enabling power: Road Traffic Regulation Act 1984, s. 14 (1) (a). – Made: 16.12.2002. Coming into force: 21.12.2002. Effect: None. Territorial extent & classification: E. Local *Unpublished*

The A2 Trunk Road (Upper Harbledown, Slip Road) (Temporary Prohibition of Traffic) Order 2002 No. 2002/2169. – Enabling power: Road Traffic Regulation Act 1984, s. 14 (1) (a). – Made: 12.08.2002. Coming into force: 16.08.2002. Effect: None. Territorial extent & classification: E. Local *Unpublished*

The A3(M) Motorway (Junction 2, Slip Road) (Temporary Prohibition of Traffic) Order 2002 No. 2002/2507. – Enabling power: Road Traffic Regulation Act 1984, s. 14 (1) (a). – Made: 30.09.2002. Coming into force: 05.10.2002. Effect: None. Territorial extent & classification: E. Local *Unpublished*

The A3 (M) Motorway (Junction 4, Slip Road) (Temporary Prohibition of Traffic) Order 2002 No. 2002/2561. – Enabling power: Road Traffic Regulation Act 1984, s. 14 (1) (a). – Made: 07.10.2002. Coming into force: 12.10.2002. Effect: None. Territorial extent & classification: E. Local *Unpublished*

The A3(M) Motorway (Junction 5) (Temporary Prohibition and Restriction of Traffic) Order 2002 No. 2002/2149. – Enabling power: Road Traffic Regulation Act 1984, s. 14 (1) (a). – Made: 12.08.2002. Coming into force: 17.08.2002. Effect: None. Territorial extent & classification: E. Local *Unpublished*

The A3(M) Motorway (Junctions 3 and 5, Southbound Exit Slip Roads) (Temporary Prohibition of Traffic) Order 2002 No. 2002/1509. – Enabling power: Road Traffic Regulation Act 1984, s. 14 (1) (a). – Made: 05.06.2002. Coming into force: 08.06.2002. Effect: None. Territorial extent & classification: E. Local *Unpublished*

The A3 Trunk Road (Copsem to Hook, Surrey) (Temporary Prohibition of Traffic) Order 2002 No. 2002/2085. – Enabling power: Road Traffic Regulation Act 1984, s. 14 (1) (a). – Made: 02.08.2002. Coming into force: 09.08.2002. Effect: None. Territorial extent & classification: E. Local *Unpublished*

The A3 Trunk Road (Hindhead and Milford) (Temporary Prohibition of Traffic) Order 2002 No. 2002/2564. – Enabling power: Road Traffic Regulation Act 1984, s. 14 (1) (a). – Made: 07.10.2002. Coming into force: 14.10.2002. Effect: None. Territorial extent & classification: E. Local *Unpublished*

The A3 Trunk Road (Hurtmore Road and Milford) (Temporary Restriction and Prohibition of Traffic) Order 2002 No. 2002/1466. – Enabling power: Road Traffic Regulation Act 1984, s. 14 (1) (a). – Made: 27.05.2002. Coming into force: 01.06.2002. Effect: None. Territorial extent & classification: E. Local *Unpublished*

The A3 Trunk Road (Hurtmore Road Junction, Slip Roads) (Temporary Prohibition of Traffic) Order 2002 No. 2002/132. – Enabling power: Road Traffic Regulation Act 1984, s. 14 (1) (a). – Made: 28.01.2002. Coming into force: 02.02.2002. Effect: None. Territorial extent & classification: E. Local *Unpublished*

The A3 Trunk Road (Longmoor and Weston Junctions) (Temporary Prohibition of Traffic) Order 2002 No. 2002/1643. – Enabling power: Road Traffic Regulation Act 1984, s. 14 (1) (a). – Made: 05.06.2002. Coming into force: 08.06.2002. Effect: None. Territorial extent & classification: E. Local *Unpublished*

The A3 Trunk Road (Midleton Road, Guildford) (Temporary Restriction and Prohibition of Traffic) Order 2002 No. 2002/1453. – Enabling power: Road Traffic Regulation Act 1984, s. 14 (1) (a). – Made: 27.05.2002. Coming into force: 01.06.2002. Effect: None. Territorial extent & classification: E. Local *Unpublished*

The A3 Trunk Road (North of Clanfield) (Temporary Restriction and Prohibition of Traffic) Order 2002 No. 2002/1345. – Enabling power: Road Traffic Regulation Act 1984, s. 14 (1) (a). – Made: 13.05.2002. Coming into force: 18.05.2002. Effect: None. Territorial extent & classification: E. Local *Unpublished*

The A3 Trunk Road (Ockham, Southbound Exit Slip Road) (Temporary Prohibition of Traffic) Order 2002 No. 2002/1464. – Enabling power: Road Traffic Regulation Act 1984, s. 14 (1) (a). – Made: 27.05.2002. Coming into force: 01.06.2002. Effect: None. Territorial extent & classification: E. Local *Unpublished*

The A3 Trunk Road (Potters Lane Junction, Slip Road) (Temporary Prohibition of Traffic) Order 2002 No. 2002/3067. – Enabling power: Road Traffic Regulation Act 1984, s. 14 (1) (a). – Made: 09.12.2002. Coming into force: 14.12.2002. Effect: None. Territorial extent & classification: E. Local *Unpublished*

The A3 Trunk Road (Ripley to Wisley) (Temporary 50 Miles Per Hour Speed Restriction) Order 2002 No. 2002/1622. – Enabling power: Road Traffic Regulation Act 1984, s. 14 (1) (a). – Made: 24.06.2002. Coming into force: 29.06.2002. Effect: None. Territorial extent & classification: E. Local *Unpublished*

The A3 Trunk Road (Sheet, Northbound Entry Slip Road) (Temporary Prohibition of Traffic) Order 2002 No. 2002/1465. – Enabling power: Road Traffic Regulation Act 1984, s. 14 (1) (a). – Made: 27.05.2002. Coming into force: 01.06.2002. Effect: None. Territorial extent & classification: E. Local *Unpublished*

The A3 Trunk Road (South of Hindhead) (Temporary Speed Restrictions) Order 2002 No. 2002/1452. – Enabling power: Road Traffic Regulation Act 1984, s. 14 (1) (a). – Made: 27.05.2002. Coming into force: 01.06.2002. Effect: None. Territorial extent & classification: E. Local *Unpublished*

The A3 Trunk Road (University Junction, Guildford) (Temporary Prohibition of Traffic) Order 2002 No. 2002/2565. – Enabling power: Road Traffic Regulation Act 1984, s. 14 (1) (a). – Made: 07.10.2002. Coming into force: 12.10.2002. Effect: None. Territorial extent & classification: E. Local *Unpublished*

The A3 Trunk Road (Various Locations, near Guidlford) (Temporary Prohibition of Traffic) Order 2002 No. 2002/2792. – Enabling power: Road Traffic Regulation Act 1984, s. 14 (1) (a). – Made: 11.11.2002. Coming into force: 16.11.2002. Effect: None. Territorial extent & classification: E. Local *Unpublished*

The A3 Trunk Road (Various Locations, Surrey) (Temporary Restriction and Prohibition of Traffic) Order 2002 No. 2002/2973. – Enabling power: Road Traffic Regulation Act 1984, s. 14 (1) (a). – Made: 02.12.2002. Coming into force: 07.12.2002. Effect: None. Territorial extent & classification: E. Local *Unpublished*

The A3 Trunk Road (Weston and Berelands Junctions) (Temporary Prohibition of Traffic) Order 2002 No. 2002/2568. – Enabling power: Road Traffic Regulation Act 1984, s. 14 (1) (a). – Made: 07.10.2002. Coming into force: 12.10.2002. Effect: None. Territorial extent & classification: E. Local *Unpublished*

The A4 Trunk Road (Colnbrook Bypass) (Temporary 40 Miles per Hour Speed Restriction)Order 2002 No. 2002/2791. – Enabling power: Road Traffic Regulation Act 1984, s. 14 (1) (a). – Made: 11.11.2002. Coming into force: 19.11.2002. Effect: None. Territorial extent & classification: E. Local *Unpublished*

The A4 Trunk Road (Crowley Way & St Brendan's Roundabout) (Temporary Prohibition of Traffic) Order 2002 No. 2002/1388. – Enabling power: Road Traffic Regulation Act 1984, s. 14 (1) (a). – Made: 17.05.2002. Coming into force: 22.05.2002. Effect: None. Territorial extent & classification: E. Local *Unpublished*

The A5 and A38 Trunk Roads (Weeford Island, Staffordshire) (Temporary 40 Miles Per Hour Speed Restriction) Order 2002 No. 2002/2500. – Enabling power: Road Traffic Regulation Act 1984, s. 14 (1) (a). – Made: 30.09.2002. Coming into force: 07.10.2002. Effect: None. Territorial extent & classification: E. Local *Unpublished*

The A5 Trunk Road and the M42 Motorway (M42 Junction 10) (Temporary Prohibition and Restriction of Traffic) Order 2002 No. 2002/2667. – Enabling power: Road Traffic Regulation Act 1984, s. 14 (1) (a). – Made: 18.10.2002. Coming into force: 25.10.2002. Effect: None. Territorial extent & classification: E. Local *Unpublished*

The A5 Trunk Road (Caddington Turn and High Street North, Dunstable) (Temporary Restriction and Prohibition of Traffic) Order 2002 No. 2002/1521. – Enabling power: Road Traffic Regulation Act 1984, s. 14 (1) (a) (7). – Made: 28.05.2002. Coming into force: 04.06.2002. Effect: None. Territorial extent & classification: E. Local *Unpublished*

The A5 Trunk Road (Daventry, Northamptonshire) (Temporary Prohibition of Traffic) Order 2002 No. 2002/2856. – Enabling power: Road Traffic Regulation Act 1984, s. 14 (1) (b). – Made: 15.11.2002. Coming into force: 22.11.2002. Effect: None. Territorial extent & classification: E. Local *Unpublished*

The A5 Trunk Road (Dordon, Grendon and Holly Lane Roundabouts, Warwickshire) (Temporary Prohibition of Traffic) Order 2002 No. 2002/2484. – Enabling power: Road Traffic Regulation Act 1984, s. 14 (1) (a). – Made: 27.09.2002. Coming into force: 04.10.2002. Effect: None. Territorial extent & classification: E. Local *Unpublished*

The A5 Trunk Road (Dordon, Warwickshire) (Temporary 50 Miles Per Hour Speed Restriction) Order 2002 No. 2002/1199. – Enabling power: Road Traffic Regulation Act 1984, s. 14 (1) (a). – Made: 25.04.2002. Coming into force: 02.05.2002. Effect: None. Territorial extent & classification: E. Local *Unpublished*

The A5 Trunk Road (Emstrey Roundabout to Preston Boats Roundabout) (Temporary Prohibition of Traffic) Order 2002 No. 2002/1. Enabling power: Road Traffic Regulation Act 1984, s. 14 (1) (a). – Made: 02.01.2002. Coming into force: 04.01.2002. Effect: None. Territorial extent & classification: E. Local *Unpublished*

The A5 Trunk Road (Gibbet Hill Roundabout, Warwickshire) (Temporary Prohibition of Traffic) Order 2002 No. 2002/2725. – Enabling power: Road Traffic Regulation Act 1984, s. 14 (1) (a). – Made: 25.10.2002. Coming into force: 01.11.2002. Effect: None. Territorial extent & classification: E. Local *Unpublished*

The A5 Trunk Road (High Street North, Dunstable, Bedfordshire) (Prohibition and Restriction of Waiting) Order 2002 No. 2002/2650. – Enabling power: Road Traffic Regulation Act 1984, ss. 1 (1), 2 (1) (2), 4 (1) (2). – Made: 18.10.2002. Coming into force: 01.11.2002. Effect: None. Territorial extent & classification: E. Local *Unpublished*

The A5 Trunk Road (Junction with A5127/A5148 Wall Island, Staffordshire) (Temporary Prohibition of Traffic) Order 2002 No. 2002/1577. – Enabling power: Road Traffic Regulation Act 1984, s. 14 (1) (a). – Made: 10.06.2002. Coming into force: 17.06.2002. Effect: None. Territorial extent & classification: E. Local *Unpublished*

The A5 Trunk Road (Junction with Leacroft Lane, Churchbridge) (Temporary Prohibition of Traffic) Order 2002 No. 2002/176. – Enabling power: Road Traffic Regulation Act 1984, s. 14 (1) (a). – Made: 25.01.2002. Coming into force: 01.02.2002. Effect: None. Territorial extent & classification: E. Local *Unpublished*

The A5 Trunk Road (Junction with Norton Lane, Great Wyrley, Staffordshire) (Temporary Prohibition of Traffic) Order 2002 No. 2002/1991. – Enabling power: Road Traffic Regulation Act 1984, s. 14 (1) (b). – Made: 08.07.2002. Coming into force: 15.07.2002. Effect: None. Territorial extent & classification: E. Local *Unpublished*

The A5 Trunk Road (Junction with Vine Lane and Delta Way, Bridgtown) (Temporary Prohibition of Traffic) Order 2002 No. 2002/2075. – Enabling power: Road Traffic Regulation Act 1984, s. 14 (1) (a). – Made: 02.08.2002. Coming into force: 09.08.2002. Effect: None. Territorial extent & classification: E. Local *Unpublished*

The A5 Trunk Road (M69 Junction 1, Hinckley, Leicestershire) (Temporary Prohibition of Traffic) Order 2002 No. 2002/2488. – Enabling power: Road Traffic Regulation Act 1984, s. 14 (1) (a). – Made: 27.09.2002. Coming into force: 04.10.2002. Effect: None. Territorial extent & classification: E. Local *Unpublished*

The A5 Trunk Road (Milton Keynes, Buckinghamshire) (Temporary Prohibition of Traffic) Order 2002 No. 2002/925. – Enabling power: Road Traffic Regulation Act 1984, s. 14 (1) (a). – Made: 25.03.2002. Coming into force: 02.04.2002. Effect: None. Territorial extent & classification: E. Local *Unpublished*

The A5 Trunk Road (Newtown, Staffordshire) (Temporary Prohibition of Traffic) Order 2002 No. 2002/2119. – Enabling power: Road Traffic Regulation Act 1984, s. 14 (1) (a). – Made: 09.08.2002. Coming into force: 16.08.2002. Effect: None. Territorial extent & classification: E. Local *Unpublished*

The A5 Trunk Road (Old Stratford, Northamptonshire) (Temporary Restriction and Prohibition of Traffic) Order 2002 No. 2002/2430. – Enabling power: Road Traffic Regulation Act 1984, s. 14 (1) (a). – Made: 20.09.2002. Coming into force: 27.09.2002. Effect: None. Territorial extent & classification: E. Local *Unpublished*

The A5 Trunk Road (Shawell, Warwickshire) (Prohibition of "U" Turns) Order 2002 No. 2002/83. – Enabling power: Road Traffic Regulation Act 1984, ss. 1 (1), 2 (1) (2). – Made: 11.01.2002. Coming into force: 25.01.2002. Effect: None. Territorial extent & classification: E. Local *Unpublished*

The A5 Trunk Road (Sheepy Road Bridge, Atherstone, Warwickshire) (Temporary Prohibition of Traffic) Order 2002 No. 2002/384. – Enabling power: Road Traffic Regulation Act 1984, s. 14 (1) (a). – Made: 18.02.2002. Coming into force: 25.02.2002. Effect: None. Territorial extent & classification: E. Local *Unpublished*

The A5 Trunk Road (Sketchley Meadow to Nutts Lane, Hinckley) (Temporary Restriction and Prohibition of Traffic) Order 2002 No. 2002/2029. – Enabling power: Road Traffic Regulation Act 1984, s. 14 (1) (a). – Made: 26.07.2002. Coming into force: 02.08.2002. Effect: None. Territorial extent & classification: E. Local *Unpublished*

The A5 Trunk Road (South of Gibbet Hill, Warwickshire) (Temporary 40 Miles Per Hour Speed Restriction) Order 2002 No. 2002/2717. – Enabling power: Road Traffic Regulation Act 1984, s. 14 (1) (a). – Made: 25.10.2002. Coming into force: 01.11.2002. Effect: None. Territorial extent & classification: E. Local *Unpublished*

The A5 Trunk Road (Tamworth, Staffordshire) (Slip Roads) (Temporary Prohibition of Traffic) Order 2002 No. 2002/2485. – Enabling power: Road Traffic Regulation Act 1984, s. 14 (1) (a). – Made: 27.09.2002. Coming into force: 04.10.2002. Effect: None. Territorial extent & classification: E. Local *Unpublished*

The A5 Trunk Road (Tebworth, Bedfordshire) (Temporary 40 Miles Per Hour Speed Restriction) Order 2002 No. 2002/2716. – Enabling power: Road Traffic Regulation Act 1984, s. 14 (1) (a). – Made: 28.10.2002. Coming into force: 04.11.2002. Effect: None. Territorial extent & classification: E. Local *Unpublished*

The A5 Trunk Road (Towcester - Weedon Bec, Northamptonshire) (Temporary Restriction and Prohibition of Traffic) Order 2002 No. 2002/2286. – Enabling power: Road Traffic Regulation Act 1984, s. 14 (1) (a). – Made: 02.09.2002. Coming into force: 09.09.2002. Effect: None. Territorial extent & classification: E. Local *Unpublished*

The A5 Trunk Road (Various Lengths, Flamstead - Catthorpe) (Temporary 40 Miles Per Hour Speed Restriction) Order 2002 No. 2002/1847. – Enabling power: Road Traffic Regulation Act 1984, s. 14 (1) (a). – Made: 12.07.2002. Coming into force: 19.07.2002. Effect: None. Territorial extent & classification: E. Local *Unpublished*

The A5 Trunk Road (Watling Street, Staffordshire) (Temporary Restriction and Prohibition of Traffic) Order 2002 No. 2002/2554. – Enabling power: Road Traffic Regulation Act 1984, s. 14 (1) (a), sch. 9, para 27 (1). – Made: 27.09.2002. Coming into force: 04.10.2002. Effect: S.I. 2001/2796 revoked. Territorial extent & classification: E. Local *Unpublished*

The A5 Trunk Road (Weedon Bec, Northamptonshire) (Temporary Restriction and Prohibition of Traffic) Order 2002 No. 2002/364. – Enabling power: Road Traffic Regulation Act 1984, s. 14 (1) (a). – Made: 18.02.2002. Coming into force: 25.02.2002. Effect: None. Territorial extent & classification: E. Local *Unpublished*

The A5 Trunk Road (Wibtoft to Smockington, Leicestershire) (Temporary Restriction and Prohibition of Traffic) Order 2002 No. 2002/2752. – Enabling power: Road Traffic Regulation Act 1984, s. 14 (1) (a). – Made: 01.11.2002. Coming into force: 08.11.2002. Effect: None. Territorial extent & classification: E. Local *Unpublished*

The A6 Trunk Road (Blackwell to Ashford in the Water, Derbyshire) (Temporary Restriction and Prohibition of Traffic) Order 2002 No. 2002/1201. – Enabling power: Road Traffic Regulation Act 1984, s. 14 (1) (a). – Made: 23.04.2002. Coming into force: 30.04.2002. Effect: None. Territorial extent & classification: E. Local *Unpublished*

The A6 Trunk Road (Clapham Bypass, Bedford Road, Milton Ernest, Bedfordshire) (One-Way) Order 2002 No. 2002/2960. – Enabling power:Road Traffic Regulation Act 1984, ss. 1 (1), 2 (1) (2). – Made: 28.11.2002. Coming into force: 12.12.2002. Effect: None. Territorial extent & classification: E. Local *Unpublished*

The A6 Trunk Road (Clapham Bypass, Bedfordshire) (24 Hours Clearway) Order 2002 No. 2002/2961. – Enabling power: Road Traffic Regulation Act 1984, ss. 1 (1), 2 (1) (2), 4 (1). – Made: 28.11.2002. Coming into force: 12.12.2002. Effect: None. Territorial extent & classification: E. Local *Unpublished*

The A6 Trunk Road (Clapham - Milton Ernest, Bedfordshire) (Temporary 40 Miles Per Hour Speed Restriction) Order 2002 No. 2002/300. – Enabling power: Road Traffic Regulation Act 1984, s. 14 (1) (a), sch. 9, para. 27 (1). – Made: 11.02.2002. Coming into force: 18.02.2002. Effect: S.I. 2001/2853 revoked. Territorial extent & classification: E. Local *Unpublished*

The A6 Trunk Road (Harborough Road, Northamptonshire) (Temporary 40 Miles Per Hour Speed Restriction) Order 2002 No. 2002/3245. – Enabling power: Road Traffic Regulation Act 1984, s. 14 (1) (a). – Made: 27.12.2002. Coming into force: 03.01.2003. Effect: None. Territorial extent & classification: E. Local *Unpublished*

The A6 Trunk Road (Higham Ferrers, Northamptonshire) (Temporary Prohibition of Traffic) Order 2002 No. 2002/2855. – Enabling power: Road Traffic Regulation Act 1984, s. 16A, 16B, 16C. – Made: 15.11.2002. Coming into force: 22.11.2002. Effect: None. Territorial extent & classification: E. Local *Unpublished*

The A6 Trunk Road (Kibworth Harcourt to Burton Overy, Leicestershire) (Temporary Prohibition of Traffic) Order 2002 No. 2002/2209. – Enabling power: Road Traffic Regulation Act 1984, s. 14 (1) (a). – Made: 23.08.2002. Coming into force: 31.08.2002. Effect: None. Territorial extent & classification: E. Local *Unpublished*

The A6 Trunk Road (Loughborough Town Centre) (Temporary Prohibition of Traffic) Order 2002 No. 2002/2754. – Enabling power: Road Traffic Regulation Act 1984, s. 14 (1) (b) (5). – Made: 01.11.2002. Coming into force: 08.11.2002. Effect: None. Territorial extent & classification: E. Local *Unpublished*

The A6 Trunk Road (Oadby to Great Glen, Leicestershire) (Temporary Restriction and Prohibition of Traffic) Order 2002 No. 2002/385. – Enabling power: Road Traffic Regulation Act 1984, s. 14 (1) (a). – Made: 18.02.2002. Coming into force: 25.02.2002. Effect: None. Territorial extent & classification: E. Local *Unpublished*

The A6 Trunk Road (Quorn Bypass, Leicestershire) (Temporary Prohibition of Traffic) Order 2002 No. 2002/1526. – Enabling power: Road Traffic Regulation Act 1984, s. 14 (1) (a). – Made: 31.05.2002. Coming into force: 07.06.2002. Effect: None. Territorial extent & classification: E. Local *Unpublished*

The A6 Trunk Road (Swan Street, Loughborough) (Temporary Prohibition of Traffic) Order 2002 No. 2002/1811. – Enabling power: Road Traffic Regulation Act 1984, s. 14 (1) (a). – Made: 08.07.2002. Coming into force: 15.07.2002. Effect: None. Territorial extent & classification: E. Local *Unpublished*

The A6 Trunk Road (Various Lengths, Bedfordshire-Northamptonshire) (Temporary 40 Miles Per Hour Speed Restriction) Order 2002 No. 2002/1749. – Enabling power: Road Traffic Regulation Act 1984, s. 14 (1) (a). – Made: 28.06.2002. Coming into force: 05.07.2002. Effect: None. Territorial extent & classification: E. Local *Unpublished*

The A7 Trunk Road (Westlinton Bridge) (Temporary Restriction and Prohibition of Traffic) Order 2002 No. 2002/162. – Enabling power: Road Traffic Regulation Act 1984, s. 14 (1) (a). – Made: 23.01.2002. Coming into force: 01.02.2002. Effect: None. Territorial extent & classification: E. Local *Unpublished*

The A10 Trunk Road (Cheshunt - Thundridge, Hertfordshire) (Temporary Prohibition of Traffic) Order 2002 No. 2002/2129. – Enabling power: Road Traffic Regulation Act 1984, s. 14 (1) (a). – Made: 09.08.2002. Coming into force: 16.08.2002. Effect: None. Territorial extent & classification: E. Local *Unpublished*

The A10 Trunk Road (Moles Interchange, Hertfordshire) (Temporary Restriction and Prohibition of Traffic) Order 2002 No. 2002/3258. – Enabling power: Road Traffic Regulation Act 1984, s. 14 (1) (a). Made: 27.12.2002. Coming into force: 03.01.2003. Effect: None. Territorial extent & classification: E. Local *Unpublished*

The A10 Trunk Road (Puckeridge - Colliers End, Hertfordshire) (Temporary 30 Miles Per Hour Speed Restriction) Order 2002 No. 2002/1582. – Enabling power: Road Traffic Regulation Act 1984, s. 14 (1) (a). – Made: 10.06.2002. Coming into force: 17.06.2002. Effect: None. Territorial extent & classification: E. Local *Unpublished*

The A10 Trunk Road (Royston to Braughing, Hertfordshire) (Temporary Restriction of Traffic) Order 2002 No. 2002/2413. – Enabling power: Road Traffic Regulation Act 1984, s. 14 (1) (a). – Made: 13.09.2002. Coming into force: 20.09.2002. Effect: None. Territorial extent & classification: E. Local *Unpublished*

The A10 Trunk Road (Thunderidge, Ware, Hertfordshire) (Temporary 30 Miles Per Hour Speed Restriction) Order 2002 No. 2002/2738. – Enabling power: Road Traffic Regulation Act 1984, s. 14 (1) (a). – Made: 01.11.2002. Coming into force: 08.11.2002. Effect: None. Territorial extent & classification: E. Local *Unpublished*

The A11 and A47 Trunk Roads (Norwich, Norwich) (Temporary 10 Miles Per Hour and 40 Miles Per Hour Speed Restriction) Order 2002 No. 2002/2131. – Enabling power: Road Traffic Regulation Act 1984, s. 14 (1) (a). – Made: 09.08.2002. Coming into force: 16.08.2002. Effect: None. Territorial extent & classification: E. Local *Unpublished*

The A11 Trunk Road (Barton Mills - Newmarket, Suffolk) (Temporary Restriction of Traffic) Order 2002 No. 2002/2395. – Enabling power: Road Traffic Regulation Act 1984, s. 14 (1) (a). – Made: 13.09.2002. Coming into force: 20.09.2002. Effect: None. Territorial extent & classification: E. Local *Unpublished*

The A11 Trunk Road (Besthorpe to Wymondham, Norfolk) (Temporary 40 Miles Per Hour Speed Restriction) Order 2002 No. 2002/168. – Enabling power: Road Traffic Regulation Act 1984, s. 14 (1) (a). – Made: 28.01.2002. Coming into force: 04.02.2002. Effect: None. Territorial extent & classification: E. Local *Unpublished*

The A11 Trunk Road (Elveden, Suffolk) (Temporary Restriction and Prohibition of Traffic) Order 2002 No. 2002/2333. – Enabling power: Road Traffic Regulation Act 1984, s. 14 (1) (a). – Made: 06.09.2002. Coming into force: 13.09.2002. Effect: None. Territorial extent & classification: E. Local *Unpublished*

The A11 Trunk Road (Six Mile Bottom, Cambridgeshire) (Temporary Restriction and Prohibition of Traffic) Order 2002 No. 2002/1531. – Enabling power: Road Traffic Regulation Act 1984, s. 14 (1) (a). – Made: 31.05.2002. Coming into force: 07.06.2002. Effect: None. Territorial extent & classification: E. Local *Unpublished*

The A11 Trunk Road (Snetterton, Norfolk) (Temporary 30 Miles Per Hour Speed Restriction) Order 2002 No. 2002/2492. – Enabling power: Road Traffic Regulation Act 1984, s. 14 (1) (a). – Made: 27.09.2002. Coming into force: 04.10.2002. Effect: None. Territorial extent & classification: E. Local *Unpublished*

The A11 Trunk Road (Thetford Bypass, Norfolk) (Temporary Restriction and Prohibition of Traffic) Order 2002 No. 2002/2140. – Enabling power: Road Traffic Regulation Act 1984, s. 14 (1) (a). – Made: 12.08.2002. Coming into force: 19.08.2002. Effect: None. Territorial extent & classification: E. Local *Unpublished*

The A11 Trunk Road (Wymondham, Norfolk) (Temporary Restriction and Prohibition of Traffic) Order 2002 No. 2002/2694. – Enabling power: Road Traffic Regulation Act 1984, s. 14 (1) (a). – Made: 25.10.2002. Coming into force: 01.11.2002. Effect: None. Territorial extent & classification: E. Local *Unpublished*

The A12 and A120 Trunk Roads (Colchester, Essex) (Temporary Restriction and Prohibition of Traffic) Order 2002 No. 2002/2009. – Enabling power: Road Traffic Regulation Act 1984, s. 14 (1) (a). – Made: 26.07.2002. Coming into force: 02.08.2002. Effect: None. Territorial extent & classification: E. Local *Unpublished*

The A12 and A120 Trunk Roads (Crown Interchange, Essex) (Temporary Prohibition of Traffic) Order 2002 No. 2002/3255. – Enabling power: Road Traffic Regulation Act 1984, s. 14 (1) (a). – Made: 30.12.2002. Coming into force: 06.01.2003. Effect: None. Territorial extent & classification: E. Local *Unpublished*

The A12 Trunk Road (Bascule Bridge, Lowestoft, Suffolk) (Temporary Prohibition of Traffic) Order 2002 No. 2002/416. – Enabling power: Road Traffic Regulation Act 1984, s. 14 (1) (a). – Made: 25.02.2002. Coming into force: 04.03.2002. Effect: None. Territorial extent & classification: E. Local *Unpublished*

The A12 Trunk Road (Blundeston Road - Market Lane, Suffolk) (Temporary Restriction and Prohibition of Traffic) Order 2002 No. 2002/2220. – Enabling power: Road Traffic Regulation Act 1984, s. 14 (1) (a). – Made: 27.08.2002. Coming into force: 03.09.2002. Effect: None. Territorial extent & classification: E. Local *Unpublished*

The A12 Trunk Road (Brentwood Bypass, Essex) (Temporary Prohibition of Traffic) Order 2002 No. 2002/2130. – Enabling power: Road Traffic Regulation Act 1984, s. 14 (1) (a). – Made: 09.08.2002. Coming into force: 16.08.2002. Effect: None. Territorial extent & classification: E. Local *Unpublished*

The A12 Trunk Road (Brentwood Bypass, Essex) (Temporary Restriction and Prohibition of Traffic) Order 2002 No. 2002/1193. – Enabling power: Road Traffic Regulation Act 1984, s. 14 (1) (a). – Made: 22.04.2002. Coming into force: 29.04.2002. Effect: None. Territorial extent & classification: E. Local *Unpublished*

The A12 Trunk Road (Breydon Bridge, Great Yarmouth, Norfolk) (Temporary Prohibition of Traffic) Order 2002 No. 2002/496. – Enabling power: Road Traffic Regulation Act 1984, s. 14 (1) (a) (7). – Made: 04.03.2002. Coming into force: 11.03.2002. Effect: None. Territorial extent & classification: E. Local *Unpublished*

The A12 Trunk Road (Brook Street Interchange - Trueloves Interchange, Brentwood, Essex) (Temporary Restriction and Prohibition of Traffic) Order 2002 No. 2002/2212. – Enabling power: Road Traffic Regulation Act 1984, s. 14 (1) (a). – Made: 23.08.2002. Coming into force: 30.08.2002. Effect: None. Territorial extent & classification: E. Local *Unpublished*

The A12 Trunk Road (Chelmsford Bypass, Essex) (Temporary 40 Miles Per Hour Speed Restriction) Order 2002 No. 2002/169. – Enabling power: Road Traffic Regulation Act 1984, s. 14 (1) (a). – Made: 28.01.2002. Coming into force: 04.02.2002. Effect: None. Territorial extent & classification: E. Local *Unpublished*

The A12 Trunk Road (Chelmsford Bypass, Essex) (Temporary Prohibition of Traffic) Order 2002 No. 2002/3256. – Enabling power: Road Traffic Regulation Act 1984, s. 14 (1) (a). – Made: 27.12.2002. Coming into force: 03.01.2003. Effect: None. Territorial extent & classification: E. Local *Unpublished*

The A12 Trunk Road (Colchester, Essex) (Temporary Restriction and Prohibition of Traffic) Order 2002 No. 2002/2412. – Enabling power: Road Traffic Regulation Act 1984, s. 14 (1) (a). – Made: 16.09.2002. Coming into force: 23.09.2002. Effect: None. Territorial extent & classification: E. Local *Unpublished*

The A12 Trunk Road (Copdock Mill Interchange, Suffolk) (Temporary 40 Miles Per Hour Speed Restriction) Order 2002 No. 2002/3254. – Enabling power: Road Traffic Regulation Act 1984, s. 14 (1) (a). – Made: 30.12.2002. Coming into force: 06.01.2003. Effect: None. Territorial extent & classification: E. Local *Unpublished*

The A12 Trunk Road (Feering, Essex) (Prohibition of "U" Turns and Right Turns) Order 2002 No. 2002/92. – Enabling power:Road Traffic Regulation Act 1984, ss. 1 (1), 2 (1) (2). – Made: 18.01.2002. Coming into force: 01.02.2002. Effect: None. Territorial extent & classification: E. Local *Unpublished*

The A12 Trunk Road (Feering to Marks Tey, Essex) (Temporary Prohibition of Traffic) Order 2002 No. 2002/61. – Enabling power: Road Traffic Regulation Act 1984, s. 14 (1) (b). – Made: 14.01.2002. Coming into force: 21.01.2002. Effect: None. Territorial extent & classification: E. Local *Unpublished*

The A12 Trunk Road (Galleywood - Margaretting, Essex) (Temporary 40 Miles Per Hour Speed Restriction) Order 2002 No. 2002/1956. – Enabling power: Road Traffic Regulation Act 1984, s. 14 (1) (a). – Made: 22.07.2002. Coming into force: 29.07.2002. Effect: None. Territorial extent & classification: E. Local *Unpublished*

The A12 Trunk Road (Great Yarmouth, Norfolk) (Temporary 10 Miles Per Hour and 30 Miles Per Hour Speed Restriction) Order 2002 No. 2002/495. – Enabling power: Road Traffic Regulation Act 1984, s. 14 (1) (a). – Made: 04.03.2002. Coming into force: 11.03.2002. Effect: None. Territorial extent & classification: E. Local *Unpublished*

The A12 Trunk Road (Lowestoft, Suffolk) (Temporary 10 Miles Per Hour and 30 Miles Per Hour Speed Restriction) Order 2002 No. 2002/170. – Enabling power: Road Traffic Regulation Act 1984, s. 14 (1) (a). – Made: 28.01.2002. Coming into force: 04.02.2002. Effect: None. Territorial extent & classification: E. Local *Unpublished*

The A12 Trunk Road (Lowestoft, Suffolk) (Temporary Restriction and Prohibition of Traffic) Order 2002 No. 2002/2219. – Enabling power: Road Traffic Regulation Act 1984, s. 14 (1) (a). – Made: 27.08.2002. Coming into force: 03.09.2002. Effect: None. Territorial extent & classification: E. Local *Unpublished*

The A12 Trunk Road (Marks Tey, Essex) (Prohibition of "U" Turns) Order 2002 No. 2002/738. – Enabling power: Road Traffic Regulation Act 1984, ss. 1 (1), 2 (1) (2). – Made: 14.03.2002. Coming into force: 28.03.2002. Effect: None. Territorial extent & classification: E. Local *Unpublished*

The A12 Trunk Road (Webbs Farm Interchange, Chelmsford, Essex) (Temporary Prohibition of Traffic) Order 2002 No. 2002/752. – Enabling power: Road Traffic Regulation Act 1984, s. 14 (1) (a). – Made: 18.03.2002. Coming into force: 25.03.2002. Effect: None. Territorial extent & classification: E. Local *Unpublished*

The A13 Trunk Road (M25 Junction 30, Slip Road) (Temporary 40 Miles Per Hour Speed Restriction) Order 2002 No. 2002/2654. – Enabling power: Road Traffic Regulation Act 1984, s. 14 (1) (b). – Made: 21.10.2002. Coming into force: 31.10.2002. Effect: None. Territorial extent & classification: E. Local *Unpublished*

The A14 and A428 Trunk Roads (Girton - Madingley, Cambridgeshire) (Temporary Prohibition of Traffic) Order 2002 No. 2002/1846. – Enabling power: Road Traffic Regulation Act 1984, s. 14 (1) (a). – Made: 12.07.2002. Coming into force: 19.07.2002. Effect: None. Territorial extent & classification: E. Local *Unpublished*

The A14 (M) Motorway (Rusts Lane, Alconbury, Cambridgeshire) (Temporary Prohibition of Traffic) Order 2002 No. 2002/1286. – Enabling power: Road Traffic Regulation Act 1984, s. 14 (1) (a). – Made: 07.05.2002. Coming into force: 14.05.2002. Effect: None. Territorial extent & classification: E. Local *Unpublished*

The A14 Trunk Road (B1106 Western Interchange, Bury St. Edmunds Bypass, Suffolk) (Temporary 50 Miles Per Hour Speed Restriction) Order 2002 No. 2002/1048. – Enabling power: Road Traffic Regulation Act 1984, s. 14 (1) (a). – Made: 02.04.2002. Coming into force: 09.04.2002. Effect: None. Territorial extent & classification: E. Local *Unpublished*

The A14 Trunk Road (Beacon Hill Interchange, Suffolk) (Temporary Restriction and Prohibition of Traffic) Order 2002 No. 2002/1800. – Enabling power: Road Traffic Regulation Act 1984, s. 14 (1) (a). – Made: 08.07.2002. Coming into force: 15.07.2002. Effect: None. Territorial extent & classification: E. Local *Unpublished*

The A14 Trunk Road (Beacon Hill, Suffolk - Histon, Cambridgeshire) (Temporary Restriction and Prohibition of Traffic) Order 2002 No. 2002/2737. – Enabling power: Road Traffic Regulation Act 1984, s. 14 (1) (a). – Made: 01.11.2002. Coming into force: 08.11.2002. Effect: None. Territorial extent & classification: E. Local *Unpublished*

The A14 Trunk Road (Bramford Road Bridge, Ipswich, Suffolk) (Temporary 40 Miles Per Hour Speed Restriction) Order 2002 No. 2002/2069. – Enabling power: Road Traffic Regulation Act 1984, s. 14 (1) (a). – Made: 02.08.2002. Coming into force: 09.08.2002. Effect: None. Territorial extent & classification: E. Local *Unpublished*

The A14 Trunk Road (Bury St. Edmunds, Slip Roads, Suffolk) (Temporary Prohibition of Traffic) Order 2002 No. 2002/1533. – Enabling power: Road Traffic Regulation Act 1984, s. 14 (1) (a). – Made: 31.05.2002. Coming into force: 07.06.2002. Effect: None. Territorial extent & classification: E. Local *Unpublished*

The A14 Trunk Road (Claydon - Bury St. Edmunds, Suffolk) (Temporary 40 Miles Per Hour Speed Restriction) Order 2002 No. 2002/1390. – Enabling power: Road Traffic Regulation Act 1984, s. 14 (1) (a). – Made: 14.05.2002. Coming into force: 21.05.2002. Effect: None. Territorial extent & classification: E. Local *Unpublished*

The A14 Trunk Road (Felixstowe, Suffolk) (Temporary Prohibition of Traffic) Order 2002 No. 2002/1812. – Enabling power: Road Traffic Regulation Act 1984, s. 14 (1) (a). – Made: 05.07.2002. Coming into force: 12.07.2002. Effect: None. Territorial extent & classification: E. Local *Unpublished*

The A14 Trunk Road (Fen Ditton, Cambridgeshire, Eastbound Slip Road) (Temporary Prohibition of Traffic) Order 2002 No. 2002/172. – Enabling power: Road Traffic Regulation Act 1984, s. 14 (1) (a). – Made: 28.01.2002. Coming into force: 04.02.2002. Effect: None. Territorial extent & classification: E. Local *Unpublished*

The A14 Trunk Road (Fen Drayton - Swavesey, Cambridgeshire) (Temporary Restriction and Prohibition of Traffic) Order 2002 No. 2002/1610. – Enabling power: Road Traffic Regulation Act 1984, s. 14 (1) (a). – Made: 17.06.2002. Coming into force: 24.06.2002. Effect: None. Territorial extent & classification: E. Local *Unpublished*

The A14 Trunk Road (Fenstanton Interchange, Westbound Exit Slip Road) (Temporary Prohibition of Traffic) Order 2002 No. 2002/1793. – Enabling power: Road Traffic Regulation Act 1984, s. 14 (1) (a). – Made: 08.07.2002. Coming into force: 15.07.2002. Effect: None. Territorial extent & classification: E. Local *Unpublished*

The A14 Trunk Road (Girton - Histon, Cambridgeshire) (Temporary Prohibition of Traffic) Order 2002 No. 2002/1194. – Enabling power: Road Traffic Regulation Act 1984, s. 14 (1) (a). Made: 22.04.2002. Coming into force: 29.04.2002. Effect: None. Territorial extent & classification: E. Local *Unpublished*

The A14 Trunk Road (Godmanchester Interchange, Cambridgeshire) (Temporary Prohibition of Traffic) Order 2002 No. 2002/1579. – Enabling power: Road Traffic Regulation Act 1984, s. 14 (1) (a). – Made: 10.06.2002. Coming into force: 17.06.2002. Effect: None. Territorial extent & classification: E. Local *Unpublished*

The A14 Trunk Road (Histon, Cambridgeshire - Whitton, Suffolk, Slip Roads) (Temporary Prohibition of Traffic) Order 2002 No. 2002/2068. – Enabling power: Road Traffic Regulation Act 1984, s. 14 (1) (a). – Made: 02.08.2002. Coming into force: 09.08.2002. Effect: None. Territorial extent & classification: E. Local *Unpublished*

The A14 Trunk Road (Huntingdon Railway Viaduct, Cambridgeshire) (Temporary Restriction and Prohibition of Traffic) Order 2002 No. 2002/2396. – Enabling power: Road Traffic Regulation Act 1984, s. 14 (1) (a). – Made: 16.09.2002. Coming into force: 23.09.2002. Effect: None. Territorial extent & classification: E. Local *Unpublished*

The A14 Trunk Road (Junction 26 Slip Roads, Fenstanton, Cambridgeshire) (Temporary Prohibition of Traffic) Order 2002 No. 2002/2546. – Enabling power: Road Traffic Regulation Act 1984, s. 14 (1) (a). – Made: 07.10.2002. Coming into force: 14.10.2002. Effect: None. Territorial extent & classification: E. Local *Unpublished*

The A14 Trunk Road (Junctions 2 - 10, Northamptonshire) (Temporary Restriction and Prohibition of Traffic) Order 2002 No. 2002/1637. – Enabling power: Road Traffic Regulation Act 1984, s. 14 (1) (a). – Made: 21.06.2002. Coming into force: 28.06.2002. Effect: None. Territorial extent & classification: E. Local *Unpublished*

The A14 Trunk Road (Junctions 9 - 10, Kettering, Northamptonshire) (Temporary Prohibition of Traffic) Order 2002 No. 2002/301. – Enabling power: Road Traffic Regulation Act 1984, s. 14 (1) (a). – Made: 11.02.2002. Coming into force: 18.02.2002. Effect: None. Territorial extent & classification: E. Local *Unpublished*

The A14 Trunk Road (Junctions 10-13, Northamptonshire) (Temporary Prohibition of Traffic) Order 2002 No. 2002/2612. – Enabling power: Road Traffic Regulation Act 1984, s. 14 (1) (a). – Made: 14.10.2002. Coming into force: 21.10.2002. Effect: None. Territorial extent & classification: E. Local *Unpublished*

The A14 Trunk Road (Keyston, Cambridgeshire) (Temporary Prohibition of Traffic) Order 2002 No. 2002/2432. – Enabling power: Road Traffic Regulation Act 1984, s. 14 (1) (a). – Made: 20.09.2002. Coming into force: 27.09.2002. Effect: None. Territorial extent & classification: E. Local *Unpublished*

The A14 Trunk Road (Levington, Seven Hills Interchange, Suffolk) (Temporary 30 Miles Per Hour Speed Restriction) Order 2002 No. 2002/497. – Enabling power: Road Traffic Regulation Act 1984, s. 14 (1) (a). – Made: 04.03.2002. Coming into force: 11.03.2002. Effect: None. Territorial extent & classification: E. Local *Unpublished*

The A14 Trunk Road (Milton - Histon Interchanges, Cambridgeshire) (Temporary 40 Miles Per Hour Speed Restriction) Order 2002 No. 2002/2699. – Enabling power: Road Traffic Regulation Act 1984, s. 14 (1) (a). – Made: 25.10.2002. Coming into force: 01.11.2002. Effect: None. Territorial extent & classification: E. Local *Unpublished*

The A14 Trunk Road (Oakington/Dry Drayton Interchange, Cambridgeshire) (Prohibition of Entry) Order 2002 No. 2002/2472. – Enabling power: Road Traffic Regulation Act 1984, s. 1 (1), 2 (1) (2). – Made: 23.09.2002. Coming into force: 07.10.2002. Effect: None. Territorial extent & classification: E. Local *Unpublished*

The A14 Trunk Road (Orwell Bridge to Copdock Interchange) (Temporary Restriction and Prohibition of Traffic) Order 2002 No. 2002/1238. – Enabling power: Road Traffic Regulation Act 1984, s. 14 (1) (a). – Made: 30.04.2002. Coming into force: 07.05.2002. Effect: None. Territorial extent & classification: E. Local *Unpublished*

The A14 Trunk Road (Rothwell, Northamptonshire) (Temporary 40 Miles Per Hour Speed Restriction) Order 2002 No. 2002/2166. – Enabling power: Road Traffic Regulation Act 1984, s. 14 (1) (a). – Made: 16.08.2002. Coming into force: 23.08.2002. Effect: None. Territorial extent & classification: E. Local *Unpublished*

The A14 Trunk Road (Rougham, Suffolk) (Prohibition of Left Turns) Order 2002 No. 2002/899. – Enabling power: Road Traffic Regulation Act 1984, ss. 1 (1), 2 (1) (2). – Made: 21.03.2002. Coming into force: 04.04.2002. Effect: None. Territorial extent & classification: E. Local *Unpublished*

The A14 Trunk Road (Rowley Mile Layby, Newmarket, Suffolk) (Prohibition of Entry) Order 2002 No. 2002/807. – Enabling power: Road Traffic Regulation Act 1984, ss. 1 (1), 2 (1) (2). – Made: 15.03.2002. Coming into force: 29.03.2002. Effect: None. Territorial extent & classification: E. Local *Unpublished*

The A14 Trunk Road (Seven Hills Interchange - Stowmarket Interchange, Suffolk) (Temporary 40 Miles Per Hour Speed Restriction) Order 2002 No. 2002/3253. – Enabling power: Road Traffic Regulation Act 1984, s. 14 (1) (a). – Made: 30.12.2002. Coming into force: 06.01.2003. Effect: None. Territorial extent & classification: E. Local *Unpublished*

The A14 Trunk Road (Spittals Interchange, Cambridgeshire) (Temporary Prohibition of Traffic) Order 2002 No. 2002/2625. – Enabling power: Road Traffic Regulation Act 1984, s. 14 (1) (a). – Made: 04.10.2002. Coming into force: 11.10.2002. Effect: None. Territorial extent & classification: E. Local *Unpublished*

The A14 Trunk Road (Stowmarket, North Interchange to Beacon Hill Interchange, Stowmarket, Suffolk) (Temporary Prohibition of Traffic) Order 2002 No. 2002/2066. – Enabling power: Road Traffic Regulation Act 1984, s. 14 (1) (a). – Made: 02.08.2002. Coming into force: 09.08.2002. Effect: None. Territorial extent & classification: E. Local *Unpublished*

The A14 Trunk Road (Trimley St. Mary, Suffolk) (Prohibition of Entry) Order 2002 No. 2002/220. – Enabling power:Road Traffic Regulation Act 1984, ss. 1 (1), 2 (1) (2). – Made: 01.02.2002. Coming into force: 15.02.2002. Effect: None. Territorial extent & classification: E. Local *Unpublished*

The A14 Trunk Road (Various Lengths, Cambridgeshire - Northamptonshire) (Temporary 40 Miles Per Hour Speed Restriction) Order 2002 No. 2002/1961. – Enabling power: Road Traffic Regulation Act 1984, s. 14 (1) (a). – Made: 22.07.2002. Coming into force: 29.07.2002. Effect: None. Territorial extent & classification: E. Local *Unpublished*

The A14 Trunk Road (Westley - Moreton Hall Interchanges, Bury St. Edmunds, Suffolk) (Temporary Restriction and Prohibition of Traffic) Order 2002 No. 2002/2734. – Enabling power: Road Traffic Regulation Act 1984, s. 14 (1) (a). – Made: 01.11.2002. Coming into force: 08.11.2002. Effect: None. Territorial extent & classification: E. Local *Unpublished*

The A14 Trunk Road (Wherstead Interchange - Copdock Interchange, Suffolk) (Temporary Prohibition of Traffic) Order 2002 No. 2002/2210. – Enabling power: Road Traffic Regulation Act 1984, s. 14 (1) (a). – Made: 23.08.2002. Coming into force: 30.08.2002. Effect: None. Territorial extent & classification: E. Local *Unpublished*

The A14 Trunk Road (Woolpit Interchange - Haughley Park Interchange, Suffolk) (Temporary Restriction and Prohibition of Traffic) Order 2002 No. 2002/3257. – Enabling power: Road Traffic Regulation Act 1984, s. 14 (1) (a). – Made: 27.12.2002. Coming into force: 03.01.2003. Effect: None. Territorial extent & classification: E. Local *Unpublished*

The A15 Trunk Road (Annual Lincolnshire Show) (Temporary Restriction and Prohibition of Traffic) Order 2002 No. 2002/1544. – Enabling power: Road Traffic Regulation Act 1984, s. 14 (1) (b). – Made: 05.06.2002. Coming into force: 12.06.2002. Effect: None. Territorial extent & classification: E. Local *Unpublished*

The A16 Trunk Road (Dalby to Ulceby Cross, Lincolnshire) (Temporary Restriction and Prohibition of Traffic) Order 2002 No. 2002/1054. – Enabling power: Road Traffic Regulation Act 1984, s. 14 (1) (a). – Made: 08.04.2002. Coming into force: 15.04.2002. Effect: None. Territorial extent & classification: E. Local *Unpublished*

The A16 Trunk Road (Holton - le - Clay, Lincolnshire) (Temporary Restriction and Prohibition of Traffic) Order 2002 No. 2002/935. – Enabling power: Road Traffic Regulation Act 1984, s. 14 (1) (a). – Made: 25.03.2002. Coming into force: 01.04.2002. Effect: None. Territorial extent & classification: E. Local *Unpublished*

The A16 Trunk Road (Policemans Corner, Deeping St. Nicholas, Lincolnshire) (Temporary 10 Miles Per Hour Speed Restriction) Order 2002 No. 2002/26. – Enabling power: Road Traffic Regulation Act 1984, s. 14 (1) (a). – Made: 07.01.2002. Coming into force: 14.01.2002. Effect: None. Territorial extent & classification: E. Local *Unpublished*

The A17 Trunk Road (Swineshead Bypass, Lincolnshire) (Temporary Restriction and Prohibition of Traffic) Order 2002 No. 2002/962. – Enabling power: Road Traffic Regulation Act 1984, s. 14 (1) (a). – Made: 02.04.2002. Coming into force: 08.04.2002. Effect: None. Territorial extent & classification: E. Local *Unpublished*

The A17 Trunk Road (Swineshead Level Crossing, Lincolnshire) (Temporary Prohibition of Traffic) Order 2002 No. 2002/516. – Enabling power: Road Traffic Regulation Act 1984, s. 14 (1) (a). – Made: 06.03.2002. Coming into force: 13.03.2002. Effect: None. Territorial extent & classification: E. Local *Unpublished*

The A19/A66 Trunk Roads (Stockton Road Interchange) (Temporary 50 Miles Per Hour Speed Restriction) Order 2002 No. 2002/3194. – Enabling power: Road Traffic Regulation Act 1984, s. 14 (1) (b). – Made: 18.12.2002. Coming into force: 19.12.2002. Effect: None. Territorial extent & classification: E. Local *Unpublished*

The A19/A66 Trunk Roads (Stockton Road Interchange) (Temporary Prohibition of Traffic) Order 2002 No. 2002/2229. – Enabling power: Road Traffic Regulation Act 1984, s. 14 (1) (a). – Made: 28.08.2002. Coming into force: 01.09.2002. Effect: None. Territorial extent & classification: E. Local *Unpublished*

The A19/A66 Trunk Roads (Tees Viaduct) (Temporary Prohibition of Traffic) Order 2002 No. 2002/18. – Enabling power: Road Traffic Regulation Act 1984, s. 14 (1) (a). – Made: 03.01.2002. Coming into force: 06.01.2002. Effect: None. Territorial extent & classification: E. Local *Unpublished*

The A19 Trunk Road and A168 Trunk Road (York Road Interchange, Thirsk) (Temporary Prohibition of Traffic) Order 2002 No. 2002/2360. – Enabling power: Road Traffic Regulation Act 1984, s. 14 (1) (a). – Made: 10.09.2002. Coming into force: 13.09.2002. Effect: None. Territorial extent & classification: E. Local *Unpublished*

The A19 Trunk Road (Catchgate Bridge) (Temporary Restriction and Prohibition of Traffic) Order 2002 No. 2002/2435. – Enabling power: Road Traffic Regulation Act 1984, s. 14 (1) (a). – Made: 19.09.2002. Coming into force: 22.09.2002. Effect: None. Territorial extent & classification: E. Local *Unpublished*

The A19 Trunk Road (Crathorne Interchange to Parkway Interchange) (Temporary Restriction and Prohibition of Traffic) Order 2002 No. 2002/2309. – Enabling power: Road Traffic Regulation Act 1984, s. 14 (1) (a). – Made: 04.09.2002. Coming into force: 08.09.2002. Effect: None. Territorial extent & classification: E. Local *Unpublished*

The A19 Trunk Road (Knayton) and the A174 Trunk Road (Acklam) (Temporary Prohibition of Traffic) Order 2002 No. 2002/2446. – Enabling power: Road Traffic Regulation Act 1984, s. 14 (1) (a). – Made: 20.09.2002. Coming into force: 24.09.2002. Effect: None. Territorial extent & classification: E. Local *Unpublished*

The A19 Trunk Road (Riccall) (Temporary 10 Miles Per Hour and 40 Miles Per Hour Speed Restriction) Order 2002 No. 2002/2260. – Enabling power: Road Traffic Regulation Act 1984, s. 14 (1) (a). – Made: 30.08.2002. Coming into force: 03.09.2002. Effect: None. Territorial extent & classification: E. Local *Unpublished*

The A19 Trunk Road (Seaton to Murton) (Temporary 50 Miles Per Hour Speed Restriction) Order 2002 No. 2002/2460. – Enabling power: Road Traffic Regulation Act 1984, s. 14 (1) (a). – Made: 19.09.2002. Coming into force: 22.09.2002. Effect: None. Territorial extent & classification: E. Local *Unpublished*

The A19 Trunk Road (Sheraton to Dalton Piercy) (Temporary Restriction and Prohibition of Traffic) Order 2002 No. 2002/1110. – Enabling power: Road Traffic Regulation Act 1984, s. 14 (1) (a). – Made: 15.04.2002. Coming into force: 15.04.2002. Effect: None. Territorial extent & classification: E. Local *Unpublished*

The A19 Trunk Road (South Kilvington Bridge and Hag Lane Bridge, Thirsk) (Temporary Prohibition of Traffic) Order 2002 No. 2002/2100. – Enabling power: Road Traffic Regulation Act 1984, s. 14 (1) (a). – Made: 07.08.2002. Coming into force: 11.08.2002. Effect: None. Territorial extent & classification: E. Local *Unpublished*

The A19 Trunk Road (Stockton Road Interchange to Parkway Interchange) (Temporary Restriction and Prohibition of Traffic) Order 2002 No. 2002/911. – Enabling power: Road Traffic Regulation Act 1984, s. 14 (1) (a). – Made: 27.03.2002. Coming into force: 02.04.2002. Effect: None. Territorial extent & classification: E. Local *Unpublished*

The A19 Trunk Road (Stockton Road Interchange to Portrack Interchange) and A66 Trunk Road (Stockton Road Interchange) (Temporary Prohibition of Traffic) Order 2002 No. 2002/2445. – Enabling power: Road Traffic Regulation Act 1984, s. 14 (1) (a). – Made: 18.09.2002. Coming into force: 22.09.2002. Effect: None. Territorial extent & classification: E. Local *Unpublished*

The A19 Trunk Road (The Tontine to South Kilvington Interchange) (Temporary 50 Miles Per Hour Speed Restriction) Order 2002 No. 2002/2461. – Enabling power: Road Traffic Regulation Act 1984, s. 14 (1) (a). – Made: 19.09.2002. Coming into force: 22.09.2002. Effect: None. Territorial extent & classification: E. Local *Unpublished*

The A19 Trunk Road (Various Locations) (Temporary 10 Miles Per Hour, 20 Miles Per Hour, 30 Miles Per Hour and 40 Miles Per Hour Speed Restriction) Order 2002 No. 2002/11. – Enabling power: Road Traffic Regulation Act 1984, s. 14 (1) (a) (b). – Made: 04.01.2002. Coming into force: 06.01.2002. Effect: None. Territorial extent & classification: E. Local *Unpublished*

The A19 Trunk Road (Wolviston Interchange to Stockton Ring Road Interchange) (Temporary Prohibition of Traffic) Order 2002 No. 2002/1249. – Enabling power: Road Traffic Regulation Act 1984, s. 14 (1) (a). – Made: 01.05.2002. Coming into force: 07.05.2002. Effect: None. Territorial extent & classification: E. Local *Unpublished*

The A20 Trunk Road (Limekiln Roundabout and the Viaduct, Dover) (Temporary Restriction of Traffic) Order 2002 No. 2002/970. – Enabling power: Road Traffic Regulation Act 1984, s. 14 (1) (a). – Made: 02.04.2002. Coming into force: 06.04.2002. Effect: None. Territorial extent & classification: E. Local *Unpublished*

The A20 Trunk Road (Roundhill Tunnels) (Temporary Prohibition of Traffic) Order 2002 No. 2002/2347. – Enabling power: Road Traffic Regulation Act 1984, s. 14 (1) (a). – Made: 09.09.2002. Coming into force: 14.09.2002. Effect: None. Territorial extent & classification: E. Local *Unpublished*

The A20 Trunk Road (The Viaduct and Lord Warden Square, Dover) (Temporary 10 Miles Per Hour Speed Restriction) Order 2002 No. 2002/2580. – Enabling power: Road Traffic Regulation Act 1984, s. 14 (1) (a). – Made: 14.10.2002. Coming into force: 19.10.2002. Effect: None. Territorial extent & classification: E. Local *Unpublished*

The A20 Trunk Road (Townwall Street, Dover) (Temporary Restriction of Traffic) Order 2002 No. 2002/1306. – Enabling power: Road Traffic Regulation Act 1984, s. 14 (1) (a). – Made: 13.05.2002. Coming into force: 18.05.2002. Effect: None. Territorial extent & classification: E. Local *Unpublished*

The A21 Trunk Road (Flimwell) (Temporary 30 Miles Per Hour Speed Restriction) Order 2002 No. 2002/31. – Enabling power: Road Traffic Regulation Act 1984, s. 14 (1) (a). – Made: 07.01.2002. Coming into force: 12.01.2002. Effect: None. Territorial extent & classification: E. Local *Unpublished*

The A21 Trunk Road (Longfield Roundabout) (Temporary 40 mph Speed Restriction) Order 2002 No. 2002/2146. – Enabling power: Road Traffic Regulation Act 1984, s. 14 (1) (a). – Made: 12.08.2002. Coming into force: 17.08.2002. Effect: None. Territorial extent & classification: E. Local *Unpublished*

The A21 Trunk Road (North of Lamberhurst) (Temporary 30 Miles Per Hour Speed Restriction) Order 2002 No. 2002/2558. – Enabling power: Road Traffic Regulation Act 1984, s. 14 (1) (a). – Made: 07.10.2002. Coming into force: 12.10.2002. Effect: None. Territorial extent & classification: E. Local *Unpublished*

The A21 Trunk Road (Sevenoaks Bypass) (Temporary Restriction and Prohibition of Traffic) Order 2002 No. 2002/740. – Enabling power: Road Traffic Regulation Act 1984, s. 14 (1) (a). – Made: 18.03.2002. Coming into force: 23.03.2002. Effect: None. Territorial extent & classification: E. Local *Unpublished*

The A21 Trunk Road (Tonbridge Bypass, Londonbound Carriageway) (Temporary Prohibition of Traffic) Order 2002 No. 2002/2459. – Enabling power: Road Traffic Regulation Act 1984, s. 14 (1) (a). – Made: 23.09.2002. Coming into force: 28.09.2002. Effect: None. Territorial extent & classification: E. Local *Unpublished*

The A21 Trunk Road (Various Locations) (Temporary Speed Restrictions) Order 2002 No. 2002/2094. – Enabling power: Road Traffic Regulation Act 1984, s. 14 (1) (a). – Made: 05.08.2002. Coming into force: 10.08.2002. Effect: None. Territorial extent & classification: E. Local *Unpublished*

The A23 Trunk Road and the M23 Motorway (Airport Way, Junction 9A and Junction 10) (Temporary 50 Miles Per Hour Speed Restriction) Order 2002 No. 2002/2698. – Enabling power: Road Traffic Regulation Act 1984, s. 14 (1) (a). – Made: 28.10.2002. Coming into force: 01.11.2002. Effect: None. Territorial extent & classification: E. Local *Unpublished*

The A23 Trunk Road (Hickstead and Pyecombe) (Temporary Restriction and Prohibition of Traffic) Order 2002 No. 2002/2913. – Enabling power: Road Traffic Regulation Act 1984, s. 14 (1) (a). – Made: 25.11.2002. Coming into force: 30.11.2002. Effect: None. Territorial extent & classification: E. Local *Unpublished*

The A26 Trunk Road (Beddingham Roundabout - The Lay) (Temporary Speed Restrictions) Order 2002 No. 2002/2582. – Enabling power: Road Traffic Regulation Act 1984, s. 14 (1) (a). – Made: 14.10.2002. Coming into force: 19.10.2002. Effect: None. Territorial extent & classification: E. Local *Unpublished*

The A26 Trunk Road (Newhaven Gateway) (Temporary Speed Restrictions) Order 2002 No. 2002/2190. – Enabling power: Road Traffic Regulation Act 1984, s. 14 (1) (a). – Made: 19.08.2002. Coming into force: 24.08.2002. Effect: None. Territorial extent & classification: E. Local *Unpublished*

The A27 Trunk Road (Adur Interchange) (Temporary Restriction and Prohibition of Traffic) Order 2002 No. 2002/1753. – Enabling power: Road Traffic Regulation Act 1984, s. 14 (1) (a). – Made: 01.07.2002. Coming into force: 06.07.2002. Effect: None. Territorial extent & classification: E. Local *Unpublished*

The A27 Trunk Road (Beddingham Level Crossing) (Temporary Prohibition of Traffic) (No. 2) Order 2002 No. 2002/1570. – Enabling power: Road Traffic Regulation Act 1984, s. 14 (1) (a) (5) (b) (7). – Made: 10.06.2002. Coming into force: 17.06.2002. Effect: None. Territorial extent & classification: E. Local *Unpublished*

The A27 Trunk Road (Beddingham Level Crossing) (Temporary Prohibition of Traffic) (No. 3) Order 2002 No. 2002/2095. – Enabling power: Road Traffic Regulation Act 1984, s. 14 (1) (a) (5) (b) (7). – Made: 05.08.2002. Coming into force: 12.08.2002. Effect: None. Territorial extent & classification: E. Local *Unpublished*

The A27 Trunk Road (Beddingham Level Crossing) (Temporary Prohibition of Traffic) Order 2002 No. 2002/665. – Enabling power: Road Traffic Regulation Act 1984, s. 14 (1) (a) (5) (b) (7). Made: 11.03.2002. Coming into force: 18.03.2002. Effect: None. Territorial extent & classification: E. Local *Unpublished*

The A27 Trunk Road (Berwick Roundabout) (Temporary 30 Miles Per Hour Speed Restriction) Order 2002 No. 2002/218. – Enabling power: Road Traffic Regulation Act 1984, s. 14 (1) (a). – Made: 04.02.2002. Coming into force: 09.02.2002. Effect: None. Territorial extent & classification: E. Local *Unpublished*

The A27 Trunk Road (Broad Marsh, Slip Road) (Temporary Prohibition of Traffic) Order 2002 No. 2002/2504. – Enabling power: Road Traffic Regulation Act 1984, s. 14 (1) (a). – Made: 30.09.2002. Coming into force: 05.10.2002. Effect: None. Territorial extent & classification: E. Local *Unpublished*

The A27 Trunk Road (Brockhampton Road Bridge) (Temporary Restriction and Prohibition of Traffic) Order 2002 No. 2002/2853. – Enabling power: Road Traffic Regulation Act 1984, s. 14 (1) (a). – Made: 18.11.2002. Coming into force: 23.11.2002. Effect: None. Territorial extent & classification: E. Local *Unpublished*

The A27 Trunk Road (Chichester Bypass, Eastbound Carriageway) (Temporary 50 Miles per Hour Speed Restriction) Order 2002 No. 2002/2809. – Enabling power: Road Traffic Regulation Act 1984, s. 14 (1) (a). – Made: 11.11.2002. Coming into force: 16.11.2002. Effect: None. Territorial extent & classification: E. Local *Unpublished*

The A27 Trunk Road (Chichester Bypass, Westbound Carriageway) (Temporary 50 Miles Per Hour Speed Restriction) Order 2002 No. 2002/2458. – Enabling power: Road Traffic Regulation Act 1984, s. 14 (1) (a). – Made: 23.09.2002. Coming into force: 28.09.2002. Effect: None. Territorial extent & classification: E. Local *Unpublished*

The A27 Trunk Road (Crossbush, Westbound Carriageway) (Temporary 40 Miles Per Hour Speed Restriction) Order 2002 No. 2002/2457. – Enabling power: Road Traffic Regulation Act 1984, s. 14 (1) (a). – Made: 23.09.2002. Coming into force: 28.09.2002. Effect: None. Territorial extent & classification: E. Local *Unpublished*

The A27 Trunk Road (Hammerpot) (Temporary 50 Miles Per Hour Speed Restriction) Order 2002 No. 2002/2341. – Enabling power: Road Traffic Regulation Act 1984, s. 14 (1) (a). – Made: 09.09.2002. Coming into force: 14.09.2002. Effect: None. Territorial extent & classification: E. Local – Revoked by S.I. 2003/1358 (unpublished) *Unpublished*

The A27 Trunk Road (Holmbush, Eastbound Exit Slip Road) (Temporary 40 Miles Per Hour Speed Restriction) Order 2002 No. 2002/1343. – Enabling power: Road Traffic Regulation Act 1984, s. 14 (1) (a). – Made: 13.05.2002. Coming into force: 18.05.2002. Effect: None. Territorial extent & classification: E. Local *Unpublished*

The A27 Trunk Road (Kingston to Hangleton) (Temporary Prohibition of Traffic) (No. 2) Order 2002 No. 2002/902. – Enabling power: Road Traffic Regulation Act 1984, s. 14 (1) (a). – Made: 25.03.2002. Coming into force: 01.04.2002. Effect: None. Territorial extent & classification: E. Local *Unpublished*

The A27 Trunk Road (Kingston to Hangleton) (Temporary Prohibition of Traffic) Order 2002 No. 2002/484. – Enabling power: Road Traffic Regulation Act 1984, s. 14 (1) (b). – Made: 04.03.2002. Coming into force: 09.03.2002. Effect: None. Territorial extent & classification: E. Local *Unpublished*

The A27 Trunk Road (Lancing) (Temporary 10 Miles Per Hour Speed Restriction) Order 2002 No. 2002/2560. – Enabling power: Road Traffic Regulation Act 1984, s. 14 (1) (a). – Made: 07.10.2002. Coming into force: 12.10.2002. Effect: None. Territorial extent & classification: E. Local *Unpublished*

The A27 Trunk Road (Lancing) (Temporary 30 Miles Per Hour Speed Restriction) Order 2002 No. 2002/1751. – Enabling power: Road Traffic Regulation Act 1984, s. 14 (1) (a). – Made: 01.07.2002. Coming into force: 06.07.2002. Effect: None. Territorial extent & classification: E. Local *Unpublished*

The A27 Trunk Road (Newmarket, Eastbound Carriageway) (Temporary 40 Miles Per Hour Speed Restriction) Order 2002 No. 2002/2191. – Enabling power: Road Traffic Regulation Act 1984, s. 14 (1) (a). – Made: 19.08.2002. Coming into force: 24.08.2002. Effect: None. Territorial extent & classification: E. Local *Unpublished*

The A27 Trunk Road (Norton - Arundel) (Temporary 40 Miles per Hour Speed Restriction) Order 2002 No. 2002/2790. – Enabling power: Road Traffic Regulation Act 1984, s. 14 (1) (a). – Made: 11.11.2002. Coming into force: 16.11.2002. Effect: None. Territorial extent & classification: E. Local *Unpublished*

The A27 Trunk Road (Old Shoreham Road and Shoreham Bypass) (Temporary Restriction of Traffic) (No. 2) Order 2002 No. 2002/2556. – Enabling power: Road Traffic Regulation Act 1984, s. 14 (1) (a). – Made: 07.10.2002. Coming into force: 12.10.2002. Effect: None. Territorial extent & classification: E. Local *Unpublished*

The A27 Trunk Road (Old Shoreham Road and Shoreham Bypass) (Temporary Restriction of Traffic) Order 2002 No. 2002/2194. – Enabling power: Road Traffic Regulation Act 1984, s. 14 (1) (b). – Made: 19.08.2002. Coming into force: 24.08.2002. Effect: None. Territorial extent & classification: E. Local *Unpublished*

The A27 Trunk Road (Poling - Hammerpot) (Temporary Speed Restrictions) Order 2002 No. 2002/2581. – Enabling power: Road Traffic Regulation Act 1984, s. 14 (1) (a). – Made: 14.10.2002. Coming into force: 19.10.2002. Effect: None. Territorial extent & classification: E. Local *Unpublished*

The A27 Trunk Road (Portfield Roundabout - Temple Bar Interchange) (Temporary 10 Miles Per Hour Speed Restriction) Order 2002 No. 2002/2511. – Enabling power: Road Traffic Regulation Act 1984, s. 14 (1) (a). – Made: 30.09.2002. Coming into force: 05.10.2002. Effect: None. Territorial extent & classification: E. Local *Unpublished*

The A27 Trunk Road (Ranscombe Hill) (Temporary 40 Miles Per Hour Speed Restriction) Order 2002 No. 2002/974. – Enabling power: Road Traffic Regulation Act 1984, s. 14 (1) (a). – Made: 02.04.2002. Coming into force: 06.04.2002. Effect: None. Territorial extent & classification: E. Local *Unpublished*

The A27 Trunk Road (Shoreham Bypass, Eastbound Carriageway) (Temporary 50 Miles Per Hour Speed Restriction) Order 2002 No. 2002/2557. – Enabling power: Road Traffic Regulation Act 1984, s. 14 (1) (a). – Made: 07.10.2002. Coming into force: 12.10.2002. Effect: None. Territorial extent & classification: E. Local *Unpublished*

The A27 Trunk Road (Temple Bar, Eastbound Carriageway) (Temporary Prohibition of Traffic) Order 2002 No. 2002/2914. – Enabling power: Road Traffic Regulation Act 1984, s. 14 (1) (a). – Made: 25.11.2002. Coming into force: 30.11.2002. Effect: None. Territorial extent & classification: E. Local *Unpublished*

The A27 Trunk Road (University of Sussex) (Temporary Restriction and Prohibition of Traffic) Order 2002 No. 2002/1633. – Enabling power: Road Traffic Regulation Act 1984, s. 14 (1) (a). – Made: 24.06.2002. Coming into force: 29.06.2002. Effect: None. Territorial extent & classification: E. Local *Unpublished*

The A27 Trunk Road (Westhampnett Bypass) (Temporary 50 Miles Per Hour Speed Restriction) Order 2002 No. 2002/1449. – Enabling power: Road Traffic Regulation Act 1984, s. 14 (1) (b). – Made: 27.05.2002. Coming into force: 31.05.2002. Effect: None. Territorial extent & classification: E. Local *Unpublished*

The A27 Trunk Road (Westhampnett Bypass) (Temporary Prohibition of Traffic) Order 2002 No. 2002/3066. – Enabling power: Road Traffic Regulation Act 1984, s. 14 (1) (a). – Made: 09.12.2002. Coming into force: 14.12.2002. Effect: None. Territorial extent & classification: E. Local *Unpublished*

The A30 Trunk Road (Bodmin Bypass) (Temporary Restriction of Traffic) Order 2002 No. 2002/1155. – Enabling power: Road Traffic Regulation Act 1984, s. 14 (1) (a). – Made: 22.04.2002. Coming into force: 26.04.2002. Effect: None. Territorial extent & classification: E. Local *Unpublished*

The A30 Trunk Road (Callywith Junction to Innis Downs Roundabout) (Temporary Prohibition of Traffic) Order 2002 No. 2002/512. – Enabling power: Road Traffic Regulation Act 1984, s. 14 (1) (a). – Made: 06.03.2002. Coming into force: 13.03.2002. Effect: None. Territorial extent & classification: E. Local *Unpublished*

The A30 Trunk Road (Helland, Near Bodmin) (Layby Closure) Order 2002 No. 2002/1936. – Enabling power: Road Traffic Regulation Act 1984, s. 1 (1), 2 (1) (2). – Made: 17.07.2002. Coming into force: 30.07.2002. Effect: None. Territorial extent & classification: E. Local *Unpublished*

The A30 Trunk Road (Honiton Bypass) (Temporary Prohibition and Restriction of Traffic) Order 2002 No. 2002/1237. – Enabling power: Road Traffic Regulation Act 1984, s. 14 (1) (a). – Made: 30.04.2002. Coming into force: 04.05.2002. Effect: None. Territorial extent & classification: E. Local *Unpublished*

The A30 Trunk Road (Innis Downs Roundabout) (Temporary Prohibition of Traffic) (No. 2) Order 2002 No. 2002/1778. – Enabling power: Road Traffic Regulation Act 1984, s. 14 (1) (b) (5) (b), sch. 9, para. 27. – Made: 10.07.2002. Coming into force: 12.07.2002. Effect: S.I. 2002/1447 revoked. Territorial extent & classification: E. Local *Unpublished*

The A30 Trunk Road (Innis Downs Roundabout) (Temporary Prohibition of Traffic) Order 2002 No. 2002/1447. – Enabling power: Road Traffic Regulation Act 1984, s. 14 (1) (b). – Made: 24.05.2002. Coming into force: 31.05.2002. Effect: None. Territorial extent & classification: E. Local – Revoked by S.I. 2002/1778 (Unpublished) *Unpublished*

The A30 Trunk Road (M25 Junction 13) (Temporary Prohibition of Traffic) Order 2002 No. 2002/2583. – Enabling power: Road Traffic Regulation Act 1984, s. 14 (1) (a). – Made: 14.10.2002. Coming into force: 19.10.2002. Effect: None. Territorial extent & classification: E. Local *Unpublished*

The A30 Trunk Road (Near Cutteridge Lane Overbridge, Near Exeter) (Temporary Restriction of Traffic) Order 2002 No. 2002/2391. – Enabling power: Road Traffic Regulation Act 1984, s. 14 (1) (a). – Made: 16.09.2002. Coming into force: 21.09.2002. Effect: None. Territorial extent & classification: E. Local *Unpublished*

The A30 Trunk Road (Temple to Bolventor) (Temporary Prohibition and Restriction of Traffic) Order 2002 No. 2002/662. – Enabling power: Road Traffic Regulation Act 1984, s. 14 (1) (a). – Made: 11.03.2002. Coming into force: 16.03.2002. Effect: None. Territorial extent & classification: E. Local *Unpublished*

The A30 Trunk Road (Tregoss Moor) (Temporary Prohibition of Traffic) Order 2002 No. 2002/2803. – Enabling power: Road Traffic Regulation Act 1984, s. 14 (1) (b). – Made: 11.11.2002. Coming into force: 15.11.2002. Effect: None. Territorial extent & classification: E. Local *Unpublished*

The A31 Trunk Road (Ashley Heath, Eastbound Exit Slip Road) (Temporary Prohibition of Traffic) Order 2002 No. 2002/1512. – Enabling power: Road Traffic Regulation Act 1984, s. 14 (1) (a). – Made: 05.06.2002. Coming into force: 08.06.2002. Effect: None. Territorial extent & classification: E. Local *Unpublished*

The A31 Trunk Road (B3074 Junction) (Temporary Speed Restrictions) Order 2002 No. 2002/2288. – Enabling power: Road Traffic Regulation Act 1984, s. 14 (1) (a). – Made: 02.09.2002. Coming into force: 07.09.2002. Effect: None. Territorial extent & classification: E. Local *Unpublished*

The A31 Trunk Road (Bere Regis - Corfe Mullen) (24 Hours Clearway) Order 2002 No. 2002/1547. – Enabling power: Road Traffic Regulation Act 1984, ss. 1 (1), 2 (1) (2), 4 (1). – Made: 05.06.2002. Coming into force: 17.06.2002. Effect: None. Territorial extent & classification: E. Local *Unpublished*

The A31 Trunk Road (Picket Post, Slip Road) (Temporary Prohibition of Traffic) Order 2002 No. 2002/1513. – Enabling power: Road Traffic Regulation Act 1984, s. 14 (1) (a). – Made: 05.06.2002. Coming into force: 08.06.2002. Effect: None. Territorial extent & classification: E. Local *Unpublished*

The A31 Trunk Road (Poulner and Verwood Road, Slip Roads) (Temporary Prohibition of Traffic) Order 2002 No. 2002/1463. – Enabling power: Road Traffic Regulation Act 1984, s. 14 (1) (a). – Made: 27.05.2002. Coming into force: 01.06.2002. Effect: None. Territorial extent & classification: E. Local *Unpublished*

The A31 Trunk Road (Ringwood) (Temporary 10 Miles Per Hour Speed Restriction) Order 2002 No. 2002/287. – Enabling power: Road Traffic Regulation Act 1984, s. 14 (1) (a). – Made: 11.02.2002. Coming into force: 16.02.2002. Effect: None. Territorial extent & classification: E. Local *Unpublished*

The A31 Trunk Road (Various Locations, Central Dorset) (Temporary Speed Restrictions) Order 2002 No. 2002/1514. – Enabling power: Road Traffic Regulation Act 1984, s. 14 (1) (a). – Made: 05.06.2002. Coming into force: 08.06.2002. Effect: None. Territorial extent & classification: E. Local *Unpublished*

The A31 Trunk Road (Various Locations, East Dorset) (Temporary Restriction of Traffic) Order 2002 No. 2002/1455. – Enabling power: Road Traffic Regulation Act 1984, s. 14 (1) (a). – Made: 27.05.2002. Coming into force: 01.06.2002. Effect: None. Territorial extent & classification: E. Local *Unpublished*

The A31 Trunk Road (Verwood Road, Slip Road) (Temporary Prohibition of Traffic) Order 2002 No. 2002/1815. – Enabling power: Road Traffic Regulation Act 1984, s. 14 (1) (a). – Made: 08.07.2002. Coming into force: 13.07.2002. Effect: None. Territorial extent & classification: E. Local *Unpublished*

The A34 Trunk Road (Beedon - Chieveley) (Temporary Prohibition of Traffic) Order 2002 No. 2002/3071. – Enabling power: Road Traffic Regulation Act 1984, s. 14 (1) (a). – Made: 09.12.2002. Coming into force: 14.12.2002. Effect: None. Territorial extent & classification: E. Local *Unpublished*

The A34 Trunk Road (Botley and Hinksey, Slip Roads) (Temporary Prohibition of Traffic) Order 2002 No. 2002/3168. Enabling power: Road Traffic Regulation Act 1984, s. 14 (1) (a). – Made: 16.12.2002. Coming into force: 21.12.2002. Effect: None. Territorial extent & classification: E. Local *Unpublished*

The A34 Trunk Road (Botley Interchange, Slip Road) (Temporary Prohibition of Traffic) Order 2002 No. 2002/969. – Enabling power: Road Traffic Regulation Act 1984, s. 14 (1) (a). – Made: 02.04.2002. Coming into force: 06.04.2002. Effect: None. Territorial extent & classification: E. Local *Unpublished*

The A34 Trunk Road (Botley Interchange, Southbound Carriageway) (Temporary Prohibition of Traffic) Order 2002 No. 2002/1159. – Enabling power: Road Traffic Regulation Act 1984, s. 14 (1) (a). – Made: 22.04.2002. Coming into force: 27.04.2002. Effect: None. Territorial extent & classification: E. Local *Unpublished*

The A34 Trunk Road (Botley Interchange) (Temporary Restriction and Prohibition of Traffic) Order 2002 No. 2002/2093. – Enabling power: Road Traffic Regulation Act 1984, s. 14 (1) (a). – Made: 05.08.2002. Coming into force: 10.08.2002. Effect: None. Territorial extent & classification: E. Local *Unpublished*

The A34 Trunk Road (Chieveley) (Temporary Speed Restrictions) Order 2002 No. 2002/2579. – Enabling power: Road Traffic Regulation Act 1984, s. 14 (1) (a). – Made: 14.10.2002. Coming into force: 19.10.2002. Effect: None. Territorial extent & classification: E. Local *Unpublished*

The A34 Trunk Road (Drayton, Southbound Carriageway) (Temporary Speed Restrictions) Order 2002 No. 2002/1454. – Enabling power: Road Traffic Regulation Act 1984, s. 14 (1) (a). – Made: 27.05.2002. Coming into force: 01.06.2002. Effect: None. Territorial extent & classification: E. Local *Unpublished*

The A34 Trunk Road (Hinksey Hill Interchange) (Temporary Restriction and Prohibition of Traffic) Order 2002 No. 2002/1462. – Enabling power: Road Traffic Regulation Act 1984, s. 14 (1) (a). – Made: 27.05.2002. Coming into force: 01.06.2002. Effect: None. Territorial extent & classification: E. Local *Unpublished*

The A34 Trunk Road (Junction with Darges Lane, Great Wyrley) (Temporary Prohibition of Traffic) Order 2002 No. 2002/1368. – Enabling power: Road Traffic Regulation Act 1984, s. 14 (1) (a). – Made: 10.05.2002. Coming into force: 17.05.2002. Effect: None. Territorial extent & classification: E. Local *Unpublished*

The A34 Trunk Road (Kidlington/Islip, Layby) (Temporary Prohibition of Traffic) Order 2002 No. 2002/3164. – Enabling power: Road Traffic Regulation Act 1984, s. 14 (1) (b). – Made: 16.12.2002. Coming into force: 24.12.2002. Effect: None. Territorial extent & classification: E. Local *Unpublished*

The A34 Trunk Road (Kidlington/Islip, Slip Road) (Temporary Prohibition of Traffic) Order 2002 No. 2002/371. – Enabling power: Road Traffic Regulation Act 1984, s. 14 (1) (a). – Made: 18.02.2002. Coming into force: 23.02.2002. Effect: None. Territorial extent & classification: E. Local *Unpublished*

The A34 Trunk Road (Marcham Interchange, Slip Roads) (Temporary Prohibition of Traffic) Order 2002 No. 2002/2449. – Enabling power: Road Traffic Regulation Act 1984, s. 14 (1) (a). – Made: 23.09.2002. Coming into force: 28.09.2002. Effect: None. Territorial extent & classification: E. Local *Unpublished*

The A34 Trunk Road (North of Bullington Cross) (Temporary Restriction and Prohibition of Traffic) Order 2002 No. 2002/2852. – Enabling power: Road Traffic Regulation Act 1984, s. 14 (1) (a). – Made: 18.11.2002. Coming into force: 23.11.2002. Effect: None. Territorial extent & classification: E. Local *Unpublished*

The A34 Trunk Road (North of Whitchurch) (Temporary Speed Restrictions) Order 2002 No. 2002/87. – Enabling power: Road Traffic Regulation Act 1984, s. 14 (1) (a). – Made: 21.01.2002. Coming into force: 26.01.2002. Effect: None. Territorial extent & classification: E. Local *Unpublished*

The A34 Trunk Road (Riverside Bridge to Gray's Bridge, Oxfordshire) (Temporary 10 mph and 40 mph Speed Restriction) Order 2002 No. 2002/2150. – Enabling power: Road Traffic Regulation Act 1984, s. 14 (1) (a). – Made: 12.08.2002. Coming into force: 17.08.2002. Effect: None. Territorial extent & classification: E. Local *Unpublished*

The A34 Trunk Road (South Wonston - M3 Junction 9) (Temporary Restriction and Prohibition of Traffic) Order 2002 No. 2002/2452. – Enabling power: Road Traffic Regulation Act 1984, s. 14 (1) (a). – Made: 23.09.2002. Coming into force: 28.09.2002. Effect: None. Territorial extent & classification: E. Local *Unpublished*

The A34 Trunk Road (Speed, Slip Road) (Temporary Prohibition of Traffic) Order 2002 No. 2002/2793. – Enabling power: Road Traffic Regulation Act 1984, s. 14 (1) (a). – Made: 11.11.2002. Coming into force: 16.11.2002. Effect: None. Territorial extent & classification: E. Local *Unpublished*

The A34 Trunk Road (Tot Hill and Bullington, Slip Roads) (Temporary Prohibition of Traffic) (No. 2) Order 2002 No. 2002/2968. – Enabling power: Road Traffic Regulation Act 1984, s. 14 (1) (a). – Made: 02.12.2002. Coming into force: 07.12.2002. Effect: None. Territorial extent & classification: E. Local *Unpublished*

The A34 Trunk Road (Tot Hill and Bullington, Slip Roads) (Temporary Prohibition of Traffic) Order 2002 No. 2002/2563. – Enabling power: Road Traffic Regulation Act 1984, s. 14 (1) (a). – Made: 07.10.2002. Coming into force: 12.10.2002. Effect: None. Territorial extent & classification: E. Local *Unpublished*

The A34 Trunk Road (Walsall Road, Cannock, Staffordshire) (Prohibition of Waiting) Order 2002 No. 2002/1370. – Enabling power: Road Traffic Regulation Act 1984, ss. 1 (1), 2 (1) (2), 4 (1) (2). – Made: 03.05.2002. Coming into force: 18.05.2002. Effect: None. Territorial extent & classification: E. Local *Unpublished*

The A35 Trunk Road (Charmouth to Chideock) (Temporary Prohibition and Restriction of Traffic) Order 2002 No. 2002/2474. – Enabling power: Road Traffic Regulation Act 1984, s. 14 (1) (a). – Made: 25.09.2002. Coming into force: 28.09.2002. Effect: None. Territorial extent & classification: E. Local *Unpublished*

The A36 Trunk Road (Brickworth Corner to Canada Common) (Temporary Prohibition of Traffic) Order 2002 No. 2002/1160. – Enabling power: Road Traffic Regulation Act 1984, s. 14 (1) (a). – Made: 18.04.2002. Coming into force: 19.04.2002. Effect: None. Territorial extent & classification: E. Local *Unpublished*

The A36 Trunk Road (Junction with A27) (Temporary Restriction of Traffic) Order 2002 No. 2002/1608. – Enabling power: Road Traffic Regulation Act 1984, s. 14 (1) (a). – Made: 17.06.2002. Coming into force: 22.06.2002. Effect: None. Territorial extent & classification: E. Local *Unpublished*

The A36 Trunk Road (Limpley Stoke) (Temporary Prohibition of Traffic) Order 2002 No. 2002/2230. – Enabling power: Road Traffic Regulation Act 1984, s. 14 (1) (a). – Made: 29.08.2002. Coming into force: 04.09.2002. Effect: None. Territorial extent & classification: E. Local *Unpublished*

The A36 Trunk Road (Plaitford, near West Wellow) (Temporary Prohibition and Restriction of Traffic) Order 2002 No. 2002/967. – Enabling power: Road Traffic Regulation Act 1984, s. 14 (1) (a). – Made: 02.04.2002. Coming into force: 06.04.2002. Effect: None. Territorial extent & classification: E. Local *Unpublished*

The A36 Trunk Road (Wilton Railway Bridge) (Temporary Prohibition of Traffic) Order 2002 No. 2002/481. – Enabling power: Road Traffic Regulation Act 1984, s. 14 (1) (a). – Made: 04.03.2002. Coming into force: 09.03.2002. Effect: None. Territorial extent & classification: E. Local *Unpublished*

The A36 Trunk Road (Wiltshire) (24 Hours Clearway) Order 2002 No. 2002/1051. – Enabling power: Road Traffic Regulation Act 1984, ss. 1 (1), 2 (1) (2), 3 (2), 4 (1), sch. 9, para. 27 (1). – Made: 08.04.2002. Coming into force: 19.04.2002. Effect: None. Territorial extent & classification: E. Local *Unpublished*

The A38 and A61 Trunk Roads (Watchorn Interchange) (Temporary 30 Miles Per Hour Speed Restriction) Order 2002 No. 2002/1088. – Enabling power: Road Traffic Regulation Act 1984, s. 14 (1) (a). – Made: 12.04.2002. Coming into force: 19.04.2002. Effect: None. Territorial extent & classification: E. Local *Unpublished*

The A38 Trunk Road (Abbey Hill, Derbyshire) (Temporary Restriction and Prohibition of Traffic) Order 2002 No. 2002/2499. – Enabling power: Road Traffic Regulation Act 1984, s. 14 (1) (a). – Made: 30.09.2002. Coming into force: 07.10.2002. Effect: None. Territorial extent & classification: E. Local *Unpublished*

The A38 Trunk Road (Ashburton) (Temporary Prohibition and Restriction of Traffic) Order 2002 No. 2002/16. – Enabling power: Road Traffic Regulation Act 1984, s. 14 (1) (a). – Made: 07.01.2002. Coming into force: 12.01.2002. Effect: None. Territorial extent & classification: E. Local *Unpublished*

The A38 Trunk Road (Avon Bridge) (Temporary Prohibition and Restriction of Traffic) Order 2002 No. 2002/2453. – Enabling power: Road Traffic Regulation Act 1984, s. 14 (1) (a). – Made: 23.09.2002. Coming into force: 28.09.2002. Effect: None. Territorial extent & classification: E. Local *Unpublished*

The A38 Trunk Road (Bittaford, Devon) (Closure of Layby) Order 2002 No. 2002/1103. – Enabling power: Road Traffic Regulation Act 1984, ss. 1 (1), 2 (1) (2). – Made: 05.04.2002. Coming into force: 15.04.2002. Effect: None. Territorial extent & classification: E. Local *Unpublished*

The A38 Trunk Road (Chudleigh Knighton) (Temporary Restriction of Traffic) Order 2002 No. 2002/2389. – Enabling power: Road Traffic Regulation Act 1984, s. 14 (1) (a). – Made: 16.09.2002. Coming into force: 21.09.2002. Effect: None. Territorial extent & classification: E. Local *Unpublished*

The A38 Trunk Road (Dobwalls) (Temporary Prohibition and Restriction of Traffic) Order 2002 No. 2002/1446. – Enabling power: Road Traffic Regulation Act 1984, s. 14 (1) (b) (5) (b). – Made: 24.05.2002. Coming into force: 31.05.2002. Effect: None. Territorial extent & classification: E. Local *Unpublished*

The A38 Trunk Road (Dobwalls Village) (Temporary Prohibition and Restriction of Traffic) Order 2002 No. 2002/2428. – Enabling power: Road Traffic Regulation Act 1984, s. 14 (1) (a). – Made: 18.09.2002. Coming into force: 21.09.2002. Effect: None. Territorial extent & classification: E. Local *Unpublished*

The A38 Trunk Road (Doublebois to Turfdown) (Temporary Prohibition of Traffic) Order 2002 No. 2002/1052. – Enabling power: Road Traffic Regulation Act 1984, s. 14 (1) (a). – Made: 08.04.2002. Coming into force: 13.04.2002. Effect: None. Territorial extent & classification: E. Local *Unpublished*

The A38 Trunk Road (Droitwich Road, Fernhill Heath) (Temporary 10 Miles Per Hour Speed Restriction) Order 2002 No. 2002/1545. – Enabling power: Road Traffic Regulation Act 1984, s. 14 (1) (a). – Made: 03.06.2002. Coming into force: 10.06.2002. Effect: None. Territorial extent & classification: E. Local *Unpublished*

The A38 Trunk Road (Drybridge Interchange) (Temporary Prohibition of Traffic) Order 2002 No. 2002/2392. – Enabling power: Road Traffic Regulation Act 1984, s. 14 (1) (a). – Made: 16.09.2002. Coming into force: 21.09.2002. Effect: None. Territorial extent & classification: E. Local *Unpublished*

The A38 Trunk Road (Junction with Little Hay Lane, Weeford, Staffordshire) (Temporary Prohibition of Traffic) Order 2002 No. 2002/2489. – Enabling power: Road Traffic Regulation Act 1984, s. 14 (1) (a). – Made: 20.09.2002. Coming into force: 27.09.2002. Effect: None. Territorial extent & classification: E. Local *Unpublished*

The A38 Trunk Road (Layby South of Findern Interchange, South West of Derby) (Temporary Prohibition of Traffic) Order 2002 No. 2002/1529. – Enabling power: Road Traffic Regulation Act 1984, s. 14 (1) (b). – Made: 31.05.2002. Coming into force: 07.06.2002. Effect: None. Territorial extent & classification: E. Local *Unpublished*

The A38 Trunk Road (Lee Mill to Ivybridge) (Temporary Restriction of Traffic) Order 2002 No. 2002/2736. – Enabling power: Road Traffic Regulation Act 1984, s. 14 (1) (a). – Made: 01.11.2002. Coming into force: 03.11.2002. Effect: None. Territorial extent & classification: E. Local *Unpublished*

The A38 Trunk Road (Liskeard Bypass) (Temporary Prohibition and Restriction of Traffic) Order 2002 No. 2002/908. – Enabling power: Road Traffic Regulation Act 1984, s. 14 (1) (a). – Made: 27.03.2002. Coming into force:30.03.2002. Effect:None. Territorial extent & classification: E. Local *Unpublished*

The A38 Trunk Road (Lower Dean Interchange) (Temporary Prohibition of Traffic) Order 2002 No. 2002/2390. – Enabling power: Road Traffic Regulation Act 1984, s. 14 (1) (a). – Made: 16.09.2002. Coming into force: 21.09.2002. Effect: None. Territorial extent & classification: E. Local *Unpublished*

The A38 Trunk Road (Monks Bridge Layby, near Clay Mills) (Temporary Restriction and Prohibition of Traffic) Order 2002 No. 2002/2137. – Enabling power: Road Traffic Regulation Act 1984, s. 14 (1) (a). – Made: 13.08.2002. Coming into force: 20.08.2002. Effect: None. Territorial extent & classification: E. Local *Unpublished*

The A38 Trunk Road (Old Newton Road) (Temporary Prohibition of Traffic) Order 2002 No. 2002/2735. – Enabling power: Road Traffic Regulation Act 1984, s. 14 (1) (a). – Made: 01.11.2002. Coming into force: 03.11.2002. Effect: None. Territorial extent & classification: E. Local *Unpublished*

The A38 Trunk Road (Pottles Lane Overbridge to Splatford Overbridge) (Temporary Prohibition and Restriction of Traffic) Order 2002 No. 2002/2804. – Enabling power: Road Traffic Regulation Act 1984, s. 14 (1) (a). – Made: 11.11.2002. Coming into force: 16.11.2002. Effect: None. Territorial extent & classification: E. Local *Unpublished*

The A38 Trunk Road (Saltash) (Temporary 30 Miles Per Hour Speed Restriction and Prohibition of Traffic) Order 2002 No. 2002/909. – Enabling power: Road Traffic Regulation Act 1984, s. 14 (1) (a), sch. 9, para. 27 (1). – Made: 27.03.2002. Coming into force: 03.04.2002. Effect: S.I. 1999/1034 revoked. Territorial extent & classification: E. Local – Revoked by S.I. 2002/2471 (unpublished) *Unpublished*

The A38 Trunk Road (Saltash Tunnel) (Temporary Prohibition and Restriction of Traffic) Order 2002 No. 2002/2471. – Enabling power: Road Traffic Regulation Act 1984, s. 14 (1) (a) (5) (a) (b) (7), sch. 9, para. 27 (1). – Made: 23.09.2002. Coming into force: 28.09.2002. Effect: S.I. 2002/909 revoked. Territorial extent & classification: E. Local *Unpublished*

The A38 Trunk Road (South of Bassetts Pole Roundabout, Warwickshire) (Temporary Restriction and Prohibition of Traffic) Order 2002 No. 2002/2718. – Enabling power: Road Traffic Regulation Act 1984, s. 14 (1) (a). – Made: 28.10.2002. Coming into force: 04.11.2002. Territorial extent & classification: E. Local *Unpublished*

The A38 Trunk Road (Tamar Bridge to Manadon Interchange) (Temporary Prohibition and Restriction of Traffic) Order 2002 No. 2002/717. – Enabling power: Road Traffic Regulation Act 1984, s. 14 (1) (a). – Made: 14.03.2002. Coming into force: 16.03.2002. Effect: None. Territorial extent & classification: E. Local *Unpublished*

The A38 Trunk Road (Watchorn Interchange) (Temporary 30 Miles Per Hour Speed Restriction) Order 2002 No. 2002/2543. – Enabling power: Road Traffic Regulation Act 1984, s. 14 (1) (a). – Made: 07.10.2002. Coming into force: 14.10.2002. Effect: None. Territorial extent & classification: E. Local *Unpublished*

The A38 Trunk Road (Weeford, Staffordshire) (Closure of Gap in the Central Reservation and Prohibition of "U" Turns) Order 2002 No. 2002/449. – Enabling power:Road Traffic Regulation Act 1984, ss. 1 (1), 2 (1) (2). – Made: 12.02.2002. Coming into force: 26.02.2002. Effect: None. Territorial extent & classification: E. Local *Unpublished*

The A39 Trunk Road (Indian Queens to Blackcross) (24 Hours Clearway) Order 2002 No. 2002/415. – Enabling power: Road Traffic Regulation Act 1984, ss. 1 (1), 2 (1) (2), 3 (2), 4 (1). – Made: 25.02.2002. Coming into force: 04.03.2002. Effect: None. Territorial extent & classification: E. Local *Unpublished*

The A39 Trunk Road (Knightsmill) (Temporary Restriction of Traffic) Order 2002 No. 2002/1056. – Enabling power: Road Traffic Regulation Act 1984, s. 14 (1) (a). – Made: 09.04.2002. Coming into force: 12.04.2002. Effect: None. Territorial extent & classification: E. Local *Unpublished*

The A40 and A48 Trunk Roads (Minsterworth, Gloucestershire) (Temporary Restriction and Prohibition of Traffic) Order 2002 No. 2002/1156. – Enabling power: Road Traffic Regulation Act 1984, s. 14 (1) (a). – Made: 22.04.2002. Coming into force: 29.04.2002. Effect: None. Territorial extent & classification: E. Local *Unpublished*

The A40 and A417 Trunk Roads (Gloucester Northern Bypass) (Temporary Restriction and Prohibition of Traffic) Order 2002 No. 2002/3246. – Enabling power: Road Traffic Regulation Act 1984, s. 14 (1) (a). – Made: 27.12.2002. Coming into force: 03.01.2003. Effect: None. Territorial extent & classification: E. Local *Unpublished*

The A40 and A417 Trunk Roads (Northern Bypass, Gloucestershire) (Temporary Restriction and Prohibition of Traffic) Order 2002 No. 2002/2074. – Enabling power: Road Traffic Regulation Act 1984, s. 14 (1) (a). – Made: 05.08.2002. Coming into force: 12.08.2002. Effect: None. Territorial extent & classification: E. Local *Unpublished*

The A40 Trunk Road (Bridstow Bridge, Herefordshire) (Temporary 50 Miles Per Hour Speed Restriction) Order 2002 No. 2002/952. – Enabling power: Road Traffic Regulation Act 1984, s. 14 (1) (a). – Made: 26.03.2002. Coming into force: 02.04.2002. Effect: None. Territorial extent & classification: E. Local *Unpublished*

The A40 Trunk Road (Cassington Halt Bridge) (Temporary Restriction of Traffic) Order 2002 No. 2002/2026. – Enabling power: Road Traffic Regulation Act 1984, s. 14 (1) (a). – Made: 15.07.2002. Coming into force: 20.07.2002. Effect: None. Territorial extent & classification: E. Local *Unpublished*

The A40 Trunk Road (Churchdown, Gloucestershire) (Closure of Gaps in the Central Reservation) Order 2002 No. 2002/1585. – Enabling power: Road Traffic Regulation Act 1984, ss. 1 (1), 2 (1) (2). – Made: 27.05.2002. Coming into force: 10.06.2002. Effect: None. Territorial extent & classification: E. Local *Unpublished*

The A40 Trunk Road (Dowdeswell Layby) (Temporary Prohibition of Traffic) Order 2002 No. 2002/1537. – Enabling power: Road Traffic Regulation Act 1984, s. 14 (1) (a). – Made: 05.06.2002. Coming into force: 08.06.2002. Effect: None. Territorial extent & classification: E. Local *Unpublished*

The A40 Trunk Road (Evenlode Layby) (Temporary Prohibition of Traffic) Order 2002 No. 2002/2993. – Enabling power: Road Traffic Regulation Act 1984, s. 14 (1) (a). – Made: 02.12.2002. Coming into force: 07.12.2002. Effect: None. Territorial extent & classification: E. Local *Unpublished*

The A40 Trunk Road (Glewstone to Wilton, Herefordshire) (Temporary 10 Miles Per Hour and 40 Miles Per Hour Speed Restriction) Order 2002 No. 2002/1525. – Enabling power: Road Traffic Regulation Act 1984, s. 14 (1) (a). – Made: 31.05.2002. Coming into force: 07.06.2002. Effect: None. Territorial extent & classification: E. Local *Unpublished*

The A40 Trunk Road (Hildersley, Herefordshire) (Temporary 30 Miles Per Hour Speed Restriction) Order 2002 No. 2002/3244. – Enabling power: Road Traffic Regulation Act 1984, s. 14 (1) (b). – Made: 27.12.2002. Coming into force: 03.01.2003. Effect: None. Territorial extent & classification: E. Local *Unpublished*

The A40 Trunk Road (Huntley, Gloucestershire) (Temporary 10 Miles Per Hour Speed Restriction) Order 2002 No. 2002/98. Enabling power: Road Traffic Regulation Act 1984, s. 14 (1) (a). – Made: 21.01.2002. Coming into force: 28.01.2002. Effect: None. Territorial extent & classification: E. Local *Unpublished*

The A40 Trunk Road (Huntley, Gloucestershire) (Temporary 30 Miles Per Hour Speed Restriction) Order 2002 No. 2002/3250. – Enabling power: Road Traffic Regulation Act 1984, s. 14 (1) (b). – Made: 27.12.2002. Coming into force: 03.01.2003. Effect: None. Territorial extent & classification: E. Local *Unpublished*

The A40 Trunk Road (Lea Village, Herefordshire) (Temporary 30 Miles Per Hour Speed Restriction) Order 2002 No. 2002/3241. – Enabling power: Road Traffic Regulation Act 1984, s. 14 (1) (b). – Made: 27.12.2002. Coming into force: 03.01.2003. Effect: None. Territorial extent & classification: E. Local *Unpublished*

The A40 Trunk Road (Near Burford) (Temporary Restriction of Traffic) Order 2002 No. 2002/1539. – Enabling power: Road Traffic Regulation Act 1984, s. 14 (1) (a). – Made: 05.06.2002. Coming into force: 08.06.2002. Effect: None. Territorial extent & classification: E. Local *Unpublished*

The A40 Trunk Road (Pencraig, Herefordshire) (Temporary 10 Miles Per Hour Speed Restriction) Order 2002 No. 2002/2077. – Enabling power: Road Traffic Regulation Act 1984, s. 14 (1) (a). – Made: 02.08.2002. Coming into force: 09.08.2002. Effect: None. Territorial extent & classification: E. Local *Unpublished*

The A40 Trunk Road (Pencraig, Herefordshire) (Temporary 50 Miles Per Hour Speed Restriction) (No. 2) Order 2002 No. 2002/2490. – Enabling power: Road Traffic Regulation Act 1984, s. 14 (1) (b), sch. 9, para. 27 (1). – Made: 19.09.2002. Coming into force: 26.09.2002. Effect: S.I. 2002/1079 revoked. Territorial extent & classification: E. Local *Unpublished*

The A40 Trunk Road (Pencraig, Herefordshire) (Temporary 50 Miles Per Hour Speed Restriction) Order 2002 No. 2002/2079. – Enabling power: Road Traffic Regulation Act 1984, s. 14 (1) (b). – Made: 02.08.2002. Coming into force: 09.08.2002. Effect: None. Territorial extent & classification: E. Local – Revoked by S.I. 2002/2490 (unpublished) *Unpublished*

The A40 Trunk Road (Pencraig, Herefordshire) (Temporary Prohibition of Waiting) Order 2002 No. 2002/2078. – Enabling power: Road Traffic Regulation Act 1984, s. 14 (1) (b). – Made: 02.08.2002. Coming into force: 09.08.2002. Effect: None. Territorial extent & classification: E. Local *Unpublished*

The A40 Trunk Road (Pencraig to Whitchurch, Herefordshire) (Temporary 10 Miles Per Hour and 40 Miles Per Hour Speed Restriction) Order 2002 No. 2002/1523. – Enabling power: Road Traffic Regulation Act 1984, s. 14 (1) (a). – Made: 30.05.2002. Coming into force: 06.06.2002. Effect: None. Territorial extent & classification: E. Local *Unpublished*

The A40 Trunk Road (Ryeford, South of Ross-on-Wye) (Temporary 40 Miles Per Hour Speed Restriction) (No. 2) Order 2002 No. 2002/3242. – Enabling power: Road Traffic Regulation Act 1984, s. 14 (1) (b). – Made: 27.12.2002. Coming into force: 03.01.2003. Effect: None. Territorial extent & classification: E. Local *Unpublished*

The A40 Trunk Road (Ryeford, South of Ross-on-Wye) (Temporary 40 Miles Per Hour Speed Restriction) Order 2002 No. 2002/1258. – Enabling power: Road Traffic Regulation Act 1984, s. 14 (1) (b). – Made: 01.05.2002. Coming into force: 08.05.2002. Effect: None. Territorial extent & classification: E. Local *Unpublished*

The A40 Trunk Road (Western Avenue, Layby) (Temporary Prohibition of Traffic) Order 2002 No. 2002/1636. – Enabling power: Road Traffic Regulation Act 1984, s. 14 (1) (a). – Made: 24.06.2002. Coming into force: 29.06.2002. Effect: None. Territorial extent & classification: E. Local *Unpublished*

The A40 Trunk Road (Wolvercote Underbridges) (Temporary Restriction of Traffic) Order 2002 No. 2002/1849. – Enabling power: Road Traffic Regulation Act 1984, s. 14 (1) (b). – Made: 15.07.2002. Coming into force: 18.07.2002. Effect: None. Territorial extent & classification: E. Local *Unpublished*

The A41 Trunk Road (Blackthorn Railway Bridge) (Temporary Restriction and Prohibition of Traffic) Order 2002 No. 2002/1757. – Enabling power: Road Traffic Regulation Act 1984, s. 14 (1) (a). – Made: 01.07.2002. Coming into force: 06.07.2002. Effect: None. Territorial extent & classification: E. Local *Unpublished*

The A41 Trunk Road (Hartspring Roundabout - Brockley Hill Roundabout) (Temporary Restriction and Prohibition of Traffic) Order 2002 No. 2002/2555. – Enabling power: Road Traffic Regulation Act 1984, s. 14 (1) (a). – Made: 07.10.2002. Coming into force: 12.10.2002. Effect: None. Territorial extent & classification: E. Local *Unpublished*

The A41 Trunk Road (Prees Heath) (Closure of Gaps in the Central Reservation) (Experimental) Order 2002 No. 2002/391. – Enabling power: Road Traffic Regulation Act 1984, ss. 9 (1) (3), 10 (2). – Made: 14.02.2002. Coming into force: 25.02.2002. Effect: None. Territorial extent & classification: E. Local *Unpublished*

The A41 Trunk Road (Two Waters - Berkhamsted) (Temporary Speed Restrictions) Order 2002 No. 2002/2450. – Enabling power: Road Traffic Regulation Act 1984, s. 14 (1) (a). – Made: 23.09.2002. Coming into force: 28.09.2002. Effect: None. Territorial extent & classification: E. Local *Unpublished*

The A42 Trunk Road (Ashby De La Zouch, Leicestershire) (Slip Roads) (Temporary Prohibition of Traffic) Order 2002 No. 2002/2858. – Enabling power: Road Traffic Regulation Act 1984, s. 14 (1) (a). – Made: 15.11.2002. Coming into force: 22.11.2002. Effect: None. Territorial extent & classification: E. Local *Unpublished*

The A42 Trunk Road (Ashby-De-La-Zouch) (Temporary Restriction and Prohibition of Traffic) Order 2002 No. 2002/2669. – Enabling power: Road Traffic Regulation Act 1984, s. 14 (1) (a). – Made: 18.10.2002. Coming into force: 25.10.2002. Effect: None. Territorial extent & classification: E. Local *Unpublished*

The A42 Trunk Road (Donington Services, Leicestershire) (Northbound Exit Slip Road) (Temporary Prohibition of Traffic) Order 2002 No. 2002/1576. – Enabling power: Road Traffic Regulation Act 1984, s. 14 (1) (a). – Made: 10.06.2002. Coming into force: 17.06.2002. Effect: None. Territorial extent & classification: E. Local *Unpublished*

The A43 Trunk Road (A413 Junction, Silverstone, Northamptonshire) (Temporary Prohibition of Traffic) Order 2002 No. 2002/1190. – Enabling power: Road Traffic Regulation Act 1984, s. 14 (1) (a). – Made: 23.04.2002. Coming into force: 30.04.2002. Effect: None. Territorial extent & classification: E. Local *Unpublished*

The A43 Trunk Road (Abthorpe Road Roundabout, Towcester) (Temporary 40 Miles Per Hour Speed Restriction) (No. 2) Order 2002 No. 2002/2653. – Enabling power: Road Traffic Regulation Act 1984, s. 14 (1) (b). – Made: 18.10.2002. Coming into force: 25.10.2002. Effect: None. Territorial extent & classification: E. Local *Unpublished*

The A43 Trunk Road (Abthorpe Road Roundabout, Towcester) (Temporary 40 Miles Per Hour Speed Restriction) Order 2002 No. 2002/1535. – Enabling power: Road Traffic Regulation Act 1984, s. 14 (1) (a). – Made: 31.05.2002. Coming into force: 07.06.2002. Effect: None. Territorial extent & classification: E. Local *Unpublished*

The A43 Trunk Road (Juniper Hill Road Junction, Oxfordshire) (Temporary Prohibition of Traffic) Order 2002 No. 2002/59. – Enabling power: Road Traffic Regulation Act 1984, s. 14 (1) (a). – Made: 14.01.2002. Coming into force: 21.01.2002. Effect: None. Territorial extent & classification: E. Local *Unpublished*

The A43 Trunk Road (Rothersthorpe, Northamptonshire) (Temporary Prohibition of Traffic) Order 2002 No. 2002/2907. – Enabling power: Road Traffic Regulation Act 1984, s. 14 (1) (a). – Made: 18.11.2002. Coming into force: 25.11.2002. Effect: None. Territorial extent & classification: E. Local *Unpublished*

The A43 Trunk Road (Silverstone Grand Prix, Northamptonshire) (Temporary Restriction and Prohibition of Traffic) Order 2002 No. 2002/1656. – Enabling power: Road Traffic Regulation Act 1984, s. 14 (1) (b). – Made: 24.06.2002. Coming into force: 01.07.2002. Effect: None. Territorial extent & classification: E. Local *Unpublished*

The A43 Trunk Road (Towcester, Northamptonshire) (Temporary Restriction and Prohibition of Traffic) Order 2002 No. 2002/1239. – Enabling power: Road Traffic Regulation Act 1984, s. 14 (1) (a). – Made: 30.04.2002. Coming into force: 07.05.2002. Effect: None. Territorial extent & classification: E. Local *Unpublished*

The A43 Trunk Road (Towcester to M40 Dualling, Northamptonshire and Oxfordshire) (24 Hours Clearway) Order 2002 No. 2002/2608. – Enabling power: Road Traffic Regulation Act 1984, ss. 1 (1), 2 (1) (2), 4 (1). – Made: 11.10.2002. Coming into force: 25.10.2002. Effect: None. Territorial extent & classification: E. Local *Unpublished*

The A43 Trunk Road (Towcester to M40 Dualling, Northamptonshire) (Prohibition of Left, Right Turns and "U" Turns) Order 2002 No. 2002/2607. – Enabling power: Road Traffic Regulation Act 1984, ss. 1 (1), 2 (1) (2). – Made: 11.10.2002. Coming into force: 25.10.2002. Effect: None. Territorial extent & classification: E. Local *Unpublished*

The A43 Trunk Road (Towcester to Whitfield Turn, Northamptonshire) (Temporary Restriction and Prohibition of Traffic) Order 2002 No. 2002/1840. – Enabling power: Road Traffic Regulation Act 1984, s. 14 (1) (a). – Made: 21.06.2002. Coming into force: 28.06.2002. Effect: None. Territorial extent & classification: E. Local *Unpublished*

The A43 Trunk Road (Various Lengths, Northamptonshire - Oxfordshire) (Temporary 40 Miles Per Hour Speed Restriction) Order 2002 No. 2002/2211. – Enabling power: Road Traffic Regulation Act 1984, s. 14 (1) (a). – Made: 23.08.2002. Coming into force: 30.08.2002. Effect: None. Territorial extent & classification: E. Local *Unpublished*

The A45 and A508 Trunk Roads (Various Lengths, Northamptonshire) (Temporary 40 Miles Per Hour Speed Restriction) Order 2002 No. 2002/2247. – Enabling power: Road Traffic Regulation Act 1984, s. 14 (1) (a). – Made: 30.08.2002. Coming into force: 06.09.2002. Effect: None. Territorial extent & classification: E. Local *Unpublished*

The A45 Trunk Road (Dodford, Northamptonshire) (Temporary 10 Miles Per Hour and 40 Miles Per Hour Speed Restriction) Order 2002 No. 2002/1574. – Enabling power: Road Traffic Regulation Act 1984, s. 14 (1) (a). – Made: 10.06.2002. Coming into force: 17.06.2002. Effect: None. Territorial extent & classification: E. Local *Unpublished*

The A45 Trunk Road (Great Billing, Northamptonshire) (Temporary Restriction and Prohibition of Traffic) Order 2002 No. 2002/2198. – Enabling power: Road Traffic Regulation Act 1984, s. 14 (1) (a). – Made: 20.08.2002. Coming into force: 27.08.2002. Effect: None. Territorial extent & classification: E. Local *Unpublished*

The A45 Trunk Road (Wellingborough and Irthlingborough, Northamptonshire) (Temporary Restriction and Prohibition of Traffic) Order 2002 No. 2002/60. – Enabling power: Road Traffic Regulation Act 1984, s. 14 (1) (a). – Made: 14.01.2002. Coming into force: 21.01.2002. Effect: None. Territorial extent & classification: E. Local *Unpublished*

The A46 Trunk Road (A50 Groby Road Interchange, Leicestershire) (Temporary Prohibition of Traffic) Order 2002 No. 2002/3263. – Enabling power: Road Traffic Regulation Act 1984, s. 14 (1) (a). – Made: 27.12.2002. Coming into force: 03.01.2003. Effect: None. Territorial extent & classification: E. Local *Unpublished*

The A46 Trunk Road (Ashchurch Village) (Temporary 30 Miles Per Hour Speed Restriction) Order 2002 No. 2002/3252. – Enabling power: Road Traffic Regulation Act 1984, s. 14 (1) (b). Made: 27.12.2002. Coming into force: 03.01.2003. Effect: None. Territorial extent & classification: E. Local *Unpublished*

The A46 Trunk Road (Ashton - Under - Hill, Worcestershire) (Temporary 10 Miles Per Hour Speed Restriction) Order 2002 No. 2002/1374. – Enabling power: Road Traffic Regulation Act 1984, s. 14 (1) (a). – Made: 14.05.2002. Coming into force: 21.05.2002. Effect: None. Territorial extent & classification: E. Local *Unpublished*

The A46 Trunk Road (Beckford, Worcestershire) (Temporary 10 Milers per House and 30 Miles per Hour Speed Restriction) Order 2002 No. 2002/2830. – Enabling power: Road Traffic Regulation Act 1984, s. 14 (1) (a). – Made: 11.11.2002. Coming into force: 18.11.2002. Effect: None. Territorial extent & classification: E. Local *Unpublished*

The A46 Trunk Road (Cheltenham Road, Little Beckford) (Temporary 10 Miles Per Hour and 30 Miles Per Hour Speed Restriction) Order 2002 No. 2002/96. – Enabling power: Road Traffic Regulation Act 1984, s. 14 (1) (a). – Made: 21.01.2002. Coming into force: 28.01.2002. Effect: None. Territorial extent & classification: E. Local *Unpublished*

The A46 Trunk Road (Cold Ashton Roundabout to London Road) (Temporary Prohibition of Traffic) Order 2002 No. 2002/1655. – Enabling power: Road Traffic Regulation Act 1984, s. 14 (1) (a). – Made: 21.06.2002. Coming into force: 26.06.2002. Effect: None. Territorial extent & classification: E. Local *Unpublished*

The A46 Trunk Road (Dyrham Park) (Temporary Restriction of Traffic) Order 2002 No. 2002/191. – Enabling power: Road Traffic Regulation Act 1984, s. 14 (1) (a). – Made: 31.01.2002. Coming into force: 05.02.2002. Effect: None. Territorial extent & classification: E. Local *Unpublished*

The A46 Trunk Road (Halfway Houses, Lincolnshire) (Temporary 40 Miles Per Hour Speed Restriction) Order 2002 No. 2002/114. – Enabling power: Road Traffic Regulation Act 1984, s. 14 (1) (a). – Made: 18.01.2002. Coming into force: 25.01.2002. Effect: None. Territorial extent & classification: E. Local *Unpublished*

The A46 Trunk Road (Junction with the M69/M6 Junction 2, Warwickshire) (Slip Road) (Temporary 40 Miles Per Hour Speed Restriction) Order 2002 No. 2002/2668. – Enabling power: Road Traffic Regulation Act 1984, s. 14 (1) (a). – Made: 10.10.2002. Coming into force: 17.10.2002. Effect: None. Territorial extent & classification: E. Local *Unpublished*

The A46 Trunk Road (Leicester Western Bypass) (Temporary Prohibition of Traffic) Order 2002 No. 2002/1517. – Enabling power: Road Traffic Regulation Act 1984, s. 14 (1) (a). – Made: 24.05.2002. Coming into force: 01.06.2002. Effect: None. Territorial extent & classification: E. Local *Unpublished*

The A46 Trunk Road (Lincoln Relief Road) (Temporary Restriction and Prohibition of Traffic) Order 2002 No. 2002/2181. – Enabling power: Road Traffic Regulation Act 1984, s. 14 (1) (a). – Made: 02.09.2002. Coming into force: 09.09.2002. Effect: None. Territorial extent & classification: E. Local *Unpublished*

The A46 Trunk Road (Little Beckford, Worcestershire) (Temporary 50 Miles Per Hour Speed Restriction) Order 2002 No. 2002/382. – Enabling power: Road Traffic Regulation Act 1984, s. 14 (1) (b). – Made: 18.02.2002. Coming into force: 25.02.2002. Effect: None. Territorial extent & classification: E. Local *Unpublished*

The A46 Trunk Road (Newark to Lincoln) (Temporary Prohibition of Traffic) Order 2002 No. 2002/2330. – Enabling power: Road Traffic Regulation Act 1984, s. 14 (1) (a). – Made: 09.09.2002. Coming into force: 16.09.2002. Effect: None. Territorial extent & classification: E. Local *Unpublished*

The A46 Trunk Road (Salford Priors Roundabout, Warwickshire) (Temporary 10 Miles Per Hour Speed Restriction) Order 2002 No. 2002/1524. – Enabling power: Road Traffic Regulation Act 1984, s. 14 (1) (a). – Made: 31.05.2002. Coming into force: 10.06.2002. Effect: None. Territorial extent & classification: E. Local *Unpublished*

The A46 Trunk Road (Sherbourne, Warwickshire) (Temporary Prohibition of Traffic) Order 2002 No. 2002/2670. – Enabling power: Road Traffic Regulation Act 1984, s. 14 (1) (a). – Made: 21.10.2002. Coming into force: 28.10.2002. Effect: None. Territorial extent & classification: E. Local *Unpublished*

The A46 Trunk Road (Swinderby, Lincolnshire) (Temporary 30 Miles Per Hour Speed Restriction) Order 2002 No. 2002/2417. – Enabling power: Road Traffic Regulation Act 1984, s. 14 (1) (a). – Made: 17.09.2002. Coming into force: 24.09.2003. Effect: None. Territorial extent & classification: E. Local *Unpublished*

The A46 Trunk Road (Swinderby to Thorpe on the Hill) (Temporary Prohibition of Traffic) Order 2002 No. 2002/2863. – Enabling power: Road Traffic Regulation Act 1984, s. 14 (1) (a). – Made: 18.11.2002. Coming into force: 25.11.2002. Effect: None. Territorial extent & classification: E. Local *Unpublished*

The A46 Trunk Road (Thorpe on the Hill, Lincolnshire) (Temporary 30 Miler per Hour Speed Restriction) Order 2002 No. 2002/2864. – Enabling power: Road Traffic Regulation Act 1984, s. 14 (1) (a). – Made: 18.11.2002. Coming into force: 25.11.2002. Effect: None. Territorial extent & classification: E. Local *Unpublished*

The A46 Trunk Road (Winthorpe, Nottinghamshire to North Hykeham, Lincolnshire) (Temporary 50 Miles Per Hour Speed Restriction) Order 2002 No. 2002/436. – Enabling power: Road Traffic Regulation Act 1984, s. 14 (1) (a). – Made: 22.02.2002. Coming into force: 01.03.2002. Effect: None. Territorial extent & classification: E. Local *Unpublished*

The A47 Trunk Road (East Dereham, Norfolk) (Temporary Restriction of Traffic) Order 2002 No. 2002/2491. – Enabling power: Road Traffic Regulation Act 1984, s. 14 (1) (a). – Made: 27.09.2002. Coming into force: 04.10.2002. Effect: None. Territorial extent & classification: E. Local *Unpublished*

The A47 Trunk Road (East Winch, Norfolk) (Temporary Restriction and Prohibition of Traffic) Order 2002 No. 2002/2334. – Enabling power: Road Traffic Regulation Act 1984, s. 14 (1) (a). – Made: 06.09.2002. Coming into force: 13.09.2002. Effect: None. Territorial extent & classification: E. Local *Unpublished*

The A47 Trunk Road (Hardwick Roundabout, Suffolk) (Temporary Restriction and Prohibition of Traffic) Order 2002 No. 2002/2213. – Enabling power: Road Traffic Regulation Act 1984, s. 14 (1) (a). – Made: 23.08.2002. Coming into force: 30.08.2002. Effect: None. Territorial extent & classification: E. Local *Unpublished*

The A47 Trunk Road (Hockering, Norfolk) (Temporary 10 Miles Per Hour and 30 Miles Per Hour Speed Restriction) Order 2002 No. 2002/270. – Enabling power: Road Traffic Regulation Act 1984, s. 14 (1) (a). – Made: 28.01.2002. Coming into force: 04.02.2002. Effect: None. Territorial extent & classification: E. Local *Unpublished*

The A47 Trunk Road (Markshall - Keswick, Norfolk) (Temporary Restriction of Traffic) Order 2002 No. 2002/2493. – Enabling power: Road Traffic Regulation Act 1984, s. 14 (1) (a). – Made: 27.09.2002. Coming into force: 04.10.2002. Effect: None. Territorial extent & classification: E. Local *Unpublished*

The A47 Trunk Road (Narborough - Necton, Norfolk) (Temporary Restriction of Traffic) Order 2002 No. 2002/2481. – Enabling power: Road Traffic Regulation Act 1984, s. 14 (1) (a). – Made: 13.09.2002. Coming into force: 20.09.2002. Effect: None. Territorial extent & classification: E. Local *Unpublished*

The A47 Trunk Road (Narborough, Norfolk) (Temporary 10 Miles Per Hour and 40 Miles Per Hour Speed Restriction) Order 2002 No. 2002/167. – Enabling power: Road Traffic Regulation Act 1984, s. 14 (1) (a). – Made: 28.01.2002. Coming into force: 04.02.2002. Effect: None. Territorial extent & classification: E. Local *Unpublished*

The A47 Trunk Road (Saddlebow Interchange, Kings Lynn, Norfolk) (Temporary Restriction and Prohibition of Traffic) Order 2002 No. 2002/1958. – Enabling power: Road Traffic Regulation Act 1984, s. 14 (1) (a). – Made: 22.07.2002. Coming into force: 29.07.2002. Effect: None. Territorial extent & classification: E. Local *Unpublished*

The A47 Trunk Road (Wansford-Sutton, City of Peterborough and Guyhirn-Wisbech, Cambridgeshire) (Temporary 10 Miles Per Hour and 40 Miles Per Hour Speed Restriction) Order 2002 No. 2002/2700. – Enabling power: Road Traffic Regulation Act 1984, s. 14 (1) (a). – Made: 25.10.2002. Coming into force: 01.11.2002. Effect: None. Territorial extent & classification: E. Local *Unpublished*

The A47 Trunk Road (Wardley Hill, Leicestershire) (Temporary Restriction and Prohibition of Traffic) Order 2002 No. 2002/934. – Enabling power: Road Traffic Regulation Act 1984, s. 14 (1) (a). – Made: 26.03.2002. Coming into force: 02.04.2002. Effect: None. Territorial extent & classification: E. Local *Unpublished*

The A47 Trunk Road (Watton Interchange - Postwick Interchange, Slip Roads, Norfolk) (Temporary Prohibition of Traffic) Order 2002 No. 2002/2414. – Enabling power: Road Traffic Regulation Act 1984, s. 14 (1) (a). – Made: 16.09.2002. Coming into force: 23.09.2002. Effect: None. Territorial extent & classification: E. Local *Unpublished*

The A47 Trunk Road (Wireless Hill, Tixover, Leicestershire) (Temporary Restriction and Prohibition of Traffic) Order 2002 No. 2002/955. – Enabling power: Road Traffic Regulation Act 1984, s. 14 (1) (a). – Made: 02.04.2002. Coming into force: 08.04.2002. Effect: None. Territorial extent & classification: E. Local *Unpublished*

The A48 Trunk Road (Aylburton, Gloucestershire) (Temporary 10 Miles Per Hour Speed Restriction) Order 2002 No. 2002/1226. – Enabling power: Road Traffic Regulation Act 1984, s. 14 (1) (a). – Made: 29.04.2002. Coming into force: 06.05.2002. Effect: None. Territorial extent & classification: E. Local *Unpublished*

The A48 Trunk Road (Broadoak, Gloucestershire) (Temporary 10 Miles Per Hour Speed Restriction) Order 2002 No. 2002/514. – Enabling power: Road Traffic Regulation Act 1984, s. 14 (1) (a). – Made: 04.03.2002. Coming into force: 11.03.2002. Effect: None. Territorial extent & classification: E. Local *Unpublished*

The A48 Trunk Road (Dinney Bank, Minsterworth, Gloucestershire) (Temporary 50 Miles Per Hour Speed Restriction) Order 2002 No. 2002/3191. – Enabling power: Road Traffic Regulation Act 1984, s. 14 (1) (b). – Made: 16.12.2002. Coming into force: 23.12.2002. Effect: None. Territorial extent & classification: E. Local *Unpublished*

The A48 Trunk Road (Minsterworth, Gloucestershire) (Temporary 50 Miles per Hour Speed Restriction) (No. 2) Order 2002 No. 2002/2829. – Enabling power: Road Traffic Regulation Act 1984, s. 14 (1) (b), sch. 9, para. 27 (1)– Made: 11.11.2002. Coming into force: 18.11.2002. Effect: S.I. 2002/1157 revoked. Territorial extent & classification: E. Local *Unpublished*

The A48 Trunk Road (Minsterworth, Gloucestershire) (Temporary 50 Miles Per Hour Speed Restriction) Order 2002 No. 2002/1157. – Enabling power: Road Traffic Regulation Act 1984, s. 14 (1) (b). – Made: 22.04.2002. Coming into force: 29.04.2002. Effect: None. Territorial extent & classification: E. Local – Revoked by S.I. 2002/2929 (unpublished) *Unpublished*

The A49 Trunk Road (Church Stretton and Leebotwood, Shropshire) (Temporary 30 and 40 Miles Per Hour Speed Restriction) Order 2002 No. 2002/3247. – Enabling power: Road Traffic Regulation Act 1984, s. 14 (1) (b). – Made: 27.12.2002. Coming into force: 03.01.2003. Effect: None. Territorial extent & classification: E. Local *Unpublished*

The A49 Trunk Road (Church Stretton, Shropshire) (Temporary Prohibition of Traffic) Order 2002 No. 2002/3249. – Enabling power: Road Traffic Regulation Act 1984, s. 14 (1) (b). – Made: 27.12.2002. Coming into force: 03.01.2003. Effect: None. Territorial extent & classification: E. Local *Unpublished*

The A49 Trunk Road (Dinmore Hill, Herefordshire) (Temporary 50 Miles Per Hour Speed Restriction) Order 2002 No. 2002/3243. – Enabling power: Road Traffic Regulation Act 1984, s. 14 (1) (b). – Made: 27.012.2002. Coming into force: 03.01.2003. Effect: None. Territorial extent & classification: E. Local *Unpublished*

The A49 Trunk Road (Dorrington Railway Bridge, Shropshire) (Temporary Restriction and Prohibition of Traffic) Order 2002 No. 2002/1332. – Enabling power: Road Traffic Regulation Act 1984, s. 14 (1) (a). – Made: 13.05.2002. Coming into force: 20.05.2002. Effect: None. Territorial extent & classification: E. Local *Unpublished*

The A49 Trunk Road (Hereford to Callow Hill) (Temporary Restriction and Prohibition of Traffic) Order 2002 No. 2002/751. – Enabling power: Road Traffic Regulation Act 1984, s. 14 (1) (a). – Made: 18.03.2002. Coming into force: 25.03.2002. Effect: None. Territorial extent & classification: E. Local *Unpublished*

The A49 Trunk Road (Holmer Road, Hereford) (Temporary 30 Miles Per Hour Speed Restriction) (No. 2) Order 2002 No. 2002/660. – Enabling power: Road Traffic Regulation Act 1984, s. 14 (1) (b). – Made: 08.03.2002. Coming into force: 15.03.2002. Effect: None. Territorial extent & classification: E. Local *Unpublished*

The A49 Trunk Road (Holmer Road, Hereford) (Temporary 30 Miles Per Hour Speed Restriction) (No. 3) Order 2002 No. 2002/1163. – Enabling power: Road Traffic Regulation Act 1984, s. 14 (1) (b). – Made: 19.04.2002. Coming into force: 26.04.2002. Effect: None. Territorial extent & classification: E. Local *Unpublished*

The A49 Trunk Road (Holmer Road, Hereford) (Temporary 30 Miles Per Hour Speed Restriction) Order 2002 No. 2002/56. – Enabling power: Road Traffic Regulation Act 1984, s. 14 (1) (b). – Made: 14.01.2002. Coming into force: 21.01.2002. Effect: None. Territorial extent & classification: E. Local *Unpublished*

The A49 Trunk Road (Holmer to Hope under Dinmore) (Temporary Prohibition of Traffic) Order 2002 No. 2002/2945. – Enabling power: Road Traffic Regulation Act 1984, s. 14 (1) (b). – Made: 25.11.2002. Coming into force: 02.12.2002. Effect: None. Territorial extent & classification: E. Local *Unpublished*

The A49 Trunk Road (Ludlow, Shropshire) (Temporary 10 Miles Per Hour Speed Restriction) Order 2002 No. 2002/953. – Enabling power: Road Traffic Regulation Act 1984, s. 14 (1) (a). – Made: 28.03.2002. Coming into force: 04.04.2002. Effect: None. Territorial extent & classification: E. Local *Unpublished*

The A49 Trunk Road (Marshbrook, Shropshire) (Temporary 10 Miles Per Hour Speed Restriction) Order 2002 No. 2002/1200. – Enabling power: Road Traffic Regulation Act 1984, s. 14 (1) (a). – Made: 25.04.2002. Coming into force: 02.05.2002. Effect: None. Territorial extent & classification: E. Local *Unpublished*

The A49 Trunk Road (Peterstow, Herefordshire) (Temporary 10 Miles Per Hour Speed Restriction) Order 2002 No. 2002/1053. – Enabling power: Road Traffic Regulation Act 1984, s. 14 (1) (a). – Made: 09.04.2002. Coming into force: 16.04.2002. Effect: None. Territorial extent & classification: E. Local *Unpublished*

The A49 Trunk Road (Redhill, Hertfordshire) (Temporary 30 Miles Per Hour Speed Restriction) Order 2002 No. 2002/1639. – Enabling power: Road Traffic Regulation Act 1984, s. 14 (1) (b). – Made: 17.06.2002. Coming into force: 24.06.2002. Effect: None. Territorial extent & classification: E. Local *Unpublished*

The A49 Trunk Road (Woofferton Railway Bridge, Shropshire) (Temporary Restriction and Prohibition of Traffic) Order 2002 No. 2002/1373. – Enabling power: Road Traffic Regulation Act 1984, s. 14 (1) (a). – Made: 13.05.2002. Coming into force: 20.05.2002. Effect: None. Territorial extent & classification: E. Local *Unpublished*

The A50 Trunk Road (Hatton, Derbyshire) (Temporary 40 Miles Per Hour Speed Restriction) Order 2002 No. 2002/171. – Enabling power: Road Traffic Regulation Act 1984, s. 14 (1) (a). – Made: 28.01.2002. Coming into force: 04.02.2002. Effect: None. Territorial extent & classification: E. Local *Unpublished*

The A50 Trunk Road (Junction with the A6, Derbyshire) (Slip Roads) (Temporary Prohibition of Traffic) Order 2002 No. 2002/2318. – Enabling power: Road Traffic Regulation Act 1984, s. 14 (1) (a). – Made: 30.08.2002. Coming into force: 06.09.2002. Effect: None. Territorial extent & classification: E. Local *Unpublished*

The A50 Trunk Road (Meir Tunnel, Staffordshire) (Temporary Prohibition of Traffic) Order 2002 No. 2002/515. – Enabling power: Road Traffic Regulation Act 1984, s. 14 (1) (a). – Made: 06.03.2002. Coming into force: 13.03.2002. Effect: None. Territorial extent & classification: E. Local *Unpublished*

The A50 Trunk Road (Uttoxeter - Blythe Bridge, Staffordshire) (Temporary 40 Miles Per Hour Speed Restriction) Order 2002 No. 2002/754. – Enabling power: Road Traffic Regulation Act 1984, s. 14 (1) (a). – Made: 18.03.2002. Coming into force: 25.03.2002. Effect: None. Territorial extent & classification: E. Local *Unpublished*

The A50 Trunk Road (Uttoxeter, Staffordshire) (Temporary 10 Miles Per Hour and 40 Miles Per Hour Speed Restriction) Order 2002 No. 2002/102. – Enabling power: Road Traffic Regulation Act 1984, s. 14 (1) (a). – Made: 21.01.2002. Coming into force: 28.01.2002. Effect: None. Territorial extent & classification: E. Local *Unpublished*

The A50 Trunk Road (Uttoxeter, Staffordshire) (Temporary 10 Miles Per Hour and 40 Miles Per Hour Speed Restriction) Order 2002 No. 2002/1106. – Enabling power: Road Traffic Regulation Act 1984, s. 14 (1) (a). – Made: 15.04.2002. Coming into force: 22.04.2002. Effect: None. Territorial extent & classification: E. Local *Unpublished*

The A50 Trunk Road (Uttoxeter - Sudbury, Staffordshire) (Temporary 10 Miles Per Hour and 40 Miles Per Hour Speed Restriction) Order 2002 No. 2002/1658. – Enabling power: Road Traffic Regulation Act 1984, s. 14 (1) (a). – Made: 24.06.2002. Coming into force: 01.07.2002. Effect: None. Territorial extent & classification: E. Local *Unpublished*

The A52 and A453 Trunk Roads (Nottingham) (Temporary Prohibition of Traffic) Order 2002 No. 2002/409. – Enabling power: Road Traffic Regulation Act 1984, s. 14 (1) (a). – Made: 22.02.2002. Coming into force: 01.03.2002. Effect: None. Territorial extent & classification: E. Local *Unpublished*

The A52 and A6514 Trunk Roads (Nottingham) (Temporary Prohibition of Traffic) Order 2002 No. 2002/2179. – Enabling power: Road Traffic Regulation Act 1984, s. 14 (1) (b). – Made: 30.08.2002. Coming into force: 06.09.2002. Effect: None. Territorial extent & classification: E. Local *Unpublished*

The A52 Trunk Road (Barrowby to Bingham) (Temporary Prohibition of Traffic) Order 2002 No. 2002/135. – Enabling power: Road Traffic Regulation Act 1984, s. 14 (1) (a). – Made: 25.01.2002. Coming into force: 01.02.2002. Effect: None. Territorial extent & classification: E. Local *Unpublished*

The A52 Trunk Road (Borrowash Bypass, Derby) (Temporary Restriction and Prohibition of Traffic) Order 2002 No. 2002/199. – Enabling power: Road Traffic Regulation Act 1984, s. 14 (1) (a). – Made: 31.01.2002. Coming into force: 07.02.2002. Effect: None. Territorial extent & classification: E. Local *Unpublished*

The A52 Trunk Road (Derby Road, Nottingham) (Bus/Cycle Lane) Order 2002 No. 2002/2359. – Enabling power: Road Traffic Regulation Act 1984, ss. 1 (1), 2 (1) (2), 4 (1) (2). – Made: 12.09.2002. Coming into force: 26.09.2002. Effect: None. Territorial extent & classification: E. Local *Unpublished*

The A52 Trunk Road (Stapleford, Nottinghamshire) (Temporary Prohibition of Traffic) Order 2002 No. 2002/27. – Enabling power: Road Traffic Regulation Act 1984, s. 14 (1) (a). – Made: 07.01.2002. Coming into force: 14.01.2002. Effect: None. Territorial extent & classification: E. Local *Unpublished*

The A55 Trunk Road (Temporary Prohibition of Traffic) (No. 2) Order 2002 No. 2002/3077. – Enabling power: Road Traffic Regulation Act 1984, s. 14 (1) (a). – Made: 12.12.2002. Coming into force: 14.12.2002. Effect: None. Territorial extent & classification: E. Local *Unpublished*

The A55 Trunk Road (Temporary Prohibition of Traffic) Order 2002 No. 2002/2910. – Enabling power: Road Traffic Regulation Act 1984, s. 14 (1) (a). – Made: 21.11.2002. Coming into force: 28.11.2002. Effect: None. Territorial extent & classification: E. Local *Unpublished*

The A56 Trunk Road (Temporary Prohibition of Traffic) Order 2002 No. 2002/3065. – Enabling power: Road Traffic Regulation Act 1984, s. 14 (1) (a). – Made: 06.12.2002. Coming into force: 09.12.2002. Effect: None. Territorial extent & classification: E. Local *Unpublished*

The A57 Trunk Road (Markham Moor to Newton on Trent, Nottinghamshire) (Temporary Restriction and Prohibition of Traffic) Order 2002 No. 2002/298. – Enabling power: Road Traffic Regulation Act 1984, ss. 3 (2), 14 (1) (a) (5) (b) (6). – Made: 11.02.2002. Coming into force: 18.02.2002. Effect: None. Territorial extent & classification: E. Local *Unpublished*

The A57 Trunk Road (Workshop Bypass, Nottinghamshire) (Temporary Restriction and Prohibition of Traffic) Order 2002 No. 2002/1217. – Enabling power: Road Traffic Regulation Act 1984, s. 14 (1) (a). – Made: 26.04.2002. Coming into force: 03.05.2002. Effect: None. Territorial extent & classification: E. Local *Unpublished*

The A58 Trunk Road (Chain Bar Roundabout) (Temporary 40 Miles Per Hour Speed Restriction) Order 2002 No. 2002/2646. – Enabling power: Road Traffic Regulation Act 1984, s. 14 (1) (a). – Made: 16.10.2002. Coming into force: 19.10.2002. Effect: None. Territorial extent & classification: E. Local *Unpublished*

The A59 Trunk Road (Bale Plantation, West Marton) (Temporary 30 Miles Per Hour Speed Restriction) Order 2002 No. 2002/2032. – Enabling power: Road Traffic Regulation Act 1984, s. 14 (1) (a). – Made: 11.07.2002. Coming into force: 14.07.2002. Effect: None. Territorial extent & classification: E. Local *Unpublished*

The A59 Trunk Road (Preston New Road, Salmesbury) (Temporary 30 Miles Per Hour Speed Limit) Order 2002 No. 2002/314. – Enabling power: Road Traffic Regulation Act 1984, s. 14 (1) (a). – Made: 07.02.2002. Coming into force: 10.02.2002. Effect: None. Territorial extent & classification: E. Local *Unpublished*

The A59 Trunk Road (Whalley Clitheroe Bypass) (Temporary Restriction and Prohibition of Traffic) Order 2002 No. 2002/1665. – Enabling power: Road Traffic Regulation Act 1984, s. 14 (1) (a). – Made: 20.06.2002. Coming into force: 23.06.2002. Effect: None. Territorial extent & classification: E. Local *Unpublished*

The A61 Trunk Road (Dronfield Bypass) (Temporary Restriction and Prohibition of Traffic) Order 2002 No. 2002/55. – Enabling power: Road Traffic Regulation Act 1984, s. 14 (1) (a). – Made: 14.01.2002. Coming into force: 21.01.2002. Effect: None. Territorial extent & classification: E. Local *Unpublished*

The A61 Trunk Road (M1 Junction 36) (Temporary Restriction and Prohibition of Traffic) Order 2002 No. 2002/54. – Enabling power: Road Traffic Regulation Act 1984, s. 14 (1) (a). – Made: 14.01.2002. Coming into force: 21.01.2002. Effect: None. Territorial extent & classification: E. Local *Unpublished*

The A63 Trunk Road (Garrison Road Roundabout) to the A1033 Trunk Road (Saltend Roundabout) (Temporary 30 Miles Per Hour Speed Restriction) Order 2002 No. 2002/2083. – Enabling power: Road Traffic Regulation Act 1984, s. 14 (1) (a). – Made: 05.08.2002. Coming into force: 08.08.2002. Effect: None. Territorial extent & classification: E. Local *Unpublished*

The A63 Trunk Road (Garrison Road) (Temporary Prohibition of Traffic) Order 2002 No. 2002/1162. – Enabling power: Road Traffic Regulation Act 1984, s. 14 (1) (a). – Made: 17.04.2002. Coming into force: 20.04.2002. Effect: None. Territorial extent & classification: E. Local *Unpublished*

The A63 Trunk Road (Garrison Road) (Temporary Restriction and Prohibition of Traffic) Order 2002 No. 2002/1993. – Enabling power: Road Traffic Regulation Act 1984, s. 14 (1) (a). – Made: 22.07.2002. Coming into force: 25.07.2002. Effect: None. Territorial extent & classification: E. Local *Unpublished*

The A63 Trunk Road (Hessle Road and Daltry Street) (Temporary Prohibition of Traffic) Order 2002 No. 2002/90. – Enabling power: Road Traffic Regulation Act 1984, s. 14 (1) (a). – Made: 17.01.2002. Coming into force: 19.01.2002. Effect: None. Territorial extent & classification: E. Local *Unpublished*

The A63 Trunk Road (Hull Road) (Temporary 10 Miles Per Hour Speed Restriction) Order 2002 No. 2002/2950. – Enabling power: Road Traffic Regulation Act 1984, s. 14 (1) (a). – Made: 27.11.2002. Coming into force: 01.12.2002. Effect: None. Territorial extent & classification: E. Local *Unpublished*

The A63 Trunk Road (Leeds Road, Selby), the A1041 Trunk Road (Bawtry Road, Selby) and the A19 Trunk Road (Barlby Road, Selby) (Temporary 40 Miles Per Hour Speed Restriction) Order 2002 No. 2002/2263. – Enabling power: Road Traffic Regulation Act 1984, ss. 14 (1) (a), 15 (2). – Made: 29.08.2002. Coming into force: 01.09.2002. Effect: None. Territorial extent & classification: E. Local *Unpublished*

The A63 Trunk Road (Melton) (Temporary Prohibition of Traffic) Order 2002 No. 2002/3030. – Enabling power: Road Traffic Regulation Act 1984, s. 14 (1) (a). – Made: 05.12.2002. Coming into force: 08.12.2002. Effect: None. Territorial extent & classification: E. Local *Unpublished*

The A63 Trunk Road (Priory Way Interchange to Brighton Street Interchange) (Temporary Prohibition of Traffic) Order 2002 No. 2002/2291. – Enabling power: Road Traffic Regulation Act 1984, s. 14 (1) (a). – Made: 30.08.2002. Coming into force: 03.09.2002. Effect: None. Territorial extent & classification: E. Local *Unpublished*

The A63 Trunk Road (Selby) (Temporary 10 Miles Per Hour Speed Restriction) Order 2002 No. 2002/2043. – Enabling power: Road Traffic Regulation Act 1984, s. 14 (1) (a). – Made: 31.07.2002. Coming into force: 04.08.2002. Effect: None. Territorial extent & classification: E. Local *Unpublished*

The A63 Trunk Road (South Cave and Western Interchanges) (Temporary Restriction and Prohibition of Traffic) Order 2002 No. 2002/2966. – Enabling power: Road Traffic Regulation Act 1984, s. 14 (1) (a). – Made: 28.11.2002. Coming into force: 01.12.2002. Effect: None. Territorial extent & classification: E. Local *Unpublished*

The A63 Trunk Road (South Cave Interchange to Welton Interchange) (Temporary Prohibition of Traffic) Order 2002 No. 2002/2206. – Enabling power: Road Traffic Regulation Act 1984, s. 14 (1) (a). – Made: 22.08.2002. Coming into force: 28.08.2002. Effect: None. Territorial extent & classification: E. Local *Unpublished*

The A63 Trunk Road (Thorpe Park Link Roads and Roundabouts) (One-Way, 24 Hours Clearway and Prohibition of Pedestrians) Order 2002 No. 2002/2515. – Enabling power: Road Traffic Regulation Act 1984, ss. 1 (1), 2 (1) (2), 122A. – Made: 26.09.2002. Coming into force: 01.10.2002. Effect: None. Territorial extent & classification: E. Local *Unpublished*

The A63 Trunk Road (Welton to Western Interchange) (Temporary Restriction and Prohibition of Traffic) Order 2002 No. 2002/15. – Enabling power: Road Traffic Regulation Act 1984, s. 14 (1) (a). – Made: 04.01.2002. Coming into force: 06.01.2002. Effect: None. Territorial extent & classification: E. Local *Unpublished*

The A63 Trunk Road (Western Interchange Road Bridge to Cliff Mill Rail Bridge) (Temporary 10 Miles Per Hour and 40 Miles Per Hour Speed Restriction) Order 2002 No. 2002/2307. – Enabling power: Road Traffic Regulation Act 1984, s. 14 (1) (a). – Made: 04.09.2002. Coming into force: 09.09.2002. Effect: None. Territorial extent & classification: E. Local *Unpublished*

The A64/A1079 Trunk Roads (Grimston Bar Interchange) and the A19/A64 Trunk Roads (Fulford Interchange) (Temporary 30 Miles Per Hour and 40 Miles Per Hour Speed Restriction) Order 2002 No. 2002/663. – Enabling power: Road Traffic Regulation Act 1984, s. 14 (1) (a) (b). – Made: 11.03.2002. Coming into force: 13.03.2002. Effect: None. Territorial extent & classification: E. Local *Unpublished*

The A64 Trunk Road (Askham Bryan) (Prohibition of Use of Gap in Central Reservation) Order 2002 No. 2002/806. – Enabling power: Road Traffic Regulation Act 1984, s. 1 (1), 2 (1) (2). – Made: 20.03.2002. Coming into force: 24.03.2002. Effect: None. Territorial extent & classification: E. Local *Unpublished*

The A64 Trunk Road (Bond Hill Eastbound Exit Slip Road) (Temporary Prohibition of Traffic) Order 2002 No. 2002/650. – Enabling power: Road Traffic Regulation Act 1984, s. 14 (1) (a). – Made: 07.03.2002. Coming into force: 11.03.2002. Effect: None. Territorial extent & classification: E. Local *Unpublished*

The A64 Trunk Road (East Heslerton to West Heslerton) (Temporary 10 Miles Per Hour and 40 Miles Per Hour Speed Restriction) Order 2002 No. 2002/1543. – Enabling power: Road Traffic Regulation Act 1984, s. 14 (1) (a). – Made: 05.06.2002. Coming into force: 09.06.2002. Effect: None. Territorial extent & classification: E. Local *Unpublished*

The A64 Trunk Road (Musley Bank Interchange) (Temporary Prohibition of Traffic) Order 2002 No. 2002/299. – Enabling power: Road Traffic Regulation Act 1984, s. 14 (1) (a). – Made: 11.02.2002. Coming into force: 11.02.2002. Effect: None. Territorial extent & classification: E. Local *Unpublished*

The A64 Trunk Road (Rillington to Sherburn) (Temporary 10 Miles Per Hour and 40 Miles Per Hour Speed Restriction) Order 2002 No. 2002/2437. – Enabling power: Road Traffic Regulation Act 1984, s. 14 (1) (a). – Made: 20.09.2002. Coming into force: 22.09.2002. Effect: None. Territorial extent & classification: E. Local *Unpublished*

The A64 Trunk Road (Tadcaster Bypass) (Temporary Prohibition of Traffic) Order 2002 No. 2002/3142. – Enabling power: Road Traffic Regulation Act 1984, s. 14 (1) (a). – Made: 16.12.2002. Coming into force: 16.12.2002. Effect: None. Territorial extent & classification: E. Local *Unpublished*

The A65 Trunk Road (Cleatop Roundabout) (Temporary 30 Miles Per Hour Speed Restriction) Order 2002 No. 2002/2542. – Enabling power: Road Traffic Regulation Act 1984, s. 14 (1) (a). – Made: 03.10.2002. Coming into force: 06.10.2002. Effect: None. Territorial extent & classification: E. Local *Unpublished*

The A65 Trunk Road (Otley Road Junction) (Temporary 10 Miles Per Hour and 40 Miles Per Hour Speed Restriction) Order 2002 No. 2002/2611. – Enabling power: Road Traffic Regulation Act 1984, s. 14 (1) (a). – Made: 14.10.2002. Coming into force: 15.10.2002. Effect: None. Territorial extent & classification: E. Local *Unpublished*

The A65 Trunk Road (Settle Roundabout to Skirbeck) (Temporary 30 Miles Per Hour Speed Restriction) Order 2002 No. 2002/3234. – Enabling power: Road Traffic Regulation Act 1984, s. 14 (1) (a). – Made: 30.12.2002. Coming into force: 07.01.2003. Effect: None. Territorial extent & classification: E. Local *Unpublished*

The A65 Trunk Road (Skipton & Addingham) and the A629 Trunk Road (Skipton) (Temporary Restriction and Prohibition of Traffic) Order 2002 No. 2002/41. – Enabling power: Road Traffic Regulation Act 1984, s. 14 (1) (a). – Made: 10.01.2002. Coming into force: 13.01.2002. Effect: None. Territorial extent & classification: E. Local *Unpublished*

The A66 Trunk Road (Appleby Bypass) (Temporary Prohibition of Traffic) Order 2002 No. 2002/1424. – Enabling power: Road Traffic Regulation Act 1984, s. 14 (1) (b) (7). – Made: 23.05.2002. Coming into force: 29.05.2002. Effect: None. Territorial extent & classification: E. Local *Unpublished*

The A66 Trunk Road (Bowes Bypass) (Temporary Restriction and Prohibition of Traffic) Order 2002 No. 2002/1375. – Enabling power: Road Traffic Regulation Act 1984, s. 14 (1) (a). – Made: 14.05.2002. Coming into force: 16.05.2002. Effect: None. Territorial extent & classification: E. Local *Unpublished*

The A66 Trunk Road (Briery Interchange) (Temporary Restriction and Prohibition of Traffic) Order 2002 No. 2002/165. – Enabling power: Road Traffic Regulation Act 1984, s. 14 (1) (a). – Made: 24.01.2002. Coming into force: 27.01.2002. Effect: None. Territorial extent & classification: E. Local *Unpublished*

The A66 Trunk Road (Brigham and Great Broughton Junctions) (Temporary 10 Miles Per Hour and 40 Miles Per Hour Speed Restriction) Order 2002 No. 2002/2253. – Enabling power: Road Traffic Regulation Act 1984, s. 14 (1) (a). – Made: 22.08.2002. Coming into force: 26.08.2002. Effect: None. Territorial extent & classification: E. Local *Unpublished*

The A66 Trunk Road (Brough Bypass, Coltsford Bridge) (Temporary 10 Miles Per Hour and 30 Miles Per Hour Speed Restriction) Order 2002 No. 2002/2409. – Enabling power: Road Traffic Regulation Act 1984, s. 14 (1) (a). – Made: 18.09.2002. Coming into force: 22.09.2002. Effect: None. Territorial extent & classification: E. Local *Unpublished*

The A66 Trunk Road (Carleton Hall) (Temporary 10 Miles Per Hour and 30 Miles Per Hour Speed Restriction) Order 2002 No. 2002/2541. – Enabling power: Road Traffic Regulation Act 1984, s. 14 (1) (a). – Made: 03.10.2002. Coming into force: 06.10.2002. Effect: None. Territorial extent & classification: E. Local *Unpublished*

The A66 Trunk Road (Crackenthorpe to Appleby Bypass) (Temporary 40 Miles Per Hour Speed Restriction) (No. 2) Order 2002 No. 2002/1448. – Enabling power: Road Traffic Regulation Act 1984, s. 14 (1) (b). – Made: 23.05.2002. Coming into force: 31.05.2002. Effect: None. Territorial extent & classification: E. Local *Unpublished*

The A66 Trunk Road (Crackenthorpe to Appleby Bypass) (Temporary 40 Miles Per Hour Speed Restriction) (No. 2) Order 2002 Amendment Order 2002 No. 2002/1607. – Enabling power: Road Traffic Regulation Act 1984, s. 14 (1) (b). – Made: 13.06.2002. Coming into force: 16.06.2002. Effect: S.I. 2002/1448 amended. Territorial extent & classification: E. Local *Unpublished*

The A66 Trunk Road (Crackenthorpe to Appleby Bypass) (Temporary Restriction and Prohibition of Traffic) Order 2002 No. 2002/480. – Enabling power: Road Traffic Regulation Act 1984, s. 14 (1) (a). – Made: 28.02.2002. Coming into force: 03.03.2002. Effect: None. Territorial extent & classification: E. Local *Unpublished*

The A66 Trunk Road (Culgaith Road Junction) (Temporary 10 Miles per Hour and 40 Miles per Hour Speed Restriction) Order 2002 No. 2002/2828. – Enabling power: Road Traffic Regulation Act 1984, s. 14 (1) (a). – Made: 13.11.2002. Coming into force: 17.11.2002. Effect: None. Territorial extent & classification: E. Local *Unpublished*

The A66 Trunk Road (Eden Bridge) (Temporary 10 Miles Per Hour and 40 Miles Per Hour Speed Restriction) Order 2002 No. 2002/161. – Enabling power: Road Traffic Regulation Act 1984, s. 14 (1) (a). – Made: 23.01.2002. Coming into force: 01.02.2002. Effect: None. Territorial extent & classification: E. Local *Unpublished*

The A66 Trunk Road (Eden Bridge) (Temporary Restriction and Prohibition of Traffic) Order 2002 No. 2002/1320. – Enabling power: Road Traffic Regulation Act 1984, s. 14 (1) (b). – Made: 10.05.2002. Coming into force: 14.05.2002. Effect: None. Territorial extent & classification: E. Local *Unpublished*

The A66 Trunk Road (Sadberge) (Prohibition of Use of Gaps in the Central Reservation) Order 2002 No. 2002/1027. – Enabling power: Road Traffic Regulation Act 1984, ss. 1 (1), 2 (1) (2). – Made: 04.04.2002. Coming into force: 09.04.2002. Effect: None. Territorial extent & classification: E. Local *Unpublished*

The A66 Trunk Road (Sadberge Village) (Temporary Restriction and Prohibition of Traffic) Order 2002 No. 2002/189. – Enabling power: Road Traffic Regulation Act 1984, s. 14 (1) (a). – Made: 31.01.2002. Coming into force: 02.02.2002. Effect: None. Territorial extent & classification: E. Local *Unpublished*

The A66 Trunk Road (Sedbury Lodge to Scotch Corner, Melsonby Crossroads and Winston Crossroads) (Temporary Restriction and Prohibition of Traffic) Order 2002 No. 2002/2144. – Enabling power: Road Traffic Regulation Act 1984, s. 14 (1) (a) (7). – Made: 13.08.2002. Coming into force: 15.08.2002. Effect: None. Territorial extent & classification: E. Local *Unpublished*

The A66 Trunk Road (Stainburn and Great Clifton Bypass) (Temporary 40 Miles Per Hour Speed Restriction) Order 2002 No. 2002/2162. – Enabling power: Road Traffic Regulation Act 1984, s. 14 (1) (a). – Made: 15.08.2002. Coming into force: 17.08.2002. Effect: None. Territorial extent & classification: E. Local *Unpublished*

The A66 Trunk Road (Stockton and Darlington) (Temporary Restriction and Prohibition of Traffic) Order 2002 No. 2002/397. – Enabling power: Road Traffic Regulation Act 1984, s. 14 (1) (a). – Made: 21.02.2002. Coming into force: 24.02.2002. Effect: None. Territorial extent & classification: E. Local *Unpublished*

The A66 Trunk Road (Surtees Bridge) (Temporary 40 Miles Per Hour Speed Restriction) Order 2002 No. 2002/2065. – Enabling power: Road Traffic Regulation Act 1984, s. 14 (1) (a). – Made: 31.07.2002. Coming into force: 04.08.2002. Effect: None. Territorial extent & classification: E. Local *Unpublished*

The A66 Trunk Road (Yarm Road Interchange) (Temporary Prohibition of Traffic) Order 2002 No. 2002/1422. – Enabling power: Road Traffic Regulation Act 1984, s. 14 (1) (a). – Made: 20.05.2002. Coming into force: 22.05.2002. Effect: None. Territorial extent & classification: E. Local *Unpublished*

The A69 Trunk Road (Acomb Junction) (One Way) Order 2002 No. 2002/109. – Enabling power: Road Traffic Regulation Act 1984, ss. 1 (1), 2 (1) (2). – Made: 22.01.2002. Coming into force: 25.01.2002. Effect: None. Territorial extent & classification: E. Local *Unpublished*

The A69 Trunk Road (Aglionby) (Temporary Restriction and Prohibition of Traffic) Order 2002 No. 2002/1645. – Enabling power: Road Traffic Regulation Act 1984, s. 14 (1) (a). – Made: 19.06.2002. Coming into force: 23.06.2002. Effect: None. Territorial extent & classification: E. Local *Unpublished*

The A69 Trunk Road (Brampton Bypass) (Temporary Restriction and Prohibition of Traffic) Order 2002 No. 2002/1247. – Enabling power: Road Traffic Regulation Act 1984, s. 14 (1) (a). – Made: 01.05.2002. Coming into force: 06.05.2002. Effect: None. Territorial extent & classification: E. Local *Unpublished*

The A69 Trunk Road (Constantius Bridge) (Temporary Restriction and Prohibition of Traffic) Order 2002 No. 2002/2097. – Enabling power: Road Traffic Regulation Act 1984, s. 14 (1) (a). – Made: 06.08.2002. Coming into force: 08.08.2002. Effect: None. Territorial extent & classification: E. Local *Unpublished*

The A69 Trunk Road (Haltwhistle to Melkridge) (Temporary Restriction and Prohibition of Traffic) Order 2002 No. 2002/2308. – Enabling power: Road Traffic Regulation Act 1984, s. 14 (1) (a). – Made: 04.09.2002. Coming into force: 08.09.2002. Effect: None. Territorial extent & classification: E. Local *Unpublished*

The A69 Trunk Road (Haydon Bridge) (Temporary Restriction and Prohibition of Traffic) Order 2002 No. 2002/977. – Enabling power: Road Traffic Regulation Act 1984, s. 14 (1) (a). – Made: 03.04.2002. Coming into force: 07.04.2002. Effect: None. Territorial extent & classification: E. Local *Unpublished*

The A69 Trunk Road (Temon Bridge) (Temporary Restriction of Traffic) Order 2002 No. 2002/2362. – Enabling power: Road Traffic Regulation Act 1984, s. 14 (1) (a). – Made: 10.09.2002. Coming into force: 15.09.2002. Effect: None. Territorial extent & classification: E. Local *Unpublished*

The A69 Trunk Road (West Rattenraw Bridge) (Temporary Restriction of Traffic) Order 2002 No. 2002/1542. – Enabling power: Road Traffic Regulation Act 1984, s. 14 (1) (a). – Made: 05.06.2002. Coming into force: 09.06.2002. Effect: None. Territorial extent & classification: E. Local *Unpublished*

The A74 Trunk Road (Floriston Overbridge) (Temporary Restriction and Prohibition of Traffic) Order 2002 No. 2002/2642. – Enabling power: Road Traffic Regulation Act 1984, s. 14 (1) (a). – Made: 17.10.2002. Coming into force: 23.10.2002. Effect: None. Territorial extent & classification: E. Local *Unpublished*

The A74 Trunk Road (Mossband Viaduct) (Temporary Restriction and Prohibition of Traffic) Order 2002 No. 2002/1161. – Enabling power: Road Traffic Regulation Act 1984, s. 14 (1) (a). – Made: 18.04.2002. Coming into force: 21.04.2002. Effect: None. Territorial extent & classification: E. Local *Unpublished*

The A160 Trunk Road (Eastfield Junction) (Temporary Prohibition of Traffic) Order 2002 No. 2002/2164. – Enabling power: Road Traffic Regulation Act 1984, s. 14 (1) (a). – Made: 15.08.2002. Coming into force: 19.08.2002. Effect: None. Territorial extent & classification: E. Local *Unpublished*

The A167 Trunk Road (Blind Lane to Hermitage Roundabout) (Temporary Restriction and Prohibition of Traffic) Order 2002 No. 2002/2228. – Enabling power: Road Traffic Regulation Act 1984, s. 14 (1) (a). – Made: 28.08.2002. Coming into force: 01.09.2002. Effect: None. Territorial extent & classification: E. Local *Unpublished*

The A174 Trunk Road and the A1053 Trunk Road (Ormesby Interchange to the A1085) (Temporary 50 Miles Per Hour Speed Restriction) Order 2002 No. 2002/2429. – Enabling power: Road Traffic Regulation Act 1984, s. 14 (1) (a). – Made: 18.09.2002. Coming into force: 19.09.2002. Effect: None. Territorial extent & classification: E. Local *Unpublished*

The A180 Trunk Road and the A160 Trunk Road (Brocklesby Interchange) (Temporary Prohibition of Traffic) Order 2002 No. 2002/1540. – Enabling power: Road Traffic Regulation Act 1984, s. 14 (1) (a). – Made: 06.06.2002. Coming into force: 09.06.2002. Effect: None. Territorial extent & classification: E. Local *Unpublished*

The A180 Trunk Road (Barnetby Interchange) (Temporary Prohibition of Traffic) Order 2002 No. 2002/91. – Enabling power: Road Traffic Regulation Act 1984, s. 14 (1) (a). – Made: 18.01.2002. Coming into force: 20.01.2002. Effect: None. Territorial extent & classification: E. Local *Unpublished*

The A180 Trunk Road (Barnetby Interchange) (Temporary Prohibition of Traffic) Order (No. 2) 2002 No. 2002/448. – Enabling power: Road Traffic Regulation Act 1984, s. 14 (1) (a). – Made: 28.02.2002. Coming into force: 03.03.2002. Effect: None. Territorial extent & classification: E. Local *Unpublished*

The A180 Trunk Road (Brocklesby Interchange) (Temporary Prohibition of Traffic) Order 2002 No. 2002/664. – Enabling power: Road Traffic Regulation Act 1984, s. 14 (1) (a). – Made: 11.03.2002. Coming into force: 14.03.2002. Effect: None. Territorial extent & classification: E. Local *Unpublished*

The A180 Trunk Road (Great Coates Interchange) (Temporary Prohibition of Traffic) Order 2002 No. 2002/1262. – Enabling power: Road Traffic Regulation Act 1984, s. 14 (1) (a). – Made: 02.05.2002. Coming into force: 07.05.2002. Effect: None. Territorial extent & classification: E. Local *Unpublished*

The A180 Trunk Road (Race Bridge) (Temporary 50 Miles Per Hour Speed Restriction) Order 2002 No. 2002/1743. – Enabling power: Road Traffic Regulation Act 1984, s. 14 (1) (a). – Made: 01.07.2002. Coming into force: 01.07.2002. Effect: None. Territorial extent & classification: E. Local *Unpublished*

The A180 Trunk Road (Stallingborough Interchange) (Temporary Prohibition of Traffic) Order 2002 No. 2002/1865. – Enabling power: Road Traffic Regulation Act 1984, s. 14 (1) (a). – Made: 16.07.2002. Coming into force: 18.07.2002. Effect: None. Territorial extent & classification: E. Local *Unpublished*

The A249 Trunk Road and the M2 Motorway (Stockbury) (Temporary 30 Miles Per Hour Speed Restriction) Order 2002 No. 2002/134. – Enabling power: Road Traffic Regulation Act 1984, s. 14 (1) (a). – Made: 28.01.2002. Coming into force: 02.02.2002. Effect: None. Territorial extent & classification: E. Local *Unpublished*

The A249 Trunk Road (Bobbing - Stockbury) (Temporary Prohibition of Traffic) Order 2002 No. 2002/2346. – Enabling power: Road Traffic Regulation Act 1984, s. 14 (1) (a). – Made: 09.09.2002. Coming into force: 14.09.2002. Effect: None. Territorial extent & classification: E. Local *Unpublished*

The A249 Trunk Road (Brielle Way, Isle of Sheppey) (Temporary Speed Restrictions) Order 2002 No. 2002/2456. – Enabling power: Road Traffic Regulation Act 1984, s. 14 (1) (a). – Made: 23.09.2002. Coming into force: 28.09.2002. Effect: None. Territorial extent & classification: E. Local *Unpublished*

The A249 Trunk Road (Cowstead Corner - Queenborough) (Temporary Speed Restrictions) Order 2002 No. 2002/2917. – Enabling power: Road Traffic Regulation Act 1984, s. 14 (1) (a). – Made: 25.11.2002. Coming into force: 30.11.2002. Effect: None. Territorial extent & classification: E. Local *Unpublished*

The A249 Trunk Road (Cowstead Corner) (Temporary 30 Miles Per Hour Speed Restriction) Order 2002 No. 2002/1634. – Enabling power: Road Traffic Regulation Act 1984, s. 14 (1) (a). – Made: 24.06.2002. Coming into force: 29.06.2002. Effect: None. Territorial extent & classification: E. Local *Unpublished*

The A249 Trunk Road (Kingsferry Roundabout - Cowstead Corner Roundabout) (Temporary Prohibition of Traffic) Order 2002 No. 2002/2348. – Enabling power: Road Traffic Regulation Act 1984, s. 14 (1) (a). – Made: 09.09.2002. Coming into force: 14.09.2002. Effect: None. Territorial extent & classification: E. Local *Unpublished*

The A259 Trunk Road (Barnhorn Road) (Temporary 40 Miles Per Hour Speed Restriction) Order 2002 No. 2002/2284. – Enabling power: Road Traffic Regulation Act 1984, s. 14 (1) (a). – Made: 02.09.2002. Coming into force: 07.09.2002. Effect: None. Territorial extent & classification: E. Local *Unpublished*

The A259 Trunk Road (Bexhill - Glyne Gap) (Temporary 10 Miles Per Hour Speed Restriction) Order 2002 No. 2002/131. – Enabling power: Road Traffic Regulation Act 1984, s. 14 (1) (a). – Made: 28.01.2002. Coming into force: 02.02.2002. Effect: None. Territorial extent & classification: E. Local *Unpublished*

The A259 Trunk Road (Brookland Level Crossing) (Temporary Prohibition of Traffic) Order 2002 No. 2002/2345. – Enabling power: Road Traffic Regulation Act 1984, s. 14 (1) (a). – Made: 09.09.2002. Coming into force: 14.09.2002. Effect: None. Territorial extent & classification: E. Local *Unpublished*

The A259 Trunk Road (Various Roads, Rye) (Temporary Prohibition of Traffic) Order 2002 No. 2002/2696. – Enabling power: Road Traffic Regulation Act 1984, s. 16A (2) (a). – Made: 28.10.2002. Coming into force: 04.11.2002. Effect: None. Territorial extent & classification: E. Local *Unpublished*

The A282 Trunk Road (Junctions 1A - 1B) (Temporary 50 Miles Per Hour Speed Restriction) Order 2002 No. 2002/1275. – Enabling power: Road Traffic Regulation Act 1984, s. 14 (1) (a). – Made: 07.05.2002. Coming into force: 11.05.2002. Effect: None. Territorial extent & classification: E. Local *Unpublished*

The A303 Trunk Road (Cartgate Roundabout to Percombe Hill Junction) (Temporary Restriction of Traffic) Order 2002 No. 2002/1553. – Enabling power: Road Traffic Regulation Act 1984, s. 14 (1) (a). – Made: 07.06.2002. Coming into force: 11.06.2002. Effect: None. Territorial extent & classification: E. Local *Unpublished*

The A303 Trunk Road (Folly Bottom, Westbound Carriageway) (Temporary Speed Restrictions) Order 2002 No. 2002/2562. – Enabling power: Road Traffic Regulation Act 1984, s. 14 (1) (a). – Made: 07.10.2002. Coming into force: 12.10.2002. Effect: None. Territorial extent & classification: E. Local *Unpublished*

The A303 Trunk Road (Marsh Interchange) (Temporary Restriction of Traffic) Order 2002 No. 2002/73. – Enabling power: Road Traffic Regulation Act 1984, s. 14 (1) (a). – Made: 16.01.2002. Coming into force: 19.01.2002. Effect: None. Territorial extent & classification: E. Local *Unpublished*

The A303 Trunk Road (Near Amesbury) (Prohibition of "U" Turns) Order 2002 No. 2002/688. – Enabling power: Road Traffic Regulation Act 1984, ss. 1 (1), 2 (1) (2). – Made: 11.03.2002. Coming into force: 27.03.2002. Effect: None. Territorial extent & classification: E. Local *Unpublished*

The A303 Trunk Road (Pill Lane to Higher Podimore) (Temporary Restriction of Traffic) Order 2002 No. 2002/2339. – Enabling power: Road Traffic Regulation Act 1984, s. 14 (1) (a). – Made: 09.09.2002. Coming into force: 13.09.2002. Effect: None. Territorial extent & classification: E. Local *Unpublished*

The A303 Trunk Road (West of Bullington Cross) (Temporary Restriction and Prohibition of Traffic) Order 2002 No. 2002/2854. – Enabling power: Road Traffic Regulation Act 1984, s. 14 (1) (a). – Made: 18.11.2002. Coming into force: 23.11.2002. Effect: None. Territorial extent & classification: E. Local *Unpublished*

The A339 Trunk Road (Newbury Road, Kingsclere) (Temporary Speed Restrictions) Order 2002 No. 2002/1606. – Enabling power: Road Traffic Regulation Act 1984, s. 14 (1) (a). – Made: 10.06.2002. Coming into force: 15.06.2002. Effect: None. Territorial extent & classification: E. Local *Unpublished*

The A339 Trunk Road (Ramsdell Junction) (Temporary Speed Restrictions) Order 2002 No. 2002/2508. – Enabling power: Road Traffic Regulation Act 1984, s. 14 (1) (a). – Made: 30.09.2002. Coming into force: 05.10.2002. Effect: None. Territorial extent & classification: E. Local *Unpublished*

The A339 Trunk Road (Ringway East, Basingstoke) (Temporary Prohibition of Traffic) Order 2002 No. 2002/2148. – Enabling power: Road Traffic Regulation Act 1984, s. 14 (1) (a). – Made: 12.08.2002. Coming into force: 17.08.2002. Effect: None. Territorial extent & classification: E. Local *Unpublished*

The A339 Trunk Road (Swan Roundabout - A34) (Temporary Restriction and Prohibition of Traffic) Order 2002 No. 2002/188. – Enabling power: Road Traffic Regulation Act 1984, s. 14 (1) (a). – Made: 28.01.2002. Coming into force: 02.02.2002. Effect: None. Territorial extent & classification: E. Local *Unpublished*

The A361 Trunk Road and the M5 Motorway (Junction 27) (Temporary Restriction of Traffic) Order 2002 No. 2002/190. – Enabling power: Road Traffic Regulation Act 1984, s. 14 (1) (a). – Made: 31.01.2002. Coming into force: 02.02.2002. Effect: None. Territorial extent & classification: E. Local *Unpublished*

The A361 Trunk Road (Bolham to Sampford Peverell) (Temporary Prohibition and Restriction of Traffic) Order 2002 No. 2002/1127. – Enabling power: Road Traffic Regulation Act 1984, s. 14 (1) (a). – Made: 02.04.2002. Coming into force: 04.04.2002. Effect: None. Territorial extent & classification: E. Local *Unpublished*

The A404 (M) Motorway and the A404 Trunk Road (Junctions 9B - 9A and Marlow - Handy Cross) (Temporary Speed Restrictions) Order 2002 No. 2002/2916. – Enabling power: Road Traffic Regulation Act 1984, s. 14 (1) (a). – Made: 25.11.2002. Coming into force: 30.11.2002. Effect: None. Territorial extent & classification: E. Local *Unpublished*

The A404(M) Motorway (Junction 9A, Southbound Slip Roads) (Temporary Prohibition of Traffic) Order 2002 No. 2002/1046. – Enabling power: Road Traffic Regulation Act 1984, s. 14 (1) (a). – Made: 08.04.2002. Coming into force: 15.04.2002. Effect: None. Territorial extent & classification: E. Local *Unpublished*

The A404(M) Motorway (Shoppenhanger's Road) (Temporary Prohibition of Traffic) Order 2002 No. 2002/2506. – Enabling power: Road Traffic Regulation Act 1984, s. 14 (1) (a). – Made: 30.09.2002. Coming into force: 05.10.2002. Effect: None. Territorial extent & classification: E. Local *Unpublished*

The A404(M) Motorway (West of Maidenhead) (Temporary Restriction and Prohibition of Traffic) Order 2002 No. 2002/1623. – Enabling power: Road Traffic Regulation Act 1984, s. 14 (1) (a) (7). – Made: 24.06.2002. Coming into force: 01.07.2002. Effect: None. Territorial extent & classification: E. Local *Unpublished*

The A404 Trunk Road (A4155 Junction - Bisham Roundabout) (Temporary Speed Restrictions) Order 2002 No. 2002/3163. – Enabling power: Road Traffic Regulation Act 1984, s. 14 (1) (a). – Made: 16.12.2002. Coming into force: 21.12.2002. Effect: None. Territorial extent & classification: E. Local *Unpublished*

The A404 Trunk Road (Bisham Roundabout - A4155 Junction) (Temporary Speed Restrictions) Order 2002 No. 2002/1938. – Enabling power: Road Traffic Regulation Act 1984, s. 14 (1) (a). – Made: 22.07.2002. Coming into force: 27.07.2002. Effect: None. Territorial extent & classification: E. Local *Unpublished*

The A404 Trunk Road (Burchett's Green - Bisham) (Temporary Speed Restrictions) Order 2002 No. 2002/2559. – Enabling power: Road Traffic Regulation Act 1984, s. 14 (1) (a). – Made: 07.10.2002. Coming into force: 12.10.2002. Effect: None. Territorial extent & classification: E. Local *Unpublished*

The A405 and the A414 Trunk Roads and the M10 Motorway (Park Street) (Temporary Restriction and Prohibition of Traffic) Order 2002 No. 2002/904. – Enabling power: Road Traffic Regulation Act 1984, s. 14 (1) (a). – Made: 25.03.2002. Coming into force: 02.04.2002. Effect: None. Territorial extent & classification: E. Local *Unpublished*

The A405 Trunk Road (Bucknalls Lane Junction) (Bus Lane) Order 2002 No. 2002/1450. – Enabling power: Road Traffic Regulation Act 1984, ss. 1 (1), 2 (1) (2), 4 (1). – Made: 27.05.2002. Coming into force: 10.06.2002. Effect: None. Territorial extent & classification: E. Local *Unpublished*

The A405 Trunk Road (North Orbital Road, Near Garston) (Temporary Restriction and Prohibition of Traffic) Order 2002 No. 2002/2134. – Enabling power: Road Traffic Regulation Act 1984, s. 14 (1) (a). – Made: 12.08.2002. Coming into force: 17.08.2002. Effect: None. Territorial extent & classification: E. Local *Unpublished*

The A414 Trunk Road (Colney Heath) (Temporary Restriction and Prohibition of Traffic) Order 2002 No. 2002/214. – Enabling power: Road Traffic Regulation Act 1984, s. 14 (1) (a). – Made: 04.02.2002. Coming into force: 09.02.2002. Effect: None. Territorial extent & classification: E. Local *Unpublished*

The A414 Trunk Road (Near London Colney) (Temporary Prohibition of Traffic) Order 2002 No. 2002/1421. – Enabling power: Road Traffic Regulation Act 1984, s. 14 (1) (a). – Made: 20.05.2002. Coming into force: 25.05.2002. Effect: None. Territorial extent & classification: E. Local *Unpublished*

The A414 Trunk Road (Park Street - London Colney) (Temporary Speed Restrictions) Order 2002 No. 2002/212. – Enabling power: Road Traffic Regulation Act 1984, s. 14 (1) (a). – Made: 04.02.2002. Coming into force: 09.02.2002. Effect: None. Territorial extent & classification: E. Local *Unpublished*

The A419 and A417 Trunk Roads (Driffield Junction to Daglingworth Quarry Junction) (Temporary Prohibition of Traffic) Order 2002 No. 2002/2262. – Enabling power: Road Traffic Regulation Act 1984, s. 14 (1) (a). – Made: 02.09.2002. Coming into force: 06.09.2002. Effect: None. Territorial extent & classification: E. Local *Unpublished*

The A419 Trunk Road (Blunsdon) (Temporary Prohibition and Restriction of Traffic) Order 2002 No. 2002/1601. – Enabling power: Road Traffic Regulation Act 1984, s. 14 (1) (a). – Made: 10.06.2002. Coming into force: 15.06.2002. Effect: None. Territorial extent & classification: E. Local *Unpublished*

The A419 Trunk Road (Commonhead Roundabout) (Temporary Restriction of Traffic) Order 2002 No. 2002/1289. – Enabling power: Road Traffic Regulation Act 1984, s. 14 (1) (a). – Made: 07.05.2002. Coming into force: 11.05.2002. Effect: None. Territorial extent & classification: E. Local *Unpublished*

The A419 Trunk Road (Cricklade Junction to Castle Eaton Junction) (Temporary Prohibition of Traffic) Order 2002 No. 2002/1814. – Enabling power: Road Traffic Regulation Act 1984, s. 14 (1) (b). – Made: 05.07.2002. Coming into force: 12.07.2002. Effect: None. Territorial extent & classification: E. Local *Unpublished*

The A419 Trunk Road (Cricklade) (Temporary Restriction of Traffic) Order 2002 No. 2002/28. – Enabling power: Road Traffic Regulation Act 1984, s. 14 (1) (a). – Made: 08.01.2002. Coming into force: 12.01.2002. Effect: None. Territorial extent & classification: E. Local *Unpublished*

The A419 Trunk Road (M4 Junction 15 to Commonhead Roundabout, Swindon) (Prohibition of Entry) Order 2002 No. 2002/3144. – Enabling power:Road Traffic Regulation Act 1984, ss. 1 (1), 2 (1), 121A (1), 122A. – Made: 10.12.2002. Coming into force: 20.12.2002. Effect: None. Territorial extent & classification: E. Local *Unpublished*

The A419 Trunk Road (Near Cricklade) (Temporary Prohibition and Restriction of Traffic) Order 2002 No. 2002/2475. – Enabling power: Road Traffic Regulation Act 1984, s. 14 (1) (a). – Made: 25.09.2002. Coming into force: 28.09.2002. Effect: None. Territorial extent & classification: E. Local *Unpublished*

The A419 Trunk Road (Turnpike Roundabout) (Temporary Restriction of Traffic) Order 2002 No. 2002/910. – Enabling power: Road Traffic Regulation Act 1984, s. 14 (1) (a). – Made: 27.03.2002. Coming into force: 03.04.2002. Effect: None. Territorial extent & classification: E. Local *Unpublished*

The A420 Trunk Road (Shrivenham/Watchfield Bypass) (Temporary Restriction of Traffic) Order 2002 No. 2002/2673. – Enabling power: Road Traffic Regulation Act 1984, s. 14 (1) (a). – Made: 21.10.2002. Coming into force: 26.10.2002. Effect: None. Territorial extent & classification: E. Local *Unpublished*

The A420 Trunk Road (Tubney Woods to Bessels Leigh) (Temporary Restriction of Traffic) Order 2002 No. 2002/2337. – Enabling power: Road Traffic Regulation Act 1984, s. 14 (1) (a). – Made: 09.09.2002. Coming into force: 14.09.2002. Effect: None. Territorial extent & classification: E. Local *Unpublished*

The A421 Trunk Road (Bedford Bypass, Bedfordshire) (Temporary Restriction and Prohibition of Traffic) Order 2002 No. 2002/2857. – Enabling power: Road Traffic Regulation Act 1984, s. 14 (1) (a). – Made: 15.11.2002. Coming into force: 22.11.2002. Effect: None. Territorial extent & classification: E. Local *Unpublished*

The A421 Trunk Road (Brogborough, Bedfordshire) (Temporary Restriction and Prohibition of Traffic) Order 2002 No. 2002/753. – Enabling power: Road Traffic Regulation Act 1984, s. 14 (1) (a). – Made: 18.03.2002. Coming into force: 25.03.2002. Effect: None. Territorial extent & classification: E. Local *Unpublished*

The A421 Trunk Road (Various Lengths, Bedfordshire) (Temporary 40 Miles Per Hour Speed Restriction) Order 2002 No. 2002/1957. – Enabling power: Road Traffic Regulation Act 1984, s. 14 (1) (a). – Made: 22.07.2002. Coming into force: 29.07.2002. Effect: None. Territorial extent & classification: E. Local *Unpublished*

The A423 Trunk Road (Oxford Southern Bypass) (Temporary Speed Restrictions) Order 2002 No. 2002/1344. – Enabling power: Road Traffic Regulation Act 1984, s. 14 (1) (a). – Made: 13.05.2002. Coming into force: 18.05.2002. Effect: None. Territorial extent & classification: E. Local *Unpublished*

The A428 Trunk Road (Cambourne, Cambridgeshire) (Temporary Restriction of Traffic) Order 2002 No. 2002/1191. – Enabling power: Road Traffic Regulation Act 1984, s. 14 (1) (a). – Made: 23.04.2002. Coming into force: 30.04.2002. Effect: None. Territorial extent & classification: E. Local *Unpublished*

The A428 Trunk Road (St. Neots Bypass, Bedfordshire) (Temporary 40 Miles Per Hour Speed Restriction) Order 2002 No. 2002/2473. – Enabling power: Road Traffic Regulation Act 1984, s. 14 (1) (a). – Made: 23.09.2002. Coming into force: 30.09.2002. Effect: None. Territorial extent & classification: E. Local *Unpublished*

The A428 Trunk Road (Various Lengths, Bedfordshire - Cambridgeshire) (Temporary 40 Miles Per Hour Speed Restriction) Order 2002 No. 2002/1959. – Enabling power: Road Traffic Regulation Act 1984, s. 14 (1) (a). – Made: 22.07.2002. Coming into force: 29.07.2002. Effect: None. Territorial extent & classification: E. Local *Unpublished*

The A435 Trunk Road (Washford to Mappleborough Green, Warwichshire) (Temporary 10 Miles per Hour Speed Restriction) Order 2002 No. 2002/2862. – Enabling power: Road Traffic Regulation Act 1984, s. 14 (1) (a). – Made: 18.11.2002. Coming into force: 25.11.2002. Effect: None. Territorial extent & classification: E. Local *Unpublished*

The A446 Trunk Road (Holly Lane/Middleton Lane to Dunton Lane, Warwickshire) (Temporary Prohibition of Traffic) Order 2002 No. 2002/2358. – Enabling power: Road Traffic Regulation Act 1984, s. 14 (1) (b). – Made: 11.09.2002. Coming into force: 18.09.2002. Effect: None. Territorial extent & classification: E. Local *Unpublished*

The A446 Trunk Road (Lichfield Road, Wishaw, Warwickshire) (Temporary 40 Miles Per Hour Speed Restriction) Order 2002 No. 2002/2672. – Enabling power: Road Traffic Regulation Act 1984, s. 14 (1) (a). – Made: 14.10.2002. Coming into force: 21.10.2002. Effect: None. Territorial extent & classification: E. Local *Unpublished*

The A449 Trunk Road (Chatley, Worcestershire) (Prohibition of U Turns) Order 2002 No. 2002/1236. – Enabling power: Road Traffic Regulation Act 1984, ss. 1 (1), 2 (1) (2). – Made: 19.04.2002. Coming into force: 03.05.2002. Effect: None. Territorial extent & classification: E. Local *Unpublished*

The A449 Trunk Road (Dunsley Bank to Lawnswood, Staffordshire) (Temporary 40 Miles Per Hour and 50 Miles Per Hour Speed Restriction) Order 2002 No. 2002/3240. – Enabling power: Road Traffic Regulation Act 1984, s. 14 (1) (b). – Made: 30.12.2002. Coming into force: 06.01.2003. Effect: None. Territorial extent & classification: E. Local *Unpublished*

The A449 Trunk Road (Junction with Bridgnorth Road, Stewponey, Staffordshire) (Temporary Prohibition of Traffic) Order 2002 No. 2002/53. – Enabling power: Road Traffic Regulation Act 1984, s. 14 (1) (b). – Made: 14.01.2002. Coming into force: 21.01.2002. Effect: None. Territorial extent & classification: E. Local *Unpublished*

The A449 Trunk Road (Kidderminster, Worcestershire) (Temporary 30 Miles Per Hour Speed Restriction) Order 2002 No. 2002/2163. – Enabling power: Road Traffic Regulation Act 1984, s. 14 (1) (b). – Made: 16.08.2002. Coming into force: 23.08.2002. Effect: None. Territorial extent & classification: E. Local *Unpublished*

The A449 Trunk Road (Low Hill, Kidderminster) (Temporary Restriction and Prohibition of Traffic) Order 2002 No. 2002/1089. – Enabling power: Road Traffic Regulation Act 1984, s. 14 (1) (a). – Made: 10.04.2002. Coming into force: 17.04.2002. Effect: None. Territorial extent & classification: E. Local *Unpublished*

The A449 Trunk Road (Penkridge, Staffordshire) (Prohibition of Waiting) Order 2002 No. 2002/954. – Enabling power: Road Traffic Regulation Act 1984, ss. 1 (1), 2 (1) (2), 4 (1) (2). – Made: 22.03.2002. Coming into force: 05.04.2002. Effect: S.I. 1984/1252 amended. Territorial extent & classification: E. Local *Unpublished*

The A449 Trunk Road (Stourton, Staffordshire) (Prohibition of Entry and "U" Turns) Order 2002 No. 2002/322. – Enabling power: Road Traffic Regulation Act 1984, ss. 1 (1), 2 (1) (2). – Made: 01.02.2002. Coming into force: 16.02.2002. Effect: None. Territorial extent & classification: E. Local *Unpublished*

The A449 Trunk Road (Waresley, Worcestershire) (Temporary 10 Miles Per Hour Speed Restriction) Order 2002 No. 2002/1365. – Enabling power: Road Traffic Regulation Act 1984, s. 14 (1) (a). – Made: 13.05.2002. Coming into force: 20.05.2002. Effect: None. Territorial extent & classification: E. Local *Unpublished*

The A449 Trunk Road (Worcester Road, Kidderminster) (Temporary 40 Miles Per Hour Speed Restriction) Order 2002 No. 2002/1519. – Enabling power: Road Traffic Regulation Act 1984, s. 14 (1) (b). – Made: 27.05.2002. Coming into force: 03.06.2002. Effect: None. Territorial extent & classification: E. Local *Unpublished*

The A452 Trunk Road (Chester Road, Walsall) (Temporary Restriction and Prohibition of Traffic) Order 2002 No. 2002/1273. – Enabling power: Road Traffic Regulation Act 1984, s. 14 (1) (a). – Made: 03.05.2002. Coming into force: 10.05.2002. Effect: None. Territorial extent & classification: E. Local *Unpublished*

The A453 Trunk Road (M1 Junction 24 to Clifton) (Temporary Prohibition of Traffic) Order 2002 No. 2002/1218. – Enabling power: Road Traffic Regulation Act 1984, s. 14 (1) (a). – Made: 26.04.2002. Coming into force: 03.05.2002. Effect: None. Territorial extent & classification: E. Local *Unpublished*

The A456 Trunk Road (Hagley Causeway, Worcestershire) (Temporary 10 Miles Per Hour Speed Restriction) Order 2002 No. 2002/1546. – Enabling power: Road Traffic Regulation Act 1984, s. 14 (1) (a). – Made: 03.06.2002. Coming into force: 10.06.2002. Effect: None. Territorial extent & classification: E. Local *Unpublished*

The A456 Trunk Road (Hayley Green, Worcestershire) (Temporary 40 Miles Per Hour Speed Restriction) Order 2002 No. 2002/2319. – Enabling power: Road Traffic Regulation Act 1984, s. 14 (1) (b). – Made: 06.09.2002. Coming into force: 13.09.2002. Effect: None. Territorial extent & classification: E. Local *Unpublished*

The A456 Trunk Road (Kidderminster Road South and Worcester Road, West Hagley) (Temporary Restriction and Prohibition of Traffic) Order 2002 No. 2002/1520. – Enabling power: Road Traffic Regulation Act 1984, s. 14 (1) (a). – Made: 28.05.2002. Coming into force: 04.06.2002. Effect: None. Territorial extent & classification: E. Local *Unpublished*

The A456 Trunk Road (West Hagley, Worcestershire) (Temporary 30 Miles Per Hour and 40 Miles Per Hour Speed Restriction) Order 2002 No. 2002/1654. – Enabling power: Road Traffic Regulation Act 1984, s. 14 (1) (b). – Made: 21.06.2002. Coming into force: 28.06.2002. Effect: None. Territorial extent & classification: E. Local *Unpublished*

The A465 Trunk Road (Belmont, Herefordshire) (Temporary 30 Miles Per Hour Speed Restriction) Order 2002 No. 2002/3251. – Enabling power: Road Traffic Regulation Act 1984, s. 14 (1) (b). – Made: 27.12.2002. Coming into force: 03.01.2003. Effect: None. Territorial extent & classification: E. Local *Unpublished*

The A465 Trunk Road (Belmont Road, Herefordshire) (Temporary 10 Miles Per Hour Speed Restriction) (No. 2) Order 2002 No. 2002/1366. – Enabling power: Road Traffic Regulation Act 1984, s. 14 (1) (a). – Made: 10.05.2002. Coming into force: 17.05.2002. Effect: None. Territorial extent & classification: E. Local *Unpublished*

The A465 Trunk Road (Belmont Road, Hereford) (Temporary Restriction and Prohibition of Traffic) Order 2002 No. 2002/235. – Enabling power: Road Traffic Regulation Act 1984, s. 14 (1) (a). – Made: 04.02.2002. Coming into force: 11.02.2002. Effect: None. Territorial extent & classification: E. Local *Unpublished*

The A465 Trunk Road (Tram Inn to Didley, Herefordshire) (Temporary 10 Miles Per Hour Speed Restriction) Order 2002 No. 2002/1224. – Enabling power: Road Traffic Regulation Act 1984, s. 14 (1) (a). – Made: 29.04.2002. Coming into force: 06.05.2002. Effect: None. Territorial extent & classification: E. Local *Unpublished*

The A500 Trunk Road (Etruria, Stoke on Trent) (Slip Road) (Temporary Prohibition of Traffic) Order 2002 No. 2002/177. – Enabling power: Road Traffic Regulation Act 1984, s. 14 (1) (a). – Made: 28.01.2002. Coming into force: 04.02.2002. Effect: None. Territorial extent & classification: E. Local *Unpublished*

The A500 Trunk Road (M6 Junction 16 to A34 Talke Interchange) (Temporary Restriction and Prohibition of Traffic) Order 2002 No. 2002/387. – Enabling power: Road Traffic Regulation Act 1984, s. 14 (1) (a). – Made: 18.02.2002. Coming into force: 25.02.2002. Effect: None. Territorial extent & classification: E. Local *Unpublished*

The A500 Trunk Road (Meremoor Moss Roundabout) (Temporary 30 Miles Per Hour Speed Limit) Order 2002 No. 2002/1552. – Enabling power: Road Traffic Regulation Act 1984, s. 14 (1) (a). – Made: 31.05.2002. Coming into force: 09.06.2002. Effect: None. Territorial extent & classification: E. Local *Unpublished*

The A516 Trunk Road (Junction with Uttoxeter Road, Derby) (Northbound Exit Slip Road) (Temporary Prohibition of Traffic) Order 2002 No. 2002/1571. – Enabling power: Road Traffic Regulation Act 1984, s. 14 (1) (a). – Made: 07.06.2002. Coming into force: 14.06.2002. Effect: None. Territorial extent & classification: E. Local *Unpublished*

The A523 Trunk Road (Flash Lane to Holehouse Lane, North of Macclesfield) (Temporary 10 Miles Per Hour and 30 Miles Per Hour Speed Restriction) Order 2002 No. 2002/1225. – Enabling power: Road Traffic Regulation Act 1984, s. 14 (1) (a). – Made: 29.04.2002. Coming into force: 06.05.2002. Effect: None. Territorial extent & classification: E. Local *Unpublished*

The A523 Trunk Road (Mill Street, Leek, Staffordshire) (Prohibition of Waiting) Order 2002 No. 2002/1081. – Enabling power: Road Traffic Regulation Act 1984, ss. 1 (1), 2 (1) (2), 4 (1) (2), sch. 9, para. 27 (1). – Made: 05.04.2002. Coming into force: 19.04.2002. Effect: S.I. 1975/506 revoked. Territorial extent & classification: E. Local *Unpublished*

The A550 Trunk Road (Welsh Road) (Temporary 30 Miles Per Hour Speed Restriction) Order 2002 No. 2002/3193. – Enabling power: Road Traffic Regulation Act 1984, s. 14 (1) (a). – Made: 17.12.2002. Coming into force: 05.01.2003. Effect: None. Territorial extent & classification: E. Local *Unpublished*

The A556 Trunk Road (Ascol Drive) (Prohibition of Right Turn) Order 2002 No. 2002/883. – Enabling power: Road Traffic Regulation Act 1984, ss. 1 (1), 2 (1) (2). – Made: 26.03.2002. Coming into force: 31.03.2002. Effect: None. Territorial extent & classification: E. Local *Unpublished*

The A556 Trunk Road (Cheshire Show) (Temporary Prohibition of Traffic) Order 2002 No. 2002/1584. – Enabling power: Road Traffic Regulation Act 1984, s. 14 (1) (b). – Made: 11.06.2002. Coming into force: 17.06.2002. Effect: None. Territorial extent & classification: E. Local *Unpublished*

The A556 Trunk Road (Mere Crossroads) (Temporary Prohibition of Right Turns) Order 2002 No. 2002/1153. – Enabling power: Road Traffic Regulation Act 1984, s. 14 (1) (b). – Made: 19.04.2002. Coming into force: 22.04.2002. Effect: None. Territorial extent & classification: E. Local *Unpublished*

The A556 Trunk Road (Plumley Moor Road) (Temporary 30 Miles Per Hour Speed Limit) Order 2002 No. 2002/22. – Enabling power: Road Traffic Regulation Act 1984, s. 14 (1) (a). – Made: 03.01.2002. Coming into force: 06.01.2002. Effect: None. Territorial extent & classification: E. Local *Unpublished*

The A556 Trunk Road (Royal Horticultural Show) (Temporary Prohibition of Traffic) Order 2002 No. 2002/1802. – Enabling power: Road Traffic Regulation Act 1984, s. 14 (1) (b). – Made: 09.07.2002. Coming into force: 16.07.2002. Effect: None. Territorial extent & classification: E. Local *Unpublished*

The A565 (Southport New Road and Gravel Lane, Banks) (Prohibition of Driving) Order 2002 No. 2002/395. – Enabling power: Road Traffic Regulation Act 1984, ss. 1 (1), 2 (1) (2). – Made: 21.02.2002. Coming into force: 25.02.2002. Effect: None. Territorial extent & classification: E. Local *Unpublished*

The A565 (Southport New Road) (Closure of Gaps in the Central Reservation, Prohibition of Entry and No "U" Turn) Order 2002 No. 2002/979. – Enabling power: Road Traffic Regulation Act 1984, ss. 1 (1), 2 (1) (2). – Made: 03.04.2002. Coming into force: 08.04.2002. Effect: None. Territorial extent & classification: E. Local *Unpublished*

The A565 Trunk Road (Formby Bypass) (Closure of Gaps in the Central Reservation) Order 2002 No. 2002/396. – Enabling power: Road Traffic Regulation Act 1984, ss. 1 (1), 2 (1) (2). – Made: 20.02.2002. Coming into force: 23.02.2002. Effect: None. Territorial extent & classification: E. Local *Unpublished*

The A565 Trunk Road (Formby Bypass, Woodvale Rally) (Temporary 40 Miles Per Hour Speed Restriction) Order 2002 No. 2002/1992. – Enabling power: Road Traffic Regulation Act 1984, s. 14 (1) (b). – Made: 24.07.2002. Coming into force: 01.08.2002. Effect: None. Territorial extent & classification: E. Local *Unpublished*

The A565 Trunk Road (Southport New Road) (Temporary 30 Miles Per Hour) Order 2002 Amendment Order 2002 No. 2002/393. – Enabling power: Road Traffic Regulation Act 1984, s. 14 (1) (a). – Made: 21.02.2002. Coming into force: 24.02.2002. Effect: S.I. 2002/6 amended. Territorial extent & classification: E. Local *Unpublished*

The A565 Trunk Road (Southport New Road) (Temporary 30 Miles Per Hour Speed Limit) Order 2002 No. 2002/6. Enabling power: Road Traffic Regulation Act 1984, s. 14 (1) (a). – Made: 02.01.2002. Coming into force: 06.01.2002. Effect: None. Territorial extent & classification: E. Local *Unpublished*

The A565 Trunk Road (Southport New Road, The Gravel) (Closure of a Gap in the Central Reservation) Order 2002 No. 2002/13. – Enabling power:Road Traffic Regulation Act 1984, ss. 1 (1), 2 (1) (2). – Made: 03.01.2002. Coming into force: 07.01.2002. Effect: None. Territorial extent & classification: E. Local *Unpublished*

The A565 Trunk Road (Southport New Road, The Gravel) (Temporary Restriction and Prohibition of Traffic) Order 2002 No. 2002/964. – Enabling power: Road Traffic Regulation Act 1984, s. 14 (1) (a). – Made: 02.04.2002. Coming into force: 06.04.2002. Effect: None. Territorial extent & classification: E. Local *Unpublished*

The A570 and A580 Trunk Roads (Temporary Restriction and Prohibition of Traffic) Order 2002 No. 2002/1316. – Enabling power: Road Traffic Regulation Act 1984, s. 14 (1) (a). – Made: 09.05.2002. Coming into force: 12.05.2002. Effect: None. Territorial extent & classification: E. Local *Unpublished*

The A570 Trunk Road (Mossborough Roundabout) (Temporary 30 Miles per Hour Speed Limit) Order 2002 No. 2002/2805. – Enabling power: Road Traffic Regulation Act 1984, s. 14 (1) (a). – Made: 07.11.2002. Coming into force: 10.11.2002. Effect: None. Territorial extent & classification: E. Local *Unpublished*

The A570 Trunk Road (Rainford Bypass) (Temporary Restriction and Prohibition of Traffic) Order 2002 No. 2002/33. – Enabling power: Road Traffic Regulation Act 1984, s. 14 (1) (a). – Made: 07.01.2002. Coming into force: 13.01.2002. Effect: None. Territorial extent & classification: E. Local *Unpublished*

The A570 Trunk Road (Southport Road, Scarisbrick) (Temporary 30 Miles Per Hour Speed Limit) Order 2002 No. 2002/5. – Enabling power: Road Traffic Regulation Act 1984, s. 14 (1) (a). – Made: 02.01.2002. Coming into force: 06.01.2002. Effect: None. Territorial extent & classification: E. Local *Unpublished*

The A570 Trunk Road (Southport Road, Scarisbrick) (Temporary 30 Miles Per Hour Speed Limit) Order 2002 No. 2002/2331. – Enabling power: Road Traffic Regulation Act 1984, s. 14 (1) (a). – Made: 04.09.2002. Coming into force: 08.09.2002. Effect: None. Territorial extent & classification: E. Local *Unpublished*

The A580 East Lancashire Road (Haydock Island) (Temporary Prohibition of Traffic) Order 2002 No. 2002/12. – Enabling power: Road Traffic Regulation Act 1984, s. 14 (1) (a). – Made: 03.01.2002. Coming into force: 06.01.2002. Effect: None. Territorial extent & classification: E. Local *Unpublished*

The A580 Trunk Road (Eastbound Entry Slip Road) (Temporary Prohibition of Traffic) Order 2002 No. 2002/372. – Enabling power: Road Traffic Regulation Act 1984, s. 14 (1) (a). – Made: 19.02.2002. Coming into force: 21.02.2002. Effect: None. Territorial extent & classification: E. Local *Unpublished*

The A580 Trunk Road (East Lancashire Road, Golborne Railway Bridge) (Temporary Prohibition of Traffic) Order 2002 No. 2002/2825. – Enabling power: Road Traffic Regulation Act 1984, s. 14 (1) (a). – Made: 13.11.2002. Coming into force: 15.11.2002. Effect: None. Territorial extent & classification: E. Local *Unpublished*

The A580 Trunk Road (East Lancashire Road) (Temporary Prohibition and Restriction of Traffic) Order 2002 No. 2002/268. – Enabling power: Road Traffic Regulation Act 1984, s. 14 (1) (a). – Made: 05.02.2002. Coming into force: 06.02.2002. Effect: None. Territorial extent & classification: E. Local *Unpublished*

The A580 Trunk Road (Golborne Island to Church Lane) (Temporary Restriction and Prohibition of Traffic) Order 2002 No. 2002/1611. – Enabling power: Road Traffic Regulation Act 1984, s. 14 (1) (a). – Made: 17.06.2002. Coming into force: 23.06.2002. Effect: None. Territorial extent & classification: E. Local *Unpublished*

The A585 Trunk Road (Amounderness Way) (Prohibition of Right Turn and Prohibition of "U" Turn) Order 2002 No. 2002/2109. – Enabling power: Road Traffic Regulation Act 1984, ss. 1 (1), 2 (1) (2). – Made: 02.08.2002. Coming into force: 12.08.2002. Effect: None. Territorial extent & classification: E. Local *Unpublished*

The A585 Trunk Road (Amounderness Way, Rossall Lane) (Temporary Prohibition of Traffic) Order 2002 No. 2002/1744. – Enabling power: Road Traffic Regulation Act 1984, s. 14 (1) (a). – Made: 04.07.2002. Coming into force: 08.07.2002. Effect: None. Territorial extent & classification: E. Local *Unpublished*

The A585 Trunk Road (Amounderness Way) (Temporary 30 Miles Per Hour Speed Limit) Order 2002 No. 2002/1867. – Enabling power: Road Traffic Regulation Act 1984, s. 14 (1) (a). – Made: 12.07.2002. Coming into force: 14.07.2002. Effect: None. Territorial extent & classification: E. Local *Unpublished*

The A585 Trunk Road (Amounderness Way, Thornton Cleveleys) (Temporary Prohibition of Traffic) (No. 2) Order 2002 No. 2002/1549. – Enabling power: Road Traffic Regulation Act 1984, s. 14 (1) (a). – Made: 05.06.2002. Coming into force: 07.06.2002. Effect: None. Territorial extent & classification: E. Local *Unpublished*

The A585 Trunk Road (Amounderness Way, Thornton Cleveleys) (Temporary Prohibition of Traffic) Order 2002 No. 2002/1303. – Enabling power: Road Traffic Regulation Act 1984, s. 14 (1) (a). – Made: 08.05.2002. Coming into force: 10.05.2002. Effect: None. Territorial extent & classification: E. Local *Unpublished*

The A585 Trunk Road (Amounderness Way, Victoria Road Roundabout) (Temporary Prohibition of Traffic) Order 2002 No. 2002/1813. – Enabling power: Road Traffic Regulation Act 1984, s. 14 (1) (a). – Made: 05.07.2002. Coming into force: 09.07.2002. Effect: None. Territorial extent & classification: E. Local *Unpublished*

The A585 Trunk Road (Fleetwood Road, Greenhalgh) (Temporary 30 Miles Per Hour Speed Limit) Order 2002 No. 2002/3233. – Enabling power: Road Traffic Regulation Act 1984, s. 14 (1) (a). – Made: 23.12.2002. Coming into force: 05.01.2003. Effect: None. Territorial extent & classification: E. Local *Unpublished*

The A590 Trunk Road (Ayside) (Temporary 10 Miles Per Hour Speed Restriction) Order 2002 No. 2002/2482. – Enabling power: Road Traffic Regulation Act 1984, s. 14 (1) (a). – Made: 26.09.2002. Coming into force: 29.09.2002. Effect: None. Territorial extent & classification: E. Local *Unpublished*

The A590 Trunk Road (Backbarrow) (Temporary 10 Miles Per Hour Speed Restriction) Order 2002 No. 2002/2410. – Enabling power: Road Traffic Regulation Act 1984, s. 14 (1) (a). – Made: 18.09.2002. Coming into force: 22.09.2002. Effect: None. Territorial extent & classification: E. Local *Unpublished*

The A590 Trunk Road (Barr End) (Temporary Restriction and Prohibition of Traffic) Order 2002 No. 2002/2383. – Enabling power: Road Traffic Regulation Act 1984, s. 14 (1) (a). – Made: 12.09.2002. Coming into force: 15.09.2002. Effect: None. Territorial extent & classification: E. Local *Unpublished*

The A590 Trunk Road (Brettargh Holt) (Temporary 10 Miles Per Hour Speed Restriction) Order 2002 No. 2002/2644. – Enabling power: Road Traffic Regulation Act 1984, s. 14 (1) (a). – Made: 17.10.2002. Coming into force: 19.10.2002. Effect: None. Territorial extent & classification: E. Local *Unpublished*

The A590 Trunk Road (Cross A Moor, Puffin Crossing) (Temporary 10 Miles Per Hour Speed Restriction) Order 2002 No. 2002/737. – Enabling power: Road Traffic Regulation Act 1984, s. 14 (1) (a). – Made: 14.03.2002. Coming into force: 17.03.2002. Effect: None. Territorial extent & classification: E. Local *Unpublished*

The A590 Trunk Road (Dalton Roundabout) (Temporary 10 Miles Per Hour Speed Restriction) Order 2002 No. 2002/2385. – Enabling power: Road Traffic Regulation Act 1984, s. 14 (1) (a). – Made: 12.09.2002. Coming into force: 15.09.2002. Effect: None. Territorial extent & classification: E. Local *Unpublished*

The A590 Trunk Road (Haverthwaite Junction) (Temporary 10 Miles Per Hour and 40 Miles Per Hour Speed Restriction) Order 2002 No. 2002/2726. – Enabling power: Road Traffic Regulation Act 1984, s. 14 (1) (a). – Made: 31.10.2002. Coming into force: 03.11.2002. Effect: None. Territorial extent & classification: E. Local *Unpublished*

The A590 Trunk Road (Lindale Hill) (Temporary 10 Miles Per Hour Speed Restriction) Order 2002 No. 2002/2483. – Enabling power: Road Traffic Regulation Act 1984, s. 14 (1) (a). – Made: 26.09.2002. Coming into force: 29.09.2002. Effect: None. Territorial extent & classification: E. Local *Unpublished*

The A590 Trunk Road (Oubas Hill) (Temporary 10 Miles Per Hour Speed Restriction) Order 2002 No. 2002/1681. – Enabling power: Road Traffic Regulation Act 1984, s. 14 (1) (a). – Made: 27.06.2002. Coming into force: 30.06.2002. Effect: None. Territorial extent & classification: E. Local *Unpublished*

The A595 Trunk Road (Bigrigg) (Temporary 10 Miles Per Hour and 40 Miles Per Hour Speed Restriction) Order 2002 No. 2002/1260. – Enabling power: Road Traffic Regulation Act 1984, s. 14 (1) (a). – Made: 01.05.2002. Coming into force: 06.05.2002. Effect: None. Territorial extent & classification: E. Local *Unpublished*

The A595 Trunk Road (Bigrigg) (Temporary Prohibition of Traffic) (No. 2) Order 2002 No. 2002/1423. – Enabling power: Road Traffic Regulation Act 1984, s. 14 (1) (a). – Made: 23.05.2002. Coming into force: 25.05.2002. Effect: None. Territorial extent & classification: E. Local *Unpublished*

The A595 Trunk Road (Broad Oak, South of Ravenglass) (Temporary 10 Miles Per Hour and 40 Miles Per Hour Speed Restriction) Order 2002 No. 2002/2408. – Enabling power: Road Traffic Regulation Act 1984, s. 14 (1) (a). – Made: 18.09.2002. Coming into force: 22.09.2002. Effect: None. Territorial extent & classification: E. Local *Unpublished*

The A595 Trunk Road (Egremont Cemetery) (Temporary Restriction and Prohibition of Traffic) Order 2002 No. 2002/2252. – Enabling power: Road Traffic Regulation Act 1984, s. 14 (1) (a). – Made: 28.08.2002. Coming into force: 01.09.2002. Effect: None. Territorial extent & classification: E. Local *Unpublished*

The A595 Trunk Road (Foxfield, Broughton in Furness) (Temporary 10 Miles Per Hour and 30 Miles Per Hour Speed Restriction) Order 2002 No. 2002/2681. – Enabling power: Road Traffic Regulation Act 1984, s. 14 (1) (a). – Made: 24.10.2002. Coming into force: 27.10.2002. Effect: None. Territorial extent & classification: E. Local *Unpublished*

The A595 Trunk Road (Hayescastle) (Temporary 10 Miles Per Hour and 30 Miles Per Hour Speed Restriction) Order 2002 No. 2002/1682. – Enabling power: Road Traffic Regulation Act 1984, s. 14 (1) (a). – Made: 26.06.2002. Coming into force: 30.06.2002. Effect: None. Territorial extent & classification: E. Local *Unpublished*

The A595 Trunk Road (Holme) (Temporary Restriction of Traffic) Order 2002 No. 2002/2514. – Enabling power: Road Traffic Regulation Act 1984, s. 14 (1) (b). – Made: 24.09.2002. Coming into force: 01.10.2002. Effect: None. Territorial extent & classification: E. Local *Unpublished*

The A595 Trunk Road (Loop Road North, Whitehaven) (Temporary 10 Miles Per Hour and 30 Miles Per Hour Speed Restriction) Order 2002 No. 2002/2678. – Enabling power: Road Traffic Regulation Act 1984, s. 14 (1) (a). – Made: 23.10.2002. Coming into force: 26.10.2002. Effect: None. Territorial extent & classification: E. Local *Unpublished*

The A595 Trunk Road (Thornhill) (Temporary 40 Miles Per Hour Speed Limit) Order 2002 No. 2002/7. – Enabling power: Road Traffic Regulation Act 1984, s. 14 (1) (a). – Made: 02.01.2002. Coming into force: 06.01.2002. Effect: None. Territorial extent & classification: E. Local *Unpublished*

The A595 Trunk Road (White Moss) (Temporary Restriction and Prohibition of Traffic) Order 2002 No. 2002/1551. – Enabling power: Road Traffic Regulation Act 1984, s. 14 (1) (a). – Made: 30.05.2002. Coming into force: 04.06.2002. Effect: None. Territorial extent & classification: E. Local *Unpublished*

The A596 Trunk Road (Aspatria) (Temporary 10 Miles Per Hour Speed Restriction) Order 2002 No. 2002/2643. – Enabling power: Road Traffic Regulation Act 1984, s. 14 (1) (a). – Made: 17.10.2002. Coming into force: 20.10.2002. Effect: None. Territorial extent & classification: E. Local *Unpublished*

The A596 Trunk Road (Birkby) (Temporary 10 Miles Per Hour Speed Restriction) Order 2002 No. 2002/2386. – Enabling power: Road Traffic Regulation Act 1984, s. 14 (1) (a). – Made: 12.09.2002. Coming into force: 15.09.2002. Effect: None. Territorial extent & classification: E. Local *Unpublished*

The A596 Trunk Road (Calva Brow, Workington) (Temporary Restriction and Prohibition of Traffic) Order 2002 No. 2002/2727. – Enabling power: Road Traffic Regulation Act 1984, s. 14 (1) (a). – Made: 31.10.2002. Coming into force: 03.11.2002. Effect: None. Territorial extent & classification: E. Local *Unpublished*

The A596 Trunk Road (Heathfield Railway Bridge) (Temporary 10 Miles Per Hour and 30 Miles Per Hour Speed Restriction) (No. 2) Order 2002 No. 2002/1866. – Enabling power: Road Traffic Regulation Act 1984, s. 14 (1) (b). – Made: 12.07.2002. Coming into force: 16.07.2002. Effect: None. Territorial extent & classification: E. Local *Unpublished*

The A596 Trunk Road (Heathfield Railway Bridge) (Temporary Restriction and Prohibition of Traffic) Order 2002 No. 2002/392. – Enabling power: Road Traffic Regulation Act 1984, s. 14 (1) (a). – Made: 21.02.2002. Coming into force: 24.02.2002. Effect: None. Territorial extent & classification: E. Local *Unpublished*

The A596 Trunk Road (Maryport New Bridge) (Temporary Prohibition of Traffic) Order 2002 No. 2002/2321. – Enabling power: Road Traffic Regulation Act 1984, s. 14 (1) (a). – Made: 05.09.2002. Coming into force: 07.09.2002. Effect: None. Territorial extent & classification: E. Local *Unpublished*

The A596 Trunk Road (Workington Bridge) (Temporary 10 Miles Per Hour Speed Restriction) Order 2002 No. 2002/160. – Enabling power: Road Traffic Regulation Act 1984, s. 14 (1) (a). – Made: 23.01.2002. Coming into force: 01.02.2002. Effect: None. Territorial extent & classification: E. Local *Unpublished*

The A596 Trunk Road (Workington) (Temporary Restriction and Prohibition of Traffic) Order 2002 No. 2002/350. – Enabling power: Road Traffic Regulation Act 1984, s. 14 (1) (a). – Made: 14.02.2002. Coming into force: 17.02.2002. Effect: None. Territorial extent & classification: E. Local *Unpublished*

The A606 Trunk Road (Melton Road, Tollerton, Nottinghamshire) (Temporary Prohibition of Traffic) Order 2002 No. 2002/1442. – Enabling power: Road Traffic Regulation Act 1984, s. 14 (1) (a). – Made: 24.05.2002. Coming into force: 31.05.2002. Effect: None. Territorial extent & classification: E. Local *Unpublished*

The A614 Trunk Road (Bothamsall Cross Roads, Nottinghamshire) (Temporary Restriction and Prohibition of Traffic) Order 2002 No. 2002/99. – Enabling power: Road Traffic Regulation Act 1984, s. 14 (1) (a). – Made: 21.01.2002. Coming into force: 28.01.2002. Effect: None. Territorial extent & classification: E. Local *Unpublished*

The A614 Trunk Road (Howden) (24 Hours Clearway) Order 2002 No. 2002/805. – Enabling power: Road Traffic Regulation Act 1984, ss. 1 (1), 2 (1) (2). – Made: 20.03.2002. Coming into force: 22.03.2002. Effect: None. Territorial extent & classification: E. Local *Unpublished*

The A616 Trunk Road (Stocksbridge Bypass, South Yorkshire) (Temporary Prohibition of Traffic) Order 2002 No. 2002/661. – Enabling power: Road Traffic Regulation Act 1984, s. 14 (1) (a). – Made: 11.03.2002. Coming into force: 18.03.2002. Effect: None. Territorial extent & classification: E. Local *Unpublished*

The A616 Trunk Road (Stocksbridge Bypass) (Temporary Restriction and Prohibition of Traffic) (No. 2) Order 2002 No. 2002/2797. – Enabling power: Road Traffic Regulation Act 1984, s. 14 (1) (a). – Made: 06.11.2002. Coming into force: 07.11.2002. Effect: None. Territorial extent & classification: E. Local *Unpublished*

The A616 Trunk Road (Stocksbridge Bypass) (Temporary Restriction and Prohibition of Traffic) Order 2002 No. 2002/2552. – Enabling power: Road Traffic Regulation Act 1984, s. 14 (1) (a). – Made: 03.10.2002. Coming into force: 06.10.2002. Effect: None. Territorial extent & classification: E. Local *Unpublished*

The A628, and A57 Trunk Roads (Market Street and Mottram Moor, Hollingworth) (Temporary Prohibition of Traffic) Order 2002 No. 2002/386. – Enabling power: Road Traffic Regulation Act 1984, s. 14 (1) (a). – Made: 18.02.2002. Coming into force: 25.02.2002. Effect: None. Territorial extent & classification: E. Local *Unpublished*

The A628 Trunk Road (Salters Brook Bridge) (Temporary 40 Miles Per Hour Speed Restriction) Order 2002 No. 2002/389. – Enabling power: Road Traffic Regulation Act 1984, s. 14 (1) (a). – Made: 15.02.2002. Coming into force: 22.02.2002. Effect: None. Territorial extent & classification: E. Local *Unpublished*

The A638 Trunk Road (Bawtry Road and Roman Road) (Temporary 40 Miles Per Hour Speed Restriction) Order 2002 No. 2002/2416. – Enabling power: Road Traffic Regulation Act 1984, ss. 14 (1) (a), 15 (2). – Made: 11.09.2002. Coming into force: 12.09.2002. Effect: None. Territorial extent & classification: E. Local *Unpublished*

The A638 Trunk Road (High Street, Bawtry) (Prohibition of Waiting) Order 2002 No. 2002/1189. – Enabling power: Road Traffic Regulation Act 1984, ss. 1 (1), 2 (1) (2). – Made: 17.04.2002. Coming into force: 22.04.2002. Effect: None. Territorial extent & classification: E. Local *Unpublished*

The A650 Trunk Road (Shipley) (Temporary Prohibition of Traffic) Order 2002 No. 2002/407. – Enabling power: Road Traffic Regulation Act 1984, s. 14 (1) (a). – Made: 22.02.2002. Coming into force: 26.02.2002. Effect: None. Territorial extent & classification: E. Local *Unpublished*

The A696 Trunk Road and the A68 Trunk Road (Various Locations: Blaxter Bends to the Scottish Border) (Temporary 10 Miles Per Hour, 30 Miles Per Hour and 40 Miles Per Hour Speed Restriction) Order 2002 No. 2002/1420. – Enabling power: Road Traffic Regulation Act 1984, s. 14 (1) (a). – Made: 17.05.2002. Coming into force: 19.05.2002. Effect: None. Territorial extent & classification: E. Local *Unpublished*

The A696 Trunk Road (Heeston Bank) (Temporary 10 Miles Per Hour, 30 Miles Per Hour and 40 Miles Per Hour Speed Restriction) Order 2002 No. 2002/1277. – Enabling power: Road Traffic Regulation Act 1984, s. 14 (1) (a). – Made: 03.05.2002. Coming into force: 06.05.2002. Effect: None. Territorial extent & classification: E. Local *Unpublished*

The A696 Trunk Road (Heeston Bank) (Temporary Restriction and Prohibition of Traffic) Order 2002 No. 2002/2647. – Enabling power: Road Traffic Regulation Act 1984, s. 14 (1) (a). – Made: 03.10.2002. Coming into force: 06.10.2002. Effect: None. Territorial extent & classification: E. Local *Unpublished*

The A696 Trunk Road (Highlander & Harnham) (Temporary 10 Miles Per Hour, 30 Miles Per Hour and 40 Miles Per Hour Speed Restriction) Order 2002 No. 2002/2501. – Enabling power: Road Traffic Regulation Act 1984, s. 14 (1) (a). – Made: 27.09.2002. Coming into force: 29.09.2002. Effect: None. Territorial extent & classification: E. Local *Unpublished*

The A696 Trunk Road (Various Locations: Ponteland to Percy's Cross) (Temporary 10 Miles Per Hour, 30 Miles Per Hour and 40 Miles Per Hour Speed Restriction) Order 2002 No. 2002/1599. – Enabling power: Road Traffic Regulation Act 1984, s. 14 (1) (a). – Made: 30.05.2002. Coming into force: 05.06.2002. Effect: None. Territorial extent & classification: E. Local *Unpublished*

The A1033 Trunk Road and South Bridge Road (Mount Pleasant Junction) (Temporary Prohibition of Traffic) Order 2002 No. 2002/1782. – Enabling power: Road Traffic Regulation Act 1984, s. 14 (1) (a). – Made: 10.07.2002. Coming into force: 13.07.2002. Effect: None. Territorial extent & classification: E. Local *Unpublished*

The A1033 Trunk Road (Mount Pleasant Roundabout to Marfleet Avenue) (Temporary Prohibition of Traffic) Order 2002 No. 2002/2944. – Enabling power: Road Traffic Regulation Act 1984, s. 14 (1) (a). – Made: 26.11.2002. Coming into force: 28.11.2002. Effect: None. Territorial extent & classification: E. Local *Unpublished*

The A1033 Trunk Road (Somerdon Road to Salt End Roundabout) (Temporary Restriction and Prohibition of Traffic) Order 2002 No. 2002/2949. – Enabling power: Road Traffic Regulation Act 1984, s. 14 (1) (a). – Made: 27.11.2002. Coming into force: 29.11.2002. Effect: None. Territorial extent & classification: E. Local *Unpublished*

The A1079 Trunk Road (Barmby Moor to Canal Head) (Temporary Restriction and Prohibition of Traffic) Order 2002 No. 2002/40. – Enabling power: Road Traffic Regulation Act 1984, s. 14 (1) (a). – Made: 11.01.2002. Coming into force: 13.01.2002. Effect: None. Territorial extent & classification: E. Local *Unpublished*

The A1079 Trunk Road (Grimston Interchange and Dunswell Lane Underpass) (Temporary 50 Miles Per Hour Speed Restriction) Order 2002 No. 2002/1430. – Enabling power: Road Traffic Regulation Act 1984, s. 14 (1) (a). – Made: 22.05.2002. Coming into force: 26.05.2002. Effect: None. Territorial extent & classification: E. Local *Unpublished*

The A4123 Trunk Road (Birmingham New Road, Dudley) (Temporary Restriction and Prohibition of Traffic) Order 2002 No. 2002/936. – Enabling power: Road Traffic Regulation Act 1984, s. 14 (1) (a). – Made: 28.03.2002. Coming into force: 05.04.2002. Effect: None. Territorial extent & classification: E. Local *Unpublished*

The A4123 Trunk Road (Birmingham New Road, Tipton) (Temporary 20 Miles Per Hour Speed Restriction) Order 2002 No. 2002/84. – Enabling power: Road Traffic Regulation Act 1984, s. 14 (1) (a). – Made: 17.01.2002. Coming into force: 24.01.2002. Effect: None. Territorial extent & classification: E. Local *Unpublished*

The A4123 Trunk Road (Causeway Green to Warley) (Temporary 10 Miles Per Hour Speed Restriction) Order 2002 No. 2002/1527. – Enabling power: Road Traffic Regulation Act 1984, s. 14 (1) (a). – Made: 31.05.2002. Coming into force: 07.06.2002. Effect: None. Territorial extent & classification: E. Local *Unpublished*

The A5092 Trunk Road (Penny Bridge) (Temporary 10 Miles Per Hour Speed Restriction) Order 2002 No. 2002/2575. Enabling power: Road Traffic Regulation Act 1984, s. 14 (1) (a). – Made: 10.10.2002. Coming into force: 12.10.2002. Effect: None. Territorial extent & classification: E. Local *Unpublished*

The A5103 Princess Parkway and A663 Broadway (Temporary Restriction and Prohibition of Traffic) Order 2002 No. 2002/2610. – Enabling power: Road Traffic Regulation Act 1984, s. 14 (1) (b). – Made: 11.10.2002. Coming into force: 13.10.2002. Effect: None. Territorial extent & classification: E. Local *Unpublished*

The A5111 Trunk Road (Harvey Road, Derby) (Temporary Prohibition of Traffic) Order 2002 No. 2002/2320. – Enabling power: Road Traffic Regulation Act 1984, s. 14 (1) (a). – Made: 30.08.2002. Coming into force: 06.09.2002. Effect: None. Territorial extent & classification: E. Local *Unpublished*

The A5111 Trunk Road (Osmaston Park Road, Derby) (Temporary Prohibition of Traffic) Order 2002 No. 2002/1572. – Enabling power: Road Traffic Regulation Act 1984, s. 14 (1) (a). – Made: 07.06.2002. Coming into force: 14.06.2002. Effect: None. Territorial extent & classification: E. Local *Unpublished*

The A5111 Trunk Road (Raynesway, Derbyshire) (Temporary 30 Miles Per Hour Speed Restriction) Order 2002 No. 2002/2250. – Enabling power: Road Traffic Regulation Act 1984, s. 14 (1) (a). – Made: 30.08.2002. Coming into force: 06.09.2002. Effect: None. Territorial extent & classification: E. Local *Unpublished*

The A5111 Trunk Road (Warwick Avenue and Kenilworth Avenue, Derby) (Temporary 10 Miles Per Hour and 30 Miles Per Hour Speed Restriction) (No. 2) Order 2002 No. 2002/750. – Enabling power: Road Traffic Regulation Act 1984, s. 14 (1) (a). – Made: 15.03.2002. Coming into force: 22.03.2002. Effect: None. Territorial extent & classification: E. Local *Unpublished*

The A5111 Trunk Road (Warwick Avenue and Kenilworth Avenue, Derby) (Temporary 10 Miles Per Hour and 30 Miles Per Hour Speed Restriction) Order 2002 No. 2002/178. – Enabling power: Road Traffic Regulation Act 1984, s. 14 (1) (a). – Made: 28.01.2002. Coming into force: 04.02.2002. Effect: None. Territorial extent & classification: E. Local *Unpublished*

The A6120 Trunk Road (East Leeds Ring Road) (Bus Lane and Prohibition and Restriction of Waiting) Order 2002 No. 2002/1425. – Enabling power: Road Traffic Regulation Act 1984, ss. 1 (1), 2 (1) (2), 4 (1). – Made: 23.05.2002. Coming into force: 31.05.2002. Effect: None. Territorial extent & classification: E. Local *Unpublished*

The A6514 Trunk Road (Queens Medical Centre Roundabout to Aspley Lane Roundabout, Nottingham) (Temporary Restriction and Prohibition of Traffic) Order 2002 No. 2002/1640. – Enabling power: Road Traffic Regulation Act 1984, s. 14 (1) (a). – Made: 17.06.2002. Coming into force: 24.06.2002. Effect: None. Territorial extent & classification: E. Local *Unpublished*

The B1172 Trunk Road (Tuttles Lane Interchange, Wymondham, Norfolk) (Temporary Prohibition of Traffic) Order 2002 No. 2002/494. – Enabling power: Road Traffic Regulation Act 1984, s. 14 (1) (a). – Made: 04.03.2002. Coming into force: 11.03.2002. Effect: None. Territorial extent & classification: E. Local *Unpublished*

The Broadgate Link Road (Prohibition of Waiting) Order 2002 No. 2002/179. – Enabling power:Road Traffic Regulation Act 1984, ss. 1 (1), 2 (1) (2). – Made: 16.01.2002. Coming into force: 18.01.2002. Effect: None. Territorial extent & classification: E. Local *Unpublished*

The City of New Sarum (Churchill Way Pedestrian Underpasses) (Prohibition of Cycling) Order 1972 (Variation) 2002 No. 2002/2732. – Enabling power: Road Traffic Regulation Act 1984, ss. 1 (1), 2 (1) (2), sch. 9, para. 27 (1). – Made: 24.09.2002. Coming into force: 04.10.2002. Effect: The City of New Sarum (Churchill Way Pedestrian Underpasses) (Prohibition of Cycling) Order 1972 amended. Territorial extent & classification: E. Local *Unpublished*

The M1 and M6 Motorways and the A14 Trunk Road (M1 Junction 19) (Temporary 50 Miles Per Hour Speed Restriction) Order 2002 No. 2002/2221. – Enabling power: Road Traffic Regulation Act 1984, s. 14 (1) (a). – Made: 23.08.2002. Coming into force: 30.08.2002. Effect: None. Territorial extent & classification: E. Local *Unpublished*

The M1 and M6 Motorways and the A14 Trunk Road (M1 Junction 19) (Temporary Prohibition of Traffic) Order 2002 No. 2002/2486. – Enabling power: Road Traffic Regulation Act 1984, s. 14 (1) (a). – Made: 27.09.2002. Coming into force: 04.10.2002. Effect: None. Territorial extent & classification: E. Local *Unpublished*

The M1 and M6 Motorways (Catthorpe Interchange, Leicestershire) (Temporary 40 Miles Per Hour Speed Restriction) Order 2002 No. 2002/1747. – Enabling power: Road Traffic Regulation Act 1984, s. 14 (1) (a). – Made: 01.07.2002. Coming into force: 08.07.2002. Effect: None. Territorial extent & classification: E. Local *Unpublished*

The M1 and M6 Motorways (Catthorpe Interchange, Leicestershire) (Temporary Restriction of Traffic) Order 2002 No. 2002/2496. – Enabling power: Road Traffic Regulation Act 1984, s. 14 (1) (a) (7). – Made: 27.09.2002. Coming into force: 04.10.2002. Effect: None. Territorial extent & classification: E. Local *Unpublished*

The M1 and M10 Motorways (St Albans, Hertfordshire) (Temporary Prohibition of Traffic) Order 2002 No. 2002/2135. – Enabling power: Road Traffic Regulation Act 1984, s. 14 (1) (a). – Made: 12.08.2002. Coming into force: 17.08.2002. Effect: None. Territorial extent & classification: E. Local *Unpublished*

The M1 (Junction 19) and M6 Motorways (River Avon Viaduct, Leicestershire) (Temporary Restriction of Traffic) Order 2002 No. 2002/2994. – Enabling power: Road Traffic Regulation Act 1984, s. 14 (1) (a) (7). – Made: 29.11.2002. Coming into force: 06.12.2002. Effect: None. Territorial extent & classification: E. Local *Unpublished*

The M1 Motorway and A631 Trunk Road (Tinsley Viaduct) (Temporary Prohibition of Traffic) (No. 2) Order 2002 No. 2002/2827. – Enabling power: Road Traffic Regulation Act 1984, s. 14 (1) (a). – Made: 13.11.2002. Coming into force: 17.11.2002. Effect: None. Territorial extent & classification: E. Local *Unpublished*

The M1 Motorway and A631 Trunk Road (Tinsley Viaduct) (Temporary Prohibition of Traffic) Order 2002 No. 2002/2648. – Enabling power: Road Traffic Regulation Act 1984, s. 14 (1) (a). – Made: 18.10.2002. Coming into force: 20.10.2002. Effect: None. Territorial extent & classification: E. Local *Unpublished*

The M1 Motorway (Junction 6A, Link Road) (Temporary Prohibition of Traffic) Order 2002 No. 2002/905. – Enabling power: Road Traffic Regulation Act 1984, s. 14 (1) (a). – Made: 25.03.2002. Coming into force: 30.03.2002. Effect: None. Territorial extent & classification: E. Local *Unpublished*

The M1 Motorway (Junction 6, Slip Roads) (Temporary Prohibition of Traffic) Order 2002 No. 2002/210. – Enabling power: Road Traffic Regulation Act 1984, s. 14 (1) (a). – Made: 04.02.2002. Coming into force: 09.02.2002. Effect: None. Territorial extent & classification: E. Local *Unpublished*

The M1 Motorway (Junction 9, Hertfordshire) (Temporary Restriction of Traffic) Order 2002 No. 2002/21. – Enabling power: Road Traffic Regulation Act 1984, s. 14 (1) (a) (7). – Made: 07.01.2002. Coming into force: 14.01.2002. Effect: None. Territorial extent & classification: E. Local *Unpublished*

The M1 Motorway (Junction 11) (Temporary 50 Miles Per Hour Speed Restriction) Order 2002 No. 2002/3009. – Enabling power: Road Traffic Regulation Act 1984, s. 14 (1) (a). – Made: 22.11.2002. Coming into force: 29.11.2002. Effect: None. Territorial extent & classification: E. Local *Unpublished*

The M1 Motorway (Junction 14) (Temporary 40 Miles Per Hour and 50 Miles Per Hour Speed Restriction) Order 2002 No. 2002/1578. – Enabling power: Road Traffic Regulation Act 1984, s. 14 (1) (a). – Made: 07.06.2002. Coming into force: 14.06.2002. Effect: None. Territorial extent & classification: E. Local *Unpublished*

The M1 Motorway (Junction 15A) and the A43 Trunk Road (Rothersthorpe, Northamptonshire) (Temporary 40 Miles Per Hour and 50 Miles Per Hour Speed Restriction) Order 2002 No. 2002/2030. – Enabling power: Road Traffic Regulation Act 1984, s. 14 (1) (a), sch. 9, para. 27 (1). – Made: 29.07.2002. Coming into force: 05.08.2002. Effect: S.I. 2002/1105 revoked. Territorial extent & classification: E. Local *Unpublished*

The M1 Motorway (Junction 15A) and the A43 Trunk Road (Rothersthorpe, Northhamptonshire) (Temporary 50 Miles Per Hour Speed Restriction) Order 2002 No. 2002/1105. – Enabling power: Road Traffic Regulation Act 1984, s. 14 (1) (a). – Made: 15.04.2002. Coming into force: 22.04.2002. Effect: None. Territorial extent & classification: E. Local – Revoked by S.I. 2002/2030 (unpublished) *Unpublished*

The M1 Motorway (Junction 15A) Southbound Entry Slip Road (Temporary Prohibition of Traffic) Order 2002 No. 2002/2287. – Enabling power: Road Traffic Regulation Act 1984, s. 14 (1) (a). – Made: 02.09.2002. Coming into force: 09.09.2002. Effect: None. Territorial extent & classification: E. Local *Unpublished*

The M1 Motorway (Junction 24A) (Southbound Exit Slip Road) (Temporary Prohibition of Traffic) Order 2002 No. 2002/97. – Enabling power: Road Traffic Regulation Act 1984, s. 14 (1) (a). – Made: 21.01.2002. Coming into force: 28.01.2002. Effect: None. Territorial extent & classification: E. Local *Unpublished*

The M1 Motorway (Junction 24A) (Southbound Exit Slip Road) (Temporary Prohibition of Traffic) Order 2002 No. 2002/3192. – Enabling power: Road Traffic Regulation Act 1984, s. 14 (1) (a). – Made: 06.12.2002. Coming into force: 13.12.2002. Effect: None. Territorial extent & classification: E. Local *Unpublished*

The M1 Motorway (Junction 32, Thurcroft) and the M18 Motorway (Temporary Prohibition of Traffic) Order 2002 No. 2002/2645. – Enabling power: Road Traffic Regulation Act 1984, s. 14 (1) (a). – Made: 16.10.2002. Coming into force: 20.10.2002. Effect: None. Territorial extent & classification: E. Local *Unpublished*

The M1 Motorway (Junction 33, Catcliffe) and the M18 Motorway (Junction 2, Wadworth) (Temporary Prohibition of Traffic) Order 2002 No. 2002/1256. – Enabling power: Road Traffic Regulation Act 1984, s. 14 (1) (a). – Made: 02.05.2002. Coming into force: 07.05.2002. Effect: None. Territorial extent & classification: E. Local *Unpublished*

The M1 Motorway (Junction 33, Catcliffe) (Temporary Prohibition of Traffic) Order 2002 No. 2002/2415. – Enabling power: Road Traffic Regulation Act 1984, s. 14 (1) (a). – Made: 12.09.2002. Coming into force: 15.09.2002. Effect: None. Territorial extent & classification: E. Local *Unpublished*

The M1 Motorway (Junction 33, Junction 34 and Junction 36) (Temporary Prohibition of Traffic) Order 2002 No. 2002/1652. – Enabling power: Road Traffic Regulation Act 1984, s. 14 (1) (a). – Made: 19.06.2002. Coming into force: 23.06.2002. Effect: None. Territorial extent & classification: E. Local *Unpublished*

The M1 Motorway (Junction 36, Tankersley) (Temporary Restriction and Prohibition of Traffic) Order 2002 No. 2002/450. – Enabling power: Road Traffic Regulation Act 1984, s. 14 (1) (a) (7). – Made: 27.02.2002. Coming into force: 03.03.2002. Effect: None. Territorial extent & classification: E. Local *Unpublished*

The M1 Motorway (Junction 36 to Junction 37) (Temporary Restriction of Traffic) Order 2002 No. 2002/2038. – Enabling power: Road Traffic Regulation Act 1984, s. 14 (1) (a) (7). – Made: 25.07.2002. Coming into force: 28.07.2002. Effect: None. Territorial extent & classification: E. Local *Unpublished*

The M1 Motorway (Junction 42, Lofthouse) (Temporary Prohibition of Traffic) Order 2002 No. 2002/1638. – Enabling power: Road Traffic Regulation Act 1984, s. 14 (1) (a). – Made: 14.06.2002. Coming into force: 16.06.2002. Effect: None. Territorial extent & classification: E. Local *Unpublished*

The M1 Motorway (Junction 44) (Temporary Prohibition of Traffic) Order 2002 No. 2002/2923. – Enabling power: Road Traffic Regulation Act 1984, s. 14 (1) (a). – Made: 25.11.2002. Coming into force: 27.11.2002. Effect: None. Territorial extent & classification: E. Local *Unpublished*

The M1 Motorway (Junction 44) (Temporary Prohibition of Traffic) Order 2002 No. 2002/3140. – Enabling power: Road Traffic Regulation Act 1984, s. 14 (1) (a). – Made: 25.11.2002. Coming into force: 27.11.2002. Effect: None. Territorial extent & classification: E. Local *Unpublished*

The M1 Motorway (Junction 45 to Junction 46) (Temporary Restriction of Traffic) Order 2002 No. 2002/1908. – Enabling power: Road Traffic Regulation Act 1984, s. 14 (1) (a) (7). – Made: 18.07.2002. Coming into force: 21.07.2002. Effect: None. Territorial extent & classification: E. Local *Unpublished*

The M1 Motorway (Junction 47, Parlington) (Temporary Prohibition of Traffic) Order 2002 No. 2002/1391. – Enabling power: Road Traffic Regulation Act 1984, s. 14 (1) (a). – Made: 16.05.2002. Coming into force: 22.05.2002. Effect: None. Territorial extent & classification: E. Local *Unpublished*

The M1 Motorway (Junctions 2 and 3, Slip Roads) (Temporary Prohibition of Traffic) Order 2002 No. 2002/903. – Enabling power: Road Traffic Regulation Act 1984, s. 14 (1) (a). – Made: 25.03.2002. Coming into force: 01.04.2002. Effect: None. Territorial extent & classification: E. Local *Unpublished*

The M1 Motorway (Junctions 6A and 8, Link and Slip Roads) (Temporary Prohibition of Traffic) Order 2002 No. 2002/211. – Enabling power: Road Traffic Regulation Act 1984, s. 14 (1) (a). – Made: 04.02.2002. Coming into force: 09.02.2002. Effect: None. Territorial extent & classification: E. Local *Unpublished*

The M1 Motorway (Junctions 8-10) Hemel Hempstead, Herfordshire - Luton, Bedfordshire (Temporary Restriction and Prohibition of Traffic) Order 2002 No. 2002/2715. – Enabling power: Road Traffic Regulation Act 1984, s. 14 (1) (a) (7). – Made: 28.10.2002. Coming into force: 04.11.2002. Effect: None. Territorial extent & classification: E. Local *Unpublished*

The M1 Motorway (Junctions 10-15) Luton, Bedfordshire - Collingtree, Northamptonshire (Temporary Restriction of Traffic) Order 2002 No. 2002/2494. – Enabling power: Road Traffic Regulation Act 1984, s. 14 (1) (a) (7). – Made: 27.09.2002. Coming into force: 04.10.2002. Effect: None. Territorial extent & classification: E. Local *Unpublished*

The M1 Motorway (Junctions 21 - 21A) (Leicestershire) (Temporary 50 Miles Per Hour Speed Restriction) Order 2002 No. 2002/1371. – Enabling power: Road Traffic Regulation Act 1984, s. 14 (1) (a). – Made: 07.05.2002. Coming into force: 14.05.2002. Effect: None. Territorial extent & classification: E. Local *Unpublished*

The M1 Motorway (Junctions 27 - 30) (Temporary Prohibition and Restriction of Traffic) Order 2002 No. 2002/517. – Enabling power: Road Traffic Regulation Act 1984, s. 14 (1) (a) (7). – Made: 04.03.2002. Coming into force: 11.03.2002. Effect: None. Territorial extent & classification: E. Local *Unpublished*

The M1 Motorway (Junctions 29-30) (Temporary Restriction and Prohibition of Traffic) Order 2002 No. 2002/2180. – Enabling power: Road Traffic Regulation Act 1984, s. 14 (1) (a) (7). – Made: 02.09.2002. Coming into force: 09.09.2002. Effect: None. Territorial extent & classification: E. Local *Unpublished*

The M1 Motorway (Junction 41, Carr Gate) (Temporary Prohibition of Traffic) Order 2002 No. 2002/1541. – Enabling power: Road Traffic Regulation Act 1984, s. 14 (1) (a). – Made: 06.06.2002. Coming into force: 09.06.2002. Effect: None. Territorial extent & classification: E. Local *Unpublished*

The M1 Motorway (Kegworth - Long Eaton) (Temporary Prohibition and Restriction of Traffic) Order 2002 No. 2002/3216. – Enabling power: Road Traffic Regulation Act 1984, s. 14 (1) (a) (7). – Made: 20.12.2002. Coming into force: 27.12.2002. Effect: None. Territorial extent & classification: E. Local *Unpublished*

The M1 Motorway (Long Eaton, Derbyshire) (Temporary 50 Miles Per Hour Speed Restriction) Order 2002 No. 2002/1367. – Enabling power: Road Traffic Regulation Act 1984, s. 14 (1) (a). – Made: 10.05.2002. Coming into force: 17.05.2002. Effect: None. Territorial extent & classification: E. Local *Unpublished*

The M1 Motorway (South of Junction 26) (Temporary Restriction and Prohibition of Traffic) Order 2002 No. 2002/103. – Enabling power: Road Traffic Regulation Act 1984, s. 14 (1) (a) (7). – Made: 21.01.2002. Coming into force: 28.01.2002. Effect: None. Territorial extent & classification: E. Local *Unpublished*

The M1 Motorway (Tinsley Viaduct, Junction 34) (Temporary 50 Miles Per Hour Speed Restriction) Order 2002 No. 2002/1139. – Enabling power: Road Traffic Regulation Act 1984, s. 14 (1) (a). – Made: 18.04.2002. Coming into force: 21.04.2002. Effect: None. Territorial extent & classification: E. Local *Unpublished*

The M2 Motorway (Farthing Corner, Slip Road) (Temporary Restriction of Traffic) Order 2002 No. 2002/2455. – Enabling power: Road Traffic Regulation Act 1984, s. 14 (1) (a). – Made: 23.09.2002. Coming into force: 28.09.2002. Effect: None. Territorial extent & classification: E. Local *Unpublished*

The M2 Motorway (Junction 1, Coastbound Slip Road) (Temporary Prohibition of Traffic) Order 2002 No. 2002/2344. – Enabling power: Road Traffic Regulation Act 1984, s. 14 (1) (a). – Made: 09.09.2002. Coming into force: 14.09.2002. Effect: None. Territorial extent & classification: E. Local *Unpublished*

The M2 Motorway (Junction 2, Londonbound Exit Slip Road) (Temporary 30 Miles Per Hour Speed Restriction) Order 2002 No. 2002/1685. – Enabling power: Road Traffic Regulation Act 1984, s. 14 (1) (a) (7). – Made: 28.06.2002. Coming into force: 02.07.2002. Effect: None. Territorial extent & classification: E. Local *Unpublished*

The M2 Motorway (Junction 2, Londonbound Exit Slip Road) (Temporary Prohibition of Traffic) Order 2002 No. 2002/1940. – Enabling power: Road Traffic Regulation Act 1984, s. 14 (1) (a). – Made: 22.07.2002. Coming into force: 29.07.2002. Effect: None. Territorial extent & classification: E. Local *Unpublished*

The M2 Motorway (Junctions 1 - 4 Junctions 3 - 4) (Temporary Prohibition of Traffic) Order 2002 No. 2002/1221. – Enabling power: Road Traffic Regulation Act 1984, s. 14 (1) (a). – Made: 29.04.2002. Coming into force: 07.05.2002. Effect: None. Territorial extent & classification: E. Local *Unpublished*

The M2 Motorway (Junctions 1 - 4, Slip Roads) (Temporary Prohibition of Traffic) Order 2002 No. 2002/2388. – Enabling power: Road Traffic Regulation Act 1984, s. 14 (1) (a). – Made: 13.09.2002. Coming into force: 14.09.2002. Effect: None. Territorial extent & classification: E. Local *Unpublished*

The M2 Motorway (Junctions 1 - 4) (Temporary Prohibition of Traffic) (No. 2) Order 2002 No. 2002/1632. – Enabling power: Road Traffic Regulation Act 1984, s. 14 (1) (a). – Made: 24.06.2002. Coming into force: 01.07.2002. Effect: None. Territorial extent & classification: E. Local *Unpublished*

The M2 Motorway (Junctions 1 - 4) (Temporary Prohibition of Traffic) (No. 3) Order 2002 No. 2002/2451. – Enabling power: Road Traffic Regulation Act 1984, s. 14 (1) (a). – Made: 23.09.2002. Coming into force: 30.09.2002. Effect: None. Territorial extent & classification: E. Local *Unpublished*

The M2 Motorway (Junctions 1 - 4) (Temporary Prohibition of Traffic) Order 2002 No. 2002/968. – Enabling power: Road Traffic Regulation Act 1984, s. 14 (1) (a). – Made: 02.04.2002. Coming into force: 08.04.2002. Effect: None. Territorial extent & classification: E. Local *Unpublished*

The M2 Motorway (Junctions 3 - 4) (Temporary Prohibition of Traffic) Order 2002 No. 2002/39. – Enabling power: Road Traffic Regulation Act 1984, s. 14 (1) (a). – Made: 14.01.2002. Coming into force: 21.01.2002. Effect: None. Territorial extent & classification: E. Local *Unpublished*

The M2 Motorway (Marker Posts 51.0 - 53.5) (Temporary Speed Restrictions) Order 2002 No. 2002/739. – Enabling power: Road Traffic Regulation Act 1984, s. 14 (1) (a) (7). – Made: 18.03.2002. Coming into force: 01.04.2002. Effect: None. Territorial extent & classification: E. Local *Unpublished*

The M2 Motorway (Marker Posts 64.0 - 84.0) (Temporary Restriction and Prohibition of Traffic) Order 2002 No. 2002/1158. – Enabling power: Road Traffic Regulation Act 1984, s. 14 (1) (a) (7). – Made: 22.04.2002. Coming into force: 06.05.2002. Effect: None. Territorial extent & classification: E. Local *Unpublished*

The M2 Motorway (Medway Bridge) (Restriction of Use of Special Track) Order 2002 No. 2002/1451. – Enabling power: Road Traffic Regulation Act 1984, ss. 1 (1), 2 (1) (2), sch. 9, para. 27 (1). – Made: 27.05.2002. Coming into force: 10.06.2002. Effect: None. Territorial extent & classification: E. Local *Unpublished*

The M2 Motorway (Medway Bridge, Special Track) (Temporary Prohibition of Traffic and Pedestrians) Order 2002 No. 2002/1510. – Enabling power: Road Traffic Regulation Act 1984, s. 14 (1) (a). – Made: 05.06.2002. Coming into force: 10.06.2002. Effect: None. Territorial extent & classification: E. Local *Unpublished*

The M3 Motorway and the A303 Trunk Road (Popham) (Temporary Speed Restrictions) Order 2002 No. 2002/2509. – Enabling power: Road Traffic Regulation Act 1984, s. 14 (1) (a). – Made: 30.09.2002. Coming into force: 05.10.2002. Effect: None. Territorial extent & classification: E. Local *Unpublished*

The M3 Motorway (Junction 5, Slip Roads) (Temporary Prohibition of Traffic) Order 2002 No. 2002/2974. – Enabling power: Road Traffic Regulation Act 1984, s. 14 (1) (a). – Made: 02.12.2002. Coming into force: 07.12.2002. Effect: None. Territorial extent & classification: E. Local *Unpublished*

The M3 Motorway (Junction 6, Black Dam) (Temporary Prohibition of Traffic) Order 2002 No. 2002/2655. – Enabling power: Road Traffic Regulation Act 1984, s. 14 (1) (a). – Made: 21.10.2002. Coming into force: 26.10.2002. Effect: None. Territorial extent & classification: E. Local *Unpublished*

The M3 Motorway (Junction 6, Westbound Slip Roads) (Temporary Prohibition of Traffic) Order 2002 No. 2002/175. – Enabling power: Road Traffic Regulation Act 1984, s. 14 (1) (a). – Made: 28.01.2002. Coming into force: 01.02.2002. Effect: None. Territorial extent & classification: E. Local *Unpublished*

The M3 Motorway (Junction 7, Slip Roads) (Temporary Prohibition of Traffic) Order 2002 No. 2002/3165. – Enabling power: Road Traffic Regulation Act 1984, s. 14 (1) (a). Made: 16.12.2002. Coming into force: 21.12.2002. Effect: None. Territorial extent & classification: E. Local *Unpublished*

The M3 Motorway (Junction 13, Slip Road) (Temporary Prohibition of Traffic) Order 2002 No. 2002/2970. – Enabling power: Road Traffic Regulation Act 1984, s. 14 (1) (a). – Made: 02.12.2002. Coming into force: 07.12.2002. Effect: None. Territorial extent & classification: E. Local *Unpublished*

The M3 Motorway (Junction 14, Southbound Carriageway) (Temporary 50 Miles Per Hour Speed Restriction) Order 2002 No. 2002/370. Enabling power: Road Traffic Regulation Act 1984, s. 14 (1) (a). – Made: 18.02.2002. Coming into force: 23.02.2002. Effect: None. Territorial extent & classification: E. Local *Unpublished*

The M3 Motorway (Junctions 1 - 2) (Temporary 50 Miles Per Hour Speed Restriction) Order 2002 No. 2002/3070. – Enabling power: Road Traffic Regulation Act 1984, s. 14 (1) (a). – Made: 09.12.2002. Coming into force: 14.12.2002. Effect: None. Territorial extent & classification: E. Local *Unpublished*

The M3 Motorway (Marker Posts 43.0 - 53.3) (Temporary Restriction and Prohibition of Traffic) Order 2002 No. 2002/2047. – Enabling power: Road Traffic Regulation Act 1984, s. 14 (1) (a) (7). – Made: 29.07.2002. Coming into force: 05.08.2002. Effect: S.I. 2002/1456 revoked. Territorial extent & classification: E. Local *Unpublished*

The M3 Motorway (Marker Posts 43.5 - 53.3) (Temporary Restriction and Prohibition of Traffic) Order 2002 No. 2002/1456. – Enabling power: Road Traffic Regulation Act 1984, s. 14 (1) (a) (7). – Made: 27.05.2002. Coming into force: 01.06.2002. Effect: None. Territorial extent & classification: E. Local – Revoked by S.I. 2002/2047 (unpublished) *Unpublished*

The M4 and M25 Motorways (Thorney Interchange) (Temporary Prohibition of Traffic) Order 2002 No. 2002/369. – Enabling power: Road Traffic Regulation Act 1984, s. 14 (1) (a). – Made: 18.02.2002. Coming into force: 23.02.2002. Effect: None. Territorial extent & classification: E. Local *Unpublished*

The M4 Motorway (Heathrow Spur and Concorde Roundabout) (Temporary Restriction of Traffic) Order 2002 No. 2002/1276. – Enabling power: Road Traffic Regulation Act 1984, s. 14 (1) (a) (7). – Made: 07.05.2002. Coming into force: 11.05.2002. Effect: None. Territorial extent & classification: E. Local *Unpublished*

The M4 Motorway (Junction 4B, Westbound Link Roads) (Temporary Prohibition of Traffic) Order 2002 No. 2002/289. – Enabling power: Road Traffic Regulation Act 1984, s. 14 (1) (a). – Made: 11.02.2002. Coming into force: 18.02.2002. Effect: None. Territorial extent & classification: E. Local *Unpublished*

The M4 Motorway (Junction 6, Slip Roads) (Temporary Prohibition of Traffic) Order 2002 No. 2002/2096. – Enabling power: Road Traffic Regulation Act 1984, s. 14 (1) (a). – Made: 05.08.2002. Coming into force: 10.08.2002. Effect: None. Territorial extent & classification: E. Local *Unpublished*

The M4 Motorway (Junction 8/9, Eastbound Slip Road) (Temporary Prohibition of Traffic) Order 2002 No. 2002/3166. – Enabling power: Road Traffic Regulation Act 1984, s. 14 (1) (a). – Made: 16.12.2002. Coming into force: 21.12.2002. Effect: None. Territorial extent & classification: E. Local *Unpublished*

The M4 Motorway (Junction 8/9) (Temporary 50 Miles Per Hour Speed Restriction) Order 2002 No. 2002/2697. – Enabling power: Road Traffic Regulation Act 1984, s. 14 (1) (a). – Made: 28.10.2002. Coming into force: 02.11.2002. Effect: None. Territorial extent & classification: E. Local *Unpublished*

The M4 Motorway (Junction 13) (Temporary 50 Miles Per Hour Speed Restriction) Order 2002 No. 2002/2510. – Enabling power: Road Traffic Regulation Act 1984, s. 14 (1) (a). – Made: 30.09.2002. Coming into force: 05.10.2002. Effect: None. Territorial extent & classification: E. Local *Unpublished*

The M4 Motorway (Junction 15) (Temporary Prohibition of Traffic) Order 2002 No. 2002/1659. – Enabling power: Road Traffic Regulation Act 1984, s. 14 (1) (a). – Made: 24.06.2002. Coming into force: 30.06.2002. Effect: None. Territorial extent & classification: E. Local *Unpublished*

The M4 Motorway (Junction 20) (Almondsbury Interchange) (Temporary Restriction of Traffic) Order 2002 No. 2002/1602. – Enabling power: Road Traffic Regulation Act 1984, s. 14 (1) (a) (7). – Made: 10.06.2002. Coming into force: 15.06.2002. Effect: None. Territorial extent & classification: E. Local *Unpublished*

The M4 Motorway (Junctions 1 - 3) (Temporary Prohibition of Traffic) Order 2002 No. 2002/777. – Enabling power: Road Traffic Regulation Act 1984, s. 14 (1) (a). – Made: 18.03.2002. Coming into force: 01.04.2002. Effect: None. Territorial extent & classification: E. Local *Unpublished*

The M4 Motorway (Junctions 4 - 4B and 5 - 4B) (Temporary 50 Miles Per Hour Speed Restriction) Order 2002 No. 2002/3068. – Enabling power: Road Traffic Regulation Act 1984, s. 14 (1) (a). – Made: 09.12.2002. Coming into force: 14.12.2002. Effect: None. Territorial extent & classification: E. Local *Unpublished*

The M4 Motorway (Junctions 4B - 5, Slip and Link Roads) (Temporary Prohibition of Traffic) Order 2002 No. 2002/2505. – Enabling power: Road Traffic Regulation Act 1984, s. 14 (1) (a). – Made: 30.09.2002. Coming into force: 05.10.2002. Effect: None. Territorial extent & classification: E. Local *Unpublished*

The M4 Motorway (Junctions 8/9, 10 and 12, Slip Roads) (Temporary Prohibition of Traffic) Order 2002 No. 2002/2042. – Enabling power: Road Traffic Regulation Act 1984, s. 14 (1) (a). – Made: 15.07.2002. Coming into force: 20.07.2002. Effect: None. Territorial extent & classification: E. Local *Unpublished*

The M4 Motorway (Junctions 8/9, 11 and 12, Slip Roads) (Temporary Prohibition of Traffic) Order 2002 No. 2002/2971. – Enabling power: Road Traffic Regulation Act 1984, s. 14 (1) (a). – Made: 02.12.2002. Coming into force: 07.12.2002. Effect: None. Territorial extent & classification: E. Local *Unpublished*

The M4 Motorway (Junctions 12 and 14, Slip Roads) (Temporary Prohibition of Traffic) Order 2002 No. 2002/2566. – Enabling power: Road Traffic Regulation Act 1984, s. 14 (1) (a). – Made: 07.10.2002. Coming into force: 12.10.2002. Effect: None. Territorial extent & classification: E. Local *Unpublished*

The M4 Motorway (Junctions 13 and 14, Slip Roads) (Temporary Prohibition of Traffic) Order 2002 No. 2002/1756. – Enabling power: Road Traffic Regulation Act 1984, s. 14 (1) (a). – Made: 01.07.2002. Coming into force: 06.07.2002. Effect: None. Territorial extent & classification: E. Local *Unpublished*

The M4 Motorway (Junctions 15-17) (Temporary Restriction of Traffic) Order 2002 No. 2002/72. – Enabling power: Road Traffic Regulation Act 1984, s. 14 (1) (a) (7). – Made: 16.01.2002. Coming into force: 19.01.2002. Effect: None. Territorial extent & classification: E. Local *Unpublished*

The M4 Motorway (Junctions 15 - 17) (Temporary Restriction of Traffic) Order 2002 No. 2002/2170. – Enabling power: Road Traffic Regulation Act 1984, s. 14 (1) (a). – Made: 19.08.2002. Coming into force: 24.08.2002. Effect: None. Territorial extent & classification: E. Local *Unpublished*

The M4 Motorway (Purley Road Overbridge) (Temporary 50 Miles Per Hour Speed Restriction) Order 2002 No. 2002/2343. – Enabling power: Road Traffic Regulation Act 1984, s. 14 (1) (a). – Made: 09.09.2002. Coming into force: 14.09.2002. Effect: None. Territorial extent & classification: E. Local *Unpublished*

The M5 Motorway (Junction 1 - M6 Junction 8), the M6 Motorway (Junctions 4 - 4A and Junctions 8 - 9) and the M42 Motorway (Junction 3A - 8) (Temporary Prohibition and Restriction of Traffic) Order 2002 No. 2002/3260. – Enabling power: Road Traffic Regulation Act 1984, s. 14 (1) (a) (7). – Made: 30.12.2002. Coming into force: 06.01.2003. Effect: None. Territorial extent & classification: E. Local *Unpublished*

The M5 Motorway (Junction 2 - Junction 5) and the M42 Motorway (M5 Motorway Junction 4A - Junction 1) (Temporary Prohibition and Restriction of Traffic) Order 2002 No. 2002/2487. – Enabling power: Road Traffic Regulation Act 1984, s. 14 (1) (a) (7). – Made: 27.09.2002. Coming into force: 04.10.2002. Effect: None. Territorial extent & classification: E. Local *Unpublished*

The M5 Motorway (Junction 4A) (Temporary Prohibition of Traffic) Order 2002 No. 2002/1575. – Enabling power: Road Traffic Regulation Act 1984, s. 14 (1) (a). – Made: 10.06.2002. Coming into force: 17.06.2002. Effect: None. Territorial extent & classification: E. Local *Unpublished*

The M5 Motorway (Junction 5) (Southbound Exit Slip Road) (Temporary Prohibition of Traffic) Order 2002 No. 2002/234. – Enabling power: Road Traffic Regulation Act 1984, s. 14 (1) (a). – Made: 06.02.2002. Coming into force: 13.02.2002. Effect: None. Territorial extent & classification: E. Local *Unpublished*

The M5 Motorway (Junction 6) (Temporary 50 Miles Per Hour Speed Restriction) Order 2002 No. 2002/1444. – Enabling power: Road Traffic Regulation Act 1984, s. 14 (1) (a). – Made: 24.05.2002. Coming into force: 31.05.2002. Effect: None. Territorial extent & classification: E. Local *Unpublished*

The M5 Motorway (Junction 6) (Temporary Prohibition of Traffic) Order 2002 No. 2002/1518. – Enabling power: Road Traffic Regulation Act 1984, s. 14 (1) (a). – Made: 28.05.2002. Coming into force: 04.06.2002. Effect: None. Territorial extent & classification: E. Local *Unpublished*

The M5 Motorway (Junction 8) (Temporary Prohibition of Traffic) Order 2002 No. 2002/1445. – Enabling power: Road Traffic Regulation Act 1984, s. 14 (1) (a) (7). – Made: 23.05.2002. Coming into force: 30.05.2002. Effect: None. Territorial extent & classification: E. Local *Unpublished*

The M5 Motorway (Junction 11a) (Temporary Prohibition of Traffic) Order 2002 No. 2002/1937. – Enabling power: Road Traffic Regulation Act 1984, s. 14 (1) (a) (7). – Made: 22.07.2002. Coming into force: 27.07.2002. Effect: None. Territorial extent & classification: E. Local *Unpublished*

The M5 Motorway (Junction 12) (Temporary Restriction of Traffic) Order 2002 No. 2002/2231. – Enabling power: Road Traffic Regulation Act 1984, ss. 14 (1) (a), 122A, sch. 9, para. 27 (1). – Made: 27.08.2002. Coming into force: 30.08.2002. Effect: S.I. 2001/3249 varied. Territorial extent & classification: E. Local *Unpublished*

The M5 Motorway (Junction 17) (Temporary Prohibition of Traffic) Order 2002 No. 2002/2340. – Enabling power: Road Traffic Regulation Act 1984, s. 14 (1) (a). – Made: 09.09.2002. Coming into force: 14.09.2002. Effect: None. Territorial extent & classification: E. Local *Unpublished*

The M5 Motorway (Junction 18a-18) and the A4 Trunk Road (Crowley Way) (Temporary Restriction of Traffic) Order 2002 No. 2002/2338. – Enabling power: Road Traffic Regulation Act 1984, s. 14 (1) (a) (7). – Made: 09.09.2002. Coming into force: 14.09.2002. Effect: None. Territorial extent & classification: E. Local *Unpublished*

The M5 Motorway (Junction 21) (Temporary Prohibition and Restriction of Traffic) Order 2002 No. 2002/1045. – Enabling power: Road Traffic Regulation Act 1984, s. 14 (1) (a). – Made: 05.04.2002. Coming into force: 11.04.2002. Effect: None. Territorial extent & classification: E. Local *Unpublished*

The M5 Motorway (Junction 22) (Temporary Prohibition of Traffic) Order 2002 No. 2002/1660. – Enabling power: Road Traffic Regulation Act 1984, s. 14 (1) (a). – Made: 24.06.2002. Coming into force: 29.06.2002. Effect: None. Territorial extent & classification: E. Local *Unpublished*

The M5 Motorway (Junction 22) (Temporary Prohibition of Traffic) Order 2002 No. 2002/2285. – Enabling power: Road Traffic Regulation Act 1984, s. 14 (1) (a). – Made: 02.09.2002. Coming into force: 07.09.2002. Effect: None. Territorial extent & classification: E. Local *Unpublished*

The M5 Motorway (Junction 25) (Temporary Prohibition of Traffic) Order 2002 No. 2002/1288. – Enabling power: Road Traffic Regulation Act 1984, s. 14 (1) (a). – Made: 07.05.2002. Coming into force: 11.05.2002. Effect: None. Territorial extent & classification: E. Local *Unpublished*

The M5 Motorway (Junctions 6 - 5) (Temporary Prohibition of Traffic) Order 2002 No. 2002/1219. – Enabling power: Road Traffic Regulation Act 1984, s. 14 (1) (a). – Made: 26.04.2002. Coming into force: 03.05.2002. Effect: None. Territorial extent & classification: E. Local *Unpublished*

The M5 Motorway (Junctions 11a-11) (Temporary Restriction of Traffic) Order 2002 No. 2002/29. – Enabling power: Road Traffic Regulation Act 1984, s. 14 (1) (a) (7). – Made: 09.01.2002. Coming into force: 11.01.2002. Effect: None. Territorial extent & classification: E. Local *Unpublished*

The M5 Motorway (Junctions 11a - 12) (Temporary Restriction of Traffic) Order 2002 No. 2002/390. – Enabling power: Road Traffic Regulation Act 1984, s. 14 (1) (a) (7). – Made: 18.02.2002. Coming into force: 23.02.2002. Effect: None. Territorial extent & classification: E. Local *Unpublished*

The M5 Motorway (Junctions 12 - 11a) (Temporary Prohibition and Restriction of Traffic) Order 2002 No. 2002/1274. – Enabling power: Road Traffic Regulation Act 1984, s. 14 (1) (a). – Made: 03.05.2002. Coming into force: 10.05.2002. Effect: None. Territorial extent & classification: E. Local *Unpublished*

The M5 Motorway (Junctions 13-14, Michaelwood Services) (Temporary Restriction of Traffic) Order 2002 No. 2002/3143. – Enabling power: Road Traffic Regulation Act 1984, s. 14 (1) (a). – Made: 12.12.2002. Coming into force: 14.12.2002. Effect: None. Territorial extent & classification: E. Local *Unpublished*

The M5 Motorway (Junctions 14-13) (Temporary Prohibition and Restriction of Traffic) Order 2002 No. 2002/973. – Enabling power: Road Traffic Regulation Act 1984, s. 14 (1) (a) (7). – Made: 02.04.2002. Coming into force: 06.04.2002. Effect: None. Territorial extent & classification: E. Local *Unpublished*

The M5 Motorway (Junctions 15-17) and the M4 Motorway (Junction 20) (Almondsbury Interchange) (Temporary Prohibition of Traffic) Order 2002 No. 2002/1154. – Enabling power: Road Traffic Regulation Act 1984, s. 14 (1) (a). – Made: 22.04.2002. Coming into force: 26.04.2002. Effect: None. Territorial extent & classification: E. Local *Unpublished*

The M5 Motorway (Junctions 18 & 18a) (Temporary Prohibition of Traffic) Order 2002 No. 2002/1952. – Enabling power: Road Traffic Regulation Act 1984, s. 14 (1) (a) (7). – Made: 23.07.2002. Coming into force: 29.07.2002. Effect: None. Territorial extent & classification: E. Local *Unpublished*

The M5 Motorway (Junctions 18a-18) (Temporary Prohibition and Restriction of Traffic) Order 2002 No. 2002/1538. – Enabling power: Road Traffic Regulation Act 1984, s. 14 (1) (a). – Made: 05.06.2002. Coming into force: 08.06.2002. Effect: None. Territorial extent & classification: E. Local *Unpublished*

The M5 Motorway (Junctions 19-20) (Temporary Prohibition and Restriction of Traffic) Order 2002 No. 2002/1107. – Enabling power: Road Traffic Regulation Act 1984, s. 14 (1) (a) (7). – Made: 15.04.2002. Coming into force: 20.04.2002. Effect: None. Territorial extent & classification: E. Local *Unpublished*

The M5 Motorway (Junctions 19-20) (Temporary Restriction of Traffic) Order 2002 No. 2002/2197. – Enabling power: Road Traffic Regulation Act 1984, s. 14 (1) (a) (7). – Made: 20.08.2002. Coming into force: 25.08.2002. Effect: None. Territorial extent & classification: E. Local *Unpublished*

The M5 Motorway (Junctions 20-19) (Temporary Restriction of Traffic) Order 2002 No. 2002/2454. – Enabling power: Road Traffic Regulation Act 1984, s. 14 (1) (a) (7). – Made: 23.09.2002. Coming into force: 28.09.2002. Effect: None. Territorial extent & classification: E. Local *Unpublished*

The M5 Motorway (Junctions 22 - 23) (Temporary Restriction of Traffic) Order 2002 No. 2002/1536. – Enabling power: Road Traffic Regulation Act 1984, s. 14 (1) (a) (7). – Made: 31.05.2002. Coming into force: 07.06.2002. Effect: None. Territorial extent & classification: E. Local *Unpublished*

The M5 Motorway (Junctions 27-28) (Temporary Prohibition and Restriction of Traffic) Order 2002 No. 2002/972. – Enabling power: Road Traffic Regulation Act 1984, s. 14 (1) (a) (7). – Made: 02.04.2002. Coming into force: 06.04.2002. Effect: None. Territorial extent & classification: E. Local *Unpublished*

The M5 Motorway (Junctions 28, 30 and 31) (Temporary Prohibition of Traffic) Order 2002 No. 2002/971. – Enabling power: Road Traffic Regulation Act 1984, s. 14 (1) (a). – Made: 02.04.2002. Coming into force: 06.04.2002. Effect: None. Territorial extent & classification: E. Local *Unpublished*

The M5 Motorway (Junctions 30 - 31) and the A38 and A30 Trunk Roads (Temporary Prohibition and Restriction of Traffic) Order 2002 No. 2002/2261. – Enabling power: Road Traffic Regulation Act 1984, s. 14 (1) (a) (7). – Made: 04.09.2002. Coming into force: 07.09.2002. Effect: None. Territorial extent & classification: E. Local *Unpublished*

The M5 Motorway (M5 Junction 1 - M6 Junction 8) (Temporary Prohibition of Traffic) Order 2002 No. 2002/1272. – Enabling power: Road Traffic Regulation Act 1984, s. 14 (1) (a) (7). – Made: 03.05.2002. Coming into force: 10.05.2002. Effect: None. Territorial extent & classification: E. Local *Unpublished*

The M6 and M56 Motorways (Lymm) (Temporary Restriction and Prohibition of Traffic) Order 2002 No. 2002/2728. – Enabling power: Road Traffic Regulation Act 1984, s. 14 (1) (a). – Made: 30.10.2002. Coming into force: 07.11.2002. Effect: None. Territorial extent & classification: E. Local *Unpublished*

The M6 and M62 Motorways (Croft) (Temporary Prohibition of Traffic) Order 2002 No. 2002/2679. – Enabling power: Road Traffic Regulation Act 1984, s. 14 (1) (a). – Made: 22.10.2002. Coming into force: 24.10.2002. Effect: None. Territorial extent & classification: E. Local *Unpublished*

The M6 Motorway and the A446 Trunk Road (M6 Junction 4) (Temporary Restriction and Prohibition of Traffic) Order 2002 No. 2002/1369. – Enabling power: Road Traffic Regulation Act 1984, s. 14 (1) (a). – Made: 10.05.2002. Coming into force: 17.05.2002. Effect: None. Territorial extent & classification: E. Local *Unpublished*

The M6 Motorway (Goodyers End - Junction 3) (Temporary Prohibition and Restriction of Traffic) Order 2002 No. 2002/2753. – Enabling power: Road Traffic Regulation Act 1984, s. 14 (1) (a) (7). – Made: 01.11.2002. Coming into force: 08.11.2002. Effect: None. Territorial extent & classification: E. Local *Unpublished*

The M6 Motorway (Junction 4A, Warwickshire) (Temporary Prohibition of Traffic) Order 2002 No. 2002/1269. – Enabling power: Road Traffic Regulation Act 1984, s. 14 (1) (a) (7). – Made: 03.05.2002. Coming into force: 10.05.2002. Effect: None. Territorial extent & classification: E. Local *Unpublished*

The M6 Motorway (Junction 8 Southbound Link Road to M5) (Temporary Prohibition of Traffic) Order 2002 No. 2002/1055. – Enabling power: Road Traffic Regulation Act 1984, s. 14 (1) (a). – Made: 05.04.2002. Coming into force: 12.04.2002. Effect: None. Territorial extent & classification: E. Local *Unpublished*

The M6 Motorway (Junction 8) (Temporary Prohibition of Traffic) Order 2002 No. 2002/2041. – Enabling power: Road Traffic Regulation Act 1984, s. 14 (1) (a). – Made: 01.07.2002. Coming into force: 08.07.2002. Effect: None. Territorial extent & classification: E. Local *Unpublished*

The M6 Motorway (Junction 8) (Temporary Prohibition of Traffic) Order 2002 No. 2002/1899. – Enabling power: Road Traffic Regulation Act 1984, s. 14 (1) (a). – Made: 01.07.2002. Coming into force: 08.07.2002. Effect: None. Territorial extent & classification: E. Local *Unpublished*

The M6 Motorway (Junction 11) (Temporary Prohibition and Restriction of Traffic) Order 2002 No. 2002/2028. – Enabling power: Road Traffic Regulation Act 1984, s. 14 (1) (a). – Made: 26.07.2002. Coming into force: 02.08.2002. Effect: None. Territorial extent & classification: E. Local *Unpublished*

The M6 Motorway (Junction 15) Slip Roads (Temporary Prohibition of Traffic) Order 2002 No. 2002/197. – Enabling power: Road Traffic Regulation Act 1984, s. 14 (1) (a). – Made: 01.02.2002. Coming into force: 08.02.2002. Effect: None. Territorial extent & classification: E. Local *Unpublished*

The M6 Motorway (Junction 18, Northbound Exit Slip Road) (Temporary Prohibition of Traffic) Order 2002 No. 2002/2958. – Enabling power: Road Traffic Regulation Act 1984, s. 14 (1) (a). – Made: 28.11.2002. Coming into force: 05.12.2002. Effect: None. Territorial extent & classification: E. Local *Unpublished*

The M6 Motorway (Junction 19, Tabley) (Temporary Restriction and Prohibition of Traffic) Order 2002 No. 2002/429. – Enabling power: Road Traffic Regulation Act 1984, s. 14 (1) (a) (7). – Made: 26.02.2002. Coming into force: 03.03.2002. Effect: None. Territorial extent & classification: E. Local *Unpublished*

The M6 Motorway (Junction 25, Slip Roads) (Temporary Prohibition of Traffic) Order 2002 No. 2002/2136. – Enabling power: Road Traffic Regulation Act 1984, s. 14 (1) (a). – Made: 12.08.2002. Coming into force: 14.08.2002. Effect: None. Territorial extent & classification: E. Local *Unpublished*

The M6 Motorway (Junction 33) (Temporary Prohibition of Traffic) Order 2002 No. 2002/20. – Enabling power: Road Traffic Regulation Act 1984, s. 14 (1) (a). – Made: 03.01.2002. Coming into force: 09.01.2002. Effect: None. Territorial extent & classification: E. Local *Unpublished*

The M6 Motorway (Junction 33) (Temporary Prohibition of Traffic) Order 2002 No. 2002/2503. – Enabling power: Road Traffic Regulation Act 1984, s. 14 (1) (a). – Made: 26.09.2002. Coming into force: 30.09.2002. Effect: None. Territorial extent & classification: E. Local *Unpublished*

The M6 Motorway (Junction 34, Slip Roads) (Temporary Prohibition of Traffic) Order 2002 No. 2002/1746. – Enabling power: Road Traffic Regulation Act 1984, s. 14 (1) (a). – Made: 02.07.2002. Coming into force: 04.07.2002. Effect: None. Territorial extent & classification: E. Local *Unpublished*

The M6 Motorway (Junction 34) (Temporary Prohibition of Traffic) Order 2002 No. 2002/1567. – Enabling power: Road Traffic Regulation Act 1984, s. 14 (1) (a). – Made: 06.06.2002. Coming into force: 13.06.2002. Effect: None. Territorial extent & classification: E. Local *Unpublished*

The M6 Motorway (Junction 37, Low Park to Low Gill) (Temporary Restriction of Traffic) Order 2002 No. 2002/1050. – Enabling power: Road Traffic Regulation Act 1984, s. 14 (1) (a) (7). – Made: 04.04.2002. Coming into force: 07.04.2002. Effect: None. Territorial extent & classification: E. Local *Unpublished*

The M6 Motorway (Junction 38, Galloper Well Bridge) (Temporary Restriction of Traffic) Order 2002 No. 2002/1742. – Enabling power: Road Traffic Regulation Act 1984, s. 14 (1) (a) (7). – Made: 04.07.2002. Coming into force: 09.07.2002. Effect: None. Territorial extent & classification: E. Local *Unpublished*

The M6 Motorway (Junction 38 Northbound) (Temporary Restriction of Traffic) Order 2002 No. 2002/1741. – Enabling power: Road Traffic Regulation Act 1984, s. 14 (1) (a) (7). – Made: 04.07.2002. Coming into force: 07.07.2002. Effect: None. Territorial extent & classification: E. Local *Unpublished*

The M6 Motorway (Junction 38, Tebay) (Temporary Restriction and Prohibition of Traffic) Order 2002 No. 2002/2251. – Enabling power: Road Traffic Regulation Act 1984, s. 14 (1) (a) (7). – Made: 22.08.2002. Coming into force: 26.08.2002. Effect: None. Territorial extent & classification: E. Local *Unpublished*

The M6 Motorway (Junction 43, Garlands Cumwhinton Bridge) (Temporary Restriction of Traffic) Order 2002 No. 2002/3. – Enabling power: Road Traffic Regulation Act 1984, s. 14 (1) (a) (7). – Made: 03.01.2002. Coming into force: 05.01.2002. Effect: None. Territorial extent & classification: E. Local *Unpublished*

The M6 Motorway (Junction 43, Rosehill Interchange) (Temporary Restriction and Prohibition of Traffic) Order 2002 No. 2002/319. – Enabling power: Road Traffic Regulation Act 1984, s. 14 (1) (a) (7). – Made: 06.02.2002. Coming into force: 16.02.2002. Effect: None. Territorial extent & classification: E. Local *Unpublished*

The M6 Motorway (Junctions 3 - 4) (Temporary Prohibition and Restriction of Traffic) Order 2002 No. 2002/900. – Enabling power: Road Traffic Regulation Act 1984, s. 14 (1) (a) (7). – Made: 21.03.2002. Coming into force: 28.03.2002. Effect: None. Territorial extent & classification: E. Local *Unpublished*

The M6 Motorway (Junctions 8-9) (Temporary Prohibition of Traffic) Order 2002 No. 2002/196. – Enabling power: Road Traffic Regulation Act 1984, s. 14 (1) (a) (7). – Made: 29.01.2002. Coming into force: 05.02.2002. Effect: None. Territorial extent & classification: E. Local *Unpublished*

The M6 Motorway (Junctions 15 - 16) (Temporary Restriction and Prohibition of Traffic) Order 2002 No. 2002/383. – Enabling power: Road Traffic Regulation Act 1984, s. 14 (1) (a) (7). – Made: 15.02.2002. Coming into force: 22.02.2002. Effect: None. Territorial extent & classification: E. Local *Unpublished*

The M6 Motorway (Junctions 22 to 23, Bridges) (Temporary Restriction of Traffic) Order 2002 No. 2002/1740. – Enabling power: Road Traffic Regulation Act 1984, s. 14 (1) (a). – Made: 02.07.2002. Coming into force: 04.07.2002. Effect: None. Territorial extent & classification: E. Local *Unpublished*

The M6 Motorway (Junctions 24 to 25) (Temporary Restriction of Traffic) Order 2002 No. 2002/353. – Enabling power: Road Traffic Regulation Act 1984, s. 14 (1) (a) (7). – Made: 13.02.2002. Coming into force: 17.02.2002. Effect: None. Territorial extent & classification: E. Local *Unpublished*

The M6 Motorway (Junctions 26 and 27, Slip Roads) (Temporary Prohibition of Traffic) Order 2002 No. 2002/2418. – Enabling power: Road Traffic Regulation Act 1984, s. 14 (1) (a). – Made: 18.09.2002. Coming into force: 23.09.2002. Effect: None. Territorial extent & classification: E. Local *Unpublished*

The M6 Motorway (Junctions 27 to 28) (Temporary Restriction of Traffic) Order 2002 No. 2002/2407. – Enabling power: Road Traffic Regulation Act 1984, s. 14 (1) (a) (7). – Made: 18.09.2002. Coming into force: 22.09.2002. Effect: None. Territorial extent & classification: E. Local *Unpublished*

The M6 Motorway (Junctions 33 to 32) (Temporary Restriction of Traffic) Order 2002 No. 2002/2112. – Enabling power: Road Traffic Regulation Act 1984, s. 14 (1) (a) (7). – Made: 02.08.2002. Coming into force: 04.08.2002. Effect: None. Territorial extent & classification: E. Local *Unpublished*

The M6 Motorway (Junctions 35 to 36) (Temporary Restriction of Traffic) Order 2002 No. 2002/1566. – Enabling power: Road Traffic Regulation Act 1984, s. 14 (1) (a) (7). – Made: 06.06.2002. Coming into force: 09.06.2002. Effect: None. Territorial extent & classification: E. Local *Unpublished*

The M6 Motorway (Junctions 36 to 38, Killington Lake) (Temporary Restriction and Prohibition of Traffic) Order 2002 No. 2002/2470. – Enabling power: Road Traffic Regulation Act 1984, s. 14 (1) (a) (7). – Made: 19.09.2002. Coming into force: 22.09.2002. Effect: None. Territorial extent & classification: E. Local *Unpublished*

The M6 Motorway (Junctions 40 to 39, Trainriggs Bridge) (Temporary Restriction and Prohibition of Traffic) Order 2002 No. 2002/2161. – Enabling power: Road Traffic Regulation Act 1984, s. 14 (1) (a) (7). – Made: 15.08.2002. Coming into force: 18.08.2002. Effect: None. Territorial extent & classification: E. Local *Unpublished*

The M6 Motorway (M1 Motorway - M42 Motorway) and the M69 Motorway (Junction 1 - M6 Motorway Junction 2) (Temporary Prohibition and Restriction of Traffic) Order 2002 No. 2002/2120. – Enabling power: Road Traffic Regulation Act 1984, s. 14 (1) (a) (7). – Made: 07.08.2002. Coming into force: 14.08.2002. Effect: None. Territorial extent & classification: E. Local *Unpublished*

The M6 Motorway (Northbound Exit Slip Road Leading to Stafford Service Area) (Temporary Prohibition of Traffic) Order 2002 No. 2002/1248. – Enabling power: Road Traffic Regulation Act 1984, s. 14 (1) (a). – Made: 30.04.2002. Coming into force: 07.05.2002. Effect: None. Territorial extent & classification: E. Local *Unpublished*

The M6 Motorway (Thelwall Viaduct) (Temporary Prohibition of Traffic) (No. 2) Order 2002 No. 2002/2826. – Enabling power: Road Traffic Regulation Act 1984, s. 14 (1) (a). – Made: 13.11.2002. Coming into force: 15.11.2002. Effect: None. Territorial extent & classification: E. Local *Unpublished*

The M6 Motorway (Thelwall Viaduct) (Temporary Restriction and Prohibition of Traffic) Order 2002 No. 2002/2196. – Enabling power: Road Traffic Regulation Act 1984, s. 14 (1) (b) (7). – Made: 14.08.2002. Coming into force: 19.08.2002. Effect: None. Territorial extent & classification: E. Local *Unpublished*

The M6 Motorway (Thelwall Viaduct) (Temporary Restriction and Prohibition of Traffic) Order 2002 Amendment Order 2002 No. 2002/2438. – Enabling power: Road Traffic Regulation Act 1984, s. 14 (1) (b) (7). – Made: 19.09.2002. Coming into force: 21.09.2002. Effect: S.I. 2002/2196 amended. Territorial extent & classification: E. Local *Unpublished*

The M6 Motorway (West of Junction 2, Coventry) (Temporary Prohibition of Traffic) Order 2002 No. 2002/1220. – Enabling power: Road Traffic Regulation Act 1984, s. 14 (1) (a) (7). – Made: 26.04.2002. Coming into force: 03.05.2002. Effect: None. Territorial extent & classification: E. Local *Unpublished*

The M11 and M25 Motorways (Theydon Interchange) (Temporary Prohibition of Traffic) Order 2002 No. 2002/2133. – Enabling power: Road Traffic Regulation Act 1984, s. 14 (1) (a). – Made: 12.08.2002. Coming into force: 17.08.2002. Effect: None. Territorial extent & classification: E. Local *Unpublished*

The M11 Motorway, A14 Trunk Road and A1307 Trunk Road (Cambridgeshire) (Temporary Restriction and Prohibition of Traffic) Order 2002 No. 2002/1287. – Enabling power: Road Traffic Regulation Act 1984, s. 14 (1) (a). – Made: 07.05.2002. Coming into force: 14.05.2002. Effect: None. Territorial extent & classification: E. Local *Unpublished*

The M11 Motorway (Junction 4, Link Roads) (Temporary Prohibition of Traffic) Order 2002 No. 2002/2084. – Enabling power: Road Traffic Regulation Act 1984, s. 14 (1) (a). – Made: 05.08.2002. Coming into force: 14.08.2002. Effect: None. Territorial extent & classification: E. Local *Unpublished*

The M11 Motorway (Junction 4, Redbridge Viaduct) (Temporary Restriction of Traffic) Order 2002 No. 2002/901. – Enabling power: Road Traffic Regulation Act 1984, s. 14 (1) (b). – Made: 22.03.2002. Coming into force: 23.03.2002. Effect: None. Territorial extent & classification: E. Local *Unpublished*

The M11 Motorway (Junction 4, Southbound) (Temporary Restriction and Prohibition of Traffic) Order 2002 No. 2002/1816. – Enabling power: Road Traffic Regulation Act 1984, s. 14 (1) (a). – Made: 08.07.2002. Coming into force: 13.07.2002. Effect: None. Territorial extent & classification: E. Local *Unpublished*

The M11 Motorway (Junction 6, Northbound Link Road) (Temporary Prohibition of Traffic) Order 2002 No. 2002/88. – Enabling power: Road Traffic Regulation Act 1984, s. 14 (1) (a). – Made: 21.01.2002. Coming into force: 26.01.2002. Effect: None. Territorial extent & classification: E. Local *Unpublished*

The M11 Motorway (Junction 6, Theydon Interchange - M25) (Temporary Prohibition of Traffic) Order 2002 No. 2002/1851. – Enabling power: Road Traffic Regulation Act 1984, s. 14 (1) (a). – Made: 15.07.2002. Coming into force: 20.07.2002. Effect: None. Territorial extent & classification: E. Local *Unpublished*

The M11 Motorway (Junction 8, Connecting Roads, Essex) (Temporary 40 Miles Per Hour and 50 Miles Per Hour Speed Restriction) Order 2002 No. 2002/2824. Enabling power: Road Traffic Regulation Act 1984, s. 14 (1) (a). – Made: 11.11.2002. Coming into force: 18.11.2002. Effect: None. Territorial extent & classification: E. Local *Unpublished*

The M11 Motorway (Junction 9, Great Chesterford, Essex) (Temporary 50 Miles Per Hour Speed Restriction) Order 2002 No. 2002/2545. Enabling power: Road Traffic Regulation Act 1984, s. 14 (1) (a). – Made: 04.10.2002. Coming into force: 11.10.2002. Effect: None. Territorial extent & classification: E. Local *Unpublished*

The M11 Motorway (Junction 14) and the A14 Trunk Road (Girton Interchange, Cambridgeshire) (Slip Roads) (Temporary Prohibition of Traffic) Order 2002 No. 2002/101. – Enabling power: Road Traffic Regulation Act 1984, s. 14 (1) (a). – Made: 21.01.2002. Coming into force: 28.01.2002. Effect: None. Territorial extent & classification: E. Local *Unpublished*

The M11 Motorway (Junctions 6 and 7, Link and Slip Roads) (Temporary Prohibition of Traffic) Order 2002 No. 2002/288. – Enabling power: Road Traffic Regulation Act 1984, s. 14 (1) (a). – Made: 11.02.2002. Coming into force: 18.02.2002. Effect: None. Territorial extent & classification: E. Local *Unpublished*

The M11 Motorway (Junctions 7 - 10, Essex) (Temporary Prohibition of Traffic) Order 2002 No. 2002/687. – Enabling power: Road Traffic Regulation Act 1984, s. 14 (1) (a). – Made: 11.03.2002. Coming into force: 18.03.2002. Effect: None. Territorial extent & classification: E. Local *Unpublished*

The M11 Motorway (Junctions 8 - 10, Essex) (Temporary Prohibition of Traffic) Order 2002 No. 2002/100. – Enabling power: Road Traffic Regulation Act 1984, s. 14 (1) (a). – Made: 21.01.2002. Coming into force: 28.01.2002. Effect: None. Territorial extent & classification: E. Local *Unpublished*

The M11 Motorway (Junctions 9 - 14, Cambridgeshire) (Temporary Restriction of Traffic) Order 2002 No. 2002/1960. – Enabling power: Road Traffic Regulation Act 1984, s. 14 (1) (a) (7). – Made: 22.07.2002. Coming into force: 29.07.2002. Effect: None. Territorial extent & classification: E. Local *Unpublished*

The M11 Motorway (Junctions 9 to 10) (Temporary Restriction) Order 2002 No. 2002/1801. – Enabling power: Road Traffic Regulation Act 1984, s. 14 (1) (a) (7). – Made: 08.07.2002. Coming into force: 15.07.2002. Effect: None. Territorial extent & classification: E. Local *Unpublished*

The M11 Motorway (Junctions 10 - 11, Cambridgeshire) (Temporary Restriction and Prohibition of Traffic) Order 2002 No. 2002/1609. – Enabling power: Road Traffic Regulation Act 1984, s. 14 (1) (a) (7). – Made: 17.06.2002. Coming into force: 24.06.2002. Effect: None. Territorial extent & classification: E. Local *Unpublished*

The M11 Motorway (Junctions 10 - 12, Cambridgeshire) (Temporary Restriction and Prohibition of Traffic) Order 2002 No. 2002/363. – Enabling power: Road Traffic Regulation Act 1984, s. 14 (1) (a) (7). – Made: 18.02.2002. Coming into force: 25.02.2002. Effect: None. Territorial extent & classification: E. Local *Unpublished*

The M11 Motorway (Junctions 12 - 11) Cambridgeshire (Temporary Prohibition of Traffic) Order 2002 No. 2002/2613. – Enabling power: Road Traffic Regulation Act 1984, s. 14 (1) (a). – Made: 11.10.2002. Coming into force: 18.10.2002. Effect: None. Territorial extent & classification: E. Local *Unpublished*

The M18 Motorway (Cantley Common) (Temporary Restriction and Prohibition of Traffic) Order 2002 No. 2002/1600. – Enabling power: Road Traffic Regulation Act 1984, s. 14 (1) (a) (7). – Made: 30.05.2002. Coming into force: 04.06.2002. Effect: None. Territorial extent & classification: E. Local *Unpublished*

The M18 Motorway (Junction 3 to Junction 4) (Temporary Restriction and Prohibition of Traffic) Order 2002 No. 2002/1604. – Enabling power: Road Traffic Regulation Act 1984, s. 14 (1) (a) (7). – Made: 11.06.2002. Coming into force: 14.06.2002. Effect: None. Territorial extent & classification: E. Local *Unpublished*

The M18 Motorway (Thurcroft Interchange and Junction 2 to Junction 5) and the A1(M) Motorway (Junction 34 to Junction 38) (Temporary Restriction and Prohibition of Traffic) Order 2002 No. 2002/1864. – Enabling power: Road Traffic Regulation Act 1984, s. 14 (1) (a) (7). – Made: 10.07.2002. Coming into force: 15.07.2002. Effect: None. Territorial extent & classification: E. Local *Unpublished*

The M20 Motorway and the A20 Trunk Road (Junction 13 - Dover) (Temporary Restriction and Prohibition of Traffic) Order 2002 No. 2002/2147. – Enabling power: Road Traffic Regulation Act 1984, s. 14 (1) (a). – Made: 12.08.2002. Coming into force: 16.08.2002. Effect: None. Territorial extent & classification: E. Local *Unpublished*

The M20 Motorway (Junction 5, Londonbound Slip Road) (Temporary Prohibition of Traffic) Order 2002 No. 2002/1511. – Enabling power: Road Traffic Regulation Act 1984, s. 14 (1) (a). – Made: 05.06.2002. Coming into force: 07.06.2002. Effect: None. Territorial extent & classification: E. Local *Unpublished*

The M20 Motorway (Junction 6, Londonbound Distributor Road) (Temporary Prohibition of Traffic) Order 2002 No. 2002/2912. – Enabling power: Road Traffic Regulation Act 1984, s. 14 (1) (a). – Made: 25.11.2002. Coming into force: 02.12.2002. Effect: None. Territorial extent & classification: E. Local *Unpublished*

The M20 Motorway (Junction 9, Slip Roads) (Temporary Prohibition of Traffic) Order 2002 No. 2002/2193. – Enabling power: Road Traffic Regulation Act 1984, s. 14 (1) (a). – Made: 19.08.2002. Coming into force: 24.08.2002. Effect: None. Territorial extent & classification: E. Local *Unpublished*

The M20 Motorway (Junctions 9 - 11) (Temporary Restriction and Prohibition of Traffic) Order 2002 No. 2002/1850. – Enabling power: Road Traffic Regulation Act 1984, s. 14 (1) (a) (7). – Made: 15.07.2002. Coming into force: 20.07.2002. Effect: None. Territorial extent & classification: E. Local *Unpublished*

The M20 Motorway (Junctions 9 - 11) (Temporary Restriction and Prohibition of Traffic) Order 2002 Variation Order 2002 No. 2002/2189. – Enabling power: Road Traffic Regulation Act 1984, s. 14 (1) (a), sch. 9, para. 27 (1). – Made: 16.08.2002. Coming into force: 19.08.2002. Effect: S.I. 2002/1850 varied. Territorial extent & classification: E. Local *Unpublished*

The M25 (Junction 16) and M40 (Junctions 1A - 4) Motorways (Temporary Restriction of Traffic) Order 2002 No. 2002/2652. – Enabling power: Road Traffic Regulation Act 1984, s. 14 (1) (a) (7). – Made: 18.10.2002. Coming into force: 25.10.2002. Effect: None. Territorial extent & classification: E. Local *Unpublished*

The M25 Motorway (Bell Common Tunnel) (Temporary Restriction and Prohibition of Traffic) Order 2002 No. 2002/2740. – Enabling power: Road Traffic Regulation Act 1984, s. 14 (1) (a) (7), sch. 9, para. 27 (1). – Made: 04.11.2002. Coming into force: 11.11.2002. Effect: S.I. 2001/3976 revoked. Territorial extent & classification: E. Local *Unpublished*

The M25 Motorway (Holmesdale Tunnel) (Temporary Restriction and Prohibition of Traffic) Order 2002 No. 2002/2741. – Enabling power: Road Traffic Regulation Act 1984, s. 14 (1) (a) (7), sch. 9, para. 27 (1). – Made: 04.11.2002. Coming into force: 11.11.2002. Effect: S.I. 2001/3977 revoked. Territorial extent & classification: E. Local *Unpublished*

The M25 Motorway (Junction 2, Southbound Entry Slip Road) (Temporary Prohibition of Traffic) Order 2002 No. 2002/1047. – Enabling power: Road Traffic Regulation Act 1984, s. 14 (1) (a). – Made: 08.04.2002. Coming into force: 13.04.2002. Effect: None. Territorial extent & classification: E. Local *Unpublished*

The M25 Motorway (Junction 9, Eastbound Slip Road) (Temporary Restriction and Prohibition of Traffic) Order 2002 No. 2002/2349. – Enabling power: Road Traffic Regulation Act 1984, s. 14 (1) (b). – Made: 09.09.2002. Coming into force: 14.09.2002. Effect: None. Territorial extent & classification: E. Local *Unpublished*

The M25 Motorway (Junction 12, Northbound Link Road) (Temporary Prohibition of Traffic) Order 2002 No. 2002/482. – Enabling power: Road Traffic Regulation Act 1984, s. 14 (1) (a). – Made: 04.03.2002. Coming into force: 08.03.2002. Effect: None. Territorial extent & classification: E. Local *Unpublished*

The M25 Motorway (Junction 13, Southbound Carriageway) (Temporary Prohibition of Traffic) Order 2002 No. 2002/2656. – Enabling power: Road Traffic Regulation Act 1984, s. 14 (1) (a). – Made: 21.10.2002. Coming into force: 26.10.2002. Effect: None. Territorial extent & classification: E. Local *Unpublished*

The M25 Motorway (Junction 15, Southbound Carriageway) (Temporary Restriction and Prohibition of Traffic) Order 2002 No. 2002/286. – Enabling power: Road Traffic Regulation Act 1984, s. 14 (1) (a) (7). – Made: 11.02.2002. Coming into force: 16.02.2002. Effect: None. Territorial extent & classification: E. Local *Unpublished*

The M25 Motorway (Junction 16, Link Road) (Temporary Prohibition of Traffic) Order 2002 No. 2002/30. – Enabling power: Road Traffic Regulation Act 1984, s. 14 (1) (a). – Made: 07.01.2002. Coming into force: 12.01.2002. Effect: None. Territorial extent & classification: E. Local *Unpublished*

The M25 Motorway (Junction 16, Southbound Slip Road) (Temporary Prohibition of Traffic) Order 2002 No. 2002/1635. – Enabling power: Road Traffic Regulation Act 1984, s. 14 (1) (a). – Made: 24.06.2002. Coming into force: 29.06.2002. Effect: None. Territorial extent & classification: E. Local *Unpublished*

The M25 Motorway (Junction 18, Slip Road) (Temporary Prohibition of Traffic) Order 2002 No. 2002/2192. – Enabling power: Road Traffic Regulation Act 1984, s. 14 (1) (a). – Made: 19.08.2002. Coming into force: 24.08.2002. Effect: None. Territorial extent & classification: E. Local *Unpublished*

The M25 Motorway (Junction 21, Eastbound Link Road) (Temporary Restriction and Prohibition of Traffic) Order 2002 No. 2002/89. – Enabling power: Road Traffic Regulation Act 1984, s. 14 (1) (a). – Made: 21.01.2002. Coming into force: 26.01.2002. Effect: None. Territorial extent & classification: E. Local *Unpublished*

The M25 Motorway (Junction 24, Slip Road) (Temporary Prohibition of Traffic) Order 2002 No. 2002/406. – Enabling power: Road Traffic Regulation Act 1984, s. 14 (1) (a). – Made: 25.02.2002. Coming into force: 02.03.2002. Effect: None. Territorial extent & classification: E. Local *Unpublished*

The M25 Motorway (Junction 24, Slip Road) (Temporary Prohibition of Traffic) Order 2002 No. 2002/1939. – Enabling power: Road Traffic Regulation Act 1984, s. 14 (1) (a). – Made: 22.07.2002. Coming into force: 27.07.2002. Effect: None. Territorial extent & classification: E. Local *Unpublished*

The M25 Motorway (Junction 26, Slip Roads) (Temporary Prohibition of Traffic) Order 2002 No. 2002/2040. – Enabling power: Road Traffic Regulation Act 1984, s. 14 (1) (a). – Made: 15.07.2002. Coming into force: 20.07.2002. Effect: None. Territorial extent & classification: E. Local *Unpublished*

The M25 Motorway (Junction 28, Slip Roads) (Temporary Prohibition of Traffic) Order 2002 No. 2002/209. – Enabling power: Road Traffic Regulation Act 1984, s. 14 (1) (a). – Made: 04.02.2002. Coming into force: 09.02.2002. Effect: None. Territorial extent & classification: E. Local *Unpublished*

The M25 Motorway (Junction 28) (Temporary Prohibition of Traffic) Order 2002 No. 2002/1942. – Enabling power: Road Traffic Regulation Act 1984, s. 14 (1) (a) (7). – Made: 22.07.2002. Coming into force: 27.07.2002. Effect: None. Territorial extent & classification: E. Local *Unpublished*

The M25 Motorway (Junctions 10, 12 and 14, Slip Roads) (Temporary Prohibition of Traffic) Order 2002 No. 2002/2132. – Enabling power: Road Traffic Regulation Act 1984, s. 14 (1) (a). – Made: 12.08.2002. Coming into force: 17.08.2002. Effect: None. Territorial extent & classification: E. Local *Unpublished*

The M25 Motorway (Junctions 17 - 22) (Temporary Restriction and Prohibition of Traffic) Order 2002 No. 2002/219. – Enabling power: Road Traffic Regulation Act 1984, s. 14 (1) (a) (7). – Made: 04.02.2002. Coming into force: 09.02.2002. Effect: None. Territorial extent & classification: E. Local *Unpublished*

The M25 Motorway (Junctions 20 - 23) (Temporary Restriction and Prohibition of Traffic) Order 2002 No. 2002/2080. – Enabling power: Road Traffic Regulation Act 1984, s. 14 (1) (a) (7). – Made: 05.08.2002. Coming into force: 10.08.2002. Effect: None. Territorial extent & classification: E. Local *Unpublished*

The M25 Motorway (Junctions 22 and 23, Slip Roads) (Temporary Prohibition of Traffic) Order 2002 No. 2002/1569. – Enabling power: Road Traffic Regulation Act 1984, s. 14 (1) (a). – Made: 10.06.2002. Coming into force: 15.06.2002. Effect: None. Territorial extent & classification: E. Local *Unpublished*

The M25 Motorway (Junctions 30 - 31, Southbound) (Temporary Prohibition of Traffic) Order 2002 No. 2002/1941. – Enabling power: Road Traffic Regulation Act 1984, s. 14 (1) (a) (7). – Made: 22.07.2002. Coming into force: 27.07.2002. Effect: None. Territorial extent & classification: E. Local *Unpublished*

The M25 Motorway (South of Junction 29) (Temporary Restriction and Prohibition of Traffic) Order 2002 No. 2002/2448. – Enabling power: Road Traffic Regulation Act 1984, s. 14 (1) (a). – Made: 23.09.2002. Coming into force: 28.09.2002. Effect: None. Territorial extent & classification: E. Local *Unpublished*

The M26 Motorway (Eastbound Carriageway) (Temporary Prohibition of Traffic) Order 2002 No. 2002/3069. – Enabling power: Road Traffic Regulation Act 1984, s. 14 (1) (a). – Made: 09.12.2002. Coming into force: 14.12.2002. Effect: None. Territorial extent & classification: E. Local *Unpublished*

The M27 Motorway (Junction 5, Slip Road) (Temporary Prohibition of Traffic) Order 2002 No. 2002/2969. – Enabling power: Road Traffic Regulation Act 1984, s. 14 (1) (a). – Made: 02.12.2002. Coming into force: 07.12.2002. Effect: None. Territorial extent & classification: E. Local *Unpublished*

The M27 Motorway (Junction 11, Slip Road) (Temporary Prohibition of Traffic) Order 2002 No. 2002/2567. – Enabling power: Road Traffic Regulation Act 1984, s. 14 (1) (a). – Made: 07.10.2002. Coming into force: 12.10.2002. Effect: None. Territorial extent & classification: E. Local *Unpublished*

The M27 Motorway (Junction 12, Eastbound Slip Road) (Temporary Prohibition of Traffic) Order 2002 No. 2002/2911. – Enabling power: Road Traffic Regulation Act 1984, s. 14 (1) (a). – Made: 25.11.2002. Coming into force: 30.11.2002. Effect: None. Territorial extent & classification: E. Local *Unpublished*

The M27 Motorway (Junctions 5 - 10, Slip Roads) (Temporary Prohibition of Traffic) Order 2002 No. 2002/2794. – Enabling power: Road Traffic Regulation Act 1984, s. 14 (1) (a). – Made: 11.11.2002. Coming into force: 16.11.2002. Effect: None. Territorial extent & classification: E. Local *Unpublished*

The M32 Motorway (Junction 2) (Temporary Prohibition and Restriction of Traffic) Order 2002 No. 2002/1906. – Enabling power: Road Traffic Regulation Act 1984, s. 14 (1) (a). – Made: 11.07.2002. Coming into force: 12.07.2002. Effect: None. Territorial extent & classification: E. Local *Unpublished*

The M32 Motorway (Junction 2) (Temporary Prohibition of Traffic) Order 2002 No. 2002/1750. – Enabling power: Road Traffic Regulation Act 1984, s. 14 (1) (a). – Made: 01.07.2002. Coming into force: 03.07.2002. Effect: None. Territorial extent & classification: E. Local *Unpublished*

The M40 Motorway (Eastbound Junctions 16-15) (Temporary Restriction and Prohibition of Traffic) Order 2002 No. 2002/2946. – Enabling power: Road Traffic Regulation Act 1984, s. 14 (1) (a) (7). – Made: 22.11.2002. Coming into force: 29.11.2002. Effect: None. Territorial extent & classification: E. Local *Unpublished*

The M40 Motorway (Junction 3, Buckinghamshire - Junction 10, Oxfordshire) (Temporary 50 Miles Per Hour Speed Restriction) Order 2002 No. 2002/2434. – Enabling power: Road Traffic Regulation Act 1984, s. 14 (1) (a). – Made: 20.09.2002. Coming into force: 27.09.2002. Effect: None. Territorial extent & classification: E. Local *Unpublished*

The M40 Motorway (Junction 5, Stokenchurch, Buckinghamshire) (Temporary Restriction of Traffic) Order 2002 No. 2002/2651. – Enabling power: Road Traffic Regulation Act 1984, s. 14 (1) (a) (7). – Made: 18.10.2002. Coming into force: 25.10.2002. Effect: None. Territorial extent & classification: E. Local *Unpublished*

The M40 Motorway (Junction 8a) Northbound Exit Slip Road (Temporary Restriction and Prohibition of Traffic) Order 2002 No. 2002/926. – Enabling power: Road Traffic Regulation Act 1984, s. 14 (1) (a). – Made: 25.03.2002. Coming into force: 02.04.2002. Effect: None. Territorial extent & classification: E. Local *Unpublished*

The M40 Motorway (Junction 8, Oxford Spur) Northbound Exit Slip Road (Temporary Prohibition of Traffic) Order 2002 No. 2002/2495. – Enabling power: Road Traffic Regulation Act 1984, s. 14 (1) (a). – Made: 27.09.2002. Coming into force: 04.10.2002. Effect: None. Territorial extent & classification: E. Local *Unpublished*

The M40 Motorway (Junction 9) (Temporary Restriction and Prohibition of Traffic) Order 2002 No. 2002/2695. – Enabling power: Road Traffic Regulation Act 1984, s. 14 (1) (a). – Made: 28.10.2002. Coming into force: 02.11.2002. Effect: None. Territorial extent & classification: E. Local *Unpublished*

The M40 Motorway (Junction 10, Ardley Interchange, Oxfordshire) (Temporary Prohibition of Traffic) Order 2002 No. 2002/686. – Enabling power: Road Traffic Regulation Act 1984, s. 14 (1) (a). – Made: 11.03.2002. Coming into force: 18.03.2002. Effect: None. Territorial extent & classification: E. Local *Unpublished*

The M40 Motorway (Junction 10) Southbound Exit Slip Road (Temporary Prohibition of Traffic) Order 2002 No. 2002/2031. – Enabling power: Road Traffic Regulation Act 1984, s. 14 (1) (a). – Made: 29.07.2002. Coming into force: 05.08.2002. Effect: None. Territorial extent & classification: E. Local *Unpublished*

The M40 Motorway (Junctions 1 to 2), the M25 Motorway (Junction 16) and the A40 Trunk Road (Buckinghamshire) (Temporary Restriction and Prohibition of Traffic) Order 2002 No. 2002/924. – Enabling power: Road Traffic Regulation Act 1984, s. 14 (1) (a) (7). – Made: 28.03.2002. Coming into force: 04.04.2002. Effect: None. Territorial extent & classification: E. Local *Unpublished*

The M40 Motorway (Junctions 4-5) Buckinghamshire (Temporary Restriction and Prohibition of Traffic) Order 2002 No. 2002/1468. – Enabling power: Road Traffic Regulation Act 1984, s. 14 (1) (a) (7). – Made: 27.05.2002. Coming into force: 03.06.2002. Effect: None. Territorial extent & classification: E. Local *Unpublished*

The M40 Motorway (Junctions 5 - 8, Buckinghamshire - Oxfordshire) (Temporary Restriction and Prohibition of Traffic) Order 2002 No. 2002/2335. – Enabling power: Road Traffic Regulation Act 1984, s. 14 (1) (a) (7). – Made: 06.09.2002. Coming into force: 13.09.2002. Effect: None. Territorial extent & classification: E. Local *Unpublished*

The M40 Motorway (Junctions 8 - 15) (Temporary Restriction and Prohibition of Traffic) Order 2002 No. 2002/2010. – Enabling power: Road Traffic Regulation Act 1984, s. 14 (1) (a) (7). – Made: 26.07.2002. Coming into force: 02.08.2002. Effect: None. Territorial extent & classification: E. Local *Unpublished*

The M40 Motorway (Junctions 12 - 13, Warwickshire) Northbound Exit Slip Roads(Temporary Restriction of Traffic) Order 2002 No. 2002/2544. – Enabling power: Road Traffic Regulation Act 1984, s. 14 (1) (a) (7). – Made: 04.10.2002. Coming into force: 11.10.2002. Effect: None. Territorial extent & classification: E. Local *Unpublished*

The M40 Motorway (Junctions 16 - 15) (Temporary Prohibition of Traffic) Order 2002 No. 2002/1528. – Enabling power: Road Traffic Regulation Act 1984, s. 14 (1) (a) (7). – Made: 31.05.2002. Coming into force: 07.06.2002. Effect: None. Territorial extent & classification: E. Local *Unpublished*

The M40 Motorway (Junction 10) Northbound Entry Slip Road (Temporary Prohibition of Traffic) Order 2002 No. 2002/2810. – Enabling power: Road Traffic Regulation Act 1984, s. 14 (1) (a). – Made: 08.11.2002. Coming into force: 15.11.2002. Effect: None. Territorial extent & classification: E. Local *Unpublished*

The M42 and M5 Motorways (M42 Southbound Link Road to M5 at Junction 4A) (Temporary Prohibition of Traffic) Order 2002 No. 2002/1271. – Enabling power: Road Traffic Regulation Act 1984, s. 14 (1) (a). – Made: 03.05.2002. Coming into force: 10.05.2002. Effect: None. Territorial extent & classification: E. Local *Unpublished*

The M42 Motorway (Junction 3A) (Temporary Prohibition of Traffic) Order 2002 No. 2002/1270. – Enabling power: Road Traffic Regulation Act 1984, s. 14 (1) (a). – Made: 03.05.2002. Coming into force: 10.05.2002. Effect: None. Territorial extent & classification: E. Local *Unpublished*

The M42 Motorway (Junction 4, Monkspath, Solihull) (Temporary Prohibition of Traffic) Order 2002 No. 2002/1268. – Enabling power: Road Traffic Regulation Act 1984, s. 14 (1) (a) (7). – Made: 03.05.2002. Coming into force: 10.05.2002. Effect: None. Territorial extent & classification: E. Local *Unpublished*

The M42 Motorway (Junction 4) (Slip Roads) (Temporary 50 Miles Per Hour Speed Restriction) Order 2002 No. 2002/3248. – Enabling power: Road Traffic Regulation Act 1984, s. 14 (1) (a). – Made: 27.12.2002. Coming into force: 03.01.2003. Effect: None. Territorial extent & classification: E. Local *Unpublished*

The M42 Motorway (Junction 4) (Temporary Restriction and Prohibition of Traffic) Order 2002 No. 2002/2076. – Enabling power: Road Traffic Regulation Act 1984, s. 14 (1) (a) (7). – Made: 02.08.2002. Coming into force: 09.08.2002. Effect: None. Territorial extent & classification: E. Local *Unpublished*

The M42 Motorway (Junctions 5 - 6) (Temporary Prohibition of Traffic) Order 2002 No. 2002/1573. – Enabling power: Road Traffic Regulation Act 1984, s. 14 (1) (a) (7). – Made: 10.06.2002. Coming into force: 17.06.2002. Effect: None. Territorial extent & classification: E. Local *Unpublished*

The M42 Motorway (Junctions 7A - 9) (Temporary Prohibition and Restriction of Traffic) (No. 2) Order 2002 No. 2002/2671. – Enabling power: Road Traffic Regulation Act 1984, s. 14 (1) (a) (7), sch. 9, para. 27 (1). – Made: 11.10.2002. Coming into force: 18.10.2002. Effect: S.I. 2002/937 revoked. Territorial extent & classification: E. Local *Unpublished*

The M42 Motorway (Junctions 7A - 9) (Temporary Prohibition and Restriction of Traffic) Order 2002 No. 2002/937. – Enabling power: Road Traffic Regulation Act 1984, s. 14 (1) (a) (7), sch. 9, para. 27 (1). – Made: 28.03.2002. Coming into force: 04.04.2002. Effect: S.I. 2001/1374 revoked. Territorial extent & classification: E. Local – Revoked by S.I. 2002/2671 (unpublished) *Unpublished*

The M42 Motorway (Junctions 10 - 11) (Temporary Prohibition and Restriction of Traffic) Order 2002 No. 2002/388. – Enabling power: Road Traffic Regulation Act 1984, s. 14 (1) (a) (7). – Made: 15.02.2002. Coming into force: 22.02.2002. Effect: None. Territorial extent & classification: E. Local *Unpublished*

The M45 Motorway (Dunchurch, Warwickshire) (Temporary Restriction and Prohibition of Traffic) Order 2002 No. 2002/1522. – Enabling power: Road Traffic Regulation Act 1984, s. 14 (1) (a) (7). – Made: 28.05.2002. Coming into force: 04.06.2002. Effect: None. Territorial extent & classification: E. Local *Unpublished*

The M48 Motorway (Junction 2) (Temporary Prohibition of Traffic) Order 2002 No. 2002/2336. – Enabling power: Road Traffic Regulation Act 1984, s. 14 (1) (a) (7). – Made: 09.09.2002. Coming into force: 12.09.2002. Effect: None. Territorial extent & classification: E. Local *Unpublished*

The M50 Motorway (Junctions 1 - 2) (Temporary Prohibition of Traffic) Order 2002 No. 2002/518. – Enabling power: Road Traffic Regulation Act 1984, s. 14 (1) (a). – Made: 02.03.2002. Coming into force: 09.03.2002. Effect: None. Territorial extent & classification: E. Local *Unpublished*

The M50 Motorway (Junctions 2 - 4) (Temporary Prohibition of Traffic) Order 2002 No. 2002/961. – Enabling power: Road Traffic Regulation Act 1984, s. 14 (1) (a). – Made: 02.04.2002. Coming into force: 08.04.2002. Effect: None. Territorial extent & classification: E. Local *Unpublished*

The M53 Motorway (Junction 2 to 1) (Temporary Restriction and Prohibition of Traffic) Order 2002 No. 2002/2756. – Enabling power: Road Traffic Regulation Act 1984, s. 14 (1) (a) (7). – Made: 01.11.2002. Coming into force: 03.11.2002. Effect: None. Territorial extent & classification: E. Local *Unpublished*

The M53 Motorway (Junction 5) and the A41 Trunk Road (Temporary 30 Miles Per Hour Speed Restriction) Order 2002 No. 2002/23. – Enabling power: Road Traffic Regulation Act 1984, s. 14 (1) (a). – Made: 03.01.2002. Coming into force: 06.01.2002. Effect: None. Territorial extent & classification: E. Local *Unpublished*

The M53 Motorway (Junction 9) (Temporary Prohibition of Traffic) Order 2002 No. 2002/1666. – Enabling power: Road Traffic Regulation Act 1984, s. 14 (1) (a). – Made: 20.06.2002. Coming into force: 23.06.2002. Effect: None. Territorial extent & classification: E. Local *Unpublished*

The M53 Motorway (Junction 12, Hoole Interchange) (Temporary Restriction and Prohibition of Traffic) Order 2002 No. 2002/2702. – Enabling power: Road Traffic Regulation Act 1984, s. 14 (1) (a) (7). – Made: 24.10.2002. Coming into force: 31.10.2002. Effect: None. Territorial extent & classification: E. Local *Unpublished*

The M53 Motorway (Junctions 2 to 3) (Temporary Restriction and Prohibition of Traffic) Order 2002 No. 2002/19. – Enabling power: Road Traffic Regulation Act 1984, s. 14 (1) (a). – Made: 03.01.2002. Coming into force: 05.01.2002. Effect: None. Territorial extent & classification: E. Local *Unpublished*

The M53 Motorway (Junctions 11 to 12) (Temporary Prohibition of Traffic) Order 2002 No. 2002/349. – Enabling power: Road Traffic Regulation Act 1984, s. 14 (1) (a). – Made: 14.02.2002. Coming into force: 17.02.2002. Effect: None. Territorial extent & classification: E. Local *Unpublished*

The M54 Motorway (Junction 2 to M6 Junction 10A) (Temporary Prohibition and Restriction of Traffic) Order 2002 No. 2002/1164. – Enabling power: Road Traffic Regulation Act 1984, s. 14 (1) (a). – Made: 19.04.2002. Coming into force: 26.04.2002. Effect: None. Territorial extent & classification: E. Local *Unpublished*

The M54 Motorway (Junction 3) - M6 Motorway (Junction 10A) (Temporary Prohibition of Traffic) Order 2002 No. 2002/2182. – Enabling power: Road Traffic Regulation Act 1984, s. 14 (1) (a). – Made: 30.08.2002. Coming into force: 06.09.2002. Effect: None. Territorial extent & classification: E. Local *Unpublished*

The M56, M60 and M67 Motorways and the A5103 Trunk Road (Temporary Prohibition of Traffic) Order 2002 No. 2002/1550. – Enabling power: Road Traffic Regulation Act 1984, s. 14 (1) (a). – Made: 30.05.2002. Coming into force: 04.06.2002. Effect: None. Territorial extent & classification: E. Local *Unpublished*

The M56, M60, M61, M62 and M602 Motorways (Loop Cutting) (Temporary Restriction and Prohibition of Traffic) Order 2002 No. 2002/360. – Enabling power: Road Traffic Regulation Act 1984, s. 14 (1) (a) (7). – Made: 15.02.2002. Coming into force: 17.02.2002. Effect: None. Territorial extent & classification: E. Local *Unpublished*

The M56 Motorway and the A550 and A5117 Trunk Roads (Temporary Restriction and Prohibition of Traffic) Order 2002 No. 2002/2795. – Enabling power: Road Traffic Regulation Act 1984, s. 14 (1) (a). – Made: 06.11.2002. Coming into force: 15.11.2002. Effect: None. Territorial extent & classification: E. Local *Unpublished*

The M56 Motorway (Junction 7, Eastbound Entry Slip Road) (Temporary Prohibition of Traffic) Order 2002 No. 2002/1428. – Enabling power: Road Traffic Regulation Act 1984, s. 14 (1) (a). – Made: 21.05.2002. Coming into force: 23.05.2002. Effect: None. Territorial extent & classification: E. Local *Unpublished*

The M56 Motorway (Junction 10, Slip Roads) (Temporary Prohibition of Traffic) Order 2002 No. 2002/2249. – Enabling power: Road Traffic Regulation Act 1984, s. 14 (1) (a). – Made: 28.08.2002. Coming into force: 30.08.2002. Effect: None. Territorial extent & classification: E. Local *Unpublished*

The M56 Motorway (Junction 12, Westbound Exit Slip Road) (Temporary Prohibition of Traffic) Order 2002 No. 2002/2909. – Enabling power: Road Traffic Regulation Act 1984, s. 14 (1) (a). – Made: 20.11.2002. Coming into force: 28.11.2002. Effect: None. Territorial extent & classification: E. Local *Unpublished*

The M56 Motorway (Junction 14) (Temporary Restriction and Prohibition of Traffic) Order 2002 No. 2002/1568. – Enabling power: Road Traffic Regulation Act 1984, s. 14 (1) (a) (7). – Made: 06.06.2002. Coming into force: 09.06.2002. Effect: None. Territorial extent & classification: E. Local *Unpublished*

The M56 Motorway (Junctions 6 to 4) and the M60 Motorway (Junction 6) (Temporary Restriction and Prohibition of Traffic) Order 2002 No. 2002/966. – Enabling power: Road Traffic Regulation Act 1984, s. 14 (1) (a) (7). – Made: 27.03.2002. Coming into force: 04.04.2002. Effect: None. Territorial extent & classification: E. Local *Unpublished*

The M56 Motorway (Junctions 6 to 7) (Temporary Restriction of Traffic) Order 2002 No. 2002/1583. – Enabling power: Road Traffic Regulation Act 1984, s. 14 (1) (a) (7). – Made: 11.06.2002. Coming into force: 13.06.2002. Effect: None. Territorial extent & classification: E. Local *Unpublished*

The M56 Motorway (Junctions 7 to 9) (Temporary Restriction of Traffic) Order 2002 No. 2002/1516. – Enabling power: Road Traffic Regulation Act 1984, s. 14 (1) (a) (7). – Made: 29.05.2002. Coming into force: 04.06.2002. Effect: None. Territorial extent & classification: E. Local *Unpublished*

The M57 Motorway and the 580 Trunk Road (Temporary Prohibition of Traffic) Order 2002 No. 2002/2609. – Enabling power: Road Traffic Regulation Act 1984, s. 14 (1) (a). – Made: 10.10.2002. Coming into force: 12.10.2002. Effect: None. Territorial extent & classification: E. Local *Unpublished*

The M57 Motorway (Junctions 1 to 7) (Temporary Restriction and Prohibition of Traffic) Order 2002 No. 2002/2067. – Enabling power: Road Traffic Regulation Act 1984, s. 14 (1) (a) (7). – Made: 31.07.2002. Coming into force: 04.08.2002. Effect: None. Territorial extent & classification: E. Local *Unpublished*

The M57 Motorway (Junctions 3 to 4) (Temporary Restriction of Traffic) Order 2002 No. 2002/352. – Enabling power: Road Traffic Regulation Act 1984, s. 14 (1) (a) (7). – Made: 13.02.2002. Coming into force: 17.02.2002. Effect: None. Territorial extent & classification: E. Local *Unpublished*

The M58 Motorway (Junction 5, Eastbound Exit Slip Road) (Temporary Prohibition of Traffic) Order 2002 No. 2002/1141. – Enabling power: Road Traffic Regulation Act 1984, s. 14 (1) (a). – Made: 19.04.2002. Coming into force: 23.04.2002. Effect: None. Territorial extent & classification: E. Local *Unpublished*

The M60 and M61 Motorways and the A580 Trunk Road (Moss Farm Footbridge and Riders Farm Bridge) (Temporary Restriction and Prohibition of Traffic) Order 2002 No. 2002/965. – Enabling power: Road Traffic Regulation Act 1984, s. 14 (1) (a) (7). – Made: 28.03.2002. Coming into force: 01.04.2002. Effect: None. Territorial extent & classification: E. Local *Unpublished*

The M60, M62, M66 and A627 (M) Motorways (Maintenance) (Temporary Restriction and Prohibition of Traffic) Order 2002 No. 2002/2205. – Enabling power: Road Traffic Regulation Act 1984, s. 14 (1) (a) (7). – Made: 20.08.2002. Coming into force: 22.08.2002. Effect: None. Territorial extent & classification: E. Local *Unpublished*

The M60, M62, M66 and A627(M) Motorways (Maintenance) (Temporary Restriction and Prohibition of Traffic) Order 2002 Variation Order 2002 No. 2002/2806. – Enabling power: Road Traffic Regulation Act 1984, s. 14 (1) (a). – Made: 08.11.2002. Coming into force: 10.11.2002. Effect: S.I. 2002/2205 amended. Territorial extent & classification: E. Local *Unpublished*

The M60 Motorway (Junction 1, Clockwise Exit Slip Road) (Temporary Prohibition of Traffic) Order 2002 No. 2002/2680. – Enabling power: Road Traffic Regulation Act 1984, s. 14 (1) (a). – Made: 22.10.2002. Coming into force: 24.10.2002. Effect: None. Territorial extent & classification: E. Local *Unpublished*

The M60 Motorway (Junction 1, Slip Roads) (Temporary Restriction and Prohibition of Traffic) Order 2002 No. 2002/2195. – Enabling power: Road Traffic Regulation Act 1984, s. 14 (1) (a). – Made: 14.08.2002. Coming into force: 18.08.2002. Effect: None. Territorial extent & classification: E. Local *Unpublished*

The M60 Motorway (Junction 1, Slip Roads) (Temporary Restriction and Prohibition of Traffic) Order 2002 Amendment Order 2002 No. 2002/2502. – Enabling power: Road Traffic Regulation Act 1984, s. 14 (1) (a). – Made: 26.09.2002. Coming into force: 28.09.2002. Effect: S.I. 2002/2195 amended. Territorial extent & classification: E. Local *Unpublished*

The M60 Motorway (Junction 3) (Temporary Prohibition of Traffic) Order 2002 No. 2002/2577. – Enabling power: Road Traffic Regulation Act 1984, s. 14 (1) (a). – Made: 09.10.2002. Coming into force: 11.10.2002. Effect: None. Territorial extent & classification: E. Local *Unpublished*

The M60 Motorway (Junction 4) (Temporary Prohibition of Traffic) Order 2002 No. 2002/2160. – Enabling power: Road Traffic Regulation Act 1984, s. 14 (1) (a). – Made: 14.08.2002. Coming into force: 16.08.2002. Effect: None. Territorial extent & classification: E. Local *Unpublished*

The M60 Motorway (Junction 5) (Temporary Prohibition of Traffic) (No. 2) Order 2002 No. 2002/2755. – Enabling power: Road Traffic Regulation Act 1984, s. 14 (1) (a). – Made: 05.11.2002. Coming into force: 07.11.2002. Effect: None. Territorial extent & classification: E. Local *Unpublished*

The M60 Motorway (Junction 5) (Temporary Prohibition of Traffic) Order 2002 No. 2002/321. – Enabling power: Road Traffic Regulation Act 1984, s. 14 (1) (a). – Made: 11.02.2002. Coming into force: 14.02.2002. Effect: None. Territorial extent & classification: E. Local *Unpublished*

The M60 Motorway (Junction 10, Anticlockwise Exit Slip Road) (Temporary Prohibition of Traffic) Order 2002 No. 2002/2947. – Enabling power: Road Traffic Regulation Act 1984, s. 14 (1) (a). – Made: 26.11.2002. Coming into force: 28.11.2002. Effect: None. Territorial extent & classification: E. Local *Unpublished*

The M60 Motorway (Junction 12, Clockwise Exit Link Road) (Temporary Prohibition of Traffic) Order 2002 No. 2002/2807. – Enabling power: Road Traffic Regulation Act 1984, s. 14 (1) (a). – Made: 12.11.2002. Coming into force: 14.11.2002. Effect: None. Territorial extent & classification: E. Local *Unpublished*

The M60 Motorway (Junction 13, Clockwise Entry Slip Road) (Temporary Prohibition of Traffic) Order 2002 No. 2002/1086. – Enabling power: Road Traffic Regulation Act 1984, s. 14 (1) (a). – Made: 08.04.2002. Coming into force: 10.04.2002. Effect: None. Territorial extent & classification: E. Local *Unpublished*

The M60 Motorway (Junction 15, Anticlockwise Exit Slip Road) (Temporary Prohibition of Traffic) Order 2002 No. 2002/1300. – Enabling power: Road Traffic Regulation Act 1984, s. 14 (1) (a). – Made: 07.05.2002. Coming into force: 10.05.2002. Effect: None. Territorial extent & classification: E. Local *Unpublished*

The M60 Motorway (Junction 15) (Temporary Prohibition of Traffic) (No. 2) Order 2002 No. 2002/2659. – Enabling power: Road Traffic Regulation Act 1984, s. 14 (1) (a). – Made: 21.10.2002. Coming into force: 23.10.2002. Effect: None. Territorial extent & classification: E. Local *Unpublished*

The M60 Motorway (Junction 15) (Temporary Restriction and Prohibition of Traffic) Order 2002 No. 2002/164. – Enabling power: Road Traffic Regulation Act 1984, s. 14 (1) (a) (7). – Made: 21.01.2002. Coming into force: 24.01.2002. Effect: None. Territorial extent & classification: E. Local *Unpublished*

The M60 Motorway (Junction 23, Anticlockwise Entry Slip Road) (Temporary Prohibition of Traffic) Order 2002 No. 2002/2921. – Enabling power: Road Traffic Regulation Act 1984, s. 14 (1) (a). – Made: 22.11.2002. Coming into force: 24.11.2002. Effect: None. Territorial extent & classification: E. Local *Unpublished*

The M60 Motorway (Junction 24, Anti-Clockwise Exit Slip Road) (Temporary Prohibition of Traffic) Order 2002 No. 2002/1389. – Enabling power: Road Traffic Regulation Act 1984, s. 14 (1) (a). – Made: 14.05.2002. Coming into force: 16.05.2002. Effect: None. Territorial extent & classification: E. Local *Unpublished*

The M60 Motorway (Junctions 1 to 2) (Temporary Restriction of Traffic) Order 2002 No. 2002/693. – Enabling power: Road Traffic Regulation Act 1984, s. 14 (1) (a) (7). – Made: 11.03.2002. Coming into force: 14.03.2002. Effect: None. Territorial extent & classification: E. Local *Unpublished*

The M60 Motorway (Junctions 1 to 2) (Temporary Restriction of Traffic) Order 2002 No. 2002/976. – Enabling power: Road Traffic Regulation Act 1984, s. 14 (1) (a) (7). – Made: 11.03.2002. Coming into force: 14.03.2002. Effect: None. Territorial extent & classification: E. Local *Unpublished*

The M60 Motorway (Junctions 8 and 7) (Temporary Prohibition of Traffic) (No. 2) Order 2002 No. 2002/32. – Enabling power: Road Traffic Regulation Act 1984, s. 14 (1) (a). – Made: 09.01.2002. Coming into force: 13.01.2002. Effect: None. Territorial extent & classification: E. Local *Unpublished*

The M60 Motorway (Junctions 8 and 7) (Temporary Prohibition of Traffic) Order 2002 No. 2002/181. – Enabling power: Road Traffic Regulation Act 1984, s. 14 (1) (a). – Made: 30.01.2002. Coming into force: 01.02.2002. Effect: None. Territorial extent & classification: E. Local *Unpublished*

The M60 Motorway (Junctions 10 to 8) (Temporary Restriction and Prohibition of Traffic) Order 2002 No. 2002/1304. – Enabling power: Road Traffic Regulation Act 1984, s. 14 (1) (a) (7). – Made: 07.05.2002. Coming into force: 09.05.2002. Effect: None. Territorial extent & classification: E. Local *Unpublished*

The M61 Motorway (Junction 1, Wardley Loop Bridge) (Temporary Prohibition of Traffic) Order 2002 No. 2002/2159. – Enabling power: Road Traffic Regulation Act 1984, s. 14 (1) (a). – Made: 14.08.2002. Coming into force: 16.08.2002. Effect: None. Territorial extent & classification: E. Local *Unpublished*

The M61 Motorway (Junction 3) (Temporary Prohibition of Traffic) Order 2002 No. 2002/323. – Enabling power: Road Traffic Regulation Act 1984, s. 14 (1) (a). – Made: 12.02.2002. Coming into force: 14.02.2002. Effect: None. Territorial extent & classification: E. Local *Unpublished*

The M61 Motorway (Junction 9) (Temporary Restriction of Traffic) Order 2002 No. 2002/2547. – Enabling power: Road Traffic Regulation Act 1984, s. 14 (1) (a) (7). – Made: 07.10.2002. Coming into force: 09.10.2002. Effect: None. Territorial extent & classification: E. Local *Unpublished*

The M61 Motorway (Junctions 6 to 8, Roscoe Lowe Bridge) (Temporary 50 Miles Per Hour Speed Restriction) Order 2002 No. 2002/394. – Enabling power: Road Traffic Regulation Act 1984, s. 14 (1) (a). – Made: 21.02.2002. Coming into force: 24.02.2002. Effect: None. Territorial extent & classification: E. Local *Unpublished*

The M61 Motorway (Junctions 6 to 8, Roscoe Lowe Bridge) (Temporary Restriction and Prohibition of Traffic) (No. 2) Order 2002 No. 2002/2384. – Enabling power: Road Traffic Regulation Act 1984, s. 14 (1) (a). – Made: 12.09.2002. Coming into force: 15.09.2002. Effect: None. Territorial extent & classification: E. Local *Unpublished*

The M61 Motorway (Junctions 8 to 9) (Temporary Restriction and Prohibition of Traffic) Order 2002 No. 2002/351. – Enabling power: Road Traffic Regulation Act 1984, s. 14 (1) (a) (7). – Made: 13.02.2002. Coming into force: 17.02.2002. Effect: None. Territorial extent & classification: E. Local *Unpublished*

The M61 Motorway (Kearsley Spur) (Temporary Prohibition of Traffic) Order 2002 No. 2002/1108. – Enabling power: Road Traffic Regulation Act 1984, s. 14 (1) (a). – Made: 12.04.2002. Coming into force: 17.04.2002. Effect: None. Territorial extent & classification: E. Local *Unpublished*

The M61 Motorway (Kearsley Spur) (Temporary Prohibition of Traffic) Order 2002 No. 2002/2908. – Enabling power: Road Traffic Regulation Act 1984, s. 14 (1) (a). – Made: 20.11.2002. Coming into force: 22.11.2002. Effect: None. Territorial extent & classification: E. Local *Unpublished*

The M61 Motorway (Tramway Link Road) (Temporary Prohibition of Traffic) Order 2002 No. 2002/2111. – Enabling power: Road Traffic Regulation Act 1984, s. 14 (1) (a). – Made: 02.08.2002. Coming into force: 06.08.2002. Effect: None. Territorial extent & classification: E. Local *Unpublished*

The M61 Motorway (Wingates Bridge) (Temporary Restriction of Traffic) Order 2002 No. 2002/163. – Enabling power: Road Traffic Regulation Act 1984, s. 14 (1) (a). – Made: 16.01.2002. Coming into force: 20.01.2002. Effect: None. Territorial extent & classification: E. Local *Unpublished*

The M62 Motorway and the M621 Motorway (Gildersome) (Temporary Restriction and Prohibition of Traffic) Order 2002 No. 2002/1314. – Enabling power: Road Traffic Regulation Act 1984, s. 14 (1) (a) (7). – Made: 09.05.2002. Coming into force: 13.05.2002. Effect: None. Territorial extent & classification: E. Local *Unpublished*

The M62 Motorway (Junction 7, Entry Slip Road) (Temporary Prohibition of Traffic) Order 2002 No. 2002/749. – Enabling power: Road Traffic Regulation Act 1984, s. 14 (1) (a). – Made: 15.03.2002. Coming into force: 18.03.2002. Effect: None. Territorial extent & classification: E. Local *Unpublished*

The M62 Motorway (Junction 8 and Junction 9) (Temporary 40 Miles Per Hour Speed Restriction) Order 2002 No. 2002/2701. – Enabling power: Road Traffic Regulation Act 1984, s. 14 (1) (a). – Made: 25.10.2002. Coming into force: 27.10.2002. Effect: None. Territorial extent & classification: E. Local *Unpublished*

The M62 Motorway (Junction 8 to Junction 9) (Temporary Restriction and Prohibition of Traffic) Order 2002 No. 2002/1084. – Enabling power: Road Traffic Regulation Act 1984, s. 14 (1) (a) (7). – Made: 08.04.2002. Coming into force: 09.04.2002. Effect: None. Territorial extent & classification: E. Local *Unpublished*

The M62 Motorway (Junction 22) (Temporary Restriction of Traffic) Order 2002 No. 2002/1255. – Enabling power: Road Traffic Regulation Act 1984, s. 14 (1) (a) (7). – Made: 02.05.2002. Coming into force: 07.05.2002. Effect: None. Territorial extent & classification: E. Local *Unpublished*

The M62 Motorway (Junction 26 to Junction 27) (Temporary Restriction and Prohibition of Traffic) Order 2002 No. 2002/2411. – Enabling power: Road Traffic Regulation Act 1984, s. 14 (1) (a) (7). – Made: 18.09.2002. Coming into force: 19.09.2002. Effect: None. Territorial extent & classification: E. Local *Unpublished*

The M62 Motorway (Junction 29, Lofthouse) (Temporary Prohibition of Traffic) Order 2002 No. 2002/2965. – Enabling power: Road Traffic Regulation Act 1984, s. 14 (1) (a). – Made: 29.11.2002. Coming into force: 01.12.2002. Effect: None. Territorial extent & classification: E. Local *Unpublished*

The M62 Motorway (Junction 29 to Junction 30) (Temporary Restriction of Traffic) Order 2002 No. 2002/1028. – Enabling power: Road Traffic Regulation Act 1984, s. 14 (1) (a) (7). – Made: 04.04.2002. Coming into force: 07.04.2002. Effect: None. Territorial extent & classification: E. Local *Unpublished*

The M62 Motorway (Junction 33, Ferrybridge) (Temporary Prohibition of Traffic) Order 2002 No. 2002/2245. – Enabling power: Road Traffic Regulation Act 1984, s. 14 (1) (a). – Made: 28.08.2002. Coming into force: 01.09.2002. Effect: None. Territorial extent & classification: E. Local *Unpublished*

The M62 Motorway (Junction 35) and the M18 Motorway (Junction 7) (Temporary Prohibition of Traffic) Order 2002 No. 2002/1508. – Enabling power: Road Traffic Regulation Act 1984, s. 14 (1) (a). – Made: 29.05.2002. Coming into force: 04.06.2002. Effect: None. Territorial extent & classification: E. Local *Unpublished*

The M62 Motorway (Junction 38, North Cave) (Temporary Prohibition of Traffic) Order 2002 No. 2002/2082. – Enabling power: Road Traffic Regulation Act 1984, s. 14 (1) (a). – Made: 05.08.2002. Coming into force: 07.08.2002. Effect: None. Territorial extent & classification: E. Local *Unpublished*

The M62 Motorway (Junctions 11 to 12) (Temporary Restriction of Traffic) Order 2002 No. 2002/1049. – Enabling power: Road Traffic Regulation Act 1984, s. 14 (1) (a) (7). – Made: 02.04.2002. Coming into force: 04.04.2002. Effect: None. Territorial extent & classification: E. Local *Unpublished*

The M62 Motorway (Junctions 12 and 11) (Temporary Restriction of Traffic) Order 2002 No. 2002/2729. – Enabling power: Road Traffic Regulation Act 1984, s. 14 (1) (a) (7). – Made: 29.10.2002. Coming into force: 31.10.2002. Effect: None. Territorial extent & classification: E. Local *Unpublished*

The M62 Motorway (River Ouse Bridge) (Temporary Restriction and Prohibition of Traffic) Order 2002 No. 2002/1140. – Enabling power: Road Traffic Regulation Act 1984, s. 14 (1) (a) (7). – Made: 18.04.2002. Coming into force: 21.04.2002. Effect: None. Territorial extent & classification: E. Local *Unpublished*

The M65 Motorway (Junction 6, Eastbound Entry Slip Road) (Temporary Prohibition of Traffic) Order 2002 No. 2002/2110. – Enabling power: Road Traffic Regulation Act 1984, s. 14 (1) (a). – Made: 07.08.2002. Coming into force: 11.08.2002. Effect: None. Territorial extent & classification: E. Local *Unpublished*

The M65 Motorway (Junctions 1 to 9) (Temporary Prohibition of Traffic) Order 2002 No. 2002/2540. – Enabling power: Road Traffic Regulation Act 1984, s. 14 (1) (a). – Made: 03.10.2002. Coming into force: 06.10.2002. Effect: None. Territorial extent & classification: E. Local *Unpublished*

The M65 Motorway (Junctions 8 to 10) (Temporary Prohibition of Traffic) Order 2002 No. 2002/1259. – Enabling power: Road Traffic Regulation Act 1984, s. 14 (1) (a). – Made: 26.04.2002. Coming into force: 27.04.2002. Effect: None. Territorial extent & classification: E. Local *Unpublished*

The M66 Motorway (Junction 4) (Temporary Prohibition of Traffic) Order 2002 No. 2002/755. – Enabling power: Road Traffic Regulation Act 1984, s. 14 (1) (a). – Made: 15.03.2002. Coming into force: 19.03.2002. Effect: None. Territorial extent & classification: E. Local *Unpublished*

The M67 Motorway (Eastbound Carriageway) (Temporary Prohibition of Traffic) Order 2002 No. 2002/1301. – Enabling power: Road Traffic Regulation Act 1984, s. 14 (1) (a). – Made: 07.05.2002. Coming into force: 09.05.2002. Effect: None. Territorial extent & classification: E. Local *Unpublished*

The M67 Motorway (Junction 1) (Temporary Restriction and Prohibition of Traffic) Order 2002 No. 2002/2948. – Enabling power: Road Traffic Regulation Act 1984, s. 14 (1) (a). – Made: 26.11.2002. Coming into force: 28.11.2002. Effect: None. Territorial extent & classification: E. Local *Unpublished*

The M67 Motorway (Junction 2 to Denton Roundabout) (Temporary Prohibition of Traffic) (No. 2) Order 2002 No. 2002/1302. – Enabling power: Road Traffic Regulation Act 1984, s. 14 (1) (a). – Made: 07.05.2002. Coming into force: 09.05.2002. Effect: None. Territorial extent & classification: E. Local *Unpublished*

The M67 Motorway (Junction 2 to Denton Roundabout) (Temporary Prohibition of Traffic) Order 2002 No. 2002/1109. – Enabling power: Road Traffic Regulation Act 1984, s. 14 (1) (a). – Made: 12.04.2002. Coming into force: 16.04.2002. Effect: None. Territorial extent & classification: E. Local *Unpublished*

The M67 Motorway (Junctions 3 to 4, Westbound Carriageway) (Temporary Restriction of Traffic) Order 2002 No. 2002/2881. – Enabling power: Road Traffic Regulation Act 1984, s. 14 (1) (a)(7). – Made: 19.11.2002. Coming into force: 21.11.2002. Effect: None. Territorial extent & classification: E. Local *Unpublished*

The M69 Motorway (M6 - Junction 1) (Temporary Prohibition and Restriction of Traffic) Order 2002 No. 2002/2831. – Enabling power: Road Traffic Regulation Act 1984, s. 14 (1) (a) (7). – Made: 11.11.2002. Coming into force: 18.11.2002. Effect: None. Territorial extent & classification: E. Local *Unpublished*

The M69 Motorway (Southbound Exit Slip Road to M6 Motorway, Junction 2) (Temporary Prohibition of Traffic) Order 2002 No. 2002/659. – Enabling power: Road Traffic Regulation Act 1984, s. 14 (1) (a). – Made: 11.03.2002. Coming into force: 18.03.2002. Effect: None. Territorial extent & classification: E. Local *Unpublished*

The M69 Motorway (South Leicester Railway Bridge) (Temporary Prohibition of Traffic) Order 2002 No. 2002/3259. – Enabling power: Road Traffic Regulation Act 1984, s. 14 (1) (b). – Made: 20.12.2002. Coming into force: 27.12.2002. Effect: None. Territorial extent & classification: E. Local *Unpublished*

The M180 Motorway (Junction 2 to Junction 3) (Temporary Restriction of Traffic) Order 2002 No. 2002/2553. – Enabling power: Road Traffic Regulation Act 1984, s. 14 (1) (a) (7). – Made: 04.10.2002. Coming into force: 04.10.2002. Effect: None. Territorial extent & classification: E. Local *Unpublished*

The M180 Motorway (Junction 3, Midmoor Interchange) (Temporary Prohibition of Traffic) Order 2002 No. 2002/1684. – Enabling power: Road Traffic Regulation Act 1984, s. 14 (1) (a). – Made: 25.06.2002. Coming into force: 27.06.2002. Effect: None. Territorial extent & classification: E. Local *Unpublished*

The M180 Motorway (Junction 4, Ermine Street) (Temporary Prohibition of Traffic) Order 2002 No. 2002/736. – Enabling power: Road Traffic Regulation Act 1984, s. 14 (1) (a). – Made: 14.03.2002. Coming into force: 16.03.2002. Effect: None. Territorial extent & classification: E. Local *Unpublished*

The M180 Motorway (Junction 4, Ermine Street) (Temporary Prohibition of Traffic) Order (No. 2) 2002 No. 2002/1192. – Enabling power: Road Traffic Regulation Act 1984, s. 14 (1) (a). – Made: 24.04.2002. Coming into force: 27.04.2002. Effect: None. Territorial extent & classification: E. Local *Unpublished*

The M180 Motorway (Junction 4 to Junction 5) (Temporary Restriction and Prohibition of Traffic) Order 2002 No. 2002/2943. – Enabling power: Road Traffic Regulation Act 1984, s. 14 (1) (a) (7). – Made: 22.11.2002. Coming into force: 24.11.2002. Effect: None. Territorial extent & classification: E. Local *Unpublished*

The M180 Motorway (Junction 4 to Junction 5) (Temporary Restriction of Traffic) Order 2002 No. 2002/2578. – Enabling power: Road Traffic Regulation Act 1984, s. 14 (1) (a) (7). – Made: 10.10.2002. Coming into force: 13.10.2002. Effect: None. Territorial extent & classification: E. Local *Unpublished*

The M180 Motorway (Junction 5, Barnetby Interchange) (Temporary Restriction and Prohibition of Traffic) Order 2002 No. 2002/1953. – Enabling power: Road Traffic Regulation Act 1984, s. 14 (1) (a) (7). – Made: 17.07.2002. Coming into force: 21.07.2002. Effect: None. Territorial extent & classification: E. Local *Unpublished*

The M271 Motorway (Redbridge Roundabout - M27 Junction 3) (Temporary Restriction of Traffic) Order 2002 No. 2002/2915. – Enabling power: Road Traffic Regulation Act 1984, s. 14 (1) (a). – Made: 25.11.2002. Coming into force: 30.11.2002. Effect: None. Territorial extent & classification: E. Local *Unpublished*

The M602 and M60 Motorways (Link Road) (Temporary 50 Miles Per Hour Speed Restriction) Order 2002 No. 2002/320. – Enabling power: Road Traffic Regulation Act 1984, s. 14 (1) (b). – Made: 07.02.2002. Coming into force: 09.02.2002. Effect: None. Territorial extent & classification: E. Local *Unpublished*

The M602 Motorway (Junctions 2 to 3) (Temporary Prohibition of Traffic) (No. 2) Order 2002 No. 2002/1429. – Enabling power: Road Traffic Regulation Act 1984, s. 14 (1) (a). – Made: 21.05.2002. Coming into force: 23.05.2002. Effect: None. Territorial extent & classification: E. Local *Unpublished*

The M602 Motorway (Junctions 2 to 3) (Temporary Prohibition of Traffic) Order 2002 No. 2002/513. – Enabling power: Road Traffic Regulation Act 1984, s. 14 (1) (a). – Made: 05.03.2002. Coming into force: 07.03.2002. Effect: None. Territorial extent & classification: E. Local *Unpublished*

The M606 Motorway and the M62 Motorway (Chain Bar Interchange) (Temporary Prohibition of Traffic) Order 2002 No. 2002/2393. – Enabling power: Road Traffic Regulation Act 1984, s. 14 (1) (a). – Made: 13.09.2002. Coming into force: 15.09.2002. Effect: None. Territorial extent & classification: E. Local *Unpublished*

The M606 Motorway (Chain Bar) and the M62 Motorway (Junction 26, Chain Bar) (Temporary Prohibition of Traffic) Order 2002 No. 2002/1954. – Enabling power: Road Traffic Regulation Act 1984, s. 14 (1) (a). – Made: 18.07.2002. Coming into force: 24.07.2002. Effect: None. Territorial extent & classification: E. Local *Unpublished*

The M606 Motorway (Junction 2, Euroway) (Temporary Restriction and Prohibition of Traffic) Order 2002 No. 2002/2920. – Enabling power: Road Traffic Regulation Act 1984, s. 14 (1) (a) (7). – Made: 21.11.2002. Coming into force: 24.11.2002. Effect: None. Territorial extent & classification: E. Local *Unpublished*

The M621 Motorway (Gildersome Interchange, Junction 2 and Junction 3) (Temporary Restriction and Prohibition of Traffic) Order 2002 No. 2002/2919. – Enabling power: Road Traffic Regulation Act 1984, s. 14 (1) (a) (7). – Made: 21.11.2002. Coming into force: 24.11.2002. Effect: None. Territorial extent & classification: E. Local *Unpublished*

The M621 Motorway (Junction 1 and Junction 4) (Temporary Prohibition of Traffic) Order 2002 No. 2002/1257. – Enabling power: Road Traffic Regulation Act 1984, s. 14 (1) (a). – Made: 02.05.2002. Coming into force: 06.05.2002. Effect: None. Territorial extent & classification: E. Local *Unpublished*

The M621 Motorway (Junction 1 to Gildersome Interchange) (Temporary Prohibition of Traffic) Order 2002 No. 2002/2922. – Enabling power: Road Traffic Regulation Act 1984, s. 14 (1) (a). – Made: 22.11.2002. Coming into force: 22.11.2002. Effect: None. Territorial extent & classification: E. Local *Unpublished*

The M621 Motorway (Junction 2, Elland Road) (Temporary Prohibition of Traffic) Order 2002 No. 2002/3141. – Enabling power: Road Traffic Regulation Act 1984, s. 14 (1) (a). – Made: 28.11.2002. Coming into force: 01.12.2002. Effect: None. Territorial extent & classification: E. Local *Unpublished*

The M621 Motorway (Junction 3, Holbeck and Junction 7, Stourton) (Temporary Prohibition of Traffic) Order 2002 No. 2002/3031. – Enabling power: Road Traffic Regulation Act 1984, s. 14 (1) (a). – Made: 05.12.2002. Coming into force: 06.12.2002. Effect: None. Territorial extent & classification: E. Local *Unpublished*

The M621 Motorway (Junction 4, Hunslet) (Temporary Prohibition of Traffic) Order 2002 No. 2002/2714. – Enabling power: Road Traffic Regulation Act 1984, s. 14 (1) (a). – Made: 24.10.2002. Coming into force: 26.10.2002. Effect: None. Territorial extent & classification: E. Local *Unpublished*

The M621 Motorway (Junction 4 to Junction 7) (Temporary Restriction and Prohibition of Traffic) Order 2002 No. 2002/1507. – Enabling power: Road Traffic Regulation Act 1984, s. 14 (1) (a) (7). – Made: 30.05.2002. Coming into force: 05.06.2002. Effect: None. Territorial extent & classification: E. Local *Unpublished*

The M621 Motorway (Junction 4 to Junction 7) (Temporary Restriction and Prohibition of Traffic) Order 2002 Amendment Order 2002 No. 2002/2551. – Enabling power: Road Traffic Regulation Act 1984, s. 14 (1) (a) (7). – Made: 04.10.2002. Coming into force: 05.10.2002. Effect: S.I. 2002/1507 amended. Territorial extent & classification: E. Local *Unpublished*

Road traffic, England

The M4 Motorway (Hillingdon and Hounslow) (Speed Limits) Regulations 2002 No. 2002/1651. – Enabling power: Road Traffic Regulation Act 1984, s. 17 (2) (3). – Issued: 03.07.2002. Made: 24.06.2002. Laid: 26.06.2002. Coming into force: 23.07.2002. Effect: S.I. 1998/1708; 1999/167 revoked. Territorial extent & classification: E. Local. – 4p.: 30 cm. – 0 11 042411 5 *£1.75*

The M4 Motorway (London Borough of Hounslow) (Bus Lane) Order 1998 (Variation) Order 2002 No. 2002/1672. – Enabling power: Road Traffic Regulation Act 1984, s. 6 (1) (3), sch. 9, part IV. – Issued: 04.07.2002. Made: 05.06.2002. Coming into force: 23.07.2002. Effect: S.I. 1998/3090 amended. Territorial extent & classification: E/W. Local. – 2p.: 30 cm. – 0 11 042415 8 *£1.50*

The M11 Motorway (Junction 8) (Speed Limit) Regulations 2002 No. 2002/2936. – Enabling power: Road Traffic Regulation Act 1984, s. 17 (2) (3). – Issued: 06.12.2002. Made: 27.11.2002. Laid: 29.11.2002. Coming into force: 20.12.2002. Effect: None. Territorial extent & classification: E. General. – 2p.: 30 cm. – 0 11 044094 3 *£1.50*

The M60 Motorway (Junction 25) (Speed Limit) Regulations 2002 No. 2002/2403. – Enabling power: Road Traffic Regulation Act 1984, s. 17 (2) (3). – Issued: 27.09.2002. Made: 18.09.2002. Laid: 23.09.2002. Coming into force: 21.10.2002. Effect: None. Territorial extent & classification: E. Local. – 2p.: 30 cm. – 0 11 042810 2 *£1.50*

The Removal and Disposal of Vehicles (Amendment) (No. 2) Regulations 2002 No. 2002/2777. – Enabling power: Road Traffic Regulation Act 1984, ss. 99, 103 (3). – Issued: 25.11.2002. Made: 07.11.2002. Laid: 11.11.2002. Coming into force: 02.12.2002. Effect: S.I. 1986/183 amended in relation to England. Territorial extent & classification: E. General. – 2p.: 30 cm. – 0 11 043044 1 *£1.50*

The Removal and Disposal of Vehicles (England) (Amendment) Regulations 2002 No. 2002/746. – Enabling power: Refuse Disposal (Amenity) Act 1978, ss. 3, 4 & Road Traffic Regulation Act 1984, ss. 99, 101. – Issued: 16.04.2002. Made: 19.03.2002. Laid: 19.03.2002. Coming into force:09.04.2002 Effect: S.I. 1986/183 amended. Territorial extent & classification: E. General. – 2p.: 25 cm. – 0 11 039757 6 *£1.50*

The Road Traffic (Permitted Parking Area and Special Parking Area) (Borough of Milton Keynes) Order 2002 No. 2002/421. – Enabling power: Road Traffic Act 1991, sch. 3, paras. 1 (1), 2 (1), 3(3). – Issued: 06.03.2002. Made: 26.02.2002. Laid: 28.02.2002. Coming into force: 25.03.2002. Effect: 1984 c. 27; 1991 c. 40 modified in relation to the parking area as specified in this order. Territorial extent & classification: E. General. – 8p.: 30 cm. – 0 11 039404 6 *£2.00*

The Road Traffic (Permitted Parking Area and Special Parking Area) (Borough of Poole) Order 2002 No. 2002/422. – Enabling power: Road Traffic Act 1991, sch. 3, paras. 1 (1), 2 (1), 3(3). – Issued: 06.03.2002. Made: 26.02.2002. Laid: 28.02.2002. Coming into force: 02.04.2002. Effect: 1984 c. 27; 1991 c. 40 modified in relation to the parking area as specified in this order. Territorial extent & classification: E. General. – 8p.: 30 cm. – 0 11 039405 4 *£2.00*

The Road Traffic (Permitted Parking Area and Special Parking Area) (City of Liverpool) Order 2002 No. 2002/1353. – Enabling power: Road Traffic Act 1991, sch. 3, paras. 1 (1), 2 (1), 3 (3). – Issued: 22.05.2002. Made: 14.05.2002. Laid: 15.05.2002. Coming into force: 01.07.2002. Effect: 1984 c. 27; 1991 c. 40 modified in relation to the parking area as specified in this order. Territorial extent & classification: E. General. – 8p.: 30 cm. – 0 11 039973 0 *£2.00*

The Road Traffic (Permitted Parking Area and Special Parking Area) (City of Nottingham) Order 2002 No. 2002/2012. – Enabling power: Road Traffic Act 1991, sch. 3, paras. 1 (1), 2 (1), 3 (3). – Issued: 08.08.2002. Made: 30.07.2002. Laid: 01.08.2002. Coming into force: 01.10.2002. Effect: 1984 c. 27; 1991 c. 40 modified in relation to the parking area as specified in this order. Territorial extent & classification: E. General. – 8p.: 30 cm. – 0 11 042620 7 *£2.00*

The Road Traffic (Permitted Parking Area and Special Parking Area) (City of Southampton) Order 2002 No. 2002/126. – Enabling power: Road Traffic Act 1991, sch. 3, paras. 1 (1), 2 (¹), 3 (3). – Issued: 07.02.2002. Made: 28.01.2002. Laid: 31.01.2002. Coming into force: 25.02.2002. Effect: 1984 c.27; 1991 c.40 modified in relation to the parking area as specified. Territorial extent & classification: E. General. – 8p.: 30 cm. – 0 11 039262 0 *£2.00*

The Road Traffic (Permitted Parking Area and Special Parking Area) (City of Sunderland) Order 2002 No. 2002/3266. – Enabling power: Road Traffic Act 1991, sch. 3, paras. 1 (1), 2 (1), 3 (3). – Issued: 22.01.2003. Made: 21.12.2002. Laid: 08.01.2003. Coming into force: 03.02.2003. Effect: 1984 c. 27; 1991 c. 40 modified in relation to the parking area as specified. Territorial extent & classification: E. General. – 8p.: 30 cm. – 0 11 044611 9 *£2.00*

The Road Traffic (Permitted Parking Area and Special Parking Area) (County of Cumbria) (District of Eden) Order 2002 No. 2002/2520. – Enabling power: Road Traffic Act 1991, sch. 3, paras 1 (1), 2 (1), 3 (3). – Issued: 14.10.2002. Made: 03.10.2002. Laid: 07.10.2002. Coming into force: 20.01.2003. Effect: 1984 c. 27; 1991 c. 40 modified in relation to the parking area as specified. Territorial extent & classification: E. General. – 8p.: 30 cm. – 0 11 042845 5 *£2.00*

The Road Traffic (Permitted Parking Area and Special Parking Area) (County of Cumbria) (District of South Lakeland) Order 2002 No. 2002/276. – Enabling power: Road Traffic Act 1991, sch. 3, paras. 1 (1), 2 (1), 3 (1). – Issued: 19.02.2002. Made: 11.02.2002. Laid: 11.02.2002. Coming into force: 04.03.2002. Effect: 1984 c. 27; 1991 c. 40 modified in relation to the parking area as specified. Territorial extent & classification: E. General. – 8p.: 30 cm. – 0 11 039320 1 *£2.00*

The Road Traffic (Permitted Parking Area and Special Parking Area) (County of Dorset) (Borough of Weymouth and Portland) Order 2002 No. 2002/2705. – Enabling power: Road Traffic Act 1991, sch. 3, paras. 1 (1), 2 (1), 3 (3). – Issued: 05.11.2002. Made: 28.10.2002. Laid: 30.10.2002. Coming into force: 25.11.2002. Effect: 1984 c. 27; 1991 c. 40 modified in relation to the parking area as specified. Territorial extent & classification: E. General. – 8p.: 30 cm. – 0 11 042938 9 *£2.00*

The Road Traffic (Permitted Parking Area and Special Parking Area) (County of Dorset) (District of East Dorset) Order 2002 No. 2002/1485. – Enabling power: Road Traffic Act 1991, sch. 3, paras. 1 (1), 2 (1), 3 (3). – Issued: 18.06.2002. Made: 10.06.2002. Laid: 10.06.2002. Coming into force: 01.07.2002. Effect: 1984 c. 27; 1991 c. 40 modified in relation to the parking area as specified. Territorial extent & classification: E. General. – 8p.: 30 cm. – 0 11 042364 X *£2.00*

The Road Traffic (Permitted Parking Area and Special Parking Area) (County of Dorset) (District of North Dorset) Order 2002 No. 2002/1504. – Enabling power: Road Traffic Act 1991, sch. 3, paras. 1 (1), 2 (1), 3 (3). – Issued: 18.06.2002. Made: 09.06.2002. Laid: 10.06.2002. Coming into force: 01.07.2002. Effect: 1984 c. 27; 1991 c. 40 modified in relation to the parking area as specified. Territorial extent & classification: E. General. – 8p.: 30 cm. – 0 11 042366 6 *£2.00*

The Road Traffic (Permitted Parking Area and Special Parking Area) (County of Dorset) (District of Purbeck) Order 2002 No. 2002/1484. – Enabling power: Road Traffic Act 1991, sch. 3, paras. 1 (1), 2 (1), 3 (3). – Issued: 20.06.2002. Made: 10.06.2002. Laid: 10.06.2002. Coming into force: 01.07.2002. Effect: 1984 c. 27; 1991 c. 40 modified in relation to the parking area as specified. Territorial extent & classification: E. General. – 8p.: 30 cm. – 0 11 042373 9 *£2.00*

The Road Traffic (Permitted Parking Area and Special Parking Area) (County of Dorset) (District of West Dorset) Order 2002 No. 2002/1486. – Enabling power: Road Traffic Act 1991, sch. 3, paras. 1 (1), 2 (1), 3 (3). – Issued: 18.06.2002. Made: 10.06.2002. Laid: 10.06.2002. Coming into force: 01.07.2002. Effect: 1984 c. 27; 1991 c. 40 modified in relation to the parking area as specified. Territorial extent & classification: E. General. – 8p.: 30 cm. – 0 11 042365 8 *£2.00*

The Road Traffic (Permitted Parking Area and Special Parking Area) (County of Essex) (Borough of Brentwood) (Amendment) Order 2002 No. 2002/2440. – Enabling power: Road Traffic Act 1991, sch. 3, paras. 1 (1), 2 (1), 3 (3). – Issued: 04.10.2002. Made: 24.09.2002. Laid: 24.09.2002. Coming into force: 30.09.2002. Effect: S.I. 2002/2183 amended. Territorial extent & classification: E. General. – This S.I. has been printed to correct errors in S.I. 2002/2183. – 2p.: 30 cm. – 0 11 042829 3 *£1.50*

The Road Traffic (Permitted Parking Area and Special Parking Area) (County of Essex) (Borough of Brentwood) Order 2002 No. 2002/2183. – Enabling power: Road Traffic Act 1991, sch. 3, paras. 1 (1), 2 (1) 3 (3). – Issued: 03.09.2002. Made: 20.08.2002. Laid: 22.08.2002. Coming into force: 01.10.2002. Effect: 1984 c. 27; 1991 c. 40 modified in relation to the parking area as specified. Territorial extent & classification: E. General. – 8p.: 30 cm. – 0 11 042705 X *£2.00*

The Road Traffic (Permitted Parking Area and Special Parking Area) (County of Essex) (Borough of Chelmsford) Order 2002 No. 2002/2184. – Enabling power: Road Traffic Act 1991, sch. 3, paras. 1 (1), 2 (1), 3(3). – Issued: 03.09.2002. Made: 20.08.2002. Laid: 22.08.2002. Coming into force: 01.10.2002. Effect: 1984 c. 27; 1991 c. 40 modified in relation to the parking area as specified. Territorial extent & classification: E. General. – 8p.: 30 cm. – 0 11 042706 8 *£2.00*

The Road Traffic (Permitted Parking Area and Special Parking Area) (County of Essex) (Borough of Colchester) Order 2002 No. 2002/2186. – Enabling power: Road Traffic Act 1991, sch. 3, paras. 1 (1), 2 (1), 3(3). – Issued: 03.09.2002. Made: 20.08.2002. Laid: 22.08.2002. Coming into force: 01.10.2002. Effect: 1984 c. 27; 1991 c. 40 modified in relation to the parking area as specified in schedules 1 & 2 of this order. Territorial extent & classification: E. General. – 8p.: 30 cm. – 0 11 042708 4 £2.00

The Road Traffic (Permitted Parking Area and Special Parking Area) (County of Essex) (District of Epping Forest) Order 2002 No. 2002/2185. – Enabling power: Road Traffic Act 1991, sch. 3, paras. 1 (1), 2 (1), 3(3). – Issued: 03.09.2002. Made: 20.08.2002. Laid: 22.08.2002. Coming into force: 01.10.2002. Effect: 1984 c. 27; 1991 c. 40 modified in relation to the parking area as specified in schedules 1 & 2 of this order. Territorial extent & classification: E. General. – 8p.: 30 cm. – 0 11 042707 6 £2.00

The Road Traffic (Permitted Parking Area and Special Parking Area) (County of Hampshire) (Borough of Basingstoke and Deane) Order 2002 No. 2002/2187. – Enabling power: Road Traffic Act 1991, sch. 3, paras. 1 (1), 2 (1), 3(3). – Issued: 03.09.2002. Made: 19.08.2002. Laid: 22.08.2002. Coming into force: 01.10.2002. Effect: 1984 c. 27; 1991 c. 40 modified in relation to the parking area as specified in schedules 1 & 2 of this order. Territorial extent & classification: E. General. – 8p.: 30 cm. – 0 11 042709 2 £2.00

The Road Traffic (Permitted Parking Area and Special Parking Area) (County of Hampshire) (Borough of Rushmoor) Order 2002 No. 2002/1352. – Enabling power: Road Traffic Act 1991, sch. 3, paras. 1 (1), 2 (1), 3 (3). – Issued: 22.05.2002. Made: 14.05.2002. Laid: 15.05.2002. Coming into force: 05.06.2002. Effect: 1984 c. 27; 1991 c. 40 modified in relation to the parking area as specified in this order. Territorial extent & classification: E. General. – 8p.: 30 cm. – 0 11 039972 2 £2.00

The Road Traffic (Permitted Parking Area and Special Parking Area) (County of Hampshire) (District of Hart) Order 2002 No. 2002/1351. – Enabling power: Road Traffic Act 1991, sch. 3, paras. 1 (1), 2 (1), 3 (3). – Issued: 22.05.2002. Made: 14.05.2002. Laid: 15.05.2002. Coming into force: 05.06.2002. Effect: 1984 c. 27; 1991 c. 40 modified in relation to the parking area as specified in this order. Territorial extent & classification: E. General. – 8p.: 30 cm. – 0 11 039971 4 £2.00

The Road Traffic (Permitted Parking Area and Special Parking Area) (County of Norfolk) (City of Norwich) Order 2002 No. 2002/37. – Enabling power: Road Traffic Act 1991, sch. 3, paras, 1 (1), 2 (1), 3 (3). – Issued: 22.01.2002. Made: 14.01.2002. Laid: 14.01.2002. Coming into force: 04.02.2002. Effect: 1984 c.27; 1991 c.40 modified in relation to the parking area as specified in sch. 1 & 2 to this order. Territorial extent & classification: E. General. – 8p.: 30 cm. – 0 11 039198 5 £2.00

The Road Traffic (Permitted Parking Area and Special Parking Area) (County of North Yorkshire) (Borough of Harrogate) Order 2002 No. 2002/1621. – Enabling power: Road Traffic Act 1991, sch. 3, paras. 1 (1), 2 (1), 3 (3). – Issued: 04.07.2002. Made: 24.06.2002. Laid: 24.06.2002. Coming into force: 15.07.2002. Effect: 1984 c. 27; 1991 c. 40 modified in relation to the parking area as specified in this order. Territorial extent & classification: E. General. – 8p.: 30 cm. – 0 11 042416 6 £2.00

The Road Traffic (Permitted Parking Area and Special Parking Area) (County of Worcestershire) (City of Worcester) Order 2002 No. 2002/3265. – Enabling power: Road Traffic Act 1991, sch. 3, paras. 1 (1), 2 (1), 3 (3). – Issued: 22.01.2003. Made: 21.12.2002. Laid: 08.01.2003. Coming into force: 03.02.2003. Effect: 1984 c. 27; 1991 c. 40 modified in relation to the parking area as specified in schedules 1 & 2 of this order. Territorial extent & classification: E. General. – 8p.: 30 cm. – 0 11 044605 4 £2.00

The Road Traffic (Permitted Parking Area and Special Parking Area) (Metropolitan Borough of Bury) Order 2002 No. 2002/2188. – Enabling power: Road Traffic Act 1991, sch. 3, paras. 1 (1), 2 (1), 3(3). – Issued: 03.09.2002. Made: 19.08.2002. Laid: 22.08.2002. Coming into force: 14.10.2002. Effect: 1984 c. 27; 1991 c. 40 modified in relation to the parking area as specified in schedules 1 & 2 of this order. Territorial extent & classification: E. General. – 8p.: 30 cm. – 0 11 042710 6 £2.00

The Road Traffic (Vehicle Emissions) (Fixed Penalty) (England) Regulations 2002 No. 2002/1808. – Enabling power: Environment Act 1995, s. 87 (1) (2) (5), sch. 11, para. 5. – Issued: 19.07.2002. Made: 11.07.2002. Coming into force: 18.07.2002. Effect: S.I. 1997/3058 revoked in relation to England. Territorial extent & classification: E. General. – 12p.: 30 cm. – Supersedes draft S.I. (ISBN 0110423887) – 0 11 042486 7 £2.50

Road traffic, England and Wales

The Goods Vehicles (Plating and Testing) (Amendment) Regulations 2002 No. 2002/487. – Enabling power: Road Traffic Act 1988, ss. 49, 51 (1), 53 (5). – Issued: 14.03.2002. Made: 06.03.2002. Laid: 07.03.2002. Coming into force: 01.04.2002. Effect: S.I. 1988/1478 amended. Territorial extent & classification: E/W. General. – 4p.: 30 cm. – 0 11 039445 3 £1.75

The International Carriage of Dangerous Goods by Road (Fees) (Amendment) Regulations 2002 No. 2002/537. – Enabling power: Finance Act 1973, s. 56 (1) (2) & S.I. 1988/643. – Issued: 19.03.2002. Made: 08.03.2002. Laid: 11.03.2002. Coming into force: 01.04.2002. Effect: S.I. 1988/370 amended. Territorial extent & classification: E/W. General. – 2p.: 30 cm. – 0 11 039486 0 £1.50

The International Transport of Goods Under Cover of TIR Carnets (Fees) (Amendment) Regulations 2002 No. 2002/539. – Enabling power: Finance Act 1973, s. 56 (1) (2) & S.I. 1988/643. – Issued: 19.03.2002. Made: 08.03.2002. Laid: 11.03.2002. Coming into force: 01.04.2002. Effect: S.I. 1988/371 amended. Territorial extent & classification: E/W. General. – 2p.: 30 cm. – 0 11 039484 4 *£1.50*

The Motor Salvage Operators Regulations 2002 No. 2002/1916. – Enabling power: Vehicles (Crime) Act 2001, ss. 2 (3), 3 (1), 7 (1) (3), 41 (2) & Local Government Act 2000, ss. 13, 105 (2). – Issued: 13.08.2002. Made: 17.07.2002. Laid: 24.07.2002. Coming into force: 21.10.2002. Effect: S.I. 2000/2853 amended. Territorial extent & classification: E/W. General. – 4p.: 30 cm. – 0 11 042635 5 *£1.75*

The Motor Vehicles (Tests) (Amendment) (No. 2) Regulations 2002 No. 2002/1698. – Enabling power: Road Traffic Act 1988, ss. 45, 46. – Issued: 09.07.2002. Made: 01.07.2002. Laid: 03.07.2002. Coming into force: 01.08.2002. Effect: S.I. 1981/1694 amended. Territorial extent classification: E/W. General. – 4p.: 30 cm. – 0 11 042434 4 *£1.75*

The Motor Vehicles (Tests) (Amendment) Regulations 2002 No. 2002/488. – Enabling power: Road Traffic Act 1988, ss. 45, 46. – Issued: 14.03.2002. Made: 06.03.2002. Laid: 07.03.2002. Coming into force: 01.04.2002. Effect: S.I. 1981/1694 amended. Territorial extent classification: E/W. General. – 8p.: 30 cm. – 0 11 039446 1 *£2.00*

The Passenger and Goods Vehicles (Recording Equipment) (Approval of Fitters and Workshops) (Fees) (Amendment) Regulations 2002 No. 2002/538. – Enabling power: Finance Act 1973, s. 56 (1) (2) & S.I. 1988/643. – Issued: 19.03.2002. Made: 08.03.2002. Laid: 11.03.2002. Coming into force: 01.04.2002. Effect: S.I. 1986/2128 amended. Territorial extent & classification: E/W. General. – 2p.: 30 cm. – 0 11 039485 2 *£1.50*

The Public Service Vehicles (Conditions of Fitness, Equipment, Use and Certification) (Amendment) Regulations 2002 No. 2002/489. – Enabling power: Public Passenger Vehicles Act 1981, ss. 10 (1), 52 (1), 60. – Issued: 14.03.2002. Made: 06.03.2002. Laid: 07.03.2002. Coming into force: 01.04.2002. Effect: S.I. 1981/257 amended. Territorial extent & classification: E/W. General. – 2p.: 30 cm. – 0 11 039447 X *£1.50*

The Road Traffic (NHS Charges) Amendment (No. 2) Regulations 2002 No. 2002/2995. – Enabling power: Road Traffic (NHS Charges) Act 1999, ss. 3 (2) (4), 16 (2), 17. – Issued: 11.12.2002. Made: 03.12.2002. Laid: 11.12.2002. Coming into force: 01.01.2003. Effect: S.I. 1999/785 amended. Territorial extent & classification: E/W. General. – 4p.: 30 cm. – 0 11 044121 4 *£1.75*

The Road Traffic (NHS Charges) Amendment Regulations 2002 No. 2002/237. – Enabling power: Road Traffic (NHS Charges) Act 1999, ss. 3 (2) (4), 16 (2), 17. – Issued: 13.03.2002. Made: 07.02.2002. Laid: 07.02.2002. Coming into force: 08.02.2002. Effect: S.I. 1999/785 amended & S.I. 2001/4030 revoked. Territorial extent & classification: E/W. General. – 2p.: 30 cm. – 0 11 039432 1 *£1.50*

The Road User Charging (Enforcement of Charging Scheme Penalty Charges) (England and Wales) Regulations 2002 No. 2002/3029. – Enabling power: Transport Act 2000, ss. 173 (4), 197 (1). – Issued: 16.12.2002. Made: 03.12.2002. Laid: 09.12.2002. Coming into force: 01.01.2003. Effect: None. Territorial extent & classification: E/W. General. – 4p.: 30 cm. – 0 11 044172 9 *£1.75*

The School Crossing Patrol Sign (England and Wales) Regulations 2002 No. 2002/3020. – Enabling power: Road Traffic Regulation Act 1984, s. 28 (4). – Issued:16.12.2002. Made: 05.12.2002. Laid 16.12.2002. Coming into force: 09.01.2003. Effect: S.I. 1994/1519 amended. Territorial extent & classification: E/W. General. – 4p., col. ill.: 30 cm. – 0 11 044164 8 *£1.75*

The Vehicles (Crime) Act 2001 (Commencement No. 3) Order 2002 No. 2002/1914 (C.59). – Enabling power: Vehicles (Crime) Act 2001, s. 44. Bringing into operation various provisions of the 2001 Act on 21.10.2002. – Issued: 13.08.2002. Made: 17.07.2002. Effect: None. Territorial extent & classification: E/W. General. – 2p.: 30 cm. – 0 11 042634 7 *£1.50*

The Vehicles (Crime) Act 2001 (Commencement No. 5) Order 2002 No. 2002/2957 (C.95). – Enabling power: Vehicles (Crime) Act 2001, s. 44. Bringing into operation various provisions of the 2001 Act on 01.12.2002. & 01.01.2003. & 01.03.2003. – Issued: 06.12.2002. Made: 29.11.2002. Effect: None. Territorial extent & classification: E/W. General. – 2p.: 30 cm. – 0 11 044109 5 *£1.50*

The Vehicles Crime (Registration of Registration Plate Suppliers) (England and Wales) Regulations 2002 No. 2002/2977. – Enabling power: Vehicles (Crime) Act 2001, ss. 17 (3), 18 (2), 19 (1) (a), 24 (1) (3), 25 (1) (2), 41 (2). – Issued: 10.02.2003. Made: 02.12.2002. Laid: 04.12.2002. Coming into force: 01.01.2003. Effect: None. Territorial extent & classification: E/W. General. – Corrected reprint. – 8p.: 30 cm. – 0 11 044117 6 *£2.00*

Road traffic, Northern Ireland

The Road Vehicles (Registration and Licensing) (Amendment) Regulations (Northern Ireland) 2002 No. 2002/2381. – Enabling power: Vehicle Excise and Registration Act 1994, ss. 22 (1) (a) (f) (h), 22A, 57 (1) (2) (3) (5). – Issued: 26.09.2002. Made: 18.09.2002. Laid: 18.09.2002. Coming into force: 09.10.2002, 07.04.2003, in accord. with art. 1 (2). Effect: SR & O (NI) 1973/490 amended. Territorial extent & classification: NI. General. – 4p.: 30 cm. – Revoked by S.I. 2002/2742 (ISBN 011042963X) – 0 11 042806 4 *£1.75*

Road traffic, Wales: Speed limits

The A5 Trunk Road (Berwyn Road, Llangollen, Denbighshire) (De-Restriction) Order 2002 No. 2002/1291 (W.128). – Enabling power: Road Traffic Regulation Act 1984, ss. 82 (2), 83 (1). – Made: 01.05.2002. Coming into force: 10.05.2002. Effect: None. Territorial extent & classification: W. Local – In English and Welsh *Unpublished*

The A40 Trunk Road (Letterston, Pembrokeshire) (40 mph and 50 mph Speed Limit) Order 2002 No. 2002/2745 (W.261). – Enabling power: Road Traffic Regulation Act 1984, s. 84 (1) (2). – Made: 28.10.2002. Coming into force: 08.11.2002. Effect: None. Territorial extent & classification: W. Local – In English and Welsh *Unpublished*

The A40 Trunk Road (Manordeilo, Carmarthenshire) (50 mph Speed Limit) Order 2002 No. 2002/2663 (W.255). – Enabling power: Road Traffic Regulation Act 1984, s. 84 (1) (2). – Made: 21.10.2002. Coming into force: 23.10.2002. Effect: None. Territorial extent & classification: W. Local – In English and Welsh *Unpublished*

The A40 Trunk Road (Square and Compass, Llangadog, Carmarthenshire) (40 mph Speed Limit) Order 2002 No. 2002/2744 (W.260). – Enabling power: Road Traffic Regulation Act 1984, s. 84 (1) (2). – Made: 29.10.2002. Coming into force: 06.11.2002. Effect: None. Territorial extent & classification: W. Local – In English and Welsh *Unpublished*

The A470 Trunk Road (Caersws, Powys) (40 MPH Speed Limit) Order 2002 No. 2002/1591 (W.156). – Enabling power: Road Traffic Regulation Act 1984, s. 84 (1) (2). – Made: 10.06.2002. Coming into force: 17.06.2002. Effect: None. Territorial extent & classification: W. Local. – In English and Welsh *Unpublished*

The A470 Trunk Road (Llanrwst, Gwynedd) (De-Restriction) Order 1995 (Variation) Order 2000 No. 2002/2585 (W.251). – Enabling power: Road Traffic Regulation Act 1984, ss. 82 (2), 83 (1), 124. – Made: 05.12.2000. Coming into force: 07.12.2000. Effect: S.I. 1995/2692 varied. Territorial extent & classification: W. Local – In English and Welsh *Unpublished*

The A477 Trunk Road (Milton Village, Pembrokeshire) (40 mph Speed Limit) Order 2002 No. 2002/2101 (W.211). – Enabling power: Road Traffic Regulation Act 1984, s. 84 (1) (2). – Made: 01.08.2002. Coming into force: 10.08.2002. Effect: None. Territorial extent & classification: W. Local – In English and Welsh *Unpublished*

The A479 Trunk Road (Cwm-du, Powys) (40 mph Speed Limit) Order 2002 No. 2002/485 (W.62). – Enabling power: Road Traffic Regulation Act 1984, s. 84 (1) (2). – Made: 25.02.2002. Coming into force: 11.03.2002. Effect: None. Territorial extent & classification: W. Local – In English and Welsh *Unpublished*

The A483 Trunk Road (Derwydd, Llandybie, Carmarthenshire) (40 mph Speed Limit) Order 2002 No. 2002/2869 (W.274). – Enabling power: Road Traffic Regulation Act 1984, s. 84 (1) (2). – Made: 14.11.2002. Coming into force: 20.11.2002. Effect: None. Territorial extent & classification: W. Local – In English and Welsh *Unpublished*

The A483 Trunk Road (Llanbadarn Fynydd, Powys) (50 mph Speed Limit) Order 2002 No. 2002/835 (W.98). – Enabling power: Road Traffic Regulation Act 1984, s. 84 (1) (2). – Made: 15.03.2002. Coming into force: 25.03.2002. Effect: None. Territorial extent & classification: W. Local – In English and Welsh *Unpublished*

The A483 Trunk Road (Southern Approach to Ty-Croes, Ammanford, Carmarthenshire) (30 mph Speed Limit) Order 2002 No. 2002/748 (W.79). – Enabling power: Road Traffic Regulation Act 1984, s. 84 (1) (2). – Made: 17.01.2002. Coming into force: 01.02.2002. Effect: None. Territorial extent & classification: W. Local – In English and Welsh *Unpublished*

The A483 Trunk Road (Southern Approach to TyCroes, Ammanford, Carmarthenshire) (40 & 50 mph Speed Limit) Order 2002 No. 2002/2664 (W.256). – Enabling power: Road Traffic Regulation Act 1984, s. 84 (1) (2). – Made: 21.10.2002. Coming into force: 23.10.2002. Effect: None. Territorial extent & classification: W. Local – In English and Welsh *Unpublished*

The A483 Trunk Road (Talhardd Villas, Ffairfach, Llandeilo, Carmarthenshire) (30 mph Speed Limit) Order 2002 No. 2002/2128 (W.215). – Enabling power: Road Traffic Regulation Act 1984, s. 84 (1) (2). – Made: 08.08.2002. Coming into force: 14.08.2002. Effect: None. Territorial extent & classification: W. Local – In English and Welsh *Unpublished*

The A487 Trunk Road (Lower Town, Fishguard, Pembrokeshire) (20 mph and 30 mph Speed Limits) Order 2002 No. 2002/2937 (W.278). – Enabling power: Road Traffic Regulation Act 1984, ss. 84 (1) (2), 124, sch. 9, para. 27. – Made: 21.11.2002. Coming into force: 29.11.2002. Effect: S.I. 1984/515 revoked. Territorial extent & classification: W. Local – In English and Welsh *Unpublished*

The A487 Trunk Road (Tanygroes, Ceredigion) (40 mph & 50 mph Speed Limit) Order 2002 No. 2002/3079 (W.290). – Enabling power: Road Traffic Regulation Act 1984, s. 84 (1) (2). – Made: 06.12.2002. Coming into force: 11.12.2002. Effect: None. Territorial extent & classification: W. Local – In English and Welsh *Unpublished*

The A4042 Trunk Road (Llanellen, Abergavenny, Monmouthshire) (40 mph Speed Limit) Order 2002 No. 2002/2549 (W.249). – Enabling power: Road Traffic Regulation Act 1984, s. 84 (1) (2). – Made: 26.09.2002. Coming into force: 03.10.2002. Effect: None. Territorial extent & classification: W. Local – In English and Welsh *Unpublished*

The A4042 Trunk Road (Penperlleni, Monmouthshire) (40 mph Speed Limit) Order 2002 No. 2002/1669 (W.160). – Enabling power: Road Traffic Regulation Act 1984, s. 84 (1) (2), 124, sch. 9, part IV, para. 27. – Made: 17.06.2002. Coming into force: 01.07.2002. Effect: None. Territorial extent & classification: W. Local – In English and Welsh *Unpublished*

Road traffic, Wales: Traffic regulation

The A40/A449 Trunk Road (Coldra to Monmouth) (Temporary Prohibition of Vehicles and 50 mph Speed Limit) Order 2002 No. 2002/478 (W.61). – Enabling power: Road Traffic Regulation Act 1984, s. 14 (1) (4). – Made: 22.02.2002. Coming into force: 28.02.2002. Effect: S.I. 1996/3246 revoked. Territorial extent & classification: W. Local – In English and Welsh *Unpublished*

The A40/A449 Trunk Road (Raglan Interchange, Monmouthshire) (Temporary 30 mph Speed Limit) Order 2002 No. 2002/1737 (W.167). – Enabling power: Road Traffic Regulation Act 1984, s. 14 (1) (4). – Made: 04.07.2002. Coming into force: 08.07.2002. Effect: None. Territorial extent & classification: W. Local – In English and Welsh *Unpublished*

The A40/A449 Trunk Road (Raglan Interchange, Monmouthshire) (Temporary Prohibition of Vehicles and 30 mph Speed Limit) Order 2002 No. 2002/2719 (W.257). – Enabling power: Road Traffic Regulation Act 1984, s. 14 (1) (4). – Made: 29.10.2002. Coming into force: 30.10.2002. Effect: None. Territorial extent & classification: W. Local – In English and Welsh *Unpublished*

The A40 Newport-Worcester Trunk Road (Gibraltar Tunnels, Monmouth, Monmouthshire) (Temporary Prohibition of Vehicles and 50 mph Speed Limit) Order 2002 No. 2002/1128 (W.116). – Enabling power: Road Traffic Regulation Act 1984, s. 14 (1) (4). – Made: 04.04.2002. Coming into force: 07.04.2002. Effect: None. Territorial extent & classification: W. Local – In English and Welsh *Unpublished*

The A40 Trunk Road (Abergavenny - Raglan Interchange, Monmouthshire) (Temporary 40 mph Speed Limit) Order 2002 No. 2002/373 (W.48). – Enabling power: Road Traffic Regulation Act 1984, s. 14 (1) (4). – Made: 06.02.2002. Coming into force: 17.02.2002. Effect: None. Territorial extent & classification: W. Local – In English and Welsh *Unpublished*

The A40 Trunk Road (Travellers' Rest, Carmarthen, Carmarthenshire) (Temporary Variable Speed Limit) Order 2002 No. 2002/613 (W.67). – Enabling power: Road Traffic Regulation Act 1984, s. 14 (1) (4). – Made: 05.03.2002. Coming into force: 06.03.2002. Effect: None. Territorial extent & classification: W. Local – In English and Welsh *Unpublished*

The A48 (M) (Junction 29 (Castleton) to Junction 29 (A) (St Mellons)) (Temporary Prohibition of Vehicles) Order (No. 2) 2002 No. 2002/1853 (W.178). – Enabling power: Road Traffic Regulation Act 1984, s. 14 (1) (4) (7). – Made: 12.07.2002. Coming into force: 15.07.2002. Effect: None. Territorial extent & classification: W. Local – In English and Welsh *Unpublished*

The A48(M) (Junction 29 (Castleton) to Junction 29(A) (St Mellons)) (Temporary Prohibition of Vehicles) Order 2002 No. 2002/541 (W.65). – Enabling power: Road Traffic Regulation Act 1984, s. 14 (1) (4) (7). – Made: 06.03.2002. Coming into force: 07.03.2002. Effect: None. Territorial extent & classification: W. Local – In English and Welsh *Unpublished*

The A55 Trunk Road (Bangor, Gwynedd) (Temporary 40 mph Speed Limit) Order 2002 No. 2002/2329 (W.234). – Enabling power: Road Traffic Regulation Act 1984, s. 14 (1) (4). – Made: 06.09.2002. Coming into force: 09.09.2002. Effect: None. Territorial extent & classification: W. Local – In English and Welsh *Unpublished*

The A55 Trunk Road (Bodelwyddan, Rhuddlan, Denbighshire) (Temporary Prohibition of Vehicles) Order 2002 No. 2002/2259 (W.223). – Enabling power: Road Traffic Regulation Act 1984, s. 14 (1) (4). – Made: 30.08.2002. Coming into force: 03.09.2002. Effect: None. Territorial extent & classification: W. Local – In English and Welsh *Unpublished*

The A55 Trunk Road (Broughton, Flintshire) (Temporary Prohibition of Vehicles and 40 mph Speed Limit) Order 2002 No. 2002/433 (W.54). – Enabling power: Road Traffic Regulation Act 1984, s. 14 (1) (4). – Made: 21.02.2002. Coming into force: 25.02.2002. Effect: None. Territorial extent & classification: W. Local – In English and Welsh *Unpublished*

The A55 Trunk Road (Colwyn Bay - Llanddulas, Conwy) (Temporary 40 mph Speed Limit) Order 2002 No. 2002/2444 (W.240). – Enabling power: Road Traffic Regulation Act 1984, s. 14 (1) (4). – Made: 19.09.2002. Coming into force: 14.10.2002. Effect: None. Territorial extent & classification: W. Local – In English and Welsh *Unpublished*

The A55 Trunk Road (Conwy Crossing Tunnel, Conwy) (Temporary Prohibition of Vehicles) Order 2002 No. 2002/374 (W.49). – Enabling power: Road Traffic Regulation Act 1984, s. 14 (1) (4). – Made: 21.01.2002. Coming into force: 22.01.2002. Effect: None. Territorial extent & classification: W. Local – In English and Welsh *Unpublished*

The A55 Trunk Road (Glan Conwy-Conwy Morfa, Conwy) (Temporary 70 mph Speed Limit) Order 2002 No. 2002/2477 (W.242). – Enabling power: Road Traffic Regulation Act 1984, s. 14 (1) (7). – Made: 25.09.2002. Coming into force: 26.09.2002. Effect: None. Territorial extent & classification: W. Local – In English and Welsh *Unpublished*

The A55 Trunk Road (Glan Llyn Junction, Rhuallt) (Closure of Central Reservation Crossing) Order 2002 No. 2002/1869 (W.182). – Enabling power: Road Traffic Regulation Act 1984, s. 1 (1), 2 (1) (2). – Made: 11.07.2002. Coming into force: 19.07.2002. Effect: S.I. 1993/1080 revoked. Territorial extent & classification: W. Local – In English and Welsh *Unpublished*

The A55 Trunk Road (Llanddulas, Conwy) (Temporary Prohibition of Vehicles) Order 2002 No. 2002/44 (W.3). – Enabling power: Road Traffic Regulation Act 1984, s. 14 (1) (4). – Made: 07.01.2002. Coming into force: 14.01.2002. Effect: None. Territorial extent & classification: W. Local – In English and Welsh *Unpublished*

The A55 Trunk Road (Llandudno Junction Interchange - Conwy Crossing Tunnel, Conwy) (Temporary 40 mph Speed Limit) Order 2002 No. 2002/2317 (W.231). – Enabling power: Road Traffic Regulation Act 1984, s. 14 (1) (4). – Made: 05.09.2002. Coming into force: 09.09.2002. Effect: None. Territorial extent & classification: W. Local – In English and Welsh *Unpublished*

The A55 Trunk Road (Mochdre, Conwy) (Temporary Prohibition of Vehicles, Contraflow & 40 mph Speed Limit) Order 2002 No. 2002/2588 (W.252). – Enabling power: Road Traffic Regulation Act 1984, s. 14 (1) (4). – Made: 11.10.2002. Coming into force: 14.10.2002. Effect: None. Territorial extent & classification: W. Local. – In English and Welsh *Unpublished*

The A55 Trunk Road (Northop Hall, Travellers Inn, Bodelwyddan and Mochdre, in the Counties of Flintshire, Denbighshire and Conwy) (Temporary 40 mph Speed Limit) Order 2002 No. 2002/1145 (W.119). – Enabling power: Road Traffic Regulation Act 1984, s. 14 (1) (4). – Made: 04.04.2002. Coming into force: 09.04.2002. Effect: None. Territorial extent & classification: W. Local – In English and Welsh *Unpublished*

The A55 Trunk Road (Penmaenbach Tunnel and Headland, Conwy) (Temporary Traffic Restrictions) Order 2002 No. 2002/747 (W.78). – Enabling power: Road Traffic Regulation Act 1984, s. 14 (1) (4) (7). – Made: 13.03.2002. Coming into force: 14.03.2002. Effect: None. Territorial extent & classification: W. Local – In English and Welsh *Unpublished*

The A55 Trunk Road (Penmaen-bach Tunnels, Conwy) (Temporary Traffic Restrictions) Order 2002 No. 2002/359 (W.47). – Enabling power: Road Traffic Regulation Act 1984, s. 14 (1) (4) (7). – Made: 07.01.2002. Coming into force: 08.01.2002. Effect: None. Territorial extent & classification: W. Local – In English and Welsh *Unpublished*

The A55 Trunk Road (Pen-y-Clip, Conwy) (Temporary Prohibition of Vehicles and Pedestrians) Order 2002 No. 2002/420 (W.51). – Enabling power: Road Traffic Regulation Act 1984, s. 14 (1) (4). – Made: 08.02.2002. Coming into force: 10.02.2002. Effect: None. Territorial extent & classification: W. Local – In English and Welsh *Unpublished*

The A55 Trunk Road (Pen-y-Clip, Conwy) (Temporary Traffic Restrictions) Order 2002 No. 2002/354 (W.46). – Enabling power: Road Traffic Regulation Act 1984, s. 14 (1) (4) (7). – Made: 08.02.2002. Coming into force: 12.02.2002. Effect: None. Territorial extent & classification: W. Local – In English and Welsh *Unpublished*

The A55 Trunk Road (Ty'r Ali, Denbighshire) (Temporary Prohibition of Vehicles) Order 2002 No. 2002/1439 (W.144). – Enabling power: Road Traffic Regulation Act 1984, s. 14 (1) (4). – Made: 28.05.2002. Coming into force: 06.06.2002 at 00.01 hours. Effect: None. Territorial extent & classification: W. Local – In English and Welsh *Unpublished*

The A458 Trunk Road (Buttington Bridge and Buttington Arches, Near Welshpool, Powys) (Temporary Prohibition of Vehicles) Order 2002 No. 2002/121 (W.15). – Enabling power: Road Traffic Regulation Act 1984, s. 14 (1) (4). – Made: 17.01.2002. Coming into force: 19.01.2002. Effect: None. Territorial extent & classification: W. Local – In English and Welsh *Unpublished*

The A458 Trunk Road (Llanerfyl, Powys) (Temporary Prohibition of Vehicles) Order 2002 No. 2002/2400 (W.239). – Enabling power: Road Traffic Regulation Act 1984, s. 14 (1) (4). – Made: 13.09.2002. Coming into force: 14.09.2002. Effect: None. Territorial extent & classification: W. Local – In English and Welsh *Unpublished*

The A458 Trunk Road (Middletown, Powys) (40 mph & 50 mph Speed Limits) Order 2002 No. 2002/477 (W.60). – Enabling power: Road Traffic Regulation Act 1984, s. 84 (1) (2), 124, sch. 9, paart IV, para. 27. – Made: 25.02.2002. Coming into force: 04.03.2002. Effect: S.I. 1998/1804 revoked. Territorial extent & classification: W. Local – In English and Welsh *Unpublished*

The A465 Heads of the Valleys Trunk Road (Gypsy Castle, Blaencarno, Caerphilly County Borough) (Temporary Prohibition of Right Hand Turn) Order 2002 No. 2002/1987 (W.205). – Enabling power: Road Traffic Regulation Act 1984, s. 14 (1) (4). – Made: 23.07.2002. Coming into force: 27.07.2002. Effect: None. Territorial extent & classification: W. Local – In English and Welsh *Unpublished*

The A465 Trunk Road (Aberbaiden Roundabout - Saleyard, Monmouthshire) (Temporary Prohibition of Cyclists and 40 mph Speed Limit) Order 2002 No. 2002/2142 (W.216). – Enabling power: Road Traffic Regulation Act 1984, s. 14 (1) (4). – Made: 15.08.2002. Coming into force: 19.08.2002. Effect: None. Territorial extent & classification: W. Local – In English and Welsh *Unpublished*

The A465 Trunk Road (Aberdulais Interchange, Neath Port Talbot) (Temporary Prohibition of Vehicles) Order 2002 No. 2002/2781 (W.265). – Enabling power: Road Traffic Regulation Act 1984, s. 14 (1) (4). – Made: 06.11.2002. Coming into force: 09.11.2002. Effect: None. Territorial extent & classification: W. Local – In English and Welsh *Unpublished*

The A465 Trunk Road (Glynneath Bypass, Rhondda Cynon Taff) (Temporary Prohibition of Vehicles and 40 mph Speed Limit) Order 2002 No. 2002/332 (W.45). – Enabling power: Road Traffic Regulation Act 1984, s. 14 (1) (4). – Made: 04.02.2002. Coming into force: 18.02.2002. Effect: None. Territorial extent & classification: W. Local. – In English and Welsh *Unpublished*

The A465 Trunk Road (Tredegar to Dowlais) (Temporary Traffic Restrictions) Order 2002 No. 2002/1146 (W.120). – Enabling power: Road Traffic Regulation Act 1984, s. 14 (1) (4). – Made: 18.04.2002. Coming into force: 22.04.2002. Effect: None. Territorial extent & classification: W. Local – In English and Welsh *Unpublished*

The A470 Trunk Road (Abercynon, Rhondda Cynon Taf-Abercanaid, Merthyr Tydfil) (Temporary Prohibition of Cyclists and 40 mph Speed Limit) Order 2002 No. 2002/2517 (W.245). – Enabling power: Road Traffic Regulation Act 1984, s. 14 (1) (4). – Made: 03.10.2002. Coming into force: 14.10.2002. Effect: None. Territorial extent & classification: W. Local. – In English and Welsh *Unpublished*

The A470 Trunk Road (Lledr Valley, Conwy County Borough) (Temporary Prohibition of Vehicles and 30 MPH Speed Limit) Order 2002 No. 2002/2512 (W.244). – Enabling power: Road Traffic Regulation Act 1984, s. 14 (1) (4). – Made: 27.09.2002. Coming into force: 01.10.2002. Effect: None. Territorial extent & classification: W. Local – In English and Welsh *Unpublished*

The A470 Trunk Road (Nantgarw Interchange) (Temporary Prohibition of Vehicles) Order 2002 No. 2002/43 (W.2). – Enabling power: Road Traffic Regulation Act 1984, s. 14 (1) (4). – Made: 02.01.2002. Coming into force: 12.01.2002. Effect: None. Territorial extent & classification: W. Local – In English and Welsh *Unpublished*

The A470 Trunk Road (Nantgarw tp Glyntaff, Rhondda Cynon Taff) (Temporary Traffic Restrictions) Order 2002 No. 2002/1976 (W.202). – Enabling power: Road Traffic Regulation Act 1984, s. 14 (1) (4). – Made: 19.07.2002. Coming into force: 29.07.2002. Effect: None. Territorial extent & classification: W. Local – In English and Welsh *Unpublished*

The A470 Trunk Road (Northbound and Southbound Slip Roads at Upper Boat Interchange, Rhondda Cynon Taff) (Temporary Prohibition of Vehicles) Order 2002 No. 2002/1978 (W.204). – Enabling power: Road Traffic Regulation Act 1984, s. 14 (1) (4). – Made: 19.07.2002. Coming into force: 29.07.2002. Effect: None. Territorial extent & classification: W. Local – In English and Welsh *Unpublished*

The A470 Trunk Road (Upper Boat Interchange, Rhondda Cynon Taff) (Temporary Prohibition of Vehicles) Order 2002 No. 2002/1977 (W.203). – Enabling power: Road Traffic Regulation Act 1984, s. 14 (1) (4). – Made: 19.07.2002. Coming into force: 29.07.2002. Effect: None. Territorial extent & classification: W. Local – In English and Welsh *Unpublished*

The A470 Trunk Road (Upper Boat Interchange) (Temporary Prohibition of Vehicles) Order 2002 No. 2002/113 (W.13). – Enabling power: Road Traffic Regulation Act 1984, s. 14 (1) (4). – Made: 02.01.2002. Coming into force: 19.01.2002. Effect: None. Territorial extent & classification: W. Local – In English and Welsh *Unpublished*

The A470 Trunk Road (Upper Boat to Pontypridd, Rhondda Cynon Taff) (Temporary 40 mph Speed Limit) Order 2002 No. 2002/1346 (W.129). – Enabling power: Road Traffic Regulation Act 1984, s. 14 (1) (4). – Made: 08.05.2002. Coming into force: 13.05.2002. Effect: None. Territorial extent & classification: W. Local – In English and Welsh *Unpublished*

The A483/A5 Trunk Road (Chirk By Pass, Wrexham) and the A483 Trunk Road (Newbridge By Pass, Wrexham) (Temporary Prohibition of Vehicles) Order 2002 No. 2002/1842 (W.177). – Enabling power: Road Traffic Regulation Act 1984, s. 14 (1) (4). – Made: 12.07.2002. Coming into force: 14.07.2002. Effect: None. Territorial extent & classification: W. Local – In English and Welsh *Unpublished*

The A483 Trunk Road (Builth Wells, Powys) (Temporary Prohibition of Vehicles) Order 2002 No. 2002/612 (W.66). – Enabling power: Road Traffic Regulation Act 1984, s. 14 (1) (4). – Made: 07.03.2002. Coming into force: 15.03.2002. Effect: None. Territorial extent & classification: W. Local – In English and Welsh *Unpublished*

The A483 Trunk Road (Gresford Interchange, Wrexham) (Temporary 40 mph Speed Limit) Order 2002 No. 2002/2571 (W.250). – Enabling power: Road Traffic Regulation Act 1984, s. 14 (1) (4). – Made: 09.10.2002. Coming into force: 14.10.2002. Effect: None. Territorial extent & classification: W. Local – In English and Welsh *Unpublished*

The A483 Trunk Road (Gresford Interchange, Wrexham) (Temporary Prohibition of Vehicles) Order 2002 No. 2002/1586 (W.155). – Enabling power: Road Traffic Regulation Act 1984, s. 14 (1) (4). – Made: 10.06.2002. Coming into force: 15.06.2002. Effect: None. Territorial extent & classification: W. Local – In English and Welsh *Unpublished*

The A483 Trunk Road (Rhostyllen - West of Wrexham) (Temporary Prohibition of Vehicles and 40 mph Speed Limit) Order 2002 No. 2002/62 (W.7). – Enabling power: Road Traffic Regulation Act 1984, s. 14 (1) (4). – Made: 02.01.2002. Coming into force: 14.01.2002. Effect: None. Territorial extent & classification: W. Local – In English and Welsh *Unpublished*

The A483 Trunk Road (Wrexham, County Borough of Wrexham) (Temporary 40 mph Speed Limit) Order 2002 No. 2002/1918 (W.200). – Enabling power: Road Traffic Regulation Act 1984, s. 14 (1) (4) (7). – Made: 15.07.2002. Coming into force: 16.07.2002. Effect: None. Territorial extent & classification: W. Local – In English and Welsh *Unpublished*

The A487 Trunk Road (Alexandra Road, Aberystwyth, Ceredigion) (Temporary Prohibition of Vehicles) Order 2002 No. 2002/540 (W.64). – Enabling power: Road Traffic Regulation Act 1984, s. 14 (1) (4). – Made: 01.03.2002. Coming into force: 11.03.2002. Effect: None. Territorial extent & classification: W. Local – In English and Welsh *Unpublished*

The A487 Trunk Road (Llwyn Mafon, Gwynedd) (Temporary 30 MPH Speed Limit) Order 2002 No. 2002/2518 (W.246). – Enabling power: Road Traffic Regulation Act 1984, s. 14 (1) (4). – Made: 03.10.2002. Coming into force: 09.10.2002. Effect: None. Territorial extent & classification: W. Local – In English and Welsh *Unpublished*

The A487 Trunk Road (Various Streets, Aberaeron, Ceredigion) (Prohibition and Restriction of Waiting) Order 2002 No. 2002/2720 (W.258). – Enabling power: Road Traffic Regulation Act 1984, s. 1(1), 2 (1) (2), 4 (2), 124, sch. 9, para. 27. – Made: 24.10.2002. Coming into force: 04.11.2002. Effect: S.I. 1982/1286 revoked. Territorial extent & classification: W. Local – In English and Welsh *Unpublished*

The A494/A550 Trunk Road (Sealand, Queensferry, Flintshire) (Temporary Prohibition of Vehicles) Order 2002 No. 2002/2356 (W.235). – Enabling power: Road Traffic Regulation Act 1984, s. 14 (1) (4). – Made: 09.09.2002. Coming into force: 16.09.2002. Effect: None. Territorial extent & classification: W. Local – In English and Welsh *Unpublished*

The A4042 Trunk Road (Grove Park, Newport) (Temporary Prohibition of Vehicles) Order 2002 No. 2002/2203 (W.220). – Enabling power: Road Traffic Regulation Act 1984, s. 14 (1) (4). – Made: 20.08.2002. Coming into force: 26.08.2002. Effect: None. Territorial extent & classification: W. Local – In English and Welsh *Unpublished*

The A4042 Trunk Road (Llanellen, Monmouthshire) (Temporary Prohibition of Vehicles) Order 2002 No. 2002/2115 (W.212). – Enabling power: Road Traffic Regulation Act 1984, s. 14 (1) (4). – Made: 08.08.2002. Coming into force: 12.08.2002. Effect: None. Territorial extent & classification: W. Local – In English and Welsh *Unpublished*

The A4060 Trunk Road (Dowlais Top, Merthyr Tydfil) (Temporary Prohibition of Cyclists and 40 mph Speed Limit) Order 2002 No. 2002/1148 (W.121). – Enabling power: Road Traffic Regulation Act 1984, s. 14 (1) (4). – Made: 18.04.2002. Coming into force: 22.04.2002. Effect: None. Territorial extent & classification: W. Local – In English and Welsh *Unpublished*

The Fishguard - Bangor Trunk Road (A487) (Bridge Street, Aberystwyth, Ceredigion) (Temporary Prohibition of Vehicles) Order 2002 No. 2002/1041 (W.112). – Enabling power: Road Traffic Regulation Act 1984, s. 14 (1) (4). – Made: 19.03.2002. Coming into force: 22.03.2002. Effect: None. Territorial extent & classification: W. Local – In English and Welsh *Unpublished*

The M4 Motorway and A4232 Trunk Road (Junction 33, Capel Llanilltern, Cardiff) (Temporary 30 mph Speed Limit) Order 2002 No. 2002/204 (W.27). – Enabling power: Road Traffic Regulation Act 1984, s. 14 (1) (4) (7). – Made: 29.01.2002. Coming into force: 03.02.2002. Effect: None. Territorial extent & classification: W. Local – In English and Welsh *Unpublished*

The M4 Motorway (Brynglas Tunnels and Junction 26 (Malpas), Newport) (Temporary Prohibition of Vehicles and 40 mph Speed Limit) Order 2002 No. 2002/2156 (W.217). – Enabling power: Road Traffic Regulation Act 1984, s. 14. – Made: 15.08.2002. Coming into force: 16.08.2002. Effect: None. Territorial extent & classification: W. Local. – In English and Welsh *Unpublished*

The M4 Motorway (Brynglas Tunnels, Newport) (Temporary Prohibition of Vehicles and 40 mph Speed Limit) (No. 2) Order 2002 No. 2002/669 (W.71). – Enabling power: Road Traffic Regulation Act 1984, s. 14 (1) (4) (7). – Made: 25.02.2002. Coming into force: 04.02.2002. Effect: None. Territorial extent & classification: W. Local – In English and Welsh *Unpublished*

The M4 Motorway (Brynglas Tunnels, Newport) (Temporary Prohibition of Vehicles and 40 mph Speed Limit) Order 2002 No. 2002/104 (W.10). – Enabling power: Road Traffic Regulation Act 1984, s. 14 (1) (4) (7). – Made: 02.01.2002. Coming into force: 11.01.2002. Effect: None. Territorial extent & classification: W. Local. – In English and Welsh *Unpublished*

The M4 Motorway (Eastbound and Westbound Entry Slip Roads, Junction 27, High Cross, Newport) (Temporary Prohibition of Vehicles) Order 2002 No. 2002/1283 (W.126). – Enabling power: Road Traffic Regulation Act 1984, s. 14 (1) (4). – Made: 30.04.2002. Coming into force: 07.05.2002. Effect: None. Territorial extent & classification: W. Local. – In English and Welsh *Unpublished*

The M4 Motorway (Eastbound and Westbound Slip Roads at Junction 45, Ynysforgan, Swansea) (Temporary Prohibition of Vehicles) Order 2002 No. 2002/2721 (W.259). – Enabling power: Road Traffic Regulation Act 1984, s. 14 (1) (4). – Made: 24.10.2002. Coming into force: 02.11.2002. Effect: None. Territorial extent & classification: W. Local – In English and Welsh *Unpublished*

The M4 Motorway (Eastbound Entry Slip Road, Junction 28, Tredegar Park, Newport) (Temporary Prohibition of Vehicles) Order 2002 No. 2002/1404 (W.141). – Enabling power: Road Traffic Regulation Act 1984, s. 14 (1) (4). – Made: 09.05.2002. Coming into force: 27.05.2002. Effect: None. Territorial extent & classification: W. Local – In English and Welsh *Unpublished*

The M4 Motorway (Junction 24, Coldra, Newport) (Temporary 50 mph Speed Limit) Order 2002 No. 2002/1972 (W.201). – Enabling power: Road Traffic Regulation Act 1984, s. 14 (1) (4) (7). – Made: 19.07.2002. Coming into force: 24.07.2002. Effect: None. Territorial extent & classification: W. Local – In English and Welsh *Unpublished*

The M4 Motorway (Junction 24, Coldra, Newport) (Temporary Prohibition of Vehicles) Order 2002 No. 2002/2328 (W.233). – Enabling power: Road Traffic Regulation Act 1984, s. 14 (1) (4) (7). – Made: 17.05.2002. Coming into force: 17.06.2002. Effect: None. Territorial extent & classification: W. Local. – In English and Welsh *Unpublished*

The M4 Motorway (Junction 24, Coldra Viaduct, Newport) (Temporary Prohibition of Vehicles) Order 2002 No. 2002/698 (W.77). – Enabling power: Road Traffic Regulation Act 1984, s. 14 (1) (4) (7). – Made: 13.03.2002. Coming into force: 17.03.2002. Effect: None. Territorial extent & classification: W. Local – In English and Welsh *Unpublished*

The M4 Motorway (Junction 25A, Grove Park, Newport County Borough) (Temporary Prohibition of Vehicles) Order 2002 No. 2002/1482 (W.150). – Enabling power: Road Traffic Regulation Act 1984, s. 14 (1) (4) (7). – Made: 31.05.2002. Coming into force: 24.06.2002. Effect: None. Territorial extent & classification: W. Local. – In English and Welsh *Unpublished*

The M4 Motorway (Junction 25, Caerleon, Newport) (Temporary Prohibition of Vehicles) Order 2002 No. 2002/154 (W.21). – Enabling power: Road Traffic Regulation Act 1984, s. 14. – Made: 10.01.2002. Coming into force: 14.01.2002. Effect: None. Territorial extent & classification: W. Local. – In English and Welsh *Unpublished*

The M4 Motorway (Junction 25, Caerleon, Newport County Borough) (Temporary Prohibition of Vehicles) Order 2002 No. 2002/1481 (W.149). – Enabling power: Road Traffic Regulation Act 1984, s. 14 (1) (4) (7). – Made: 31.05.2002. Coming into force: 10.06.2002. Effect: None. Territorial extent & classification: W. Local – In English and Welsh *Unpublished*

The M4 Motorway (Junction 26, Malpas, Newport) (Temporary Prohibition of Vehicles) Order 2002 No. 2002/1557 (W.154). – Enabling power: Road Traffic Regulation Act 1984, s. 14 (1) (4). – Made: 06.06.2002. Coming into force: 10.06.2002. Effect: None. Territorial extent & classification: W. Local – In English and Welsh *Unpublished*

The M4 Motorway Junction 27 Highcross and Junction 28 Tredegar Park, Newport) (Temporary Prohibition of Vehicles) Order 2002 No. 2002/474 (W.59). – Enabling power: Road Traffic Regulation Act 1984, s. 14 (1) (4). – Made: 26.02.2002. Coming into force: 01.03.2002, at 20.00 hours. Effect: None. Territorial extent & classification: W. Local – In English and Welsh *Unpublished*

The M4 Motorway (Junction 30, Pentwyn, Cardiff) (Temporary Prohibition of Vehicles) Order 2002 No. 2002/2519 (W.247). – Enabling power: Road Traffic Regulation Act 1984, s. 14 (1) (4). – Made: 03.10.2002. Coming into force: 08.10.2002. Effect: None. Territorial extent & classification: W. Local – In English and Welsh *Unpublished*

The M4 Motorway (Junction 33, Capel Llanilltern, Cardiff) (Temporary Prohibition of Vehicles) Order 2002 No. 2002/278 (W.31). – Enabling power: Road Traffic Regulation Act 1984, s. 14 (1) (4). – Made: 29.01.2002. Coming into force: 03.02.2002. Effect: None. Territorial extent & classification: W. Local. – In English and Welsh *Unpublished*

The M4 Motorway (Junction 34, Miskin Interchange, Rhondda Cynon Taff) (Temporary Prohibition of Vehicles) Order 2002 No. 2002/106 (W.11). – Enabling power: Road Traffic Regulation Act 1984, s. 14 (1) (4). – Made: 02.01.2002. Coming into force: 12.01.2002. Effect: None. Territorial extent & classification: W. Local. – In English and Welsh *Unpublished*

The M4 Motorway (Junction 41, Pentyla, Neath Port Talbot) (Temporary Prohibition of Vehicles) Order 2002 No. 2002/310 (W.36). – Enabling power: Road Traffic Regulation Act 1984, s. 14 (1) (4). – Made: 07.02.2002. Coming into force: 17.02.2002. Effect: None. Territorial extent & classification: W. Local – In English and Welsh *Unpublished*

The M4 Motorway (Junction 43 Eastbound On-slip Road, Llandarcy, Neath Port Talbot) (Temporary Prohibition of Vehicles) Order 2002 No. 2002/2465 (W.241). – Enabling power: Road Traffic Regulation Act 1984, s. 14 (1) (4). – Made: 24.09.2002. Coming into force: 28.09.2002. Effect: None. Territorial extent & classification: W. Local. – In English and Welsh *Unpublished*

The M4 Motorway (Junction 43, Llandarcy, Neath Port Talbot) (Temporary Prohibition of Vehicles) Order 2002 No. 2002/2365 (W.236). – Enabling power: Road Traffic Regulation Act 1984, s. 14 (1) (4) (7). – Made: 12.09.2002. Coming into force: 14.09.2002. Effect: None. Territorial extent & classification: W. Local – In English and Welsh *Unpublished*

The M4 Motorway (Junction 44, Lon-Las, City and County of Swansea) (Temporary Prohibition of Vehicles and 30 mph Speed Limit) Order 2002 No. 2002/2305 (W.230). – Enabling power: Road Traffic Regulation Act 1984, s. 14 (1) (4) (7). – Made: 05.09.2002. Coming into force: 15.09.2002. Effect: None. Territorial extent & classification: W. Local – In English and Welsh *Unpublished*

The M4 Motorway (Junction 45, Swansea) (Temporary 30 mph Speed Limit) Order 2002 No. 2002/2399 (W.238). – Enabling power: Road Traffic Regulation Act 1984, s. 14 (1) (4) (7). – Made: 13.09.2002. Coming into force: 15.09.2002. Effect: None. Territorial extent & classification: W. Local – In English and Welsh *Unpublished*

The M4 Motorway (Westbound Entry Slip Road, Junction 28, Tredegar Park, Newport) (Temporary Prohibition of Vehicles) Order 2002 No. 2002/1284 (W.127). – Enabling power: Road Traffic Regulation Act 1984, s. 14 (1) (4). – Made: 30.04.2002. Coming into force: 20.05.2002. Effect: None. Territorial extent & classification: W. Local. – In English and Welsh *Unpublished*

The Shrewsbury - Dolgellau Trunk Road (A458) (Cefn Railway Bridge, Tre-Wern, Powys) (Temporary Prohibition of Vehicles) Order 2002 No. 2002/239 (W.28). – Enabling power: Road Traffic Regulation Act 1984, s. 14 (1) (4). – Made: 05.02.2002. Coming into force: 11.02.2002. Effect: None. Territorial extent & classification: W. Local – In English and Welsh *Unpublished*

The A470 Trunk Road (Llan Ffestiniog, Gwynedd) (Temporary Prohibition of Vehicles) Order 2002 No. 2002/2751 (W.262). – Enabling power: Road Traffic Regulation Act 1984, s. 16A (2) (5) (9). – Made: 04.11.2002. Coming into force: 12.11.2002. Effect: None. Territorial extent & classification: W. Local – In English and Welsh *Unpublished*

The M4 Motorway (Junction 46, Pant Lasau Bridge, Neath Port Talbot) (Temporary Prohibition of Vehicles and 50 mph Speed Limit) Order 2002 No. 2002/2378 (W.237). – Enabling power: Road Traffic Regulation Act 1984, s. 14 (1) (4) (7). – Made: 13.09.2002. Coming into force: 14.09.2002. Effect: None. Territorial extent & classification: W. Local – In English and Welsh *Unpublished*

Sea fisheries, England

The Sea Fishing (Enforcement of Community Conservation Measures) (Amendment) Order 2002 No. 2002/426. – Enabling power: Fisheries Act 1981, s. 30 (2). – Issued: 18.03.2002. Made: 21.02.2002. Laid: 04.03.2002. Coming into force: 26.03.2002. Effect: S.I. 2000/1081 amended. Territorial extent & classification:E/NI. General. – 4p.: 30 cm. – EC note: This Order updates the definition of "the Council Regulation" in the 2000 Order to take account of the amendment of REG 850/98 by 812/2000, 1298/2000 and 724/2000 and also makes provision for the enforcement of art. 2 of REG 2549/2000 concerning technical measures for the recovery of the stock of cod in the Irish Sea (ICES Division VIIa), as amended by 1456/2001 and arts. 4 to 8 of 2056/2001 – 0 11 039461 5 *£1.75*

The Sea Fishing (Enforcement of Community Quota and Third Country Fishing Measures) Order 2002 No. 2002/272. – Enabling power: Fisheries Act 1981, s. 30 (2). – Issued: 12.03.2002. Made: 08.02.2002. Laid: 13.02.2002. Coming into force: 08.03.2002. Effect: S.I. 2001/1631 revoked except insofar as they form part of the law of Scotland or have effect in relation to Wales. Territorial extent & classification: E/NI. General. – With correction slip dated March 2002. – EC note: Makes provision for enforcement of certain enforceable Community restrictions & other obligations relating to sea fishing by both Community & third country vessels set out in Reg. No. 2555/2001. – 12p.: 30 cm. – Revoked by S.I. 2003/772 (ISBN 0110454685) in relation to England – 0 11 039425 9 *£2.50*

The A4060 Trunk Road (Dowlais Top, Merthyr Tydfil) (Temporary Prohibition of Cyclists and 40 mph Speed Limit) Order 2002 No. 2002/1148 (W.121). – Enabling power: Road Traffic Regulation Act 1984, s. 14 (1) (4). – Made: 18.04.2002. Coming into force: 22.04.2002. Effect: None. Territorial extent & classification: W. Local – In English and Welsh *Unpublished*

The Fishguard - Bangor Trunk Road (A487) (Bridge Street, Aberystwyth, Ceredigion) (Temporary Prohibition of Vehicles) Order 2002 No. 2002/1041 (W.112). – Enabling power: Road Traffic Regulation Act 1984, s. 14 (1) (4). – Made: 19.03.2002. Coming into force: 22.03.2002. Effect: None. Territorial extent & classification: W. Local – In English and Welsh *Unpublished*

The M4 Motorway and A4232 Trunk Road (Junction 33, Capel Llanilltern, Cardiff) (Temporary 30 mph Speed Limit) Order 2002 No. 2002/204 (W.27). – Enabling power: Road Traffic Regulation Act 1984, s. 14 (1) (4) (7). – Made: 29.01.2002. Coming into force: 03.02.2002. Effect: None. Territorial extent & classification: W. Local – In English and Welsh *Unpublished*

The M4 Motorway (Brynglas Tunnels and Junction 26 (Malpas), Newport) (Temporary Prohibition of Vehicles and 40 mph Speed Limit) Order 2002 No. 2002/2156 (W.217). – Enabling power: Road Traffic Regulation Act 1984, s. 14. – Made: 15.08.2002. Coming into force: 16.08.2002. Effect: None. Territorial extent & classification: W. Local. – In English and Welsh *Unpublished*

The M4 Motorway (Brynglas Tunnels, Newport) (Temporary Prohibition of Vehicles and 40 mph Speed Limit) (No. 2) Order 2002 No. 2002/669 (W.71). – Enabling power: Road Traffic Regulation Act 1984, s. 14 (1) (4) (7). – Made: 25.02.2002. Coming into force: 04.02.2002. Effect: None. Territorial extent & classification: W. Local – In English and Welsh *Unpublished*

The M4 Motorway (Brynglas Tunnels, Newport) (Temporary Prohibition of Vehicles and 40 mph Speed Limit) Order 2002 No. 2002/104 (W.10). – Enabling power: Road Traffic Regulation Act 1984, s. 14 (1) (4) (7). – Made: 02.01.2002. Coming into force: 11.01.2002. Effect: None. Territorial extent & classification: W. Local. – In English and Welsh *Unpublished*

The M4 Motorway (Eastbound and Westbound Entry Slip Roads, Junction 27, High Cross, Newport) (Temporary Prohibition of Vehicles) Order 2002 No. 2002/1283 (W.126). – Enabling power: Road Traffic Regulation Act 1984, s. 14 (1) (4). – Made: 30.04.2002. Coming into force: 07.05.2002. Effect: None. Territorial extent & classification: W. Local. – In English and Welsh *Unpublished*

The M4 Motorway (Eastbound and Westbound Slip Roads at Junction 45, Ynysforgan, Swansea) (Temporary Prohibition of Vehicles) Order 2002 No. 2002/2721 (W.259). – Enabling power: Road Traffic Regulation Act 1984, s. 14 (1) (4). – Made: 24.10.2002. Coming into force: 02.11.2002. Effect: None. Territorial extent & classification: W. Local – In English and Welsh *Unpublished*

The M4 Motorway (Eastbound Entry Slip Road, Junction 28, Tredegar Park, Newport) (Temporary Prohibition of Vehicles) Order 2002 No. 2002/1404 (W.141). – Enabling power: Road Traffic Regulation Act 1984, s. 14 (1) (4). – Made: 09.05.2002. Coming into force: 27.05.2002. Effect: None. Territorial extent & classification: W. Local – In English and Welsh *Unpublished*

The M4 Motorway (Junction 24, Coldra, Newport) (Temporary 50 mph Speed Limit) Order 2002 No. 2002/1972 (W.201). – Enabling power: Road Traffic Regulation Act 1984, s. 14 (1) (4) (7). – Made: 19.07.2002. Coming into force: 24.07.2002. Effect: None. Territorial extent & classification: W. Local – In English and Welsh *Unpublished*

The M4 Motorway (Junction 24, Coldra, Newport) (Temporary Prohibition of Vehicles) Order 2002 No. 2002/2328 (W.233). – Enabling power: Road Traffic Regulation Act 1984, s. 14 (1) (4) (7). – Made: 17.05.2002. Coming into force: 17.06.2002. Effect: None. Territorial extent & classification: W. Local. – In English and Welsh *Unpublished*

The M4 Motorway (Junction 24, Coldra Viaduct, Newport) (Temporary Prohibition of Vehicles) Order 2002 No. 2002/698 (W.77). – Enabling power: Road Traffic Regulation Act 1984, s. 14 (1) (4) (7). – Made: 13.03.2002. Coming into force: 17.03.2002. Effect: None. Territorial extent & classification: W. Local – In English and Welsh *Unpublished*

The M4 Motorway (Junction 25A, Grove Park, Newport County Borough) (Temporary Prohibition of Vehicles) Order 2002 No. 2002/1482 (W.150). – Enabling power: Road Traffic Regulation Act 1984, s. 14 (1) (4) (7). – Made: 31.05.2002. Coming into force: 24.06.2002. Effect: None. Territorial extent & classification: W. Local. – In English and Welsh *Unpublished*

The M4 Motorway (Junction 25, Caerleon, Newport) (Temporary Prohibition of Vehicles) Order 2002 No. 2002/154 (W.21). – Enabling power: Road Traffic Regulation Act 1984, s. 14. – Made: 10.01.2002. Coming into force: 14.01.2002. Effect: None. Territorial extent & classification: W. Local. – In English and Welsh *Unpublished*

The M4 Motorway (Junction 25, Caerleon, Newport County Borough) (Temporary Prohibition of Vehicles) Order 2002 No. 2002/1481 (W.149). – Enabling power: Road Traffic Regulation Act 1984, s. 14 (1) (4) (7). – Made: 31.05.2002. Coming into force: 10.06.2002. Effect: None. Territorial extent & classification: W. Local – In English and Welsh *Unpublished*

The M4 Motorway (Junction 26, Malpas, Newport) (Temporary Prohibition of Vehicles) Order 2002 No. 2002/1557 (W.154). – Enabling power: Road Traffic Regulation Act 1984, s. 14 (1) (4). – Made: 06.06.2002. Coming into force: 10.06.2002. Effect: None. Territorial extent & classification: W. Local – In English and Welsh *Unpublished*

The M4 Motorway Junction 27 Highcross and Junction 28 Tredegar Park, Newport) (Temporary Prohibition of Vehicles) Order 2002 No. 2002/474 (W.59). – Enabling power: Road Traffic Regulation Act 1984, s. 14 (1) (4). – Made: 26.02.2002. Coming into force: 01.03.2002, at 20.00 hours. Effect: None. Territorial extent & classification: W. Local – In English and Welsh *Unpublished*

The M4 Motorway (Junction 30, Pentwyn, Cardiff) (Temporary Prohibition of Vehicles) Order 2002 No. 2002/2519 (W.247). – Enabling power: Road Traffic Regulation Act 1984, s. 14 (1) (4). – Made: 03.10.2002. Coming into force: 08.10.2002. Effect: None. Territorial extent & classification: W. Local – In English and Welsh *Unpublished*

The M4 Motorway (Junction 33, Capel Llanilltern, Cardiff) (Temporary Prohibition of Vehicles) Order 2002 No. 2002/278 (W.31). – Enabling power: Road Traffic Regulation Act 1984, s. 14 (1) (4). – Made: 29.01.2002. Coming into force: 03.02.2002. Effect: None. Territorial extent & classification: W. Local. – In English and Welsh *Unpublished*

The M4 Motorway (Junction 34, Miskin Interchange, Rhondda Cynon Taff) (Temporary Prohibition of Vehicles) Order 2002 No. 2002/106 (W.11). – Enabling power: Road Traffic Regulation Act 1984, s. 14 (1) (4). – Made: 02.01.2002. Coming into force: 12.01.2002. Effect: None. Territorial extent & classification: W. Local. – In English and Welsh *Unpublished*

The M4 Motorway (Junction 41, Pentyla, Neath Port Talbot) (Temporary Prohibition of Vehicles) Order 2002 No. 2002/310 (W.36). – Enabling power: Road Traffic Regulation Act 1984, s. 14 (1) (4). – Made: 07.02.2002. Coming into force: 17.02.2002. Effect: None. Territorial extent & classification: W. Local – In English and Welsh *Unpublished*

The M4 Motorway (Junction 43 Eastbound On-slip Road, Llandarcy, Neath Port Talbot) (Temporary Prohibition of Vehicles) Order 2002 No. 2002/2465 (W.241). – Enabling power: Road Traffic Regulation Act 1984, s. 14 (1) (4). – Made: 24.09.2002. Coming into force: 28.09.2002. Effect: None. Territorial extent & classification: W. Local. – In English and Welsh *Unpublished*

The M4 Motorway (Junction 43, Llandarcy, Neath Port Talbot) (Temporary Prohibition of Vehicles) Order 2002 No. 2002/2365 (W.236). – Enabling power: Road Traffic Regulation Act 1984, s. 14 (1) (4) (7). – Made: 12.09.2002. Coming into force: 14.09.2002. Effect: None. Territorial extent & classification: W. Local – In English and Welsh *Unpublished*

The M4 Motorway (Junction 44, Lon-Las, City and County of Swansea) (Temporary Prohibition of Vehicles and 30 mph Speed Limit) Order 2002 No. 2002/2305 (W.230). – Enabling power: Road Traffic Regulation Act 1984, s. 14 (1) (4) (7). – Made: 05.09.2002. Coming into force: 15.09.2002. Effect: None. Territorial extent & classification: W. Local – In English and Welsh *Unpublished*

The M4 Motorway (Junction 45, Swansea) (Temporary 30 mph Speed Limit) Order 2002 No. 2002/2399 (W.238). – Enabling power: Road Traffic Regulation Act 1984, s. 14 (1) (4) (7). – Made: 13.09.2002. Coming into force: 15.09.2002. Effect: None. Territorial extent & classification: W. Local – In English and Welsh *Unpublished*

The M4 Motorway (Westbound Entry Slip Road, Junction 28, Tredegar Park, Newport) (Temporary Prohibition of Vehicles) Order 2002 No. 2002/1284 (W.127). – Enabling power: Road Traffic Regulation Act 1984, s. 14 (1) (4). – Made: 30.04.2002. Coming into force: 20.05.2002. Effect: None. Territorial extent & classification: W. Local. – In English and Welsh *Unpublished*

The Shrewsbury - Dolgellau Trunk Road (A458) (Cefn Railway Bridge, Tre-Wern, Powys) (Temporary Prohibition of Vehicles) Order 2002 No. 2002/239 (W.28). – Enabling power: Road Traffic Regulation Act 1984, s. 14 (1) (4). – Made: 05.02.2002. Coming into force: 11.02.2002. Effect: None. Territorial extent & classification: W. Local – In English and Welsh *Unpublished*

The A470 Trunk Road (Llan Ffestiniog, Gwynedd) (Temporary Prohibition of Vehicles) Order 2002 No. 2002/2751 (W.262). – Enabling power: Road Traffic Regulation Act 1984, s. 16A (2) (5) (9). – Made: 04.11.2002. Coming into force: 12.11.2002. Effect: None. Territorial extent & classification: W. Local – In English and Welsh *Unpublished*

The M4 Motorway (Junction 46, Pant Lasau Bridge, Neath Port Talbot) (Temporary Prohibition of Vehicles and 50 mph Speed Limit) Order 2002 No. 2002/2378 (W.237). – Enabling power: Road Traffic Regulation Act 1984, s. 14 (1) (4) (7). – Made: 13.09.2002. Coming into force: 14.09.2002. Effect: None. Territorial extent & classification: W. Local – In English and Welsh *Unpublished*

Sea fisheries, England

The Sea Fishing (Enforcement of Community Conservation Measures) (Amendment) Order 2002 No. 2002/426. – Enabling power: Fisheries Act 1981, s. 30 (2). – Issued: 18.03.2002. Made: 21.02.2002. Laid: 04.03.2002. Coming into force: 26.03.2002. Effect: S.I. 2000/1081 amended. Territorial extent & classification:E/NI. General. – 4p.: 30 cm. – EC note: This Order updates the definition of "the Council Regulation" in the 2000 Order to take account of the amendment of REG 850/98 by 812/2000, 1298/2000 and 724/2000 and also makes provision for the enforcement of art. 2 of REG 2549/2000 concerning technical measures for the recovery of the stock of cod in the Irish Sea (ICES Division VIIa), as amended by 1456/2001 and arts. 4 to 8 of 2056/2001 – 0 11 039461 5 *£1.75*

The Sea Fishing (Enforcement of Community Quota and Third Country Fishing Measures) Order 2002 No. 2002/272. – Enabling power: Fisheries Act 1981, s. 30 (2). – Issued: 12.03.2002. Made: 08.02.2002. Laid: 13.02.2002. Coming into force: 08.03.2002. Effect: S.I. 2001/1631 revoked except insofar as they form part of the law of Scotland or have effect in relation to Wales. Territorial extent & classification: E/NI. General. – With correction slip dated March 2002. – EC note: Makes provision for enforcement of certain enforceable Community restrictions & other obligations relating to sea fishing by both Community & third country vessels set out in Reg. No. 2555/2001. – 12p.: 30 cm. – Revoked by S.I. 2003/772 (ISBN 0110454685) in relation to England – 0 11 039425 9 *£2.50*

Sea fisheries, England: Conservation of sea fish

The Shrimp Fishing Nets Order 2002 No. 2002/2870. – Enabling power: Sea Fish (Conservation) Act 1967, ss. 3 (1), 15 (3). – Issued: 04.12.2002. Made: 18.11.2002. Laid: 21.11.2002. Coming into force: 01.01.2003. Effect: None. Territorial extent and classification: E. General– 4p.: 30 cm. – EC note: Regulates the carriage and use of any fishing nets with mesh size between 16 and 31 mm., measured in accordance with Commission Regulation (EEC) No. 2108/1984. It also sets out the national provisions called for by Article 25 of Council Regulation (EC) No. 850/98 by specifying veil nets and sorting grids as the types of device required to be used – 0 11 044081 1   £1.75

Sea fisheries, England and Wales

The Diseases of Fish (Control) (Amendment) (England and Wales) Regulations 2002 No. 2002/284. – Enabling power: European Communities Act 1972, s. 2 (2). – Issued: 22.03.2002. Made: 11.02.2002. Laid: 12.02.2002. Coming into force: 10.03.2002. Effect: S.I. 1994/1447 amended. Territorial extent & classification: E/W. General. – 8p.: 30 cm. – EC note: Implement in relation to England and Wales amendments to "the directive" (Dir. 93/53/EEC) made by directive 2000/27/EC – 0 11 039529 8   £2.00

Sea fisheries, Northern Ireland

The Sea Fisheries (Northern Ireland) Order 2002 No. 2002/790. – Enabling power: Northern Ireland Act 1998, ss. 6 (4), 86 (1) (3) (4) (5). – Issued: 09.04.2002. Made: 26.03.2002. Coming into force: 28.03.2002. Effect: 1962 c.31; 1966 c.17 (NI); 1968 c.77; 1976 c.86; 1981 c.29; S.I. 1981/227 (NI); 1983 c. 8 modified. Territorial extent & classification: NI. General. – Supersedes draft S.I. (ISBN 0110392442) issued 07/02/2002. – 12p.: 30 cm. – 0 11 039631 6   £2.50

The Sea Fishing (Enforcement of Community Conservation Measures) (Amendment) Order 2002 No. 2002/426. – Enabling power: Fisheries Act 1981, s. 30 (2). – Issued: 18.03.2002. Made: 21.02.2002. Laid: 04.03.2002. Coming into force: 26.03.2002. Effect: S.I. 2000/1081 amended. Territorial extent & classification:E/NI. General. – 4p.: 30 cm. – EC note: This Order updates the definition of "the Council Regulation" in the 2000 Order to take account of the amendment of REG 850/98 by 812/2000, 1298/2000 and 724/2000 and also makes provision for the enforcement of art. 2 of REG 2549/2000 concerning technical measures for the recovery of the stock of cod in the Irish Sea (ICES Division VIIa), as amended by 1456/2001 and arts. 4 to 8 of 2056/2001 – 0 11 039461 5   £1.75

The Sea Fishing (Enforcement of Community Quota and Third Country Fishing Measures) Order 2002 No. 2002/272. – Enabling power: Fisheries Act 1981, s. 30 (2). – Issued: 12.03.2002. Made: 08.02.2002. Laid: 13.02.2002. Coming into force: 08.03.2002. Effect: S.I. 2001/1631 revoked except insofar as they form part of the law of Scotland or have effect in relation to Wales. Territorial extent & classification: E/NI. General. – With correction slip dated March 2002. – EC note: Makes provision for enforcement of certain enforceable Community restrictions & other obligations relating to sea fishing by both Community & third country vessels set out in Reg. No. 2555/2001. – 12p.: 30 cm. – Revoked by S.I. 2003/772 (ISBN 0110454685) in relation to England – 0 11 039425 9   £2.50

Sea fisheries, Wales

The Sea Fishing (Enforcement of Community Satellite Monitoring Measures) (Wales) Order 2000 Amendment Regulations 2002 No. 2002/677 (W.74). – Enabling power: European Communities Act 1972, s. 2 (2). – Issued: 05.04.2002. Made: 12.03.2002. Coming into force: 01.04.2002. Effect: S.I. 2000/1078 (W.71) amended. Territorial extent & classification: W. General. – 8p.: 30 cm. – In English & Welsh. Welsh title: Rheoliadau Diwygio Gorchymyn Pysgota Môr (Gorfodi Mesurau Cymunedol ar gyfer Monitro â Lloeren) (Cymru) 2000 2002 – 0 11 090454 0   £2.00

Sea fisheries, Wales: Conservation of sea fish

The Lobsters and Crawfish (Prohibition of Fishing and Landing) (Wales) Order 2002 No. 2002/676 (W.73). – Enabling power: Sea Fish (Conservation) Act 1967, ss. 5 (1), 6 (1), 15 (3). – Issued: 03.05.2002. Made: 12.03.2002. Coming into force: 01.04.2002. Effect: None. Territorial extent & classification: W. General. – 8p.: 30 cm. – In English & Welsh. Welsh title: Gorchymyn Cimychiaid a Chimychiaid Cochion (Gwahardd eu Pysgota a'u Glanio) (Cymru) 2002 – 0 11 090476 1   £2.00

The Undersized Spider Crabs (Wales) Order 2002 No. 2002/1897 (W.198). – Enabling power: Sea Fish (Conservation) Act 1967, ss. 1 (1) (6), 15 (3). – Issued: 12.08.2002. Made: 18.07.2002. Coming into force: 05.08.2002. Effect: None. Territorial extent & classification: W. General. – In English and Welsh. Welsh title: Gorchymyn Crancod Heglog Rhy Fach (Cymru) 2002. – 8p., ill.: 30 cm. – EC note: Made in reliance on art. 46 (1) of REG (EC) 850/98 – 0 11 090543 1   £2.00

Sea fisheries, Wales: Sea fish industry

The Fisheries and Aquaculture Structures (Grants) (Wales) Regulations 2002 No. 2002/675 (W.72). – Enabling power: European Communities Act 1972, s. 2 (2). – Issued: 19.04.2002. Made: 12.03.2002. Coming into force: 13.03.2002. Effect: None. Territorial extent & classification: W. General. – 20p.: 30 cm. – In English & Welsh. Welsh title: Rheoliadau Strwythurau Pysgodfeydd a Dyframaethu (Grantiau) (Cymru) 2002 – 0 11 090463 X *£3.50*

Sea fisheries, Wales: Shellfish

The Shellfish (Specification of Crustaceans) (Wales) Regulations 2002 No. 2002/1885 (W.194). – Enabling power: Sea Fisheries (Shellfish) Act 1967, s. 1 (1). – Issued: 22.08.2002. Made: 18.07.2002. Coming into force: 05.08.2002. Effect: None. Territorial extent & classification: W. General. – 4p.: 30 cm. – In English and Welsh. - Welsh title: Rheoliadau Pysgod Cregyn (Dynodi Cramenogion) (Cymru) 2002 – 0 11 090557 1 *£1.75*

The Swansea Bay (Deepdock Limited) Mussel Fishery Order 2002 No. 2002/469 (W.58). – Enabling power: Sea Fisheries (Shellfish) Act 1967, s. 1. – Made: 14.02.2002. Coming into force: 18.02.2002. Effect: None. Territorial extent & classification: W. Local – In English and Welsh *Unpublished*

The Swansea Bay Mussel Fishery (C V and D M Thomas) Order 2002 No. 2002/2226 (W.221). – Enabling power: Sea Fisheries (Shellfish) Act 1967, s. 1. – Made: 28.08.2002. Coming into force: 18.09.2002. Effect: None. Territorial extent & classification: W. Local – In English and Welsh *Unpublished*

Seeds

The Forest Reproductive Material (Great Britain) Regulations 2002 No. 2002/3026. – Enabling power: European Communities Act 1972, s. 2 (2). – Issued: 07.03.2003. Made: 04.12.2002. Laid: 09.12.2002. Coming into force: 01.01.2003. Effect: S.I. 1977/891, 1264; 1992/3078 revoked. Territorial extent & classification: GB. General. – 40p.: 30 cm. – EC note: Implements in Great Britain Council Directive 1999/105/EC on the marketing of forest reproductive material. The Directive replaces Directive 66/404/EEC and Council Directive 71/161/EEC – 0 11 044565 1 *£6.50*

Seeds, England

The Beet Seed (England) Regulations 2002 No. 2002/3171. – Enabling power: Plant Varieties and Seeds Act 1964, ss. 16 (1) (1A) (2) (3) (4) (5) (5A), 36. – Issued: 18.12.2002. Laid: 20.12.2002. Coming into force: 31.01.2003. Effect: S.I. 1993/2006; 1999/1861 revoked in relation to England; S.I. 1985/981 revoked insofar as they apply to England in relation to matters arising under S.I. 1993/2006; S.I. 2002/1563 in relation to matters arising under S.I. 1993/2006; S.I. 2000/1791 revoked. Territorial extent & classification: E. General. – 54p.: 30 cm. – EC note: Implements the provisions of Council Directive 2002/54/EC on the marketing of beet seed, which amended Council Directive 66/400/EEC – 0 11 044855 3 *£7.50*

The Cereal Seed (England) Regulations 2002 No. 2002/3173. – Enabling power: Plant Varieties and Seeds Act 1964, ss. 16 (1) (1A) (2) (3) (4) (5) (5A), 36. – Issued: 19.02.2003. Made: 18.12.2002. Laid: 20.12.2002. Coming into force: 31.01.2003. Effect: S.I. 1993/2005; 1995/1482; 1997/616; 1999/1860 revoked in relation to England; S.I. 1985/981 revoked in so far as they apply to England in relation to matters arising under S.I. 1993/2005; S.I. 2002/1563 revoked in relation to matters arising under S.I. 1993/2005; S.I. 1999/2196; 2000/1793 revoked. Territorial extent & classification: E. General. – 86p.: 30 cm. – EC note: These Regulations continue to implement the provisions of Council Directive 66/402/EEC on the marketing of cereal seed, as last amended by Council Directive 2001/64/EC – 0 11 044857 X *£9.00*

The Fodder Plant Seed (England) Regulations 2002 No. 2002/3172. – Enabling power: Plant Varieties and Seeds Act 1964, ss. 16 (1) (1A) (2) (3) (4) (5) (5A), 36. – Issued: 19.02.2003. Made: 18.12.2002. Laid: 20.12.2002. Coming into force: 31.01.2003. Effect: S.I. 1993/2009, 2529; 1996/1453; 1999/1864 revoked in relation to England; S.I. 1985/981 revoked insofar as they apply to England in relation to matters arising under S.I. 1993/2009; S.I. 2002/1563 revoked in relation to matters arising under S.I. 1993/2009; S.I. 2000/1792 revoked. Territorial extent & classification: E. General. – EC note: These Regulations continue to implement Council Directive 66/401/EEC on the marketing of fodder plant seed, as last amended by Council Directive 2001/64/EC. – 108p.: 30 cm. – 0 11 044856 1 *£10.50*

The Oil and Fibre Plant Seed (England) Regulations 2002 No. 2002/3174. – Enabling power: Plant Varieties and Seeds Act 1964, ss. 16 (1) (1A) (2) (3) (4) (5) (5A), 36. – Issued: 19.02.2003. Made: 18.12.2002. Laid: 20.12.2002. Coming into force: 31.01.2003. Effect: S.I. 1993/2007; 1994/1423; 1996/1451; 1999/1862 revoked in relation to England; S.I. 1985/981 revoked insofar as they apply to England in relation to matters arising under S.I. 1993/2007; S.I. 2002/1563 revoked in relation to matters arising under S.I. 1993/2007; S.I. 2000/1789 revoked. Territorial extent & classification: E. General. – EC note: These Regulations implement Council Directive 2002/57/EC on the marketing of seed of oil and fibre plants, which replaced Council Directive 69/208/EEC. – 86p.: 30 cm. – 0 11 044858 8 *£9.00*

The Seed (Registration, Licensing and Enforcement) (England) Regulations 2002 No. 2002/3176. – Enabling power: Plant Varieties and Seeds Act 1964, ss. 16 (1) (1A) (2) (3) (4) (5A), 24 (5), 26 (2) (3), 36. – Issued: 05.03.2003. Made: 18.12.2002. Laid: 20.12.2002. Coming into force: 31.01.2003. Effect: S.I. 1985/980 revoked in relation to England & 1985/981 revoked in relation to matters arising under S.I. 1985/980 as applied to England. (These revocations do not apply in relation to seed harvested on or before 31.12.2002. until 01.07.2003). Territorial extent & classification: E. General. – 40p.: 30 cm. – 0 11 044992 4 £6.50

The Seeds (Fees) (Amendment) (England) Regulations 2002 No. 2002/1563. – Enabling power: Plant Varieties and Seeds Act 1964, ss. 16 (1) (1A) (e), 36. – Issued: 12.07.2002. Made: 12.06.2002. Laid: 28.06.2002. Coming into force: 23.07.2002. Effect: S.I. 1985/981 amended. Territorial extent & classification: E. General. – 12p.: 30 cm. – Revoked by S.I. 2002/3171 (ISBN 0110448553) in relation to matters arising under S.I. 1993/2006 & Revoked by S.I. 2002/3172 (ISBN 0110448561) in relation to matters arising under S.I. 1993/2009 & Revoked by S.I. 2002/3173 (ISBN 011044857X) in relation to matters arising under S.I. 1993/2005 & Revoked by S.I. 2002/3174 (ISBN 0110448588) in relation to matters arising under S.I. 1993/2007 & Revoked by S.I. 2002/3175 (ISBN 011044860X) in relation to matters arising under S.I. 1993/2008 – 0 11 042451 4 £2.50

The Vegetable Seed (England) Regulations 2002 No. 2002/3175. – Enabling power: Plant Varieties and Seeds Act 1964, ss. 16 (1) (1A) (2) (3) (4) (5) (5A), 36. – Issued: 19.02.2003. Made: 18.12.2002. Laid: 20.12.2002. Coming into force: 31.01.2003. Effect: S.I. 1993/2008; 1996/1452; 1999/1863 revoked in relation to England; S.I. 1985/981 revoked in so far as they apply to England in relation to matters arising under S.I. 1993/2008; S.I. 2002/1563 revoked in relation to matters arising under S.I. 1993/2008; S.I. 2000/1790 revoked. Territorial extent & classification: E. General. – 64p.: 30 cm. – EC note: These Regulations implement the provisions of Council Directive 2002/55/EC on the marketing of vegetable seed, which replaced Council Directive 70/458/EEC – 0 11 044860 X £7.50

Seeds, England and Wales

The Plant Varieties and Seeds Tribunal (Amendment) (England and Wales) Rules 2002 No. 2002/3198. – Enabling power: Plant Varieties Act 1997, s. 42, sch. 3, para. 13. – Issued: 29.01.2003. Made: 18.12.2002. Laid: 20.12.2002. Coming into force: 27.01.2003. Effect: S.I. 1974/1136 amended in relation to England & Wales. Territorial extent & classification: E/W. General. – 4p.: 30 cm. – 0 11 044660 7 £1.75

Seeds, Wales

The Seeds (Fees) (Amendment) (Wales) (No. 2) Regulations 2002 No. 2002/1870 (W.183). – Enabling power: Plant Varieties and Seeds Act 1964, ss. 16 (1) (1A) (e), 36. – Issued: 12.08.2002. Made: 18.07.2002. Coming into force: 23.07.2002. Effect: S.I. 1985/981 amended in relation to Wales. Territorial extent & classification: W. General. – In English and Welsh. Welsh title: Rheoliadau Hadau (Ffioedd) (Diwygio) (Cymru) (Rhif 2) 2002. – 16p.: 30 cm. – 0 11 090542 3 £3.00

The Seeds (Fees) (Amendment) (Wales) Regulations 2002 No. 2002/1554 (W.152). – Enabling power: Plant Varieties and Seeds Act 1964, ss. 16 (1) (1A) (e), 36. – Issued: 27.06.2002. Made: 11.06.2002. Coming into force: 09.07.2002. Effect: S.I. 1985/981 amended. Territorial extent & classification: W. General. – In English and Welsh. Welsh title: Rheoliadau Hadau (Ffioedd) (Diwygio) (Cymru) 2002. – 4p.: 30 cm. – 0 11 090511 3 £1.75

Social care

The Abolition of the Central Council for Education and Training in Social Work Order 2002 No. 2002/797. – Enabling power: Care Standards Act 2000, ss. 70 (2) to (4), 118 (4) to (6). – Issued: 05.04.2002. Made: 26.03.2002. Coming into force: 01.04.2002. Effect: 1993 c.41; 1998 c.39; 2000 c.36 & S.I. 2001/2561 amended. Territorial extent & classification: EW/S/NI. General. – 2p.: 30 cm. – 0 11 039637 5 £1.50

The Health and Social Care Act 2001 (Commencement No. 9) Order 2002 No. 2002/1312 (C.36). – Enabling power: Health and Social Care Act 2001, s. 70 (2). Bringing into force various provisions of the 2001 Act on 15.04.2002 in accord. with arts. 2, 3. – Issued: 20.05.2002. Made: 14.04.2002. Effect: None. Territorial extent & classification: E/W/S. General. – 4p.: 30 cm. – 0 11 039943 9 £1.75

Social care, England

The Care Standards Act 2000 (Commencement and Transitional Provisions) (Amendment) (England) Order 2002 No. 2002/2001 (C.67). – Enabling power: Care Standards Act 2000, ss. 118 (5) to (7), 122. – Issued: 06.08.2002. Made: 29.07.2002. Effect: S.I. 2001/3852, 4150 amended. Territorial extent & classification: E. General. – The dates appointed for the coming into force of certain provisions of the Act are altered. • The (0.67) part of the number is missing on the document. – [12]p.: 30 cm. – 0 11 042591 X £2.50

The Care Standards Act 2000 (Commencement and Transitional Provisions) (Amendment No. 2) (England) Order 2002 No. 2002/3210 (C.109). – Enabling power: Care Standards Act 2000, ss. 118 (5) to (7), 122. Bringing into operation various provisions of the 2000 Act in accord.with art. 2. – Issued: 17.01.2003. Made: 19.12.2002. Effect: S.I. 2001/3852, 4150 amended. Territorial extent & classification: E. General. – 12p.: 30 cm. – 0 11 044599 6 £2.50

The Care Standards Act 2000 (Commencement No. 12) (England) Order 2002 No. 2002/1245 (C.33). – Enabling power: Care Standards Act 2000, ss. 118 (4) to (6), 122. Bringing into operation various provisions of the 2000 Act on 25.03.2002, 01.04.2002, in accord. with art. 2 (1) (2). – Issued: 10.05.2002. Made: 24.03.2002. Effect: None. Territorial extent & classification: E. General. – 8p.: 30 cm. – 0 11 039910 2 *£2.00*

The Care Standards Act 2000 (Commencement No. 14 (England) and Transitional, Savings and Amendment Provisions) Order 2002 No. 2002/1493 (C.43). – Enabling power: Care Standards Act 2000, ss. 118 (5) to (7), 122. Bringing into operation various provisions of the 2000 Act on 01.04.2002. – Issued: 14.06.2002. Made: 27.03.2002. Effect: S.I. 2001/3852, 4150 amended. Territorial extent & classification: E. General. – 12p.: 30 cm. – 0 11 042340 2 *£2.50*

The Care Standards Act 2000 (Commencement No. 15 (England) and Transitional Provisions) (Amendment) Order 2002 No. 2002/1790 (C.55). – Enabling power: Care Standards Act 2000, ss. 118 (5) to (7), 122. – Issued: 24.07.2002. Made: 31.05.2002. Effect: S.I. 2001/3852, 4150 amended. Territorial extent & classification: E. General. – The dates appointed for the coming into force of certain provisions of the Act are altered. – 8p.: 30 cm. – 0 11 042474 3 *£2.00*

The Care Standards Act 2000 (Establishments and Agencies) (Miscellaneous Amendments) Regulations 2002 No. 2002/865. – Enabling power: Care Standards Act 2000, ss. 12 (2), 22 (1) (2) (a) to (d) (5) (c) (7) (c), 25 (1), 36 (3), 48 (1), 118 (5) to (7) & Children Act 1989, ss. 23 (2) (a) (9), 59 (2), sch. 2, para. 12. – Issued: 09.05.2002. Made: 27.03.2002. Laid: 28.03.2002. Coming into force: 18.04.2002. Effect: S.I. 2001/3965, 3967, 3968, 3969; 2002/57 amended. Territorial extent & classification: E. General. – 8p.: 30 cm. – 0 11 039888 2 *£2.00*

The Domiciliary Care Agencies Regulations 2002 No. 2002/3214. – Enabling power: Care Standards Act 2000, ss. 4 (6), 22 (1) (2) (a) to (d) (f) to (j) (5) (a) (7) (a) to (h) (j), 25, 34 (1), 35, 118 (5) to (7). – Issued: 17.01.2003. Made: 21.12.2002. Laid: 23.12.2002. Coming into force: 01.04.2003. Effect: None. Territorial extent & classification: E. General. – 16p.: 30 cm. – 0 11 044603 8 *£3.00*

The Fostering Services Regulations 2002 No. 2002/57. – Enabling power: Care Standards Act 2000, ss. 22 (1) (2) (a) to (c) (e) to (j) (6) (7) (a) to (h) (j), 25 (1), 34 (1), 48 (1), 52 (1), 118 (5) to (7) & Children Act 1989 ss. 23 (2) (a) (9), 59 (2), 62 (3), sch. 2, para. 12. – Issued: 26.02.2002. Made: 14.01.2002. Laid: 15.01.2002. Coming into force: 01.04.2002. Effect: S.I. 1995/2015; 1997/2308; 1999/2768; 2001/2992 amended & S.I. 1991/910 revoked. Territorial extent & classification: E. General. – 35p.: 30 cm. – 0 11 039364 3 *£6.50*

The National Care Standards Commission (Children's Rights Director) Regulations 2002 No. 2002/1250. – Enabling power: Care Standards Act 2000, sch. 1, para. 10 (2). – Issued: 16.05.2002. Made: 01.05.2002. Laid: 03.05.2002. Coming into force: In accord. with reg. 1 (1). Effect: None. Territorial extent & classification: E. General. – 4p.: 30 cm. – 0 11 039934 X *£1.75*

The National Care Standards Commission (Fees and Frequency of Inspections) (Amendment) (No. 2) Regulations 2002 No. 2002/2070. – Enabling power: Care Standards Act 2000, ss. 12 (2), 16 (3), 31 (7), 118 (5) to (7). – Issued: 12.08.2002. Made: 05.08.2002. Laid: 06.08.2002. Coming into force: 01.09.2002. Effect: S.I. 2001/3980 amended. Territorial extent & classification: E. General. – 2p.: 30 cm. – 0 11 042638 X *£1.50*

The National Care Standards Commission (Fees and Frequency of Inspections) Amendment (No. 3) Regulations 2002 No. 2002/3211. – Enabling power: Care Standards Act 2000, ss. 12 (2), 16 (3), 31 (7), 118 (5) to (7). – Issued: 17.01.2003. Made: 21.12.2002. Laid: 23.12.2002. Coming into force: 01.01.2003. Effect: S.I. 2001/3980 amended. Territorial extent & classification: E. General. – 4p.: 30 cm. – 0 11 044600 3 *£1.75*

The National Care Standards Commission (Fees and Frequency of Inspections) (Amendment) Regulations 2002 No. 2002/1505. – Enabling power: Care Standards Act 2000, ss. 12 (2), 16 (3), 31 (7), 118 (5) to (7). – Issued: 28.06.2002. Made: 10.06.2002. Laid: 10.06.2002. Coming into force: 01.07.2002. Effect: S.I. 2001/3980 amended. Territorial extent & classification: E. General. – 2p.: 30 cm. – 0 11 042390 9 *£1.50*

The Residential Family Centres Regulations 2002 No. 2002/3213. – Enabling power: Care Standards Act 2000, ss. 4 (6), 22 (1) (2) (a) to (d) (f) to (j) (5) (a) to (c) (7) (a) to (j), 25 (1), 34 (1), 35 (1), 118 (5) to (7). – Issued: 16.01.2003. Made: 21.12.2002. Laid: 23.12.2002. Coming into force: 01.04.2003. Effect: None. Territorial extent & classification: E. General. – 24p.: 30 cm. – 0 11 044588 0 *£4.00*

Social care, England and Wales

The Care Standards Act 2000 (Commencement No. 11) Order 2002 No. 2002/629 (C.19). – Enabling power: Care Standards Act 2000, ss. 118 (7), 122. Bringing into operation various provisions of the 2000 Act on 18.03.2002, 01.04.2002, in accord. with art. 2 (2) (3). – Issued: 06.06.2002. Made: 15.03.2002. Effect: None. Territorial extent & classification: E/W. General. – 8p.: 30 cm. – 0 11 042304 6 *£2.00*

The Protection of Children and Vulnerable Adults and Care Standards Tribunal Regulations 2002 No. 2002/816. – Enabling power: Protection of Children Act 1999, s. 9 (2) to (4), sch. para. 2 (4). – Issued: 17.05.2002. Made: 25.03.2002. Laid: 25.03.2002. Coming into force: in accordance with reg. 1 (1). Effect: S.I. 2000/2619 revoked. Territorial extent & classification: E/W. General. – 36p.: 30 cm. – 0 11 039942 0 *£6.50*

Social care, Wales

The Care Homes (Wales) Regulations 2002 No. 2002/324 (W.37). – Enabling power: Care Standards Act 2000, ss. 3 (3), 22 (1) (2) (a) to (d) (f) to (j) (5) (7) (a) to (j) (l), 25 (1), 33, 34 (1), 35, 118 (5) to (7). – Issued: 03.04.2002. Made: 12.02.2002. Coming into force: 01.04.2002. Effect: S.I. 1984/1345, 1578 revoked in relation to Wales. Territorial extent & classification: W. General. – In English & Welsh. Welsh title: Rheoliadau Cartrefi Gofal (Cymru) 2002. – 48p.: 30 cm. – 0 11 090452 4 *£6.50*

The Care Standards Act 2000 (Commencement No. 8 (Wales) and Transitional, Savings and Consequential Provisions) Order 2002 No. 2002/920 (W.108) (C.24). – Enabling power: Care Standards Act 2000, ss. 118 (5) to (7), 119, 122. Bringing into operation various provisions of the 2000 Act on 01.04.2002, in accord. with arts. 2, 3. – Issued: 24.06.2002. Made: 28.03.2002. Effect: S.I. 1996/708 amended. Territorial extent & classification: W. General. – 24p.: 30 cm. – 0 11 090509 1 *£4.00*

The Care Standards Act 2000 (Commencement No. 9) (Wales) Order 2002 No. 2002/1175 (W.123) (C.31). – Enabling power: Care Standards Act 2000, ss 118 (5) (6), 122. Bringing into operation various provisions of the 2000 Act on 30.04.2002. – Issued: 19.06.2002. Made: 25.04.2002. Effect: None. Territorial extent & classification: W. General. – 8p.: 30 cm. – In English and Welsh. Welsh title: Gorchymyn Deddf Safonau Gofal 2000 (Cychwyn Rhif 9) (Cymru) 2002 – 0 11 090504 0 *£2.00*

The Care Standards Act 2000 (Extension of Meaning of "Social Care Worker") (Wales) Regulations 2002 No. 2002/1176 (W.124). – Enabling power: Care Standards Act 2000, ss. 55 (3), 118 (5) (6). – Issued: 20.06.2002. Made: 25.04.2002. Coming into force: 30.04.2002. Effect: None. Territorial extent & classification: W. General. – In English & Welsh. Welsh title: Rheoliadau Deddf Safonau Gofal 2000 (Ehangu Ystyr "Gweithiwr Gofal Cymdeithasol") (Cymru) 2002. – 4p.: 30 cm. – 0 11 090508 3 *£1.75*

The Child Minding and Day Care (Wales) (Amendment) Regulations 2002 No. 2002/2171 (W.218). – Enabling power: Children Act 1989, ss. 79C, 79E, 104 (4). Issued: 29.08.2002. Made: 22.07.2002 at 11.45 am. Coming into force: 22.07.2002 at 12 noon. Effect: S.I. 2002/812, 919 amended. Territorial extent & classification: W. General. – In English & Welsh. Welsh title: Rheoliadau Gwarchod Plant a Gofal Dydd (Cymru) (Diwygio) 2002. – [8]p.: 30 cm. – Revoked by S.I. 2002/2622 (W.254) (ISBN 0110905784) – 0 11 090561 X *£2.00*

The Child Minding and Day Care (Wales) Regulations 2002 No. 2002/812 (W.92). – Enabling power: Children Act 1989, ss. 79C, 104 (4). – Issued: 01.05.2002. Made: 21.03.2002 at 1600 hours. Coming into force: 01.04.2002. Effect: None. Territorial extent & classification: W. General. – In English & Welsh. Welsh title: Rheoliadau Gwarchod Plant a Gofal Dydd (Cymru) 2002. – 28p.: 30 cm. – 0 11 090477 X *£4.50*

The Children Act 1989 and the Care Standards Act 2000 (Miscellaneous Regulations) (Amendment) (Wales) (No. 2) Regulations 2002 No. 2002/2935 (W.277). – Enabling power: Children Act 1989, ss. 23 (2) (a) (f) (5) (9), 23A (3), 25 (2) (7), 26 (1) (2) (5) (6), 51 (4), 59 (2) to (5), 104 (4), sch. 2, paras. 13, 14, sch. 4, para. 4 (1) (a), sch. 5, para. 7 (1) (a), sch. 6, para. 10 (1) (a) (2) (l) & Care Standards Act 2000, ss. 3 (3), 12 (2) (a), 16 (1) (a) (3), 22 (1), 118 (6). – Issued: 20.12.2002. Made: 27.11.2002. Coming into force: 31.12.2002. Effect: S.I. 1991/890, 893, 894, 895, 1505, 1507, 2034; 2001/2189; 2002/324, 919, 921 amended. Territorial extent & classification: W. General. – 8p.: 30 cm. – In English and Welsh. Welsh title: Rheoliadau Deddf Plant 1989 a Deddf Safonau Gofal 2000 (Rheoliadau Amrywiol) (Diwygio) (Cymru) (Rhif 2) 2002 – 0 11 090601 2 *£2.00*

The Children Act 1989 and the Care Standards Act 2000 (Miscellaneous Regulations) (Amendment) (Wales) Regulations 2002 No. 2002/2622 (W.254). – Enabling power: Care Standards Act 2000, ss. 12 (2) (a), 16 (1) (a), 22 (1), (2) (a) (b), (7) (c), 118 (5) (6) & Children Act 1989, ss. 79C (2) (3) (b) (f) (g), 79E (2) (a), 104 (4). – Issued: 19.11.2002. Made: 17.10.2002. Coming into force: 18.10.2002. Effect: S.I. 2002/324 (W.37), 325 (W.38), 327 (W.40), 812 (W.192), 919 (W.107) amended & S.I. 2002/2171 (W.218) revoked. Territorial extent & classification: W. General. – 16p.: 30 cm. – 0 11 090578 4 *£3.00*

The Children's Homes (Wales) Regulations 2002 No. 2002/327 (W.40). – Enabling power: Care Standards Act 2000, ss. 1 (4), 22 (1) (2) (a) to (d) (f) to (j) (5) (a) (c) (7) (a) to (h) (j) (8) (c), 25 (1), 33, 34 (1), 35, 118 (5) to (7). – Issued: 28.03.2002. Made: 12.02.2002. Coming into force: 01.04.2002. Effect: S.I. 1993/3069; 1997/2308 amended & 1991/1506; 1994/1511 revoked in relation to Wales & S.I. 2001/140 revoked. Territorial extent & classification: W. General. – In English & Welsh. Welsh title: Rheoliadau Cartrefi Plant (Cymru) 2002. – 48p.: 30 cm. – 0 11 090448 6 *£6.50*

The Inspection of Boarding Schools and Colleges (Powers and Fees) (Wales) Regulations 2002 No. 2002/3161 (W.296). – Enabling power: Children Act 1989, ss. 87 (6), 87D (2), 104 (4). – Issued: 15.01.2003. Made: 17.12.2002. Coming into force: 01.02.2003. Effect: S.I. 2002/921 (W.109) amended & S.I. 1991/975 revoked in relation to Wales. Territorial extent & classification: W. General. – 8p.: 30 cm. – In English and Welsh. Welsh title: Rheoliadau Arolygu Ysgolion a Cholegau Preswyl (Pwerau a Ffioedd) (Cymru) 2002 – 0 11 090616 0 *£2.00*

The Registration of Social Care and Independent Healthcare (Fees) (Wales) Regulations 2002 No. 2002/921 (W.109). – Enabling power: Care Standards Act 2000, ss. 12 (2), 15 (3), 16 (3), 118 (5) to (7) & Children Act 1989, ss. 79F, 104 (4), sch. 9A, para. 7. – Issued: 20.06.2002. Made: 28.03.2002. Coming into force: 01.04.2002. Effect: None. Territorial extent & classification: W. General. – 8p.: 30 cm. – 0 11 090507 5 *£2.00*

The Registration of Social Care and Independent Health Care (Wales) Regulations 2002 No. 2002/919 (W.107). – Enabling power: Care Standards Act 2000, ss. 12 (2), 14 (1) (d), 15 (3), 16 (1), 25 (1), 118 (5) to (7) & Children Act 1989, ss. 79E (2), 104 (4), sch. 9A, para. 6 (2). – Issued: 21.06.2002. Made: 28.03.2002. Coming into force: 01.04.2002. Effect: None. Territorial extent & classification: W. General. – 24p.: 30 cm. – 0 11 090506 7 £4.00

Social security

The Contracting Out (Functions of Local Authorities: Income-related Benefits) Order 2002 No. 2002/1888. – Enabling power: Deregulation and Contracting Out Act 1994, ss. 69, 70 (2) (4), 77 (1). – Issued: 26.07.2002. Made: 18.07.2002. Coming into force: 25.07.2002. Effect: None. Territorial extent & classification: E/W/S. General. – Supersedes draft S.I. (ISBN 011042395X) issued 26 June 2002. – 4p.: 30 cm. – 0 11 042524 3 £1.75

The Employment Act 2002 (Commencement No. 2) Order 2002 No. 2002/2256 (C.73). – Enabling power: Employment Act 2002, s. 55 (2). Bringing into operation various provisions of the 2002 Act on 09.09.2002. – Issued: 09.09.2002. Made: 30.08.2002. Effect: None. Territorial extent & classification: E/W/S/NI. General. – 2p.: 30 cm. – With correction slip dated April 2003 – 0 11 042733 5 £1.50

The Employment Act 2002 (Commencement No. 3 and Transitional and Saving Provisions) Order 2002 No. 2002/2866 (C.91). – Enabling power: Employment Act 2002, s. 55 (2) (3). Bringing into operation various provisions of the 2002 Act in accord. with art. 2. – Issued: 02.12.2002. Made: 18.11.2002. Effect: 1992 c. 4, 5 (24.11.2002) & 1996 c. 17; 1999 c. 2, 30 (06.04.2003) & S.I. 1999/671 (06.04.2003) amended. Territorial extent & classification: E/W/S. General. – 8p.: 30 cm. – 0 11 044073 0 £2.00

The General Commissioners and Special Commissioners (Jurisdiction and Procedure) (Amendment) Regulations 2002 No. 2002/2976. – Enabling power: Taxes Management Act 1970, ss. 46A (1) (a) (1A) to (3), 56B & Social Security Contributions (Transfer of Functions etc.) Act 1999, s. 13 (3) & S.I.1999/671, art. 12 (3). – Issued: 10.12.2002. Made: 25.11.2002. Laid: 03.12.2002. Coming into force: 31.12.2002. Effect: S.I. 1994/1811, 1812 amended. Territorial extent & classification: E/W/S/NI. General. – 8p.: 30 cm. – This S.I. has been reprinted (23.12.2002.) to incorporate text omitted from the original and is being issued free of charge to all known recipients – 0 11 044116 8 £2.00

The Housing Benefit and Council Tax Benefit (Child Care Charges) Regulations 2002 No. 2002/499. – Enabling power: Social Security Contributions and Benefits Act 1992, ss. 123 (1) (d) (e), 136 (3) (5) (b), 137 (1), 175 (1) (3). – Issued: 08.03.2002. Made: 05.03.2002. Laid: 08.03.2002. Coming into force: 01.04.2002. Effect: S.I. 1987/1971; 1992/1814 amended. Territorial extent & classification: E/W/S. General. – 2p.: 30 cm. – 0 11 039434 8 £1.50

The Housing Benefit (General) Amendment Regulations 2002 No. 2002/2322. – Enabling power: Social Security Contributions and Benefits Act 1992, ss. 123 (1) (d), 130 (4), 137 (1), 175 (1) (3) to (5) & Housing Act 1996, s. 122 (3) (5). – Issued: 13.09.2002. Made: 09.09.2002. Laid: 13.09.2002. Coming into force: 07.10.2002. Effect: S.I. 1987/1971 amended. Territorial extent & classification: E/W/S. General. – 2p.: 30 cm. – 0 11 042749 1 £1.50

The Income-related Benefits and Jobseeker's Allowance (Working Tax Credit and Child Tax Credit) (Amendment) Regulations 2002 No. 2002/2402. – Enabling power: Social Security Contributions and Benefits Act 1992, ss. 123 (1) (a) (d) (e), 135 (1), 136 (3) (4) (5) (a) (b), 137 (1) (2) (m), 175 (1) (3) to (5) & Jobseekers Act 1995, ss. 12 (2) (3) (4) (b), 35 (1), 36 (2) (4), sch. 1, para. 13. – Issued: 27.09.2002. Made: 19.09.2002. Laid: 27.09.2002. Coming into force: In accord. with regs. 1 (2) to (6). Effect: S.I. 1987/1967, 1971; 1992/1814; 1996/207 amended. Territorial extent & classification: E/W/S. General. – 12p.: 30 cm. – 0 11 042802 1 £2.50

The Income-related Benefits (Subsidy to Authorities) Amendment (No. 2) Order 2002 No. 2002/3116. – Enabling power: Social Security Administration Act 1992, ss. 140B (1) (3) (4), 140F (2), 189 (1) (4) to (7). – Issued: 23.12.2002. Made: 16.12.2002. Laid: 23.12.2002. Coming into force: 13.01.2003. Effect: S.I. 1998/562 amended (from 01.04.2001.). Territorial extent & classification: E/W/S. General. – 4p.: 30 cm. – 0 11 044236 9 £1.75

The Income-Related Benefits (Subsidy to Authorities) Amendment Order 2002 No. 2002/1859. – Enabling power: Social Security Administration Act 1992, ss. 140B (1) (3) (4), 140F (2), 189 (1) (4) to (7). – Issued: 23.07.2002. Made: 17.07.2002. Laid: 23.07.2002. Coming into force: 17.08.2002. Effect: S.I. 1998/562 amended. Territorial extent & classification: E/W/S. General. – 32p.: 30 cm. – 0 11 042519 7 £6.00

The Income Support (General) and Jobseeker's Allowance Amendment Regulations 2002 No. 2002/1411. – Enabling power: Social Security Contributions and Benefits Act 1992, ss. 123 (1) (a), 136 (3), 137 (1), 175 (1) (3) to (5) & Jobseekers Act 1995, ss. 12 (1), 35 (1), 36 (2) (4). – Issued: 27.05.2002. Made: 24.05.2002. Laid: 27.05.2002. Coming into force: 17.06.2002. Effect: S.I. 1987/1967; 1996/207 amended. Territorial extent & classification: E/W/S. General. – 2p.: 30 cm. – 0 11 042263 5 £1.50

The Income Support (General) (Standard Interest Rate Amendment) (No. 2) Regulations 2002 No. 2002/338. – Enabling power: Social Security Contributions and Benefits Act 1992, ss. 123 (1) (a), 135 (1), 137 (1), 175 (1) (3) to (5). – Issued: 22.02.2002. Made: 16.02.2002. Laid: 22.02.2002. Coming into force: 17.03.2002. Effect: S.I. 1987/1967 amended & S.I. 2002/105 revoked (with saving). Territorial extent & classification: E/W/S. General. – 2p.: 30 cm. – 0 11 039353 8 £1.50

The Income Support (General) (Standard Interest Rate Amendment) Regulations 2002 No. 2002/105. – Enabling power: Social Security Contributions and Benefits Act 1992, ss. 123 (1) (a), 135 (1), 137 (1), 175 (1) (3) to (5). – Issued: 25.01.2002. Made: 22.01.2002. Laid: 25.01.2002. Coming into force: 17.02.2002. Effect: S.I. 1987/1967 amended & S.I. 2001/3721 revoked (with saving). Territorial extent & classification: E/W/S. General. – 2p.: 30 cm. – Revoked by S.I. 2002/338 (ISBN 0110393538) with saving – 0 11 039223 X £1.50

The Jobseeker's Allowance (Amendment) Regulations 2002 No. 2002/3072. – Enabling power: Jobseekers Act 1995, ss. 6 (4), 8 (1) (a) (2) (d) (ii), 35 (1), 36 (2) (4). – Issued: 18.12.2002. Made: 12.12.2002. Coming into force: 13.12.2002, 01.01.2003, in accord. with reg 1. Effect: S.I. 1996/207 amended. Territorial extent & classification: E/W/S. General. – 4p.: 30 cm. – Supersedes draft S.I. (ISBN 0110429966) issued on 20.11.2002 – 0 11 044185 0 £1.75

The Jobseeker's Allowance (Joint Claims) Amendment Regulations 2002 No. 2002/1701. – Enabling power: Jobseekers Act 1995, ss. 1 (2C) (4), 35 (1), 36 (2) (4). – Issued: 09.07.2002. Made: 02.07.2002. Laid: 09.07.2002. Coming into force: 28.10.2002. Effect: S.I. 1996/207 amended. Territorial extent & classification: E/W/S. General. – 2p.: 30 cm. – 0 11 042436 0 £1.50

The Northern Ireland Act 1998 (Modification) Order 2002 No. 2002/265. – Enabling power: Northern Ireland Act 1998, s. 87 (7). – Issued: 22.02.2002. Made: 12.02.2002. Laid: 22.02.2002. Coming into force: 15.03.2002. Effect: 1998 c. 47 modified. Territorial extent & classification: E/W/S/NI. General. – 2p.: 30 cm. – 0 11 039334 1 £1.50

The Regulatory Reform (Carer's Allowance) Order 2002 No. 2002/1457. – Enabling power: Regulatory Reform Act 2001, s. 1. – Issued: 06.06.2002. Made: 29.05.02. Coming into force: 01.09.2002, 28.10.2002, 01.04.2002 in accord with arts. 1 & 2. Effect: 1992 c. 4 amended. Territorial extent and classification: E/W/S. General. – 4p.: 30 cm. – Supersedes draft S.I. (ISBN 0110399749) published on 22.05.02 – 0 11 042321 6 £1.75

The Social Fund Cold Weather Payments (General) Amendment Regulations 2002 No. 2002/2524. – Enabling power: Social Security Contributions and Benefits Act 1992, ss. 138 (2) (4), 175 (1) (3) (4). – Issued: 10.10.2002. Made: 05.10.2002. Laid: 10.10.2002. Coming into force: 01.11.2002. Effect: S.I. 1988/1724 amended. Territorial extent & classification: E/W/S. General. – 4p.: 30 cm. – 0 11 042843 9 £1.75

The Social Fund Maternity and Funeral Expenses (General) Amendment (No. 2) Regulations 2002 No. 2002/470. – Enabling power: Social Security Contributions and Benefits Act 1992, ss. 138 (1) (a) (4), 175 (1) (3) (4). – Issued: 08.03.2002. Made: 04.03.2002. Laid: 08.03.2002. Coming into force: 30.03.2002. Effect: S.I. 2002/79 amended. Territorial extent & classification: E/W/S. General. – 2p.: 30 cm. – 0 11 039424 0 £1.50

The Social Fund Maternity and Funeral Expenses (General) Amendment Regulations 2002 No. 2002/79. – Enabling power: Social Security Contributions and Benefits Act 1992, ss. 138 (1) (a) (4), 175 (1) (3) (4) & Social Security Act 1998, s. 9 (1) (a). – Issued: 24.01.2002. Made: 16.01.2002. Laid: 24.01.2002. Coming into force: 31.03.2002. Effect: S.I. 1987/481 amended. Territorial extent & classification: E/W/S. General. – 4p.: 30 cm. – 0 11 039213 2 £1.75

The Social Fund (Miscellaneous Amendments) Regulations 2002 No. 2002/2323. – Enabling power: Social Security Contributions and Benefits Act 1992, ss. 138 (1) (a) (4), 175 (3) & Social Security Administration Act 1992, ss. 12 (1) (2) (a) (b), 189 (4) (6), 191. – Issued: 13.09.2002. Made: 08.09.2002. Laid: 13.09.2002. Coming into force: 01.10.2002. Effect: S.I. 1987/481; 1988/524 amended. Territorial extent & classification: E/W/S. General. – 4p.: 30 cm. – 0 11 042747 5 £1.75

The Social Security Administration Act 1992 (Amendment) Order 2002 No. 2002/817. – Enabling power: Social Security Administration Act 1992, ss. 109B (6) (a) (b), 189 (1) (4) (5). – Issued: 28.03.2002. Made: 25.03.2002. Coming into force: 01.04.2002. Effect: 1992 c. 5 amended. Territorial extent & classification: E/W/S. General. – Supersedes draft S.I. (ISBN 0110393961) issued 28 February 2002. – 4p.: 30 cm. – 0 11 039617 0 £1.75

The Social Security Amendment (Carer Premium) Regulations 2002 No. 2002/2020. – Enabling power: Social Security Contributions and Benefits Act 1992, ss. 123 (1) (a) (d) (e), 135 (1), 137 (1), 175 (1) (3) (4) & Jobseekers Act 1995, ss. 4 (5), 35 (1), 36 (2) (4). – Issued: 07.08.2002. Made: 30.07.2002. Laid: 07.08.2002. Coming into force: 28.10.2002. Effect: S.I. 1987/1967, 1971; 1992/1814; 1996/207 amended. Territorial extent & classification: E/W/S. General. – 4p.: 30 cm. – 0 11 042609 6 £1.75

The Social Security Amendment (Carer Premium) Regulations 2002 No. 2002/2020. – Enabling power: Social Security Contributions and Benefits Act 1992, ss. 123 (1) (a) (d) (e), 135 (1), 137 (1), 175 (1) (3) (4) & Jobseekers Act 1995, ss. 4 (5), 35 (1), 36 (2) (4). – Issued: 01.11.2002. Made: 30.07.2002. Laid: 07.00.2002. Coming into force: 28.10.2002. Effect: S.I. 1987/1967, 1971; 1992/1814; 1996/207 amended. Territorial extent & classification: E/W/S. General. – 4p.: 30 cm. – This statutory instrument replaces the S.I. of same number (but different ISBN 0110426096) issued on 07.08.2002, and is being issued free of charge to all known recipients of that instrument – 0 11 042891 9 £1.75

The Social Security Amendment (Carer's Allowance) Regulations 2002 No. 2002/2497. – Enabling power: Child Support Act 1991, sch. 1, para. 4 (1) (b) (c) (2) & Social Security Contributions and Benefits Act 1992, ss. 22 (5), 70, 79 (2), 90, 113, 124 (1) (e), 135 (1), 136 (3) (5) (b), 138 (2) (4), 175 (1) (4), sch. 3, para. 2 (8) & Social Security Administration Act 1992, ss. 2A, 5 (1), 7A, 73, 78 (2), 107 (1), 189 (1) (4) (5) & Social Security (Consequential Provisions) Act 1992, s. 5, sch. 3, para. 12 & Jobseekers Act 1995, ss. 26 (1), 40 & Child Support Act 1995, ss. 10, 26 (1) (3) & Welfare Reform and Pensions Act 1999, ss. 72, 83 (1) (4) (8) & Immigration and Asylum Act 1999, s. 115 (3) (4) (5). – Issued: 04.10.2002. Made: 27.09.2002. Laid: 04.10.2002. Coming into force: 01.04.2003, for the purposes of reg. 3; 28.10.002, except for the purposes of reg. 3, in accord. with reg. 1. Effect: S.I. 1975/563, 1483; 1976/409; 1977/343; 1979/597, 642; 1987/1967, 1968, 1971; 1988/35; 1990/1777; 1992/1814; 1994/2946; 1996/2567, 2570, 2744, 3195; 1999/3108; 2000/636; 2001/155; 2002/1703 amended. Territorial extent & classification: E/W/S. General. – 8p.: 30 cm. – 0 11 042837 4 *£2.00*

The Social Security Amendment (Employment Programme) Regulations 2002 No. 2002/2314. – Enabling power: Social Security Contributions and Benefits Act 1992, ss. 123 (1) (a) (d) (e), 136 (3) (5) (b), 137 (1), 175 (1) (3) (4) & Jobseekers Act 1995, ss. 12 (1) (4) (b), 19 (10) (c), 35 (1), 36 (2) (4), sch. 1, para. 3 (b)– Issued: 12.09.2002. Made: 05.09.2002. Laid: 12.09.2002. Coming into force: 14.10.2002. Effect: S.I. 1987/1967, 1971; 1992/1814 ; 1996/207 amended. Territorial extent & classification:E/W/S. General. – 4p.: 30 cm. – 0 11 042745 9 *£1.75*

The Social Security Amendment (Intercalating Students) Regulations 2002 No. 2002/1763. – Enabling power: Social Security Contributions and Benefits Act 1992, ss. 123 (1) (d) (e), 131 (3) (b), 137 (1) (2) (j), 175 (1) (3) (4) & Jobseekers Act 1995, ss. 6 (4), 35 (1), 36 (2). – Issued: 16.07.2002. Made: 10.07.2002. Coming into force: 01.08.2002. Effect: S.I. 1987/1971; 1992/1814; 1996/207 amended. Territorial extent & classification: E/W/S. General. – Supersedes draft S.I. issued 12 June 2002 (ISBN 0110423267). – 2p.: 30 cm. – 0 11 042461 1 *£1.50*

The Social Security Amendment (Personal Allowances for Children and Young Persons) Regulations 2002 No. 2002/2019. – Enabling power: Social Security Contributions and Benefits Act 1992, ss. 123 (1) (a) (d) (e), 135 (1), 137 (1), 175 (1) (3) & Jobseekers Act 1995, ss. 4 (5), 35 (1), 36 (2). – Issued: 07.08.2002. Made: 30.07.2002. Laid: 07.08.2002. Coming into force: 14.10.2002. Effect: S.I. 1987/1967, 1971; 1992/1814; 1996/207 amended. Territorial extent & classification: E/W/S. General. – 4p.: 30 cm. – 0 11 042611 8 *£1.75*

The Social Security Amendment (Personal Injury Payments) Regulations 2002 No. 2002/2442. – Enabling power: Social Security Contributions and Benefits Act 1992, ss. 123 (1) (a) (d) (e), 136 (5) (b) (d), 137 (1), 175 (3) (4) & Jobseekers Act 1995, ss. 12 (4) (b) (d), 35 (1), 36 (2). – Issued: 27.09.2002. Made: 23.09.2002. Laid: 27.09.2002. Coming into force: 28.10.2002. Effect: S.I. 1987/1967, 1971; 1992/1814; 1996/207 amended. Territorial extent & classification: E/W/S. General. – 4p.: 30 cm. – 0 11 042817 X *£1.75*

The Social Security Amendment (Residential Care and Nursing Homes) Regulations 2002 No. 2002/398. – Enabling power: Social Security Contributions and Benefits Act 1992, ss. 123 (1) (a), 135 (1), 137 (1), 175 (1) (3) (4) & Social Security Administration Act 1992, ss. 5 (1) (p), 189 (4) & Jobseekers Act 1995, ss. 4 (5), 35 (1), 36 (1) (2) & Social Security Act 1998, ss. 10 (6), 84. – Issued: 27.02.2002. Made: 21.02.2002. Laid: 27.02.2002. Coming into force: 08.04.2002. Effect: S.I. 1987/1968; 1999/991; 2001/3767 amended. Territorial extent & classification: E/W/S. General. – 4p.: 30 cm. – 0 11 039389 9 *£1.75*

The Social Security Amendment (Students and Income-related Benefits) (No. 2) Regulations 2002 No. 2002/2207. – Enabling power: Social Security Contributions and Benefits Act 1992, ss. 123 (1) (a) (d) (e), 136 (5) (b), 137 (1), 175 (1) (3) & Jobseekers Act 1995, ss. 12 (4) (b), 35 (1), 36 (2). – Issued: 29.08.2002. Made: 23.08.2002. Laid: 29.08.2002. Coming into force: 02.09.2002. Effect: S.I. 1987/1967, 1971; 1992/1814; 1996/207 amended in so far as they apply to students. Territorial extent & classification: E/W/S. General. – 2p.: 30 cm. – 0 11 042704 1 *£1.50*

The Social Security Amendment (Students and Income-related Benefits) Regulations 2002 No. 2002/1589. – Enabling power: Social Security Contributions and Benefits Act 1992, ss. 123 (1) (a) (d) (e), 130 (2), 136 (3) (5) (b), 137 (1), 175 (1) (3) (4) & Jobseekers Act 1995, ss. 12 (1) (4) (b), 35 (1), 36 (2). – Issued: 21.06.2002. Made: 13.06.2002. Laid: 21.06.2002. Coming into force: In accord. with reg. 1 (1). Effect: S.I. 1987/1967, 1971; 1992/1814; 1996/207 amended. Territorial extent & classification: E/W/S. General. – 8p.: 30 cm. – 0 11 042375 5 *£2.00*

The Social Security (Attendance Allowance and Disability Living Allowance) (Amendment) (No. 2) Regulations 2002 No. 2002/1406. – Enabling power: Social Security Contributions and Benefits Act 1992, ss. 67 (2), 72 (8), 175 (1) (3) (4). – Issued: 30.05.2002. Made: 22.05.2002. Laid: 30.05.2002. Coming into force: 01.07.2002. Effect: S.I. 1991/2740, 2890 amended. Territorial extent and classification: E/W/S. General. – 2p.: 25 cm. – 0 11 042257 0 *£1.50*

The Social Security (Attendance Allowance and Disability Living Allowance) (Amendment) Regulations 2002 No. 2002/208. – Enabling power: Social Security Contributions and Benefits Act 1992, ss. 67 (2), 72 (8), 175 (1) (3) (4). – Issued: 08.02.2002. Made: 05.02.2002. Laid: 08.02.2002. Coming into force: 01.03.2002. Effect: S.I 1991/2740, 2890 amended. Territorial extent and classification: E/W/S. General. – 2p.: 25 cm. – 0 11 039285 X *£1.50*

The Social Security Benefit (Computation of Earnings) (Amendment) Regulations 2002 No. 2002/2823. – Enabling power: Social Security Contributions and Benefits Act 1992, s. 3 (2) (3). – Issued: 28.11.2002. Made: 14.11.2002. Laid: 15.11.2002. Coming into force: 08.12.2002. & 01.04.2003. in accord.with art. 1. Effect: S.I. 1996/2745 amended. Territorial extent & classification: E/W/S. General. – 4p.: 30 cm. – 0 11 043949 X *£1.75*

The Social Security Benefit (Computation of Earnings) (Child Care Charges) Regulations 2002 No. 2002/842. – Enabling power: Social Security Contributions and Benefits Act 1992, ss. 3 (2) (3), 175 (3). – Issued: 10.07.2002. Made: 26.03.2002. Laid: 27.03.2002. Coming into force: 01.04.2002. Effect: S.I. 1996/2745 amended. Territorial extent & classification: E/W/S/NI. General. – 2p.: 30 cm. – 0 11 042443 3 £1.50

The Social Security Benefits Up-rating Order 2002 No. 2002/668. – Enabling power: Social Security Administration Act 1992, ss. 150, 151, 189 (1) (3) (4) (5). – Issued: 20.03.2002. Made: 12.03.2002. Coming into force: In accord. with art. 1 (2). Effect: 1965 c. 51; 1992 c. 4; 1993 c. 48 & S.I. 1976/1267; 1978/393; 1986/1960; 1987/1967, 1969, 1971; 1991/2890; 1992/1814; 1994/2946; 1995/310; 1996/207 amended & S.I. 2001/207 revoked (01.04.2002). Territorial extent & classification: E/W/S. General. – 54p.: 30 cm. – Revoked by S.I. 2003/526 (ISBN 0110451732) – 0 11 039490 9 £7.50

The Social Security Benefits Up-rating Regulations 2002 No. 2002/684. – Enabling power: Social Security Contributions and Benefits Act 1992, ss. 30E (1), 90, 113 (1), 122 (1), 171D, 171G (2), 175 (1) to (4), sch. 7, para. 2 (3) & Social Security Administration Act 1992, ss. 155 (3), 189 (1) (3) (4), 191. – Issued: 18.03.2002. Made: 13.03.2002. Laid: 18.03.2002. Coming into force: 08.04.2002. Effect: S.I. 1977/343; 2001/910 amended. Territorial extent & classification: E/W/S. General. – 2p.: 30 cm. – Revoked by S.I. 2003/601 (ISBN 0110452089) 0 11 039497 6 £1.50

The Social Security (Claims and Information) (Housing Benefit and Council Tax Benefit) Regulations 2002 No. 2002/1132. – Enabling power: Social Security Administration Act 1992, ss. 7A (2) (b) (c) (3) (6), 189 (1) (4) (5), 191. – Issued: 24.04.2002. Made: 17.04.2002. Laid: 24.04.2002. Coming into force: 17.05.2002. Effect: None. Territorial extent & classification: E/W/S. General. – 4p.: 30 cm. – 0 11 039813 0 £1.75

The Social Security (Claims and Payments) Amendment (No. 2) Regulations 2002 No. 2002/1950. – Enabling power: Social Security Administration Act 1992, ss. 5 (1) (l) (p), 189 (1) (5) (6) & Child Support Act 1991, s. 43 (2). – Issued: 30.07.2002. Made: 24.07.2002. Laid: 30.07.2002. Coming into force: In accord. with reg. 1 (2). Effect: S.I. 1987/1968 amended. Territorial extent & classification: E/W/S. General. – 2p.: 30 cm. – Revoked by S.I. 2003/492 (ISBN 0110451309) – 0 11 042551 0 £1.50

The Social Security (Claims and Payments) Amendment Regulations 2002 No. 2002/355. – Enabling power: Social Security Administration Act 1992, ss. 15A (2) (b), 189 (1). – Issued: 25.02.2002. Made: 18.02.2002. Laid: 25.02.2002. Coming into force: 01.04.2002. Effect: S.I. 1987/1968 amended. Territorial extent & classification: E/W/S. General. – 2p.: 30 cm. – Revoked by S.I. 2003/492 (ISBN 0110451309) – 0 11 039363 5 £1.50

The Social Security (Claims and Payments and Miscellaneous Amendments) (No. 2) Regulations 2002 No. 2002/2441. – Enabling power: Social Security Administration Act 1992, ss. 5 (1) (i) (m) (p) (q), 15 (A) (2) (a), 71 (6) (8), 189 (1) (4) (6), 191. – Issued: 27.09.2002. Made: 23.09.2002. Laid: 27.09.2002. Coming into force: In accord. with reg. 1 (1). Effect: S.I. 1987/1968; 1988/664 amended. Territorial extent & classification: E/W/S. General. – 4p.: 30 cm. – Revoked by S.I. 2003/492 (ISBN 0110451309) – 0 11 042818 8 £1.75

The Social Security (Claims and Payments and Miscellaneous Amendments) (No. 3) Regulations 2002 No. 2002/2660. – Enabling power: Social Security Contributions and Benefits Act 1992, ss. 138 (2) (4), 175 (1) (3) & Social Security Administration Act 1992, ss. 5 (1) (a) (p), 189 (1) (4) (5). – Issued: 24.10.2002. Made: 22.10.2002. Laid: 24.10.2002. Coming into force: 02.11.2002 & 01.04.2003 in accord. with reg. 1 (1). Effect: S.I. 1987/1968, 2000/729 amended. Territorial extent & classification: E/W/S. General. – 2p.: 30 cm. – 0 11 042890 0 £1.50

The Social Security (Claims and Payments and Miscellaneous Amendments) Regulations 2002 No. 2002/428. – Enabling power: Social Security Administration Act 1992, ss. 5 (1) (a) (b), 191 & Social Security Act 1998, ss. 9 (1), 10 (3) (6), 84. – Issued: 05.03.2002. Made: 26.02.2002. Laid: 05.03.2002. Coming into force: 02.04.2002. Effect: S.I. 1987/1968; 1999/991 amended. Territorial extent & classification: E/W/S. General. – 4p.: 30 cm. – 0 11 039402 X £1.75

The Social Security Commissioners (Procedure) (Tax Credits Appeals) Regulations 2002 No. 2002/3237. – Enabling power: Social Security Act 1998, ss. 14, 15, 16, 28, 39, 79 (2), 84, sch. 4, 5. – Issued: 13.01.2003. Made: 18.12.2002. Laid: 28.11.2002. Coming into force: 01.01.2003. Effect: None. Territorial extent & classification: E/W/S. General. – 12p.: 30 cm. – 0 11 044031 5 £2.50

The Social Security (Contributions) (Amendment No. 2) Regulations 2002 No. 2002/307. – Enabling power: Social Security Contributions and Benefits Act 1992, ss. 3 (2) (3), 4 (6) (7) & Social Security Contributions and Benefits (Northern Ireland) Act 1992, ss. 3 (2) (3), 4 (6) (7). – Issued: 22.03.2002. Made: 13.02.2002. Laid: 13.02.2002. Coming into force: 06.04.2002. Effect: S.I. 2001/1004 amended. Territorial extent & classification: E/W/S/NI. General. – 8p.: 30 cm. – 0 11 039557 3 £2.00

The Social Security (Contributions) (Amendment No. 3) Regulations 2002 No. 2002/2366. – Enabling power: Social Security Contributions and Benefits Act 1992, ss. 3 (2), 17 (3), 119, sch. 1, paras 2, 4, 8 & Social Security Contributions and Benefits (Northern Ireland) Act 1992, ss. 3 (2), 17 (3), 119, sch. 1, paras 2, 4, 8 & Social Security Contributions (Transfer of Functions, etc.) Act 1999, ss. 8 (1) (m), 25 (5) & S.I. 1999/671, arts 7 (1) (m), 23 (7). – Issued: 11.10.2002. Made: 16.09.2002. Laid: 17.09.2002. Coming into force: 08.10.2002. Effect: S.I. 2001/769, 1004; S.R. 2001/102 amended. Territorial extent & classification: E/W/S/NI. General. – 12p.: 30 cm. – 0 11 042841 2 £2.50

The Social Security (Contributions) (Amendment No. 4) Regulations 2002 No. 2002/2924. – Enabling power: Social Security Contributions and Benefits Act 1992, ss. 3 (2) (3). – Issued: 11.12.2002. Made: 26.11.2002. Laid: 26.11.2002. Coming into force: 17.12.2002. Effect: S.I. 2001/1004 amended. Territorial extent & classification: E/W/S/NI. General. – 2p.: 30 cm. – 0 11 044146 X *£1.50*

The Social Security (Contributions) (Amendment No. 5) Regulations 2002 No. 2002/2929. – Enabling power: Social Security Contributions and Benefits Act 1992, sch. 1, para. 6 (1) (2) & Social Security Contributions and Benefits (Northern Ireland) Act 1992, sch. 1, para. 6 (1) (2). – Issued: 03.12.2002. Made: 27.11.2002. Laid: 27.11.2002. Coming into force: 28.11.2002. Effect: S.I. 2001/1004 amended. Territorial extent & classification: E/W/S/NI. General. – 4p.: 30 cm. – 0 11 044079 X *£1.75*

The Social Security (Contributions) (Amendment) Regulations 2002 No. 2002/238. – Enabling power: Social Security Contributions and Benefits Act 1992, ss. 5, 175 (3) (4) & Social Security Contributions and Benefits (Northern Ireland) Act 1992, ss. 5, 171 (3) (4) (10). – Issued: 06.03.2002. Made: 07.02.2002. Laid: 07.02.2002. Coming into force: 06.04.2002. Effect: S.I. 2001/1004 amended. Territorial extent & classification: E/W/S/NI. General. – 2p.: 30 cm. – 0 11 039408 9 *£1.50*

The Social Security Contributions (Decisions and Appeals) (Amendment) Regulations 2002 No. 2002/3120. – Enabling power: Social Security Contributions (Transfer of Functions, etc.) Act 1999, ss. 9, 11, 13, 24, 25 (3) & S.I. 1999/1027, arts. 8, 10, 12, 23 (5). – Issued: 20.12.2002. Made: 16.12.2002. Laid: 17.12.2002. Coming into force: 07.01.2003. Effect: S.I. 1999/1027 amended. Territorial extent & classification: E/W/S/NI. General. – 2p.: 30 cm. – 0 11 044239 3 *£1.50*

The Social Security Contributions (Intermediaries) (Amendment) Regulations 2002 No. 2002/703. – Enabling power: Social Security Contributions and Benefits Act 1992, ss. 4A, 122 (1), 175 (1A) (2) to (4). – Issued: 05.04.2002. Made: 14.03.2002. Laid: 15.03.2002. Coming into force: 06.04.2002. Effect: S.I. 2000/727 amended. Territorial extent & classification: E/W/S. General. – 4p.: 30 cm. – 0 11 039649 9 *£1.75*

The Social Security (Contributions) (Re-rating and National Insurance Funds Payments) Order 2002 No. 2002/830. – Enabling power: Social Security Administration Act 1992, ss. 141 (4) (5), 142 (2) (3), 143 (1) (4), 144 (2), 189 (3) & Social Security Administration (Northern Ireland) Act 1992, ss. 129, 165 (11A) & Social Security Act 1993, ss. 2 (2) (8) & S.I. 1993/592 (NI. 2), art. 4 (3) (8). – Issued: 05.04.2002. Made: 26.03.2002. Coming into force: 06.04.2002. Effect: 1992 c.4, c.7 amended. Territorial extent & classification: E/W/S/NI. General. – 4p.: 30 cm. – Supersedes draft S.I. (ISBN 0110393503) issued on 21.02.2002 – 0 11 039653 7 *£1.75*

The Social Security (Disability Living Allowance) (Amendment) Regulations 2002 No. 2002/648. – Enabling power: Social Security Contributions and Benefits Act 1992, ss. 73 (5), 175 (3). – Issued: 15.03.2002. Made: 11.03.2002. Laid: 15.03.2002. Coming into force: 08.04.2002. Effect: S.I. 1991/2890 amended. Territorial extent and classification: E/W/S. General. – 2p.: 25 cm. – 0 11 039459 3 *£1.50*

The Social Security (Electronic Communications) (Child Benefit) Order 2002 No. 2002/1789. – Enabling power: Electronic Communications Act 2000, ss. 8, 9. – Issued: 18.07.2002. Made: 10.07.2002. Laid:-. Coming into force: 28.10.2002. Effect: S.I. 1975/515; 1976/965; 1987/1968; 2001/3252 amended. Territorial extent & classification: E/W/S. General. – Supersedes draft S.I. (ISBN 0110398564). – 8p.: 30 cm. – 0 11 042471 9 *£2.00*

The Social Security Fraud Act 2001 (Commencement No. 3) Order 2002 No. 2002/117 (C. 2). – Enabling power: Social Security Fraud Act 2001, s. 20 (1). Bringing into operation various provisions of the 2001 Act on 28.01.2002. – Issued: 31.01.2002. Made: 24.01.2002 Effect: None. Territorial extent & classification: E/W/S. General. – 2p.: 30 cm. – 0 11 039234 5 *£1.50*

The Social Security Fraud Act 2001 (Commencement No. 4) Order 2002 No. 2002/403 (C.10). – Enabling power: Social Security Fraud Act 2001, s. 20 (1). Bringing into operation various provisions of the 2001 Act on 26.02.2002. – Issued: 05.03.2002. Made: 24.01.2002 Effect: None. Territorial extent & classification: E/W/S. General. – 2p.: 30 cm. – 0 11 039391 0 *£1.50*

The Social Security Fraud Act 2001 (Commencement No. 5) Order 2002 No. 2002/1222 (C.32). – Enabling power: Social Security Fraud Act 2001, s. 20 (1). Bringing into operation various provisions of the 2001 Act on 30.04.2002. – Issued: 03.05.2002. Made: 29.04.2002 Effect: None. Territorial extent & classification: E/W/S. General. – 2p.: 30 cm. – 0 11 039879 3 *£1.50*

The Social Security (Guardian's Allowances) Amendment Regulations 2002 No. 2002/492. – Enabling power: Social Security Contributions and Benefits Act 1992, ss. 77 (8) (b), 122 (1), 175 (1) (3) (4). – Issued: 08.03.2002. Made: 05.03.2002. Laid: 08.03.2002. Coming into force: 01.04.2002. Effect: S.I. 1975/515 amended. Territorial extent & classification:E/W/S. General. – 4p.: 30 cm. – Revoked by S.I. 2003/495 (ISBN 0110451325) – 0 11 039433 X *£1.75*

The Social Security (Hospital In-patients) Amendment Regulations 2002 No. 2002/685. – Enabling power: Social Security Administration Act 1992, ss. 73 (1) (b), 189 (1) (4), 191. – Issued: 18.03.2002. Made: 13.03.2002. Laid: 18.03.2002. Coming into force: 08.04.2002. Effect: S.I. 1975/555 amended. Territorial extent & classification: E/W/S. General. – 2p.: 30 cm. – 0 11 039498 4 *£1.50*

The Social Security (Incapacity) (Miscellaneous Amendments) (No. 2) Regulations 2002 No. 2002/2311. – Enabling power: Social Security Contributions and Benefits Act 1992, ss. 30A (6), 30E, 122 (1), 171D (2), 171G (2), 175 (1) to (4), sch. 7, para. 2 (3). – Issued: 10.09.2002. Made: 05.09.2002. Laid: 10.09. 2002. Coming into force: 01.10.2002 & 01.01.2003 in accord.with reg. 1. Effect: S.I. 1982/1408; 1994/2946; 1995/311 amended. Territorial extent & classification: E/W/S. General. – 2p.: 30 cm. – 0 11 042743 2 *£1.50*

The Social Security (Incapacity) (Miscellaneous Amendments) Regulations 2002 No. 2002/491. – Enabling power: Social Security Contributions and Benefits Act 1992, ss. 171D, 171G (2), 175 (1) to (4) & Social Security (Incapacity for Work) Act 1994, s. 4 (1) (6) & Welfare Reform and Pensions Act 1999, s. 85 (6). – Issued: 12.03.2002. Made: 05.03.2002. Laid: 12.03.2001. Coming into force: 05.04.2002. for reg. 4 & 08.04.2002. for all other purposes. Effect: S.I. 1994/2946; 1995/310, 311 amended. Territorial extent & classification: E/W/S. General. – 8p.: 30 cm. – 0 11 039431 3 *£2.00*

The Social Security (Industrial Injuries) (Dependency) (Permitted Earnings Limits) Order 2002 No. 2002/683. – Enabling power: Social Security Contributions and Benefits Act 1992, s. 175 (1) (3), sch. 7, para. 4 (5). – Issued: 18.03.2002. Made: 13.03.2002. Laid: 18.03.2002. Coming into force: 08.04.2002. Effect: S.I. 2001/911 amended. Territorial extent & classification: E/W/S. General. – 2p.: 30 cm. – 0 11 039496 8 *£1.50*

The Social Security (Industrial Injuries) (Prescribed Diseases) Amendment Regulations 2002 No. 2002/1717. – Enabling power: Social Security Contributions and Benefits Act 1992, ss. 109 (2), 122 (1), 175 (1) (4), sch. 6, para. 1 (d). – Issued: 08.07.2002. Made: 02.07.2002. Laid: 08.07.2002. Coming into force: 29.07.2002. Effect: S.I. 1985/967 amended. Territorial extent & classification: E/W/S. General. – 2p.: 30 cm. – 0 11 042440 9 *£1.50*

The Social Security (Jobcentre Plus Interviews) Regulations 2002 No. 2002/1703. – Enabling power: Social Security Administration Act 1992, ss. 2A (1) (3) to (6) (8), 2B (6) (7), 5 (1) (a) (b), 6 (1) (a) (b), 189 (1) (4) (5), 191 & Child Support, Pensions and Social Security Act 2000, sch. 7, paras. 3 (1), 4 (4), 8 (8), 20 (3), 23 (1). – Issued: 08.07.2002. Made: 03.07.2002. Laid: 08.07.2002. Coming into force: 30.09.2002. Effect: S.I. 1987/1968, 1971; 1992/1813, 1814; 1996/2907; 1999/991; 2000/897, 1926; 2001/1002, 3210 amended. Territorial extent & classification: E/W/S. General. – 16p.: 30 cm. – 0 11 042438 7 *£3.00*

The Social Security (Loss of Benefit) (Amendment) Regulations 2002 No. 2002/486. – Enabling power: Social Security Fraud Act 2001, ss. 7 (6), 11 (1). – Issued: 08.03.2002. Made: 05.03.2002. Laid: 08.03.2002. Coming into force: 01.04.2002. Effect: S.I. 2001/4022 amended. Territorial extent & classification: E/W/S. General. – 2p.: 30 cm. – 0 11 039430 5 *£1.50*

The Social Security (Loss of Benefit) (Consequential Amendments) Regulations 2002 No. 2002/490. – Enabling power: Social Security Contributions and Benefits Act 1992, ss. 22 (5), 122 (1), 123 (1) (a) (d) (e), 124 (1) (e), 135 (1), 137 (1), 175 (1) (3) & Jobseekers Act 1995, ss. 5 (3), 26 (1) (4) (d), 35 (1), 36 (1) (2) (4) & Social Security Act 1998, ss. 9 (1), 10 (3) (6), 79 (1), 84 & Child Support, Pensions and Social Security Act 2000, ss. 62 (3), 65 (1), 69 (1) (2) (a) (7), sch. 7, paras. 3 (1), 4 (4) (6), 23 (1). – Issued: 08.03.2002. Made: 05.03.2002. Laid: 08.03.2002. Coming into force: 01.04.2002. Effect: S.I. 1975/556; 1987/1967, 1971; 1992/1814; 1996/207, 2570; 1999/991; 2001/1002, 1167, 1395 amended. Territorial extent & classification: E/W/S. General. – [8]p.: 30 cm. – 0 11 039427 5 *£2.00*

The Social Security (Miscellaneous Amendments) (No. 2) Regulations 2002 No. 2002/2380. – Enabling power: Social Security Contributions and Benefits Act 1992, ss. 123 (1) (a) (d) (e), 136 (3) (5) (b), 137 (1), 175 (1) (3) (4) & Jobseekers Act 1995, ss. 4 (5), 12 (1) (4) (b), 35 (1), 36 (2) (4). – Issued: 20.09.2002. Made: 17.09.2002. Laid: 20.09.2002. Coming into force: 14.10.2002, 28.10.2002, in accord. with art. 1. Effect: S.I. 1987/1967, 1971; 1992/1814; 1996/207 amended. Territorial extent & classification: E/W/S. General. – 8p.: 30 cm. – 0 11 042793 9 *£2.00*

The Social Security (Miscellaneous Amendments) Regulations 2002 No. 2002/841. – Enabling power: Social Security Contributions and Benefits Act 1992, ss. 123 (1) (a) (d) (e), 135 (1), 136 (3) (5) (b), 137 (1), 175 (1) (3) (4) & Jobseekers Act 1995, ss. 4 (5), 12 (1) (4) (b), 35 (1), 36 (2) (4) & Social Security Administration Act 1992, ss. 134 (8) (b), 139 (6) (b). – Issued: 02.04.2002. Made: 26.03.2002. Laid: 02.04.2002. Coming into force: 08.04.2002. Effect: S.I. 1987/1967, 1971; 1992/1814; 1996/207 amended. Territorial extent & classification: E/W/S. General. – 4p.: 30 cm. – 0 11 039627 8 *£1.75*

The Social Security (Paternity and Adoption) Amendment Regulations 2002 No. 2002/2689. – Enabling power: Social Security Contributions and Benefits Act 1992, ss. 123 (1) (a) (d) (e), 124 (1) (e), 136 (3) (5) (b), 137 (1) (2) (d), 175 (1) (3) (4) & Jobseekers Act 1995, ss. 1 (2C), 12 (1) (4) (b), 35 (1), 36 (2) (4), sch. 1, para. 1. – Issued: 01.11.2002. Made: 29.10.2002. Laid: 01.11.2002. Coming into force: In accord. with reg. 1 (1). Effect: S.I. 1987/1967, 1971; 1992/1814; 1996/207 amended. Territorial extent & classification: E/W/S. General. – 8p.: 30 cm. – 0 11 042930 3 *£2.00*

The Social Security Pensions (Low Earnings Threshold) Order 2002 No. 2002/36. – Enabling power: Social Security Administration Act 1992, s. 148A. – Issued: 17.01.2002. Made: 09.01.2002. Laid: 17.01.2002. Coming into force: 06.04.2002. Effect: None. Territorial extent & classification: E/W/S. General. – 2p.: 30 cm. – 0 11 039184 5 *£1.50*

The Social Security Revaluation of Earnings Factors Order 2002 No. 2002/519. – Enabling power: Social Security Administration Act 1992, ss. 148 (3) (4), 189 (1) (3) (4) (5). – Issued: 13.03.2002. Made: 07.03.2002. Laid: 13.03.2002. Coming into force: 06.04.2002. Effect: None. Territorial extent & classification: E/W/S. General. – 4p.: 30 cm. – 0 11 039440 2 *£1.75*

The Social Security, Statutory Maternity Pay and Statutory Sick Pay (Miscellaneous Amendments) Regulations 2002 No. 2002/2690. – Enabling power: Social Security Contributions and Benefits Act 1992, ss. 35 (3), 35A (4) (5) (a) (d), 153 (6), 163 (1) (3), 164 (9) (c) (ea), 165 (1) (3) (7), 166 (1) (b), 171 (1) (3) (b) to (d) (5), 171ZP (2) (3), 171ZS (1), 175 (1) to (4), sch. 11, paras 1, 1A, sch. 13, para. 2 & Social Security Administration Act 1992, ss. 5 (1) (I), 132 (1) (2), 189 (1) (191). – Issued: 01.11.2002. Made: 30.10.2002. Laid: 01.11.2002. Coming into force: In accord. with reg. 1 (1). Effect: S.I. 1982/894; 1986/1960; 1987/416; 1991/590; 1994/2946; 2000/688 amended. Territorial extent & classification: E/W/S. General. – 12p.: 30 cm. – 0 11 042935 4 *£2.50*

The Social Security (Work-focused Interviews for Lone Parents) Amendment Regulations 2002 No. 2002/670. – Enabling power: Social Security Administration Act 1992, ss. 2A (1) (3) (b) to (f) (4) (5) (a) (b) (6) (7) (8), 189 (1) (4) to (6) (7A), 191. – Issued: 15.03.2002. Made: 12.03.2002. Laid: 15.03.2002. Coming into force: 08.04.2002. Effect: S.I. 2000/1926 amended. Territorial extent & classification: E/W/S. General. – 4p.: 30 cm. – 0 11 039469 0 *£1.75*

The State Pension Credit Act 2002 (Commencement No. 1) Order 2002 No. 2002/1691 (C.51). – Enabling power: State Pension Credit Act 2002, s. 22 (3). Bringing into force various provisions of the 2002 Act on 02.07.2002. – Issued: 04.07.2002. Made: 01.07.2002. Effect: None. Territorial extent & classification: E/W/S. General. – With correction slip dated July 2002 adding the C. 51 number. – 2p.: 30 cm. – 0 11 042426 3 *£1.50*

The State Pension Credit Act (Commencement No. 2) Order 2002 No. 2002/2248 (C.72). – Enabling power: State Pension Credit Act 2002, s. 22 (3). Bringing into force various provisions of the 2002 Act on 03.09.2002. – Issued: 06.09.2002. Made: 30.08.2002. Effect: None. Territorial extent & classification: E/W/S. General. – 2p.: 30 cm. – 0 11 042731 9 *£1.50*

The State Pension Credit (Consequential, Transitional and Miscellaneous Provisions) (No. 2) Regulations 2002 No. 2002/3197. – Enabling power: Social Security Contributions and Benefits Act 1992, ss. 3 (2), 175 (3) to (5) & Social Security Administration Act 1992, ss. 5 (1) (p), 15A (2) (aa), 189 (4) to (6), 191 & Jobseekers Act 1995, ss. 26 (1) (4) (a), 35 (1), 36 (2) & Child Support Act 1995, ss. 10 (1) (5) (a), 26 (3) & Social Security Act 1998, ss. 10 (3) (6), 79 (4), 84 & State Pension Credit Act 2002, ss. 2 (3) (b) (6), 12 (2) (b), 13, 15 (3) (6) (a) (b), 16 (2) (a), 17 (2) (a). – Issued: 23.12.2002. Made: 19.12.2002. Laid:23.12.2002. Coming into force: 07.04.2003. & 06.10.2003. Effect: S.I. 1987/1968; 1989/507; 1996/2570, 3195; 1999/991; 2002/1792, 3019 amended. Territorial extent & classification: E/W/S. General. – 12p.: 30 cm. – 0 11 044278 4 *£2.50*

The State Pension Credit (Consequential, Transitional and Miscellaneous Provisions) Regulations 2002 No. 2002/3019. – Enabling power: Social Security Administration Act 1992, ss. 5 (1) (a) to (e) (h) to (l) (p) (3A), 7A, 15A, 159B (1), 189 (4) to (6) & Social Security Contributions and Benefits Act 1992, ss. 3 (2), 138 (1) (a), 175 (3) to (5) & Social Security Act 1998, ss. 10 (3) (6), 18, 79 (4) & State Pension Credit Act 2002, ss. 1 (5) (b), 2 (3) (b), 3 (5), 7 (4), 12 (2), 13, 15 (1) (j) (3) (6) (b), 17 (2) (a), sch. 1, para. 13. – Issued: 10.12.2002. Made: 04.12.2002. Laid: 10.12.2002. Coming into force: 07.04.2003 for the purposes of Parts I, II, III, VII; 06.10.2003, for all other purposes. Effect: S.I. 1987/487, 1967, 1968; 1988/664; 1989/507; 1990/545; 1991/2740, 2890; 1992/1816, 2182; 1993/494; 1996/207; 1999/911; 2001/155; 2002/1792 amended. Territorial extent & classification: E/W/S. General. – 36p.: 30 cm. – 0 11 044163 X *£6.50*

The State Pension Credit Regulations 2002 No. 2002/1792. – Enabling power: Social Security Contributions and Benefits Act 1992, s, 175 (3) to (5) & Social Security Fraud Act 2001, ss. 7 (4A), 9 (4A), 11 (1) (4) & State Pension Credit Act 2002, ss. 1 (5), 2 (3) (4) (6), 3 (4) to (8), 4 (3), 5, 6 (2), 7 (4) (7), 9 (4) (5), 12 (2) (3), 15, 16 (2), 17 (1) (2). – Issued: 19.07.2002. Made: 11.07.2002. Coming into force: 06.10.2003. Effect: 2002 c. 16; S.I. 2001/4022 amended. Territorial extent & classification: E/W/S. General. – 42p.: 30 cm. – Supersedes draft S.I. (ISBN 0110424395) – 0 11 042475 1 *£6.50*

The Statutory Maternity Pay (Compensation of Employers) Amendment Regulations 2002 No. 2002/225. – Enabling power: Social Security Contributions and Benefits Act 1992, ss. 167 (1) (c) (1B) (a), 171 (1), 175 (1) to (3) & Social Security Contributions and Benefits (Northern Ireland) Act 1992, s. 163 (1) (c) (1B) (a) (5), 171 (1) (3) (10). – Issued: 08.02.2002. Made: 05.02.2002. Laid: 08.02.2002. Coming into force: 06.04.2002. Effect: S.I. 1994/1882; S.R. 1994/271 amended. Territorial extent & classification:E/W/S. General. – 4p.: 30 cm. – 0 11 039283 3 *£1.75*

The Statutory Paternity Pay and Statutory Adoption Pay (Administration) Regulations 2002 No. 2002/2820. – Enabling power: Employment Act 2002, ss. 7 (1) (2) (a) (b) (4) (a) (b) (c) (5), 8 (1) (2) (a) (b) (c), 10 (1) (2), 51 (1) & Social Security Contributions (Transfer of Functions etc.) Act 1999, ss. 8 (1) (f) (ga), 25. – Issued: 29.11.2002. Made: 13.11.2002. Laid: 15.11.2002. Coming into force: 08.12.2002. Effect: None. Territorial extent & classification: E/W/S. General. – 8p.: 30 cm. – 0 11 044026 9 *£2.00*

The Statutory Payment Schemes (Electronic Communications) Regulations 2002 No. 2002/3047. – Enabling power: Finance Act 1999, ss. 132, 133 (2). – Issued: 16.12.2002. Made: 11.12.2002. Laid: 11.12.2002. Coming into force: 01.01.2003. Effect: None. Territorial extent & classification: E/W/S/NI. General. – 4p.: 30 cm. – 0 11 044179 6 *£1.75*

The Tax Credits (Appeals) (No. 2) Regulations 2002 No. 2002/3196. – Enabling power: Social Security Act 1998, ss. 7 (6), 12 (2) (7), 14 (10) (11), 16 (1), 28 (1), 39 (1), 79 (1) (3) to (7), 84, sch. 1, paras. 11, 12, sch 5. – Issued: 27.12.2002. Made: 18.12.2002. Coming into force: 01.01.2003. Effect: None. Territorial extent & classification: E/W/S. General. – 20p.: 30 cm. – Supersedes draft S.I. (ISBN 0110439430) issued on 02.12.2002 – 0 11 044385 3 £3.50

The Tax Credits (Miscellaneous Amendments No. 2) Regulations 2002 No. 2002/525. – Enabling power: Social Security Contributions and Benefits Act 1992, ss. 123 (1) (b) (c), 128 (5), 129 (8), 136 (5) (b), 137 (1), 175 (1) & Tax Credits Act 1999, s. 2 (1) (a), sch. 2, paras. 1 (b) (c) (d) (g), 20 (a). – Issued: 28.03.2002. Made: 07.03.2002. Laid: 08.03.2002. Coming into force: 02.04.2002. Effect: S.I. 1987/1973; 1991/2887 amended. Territorial extent & classification: E/W/S/NI. General. – 2p.: 30 cm. – 0 11 039609 X £1.75

The Tax Credits (Miscellaneous Amendments No. 3) Regulations 2002 No. 2002/1333. – Enabling power: Social Security Contributions and Benefits Act 1992, ss. 128 (5), 129 (8), 136 (3) (5) (a) (b), 137 (1), 175 (1) (3) & Tax Credits Act 1999, s. 2 (1) (a), sch. 2, paras. 1 (c) (d) (g), 20 (a). – Issued: 19.06.2002. Made: 14.05.2002. Laid: 14.05.2002. Coming into force: In accordance with reg. 1(1). Effect: S.I. 1987/1973; 1991/2887 amended. Territorial extent & classification: E/W/S/NI. General. – 4p.: 30 cm. – 0 11 042355 0 £1.75

The Tax Credits (Miscellaneous Amendments No. 4) Regulations 2002 No. 2002/1696. – Enabling power: Social Security Contributions and Benefits Act 1992, ss. 128 (5), 136 (3), 137 (1) (2) (a), 175 (1) (3) (4) & Tax Credits Act 1999, s. 2 (1) (a) (c), sch. 2, paras. 1 (c) (g), 7 (b), 20 (a) & Social Security Administration Act 1992, 1 (1C) (b), 5 (1) (a), 189 (1) (4) (5). – Issued: 01.08.2002. Made: 01.07.2002. Laid: 02.07.2002. Coming into force: 23.07.2002. Effect: S.I. 1987/1968, 1973; 1991/2887 amended. Territorial extent & classification: E/W/S/NI. General. – 4p.: 30 cm. – 0 11 042573 1 £1.75

The Tax Credits (Miscellaneous Amendments) Regulations 2002 No. 2002/14. – Enabling power: Social Security Contributions and Benefits Act 1992, ss. 128 (5), 129 (8), 136 (5) (b), 137 (1), 175 (1) & Tax Credits Act 1999, s. 2 (1) (a), sch. 2, paras. 1 (c) (d) (g), 20 (a). – Issued: 08.02.2002. Made: 08.01.2002. Laid: 08.01.2002. Coming into force: 29.01.2002. Effect: S.I. 1987/1973; 1991/2887 amended. Territorial extent & classification: E/W/S/NI. General. – 2p.: 30 cm. – 0 11 039270 1 £1.75

The Tax Credits (Prescribed Periods of Awards) Regulations 2002 No. 2002/1334. – Enabling power: Social Security Contributions and Benefits Act 1992, ss. 128 (3), 129 (6), 137 (1), 175 (1) & Tax Credits Act 1999, s. 2 (1) (a), sch. 2, paras. 1 (c) (d), 20 (a). – Issued: 19.06.2002. Made: 14.05.2002. Laid: 14.05.2002. Coming into force: 04.06.2002. Effect: None. Territorial extent & classification: E/W/S/NI. General. – 2p.: 30 cm. – 0 11 042356 9 £1.50

The Tax Credits Up-rating Order 2002 No. 2002/829. – Enabling power: Social Security Administration Act 1992, ss. 150, 189 (4) & Social Security Administration (Northern Ireland) Act 1992, s. 132 & Tax Credits Act 1999, s. 2 (1) (a) (4), sch. 2, paras. 2, 4, 20 (f). – Issued: 05.04.2002. Made: 26.03.2002. Coming into force: 09.04.2002. Effect: None. Territorial extent & classification: E/W/S/NI. General. – 4p.: 30 cm. – Supersedes draft S.I. (ISBN 0110394070) previously published on 06.03.2002 – 0 11 039652 9 £1.75

The Workmen's Compensation (Supplementation) (Amendment) Scheme 2002 No. 2002/718. – Enabling power: Social Security Contributions and Benefits Act 1992, sch. 8, para. 2 & Social Security Administration Act 1992, sch. 9, para. 1. – Issued: 20.03.2002. Made: 15.03.2002. Laid: 20.03.2002. Coming into force: 10.04.2002. Effect: S.I. 1982/1489 amended. Territorial extent & classification: E/W/S. General. – 4p.: 30 cm. – 0 11 039517 4 £1.75

Social security: Child support

The Social Security and Child Support (Decisions and Appeals) (Miscellaneous Amendments) Regulations 2002 No. 2002/1379. – Enabling power: Vaccine Damage Payments Act 1979, s. 4 (2) (3) & Child Support Act 1991, s. 20 (4) (5) (6) & Jobseekers Act 1995, ss. 31, 35 (1), sch. 1, para. 4 & Social Security (Recovery of Benefits) Act 1997, s. 11 (5) (a) (b) & Social Security Act 1998, ss. 6 (3), 9 (1), 10A (1), 12 (2) (7), 14 (11), 16 (1), 24A (I), (2) (a), 28 (1), 79 (1) (3) (4) (6) (7), 84, sch. 1, para. 12 (1), sch. 2, para. 9, sch. 5, paras. 1 to 4, 6, 7 & Child Support, Pensions, and Social Security Act 2000, s. 68, sch. 7, paras. 3 (1), 6 (7) (8), 10 (1), 19 (1), 20 (1) (3), 23 (1). – Issued: 10.04.2002. Made: 15.05.2002Coming into force: 20.05.2002. Effect: S.I. 1999/991; 2001/1002 amended. Territorial extent & classification: E/W/S. General. – Supersedes draft S.I. (ISBN 0110397258) issued 10 April 2002. – 16p.: 30 cm. – 0 11 039975 7 £3.00

Social security, Northern Ireland

The Social Security Benefit (Computation of Earnings) (Amendment) (Northern Ireland) Regulations 2002 No. 2002/2925. – Enabling power: Social Security Contributions and Benefits (Northern Ireland) Act 1992, ss. 3 (2) (3). – Issued: 11.12.2002. Made: 26.11.2002. Laid: 26.11.2002. Coming into force: 08.12.2002 & 01.04.2003 in accordance with art. 1. Effect: S.R. 1996/520 amended. Territorial extent & classification: NI. General. – 4p.: 30 cm. – 0 11 044144 3 £1.75

The Social Security Contributions (Intermediaries) (Northern Ireland) (Amendment) Regulations 2002 No. 2002/705. – Enabling power: Social Security Contributions and Benefits (Northern Ireland) Act 1992, ss. 4A, 122 (1), 171 (3) (4) (10). – Issued: 05.04.2002. Made: 14.03.2002. Laid: 15.03.2002. Coming into force: 06.04.2002. Effect: S.I. 2000/728 amended. Territorial extent & classification: NI. General. – 4p.: 30 cm. – 0 11 039650 2 £1.75

The Tax Credits (Claims and Payments and Miscellaneous Amendments) (Northern Ireland) Regulations 2002 No. 2002/527. – Enabling power: Social Security Administration (Northern Ireland) Act 1992, ss. 5 (1) (a) (b), 167 (1) & S.I. 1998/1506 (NI. 10), arts. 2 (2), 10 (1), 11 (3). – Issued: 16.04.2002. Made: 07.03.2002. Laid: 08.03.2002. Coming into force: 02.04.2002. Effect: S.R. 1987/465; 1999/162 amended. Territorial extent & classification: NI. General. – 4p.: 30 cm. – 0 11 039745 2 *£1.75*

The Tax Credits (Decisions and Appeals) (Northern Ireland) (Amendment) Regulations 2002 No. 2002/1378. – Enabling power: S.I. 1998/1506 (N.I. 10), arts. 2 (2), 10 (1), 13 (2) (7), 15 (11), 16 (1), 28 (1), 74 (1) (3) (5) (6), sch. 2, para. 9, sch. 4, paras. 1, 2, 4, 6, 7 & Tax Credits Act 1999, s. 2 (1) (c) (4), sch. 2, paras. 8 (b), 9, 22 (c), 36. – Issued: 21.05.2002. Made: 15.05.2002. Coming into force: 21.05.2002. Effect: S.R. 1999/162 amended. Territorial extent & classification: NI. General. – 12p.: 30 cm. – Supersedes draft (ISBN 0110398068) – 0 11 039970 6 *£2.50*

The Tax Credits (Miscellaneous Amendments No. 2) (Northern Ireland) Regulations 2002 No. 2002/1340. – Enabling power: Social Security Contributions and Benefits (Northern Ireland) Act 1992, ss. 127 (5), 128 (8), 132 (3) (4) (a) (b), 133 (1), 171 (1) (3) & Tax Credits Act 1999, s. 2 (1) (a), sch. 2, paras. 3 (c) (d) (g), 22 (a). – Issued: 19.06.2002. Made: 14.05.2002. Laid: 14.05.2002. Coming into force: In accordance with reg. 1(1). Effect: S.R. 1987/463; 1992/78 amended. Territorial extent & classification: NI. General. – 4p.: 30 cm. – 0 11 042358 5 *£1.75*

The Tax Credits (Miscellaneous Amendments No. 3) (Northern Ireland) Regulations 2002 No. 2002/1697. – Enabling power: Social Security Contributions and Benefits (Northern Ireland) Act 1992, ss. 127 (5) & Tax Credits Act 1999, s. 2 (1) (a), sch. 6, paras. 3 (c), 22 (a). – Issued: 01.08.2002. Made: 01.07.2002. Laid: 02.07.2002. Coming into force: 23.07.2002. Effect: S.R. 1987/463; 1992/78 amended. Territorial extent & classification: NI. General. – 2p.: 30 cm. – 0 11 042574 X *£1.50*

The Tax Credits (Miscellaneous Amendments) (Northern Ireland) Regulations 2002 No. 2002/524. – Enabling power: Social Security Contributions and Benefits (Northern Ireland) Act 1992, ss. 122 (1) (b) (c), 132 (4) (b), 133 (1), 171 (1) & Tax Credits Act 1999, s. 2 (1) (a), sch. 2, paras. 3 (b) (g), 22 (a). – Issued: 28.03.2002. Made: 07.03.2002. Laid: 08.03.2002. Coming into force: 02.04.2002. Effect: S.R. 1987/463; 1992/78 amended. Territorial extent & classification: NI. General. – 2p.: 30 cm. – 0 11 039608 1 *£1.50*

The Tax Credits (Prescribed Period of Awards) (Northern Ireland) Regulations 2002 No. 2002/1339. – Enabling power: Social Security Contributions and Benefits (Northern Ireland) Act 1992, ss. 127 (3), 128 (6), 133 (1), 171 (1) & Tax Credits Act 1999, s. 2 (1) (a), sch. 2, paras. 3 (c) (d), 22 (a). – Issued: 19.06.2002. Made: 14.05.2002. Laid: 14.05.2002. Coming into force: 04.06.2002. Effect: None. Territorial extent & classification: NI. General. – 2p.: 30 cm. – 0 11 042357 7 *£1.50*

Sports grounds and sporting events, England

The Safety of Sports Grounds (Designation) (No. 2) Order 2002 No. 2002/2893. – Enabling power: Safety of Sports Grounds Act 1975, ss. 1 (1), 18 (2). – Issued: 27.11.2002. Made: 21.11.2002. Laid: 21.11.2002. Coming into force: 16.12.2002. Effect: None. Territorial extent & classification: E. General. – 2p.: 30 cm. – 0 11 043946 5 *£1.50*

The Safety of Sports Grounds (Designation) Order 2002 No. 2002/1754. – Enabling power: Safety of Sports Grounds Act 1975, ss. 1 (5), 18 (2). – Issued: 22.07.2002. Made: 08.07.2002. Laid: 09.07.2002. Coming into force: 31.07.2002. Effect: None. Territorial extent & classification: E. General. – 2p.: 30 cm. – 0 11 042492 1 *£1.50*

Sports grounds and sporting events, England and Wales

The Football (Disorder) (Amendment) Act 2002 (Commencement) Order 2002 No. 2002/2200 (C.68). – Enabling power: Football (Disorder) (Amendment) Act 2002, s. 3 (2). Bringing into operation various provisions of the Act on 28.08.2002. – Issued: 06.09.2002. Made: 22.08.2002. Effect: None. Territorial extent & classification: E/W. General. – 2p.: 30 cm. – 0 11 042732 7 *£1.50*

The Football Spectators (Seating) Order 2002 No. 2002/1755. – Enabling power: Football Spectators Act 1989, s. 11 (1) to (3). – Issued: 22.07.2002. Made: 08.07.02. Laid: 09.07.2002. Coming into force: 31.07.2002. Effect: None. Territorial extent & classification: E/W. General. – 4p.: 30 cm. – 0 11 042493 X *£1.75*

The Football Spectators (World Cup Control Period) (No. 2) Order 2002 No. 2002/1143. – Enabling power: Football Spectators Act 1989, s. 14 (6). – Issued: 03.05.2002. Made: 22.04.2002. Laid: 24.04.2002. Coming into force: 15.05.2002. Effect: S.I. 2002/1096 revoked. Territorial extent & classification: E/W. General. – 2p.: 30 cm. – 0 11 039874 2 *£1.50*

Statistics of trade

The Statistics of Trade (Customs and Excise) (Amendment) Regulations 2002 No. 2002/2498. – Enabling power: European Communities Act 1972, s. 2 (2). – Issued: 09.10.2002. Made: 02.10.2002. Laid: 04.10.2002. Coming into force: 28.10.2002. Effect: S.I. 1992/2790 amended & S.I. 2001/3887 revoked. Territorial extent & classification: E/W/S/NI. General. – 2p.: 30 cm. – This S.I. has been made in consequence of a defect in S.I. 2001/3887 and is being issued free of charge to all known recipients of that S.I. – 0 11 042839 0 *£1.50*

Summer time

The Summer Time Order 2002 No. 2002/262. – Enabling power: European Communities Act 1972, s. 2 (2). – Issued: 20.02.2002. Made: 12.02.2002. Laid: 18.02.2002. Coming into force: 11.03.2002. Effect: 1972 c. 6 amended. Territorial extent & classification: E/W/S/NI. General. – 2p.: 30 cm. – EC note: Implements DIR 2000/84/EC – 0 11 039331 7 *£1.50*

Supreme Court of England and Wales

The Civil Procedure (Amendment No. 2) Rules 2002 No. 2002/3219 (L.18). – Enabling power: Civil Procedure Act 1997, s. 2 (6) (a). – Issued: 03.01.2003. Made: 14.12.2002. Laid: 24.12.2002. Coming into force: 01.04.2003. in accord. with rule 1. Effect: S.I. 1998/3132 amended in relation to England and Wales. Territorial extent & classification: E/W. General. – 8p.: 30 cm. – 0 11 044429 9 *£2.00*

The Civil Procedure (Amendment) Rules 2002 No. 2002/2058 (L.10). – Enabling power: Civil Procedure Act 1997, s. 2. – Issued: 13.08.2002. Made: 23.07.2002. Laid: 06.08.2002. Coming into force: 01.10.2002, 02.12.2002, in accord., with rule 1. Effect: S.I. 1998/3132 amended in relation to England and Wales. Territorial extent & classification: E/W. General. – 36p.: 30 cm. – 0 11 042632 0 *£6.50*

The Civil Procedure (Modification of Enactments) Order 2002 No. 2002/439. – Enabling power: Civil Procedure Act 1997, s. 4 (1). – Issued: 08.03.2002. Made: 28.02.2002. Laid: 01.03.2002. Coming into force: 25.03.2002. Effect: 1869 c. 62 (32 & 33 Vict); 1979 c. 53; 1981 c. 54; 1984 c. 28; S.I. 1991/1222; 1996/3215; 2000/1071 amended. Territorial extent & classification: E/W. General. – 4p.: 30 cm. – 0 11 039415 1 *£1.75*

Court of Appeal (Appeals from Pathogens Access Appeal Commission) Rules 2002 No. 2002/1844 (L.8). – Enabling power: Anti-Terrorism, Crime and Security Act 2001, sch. 6, para. 5. – Issued: 22.07.2002. Made: 16.07.2002. Coming into force: 23.07.2002. Effect: None. Territorial extent & classification: E/W. General. – 2p.: 30 cm. – 0 11 042516 2 *£1.50*

The Court of Appeal (Appeals from Proscribed Organisations Appeal Commission) Rules 2002 No. 2002/1843 (L.7). – Enabling power: Terrorism Act 2000, sch. 3, para. 5. – Issued: 22.07.2002. Made: 16.07.2002. Coming into force: 23.07.2002. Effect: None. Territorial extent & classification: E/W. General. – 2p.: 30 cm. – 0 11 042515 4 *£1.50*

The Crown Court (Amendment) (No. 2) Rules 2002 No. 2002/2997 (L.16). – Enabling power: Supreme Court Act 1981, ss. 84 (1), 86. – Issued: 19.12.2002. Made: 02.12.2002. Laid: 09.12.2002. Coming into force: 30.12.2002. Effect: S.I. 1982/1109 amended. Territorial extent & classification: E/W. General. – 2p.: 30 cm. – 0 11 044199 0 *£1.50*

The Crown Court (Amendment) Rules 2002 No. 2002/2783 (L.13). – Enabling power: Supreme Court Act 1981, ss. 84 (1), 86. – Issued: 21.11.2002. Made: 08.11.2002. Laid: 11.11.2002. Coming into force: 02.12.2002. Effect: S.I. 1982/1109 amended. Territorial extent & classification: E/W. General. – 4p.: 30 cm. – 0 11 042988 5 *£1.75*

The Crown Court (Special Measures Directions and Directions Prohibiting Cross-examination) Rules 2002 No. 2002/1688 (L.5). – Enabling power: Supreme Court Act 1981, ss. 84 (1), 86 & Youth Justice and Criminal Evidence Act 1999, ss. 20 (6), 37 (5), 38 (6), 65 (1). – Issued: 05.07.2002. Made: 28.06.2002. Laid: 01.07.2002. Coming into force: 24.07.2002. Effect: S.I. 1982/1109 amended & S.I. 1992/1847 revoked. Territorial extent & classification: E/W. General. – 13p.: 30 cm. – 0 11 042430 1 *£3.00*

The Maximum Number of Judges Order 2002 No. 2002/2837. – Enabling power: Supreme Court Act 1981, s. 2 (4). – Issued: 27.11.2002. Made: 20.11.2002. Coming into force: 21.11.2002. Effect: 1981 c. 54 amended. Territorial extent & classification: E/W General. – 2p.: 30 cm. – Supersedes draft. S.I. (ISBN 0110428501) published on 15th October 2002 – 0 11 043049 2 *£1.50*

The Supreme Court Fees (Amendment) Order 2002 No. 2002/222 (L.2). – Enabling power: Supreme Court Act 1981, s. 130. – Issued: 13.02.2002. Made: 06.02.2002. Laid: 07.02.2002. Coming into force: 01.03.2002, 25.03.2002, in accord. with art. 1. Effect: S.I. 1999/687 amended. Territorial extent & classification: E/W. General. – 2p.: 30 cm. – 0 11 039295 7 *£1.50*

Tax credits

The Child Tax Credit Regulations 2002 No. 2002/2007. – Enabling power: Tax Credits Act 2002, ss. 8, 9, 65, 67. – Issued: 07.08.2002. Made: 30.07.2002. Laid:-. Coming into force: in accordance with regulation 1. Effect: None. Territorial extent & classification: E/W/S/NI. General. – 8p.: 30 cm. – 0 11 042613 4 *£2.00*

The Tax Credits Act 2002 (Commencement No. 1) Order 2002 No. 2002/1727 (C.52). – Enabling power: Tax Credits Act 2002, ss. 61, 62. Bringing into force various provisions of the Act on 09.07.2002, 01.08.2002, 01.01.2003, 06.04.2003. – Issued: 01.08.2002. Made: 08.07.2002. Effect: None. Territorial extent & classification: E/W/S/NI. General. – 16p.: 30 cm. – 0 11 042575 8 *£3.00*

The Tax Credits (Administrative Arrangements) Regulations 2002 No. 2002/3036. – Enabling power: Tax Credits Act 2002, ss. 58, 65 (1) (2) (7) (9). – Issued: 16.12.2002. Made: 09.12.2002. Laid: 10.12.2002. Coming into force: 01.01.2003. Effect: None. Territorial extent & classification: E/W/S/NI. General. – 4p.: 30 cm. – 0 11 044173 7 *£1.75*

The Tax Credits (Appeals) (No. 2) Regulations 2002 No. 2002/3196. – Enabling power: Social Security Act 1998, ss. 7 (6), 12 (2) (7), 14 (10) (11), 16 (1), 28 (1), 39 (1), 79 (1) (3) to (7), 84, sch. 1, paras. 11, 12, sch 5. – Issued: 27.12.2002. Made: 18.12.2002. Coming into force: 01.01.2003. Effect: None. Territorial extent & classification: E/W/S. General. – 20p.: 30 cm. – Supersedes draft S.I. (ISBN 0110439430) issued on 02.12.2002 – 0 11 044385 3 *£3.50*

The Tax Credits (Appeals) Regulations 2002 No. 2002/2926. – Enabling power: Tax Credits Act 2002, ss. 63 (8), 65 (2) (6). – Issued: 03.12.2002. Made: 26.11.2002. Laid: 26.11.2002. Coming into force: 17.12.2002. Effect: None. Territorial extent & classification: E/W/S/NI. General. – 8p.: 30 cm. – 0 11 044075 7 *£2.00*

The Tax Credits (Claims and Notifications) Regulations 2002 No. 2002/2014. – Enabling power: Tax Credits Act 2002, ss. 4 (1), 6, 14 (2), 15 (2), 16 (3), 17 (10), 19 (2), 22 (1) (b) (2), 65 (1) (2) (7), 67. – Issued: 03.09.2002. Made: 31.07.2002. Laid: 31.07.2002. Coming into force: 12.08.2002. Effect: None. Territorial extent & classification: E/W/S/NI. General. – 16p.: 30 cm. – 0 11 042711 4 *£3.00*

The Tax Credits (Definition and Calculation of Income) Regulations 2002 No. 2002/2006. – Enabling power: Tax Credits Act 2002, ss. 7 (8) (9), 65 (1) (7) (9), 67. – Issued: 07.08.2002. Made: 30.07.2002. Laid:-. Coming into force: in accordance with regulation 1. Effect: None. Territorial extent & classification: E/W/S/NI. General. – 24p.: 30 cm. – 0 11 042612 6 *£4.00*

The Tax Credits (Income Thresholds and Determination of Rates) Regulations 2002 No. 2002/2008. – Enabling power: Tax Credits Act 2002, ss. 8 (1) to (3), 13 (2) (3), 65 (1) (7), 67. – Issued: 07.08.2002. Made: 30.07.2002. Laid:-. Coming into force: in accordance with regulation 1. Effect: None. Territorial extent & classification: E/W/S/NI. General. – 8p.: 30 cm. – 0 11 042614 2 *£2.00*

The Tax Credits (Notice of Appeal) Regulations 2002 No. 2002/3119. – Enabling power: Tax Credits Act 2002, ss. 39 (1), 65 (2), 67. – Issued: 20.12.2002. Made: 17.12.2002. Laid: 17.12.2002. Coming into force: 07.01.2003. Effect: None. Territorial extent & classification: E/W/S/NI. General. – 2p.: 30 cm. – 0 11 044237 7 *£1.50*

The Tax Credits (Payments by the Board) Regulations 2002 No. 2002/2173. – Enabling power: Tax Credits Act 2002, ss. 24 (2) (3) (4) (7) (8), 65 (1) (2) (7), 67. – Issued: 09.09.2002. Made: 20.08.2002. Laid: 21.08.2002. Coming into force: 06.04.2003. Effect: None. Territorial extent & classification: E/W/S/NI. General. – 8p.: 30 cm. – 0 11 042729 7 *£2.00*

The Tax Credits (Transitional Provision) (Amendment) Order 2002 No. 2002/2158. – Enabling power: Tax Credits Act 2002, s. 62 (2). – Issued: 27.09.2002. Made: 20.08.2002. Coming into force: 21.08.2002. Effect: S.I. 2002/1727 (C.52) amended. Territorial extent & classification: E/W/S/NI. General. – This instrument has been made in consequence of a defect in S.I. 2002/1727 (C.52) (ISBN 0110425758) and is being issued free of charge to all known recipients of that statutory instrument. – 2p.: 30 cm. – 0 11 042815 3 *£1.50*

The Working Tax Credit (Entitlement and Maximum Rate) Regulations 2002 No. 2002/2005. – Enabling power: Tax Credits Act 2002, ss. 10, 11, 12, 65 (1) (7), 67. – Issued: 07.08.2002. Made: 30.07.2002. Laid:-. Coming into force: in accordance with regulation 1. Effect: None. Territorial extent & classification: E/W/S/NI. General. – 20p.: 30 cm. – 0 11 042615 0 *£3.50*

The Working Tax Credit (Payment by Employers) Regulations 2002 No. 2002/2172. – Enabling power: Tax Credits Act 2002, ss. 25 (1) (2), 65, 67. – Issued: 09.09.2002. Made: 20.08.2002. Laid: 21.08.2002. Coming into force: 01.03.2003. Effect: None. Territorial extent & classification: E/W/S/NI. General. – 12p.: 30 cm. – 0 11 042728 9 *£2.50*

Taxes

The Capital Gains Tax (Annual Exempt Amount) Order 2002 No. 2002/702. – Enabling power: Taxation of Chargeable Gains Act 1992, s. 3 (4). – Issued: 12.04.2002 Made: 15.03.2002. Coming into force: 15.03.2002. Effect: None. Territorial extent & classification: E/W/S/NI. General. – 2p.: 30 cm. – 0 11 039728 2 *£1.50*

The Capital Gains Tax (Gilt-edged Securities) Order 2002 No. 2002/2849. – Enabling power: Taxation of Chargeable Gains Act 1992, sch. 9, para. 1. – Issued: 28.11.2002. Made: 18.11.2002. Coming into force: 18.11.2002. Effect: None. Territorial extent & classification: E/W/S/NI. General. – 8p.: 30 cm. – 0 11 043984 8 *£2.00*

The European Single Currency (Taxes) (Amendment) Regulations 2002 No. 2002/1971. – Enabling power: Finance Act 1998, s. 163. – Issued: 16.08.2002. Made: 25.07.2002. Laid: 25.07.2002. Coming into force: 01.10.2002. Effect: S.I. 1998/3177 amended. Territorial extent & classification: E/W/S/NI. General. – 2p.: 30 cm. – 0 11 042658 4 *£1.50*

The General Commissioners and Special Commissioners (Jurisdiction and Procedure) (Amendment) Regulations 2002 No. 2002/2976. – Enabling power: Taxes Management Act 1970, ss. 46A (1) (a) (1A) to (3), 56B & Social Security Contributions (Transfer of Functions etc.) Act 1999, s. 13 (3) & S.I.1999/671, art. 12 (3). – Issued: 10.12.2002. Made: 25.11.2002. Laid: 03.12.2002. Coming into force: 31.12.2002. Effect: S.I. 1994/1811, 1812 amended. Territorial extent & classification: E/W/S/NI. General. – 8p.: 30 cm. – This S.I. has been reprinted (23.12.2002.) to incorporate text omitted from the original and is being issued free of charge to all known recipients – 0 11 044116 8 *£2.00*

The Life Assurance and Other Policies (Keeping of Information and Duties of Insurers) (Amendment) Regulations 2002 No. 2002/444. – Enabling power: Income and Corporation Taxes Act 1988, s. 552ZA (6) to (8). – Issued: 20.03.2002. Made: 28.02.2002. Laid: 01.03.2002. Coming into force: 06.04.2002. Effect: S.I. 1997/265 amended. Territorial extent & classification: E/W/S/NI. General. – With correction slip dated April 2002. – 2p.: 30 cm. – 0 11 039495 X *£1.50*

The Overseas Insurers (Tax Representatives) (Amendment) Regulations 2002 No. 2002/443. – Enabling power: Income and Corporation Taxes Act 1988, s. 552A (7) (9) & Finance Act 1999, s. 133. – Issued: 20.03.2002. Made: 28.02.2002. Laid: 01.03.2002. Coming into force: 06.04.2002. Effect: S.I. 1999/881 amended. Territorial extent & classification: E/W/S/NI. General. – With correction slip dated April 2002. – 4p.: 30 cm. – 0 11 039494 1 *£1.75*

The Personal Portfolio Bonds (Tax) (Amendment) Regulations 2002 No. 2002/455. – Enabling power: Income and Corporation Taxes Act 1988, s. 553C. – Issued: 22.03.2002. Made: 28.02.2002. Laid: 04.03.2002. Coming into force: 06.04.2002. Effect: S.I. 1999/1029 amended. Territorial extent and classification: E/W/S/NI. General. – 4p.: 30 cm. – 0 11 039559 X *£1.75*

The Relief for Community Amateur Sports Clubs (Designation) Order 2002 No. 2002/1966. – Enabling power: Finance Act 2002, sch. 18, para. 14 (1). – Issued: 02.09.2002. Made: 25.07.2002. Laid: 25.07.2002. Coming into force: 15.08.2002. Effect: None. Territorial extent & classification: E/W/S/NI. General. – 2p.: 30 cm. – 0 11 042701 7 *£1.50*

The Scottish Water (Transfer of Functions, etc.) (Tax Provisions) Order 2002 No. 2002/653. – Enabling power: Scotland Act 1998, ss. 104 (1), 112 (1) (5), 126 (1). – Issued: 12.04.2002. Made: 11.03.2002. Laid: 11.03.2002. Coming into force: 01.04.2002. Effect: None. Territorial extent & classification: UK. General. – 4p.: 30 cm. – 0 11 039726 6 *£1.75*

The Stamp Duty and Stamp Duty Reserve Tax (Extension of Exceptions Relating to Recognised Exchanges) Regulations 2002 No. 2002/1975. – Enabling power: Finance Act 2002, s. 117 (1). – Issued: 16.08.2002. Made: 25.07.2002. Laid: 25.07.2002. Coming into force: 26.07.2002. Effect: None. Territorial extent & classification: E/W/S/NI. General. – 2p.: 30 cm. – 0 11 042660 6 *£1.50*

The Tax Credit (New Category of Child Care Provider) Regulations 2002 No. 2002/1417. – Enabling power: Tax Credits Act 1999, s. 15 (1) (2) (4). – Issued: 31.05.2002. Made: 22.05.2002. Laid: 29.05.2002. Coming into force: 20.06.2002. Effect: None. Territorial extent & classification: E/S/W/NI. General. – 8p.: 30 cm. – 0 11 042296 1 *£2.00*

The Tax Credits (Miscellaneous Amendments No. 2) Regulations 2002 No. 2002/525. – Enabling power: Social Security Contributions and Benefits Act 1992, ss. 123 (1) (b) (c), 128 (5), 129 (8), 136 (5) (b), 137 (1), 175 (1) & Tax Credits Act 1999, s. 2 (1) (a), sch. 2, paras. 1 (b) (c) (d) (g), 20 (a). – Issued: 28.03.2002. Made: 07.03.2002. Laid: 08.03.2002. Coming into force: 02.04.2002. Effect: S.I. 1987/1973; 1991/2887 amended. Territorial extent & classification: E/W/S/NI. General. – 2p.: 30 cm. – 0 11 039609 X *£1.75*

The Tax Credits (Miscellaneous Amendments No. 3) Regulations 2002 No. 2002/1333. – Enabling power: Social Security Contributions and Benefits Act 1992, ss. 128 (5), 129 (8), 136 (3) (5) (a) (b), 137 (1), 175 (1) (3) & Tax Credits Act 1999, s. 2 (1) (a), sch. 2, paras. 1 (c) (d) (g), 20 (a). – Issued: 19.06.2002. Made: 14.05.2002. Laid: 14.05.2002. Coming into force: In accordance with reg. 1(1). Effect: S.I. 1987/1973; 1991/2887 amended. Territorial extent & classification: E/W/S/NI. General. – 4p.: 30 cm. – 0 11 042355 0 *£1.75*

The Tax Credits (Miscellaneous Amendments No. 4) Regulations 2002 No. 2002/1696. – Enabling power: Social Security Contributions and Benefits Act 1992, ss. 128 (5), 136 (3), 137 (1) (2) (a), 175 (1) (3) (4) & Tax Credits Act 1999, s. 2 (1) (a) (c), sch. 2, paras. 1 (c) (g), 7 (b), 20 (a) & Social Security Administration Act 1992, 1 (1C) (b), 5 (1) (a), 189 (1) (4) (5). – Issued: 01.08.2002. Made: 01.07.2002. Laid: 02.07.2002. Coming into force: 23.07.2002. Effect: S.I. 1987/1968, 1973; 1991/2887 amended. Territorial extent & classification: E/W/S/NI. General. – 4p.: 30 cm. – 0 11 042573 1 *£1.75*

The Tax Credits (Miscellaneous Amendments) Regulations 2002 No. 2002/14. – Enabling power: Social Security Contributions and Benefits Act 1992, ss. 128 (5), 129 (8), 136 (5) (b), 137 (1), 175 (1) & Tax Credits Act 1999, s. 2 (1) (a), sch. 2, paras. 1 (c) (d) (g), 20 (a). – Issued: 08.02.2002. Made: 08.01.2002. Laid: 08.01.2002. Coming into force: 29.01.2002. Effect: S.I. 1987/1973; 1991/2887 amended. Territorial extent & classification: E/W/S/NI. General. – 2p.: 30 cm. – 0 11 039270 1 *£1.75*

The Tax Credits (Prescribed Periods of Awards) Regulations 2002 No. 2002/1334. – Enabling power: Social Security Contributions and Benefits Act 1992, ss. 128 (3), 129 (6), 137 (1), 175 (1) & Tax Credits Act 1999, s. 2 (1) (a), sch. 2, paras. 1 (c) (d), 20 (a). – Issued: 19.06.2002. Made: 14.05.2002. Laid: 14.05.2002. Coming into force: 04.06.2002. Effect: None. Territorial extent & classification: E/W/S/NI. General. – 2p.: 30 cm. – 0 11 042356 9 *£1.50*

The Tax Credits Up-rating Order 2002 No. 2002/829. – Enabling power: Social Security Administration Act 1992, ss. 150, 189 (4) & Social Security Administration (Northern Ireland) Act 1992, s. 132 & Tax Credits Act 1999, s. 2 (1) (a) (4), sch. 2, paras. 2, 4, 20 (f). – Issued: 05.04.2002. Made: 26.03.2002. Coming into force: 09.04.2002. Effect: None. Territorial extent & classification: E/W/S/NI. General. – 4p.: 30 cm. – Supersedes draft S.I. (ISBN 0110394070) previously published on 06.03.2002 – 0 11 039652 9 *£1.75*

Taxes: Child support

The Social Security and Child Support (Decisions and Appeals) (Miscellaneous Amendments) Regulations 2002 No. 2002/1379. – Enabling power: Vaccine Damage Payments Act 1979, s. 4 (2) (3) & Child Support Act 1991, s. 20 (4) (5) (6) & Jobseekers Act 1995, ss. 31, 35 (1), sch. 1, para. 4 & Social Security (Recovery of Benefits) Act 1997, s. 11 (5) (a) (b) & Social Security Act 1998, ss. 6 (3), 9 (1), 10A (1), 12 (2) (7), 14 (11), 16 (1), 24A (I), (2) (a), 28 (1), 79 (1) (3) (4) (6) (7), 84, sch. 1, para. 12 (1), sch. 2, para. 9, sch. 5, paras. 1 to 4, 6, 7 & Child Support, Pensions, and Social Security Act 2000, s. 68, sch. 7, paras. 3 (1), 6 (7) (8), 10 (1), 19 (1), 20 (1) (3), 23 (1). – Issued: 10.04.2002. Made: 15.05.2002Coming into force: 20.05.2002. Effect: S.I. 1999/991; 2001/1002 amended. Territorial extent & classification: E/W/S. General. – Supersedes draft S.I. (ISBN 0110397258) issued 10 April 2002. – 16p.: 30 cm. – 0 11 039975 7 £3.00

Taxes: Tonnage tax

The Tonnage Tax (Training Requirement) (Amendment) Regulations 2002 No. 2002/2265. – Enabling power: Finance Act 2000, sch. 22, paras, 29, 31, 36. – Issued: 12.09.2002. Made: 04.09.2002. Laid: 05.09.2002. Coming into force: 01.10.2002. Effect: S.I. 2000/2129 amended. Territorial extent & classification: E/W/S/NI. General. – 2p.: 30 cm. – 0 11 042742 4 £1.50

Taxes, Northern Ireland

The Tax Credits (Claims and Payments and Miscellaneous Amendments) (Northern Ireland) Regulations 2002 No. 2002/527. – Enabling power: Social Security Administration (Northern Ireland) Act 1992, ss. 5 (1) (a) (b), 167 (1) & S.I. 1998/1506 (NI. 10), arts. 2 (2), 10 (1), 11 (3). – Issued: 16.04.2002. Made: 07.03.2002. Laid: 08.03.2002. Coming into force: 02.04.2002. Effect: S.R. 1987/465; 1999/162 amended. Territorial extent & classification: NI. General. – 4p.: 30 cm. – 0 11 039745 2 £1.75

The Tax Credits (Decisions and Appeals) (Northern Ireland) (Amendment) Regulations 2002 No. 2002/1378. – Enabling power: S.I. 1998/1506 (N.I. 10), arts. 2 (2), 10 (1), 13 (2) (7), 15 (11), 16 (1), 28 (1), 74 (1) (3) (5) (6), sch. 2, para. 9, sch. 4, paras. 1, 2, 4, 6, 7 & Tax Credits Act 1999, s. 2 (1) (c) (4), sch. 2, paras. 8 (b), 9, 22 (c), 36. – Issued: 21.05.2002. Made: 15.05.2002. Coming into force: 21.05.2002. Effect: S.R. 1999/162 amended. Territorial extent & classification: NI. General. – 12p.: 30 cm. – Supersedes draft (ISBN 0110398068) – 0 11 039970 6 £2.50

The Tax Credits (Miscellaneous Amendments No. 2) (Northern Ireland) Regulations 2002 No. 2002/1340. – Enabling power: Social Security Contributions and Benefits (Northern Ireland) Act 1992, ss. 127 (5), 128 (8), 132 (3) (4) (a) (b), 133 (1), 171 (1) (3) & Tax Credits Act 1999, s. 2 (1) (a), sch. 2, paras. 3 (c) (d) (g), 22 (a). – Issued: 19.06.2002. Made: 14.05.2002. Laid: 14.05.2002. Coming into force: In accordance with reg. 1(1). Effect: S.R. 1987/463; 1992/78 amended. Territorial extent & classification: NI. General. – 4p.: 30 cm. – 0 11 042358 5 £1.75

The Tax Credits (Miscellaneous Amendments No. 3) (Northern Ireland) Regulations 2002 No. 2002/1697. – Enabling power: Social Security Contributions and Benefits (Northern Ireland) Act 1992, ss. 127 (5) & Tax Credits Act 1999, s. 2 (1) (a), sch. 6, paras. 3 (c), 22 (a). – Issued: 01.08.2002. Made: 01.07.2002. Laid: 02.07.2002. Coming into force: 23.07.2002. Effect: S.R. 1987/463; 1992/78 amended. Territorial extent & classification: NI. General. – 2p.: 30 cm. – 0 11 042574 X £1.50

The Tax Credits (Miscellaneous Amendments) (Northern Ireland) Regulations 2002 No. 2002/524. – Enabling power: Social Security Contributions and Benefits (Northern Ireland) Act 1992, ss. 122 (1) (b) (c), 132 (4) (b), 133 (1), 171 (1) & Tax Credits Act 1999, s. 2 (1) (a), sch. 2, paras. 3 (b) (g), 22 (a). – Issued: 28.03.2002. Made: 07.03.2002. Laid: 08.03.2002. Coming into force: 02.04.2002. Effect: S.R. 1987/463; 1992/78 amended. Territorial extent & classification: NI. General. – 2p.: 30 cm. – 0 11 039608 1 £1.50

The Tax Credits (Prescribed Period of Awards) (Northern Ireland) Regulations 2002 No. 2002/1339. – Enabling power: Social Security Contributions and Benefits (Northern Ireland) Act 1992, ss. 127 (3), 128 (6), 133 (1), 171 (1) & Tax Credits Act 1999, s. 2 (1) (a), sch. 2, paras. 3 (c) (d), 22 (a). – Issued: 19.06.2002. Made: 14.05.2002. Laid: 14.05.2002. Coming into force: 04.06.2002. Effect: None. Territorial extent & classification: NI. General. – 2p.: 30 cm. – 0 11 042357 7 £1.50

Telecommunications

The Mobile Telephones (Re-programming) Act 2002 (Commencement) Order 2002 No. 2002/2294 (C.74). – Enabling power: Mobile Telephones (Re-progamming) Act 2002. s. 3 (2). Bringing into operation various provisions of the 2002 Act on 04.10.2002. – Issued: 16.09.2002. Made: 05.09.2002. Effect: None. Territorial extent & classification: UK. General. – 2p.: 30 cm. – 0 11 042751 3 £1.50

The Public Telecommunication System Designation (AT&T Global Network Services (UK) B.V.) Order 2002 No. 2002/1376. – Enabling power: Telecommunications Act 1984, s. 9. – Issued: 22.05.2002. Made: 14.05.2002. Laid: 16.05.2002. Coming into force: 14.06.2002. Effect: None. Territorial extent & classification: E/W/S/NI. General. – 2p.: 30 cm. – 0 11 039981 1 £1.50

The Public Telecommunication System Designation (Companhia Portuguesa Radio Marconi SA) Order 2002 No. 2002/1560. – Enabling power: Telecommunications Act 1984, s. 9. – Issued: 30.07.2002. Made: 11.06.2002. Laid: 13.06.2002. Coming into force: 12.07.2002. Effect: None. Territorial extent & classification: E/W/S/NI. General. – 2p.: 30 cm. – 0 11 042554 5 *£1.50*

The Public Telecommunication System Designation (Econet Satellite Services Limited) Order 2002 No. 2002/2657. – Enabling power: Telecommunications Act 1984, s. 9. – Issued: 04.11.2002. Made: 21.10.2002. Laid: 28.10.2002. Coming into force: 26.11.2002. Effect: None. Territorial extent & classification: E/W/S/NI. General. – 2p.: 30 cm. – 0 11 042924 9 *£1.50*

The Public Telecommunication System Designation (Eurocall Limited) Order 2002 No. 2002/1071. – Enabling power: Telecommunications Act 1984, s. 9. – Issued: 24.04.2002. Made: 14.04.2002. Laid: 18.04.2002. Coming into force: 17.05.2002. Effect: None. Territorial extent & classification: E/W/S/NI. General. – 2p.: 30 cm. – 0 11 039809 2 *£1.50*

The Public Telecommunication System Designation (Fibernet UK Limited) Order 2002 No. 2002/1070. – Enabling power: Telecommunications Act 1984, s. 9. – Issued: 24.04.2002. Made: 14.04.2002. Laid: 18.04.2002. Coming into force: 17.05.2002. Effect: None. Territorial extent & classification: E/W/S/NI. General. – 2p.: 30 cm. – 0 11 039808 4 *£1.50*

The Public Telecommunication System Designation (France Telecom Network Services-UK Ltd) Order 2002 No. 2002/400. – Enabling power: Telecommunications Act 1984, s. 9. – Issued: 01.03.2002. Made: 18.02.2002. Laid: 25.02.2002. Coming into force: 26.03.2002. Effect: None. Territorial extent & classification: E/W/S/NI. General. – 2p.: 30 cm. – 0 11 039393 7 *£1.50*

The Public Telecommunication System Designation (Gamma Telecommunications Limited) Order 2002 No. 2002/2658. – Enabling power: Telecommunications Act 1984, s. 9. – Issued: 04.11.2002. Made: 21.10.2002. Laid: 28.10.2002. Coming into force: 26.11.2002. Effect: None. Territorial extent & classification: E/W/S/NI. General. – 2p.: 30 cm. – 0 11 042923 0 *£1.50*

The Public Telecommunication System Designation (Severn Trent Retail Services Limited) Order 2002 No. 2002/1947. – Enabling power: Telecommunications Act 1984, s. 9. – Issued: 30.07.2002. Made: 22.07.2002. Laid: 24.07.2002. Coming into force: 22.08.2002. Effect: None. Territorial extent & classification: E/W/S/NI. General. – 2p.: 30 cm. – 0 11 042557 X *£1.50*

The Public Telecommunication System Designation (Telekom Malaysia (UK) Limited) Order 2002 No. 2002/399. – Enabling power: Telecommunications Act 1984, s. 9. – Issued: 01.03.2002. Made: 18.02.2002. Laid: 25.02.2002. Coming into force: 26.03.2002. Effect: None. Territorial extent & classification: E/W/S/NI. General. – 2p.: 30 cm. – 0 11 039392 9 *£1.50*

The Public Telecommunication System Designation (T-Systems Limited) Order 2002 No. 2002/1562. – Enabling power: Telecommunications Act 1984, s. 9. – Issued: 30.07.2002. Made: 11.06.2002. Laid: 13.06.2002. Coming into force: 12.07.2002. Effect: None. Territorial extent & classification: E/W/S/NI. General. – 2p.: 30 cm. – 0 11 042556 1 *£1.50*

The Public Telecommunication System Designation (Tweedwind Limited) Order 2002 No. 2002/1949. – Enabling power: Telecommunications Act 1984, s. 9. – Issued: 30.07.2002. Made: 22.07.2002. Laid: 24.07.2002. Coming into force: 22.08.2002. Effect: None. Territorial extent & classification: E/W/S/NI. General. – 2p.: 30 cm. – 0 11 042559 6 *£1.50*

The Public Telecommunication System Designation (United Networks Limited) Order 2002 No. 2002/1561. – Enabling power: Telecommunications Act 1984, s. 9. – Issued: 30.07.2002. Made: 11.06.2002. Laid: 13.06.2002. Coming into force: 12.07.2002. Effect: None. Territorial extent & classification: E/W/S/NI. General. – 2p.: 30 cm. – 0 11 042555 3 *£1.50*

The Public Telecommunication System Designation (VTL (UK) Limited) Order 2002 No. 2002/1948. – Enabling power: Telecommunications Act 1984, s. 9. – Issued: 30.07.2002. Made: 22.07.2002. Laid: 24.07.2002. Coming into force: 22.08.2002. Effect: None. Territorial extent & classification: E/W/S/NI. General. – 2p.: 30 cm. – 0 11 042558 8 *£1.50*

Telegraphs

The Wireless Telegraphy (Exemption) (Amendment) Regulations 2002 No. 2002/1590. – Enabling power: Wireless Telegraphy Act 1949, s. 1 (1). – Issued: 27.06.2002. Made: 17.06.2002. Laid: 17.06.2002. Coming into force: 08.07.2002. Effect: S.I. 1999/930 amended. Territorial extent & classification: E/W/S/NI. General. – 2p.: 30 cm. – Revoked by S.I. 2003/74 (ISBN 0110446534) – 0 11 042396 8 *£1.50*

The Wireless Telegraphy (Licence Charges) Regulations 2002 No. 2002/1700. – Enabling power: Wireless Telegraphy Act 1998, s. 1. – Issued: 11.07.2002. Made: 02.07.2002. Laid: 04.07.2002. Coming into force: 26.07.2002. Effect: S.I. 1999/1774, 3243; 2000/1678; 2001/2265 revoked. Territorial extent & classification: E/W/S/NI/IoM/CI. General. – 32p.: 30 cm. – 0 11 042447 6 *£6.00*

The Wireless Telegraphy (Public Fixed Wireless Access Licences) Regulations 2002 No. 2002/1911. – Enabling power: Wireless Telegraphy Act 1998, ss. 3, 6. – Issued: 31.07.2002. Made: 22.07.2002. Laid: 22.07.2002. Coming into force: 12.08.2002. Effect: None. Territorial extent & classification: E/W/S/NI. General. – 8p.: 30 cm. – 0 11 042571 5 *£2.00*

The Wireless Telegraphy (Television Licence Fees) (Amendment) Regulations 2002 No. 2002/641. – Enabling power: Wireless Telegraphy Act 1949, s. 2. – Issued: 21.03.2002. Made: 06.03.2002. Laid: 11.03.2002. Coming into force: 01.04.2002. Effect: S.I. 1997/290 amended. Territorial extent & classification: E/W/S/NI. General. – 4p.: 30 cm. – 0 11 039512 3 *£1.75*

Terms and conditions of employment

The Employment Act 2002 (Commencement No. 1) Order 2002 No. 2002/1989 (C.62). – Enabling power: Employment Act 2002, s. 55 (2). Bringing into operation various provisions of the 2001 Act on 31.07.2002. – Issued: 16.08.2002. Made: 15.07.2002. Effect: None. Territorial extent & classification: E/W/S/NI. General. – 2p.: 30 cm. – 0 11 042663 0 *£1.50*

The Employment Act 2002 (Commencement No. 3 and Transitional and Saving Provisions) Order 2002 No. 2002/2866 (C.91). – Enabling power: Employment Act 2002, s. 55 (2) (3). Bringing into operation various provisions of the 2002 Act in accord. with art. 2. – Issued: 02.12.2002. Made: 18.11.2002. Effect: 1992 c. 4, 5 (24.11.2002) & 1996 c. 17; 1999 c. 2, 30 (06.04.2003) & S.I. 1999/671 (06.04.2003) amended. Territorial extent & classification: E/W/S. General. – 8p.: 30 cm. – 0 11 044073 0 *£2.00*

The Employment Rights (Increase of Limits) (No. 2) Order 2002 No. 2002/2927. – Enabling power: Employment Relations Act 1999, s. 34. – Issued: 03.12.2002. Made: 25.11.2002. Laid: 27.11.2002. Coming into force: 01.02.2003. Effect: S.I. 2002/10 revoked with savings. Territorial extent & classification: E/W/S. General. – 4p.: 30 cm. – 0 11 044076 5 *£1.75*

Employment Rights (Increase of Limits) Order 2002 No. 2002/10. – Enabling power: Employment Relations Act 1999, s. 34. – Issued: 14.01.2002. Made: 07.01.2002. Laid: 08.01.2002. Coming into force: 01.02.2002. Effect: S.I. 2001/21 revoked with savings. Territorial extent & classification: E/W/S. General. – 4p.: 30 cm. – Revoked by S.I. 2002/2927 (ISBN 0110440765) with savings – 0 11 039144 6 *£1.75*

The Fixed-term Employees (Prevention of Less Favourable Treatment) Regulations 2002 No. 2002/2034. – Enabling power: Employment Act 2002, ss. 45, 51 (1). – Issued: 12.08.2002. Made: 30.07.2002. Coming into force: 01.10.2002. Effect: 1992 c. 4; 1996 c. 17, 18 amended. Territorial extent & classification: E/W/S. General. – 16p.: 30 cm. – EC note: Implements DIR 99/70/EC (the Fixed-term Work Directive) in England , Wales and Scotland – 0 11 042626 6 *£3.00*

The Flexible Working (Eligibility, Complaints and Remedies) Regulations 2002 No. 2002/3236. – Enabling power: Employment Rights Act 1996, ss. 80F (1) (b) (5) (8) (a), 80H (3) (b), 80I (3). – Issued: 09.01.2003. Made: 31.12.2002. Laid: 03.01.2003. Coming into force: 06.04.2003. Effect: None. Territorial extent & classification: E/W/S. General. – 4p.: 30 cm. – 0 11 044463 9 *£1.75*

The Flexible Working (Procedural Requirements) Regulations 2002 No. 2002/3207. – Enabling power: Employment Rights Act 1996, s. 80G (2) (3). – Issued: 07.01.2003. Made: 20.12.2002. Coming into force: 06.04.2003. Effect: None. Territorial extent & classification: E/W/S. General. – 8p.: 30 cm. – Supersedes draft (ISBN 0110441087) issued on 04.12.2002 – 0 11 044455 8 *£2.00*

The Maternity and Parental Leave (Amendment) Regulations 2002 No. 2002/2789. – Enabling power: Employment Rights Act 1996, ss. 47C (2), 71 (1) to (4) (6) (7), 73 (1) (2) (4) (7), 74 (4), 75 (1), 76, 99 (1). – Issued: 21.11.2002. Made: 11.11.2002. Coming into force: 24.11.2002. Effect: S.I. 1999/3312 amended. Territorial extent & classification: E/W/S. General. – EC note: Implements (in part) provisions of Council Directive 92/85/EEC relating to the safety and health of pregnant workers and workers who have recently given birth or are breastfeeding, and provisions of the Framework Agreement on Parental Leave annexed to Council Directive 96/34/EC. – 8p.: 30 cm. – Supersedes draft S.I. (ISBN 0110429109) issued on 30.10.2002 – 0 11 042973 7 *£2.00*

The National Minimum Wage Regulations 1999 (Amendment) Regulations 2002 No. 2002/1999. – Enabling power: National Minimum Wage Act 1998, ss. 1 (3), 2, 3, 51. – Issued: 01.08.2002. Made: 25.07.2002. Coming into force: 01.10.2002. Effect: S.I. 1999/584; 2000/1989; 2001/2763 amended & S.I. 2000/1411 revoked. Territorial extent & classification: E/W/S/NI. General. – 4p.: 30 cm. – 0 11 042589 8 *£1.75*

The Part-time Workers (Prevention of Less Favourable Treatment) Regulations 2000 (Amendment) Regulations 2002 No. 2002/2035. – Enabling power: Employment Relations Act 1999, s. 19. – Issued: 09.08.2002. Made: 30.07.2002. Coming into force: 01.10.2002. Effect: S.I. 2000/1551 amended. Territorial extent & classification: E/W/S. General. – 2p.: 30 cm. – 0 11 042628 2 *£1.50*

The Paternity and Adoption Leave Regulations 2002 No. 2002/2788. – Enabling power: Employment Rights Act 1996, ss. 47C(2), 75A (1) to (3) (6) (7), 75B (1) (2) (4) (8), 75C (1) (2), 75D (1), 80A (1) (2) (5), 80B (1) (2) (5), 80C (1) (6), 80D (1), 80E, 99 (1). – Issued: 21.11.2002. Made: 11.11.2002. Coming into force: 08.12.2002. Effect: None. Territorial extent & classification: E/W/S. General. – [20]p.: 30 cm. – Supersedes draft S.I. (ISBN 0110429222) issued on 31.10.2002 – 0 11 042972 9 *£3.50*

The Recognition and Derecognition Ballots (Qualified Persons) Order 2000 (Amendment) Order 2002 No. 2002/2268. – Enabling power: Trade Union and Labour Relations (Consolidation) Act 1992, sch. A1, paras. 25 (7) (a), 117 (9) (a). – Issued: 03.10.2002. Made: 03.09.2002. Laid: 05.09.2002. Coming into force: 01.10.2002. Effect: S.I. 2000/1306 amended. Territorial extent & classification: E/W/S. General. – 2p.: 30 cm. – 0 11 042827 7 *£1.50*

The Redundancy Payments (Continuity of Employment in Local Government, etc.) (Modification) (Amendment) Order 2002 No. 2002/532. – Enabling power: Employment Rights Act 1996, ss. 209 (1) (b), 236. – Issued: 20.03.2002. Made: 07.03.2002. Laid: 08.03.2002. Coming into force: 01.04.2002. Effect: S.I. 1999/2277 amended. Territorial extent & classification: E/W/S. General. – 2p.: 30 cm. – 0 11 039507 7 *£1.50*

The Social Security Benefits Up-rating Order 2002 No. 2002/668. – Enabling power: Social Security Administration Act 1992, ss. 150, 151, 189 (1) (3) (4) (5). – Issued: 20.03.2002. Made: 12.03.2002. Coming into force: In accord. with art. 1 (2). Effect: 1965 c. 51; 1992 c. 4; 1993 c. 48 & S.I. 1976/1267; 1978/393; 1986/1960; 1987/1967, 1969, 1971; 1991/2890; 1992/1814; 1994/2946; 1995/310; 1996/207 amended & S.I. 2001/207 revoked (01.04.2002). Territorial extent & classification: E/W/S. General. – 54p.: 30 cm. – Revoked by S.I. 2003/526 (ISBN 0110451732) – 0 11 039490 9 *£7.50*

The Social Security, Statutory Maternity Pay and Statutory Sick Pay (Miscellaneous Amendments) Regulations 2002 No. 2002/2690. – Enabling power: Social Security Contributions and Benefits Act 1992, ss. 35 (3), 35A (4) (5) (a) (d), 153 (6), 163 (1) (3), 164 (9) (c) (ea), 165 (1) (3) (7), 166 (1) (b), 171 (1) (3) (b) to (d) (5), 171ZP (2) (3), 171ZS (1), 175 (1) to (4), sch. 11, paras 1, 1A, sch. 13, para. 2 & Social Security Administration Act 1992, ss. 5 (1) (I), 132 (1) (2), 189 (1) (191). – Issued: 01.11.2002. Made: 30.10.2002. Laid: 01.11.2002. Coming into force: In accord. with reg. 1 (1). Effect: S.I. 1982/894; 1986/1960; 1987/416; 1991/590; 1994/2946; 2000/688 amended. Territorial extent & classification: E/W/S. General. – 12p.: 30 cm. – 0 11 042935 4 *£2.50*

The Statutory Maternity Pay (Compensation of Employers) Amendment Regulations 2002 No. 2002/225. – Enabling power: Social Security Contributions and Benefits Act 1992, ss. 167 (1) (c) (1B) (a), 171 (1), 175 (1) to (3) & Social Security Contributions and Benefits (Northern Ireland) Act 1992, s. 163 (1) (c) (1B) (a) (5), 171 (1) (3) (10). – Issued: 08.02.2002. Made: 05.02.2002. Laid: 08.02.2002. Coming into force: 06.04.2002. Effect: S.I. 1994/1882; S.R. 1994/271 amended. Territorial extent & classification:E/W/S. General. – 4p.: 30 cm. – 0 11 039283 3 *£1.75*

The Statutory Paternity Pay and Statutory Adoption Pay (Administration) Regulations 2002 No. 2002/2820. – Enabling power: Employment Act 2002, ss. 7 (1) (2) (a) (b) (4) (a) (b) (c) (5), 8 (1) (2) (a) (b) (c), 10 (1) (2), 51 (1) & Social Security Contributions (Transfer of Functions etc.) Act 1999, ss. 8 (1) (f) (ga), 25. – Issued: 29.11.2002. Made: 13.11.2002. Laid: 15.11.2002. Coming into force: 08.12.2002. Effect: None. Territorial extent & classification: E/W/S. General. – 8p.: 30 cm. – 0 11 044026 9 *£2.00*

The Statutory Paternity Pay and Statutory Adoption Pay (General) Regulations 2002 No. 2002/2822. – Enabling power: Social Security Contributions and Benefits Act 1992, ss. 171ZA (2) (a), 171ZB (2) (a), 171ZC (3) (a) (c) (d) (f) (g), 171ZD (2) (3), 171ZE (2) (a) (b) (i) (3) (7) (8), 171ZG (3), 171ZJ (1) (3) (4) (7) (8), 171ZL (8) (b) to (d) (f) (g), 171ZM (2) (3), 171ZN (2) (5) (6), 171ZP (6), 171ZS (1) (3) (4) (7) (8), 175 (4) & Social Security Administration Act 1992, s. 5 (1) (g) (i) (p). – Issued: 06.12.2002. Made: 13.11.2002. Laid: 15.11.2002. Coming into force: 08.12.2002. Effect: None. Territorial extent & classification: E/W/S. General. – 20p.: 30 cm. – 0 11 044100 1 *£3.50*

The Statutory Paternity Pay and Statutory Adoption Pay (National Health Service Employees) Regulations 2002 No. 2002/2819. – Enabling power: Social Security Contributions and Benefits Act 1992, ss. 171ZJ (9) (10), 171ZS (9) (10). – Issued: 29.11.2002. Made: 13.11.2002. Laid: 15.11.2002. Coming into force: 08.12.2002. Effect: None. Territorial extent & classification: E/W/S. General. – 4p.: 30 cm. – 0 11 043996 1 *£1.75*

The Statutory Paternity Pay and Statutory Adoption Pay (Persons Abroad and Mariners) Regulations 2002 No. 2002/2821. – Enabling power: Social Security Contributions and Benefits Act 1992, ss. 171ZI, 171ZJ (1), 171ZR, 171ZS (1). – Issued: 29.11.2002. Made: 13.11.2002. Laid: 15.11.2002. Coming into force: 08.12.2002. Effect: None. Territorial extent & classification: E/W/S. General. – 4p.: 30 cm. – 0 11 044027 7 *£1.75*

The Statutory Paternity Pay and Statutory Adoption Pay (Weekly Rates) Regulations 2002 No. 2002/2818. – Enabling power: Social Security Contributions and Benefits Act 1992, ss. 171ZE (1), 171ZN (1) & Social Security Administration Act 1992, s. 5 (1) (I). – Issued: 21.11.2002. Made: 11.11.2002. Coming into force: 08.12.2002. Effect: None. Territorial extent & classification: E/W/S. General. – 2p.: 30 cm. – Supersedes draft S.I. (ISBN 0110429095) issued on 30.10.2002 – 0 11 042992 3 *£1.50*

The Working Time (Amendment) Regulations 2002 No. 2002/3128. – Enabling power: European Communities Act 1972, s. 2 (2). Issued: 10.01.2003. Made: 16.12.2002. Laid: 18.12.2002. Coming into force: 06.04.2003. Effect: S.I. 1998/1833 amended. Territorial extent & classification: E/W/S. General. – 4p.: 30 cm. – EC note: Implement certain provisions of Council directive 94/33/EC on the protection of young people at work – 0 11 044467 1 *£1.75*

Territorial sea

The Territorial Sea Act 1987 (Jersey) (Amendment) Order 2002 No. 2002/250. – Enabling power: Territorial Sea Act 1987, s. 4 (4). – Issued: 20.02.2002. Made: 12.02.2002. Coming into force: In accord. with art. 1. Effect: S.I. 1997/278 amended. Territorial extent & classification: E/W/S/NI. General. – 2p.: 30 cm. – 0 11 039327 9 *£1.50*

Territorial waters

The National Heritage (Territorial Waters Adjacent to England) Order 2002 No. 2002/2427. – Enabling power: National Heritage Act 1983, s. 33 (10). – Issued: 30.09.2002. Made: 18.09.2002. Laid: 23.09.2002. Coming into force: 15.10.2002. Effect: None. Territorial extent & classification: E. General. – With correction slip dated October 2002. – 4p.: 30 cm. – 0 11 042816 1 *£1.75*

Terrorism, Northern Ireland

The Terrorism Act 2000 (Cessation of Effect of Section 76) Order 2002 No. 2002/2141. – Enabling power: Terrorism Act 2000, s. 112 (2) (b). – Issued: 22.08.2002. Made: 25.07.2002. Coming into force: 26.07.2002. Effect: 2000 c. 11 amended. Territorial extent & classification: NI. General. – 2p.: 30 cm. – Supersedes draft S.I. (ISBN 0110424204) issued on 04.07.2002 – 0 11 042674 6 *£1.50*

The Terrorism Act 2000 (Continuance of Part VII) Order 2002 No. 2002/365. – Enabling power: Terrorism Act 2000, s. 112 (2) (a). – Issued: 26.02.2002. Made: 18.02.2002. Coming into force: 19.02.2002. Effect: None. Territorial extent & classification: NI. General. – Supersedes draft S.I. (ISBN 0110392361) issued 31.01.2002. – 2p.: 30 cm. – 0 11 039367 8 *£1.50*

Town and country planning, England

The Planning and Compensation Act 1991 (Amendment of Schedule 18) (England) Order 2002 No. 2002/116. – Enabling power: Planning and Compensation Act 1991, s. 80 (4). – Issued: 31.01.2002. Made: 24.01.2002. Laid: 31.01.2002. Coming into force: 22.02.2002. Effect: 1991 c.34 amended. Territorial extent & classification: E. General. – 2p.: 30 cm. – 0 11 039232 9 *£1.50*

The Town and Country Planning (Costs of Inquiries etc.) (Standard Daily Amount) (England) Regulations 2002 No. 2002/452. – Enabling power: Town and Country Planning Act 1990, s. 303A (5). – Issued: 08.03.2002. Made: 01.03.2002. Laid: 08.03.2002. Coming into force: 31.03.2002. Effect: None. Territorial extent & classification: E. General. – 4p.: 30 cm. – 0 11 039420 8 *£1.75*

The Town and Country Planning (Enforcement Notices and Appeals) (England) Regulations 2002 No. 2002/2682. – Enabling power: Town and Country Planning Act 1990, ss. 173 (10), 174 (4), 175 (1) & Planning (Listed Buildings and Conservation Areas) Act 1990, ss. 39 (4), 40 (1), 42 (5), 91 (1) (a). – Issued: 01.11.2002. Made: 23.10.2002. Laid: 01.11.2002. Coming into force: 23.12.2002. Effect: S.I. 1991/2804 (with saving); 1992/1904 revoked in relation to England. Territorial extent & classification: E. General. – 8p.: 30 cm. – 0 11 042912 5 *£2.00*

The Town and Country Planning (Enforcement) (Written Representations Procedure) (England) Regulations 2002 No. 2002/2683. – Enabling power: Town and Country Planning Act 1990, ss. 175, 323. – Issued: 01.11.2002. Made: 23.10.2002. Laid: 01.11.2002. Coming into force: 23.12.2002. Effect: None. Territorial extent & classification: E. General. – [8]p.: 30 cm. – 0 11 042913 3 *£2.00*

The Town and Country Planning (Fees for Applications and Deemed Applications) (Amendment) (England) Regulations 2002 No. 2002/768. – Enabling power: Town and Country Planning Act 1990, s. 303. – Issued: 27.03.2002. Made: 20.03.2002. Coming into force: 01.04.2002. Effect: S.I. 1989/193; 1997/37 amended in relation to England. Territorial extent & classification: E. General. – Supersedes draft S.I. (ISBN 0110392930) issued 12 February 2002. – 8p.: 30 cm. – 0 11 039592 1 *£2.00*

The Town and Country Planning (General Development Procedure) (Amendment) (England) Order 2002 No. 2002/828. – Enabling power: Town and Country Planning Act 1990, ss. 59, 69, 333 (7). – Issued: 28.03.2002. Made: 26.03.2002. Laid: 28.03.2002. Coming into force: 01.07.2002. Effect: S.I. 1995/419 amended in relation to England. Territorial extent & classification: E. General. – 4p.: 30 cm. – 0 11 039628 6 *£1.75*

Town and country planning, Wales

The Town and Country Planning (Costs of Inquiries etc.) (Standard Daily Amount) (Wales) Regulations 2002 No. 2002/2801 (W.269). – Enabling power: Town and Country Planning Act 1990, s. 303A (5). – Issued: 22.11.2002. Made: 12.11.2002. Coming into force: 01.04.2003. Effect: None. Territorial extent & classification: W. General. – 4p.: 30 cm. – In English & Welsh. Welsh title: Rheoliadau Cynllunio Gwlad a Thref (Costau Ymchwiliadau etc.) (Swm Dyddiol Safonol) (Cymru) 2002 – 0 11 090581 4 *£1.75*

The Town and Country Planning (Fees for Applications and Deemed Applications) (Amendment No. 2) (Wales) Regulations 2002 No. 2002/2258 (W.222). – Enabling power: Town and Country Planning Act 1990, s. 303. – Issued: 09.09.2002. Made: 03.09.2002. Coming into force: 04.09.2002. Effect: S.I. 1989/193 amended in relation to Wales. Territorial extent & classification: W. General. – 8p.: 30 cm. – In English & Welsh. Welsh title: Rheoliadau Cynllunio Gwlad a Thref (Ffioedd ar gyfer Ceisiadau a Cheisiadau Tybiedig) (Diwygio Rhif 2) (Cymru) 2002 – 0 11 090567 9 *£2.00*

The Town and Country Planning (Fees for Applications and Deemed Applications) (Amendment) (Wales) Regulations 2002 No. 2002/1876 (W.185). – Enabling power: Town and Country Planning Act 1990, s. 303. – Issued: 02.08.2002. Made: 18.07.2002. Coming into force: 01.08.2002. Effect: S.I. 1989/193 amended in relation to Wales. Territorial extent & classification: W. General. – 4p.: 30 cm. – In English & Welsh. Welsh title: Rheoliadau Cynllunio Gwlad a Thref (Ffioedd ar gyfer Ceisiadau a Chesiadau Tybiedig) (Diwygio) (Cymru) 2002 – 0 11 090537 7 *£1.75*

The Town and Country Planning (General Development Procedure) (Amendment) (Wales) Order 2002 No. 2002/1877 (W.186). – Enabling power: Town and Country Planning Act 1990, ss. 59, 61 (1), 65, 69, 71, 73 (3), 74, 77 (4), 78, 79 (4), 188, 193, 196 (4), 333 (7), sch. 1, paras. 5, 6, 7 (6), 8 (6). – Issued: 02.08.2002. Made: 18.07.2002. Coming into force: 01.08.2002. Effect: S.I. 1995/419 amended. Territorial extent & classification: W. General. – 4p.: 30 cm. – In English and Welsh. Welsh title: Gorchymyn Cynllunio Gwlad a Thref (Gweithdrefn Datblygu Cyffredinol) (Diwygio) (Cymru) 2002 – 0 11 090536 9 *£1.75*

The Town and Country Planning (General Permitted Development) (Amendment) (Wales) Order 2002 No. 2002/1878 (W.187). – Enabling power: Town and Country Planning Act 1990, ss. 59, 60, 61 (1), 333 (7). – Issued: 02.08.2002. Made: 18.07.2002. Coming into force: 01.08.2002. Effect: S.I. 1995/418; 1998/462; 1999/1661 amended in relation to Wales. Territorial extent & classification: W. General. – 12p.: 30 cm. – In English and Welsh. Welsh title: Gorchymyn Cynllunio Gwlad a Thref (Datblygu Cyffredinol a Ganiateir) (Diwygio) (Cymru) 2002 – 0 11 090535 0 *£2.50*

The Town and Country Planning (Use Classes) (Amendment) (Wales) Order 2002 No. 2002/1875 (W.184). – Enabling power: Town and Country Planning Act 1990, ss. 55 (2) (f), 333 (7). – Issued: 06.08.2002. Made: 18.07.2002. Coming into force: 12.08.2002. Effect: S.I. 1987/764 amended in relation to Wales. Territorial extent & classification: W. General. – In English and Welsh. Welsh title: Gorchymyn Cynllunio Gwlad a Thref (Dosbarthiadau Defnydd) (Diwygio) (Cymru) 2002. – 4p.: 30 cm. – 0 11 090534 2 *£1.75*

Tractors

The Agricultural or Forestry Tractors and Tractor Components (Type Approval) (Amendment) Regulations 2002 No. 2002/1890. – Enabling power: European Communities Act 1972, s. 2 (2). – Issued: 31.07.2002. Made: 17.07.2002. Laid: 22.07.2002. Coming into force: 12.08.2002. Effect: S.I. 1988/1567 amended. Territorial extent & classification: E/W/S/NI. General. – 2p.: 30 cm. – EC note: These Regs. amend the 1988 Regs. in consequence of the implementation by S.I. 2002/1891 of articles 4.3 to 4.5 of DIR 2000/25 – 0 11 042547 2 *£1.50*

Trade marks

The Copyright, etc. and Trade Marks (Offences and Enforcement) Act 2002 (Commencement) Order 2002 No. 2002/2749 (C.84). – Enabling power: Copyright, etc. and Trade Marks (Offences and Enforcement) Act 2002, s. 7 (2). Bringing into operation various provisions of the 2002 Act on 20.11.2002. – Issued: 12.11.2002. Made: 05.11.2002. Effect: None. Territorial extent & classification:E/W/S/NI. General. – 2p.: 30 cm. – 0 11 042949 4 *£1.50*

The Trade Marks Act 1994 (Isle of Man) (Amendment) Order 2002 No. 2002/3148. – Enabling power: Trade Marks Act 1994, s. 108 (2). – Issued: 24.12.2002. Made: 17.12.2002. Coming into force: 24.12.2002. Effect: S.I. 1996/729 amended. Territorial extent & classification: IoM. General. – 2p.: 30 cm. – 0 11 044275 X *£1.50*

The Trade Marks (International Registration) (Amendment) Order 2002 No. 2002/692. – Enabling power: Trade Marks Act 1994, s. 54. – Issued: 08.04.2002. Made: 14.03.2002. Laid: 14.03.2002. Coming into force: 04.04.2002. Effect: S.I. 1996/714 amended. Territorial extent & classification:E/W/S/NI/IoM. General. – 8p.: 30 cm. – 0 11 039667 7 *£2.00*

Trade unions

The Trade Union Ballots and Elections (Independent Scrutineer Qualifications) Order 1993 (Amendment) Order 2002 No. 2002/2267. – Enabling power: Trade Union and Labour Relations (Consolidation) Act 1992, ss. 49 (2), 75 (2), 100A (2), 226B (2). – Issued: 04.10.2002. Made: 03.09.2002. Laid: 05.09.2002. Coming into force: 01.10.2002. Effect: S.I. 1993/1909 amended. Territorial extent & classification: E/W/S. General. – 2p.: 30 cm. – 0 11 042833 1 *£1.50*

Transport

The Merseyrail Electrics Network Order 2002 No. 2002/1946. – Enabling power: Railways Act 1993, ss. 24 (1) (2) (12), 49 (2) to (5), 151 (5). – Issued: 06.08.2002. Made: 18.07.2002. Laid: 24.07.2002. Coming into force: 20.07.2003. Effect: None. Territorial extent & classification: E/W.S. General. – 4p.: 30 cm. – 0 11 042584 7 *£1.75*

The Public Service Vehicles Accessibility (Amendment) Regulations 2002 No. 2002/2981. – Enabling power: Disability Discrimination Act 1995, ss. 40 (1) (2) (6) (7), 67 (2). – Issued: 11.12.2002. Made: 03.12.2002. Laid: 05.12.2002. Coming into force: 31.12.2002. Effect: S.I. 2000/1970 amended. Territorial extent & classification: E/W/S. General. – 2p.: 30 cm. – 0 11 044132 X *£1.50*

The Rail Vehicle Accessibility (C2C Class 357/0 Vehicles) Exemption (Amendment) Order 2002 No. 2002/3002. – Enabling power: Disability Discrimination Act 1995, s. 47. – Issued: 12.12.2002. Made: 04.12.2002. Laid: 05.12.2002. Coming into force: 01.01.2003. Effect: S.I. 2001/3955 amended. Territorial extent & classification: E/W/S/NI. General. – 2p.: 30 cm. – 0 11 044136 2 *£1.50*

The Rail Vehicle Accessibility (Cairngorm Funicular Railway) Exemption Order 2002 No. 2002/657. – Enabling power: Disability Discrimination Act 1995, s. 47 (1) (3) (4). – Issued: 19.03.2002. Made: 08.03.2002. Laid: 13.03.2002. Coming into force: 03.04.2002. Effect: None. Territorial extent & classification: E/W/S/NI. General. – 4p.: 30 cm. – 0 11 039483 6 *£1.75*

The Rail Vehicle Accessibility (Croydon Tramlink Class CR4000 Vehicles) Exemption (Amendment) Order 2002 No. 2002/3001. – Enabling power: Disability Discrimination Act 1995, s. 47. – Issued: 12.12.2002. Made: 04.12.2002. Laid: 05.12.2002. Coming into force: 01.01.2003. Effect: S.I. 2001/3952 amended. Territorial extent & classification: E/W/S/NI. General. – 2p.: 30 cm. – 0 11 044166 4 £1.50

The Rail Vehicle Accessibility (East Hayling Light Railway Vehicles) Exemption Order 2002 No. 2002/285. – Enabling power: Disability Discrimination Act 1995, s. 47 (1). – Issued: 20.02.2002. Made: 11.02.2002. Laid: 13.02.2002. Coming into force: 07.03.2002. Effect: None. Territorial extent & classification: E/W/S. General. – 8p., ill.: 30 cm. – 0 11 039335 X £2.00

The Rail Vehicle Accessibility (Isle of Wight Railway LCDR No. 2515 Vehicle) Exemption Order 2002 No. 2002/1694. – Enabling power: Disability Discrimination Act 1995, s. 47 (1) (3) (4). – Issued: 09.07.2002. Made: 28.06.2002. Laid: 03.07.2002. Coming into force: 31.07.2002. Effect: None. Territorial extent & classification: E/W/S/NI. General. – 4p.: 30 cm. – 0 11 042433 6 £1.75

The Rail Vehicle Accessibility (Middleton Railway Drewry Car) Exemption Order 2002 No. 2002/1188. – Enabling power: Disability Discrimination Act 1995, s. 47 (1) (3) (4). – Issued: 07.05.2002. Made: 25.04.2002. Laid: 30.04.2002. Coming into force: 22.05.2002. Effect: None. Territorial extent & classification: E/W/S/NI. General. – 4p.: 30 cm. – 0 11 039894 7 £1.75

The Rail Vehicle Accessibility (South Central Class 375/3 Vehicles) Exemption Order 2002 No. 2002/1617. – Enabling power: Disability Discrimination Act 1995, s. 47 (1) (3) (4). – Issued: 11.07.2002. Made: 23.06.2002. Laid: 24.06.2002. Coming into force: 16.07.2002. Effect: None. Territorial extent & classification: E/W/S/NI. General. – 4p.: 30 cm. – 0 11 042450 6 £1.75

The Rail Vehicle Accessibility (South West Trains Class 458 Vehicles) Exemption (Amendment) Order 2002 No. 2002/1762. – Enabling power: Disability Discrimination Act 1995, s. 47. – Issued: 24.07.2002. Made: 10.07.2002. Laid: 10.07.2002. Coming into force: 31.07.2002. Effect: S.I. 2002/656 amended. Territorial extent & classification: E/W/S/NI. General. – 4p.: 30 cm. – 0 11 042518 9 £1.75

The Rail Vehicle Accessibility (South West Trains Class 458 Vehicles) Exemption Order 2002 No. 2002/656. – Enabling power: Disability Discrimination Act 1995, s. 47. – Issued: 19.03.2002. Made: 08.03.2002. Laid: 13.03.2002. Coming into force: 03.04.2002. Effect: S.I. 2001/848 revoked. Territorial extent & classification: E/W/S/NI. General. – 4p.: 30 cm. – 0 11 039482 8 £1.75

The Rail Vehicle Accessibility (Summerlee Tramcar No. 392) Exemption Order 2002 No. 2002/2873. – Enabling power: Disability Discrimination Act 1995, s. 47 (1) (3) (4). – Issued: 28.11.2002. Made: 20.11.2002. Laid: 21.11.2002. Coming into force: 15.12.2002 Effect: None. Territorial extent & classification: E/W/S/NI. General. – 4p.: 30 cm. – 0 11 043698 9 £1.75

The Rail Vehicle Accessibility (Virgin West Coast Class 390 Vehicles) Exemption Order 2002 No. 2002/1699. – Enabling power: Disability Discrimination Act 1995, s. 47 (1) (3) (4). – Issued: 18.07.2002. Made: 28.06.2002. Laid: 03.07.2002. Coming into force: 22.07.2002. Effect: None. Territorial extent & classification: E/W/S. General. – 4p.: 30 cm. – 0 11 042466 2 £1.75

The Transport Act 2000 (Commencement No. 8 and Transitional Provisions) (Amendment) Order 2002 No. 2002/846 (C.23). – Enabling power: Transport Act 2000, s. 275 (1). – Issued: 04.04.2002. Made: 27.03.2002. Effect: S.I. 2002/658 (C. 16) amended. Territorial extent & classification: E/W/S. General. – This Statutory Instrument has been made in consequence of a defect in S.I. 2002/658 (C. 16) and is being issued free of charge to all known recipients of that SI. – 2p.: 30 cm. – 0 11 039654 5 £1.50

The Transport Act 2000 (Commencement No. 8 and Transitional Provisions) Order 2002 No. 2002/658 (C.16). – Enabling power: Transport Act 2000, ss. 275 (1) (2), 276. Bringing into operation various provisions of the 2000 Act on 01.04.2002. – Issued: 20.03.2002. Made: 10.03.2002. Effect: None. Territorial extent & classification: E/W/S. General. – 8p.: 30 cm. – 0 11 039499 2 £2.00

The Transport Tribunal (Amendment) Rules 2002 No. 2002/643. – Enabling power: Transport Act 1985, sch. 4, para. 11 (1) (2) (d). – Issued: 20.03.2002. Made: 08.03.2002. Laid: 11.03.2002. Coming into force: 01.04.2002. Effect: S.I. 2000/3226 amended. Territorial extent & classification: E/W/S. General. – 4p.: 30 cm. – 0 11 039503 4 £1.75

Transport: Railways

The Railways (Interoperability) (High-Speed) Regulations 2002 No. 2002/1166. – Enabling power: European Communities Act 1972, s. 2 (2) & Transport Act 2000, s. 247. – Issued: 02.05.2002. Made: 24.04.2002. Laid: 25.04.2002. Coming into force: 16.05.2002. Effect: S.I. 1994/157 amended & S.I. 2000/1674 revoked with saving. Territorial extent & classification: EW/S/NI. General. – EC note: Implements, for the UK, DIR 96/48/EC on the interoperability of the trans-European high-speed rail system. – 37p.: 30 cm. – 0 11 039857 2 £6.50

Transport and works, England

The Bitton Railway Order 2002 No. 2002/366. – Enabling power: Transport and Works Act 1992, ss. 1, 5, sch. 1, paras. 1, 7, 16, 17. – Issued: 26.02.2002. Made: 22.01.2002. Coming into force: 12.02.2002. Effect: None. Territorial extent & classification: E. General. – 12p.: 30 cm. – In the areas of the Councils of South Gloucestershire and of Bath and North East Somerset – 0 11 039368 6 £2.50

The Channel Tunnel Rail Link (Thames Tunnel Approach) Order 2002 No. 2002/1943. – Enabling power: Transport and Works Act 1992, ss. 1, 5, sh. 1, paras. 4, 7, 8, 10, 11, 15 to 17. – Issued: 30.07.2002. Made: 22.07.2002. Coming into force: 12.08.2002. Effect: None. Territorial extent & classification: E. General. – 8p.: 30 cm. – 0 11 042560 X £2.00

The Chester Guided Busway Order 2002 No. 2002/412. – Enabling power: Transport and Works Act 1992, ss. 1, 5, sch. 1, paras. 1 to 5, 7 to 13, 15 to 17. – Issued: 04.03.2002. Made: 21.02.2002. Coming into force: 14.03.2002. Effect: 1965 c. 56; 1973 c. 26 modified. Territorial extent & classification: E. General. – 37p.: 30 cm. – 0 11 039394 5 £6.50

The Docklands Light Railway (Silvertown and London City Airport Extension) Order 2002 No. 2002/1066. – Enabling power: Transport and Works Act 1992, ss. 1, 5, sch. 1, paras. 1 to 4, 7, 8, 10, 11, 15 to 17. – Issued: 22.04.2002. Made: 09.04.2002. Coming into force: 30.04.2002. Effect: 1965 c. 56; 1973 c. 26 modified. Territorial extent & classification: E. General. – 50p.: 30 cm. – 0 11 039768 1 £7.50

The Greater Manchester (Light Rapid Transit System) (Trafford Depot) Order 2002 No. 2002/1327. – Enabling power: Transport and Works Act 1992, ss. 1, 5, sch. 1, paras. 1 to 4, 7 to 13, 15 to 17. – Issued: 20.05.2002. Made: 10.05.2002. Coming into force: 31.05.2002. Effect: 1965 c. 56; 1973 c. 26; 1981 c. 66 modified. Territorial extent & classification: E. General. – 23p.: 30 cm. – 0 11 039953 6 £4.00

The Heathrow Express Railway Extension Order 2002 No. 2002/1064. – Enabling power: Transport and Works Act 1992, ss. 1, 5, sch. 1, paras 1 to 5, 7 to 11, 13, 15, 16. – Issued: 01.05.2002. Made: 09.04.2002. Coming into force: 30.04.2002. Effect: 1965 c. 56; 1991 c.viii amended. Territorial extent & classification: E. General. – 28p.: 30 cm. – 0 11 039832 7 £4.50

The Piccadilly Line (Heathrow T5 Extension) Order 2002 No. 2002/1065. – Enabling power: Transport and Works Act 1992, ss. 1, 5, sch. 1, paras 1 to 5, 7, 10, 11, 15 to 17. – Issued: 01.05.2002. Made: 09.04.2002. Coming into force: 30.04.2002. Effect: 1965 c.56 amended. Territorial extent & classification: E. General. – 20p.: 30 cm. – 0 11 039833 5 £4.50

The Strand Road, Preston Railway Order 2002 No. 2002/2398. – Enabling power: Transport and Works Act 1992, ss. 1, 5, sch. 1, paras. 1, 3, 8, 15, 17. – Issued: 25.09.2002. Made: 03.09.2002. Coming into force: 24.09.2002. Effect: None. Territorial extent & classification: E. General. – 8p.: 30 cm. – In the area of Preston City Council – 0 11 042798 X £2.00

The Wear Valley Railway Order 2002 No. 2002/1997. – Enabling power: Transport and Works Act 1992, ss. 1, 5, , sch. 1, paras. 1, 15. – Issued: 05.08.2002. Made: 22.07.2002. Coming into force: 12.08.2002. Effect: None. Territorial extent & classification: E. General. – 8p.: 30 cm. – 0 11 042583 9 £2.00

Transport and works, England and Wales

The Transport and Works (Applications and Objections Procedure) (England and Wales) (Amendment) Rules 2002 No. 2002/1965. – Enabling power: Transport and Works Act 1992, s. 6 (4) (5). – Issued: 07.08.2002. Made: 24.07.2002. Laid: 25.07.2002. Coming into force: 22.08.2002. Effect: S.I. 2000/2190 amended. Territorial extent & classification: E/W. General. – 4p.: 30 cm. – 0 11 042606 1 £1.75

The Wye Navigation Order 2002 No. 2002/1998. – Enabling power: Transport and Works Act 1992, ss. 3, 5, sch. 1, paras 1, 2, 4, 7, 8, 12, 13, 16. – Issued: 05.08.2002. Made: 25.07.2002. Coming into force: 15.08.2002. Effect: 1985 c. xlii amended & 1662 (13 & 14 Cha. 2) c. xiv; 1695 (7 & 8 Will. 3) c. 14; 1727 (13 Geo. 1) c. 34; 1809 (49 Geo. 3) c. lxxviii repealed (with savings). Territorial extent & classification: E/W. General. – 29p., map: 30 cm. – With correction slip, dated August 2002 – 0 11 042582 0 £6.50

Transport, England

The Bitton Railway Order 2002 No. 2002/366. – Enabling power: Transport and Works Act 1992, ss. 1, 5, sch. 1, paras. 1, 7, 16, 17. – Issued: 26.02.2002. Made: 22.01.2002. Coming into force: 12.02.2002. Effect: None. Territorial extent & classification: E. General. – 12p.: 30 cm. – In the areas of the Councils of South Gloucestershire and of Bath and North East Somerset – 0 11 039368 6 £2.50

The Channel Tunnel Rail Link (Thames Tunnel Approach) Order 2002 No. 2002/1943. – Enabling power: Transport and Works Act 1992, ss. 1, 5, sh. 1, paras. 4, 7, 8, 10, 11, 15 to 17. – Issued: 30.07.2002. Made: 22.07.2002. Coming into force: 12.08.2002. Effect: None. Territorial extent & classification: E. General. – 8p.: 30 cm. – 0 11 042560 X £2.00

The Chester Guided Busway Order 2002 No. 2002/412. – Enabling power: Transport and Works Act 1992, ss. 1, 5, sch. 1, paras. 1 to 5, 7 to 13, 15 to 17. – Issued: 04.03.2002. Made: 21.02.2002. Coming into force: 14.03.2002. Effect: 1965 c. 56; 1973 c. 26 modified. Territorial extent & classification: E. General. – 37p.: 30 cm. – 0 11 039394 5 £6.50

The Docklands Light Railway (Silvertown and London City Airport Extension) Order 2002 No. 2002/1066. – Enabling power: Transport and Works Act 1992, ss. 1, 5, sch. 1, paras. 1 to 4, 7, 8, 10, 11, 15 to 17. – Issued: 22.04.2002. Made: 09.04.2002. Coming into force: 30.04.2002. Effect: 1965 c. 56; 1973 c. 26 modified. Territorial extent & classification: E. General. – 50p.: 30 cm. – 0 11 039768 1 £7.50

The East Lancashire (Heywood Extension) Light Railway Order 2002 No. 2002/1384. – Enabling power: Light Railways Act 1896, s. 7, 10 to 12 and Transport Act 1968 s. 121 (4). – Issued: 24.05.2002. Made: 15.05.2002. Coming into force: 16.05.2002. Effect: None. Territorial extent & classification: E. General. – 8p.: 30 cm. – 0 11 039978 1 £2.00

The Greater Manchester (Light Rapid Transit System) (Trafford Depot) Order 2002 No. 2002/1327. – Enabling power: Transport and Works Act 1992, ss. 1, 5, sch. 1, paras. 1 to 4, 7 to 13, 15 to 17. – Issued: 20.05.2002. Made: 10.05.2002. Coming into force: 31.05.2002. Effect: 1965 c. 56; 1973 c. 26; 1981 c. 66 modified. Territorial extent & classification: E. General. – 23p.: 30 cm. – 0 11 039953 6 £4.00

The Heathrow Express Railway Extension Order 2002 No. 2002/1064. – Enabling power: Transport and Works Act 1992, ss. 1, 5, sch. 1, paras 1 to 5, 7 to 11, 13, 15, 16. – Issued: 01.05.2002. Made: 09.04.2002. Coming into force: 30.04.2002. Effect: 1965 c. 56; 1991 c.viii amended. Territorial extent & classification: E. General. – 28p.: 30 cm. – 0 11 039832 7 £4.50

The Piccadilly Line (Heathrow T5 Extension) Order 2002 No. 2002/1065. – Enabling power: Transport and Works Act 1992, ss. 1, 5, sch. 1, paras 1 to 5, 7, 10, 11, 15 to 17. – Issued: 01.05.2002. Made: 09.04.2002. Coming into force: 30.04.2002. Effect: 1965 c.56 amended. Territorial extent & classification: E. General. – 28p.: 30 cm. – 0 11 039833 5 £4.50

The Railways (Heathrow Express) (Exemptions) (Amendment) Order 2002 No. 2002/2703. – Enabling power: Railways Act 1993, ss. 49 (2), 143 (4), 151 (5). – Issued: 05.11.2002. Made: 24.10.2002. Laid: 01.11.2002. Coming into force: 01.12.2002. Effect: S.I. 1994/574 amended. Territorial extent & classification: E. General. – 2p.: 30 cm. – 0 11 042937 0 £1.50

The Service Subsidy Agreements (Tendering) (England) Regulations 2002 No. 2002/2090. – Enabling power: Transport Act 1985, ss. 90 (2) (3), 91 (1) (7), 134 (5). – Issued: 15.08.2002. Made: 06.08.2002. Laid: 08.08.2002. Coming into force: 02.09.2002. Effect: S.I. 1985/1921; 1989/464; 1994/1227; 1998/2197 revoked in relation to England & 1985 c.67 excludes from s. 89 (1) various agreements that provide for the payment of service subsidies as part of the provision of a local service. Territorial extent & classification: E. General. – 8p.: 30 cm. – 0 11 042646 0 £2.00

The Strand Road, Preston Railway Order 2002 No. 2002/2398. – Enabling power: Transport and Works Act 1992, ss. 1, 5, sch. 1, paras. 1, 3, 8, 15, 17. – Issued: 25.09.2002. Made: 03.09.2002. Coming into force: 24.09.2002. Effect: None. Territorial extent & classification: E. General. – 8p.: 30 cm. – In the area of Preston City Council – 0 11 042798 X £2.00

The Travel Concessions (Eligibility) Act 2002 (Commencement) (England) Order 2002 No. 2002/673 (C.17). – Enabling power: Travel Concessions (Eligibility) Act 2002, s. 2 (1). Bringing into operation various provisions of the 2000 Act on 01.04.2003 with regards to England. – Issued: 20.03.2002. Made: 12.03.2002. Effect: None. Territorial extent & classification: E. General. – 2p.: 30 cm. – 0 11 039500 X £1.50

The Wear Valley Railway Order 2002 No. 2002/1997. – Enabling power: Transport and Works Act 1992, ss. 1, 5, , sch. 1, paras. 1, 15. – Issued: 05.08.2002. Made: 22.07.2002. Coming into force: 12.08.2002. Effect: None. Territorial extent & classification: E. General. – 8p.: 30 cm. – 0 11 042583 9 £2.00

Transport, England and Wales

The Transport and Works (Applications and Objections Procedure) (England and Wales) (Amendment) Rules 2002 No. 2002/1965. – Enabling power: Transport and Works Act 1992, s. 6 (4) (5). – Issued: 07.08.2002. Made: 24.07.2002. Laid: 25.07.2002. Coming into force: 22.08.2002. Effect: S.I. 2000/2190 amended. Territorial extent & classification: E/W. General. – 4p.: 30 cm. – 0 11 042606 1 £1.75

Transport, Wales

The Service Subsidy Agreements (Tendering) (Amendment) (Wales) Regulations 2002 No. 2002/520 (W.63). – Enabling power: Transport Act 1985, s. 91 (1). – Issued: 03.04.2002. Made: 05.03.2002. Coming into force: 01.04.2002. Effect: S.I. 1985/1921 amended in relation to Wales. Territorial extent & classification: W. General. – In English and Welsh. Welsh title: Rheoliadau Cytundebau Cymhorthdal Gwasanaeth (Tendro) (Diwygio) (Cymru) 2002. – 4p.: 30 cm. – 0 11 090449 4 £1.75

The Transport Act 2000 (Commencement No. 2) (Wales) Order 2002 No. 2002/2024 (W.208) (C.65). – Enabling power: Transport Act 2000, s. 275 (2). Bringing into operation for Wales various provisions of the 2000 Act on 14.08.2002. – Issued: 16.08.2002. Made: 31.07.2002. Effect: None. Territorial extent & classification: W. General. – 8p.: 30 cm. – 0 11 090552 0 £2.00

The Travel Concessions (Eligibility) Act 2002 (Commencement) (Wales) Order 2002 No. 2002/3014 (W.286) (C.97). – Enabling power: Travel Concessions (Eligibility) Act 2002, s. 2 (1). Bringing into operation various provisions of the 2002 Act on 01.04.2003, in accord. with art. 2. – Issued: 16.12.2002. Made: 04.12.2002. Effect: None. Territorial extent & classification: W. General. – 4p.: 30 cm. – 0 11 090596 2 £1.75

Treasure

The Treasure (Designation) Order 2002 No. 2002/2666. – Enabling power: Treasure Act 1996, s. 2 (1) (3). – Issued: 29.10.2002. Made: 21.10.2002. Coming into force: 01.01.2003. Effect: None. Territorial extent & classification: E/W/NI. General. – 2p.: 30 cm. – Supersedes draft S.I. (ISBN 0110424700) issued on 18.07.2002 – 0 11 042908 7 £1.50

Tribunals and inquiries, England

The Town and Country Planning (Costs of Inquiries etc.) (Standard Daily Amount) (England) Regulations 2002 No. 2002/452. – Enabling power: Town and Country Planning Act 1990, s. 303A (5). – Issued: 08.03.2002. Made: 01.03.2002. Laid: 08.03.2002. Coming into force: 31.03.2002. Effect: None. Territorial extent & classification: E. General. – 4p.: 30 cm. – 0 11 039420 8 £1.75

The Town and Country Planning (Enforcement) (Determination by Inspectors) (Inquiries Procedure) (England) Rules 2002 No. 2002/2685. – Enabling power: Tribunals and Inquiries Act 1992, s. 9. – Issued: 01.11.2002. Made: 23.10.2002. Laid: 01.11.2002. Coming into force: 23.12.2002. Effect: None. Territorial extent & classification: E. General. – 13p.: 30 cm. – 0 11 042915 X £3.00

The Town and Country Planning (Enforcement) (Hearings Procedure) (England) Rules 2002 No. 2002/2684. – Enabling power: Tribunals and Inquiries Act 1992, s. 9. – Issued: 01.11.2002. Made: 23.10.2002. Laid: 01.11.2002. Coming into force: 23.12.2002. Effect: None. Territorial extent & classification: E. General. – 12p.: 30 cm. – 0 11 042914 1 £2.50

The Town and Country Planning (Enforcement) (Inquiries Procedure) (England) Rules 2002 No. 2002/2686. – Enabling power: Tribunals and Inquiries Act 1992, s. 9. – Issued: 01.11.2002. Made: 23.10.2002. Laid: 01.11.2002. Coming into force: 23.12.2002. Effect: S.I. 1992/1903 revoked (with saving) in relation to England. Territorial extent & classification: E. General. – 16p.: 30 cm. – 0 11 042916 8 £3.00

The Town and Country Planning (Major Infrastructure Project Inquiries Procedure) (England) Rules 2002 No. 2002/1223. – Enabling power: Tribunals and Inquiries Act 1992, s. 9. – Issued: 13.05.2002. Made: 26.04.2002. Laid: 13.05.2002. Coming into force: 07.06.2002. Effect: None. Territorial extent & classification: E. General. – 18, [1]p.: 30 cm. – 0 11 039916 1 £3.50

Tribunals and inquiries, Wales

The Fees for Inquiries (Standard Daily Amount) (Wales) Regulations 2002 No. 2002/2780 (W.264). – Enabling power: Housing and Planning Act 1986, s. 42 (4). – Issued: 22.11.2002. Made: 08.11.2002. Coming into force: 29.11.2002. Effect: None. Territorial extent & classification: W. General. – 4p.: 30 cm. – In English & Welsh. Welsh title: Rheoliadau Ffioedd Ymchwiliadau (Swm Dyddiol Safonol) (Cymru) 2002 – 0 11 090580 6 £1.75

Trustees, England and Wales

The Public Trustee (Fees) (Amendment) Order 2002 No. 2002/2232. – Enabling power: Public Trustee Act 1906, s. 9. – Issued: 09.09.2002. Made: 27.08.2002. Coming into force: 27.09.2002. Effect: S.I. 1999/855 amended. Territorial extent & classification: E/W. General. – 2p.: 30 cm. – 0 11 042727 0 £1.50

United Nations

The Al-Qa'ida and Taliban (United Nations Measures) (Amendment) Order 2002 No. 2002/251. – Enabling power: United Nations Act 1946, s. 1. – Issued: 19.02.2002. Made: 12.02.2002. Laid: 13.02.2002. Coming into force: 14.02.2002. Effect: S.I. 2002/111 amended. Territorial extent & classification: E/W/S/NI. General. – 2p.: 30 cm. – 0 11 039317 1 £1.50

The Al-Qa'ida and Taliban (United Nations Measures) (Channel Islands) Order 2002 No. 2002/258. – Enabling power: United Nations Act 1946, s. 1. – Issued: 14.02.2002. Made: 12.02.2002. Laid: 13.02.2002. Coming into force: 14.02.2002. Effect: S.I. 2001/3363 amended & S.I. 2001/393, 2562 revoked. Territorial extent & classification: Channel Islands. General. – 16p.: 30 cm. – 0 11 039313 9 £3.00

The Al-Qa'ida and Taliban (United Nations Measures) (Isle of Man) Order 2002 No. 2002/259. – Enabling power: United Nations Act 1946, s. 1. – Issued: 14.02.2002. Made: 12.02.2002. Laid: 13.02.2002. Coming into force: 14.02.2002. Effect: S.I. 2001/3364 amended & S.I. 2001/394, 2566 revoked. Territorial extent & classification: Isle of Man. General. – 16p.: 30 cm. – 0 11 039314 7 £3.00

The Al-Qa'ida and Taliban (United Nations Measures) Order 2002 No. 2002/111. – Enabling power: United Nations Act 1946, s. 1. – Issued: 14.02.2002. Made: 23.01.2002. Laid: 24.01.2002. Coming into force: 25.01.2002. Effect: None. Territorial extent & classification: E/W/S/NI. General. – 16p.: 30 cm. – 0 11 039298 1 £3.00

The Al-Qa'ida and Taliban (United Nations Measures) (Overseas Territories) (Amendment) Order 2002 No. 2002/266. – Enabling power: United Nations Act 1946, s. 1 (1). – Issued: 19.02.2002. Made: 12.02.2002. Laid: 13.02.2002. Coming into force: 14.02.2002. Effect: S.I. 2002/112 amended. Territorial extent & classification: E/W/S/NI. General. – 4p.: 30 cm. – 0 11 039318 X £1.75

The Al-Qa'ida and Taliban (United Nations Measures) (Overseas Territories) Order 2002 No. 2002/112. – Enabling power: United Nations Act 1946, s. 1. – Issued: 14.02.2002. Made: 23.01.2002. Laid: 24.01.2002. Coming into force: 25.01.2002. Effect: None. Territorial extent & classification: E/W/S/NI. General. – 16p.: 30 cm. – 0 11 039299 X £3.00

The Somalia (United Nations Sanctions) (Channel Islands) Order 2002 No. 2002/2629. – Enabling power: United Nations Act 1946, s. 1. – Issued: 23.10.2002. Made: 22.10.2002. Laid: 23.10.2002. Coming into force: 24.10.2002. Effect: S.I. 1996/3154 amended. Territorial extent & classification: CI. General. – 16p.: 30 cm. – 0 11 042888 9 £3.00

The Somalia (United Nations Sanctions) (Isle of Man) Order 2002 No. 2002/2630. – Enabling power: United Nations Act 1946, s. 1. – Issued: 23.10.2002. Made: 22.10.2002. Laid: 23.10.2002. Coming into force: 24.10.2002. Effect: S.I. 1996/3153 amended. Territorial extent & classification: IoM. General. – 16p.: 30 cm. – 0 11 042889 7 £3.00

The Somalia (United Nations Sanctions) Order 2002 No. 2002/2628. – Enabling power: United Nations Act 1946, s. 1. – Issued: 28.10.2002. Made: 22.10.2002. Laid: 23.10.2002. Coming into force: 24.10.2002. Effect: None. Territorial extent & classification: E/W/S/NI. General. – 12p.: 30 cm. – 0 11 042893 5 £2.50

The Somalia (United Nations Sanctions) (Overseas Territories) Order 2002 No. 2002/2631. – Enabling power: United Nations Act 1946, s. 1. – Issued: 28.10.2002. Made: 22.10.2002. Laid: 23.10.2002. Coming into force: 24.10.2002. Effect: None. Territorial extent & classification: E/W/S/NI. General. – 16p.: 30 cm. – 0 11 042894 3 £3.00

Value added tax

The Finance Act 2002, section 22, (Appointed Day) Order 2002 No. 2002/3028 (C.99). – Enabling power: Finance Act 2002, s. 22 (3). Bringing into force various provisions of the 2002 Act on 01.01.2003. – Issued: 12.12.2002. Made: 06.12.2002. Effect: None.Territorial extent & classification: E/W/S/NI. General. – 2p.: 30 cm. – 0 11 044169 9 £1.50

The Value Added Tax (Acquisitions) Relief Order 2002 No. 2002/1935. – Enabling power: Value Added Tax Act 1994, s. 36A. – Issued: 16.08.2002. Made: 25.07.2002. Laid: 25.07.2002. Coming into force: 15.08.2002. Effect: None. Territorial extent & classification: E/W/S/NI. General. – 2p.: 30 cm. – 0 11 042654 1 £1.50

The Value Added Tax (Amendment) (No. 2) Regulations 2002 No. 2002/1142. – Enabling power: Value Added Tax Act 1994, ss. 25 (1), 26B, sch. 11, para. s 2 (1) (11). – Issued: 22.05.2002. Made: 24.04.2002. Laid: 24.04.2002. Coming into force: 25.04.2002. Effect: S.I. 1995/2518 amended. Territorial extent & classification: E/W/S/NI. General. – 12p.: 30 cm. – 0 11 039982 X £2.50

The Value Added Tax (Amendment) (No. 3) Regulations 2002 No. 2002/2918. – Enabling power: Value Added Tax Act 1994, s. 6 (14). – Issued: 18.12.2002. Made: 25.11.2002. Laid: 27.11.2002. Coming into force: 28.11.2002. Effect: S.I. 1995/2518 amended. Territorial extent & classification: E/W/S/NI. General. – 4p.: 30 cm. – 0 11 044193 1 £1.75

The Value Added Tax (Amendment) (No. 4) Regulations 2002 No. 2002/3027. – Enabling power: Value Added Tax Act 1994, ss. 26A (3) (4) (5), 36 (5) (6) (7). – Issued: 12.12.2002. Made: 06.12.2002. Laid: 09.12.2002. Coming into force: 01.01.2003. Effect: S.I. 1995/2518 amended. Territorial extent & classification: E/W/S/NI. General. – 4p.: 30 cm. – 0 11 044171 0 £1.75

The Value Added Tax (Amendment) Regulations 2002 No. 2002/1074. – Enabling power: Value Added Tax Act 1994, s. 26 (1) (3) (4). – Issued: 14.05.2002. Made: 16.04.2002. Laid: 17.04.2002. Coming into force: 18.04.2002. Effect: S.I. 1995/2518 amended. Territorial extent & classification: E/W/S/NI. General. – 4p.: 30 cm. – 0 11 039925 0 £1.75

The Value Added Tax (Buildings and Land) Order 2002 No. 2002/1102. – Enabling power: Value Added Tax Act 1994, s. 51 (2). – Issued: 15.05.2002. Made: 17.04.2002. Laid: 17.04.2002. Coming into force: 01.06.2002. Effect: 1994 c. 23 amended. Territorial extent & classification: E/W/S/NI. General. – 2p.: 30 cm. – Superseded by S.I. of same number (ISBN 0110422473) – 0 11 039930 7 £1.50

The Value Added Tax (Buildings and Land) Order 2002 No. 2002/1102. – Enabling power: Value Added Tax Act 1994, s. 51 (2). – Issued: 29.05.2002. Made: 17.04.2002. Laid: 17.04.2002. Coming into force: 01.06.2002. Effect: 1994 c. 23 amended. Territorial extent & classification: E/W/S/NI. General. – 2p.: 30 cm. – Supersedes S.I. of same number (ISBN 0110399307) – 0 11 042247 3 £1.50

The Value Added Tax (Cars) (Amendment) Order 2002 No. 2002/1502. – Enabling power: Value Added Tax Act 1994, s. 50A (1) (5) (8). – Issued: 19.06.2002. Made: 10.06.2002. Laid: 10.06.2002. Coming into force: 01.07.2002. Effect: S.I. 1992/3122 amended. Territorial extent & classification: E/W/S/NI. General. – 4p.: 30 cm. – 0 11 042361 5 £1.75

The Value Added Tax (Consideration for Fuel Provided for Private Use) Order 2002 No. 2002/1099. – Enabling power: Value Added Tax Act 1994, s. 57 (4). – Issued: 15.05.2002. Made: 17.04.2002. Laid: 17.04.2002. Coming into force: 01.05.2002. Effect: 1994 c. 23 amended. Territorial extent & classification: E/W/S/NI. General. – 2p.: 30 cm. – 0 11 039927 7 £1.50

The Value Added Tax (Construction of Buildings) Order 2002 No. 2002/1101. – Enabling power: Value Added Tax Act 1994, s. 30 (4). – Issued: 15.05.2002. Made: 17.04.2002. Laid: 17.04.2002. Coming into force: 01.06.2002. Effect: 1994 c. 23 amended. Territorial extent & classification: E/W/S/NI. General. – 2p.: 30 cm. – 0 11 039929 3 £1.50

The Value Added Tax (Drugs, Medicines, Aids for the Handicapped and Charities etc) Order 2002 No. 2002/2813. – Enabling power: Value Added Tax Act 1994, ss. 30 (4), 96 (9). – Issued: 10.01.2003. Made: 14.11.2002. Laid: 14.11.2002. Coming into force: 05.12.2002. Effect: 1994 c. 23 amended. Territorial extent & classification: E/W/S/NI. General. – 2p.: 30 cm. – 0 11 044459 0 £1.50

The Value Added Tax (Equipment in Lifeboats) Order 2002 No. 2002/456. – Enabling power: Value Added Tax Act 1994, s. 30 (4). – Issued: 19.03.2002. Made: 28.02.2002. Laid: 04.03.2002. Coming into force: 01.04.2002. Effect: 1994 c. 23 amended. Territorial extent & classification: E/W/S/NI. General. – EC note: The Order gives effect to art. 15.5 of DIR 77/388/9/EEC in relation to the supply of equipment that is to be incorporated or used in a vessel used for rescue or assistance at sea. – 2p.: 30 cm. – 0 11 039493 3 *£1.50*

The Value Added Tax (Health and Welfare) Order 2002 No. 2002/762. – Enabling power: Value Added Tax Act 1994, s. 31 (2). – Issued: 20.03.2002. Made: 20.03.2002. Laid: 20.03.2002. Coming into force: 20.03.2002. Effect: 1994 c. 23 amended. Territorial extent & classification: E/W/S/NI. General. – 4p.: 30 cm. – 0 11 039610 3 *£1.75*

The Value Added Tax (Increase of Registration Limits) Order 2002 No. 2002/1098. – Enabling power: Value Added Tax Act 1994, sch. 1, para. 15, sch. 3, para. 9. – Issued: 15.05.2002. Made: 17.04.2002. Laid: 17.04.2002. Coming into force: 25.04.2002. Effect:1994 c. 23 amended. Territorial extent & classification: E/W/S/NI. General. – 2p.: 30 cm. – 0 11 039926 9 *£1.50*

The Value Added Tax (Reduced Rate) Order 2002 No. 2002/1100.   Enabling power: Value Added Tax Act 1994, s. 29A. – Issued: 15.05.2002. Made: 17.04.2002. Laid: 17.04.2002. Coming into force: 01.06.2002. Effect: 1994 c. 23 amended. Territorial extent & classification: E/W/S/NI. General. – 8p.: 30 cm. – 0 11 039928 5 *£2.00*

The Value Added Tax (Special Provisions) (Amendment) (No. 2) Order 2002 No. 2002/1503. – Enabling power: Value Added Tax Act 1994, s. 50A (1) (5) (8). – Issued: 19.06.2002. Made: 10.06.2002. Laid: 10.06.2002. Coming into force: 01.07.2002. Effect: S.I. 1995/1268 amended. Territorial extent & classification: E/W/S/NI. General. – 4p.: 30 cm. – 0 11 042362 3 *£1.75*

The Value Added Tax (Special Provisions) (Amendment) Order 2002 No. 2002/1280. – Enabling power: Value Added Tax Act 1994, ss. 5 (5), 43 (2). – Issued: 16.05.2002. Made: 08.05.2002. Laid: 09.05.2002. Coming into force: 01.06.2002. Effect: S.I. 1995/1268 amended. Territorial extent & classification: E/W/S/NI. General. – 2p.: 30 cm. – 0 11 039945 5 *£1.50*

The Value Added Tax (Transport) Order 2002 No. 2002/1173. – Enabling power: Value Added Tax Act 1994, ss. 30 (4), 96 (9). – Issued: 15.05.2002. Made: 24.04.2002. Laid: 25.04.2002. Coming into force: 01.06.2002. Effect: 1994 c. 23 amended. Territorial extent & classification: E/W/S/NI. General. – 2p.: 30 cm. – 0 11 039931 5 *£1.50*

Value added tax, England and Wales

The Value Added Tax Tribunals (Amendment) Rules 2002 No. 2002/2851. – Enabling power: Value Added Tax Act 1994, sch. 12, para. 9. – Issued: 27.11.2002. Made: 16.11.2002. Laid: 18.11.2002. Coming into force: 09.12.2002. Effect: S.I. 1986/590 amended. Territorial extent & classification: E/W. General. – 2p.: 30 cm. – 0 11 043009 3 *£1.50*

Veterinary surgeons

The Veterinary Surgeons Act 1966 (Schedule 3 Amendment) Order 2002 No. 2002/1479. – Enabling power: Veterinary Surgeons Act 1966, s. 19 (5). – Issued: 21.03.2002. Made: 06.06.2002. Approved by both Houses of Parliament. Coming into force: 10.06.2002. Effect: 1966 c. 36 amended. Territorial extent & classification: E/W/S/NI. General. – Supersedes draft S.I. issued 21 March 2002 (ISBN 0110395271). – 4p.: 30 cm. – 0 11 042335 6 *£1.75*

The Veterinary Surgery (Rectal Ultrasound Scanning of Bovines) Order 2002 No. 2002/2584. – Enabling power: Veterinary Surgeons Act 1966, s. 19 (4) (e). – Issued: 05.11.2002. Made: 11.10.2002. Laid: 15.10.2002. Coming into force: 05.11.2002. Effect: None. Territorial extent & classification: E/W/S/NI. General. – 4p.: 30 cm. – 0 11 042931 1 *£1.75*

Water, England

The Nitrate Vulnerable Zones (Additional Designations) (England) (No. 2) Regulations 2002 No. 2002/2614. – Enabling power: European Communities Act 1972, s. 2 (2). – Issued: 05.11.2002. Made: 15.10.2002. Laid: 17.10.2002. Coming into force: 19.12.2002 for reg. 18.10.2002 for remainder, in accord. with reg. 1(2). Effect: S.I. 1996/888; 1998/1202 amended in relation to England; S.I. 2000/2911 amended & S.I. 2002/2525 revoked. Territorial extent & classification: E. General.   EC note: These regs designate additional nitrate vulnerable zones and make provision for the purpose of implementing in England Council DIR 91/676, concerning the protection of waters against nitrate pollution caused by nitrates from agricultural sources. – 8p.: 30 cm. – 0 11 042932 X *£2.00*

Water, Scotland

The Water Industry (Scotland) Act 2002 (Directions in the Interests of National Security) Order 2002 No. 2002/1264 (S.4). – Enabling power: Scotland Act 1998, ss. 104, 112 (1), 113. – Issued: 21.05.2002. Made: 01.05.2002 Laid: 08.05.2002. Coming into force: 31.05.2002. Effect: None. Territorial extent & classification: S. General. – 4p.: 30 cm. – 0 11 061412 7 *£1.75*

Water, Wales

The Protection of Water Against Agricultural Nitrate Pollution (Amendment) (Wales) Regulations 2002 No. 2002/2297 (W.226). – Enabling power: European Communities Act 1972, s. 2 (2). – Issued: 12.09.2002. Made: 05.09.2002. Laid:-. Coming into force: 11.09.2002. Effect: S.I. 1996/888 amended in relation to Wales. Territorial extent & classification: W. General. – EC note: These regs. make further provision relating to the implementation of DIR 91/676 EEC concerning the protection of waters against pollution caused by nitrates from agricultural sources. – 8p.: 30 cm. – 0 11 090568 7 *£2.00*

Welsh language

The Welsh Language Schemes (Public Bodies) Order 2002 No. 2002/1441 (W.145). – Enabling power: Welsh Language Act 1993, s. 6 (1). – Issued: 19.06.2002. Made: 28.05.2002. Coming into force: 25.06.2002. Effect: None. Territorial extent & classification: W. General. – 4p.: 30 cm. – In English & Welsh. Welsh title: Gorchymyn Cynlluniau Iaith Gymraeg (Cyrff Cyhoeddus) 2002 – 0 11 090505 9   £1.75

Young offender institutions, England and Wales

The Young Offender Institution (Amendment) Rules 2002 No. 2002/2117. – Enabling power: Prison Act 1952, s. 47. – Issued: 09.09.2002. Made: 14.08.2002. Laid: 14.08.2002. Coming into force: 15.08.2002. Effect: S.I. 2000/3371 amended. Territorial extent & classification: E/W. General. – 4p.: 30 cm. – 0 11 042738 6   £1.75

Zoos, England and Wales

The Zoo Licensing Act 1981 (Amendment) (England and Wales) Regulations 2002 No. 2002/3080. – Enabling power: European Communities Act 1972, s. 2 (2). – Issued: 19.12.2002. Made: 11.12.2002. Laid: 16.12.2002. Coming into force: 08.01.2003. Effect: 1981 c.37 amended in relation to England and Wales. Territorial extent & classification: E/W. General. – 20p.: 30 cm. – EC note: These Regs. contain provisions implementing DIR 1999/22/EC relating to the keeping of wild animals in zoos. For this purpose they amend the 1981 Act in relation to zoos in England only – 0 11 044222 9   £3.50

Statutory Instruments 2002

Arranged by Number

1	Landfill tax
2	Animals, England
3	Road traffic
4	Road traffic
5	Road traffic
6	Road traffic
7	Road traffic
8 (W.1)	Animals, Wales
9	Immigration
10	Terms and conditions of employment
11	Road traffic
12	Road traffic
13	Road traffic
14	Social security
	Taxes
15	Road traffic
16	Road traffic
17	Road traffic
18	Road traffic
19	Road traffic
20	Road traffic
21	Road traffic
22	Road traffic
23	Road traffic
24	Civil aviation
25	Civil aviation
26	Road traffic
27	Road traffic
28	Road traffic
29	Road traffic
30	Road traffic
31	Road traffic
32	Road traffic
33	Road traffic
34	National Health Service, England
35	National Health Service, England
36	Social security
37	Road traffic, England
38	National Health Service, England
39	Road traffic
40	Road traffic
41	Road traffic
42	European Communities
43 (W.2)	Road traffic, Wales
44 (W.3)	Road traffic, Wales
45 (W.4)	Education, Wales
46 (W.5)	Education, Wales
47 (W.6)	Food, Wales
48	Local government, England
49	Local government, England
50	Customs and excise
51	Civil aviation
52	Civil aviation
53	Road traffic
54	Road traffic
55	Road traffic
56	Road traffic
57	Social care, England
	Children and young persons, England
58	Road traffic
59	Road traffic
60	Road traffic
61	Road traffic
62 (W.7)	Road traffic, Wales
63	Health and safety
64	National Health Service, England
65	National Health Service, England
66	National Health Service, England

67	National Health Service, England	103	Road traffic
68	National Health Service, England	104 (W.10)	Road traffic, Wales
69	National Health Service, England	105	Social security
70	National Health Service, England	106 (W.11)	Road traffic, Wales
71	National Health Service, England	107 (W.12)	Education, Wales
72	Road traffic	108	Competition
73	Road traffic	109	Road traffic
74 (W.8) (C.1)	Education, Wales	110	Local government, England
75	Highways, England and Wales	111	United Nations
76	Animals, England	112	United Nations
77	Prisons, England and Wales	113 (W.13)	Road traffic, Wales
78	Prisons, England and Wales	114	Road traffic
79	Social security	115	Energy conservation, England
80	Countryside, England	116	Town and country planning, England
81	Local government, England	117 (C. 2)	Social security
82	Nurses, midwives and health visitors, England and Wales	118	Food, England
		119	Animals, England
83	Road traffic	120 (W.14)	Plant health, Wales
84	Road traffic	121 (W.15)	Road traffic, Wales
85 (W.9)	Animals, Wales	122 (W.16)	Education, Wales
86	Housing, England	123	Highways, England and Wales
87	Road traffic	124	Highways, England and Wales
88	Road traffic	125	Postal services
89	Road traffic	126	Road traffic, England
90	Road traffic	127	Arms and ammunition
91	Road traffic	128	Agriculture, England and Wales
92	Road traffic	129 (W.17)	Food, Wales
93	Electricity	130 (W.18)	Animals, Wales
94	Animals, England	131	Road traffic
95	Animals, England	132	Road traffic
96	Road traffic	133	Road traffic
97	Road traffic	134	Road traffic
98	Road traffic	135	Road traffic
99	Road traffic	136 (W.19)	Education, Wales
100	Road traffic	137	National Health Service, England
101	Road traffic	138	National Health Service, England
102	Road traffic	139	National Health Service, England

140	National Health Service, England	177	Road traffic
141	National Health Service, England	178	Road traffic
142	National Health Service, England	179	Road traffic
143	National Health Service, England	180	Council tax, England
144	National Health Service, England		Rating and valuation, England
145	National Health Service, England	181	Road traffic
146	National Health Service, England	182	Public passenger transport, England and Wales
147	National Health Service, England	183	Food, England
148	National Health Service, England		Agriculture, England
149	National Health Service, England	184 (W.24)	*Cancelled*
150	National Health Service, England	185	Local government, England and Wales
151	Industrial development	186 (W.25)	National Health Service, Wales
152 (W.20)	Education, Wales	187	Local government, England
153 (C.3)	Pensions	188	Road traffic
154 (W.21)	Road traffic, Wales	189	Road traffic
155	Local government, England	190	Road traffic
156 (W.22)	Education, Wales	191	Road traffic
157 (W.23)	Education, Wales	192	Immigration
158	Local government, England	193	Justices of the Peace, England and Wales
159	Local government, England	194 (L.1)	Magistrates' courts, England and Wales
160	Road traffic	195	Education, England and Wales
161	Road traffic	196	Road traffic
162	Road traffic	197	Road traffic
163	Road traffic	198	Road traffic
164	Road traffic	199	Road traffic
165	Road traffic	200	Postal services
166	National Health Service, England	201	Defence
167	Road traffic	202	Animals, England
168	Road traffic	203 (W.26)	Food, Wales
169	Road traffic		Agriculture, Wales
170	Road traffic	204 (W.27)	Road traffic, Wales
171	Road traffic	205	Income tax
172	Road traffic	206	Pensions, England and Wales
173	Education, England and Wales	207	Highways, England and Wales
174	Education, England and Wales	208	Social security
175	Road traffic		
176	Road traffic		

209	Road traffic	**241**	Animals, England
210	Road traffic	**242**	Animals, England
211	Road traffic	**243**	Education, England
212	Road traffic	**244**	Education, England
213	Road traffic	**245**	Education, England
214	Road traffic	**246**	Education, England
215	Highways, England and Wales	**247**	Patents
216	Highways, England and Wales		Plant breeders' rights
217	Highways, England and Wales	**248**	European Communities
	Trunk roads: A44: London to Aberystwyth	**249**	Pitcairn Islands
218	Road traffic	**250**	Territorial sea
219	Road traffic	**251**	United Nations
220	Road traffic	**252**	Education, England
221	Animals, England	**253**	Nurses and midwives
222 (L.2)	Supreme Court of England and Wales	**254**	Health care and associated professions
223 (L.3)	County courts, England and Wales	**255**	Criminal law, England and Wales
224	Representation of the people		Criminal law, Northern Ireland
225	Social security	**256**	Criminal law, England and Wales
	Terms and conditions of employment	**257**	Criminal law, England and Wales
226	Forestry, England and Wales	**258**	United Nations
227	Road traffic	**259**	United Nations
228 (C.4)	Criminal law, England and Wales	**260**	Education, Wales
	Criminal law, Northern Ireland	**261 (S.1)**	Constitutional law
229	Defence		Devolution, Scotland
230	Defence	**262**	Summer time
231	Defence	**263**	Civil aviation
232	Education, England and Wales	**264**	Civil aviation
233	Police, England and Wales	**265**	Northern Ireland
234	Road traffic		Social security
235	Road traffic	**266**	United Nations
236	Medicines	**267**	London government
237	National Health Service, England and Wales	**268**	Road traffic
		269	Medicines
	Road traffic, England and Wales	**270**	Road traffic
238	Social security	**271**	Agriculture, England
239 (W.28)	Road traffic, Wales	**272**	Sea fisheries, England
240	Animals, England		Sea fisheries, Northern Ireland

273 (W.29)	Animals, Wales	306	Harbours, docks, piers and ferries
274 (W.30)	Animals, Wales	307	Social security
275	Environmental protection, England and Wales	308	National Health Service, England
276	Road traffic, England	309	Highways, England and Wales
277	Animals, England and Wales	310 (W.36)	Road traffic, Wales
278 (W.31)	Road traffic, Wales	311	Harbours, docks, piers and ferries
279 (C. 5)	Education, England and Wales	312 (C.6)	Chiropractors
	Employment and training, England and Wales	313	Criminal law
		314	Road traffic
280 (W.32)	Animals, Wales	315	Customs and excise
281 (W.33)	Animals, Wales	316	Customs and excise
282	Health and safety	317	Companies
283 (W.34)	Animals, Wales	318	Electronic communications
284	River, England and Wales	319	Road traffic
	Sea fisheries, England and Wales	320	Road traffic
285	Disabled persons	321	Road traffic
	Transport	322	Road traffic
286	Road traffic	323	Road traffic
287	Road traffic	324 (W.37)	Social care, Wales
288	Road traffic		Children and young persons, Wales
289	Road traffic	325 (W.38)	Public health, Wales
290	Civil aviation	326 (W.39)	Education, Wales
291	Civil aviation	327 (W.40)	Social care, Wales
292	Civil aviation		Children and young persons, Wales
293	Civil aviation	328 (W.41)	Local government, Wales
294	Civil aviation	329 (W.42)	Food, Wales
295	Plant health	330 (W.43)	Food, Wales
296	Plant health, England and Wales	331 (W.44)	Rating and valuation, Wales
297	Road traffic	332 (W.45)	Road traffic, Wales
298	Road traffic	333	Food, England and Wales
299	Road traffic	334	Food, England
300	Road traffic	335	Road traffic
301	Road traffic	336	Civil aviation
302	Employment and training	337	Landlord and tenant, England
303	Employment and training	338	Social security
304 (W.35)	Animals, Wales	339	Local government, England and Wales
305	Local government, England and Wales	340	Highways, England and Wales

341	Highways, England and Wales	376	Partnership
342	Highways, England and Wales	377	Education, England
343	Highways, England and Wales	378	Education, England and Wales
344 (C.7)	Criminal law	379	Food, England
	Police	380	Pensions
345 (C.8)	Defence	381 (C.9)	Pensions
346	Pensions	382	Road traffic
347	Road traffic	383	Road traffic
348	Road traffic	384	Road traffic
349	Road traffic	385	Road traffic
350	Road traffic	386	Road traffic
351	Road traffic	387	Road traffic
352	Road traffic	388	Road traffic
353	Road traffic	389	Road traffic
354 (W.46)	Road traffic, Wales	390	Road traffic
355	Social security	391	Road traffic
356	National Health Service, England	392	Road traffic
357	National Health Service, England	393	Road traffic
358	National Health Service, England	394	Road traffic
359 (W.47)	Road traffic, Wales	395	Road traffic
360	Road traffic	396	Road traffic
361	Road traffic	397	Road traffic
362	Road traffic	398	Social security
363	Road traffic	399	Telecommunications
364	Road traffic	400	Telecommunications
365	Terrorism, Northern Ireland	401	Fees and charges
366	Transport and works, England	402 (W.50)	Food, Wales
	Transport, England	403 (C.10)	Social security
367	Deregulation, England and Wales	404	Road traffic
368	Civil aviation	405	Road traffic
369	Road traffic	406	Road traffic
370	Road traffic	407	Road traffic
371	Road traffic	408	Education, Wales
372	Road traffic	409	Road traffic
373 (W.48)	Road traffic, Wales	410	National assistance services, England
374 (W.49)	Road traffic, Wales	411	National assistance services, England
375	Local government, England	412	Transport and works, England

	Transport, England	444	Taxes
413 (C.11)	Police, England and Wales	445	Contracting out, England
414	Registration of political parties	446	Police, England and Wales
415	Road traffic	447 (C.13)	Criminal law
416	Road traffic	448	Road traffic
417	Civil aviation	449	Road traffic
418	Civil aviation	450	Road traffic
419	Extradition	451	Local government, England
420 (W.51)	Road traffic, Wales	452	Town and country planning, England
421	Road traffic, England		Tribunals and inquiries, England
422	Road traffic, England	453	Income tax
423	Education, England	454	Government resources and accounts
424	Environmental protection, England	455	Taxes
425	Environmental protection, England	456	Value added tax
426	Sea fisheries, England	457	Food
	Sea fisheries, Northern Ireland	458	Food
427	Pensions	459	Pensions
	Insolvency	460	Deregulation
428	Social security	461	Public health, England
429	Road traffic	462	Road traffic
430 (W.52)	Animals, Wales	463	Civil aviation
431 (W.53)	Animals, Wales	464	Civil aviation
432 (W.55)	Education, Wales	465	Civil aviation
433 (W.54)	Road traffic, Wales	466	Civil aviation
434	Highways, England and Wales	467	Animals, England
435	Education, England and Wales	468	Animals, England
	Education, Northern Ireland	469 (W.58)	Sea fisheries, Wales
436	Road traffic	470	Social security
437 (C.12)	Pensions	471	Immigration
438 (W.56)	Education, Wales	472	Immigration
439	Supreme Court of England and Wales	473	Animals
	County courts, England and Wales	474 (W.59)	Road traffic, Wales
440	Building and buildings, England and Wales	475	Gas
441	Rehabilitation of offenders, England and Wales	476	Electricity
		477 (W.60)	Road traffic, Wales
442 (W.57)	National Health Service, Wales	478 (W.61)	Road traffic, Wales
443	Taxes	479	Education, England

480	Road traffic	517	Road traffic
481	Road traffic	518	Road traffic
482	Road traffic	519	Social security
483	Road traffic	520 (W.63)	Transport, Wales
484	Road traffic	521	Local government, England
485 (W.62)	Road traffic, Wales	522	Local government, England
486	Social security	523	Local government, England and Wales
487	Road traffic, England and Wales	524	Social security, Northern Ireland
488	Road traffic, England and Wales		Taxes, Northern Ireland
489	Road traffic, England and Wales	525	Social security
490	Social security		Taxes
491	Social security	526	Pesticides, England and Wales
492	Social security	527	Social security, Northern Ireland
493	Deregulation, England and Wales		Taxes, Northern Ireland
494	Road traffic	528	Environmental protection
495	Road traffic	529	Patents
496	Road traffic	530	Housing, England
497	Road traffic	531	Environmental protection, England
498	Rating and valuation, England	532	Terms and conditions of employment
499	Social security	533 (C.15)	Police
500 (C.14)	Osteopaths		Companies
501	Customs and excise	534	Police
502	Companies	535	Education, England
503	Partnership	536	Education, England
504	Merchant shipping	537	Road traffic, England and Wales
505	Electoral Commission	538	Road traffic, England and Wales
506	Hallmark	539	Road traffic, England and Wales
507	Education, England	540 (W.64)	Road traffic, Wales
508	Education, England	541 (W.65)	Road traffic, Wales
509	Education, England	542	Medicines
510	Education, England		Fees and charges
511	Fees and charges	543	National Health Service, England
512	Road traffic	544	National Health Service, England
513	Road traffic	545	National Health Service, England
514	Road traffic	546	Children and young persons, England
515	Road traffic	547	National Health Service, England
516	Road traffic	548	National Health Service, England

549	Medicines	585	National Health Service, England
550	Food	586	National Health Service, England
551	National Health Service, England	587	National Health Service, England
552	Children and young persons, England	588	National Health Service, England
553	National Health Service, England	589	National Health Service, England
554	National Health Service, England	590	National Health Service, England
555	National Health Service, England	591	National Health Service, England
556	National Health Service, England	592	National Health Service, England
557	National Health Service, England	593	National Health Service, England
558	National Health Service, England	594	National Health Service, England
559	National Health Service, England	595	National Health Service, England
560	National Health Service, England	596	National Health Service, England
561	National Health Service, England and Wales	597	National Health Service, England
		598	National Health Service, England
562	National Health Service, England	599	National Health Service, England
563	National Health Service, England	600	National Health Service, England
564	National Health Service, England	601	National Health Service, England
565	National Health Service, England	602	Food, England
566	National Health Service, England	603	Public health, England
567	National Health Service, England	604	National Health Service, England
568	National Health Service, England	605	National Health Service, England
569	National Health Service, England	606	National Health Service, England
570	National Health Service, England	607	National Health Service, England
571	National Health Service, England	608	National Health Service, England
572	National Health Service, England	609	National Health Service, England
573	National Health Service, England	610	National Health Service, England and Wales
574	National Health Service, England		
575	National Health Service, England	611	Road traffic
576	National Health Service, England	612 (W.66)	Road traffic, Wales
577	National Health Service, England	613 (W.67)	Road traffic, Wales
578	National Health Service, England	614	London government
579	National Health Service, England		Public passenger transport, England
580	National Health Service, England	615	Police, England and Wales
581	National Health Service, England	616	National Health Service, England
582	National Health Service, England	617	National Health Service, England
583	National Health Service, England	618	Consumer protection
584	National Health Service, England	619	National Health Service, England

620	National Health Service, England		Taxes
621	National Health Service, England	654 (W.70)	Local government, Wales
622	National Health Service, England	655	Health and safety
623	National Health Service, England	656	Disabled persons
624	National Health Service, England		Transport
625	National Health Service, England	657	Disabled persons
626	National Health Service, England		Transport
627	National Health Service, England	658 (C.16)	Transport
628	National Health Service, England		London government
629 (C.19)	Social care, England and Wales	659	Road traffic
	Children and young persons, England and Wales	660	Road traffic
		661	Road traffic
	Public health, England and Wales	662	Road traffic
630	National Health Service, England	663	Road traffic
631	National Health Service, England	664	Road traffic
632	National Health Service, England	665	Road traffic
633	National Health Service, England	666	Housing, England
634	National Health Service, England	667	Housing, England
635	Children and young persons, England	668	Social security
636	National Health Service, England		Terms and conditions of employment
637	Betting, gaming and lotteries, England and Wales	669 (W.71)	Road traffic, Wales
638	National lottery, Enlgand	670	Social security
639	Betting, gaming and lotteries	671	Pensions
640	Betting, gaming and lotteries	672	Pensions
641	Telegraphs	673 (C.17)	Transport, England
642	Betting, gaming and lotteries	674	Environmental protection, England
643	Transport	675 (W.72)	Sea fisheries, Wales
644	Damages, England and Wales		Fish farming, Wales
645	Damages, Northern Ireland	676 (W.73)	Sea fisheries, Wales
646	Agriculture, England	677 (W.74)	Sea fisheries, Wales
647	National Health Service, England	678 (W.75)	Local government, Wales
648	Social security	679 (W.76)	Education, Wales
649	Pensions	680	Income tax
650	Road traffic	681	Pensions
651 (W.68)	Local government, Wales	682	Financial services and markets
652 (W.69)	Local government, Wales	683	Social security
653	Income tax	684	Social security

685	Social security	718	Social security
686	Road traffic	719	Government trading funds
687	Road traffic	720	Disabled persons
688	Road traffic	721	Disabled persons
689	Companies	722	National Health Service, England
690	Partnership	723	National Health Service, England
691	Companies	724	National Health Service, England
692	Trade marks	725	National Health Service, England
693	Road traffic	726	National Health Service, England
694	Local government, England and Wales	727	National Health Service, England
	Police, England and Wales	728	National Health Service, England
695	Police, England and Wales	729	National Health Service, England
696	Agriculture	730	National Health Service, England
697	Medicines	731	National Health Service, England
698 (W.77)	Road traffic, Wales	732	Environmental protection, England
699	Pensions	733	Civil aviation
700	Income tax	734	Civil aviation
701	Inheritance tax	735	Civil aviation
702	Taxes	736	Road traffic
703	Social security	737	Road traffic
704	Financial services and markets	738	Road traffic
705	Social security, Northern Ireland	739	Road traffic
706	Income tax	740	Road traffic
707	Income tax	741	Gas
708	Nurses, midwives and health visitors, England and Wales	742	Electricity
709	Legal Services Commission, England and Wales	743	Local government, England and Wales
		744	Agriculture, England
710	Legal aid and advice, England and Wales	745	Road traffic
711	Legal aid and advice, England and Wales	746	Road traffic, England
		747 (W.78)	Road traffic, Wales
712	Legal Services Commission, England and Wales	748 (W.79)	Road traffic, Wales
713	Legal Services Commission, England and Wales	749	Road traffic
		750	Road traffic
714	Legal Services Commission, England and Wales	751	Road traffic
715	Local government, England	752	Road traffic
716	Local government, England	753	Road traffic
717	Road traffic	754	Road traffic

755	Road traffic			Sea fisheries, Northern Ireland
756	Education, England	791		Constitutional law
757 (W.80)	Local government, Wales			Northern Ireland
758 (W.81) (C.18)	Energy conservation, Wales	792		Pensions
759	Road traffic	793		International immunities and privileges
760	Road traffic	794		Ministers of the Crown
761	Aggregates levy	795		Immigration
762	Value added tax	796 (N.I. 1)		Northern Ireland
763 (W.82)	Housing, Wales	797		Social care
764	Animals, England	798		Civil aviation
765	Financial services and markets	799		Post office
	Banks and banking	800 (S.2)		Constitutional law
766	*Cancelled*			Devolution, Scotland
767	Police, England and Wales	801 (S.3)		Constitutional law
768	Town and country planning, England			Devolution, Scotland
769	Pensions, England and Wales	802 (W.87)		Local government, Wales
770	Lands tribunal, England and Wales	803 (W.88)		Local government, Wales
771	Family law	804		Road traffic
772	Education, England	805		Road traffic
773	Food, England	806		Road traffic
774	Food. England	807		Road traffic
775	Opticians	808 (W.89)		Local government, Wales
776	Civil aviation	809 (C.20)		Aggregates levy
777	Road traffic	810 (W.90)		Local government, Wales
778	Police	811 (W.91)		Animals, Wales
779	Police, England and Wales	812 (W.92)		Social care, Wales
780	Highways, England and Wales			Children and young persons, Wales
781	Highways, England and Wales	813 (W.93)		Environmental protection, Wales
782	Immigration	814 (W.94)		National assistance services, Wales
783 (W.84)	Local government, Wales	815 (W.95)		National assistance services, Wales
784 (W.85)	Environmental protection, Wales	816		Social care, England and Wales
785 (W.86)	Local government, Wales			Children and young persons, England and Wales
786	Highways, England and Wales			Public health, England and Wales
787	Agriculture	817		Social security
788	Maintenance of dependants	818 (C.21)		Pensions
789	Maintenance of dependants	819		Pensions, England and Wales
790	Northern Ireland	820 (W.96)		Food, Wales

821 (W.97)	Food, Wales	**851**	National Health Service, England
822	International criminal court, England and Wales	**852**	National Health Service, England
		853	National Health Service, England
	International criminal court, Northern Ireland	**854**	National Health Service, England
823	Electricity, England and Wales	**855**	National Health Service, England
824	Agriculture, England	**856**	National Health Service, England
825	Immigration	**857**	National Health Service, England
826	Criminal law	**858**	National Health Service, England
827	Osteopaths	**859**	National Health Service, England
828	Town and country planning, England	**860**	*Cancelled*
829	Social security	**861**	National Health Service, England
	Taxes	**862**	National Health Service, England
830	Social security	**863**	National Health Service, England
831	Government trading funds	**864**	National Health Service, England
832	Powers of attorney, England and Wales	**865**	Social care, England
	Mental health, England and Wales		Children and young persons, England
833	Mental health, England and Wales		Public health, England
834	Constitutional law	**866**	National Health Service, England
	Devolution, Wales	**867**	National Health Service, England
	Representation of the people, Wales	**868**	Customs and excise
835 (W.98)	Road traffic, Wales	**869**	National Health Service, England
836	Pensions	**870**	National Health Service, England
	Insolvency	**871**	National Health Service, England
837 (W.99)	Housing, Wales	**872**	National Health Service, England
838	Education, England and Wales	**873**	National Health Service, England
839 (C.22)	Children and young persons, England	**874**	National Health Service, England
840	Education, England	**875**	National Health Service, England
841	Social security	**876**	National Health Service, England
842	Social security	**877**	National Health Service, England
843	Animals, England	**878**	National Health Service, England
844	Criminal law, England and Wales	**879**	National Health Service, England
845	Children and young persons, England and Wales	**880**	Health care and associated professions
846 (C.23)	Transport	**881**	Nurses and midwives
847	National Health Service, England	**882**	Animals, Wales
848	National Health Service, England	**883**	Road traffic
849	Medical profession	**884**	Road traffic
850	National Health Service, England	**885 (W.100)**	Local government, Wales

886 (W.101)	Local government, Wales
887	Medical profession, England
888	National Health Service, England
889	Food, England
890	Food, England
891	National Health Service, England
892	Agriculture, England
893	National Health Service, England
894	National Health Service, England
895	National Health Service, England
896 (W.102)	Children and young persons, Wales
897 (W.103)	Food, Wales
898	Highways, England and Wales
899	Road traffic
900	Road traffic
901	Road traffic
902	Road traffic
903	Road traffic
904	Road traffic
905	Road traffic
906	Education, England
	Regulatory reform, England
907	Animals, England
908	Road traffic
909	Road traffic
910	Road traffic
911	Road traffic
912	Companies
913	Partnership
	Limited liability partnerships
914	Electricity, England and Wales
915	Partnership
	Limited liability partnerships
916 (W.104)	National Health Service, Wales
917 (W.105)	National Health Service, Wales
918 (W.106)	National Health Service, Wales
919 (W.107)	Social care, Wales
	Children and young persons, Wales
	Public health, Wales
920 (W.108) (C.24)	Social care, Wales
	Children and young persons, Wales
	Public health, Wales
921 (W.109)	Social care, Wales
	Children and young persons, Wales
	Public health, Wales
922	Health care and associated professions
923	Nurses and midwives
924	Road traffic
925	Road traffic
926	Road traffic
927	Plant health
928	Contracting out, England
929	Civil aviation
930	Civil aviation
931	Food, England
932	Civil aviation
933	Medicines
934	Road traffic
935	Road traffic
936	Road traffic
937	Road traffic
938	National Health Service, England
939	National Health Service, England
940	National Health Service, England
941	National Health Service, England
942	National Health Service, England
943	National Health Service, England
944	National Health Service, England
945	National Health Service, England
946	National Health Service, England
947	National Health Service, England
948	National Health Service, England
949	National Health Service, England
950	National Health Service, England

951	National Health Service, England	988	National Health Service, England
952	Road traffic	989	National Health Service, England
953	Road traffic	990	National Health Service, England
954	Road traffic	991	National Health Service, England
955	Road traffic	992	National Health Service, England
956	Animals, England	993	National Health Service, England
957	National Health Service, England	994	National Health Service, England
958	National Health Service, England	995	National Health Service, England
959	National Health Service, England	996	National Health Service, England
960	National Health Service, England	997	National Health Service, England
961	Road traffic	998	National Health Service, England
962	Road traffic	999	National Health Service, England
963	Road traffic	1000	National Health Service, England
964	Road traffic	1001	National Health Service, England
965	Road traffic	1002	National Health Service, England
966	Road traffic	1003	National Health Service, England
967	Road traffic	1004	National Health Service, England
968	Road traffic	1005	National Health Service, England
969	Road traffic	1006	National Health Service, England
970	Road traffic	1007	National Health Service, England
971	Road traffic	1008	National Health Service, England
972	Road traffic	1009	National Health Service, England
973	Road traffic	1010	National Health Service, England
974	Road traffic	1011	Animals, England
975	Local government, England	1012	*Cancelled*
976	Road traffic	1013	*Cancelled*
977	Road traffic	1014 (C.25)	Public passenger transport, England
978	Road traffic		Road traffic
979	Road traffic	1015	Public passenger transport, England
980	National Health Service, England	1016	Public passenger transport, England
981	National Health Service, England	1017	Civil aviation
982	National Health Service, England	1018	Civil aviation
983	National Health Service, England	1019	Civil aviation
984	National Health Service, England	1020	Civil aviation
985	National Health Service, England	1021	Civil aviation
986	National Health Service, England	1022	Civil aviation
987	National Health Service, England	1023	Civil aviation

1024	Civil aviation
1025	Civil aviation
1026	Civil aviation
1027	Road traffic
1028	Road traffic
1029	Highways, England and Wales
1030	Highways, England and Wales
1031	Local government, England
1032	Local government, England
1033	Local government, England
1034	Local government, England
1035	Local government, England
1036	Local government, England
1037	Insolvency
1038 (W.110)	Animals, Wales
1039 (W.111)	Animals, Wales
1040	Highways, England and Wales
1041 (W.112)	Road traffic, Wales
1042 (W.113)	Protection of wrecks, Wales
1043	London government
	Pensions
1044	London government
1045	Road traffic
1046	Road traffic
1047	Road traffic
1048	Road traffic
1049	Road traffic
1050	Road traffic
1051	Road traffic
1052	Road traffic
1053	Road traffic
1054	Road traffic
1055	Road traffic
1056	Road traffic
1057	Local government, England
1058	Highways, England and Wales
1059	Local government, England
1060	Local government, England
1061	Local government, England
1062	Regulatory reform, England and Wales
1063	Offshore installations
1064	Transport and works, England
	Transport, England
1065	Transport and works, England
	Transport, England
1066	Transport and works, England
	Transport, England
1067	Plant health, England
1068	Local government, England
1069	Police, England and Wales
1070	Telecommunications
1071	Telecommunications
1072	Road traffic
1073	National Health Service, England
1074	Value added tax
1075	Civil aviation
1076	Geneva conventions
1077	Overseas territories
1078	Civil aviation
1079	Education, Wales
1080	European Communities
1081	Road traffic
1082	Road traffic
1083	Road traffic
1084	Road traffic
1085	Road traffic
1086	Road traffic
1087 (W.114)	Environmental protection, Wales
1088	Road traffic
1089	Road traffic
1090 (W.115)	Food, Wales
1091	Housing, England
1092	Atomic energy and radioactive substances

1093	Atomic energy and radioactive substances
1094	Education, England
1095 (C.26)	Medicines
	National Health Service
1096	*Cancelled*
1097 (C.27)	Criminal law, England and Wales
1098	Value added tax
1099	Value added tax
1100	Value added tax
1101	Value added tax
1102	Value added tax
1103	Road traffic
1104	Road traffic
1105	Road traffic
1106	Road traffic
1107	Road traffic
1108	Road traffic
1109	Road traffic
1110	Road traffic
1111	Electricity
	Gas
1112	National Health Service, England
1113	National Health Service, England
1114	National Health Service, England
1115	National Health Service, England
1116	National Health Service, England
1117	National Health Service, England
1118	National Health Service, England
1119	National Health Service, England
1120	National Health Service, England
1121	National Health Service, England
1122	National Health Service, England
1123	National Health Service, England
1124	Health care and associated professions
1125	Nurses and midwives
1126	Road traffic
1127	Road traffic
1128 (W.116)	Road traffic, Wales
1129 (W.117)	Local government, Wales
1130	Betting, gaming and lotteries
1131 (W.118)	Agriculture, Wales
1132	Social security
1133	National Health Service, England
1134	Highways, England and Wales
1135	Magistrates' courts, England and Wales
1136	Education, England and Wales
1137	Education, England
1138	Road traffic
1139	Road traffic
1140	Road traffic
1141	Road traffic
1142	Value added tax
1143	Sports grounds and sporting events, England and Wales
1144	Consumer protection
	Health and safety
1145 (W.119)	Road traffic, Wales
1146 (W.120)	Road traffic, Wales
1147	Immigration
1148 (W.121)	Road traffic, Wales
1149 (C.28)	Criminal law, England and Wales
1150	Police, England and Wales
1151	Atomic energy and radioactive substances
	Police
1152	Climate change levy
1153	Road traffic
1154	Road traffic
1155	Road traffic
1156	Road traffic
1157	Road traffic
1158	Road traffic
1159	Road traffic

Number	Subject	Number	Subject
1160	Road traffic	1194	Road traffic
1161	Road traffic	1195	Road traffic
1162	Road traffic	1196	Road traffic
1163	Road traffic	1197	Road traffic
1164	Road traffic	1198	Road traffic
1165	Civil aviation	1199	Road traffic
1166	Transport	1200	Road traffic
1167 (C.29)	Health care and associated professions	1201	Road traffic
1168	Highways, England and Wales	1202	Road traffic
1169	Nurses, midwives and health visitors	1203	Road traffic
1170 (C.30)	Medicines, England and Wales	1204	Family law
	National Health Service, England and Wales	1205	Highways, England and Wales
1171	Education, England	1206	Highways, England and Wales
1172	Education, England	1207	Highways, England and Wales
1173	Value added tax	1208	Highways, England and Wales
1174 (W.122)	Agriculture, Wales	1209	Highways, England and Wales
1175 (W.123) (C.31)	Social care, Wales	1210	Highways, England and Wales
1176 (W.124)	Social care, Wales	1211	Highways, England and Wales
1177	Atomic energy and radioactive substances	1212	Highways, England and Wales
		1213	Highways, England and Wales
1178	Highways, England and Wales	1214	Highways, England and Wales
1179	Highways, England and Wales	1215	Highways, England and Wales
1180	Highways, England and Wales	1216	Local government, England
1181	Highways, England and Wales	1217	Road traffic
1182	Highways, England and Wales	1218	Road traffic
1183	Highways, England and Wales	1219	Road traffic
1184	Highways, England and Wales	1220	Road traffic
1185	Highways, England and Wales	1221	Road traffic
1186	Highways, England and Wales	1222 (C.32)	Social security
1187 (W.125)	Education, Wales	1223	Tribunals and inquiries, England
1188	Disabled persons	1224	Road traffic
	Transport	1225	Road traffic
1189	Road traffic	1226	Road traffic
1190	Road traffic	1227	Agriculture, England
1191	Road traffic	1228	Civil aviation
1192	Road traffic	1229	Civil aviation
1193	Road traffic	1230	Civil aviation

1231	Civil aviation
1232	Civil aviation
1233	Civil aviation
1234	National Health Service, England
1235	National Health Service, England
1236	Road traffic
1237	Road traffic
1238	Road traffic
1239	Road traffic
1240	Insolvency
	Companies
1241	Immigration
1242	Financial services and markets
1243	National Health Service, England
1244	National Health Service, England
1245 (C.33)	Social care, England
1246	Road traffic
1247	Road traffic
1248	Road traffic
1249	Road traffic
1250	Social care, England
	Children and young persons, England
1251	National Health Service, England
1252 (C.34)	British overseas territories
	British nationality
1253	Animals, England
1254	Education, England
1255	Road traffic
1256	Road traffic
1257	Road traffic
1258	Road traffic
1259	Road traffic
1260	Road traffic
1261	Road traffic
1262	Road traffic
1263	Chiropractors
1264 (S.4)	Constitutional law
	Water, Scotland
	Devolution, Scotland
1265	Customs and excise
1266	Police, England and Wales
1267	Health and safety
1268	Road traffic
1269	Road traffic
1270	Road traffic
1271	Road traffic
1272	Road traffic
1273	Road traffic
1274	Road traffic
1275	Road traffic
1276	Road traffic
1277	Road traffic
1278	Coast protection, England
1279 (C.35)	Prevention and suppression of terrorism
1280	Value added tax
1281	Prevention and suppression of terrorism
1282	Police, England and Wales
1283 (W.126)	Road traffic, Wales
1284 (W.127)	Road traffic, Wales
1285	Road traffic
1286	Road traffic
1287	Road traffic
1288	Road traffic
1289	Road traffic
1290	Civil aviation
1291 (W.128)	Road traffic, Wales
1292	Civil aviation
1293	National Health Service, England
1294	National Health Service, England
1295	National Health Service, England
1296	National Health Service, England
1297	National Health Service, England
1298	Investigatory powers

1299	Plant health, England	1332	Road traffic
1300	Road traffic	1333	Social security
1301	Road traffic		Taxes
1302	Road traffic	1334	Social security
1303	Road traffic		Taxes
1304	Road traffic	1335	National Health Service, England
1305	Road traffic	1336	National Health Service, England
1306	Road traffic	1337	National Health Service, England
1307	Insolvency, England and Wales	1338	National Health Service, England
1308	Insolvency, England and Wales	1339	Social security, Northern Ireland
1309	Insolvency, England and Wales		Taxes, Northern Ireland
1310	Financial services and markets	1340	Social security, Northern Ireland
1311	National Health Service, England and Wales		Taxes, Northern Ireland
1312 (C.36)	Chronically sick and disabled persons	1341	National Health Service, England
	Social care	1342	National Health Service, England
1313	National Health Service, England	1343	Road traffic
1314	Road traffic	1344	Road traffic
1315	Highways, England and Wales	1345	Road traffic
1316	Road traffic	1346 (W.129)	Road traffic, Wales
1317	Road traffic	1347	Pensions
1318	Education, England and Wales	1348	Animals, England
1319	Road traffic	1349	Animals, England
1320	Road traffic	1350 (W.130)	Plant health, Wales
1321	Road traffic	1351	Road traffic, England
1322	National Health Service, England	1352	Road traffic, England
1323	National Health Service, England	1353	Road traffic, England
1324	National Health Service, England	1354 (W.131)	Animals, Wales
1325	National Health Service, England	1355	Environmental protection
1326	National Health Service, England	1356 (W.132)	Animals, Wales
1327	Transport and works, England	1357 (W.133)	Animals, Wales
	Transport, England	1358 (W.134)	Animals, Wales
1328	Animals, England	1359 (C.37)	Local government, Wales
1329	Education, England and Wales	1360	National Health Service, England
1330	Education, England and Wales	1361	National Health Service, England
1331	Education, England and Wales	1362	National Health Service, England
	Education, Northern Ireland	1363	National Health Service, England
		1364	National Health Service, England

1365	Road traffic	**1399**	Dentists
1366	Road traffic	**1400 (W.139)**	Education, Wales
1367	Road traffic	**1401 (W.140)**	Education, Wales
1368	Road traffic	**1402**	Education, England
1369	Road traffic	**1403**	Education, England
1370	Road traffic	**1404 (W.141)**	Road traffic, Wales
1371	Road traffic	**1405**	National Health Service, England
1372	Criminal law, England and Wales	**1406**	Social security
1373	Road traffic	**1407**	Betting, gaming and lotteries
1374	Road traffic	**1408 (C.39)**	International development
1375	Road traffic	**1409**	Financial services and markets
1376	Telecommunications	**1410**	Betting, gaming and lotteries
1377	Education, England	**1411**	Social security
1378	Social security, Northern Ireland	**1412**	Civil aviation
	Taxes, Northern Ireland	**1413**	Civil aviation
1379	Social security	**1414**	Civil aviation
	Taxes	**1415**	Road traffic
	Family law	**1416 (W.142)**	Animals, Wales
1380	Civil aviation	**1417**	Taxes
1381	Civil aviation	**1418**	Customs and excise, England
1382	Civil aviation	**1419**	Deregulation
1383	Pensions	**1420**	Road traffic
1384	Transport, England	**1421**	Road traffic
1385 (W.135)	Local government, Wales	**1422**	Road traffic
1386	National Health Service, England	**1423**	Road traffic
1387 (W.136)	Agriculture, Wales	**1424**	Road traffic
1388	Road traffic	**1425**	Road traffic
1389	Road traffic	**1426**	Road traffic
1390	Road traffic	**1427**	Road traffic
1391	Road traffic	**1428**	Road traffic
1392	National Health Service, England	**1429**	Road traffic
1393	National Health Service, England	**1430**	Road traffic
1394 (W.137)	Education, Wales	**1431**	Road traffic
1395	Highways, England and Wales	**1432 (W.143)**	Local government, Wales
1396 (W.138)	Education, Wales	**1433**	Education, England and Wales
1397	Ministers of the Crown	**1434**	Education, England
1398	Cinemas and films	**1435**	Race relations

1436 (C. 40)	Children and young persons, England and Wales	1468	Road traffic
1437	National Health Service, England	1469	Civil aviation
1438	National Health Service, England and Wales	1470	Civil aviation
		1471	Customs and excise
1439 (W.144)	Road traffic, Wales	1472 (W.146)	Food, Wales
1440	Justices of the Peace, England and Wales	1473	Merchant shipping
		1474	Road traffic
1441 (W.145)	Welsh language	1475 (W.147) (C.41)	National Health Service, Wales
1442	Road traffic	1476 (W.148)	Food, Wales
1443	Road traffic	1477	Education, England
1444	Road traffic	1478	Plant health
1445	Road traffic	1479	Veterinary surgeons
1446	Road traffic	1480	Pensions
1447	Road traffic	1481 (W.149)	Road traffic, Wales
1448	Road traffic	1482 (W.150)	Road traffic, Wales
1449	Road traffic	1483 (C.42)	Electronic communications
1450	Road traffic	1484	Road traffic, England
1451	Road traffic	1485	Road traffic, England
1452	Road traffic	1486	Road traffic, England
1453	Road traffic	1487	Highways, England and Wales
1454	Road traffic	1488	Gas
1455	Road traffic	1489	National Health Service, England
1456	Road traffic	1490	National Health Service, England
1457	Regulatory reform	1491	National Health Service, England
	Social security	1492	National Health Service, England
1458	Disabled persons	1493 (C.43)	Children and young persons, England
	Education		Public health, England
1459	Disabled persons		Social care, England
	Education		
1460	Pesticides, England and Wales	1494	National Health Service, England
1461	Agriculture	1495	National Health Service, England
1462	Road traffic	1496	National Health Service, England
1463	Road traffic	1497	National Health Service, England
1464	Road traffic	1498	National Health Service, England
1465	Road traffic	1499	National Health Service, England
1466	Road traffic	1500	National Health Service, England
1467	Road traffic	1501	Financial services and markets
		1502	Value added tax

1503	Value added tax	**1539**	Road traffic
1504	Road traffic, England	**1540**	Road traffic
1505	Public health, England	**1541**	Road traffic
	Social care, England	**1542**	Road traffic
1506 (W.151)	National Health Service, Wales	**1543**	Road traffic
1507	Road traffic	**1544**	Road traffic
1508	Road traffic	**1545**	Road traffic
1509	Road traffic	**1546**	Road traffic
1510	Road traffic	**1547**	Road traffic
1511	Road traffic	**1548**	Road traffic
1512	Road traffic	**1549**	Road traffic
1513	Road traffic	**1550**	Road traffic
1514	Road traffic	**1551**	Road traffic
1515	Road traffic	**1552**	Road traffic
1516	Road traffic	**1553**	Road traffic
1517	Road traffic	**1554 (W.152)**	Seeds, Wales
1518	Road traffic	**1555**	Financial services and markets
1519	Road traffic	**1556 (W.153)**	Education, Wales
1520	Road traffic	**1557 (W.154)**	Road traffic, Wales
1521	Road traffic	**1558 (C.44)**	Prevention and suppression of terrorism
1522	Road traffic	**1559**	Environmental protection, England and Wales
1523	Road traffic		
1524	Road traffic	**1560**	Telecommunications
1525	Road traffic	**1561**	Telecommunications
1526	Road traffic	**1562**	Telecommunications
1527	Road traffic	**1563**	Seeds, England
1528	Road traffic	**1564**	Civil aviation
1529	Road traffic	**1565**	Road traffic
1530	Road traffic	**1566**	Road traffic
1531	Road traffic	**1567**	Road traffic
1532	Road traffic	**1568**	Road traffic
1533	Road traffic	**1569**	Road traffic
1534	Road traffic	**1570**	Road traffic
1535	Road traffic	**1571**	Road traffic
1536	Road traffic	**1572**	Road traffic
1537	Road traffic	**1573**	Road traffic
1538	Road traffic	**1574**	Road traffic

1575	Road traffic	1611	Road traffic
1576	Road traffic	1612	Road traffic
1577	Road traffic	1613	Road traffic
1578	Road traffic	1614	Food, England
1579	Road traffic		Agriculture, England
1580	Road traffic	1615	National Health Service, England
1581	Road traffic	1616 (C.45)	National Health Service, England
1582	Road traffic	1617	Disabled persons
1583	Road traffic		Transport
1584	Road traffic	1618	Fees and charges
1585	Road traffic	1619	Food, England
1586 (W.155)	Road traffic, Wales	1620	Legal Services Commission, England and Wales
1587	Merchant shipping	1621	Road traffic, England
1588	Coroners	1622	Road traffic
1589	Social security	1623	Road traffic
1590	Telegraphs	1624	Road traffic
1591 (W.156)	Road traffic, Wales	1625	Dentists
1592	Regulatory reform	1626	Charities, England and Wales
	Public health	1627	Diplomatic service
1593	Road traffic	1628	Civil aviation
1594	Highways, England and Wales	1629 (S.5)	Constitutional law
1595	Highways, England and Wales		Devolution, Scotland
1596	Income tax	1630 (S.6)	Constitutional law
1597	Professional qualifications		Devolution, Scotland
1598	Charities, England and Wales	1631	Road traffic
1599	Road traffic	1632	Road traffic
1600	Road traffic	1633	Road traffic
1601	Road traffic	1634	Road traffic
1602	Road traffic	1635	Road traffic
1603	Road traffic	1636	Road traffic
1604	Road traffic	1637	Road traffic
1605	Road traffic	1638	Road traffic
1606	Road traffic	1639	Road traffic
1607	Road traffic	1640	Road traffic
1608	Road traffic	1641	Road traffic
1609	Road traffic	1642	Road traffic
1610	Road traffic		

1643	Road traffic	**1675**	Contracts, England and Wales
1644	Road traffic		Contracts, Northern Ireland
1645	Road traffic	**1676**	Industrial organisation and development
1646	Animals, England		
1647 (C.49)	Disabled persons, England and Wales	**1677**	Plant breeders' rights
	Education, England and Wales	**1678**	Highways, England and Wales
		1679	Highways, England and Wales
1648 (C.46)	Representation of the people, Northern Ireland	**1680**	Education, England
1649	Environmental protection	**1681**	Road traffic
1650	Merchant shipping	**1682**	Road traffic
1651	Road traffic, England	**1683**	Road traffic
1652	Road traffic	**1684**	Road traffic
1653	Road traffic	**1685**	Road traffic
1654	Road traffic	**1686**	Environmental protection, England and Wales
1655	Road traffic	**1687 (L.4)**	Magistrates' courts, England and Wales
1656	Road traffic		
1657	Road traffic	**1688 (L.5)**	Supreme Court of England and Wales
1658	Road traffic	**1689**	Health and safety
1659	Road traffic	**1690**	National Health Service, England
1660	Road traffic	**1691 (C.51)**	Social security
1661 (W.157)	Education, Wales	**1692**	National Health Service, England
1662	Extradition	**1693**	Investigatory powers
1663 (W.158)	Education, Wales	**1694**	Disabled persons
1664	Highways, England and Wales		Transport
1665	Road traffic	**1695**	Education, England
1666	Road traffic	**1696**	Social security
1667 (W.159)	Education, Wales		Taxes
1668	Criminal law, England and Wales	**1697**	Social security, Northern Ireland
	Criminal law, Northern Ireland		Taxes, Northern Ireland
1669 (W.160)	Road traffic, Wales	**1698**	Road traffic, England and Wales
1670	Local government, England	**1699**	Disabled persons
1671	Dentists, England		Transport
1672	Road traffic, England	**1700**	Telegraphs
1673 (C.47)	Contracts, England and Wales	**1701**	Social security
	Contracts, Northern Ireland	**1702**	Environmental protection, England and Wales
1674	Contracts, England and Wales	**1703**	Social security
	Contracts, Northern Ireland	**1704**	Civil aviation

1705	Civil aviation	**1740**	Road traffic
1706	Civil aviation	**1741**	Road traffic
1707	Civil aviation	**1742**	Road traffic
1708	Civil aviation	**1743**	Road traffic
1709	Civil aviation	**1744**	Road traffic
1710	Countryside, England	**1745**	Road traffic
1711	Countryside, England	**1746**	Road traffic
1712	Civil aviation	**1747**	Road traffic
1713	Civil aviation	**1748**	Road traffic
1714	Education, England	**1749**	Road traffic
1715	Landlord and tenant, England	**1750**	Road traffic
1716	Immigration and asylum	**1751**	Road traffic
1717	Social security	**1752**	Road traffic
1718 (C. 48)	Local government, England and Wales	**1753**	Road traffic
1719	Local government, England and Wales	**1754**	Sports grounds and sporting events, England
1720	Education, England	**1755**	Sports grounds and sporting events, England and Wales
1721 (C.50)	Disabled persons, England and Wales		
	Education, England and Wales	**1756**	Road traffic
1722	Education, England	**1757**	Road traffic
1723	Local government, England and Wales	**1758**	Police, England and Wales
1724	Public passenger transport	**1759**	National Health Service, England and Wales
1725	Civil aviation	**1760**	National Health Service, England and Wales
1726 (W.161)	Food, Wales		
1727 (C.52)	Tax credits	**1761**	Defence
1728 (W.162)	Food, Wales	**1762**	Disabled persons
1729 (W.163)	Local government, Wales		Transport
1730 (W.164)	Environmental protection, Wales	**1763**	Social security
1731	Inheritance tax	**1764**	Animals, England
1732	Inheritance tax	**1765**	Animals, England
1733	Inheritance tax	**1766**	Legal Services Commission, England and Wales
1734 (L.6)	Magistrates' courts, England and Wales	**1767**	Agriculture
1735 (W.165)	Rating and valuation, Wales	**1768**	National Health Service, England
1736 (W.166) (C.53)	Housing, Wales	**1769**	Housing, England
1737 (W.167)	Road traffic, Wales	**1770**	Consumer protection
1738	Education, England	**1771**	*Cancelled*
1739 (C.54)	Criminal law, England and Wales	**1772 (W.168)**	Countryside, Wales

1773	Customs and excise	**1805 (W.175)**	Plant health, Wales
1774	Local government, England	**1806 (W.176)**	Agriculture, Wales
1775	Financial services and markets	**1807**	Parliament
	Electronic communications	**1808**	Road traffic, England
1776	Financial services and markets	**1809**	Highways, England and Wales
	Electronic communications	**1810**	Highways, England and Wales
1777	Financial services and markets	**1811**	Road traffic
1778	Road traffic	**1812**	Road traffic
1779	Road traffic	**1813**	Road traffic
1780	Companies	**1814**	Road traffic
1781	Local government, England	**1815**	Road traffic
1782	Road traffic	**1816**	Road traffic
1783	Local government, England	**1817**	Food, England
1784	Local government, England	**1818**	Income tax
1785	Local government, England	**1819**	European Communities
1786	Local government, England	**1820**	Defence
1787	Local government, England	**1821**	Education, England
1788	Local government, England	**1822**	Overseas territories
1789	Social security	**1823**	Extradition
1790 (C.55)	Children and young persons, England	**1824**	Extradition
	Public health, England		Hong Kong
	Social care, England	**1825**	Extradition
1791	National Health Service, England		Hong Kong
1792	Social security	**1826**	International immunities and privileges
1793	Road traffic	**1827**	International immunities and privileges
1794 (W.169)	Countryside, Wales	**1828**	International immunities and privileges
1795 (W.170)	Public health, Wales	**1829**	Extradition
1796 (W.171)	Countryside, Wales	**1830**	Extradition
1797 (W.172)	Agriculture, Wales	**1831**	Extradition
1798 (W.173)	Food, Wales	**1832**	Immigration
	Agriculture, Wales	**1833**	*Cancelled*
1799 (C.56)	Housing, England	**1834**	Companies
1800	Road traffic	**1835**	Road traffic
1801	Road traffic	**1836**	Countryside, England
1802	Road traffic	**1837**	Criminal law, England and Wales
1803	*Cancelled*	**1838**	Criminal law, England and Wales
1804 (W.174)	National Health Service, Wales	**1839**	Civil aviation

1840	Road traffic	**1874**	Insider dealing
1841	Education, England	**1875 (W.184)**	Town and country planning, Wales
1842 (W.177)	Road traffic, Wales	**1876 (W.185)**	Town and country planning, Wales
1843 (L.7)	Supreme Court of England and Wales	**1877 (W.186)**	Town and country planning, Wales
1844 (L.8)	Supreme Court of England and Wales	**1878 (W.187)**	Town and country planning, Wales
1845	Prevention and suppression of terrorism	**1879 (W.188)**	Education, Wales
1846	Road traffic	**1880 (W.189)**	Education, Wales
1847	Road traffic	**1881 (W.190)**	National Health Service, Wales
1848	Road traffic	**1882 (W.191)**	National Health Service, Wales
1849	Road traffic	**1883 (W.192)**	National Health Service, Wales
1850	Road traffic	**1884 (W.193)**	Local government, Wales
1851	Road traffic	**1885 (W.194)**	Sea fisheries, Wales
1852	Pensions, England and Wales	**1886 (W.195)**	Food, Wales
1853 (W.178)	Road traffic, Wales	**1887**	Parliament
1854	Family law	**1888**	Contracting out
1855 (W.179)	Children and young persons, Wales		Social security
1856 (W.180)	Education, Wales	**1889**	Companies
1857 (W.181)	Education, Wales	**1890**	Tractors
1858	Protection of wrecks, England	**1891**	Environmental protection
1859	Social security	**1892**	Ecclesiastical law, England
1860	Housing, England and Wales	**1893**	Ecclesiastical law, England
	Regulatory reform, England and Wales	**1894**	Ecclesiastical law, England
1861	Environmental protection	**1895 (W.196)**	Local government, Wales
1862 (C.57)	Criminal law, England and Wales	**1896 (W.197)**	National Health Service, Wales
1863	Police, England and Wales	**1897 (W.198)**	Sea fisheries, Wales
1864	Road traffic	**1898 (W.199)**	Animals, Wales
1865	Road traffic	**1899**	Road traffic
1866	Road traffic	**1900**	Local government, England
1867	Road traffic	**1901**	Betting, gaming and lotteries
1868	Highways, England and Wales	**1902**	Betting, gaming and lotteries
1869 (W.182)	Road traffic, Wales	**1903**	Cinemas and films, England and Wales
1870 (W.183)	Seeds, Wales	**1904**	Betting, gaming and lotteries
1871	Representation of the people, England and Wales	**1905**	Road traffic
1872 (S.7)	Representation of the people, Scotland	**1906**	Road traffic
1873	Representation of the people, Northern Ireland	**1907**	Road traffic
		1908	Road traffic
		1909	Betting, gaming and lotteries

1910	Betting, gaming and lotteries, England and Wales	1944	Powers of attorney, England and Wales
1911	Telegraphs		Mental health, England and Wales
1912 (C.58)	Housing, England	1945	Prevention and suppression of terrorism
1913	Pensions	1946	Transport
1914 (C.59)	Road traffic, England and Wales	1947	Telecommunications
1915 (L.9)	Family law, England and Wales	1948	Telecommunications
1916	Road traffic, England and Wales	1949	Telecommunications
1917	Criminal law, England and Wales	1950	Social security
1918 (W.200)	Road traffic, Wales	1951	Government trading funds
1919 (C.60)	National Health Service, Wales	1952	Road traffic
1920	National Health Service, England and Wales	1953	Road traffic
1921	National Health Service, England and Wales	1954	Road traffic
		1955	Road traffic
1922	Food, England	1956	Road traffic
1923	Food, England	1957	Road traffic
1924	Agriculture	1958	Road traffic
1925	Landlord and tenant, England	1959	Road traffic
1926 (C.61)	Customs and excise	1960	Road traffic
1927	Aggregates levy	1961	Road traffic
1928	Customs and excise	1962	Local government, England
1929	Aggregates levy	1963	Income tax
1930	Betting, gaming and lotteries	1964	Northern Ireland
1931	Investigatory powers	1965	Transport and works, England and Wales
1932	Investigatory powers		
1933	Investigatory powers		Transport, England and Wales
1934	Criminal law, England and Wales		Canals and inland waterways, England and Wales
1935	Value added tax	1966	Taxes
1936	Road traffic	1967	Income tax
1937	Road traffic	1968	Income tax
1938	Road traffic	1969	Income tax
1939	Road traffic	1970	Income tax
1940	Road traffic	1971	Taxes
1941	Road traffic	1972 (W.201)	Road traffic, Wales
1942	Road traffic	1973	Income tax
1943	Transport and works, England	1974	Income tax
	Transport, England	1975	Taxes

1976 (W.202)	Road traffic, Wales	2008	Tax credits
1977 (W.203)	Road traffic, Wales	2009	Road traffic
1978 (W.204)	Road traffic, Wales	2010	Road traffic
1979	Education, England	2011	Immigration
1980	Disabled persons	2012	Road traffic, England
1981	Disabled persons, England	2013	Electronic communications
1982	Education, England	2014	Tax credits
1983	Education, England	2015	Financial services and markets
1984	Education, England		Electronic communications
1985	Disabled persons, England and Wales	2016	National Health Service, England
	Education, England and Wales	2017	Education, England
1986	Companies	2018 (C.64)	Education, England
1987 (W.205)	Road traffic, Wales	2019	Social security
1988	Road traffic	2020	Social security
1989 (C.62)	Terms and conditions of employment	2021	Environmental protection, England and Wales
1990	Insolvency	2022 (W.206)	Public passenger transport, Wales
1991	Road traffic	2023 (W.207)	Public passenger transport, Wales
1992	Road traffic	2024 (W.208) (C.65)	Transport, Wales
1993	Road traffic	2025	National Health Service, England
1994	Education, England	2026	Road traffic
1995	Civil aviation	2027	Road traffic
1996	Civil aviation	2028	Road traffic
1997	Transport and works, England	2029	Road traffic
	Transport, England	2030	Road traffic
1998	Transport and works, England and Wales	2031	Road traffic
	Canals and inland waterways, England and Wales	2032	Road traffic
		2033	Customs and excise
1999	Terms and conditions of employment	2034	Terms and conditions of employment
2000	Port health authorities, England and Wales	2035	Terms and conditions of employment
2001 (C.67)	Social care, England	2036	Professional qualifications
2002 (C.63)	Education, England	2037	Legal services, England and Wales
2003	Education, England	2038	Road traffic
2004	Education, England	2039	Road traffic
2005	Tax credits	2040	Road traffic
2006	Tax credits	2041	Road traffic
2007	Tax credits	2042	Road traffic

2043	Road traffic	2076	Road traffic
2044	Road traffic	2077	Road traffic
2045	Road traffic	2078	Road traffic
2046	Road traffic	2079	Road traffic
2047	Road traffic	2080	Road traffic
2048	Education, England	2081	Road traffic
2049	Education, England	2082	Road traffic
2050 (C.66)	Criminal law, England and Wales	2083	Road traffic
	Police	2084	Road traffic
2051	Housing, England	2085	Road traffic
2052	Justices of the Peace, England and Wales	2086	Education, England and Wales
		2087	Education, England and Wales
2053	Derelict land, England	2088	Education, England and Wales
2054	Antarctica	2089	Education, England and Wales
2055	Merchant shipping	2090	Transport, England
2056	Civil aviation	2091	Highways, England and Wales
2057	Civil aviation	2092	Highways, England and Wales
2058 (L.10)	Supreme Court of England and Wales	2093	Road traffic
	County Courts, England and Wales	2094	Road traffic
2059	Customs and excise	2095	Road traffic
2060 (W.209)	Animals, Wales	2096	Road traffic
2061 (W.210)	Animals, Wales	2097	Road traffic
2062	Education, England	2098	Pensions
2063	Education, England	2099	Health and safety
2064	Education, England	2100	Road traffic
2065	Road traffic	2101 (W.211)	Road traffic, Wales
2066	Road traffic	2102	Environmental protection, England
2067	Road traffic	2103	Education, England and Wales
2068	Road traffic	2104	Education, England and Wales
2069	Road traffic	2105	Education, England
2070	Public health, England	2106	National Health Service, England
	Social care, England	2107	Highways, England and Wales
2071	Education, England	2108	Highways, England and Wales
2072	Education, England	2109	Road traffic
2073	National Health Service, England	2110	Road traffic
2074	Road traffic	2111	Road traffic
2075	Road traffic	2112	Road traffic

2113	Education, England	2148	Road traffic
2114	Education, England	2149	Road traffic
2115 (W.212)	Road traffic, Wales	2150	Road traffic
2116	Prisons, England and Wales	2151	Food, England
2117	Young offender institutions, England and Wales		Agriculture, England
		2152	Animals, England
2118 (W.213)	Local government, Wales	2153	Animals, England
2119	Road traffic	2154	Animals, England
2120	Road traffic	2155	Immigration
2121	Civil aviation	2156 (W.217)	Road traffic, Wales
2122	Education, England	2157	Financial services and markets
2123	Education, England		Electronic communications
2124	Education, England	2158	Tax credits
2125	Merchant shipping	2159	Road traffic
2126	Road traffic	2160	Road traffic
2127 (W.214)	Agriculture, Wales	2161	Road traffic
2128 (W.215)	Road traffic, Wales	2162	Road traffic
2129	Road traffic	2163	Road traffic
2130	Road traffic	2164	Road traffic
2131	Road traffic	2165	Road traffic
2132	Road traffic	2166	Road traffic
2133	Road traffic	2167	Civil aviation
2134	Road traffic	2168	Civil aviation
2135	Road traffic	2169	Road traffic
2136	Road traffic	2170	Road traffic
2137	Road traffic	2171 (W.218)	Social care, Wales
2138	Civil aviation		Children and young persons, Wales
2139	Civil aviation	2172	Tax credits
2140	Road traffic	2173	Tax credits
2141	Terrorism, Northern Ireland	2174	Health and safety
2142 (W.216)	Road traffic, Wales	2175	Health and safety
2143	Magistrates' courts, England and Wales	2176	Health and safety
	Pensions, England and Wales	2177	Road traffic
2144	Road traffic	2178	Road traffic
2145	Road traffic	2179	Road traffic
2146	Road traffic	2180	Road traffic
2147	Road traffic	2181	Road traffic

2182	Road traffic	2217 (C.71)	Disabled persons, England and Wales
2183	Road traffic, England		Education, England and Wales
2184	Road traffic, England	2218	Civil aviation
2185	Road traffic, England	2219	Road traffic
2186	Road traffic, England	2220	Road traffic
2187	Road traffic, England	2221	Road traffic
2188	Road traffic, England	2222	Civil aviation
2189	Road traffic	2223	Education, England and Wales
2190	Road traffic	2224	Local government, England
2191	Road traffic	2225	Income tax
2192	Road traffic	2226 (W.221)	Sea fisheries, Wales
2193	Road traffic	2227	Landlord and tenant, England
2194	Road traffic	2228	Road traffic
2195	Road traffic	2229	Road traffic
2196	Road traffic	2230	Road traffic
2197	Road traffic	2231	Road traffic
2198	Road traffic	2232	Trustees, England and Wales
2199 (W.219)	National Health Service, Wales	2233	National Health Service, England
2200 (C.68)	Sports grounds and sporting events, England and Wales	2234	Local government, England
		2235	Local government, England
2201	Merchant shipping	2236	Local government, England
2202 (C.69)	Health care and associated professions	2237	Local government, England
	National Health Service, England	2238	Local government, England
2203 (W.220)	Road traffic, Wales	2239	Local government, England
2204	Road traffic	2240	Local government, England
2205	Road traffic	2241	Local government, England
2206	Road traffic	2242	Local government, England
2207	Social security	2243	Local government, England
2208	Civil aviation	2244	Local government, England
2209	Road traffic	2245	Road traffic
2210	Road traffic	2246	Highways, England and Wales
2211	Road traffic	2247	Road traffic
2212	Road traffic	2248 (C.72)	Social security
2213	Road traffic	2249	Road traffic
2214	Education, England	2250	Road traffic
2215 (C.70)	Children and young persons, England	2251	Road traffic
2216	Disabled persons	2252	Road traffic

2253	Road traffic	2288	Road traffic
2254	Civil aviation	2289	Road traffic
2255	Civil aviation	2290	Road traffic
2256 (C.73)	Social security	2291	Road traffic
2257	Coroners	2292	Road traffic
2258 (W.222)	Town and country planning, Wales	2293	Civil aviation
2259 (W.223)	Road traffic, Wales	2294 (C.74)	Telecommunications
2260	Road traffic		Criminal law
2261	Road traffic	2295 (W.224)	Food, Wales
2262	Road traffic	2296 (W.225)	Food, Wales
2263	Road traffic	2297 (W.226)	Water, Wales
2264 (S.8)	Constitutional law	2298	Local government, England
	Devolution, Scotland	2299	Local government, England
	Housing, Scotland	2300	Animals, England
2265	Taxes	2301	Education, England
2266	Customs and excise	2302 (W.227)	Animals, Wales
2267	Trade unions	2303 (W.228)	Animals, Wales
2268	Terms and conditions of employment	2304 (W.229)	Animals, Wales
2269	National Health Service, England	2305 (W.230)	Road traffic, Wales
2270	National Health Service, England	2306 (C.75)	Police
2271	National Health Service, England	2307	Road traffic
2272	National Health Service, England	2308	Road traffic
2273	National Health Service, England	2309	Road traffic
2274	National Health Service, England	2310	Customs and excise
2275	National Health Service, England	2311	Social security
2276	National Health Service, England	2312	Police, England and Wales
2277	National Health Service, England	2313	Police, England and Wales
2278	National Health Service, England	2314	Social security
2279	National Health Service, England	2315	Agriculture, England
2280	National Health Service, England	2316	Education, England
2281	National Health Service, England	2317 (W.231)	Road traffic, Wales
2282	National Health Service, England	2318	Road traffic
2283	National Health Service, England	2319	Road traffic
2284	Road traffic	2320	Road traffic
2285	Road traffic	2321	Road traffic
2286	Road traffic	2322	Social security
2287	Road traffic	2323	Social security

2324 (C.76)	Housing, England
2325 (W.232)	Agriculture, Wales
2326	Criminal law, England and Wales
2327	Pensions
2328 (W.233)	Road traffic, Wales
2329 (W.234)	Road traffic, Wales
2330	Road traffic
2331	Road traffic
2332	Road traffic
2333	Road traffic
2334	Road traffic
2335	Road traffic
2336	Road traffic
2337	Road traffic
2338	Road traffic
2339	Road traffic
2340	Road traffic
2341	Road traffic
2342	Road traffic
2343	Road traffic
2344	Road traffic
2345	Road traffic
2346	Road traffic
2347	Road traffic
2348	Road traffic
2349	Road traffic
2350	Food, England
2351	Food, England
2352	National Health Service, England
2353	National Health Service, England
2354	Customs and excise
2355	Customs and excise
2356 (W.235)	Road traffic, Wales
2357	Agriculture, England
2358	Road traffic
2359	Road traffic
2360	Road traffic
2361	Road traffic
2362	Road traffic
2363 (C.77)	National Health Service, England
2364	Food, England
2365 (W.236)	Road traffic, Wales
2366	Social security
2367 (S.9)	Housing, Scotland
2368	Local government, England
2369	Local government, England
2370	Local government, England
2371	Local government, England
2372	Local government, England
2373	Local government, England
2374	Local government, England
2375	National Health Service, England
2376	Health care and associated professions
2377 (C.78)	Road traffic
2378 (W.237)	Road traffic, Wales: Traffic regulation
2379	Road traffic
2380	Social security
2381	Road traffic, Northern Ireland
2382	Road traffic
2383	Road traffic
2384	Road traffic
2385	Road traffic
2386	Road traffic
2387	Justices of the Peace, England and Wales
2388	Road traffic
2389	Road traffic
2390	Road traffic
2391	Road traffic
2392	Road traffic
2393	Road traffic
2394	Road traffic
2395	Road traffic
2396	Road traffic

2397	National Health Service, England	2433	Road traffic
2398	Transport and works, England	2434	Road traffic
	Transport, England	2435	Road traffic
2399 (W.238)	Road traffic, Wales	2436	Road traffic
2400 (W.239)	Road traffic, Wales	2437	Road traffic
2401	Coroners	2438	Road traffic
2402	Social security	2439 (C.79)	Education, England and Wales
2403	Road traffic, England	2440	Road traffic, England
2404	International development	2441	Social security
2405	International development	2442	Social security
2406	Income tax	2443	Environmental protection
2407	Road traffic	2444 (W.240)	Road traffic, Wales
2408	Road traffic	2445	Road traffic
2409	Road traffic	2446	Road traffic
2410	Road traffic	2447	Road traffic
2411	Road traffic	2448	Road traffic
2412	Road traffic	2449	Road traffic
2413	Road traffic	2450	Road traffic
2414	Road traffic	2451	Road traffic
2415	Road traffic	2452	Road traffic
2416	Road traffic	2453	Road traffic
2417	Road traffic	2454	Road traffic
2418	Road traffic	2455	Road traffic
2419	National Health Service, England	2456	Road traffic
2420	National Health Service, England	2457	Road traffic
2421	Civil aviation	2458	Road traffic
2422	Highways, England and Wales	2459	Road traffic
2423	Highways, England and Wales	2460	Road traffic
2424	Highways, England and Wales	2461	Road traffic
2425	Highways, England and Wales	2462	Road traffic
2426	Road traffic	2463	Dentists
2427	Territorial waters	2464	Dentists
2428	Road traffic	2465 (W.241)	Road traffic, Wales
2429	Road traffic	2466	Education, England
2430	Road traffic	2467	Offshore installations
2431	Road traffic	2468	Police, England and Wales
2432	Road traffic		Pensions, England and Wales

2469	National Health Service, England	2504	Road traffic
2470	Road traffic	2505	Road traffic
2471	Road traffic	2506	Road traffic
2472	Road traffic	2507	Road traffic
2473	Road traffic	2508	Road traffic
2474	Road traffic	2509	Road traffic
2475	Road traffic	2510	Road traffic
2476	Harbours, docks, piers and ferries	2511	Road traffic
2477 (W.242)	Road traffic, Wales	2512 (W.244)	Road traffic, Wales
2478 (C.80)	National Health Service, England and Wales	2513	Education, England and Wales
		2514	Road traffic
	Health care and associated professions	2515	Road traffic
2479	Consumer protection	2516	Local government, England
2480 (W.243)	Animals, Wales	2517 (W.245)	Road traffic, Wales
2481	Road traffic	2518 (W.246)	Road traffic, Wales
2482	Road traffic	2519 (W.247)	Road traffic, Wales
2483	Road traffic	2520	Road traffic, England
2484	Road traffic	2521	National debt
2485	Road traffic	2522	Education, England
2486	Road traffic	2523	Education, England
2487	Road traffic	2524	Social security
2488	Road traffic	2525	*Cancelled*
2489	Road traffic	2526	Police, England and Wales
2490	Road traffic	2527	Police, England and Wales
2491	Road traffic	2528	Environmental protection, England and Wales
2492	Road traffic	2529	Police, England and Wales
2493	Road traffic	2530	Criminal law
2494	Road traffic	2531	National assistance services, England
2495	Road traffic	2532 (W.248) (C.81)	National Health Service, Wales
2496	Road traffic	2533	Atomic energy and radioactive substances
2497	Social security		
2498	Statistics of trade	2534	Public passenger transport
2499	Road traffic	2535	Public passenger transport
2500	Road traffic	2536	Public passenger transport, England and Wales
2501	Road traffic		
2502	Road traffic	2537	Public passenger transport
2503	Road traffic	2538	Immigration

2539 (L.11)	Land registration, England and Wales	2575	Road traffic
2540	Road traffic	2576	Road traffic
2541	Road traffic	2577	Road traffic
2542	Road traffic	2578	Road traffic
2543	Road traffic	2579	Road traffic
2544	Road traffic	2580	Road traffic
2545	Road traffic	2581	Road traffic
2546	Road traffic	2582	Road traffic
2547	Road traffic	2583	Road traffic
2548	National Health Service, England	2584	Veterinary surgeons
2549 (W.249)	Road traffic, Wales	2585 (W.251)	Road traffic, Wales
2550	Education, England	2586	Harbours, docks, piers and ferries
2551	Road traffic	2587	Northern Ireland
2552	Road traffic		Constitutional law
2553	Road traffic	2588 (W.252)	Road traffic, Wales
2554	Road traffic	2589	Plant health
2555	Road traffic	2590	Road traffic
2556	Road traffic	2591	Civil aviation
2557	Road traffic	2592	Civil aviation
2558	Road traffic	2593	Local government, England
2559	Road traffic	2594	Local government, England
2560	Road traffic	2595	Local government, England
2561	Road traffic	2596	Local government, England
2562	Road traffic	2597	Local government, England
2563	Road traffic	2598	Local government, England
2564	Road traffic	2599	Local government, England
2565	Road traffic	2600	Local government, England
2566	Road traffic	2601	Local government, England
2567	Road traffic	2602	Local government, England
2568	Road traffic	2603	Local government, England
2569	Medicines	2604	Local government, England
2570	Agriculture, England	2605	Road traffic
2571 (W.250)	Road traffic, Wales	2606	Road traffic
2572	Medical profession	2607	Road traffic
2573	Plant health, England	2608	Road traffic
2574	Northern Ireland	2609	Road traffic
	Constitutional law	2610	Road traffic

2611	Road traffic	2644	Road traffic
2612	Road traffic	2645	Road traffic
2613	Road traffic	2646	Road traffic
2614	Agriculture, England	2647	Road traffic
	Water, England	2648	Road traffic
2615 (W.253) (C.82)	Countryside, Wales	2649	Road traffic
2616	National Health Service, England	2650	Road traffic
2617	National Health Service, England	2651	Road traffic
2618	Harbours, docks, piers and ferries	2652	Road traffic
2619	Immigration	2653	Road traffic
2620	Local government, England	2654	Road traffic
2621	National Health Service, England	2655	Road traffic
2622 (W.254)	Social care, Wales	2656	Road traffic
	Children and young persons, Wales	2657	Telecommunications
	Public health, Wales	2658	Telecommunications
2623	Freedom of information	2659	Road traffic
2624	Local government, England	2660	Social security
2625	Road traffic	2661	Income tax
2626	Ministers of the Crown, England and Wales	2662	Justices of the Peace, England and Wales
2627	Overseas territories	2663 (W.255)	Road traffic, Wales
2628	United Nations	2664 (W.256)	Road traffic, Wales
2629	United Nations	2665	Electricity
2630	United Nations	2666	Treasure
2631	United Nations	2667	Road traffic
2632	Education, Wales	2668	Road traffic
2633	Ministers of the Crown	2669	Road traffic
2634	Diplomatic service	2670	Road traffic
2635	Cinemas and films	2671	Road traffic
2636	Constitutional law	2672	Road traffic
2637	Caribbean and North Atlantic territories	2673	Road traffic
2638	Pitcairn Islands	2674	Road traffic
2639	Agriculture, England	2675	Health and safety
2640	Road traffic	2676	Health and safety
2641	Road traffic	2677	Health and safety
2642	Road traffic	2678	Road traffic
2643	Road traffic	2679	Road traffic

2680	Road traffic	2714	Road traffic
2681	Road traffic	2715	Road traffic
2682	Town and country planning, England	2716	Road traffic
2683	Town and country planning, England	2717	Road traffic
2684	Tribunals and inquiries, England	2718	Road traffic
2685	Tribunals and inquiries, England	2719 (W.257)	Road traffic, Wales
2686	Tribunals and inquiries, England	2720 (W.258)	Road traffic, Wales
2687	Road traffic	2721 (W.259)	Road traffic, Wales
2688	Environmental protection, England and Wales	2722	Data protection, England and Wales
2689	Social security		Freedom of Information, England and Wales
2690	Social security	2723	Agriculture, England and Wales
	Terms and conditions of employment		Pesticides, England and Wales
2691	Customs and excise	2724	Prevention and suppression of terrorism
2692	Customs and excise	2725	Road traffic
2693	Channel Tunnel	2726	Road traffic
2694	Road traffic	2727	Road traffic
2695	Road traffic	2728	Road traffic
2696	Road traffic	2729	Road traffic
2697	Road traffic	2730	Harbours, docks, piers and ferries
2698	Road traffic	2731	Immigration
2699	Road traffic	2732	Road traffic
2700	Road traffic	2733	Pesticides
2701	Road traffic		Fees and charges
2702	Road traffic	2734	Road traffic
2703	Transport, England	2735	Road traffic
2704	Chiropractors	2736	Road traffic
2705	Road traffic, England	2737	Road traffic
2706	Financial services and markets	2738	Road traffic
2707	Financial services and markets	2739	Road traffic
2708	Insolvency, England and Wales	2740	Road traffic
2709 (S.10)	Insolvency, Scotland	2741	Road traffic
	Companies, Scotland	2742	Road traffic
2710	Insolvency	2743	Road traffic
2711 (C.83)	Insolvency	2744 (W.260)	Road traffic, Wales
2712	Insolvency, England and Wales	2745 (W.261)	Road traffic, Wales
2713	Education, England	2746	Civil aviation

2747	Civil aviation	2780 (W.264)	Tribunals and inquiries, Wales
2748	Insolvency	2781 (W.265)	Road traffic, Wales
2749 (C.84)	Copyright	2782 (L.12)	Magistrates' courts, England and Wales
	Trade marks	2783 (L.13)	Supreme Court of England and Wales
	Criminal law	2784 (L.14)	Magistrates' courts, England and Wales
2750 (C.85)	Police		
2751 (W.262)	Road traffic, Wales: Traffic regulation	2785	Legal Services Commission, England and Wales
2752	Road traffic	2786	Civil aviation
2753	Road traffic	2787	Education, England and Wales
2754	Road traffic	2788	Terms and conditions of employment
2755	Road traffic	2789	Terms and conditions of employment
2756	Road traffic	2790	Road traffic
2757	Highways, England and Wales	2791	Road traffic
2758	Immigration	2792	Road traffic
2759	National Health Service, England and Wales	2793	Road traffic
2760	Education, England	2794	Road traffic
2761	Agriculture	2795	Road traffic
2762 (W.263)	Plant health, Wales	2796	Road traffic
2763	Education, England	2797	Road traffic
2764	Education, England	2798 (W.266)	Housing, Wales
2765	Education, England	2799 (W.267)	Housing, Wales
2766	Education, England	2800 (W.268)	Housing, Wales
2767	Education, England	2801 (W.269)	Town and country planning, Wales
2768	Education, England	2802 (W.270)	National Health Service, Wales
2769	Education, England	2803	Road traffic
2770	Education, England	2804	Road traffic
2771	Education, England	2805	Road traffic
2772	Education, England	2806	Road traffic
2773	Education, England	2807	Road traffic
2774	Education, England	2808	Road traffic
2775	Education, England	2809	Road traffic
2776	Health and safety	2810	Road traffic
2777	Road traffic, England	2811 (C.87)	Immigration
2778	Road traffic	2812 (C.86)	Freedom of information, England and Wales
2779 (S.11)	Constitutional law		
	Devolution, Scotland	2813	Value added tax
		2814 (W.271)	Education, Wales

2815 (C.88)	Immigration	2850	Animals, England
2816	Immigration and asylum	2851	Value added tax, England and Wales
2817	Immigration and asylum	2852	Road traffic
2818	Terms and conditions of employment	2853	Road traffic
2819	Terms and conditions of employment	2854	Road traffic
2820	Terms and conditions of employment	2855	Road traffic
	Social security	2856	Road traffic
2821	Terms and conditions of employment	2857	Road traffic
2822	Terms and conditions of employment	2858	Road traffic
2823	Social security	2859	Education
2824	Road traffic	2860	Animals, England
2825	Road traffic	2861	National Health Service, England
2826	Road traffic	2862	Road traffic
2827	Road traffic	2863	Road traffic
2828	Road traffic	2864	Road traffic
2829	Road traffic	2865 (C.90)	Consumer protection, England and Wales
2830	Road traffic		Consumer protection, Northern Ireland
2831	Road traffic	2866 (C.91)	Social security
2832	Freedom of information		Terms and conditions of employment
2833 (C.89)	Rights of way, England	2867 (C. 92)(W.273)	Cancelled
2834 (W.272)	Food, Wales	2868	Education, England
2835	Northern Ireland	2869 (W.274)	Road traffic, Wales
2836 (N.I.2)	Northern Ireland	2870	Sea fisheries, England
2837	Supreme Court of England and Wales	2871	Building and buildings, England and Wales
2838	Maintenance of dependants		
2839	Maintenance of dependants	2872	Building and buildings, England and Wales
2840	European Communities	2873	Disabled persons
2841	European Communities		Transport
2842	Architects	2874	Pesticides, England and Wales
2843	Northern Ireland	2875	Animals, England
2844	Criminal law, England and Wales	2876	Local government, England
2845	Criminal law, England and Wales	2877	Local government, England
	Criminal law, Northern Ireland	2878	Local government, England
2846	Criminal law, England and Wales	2879 (W.275)	Medical profession, Wales
2847	Income tax	2880 (W.276)	Local government, Wales
2848	Income tax	2881	Road traffic
2849	Taxes		

2882	Local government, England	2918	Value added tax
2883	Local government, England	2919	Road traffic
2884	Local government, England	2920	Road traffic
2885	Local government, England	2921	Road traffic
2886	Local government, England	2922	Road traffic
2887	Local government, England	2923	Road traffic
2888	Local government, England	2924	Social security
2889	Local government, England	2925	Social security, Northern Ireland
2890	Local government, England	2926	Tax credits
2891	Local government, England	2927	Terms and conditions of employment
2892	Local government, England	2928	Fees and charges
2893	Sports grounds and sporting events, England	2929	Social security
2894	Companies	2930	Income tax
2895	Partnership	2931	Income tax
2896	Education, England	2932	National Health Service, England and Wales
2897	Education, England	2933	Prisons, England and Wales
2898	Education, England	2934	Professional qualifications
2899	Education, England	2935 (W.277)	Children and young persons, Wales
2900	Education, England		Social care, Wales
2901	Education, England	2936	Road traffic, England
2902	Plant health, England	2937 (W.278)	Road traffic, Wales
2903	Education, England	2938 (W.279)	Education, Wales
2904	Education, England	2939 (W.280)	Food, Wales
2905	Data protection	2940 (W.281)	Education, Wales
2906	Road traffic	2941 (W.282)	Local government, Wales
2907	Road traffic	2942	Fees and charges
2908	Road traffic	2943	Road traffic
2909	Road traffic	2944	Road traffic
2910	Road traffic	2945	Road traffic
2911	Road traffic	2946	Road traffic
2912	Road traffic	2947	Road traffic
2913	Road traffic	2948	Road traffic
2914	Road traffic	2949	Road traffic
2915	Road traffic	2950	Road traffic
2916	Road traffic	2951	Pensions
2917	Road traffic	2952 (C.93)	Education, England

2953	Education, England
2954	Local government, England
2955 (C.94)	Electronic communications
2956	Electronic communications
2957 (C.95)	Road traffic, England and Wales
2958	Road traffic
2959	Road traffic
2960	Road traffic
2961	Road traffic
2962	Road traffic
2963	Road traffic
2964	Road traffic
2965	Road traffic
2966	Road traffic
2967	Road traffic
2968	Road traffic
2969	Road traffic
2970	Road traffic
2971	Road traffic
2972 (S.12)	Employment tribunals, Scotland
2973	Road traffic
2974	Road traffic
2975	Police, England and Wales
2976	Income tax
	Inheritance tax
	Taxes
	Social security
2977	Road traffic, England and Wales
2978	Education, England
2979	Health and safety
2980	Environmental protection, England and Wales
2981	Disabled persons
	Transport
2982	Local government, England
2983	Local government, England
2984	Local government, England
2985	Local government, England
2986	Local government, England
2987	Local government, England
2988	Local government, England
2989	Local government, England
2990	Local government, England
2991	Local government, England
2992	Local government, England
2993	Road traffic
2994	Road traffic
2995	National Health Service, England and Wales
	Road traffic, England and Wales
2996	Education, England
2997 (L.16)	Supreme Court of England and Wales
2998 (L.17)	Magistrates' courts, England and Wales
2999	Local government, England
3000	Local government, England
3001	Disabled persons
	Transport
3002	Disabled persons
	Transport
3003	Education, England
3004	Highways, England and Wales
3005	Education, England
3006	Income tax
3007	National Health Service, England
3008	Food, England
3009	Road traffic
3010	Consumer protection
3011 (W.283)	Agriculture, Wales
3012 (W.284) (C.96)	Housing, Wales
3013 (W.285)	Children and young persons, Wales
3014 (W.286) (C.97)	Transport, Wales
3015 (C.98)	Proceeds of crime
3016	Proceeds of crime
3017 (W.287)	Public passenger transport, Wales

3018	Immigration	3051	Professional qualifications
3019	Social security	3052	Contracting out
3020	Road traffic, England and Wales	3053 (W.288)	Representation of the people, Wales
3021	Rating and valuation, England	3054 (W.289)	Rating and valuation, Wales
3022	Local government, England	3055 (C.102)	Proceeds of crime
3023	Local government, England	3056 (C.103)	Customs and excise
3024	Medicines, England	3057	Customs and excise
	Medicines, Northern Ireland	3058	Education, England and Wales
3025	Immigration	3059	Education, England and Wales
3026	Seeds	3060	Education, England and Wales
3027	Value added tax	3061	Road traffic
3028 (C.99)	Value added tax	3062	Industrial organisation and development
3029	Road traffic, England and Wales	3063	Education, England
3030	Road traffic	3064	Road traffic
3031	Road traffic	3065	Road traffic
3032 (C.100)	Criminal law, England and Wales	3066	Road traffic
	Police, England and Wales	3067	Road traffic
3033	Legal aid and advice, England and Wales	3068	Road traffic
3034	Road traffic	3069	Road traffic
3035	Local government, England	3070	Road traffic
3036	Tax credits	3071	Road traffic
3037	Pilotage	3072	Social security
3038	National Health Service, England	3073	Civil aviation
3039	National Health Service, England	3074	Civil aviation
3040	National Health Service, England	3075	Police, England and Wales
3041	Consumer protection	3076	Registration of births, deaths, marriages, etc., England and Wales
3042	Customs and excise	3077	Road traffic
3043	Environmental protection, England	3078	Immigration
3044 (C.101)	Animals, England	3079 (W.290)	Road traffic, Wales
3045	Consumer protection	3080	Zoos, England and Wales
3046	Clean air, England	3081	Companies
3047	Social security	3082	Electricity
	Electronic communications	3083	Pensions, England and Wales
3048	National Health Service, England	3084	Coroners
3049	Police, England and Wales	3085	Education, England
3050	Postal services	3086	Education, England

3087	Education, England	3123	Libraries
3088	Education, England	3124	National lottery
3089	Education, England	3125 (C.105)	Private security industry
3090	Education, England	3126	Northern Ireland
3091	Education, England	3127	Harbours, docks, piers and ferries
3092	Education, England	3128	Terms and conditions of employment
3093	Education, England	3129	Electricity
3094	Education, England	3130	Gas
3095	Education, England	3131	Clerk of the Crown in Chancery
3096	Education, England	3132	Merchant shipping
3097	Education, England	3133	Proceeds of crime
3098	Education, England	3134	Dentists
3099	Education, England	3135	Health care and associated professions
3100	Education, England	3136	Health care and associated professions
3101	Education, England	3137	Income tax
3102	Education, England	3138	Income tax
3103	Education, England	3139	European Communities
3104	Education, England	3140	Road traffic
3105	Education, England	3141	Road traffic
3106	Education, England	3142	Road traffic
3107	Education, England	3143	Road traffic
3108	Education, England	3144	Road traffic
3109	Education, England	3145 (C.106)	Proceeds of crime
3110	Immigration	3146 (W.292)	Constitutional law
3111 (S.13)	Race relations, Scotland	3147	Merchant shipping
3112	Education, England	3148	Trade marks
3113	Road traffic	3149 (N.I.3)	Northern Ireland
3114 (C.104)	Housing, England	3150 (N.I.4)	Northern Ireland
3115	Proceeds of crime	3151 (N.I.5)	Northern Ireland
3116	Social security	3152 (N.I.6)	Northern Ireland
3117	Environmental protection, England	3153 (N.I.7)	Northern Ireland
3118	Environmental protection	3154 (N.I.8)	Northern Ireland
3119	Tax credits	3155 (N.I.9)	Northern Ireland
3120	Social security	3156	Education, England
3121 (W.291)	Education, Wales	3157 (W.293)	Food, Wales
3122	Registration of births, deaths, marriages, etc	3158	Income tax
		3159 (W.294)	Agriculture, Wales

3160 (W.295)	Clean air, Wales	3194	Road traffic
3161 (W.296)	Social care, Wales	3195	*Cancelled*
	Children and young persons, Wales	3196	Social security
3162	Police, England and Wales		Tax credits
3163	Road traffic	3197	Social security
3164	Road traffic	3198	Seeds, England and Wales
3165	Road traffic	3199	Education, England
3166	Road traffic	3200	Education, England and Wales
3167	Road traffic	3201	Local government, England
3168	Road traffic	3202	Police, England and Wales
3169	Food, England		Pensions, England and Wales
3170	Medicines, England	3203	Regulatory reform
	Medicines, Northern Ireland	3204	Competition
3171	Seeds, England	3205	Regulatory reform, England and Wales
3172	Seeds, England	3206	Agriculture, England
3173	Seeds, England	3207	Terms and conditions of employment
3174	Seeds, England	3208	Landlord and tenant, England
3175	Seeds, England	3209	Landlord and tenant, England
3176	Seeds, England	3210 (C.109)	Social care, England
3177	Education, England	3211	Public health, England
3178	Education, England		Social care, England
3179	Education, England	3212	Nurses, midwives and health visitors, England
3180	Police, England and Wales	3213	Children and young persons, England
3181 (W.297)	Highways, Wales		Social care, England
3182 (W.298)	Environmental protection, Wales	3214	Social care, England
3183 (W.299)	Environmental protection, Wales	3215	Animals, England
3184 (W.300)	Education, Wales	3216	Road traffic
3185 (W.301) (C.107)	Education, Wales	3217	Highways, England and Wales
3186 (W.302)	Rating and valuation, Wales	3218	Local government, England
3187 (W.303)	Landlord and tenant, Wales	3219 (L.18)	Supreme Court of England and Wales
3188 (W.304)	Environmental protection, Wales		County Courts, England and Wales
3189 (W.305)	National Health Service, Wales	3220	Children and young persons, England and Wales
3190 (C.108)	National Health Service, England and Wales	3221	Local government, England
3191	Road traffic	3222	Local government, England
3192	Road traffic	3223	Local government, England
3193	Road traffic	3224	Local government, England

3225	Local government, England
3226 (W.306)	Plant health, Wales
3227	Local government, England
3228	Local government, England
3229	Animals, England
3230 (W.307)	Agriculture, Wales
3231	Food, England
3232	Electricity
3233	Road traffic
3234	Road traffic
3235	Legal services, England and Wales
3236	Terms and conditions of employment
3237	Social security
3238	Highways, England and Wales
3239	Highways, England and Wales
3240	Road traffic
3241	Road traffic
3242	Road traffic
3243	Road traffic
3244	Road traffic
3245	Road traffic
3246	Road traffic
3247	Road traffic
3248	Road traffic
3249	Road traffic
3250	Road traffic
3251	Road traffic
3252	Road traffic
3253	Road traffic
3254	Road traffic
3255	Road traffic
3256	Road traffic
3257	Road traffic
3258	Road traffic
3259	Road traffic
3260	Road traffic
3261	Road traffic
3262	Road traffic
3263	Road traffic
3264	Housing, England
3265	Road traffic, England
3266	Road traffic, England
3267 (C.110)	Highways, England and Wales
3268	Harbours, docks, piers and ferries
3269	Harbours, docks, piers and ferries
3270 (W.308)	Local government, Wales
3271 (W.309)	Local government, Wales
3272 (W.310)	Local government, Wales
3273 (W.311)	Local government, Wales
3274 (W.312)	Local government, Wales
3275 (W.313)	Local government, Wales
3276 (W.314)	Local government, Wales
3277 (W.315)	Local government, Wales
3278 (W.316)	Local government, Wales
3279 (W.317)	Local government, Wales
Draft (N.I.)	Northern Ireland
Unnumbered	Police, England and Wales
Unnumbered	Police, England and Wales

Subsidiary Numbers

Commencement orders (bring an act or part of an act into operation) 2002

74 (W.8) (C.1)

117 (C.2)

153 (C.3)

228 (C.4)

279 (C.5)

312 (C.6)

344 (C.7)

345 (C.8)

381 (C.9)
403 (C.10)
413 (C.11)
437 (C.12)
447 (C.13)
500 (C.14)
533 (C.15)
629 (C.19)
658 (C.16)
673 (C.17)
758 (W.81) (C.18)
809 (C.20)
818 (C.21)
839 (C.22)
846 (C.23)
920 (W.108) (C.24)
1014 (C.25)
1095 (C.26)
1097 (C.27)
1149 (C.28)
1167 (C.29)
1170 (C.30)
1175 (W.123) (C.31)
1222 (C.32)
1245 (C.33)
1252 (C.34)
1279 (C.35)
1312 (C.36)
1359 (C.37)
1400 (C.38)
1436 (C.40)
1475 (W.147) (C.41)
1483 (C.42)
1493 (C.43)
1558 (C.44)
1616 (C.45)
1647 (C.49)

1648 (C.46)
1673 (C.47)
1691 (C.51)
1691 (C.51)
1718 (C.48)
1721 (C.50)
1727 (C.52)
1736 (W.166) (C.53)
1739 (C.54)
1790 (C.55)
1799 (C.56)
1862 (C.57)
1912 (C.58)
1914 (C.59)
1919 (C.60)
1926 (C.61)
1989 (C.62)
2001 (C.67)
2002 (C.63)
2018 (C.64)
2018 (C.64)
2024 (W.208) (C.65)
2050 (C.66)
2200 (C.68)
2202 (C.69)
2215 (C.70)
2217 (C.71)
2248 (C.72)
2256 (C.73)
2266 (C.77)
2294 (C.74)
2306 (C.75)
2324 (C.76)
2363 (C.77)
2377 (C.78)
2439 (C.79)
2478 (C.80)

2532 (W.248) (C.81)

2615 (W.253) (C.82)

2711 (C.83)

2749 (C.84)

2750 (C.85)

2811 (C.87)

2812 (C.86)

2815 (C.88)

2833 (C.89)

2865 (C.90)

2866 (C.91)

2867 (C.92) (W.273)*[Cancelled]*

2952 (C.93)

2955 (C.94)

2957 (C.95)

3012 (W.284) (C.96)

3014 (W.286) (C.97)

3015 (C.98)

3028 (C.99)

3032 (C.100)

3044 (C.101)

3055 (C.102)

3056 (C.103)

3114 (C.104)

3125 (C.105)

3145 (C.106)

3185 (W.301) (C.107)

3190 (C.108)

3210 (C.109)

3267 (C.110)

Instruments relating to fees or procedure in courts in England and Wales 2002

194 (L.1)

222 (L.2)

223 (L.3)

1687 (L.4)

1688 (L.5)

1734 (L.6)

1734 (L.6)

1843 (L.7)

1844 (L.8)

1915 (L.9)

2058 (L.10)

2539 (L.11)

2782 (L.12)

2783 (L.13)

2784 (L.14)

2997 (L.16)

2998 (L.17)

3219 (L.18)

Certain orders in Council relating to Northern Ireland 2002

796 (N.I.1)

2836 (N.I.2)

3149 (N.I.3)

3150 (N.I.4)

3151 (N.I.5)

3152 (N.I.6)

3153 (N.I.7)

3154 (N.I.8)

3155 (N.I.9)

Instruments that extend only to Scotland 2002

261 (S.1)

800 (S.2)

801 (S.3)

1264 (S.4)

1629 (S.5)

1630 (S.6)

1872 (S.7)

2264 (S.8)

2367 (S.9)

2709 (S.10)

2779 (S.11)

2972 (S.12)

3111 (S.13)

Instruments that extend only to Wales 2002

8 (W.1)

43 (W.2)

44 (W.3)

45 (W.4)

46 (W.5)

47 (W.6)

62 (W.7)

74 (W.8) (C.1)

85 (W.9)

104 (W.10)

106 (W.11)

107 (W.12)

113 (W.13)

120 (W.14)

121 (W.15)

122 (W.16)

129 (W.17)

130 (W.18)

136 (W.19)

152 (W.20)

154 (W.21)

156 (W.22)

157 (W.23)

184 (W.24) [*Cancelled*]

186 (W.25)

203 (W.26)

204 (W.27)

239 (W.28)

273 (W.29)

274 (W.30)

278 (W.31)

280 (W.32)

281 (W.33)

283 (W.34)

304 (W.35)

310 (W.36)

324 (W.37)

325 (W.38)

326 (W.39)

327 (W.40)

328 (W.41)

329 (W.42)

330 (W.43)

331 (W.44)

332 (W.45)

354 (W.46)

359 (W.47)

373 (W.48)

374 (W.49)

402 (W.50)

420 (W.51)

430 (W.52)

431 (W.53)

432 (W.55)

433 (W.54)

438 (W.56)

442 (W.57)

469 (W.58)

474 (W.59)

477 (W.60)

478 (W.61)

485 (W.62)

520 (W.63)

540 (W.64)

541 (W.65)

612 (W.66)

613 (W.67)

651 (W.68)	918 (W.106)
652 (W.69)	919 (W.107)
654 (W.70)	920 (W.108) (C.24)
669 (W.71)	921 (W.109)
675 (W.72)	1038 (W.110)
676 (W.73)	1039 (W.111)
677 (W.74)	1041 (W.112)
678 (W.75)	1042 (W.113)
679 (W.76)	1087 (W.114)
698 (W.77)	1090 (W.115)
747 (W.78)	1128 (W.116)
748 (W.79)	1129 (W.117)
757 (W.80)	1131 (W.118)
758 (W.81) (C.18)	1145 (W.119)
763 (W.82)	1146 (W.120)
783 (W.84)	1148 (W.121)
784 (W.85)	1174 (W.122)
785 (W.86)	1175 (W.123) (C.31)
802 (W.87)	1176 (W.124)
803 (W.88)	1187 (W.125)
808 (W.89)	1283 (W.126)
810 (W.90)	1284 (W.127)
811 (W.91)	1291 (W.128)
812 (W.92)	1346 (W.129)
813 (W.93)	1350 (W.130)
814 (W.94)	1354 (W.131)
815 (W.95)	1356 (W.132)
820 (W.96)	1357 (W.133)
821 (W.97)	1358 (W.134)
835 (W.98)	1385 (W.135)
837 (W.99)	1387 (W.136)
885 (W.100)	1394 (W.137)
886 (W.101)	1396 (W.138)
896 (W.102)	1400 (W.139)
897 (W.103)	1401 (W.140)
916 (W.104)	1404 (W.141)
917 (W.105)	1416 (W.142)

1432 (W.143)	1856 (W.180)
1439 (W.144)	1857 (W.181)
1441 (W.145)	1869 (W.182)
1472 (W.146)	1870 (W.183)
1475 (W.147) (C.41)	1875 (W.184)
1476 (W.148)	1876 (W.185)
1481 (W.149)	1877 (W.186)
1482 (W.150)	1878 (W.187)
1506 (W.151)	1879 (W.188)
1554 (W.152)	1880 (W.189)
1556 (W.153)	1881 (W.190)
1557 (W.154)	1882 (W.191)
1586 (W.155)	1883 (W.192)
1591 (W.156)	1884 (W.193)
1661 (W.157)	1885 (W.194)
1663 (W.158)	1886 (W.195)
1667 (W.159)	1895 (W.196)
1669 (W.160)	1896 (W.197)
1726 (W.161)	1897 (W.198)
1728 (W.162)	1898 (W.199)
1729 (W.163)	1918 (W.200)
1730 (W.164)	1972 (W.201)
1735 (W.165)	1976 (W.202)
1736 (W.166) (C.53)	1977 (W.203)
1737 (W.167)	1978 (W.204)
1772 (W.168)	1987 (W.205)
1794 (W.169)	2022 (W.206)
1795 (W.170)	2023 (W.207)
1796 (W.171)	2024 (W.208) (C.65)
1797 (W.172)	2060 (W.209)
1798 (W.173)	2061 (W.210)
1804 (W.174)	2101 (W.211)
1805 (W.175)	2115 (W.212)
1806 (W.176)	2118 (W.213)
1842 (W.177)	2127 (W.214)
1853 (W.178)	2128 (W.215)
1855 (W.179)	2142 (W.216)

2156 (W.217)

2171 (W.218)

2199 (W.219)

2203 (W.220)

2226 (W.221)

2258 (W.222)

2259 (W.223)

2295 (W.224)

2296 (W.225)

2297 (W.226)

2302 (W.227)

2303 (W.228)

2304 (W.229)

2305 (W.230)

2317 (W.231)

2325 (W.232)

2328 (W.233)

2329 (W.234)

2356 (W.235)

2365 (W.236)

2378 (W.237)

2399 (W.238)

2400 (W.239)

2444 (W.240)

2465 (W.241)

2477 (W.242)

2480 (W.243)

2512 (W.244)

2517 (W.245)

2518 (W.246)

2519 (W.247)

2532 (W.248) (C.81)

2549 (W.249)

2571 (W.250)

2585 (W.251)

2588 (W.252)

2615 (W.253) (C.82)

2622 (W.254)

2663 (W.255)

2664 (W.256)

2719 (W.257)

2720 (W.258)

2721 (W.259)

2744 (W.260)

2745 (W.261)

2751 (W.262)

2762 (W.263)

2780 (W.264)

2781 (W.265)

2798 (W.266)

2799 (W.267)

2800 (W.268)

2801 (W.269)

2802 (W.270)

2814 (W.271)

2834 (W.272)

2867 (W.273) [Cancelled]

2869 (W.274)

2879 (W.275)

2880 (W.276)

2935 (W.277)

2937 (W.278)

2938 (W.279)

2939 (W.280)

2940 (W.281)

2941 (W.282)

3011 (W.283)

3012 (W.284) (C.96)

3013 (W.285)

3014 (W.286) (C.97)

3017 (W.287)

3053 (W.288)

3054 (W.289)

3079 (W.290)

3121 (W.291)

3146 (W.292)

3157 (W.293)

3159 (W.294)

3160 (W.295)

3161 (W.296)

3181 (W.297)

3182 (W.298)

3183 (W.299)

3184 (W.300)

3185 (W.301) (C.107)

3186 (W.302)

3187 (W.303)

3188 (W.304)

3189 (W.305)

3226 (W.306)

3230 (W.307)

3270 (W.308)

3271 (W.309)

3272 (W.310)

3273 (W.311)

3274 (W.312)

3275 (W.313)

3276 (W.314)

3277 (W.315)

3278 (W.316)

3279 (W.317)

Scottish Legislation

Acts of the Scottish Parliament

Acts of the Scottish Parliament 2002

Budget (Scotland) Act 2002: Elizabeth II. 2002 asp 7. – ii, 21p.: 30 cm. – Royal assent, 15th March 2002. – 0 10 590031 1 £5.00

Community Care and Health (Scotland) Act 2002: Elizabeth II 2002 asp 5. – ii, 24 [1]p.: 30 cm. – Royal assent, 12th March 2002. – Explanatory notes have been produced to assist in the understanding of this Act and are available separately (ISBN 0105910252). – 0 10 590030 3 £5.65

Criminal Procedure (Amendment) (Scotland) Act 2002: Elizabeth II. 2002 asp 4. – [8]p.: 30 cm. – Royal assent, 8th March 2002. – Explanatory notes have been produced to assist in the understanding of this Act and are available separately (ISBN 0105910236). – 0 10 590029 X £1.55

Debt Arrangement and Attachment (Scotland) Act 2002: Elizabeth II. 2002 asp 17. – iii, 46p.: 30 cm. – Royal assent, 17th December 2002. - An Act .. to provide a scheme under which individuals may arrange for their debts to be paid under payment programmes; to create a new diligence in relation to corporeal moveable property owned by a debtor; to make special provision for the use of that diligence in relation to property kept in dwellinghouses; to abolish poindings and warrant sales. – Explanatory notes to assist in the understanding of this Act are available separately (ASP 17 EN) (ISBN 0105910376). – With correction slips dated March 2003 and June 2003. – 0 10 590042 7 £7.65

Education (Disability Strategies and Pupils' Educational Records) (Scotland) Act 2002: Elizabeth II. 2002 asp 12. – [1], i, [4]p.: 30 cm. – Royal assent, 30th April 2002. – Explanatory notes have been produced to assist in the understanding of this Act and are available separately (ISBN 0105910287). – 0 10 590037 0 £2.50

Freedom of Information (Scotland) Act 2002: Elizabeth II. 2002 asp 13. – iii, 48p.: 30 cm. – Royal assent, 28th May 2002. - An Act of the Scottish Parliament to make provision for the disclosure of information held by Scottish public authorities or by persons providing services for them. – Explanatory notes to assist in the understanding of this Act are available separately (ISBN 0105910368). – 0 10 590038 9 £7.65

Fur Farming (Prohibition) (Scotland) Act 2002: Elizabeth II. 2002 asp 10. – [8]p.: 30 cm. – Royal assent, 11th April 2002. – Explanatory notes have been produced to assist in the understanding of this Act and are available separately (ISBN 0105910309). – 0 10 590034 6 £2.00

Marriage (Scotland) Act 2002: Elizabeth II. 2002 asp 8. – [8]p.: 30 cm. – Royal assent, 4th April 2002. – Explanatory notes have been produced to assist in the understanding of this Act and are available separately (ISBN 0105910260). – 0 10 590033 8 £1.55

Protection of Wild Mammals (Scotland) Act 2002: Elizabeth II. 2002 asp 6. – [2], 7p.: 30 cm. – Royal assent, 15th March 2002. – 0 10 590032 X £3.00

School Education (Amendment) (Scotland) Act 2002: Elizabeth II. 2002 asp 2. – [8]p.: 30 cm. – Royal assent, 22nd January 2002. – Explanatory notes have been produced to assist in the understanding of this Act and are available separately (ISBN 0105910228). – 0 10 590027 3 £1.55

Scottish Local Government (Elections) Act 2002: Elizabeth II. 2002 asp 1. – [12]p.: 30 cm. – Royal assent, 22nd January 2002. – Explanatory notes have been produced to assist in the understanding of this Act and are available separately (ISBN 0105910201). – 0 10 590026 5 £3.00

Scottish Parliamentary Standards Commissioner Act 2002: Elizabeth II. 2002 asp 16. – ii, 14p.: 30 cm. – Royal assent, 30th July 2002. - An Act .. to establish a Scottish Parliamentary Standards Commissioner to investigate complaints about the conduct of members of the Parliament and to report upon the outcome of such investigations to the Parliament. – Explanatory notes to assist in the understanding of this Act are available separately (ISBN 0105910333). – 0 10 590041 9 £4.00

Scottish Public Services Ombudsman Act 2002: Elizabeth II. 2002 asp 11. – ii, 38p.: 30 cm. – Royal assent, 23rd April 2002. – Explanatory notes have been produced to assist in the understanding of this Act and are available separately (ISBN 0105910279). – 0 10 590036 2   £6.95

Scottish Qualifications Authority Act 2002: Elizabeth II. 2002 asp 14. – [2], 4. [1]p.: 30 cm. – Royal assent, 6th June 2002. - An Act ... to make provision in relation to the members of the Scottish Qualifications Authority; to confer power on the Scottish Ministers to regulate the procedure of that Authority; to provide for the establishment of a committee to consider and advise on matters relating to qualifications awarded by, and the functions and procedures of that Authority. – Explanatory notes to assist in the understanding of this Act are available separately (ISBN 0105910317). – 0 10 590039 7   £2.00

Sexual Offences (Procedure and Evidence) (Scotland) Act 2002: Elizabeth II. 2002 asp 9. – 18p.: 30 cm. – Royal assent, 11th April 2002. – Explanatory notes have been produced to assist in the understanding of this Act and are available separately (ISBN 0105910295). – 0 10 590035 4   £4.45

University of St. Andrews (Postgraduate Medical Degrees) Act 2002: Elizabeth II. 2002 asp 15. – [4]p.: 30 cm. – Royal assent, 30th July 2002. - An Act ... to permit the University of St. Andrews to grant postgraduate research degrees in medicine to qualified medical practitioners. – Explanatory notes to assist in the understanding of this Act are available separately (ISBN 0105910325). – 0 10 590040 0   £1.15

Water Industry (Scotland) Act 2002: Elizabeth II. 2002 asp 3. – iii, 82p.: 30 cm. – Royal assent, 1st March 2002. – Explanatory notes have been produced to assist in the understanding of this Act and are available separately (ISBN 0105910244). – 0 10 590028 1   £10.00

Acts of the Scottish Parliament - Explanatory notes 2002

Community Care and Health (Scotland) Act 2002 (asp 5): explanatory notes. – 24p.: 30 cm. – These notes refer to the Community Care and Health (Scotland) Act 2002 (asp 5) (ISBN 0105900303) which received Royal Assent on 12 March 2002. – 0 10 591025 2   £5.00

Criminal Procedure (Amendment) (Scotland) Act 2002 (asp 4): explanatory notes. – [8]p.: 30 cm. – These notes refer to the Criminal Procedure (Amendment) (Scotland) Act 2002 (asp 4) (ISBN 010590029X) which received Royal Assent on 8th March 2002. – 0 10 591023 6   £1.55

Debt Arrangement and Attachment (Scotland) Act 2002 (asp 17): explanatory notes. – [1], 18p.: 30 cm. – These notes refer to the Debt Arrangement and Attachment (Scotland) Act 2002 (asp 17) (ISBN 0105900427) which received Royal Assent on 17 December 2002. – 0 10 591037 6   £4.45

Education (Disability Strategies and Pupils' Educational Records) (Scotland) Act 2002 (asp 12): explanatory notes. – [8]p.: 30 cm. – These notes refer to the Education (Disability Strategies and Pupils' Educational Records) (Scotland) Act 2002 (asp 12) (ISBN 0105900370) which received Royal Assent on 30 April 2002. – 0 10 591028 7   £2.00

Freedom of Information (Scotland) Act 2002 (asp 13): explanatory notes. – 27, [2]p.: 30 cm. – These notes refer to the Freedom of Information (Scotland) Act 2002 (asp 13) (ISBN 0105900389) which received Royal Assent on 28 May 2002. – 0 10 591036 8   £5.65

Fur Farming (Prohibition) (Scotland) Act 2002 (asp 10): explanatory notes. – 7, [1]p.: 30 cm. – These notes refer to the Fur Farming (Prohibition) (Scotland) Act 2002 (asp 10) (ISBN 0105900346) which received Royal Assent on 11 April 2002. – 0 10 591030 9   £2.00

Marriage (Scotland) Act 2002 (asp 8): explanatory notes. – [8]p.: 30 cm. – These notes refer to the Marriage (Scotland) Act 2002 (asp 8) (ISBN 0105900338) which received Royal Assent on 4 April 2002. – 0 10 591026 0   £2.00

School Education (Amendment) (Scotland) Act 2002 (asp 2): explanatory notes. – [8]p.: 30 cm. – These notes refer to the School Education (Amendment) (Scotland) Act 2002 (asp 2) (ISBN 0105900273) which received Royal Assent on 22nd January 2002. – 0 10 591022 8   £1.55

Scottish Local Government (Elections) Act 2002 (asp 1): explanatory notes. – [8]p.: 30 cm. – These notes refer to the Scottish Local Government (Elections) Act 2002 (asp 1) (ISBN 0105900265) which received Royal assent on 22 January 2002. – 0 10 591020 1   £2.00

Scottish Parliamentary Standards Commissioner Act 2002 (asp 16): explanatory notes. – [1], 20p.: 30 cm. – These notes refer to the Scottish Parliamentary Standards Commissioner Act 2002 (asp 16) (ISBN 0105900419) which received Royal Assent on 30 July 2002. – 0 10 591033 3   £4.45

Scottish Public Services Ombudsman Act 2002 (asp 11): explanatory notes. – 14p.: 30 cm. – These notes refer to the Scottish Public Services Ombudsman Act 2002 (asp 11) (ISBN 0105900362) which received Royal Assent on 23 April 2002. – 0 10 591027 9   £4.00

Scottish Qualifications Authority Act 2002 (asp 14): explanatory notes. – [8]p.: 30 cm. – These notes refer to the Scottish Qualifications Authority Act 2002 (asp 14) (ISBN 0105900397) which received Royal Assent on 6 June 2002. – 0 10 591031 7 £2.00

Sexual Offences (Procedure and Evidence) (Scotland) Act 2002 (asp 9): explanatory notes. – 12p.: 30 cm. – These notes refer to the Sexual Offences (Procedure and Evidence) (Scotland) Act 2002 (asp 9) (ISBN 0105900354) which received Royal Assent on 11 April 2002. – 0 10 591029 5 £3.40

University of St. Andrews (Postgraduate Medical Degrees) Act 2002 (asp 15): explanatory notes. – [8]p.: 30 cm. – These notes refer to the University of St. Andrews (Postgraduate Medical Degrees) Act 2002 (asp 15) (ISBN 0105900400) which received Royal Assent on 30 July 2002. – 0 10 591032 5 £2.00

Water Industry (Scotland) Act 2002 (asp 3): explanatory notes. – 28p.: 30 cm. – These notes relate to the Water Industry (Scotland) Act 2002 (asp 3) (ISBN 010590281) which received Royal Assent on 1 March 2002. – 0 10 591024 4 £5.65

Scottish Statutory Instruments

By Subject Heading

Adults with incapacity

The Adults with Incapacity (Ethics Committee) (Scotland) Regulations 2002 No. 2002/190. – Enabling power: Adults with Incapacity (Scotland) Act 2000, ss. 51 (6) (7), 86 (2). – Issued: 02.05.2002. Made: 15.04.2002. Laid before the Scottish Parliament: 17.04.2002. Coming into force: 01.07.2002. Effect: None. Territorial extent & classification: S. General. – 4p.: 30 cm. – 0 11 061395 3 £1.75

The Adults with Incapacity (Medical Treatment Certificates) (Scotland) Regulations 2002 No. 2002/208. – Enabling power: Adults with Incapacity (Scotland) Act 2000, s. 47 (5). – Issued: 15.05.2002. Made: 30.04.2002. Laid before the Scottish Parliament: 03.05.2002. Coming into force: 01.07.2002. Effect: None. Territorial extent & classification: S. General. – 4p.: 30 cm. – 0 11 061411 9 £1.75

The Adults with Incapacity (Non-compliance with Decisions of Welfare Guardians) (Scotland) Regulations 2002 No. 2002/98. – Enabling power: Adults with Incapacity (Scotland) Act 2000, s. 70 (3). – Issued: 22.04.2002. Made: 05.03.2002. Laid before the Scottish Parliament: 07.03.2002. Coming into force: 01.04.2002. Effect: None. Territorial extent & classification: S. General. – 4p.: 30 cm. – 0 11 061357 0 £1.75

The Adults with Incapacity (Public Guardian's Fees) (Scotland) Amendment Regulations 2002 No. 2002/131. – Enabling power: Adults with Incapacity (Scotland) Act 2000, ss. 7 (2), 86 (2). – Issued: 28.03.2002. Made: 14.03.2002. Laid before the Scottish Parliament: 14.03.2002. Coming into force: 22.04.2002. Effect: S.S.I. 2001/75 amended. Territorial extent & classification: S. General. – 4p.: 30 cm. – 0 11 061241 8 £1.75

The Adults with Incapacity (Recall of Guardians' Powers) (Scotland) Regulations 2002 No. 2002/97. – Enabling power: Adults with Incapacity (Scotland) Act 2000, ss. 73 (5) (7) (10), 86 (2). – Issued: 15.04.2002. Made: 05.03.2002. Laid before the Scottish Parliament: 07.03.2002. Coming into force: 01.04.2002. Effect: None. Territorial extent & classification: S. General. – 38p.: 30 cm. – 0 11 061302 3 £6.50

The Adults with Incapacity (Reports in Relation to Guardianship and Intervention Orders) (Scotland) Regulations 2002 No. 2002/96. – Enabling power: Adults with Incapacity (Scotland) Act 2000, ss. 57 (3), 86 (2). – Issued: 15.04.2002. Made: 05.03.2002. Laid before the Scottish Parliament: 07.03.2002. Coming into force: 01.04.2002. Effect: None. Territorial extent & classification: S. General. – 107p.: 30 cm. – With correction slip. – 0 11 061305 8 £10.50

The Adults with Incapacity (Scotland) Act 2000 (Commencement No. 1) (Amendment) Order 2002 No. 2002/172 (C.11). – Enabling power: Adults with Incapacity (Scotland) Act 2000, s. 89 (2). Bringing into operation various provisions of the 2000 Act on 02.04.2001 & 01.04.2002. – Issued: 16.04.2002. Made: 28.03.2002. Effect: S.S.I 2001/8 amended. Territorial extent & classification: S. General. – 2p.: 30 cm. – 0 11 061337 6 £1.00

The Adults with Incapacity (Scotland) Act 2000 (Commencement No. 2) Order 2002 No. 2002/189 (C.14). – Enabling power: Adults with Incapacity (Scotland) Act 2000, s. 89 (2). Bringing into operation various provisions of the 2000 Act on 01.07.2002. – Issued: 02.05.2002. Made: 15.04.2002. Effect: None. Territorial extent & classification: S. General. – 2p.: 30 cm. – 0 11 061391 0 £1.50

The Adults with Incapacity (Specified Medical Treatments) (Scotland) Amendment Regulations 2002 No. 2002/302. – Enabling power: Adults with Incapacity (Scotland) Act 2000, s. 48 (2) (3). – Issued: 11.07.2002. Made: 21.06.2002. Laid before the Scottish Parliament: 24.06.2002. Coming into force: 01.07.2002. Effect: S.S.I. 2002/275 amended. Territorial extent & classification: S. General. – 2p.: 30 cm. – 0 11 061513 1 £1.50

The Adults with Incapacity (Specified Medical Treatments) (Scotland) Regulations 2002 No. 2002/275. – Enabling power: Adults with Incapacity (Scotland) Act 2000, s. 48 (2) (3). – Issued: 21.06.2002. Made: 06.06.2002. Laid before the Scottish Parliament: 07.06.2002. Coming into force: 01.07.2002. Effect: None. Territorial extent & classification: S. General. – 8p.: 30 cm. – 0 11 061478 X *£2.00*

The Adults with Incapacity (Supervision of Welfare Guardians etc. by Local Authorities) (Scotland) Regulations 2002 No. 2002/95. – Enabling power: Adults with Incapacity (Scotland) Act 2000, ss. 10 (3) (a) (b) (i), 86 (2). – Issued: 28.03.2002. Made: 05.03.2002. Laid before the Scottish Parliament: 07.03.2002. Coming into force: 01.04.2002. Effect: S.I. 1984/1494 amended. Territorial extent & classification: S. General. – 4p.: 30 cm. – 0 11 061228 0 *£1.75*

Agriculture

The Bovines and Bovine Products (Trade) Amendment (Scotland) Regulations 2002 No. 2002/449. – Enabling power: European Communities Act 1972, s. 2 (2). – Issued: 18.10.2002. Made: 03.10.2002. Laid before the Scottish Parliament: 04.10.2002. Coming into force: 07.10.2002. Effect: S.I. 1999/1103 amended in relation to Scotland & S.S.I. 2000/184 amended. – EC note: Gives effect to DEC 2002/670/EC which amends 98/256/EC to enable the despatch from Scotland of bovine embryos and bone in veal carcases from calves between 6 and 9 months exported from the Date Based Export Scheme (DBES). – 12p.: 30 cm. – 0 11 061666 9 *£2.50*

The Common Agricultural Policy (Wine) (Scotland) Regulations 2002 No. 2002/325. – Enabling power: European Communities Act 1972, s. 2 (2). – Issued: 17.07.2002. Made: 27.06.2002. Laid before the Scottish Parliament: 28.06.2002. Coming into force: 23.09.2002. Effect: S.I. 1996/696; 1997/542; 1998/453; 1999/482 revoked in relation to Scotland. Territorial extent & classification: S. General. – 26p.: 30 cm. – 0 11 061560 3 *£4.50*

The Environmental Impact Assessment (Uncultivated Land and Semi-natural Areas) (Scotland) Regulations 2002 No. 2002/6. – Enabling power: European Communities Act 1972, s. 2 (2). – Issued: 22.02.2002. Made: 14.01.2002. Laid before the Scottish Parliament: 14.01.2002. Coming into force: 04.02.2002. Effect: None. Territorial extent & classification: S. General. – EC note: Implement DIR 85/337/EEC (as amended by 97/11/EEC). – 24p.: 30 cm. – 0 11 059998 5 *£4.00*

The Extensification Payment (Scotland) Regulations 2002 No. 2002/278. – Enabling power: European Communities Act 1972, s. 2 (2). – Issued: 20.06.2002. Made: 07.06.2002. Laid before the Scottish Parliament: 07.06.2002. Coming into force: 28.06.2002. Effect: None. Territorial extent & classification: S. General. – EC note: Implements art. 13 of REG (EC) 1254/1999 on the common organisation of the market in beef and veal, for beef producers who comply with certain stocking density requirements, and also confers powers of entry and inspection on and permits collection of evidence by authorised persons as required by REG (EC) 2419/2001. – 8p.: 30 cm. – 0 11 061452 6 *£2.00*

The Feeding Stuffs Amendment (Scotland) Regulations 2002 No. 2002/285. – Enabling power: Agriculture Act 1970, ss. 66 (1), 68 (1) (1A), 69 (1) 74A, 75 (1), 76 (1), 77 (4), 78 (6), 79 (1), 84 & European Communities Act 1972, s. 2 (2). – Issued: 21.06.2002. Made: 07.06.2002. Laid before the Scottish Parliament: 10.06.2002. Coming into force: 01.07.2002. Effect: S.I. 1999/1663, 2325 & S.S.I. 2000/453 amended. Territorial extent & classification: S. General. – 12p.: 30 cm. – 0 11 061475 5 *£2.50*

The Food and Animal Feedingstuffs (Products of Animal Origin from China) (Control) (Scotland) Regulations 2002 No. 2002/36. – Enabling power: European Communities Act 1972, s. 2 (2). – Issued: 20.02.2002. Made: 01.02.2002. Laid before the Scottish Parliament: 05.02.2002. Coming into force: 02.02.2002. Effect: None. Territorial extent & classification: S. General. – 8p.: 30 cm. – 0 11 059986 1 *£2.00*

The Food and Animal Feedingstuffs (Products of Animal Origin from China) (Emergency Control) (Scotland) Amendment Regulations 2002 No. 2002/356. – Enabling power: European Communities Act 1972, s. 2 (2). – Issued: 06.08.2002. Made: 29.07.2002. Laid before the Scottish Parliament: 30.07.2002. Coming into force: 31.07.2002. Effect: S.S.I. 2002/300 amended. Territorial extent & classification: S. General. – 2p.: 30 cm. – 0 11 061578 6 *£1.50*

The Food and Animal Feedingstuffs (Products of Animal Origin from China) (Emergency Control) (Scotland) Regulations 2002 No. 2002/300. – Enabling power: European Communities Act 1972, s. 2 (2). – Issued: 11.07.2002. Made: 19.06.2002. Laid before the Scottish Parliament: 24.06.2002. Coming into force: 20.06.2002. Effect: S.S.I. 2002/36 revoked. Territorial extent & classification: S. General. – [8]p.: 30 cm. – 0 11 061514 X *£2.00*

The Less Favoured Area Support Scheme (Scotland) Regulations 2002 No. 2002/139. – Enabling power: European Communities Act 1972, s. 2 (2). – Issued: 12.04.2002. Made: 21.03.2002. Laid before the Scottish Parliament: 21.03.2002. Coming into force: 22.03.2002. Effect: S.S.I. 2000/347 amended & S.S.I. 2001/50 revoked with saving. Territorial extent & classification: S. General. – 20p.: 30 cm. – 0 11 061318 X *£3.50*

The Pesticides (Maximum Residue Levels in Crops, Food and Feeding Stuffs) (Scotland) Amendment (No. 2) Regulations 2002 No. 2002/489. – Enabling power: European Communities Act 1972, s. 2 (2). – Issued: 28.11.2002. Made: 04.11.2002. Laid before the Scottish Parliament: 06.11.2002. Coming into force: 30.11.2002. Effect: S.S.I. 2000/22; 2001/84, 221, 271, 435; 2002/271 amended. Territorial extent & classification: S. General. – 118, [1]p.: 30 cm. – 0 11 061698 7 *£10.50*

The Pig Industry Restructuring (Capital Grant) (Scotland) Scheme 2002 No. 2002/43. – Enabling power: Agriculture Act 1970, s. 29. – Issued: 12.04.2002. Made: 06.02.2002. Laid before the Scottish Parliament: 07.02.2002. Coming into force: 29.03.2002. Effect: None. Territorial extent and classification: S. General. – 4p.: 30 cm. – 0 11 061316 3 *£1.75*

The Pig Industry Restructuring (Non-capital Grant) (Scotland) Scheme 2002 No. 2002/44. – Enabling power: Farm Land and Rural Development Act 1988, s. 1. – Issued: 28.02.2002. Made: 06.02.2002. Laid before the Scottish Parliament: 07.02.2002. Coming into force: 29.03.2002. Effect: None. Territorial extent and classification: S. General. – 4p.: 30 cm. – 0 11 061022 9 *£1.75*

The Products of Animal Origin (Third Country Imports) (Scotland) Amendment Regulations 2002 No. 2002/565. – Enabling power: European Communities Act 1972, s. 2 (2). – Issued: 10.01.2003. Made: 19.12.2002. Laid before the Scottish Parliament: 23.12.2002. Coming into force: 01.01.2003. Effect: S.S.I. 2002/445 amended. Territorial extent & classification: S. General. – 4p.: 30 cm. – 0 11 061841 6 *£1.75*

The Products of Animal Origin (Third Country Imports) (Scotland) Regulations 2002 No. 2002/445. – Enabling power: European Communities Act 1972, s. 2 (2). – Issued: 17.10.2002. Made: 29.09.2002. Laid before the Scottish Parliament: 30.09.2002. Coming into force: 01.10.2002. Effect: S.I. 1980/14; 1995/1372; 1996/3124, 3125; 1997/2537; 1999/157 amended in relation to Scotland & S.I. 1985/913 revoked & S.S.I. 2000/62; 2001/257 amended. – 60p.: 30 cm. – 0 11 061656 1 *£7.50*

Agriculture: Livestock industries

The Artificial Insemination of Cattle (Animal Health) (Scotland) Amendment Regulations 2002 No. 2002/191. – Enabling power: Animal Health and Welfare Act 1984, s. 10 (1) (2) (a). – Issued: 26.04.2002. Made: 17.04.2002. Laid before the Scottish Parliament: 17.04.2002. Coming into force: 18.04.2002. Effect: S.I. 1985/1857 amended. Territorial extent & classification: S. General. – 4p.: 30 cm. – 0 11 061381 3 *£1.75*

Agriculture: Pesticides

The Pesticides (Maximum Residue Levels in Crops, Food and Feeding Stuffs) (Scotland) Amendment Regulations 2002 No. 2002/271. – Enabling power: European Communities Act 1972, s. 2 (2). – Issued: 20.06.2002. Made: 05.06.2002. Laid before the Scottish Parliament: 07.06.2002. Coming into force: 01.09.2002. Effect: S.S.I. 2000/22; 2001/221, 435 amended. Territorial extent & classification: S. General. – 16p.: 30 cm. – 0 11 061448 8 *£3.00*

Animals

The Animals and Animal Products (Import and Export) (Scotland) Amendment (No. 2) Regulations 2002 No. 2002/196. – Enabling power: European Communities Act 1972, s. 2 (2). – Issued: 30.04.2002. Made: 17.04.2002. Laid before the Scottish Parliament: 19.04.2002. Coming into force: 20.04.2002. Effect: S.S.I. 2000/216 amended. – 4p.: 30 cm. – 0 11 061387 2 *£1.75*

The Animals and Animal Products (Import and Export) (Scotland) Amendment Regulations 2002 No. 2002/125. – Enabling power: European Communities Act 1972, s. 2 (2). – Issued: 11.04.2002. Made: 07.03.2002. Laid before the Scottish Parliament: 13.03.2002. Coming into force: 07.03.2002 at 5.00 pm. Effect: S.S.I. 2000/216 amended. – 4p.: 30 cm. – 0 11 061301 5 *£1.75*

The Fur Farming (Prohibition) (Scotland) Act 2002 (Commencement) Order 2002 No. 2002/519 (C.27). – Enabling power: Fur Farming (Prohibition) (Scotland) Act 2002, s. 6 (1). Bringing into force various provisions of the 2002 Act on 01.01.2003. – Issued: 06.12.2002. Made: 25.11.2002. Effect: None. Territorial extent & classification: S. General. – 2p.: 30 cm. – 0 11 061729 0 *£1.50*

The Protection of Wild Mammals (Scotland) Act 2002 (Commencement) Order 2002 No. 2002/181 (C.12). – Enabling power: Protection of Wild Mammals (Scotland) Act 2002, s. 12 (2). Bringing into force the 2002 Act on 01.08.2002 in accord. with art. 2. – Issued: 24.04.2002. Made: 09.04.2002. Effect: None. Territorial extent & classification: S. General. – 2p.: 30 cm. – 0 11 061369 4 *£1.50*

Animals: Animal health

The BSE Monitoring (Scotland) Amendment Regulations 2002 No. 2002/1. – Enabling power: European Communities Act 1972, s. 2 (2). – Issued: 23.01.2002. Made: 08.01.2002. Laid before the Scottish Parliament: 09.01.2002. Coming into force: 30.01.2002. Effect: S.I. 1998/871 amended in relation to Scotland & S.S.I. 2001/1, 231 amended. Territorial extent & classification: S. General. – 4p.: 30 cm. – 0 11 059969 1 *£1.75*

The Cattle Identification (Notification of Movement) (Scotland) Amendment Regulations 2002 No. 2002/22. – Enabling power: European Communities Act 1972, s. 2 (2). – Issued: 06.02.2002. Made: 24.01.2002. Laid before the Scottish Parliament: 25.01.2002. Coming into force: 18.02.2002. Effect: S.I. 1998/1796 (in relation to Scotland); S.S.I. 2001/1 amended. Territorial extent & classification: S. General. – 2p.: 30 cm. – 0 11 059981 0 *£1.50*

The Disease Control and Animal Movements (Interim Measures) (Scotland) Amendment Order 2002 No. 2002/221. – Enabling power: Animal Health Act 1981, ss. 1, 7, 8 (1). – Issued: 21.05.2002. Made: 08.05.2002. Coming into force: 09.05.2002. Effect: S.I. 1995/11 amended (in relation to Scotland); S.S.I 2002/34, 38 amended. Territorial extent & classification: S. General. – 12p.: 30 cm. – 0 11 061418 6 *£2.50*

The Disease Control (Interim Measures) (Scotland) Amendment (No. 2) Order 2002 No. 2002/530. – Enabling power: Animal Health Act 1981, ss. 1, 7, 8 (1). – Issued: 12.12.2002. Made: 28.11.2002. Coming into force: 01.01.2003. Effect: S.S.I. 2002/34 amended. Territorial extent & classification: S. General. – 2p.: 30 cm. – 0 11 061740 1 *£1.50*

The Disease Control (Interim Measures) (Scotland) Amendment Order 2002 No. 2002/369. – Enabling power: Animal Health Act 1981, ss. 1, 7, 8 (1). – Issued: 20.08.2002. Made: 12.08.2002. Coming into force: 13.08.2002. Effect: S.S.I. 2002/34 amended. Territorial extent & classification: S. General. – 4p.: 30 cm. – 0 11 061582 4 *£1.75*

The Disease Control (Interim Measures) (Scotland) Order 2002 No. 2002/34. – Enabling power: Animal Health Act 1981, ss. 1, 7, 8 (1), 83 (2). – Issued: 21.02.2002. Made: 01.02.2002. Coming into force: 18.02.2002. Effect: S.I. 1995/11 amended. Territorial extent & classification: S. General. – 16p.: 30 cm. – 0 11 059994 2 *£3.00*

The Foot-and-Mouth Disease Declaratory (Controlled Area) (Scotland) Amendment and Revocation Order 2002 No. 2002/54. – Enabling power: S.I. 1983/1950, art. 30 (1). – Issued: 06.03.2002. Made: 11.02.2002. Coming into force: 11.02.2002, 18.02.2002, in accord. with art. 1 (2). Effect: S.S.I. 2001/66, 90, 111, 146, 150, 159, 170, 187, 204, 246, 290, 481 revoked with savings (18.02.2002). Territorial extent & classification: S. General. – 8p.: 30 cm. – 0 11 061091 1 *£2.00*

The Import and Export Restrictions (Foot-and-Mouth Disease) (Scotland) (No. 3) Amendment (No. 2) Amendment Regulations 2002 No. 2002/169. – Enabling power: European Communities Act 1972, s. 2 (2). – Issued: 24.04.2002. Made: 28.03.2002. Laid before the Scottish Parliament: 04.04.2002. Coming into force: 29.03.2002. Effect: S.S.I. 2002/35 amended. Territorial extent & classification: S. General. – 2p.: 30 cm. – 0 11 061368 6 *£1.50*

The Import and Export Restrictions (Foot-and-Mouth Disease) (Scotland) (No. 3) Amendment (No. 2) Regulations 2002 No. 2002/35. – Enabling power: European Communities Act 1972, s. 2 (2). – Issued: 21.02.2002. Made: 01.02.2002. Laid before the Scottish Parliament: 01.02.2002. Coming into force: 01.02.2002 at 12.00 noon. Effect: S.I. 1994/3082; 1995/539, 3205 & S.S.I. 2001/160, 394, 429, 455, 483 amended & S.S.I. 2001/358; 2002/21 revoked. Territorial extent & classification: S. General. – EC note: These Regs. implement in Scotland DEC 2001/911/EC amending for the 4th time DEC 2001/740/EC – 8p.: 30 cm. – 0 11 059995 0 *£2.00*

The Import and Export Restrictions (Foot-and-Mouth Disease) (Scotland) (No. 3) Amendment Regulations 2002 No. 2002/21. – Enabling power: European Communities Act 1972, s. 2 (2). – Issued: 21.02.2002. Made: 18.01.2002. Laid before the Scottish Parliament: 25.01.2002. Coming into force: 18.01.2002 at 5.00 p.m. Effect: S.S.I. 2001/429 amended. Territorial extent & classification: S. General. – 2p.: 30 cm. – 0 11 059992 6 *£1.50*

The Import and Export Restrictions (Foot-and-Mouth Disease) (Scotland) (No. 3) Revocation Regulations 2002 No. 2002/109. – Enabling power: European Communities Act 1972, s. 2 (2). – Issued: 11.04.2002. Made: 06.03.2002. Laid before the Scottish Parliament: 13.03.2002. Coming into force: 07.03.2002. Effect: S.S.I 2002/35 amended & S.S.I 2001/429, 455, 483 revoked. Territorial extent & classification: S. General. – EC note: These Regs. implement in Scotland art. 3 of DEC 2002/153/EC concerning certain protection measures with regard to foot-and-mouth disease in the United Kingdom, repealing DEC 2001/740/EC & amending for the 8th time EC DEC 2001/327/EC. – 4p.: 30 cm. – 0 11 061014 8 *£1.75*

The Pigs (Records, Identification and Movement) (Scotland) Amendment Order 2002 No. 2002/540. – Enabling power: Animal Health Act 1981, ss. 1, 8 (1), 83 (2). – Issued: 13.12.2002. Made: 02.12.2002. Coming into force: 31.12.2002. Effect: S.I. 1995/11 amended in relation to Scotland. Territorial extent & classification: S. General. – EC note: Implements in Scotland, Council Directive 2000/15/EC amending Council Directive 64/432/EEC on health problems affecting intra-Community trade in bovine animals and swine. – 4p.: 30 cm. – 0 11 061751 7 *£1.75*

The Poultry Breeding Flocks, Hatcheries and Animal By-Products (Fees) (Scotland) Order 2002 No. 2002/529. – Enabling power: Animal Health Act 1981, s. 84 (1). – Issued: 10.12.2002. Made: 29.11.2002. Laid before the Scottish Parliament: 02.12.2002. Coming into force: 01.01.2003. Effect: S.I. 1993/1990 revoked in relation to Scotland. Territorial extent & classification: S. General. – 4p.: 30 cm. – 0 11 061735 5 *£1.75*

The Sheep and Goats Identification (Scotland) Amendment (No. 2) Regulations 2002 No. 2002/531. – Enabling power: European Communities Act 1972, s. 2 (2). – Issued: 12.12.2002. Made: 28.11.2002. Laid before the Scottish Parliament: 02.12.2002. Coming into force: 01.01.2003. Effect: S.S.I. 2000/418 amended. Territorial extent & classification: S. General. – 4p.: 30 cm. – 0 11 061746 0 *£1.75*

The Sheep and Goats Identification (Scotland) Amendment Regulations 2002 No. 2002/39. – Enabling power: European Communities Act 1972, s. 2 (2). – Issued: 22.02.2002. Made: 04.02.2002. Laid before the Scottish Parliament: 05.02.2002. Coming into force: 18.02.2002. Effect: S.S.I. 2001/418 amended. Territorial extent & classification: S. General. – [8]p.: 30 cm. – 0 11 059997 7 *£2.00*

The Sheep and Goats Movement (Interim Measures) (Scotland) Order 2002 No. 2002/38. – Enabling power: Animal Health Act 1981, ss. 1, 8 (1). – Issued: 22.02.2002. Made: 04.02.2002. Coming into force: 18.02.2002. Effect: None. Territorial extent & classification: S. General. – 4p.: 30 cm. – 0 11 059996 9 *£1.75*

The TSE (Scotland) Regulations 2002 No. 2002/255. – Enabling power: European Communities Act 1972, s. 2 (2). – Issued: 13.06.2002. Made: 27.05.2002. Laid before the Scottish Parliament: 28.05.2002. Coming into force: 19.06.2002. Effect: S.I. 1995/539; 1997/2964; 1998/871; 1999/646; 2001/231 amended in relation to Scotland & S.S.I. 2000/62, 344, 453; 2001/1, 189, 276, 383; 2002/1 amended & S.I. 1996/3183, 3184; 1997/2365, 2387, 2965, 3062; 1998/954, 955, 1645, 1646, 1647, 2405, 2431, 3070, 3071; 1999/539, 882, 921 revoked in relation to Scotland & S.S.I. 2000/345; 2001/3, 73, 86, 288, 458 revoked. Territorial extent & classification: S. General. – [100]p.: 30 cm. – 0 11 061439 9 *£10.50*

Animals: Prevention of cruelty

The Welfare of Animals (Slaughter or Killing) Amendment (Scotland) Regulations 2002 No. 2002/238. – Enabling power: European Communities Act 1972, s. 2 (2). – Issued: 10.06.2002. Made: 17.05.2002. Laid before the Scottish Parliament: 21.05.2002. Coming into force: 10.06.2002. Effect: S.I. 1995/731 amended in relation to Scotland. Territorial extent & classification: S. General– 4p.: 30 cm. – 0 11 061434 8 *£1.75*

The Welfare of Farmed Animals (Scotland) Amendment Regulations 2002 No. 2002/334. – Enabling power: Agriculture (Miscellaneous Provisions) Act 1968, s. 2. – Issued: 15.07.2002. Made: 02.07.2002. Coming into force: 03.07.2002, 01.01.2003 in accord. with reg. 1. Effect: S.S.I. 2000/442 amended. Territorial extent & classification: S. General. – EC note: Amendments give effect to EC DIR 99/74/EC laying down minimum standards for the protection of laying hens. – 8p.: 30 cm. – 0 11 061557 3 *£2.00*

Betting, gaming and lotteries

The Gaming Act (Variation of Fees) (Scotland) Order 2002 No. 2002/281. – Enabling power: Gaming Act 1968, ss. 48 (5), 51 (4). – Issued: 21.06.2002. Made: 06.06.2002. Laid before the Scottish Parliament: 10.06.2002. Coming into force: 15.07.2002. Effect: S.S.I. 2001/83, 230 revoked. Territorial extent & classification: S. General. – 4p.: 30 cm. – 0 11 061481 X *£1.75*

Building and buildings

The Buildings Standards (Scotland) Amendment Regulations 2001 Amendment Regulations 2002 No. 2002/40. – Enabling power: Building (Scotland) Act 1959, ss. 3, 24 (1) (b), 29 (1), sch. 4. – Issued: 28.02.2002. Made: 04.02.2002. Laid before the Scottish Parliament: 06.02.2002. Coming into force: 03.03.2002. Effect: S.S.I. 2001/320 amended. Territorial extent & classification: S. General. – 4p.: 30 cm. – 0 11 061021 0 *£1.75*

Children and young persons

The Adoption (Intercountry Aspects) Act 1999 (Commencement No. 7) (Scotland) Order 2002 No. 2002/562 (C.28). – Enabling power: Adoption (Intercountry Aspects) Act 1999, s. 18 (3). Bringing into operation for Scotland various provisions of the 1999 Act on 14.01.2003. – Issued: 09.01.2003. Made: 18.12.2002. Effect: None. Territorial extent & classification: S. General. – 2p.: 30 cm. – 0 11 061828 9 *£1.50*

The Children (Scotland) Act 1995 (Commencement No. 5) Order 2002 No. 2002/12 (C.1). – Enabling power: Children (Scotland) Act 1995, s. 105 (1). Bringing into force various provisions of the 1995 Act on 22.01.2002. – Issued: 01.02.2002. Made: 21.01.2002. Effect: None. Territorial extent & classification: S. General. – 2p.: 30 cm. – 0 11 059979 9 *£1.50*

The Children's Hearings (Legal Representation) (Scotland) Amendment Rules 2002 No. 2002/30. – Enabling power: Children (Scotland) Act 1995, s. 42 (1) (2) (a) (b) (d) (i). – Issued: 28.02.2002. Made: 25.01.2002. Laid before the Scottish Parliament: 30.01.2002. Coming into force: 22.02.2002. Effect: S.S.I. 2001/478 amended.Territorial extent & classification: S. General. – 2p.: 30 cm. – 0 11 061010 5 *£1.50*

The Children's Hearings (Legal Representation) (Scotland) Rules 2002 No. 2002/63. – Enabling power: Children (Scotland) Act 1995, ss. 42 (1) (2) (a) (b) (d) (i), 103 (3). – Issued: 28.02.2002. Made: 14.02.2002. Laid before the Scottish Parliament: 15.02.2002. Coming into force: 23.02.2002. Effect: S.S.I. 2001/478; 2002/30 revoked. Territorial extent & classification: S. General. – 4p.: 30 cm. – 0 11 061008 3 *£1.75*

Clean air

The Smoke Control Areas (Authorised Fuels) (Scotland) Amendment Regulations 2002 No. 2002/527. – Enabling power: Clean Air Act 1993, ss. 20 (6), 63 (1). – Issued: 12.12.2002. Made: 28.11.2002. Laid before the Scottish Parliament: 02.12.2002. Coming into force: 23.12.2002. Effect: S.S.I. 2001/433 amended. Territorial extent & classification: S. General. – 4p.: 30 cm. – 0 11 061747 9 *£1.75*

Consumer protection

The Tobacco Advertising and Promotion Act 2002 (Commencement) (Scotland) Order 2002 No. 2002/512 (C.26). – Enabling power: Tobacco Advertising and Promotion Act 2002, s. 22 (1) to (3). Bringing into force various provisions of the 2002 Act in accordance with reg. 2. – Issued: 06.12.2002. Made: 19.11.2002. Effect: None. Territorial extent & classification: S. General. – 4p.: 30 cm. – 0 11 061727 4 *£1.75*

Contracts

The Late Payment of Commercial Debts (Interest) Act 1998 (Commencement No. 6) (Scotland) Order 2002 No. 2002/337 (C.17). – Enabling power: Late Payment of Commercial Debts (Interest) Act 1998, s. 17 (2). Bringing into operation various provisions of the 1998 Act on 07.08.2002. – Issued: 15.07.2002. Made: 02.07.2002. Effect: None. Territorial extent and classification: S. General. – EC note: This Order partially implements EC DIR 2000/35/EC. – 2p.: 30 cm. – 0 11 061540 9 *£1.50*

The Late Payment of Commercial Debts (Rate of Interest) (Scotland) Order 2002 No. 2002/336. – Enabling power: Late Payment of Commercial Debts (Interest) Act 1998, s. 6. – Issued: 15.07.2002. Made: 02.07.2002. Laid before the Scottish Parliament: 04.07.2002. Coming into force: 07.08.2002. Effect: S.I. 1998/2765 revoked. Territorial extent and classification: S. General. – 4p.: 30 cm. – 0 11 061555 7 *£1.75*

The Late Payment of Commercial Debts (Scotland) Regulations 2002 No. 2002/335. – Enabling power: European Communities Act 1972, ss. 2 (2). – Issued: 15.07.2002. Made: 02.07.2002. Laid before the Scottish Parliament: 04.07.2002. Coming into force: 07.08.2002. Effect: 1998 c.20 amended. Territorial extent and classification: S. General. – EC note: Partially implements EC DIR 2000/35/EC. – 4p.: 30 cm. – 0 11 061556 5 *£1.75*

Council tax

The Council Tax (Dwellings and Part Residential Subjects) (Scotland) Amendment Regulations 2002 No. 2002/102. – Enabling power: Local Government Finance Act 1992, ss. 72 (4), 99 (1), 116 (1). – Issued: 28.03.2002. Made: 07.03.2002. Laid before the Scottish Parliament: 08.03.2002. Coming into force: 01.04.2002. Effect: S.I. 1992/2955 amended. Territorial extent & classification: S. General. – 4p.: 30 cm. – 0 11 061232 9 *£1.75*

The Council Tax (Exempt Dwellings) (Scotland) Amendment Order 2002 No. 2002/101. – Enabling power: Local Government Finance Act 1992, s. 72 (6) (7). – Issued: 28.03.2002. Made: 07.03.2002. Laid before the Scottish Parliament: 08.03.2002. Coming into force: 01.04.2002. Effect: S.I. 1997/728 amended. Territorial extent & classification: S. General. – 2p.: 30 cm. – 0 11 061231 0 *£1.50*

Countryside

The Fur Farming (Prohibition) (Scotland) Act 2002 (Commencement) Order 2002 No. 2002/519 (C.27). – Enabling power: Fur Farming (Prohibition) (Scotland) Act 2002, s. 6 (1). Bringing into force various provisions of the 2002 Act on 01.01.2003. – Issued: 06.12.2002. Made: 25.11.2002. Effect: None. Territorial extent & classification: S. General. – 2p.: 30 cm. – 0 11 061729 0 *£1.50*

The Loch Lomond and the Trossachs National Park Designation, Transitional and Consequential Provisions (Scotland) Order 2002 No. 2002/201. – Enabling power: National Parks (Scotland) Act 2000, ss. 6 (1), 7 (1) (2) (4), 9 (2) (d), 10 (1), 33, 34 (2) (3) (4), sch. 1, paras. 3, 4, 16 (3). – Issued: 03.05.2002. Made: 24.04.2002. Coming into force: In accord. with art. 1. Effect: 2000 asp 7 amended. Territorial extent & classification: S. General. – 12p.: 30 cm. – 0 11 061405 4 *£2.50*

The Loch Lomond and the Trossachs National Park Elections (Scotland) Order 2002 No. 2002/202. – Enabling power: National Parks (Scotland) Act 2000, sch. 1, para. 4. – Issued: 03.05.2002. Made: 24.04.2002. Coming into force: In accord. with art. 1. Effect: None. Territorial extent & classification: S. General. – 16p.: 30 cm. – 0 11 061404 6 *£3.00*

The Protection of Wild Mammals (Scotland) Act 2002 (Commencement) Order 2002 No. 2002/181 (C.12). – Enabling power: Protection of Wild Mammals (Scotland) Act 2002, s. 12 (2). Bringing into force the 2002 Act on 01.08.2002 in accord. with art. 2. – Issued: 24.04.2002. Made: 09.04.2002. Effect: None. Territorial extent & classification: S. General. – 2p.: 30 cm. – 0 11 061369 4 *£1.50*

Court of Session

Act of Sederunt (Fees of Messengers-at-Arms) 2002 No. 2002/513. – Enabling power: Execution of Diligence (Scotland) Act 1926, s. 6 & Court of Session Act 1988, s. 5. – Issued: 02.12.2002. Made: 21.11.2002. Coming into force: 01.01.2003. Effect: S.I. 1994/391 amended. Territorial extent and classification: S. General. – 8p.: 30 cm. – 0 11 061720 7 *£2.00*

Act of Sederunt (Fees of Messengers-at-Arms) (No. 2) 2002 No. 2002/566. – Enabling power: Execution of Diligence (Scotland) Act 1926, s. 6 & Court of Session Act 1988, s. 5. – Issued: 13.01.2003. Made: 20.12.2002. Coming into force: 30.12.2002. Effect: S.I. 1994/391 (with saving), 3268; 1995/3094; 1996/2855; 1997/2825; 1998/2668, 3256; 1999/351; 2000/421; 2001/440; 2002/513 revoked. Territorial extent and classification: S. General. – 12p.: 30 cm. – 0 11 061852 1 *£2.50*

Act of Sederunt (Lands Valuation Appeal Court) 2002 No. 2002/340. – Enabling power: Valuation of Lands (Scotland) Amendment Act 1879, s. 7. – Issued: 19.07.2002. Made: 09.07.2002. Coming into force: 01.08.2002. Effect: S.I. 1997/378 revoked. Territorial extent & classification: S. General. – 2p.: 30 cm. – 0 11 061561 1 *£1.50*

Act of Sederunt (Rules of the Court of Session Amendment) (Fees of Solicitors, Shorthand Writers and Witnesses) 2002 No. 2002/301. – Enabling power: Court of Session Act 1988, s. 5. – Issued: 03.07.2002. Made: 18.06.2002. Coming into force: 01.07.2002. Effect: S.I. 1994/1443 amended. Territorial extent & classification: S. General. – 8p.: 30 cm. – 0 11 061490 9 £2.00

Act of Sederunt (Rules of the Court of Session Amendment No. 2) (Applications under the Protection from Abuse (Scotland) Act 2001) 2002 No. 2002/514. – Enabling power: Court of Session Act 1988, s. 5 & Protection from Abuse (Scotland) Act 2001, ss. 2 (1), 3 (1), 5 (a). – Issued: 02.12.2002. Made: 21.11.2002. Coming into force: 01.12.2002. Effect: S.I. 1994/1443 amended. Territorial extent & classification: S. General. – 8p.: 30 cm. – 0 11 061721 5 £2.00

Act of Sederunt (Rules of the Court of Session Amendment No. 2) (Personal Injuries Actions) 2002 No. 2002/570. – Enabling power: Court of Session Act 1988, s. 5. – Issued: 10.01.2003. Made: 23.12.2002. Coming into force: 01.04.2003. Effect: S.I. 1994/1443 amended. Territorial extent & classification: S. General. – 24p.: 30 cm. – 0 11 061845 9 £4.00

The Court of Session etc. Fees Amendment Order 2002 No. 2002/270. – Enabling power: Courts of Law Fees (Scotland) Act 1895, s. 2. – Issued: 20.06.2002. Made: 05.06.2002. Laid before the Scottish Parliament: 07.06.2002. Coming into force: 01.07.2002. Effect: S.I. 1997/688 amended. Territorial extent and classification: S. General. – 12p.: 30 cm. – 0 11 061463 1 £2.50

Criminal law

The Criminal Justice Act 1988 (Offensive Weapons) Amendment (Scotland) Order 2002 No. 2002/323. – Enabling power: Criminal Justice Act 1988, s. 141 (2). – Issued: 12.07.2002. Made: 21.06.2002. Coming into force: 22.06.2002. Effect: S.I. 1988/2019 amended. Territorial extent & classification: S. General. – 2p.: 30 cm. – 0 11 061523 9 £1.50

The Restriction of Liberty Order (Scotland) Amendment Regulations 2002 No. 2002/119. – Enabling power: Criminal Procedure (Scotland) Act 1995, ss. 245A (8), 245C (3). – Issued: 28.03.2002. Made: 11.03.2002. Laid before the Scottish Parliament: 11.03.2002. Coming into force: 16.04.2002 for the purposes of reg. 4 (a) & 01.05.2002 for all other purposes. Effect: S.I. 1998/1802 amended. Territorial extent & classification: S. General. – 4p.: 30 cm. – 0 11 061195 0 £1.75

The Sexual Offences (Procedure and Evidence) (Scotland) Act 2002 (Commencement and Transitional Provisions) Order 2002 No. 2002/443 (C.24). – Enabling power: Sexual Offences (Amendment) Act 2000, s. 11(2) (3). Bringing into operation various provisions of the 2002 Act on 01.11.2002, in accord. with art. 3. – Issued: 04.10.2002. Made: 25.09.2002. Effect: None. Territorial extent & classification: S. General. – 4p.: 30 cm. – 0 11 061650 2 £1.75

Damages

The Damages (Personal Injury) (Scotland) Order 2002 No. 2002/46. – Enabling power: Damages Act 1996, s. 1 (1) (4). – Issued: 28.02.2002. Made: 06.02.2002. Laid before the Scottish Parliament: 07.02.2002. Coming into force: 08.02.2002. Effect: None. Territorial extent & classification: S. General. – 2p.: 30 cm. – 0 11 061020 2 £1.50

Education

The Advisory Council (Establishment) (Scotland) Regulations 2002 No. 2002/293. – Enabling power: Scottish Qualifications Authority Act 2002, s. 3. – Issued: 26.06.2002. Made: 10.06.2002. Laid before the Scottish Parliament: 10.06.2002. Coming into force: 07.08.2002. Effect: None. Territorial extent & classification: S. General. – 4p.: 30 cm. – 0 11 061487 9 £1.75

The Education (Assisted Places) (Scotland) Amendment Regulations 2002 No. 2002/249. – Enabling power: Education (Scotland) Act 1980, ss. 75A (9) (10), 75B. – Issued: 12.06.2002. Made: 21.05.2002. Laid before the Scottish Parliament: 27.05.2002. Coming into force: 01.08.2002. Effect: S.S.I. 2201/222 amended. Territorial extent & classification: S. General. – 4p.: 30 cm. – 0 11 061442 9 £1.75

The Education (Disability Strategies and Pupils' Educational Records) (Scotland) Act 2002 (Commencement) Order 2002 No. 2002/367 (C.19). – Enabling power: Education (Disability Strategies and Pupils' Educational Records) (Scotland) Act 2002, s. 7. Bringing into force various provisions of the 2002 Act on 15.08.2002. – Issued: 19.08.2002. Made: 08.08.2002. Effect: None. Territorial extent & classification: S. General. – 2p.: 30 cm. – 0 11 061581 6 £1.50

The Education (Disability Strategies) (Scotland) Regulations 2002 No. 2002/391. – Enabling power: Education (Disability Strategies and Pupils' Educational Records) (Scotland) Act 2002, ss. 1 (1) (2), 2 (1), 3 (6), 5. – Issued: 05.09.2002. Made: 27.08.2002. Laid before the Scottish Parliament: 28.08.2002. Coming into force: 01.10.2002. Effect: None. Territorial extent & classification: S. General. – 4p.: 30 cm. – 0 11 061585 9 £1.75

The Education (Listed Bodies) (Scotland) Order 2002 No. 2002/406. – Enabling power: Education Reform Act 1988, s.216 (2). – Issued: 12.09.2002. Made: 03.09.2002. Coming into force: 26.09.2002. Effect: S.S.I. 2000/293 revoked. Territorial extent & classification: S. General. – 16p.: 30 cm. – 0 11 061610 3 £3.00

The Education (Student Loans) Amendment (Scotland) Regulations 2002 No. 2002/282. – Enabling power: Education (Scotland) Act 1990, s. 1 (2) (b) (7), sch. 2, para. 1 (1). – Issued: 21.06.2002. Made: 07.06.2002. Laid before the Scottish Parliament: 10.06.2002. Coming into force: 01.08.2002. Effect: S.I. 1998/211 amended in relation to Scotland. Territorial extent & classification: S. General. – 4p.: 30 cm. – 0 11 061483 6 £1.75

The Nursing and Midwifery Student Allowances (Scotland) Amendment Regulations 2002 No. 2002/423. – Enabling power: Education (Scotland) Act 1980, ss. 73 (f), 74 (1). – Issued: 23.09.2002. Made: 11.09.2002. Laid before the Scottish Parliament: 13.09.2002. Coming into force: 04.10.2002. Effect: S.I. 1992/580 amended. Territorial extent & classification: S. General. – 8p.: 30 cm. – 0 11 061636 7 £2.00

The Provision of School Education for Children under School Age (Prescribed Children) (Scotland) Order 2002 No. 2002/90. – Enabling power: Education (Scotland) Act 1980, ss. 1 (1A) (1B). – Issued: 21.03.2002. Made: 04.03.2002. Laid before the Scottish Parliament: 07.03.2002. Coming into force: 01.04.2002. Effect: None. Territorial extent & classification: S. General. – 4p.: 30 cm. – 0 11 061174 8 £1.75

The School Education (Amendment) (Scotland) Act 2002 (Commencement) Order 2002 No. 2002/74 (C.3). – Enabling power: School Education (Amendment) (Scotland) Act 2002, s. 3. Bringing into force various provisions of the 2002 Act on 26.02.2002. & 22.03.2002. – Issued: 12.03.2002. Made: 25.02.2002. Effect: None. Territorial extent & classification: S. General. – 2p.: 30 cm. – 0 11 061106 3 £1.50

The Scottish Qualifications Authority Act 2002 (Commencement No. 1) Order 2002 No. 2002/355 (C.18). – Enabling power: Scottish Qualifications Authority Act 2002, s. 6 (2) (3). Bringing into force various provisions of the 2002 Act on 07.08.2002 & 19.08.2002, in accord. with art. 3. – Issued: 06.08.2002. Made: 26.07.2002. Effect: None. Territorial extent & classification: S. General. – 2p.: 30 cm. – 0 11 061579 4 £1.50

The Standards in Scotland's Schools etc. Act 2000 (Commencement No. 5) Order 2002 No. 2002/72 (C.2). – Enabling power: Standards in Scotland's Schools etc. Act 2000, s. 61 (2). Bringing into force various provisions of the Act on 04.03.2002. & 01.04.2002. – Issued: 11.03.2002. Made: 25.02.2002. Effect: None. Territorial extent and classification: S. General. – 4p.: 30 cm. – 0 11 061105 5 £1.75

The St Mary's Music School (Aided Places) (Scotland) Amendment Regulations 2002 No. 2002/248. – Enabling power: Education (Scotland) Act 1980, ss. 73(f), 74 (1). – Issued: 12.06.2002. Made: 21.05.2002. Laid before the Scottish Parliament: 27.05.2002. Coming into force: 01.08.2002. Effect: S.S.I 2001/223 amended. Territorial extent & classification: S. General. – 4p.: 30 cm. 0 11 061441 0 £1.75

Electricity

The Electricity Act 1989 (Requirement of Consent for Offshore Generating Stations) (Scotland) Order 2002 No. 2002/407. – Enabling power: Electricity Act 1989, ss. 36 (2) (3), 111 (2). – Issued: 12.09.2002. Made: 02.09.2002. Laid before the Scottish Parliament: 04.09.2002. Coming into force: 26.09.2002. Effect: 1989 c.29 modified. Territorial extent and classification: S. General. – 4p.: 30 cm. – 0 11 061609 X £1.75

The Electricity from Non-Fossil Fuel Sources (Locational Flexibility) (Scotland) Order 2002 No. 2002/92. – Enabling power: Utilities Act 2000, s. 67. – Issued: 28.03.2002. Made: 06.03.2002. Laid before the Scottish Parliament: 07.03.2002. Coming into force: 31.03.2002. Effect: 1989 c. 29 modified. Territorial extent & classification: S. General. – 4p.: 30 cm. – 0 11 061220 5 £1.75

The Electricity from Non-Fossil Fuel Sources (Scotland) Saving Arrangements (Modification) Order 2002 No. 2002/93. – Enabling power: Utilities Act 2000, s. 67 (1) (c). – Issued: 08.04.2002. Made: 06.03.2002. Laid before the Scottish Parliament: 07.03.2002. Coming into force: 31.03.2002. Effect: S.I. 2001/3269 modified. Territorial extent & classification: S. General. – 4p.: 30 cm. – 0 11 061259 0 £1.75

The Fossil Fuel Levy (Scotland) Amendment Regulations 2002 No. 2002/94. – Enabling power: Electricity Act 1989, ss. 33, 60. – Issued: 08.04.2002. Made: 06.03.2002. Laid before the Scottish Parliament: 07.03.2002. Coming into force: 31.03.2002. Effect: S.I. 1996/293 amended. Territorial extent & classification: S. General. – 2p.: 30 cm. – 0 11 061260 4 £1.50

The Renewables Obligation (Scotland) Order 2002 No. 2002/163. – Enabling power: Electricity Act 1989, ss. 32 to 32C. – Issued: 17.04.2002. Made: 26.03.2002. Coming into force: 01.04.2002. Effect: None. Territorial extent & classification: S. General. – 16p.: 30 cm. – 0 11 061346 5 £3.00

Environmental protection

The Air Quality Limit Values (Scotland) Amendment Regulations 2002 No. 2002/556. – Enabling power: European Communities Act 1972, s. 2 (2). – Issued: 09.01.2003. Made: 17.12.2002. Laid before the Scottish Parliament: 17.12.2002. Coming into force: 19.01.2003. Effect: S.S.I. 2001/224 amended. Territorial extent & classification: S. General. – This Scottish Statutory Instrument has been printed in substitution of the S.S.I. of the same number and is being issued free of charge to all known recipients of that SI. –Revoked by S.S.I. 2003/428 (ISBN 0110624556). EC note: These Regs were made in implementation of EC DIR 2000/69/EC. Reg. 2 amends the principal regulations which implement EC DIR 96/62/EC on ambient air quality assessment and management and Council DIR 1999/30/EC relating to limit values for sulphur dioxide, nitrogen dioxide and oxides of nitrogen, particulate matter and lead in ambient air (known as "the First Daughter Directive"). – 8p.: 30 cm. – 0 11 061817 3 £2.00

The Air Quality (Scotland) Amendment Regulations 2002 No. 2002/297. – Enabling power: Environment Act 1995, ss. 87 (1) (2) (b) (h) (3) (5), 91 (1). – Issued: 24.06.2002. Made: 11.06.2002. Coming into force: 12.06.2002. Effect: S.S.I. 2000/97 amended. – 4p.: 30 cm. – 0 11 061468 2 £1.75

The Financial Assistance for Environmental Purposes (Scotland) Order 2002 No. 2002/83. – Enabling power: Environmental Protection Act 1990, s. 153 (4). – Issued: 13.03.2002. Made: 05.03.2002. Laid before the Scottish Parliament: 05.03.2002. Coming into force: 26.03.2002. Effect: 1990 c.43 amended. Territorial extent & classification: S. General. – 2p.: 30 cm. – 0 11 061116 0 *£1.50*

The Genetically Modified Organisms (Deliberate Release) (Scotland) Regulations 2002 No. 2002/541. – Enabling power: European Communities Act 1972, s. 2 (2). – Issued: 16.12.2002. Made: 04.12.2002. Coming into force: In accord.with reg. 1 (1). Effect: S.I. 1997/1900; 2000/2831; 2002/800 amended & S.I. 1993/152; 1995/304 revoked in relation to Scotland & S.I.1992/3280 revoked with saving. – EC note: Implements in respect of Scotland, Directive 2001/18/EC on the deliberate release into the environment of genetically modified organisms which replaced Directive 1990/220/EEC (as amended). – 40p.: 30 cm. – 0 11 061760 6 *£6.50*

The Large Combustion Plants (Scotland) Regulations 2002 No. 2002/493. – Enabling power: Pollution Prevention and Control Act 1999, s. 2, sch. 1, part 1, para. 20 (2) (c). – Issued: 14.11.2002. Made: 06.11.2002. Laid before the Scottish Parliament: 06.11.2002. Coming into force: 27.11.2002. Effect: S.S.I 2000/323 amended. Territorial extent & classification: S. General. – 4p.: 30 cm. – 0 11 061699 5 *£1.75*

The Pollution Prevention and Control (Designation of Council Directives on Large Combustion Plants and National Emission Ceilings) (Scotland) Order 2002 No. 2002/488. – Enabling power: Pollution Prevention and Control Act 1999, sch. 1, part 1, para. 20 (2) (c). – Issued: 13.11.2002. Made: 03.11.2002. Laid before the Scottish Parliament: -.Coming into force: 04.11.2002. Effect: None. Territorial extent & classification: S. General. – 2p.: 30 cm. – 0 11 061697 9 *£1.50*

The Producer Responsibility Obligations (Packaging Waste) Amendment (Scotland) Regulations 2002 No. 2002/147. – Enabling power: Environment Act 1995, ss. 93, 94 (1) (c). – Issued: 12.04.2002. Made: 25.03.2002. Laid before the Scottish Parliament: 25.03.2002. Coming into force: 26.03.2002. Effect: S.I. 1997/648 amended (in relation to Scotland). Territorial extent & classification: S. General. – 4p.: 30 cm. – 0 11 061309 0 *£1.75*

Fire services

The Combined Fire Services Area Administration Schemes (Variation) (Scotland) Order 2002 No. 2002/141. – Enabling power: Fire Services Act 1947, s. 36 (8). – Issued: 12.04.2002. Made: 22.03.2002. Laid before the Scottish Parliament: 22.03.2002. Coming into force: 31.03.2002. Effect: S.I. 1995/2632, 2633, 2634, 2635, 2636, 2637 amended. Territorial extent & classification: S. General. – 4p.: 30 cm. – 0 11 061312 0 *£1.75*

The Police and Fire Services (Finance) (Scotland) Act 2001 (Commencement) Order 2002 No. 2002/84 (C.5). – Enabling power: Police and Fire Services (Finance) (Scotland) Act 2001, s. 3 (2). Bringing into force various provisions of the 2001 Act on 11.03.2002. – Issued: 21.03.2002. Made: 04.03.2002. Effect: None. Territorial extent & classification: S. General. – 2p.: 30 cm. – 0 11 061164 0 *£1.50*

Food

The Animal By-products (Identification) Amendment (Scotland) Regulations 2002 No. 2002/283. – Enabling power: Food Safety Act 1990, ss. 6 (4), 16 (1) (c) (d) (f) (3), 26 (3), 48 (1), sch. 1, para. 3. – Issued: 21.06.2002. Made: 07.06.2002. Laid before the Scottish Parliament: 10.06.2002. Coming into force: 01.07.2002. Effect: S.I. 1995/614 amended. Territorial extent & classification: S. General. – 8p.: 30 cm. – 0 11 061477 1 *£2.00*

The Contaminants in Food (Scotland) (Amendment) Regulations 2002 No. 2002/349. – Enabling power: Food Safety Act 1990, ss. 6 (4), 16 (1) (a) (f), 17 (2), 26 (1) (a) (3), 48 (1). – Issued: 05.08.2002. Made: 23.07.2002. Laid before the Scottish Parliament: 23.07.2002. Coming into force: 24.07.2002. Effect: S.I. 1983/270; 1985/1068; S.S.I. 2002/267 amended & S.I. 1985/1438 revoked. Territorial extent & classification: S. General. – EC note: The Contaminants in Food (Scotland) Regulations 2002 make provision for the enforcement and execution of EC Reg 466/2001 setting maximum levels for certain contaminants. –This S.S.I. has been made in consequence of the correction of a defect in Commission Regulation (EC) No. 563/2002 which was reflected in S.S.I. 2002/267 and is being issued free of charge to all known recipients of that instrument. – 4p.: 30 cm. – 0 11 061575 1 *£1.75*

The Contaminants in Food (Scotland) Regulations 2002 No. 2002/267. – Enabling power: Food Safety Act 1990, ss. 6 (4), 16 (1) (a) (f), 17 (2), 26 (1) (a) (3), 48 (1). – Issued: 21.06.2002. Made: 06.06.2002. Laid before the Scottish Parliament: 07.06.2002. Coming into force: 01.07.2002. Effect: 1990 c.16 modified & S.I. 1990/2463, 2625; 1991/1476; 1992/1971; 1995/3124, 3267 amended & S.I. 1979/1641; 1997/1499; 1999/1603, S.S.I. 1999/171 revoked. Territorial extent & classification: S. General. – EC note: Extending to Scotland only these regs. make provision for the enforcement and execution of EC Regs 466/2001 as amended by Reg. 2375/2001, 221/2002, 257/2002, 472/2002 & 563/2002 and implements the following Commission directives - 98/53/EC, 2001/22/EC, 2002/26/EC & 2002/27/EC amending 98/53/EC. – 12p.: 30 cm. – 0 11 061445 3 *£2.50*

The Dairy Produce Quotas (Scotland) Amendment Regulations 2002 No. 2002/228. – Enabling power: European Communities Act 1972, s. 2 (2). – Issued: 27.05.2002. Made: 13.05.2002. Laid before the Scottish Parliament: 14.05.2002. Coming into force: 05.06.2002. Effect: S.S.I. 2000/347; 2002/110 amended. Territorial extent & classification: S. General. – 4p.: 30 cm. – 0 11 061426 7 *£1.75*

The Dairy Produce Quotas (Scotland) Regulations 2002 No. 2002/110. – Enabling power: European Communities Act 1972, s. 2 (2). – Issued: 08.04.2002. Made: 07.03.2002. Laid before the Scottish Parliament: 08.03.2002. Coming into force: 31.03.2002. Effect: S.S.I. 2001/390 amended & S.I. 1997/733 (with saving), 1093 revoked in relation to Scotland & S.S.I. 2000/52, 391 revoked. Territorial extent & classification: S. General. – EC note: These Regs. implement, for Scotland, Council Reg. 3950/92 & Reg. 1392/2001. – 32p.: 30 cm. – 0 11 061270 1 *£6.00*

The Food and Animal Feedingstuffs (Products of Animal Origin from China) (Control) (Scotland) Regulations 2002 No. 2002/36. – Enabling power: European Communities Act 1972, s. 2 (2). – Issued: 20.02.2002. Made: 01.02.2002. Laid before the Scottish Parliament: 05.02.2002. Coming into force: 02.02.2002. Effect: None. Territorial extent & classification: S. General. – 8p.: 30 cm. – 0 11 059986 1 *£2.00*

The Food and Animal Feedingstuffs (Products of Animal Origin from China) (Emergency Control) (Scotland) Amendment Regulations 2002 No. 2002/356. – Enabling power: European Communities Act 1972, s. 2 (2). – Issued: 06.08.2002. Made: 29.07.2002. Laid before the Scottish Parliament: 30.07.2002. Coming into force: 31.07.2002. Effect: S.S.I. 2002/300 amended. Territorial extent & classification: S. General. – 2p.: 30 cm. – 0 11 061578 6 *£1.50*

The Food and Animal Feedingstuffs (Products of Animal Origin from China) (Emergency Control) (Scotland) Regulations 2002 No. 2002/300. – Enabling power: European Communities Act 1972, s. 2 (2). – Issued: 11.07.2002. Made: 19.06.02. Laid before the Scottish Parliament: 24.06.02. Coming into force: 20.06.02. Effect: S.S.I. 2002/36 revoked. Territorial extent & classification: S. General. – [8]p.: 30 cm. – 0 11 061514 X *£2.00*

The Food (Control of Irradiation) Amendment (Scotland) Regulations 2002 No. 2002/284. – Enabling power: Food Safety Act 1990, ss. 6 (4), 16 (1) (3), 17 (1), 18 (1), 19 (1) (b), 26 (1), 48 (1), sch. 1, paras. 1, 4 (b). – Issued: 21.06.2002. Made: 07.06.2002. Laid before the Scottish Parliament: 10.06.2002. Coming into force: 01.07.2002. Effect: S.I. 1990/2490 amended in relation to Scotland. Territorial extent & classification: S. General– EC note: These amendments to the 1990 Regs are in accordance with the provisions of Directive 1999/2/EC and Directive 1999/3/EC in relation to Scotland only. – 4p.: 30 cm. – 0 11 061476 3 *£1.75*

The Food (Figs, Hazelnuts and Pistachios from Turkey) (Emergency Control) (Scotland) (No. 2) Regulations 2002 No. 2002/424. – Enabling power: European Communities Act 1972, s. 2 (2). – Issued: 27.09.2002. Made: 12.09.2002. Laid before the Scottish Parliament: 13.09.2002. Coming into force: 13.09.2002. Effect: S.S.I. 2002/148 revoked. Territorial extent and classification: S. General. – EC note: These Regs. revoke and re-enact S.S.I. 2002/148, implementing, for Scotland, DEC 2002/80/EC as amended by 2002/233/EC and by 2002/679/EC. – 8p.: 30 cm. – 0 11 061631 6 *£2.00*

The Food (Figs, Hazelnuts and Pistachios from Turkey) (Emergency Control) (Scotland) Regulations 2002 No. 2002/148. – Enabling power: European Communities Act 1972, s. 2 (2). – Issued: 24.04.2002. Made: 25.03.2002. Laid before the Scottish Parliament: 25.03.2002. Coming into force: 17.00 hours on 25.03.2002. Effect: None. Territorial extent and classification: S. General. – EC note: Implements, for Scotland, DEC 2002/80/EC as amended by 2002/233/EC. – 8p.: 30 cm. – 0 11 061360 0 *£2.00*

The Food for Particular Nutritional Uses (Addition of Substances for Specific Nutritional Purposes) (Scotland) Regulations 2002 No. 2002/397. – Enabling power: Food Safety Act 1990, ss. 6 (4), 16 (1) (a) (f), 17 (1), 26 (1) (a) (3), 48 (1). – Issued: 10.09.2002. Made: 30.08.2002. Laid before the Scottish Parliament: 02.09.2002. Coming into force: 23.09.2002 & 01.04.2004 in accordance with reg. 1 (2) (3). Effect: S.I. 1990/1972 amended. Territorial extent and classification: S. General. – 12p.: 30 cm. – 0 11 061598 0 *£2.50*

The Food (Jelly Confectionery) (Emergency Control) (Scotland) Regulations 2002 No. 2002/179. – Enabling power: European Communities Act 1972, s. 2 (2). – Issued: 24.04.2002. Made: 03.04.2002. Laid before the Scottish Parliament: 04.04.2002. Coming into force: 04.04.2002. Effect: S.I. 1990/2463 amended in relation to Scotland. Territorial extent and classification: S. General. – EC note: Implement DEC 2002/247/EC suspending the placing on the market and import of jelly confectionery containing the food additive E 425 Konjac. – 8p.: 30 cm. – 0 11 061371 6 *£2.00*

The Food Labelling Amendment (Scotland) Regulations 2002 No. 2002/524. – Enabling power: Food Safety Act 1990, ss. 6 (4), 16 (1) (e) (f), 17 (1), 26 (1) (3), 48 (1). – Issued: 10.12.2002. Made: 28.11.2002. Laid before the Scottish Parliament: 02.12.2002. Coming into force: 01.01.2003. Effect: S.I. 1996/1489 amended. – EC note: Implements EC DIR 2001/101/EC; 2002/86/EC which amends 2000/13/EC. – 4p.: 30 cm. – 0 11 061733 9 *£1.75*

The Food (Peanuts from China) (Emergency Control) (Scotland) (No. 2) Regulations 2002 No. 2002/425. – Enabling power: European Communities Act 1972, s. 2 (2). – Issued: 27.09.2002. Made: 12.09.2002. Laid before the Scottish Parliament: 13.09.2002. Coming into force: 13.09.2002. Effect: S.S.I. 2002/149 revoked. Territorial extent & classification: S. General. – EC note: These Regs. revoke and re-enact S.S.I. 2002/149, implementing, for Scotland, DEC 2002/79/EC as amended by 2002/233/EC and by 2002/678/EC. – 8p.: 30 cm. – 0 11 061630 8 *£2.00*

The Food (Peanuts from China) (Emergency Control) (Scotland) Regulations 2002 No. 2002/149. – Enabling power: European Communities Act 1972, s. 2 (2). – Issued: 24.04.2002. Made: 25.03.2002. Laid before the Scottish Parliament: 25.03.2002. Coming into force: 17.00 hours on 25.03.2002. Effect: None. Territorial extent & classification: S. General. – EC note: Implement for Scotland DEC 2002/79, as amended by DEC 2002/233/EC. – 8p.: 30 cm. – 0 11 061361 9 *£2.00*

The Food (Star Anise from Third Countries) (Emergency Control) (Scotland) Order 2002 No. 2002/64. – Enabling power: Food Safety Act 1990, ss. 6 (4), 13 (1), 48 (1). – Issued: 06.03.2002. Made: 15.02.2002. Laid before the Scottish Parliament: 15.02.2002. Coming into force: 16.02.2002. Effect: None. Territorial extent and classification: S. General. – 4p.: 30 cm. – 0 11 061079 2 £1.75

The Import and Export Restrictions (Foot-and-Mouth Disease) (Scotland) (No. 3) Amendment (No. 2) Amendment Regulations 2002 No. 2002/169. – Enabling power: European Communities Act 1972, s. 2 (2). – Issued: 24.04.2002. Made: 28.03.2002. Laid before the Scottish Parliament: 04.04.2002. Coming into force: 29.03.2002. Effect: S.S.I. 2002/35 amended. Territorial extent & classification: S. General. – 2p.: 30 cm. – 0 11 061368 6 £1.50

The Kava-kava in Food (Scotland) Regulations 2002 No. 2002/523. – Enabling power: Food Safety Act 1990, ss. 6 (4), 16 (1) (a) (e) (f), 18 (1) (c), 26 (1) (3), 48 (1). – Issued: 10.12.2002. Made: 28.11.2002. Laid before the Scottish Parliament: 02.12.2002. Coming into force: 01.01.2003. Effect: None. Territorial extent and classification: S. General. – 4p.: 30 cm. – 0 11 061734 7 £1.75

The Meat (Hazard Analysis and Critical Control Point) (Scotland) Regulations 2002 No. 2002/234. – Enabling power: Food Safety Act 1990, ss. 6 (4), 16 (1) (b) (d) (f), 17 (1), 26 (2) (a), 48 (1). – Issued: 27.05.2002. Made: 16.05.2002. Laid before the Scottish Parliament: 16.05.2002. Coming into force: 07.06.2002, in accord. with reg. 3. Effect: S.I. 1995/539, 540; 1996/3124 amended in relation to Scotland. Territorial extent & classification: S. General. – 16p.: 30 cm. – 0 11 061427 5 £3.00

The Notification of Marketing of Food for Particular Nutritional Uses (Scotland) Regulations 2002 No. 2002/50. – Enabling power: Food Safety Act 1990, ss. 6 (4), 17 (1), 26 (1) (a) (3), 48 (1). – Issued: 28.02.2002. Made: 08.02.2002. Laid before the Scottish Parliament: 08.02.2002. Coming into force: 08.03.2002. Effect: None. Territorial extent and classification: S. General. – 4p.: 30 cm. – 0 11 061033 4 £1.75

The Plastic Materials and Articles in Contact with Food (Amendment) (Scotland) Regulations 2002 No. 2002/498. – Enabling power: Food Safety Act 1990, ss. 6 (4), 16 (2), 17 (1), 26 (1) (a) (3), 31, 48 (1). – Issued: 20.11.2002. Made: 07.11.2002. Laid before the Scottish Parliament: 08.11.2002. Coming into force: 30.11.2002. Effect: S.I. 1998/1376 amended in relation to Scotland. Territorial extent & classification: S. General. – 28p.: 30 cm. – 0 11 061713 4 £4.50

The Poultry Meat, Farmed Game Bird Meat and Rabbit Meat (Hygiene and Inspection) Amendment (Scotland) Regulations 2002 No. 2002/87. – Enabling power: Food Safety Act 1990, ss. 16 (1) (b) (c) (d) (e) (f) (3), 17 (1), 19 (1) (b), 26, 48 (1), sch. 1, paras. 5 (1) (a) (2) (a), 6 (1) (a) & European Communities Act 1972, s. 2 (2). – Issued: 20.03.2001. Made: 05.03.2002. Laid before the Scottish Parliament: 06.03.2002. Coming into force: 01.04.2002 except for reg. 2 (2) (3) (4) (5) (6) which come into force on 01.12.2002. Effect: S.I. 1995/540; 1996/3124 amended in relation to Scotland only. Territorial extent & classification: S. General. – 4p.: 30 cm. – 0 11 061143 8 £1.75

The Sweeteners in Food Amendment (Scotland) Regulations 2002 No. 2002/61. – Enabling power: Food Safety Act 1990, ss. 16 (1) (a) (e), 17 (1), 48 (1), sch. 1, para. 1. – Issued: 28.02.2002. Made: 14.02.2002. Laid before the Scottish Parliament: 15.02.2002. Coming into force: 15.03.2002. Effect: S.I. 1995/3123 amended. Territorial extent & classification: S. General. – EC note: These Regs bring up to date, in relation to Scotland, the definition of DIR 95/31 so as to cover its amendment by DIR 2001/52/EC to substitute new purity criteria for two permitted sweeteners and grant provisional authorisation for the marketing and use as a sweetener of sucralose, as permitted by Art. 5 of Dir 89/107/EEC . – 8p.: 30 cm. – 0 11 061011 3 £2.00

Freedom of information

The Freedom of Information (Scotland) Act 2002 (Commencement No. 1) Order 2002 No. 2002/437 (C.23). – Enabling power: Freedom of Information (Scotland) Act 2002, s. 75 (1). Bringing into force various provisions of the 2001 Act on 30.09.2002 in accord. with art. 2. – Issued: 03.10.2002. Made: 24.09.2002. Effect: None. Territorial extent & classification: S. General. – 2p.: 30 cm. – 0 11 061649 9 £1.50

Harbours, docks, piers and ferries

The Aberdeen Harbour Revision (Constitution) Order 2002 No. 2002/310. – Enabling power: Harbours Act 1964, s.14. – Issued: 11.07.2002. Made: 24.06.2002. Coming into force: 25.06.2002. Effect: 1960 c. i; 1987 c. xxi amended & S.I. 1972/275, 1704; 1976/817; 1990/2359 revoked. Territorial extent & classification: S. Local. – 12p.: 30 cm. – 0 11 061511 5 £2.50

Clydeport (Closure of Yorkhilll Basin) Harbour Revision Order 2002 No. 2002/121. – Enabling power: Harbours Act 1964, s. 14. – Issued: 21.03.2002. Made: 11.03.2002. Coming into force: 12.03.2002. Effect: None. Territorial extent & classification: S. Local. – 4p.: 30 cm. – 0 11 061185 3 £1.75

The Comhairle nan Eilean Siar (Various Harbours) Harbour Revision Order 2002 No. 2002/410. – Enabling power: Harbours Act 1964, s. 14. – Issued: 23.12.2002. Made: 04.09.2002. Coming into force: 05.09.2002. Effect: 1878 c. cxv; 1980 c. i, c.xxvii; 1982 c. ii; 1984 c. ii, c. xxx; 1986 c. xix; S.I. 1949/1516 (S.107); 1951/1866 (S.94); 1992/1975 (S.202), 1976 (S.208); 1993/2908 (S.259); 1995/2971 (S.214); S.S.I. 2001/262 amended & S.I. 1995/2007 (S.146); S.S.I. 2000/233 revoked. Territorial extent & classification: S. Local. –This S.S.I. has been printed in substitution of the S.S.I. with the same number and ISBN (originally issued 18.09.2002) and is being issued free of charge to all known recipients of that S.S.I. – 34p.: 30 cm. – 0 11 061622 7 £6.50

The Inverness Harbour Revision (Constitution) Order 2002 No. 2002/557. – Enabling power: Harbours Act 1964, s.14. – Issued: 09.01.2003. Made: 12.12.2002. Coming into force: 13.12.2002. Effect: Inverness Harbour Act, 1899; 1911 1&2 Geo 5 (Ch.Cxxi) amended. Territorial extent & classification: S. Local. – 12p.: 30 cm. – 0 11 061822 X £2.50

The Peterhead Bay Authority (Constitution) Revision Order 2002 No. 2002/294. – Enabling power: Harbours Act 1964, s.14. – Issued: 11.07.2002. Made: 05.06.02. Coming into force: 10.06.02. Effect: S.I. 1983/316 amended. Territorial extent & classification. S. Local. – 12p.: 30 cm. – 0 11 061472 0 £2.50

Peterhead Harbours Revision (Constitution) Order 2002 No. 2002/504. – Enabling power: Harbours Act 1964, s. 14. – Issued: 20.02.2003. Made: 28.10.2002. Coming into force: 31.10.2002. Effect: Peterhead Harbours Order Confirmation Act 1992 amended. Territorial extent & classification: S. Local. –This S.S.I. has been printed in substitution of the S.S.I. of the same number and is being issued free of charge to all known recipients of that SSI. – 12p.: 30 cm. – 0 11 061715 0 £2.50

High Court of Justiciary

Act of Adjournal (Criminal Appeals) 2002 No. 2002/387. – Enabling power: Criminal Procedure (Scotland) Act 1995, s. 305. – Issued: 09.09.2002. Made: 23.08.2002. Coming into force: 26.08.2002. & 23.09.2002 in acc.with para. 1 (2). Effect: 1995 c.46 & S.I. 1996/513 amended. Territorial extent & classification: S. General. – 8p.: 30 cm. – 0 11 061589 1 £2.00

Act of Adjournal (Criminal Procedure Rules Amendment) (Convention Rights (Compliance) (Scotland) Act 2001) 2002 No. 2002/137. – Enabling power: Criminal Procedure (Scotland) Act 1995, s. 305. – Issued: 12.04.2002. Made: 01.03.2002. Coming into force: 04.03.2002. Effect: S.I. 1996/513 amended. Territorial extent & classification: S. General. – 4p.: 30 cm. – 0 11 061319 8 £1.75

Act of Adjournal (Criminal Procedure Rules Amendment No. 3) (Sexual Offences) (Procedure and Evidence) (Scotland) Act 2002) 2002 No. 2002/454. – Enabling power: Criminal Procedure (Scotland) Act 1995, s. 305. – Issued: 24.10.2002. Made: 07.10.2002. Coming into force: 01.11.2002. Effect: S.I. 1996/513 amended. Territorial extent & classification: S. General. – [12]p.: 30 cm. – 0 11 061668 5 £2.50

Act of Adjournal (Criminal Procedure Rules Amendment No. 4) (Extradition) 2002 No. 2002/517. – Enabling power: Extradition Act 1989 s. 14A (6) & Criminal Procedure (Scotland) Act 1995, s. 305. – Issued: 02.12.2002. Made: 21.11.2002. Coming into force: 01.12.2002. Effect: S.I. 1996/513 amended. Territorial extent & classification: S. General. – 4p.: 30 cm. – 0 11 061724 X £1.75

Housing

The Civic Government (Scotland) Act 1982 (Licensing of Houses in Multiple Occupation) Amendment Order 2002 No. 2002/161. – Enabling power: Civic Government (Scotland) Act 1982, s. 44 (1) (b) (2). – Issued: 24.04.2002. Made: 26.03.2002. Coming into force: 01.04.2002. Effect: S.S.I. 2000/177 amended. Territorial extent & classification: S. General. – 4p.: 30 cm. – 0 11 061365 1 £1.75

The Homeless Persons Advice and Assistance (Scotland) Regulations 2002 No. 2002/414. – Enabling power: Housing (Scotland) Act 1987, ss. 31 (3) (b), 32 (3) (6). – Issued: 18.09.2002. Made: 05.09.2002. Laid before the Scottish Parliament: 09.09.2002. Coming into force: 30.09.2002. Effect: None. Territorial extent & classification: S. General. – 4p.: 30 cm. – 0 11 061615 4 £1.75

The Homeless Persons Interim Accommodation (Scotland) Regulations 2002 No. 2002/412. – Enabling power: Housing (Scotland) Act 1987, s. 32A (1). – Issued: 18.09.2002. Made: 05.09.2002. Laid before the Scottish Parliament: 09.09.2002. Coming into force: 30.09.2002. Effect: None. Territorial extent & classification: S. General. – 4p.: 30 cm. – 0 11 061613 8 £1.75

The Housing Revenue Account General Fund Contribution Limits (Scotland) Order 2002 No. 2002/45. – Enabling power: Housing (Scotland) Act 1987, s. 204. – Issued: 28.02.2002. Made: 05.02.2002. Laid before the Scottish Parliament: 07.02.2002. Coming into force: 11.03.2002. Effect: None. Territorial extent & classification: S. General. – 2p.: 30 cm. – 0 11 061023 7 £1.50

The Housing (Right to Buy) (Houses Liable to Demolition) (Scotland) Order 2002 No. 2002/317. – Enabling power: Housing (Scotland) Act 1987, ss. 70A (3). – Issued: 15.07.2002. Made: 26.06.2002. Laid before the Scottish Parliament: 27.06.2002. Coming into force: 30.09.2002. Effect: None. Territorial extent & classification: S. General. – 4p.: 30 cm. – 0 11 061535 2 £1.75

The Housing (Scotland) Act 2001 (Appointment of Arbiter) Order 2002 No. 2002/413. – Enabling power: Housing (Scotland) Act 2001, ss. 6 (1) (c), 110. – Issued: 18.09.2002. Made: 05.09.2002. Laid before the Scottish Parliament: 09.09.2002. Coming into force: 30.09.2002. Effect: None. Territorial extent & classification: S. General. – 2p.: 30 cm. – 0 11 061614 6 *£1.50*

The Housing (Scotland) Act 2001 (Commencement No. 4, Transitional Provisions and Savings) Order 2002 No. 2002/168 (C.9). – Enabling power: Housing (Scotland) Act 2001, ss. 109 (2), 113 (1) (2). Bringing into force various provisions of the 2001 Act on 01.04.2002 in accord. with art. 2. – Issued: 24.04.2002. Made: 26.03.2002. Effect: 1987 c. 26; 1992 c. 5; 1993 c. 28 modified. Territorial extent & classification: S. General. – 8p.: 30 cm. – 0 11 061372 4 *£2.00*

The Housing (Scotland) Act 2001 (Commencement No. 5, Transitional Provisions and Savings) Order 2002 No. 2002/321 (C.16). – Enabling power: Housing (Scotland) Act 2001, ss. 109 (2), 113 (1) (2). Bringing into force various provisions of the 2001 Act on 30.09.2002 in accord. with arts 2 to 5. – Issued: 12.07.2002. Made: 26.06.2002. Effect: None. Territorial extent & classification: S. General. – 8p.: 30 cm. – 0 11 061515 8 *£2.00*

The Housing (Scotland) Act 2001 (Commencement No. 6 and Amendment) Order 2002 No. 2002/433 (C.22). – Enabling power: Housing (Scotland) Act 2001, s. 113 (1) (2). Bringing into force various provisions of the 2001 Act on 30.09.2002 in accord. with art. 2. – Issued: 30.09.2002. Made: 19.09.2002. Effect: S.S.I. 2002/321 amended. Territorial extent & classification: S. General. – 8p.: 30 cm. – 0 11 061639 1 *£2.00*

The Housing (Scotland) Act 2001 (Housing Support Services) Regulations 2002 No. 2002/444. – Enabling power: Housing (Scotland) Act 2001, ss. 91 (8) (9), 109 (2). – Issued: 04.10.2002. Made: 26.09.2002. Laid before the Scottish Parliament: 27.09.2002. Coming into force: 31.10.2002. Effect: None. Territorial extent & classification: S. General. – 4p.: 30 cm. – 0 11 061654 5 *£1.75*

The Housing (Scotland) Act 2001 (Registered Social Landlords) Order 2002 No. 2002/411. – Enabling power: Housing (Scotland) Act 2001, s. 57 (3) (b). – Issued: 18.09.2002. Made: 05.09.2002. Laid before the Scottish Parliament: 09.09.2002. Coming into force: 30.09.2002. Effect: None. Territorial extent & classification: S. General. – 4p.: 30 cm. – 0 11 061612 X *£1.75*

The Housing (Scotland) Act 2001 (Registration of Tenant Organisations) Order 2002 No. 2002/416. – Enabling power: Housing (Scotland) Act 2001, s. 53 (4). – Issued: 19.09.2002. Made: 05.09.2002. Laid before the Scottish Parliament: 09.09.2002. Coming into force: 30.09.2002. Effect: None. Territorial extent & classification: S. General. – 8p.: 30 cm. – 0 11 061617 0 *£2.00*

The Housing (Scotland) Act 2001 (Scottish Secure Tenancy etc.) Amendment Order 2002 No. 2002/415. – Enabling power: Housing (Scotland) Act 2001, ss. 11 (1), 109 (2). – Issued: 19.09.2002. Made: 05.09.2002. Laid before the Scottish Parliament: 09.09.2002. Coming into force: 30.09.2002. Effect: S.S.I. 2002/318 amended. Territorial extent & classification: S. General. –This S.I. has been printed to correct errors in S.S.I. 2002/318 and is being issued free of charge to all known recipients of that instrument. – 4p.: 30 cm. – 0 11 061616 2 *£1.75*

The Housing (Scotland) Act 2001 (Scottish Secure Tenancy etc.) Order 2002 No. 2002/318. – Enabling power: Housing (Scotland) Act 1987, ss. 61A (2) (c) & Housing (Scotland) Act 2001, ss. 11 (1) (2), 109 (2), 110. – Issued: 15.07.2002. Made: 26.06.2002. Laid before the Scottish Parliament: 27.06.2002. Coming into force: 30.09.2002. Effect: None. Territorial extent & classification: S. General. – 4p.: 30 cm. – 0 11 061534 4 *£1.75*

The Housing Support Grant (Scotland) Order 2002 No. 2002/171. – Enabling power: Housing (Scotland) Act 1987, ss. 191, 192. – Issued: 17.04.2002. Made: 27.03.2002. Coming into force: 01.04.2002. Effect: None. Territorial extent & classification: S. General. – 8p.: 30 cm. – 0 11 061348 1 *£2.00*

The Right to Purchase (Application Form) (Scotland) Order 2002 No. 2002/322. – Enabling power: Housing (Scotland) Act 1987, s. 63 (1). – Issued: 12.07.2002. Made: 26.06.2002. Coming into force: 30.09.2002. Effect: S.I. 2000/120 revoked. Territorial extent & classification: S. General. – 16p.: 30 cm. – 0 11 061516 6 *£3.00*

The Scottish Secure Tenancies (Abandoned Property) Order 2002 No. 2002/313. – Enabling power: Housing (Scotland) Act 2001, ss. 18 (4), 109 (2). – Issued: 15.07.2002. Made: 26.06.2002. Laid before the Scottish Parliament: 27.06.2002. Coming into force: 30.09.2002. Effect: None. Territorial extent & classification: S. General. – 4p.: 30 cm. – 0 11 061528 X *£1.75*

The Scottish Secure Tenancies (Exceptions) Amendment Regulations 2002 No. 2002/434. – Enabling power: Housing (Scotland) Act 2001, ss. 109 (2), sch. 1, para. 3 (2). – Issued: 04.10.2002. Made: 19.09.2002. Laid before the Scottish Parliament: 23.09.2002. Coming into force: 30.09.2002. Effect: S.S.I. 2002/314 amended. Territorial extent & classification: S. General. –This S.S.I. has been made in consequence of a defect in S.S.I. 2002/314 and is being issued free of charge to all known recipients of that instrument. – 2p.: 30 cm. – 0 11 061655 3 *£1.50*

The Scottish Secure Tenancies (Exceptions) Regulations 2002 No. 2002/314. – Enabling power: Housing (Scotland) Act 2001, ss. 109 (2), sch. 1, para. 3 (2). – Issued: 15.07.2002. Made: 26.06.2002. Laid before the Scottish Parliament: 27.06.2002. Coming into force: 30.09.2002. Effect: None. Territorial extent & classification: S. General. – 4p.: 30 cm. – 0 11 061526 3 *£1.75*

The Scottish Secure Tenancies (Proceedings for Possession) Regulations 2002 No. 2002/320. – Enabling power: Housing (Scotland) Act 2001, ss. 14 (4), 109 (2). – Issued: 15.07.2002. Made: 26.06.2002. Laid before the Scottish Parliament: 27.06.2002. Coming into force: 30.09.2002. Effect: None. Territorial extent & classification: S. General. – 8p.: 30 cm. – 0 11 061536 0 *£2.00*

The Scottish Secure Tenants (Compensation for Improvements) Regulations 2002 No. 2002/312. – Enabling power: Housing (Scotland) Act 2001, ss. 30, 109 (2). – Issued: 15.07.2002. Made: 26.06.2002. Laid before the Scottish Parliament: 27.06.2002. Coming into force: 30.09.2002. Effect: None. Territorial extent & classification: S. General. – 8p.: 30 cm. – 0 11 061529 8 *£2.00*

The Scottish Secure Tenants (Right to Repair) Regulations 2002 No. 2002/316. – Enabling power: Housing (Scotland) Act 2001, ss. 27, 109 (2). – Issued: 15.07.2002. Made: 26.06.2002. Laid before the Scottish Parliament: 27.06.2002. Coming into force: 30.09.2002. Effect: None. Territorial extent & classification: S. General. – 8p.: 30 cm. – 0 11 061538 7 *£2.00*

The Short Scottish Secure Tenancies (Notices) Regulations 2002 No. 2002/315. – Enabling power: Housing (Scotland) Act 2001, ss. 34 (4), 109 (2). – Issued: 15.07.2002. Made: 26.06.2002. Laid before the Scottish Parliament: 27.06.2002. Coming into force: 30.09.2002. Effect: None. Territorial extent & classification: S. General. – 8p.: 30 cm. – 0 11 061539 5 *£2.00*

The Short Scottish Secure Tenancies (Proceedings for Possession) Regulations 2002 No. 2002/319. – Enabling power: Housing (Scotland) Act 2001, ss. 36 (3), 109 (2). – Issued: 15.07.2002. Made: 26.06.2002. Laid before the Scottish Parliament: 27.06.2002. Coming into force: 30.09.2002. Effect: None. Territorial extent & classification: S. General. – 4p.: 30 cm. – 0 11 061537 9 *£1.75*

Investigatory powers

The Regulation of Investigatory Powers (Cancellation of Authorisations) (Scotland) Regulations 2002 No. 2002/207. – Enabling power: Regulation of Investigatory Powers (Scotland) Act 2000, s. 20 (4) (5) – Issued: 08.05.2002. Made: 26.04.2002. Laid before the Scottish Parliament: 27.04.2002. Coming into force: 20.05.2002. Effect: None. Territorial extent & classification: S. General. – 2p.: 30 cm. 0 11 061406 2 *£1.50*

The Regulation of Investigatory Powers (Juveniles) (Scotland) Order 2002 No. 2002/206. – Enabling power: Regulation of Investigatory Powers (Scotland) Act 2000, ss. 7 (2) (c) (4) (a) (b), 19 (8). – Issued: 08.05.2002. Made: 26.04.2002. Laid before Parliament: 29.04.2002. Coming into force: 20.05.2002. Effect: None. Territorial extent & classification: S. General. – 4p.: 30 cm. – 0 11 061408 9 *£1.75*

The Regulation of Investigatory Powers (Source Records) (Scotland) Regulations 2002 No. 2002/205. – Enabling power: Regulation of Investigatory Powers (Scotland) Act 2000, s. 7 (6) (d). – Issued: 08.05.2002. Made: 26.04.2002. Laid before the Scottish Parliament: 29.04.2002. Coming into force: 20.05.2002. Effect: None. Territorial extent & classification: S. General. – 4p.: 30 cm. – 0 11 061409 7 *£1.75*

Land drainage

The Environmental Impact Assessment (Scotland) Amendment Regulations 2002 No. 2002/324. – Enabling power: European Communities Act 1972, s. 2 (2) & Town & Country Planning (Scotland) Act 1997, s. 40. – Issued: 17.07.2002. Made: 27.06.2002. Laid before the Scottish Parliament: 28.06.2002. Coming into force: 23.09.2002. Effect: S.S.I. 1999/1 amended. Territorial extent & classification: S. General. – EC note: Implement in Scotland DIR 85/337/EEC (as amended by 97/11/EEC), in relation to applications to planning authorities to determine the revised conditions to which an existing minerals planning permission should be subjected. – 8p.: 30 cm. – 0 11 061558 1 *£2.00*

Land registration

The Land Registration (Scotland) Act 1979 (Commencement No. 16) Order 2002 No. 2002/432 (C.21). – Enabling power: Land Registration (Scotland) Act 1979, s. 30 (2). Bringing into force various provisions of the Act on 01.04.2003 in accord. with art. 2. – Issued: 30.09.2002. Made: 12.09.2002. Effect: None. Territorial extent & classification: S. General. – 2p.: 30 cm. – 0 11 061637 5 *£1.50*

Legal aid and advice

The Advice and Assistance (Assistance by Way of Representation) (Scotland) Amendment Regulations 2002 No. 2002/37. – Enabling power: Legal Aid (Scotland) Act 1986, ss. 9 (1) (2) (a) (dd) (de), 37 (1). – Issued: 22.02.2002. Made: 04.02.2002. Coming into force: 06.02.2002. Effect: S.I. 1997/3070 amended. Territorial extent & classification: S. General. – 4p.: 30 cm. – 0 11 059999 3 *£1.75*

The Advice and Assistance (Financial Conditions) (Scotland) (No. 2) Regulations 2002 No. 2002/329. – Enabling power: Legal Aid (Scotland) Act 1986, s. 36 (1) (2) (b) – Issued: 11.07.2002. Made: 24.06.02. Coming into force: 01.07.02. Effect: 1986 c. 47 & S.I. 1992/1587 amended. Territorial extent & classification: S. General. – 2p.: 30 cm. – 0 11 061508 5 *£1.50*

The Advice and Assistance (Financial Conditions) (Scotland) Regulations 2002 No. 2002/144. – Enabling power: Legal Aid (Scotland) Act 1986, ss. 11 (2), 36 (1) (2) (b), 37 (1). – Issued: 08.04.2002. Made: 19.03.2002. Coming into force: 08.04.2002. Effect: 1986 c. 47 amended & S.S.I. 2001/124 revoked with saving. Territorial extent & classification: S. General. – 4p.: 30 cm. – 0 11 061278 7 *£1.75*

The Advice and Assistance (Scotland) Amendment Regulations 2002 No. 2002/495. – Enabling power: Legal Aid (Scotland) Act 1986, ss. 12 (3), 37 (1). – Issued: 18.11.2002. Made: 06.11.2002. Laid before the Scottish Parliament: 07.11.2002. Coming into force: 01.12.2002. Effect: S.I. 1996/2447 amended. – 2p.: 30 cm. – 0 11 061710 X *£1.50*

The Civil Legal Aid (Financial Conditions) (Scotland) (No. 2) Regulations 2002 No. 2002/330. – Enabling power: Legal Aid (Scotland) Act 1986, s. 36 (1) (2) (b). – Issued: 11.07.2002. Made: 26.06.02. Coming into force: 01.07.02. Effect: 1986 c. 47 & S.S.I. 1996/1012 amended. Territorial extent & classification: S. General. – 2p.: 30 cm. – 0 11 061509 3 *£1.50*

The Civil Legal Aid (Financial Conditions) (Scotland) Regulations 2002 No. 2002/145. – Enabling power: Legal Aid (Scotland) Act 1986, s. 36 (1) (2) (b). – Issued: 08.04.2002. Made: 19.03.2002. Coming into force: 08.04.2002. Effect: 1986 c.47 amended & S.S.I. 2001/123 revoked with saving. Territorial extent & classification: S. General. – 4p.: 30 cm. – 0 11 061276 0 *£1.75*

The Civil Legal Aid (Scotland) Amendment (No. 2) Regulations 2002 No. 2002/254. – Enabling power: Legal Aid (Scotland) Act 1986, s. 36 (1) (2) (h) (3) (bb). – Issued: 12.06.2002. Made: 24.05.2002. Laid before the Scottish Parliament: 28.05.2002. Coming into force: 01.07.2002. Effect: S.I. 1996/2444 amended. Territorial extent & classification: S. General. – 2p.: 30 cm. – 0 11 061443 7 *£1.50*

The Civil Legal Aid (Scotland) Amendment Regulations 2002 No. 2002/88. – Enabling power: Legal Aid (Scotland) Act 1986, s. 36 (1) (2) (h) (3) (bb). – Issued: 20.03.2002. Made: 05.03.2002. Laid before the Scottish Parliament: 06.03.2002. Coming into force: 01.04.2002. Effect: S.I. 1996/2444 amended. Territorial extent & classification: S. General. – 2p.: 30 cm. – 0 11 061144 6 *£1.50*

The Civil Legal Aid (Scotland) (Fees) Amendment Regulations 2002 No. 2002/496. – Enabling power: Legal Aid (Scotland) Act 1986, s. 33 (2) (a) (3). – Issued: 18.11.2002. Made: 06.11.2002. Laid before the Scottish Parliament: 07.11.2002. Coming into force: 01.12.2002. Effect: S.I. 1989/1490 (S.119) amended. Territorial extent & classification: S. General. – 4p.: 30 cm. – 0 11 061703 7 *£1.75*

The Civil Legal Aid (Scotland) Regulations 2002 No. 2002/494. – Enabling power: Legal Aid (Scotland) Act 1986, ss. 17 (2B), 19 (4), 20 (4), 36 (1) (2) (a) (c) to (h) (3) (bb) (e) (f) (4), 37 (1) (3), 42. – Issued: 18.11.2002. Made: 06.11.2002. Laid before the Scottish Parliament: 07.11.2002. Coming into force: 01.12.2002. Effect: S.I. 1996/2444; 1997/727; 1998/725; S.S.I. 2000/182; 2001/82; 2002/88, 254 revoked (with saving). Territorial extent & classification: S. General. – 29p.: 30 cm. – 0 11 061700 2 *£6.00*

The Criminal Legal Aid (Fixed Payments) (Scotland) Amendment (No. 2) Regulations 2002 No. 2002/442. – Enabling power: Legal Aid (Scotland) Act 1986, ss. 33, 41A. – Issued: 04.10.2002. Made: 25.09.2002. Laid before the Scottish Parliament: 27.09.2002. Coming into force: 01.11.2002. Effect: S.I. 1999/491 amended. Territorial extent & classification: S. General. – 2p.: 30 cm. – 0 11 061653 7 *£1.50*

The Criminal Legal Aid (Fixed Payments) (Scotland) Amendment Regulations 2002 No. 2002/247. – Enabling power: Legal Aid (Scotland) Act 1986, ss. 33 (3A), (3AA), (3C) to (3H) (3K), 36 (1) (2) (a) (e). – Issued: 10.06.2002. Made: 21.05.2002. Laid before the Scottish Parliament: 23.05.2002. Coming into force: 17.06.2002. Effect: S.I. 1999/491 amended. Territorial extent & classification: S. General. – 4p.: 30 cm. – 0 11 061428 3 *£1.75*

The Criminal Legal Aid (Scotland) Amendment Regulations 2002 No. 2002/441. – Enabling power: Legal Aid (Scotland) Act 1986, s. 36 (1) (2) (a). – Issued: 04.10.2002. Made: 25.09.2002. Laid before the Scottish Parliament: 27.09.2002. Coming into force: 01.11.2002. Effect: S.I. 1996/2555 amended. Territorial extent & classification: S. General. – 2p.: 30 cm. – 0 11 061651 0 *£1.50*

The Criminal Legal Aid (Scotland) (Fees) Amendment (No. 2) Regulations 2002 No. 2002/440. – Enabling power: Legal Aid (Scotland) Act 1986, s. 33 (2) (a). – Issued: 04.10.2002. Made: 25.09.2002. Laid before the Scottish Parliament: 27.09.2002. Coming into force: 01.11.2002. Effect: S.I. 1989/1491 amended. Territorial extent & classification: S. General. – 2p.: 30 cm. – 0 11 061652 9 *£1.50*

The Criminal Legal Aid (Scotland) (Fees) Amendment Regulations 2002 No. 2002/246. – Enabling power: Legal Aid (Scotland) Act 1986, ss. 33 (2) (a) (3) (b). – Issued: 10.06.2002. Made: 21.05.2002. Laid before the Scottish Parliament: 23.05.2002. Coming into force: 17.06.2002. Effect: S.I. 1989/1491 amended. Territorial extent & classification: S. General. – 2p.: 30 cm. – 0 11 061429 1 *£1.50*

The Legal Aid (Scotland) Act 1986 Amendment Regulations 2002 No. 2002/532. – Enabling power: Legal Aid (Scotland) Act 1986, ss. 13 (4), 37 (1). – Issued: 10.12.2002. Made: 28.11.2002. Coming into force: 01.12.2002. Effect: 1986 c. 47 amended. Territorial extent & classification: S. General. – 2p.: 30 cm. – 0 11 061739 8 *£1.50*

Legal services

The Scottish Legal Services Ombudsman (Compensation) (Prescribed Amount) Order 2002 No. 2002/32. – Enabling power: Law Reform (Miscellaneous Provisions) (Scotland) Act 1990, s. 34A (10). – Issued: 11.02.2002. Made: 29.01.2002 Laid before the Scottish Parliament: 31.01.2002. Coming into force: 28.02.2002. Effect: None. Territorial extent & classification: S. General. – 2p.: 30 cm. – 0 11 059985 3 *£1.50*

Licences and licensing

The Civic Government (Scotland) Act 1982 (Licensing of Houses in Multiple Occupation) Amendment Order 2002 No. 2002/161. – Enabling power: Civic Government (Scotland) Act 1982, s. 44 (1) (b) (2). – Issued: 24.04.2002. Made: 26.03.2002. Coming into force: 01.04.2002. Effect: S.S.I. 2000/177 amended. Territorial extent & classification: S. General. – 4p.: 30 cm. – 0 11 061365 1 *£1.75*

The Taxi Drivers' Licences (Carrying of Guide Dogs and Hearing Dogs) (Scotland) Amendment Regulations 2002 No. 2002/521. – Enabling power: Civic Government (Scotland) Act 1982, s. 20 (1) (2A). – Issued: 09.12.2002. Made: 27.11.2002. Laid before the Scottish Parliament: 27.11.2002. Coming into force: 02.12.2002. Effect: S.S.I. 2002/500 amended. Territorial extent & classification: S. General. – 4p.: 30 cm. – 0 11 061730 4 *£1.75*

The Taxi Drivers' Licences (Carrying of Guide Dogs and Hearing Dogs) (Scotland) Regulations 2002 No. 2002/500. – Enabling power: Civic Government (Scotland) Act 1982, s. 20 (1) (2A). – Issued: 19.11.2002. Made: 11.11.2002. Laid before the Scottish Parliament: 11.11.2002. Coming into force: 02.12.2002, 03.03.2003, in accord. with reg. 1. Effect: None. Territorial extent & classification: S. General. – 8p.: 30 cm. – 0 11 061711 8 *£2.00*

Local government

The Aberdeen City Council and Aberdeenshire Council Boundaries (Blackburn) Amendment Order 2002 No. 2002/154. – Enabling power: Local Government (Scotland) Act 1973, s.17 (2). – Issued: 17.04.2002. Made: 25.03.2002. Laid before the Scottish Parliament: 26.03.2002. Coming into force: 01.06.2002. Effect: None. Territorial extent & classification: S. General. – 8p., col. map: 30 cm. – 0 11 061351 1 *£2.00*

The Argyll and Bute Council and West Dunbartonshire Council Boundaries (Ardoch Sewage Works) Amendment Order 2002 No. 2002/155. – Enabling power: Local Government (Scotland) Act 1973, s.17 (2). – Issued: 17.04.2002. Made: 25.03.2002. Laid before the Scottish Parliament: 26.03.2002. Coming into force: 01.06.2002. Effect: None. Territorial extent & classification: S. General. – 8p., col. map: 30 cm. – 0 11 061350 3 *£2.00*

The City of Edinburgh Council and West Lothian Council Boundaries (West Farm, Broxburn) Amendment Order 2002 No. 2002/157. – Enabling power: Local Government (Scotland) Act 1973, s.17 (2). – Issued: 17.04.2002. Made: 25.03.2002. Coming into force: 26.03.2002. Effect: None. territorial extent & classification: S. General. – 8p., col. map: 30 cm. – 0 11 061352 X *£2.00*

The Ethical Standards in Public Life etc. (Scotland) Act 2000 (Stipulated Time Limit) Order 2002 No. 2002/55. – Enabling power: Ethical Standards in Public Life etc. (Scotland) Act 2000, s. 3 (2). – Issued: 06.03.2002. Made: 11.02.2002. Laid before the Scottish Parliament: 12.02.2002. Coming into force: 11.03.2002. Effect: None. Territorial extent and classification: S. General. – 2p.: 30 cm. – 0 11 061092 X *£1.50*

The Glasgow City Council and Renfrewshire Council Boundaries (Braehead) Amendment Order 2002 No. 2002/156. – Enabling power: Local Government (Scotland) Act 1973, s.17 (2). – Issued: 17.04.2002. Made: 25.03.2002. Laid before the Scottish Parliament: 26.03.2002. Coming into force: 01.06.2002. Effect: None. Territorial extent & classification: S. General. – 8p., col. map: 30 cm. – 0 11 061349 X *£2.00*

The Local Authorities Etc. (Allowances) (Scotland) Amendment Regulations 2002 No. 2002/15. – Enabling power: Local Government (Scotland) Act 1973, ss. 45 (4), 47, 235 (1) & Local Government and Housing Act 1989, ss. 18, 190 (1). – Issued: 04.02.2002. Made: 23.01.2002. Laid before the Scottish Parliament: 24.01.2002. Coming into force: 15.02.2002. Effect: S.I. 1995/912 amended & 1998/3219 (S.197) revoked. Territorial extent & classification: S. General. – 4p.: 30 cm. – 0 11 059980 2 *£1.75*

The Local Government Finance (Scotland) (No. 2) Order 2002 No. 2002/230. – Enabling power: Local Government Finance Act 1992, sch. 12, paras. 1, 9 (4). – Issued: 12.07.2002. Made: 14.05.2002. Laid before the Scottish Parliament: 15.05.2002. Coming into force: 21.06.2002. Effect: S.S.I. 2002/70 amended. Territorial extent & classification: S. General. – 8p.: 30 cm. – 0 11 061524 7 *£2.00*

The Local Government Finance (Scotland) Order 2002 No. 2002/70. – Enabling power: Local Government Finance Act 1992, sch. 12, paras. 1, 9 (4). – Issued: 11.03.2002. Made: 22.01.2002. Laid before the Scottish Parliament: 24.01.2002. Coming into force: 01.02.2002. Effect: S.S.I. 2001/260 amended. Territorial extent & classification: S. General. – 8p.: 30 cm. – 0 11 061096 2 *£2.00*

Marriage

The Births, Deaths, Marriages and Divorces (Fees) (Scotland) Amendment Regulations 2002 No. 2002/390. – Enabling power: Registration of Births, Deaths and Marriages (Scotland) Act 1965, ss. 28A (4), 37 (2) (3), 38 (2) (3), 40 (1), 43 (8), 47, 54 (1), 56 & Marriage (Scotland) Act 1977, ss. 3 (1), 25, 26. – Issued: 05.09.2002. Made: 26.08.2002. Laid before the Scottish Parliament: 28.08.2002. Coming into force: 01.10.2002. Effect: S.I. 1998/643 amended. Territorial extent & classification: S. General. – 4p.: 30 cm. – 0 11 061587 5 *£1.75*

The Marriage (Approval of Places) (Scotland) Regulations 2002 No. 2002/260. – Enabling power: Marriage (Scotland) Act 1977, s. 18A (1) (2). – Issued: 10.06.2002. Made: 30.05.2002. Coming into force: 10.06.2002. Effect: None. Territorial extent & classification: S. General. – 8p.: 30 cm. – 0 11 061437 2 *£2.00*

The Marriage (Scotland) Act 2002 (Commencement) Order 2002 No. 2002/184 (C.13). – Enabling power: Marriage (Scotland) Act 2002, s. 2 (2). Bringing into force various provisions of the 2002 Act on 25.04.2002, in accord. with art. 2. – Issued: 24.04.2002. Made: 11.04.2002. Effect: None. Territorial extent & classification: S. General. – 2p.: 30 cm. – 0 11 061373 2 £1.50

National assistance services

The National Assistance (Sums for Personal Requirements) (Scotland) Regulations 2002 No. 2002/85. – Enabling power: National Assistance Act 1948, s. 22 (4). – Issued: 21.03.2002. Made: 04.03.2002. Laid before the Scottish Parliament: 06.03.2002. Coming into force: 08.04.2002. Effect: None. Territorial extent & classification: S. General. – 4p.: 30 cm. – 0 11 061166 7 £1.75

National Health Service

The National Health Service (Charges for Drugs and Appliances) (Scotland) Amendment Regulations 2002 No. 2002/100. – Enabling power: National Health Service (Scotland) Act 1978, ss. 19 (2), 25 (2), 27 (2), 69 (1) (2), 105 (7), 108 (1). – Issued: 28.03.2002. Made: 06.03.2002. Laid before the Scottish Parliament: 08.03.2002. Coming into force: 01.04.2002. Effect: S.S.I. 2001/430 amended. Territorial extent & classification: S. General. – 8p.: 30 cm. – 0 11 061230 2 £2.00

The National Health Service (Clinical Negligence and Other Risks Indemnity Scheme) (Scotland) Amendment Regulations 2002 No. 2002/239. – Enabling power: National Health Service (Scotland) Act 1978, ss. 2 (5), 85B, 105 (7), 108 (1). – Issued: 10.06.2002. Made: 20.05.2002. Laid before the Scottish Parliament: 22.05.2002. Coming into force: 14.06.2002. Effect: S.S.I. 2000/54 amended. Territorial extent & classification: S. General. – 4p.: 30 cm. – 0 11 061435 6 £1.75

The National Health Service (General Dental Services and Dental Charges) (Scotland) Amendment Regulations 2002 No. 2002/99. – Enabling power: National Health Service (Scotland) Act 1978, ss. 2 (5), 25 (2) (2B), 70 (1A), 71 (1), 71A, 105 (7), 108 (1). – Issued: 28.03.2002. Made: 06.03.2002. Laid before the Scottish Parliament: 08.03.2002. Coming into force: 01.04.2002. Effect: S.I. 1989/363; 1996/177 amended. Territorial extent & classification: S. General. – 4p.: 30 cm. – 0 11 061229 9 £1.75

The National Health Service (General Dental Services) (Scotland) Amendment (No. 2) Regulations 2002 No. 2002/268. – Enabling power: National Health Service (Scotland) Act 1978, ss. 2 (5), 25 (2), 105 (7), 108 (1). – Issued: 21.06.2002. Made: 05.06.2002. Laid before the Scottish Parliament: 07.06.2002. Coming into force: 01.08.2002. Effect: S.I. 1996/177 amended. Territorial extent & classification: S. General. – 2p.: 30 cm. – 0 11 061444 5 £1.50

The National Health Service (General Dental Services) (Scotland) Amendment Regulations 2002 No. 2002/192. – Enabling power: National Health Service (Scotland) Act 1978, ss. 2 (5), 25 (2), 105 (7), 108 (1). – Issued: 26.04.2002. Made: 16.04.2002. Laid before the Scottish Parliament: 18.04.2002. Coming into force: 10.05.2002. Effect: S.I. 1996/177 amended. Territorial extent & classification: S. General. – 2p.: 30 cm. – 0 11 061384 8 £1.50

The National Health Service (General Medical Services and Pharmaceutical Services) (Scotland) Amendment (No. 2) Regulations 2002 No. 2002/153. – Enabling power: National Health Service (Scotland) Act 1978, ss. 2 (5), 19, 27 (2), 28 (1), 28A, 105 (7), 106 (a), 108 (1), sch. 1, para. 11 (c). – Issued: 16.04.2002. Made: 22.03.2002. Laid before the Scottish Parliament: 26.03.2002. Coming into force: 31.03.2002. Effect: S.S.I. 2002/111 amended. Territorial extent & classification: S. General. –This S.S.I. has been made in consequence of defects in S.S.I. 2002/111 (ISBN 0110611942) and is being issued free of charge to all known recipients of that instrument. – 4p.: 30 cm. – 0 11 061336 8 £1.75

The National Health Service (General Medical Services and Pharmaceutical Services) (Scotland) Amendment Regulations 2002 No. 2002/111. – Enabling power: National Health Service (Scotland) Act 1978, ss. 2 (5), 19, 27 (2), 28 (1), 28A, 105 (7), 106 (a), 108 (1), sch. 1, para. 11 (c). – Issued: 28.03.2002. Made: 06.03.2002. Laid before the Scottish Parliament: 08.03.2002. Coming into force: 01.04.2002. Effect: S.I. 1995/414, 416 amended. Territorial extent & classification: S. General. – 8p.: 30 cm. – 0 11 061194 2 £2.00

The National Health Service (General Medical Services) (Scotland) Amendment Regulations 2002 No. 2002/438. – Enabling power: National Health Service (Scotland) Act 1978, ss. 19, 105 (7), 108 (1). – Issued: 03.10.2002. Made: 24.09.2002. Laid before the Scottish Parliament: 26.09.2002. Coming into force: 31.10.2002. Effect: S.I. 1995/416 amended. Territorial extent & classification: S. General. – 4p.: 30 cm. – 0 11 061648 0 £1.75

The National Health Service (Optical Charges and Payments) and (General Ophthalmic Services) (Scotland) Amendment Regulations 2002 No. 2002/86. – Enabling power: National Health Service (Scotland) Act 1978, ss. 26. 70 (1), 73 (a), 74 (a), 105 (7), 108 (1), sch. 11, paras. 2, 2A. – Issued: 21.03.2002. Made: 05.03.2002. Laid before the Scottish Parliament: 06.03.2002. Coming into force: 01.04.2002, 09.04.2002, in acc. with reg. 1 (2) (3). Effect: S.I. 1998/642 amended (09.04.2002). Territorial extent & classification: S. General. – 8p.: 30 cm. – 0 11 061165 9 £2.00

The National Health Service (Optical Charges and Payments) (Scotland) Amendment (No. 2) Regulations 2002 No. 2002/224. – Enabling power: National Health Service (Scotland) Act 1978, ss. 26, 70 (1), 105 (7), 108 (1), sch. 11, paras. 2, 2A. – Issued: 21.05.2002. Made: 08.05.2002. Laid before the Scottish Parliament: 10.05.2002. Coming into force: 03.06.2002. Effect: S.I. 1998/642 amended. Territorial extent & classification: S. General. – 4p.: 30 cm. – 0 11 061422 4 £1.75

The National Health Service (Optical Charges and Payments) (Scotland) Amendment Regulations 2002 No. 2002/17. – Enabling power: National Health Service (Scotland) Act 1978, ss. 26, 70 (1), 105 (7), 108 (1), sch. 11, paras. 2, 2A. – Issued: 06.02.2002. Made: 22.01.2002. Laid before the Scottish Parliament: 25.01.2002. Coming into force: 15.02.2002. Effect: S.I. 1998/642 amended. Territorial extent & classification: S. General. – 2p.: 30 cm. – 0 11 059982 9 £1.50

The National Waiting Times Centre Board (Scotland) Order 2002 No. 2002/305. – Enabling power: National Health Service (Scotland) Act 1978, ss. 2 (1) (b) (1A) (1B) (1C), 105 (7). – Issued: 11.07.2002. Made: 24.06.02. Laid before the Scottish Parliament: 25.06.02. Coming into force: 27.06.02. Effect: 1978 c. 29 amended & S.I. 1974/468 modified. Territorial extent & classification: S. General. – [12]p.: 30 cm. – 0 11 061512 3 £2.50

The NHS Education for Scotland Order 2002 No. 2002/103. – Enabling power: National Health Service (Scotland) Act 1978, ss. 2 (1) (b) (1A) (1B) (1C), 105 (6) (7). – Issued: 28.03.2002. Made: 05.03.2002. Laid before the Scottish Parliament: 08.03.2002. Coming into force: 31.03.2002. & 01.04.2002. in accord. with art. 1 (2) (3). Effect: S.I. 1993/577 revoked (01.04.2002.). Territorial extent & classification: S. General. – 12p.: 30 cm. – 0 11 061186 1 £2.50

The NHS Quality Improvement Scotland Order 2002 No. 2002/534. – Enabling power: National Health Service (Scotland) Act 1978, ss. 2 (1) (b) (1A) (1B) (1C), 105 (6) (7) – Issued: 12.12.2002. Made: 30.11.2002. Laid before the Scottish Parliament: 02.12.2002. Coming into force: 01.01.2003 & 02.01.2003 in accordance with art. 1 (2) (3). Effect: S.I. 1999/726 revoked and S.S.I. 2000/47 revoked (02.01.2003.). Territorial extent & classification: S. General. – [12]p.: 30 cm. – 0 11 061749 5 £2.50

The NHS Quality Improvement Scotland (Transfer of Officers) Regulations 2002 No. 2002/535. – Enabling power: National Health Service (Scotland) Act 1978, ss. 105 (7), 108 (1), sch. 1, para. 7A, sch. 5, para. 7B. – Issued: 12.12.2002. Made: 30.11.2002. Laid before the Scottish Parliament: 02.12.2002. Coming into force: 01.01.2003. Effect: None. Territorial extent & classification: S. General. – 4p.: 30 cm. – 0 11 061748 7 £1.75

The Road Traffic (NHS Charges) Amendment (No. 2) (Scotland) Regulations 2002 No. 2002/528. – Enabling power: Road Traffic (NHS Charges) Act 1999, ss. 3 (2) (4), 16 (2) (a) (b). – Issued: 10.12.2002. Made: 29.11.2002. Laid before the Scottish Parliament: 02.12.2002. Coming into force: 01.01.2003. Effect: S.I. 1999/785 amended (in relation to Scotland). – 4p.: 30 cm. – 0 11 061738 X £1.75

The Road Traffic (NHS Charges) Amendment (Scotland) Regulations 2002 No. 2002/56. – Enabling power: Road Traffic (NHS Charges) Act 1999, ss. 3 (2) (4), 16 (2) (a) (b), 17. – Issued: 01.03.2002. Made: 12.02.2002. Laid before the Scottish Parliament: 13.02.2002. Coming into force: 14.02.2002. Effect: S.I. 1999/785 amended (in relation to Scotland). – 4p.: 30 cm. – 0 11 061059 8 £1.75

The Scottish Council for Postgraduate Medical and Dental Education and NHS Education for Scotland (Transfer of Staff) Regulations 2002 No. 2002/105. – Enabling power: National Health Service (Scotland) Act 1978, ss. 105 (7), 108 (1), sch. 1, para. 7A. – Issued: 28.03.2002. Made: 05.03.2002. Laid before the Scottish Parliament: 08.03.2002. Coming into force: 31.03.2002. Effect: None. Territorial extent & classification: S. General. – 4p.: 30 cm. – 0 11 061187 X £1.75

Nurses, midwives and health visitors

The Nurses, Midwives and Health Visitors (Professional Conduct) (Amendment) (No. 2) Rules 2002 Approval (Scotland) Order 2002 No. 2002/142. – Enabling power: Nurses, Midwives and Health Visitors Act 1997, s. 19 (5). – Issued: 12.04.2002. Made: 19.03.2002. Coming into force: 31.03.2002. Effect: S.I. 1993/893 amended (in relation to Scotland). Territorial extent and classification: S. General. – 8p.: 30 cm. – 0 11 061310 4 £2.00

The Nurses, Midwives and Health Visitors (Professional Conduct) (Amendment) Rules 2002 Approval (Scotland) Order 2002 No. 2002/59. – Enabling power: Nurses, Midwives and Health Visitors Act 1997, s. 19 (5). – Issued: 01.03.2002. Made: 08.02.2002. Coming into force: 18.02.2002. Effect: S.I. 1993/893 amended. Territorial extent and classification: S. General. – 4p.: 30 cm. – 0 11 061058 X £1.75

Pensions

The Local Government Pension Scheme (Scotland) Amendment Regulations 2002 No. 2002/311. – Enabling power: Superannuation Act 1972, ss. 7, 12. – Issued: 12.07.2002. Made: 25.06.2002. Laid before the Scottish Parliament: 27.06.2002. Coming into force: 23.09.2002. Effect: S.I. 1998/366 amended. Territorial extent & classification: S. General. – 4p.: 30 cm. – 0 11 061518 2 £1.75

The Teachers' Superannuation (Scotland) Amendment Regulations 2002 No. 2002/288. – Enabling power: Superannuation Act 1972, ss. 9, 12, sch. 3. – Issued: 24.06.2002. Made: 10.06.2002. Laid before the Scottish Parliament: 10.06.2002. Coming into force: 01.07.2002. Effect: S.I. 1992/280 amended. Territorial extent & classification: S. General. – 8p.: 30 cm. – 0 11 061474 7 £2.00

Pesticides

The Pesticides (Maximum Residue Levels in Crops, Food and Feeding Stuffs) (Scotland) Amendment (No. 2) Regulations 2002 No. 2002/489. – Enabling power: European Communities Act 1972, s. 2 (2). – Issued: 28.11.2002. Made: 04.11.2002. Laid before the Scottish Parliament: 06.11.2002. Coming into force: 30.11.2002. Effect: S.S.I. 2000/22; 2001/84, 221, 271, 435; 2002/271 amended. Territorial extent & classification: S. General. – 118, [1]p.: 30 cm. – 0 11 061698 7 £10.50

The Plant Protection Products Amendment (No. 2) (Scotland) Regulations 2002 No. 2002/279. – Enabling power: European Communities Act 1972, s. 2 (2). – Issued: 20.06.2002. Made: 06.06.2002. Laid before the Scottish Parliament: 07.06.2002. Coming into force: 01.07.2002. Effect: S.I. 1995/887 amended in relation to Scotland & S.S.I. 2001/454; 2002/117 amended. Territorial extent & classification: S. General. – 4p.: 30 cm. – 0 11 061453 4 £1.75

The Plant Protection Products Amendment (No. 3) (Scotland) Regulations 2002 No. 2002/537. – Enabling power: European Communities Act 1972, s. 2 (2). – Issued: 12.12.2002. Made: 02.12.2002. Laid before the Scottish Parliament: 02.12.2002. Coming into force: 31.12.2002. Effect: S.I. 1995/887 amended in relation to Scotland. Territorial extent & classification: S. General. – 4p.: 30 cm. – 0 11 061741 X £1.75

The Plant Protection Products Amendment (Scotland) Regulations 2002 No. 2002/117. – Enabling power: European Communities Act 1972, s. 2 (2). – Issued: 08.04.2002. Made: 05.03.2002. Laid before the Scottish Parliament: 08.03.2002. Coming into force: 30.03.2002. Effect: S.I. 1995/887; 1997/7 amended in relation to Scotland. Territorial extent & classification: S. General. – 4p.: 30 cm. – 0 11 061280 9 £1.75

Plant health

The Plant Health (Great Britain) (Amendment) (Scotland) Order 2002 No. 2002/164. – Enabling power: European Communities Act 1972, s. 2 (2). – Issued: 16.04.2002. Made: 27.03.2002. Laid before the Scottish Parliament: 28.03.2002. Coming into force: 01.04.2002. Effect: S.I. 1993/1320 amended in relation in Scotland; S.S.I. 2001/249 amended. Territorial extent & classification: S. General. – EC note: This Order amends S.I. 1993/1320 in relation to Scotland so as to implement certain elements of Commission Directives 2002/28/EC (O.J. No. L 77 20.3.02, p.23) and 2002/29/EC – 4p.: 30 cm. – 0 11 061320 1 £1.75

The Plant Health (Phytophthora ramorum) (Scotland) (No. 2) Order 2002 No. 2002/483. – Enabling power: Plant Health Act 1967, ss. 2, 3 (1) (2) (b) (3) (4), 4 (1) (b). – Issued: 05.11.2002. Made: 29.10.2002. Laid before the Scottish Parliament: 29.10.2002. Coming into force: 01.11.2002. Effect: S.S .I. 2002/223 revoked with saving. Territorial extent & classification: S. General. – 8p.: 30 cm. – 0 11 061688 X £2.00

The Plant Health (Phytophthora ramorum) (Scotland) Order 2002 No. 2002/223. – Enabling power: Plant Health Act 1967, ss. 2, 3 (1) (2) (b) (4), 4 (1) (b). – Issued: 21.05.2002. Made: 09.05.2002. Laid before the Scottish Parliament: 10.05.2002. Coming into force: 13.05.2002. Effect: None. Territorial extent & classification: S. General. – 8p.: 30 cm. – 0 11 061423 2 £2.00

The Potatoes Originating in Egypt (Scotland) Amendment Regulations 2002 No. 2002/518. – Enabling power: European Communities Act 1972, s. 2 (2). – Issued: 05.12.2002. Made: 21.11.2002. Laid before the Scottish Parliament: 22.11.2002. Coming into force: 13.12.2002. Effect: S.S.I. 2001/421 amended. Territorial extent and classification: S. General. – 2p.: 30 cm. – 0 11 061725 8 £1.50

Police

The Combined Police Area Amalgamation Schemes 1995 Amendment (No. 2) (Scotland) Order 2002 No. 2002/458. – Enabling power: Police (Scotland) Act 1967, ss. 20, 21 (1) (b). – Issued: 16.10.2002. Made: 07.10.2002. Laid before the Scottish Parliament: 09.10.2002. Coming into force: 08.10.2002. Effect: S.I. 1995/2638, 2639, 2640, 2641, 2642, 2643 amended. Territorial extent & classification: S. General. – 12p.: 30 cm. – 0 11 061662 6 £2.50

The Combined Police Area Amalgamation Schemes 1995 (Amendment) (Scotland) Order 2002 No. 2002/140. – Enabling power: Police (Scotland) Act 1967, ss. 20, 21 (1) (b). – Issued: 12.04.2002. Made: 22.03.2002. Laid before the Scottish Parliament: 22.03.2002. Coming into force: 31.03.2002. Effect: S.I. 1995/2638, 2639, 2640, 2641, 2642, 2643 amended. Territorial extent & classification: S. General. – 12p.: 30 cm. – 0 11 061313 9 £2.50

The Police Act 1997 (Commencement No. 10) (Scotland) Order 2002 No. 2002/124 (C.7). – Enabling power: Police Act 1997, s. 135 (1) (2) (a). Bringing into operation various provisions of the 1997 Act on 11.03.2002. & 25.04.2002. & 31.07.2002. – Issued: 28.03.2002. Made: 11.03.2002. Effect: None. Territorial extent & classification: S. General. – 4p.: 30 cm. – 0 11 061233 7 £1.75

The Police Act 1997 (Criminal Records) (Registration) (Scotland) Regulations 2002 No. 2002/23. – Enabling power: Police Act 1997, s. 120 (3). – Issued: 06.02.2002. Made: 23.01.2002. Laid before the Scottish Parliament: 28.01.2002. Coming into force: 18.02.2002. Effect: None. Territorial extent & classification: S. General. – 4p.: 30 cm. – 0 11 059984 5 £1.75

The Police Act 1997 (Criminal Records) (Scotland) Regulations 2002 No. 2002/143. – Enabling power: Police Act 1997, ss. 112 (1) (b), 113 (1) (b), 114 (1) (b), 115 (1) (b) (10), 116 (1) (b), 118 (3), 125 (5). – Issued: 22.04.2002. Made: 22.03.2002. Laid before the Scottish Parliament: 22.03.2002. Coming into force: 28.04.2002, 29.07.2002, in accord. with reg. 1 (2). Effect: None. Territorial extent & classification: S. General. – 12p.: 30 cm. – 0 11 061358 9 £2.50

The Police Act 1997 (Enhanced Criminal Record Certificates) (Protection of Vulnerable Adults) (Scotland) Regulations 2002 No. 2002/217. – Enabling power: Police Act 1997, s. 115 (4). – Issued: 21.05.2002. Made: 02.05.2002. Coming into force: 03.05.2002. Effect: None. Territorial extent & classification: S. General. – 4p.: 30 cm. – With correction slip – 0 11 061413 5 £1.75

The Police and Fire Services (Finance) (Scotland) Act 2001 (Commencement) Order 2002 No. 2002/84 (C.5). – Enabling power: Police and Fire Services (Finance) (Scotland) Act 2001, s. 3 (2). Bringing into force various provisions of the 2001 Act on 11.03.2002. – Issued: 21.03.2002. Made: 04.03.2002. Effect: None. Territorial extent & classification: S. General. – 2p.: 30 cm. – 0 11 061164 0 *£1.50*

The Police Grant (Scotland) Order 2002 No. 2002/116. – Enabling power: Police (Scotland) Act 1967, s. 32 (3) (5). – Issued: 08.04.2002. Made: 07.03.2002. Laid before the Scottish Parliament: 08.03.2002. Coming into force: 01.04.2002. Effect: None. Territorial extent & classification: S. General. – 4p.: 30 cm. – 0 11 061258 2 *£1.75*

The Police Reform Act 2002 (Commencement No. 2) (Scotland) Order 2002 No. 2002/420 (C.20). – Enabling power: Police Reform Act 2002, s. 108 (5). Bringing into operation various provisions of the 2002 Act on 01.10.2002. – Issued: 20.09.2002. Made: 10.09.2002. Effect: None. Territorial extent & classification: S. General. – 2p.: 30 cm. – 0 11 061625 1 *£1.50*

Prisons

The Discontinuance of Legalised Police Cells (Ayr) Rules 2002 No. 2002/472. – Enabling power: Prisons (Scotland) Act 1989, ss. 14, 39. – Issued: 01.11.2002. Made: 22.10.2002. Laid before the Scottish Parliament: 25.10.2002. Coming into force: 30.11.2002. Effect: S.R. & O. 1927/448 revoked. Territorial extent & classification: S. General. – 4p.: 30 cm. – 0 11 061686 3 *£1.75*

The Prisons and Young Offenders Institutions (Scotland) Amendment Rules 2002 No. 2002/107. – Enabling power: Prisons (Scotland) Act 1989, s. 39. – Issued: 11.04.2002. Made: 06.03.2002. Laid before the Scottish Parliament: 08.04.2002. Coming into force: 01.04.2002. Effect: S.I. 1994/1931 amended. – 12p.: 30 cm. – 0 11 060990 5 *£2.50*

Proceeds of Crime

The Proceeds of Crime Act 2002 (Cash Searches: Constables in Scotland: Code of Practice) Order 2002 No. 2002/569. – Enabling power: Proceeds of Crime Act 2002, s. 293 (4). – Issued: 14.01.2003. Made: 19.12.2002. Coming into force: In accord. with art. 1. Effect: None. Territorial extent & classification: S. General. – 4p.: 30 cm. 0 11 061855 6 *£1.75*

Public finance and accountability

The Budget (Scotland) 2002 Amendment Order 2002 No. 2002/542. – Enabling power: Budget (Scotland) Act 2002, s. 7 (1). – Issued: 23.12.2002. Made: 28.11.2002. Coming into force: 29.11.2002. Effect: 2002 asp 7 amended. Territorial extent & classification: S. General– 4p.: 30 cm. – 0 11 061805 X *£1.75*

The Budget (Scotland) Act 2001 (Amendment) Order 2002 No. 2002/134. – Enabling power: Budget (Scotland) Act 2001, s. 7 (1). – Issued: 28.03.2002. Made: 12.03.2002. Coming into force: 13.03.2002. Effect: 2001 asp 4 amended. Territorial extent & classification: S. General– 8p.: 30 cm. – 0 11 061235 3 *£2.00*

The Public Finance and Accountability (Scotland) Act 2000 (Access to Documents and Information) (Relevant Persons) Order 2002 No. 2002/78. – Enabling power: Public Finance and Accountability (Scotland) Act 2000, s. 24 (5). – Issued: 20.03.2002. Made: 28.02.2002. Laid before the Scottish Parliament: 04.03.2002. Coming into force: 01.04.2002. Effect: None. Territorial extent & classification: S. General. – 4p.: 30 cm. – 0 11 061123 3 *£1.75*

The Public Finance and Accountability (Scotland) Act 2000 (Consequential Modifications) Order 2002 No. 2002/176. – Enabling power: Public Finance and Accountability (Scotland) Act 2000, s. 26 (2). – Issued: 17.04.2002. Made: 27.03.2002. Coming into force: 01.04.2002. Effect: 1968 c. 4; 1969 c. 51; 1978 c. 29; 1990 c. 19; 1992 c. 14 amended. Territorial extent & classification: S. General. – 4p.: 30 cm. – 0 11 061347 3 *£1.75*

The Public Finance and Accountability (Scotland) Act 2000 (Economy, Efficiency and Effectiveness Examinations) (Specified bodies etc.) Order 2002 No. 2002/77. – Enabling power: Public Finance and Accountability (Scotland) Act 2000, s. 23 (2) (b) (3). – Issued: 20.03.2002. Made: 28.02.2002. Laid before the Scottish Parliament: 04.03.2002. Coming into force: 01.04.2002. Effect: None. Territorial extent & classification: S. General. – 4p.: 30 cm. – 0 11 061122 5 *£1.75*

Public health

The Control of Noise (Codes of Practice for Construction and Open Sites) (Scotland) Order 2002 No. 2002/104. – Enabling power: Control of Pollution Act 1974, ss. 71, 104 (1). – Issued: 08.04.2002. Made: 07.03.2002. Laid before the Scottish Parliament: 08.03.2002. Coming into force: 29.03.2002. Effect: S.I. 1985/145 revoked & S.I. 1987/1730 revoked in relation to Scotland. Territorial extent & classification: S. General. – 4p.: 30 cm. – 0 11 061261 2 *£1.75*

Public health: Contamination of food

The Food Protection (Emergency Prohibitions) (Amnesic, Paralytic and Diarrhetic Shellfish Poisoning) (Orkney) (Scotland) Revocation Order 2002 No. 2002/197. – Enabling power: Food and Environment Protection Act 1985, s. 1 (1) (2). – Issued: 02.05.2002. Made: 19.04.2002. Laid before the Scottish Parliament: 23.04.2002. Coming into force: 19.04.2002 at 1600 hours, in accord. with art. 1. Effect: S.S.I. 2001/282, 463 revoked. Territorial extent and classification: S. General. – 2p.: 30 cm. – 0 11 061390 2 *£1.50*

The Food Protection (Emergency Prohibitions) (Amnesic Shellfish Poisoning) (Orkney) (No. 2) (Scotland) Order 2002 No. 2002/353. – Enabling power: Food and Environment Protection Act 1985, ss. 1 (1) (2), 24 (3). – Issued: 01.08.2002. Made: 23.07.2002. Laid before the Scottish Parliament: 25.07.02002. Coming into foce: 23.07.2002 at 1700 hours, in accord. with art. 1(1). Effect: None. Territorial extent and classification: S. General. – 4p.: 30 cm. – 0 11 061577 8 *£1.75*

The Food Protection (Emergency Prohibitions) (Amnesic Shellfish Poisoning) (Orkney) (No. 2) (Scotland) Revocation Order 2002 No. 2002/403. – Enabling power: Food and Environment Protection Act 1985, s. 1 (1) (2). – Issued: 11.09.2002. Made: 30.08.2002. Laid before the Scottish Parliament: 03.09.02002. Coming into force: 1600 hours on 30.08.2002, in accord. with art. 1. Effect: S.S.I. 2002/353 revoked. Territorial extent and classification: S. General. – 2p.: 30 cm. – 0 11 061603 0 *£1.50*

The Food Protection (Emergency Prohibitions) (Amnesic Shellfish Poisoning) (Orkney) (No. 3) (Scotland) Order 2002 No. 2002/408. – Enabling power: Food and Environment Protection Act 1985, ss. 1 (1) (2), 24 (3). – Issued: 18.09.2002. Made: 04.09.2002. Laid before the Scottish Parliament: 05.09.02002. Coming into force: 04.09.2002 at 1700 hours, in accord. with art. 1(1). Effect: None. Territorial extent & classification: S. General. –Revoked by S.S.I. 2003/197 (ISBN 0110622936) at 1500 hours on 13.03.2003. Partially revoked by S.S.I. 2002/558 (ISBN 0110618106) at 1200 hours on 17.12.2002. – 4p.: 30 cm. – 0 11 061618 9 *£1.75*

The Food Protection (Emergency Prohibitions) (Amnesic Shellfish Poisoning) (Orkney) (No. 3) (Scotland) Partial Revocation Order 2002 No. 2002/558. – Enabling power: Food and Environment Protection Act 1985, ss. 1 (1) (2), 24 (3). – Issued: 10.01.2002. Made: 17.12.2002. Laid before the Scottish Parliament: 18.12.2002. Coming into force: 17.12.2002 at 1200 hours, in accord. with art. 1. Effect: S.S.I. 2002/408 partially revoked. Territorial extent & classification: S. General. – 4p.: 30 cm. – 0 11 061810 6 *£1.75*

The Food Protection (Emergency Prohibitions) (Amnesic Shellfish Poisoning) (Orkney) (Scotland) Order 2002 No. 2002/345. – Enabling power: Food and Environment Protection Act 1985, ss. 1 (1) (2), 24 (3). – Issued: 22.07.2002. Made: 12.07.2002. Laid before the Scottish Parliament: 15.07.2002. Coming into force: 1600 hours on 12.07.2002, in accord. with art. 1 (1). Effect: None. Territorial extent and classification: S. General. – 4p.: 30 cm. – 0 11 061567 0 *£1.75*

The Food Protection (Emergency Prohibitions) (Amnesic Shellfish Poisoning) (Orkney) (Scotland) Revocation Order 2002 No. 2002/402. – Enabling power: Food and Environment Protection Act 1985, s. 1 (1) (2). – Issued: 11.09.2002. Made: 30.08.2002. Laid before the Scottish Parliament: 03.09.2002. Coming into force: 30.08.2002 at 1600 hours in accord. with art. 1. Effect: S.S.I. 2002/345 revoked. Territorial extent and classification: S. General. – 2p.: 30 cm. – 0 11 061607 3 *£1.50*

The Food Protection (Emergency Prohibitions) (Amnesic Shellfish Poisoning) (West Coast) (No. 2) (Scotland) Order 2001 Revocation Order 2002 No. 2002/182. – Enabling power: Food and Environment Protection Act 1985, s. 1 (1) (2). – Issued: 24.04.2002. Made: 10.04.2002. Laid before the Scottish Parliament: 12.04.2002. Coming into force: 16.00 hours on 10.04.2002 in accord. with art. 1. Effect: S.S.I. 2001/281, 434; 2002/67 revoked. Territorial extent and classification: S. General. – 2p.: 30 cm. – 0 11 061375 9 *£1.50*

The Food Protection (Emergency Prohibitions) (Amnesic Shellfish Poisoning) (West Coast) (No. 2) (Scotland) Order 2002 No. 2002/65. – Enabling power: Food and Environment Protection Act 1985, ss. 1 (1) (2), 24 (3). – Issued: 06.03.2002. Made: 20.02.2002. Laid before the Scottish Parliament: 22.02.2002. Coming into force: 20.02.2002 at 1600 hours in accord. with art. 1 (1). Effect: None. Territorial extent and classification: S. General. – 4p.: 30 cm. – 0 11 061072 5 *£1.75*

The Food Protection (Emergency Prohibitions) (Amnesic Shellfish Poisoning) (West Coast) (No. 2) (Scotland) Partial Revocation Order 2002 No. 2002/67. – Enabling power: Food and Environment Protection Act 1985, ss. 1 (1) (2), 24 (3). – Issued: 20.03.2002. Made: 21.02.2002. Laid before the Scottish Parliament: 22.02.2002. Coming into force: 21.02.2002 at 1400 hours in accord. with art. 1 (1). Effect: S.S.I. 2001/281 amended. Territorial extent and classification: S. General. – 4p.: 30 cm. – 0 11 061147 0 *£1.75*

The Food Protection (Emergency Prohibitions) (Amnesic Shellfish Poisoning) (West Coast) (No. 2) (Scotland) Revocation Order 2002 No. 2002/183. – Enabling power: Food and Environment Protection Act 1985, s. 1 (1) (2). – Issued: 24.04.2002. Made: 10.04.2002. Laid before the Scottish Parliament: 12.04.2002. Coming into force: 16.00 hours on 10.04.2002 in accord. with art. 1. Effect: S.S.I. 2002/65 revoked. Territorial extent and classification: S. General. – 2p.: 30 cm. – 0 11 061374 0 *£1.50*

The Food Protection (Emergency Prohibitions) (Amnesic Shellfish Poisoning) (West Coast) (No. 3) (Scotland) Order 2002 No. 2002/80. – Enabling power: Food and Environment Protection Act 1985, ss. 1 (1) (2), 24 (3). – Issued: 20.03.2002. Made: 01.03.2002. Laid before the Scottish Parliament: 05.03.2002. Coming into force: 01.03.2002 at 1700 hours in accord. with art. 1 (1). Effect: None. Territorial extent and classification: S. General. – 4p.: 30 cm. – 0 11 061146 2 *£1.75*

The Food Protection (Emergency Prohibitions) (Amnesic Shellfish Poisoning) (West Coast) (No. 3) (Scotland) (Revocation) Order 2002 No. 2002/218. – Enabling power: Food and Environment Protection Act 1985, s. 1 (1) (2). – Issued: 21.05.2002. Made: 07.05.2002. Laid before the Scottish Parliament: 08.05.2002. Coming into force: 07.05.2002 at 1600 hours in accord. with art. 1 (1). Effect: S.S.I. 2002/80 revoked. Territorial extent and classification: S. General. – 2p.: 30 cm. – 0 11 061414 3 *£1.50*

The Food Protection (Emergency Prohibitions) (Amnesic Shellfish Poisoning) (West Coast) (No. 4) (Scotland) Order 2002 No. 2002/231. – Enabling power: Food and Environment Protection Act 1985, ss. 1 (1) (2), 24 (3). – Issued: 27.05.2002. Made: 14.05.2002. Laid before the Scottish Parliament: 15.05.2002. Coming into force: 14.05.2002 at 1600 hours, in accord. with art. 1 (1). Effect: None. Territorial extent and classification: S. General. – 4p.: 30 cm. – 0 11 061424 0 *£1.75*

The Food Protection (Emergency Prohibitions) (Amnesic Shellfish Poisoning) (West Coast) (No. 4) (Scotland) Order 2002 Revocation Order 2002 No. 2002/550. – Enabling power: Food and Environment Protection Act 1985, s. 1 (1) (2). – Issued: 10.01.2003. Made: 16.12.2002. Laid before the Scottish Parliament: 18.12.2002. Coming into force: 16.12.2002. at 1700 hours in accord. with art. 1. Effect: S.S.I. 2002/231 revoked. Territorial extent and classification: S. General. – 2p.: 30 cm. – 0 11 061816 5 *£1.50*

The Food Protection (Emergency Prohibitions) (Amnesic Shellfish Poisoning) (West Coast) (No. 4) (Scotland) Partial Revocation (No. 2) Order 2002 No. 2002/19. – Enabling power: Food and Environment Protection Act 1985, ss. 1 (1) (2), 24 (3). – Issued: 20.02.2002. Made: 24.01.2002. Laid before the Scottish Parliament: 25.01.2002. Coming into force: 24.01.2002 at 1600 hours in accord. with art. 1. Effect: S.S.I. 2001/289 amended. Territorial extent and classification: S. General. – 2p.: 30 cm. – 0 11 059990 X *£1.50*

The Food Protection (Emergency Prohibitions) (Amnesic Shellfish Poisoning) (West Coast) (No. 4) (Scotland) Revocation Order 2002 No. 2002/160. – Enabling power: Food and Environment Protection Act 1985, s. 1 (1) (2). – Issued: 24.04.2002. Made: 26.03.2002. Laid before the Scottish Parliament: 27.03.2002. Coming into force: 17.00 hours on 26.03.2002. Effect: S.S.I. 2001/289, 473; 2002/19 revoked. Territorial extent and classification: S. General. – 2p.: 30 cm. – 0 11 061364 3 *£1.50*

The Food Protection (Emergency Prohibitions) (Amnesic Shellfish Poisoning) (West Coast) (No. 5) (Scotland) Order 2002 No. 2002/306. – Enabling power: Food and Environment Protection Act 1985, s. 1 (1) (2), 24 (3). – Issued: 15.07.2002. Made: 24.06.2002. Laid before the Scottish Parliament: 25.06.2002. Coming into force: 24.06.2002, at 16.30 hrs in accord. with art 1 (1), . Effect: None. Territorial extent and classification: S. General. – 4p.: 30 cm. – 0 11 061531 X *£1.75*

The Food Protection (Emergency Prohibitions) (Amnesic Shellfish Poisoning) (West Coast) (No. 5) (Scotland) Partial Revocation (No. 2) Order 2002 No. 2002/409. Enabling power: Food and Environment Protection Act 1985, ss. 1 (1) (2), 24 (3). – Issued: 18.09.2002. Made: 04.09.2002. Laid before the Scottish Parliament: 05.09.2002. Coming into force: 04.09.2002 at 1630 hours in accord. with art. 1. Effect: S.S.I. 2002/306 partially revoked. Territorial extent and classification: S. General. – 2p.: 30 cm. – 0 11 061619 7 *£1.50*

The Food Protection (Emergency Prohibitions) (Amnesic Shellfish Poisoning) (West Coast) (No. 5) (Scotland) Partial Revocation Order 2002 No. 2002/383. – Enabling power: Food and Environment Protection Act 1985, ss. 1 (1) (2), 24 (3). – Issued: 09.09.2002. Made: 21.08.2002. Laid before the Scottish Parliament: 22.08.2002. Coming into force: 21.08.2002 at 1600 hours in accord. with art. 1. Effect: S.S.I. 2002/306 partially revoked. Territorial extent and classification: S. General. – 2p.: 30 cm. – 0 11 061592 1 *£1.50*

The Food Protection (Emergency Prohibitions) (Amnesic Shellfish Poisoning) (West Coast) (No. 5) (Scotland) Revocation Order 2002 No. 2002/126. – Enabling power: Food and Environment Protection Act 1985, s. 1 (1) (2). – Issued: 11.04.2002. Made: 08.03.2002. Laid before the Scottish Parliament: 13.03.2002. Coming into force: 08.03.2002 at 14.00 hrs, in accord. with art. 1. Effect: S.S.I. 2001/295 revoked. Territorial extent and classification: S. General. – 2p.: 30 cm. – 0 11 061293 0 *£1.50*

The Food Protection (Emergency Prohibitions) (Amnesic Shellfish Poisoning) (West Coast) (No. 5) (Scotland) Revocation Order 2002 No. 2002/431. – Enabling power: Food and Environment Protection Act 1985, s. 1 (1) (2). – Issued: 30.09.2002. Made: 18.09.2002. Laid before the Scottish Parliament: 19.09.2002. Coming into force: 18.09.2002 at 1600 hours in accord. with art. 1. Effect: S.S.I. 2002/306, 383, 409 revoked. Territorial extent and classification: S. General. – 2p.: 30 cm. – 0 11 061647 2 *£1.50*

The Food Protection (Emergency Prohibitions) (Amnesic Shellfish Poisoning) (West Coast) (No.6) (Scotland) Order 2002 No. 2002/307. – Enabling power: Food and Environment Protection Act 1985, ss. 1 (1) (2), 24 (3). – Issued: 15.07.2002. Made: 24.06.2002. Laid before the Scottish Parliament: 25.06.2002. Coming into force: In accord. with art. 1 (1), 24.06.2002, at 16.30 hrs. Effect: None. Territorial extent and classification: S. General. – 4p.: 30 cm. – 0 11 061530 1 *£1.75*

The Food Protection (Emergency Prohibitions) (Amnesic Shellfish Poisoning) (West Coast) (No. 6) (Scotland) Partial Revocation Order 2002 No. 2002/551. – Enabling power: Food and Environment Protection Act 1985, ss. 1 (1) (2), 24 (3). – Issued: 10.01.2003. Made: 16.12.2002. Laid before the Scottish Parliament: 18.12.2002. Coming into force: 16.12.2002. at 1700 hours in accord. with art. 1. Effect: S.S.I. 2002/307 partially revoked. Territorial extent and classification: S. General. – 2p.: 30 cm. – 0 11 061815 7 *£1.50*

The Food Protection (Emergency Prohibitions) (Amnesic Shellfish Poisoning) (West Coast) (No. 7) (Scotland) Order 2002 No. 2002/332. – Enabling power: Food and Environment Protection Act 1985, s. 1 (1) (2), 24 (3). – Issued: 19.07.2002. Made: 03.07.2002. Laid before the Scottish Parliament: 04.07.2002. Coming into force: 03.07.2002 at 1500 hours, in accord. with art. 1 (1). Effect: None. Territorial extent and classification: S. General. – 4p.: 30 cm. – 0 11 061565 4 *£1.75*

The Food Protection (Emergency Prohibitions) (Amnesic Shellfish Poisoning) (West Coast) (No. 7) (Scotland) Order 2002 Revocation Order 2002 No. 2002/422. – Enabling power: Food and Environment Protection Act 1985, ss. 1 (1) (2). – Issued: 23.09.2002. Made: 11.09.2002. Laid before the Scottish Parliament: 13.09.2002. Coming into force: 11.09.2002 at 1600 hours in accord. with art. 1. Effect: S.S.I. 2002/332 revoked. Territorial extent and classification: S. General. – 2p.: 30 cm. – 0 11 061629 4 £1.50

The Food Protection (Emergency Prohibitions) (Amnesic Shellfish Poisoning) (West Coast) (No. 7) (Scotland) Revocation Order 2002 No. 2002/20. – Enabling power: Food and Environment Protection Act 1985, s. 1 (1) (2). – Issued: 21.02.2002. Made: 24.01.2002. Laid before the Scottish Parliament: 25.01.2002. Coming into force: 24.01.2002 at 1600 hours in accord. with art. 1. Effect: S.S.I. 2001/322 revoked. Territorial extent and classification: S. General. – 2p.: 30 cm. – 0 11 059991 8 £1.50

The Food Protection (Emergency Prohibitions) (Amnesic Shellfish Poisoning) (West Coast) (No. 8) (Scotland) Order 2002 No. 2002/333. – Enabling power: Food and Environment Protection Act 1985, s. 1 (1) (2), 24 (3). – Issued: 19.07.2002. Made: 03.07.2002. Laid before the Scottish Parliament: 04.07.2002. Coming into force: 03.07.2002 at 1500 hours, in accord. with art. 1 (1). Effect: None. Territorial extent and classification: S. General. –4p.: 30 cm. – 0 11 061566 2 £1.75

The Food Protection (Emergency Prohibitions) (Amnesic Shellfish Poisoning) (West Coast) (No. 8) (Scotland) Revocation Order 2002 No. 2002/127. – Enabling power: Food and Environment Protection Act 1985, s. 1 (1) (2). – Issued: 11.04.2002. Made: 08.03.2002. Laid before the Scottish Parliament: 13.03.2002. Coming into force: 08.03.2002 at 18.00 hrs, in accord. with art. 1. Effect: S.S.I. 2001/374 revoked. Territorial extent and classification: S. General. – 2p.: 30 cm. – 0 11 061299 X £1.50

The Food Protection (Emergency Prohibitions) (Amnesic Shellfish Poisoning) (West Coast) (No. 8) (Scotland) Revocation Order 2002 No. 2002/384. – Enabling power: Food and Environment Protection Act 1985, s. 1 (1) (2). – Issued: 09.09.2002. Made: 21.08.2002. Laid before the Scottish Parliament: 22.08.2002. Coming into force: 21.08.2002 at 1600 hours in accord. with art. 1. Effect: S.S.I. 2002/333 revoked. Territorial extent and classification: S. General. – 2p.: 30 cm. – 0 11 061591 3 £1.50

The Food Protection (Emergency Prohibitions) (Amnesic Shellfish Poisoning) (West Coast) (No. 9) (Scotland) Order 2002 No. 2002/350. – Enabling power: Food and Environment Protection Act 1985, s. 1 (1) (2), 24 (3). – Issued: 02.08.2002. Made: 22.07.2002. Laid before the Scottish Parliament: 23.07.2002. Coming into force: 22.07.2002 at 1600 hours, in accord. with art. 1 (1). Effect: None. Territorial extent and classification: S. General. – 4p.: 30 cm. – 0 11 061576 X £1.75

The Food Protection (Emergency Prohibitions) (Amnesic Shellfish Poisoning) (West Coast) (No. 9) (Scotland) Revocation Order 2002 No. 2002/9. – Enabling power: Food and Environment Protection Act 1985, s. 1 (1) (2). – Issued: 20.02.2002. Made: 14.01.2002. Laid before the Scottish Parliament: 16.01.2002. Coming into force: 14.01.2002 at 1600 hours in accord. with art. 1. Effect: S.S.I. 2001/388, 469 revoked. Territorial extent and classification: S. General. – 2p.: 30 cm. – 0 11 059987 X £1.50

The Food Protection (Emergency Prohibitions) (Amnesic Shellfish Poisoning) (West Coast) (No. 9) (Scotland) Revocation Order 2002 No. 2002/401. – Enabling power: Food and Environment Protection Act 1985, s. 1 (1) (2). – Issued: 11.09.2002. Made: 30.08.2002. Laid before the Scottish Parliament: 03.09.2002. Coming into force: 30.08.2002 at 1600 hours in accord. with art. 1 (1). Effect: S.S.I. 2002/350 revoked. Territorial extent and classification: S. General. – 2p.: 30 cm. – 0 11 061608 1 £1.50

The Food Protection (Emergency Prohibitions) (Amnesic Shellfish Poisoning) (West Coast) (No. 10) (Scotland) Order 2002 No. 2002/357. – Enabling power: Food and Environment Protection Act 1985, ss. 1 (1) (2), 24 (3). – Issued: 14.08.2002. Made: 30.07.2002. Laid before the Scottish Parliament: 31.07.2002. Coming into force: 30.07.2002 at 1600 hours in accord. with art. 1 (1). Effect: None. Territorial extent & classification: S. General. – 4p.: 30 cm. – 0 11 061580 8 £1.75

The Food Protection (Emergency Prohibitions) (Amnesic Shellfish Poisoning) (West Coast) (No. 10) (Scotland) Partial Revocation Order 2002 No. 2002/421. – Enabling power: Food and Environment Protection Act 1985, ss. 1 (1) (2), 24 (3). – Issued: 23.09.2002. Made: 11.09.2002. Laid before the Scottish Parliament: 13.09.2002. Coming into force: 11.09.2002 at 1600 hours in accord. with art. 1. Effect: S.S.I. 2002/357 partially revoked. Territorial extent and classification: S. General. – 2p.: 30 cm. – 0 11 061627 8 £1.50

The Food Protection (Emergency Prohibitions) (Amnesic Shellfish Poisoning) (West Coast) (No. 10) (Scotland) Revocation Order 2002 No. 2002/510. – Enabling power: Food and Environment Protection Act 1985, s. 1 (1) (2), 24 (3). – Issued: 28.11.2002. Made: 19.11.2002. Laid before the Scottish Parliament: 20.11.2002. Coming into force: 19.11.2002 at 1700 hours in accord. with art. 1. Effect: S.S.I. 2002/357, 421 revoked. Territorial extent and classification: S. General. – 2p.: 30 cm. – 0 11 061719 3 £1.50

The Food Protection (Emergency Prohibitions) (Amnesic Shellfish Poisoning) (West Coast) (No. 11) (Scotland) Order 2002 No. 2002/388. – Enabling power: Food and Environment Protection Act 1985, ss. 1 (1) (2), 24 (3). – Issued: 09.09.2002. Made: 26.08.2002. Laid before the Scottish Parliament: 28.08.2002. Coming into force: 26.08.2002 at 1600 hours in accord. with art. 1. Effect: None. Territorial extent and classification: S. General. – 4p.: 30 cm. – 0 11 061590 5 £1.75

The Food Protection (Emergency Prohibitions) (Amnesic Shellfish Poisoning) (West Coast) (No. 11) (Scotland) Partial Revocation Order 2002 No. 2002/545. – Enabling power: Food and Environment Protection Act 1985, ss. 1 (1) (2), 24 (3). – Issued: 23.12.2002. Made: 09.12.2002. Laid before the Scottish Parliament: 11.12.2002. Coming into force: 09.12.2002 at 1600 hours in accord. with art. 1. Effect: S.S.I. 2002/388 partially revoked. Territorial extent and classification: S. General. – 2p.: 30 cm. – 0 11 061803 3 £1.50

The Food Protection (Emergency Prohibitions) (Amnesic Shellfish Poisoning) (West Coast) (No. 12) (Scotland) Order 2002 No. 2002/430. – Enabling power: Food and Environment Protection Act 1985, ss. 1 (1) (2), 24 (3). – Issued: 30.09.2002. Made: 18.09.2002. Laid before the Scottish Parliament: 19.09.2002. Coming into force: 18.09.2002 at 1600 hours in accord. with art. 1 (1). Effect: None. Territorial extent and classification: S. General. – 4p.: 30 cm. – 0 11 061642 1 £1.75

The Food Protection (Emergency Prohibitions) (Amnesic Shellfish Poisoning) (West Coast) (No.12) (Scotland) Partial Revocation Order 2002 No. 2002/66. – Enabling power: Food and Environment Protection Act 1985, s. 1 (1) (2), 24 (3). – Issued: 06.03.2002. Made: 20.02.2002. Laid before the Scottish Parliament: 22.02.2002. Coming into force: 20.02.2002 at 1600 hours, in accord. with art. 1. Effect: S.S.I. 2001/423 amended. Territorial extent and classification: S. General. – 4p.: 30 cm. – 0 11 061074 1 £1.75

The Food Protection (Emergency Prohibitions) (Amnesic Shellfish Poisoning) (West Coast) (No. 12) (Scotland) Partial Revocation Order 2002 No. 2002/552. – Enabling power: Food and Environment Protection Act 1985, ss. 1 (1) (2), 24 (3). – Issued: 10.01.2003. Made: 16.12.2002. Laid before the Scottish Parliament: 18.12.2002. Coming into force: 16.12.2002. at 1700 hours in accord. with art. 1. Effect: S.S.I. 2002/430 partially revoked. Territorial extent and classification: S. General. – 2p.: 30 cm. – 0 11 061814 9 £1.50

The Food Protection (Emergency Prohibitions) (Amnesic Shellfish Poisoning) (West Coast) (No. 12) (Scotland) Revocation Order 2002 No. 2002/198. – Enabling power: Food and Environment Protection Act 1985, s. 1 (1) (2). – Issued: 01.05.2002. Made: 19.04.2002. Laid before the Scottish Parliament: 23.04.2002. Coming into force: 19.04.2002 at 1600 hours, in accord. with art. 1. Effect: S.S.I. 2001/423; 2002/66 revoked. Territorial extent and classification: S. General. – 2p.: 30 cm. – 0 11 061388 0 £1.50

The Food Protection (Emergency Prohibitions) (Amnesic Shellfish Poisoning) (West Coast) (No. 13) (Scotland) Order 2002 No. 2002/465. – Enabling power: Food and Environment Protection Act 1985, ss. 1 (1) (2), 24 (3). – Issued: 24.10.2002. Made: 15.10.2002. Laid before the Scottish Parliament: 17.10.2002. Coming into force: 15.10.2002 at 1600 hours in accord. with art. 1 (1). Effect: None. Territorial extent and classification: S. General. – [8]p.: 30 cm. – 0 11 061671 5 £2.00

The Food Protection (Emergency Prohibitions) (Amnesic Shellfish Poisoning) (West Coast) (No. 14) (Scotland) Order 2002 No. 2002/482. – Enabling power: Food and Environment Protection Act 1985, ss. 1 (1) (2), 24 (3). – Issued: 06.11.2002. Made: 25.10.2002. Laid before the Scottish Parliament: 29.10.2002. Coming into force: 25.10.2002 at 1400 hours in accord. with art. 1 (1). Effect: None. Territorial extent and classification: S. General. – 4p.: 30 cm. – 0 11 061696 0 £1.75

The Food Protection (Emergency Prohibitions) (Amnesic Shellfish Poisoning) (West Coast) (No. 14) (Scotland) Partial Revocation Order 2002 No. 2002/553. – Enabling power: Food and Environment Protection Act 1985, ss. 1 (1) (2), 24 (3). – Issued: 10.01.2003. Made: 16.12.2002. Laid before the Scottish Parliament: 18.12.2002. Coming into force: 16.12.2002. at 1700 hours in accord. with art. 1. Effect: S.S.I. 2002/482 partially revoked. Territorial extent and classification: S. General. – 2p.: 30 cm. – 0 11 061811 4 £1.50

The Food Protection (Emergency Prohibitions) (Amnesic Shellfish Poisoning) (West Coast) (No. 14) (Scotland) Revocation Order 2002 No. 2002/48. – Enabling power: Food and Environment Protection Act 1985, s. 1 (1) (2). – Issued: 28.02.2002. Made: 07.02.2002. Laid before the Scottish Parliament: 08.02.2002. Coming into force: 07.02.2002 at 1700 hours in accord. with art. 1. Effect: S.S.I. 2001/451 revoked. Territorial extent and classification: S. General. – 2p.: 30 cm. – 0 11 061024 5 £1.50

The Food Protection (Emergency Prohibitions) (Amnesic Shellfish Poisoning) (West Coast) (No. 15) (Scotland) Order 2002 No. 2002/511. – Enabling power: Food and Environment Protection Act 1985, ss. 1 (1) (2), 24 (3). – Issued: 28.11.2002. Made: 19.11.2002. Laid before the Scottish Parliament: 20.11.2002. Coming into force: 19.11.2002 at 1700 hours in accord. with art. 1. Effect: None. Territorial extent and classification: S. General. – 4p.: 30 cm. – 0 11 061718 5 £1.75

The Food Protection (Emergency Prohibitions) (Amnesic Shellfish Poisoning) (West Coast) (No. 16) (Scotland) Order 2002 No. 2002/544. – Enabling power: Food and Environment Protection Act 1985, ss. 1 (1) (2), 24 (3). – Issued: 23.12.2002. Made: 09.12.2002. Laid before the Scottish Parliament: 11.12.2002. Coming into force: 09.12.2002 at 1700 hours in accord. with art. 1 (1). Effect: None. Territorial extent and classification: S. General. – 4p.: 30 cm. – 0 11 061804 1 £1.75

The Food Protection (Emergency Prohibitions) (Amnesic Shellfish Poisoning) (West Coast) (Scotland) Order 2002 No. 2002/49. – Enabling power: Food and Environment Protection Act 1985, ss. 1 (1) (2), 24 (3). – Issued: 28.02.2002. Made: 07.02.2002. Laid before the Scottish Parliament: 08.02.2002. Coming into force: 07.02.2002 at 1700 hours in accord. with art. 1 (1). Effect: None. Territorial extent and classification: S. General. – 4p.: 30 cm. – 0 11 061025 3 £1.75

The Food Protection (Emergency Prohibitions) (Amnesic Shellfish Poisoning) (West Coast) (Scotland) Revocation Order 2002 No. 2002/152. – Enabling power: Food and Environment Protection Act 1985, s. 1 (1) (2). – Issued: 16.04.2002. Made: 20.03.2002. Laid before the Scottish Parliament: 26.03.2002. Coming into force: 20.03.2002, 16.00 hrs, in accord. with art. 1. Effect: S.S.I. 2002/49 revoked. Territorial extent and classification: S. General. – 2p.: 30 cm. – 0 11 061335 X *£1.50*

The Food Protection (Emergency Prohibitions) (Diarrhetic Shellfish Poisoning) (Orkney) (Scotland) Revocation Order 2002 No. 2002/57. – Enabling power: Food and Environment Protection Act 1985, s. 1 (1) (2). – Issued: 06.03.2002. Made: 12.02.2002. Laid before the Scottish Parliament: 13.02.2002. Coming into force: 12.02.2002 at 1600 hours, in accord, with art.1. Effect: S.S.I. 2001/391 revoked. Territorial extent and classification: S. General. – 2p.: 30 cm. – 0 11 061086 5 *£1.50*

The Food Protection (Emergency Prohibitions) (Paralytic Shellfish Poisoning) (Orkney) (No. 3) (Scotland) Revocation Order 2002 No. 2002/82. – Enabling power: Food and Environment Protection Act 1985, s. 1 (1) (2). – Issued: 13.03.2002. Made: 04.03.2002. Laid before the Scottish Parliament: 05.03.2002. Coming into force: 04.03.2002 at 1600 hours, in accord. with art. 1. Effect: S.S.I. 2001/255 revoked. Territorial extent and classification: S. General. – 2p.: 30 cm. – 0 11 061115 2 *£1.50*

Public passenger transport

The Public Service Vehicles (Registration of Local Services) (Scotland) Amendment Regulations 2002 No. 2002/548. – Enabling power: Public Service Vehicles Act 1981, s. 60 (1) (e). – Issued: 23.12.2002. Made: 12.12.2002. Laid before the Scottish Parliament: 13.12.2002. Coming into force: 15.01.2003. Effect: S.S.I. 2001/219 amended. Territorial extent & classification: S. General. – 2p.: 30 cm. – 0 11 061765 7 *£1.50*

Race relations

The Race Relations Act 1976 (Statutory Duties) (Scotland) Order 2002 No. 2002/62. – Enabling power: Race Relations Act 1976, s. 71 (2) (3). – Issued: 06.03.2002. Made: 14.02.2002. Laid before the Scottish Parliament: 15.02.2002. Coming into force: 13.03.2002. Effect: None. Territorial extent & classification: S. General. – 8p.: 30 cm. – 0 11 061085 7 *£2.00*

Rating and valuation

The Electricity Lands and Generators (Rateable Values) (Scotland) Variation Order 2002 No. 2002/158. – Enabling power: Local Government (Scotland) Act 1975, ss. 6, 35 (2), 37 (1). – Issued: 16.04.2002. Made: 22.03.2002. Coming into force: 31.03.2002. Effect: 1975 c.30; S.S.I. 2000/86, 88 amended. Territorial extent and classification: S. General. – 8p.: 30 cm. – 0 11 061334 1 *£2.00*

The Non-domestic Rate (Scotland) Order 2002 No. 2002/89. – Enabling power: Local Government (Scotland) Act 1975, ss. 7B (1), 37 (1). – Issued: 21.03.2002. Made: 28.02.2002. Laid before the Scottish Parliament: 07.03.2002. Coming into force: 01.04.2002. Effect: None. Territorial extent & classification: S. General. – 2p.: 30 cm. – 0 11 061169 1 *£1.50*

The Non-domestic Rates (Levying) (Scotland) Regulations 2002 No. 2002/91. – Enabling power: Local Government etc. (Scotland) Act 1994, s. 153. – Issued: 21.03.2002. Made: 05.03.2002. Laid before the Scottish Parliament: 07.03.2002. Coming into force: 01.04.2002. Effect: S.S.I. 2001/71 revoked with savings. Territorial extent & classification: S. General. – 12p.: 30 cm. – 0 11 061178 0 *£2.50*

The Valuation for Rating (Exempted Classes) (Scotland) Order 2002 No. 2002/262. – Enabling power: The Valuation and Rating (Exempted Classes) (Scotland) Act 1976, s. 1. – Issued: 12.06.2002. Made: 29.05.2002. Laid before the Scottish Parliament: - Coming into force: 01.06.2002. Effect: None. Territorial extent & classification: S. General. – 4p.: 30 cm. – 0 11 061438 0 *£1.75*

The Water Undertakings (Rateable Values) (Scotland) Variation Order 2002 No. 2002/159. – Enabling power: Local Government (Scotland) Act 1975, ss. 6, 35, 37 (1). – Issued: 16.04.2002. Made: 22.03.2000. Laid:-. Coming into force: 31.03.2002. Effect: S.S.I. 2000/90 amended. –This S.S.I. has been printed to correct an error in S.S.I. 2000/90 (ISBN 0110593197) and is being issued free of charge to all known recipients of that instrument. – 4p.: 30 cm. – 0 11 061321 X *£1.75*

Registration of births, deaths, marriages, etc.

The Births, Deaths, Marriages and Divorces (Fees) (Scotland) Amendment Regulations 2002 No. 2002/390. – Enabling power: Registration of Births, Deaths and Marriages (Scotland) Act 1965, ss. 28A (4), 37 (2) (3), 38 (2) (3), 40 (1), 43 (8), 47, 54 (1), 56 & Marriage (Scotland) Act 1977, ss. 3 (1), 25, 26. – Issued: 05.09.2002. Made: 26.08.2002. Laid before the Scottish Parliament: 28.08.2002. Coming into force: 01.10.2002. Effect: S.I. 1998/643 amended. Territorial extent & classification: S. General. – 4p.: 30 cm. – 0 11 061587 5 *£1.75*

The Registration of Births, Deaths and Marriages (Fees) (Scotland) Order 2002 No. 2002/389. – Enabling power: Public Expenditure and Receipts Act 1968, s. 5 (1) (2), sch. 3, para. 1 (b). – Issued: 05.09.2002. Made: 26.08.2002. Laid before the Scottish Parliament: 28.08.2002. Coming into force: 01.10.2002. Effect: S.I. 1997/717 revoked. Territorial extent & classification: S. General. – 4p.: 30 cm. – 0 11 061588 3 *£1.75*

Representation of the people

The Scottish Local Government Elections Amendment Rules 2002 No. 2002/522. – Enabling power: Representation of the People Act 1983, s. 42. – Issued: 09.12.2002. Made: 28.11.2002. Laid before the Scottish Parliament: 28.11.2002. Coming into force: 19.12.2002. Effect: S.S.I. 2002/457 amended. Territorial extent & classification: S. General. – 4p.: 30 cm. – 0 11 061731 2 £1.75

The Scottish Local Government Elections Regulations 2002 No. 2002/561. – Enabling power: Representation of the People Act 1983, s. 53 (1) (c) (3), sch. 2. – Issued: 09.01.2003. Made: 19.12.2002. Coming into force: In accord. with art. 1. Effect: None. Territorial extent & classification: S. General. – 12p.: 30 cm. – 0 11 061827 0 £2.50

The Scottish Local Government Elections Rules 2002 No. 2002/457. – Enabling power: Representation of the People Act 1983, s. 42. – Issued: 18.10.2002. Made: 08.10.2002. Laid before the Scottish Parliament: 09.10.2002. Coming into force: 13.11.2002, in accord. with rule 1 (2). Effect: S.I. 1986/2213; 1999/492 revoked. Territorial extent & classification: S. General. – 52p.: 30 cm. – 0 11 061667 7 £7.50

River: Salmon and freshwater fisheries

The Conservation of Salmon (Prohibition of Sale) (Scotland) Regulations 2002 No. 2002/418. – Enabling power: Salmon Act 1986, s. 10A (3) (b). – Issued: 20.09.2002. Made: 10.09.2002. Laid before the Scottish Parliament: 10.09.2002. Coming into force: 01.10.2002. Effect: None. Territorial extent and classification: S. General. – 2p.: 30 cm. – 0 11 061623 5 £1.50

The Mull Salmon Fishery District Designation (Scotland) Order 2002 No. 2002/138. – Enabling power: Salmon Act 1986, ss. 1 (2), 2. – Issued: 28.03.2002. Made: 14.03.2002. Coming into force: 20.03.2002. Effect: None. Territorial extent & classification: S. General. – 8p.: 30 cm. – 0 11 061239 6 £2.00

The Registration of Fish Farming and Shellfish Farming Businesses Amendment (No. 2) (Scotland) Order 2002 No. 2002/220. – Enabling power: Diseases of Fish Act 1983, s. 7 (1) (2) (3). – Issued: 21.05.2002. Made: 08.05.2002. Laid before the Scottish Parliament: 08.05.2002. Coming into force: 10.05.2002. Effect: S.S.I. 2002/193 amended. Territorial extent and classification: S. General. –This S.S.I. has been made in consequence of a drafting defect in S.S.I. 2002/193 and is being issued free of charge to all known recipients of that instrument. – 2p.: 30 cm. – 0 11 061415 1 £1.50

The Registration of Fish Farming and Shellfish Farming Businesses Amendment (Scotland) Order 2002 No. 2002/193. – Enabling power: Diseases of Fish Act 1983, s. 7 (1) (2) (3). – Issued: 30.04.2002. Made: 17.04.2002. Laid before the Scottish Parliament: 19.04.2002. Coming into force: 10.05.2002. Effect: S.I. 1985/1391 amended in relation to Scotland. Territorial extent and classification: S. General. – 8p.: 30 cm. – 0 11 061386 4 £2.00

The River Dee (Kirkcudbright) Salmon Fishery District (Baits and Lures) Regulations 2002 No. 2002/11. – Enabling power: Salmon Act 1986, s. 8. – Issued: 31.01.2002. Made: 07.01.2002. Coming into force: 01.02.2002. Effect: None. Territorial extent & classification: S. General. – 2p.: 30 cm. – 0 11 059978 0 £1.50

Roads and bridges

The A75 Trunk Road (Cairntop Cottages to Barlae Improvement) (Side Roads) Order 2002 No. 2002/426. – Enabling power: Roads (Scotland) Act 1984, s. 12 (1). – Made: 19.19.2002. Coming into force: 27.09.2002. Effect: None. Territorial extent & classification: S. Local *Unpublished*

The A78 Trunk Road (Ardrossan, Saltcoats and Stevenson Bypass) Order 2002 No. 2002/347. – Enabling power: Roads (Scotland) Act 1984, ss. 5 (2), 143 (1). – Made: 12.07.2002. Coming into force: 19.07.2002. Effect: None. Territorial extent & classification: S. Local *Unpublished*

The A78 Trunk Road (Ardrossan, Saltcoats and Stevenson Bypass) Side Roads Order 2002 No. 2002/348. – Enabling power: Roads (Scotland) Act 1984, s. 12 (1) (c). – Made: 12.07.2002. Coming into force: 19.07.2002. Effect: None. Territorial extent & classification: S. Local *Unpublished*

The A78 Trunk Road (Inverkip Road, Greenock) (Redetermination of Means of Exercise of Public Right of Passage) Order 2002 No. 2002/210. – Enabling power: Roads (Scotland) Act 1984, ss. 2 (1), 152 (2). – Made: 30.04.2002. Coming into force: 17.05.2002. Effect: None. Territorial extent & classification: S. Local *Unpublished*

The A83 Trunk Road (Tarbert) (Temporary Prohibition of Waiting) Order 2002 No. 2002/237. – Enabling power: Roads (Scotland) Act 1984, s. 62. – Made: 17.05.2002. Coming into force: 30.05.2002. Effect: None. Territorial extent & classification: S. Local *Unpublished*

The A90 Trunk Road (Hatton Bends Improvement) Order 2002 No. 2002/501. – Enabling power: Roads (Scotland) Act 1984, s.5 (2). – Made: 08.11.2002. Coming into force: 19.11.2002. Effect: None. Territorial extent & classification: S. Local *Unpublished*

The A90 Trunk Road (Hatton Bends Improvement) (Side Roads) Order 2002 No. 2002/502. – Enabling power: Roads (Scotland) Act 1984, s.12 (1). – Made: 08.11.2002. Coming into force: 19.11.2002. Effect: None. Territorial extent & classification: S. Local *Unpublished*

The A92 Trunk Road (Markinch Junction Improvement) (Side Roads) Order 2002 No. 2002/370. – Enabling power: Roads (Scotland) Act 1984, s. 12 (1). – Made: 16.08.2002. Coming into force: 30.08.2002. Effect: None. Territorial extent & classification: S. Local *Unpublished*

The A95 Trunk Road (Kinveachy Junction Improvement) Order 2002 No. 2002/460. – Enabling power: Roads (Scotland) Act 1984, s. 5 (2). – Made: 09.10.2002. Coming into force: 25.10.2002. Effect: None. Territorial extent & classification: S. Local *Unpublished*

The A985 Trunk Road (Kincardine Eastern Link Road) Order 2002 No. 2002/273. – Enabling power: Roads (Scotland) Act 1984, s. 5 (2). – Made: 05.07.2002. Coming into force: 19.07.2002. Effect: None. Territorial extent & classification: S. Local *Unpublished*

The A985 Trunk Road (Kincardine Eastern Link Road) (Side Roads) Order 2002 No. 2002/342. – Enabling power: Roads (Scotland) Act 1984, s. 12 (1). – Made: 05.07.2002. Coming into force: 19.07.2002. Effect: None. Territorial extent & classification: S. Local *Unpublished*

The Environmental Impact Assessment (Scotland) Amendment Regulations 2002 No. 2002/324. – Enabling power: European Communities Act 1972, s. 2 (2) & Town & Country Planning (Scotland) Act 1997, s. 40. – Issued: 17.07.2002. Made: 27.06.2002. Laid before the Scottish Parliament: 28.06.2002. Coming into force: 23.09.2002. Effect: S.S.I. 1999/1 amended. Territorial extent & classification: S. General. – EC note: Implement in Scotland DIR 85/337/EEC (as amended by 97/11/EEC), in relation to applications to planning authorities to determine the revised conditions to which an existing minerals planning permission should be subjected. – 8p.: 30 cm. – 0 11 061558 1 *£2.00*

The Forth Estuary Transport Authority Order 2002 No. 2002/178. – Enabling power: Transport (Scotland) Act 2001, s. 69 (1) (2), 81 (2). – Issued: 22.04.2002. Made: 28.03.2002. Coming into force: 01.04.2002. Effect: 1947 c. iv; 1958 c. vi; 1960 c. iii; Forth Road Bridge (Toll Period) Extension Order 1997 dated 30 January 1997, modified & 1950 c. xxiv; 1954 c. xx; 1961 c. xxi revoked. Territorial extent & classification: S. General. – 12p.: 30 cm. – 0 11 061353 8 *£2.50*

The Glasgow-Monkland Motorway (Stage II) (Connecting Roads) Special Roads (Variation) Scheme 2002 No. 2002/363. – Enabling power: Roads (Scotland) Act 1984, ss. 7, 143 (1), 145. – Made: 31.07.2002. Coming into force: 13.08.2002. Effect: S.I. 1974/2007 varied. Territorial extent & classification: S. Local *Unpublished*

The M8 Motorway (Westerhouse Road Eastbound Slip Roads at Junction 10) (Stopping Up) Order 2002 No. 2002/362. – Enabling power: Roads (Scotland) Act 1984, s. 9. – Made: 31.07.2002. Coming into force: 13.08.2002. Effect: None. Territorial extent and classification: S. Local *Unpublished*

The M77 (Fenwick to Malletsheugh) Special Road Scheme 2002 No. 2002/244. – Enabling power: Roads (Scotland) Act 1984, s. 7. – Made: 13.05.2002. Coming into force: 31.05.2002. Effect: None. Territorial extent & classification: S. Local *Unpublished*

The M77 Special Road (Fenwick to Floak) Side Roads (No. 3) Order 2002 No. 2002/240. – Enabling power: Roads (Scotland) Act 1984, s. 9 (1) (c). – Made: 13.05.2002. Coming into force: 31.05.2002. Effect: S.S.I. 1999/179, 180 revoked. Territorial extent & classification: S. Local *Unpublished*

The M77 Special Road (Fenwick to Malletsheugh) Appropriation Order 2002 No. 2002/243. – Enabling power: Roads (Scotland) Act 1984, ss. 9 (1) (a), 143 (1). – Made: 13.05.2002. Coming into force: 31.05.2002. Effect: None. Territorial extent & classification: S. Local *Unpublished*

The M77 Special Road (Fenwick to Malletsheugh) Side Roads Order 2002 No. 2002/245. – Enabling power: Roads (Scotland) Act 1984, s. 9 (1) (c). – Made: 13.05.2002. Coming into force: 31.05.2002. Effect: None. Territorial extent & classification: S. Local *Unpublished*

The M77 Special Road (Floak to Malletsheugh) Side Roads (No. 2) Order 2002 No. 2002/241. – Enabling power: Roads (Scotland) Act 1984, s. 9 (1) (c). – Made: 13.05.2002. Coming into force: 31.05.2002. Effect: S.S.I. 1999/184 revoked. Territorial extent & classification: S. Local *Unpublished*

The Road Humps and Traffic Calming (Scotland) Amendment Regulations 2002 No. 2002/419. – Enabling power: Roads (Scotland) Act 1984, ss. 38 (1), 39B, 143 (1). – Issued: 20.09.2002. Made: 09.09.2002. Laid before the Scottish Parliament: 10.09.2002. Coming into force: 01.10.2002. Effect: S.I. 1994/2488; 1998/1448 amended. Territorial extent & classification: S. General. – 4p.: 30 cm. – 0 11 061624 3 *£1.75*

The Road Works (Inspection Fees) (Scotland) Amendment Regulations 2002 No. 2002/13. – Enabling power: New Roads and Street Works Act 1991, ss. 134, 163 (1). – Issued: 20.02.2002. Made: 17.01.2002. Laid before the Scottish Parliament: 22.01.2002. Coming into force: 01.03.2002. Effect: S.I. 1992/1676 amended & S.I. 1998/1029 revoked. Territorial extent & classification: S. General. – 2p.: 30 cm. – 0 11 059988 8 *£1.50*

Road traffic

The A9 Trunk Road (Ballinluig) (Temporary 50mph Speed Limit) (Continuation) Order 2002 No. 2002/371. – Enabling power: Road Traffic Regulation Act 1984, s. 88 (4). – Issued: 27.08.2002. Made: 14.08.2002. Laid before the Scottish Parliament: 16.08.2002. Coming into force: 02.09.2002. Effect: None. Territorial extent & classification: S. General. – 2p.: 30 cm. – 0 11 061583 2 *£1.50*

The Disabled Persons (Badges for Motor Vehicles) (Scotland) Amendment Regulations 2002 No. 2002/451. – Enabling power: Chronically Sick and Disabled Persons Act 1970, s. 21 (7F). – Issued: 18.10.2002. Made: 03.10.2002. Laid before the Scottish Parliament: 04.10.2002. Coming into force: 08.11.2002. Effect: S.S.I. 2000/59 amended. Territorial extent & classification: S. General. – 2p.: 30 cm. – 0 11 061663 4 *£1.50*

The Local Authorities' Traffic Orders (Exemptions for Disabled Persons) (Scotland) Amendment Regulations 2002 No. 2002/547. – Enabling power: Road Traffic Regulation Act 1984, s. 124, sch. 9, pt. III, paras. 21, 22 (1) (d), 25. – Issued: 23.12.2002. Made: 12.12.2002. Laid before the Scottish Parliament: 13.12.2002. Coming into force: 15.01.2003. Effect: S.S.I. 2002/450 amended. Territorial extent & classification: S. General. – 4p.: 30 cm. – 0 11 061793 2 *£1.75*

The Local Authorities' Traffic Orders (Exemptions for Disabled Persons) (Scotland) Regulations 2002 No. 2002/450. – Enabling power: Road Traffic Regulation Act 1984, s. 124, sch. 9, pt. III, paras. 21, 22 (1) (d), 25. – Issued: 18.10.2002. Made: 03.10.2002. Laid before the Scottish Parliament: 04.10.2002. Coming into force: 08.11.2002. Effect: S.S.I. 2000/60 revoked. – 4p.: 30 cm. – 0 11 061665 0 £1.75

The Local Authorities' Traffic Orders (Procedure) (Scotland) Amendment Regulations 2002 No. 2002/31. – Enabling power: Road Traffic Regulation Act 1984, s. 124, sch. 9, part III. – Issued: 28.02.2002. Made: 21.01.2002. Laid before the Scottish Parliament: 29.01.2002. Coming into force: 01.03.2002. Effect: S.I. 1999/614 amended. Territorial extent & classification: S. General. – 4p.: 30 cm. – 0 11 061009 1 £1.75

The Motor Vehicles (Competitions and Trials) (Scotland) Amendment Regulations 2002 No. 2002/14. – Enabling power: Road Traffic Act 1988, s. 13 (2). – Issued: 20.02.2002. Made: 17.01.2002. Laid before the Scottish Parliament: 22.01.2002. Coming into force: 01.03.2002. Effect: S.I. 1976/2019 amended & S.I. 1992/747 revoked. – 2p.: 30 cm. – 0 11 059989 6 £1.50

The Parking Attendants (Wearing of Uniforms) (Perth and Kinross Council Parking Area) Regulations 2002 No. 2002/399. – Enabling power: Road Traffic Regulation Act 1984, s. 63A. – Issued: 11.09.2002. Made: 02.09.2002. Laid before the Scottish Parliament: 03.09.2002. Coming into force: 01.10.2002. Effect: None. Territorial extent & classification: S. General. – 4p.: 30 cm. – 0 11 061601 4 £1.75

The Removal and Disposal of Vehicles Amendment (Scotland) Regulations 2002 No. 2002/538. – Enabling power: Refuse Disposal (Amenity) Act 1978, ss. 3, 4 & Road Traffic Regulation Act 1984, ss. 99, 101. – Issued: 13.12.2002. Made: 29.11.2002. Laid before the Scottish Parliament: 04.12.2002. Coming into force: 15.01.2003. Effect: S.I. 1986/183 amended in relation to Scotland. Territorial extent & classification: S. General. – 4p.: 30 cm. – 0 11 061754 1 £1.75

The Road Traffic (NHS Charges) Amendment (No. 2) (Scotland) Regulations 2002 No. 2002/528. Enabling power: Road Traffic (NHS Charges) Act 1999, ss. 3 (2) (4), 16 (2) (a) (b). – Issued: 10.12.2002. Made: 29.11.2002. Laid before the Scottish Parliament: 02.12.2002. Coming into force: 01.01.2003. Effect: S.I. 1999/705 amended (in relation to Scotland). – 4p.: 30 cm. – 0 11 061738 X £1.75

The Road Traffic (NHS Charges) Amendment (Scotland) Regulations 2002 No. 2002/56. – Enabling power: Road Traffic (NHS Charges) Act 1999, ss. 3 (2) (4), 16 (2) (a) (b), 17. – Issued: 01.03.2002. Made: 12.02.2002. Laid before the Scottish Parliament: 13.02.2002. Coming into force: 14.02.2002. Effect: S.I. 1999/785 amended (in relation to Scotland). – 4p.: 30 cm. – 0 11 061059 8 £1.75

The Road Traffic (Parking Adjudicators) (Perth and Kinross Council) Regulations 2002 No. 2002/400. – Enabling power: Road Traffic Act 1991, s. 73 (11) (12). – Issued: 11.09.2002. Made: 02.09.2002. Laid before the Scottish Parliament: 03.09.2002. Coming into force: 01.10.2002. Effect: None. Territorial extent & classification: S. General. – 12p.: 30 cm. – 0 11 061602 2 £2.50

The Road Traffic (Permitted Parking Area and Special Parking Area) (City of Edinburgh) Designation Amendment Order 2002 No. 2002/188. – Enabling power: Road Traffic Act 1991, sch. 3, paras. 1 (1), 2 (1), 3 (3)– Issued: 03.05.2002. Made: 16.04.2002. Laid before the Scottish Parliament: 17.04.2002. Coming into force: 17.05.2002. Effect: S.I. 1998/1539 amended. Territorial extent & classification: S. General. – 2p.: 30 cm. – 0 11 061398 8 £1.50

The Road Traffic (Permitted Parking Area and Special Parking Area) (City of Glasgow) Designation Amendment Order 2002 No. 2002/187. – Enabling power: Road Traffic Act 1991, sch. 3, paras. 1 (1), 2 (1), 3 (3)– Issued: 03.05.2002. Made: 16.04.2002. Laid before the Scottish Parliament: 17.04.2002. Coming into force: 17.05.2002. Effect: S.S.I. 1999/59 amended. Territorial extent & classification: S. General. – 2p.: 30 cm. – 0 11 061402 X £1.50

The Road Traffic (Permitted Parking Area and Special Parking Area) (Perth and Kinross Council) Designation Order 2002 No. 2002/398. – Enabling power: Road Traffic Act 1991, sch. 3, paras. 1 (1), 2 (1), 3 (3)– Issued: 11.09.2002. Made: 02.09.2002. Laid before the Scottish Parliament: 03.09.2002. Coming into force: 01.10.2002. Effect: 1984, c. 27; 1991 c. 40 modified. Territorial extent & classification: S. General. – 12p.: 30 cm. – 0 11 061599 9 £2.50

The School Crossing Patrol Sign (Scotland) Regulations 2002 No. 2002/549. – Enabling power: Road Traffic Regulation Act 1984, s. 28 (4). – Issued: 23.12.2002. Made: 12.12.2002. Laid before the Scottish Parliament: 13.12.2002. Coming into force: 15.01.2003. Effect: S.I. 1994/1519 amended in relation to Scotland. Territorial extent & classification: S. General. – 4p., col. ill.: 30 cm. – 0 11 061761 4 £1.75

Road traffic: Speed limits

The A9 Trunk Road (Ballinluig) (50mph Speed Limit) Order 2002 No. 2002/464. – Enabling power: Road Traffic Regulation Act 1984, s. 84 (1) (a). – Made: 10.10.2002. Coming into force: 24.10.2002. Effect: None. Territorial extent & classification: S. Local *Unpublished*

The A9 Trunk Road (Golspie) (30mph Speed Limit) Order 2002 No. 2002/394. – Enabling power: Road Traffic Regulation Act 1984, ss. 82 (2) (a), 83 (1), 84 (1) (a). – Made: 21.08.2002. Coming into force: 04.09.2002. Effect: S.I. 1975/819 amended & S.I. 1995/1586 revoked. Territorial extent & classification: S. Local *Unpublished*

The A82 Trunk Road (Loch Lomond World Invitation Golf Tournament) (Temporary 30 mph Speed Limit) Order 2002 No. 2002/331. – Enabling power: Road Traffic Regulation Act 1984, s. 88 (1) (a). – Made: 02.07.2002. Coming into force: 09.07.2002. Effect: None. Territorial extent & classification: S. Local *Unpublished*

The A85 Trunk Road (Crieff) (30mph Speed Limit) Order 2002 No. 2002/392. – Enabling power: Road Traffic Regulation Act 1984, s. 84 (1) (a). – Made: 27.08.2002. Coming into force: 10.09.2002. Effect: Tayside Region (Restricted Roads) Order 1988 amended. Territorial extent & classification: S. Local *Unpublished*

The A86 Trunk Road (Newtonmore) (30mph Speed Limit) Order 2002 No. 2002/53. – Enabling power: Road Traffic Regulation Act 1984, ss. 82 (2) (b), 83 (1), 84 (1) (a), 124 (1) (d). – Made: 06.02.2002. Coming into force: 20.02.2002. Effect: The Highland Regional Council (A86 Newtonmore) (Restricted Road) Order 1989 revoked. Territorial extent & classification: S. Local *Unpublished*

The A86 Trunk Road (Spean Bridge) (30mph Speed Limit) Order 2002 No. 2002/377. – Enabling power: Road Traffic Regulation Act 1984, ss. 82 (2) (b), 83 (1), 84 (1) (a), 124 (1) (d). – Made: 14.08.2002. Coming into force: 28.08.2002. Effect: The County Council of Inverness (Restricted Roads) (No. 2) Order 1967 & The Highland Regional Council Transitional Order 1994 - Restricted and Non-Restricted Roads varied. Territorial extent & classification: S. Local *Unpublished*

The A92 Trunk Road (Balfarg Junction, Glenrothes) (50mph Speed Limit) Order 2002 No. 2002/27. – Enabling power: Road Traffic Regulation Act 1984, ss. 84 (1) (a), 124 (2). – Made: 25.01.2002. Coming into force: 08.02.2002. Effect: None. Territorial extent & classification: S. Local *Unpublished*

The A876 Trunk Road (Kincardine Bridge) (30mph Speed Limit) Order 2002 No. 2002/405. – Enabling power: Road Traffic Regulation Act 1984, ss. 84 (1) (a), 124 (2). – Made: 29.08.2002. Coming into force: 20.09.2002. Effect: S.I. 1965/1336 revoked. Territorial extent & classification: S. Local *Unpublished*

Road traffic: Traffic regulation

The A1 Trunk Road (Off Slip Westbound to the A6094) (Temporary Prohibition of Traffic) Order 2002 No. 2002/204. – Enabling power: Road Traffic Regulation Act 1984, s. 14 (1) (a). – Made: 24.04.2002. Coming into force: 03.05.2002. Effect: None. Territorial extent & classification: S. Local *Unpublished*

The A7 Trunk Road (Hoghill Farm to Kirkstile Bridge) (Temporary Prohibition of Traffic) Order 2002 No. 2002/446. – Enabling power: Road Traffic Regulation Act 1984, s. 14 (1) (a). – Made: 30.09.2002. Coming into force: 04.10.2002. Effect: None. Territorial extent & classification: S. Local *Unpublished*

The A7 Trunk Road (West Port to Raeburn Place, Selkirk) (Temporary Prohibition of Traffic and Temporary Prohibition of Specified Turns) Order 2002 No. 2002/250. – Enabling power: Road Traffic Regulation Act 1984, s. 14 (1) (a). – Made: 22.05.2002. Coming into force: 29.05.2002. Effect: None. Territorial extent & classification: S. Local *Unpublished*

The A7 Trunk Road (West Port to Raeburn Place, Selkirk) (Temporary Prohibition of Traffic) Order 2002 No. 2002/309. – Enabling power: Road Traffic Regulation Act 1984, s. 14 (1) (a). – Made: 24.06.2002. Coming into force: 01.07.2002. Effect: None. Territorial extent & classification: S. Local *Unpublished*

The A7 Trunk Road (West Port to Raeburn Place, Selkirk) (Temporary Prohibition of Traffic) Order 2002 No. 2002/251. – Enabling power: Road Traffic Regulation Act 1984, s. 14 (1) (a). – Made: 23.05.2002. Coming into force: 04.06.2002. Effect: None. Territorial extent & classification: S. Local *Unpublished*

The A8/M8 Trunk Road (Junction 6 (Newhouse to Junction 31 (West Ferry)) (Temporary Prohibition of Traffic) Order 2002 No. 2002/211. – Enabling power: Road Traffic Regulation Act 1984, s. 14 (1) (a). – Made: 03.05.2002. Coming into force: 10.05.2002. Effect: None. Territorial extent & classification: S. Local *Unpublished*

The A8 Trunk Road (Baillieston to Newhouse) (Temporary Prohibition of Specified Turns) Order 2002 No. 2002/41. – Enabling power: Road Traffic Regulation Act 1984, ss.1 (1), 2 (1) (2). – Made: 07.02.2002. Coming into force: 15.02.2002. Effect: None. Territorial extent & classification: S. Local *Unpublished*

The A8 Trunk Road (Bargeddie Railway Bridge) (Temporary Prohibition of Traffic) Order 2002 No. 2002/554. – Enabling power: Road Traffic Regulation Act 1984, s. 14 (1) (a). – Made: 16.12.2002. Coming into force: 28.12.2002. Effect: None. Territorial extent & classification: S. Local *Unpublished*

The A8 Trunk Road/M73 Motorway (Baillieston Roundabout) (Temporary Prohibition of Traffic) (No. 2) Order 2002 No. 2002/364. – Enabling power: Road Traffic Regulation Act 1984, s. 14 (1) (a). – Made: 31.07.2002. Coming into force: 02.08.2002. Effect: None. Territorial extent & classification: S. Local *Unpublished*

The A8 Trunk Road/M73 Motorway (Baillieston Roundabout) (Temporary Prohibition of Traffic) Order 2002 No. 2002/256. – Enabling power: Road Traffic Regulation Act 1984, s. 14 (1) (a). – Made: 24.05.2002. Coming into force: 02.06.2002. Effect: None. Territorial extent & classification: S. Local *Unpublished*

The A8 Trunk Road (Sinclair Street to Cartsdyke Roundabout, Greenock) (Temporary Prohibition of Specified Turns) Order 2002 No. 2002/344. – Enabling power: Road Traffic Regulation Act 1984, s. 14 (1) (a). – Made: 10.07.2002. Coming into force: 19.07.2002. Effect: None. Territorial extent & classification: S. Local *Unpublished*

The A9 Trunk Road (Auchterarder to Blackford) (Temporary Prohibition of Specified Turns) Order 2002 No. 2002/459. – Enabling power: Road Traffic Regulation Act 1984, s.14 (1) (a). – Made: 08.10.2002. Coming into force: 21.10.2002. Effect: None. Territorial extent & classification: S. Local *Unpublished*

The A9 Trunk Road (Blackford) (Temporary Prohibition of Specified Turns) Order 2002 No. 2002/79. – Enabling power: Road Traffic Regulation Act 1984, s.14 (1) (a). – Made: 26.02.2002. Coming into force: 11.03.2002. Effect: None. Territorial extent & classification: S. Local *Unpublished*

The A68 Trunk Road (Harryburn to Newmills) (Temporary Prohibition of Traffic) (No. 2) Order 2002 No. 2002/452. – Enabling power: Road Traffic Regulation Act 1984, s. 14 (1) (a). – Made: 03.10.2002. Coming into force: 18.10.2002. Effect: None. Territorial extent & classification: S. Local *Unpublished*

The A68 Trunk Road (Harryburn to Newmills) (Temporary Prohibition of Traffic) Order 2002 No. 2002/327. – Enabling power: Road Traffic Regulation Act 1984, s. 14 (1) (a). – Made: 27.06.2002. Coming into force: 08.07.2002. Effect: None. Territorial extent & classification: S. Local *Unpublished*

The A68 Trunk Road (West High Street, Market Place and East High Street, Lauder) (Special Event) (Temporary Prohibition of Traffic) Order 2002 No. 2002/257. – Enabling power: Road Traffic Regulation Act 1984, s. 16A. – Made: 24.05.2002. Coming into force: 28.05.2002 at 23:00 hours. Effect: None. Territorial extent & classification: S. Local *Unpublished*

The A68 Trunk Road (West High Street, Market Place and East High Street, Lauder) (Special Event) Temporary Prohibition of Traffic) Order 2002 No. 2002/259. – Enabling power: Road Traffic Regulation Act 1984, s. 16A. – Made: 28.05.2002. Coming into force: 29.05.2002. Effect: None. Territorial extent & classification: S. Local *Unpublished*

The A74 (M) Motorway, Junction 19 (Ecclefechan) Southbound On-Slip Road (Temporary Prohibition of Traffic) Order 2002 No. 2002/180. – Enabling power: Road Traffic Regulation Act 1984, s. 14 (1) (a). – Made: 05.04.2002. Coming into force: 13.04.2002. Effect: None. Territorial extent & classification: S. Local *Unpublished*

The A75 Trunk Road (Challoch Bridge at Dunragit) (Temporary Prohibition of Traffic) Order 2002 No. 2002/8. Enabling power: Road Traffic Regulation Act 1984, s. 14 (1) (a). – Made: 11.01.2002. Coming into force: 19.01.2002. Effect: None. Territorial extent & classification: S. Local *Unpublished*

The A75 Trunk Road (College Road Footbridge, Dumfries) (Temporary Prohibition) Order 2002 No. 2002/71. – Enabling power: Road Traffic Regulation Act 1984, s. 14 (1) (a). – Made: 22.02.2002. Coming into force: 01.03.2002. Effect: None. Territorial extent & classification: S. Local *Unpublished*

The A75 (T) Trunk Road (Southbound On-Slip Road to the A74 (M) Motorway at Gretna) (Temporary Prohibition of Traffic) Order 2002 No. 2002/286. – Enabling power: Road Traffic Regulation Act 1984, s. 14 (1) (a). – Made: 27.05.2002. Coming into force: 08.06.2002. Effect: None. Territorial extent & classification: S. Local *Unpublished*

The A76 Trunk Road (Carronbridge) (Temporary Prohibition of Traffic) Order 2002 No. 2002/296. – Enabling power: Road Traffic Regulation Act 1984, s. 14 (1) (a). – Made: 07.06.2002. Coming into force: 15.06.2002. Effect: None. Territorial extent & classification: S. Local *Unpublished*

The A77 Trunk Road (Dalrymple Street, Girvan) (Special Event) (Temporary Prohibition of Traffic) Order 2002 No. 2002/543. – Enabling power: Road Traffic Regulation Act 1984, s. 16A. – Made: 05.12.2002. Coming into force: 06.12.2002. Effect: None. Territorial extent & classification: S. Local *Unpublished*

The A77 Trunk Road (Dalrymple Street, Girvan) (Temporary Prohibition of Traffic) Order 2002 No. 2002/386. – Enabling power: Road Traffic Regulation Act 1984, s. 14 (1) (a). – Made: 21.08.2002. Coming into force: 02.09.2002. Effect: None. Territorial extent & classification: S. Local *Unpublished*

The A77 Trunk Road (Dutchhouse Roundabout to Symington) (Temporary Prohibition of Traffic and Temporary Prohibition of Specified Turns) (No. 2) Order 2002 No. 2002/298. – Enabling power: Road Traffic Regulation Act 1984, s. 14 (1) (a). – Made: 12.06.2002. Coming into force: 21.06.2002. Effect: None. Territorial extent & classification: S. Local *Unpublished*

The A77 Trunk Road (Dutchhouse Roundabout to Symington) (Temporary Prohibition of Traffic and Temporary Prohibition of Specified Turns) Order 2002 No. 2002/209. – Enabling power: Road Traffic Regulation Act 1984, s.14 (1) (a). – Made: 30.04.2002. Coming into force: 07.05.2002. Effect: None. Territorial extent & classification: S. Local *Unpublished*

The A77 Trunk Road (Hansel Village, Symington) (Temporary Prohibition of Specified Turns) Order 2002 No. 2002/5. – Enabling power: Road Traffic Regulation Act 1984, s.14 (1) (a). – Made: 04.01.2002. Coming into force: 12.01.2002. Effect: None. Territorial extent & classification: S. Local *Unpublished*

The A77 Trunk Road (Hansel Village, Symington) (Temporary Prohibition of Traffic) Order 2002 No. 2002/52. – Enabling power: Road Traffic Regulation Act 1984, s. 14 (1) (a). – Made: 08.02.2002. Coming into force: 16.02.2002. Effect: None. Territorial extent & classification: S. Local *Unpublished*

The A77 Trunk Road (Vicarton Street, Girvan) (Temporary Prohibition of Traffic) Order 2002 No. 2002/476. – Enabling power: Road Traffic Regulation Act 1984, s. 14 (1) (a). – Made: 23.10.2002. Coming into force: 03.11.2002. Effect: None. Territorial extent & classification: S. Local *Unpublished*

The A77 Trunk Road (Whitletts Roundabout to Dutch House Roundabout) (Temporary Prohibition of Specified Turns) Order 2002 No. 2002/222. – Enabling power: Road Traffic Regulation Act 1984, s.14 (1) (a). – Made: 08.05.2002. Coming into force: 17.05.2002. Effect: None. Territorial extent & classification: S. Local *Unpublished*

The A78 Trunk Road (Access to Nos 90, 92 and 94 Inverkip Road, Greenock) (One-Way Traffic) Order 2002 No. 2002/212. – Enabling power: Road Traffic Regulation Act 1984, ss. 1 (1), 2 (1) (2). – Made: 01.05.2002. Coming into force: 15.05.2002. Effect: None. Territorial extent & classification: S. Local *Unpublished*

The A78 Trunk Road (Ardgowan Road to Wemyss Bay Road, Wemyss Bay) (Temporary Prohibition of Specified Turns) Order 2002 No. 2002/466. – Enabling power: Road Traffic Regulation Act 1984, s. 14 (1) (a). – Made: 11.10.2002. Coming into force: 19.10.2002. Effect: None. Territorial extent & classification: S. Local *Unpublished*

The A78 Trunk Road (Dunlop Street Roundabout to South Street Roundabout, Greenock) (Temporary Prohibition of Traffic, Temporary Prohibition of Specified Turns and Temporary Prohibition of Waiting) Order 2002 No. 2002/436. – Enabling power: Road Traffic Regulation Act 1984, s. 14 (1) (a). – Made: 19.09.2002. Coming into force: 27.09.2002. Effect: None. Territorial extent & classification: S. Local *Unpublished*

The A78 Trunk Road (Dutch House Roundabout to Monktonhead Roundabout) (Prohibition of Specified Turns) Order 2002 No. 2002/525. – Enabling power: Road Traffic Regulation Act 1984, s. 1 (1). – Made: 27.11.2002. Coming into force: 11.12.2002. Effect: None. Territorial extent & classification: S. Local *Unpublished*

The A78 Trunk Road (Inverkip Road, Greenock) (Prohibition of Specified Turns) Order 2002 No. 2002/213. – Enabling power: Road Traffic Regulation Act 1984, ss. 1 (1), 2 (1) (2). – Made: 01.05.2002. Coming into force: 15.05.2002. Effect: None. Territorial extent & classification: S. Local *Unpublished*

The A78 Trunk Road (Inverkip Road, Greenock) (Temporary Prohibition of Specified Turns) Order 2002 No. 2002/381. – Enabling power: Road Traffic Regulation Act 1984, s. 14 (1) (a). – Made: 09.08.2002. Coming into force: 19.08.2002. Effect: None. Territorial extent & classification: S. Local *Unpublished*

The A78 Trunk Road (Irvine Road and Main Street, Largs) (Temporary Prohibition of Waiting and Loading) Order 2002 No. 2002/380. – Enabling power: Road Traffic Regulation Act 1984, s. 14 (1) (a). – Made: 09.08.2002. Coming into force: 17.08.2002. Effect: None. Territorial extent & classification: S. Local *Unpublished*

The A78 Trunk Road (Main Street and Irvine Road, Largs) (Temporary Prohibition of Waiting) (No. 2) Order 2002 No. 2002/351. – Enabling power: Roads (Scotland) Act 1984, s. 62. – Made: 19.07.2002. Coming into force: 26.07.2002. Effect: None. Territorial extent & classification: S. Local *Unpublished*

The A78 Trunk Road (Main Street and Irvine Road, Largs) (Temporary Prohibition of Waiting) Order 2002 No. 2002/308. – Enabling power: Roads (Scotland) Act 1984, s. 62. – Made: 21.06.2002. Coming into force: 29.06.2002. Effect: None. Territorial extent & classification: S. Local *Unpublished*

The A80 Trunk Road (Auchenkilns Roundabout) (Temporary Prohibition of Traffic and Temporary Prohibition of Specified Turns) Order 2002 No. 2002/343. – Enabling power: Road Traffic Regulation Act 1984, s. 14 (1) (a). – Made: 10.07.2002. Coming into force: 19.07.2002. Effect: None. Territorial extent & classification: S. Local *Unpublished*

The A80 Trunk Road (Moodiesburn) (Temporary Prohibition of Specified Turns) Order 2002 No. 2002/2. – Enabling power: Road Traffic Regulation Act 1984, s.14 (1) (a). – Made: 03.01.2002. Coming into force: 11.01.2002. Effect: None. Territorial extent & classification: S. Local *Unpublished*

The A80 Trunk Road (Muirhead North Junction) (Temporary Prohibition of Specified Turns) Order 2002 No. 2002/16. – Enabling power: Road Traffic Regulation Act 1984, s.14 (1) (a). – Made: 18.01.2002. Coming into force: 01.02.2002. Effect: None. Territorial extent & classification: S. Local *Unpublished*

The A80 Trunk Road (Muirhead South Junction) (Temporary Prohibition of Specified Turns) Order 2002 No. 2002/24. – Enabling power: Road Traffic Regulation Act 1984, s.14 (1) (a). – Made: 25.01.2002. Coming into force: 08.02.2002. Effect: None. Territorial extent & classification: S. Local *Unpublished*

The A80 Trunk Road (Old Inns A8011 Junction) (Temporary Prohibition of Traffic) Order 2002 No. 2002/378. – Enabling power: Road Traffic Regulation Act 1984, s. 14 (1) (a). – Made: 12.08.2002. Coming into force: 16.08.2002. Effect: None. Territorial extent & classification: S. Local *Unpublished*

The A80 Trunk Road (On and Off Slip Roads at Old Inns Interchange) (Temporary Prohibition of Traffic) Order 2002 No. 2002/503. – Enabling power: Road Traffic Regulation Act 1984, s. 14 (1) (a). – Made: 15.11.2002. Coming into force: 22.11.2002. Effect: None. Territorial extent & classification: S. Local *Unpublished*

The A80 Trunk Road (Slip Roads at Cumbernauld Road) (Temporary Prohibition of Traffic) Order 2002 No. 2002/395. – Enabling power: Road Traffic Regulation Act 1984, s. 14 (1) (a). – Made: 28.08.2002. Coming into force: 06.09.2002. Effect: None. Territorial extent & classification: S. Local *Unpublished*

The A80 Trunk Road (Woodhead Road Junction, Muirhead) (Temporary Prohibition of Specified Turns) Order 2002 No. 2002/25. – Enabling power: Road Traffic Regulation Act 1984, s.14 (1) (a). – Made: 25.01.2002. Coming into force: 08.02.2002. Effect: None. Territorial extent & classification: S. Local *Unpublished*

The A82 Trunk Road (Gavinburn to Dunglass) (Temporary Prohibition of Specified Turns) Order 2002 No. 2002/214. – Enabling power: Road Traffic Regulation Act 1984, s.14 (1) (a). – Made: 03.05.2002. Coming into force: 10.05.2002. Effect: None. Territorial extent & classification: S. Local *Unpublished*

The A82 Trunk Road (Junction with Colquhoun Road, Milton) (Temporary Prohibition of Specified Turns) Order 2002 No. 2002/26. – Enabling power: Road Traffic Regulation Act 1984, s.14 (1) (a). – Made: 25.01.2002. Coming into force: 05.02.2002. Effect: None. Territorial extent & classification: S. Local *Unpublished*

The A82 Trunk Road (Tarbet to Crianlarich) (Temporary Prohibition of Traffic) Order 2002 No. 2002/555. – Enabling power: Road Traffic Regulation Act 1984, s. 14 (1) (a). – Made: 13.12.2002. Coming into force: 06.01.2003. Effect: None. Territorial extent & classification: S. Local *Unpublished*

The A85 Trunk Road (Crieff Road, Perth) (Temporary Prohibition of Specified Turns) Order 2002 No. 2002/481. – Enabling power: Road Traffic Regulation Act 1984, s. 14 (1) (a). – Made: 25.10.2002. Coming into force: 07.11.2002. Effect: None. Territorial extent & classification: S. Local *Unpublished*

The A90 Trunk Road (Cross Street, Fraserburgh) (Temporary Prohibition of Traffic) Order 2002 No. 2002/287. – Enabling power: Road Traffic Regulation Act 1984, s. 14 (1) (a). – Made: 05.06.2002. Coming into force: 16.06.2002. Effect: None. Territorial extent & classification: S. Local *Unpublished*

The A90 Trunk Road (Dubton Cottages to North Water Bridge, Laurencekirk) (Temporary Prohibition of Specified Turns) (No. 2) Order 2002 No. 2002/559. – Enabling power: Road Traffic Regulation Act 1984, s.14 (1) (a). – Made: 17.12.2002. Coming into force: 01.01.2003. Effect: None. Territorial extent & classification: S. Local *Unpublished*

The A90 Trunk Road (Dubton Cottages to North Water Bridge, Laurencekirk) (Temporary Prohibition of Specified Turns) Order 2002 No. 2002/470. – Enabling power: Road Traffic Regulation Act 1984, s.14 (1) (a). – Made: 21.10.2002. Coming into force: 04.11.2002. Effect: None. Territorial extent & classification: S. Local *Unpublished*

The A90 Trunk Road (Glencarse Village, by Perth) (Temporary Prohibition of Traffic and Temporary Prohibition of Specified Turns) Order 2002 No. 2002/486. – Enabling power: Road Traffic Regulation Act 1984, s.14 (1) (a). – Made: 28.10.2002. Coming into force: 11.11.2002. Effect: None. Territorial extent & classification: S. Local *Unpublished*

The A90 Trunk Road (Kingsway West, Dundee) (Temporary Prohibition of Traffic) Order 2002 No. 2002/366. – Enabling power: Road Traffic Regulation Act 1984, s. 14 (1) (a). – Made: 29.07.2002. Coming into force: 12.08.2002. Effect: None. Territorial extent & classification: S. Local *Unpublished*

The A90 Trunk Road (Kirriemuir Junction, near Forfar) (Temporary Prohibition of Traffic) Order 2002 No. 2002/485. – Enabling power: Road Traffic Regulation Act 1984, s. 14 (1) (a). – Made: 28.10.2002. Coming into force: 11.11.2002. Effect: None. Territorial extent & classification: S. Local *Unpublished*

The A90 Trunk Road (Milton of Philorth, Near Fraserburgh) (Temporary Prohibition of Traffic) Order 2002 No. 2002/215. – Enabling power: Road Traffic Regulation Act 1984, s. 14 (1) (a). – Made: 03.05.2002. Coming into force: 13.05.2002. Effect: None. Territorial extent & classification: S. Local *Unpublished*

The A90 Trunk Road (Muchalls to Westport) (Temporary Prohibition of Specified Turns) Order 2002 No. 2002/471. – Enabling power: Road Traffic Regulation Act 1984, s.14 (1) (a). – Made: 22.10.2002. Coming into force: 30.10.2002. Effect: None. Territorial extent & classification: S. Local *Unpublished*

The A90 Trunk Road (Shielhill to North Powrie Farm, North of Dundee) (Temporary Prohibition of Specified Turns) Order 2002 No. 2002/376. – Enabling power: Road Traffic Regulation Act 1984, s.14 (1) (a). – Made: 15.08.2002. Coming into force: 23.08.2002. Effect: None. Territorial extent & classification: S. Local *Unpublished*

The A92 Trunk Road (Forgan Roundabout, near Newport-on-Tay) (Temporary Prohibition of Traffic and Temporary Prohibition of Specified Turns) (No. 2) Order 2002 No. 2002/492. – Enabling power: Road Traffic Regulation Act 1984, s. 14 (1) (a). – Made: 31.10.2002. Coming into force: 12.11.2002. Effect: None. Territorial extent & classification: S. Local *Unpublished*

The A92 Trunk Road (Forgan Roundabout, near Newport-on-Tay) (Temporary Prohibition of Traffic and Temporary Prohibition of Specified Turns) Order 2002 No. 2002/439. – Enabling power: Road Traffic Regulation Act 1984, s. 14 (1) (a). – Made: 24.09.2002. Coming into force: 07.10.2002. Effect: None. Territorial extent & classification: S. Local *Unpublished*

The A92 Trunk Road (Forgan Roundabout, near Tayport) (Temporary Prohibition of Traffic and Temporary Prohibition of Specified Turns) Order 2002 No. 2002/346. – Enabling power: Road Traffic Regulation Act 1984, s. 14 (1) (a). – Made: 15.07.2002. Coming into force: 29.07.2002. Effect: None. Territorial extent & classification: S. Local *Unpublished*

The A92 Trunk Road (Preston Roundabout, Glenrothes) (Temporary Prohibition of Traffic) Order 2002 No. 2002/194. – Enabling power: Road Traffic Regulation Act 1984, s. 14 (1) (a). – Made: 17.04.2002. Coming into force: 26.04.2002. Effect: None. Territorial extent & classification: S. Local *Unpublished*

The A95 Trunk Road (Auchlunkart, Near Keith) Order 2002 No. 2002/574. – Enabling power: Road Traffic Regulation Act 1984, s. 14 (1) (a). – Made: 20.12.2002. Coming into force: 03.01.2003. Effect: None. Territorial extent & classification: S. Local *Unpublished*

The A96 Trunk Road (Alexandra Road, Elgin) (Temporary Prohibition of Traffic) Order 2002 No. 2002/571. – Enabling power: Road Traffic Regulation Act 1984, s. 14 (1) (a). – Made: 27.12.2002. Coming into force: 13.01.2003. Effect: None. Territorial extent & classification: S. Local *Unpublished*

The A96 Trunk Road (Inveramsay Bridge, Milton of Inveramsay, Near Inverurie) (Temporary Prohibition of Traffic) Order 2002 No. 2002/261. – Enabling power: Road Traffic Regulation Act 1984, s. 14 (1) (a). – Made: 29.05.2002. Coming into force: 11.06.2002. Effect: None. Territorial extent & classification: S. Local *Unpublished*

The A96 Trunk Road (South College Street, Dr Gray's Roundabout to River Lossie Bridge and High Street, Elgin) (Temporary Prohibition of Traffic) (No. 2) Order 2002 No. 2002/427. – Enabling power: Road Traffic Regulation Act 1984, s. 14 (1) (a). – Made: 10.09.2002. Coming into force: 24.09.2002. Effect: None. Territorial extent & classification: S. Local *Unpublished*

The A96 Trunk Road (South College Street, Dr Gray's Roundabout to River Lossie Bridge and High Street, Elgin) (Temporary Prohibition of Traffic) (No. 3) Order 2002 No. 2002/455. – Enabling power: Road Traffic Regulation Act 1984, s. 14 (1) (a). – Made: 04.10.2002. Coming into force: 16.10.2002. Effect: None. Territorial extent & classification: S. Local *Unpublished*

The A96 Trunk Road (South College Street, Dr Gray's Roundabout to River Lossie Bridge and High Street, Elgin) (Temporary Prohibition of Traffic) Order 2002 No. 2002/361. – Enabling power: Road Traffic Regulation Act 1984, s. 14 (1) (a). – Made: 01.08.2002. Coming into force: 08.08.2002. Effect: None. Territorial extent & classification: S. Local *Unpublished*

The A702 Trunk Road (Edmonston Brae, Biggar) (Temporary Prohibition of Traffic) Order 2002 No. 2002/428. – Enabling power: Road Traffic Regulation Act 1984, s. 14 (1) (a). – Made: 13.09.2002. Coming into force: 23.09.2002. Effect: None. Territorial extent & classification: S. Local *Unpublished*

The A725 Trunk Road (Eastbound and Westbound Slip Roads from Glasgow Road to Douglas Street, Blantyre) (Temporary Prohibition of Traffic) Order 2002 No. 2002/375. – Enabling power: Road Traffic Regulation Act 1984, s. 14 (1) (a). – Made: 15.08.2002. Coming into force: 25.08.2002. Effect: None. Territorial extent & classification: S. Local *Unpublished*

The A725 Trunk Road (Eastbound between Shawhead and Diamond Interchange) (Temporary Prohibition of Traffic) Order 2002 No. 2002/539. – Enabling power: Road Traffic Regulation Act 1984, s. 14 (1) (a). – Made: 29.11.2002. Coming into force: 03.12.2002. Effect: None. Territorial extent & classification: S. Local *Unpublished*

The A725 Trunk Road (Eastbound Glasgow Road to Whistleberry) (Temporary Prohibition of Traffic) Order 2002 No. 2002/477. – Enabling power: Road Traffic Regulation Act 1984, s. 14 (1) (a). – Made: 24.10.2002. Coming into force: 02.11.2002. Effect: None. Territorial extent & classification: S. Local *Unpublished*

The A725 Trunk Road (Eastbound Off Slip Road and the Westbound On Slip Road at Bellziehill Interchange, Bellshill) (Temporary Prohibition of Traffic) Order 2002 No. 2002/258. – Enabling power: Road Traffic Regulation Act 1984, s. 14 (1) (a). – Made: 24.05.2002. Coming into force: 02.06.2002. Effect: None. Territorial extent & classification: S. Local *Unpublished*

The A725 Trunk Road (Eastbound On Slip Road at Glasgow Road and Eastbound Off Slip Road at Craighead) (Temporary Prohibition of Traffic) Order 2002 No. 2002/236. – Enabling power: Road Traffic Regulation Act 1984, s. 14 (1) (a). – Made: 16.05.2002. Coming into force: 19.05.2002. Effect: None. Territorial extent & classification: S. Local *Unpublished*

The A725 Trunk Road (Eastbound on Slip Road from Main Street, High Blantyre) (Temporary Prohibition of Traffic) Order 2002 No. 2002/326. – Enabling power: Road Traffic Regulation Act 1984, s. 14 (1) (a). – Made: 27.06.2002. Coming into force: 05.07.2002. Effect: None. Territorial extent & classification: S. Local *Unpublished*

The A725 Trunk Road (Shawhead to Diamond Interchange) (Temporary Prohibition of Traffic) Order 2002 No. 2002/173. – Enabling power: Road Traffic Regulation Act 1984, s. 14 (1) (a). – Made: 28.03.2002. Coming into force: 08.04.2002. Effect: None. Territorial extent & classification: S. Local *Unpublished*

The A725 Trunk Road (Slip Roads at Belziehill Interchange, Bellshill) (Temporary Prohibition of Traffic) Order 2002 No. 2002/360. – Enabling power: Road Traffic Regulation Act 1984, s. 14 (1) (a). – Made: 01.08.2002. Coming into force: 10.08.2002. Effect: None. Territorial extent & classification: S. Local *Unpublished*

The A725 Trunk Road (The Link Road between Mavor Roundabout on Kingsway (A749) East Kilbride to the Junction with Hamilton Road (A725) East Kilbride) (Temporary Prohibition of Traffic) Order 2002 No. 2002/536. – Enabling power: Road Traffic Regulation Act 1984, s. 14 (1) (a). – Made: 29.11.2002. Coming into force: 06.12.2002. Effect: None. Territorial extent & classification: S. Local *Unpublished*

The A725 Trunk Road (Westbound between Douglas Street, Blantyre Off and On Slip Roads) (Temporary Prohibition of Traffic) Order 2002 No. 2002/505. – Enabling power: Road Traffic Regulation Act 1984, s. 14 (1) (a). – Made: 15.11.2002. Coming into force: 25.11.2002. Effect: None. Territorial extent & classification: S. Local *Unpublished*

The A725 Trunk Road (Westbound between Shawhead and Diamond Interchange) (Temporary Prohibition of Traffic) Order 2002 No. 2002/479. – Enabling power: Road Traffic Regulation Act 1984, s. 14 (1) (a). – Made: 24.10.2002. Coming into force: 04.11.2002. Effect: None. Territorial extent & classification: S. Local *Unpublished*

The A725 Trunk Road (Westbound Carriageway between Shawhead and Diamond Interchange) (Temporary Prohibition of Traffic) Order 2002 No. 2002/374. – Enabling power: Road Traffic Regulation Act 1984, s. 14 (1) (a). – Made: 15.08.2002. Coming into force: 22.08.2002. Effect: None. Territorial extent & classification: S. Local *Unpublished*

The A725 Trunk Road (Whirlies to Crossbaskets) (Temporary Prohibition of Traffic and Temporary Prohibition of Specified Turns) Order 2002 No. 2002/135. – Enabling power: Road Traffic Regulation Act 1984, s.14 (1) (a). – Made: 14.03.2002. Coming into force: 23.03.2002. Effect: None. Territorial extent & classification: S. Local *Unpublished*

The A725 Trunk Road (Whistleberry Road to Glasgow Road, Blantyre) (Temporary Prohibition of Traffic) Order 2002 No. 2002/359. – Enabling power: Road Traffic Regulation Act 1984, s. 14 (1) (a). – Made: 01.08.2002. Coming into force: 09.08.2002. Effect: None. Territorial extent & classification: S. Local *Unpublished*

The A725 Trunk Road (Whistleberry Toll to Whistleberry Road, Blantyre) (Temporary Prohibition of Traffic) Order 2002 No. 2002/461. – Enabling power: Road Traffic Regulation Act 1984, s. 14 (1) (a). – Made: 10.10.2002. Coming into force: 26.10.2002. Effect: None. Territorial extent & classification: S. Local *Unpublished*

The A725 Trunk Road (Whitemoss Roundabout to Whirlies Roundabout) (Temporary Prohibition of Traffic) Order 2002 No. 2002/28. – Enabling power: Road Traffic Regulation Act 1984, s. 14 (1) (a). – Made: 24.01.2002. Coming into force: 01.02.2002. Effect: None. Territorial extent & classification: S. Local *Unpublished*

The A726 Trunk Road (BSR Footbridge, East Kilbride) (Temporary Prohibition) Order 2002 No. 2002/462. – Enabling power: Road Traffic Regulation Act 1984, s. 14 (1) (a). – Made: 09.10.2002. Coming into force: 22.10.2002. Effect: None. Territorial extent & classification: S. Local *Unpublished*

The A726 Trunk Road (Lindores Drive Footbridge, East Kilbride) (Temporary Prohibition) Order 2002 No. 2002/123. – Enabling power: Road Traffic Regulation Act 1984, s. 14 (1) (a). – Made: 11.03.2002. Coming into force: 14.03.2002. Effect: None. Territorial extent & classification: S. Local *Unpublished*

The A726 Trunk Road (Righead Roundabout to Eaglesham Road Roundabout) (Temporary Prohibition of Traffic) Order 2002 No. 2002/229. – Enabling power: Road Traffic Regulation Act 1984, s. 14 (1) (a). – Made: 10.05.2002. Coming into force: 17.05.2002. Effect: None. Territorial extent & classification: S. Local *Unpublished*

The A726 Trunk Road (West Mains Roundabout to Peel Park Roundabout, East Kilbride) (Temporary Prohibition and Temporary Prohibitions of Specified Turns) Order 2002 No. 2002/368. – Enabling power: Road Traffic Regulation Act 1984, s. 14 (1) (a). – Made: 07.08.2002. Coming into force: 19.08.2002. Effect: None. Territorial extent & classification: S. Local *Unpublished*

The A737 Trunk Road (Dalry) (Temporary Prohibition of Traffic) Order 2002 No. 2002/29. – Enabling power: Road Traffic Regulation Act 1984, s. 14 (1) (a). – Made: 24.01.2002. Coming into force: 02.02.2002. Effect: None. Territorial extent & classification: S. Local *Unpublished*

The A823(M) Motorway (Pitreavie Spur) and M90 Motorway (Junction 1) (Temporary Prohibition of Traffic) Order 2002 No. 2002/338. – Enabling power: Road Traffic Regulation Act 1984, s. 14 (1) (a). – Made: 04.07.2002. Coming into force: 12.07.2002. Effect: None. Territorial extent & classification: S. Local *Unpublished*

The A828 Trunk Road (Connel Bridge, Near Oban) (Temporary Prohibition of Traffic) (No. 2) Order 2002 No. 2002/385. – Enabling power: Road Traffic Regulation Act 1984, s. 14 (1) (a). – Made: 15.08.2002. Coming into force: 26.08.2002. Effect: None. Territorial extent & classification: S. Local *Unpublished*

The A828 Trunk Road (Connel Bridge, Near Oban) (Temporary Prohibition of Traffic) (No. 3) Order 2002 No. 2002/474. – Enabling power: Road Traffic Regulation Act 1984, s. 14 (1) (a). – Made: 24.10.2002. Coming into force: 01.11.2002. Effect: None. Territorial extent & classification: S. Local *Unpublished*

The A828 Trunk Road (Connel Bridge, Near Oban) (Temporary Prohibition of Traffic) Order 2002 No. 2002/216. – Enabling power: Road Traffic Regulation Act 1984, s. 14 (1) (a). – Made: 02.05.2002. Coming into force: 13.05.2002. Effect: None. Territorial extent & classification: S. Local *Unpublished*

The A830 Trunk Road (West of Lochailort to Kinsadel, Near Morar) (Temporary Prohibition of Traffic) Order 2002 No. 2002/453. – Enabling power: Road Traffic Regulation Act 1984, s. 14 (1) (a). – Made: 03.10.2002. Coming into force: 14.10.2002. Effect: None. Territorial extent & classification: S. Local *Unpublished*

The A898 Erskine Bridge Trunk Road (Off and On Slip Roads at Dalnottar Interchange) (Temporary Prohibition of Traffic) Order 2002 No. 2002/490. – Enabling power: Road Traffic Regulation Act 1984, s. 14 (1) (a). – Made: 01.11.2002. Coming into force: 11.11.2002. Effect: None. Territorial extent & classification: S. Local *Unpublished*

The A898 Erskine Bridge Trunk Road (Slip Roads at Dalnottar) (Temporary Prohibition of Traffic) Order 2002 No. 2002/480. – Enabling power: Road Traffic Regulation Act 1984, s. 14 (1) (a). – Made: 24.10.2002. Coming into force: 01.11.2002. Effect: None. Territorial extent & classification: S. Local *Unpublished*

The A898 Erskine Bridge Trunk Road (Southbound On Slip Road from the A82 Eastbound) (Temporary Prohibition of Traffic) Order 2002 No. 2002/295. – Enabling power: Road Traffic Regulation Act 1984, s. 14 (1) (a). – Made: 10.06.2002. Coming into force: 24.06.2002. Effect: None. Territorial extent & classification: S. Local *Unpublished*

The A898 Erskine Bridge Trunk Road (Southbound On Slip Road from the A82 Westbound) (Temporary Prohibition of Traffic) (No. 2) Order 2002 No. 2002/352. – Enabling power: Road Traffic Regulation Act 1984, s. 14 (1) (a). – Made: 22.07.2002. Coming into force: 31.07.2002. Effect: None. Territorial extent & classification: S. Local *Unpublished*

The A898 Erskine Bridge Trunk Road (Southbound on Slip Road from the A82 Westbound) (Temporary Prohibition of Traffic) Order 2002 No. 2002/219. – Enabling power: Road Traffic Regulation Act 1984, s. 14 (1) (a). – Made: 07.05.2002. Coming into force: 15.05.2002. Effect: None. Territorial extent & classification: S. Local *Unpublished*

The A898 Trunk Road (Slip Roads at Dalnottar Interchange) (Temporary Prohibition of Traffic) Order 2002 No. 2002/68. – Enabling power: Road Traffic Regulation Act 1984, s. 14 (1) (a). – Made: 21.02.2002. Coming into force: 01.03.2002. Effect: None. Territorial extent & classification: S. Local *Unpublished*

The A985 Trunk Road (Admiralty Road, Rosyth) M90 Motorway (Junction 1, Admiralty Interchange, Rosyth) (Temporary Prohibition of Traffic and Temporary Prohibition of Specified Turns) Order 2002 No. 2002/174. – Enabling power: Road Traffic Regulation Act 1984, s. 14 (1) (a). – Made: 02.04.2002. Coming into force: 08.04.2002. Effect: None. Territorial extent & classification: S. Local *Unpublished*

The M8 Motorway (Eastbound Off Slip to A720 at Junction 1, Hermiston Interchange) (Temporary Prohibition of Traffic) Order 2002 No. 2002/10. – Enabling power: Road Traffic Regulation Act 1984, s. 14 (1) (a). – Made: 16.01.2002. Coming into force: 28.01.2002. Effect: None. Territorial extent & classification: S. Local *Unpublished*

The M8 Motorway (Eastbound On-Slip Road at A899, Junction 3) (Temporary Prohibition of Traffic) Order 2002 No. 2002/227. – Enabling power: Road Traffic Regulation Act 1984, s. 14 (1) (a). – Made: 10.05.2002. Coming into force: 20.05.2002. Effect: None. Territorial extent & classification: S. Local *Unpublished*

The M8 Motorway (Eastbound On-Slip Road at Junction 3) (Temporary Prohibition of Traffic) Order 2002 No. 2002/417. – Enabling power: Road Traffic Regulation Act 1984, s. 14 (1) (a). – Made: 05.09.2002. Coming into force: 16.09.2002. Effect: None. Territorial extent & classification: S. Local *Unpublished*

The M8 Motorway (Kingston Bridge) (Temporary Prohibition of Traffic) Order 2002 No. 2002/195. – Enabling power: Road Traffic Regulation Act 1984, s. 14 (1) (a). – Made: 16.04.2002. Coming into force: 19.04.2002. Effect: None. Territorial extent & classification: S. Local *Unpublished*

The M8 Motorway (Slip Roads at Junction 4) (Temporary Prohibition of Traffic) Order 2002 No. 2002/506. – Enabling power: Road Traffic Regulation Act 1984, s. 14 (1) (a). – Made: 14.11.2002. Coming into force: 25.11.2002. Effect: None. Territorial extent & classification: S. Local *Unpublished*

The M8 Motorway (Westbound Carriageway from Junction 22 (Plantation) to Junction 26 (Hillington)) (Temporary Prohibition of Traffic) Order 2002 No. 2002/203. – Enabling power: Road Traffic Regulation Act 1984, s. 14 (1) (a). – Made: 24.04.2002. Coming into force: 27.04.2002. Effect: None. Territorial extent & classification: S. Local *Unpublished*

The M8 Motorway (Westbound Off-Slip Road at Junction 3) (Temporary Prohibition of Traffic) Order 2002 No. 2002/396. – Enabling power: Road Traffic Regulation Act 1984, s. 14 (1) (a). – Made: 28.08.2002. Coming into force: 07.09.2002. Effect: None. Territorial extent & classification: S. Local *Unpublished*

The M9 Motorway (Craigforth Interchange Junction 10 Southbound On Slip) (Temporary Prohibition of Traffic) Order 2002 No. 2002/252. – Enabling power: Road Traffic Regulation Act 1984, s. 14 (1) (a). – Made: 22.05.2002. Coming into force: 01.06.2002. Effect: None. Territorial extent & classification: S. Local *Unpublished*

The M9 Motorway (Eastbound Off Slip at Junction 2, Philipstoun) (Temporary Prohibition of Traffic) Order 2002 No. 2002/372. – Enabling power: Road Traffic Regulation Act 1984, s. 14 (1) (a). – Made: 07.08.2002. Coming into force: 16.08.2002. Effect: None. Territorial extent & classification: S. Local *Unpublished*

The M9 Motorway (Eastbound Off Slip at Junction 4) (Temporary Prohibition of Traffic) Order 2002 No. 2002/497. – Enabling power: Road Traffic Regulation Act 1984, s. 14 (1) (a). – Made: 06.11.2002. Coming into force: 15.11.2002. Effect: None. Territorial extent & classification: S. Local *Unpublished*

The M9 Motorway (Lathallan Interchange Junction 4 Westbound On Slip) (Temporary Prohibition of Traffic) Order 2002 No. 2002/226. – Enabling power: Road Traffic Regulation Act 1984, s. 14 (1) (a). – Made: 10.05.2002. Coming into force: 20.05.2002. Effect: None. Territorial extent & classification: S. Local *Unpublished*

The M9 Motorway (Northbound On Slip Road at A904, West Mains) (Temporary Prohibition of Traffic) Order 2002 No. 2002/225. – Enabling power: Road Traffic Regulation Act 1984, s. 14 (1) (a). – Made: 10.5.2002. Coming into force: 20.05.2002. Effect: None. Territorial extent & classification: S. Local *Unpublished*

The M9 Motorway (Northbound On Slip Road at Junction 4, Lathallan) (Temporary Prohibition of Traffic) Order 2002 No. 2002/373. – Enabling power: Road Traffic Regulation Act 1984, s. 14 (1) (a). – Made: 07.08.2002. Coming into force: 16.08.2002. Effect: None. Territorial extent & classification: S. Local *Unpublished*

The M9 Motorway (Slip roads at Junction 5) (Temporary Prohibition of Traffic) Order 2002 No. 2002/507. – Enabling power: Road Traffic Regulation Act 1984, s. 14 (1) (a). – Made: 13.11.2002. Coming into force: 22.11.2002. Effect: None. Territorial extent & classification: S. Local *Unpublished*

The M9 Motorway (Slip roads at Junction 9) (Temporary Prohibition of Traffic) Order 2002 No. 2002/509. – Enabling power: Road Traffic Regulation Act 1984, s. 14 (1) (a). – Made: 13.11.2002. Coming into force: 24.11.2002. Effect: None. Territorial extent & classification: S. Local *Unpublished*

The M9 Motorway (Southbound Off Slip at Junction 6) (Temporary Prohibition of Traffic) Order 2002 No. 2002/508. – Enabling power: Road Traffic Regulation Act 1984, s. 14 (1) (a). – Made: 14.11.2002. Coming into force: 24.11.2002. Effect: None. Territorial extent & classification: S. Local *Unpublished*

The M73 Motorway (Junction 2 (Baillieston) to Junction 2A (Gartcosh)) (Temporary Prohibition of Traffic) Order 2002 No. 2002/200. – Enabling power: Road Traffic Regulation Act 1984, s. 14 (1) (a). – Made: 23.04.2002. Coming into force: 29.04.2002. Effect: None. Territorial extent & classification: S. Local *Unpublished*

The M73 Motorway (Northbound Off Slip Road to the M8 at Junction 2 (Baillieston)) (Temporary Prohibition of Traffic) Order 2002 No. 2002/354. – Enabling power: Road Traffic Regulation Act 1984, s. 14 (1) (a). – Made: 24.07.2002. Coming into force: 02.08.2002. Effect: None. Territorial extent & classification: S. Local *Unpublished*

The M73 Motorway (Northbound On Slip Road and Southbound Off Slip Road at Junction 2 (Baillieston)) (Temporary Prohibition of Traffic) Order 2002 No. 2002/3. – Enabling power: Road Traffic Regulation Act 1984, s. 14 (1) (a). – Made: 04.01.2002. Coming into force: 11.01.2002. Effect: None. Territorial extent & classification: S. Local *Unpublished*

The M73 Motorway (Northbound On Slip Road and Southbound Off Slip Road at Junction 2 (Baillieston)) (Temporary Prohibition of Traffic) Order 2002 No. 2002/475. – Enabling power: Road Traffic Regulation Act 1984, s. 14 (1) (a). – Made: 23.10.2002. Coming into force: 04.11.2002. Effect: None. Territorial extent & classification: S. Local *Unpublished*

The M73 Motorway (Southbound On Slip Road at Junction 2A (Gartcosh)) (Temporary Prohibition of Traffic) Order 2002 No. 2002/365. – Enabling power: Road Traffic Regulation Act 1984, s. 14 (1) (a). – Made: 05.08.2002. Coming into force: 12.08.2002. Effect: None. Territorial extent & classification: S. Local *Unpublished*

The M73 Motorway (Southbound On Slip Road to Northbound M74 Motorway at Junction 1 (Maryville)) (Temporary Prohibition of Traffic) Order 2002 No. 2002/341. – Enabling power: Road Traffic Regulation Act 1984, s. 14 (1) (a). – Made: 09.07.2002. Coming into force: 15.07.2002. Effect: None. Territorial extent & classification: S. Local *Unpublished*

The M74 Motorway (Junction 1 (Fullarton) to Junction 4 (Maryville Interchange)) (Temporary Prohibition of Traffic) Order 2002 No. 2002/429. – Enabling power: Road Traffic Regulation Act 1984, s. 14 (1) (a). – Made: 12.09.2002. Coming into force: 22.09.2002. Effect: None. Territorial extent & classification: S. Local *Unpublished*

The M74 Motorway (Northbound Off Slip Road at Junction 4 (Maryville)) (Temporary Prohibition of Traffic) Order 2002 No. 2002/175. – Enabling power: Road Traffic Regulation Act 1984, s. 14 (1) (a). – Made: 28.03.2002. Coming into force: 08.04.2002. Effect: None. Territorial extent & classification: S. Local *Unpublished*

The M74 Motorway (Northbound Off Slip Road at Junction 8 (Canderside)) (Temporary Prohibition of Traffic) Order 2002 No. 2002/358. – Enabling power: Road Traffic Regulation Act 1984, s. 14 (1) (a). – Made: 01.08.2002. Coming into force: 12.08.2002. Effect: None. Territorial extent & classification: S. Local *Unpublished*

The M74 Motorway (Northbound On Slip Road at Junction 7 (Merryton)) (Temporary Prohibition of Traffic) Order 2002 No. 2002/487. – Enabling power: Road Traffic Regulation Act 1984, s. 14 (1) (a). – Made: 31.10.2002. Coming into force: 09.11.2002. Effect: None. Territorial extent & classification: S. Local *Unpublished*

The M74 Motorway (Northbound On Slip Road at Junction 8 (Canderside)) (Temporary Prohibition of Traffic) Order 2002 No. 2002/456. – Enabling power: Road Traffic Regulation Act 1984, s. 14 (1) (a). – Made: 04.10.2002. Coming into force: 14.10.2002. Effect: None. Territorial extent & classification: S. Local *Unpublished*

The M74 Motorway (Northbound On Slip Road at Junction 10 (Wellburn)) (Temporary Prohibition of Traffic) Order 2002 No. 2002/4. – Enabling power: Road Traffic Regulation Act 1984, s. 14 (1) (a). – Made: 04.01.2002. Coming into force: 11.01.2002. Effect: None. Territorial extent & classification: S. Local *Unpublished*

The M74 Motorway (On Slip Roads at Junction 6 (Hamilton) and Junction 7 (Merryton)) (Temporary Prohibition of Traffic) Order 2002 No. 2002/253. – Enabling power: Road Traffic Regulation Act 1984, s. 14 (1) (a). – Made: 23.05.2002. Coming into force: 01.06.2002. Effect: None. Territorial extent & classification: S. Local *Unpublished*

The M74 Motorway (Slip Roads at Junction 8 (Canderside)) (Temporary Prohibition of Traffic) Order 2002 No. 2002/242. – Enabling power: Road Traffic Regulation Act 1984, s. 14 (1) (a). – Made: 21.05.2002. Coming into force: 27.05.2002. Effect: None. Territorial extent & classification: S. Local *Unpublished*

The M74 Motorway (Slip Roads at Maryville Interchange) (Temporary Prohibition of Traffic) Order 2002 No. 2002/447. – Enabling power: Road Traffic Regulation Act 1984, s. 14 (1) (a). – Made: 01.10.2002. Coming into force: 07.10.2002. Effect: None. Territorial extent & classification: S. Local *Unpublished*

The M74 Motorway (Southbound Off Slip Road at Junction 5 (Raith Interchange)) (Temporary Prohibition of Traffic) Order 2002 No. 2002/478. – Enabling power: Road Traffic Regulation Act 1984, s. 14 (1) (a). – Made: 25.10.2002. Coming into force: 02.11.2002. Effect: None. Territorial extent & classification: S. Local *Unpublished*

The M74 Motorway (Southbound Off Slip Road at Junction 9 (Draffan)) (Temporary Prohibition of Traffic) (No. 2) Order 2002 No. 2002/448. – Enabling power: Road Traffic Regulation Act 1984, s. 14 (1) (a). – Made: 01.10.2002. Coming into force: 07.10.2002. Effect: None. Territorial extent & classification: S. Local *Unpublished*

The M74 Motorway (Southbound Off Slip Road at Junction 9 (Draffan)) (Temporary Prohibition of Traffic) Order 2002 No. 2002/339. – Enabling power: Road Traffic Regulation Act 1984, s. 14 (1) (a). – Made: 04.07.2002. Coming into force: 15.07.2002. Effect: None. Territorial extent & classification: S. Local *Unpublished*

The M74 Motorway (Southbound Off Slip Road to Canderside at Junction 8) (Temporary Prohibition of Traffic) Order 2002 No. 2002/232. – Enabling power: Road Traffic Regulation Act 1984, s. 14 (1) (a). – Made: 07.11.2002. Coming into force: 16.11.2002. Effect: None. Territorial extent & classification: S. Local *Unpublished*

The M74 Motorway (Southbound Off Slip Road to Motherwell at Junction 6 (Hamilton Interchange)) (Temporary Prohibition of Traffic) Order 2002 No. 2002/232. – Enabling power: Road Traffic Regulation Act 1984, s. 14 (1) (a). – Made: 14.05.2002. Coming into force: 18.05.2002. Effect: None. Territorial extent & classification: S. Local *Unpublished*

The M74 Motorway (Southbound On Slip Road at Junction 4 (Maryville Interchange)) (Temporary Prohibition of Traffic) Order 2002 No. 2002/299. – Enabling power: Road Traffic Regulation Act 1984, s. 14 (1) (a). – Made: 19.06.2002. Coming into force: 29.06.2002. Effect: None. Territorial extent & classification: S. Local *Unpublished*

The M74 Motorway (Various On Slip Roads at Junction 6 (Hamilton) (Temporary Prohibition of Traffic) Order 2002 No. 2002/463. – Enabling power: Road Traffic Regulation Act 1984, s. 14 (1) (a). – Made: 10.10.2002. Coming into force: 21.10.2002. Effect: None. Territorial extent & classification: S. Local *Unpublished*

The M77 Motorway (Northbound On Slip Road at Junction 1 (Dumbreck)) (Temporary Prohibition of Traffic) Order 2002 No. 2002/42. – Enabling power: Road Traffic Regulation Act 1984, s. 14 (1) (a). – Made: 01.02.2002. Coming into force: 08.02.2002. Effect: None. Territorial extent & classification: S. Local *Unpublished*

The M80 Motorway (Northbound Carriageway Off and On Slip Roads at Junction 4, Haggs) (Temporary Prohibition of Traffic) (No. 2) Order 2002 No. 2002/150. – Enabling power: Road Traffic Regulation Act 1984, s. 14 (1) (a). – Made: 20.03.2002. Coming into force: 01.04.2002. Effect: None. Territorial extent & classification: S. Local *Unpublished*

The M80 Motorway (Northbound Carriageway Off and On Slip Roads at Junction 4, Haggs) (Temporary Prohibition of Traffic) Order 2002 No. 2002/73. – Enabling power: Road Traffic Regulation Act 1984, s. 14 (1) (a). – Made: 15.02.2002. Coming into force: 01.03.2002. Effect: None. Territorial extent & classification: S. Local *Unpublished*

The M80 Motorway (Northbound Carriageway Slip Roads at Junction 4, Haggs) (Temporary Prohibition of Traffic) Order 2002 No. 2002/393. – Enabling power: Road Traffic Regulation Act 1984, s. 14 (1) (a). – Made: 26.08.2002. Coming into force: 30.08.2002. Effect: None. Territorial extent & classification: S. Local *Unpublished*

The M90 Motorway (Junction 4, Cocklaw Interchange, Kelty)/ The A823(M) Trunk Road (Northbound and Southbound On Slip Roads) (Temporary Prohibition of Traffic) Order 2002 No. 2002/572. – Enabling power: Road Traffic Regulation Act 1984, s. 14 (1) (a). – Made: 27.12.2002. Coming into force: 06.01.2003. Effect: None. Territorial extent & classification: S. Local *Unpublished*

The M90 Motorway (Junction 10, Craigend, Southbound On Slip Road) (Temporary Prohibition of Traffic) Order 2002 No. 2002/575. – Enabling power: Road Traffic Regulation Act 1984, s. 14 (1) (a). – Made: 23.12.2002. Coming into force: 06.01.2003. Effect: None. Territorial extent & classification: S. Local *Unpublished*

The M90 Motorway (Southbound Off Slip Road at Junction 10 Craigend) (Temporary Prohibition of Traffic) (No. 2) Order 2002 No. 2002/573. – Enabling power: Road Traffic Regulation Act 1984, s. 14 (1) (a). – Made: 24.12.2002. Coming into force: 03.01.2003. Effect: None. Territorial extent & classification: S. Local *Unpublished*

The M90 Motorway (Southbound Off Slip Road at Junction 10 Craigend) (Temporary Prohibition of Traffic) Order 2002 No. 2002/484. – Enabling power: Road Traffic Regulation Act 1984, s. 14 (1) (a). – Made: 29.10.2002. Coming into force: 11.11.2002. Effect: None. Territorial extent & classification: S. Local *Unpublished*

The M876 Motorway (Off and On Slip Roads at Junction 1, A883 Interchange) (Temporary Prohibition of Traffic) Order 2002 No. 2002/379. – Enabling power: Road Traffic Regulation Act 1984, s. 14 (1) (a). – Made: 13.08.2002. Coming into force: 19.08.2002. Effect: None. Territorial extent & classification: S. Local *Unpublished*

The M876 Motorway (Westbound On Slip at Junction 8) (Temporary Prohibition of Traffic) Order 2002 No. 2002/435. – Enabling power: Road Traffic Regulation Act 1984, s. 14 (1) (a). – Made: 18.09.2002. Coming into force: 27.09.2002. Effect: None. Territorial extent & classification: S. Local *Unpublished*

The M898/A898 Erskine Bridge Trunk Road/M8 Motorway (Slip Roads from A82, A898/M898 Southbound Carriageway, On/Off Erskine Roundabout (East) Slip Roads and M8 Slip Roads from M898) (Temporary Prohibition of Traffic) Order 2002 No. 2002/491. – Enabling power: Road Traffic Regulation Act 1984, s. 14 (1) (a). – Made: 01.11.2002. Coming into force: 11.11.2002. Effect: None. Territorial extent & classification: S. Local *Unpublished*

The Trunk Roads in Scotland (Temporary Prohibitions and Temporary Speed Restrictions) Order 2002 No. 2002/151. – Enabling power: Road Traffic Regulation Act 1984, s. 14 (1) (4). – Made: 19.03.2002. Coming into force: 01.04.2002. Effect: None. Territorial extent & classification: S. Local *Unpublished*

Scottish Public Services Ombudsman

The Scottish Public Services Ombudsman Act 2002 (Amendment) Order 2002 No. 2002/468. – Enabling power: Scottish Public Services Ombudsman Act 2002, s. 3 (2) (b). – Issued: 30.10.2002. Made: 22.10.2002 Coming into operation: 23.10.2002. Effect: 2002 asp 11 amended. Territorial extent & classification: S. General. – 2p.: 30 cm. – 0 11 061673 1 £1.50

The Scottish Public Services Ombudsman Act 2002 (Commencement and Revocation of Transitory and Transitional Provisions) Order 2002 No. 2002/467 (C.25). – Enabling power: Scottish Public Services Ombudsman Act 2002, s. 27 (1) (2). Bringing into operation various provisions of the Act on 23.10.2002. – Issued: 30.10.2002. Made: 22.10.2002. Effect: S.I. 1999/1351 revoked. Territorial extent & classification: S. General. – 2p.: 30 cm. – 0 11 061672 3 £1.50

The Scottish Public Services Ombudsman Act 2002 (Transitory and Transitional Provisions) Order 2002 No. 2002/469. – Enabling power: Scottish Public Services Ombudsman Act 2002, s. 26 (2). – Issued: 30.10.2002. Made: 22.10.2002. Laid before the Scottish Parliament: 23.10.2002. Coming into force: 23.10.2002. Effect: None. The Order, unless previously revoked by Her Majesty by Order in Council, shall cease to have effect on 31st December 2003. Territorial extent & classification: S. General. – 4p.: 30 cm. – 0 11 061684 7 £1.75

Sea fisheries

The Conservation of Seals (Scotland) Order 2002 No. 2002/404. – Enabling power: Conservation of Seals Act 1970, s. 3 (1). – Issued: 10.09.2002. Made: 02.09.2002. Laid before the Scottish Parliament: 03.09.2002. Coming into force: 04.09.2002. Effect: None. Territorial extent & classification: S. General. – 2p.: 30 cm. – 0 11 061594 8 £1.50

The Sea Fishing (Enforcement of Community Conservation Measures) (Scotland) Amendment Order 2002 No. 2002/81. Enabling power: Fisheries Act 1981, s. 30 (2) – Issued: 20.03.2002. Made: 04.03.2002. Laid: 05.03.2002. Coming into force: 26.03.2002. Effect: S.S.I. 2001/53 amended. Territorial extent & classification: S. General. – 8p.: 30 cm. – 0 11 061139 X £2.00

The Sea Fishing (Enforcement of Community Quota and Third Country Fishing Measures) (Scotland) Order 2002 No. 2002/51. – Enabling power: Fisheries Act 1981, s. 30 (2). – Issued: 01.03.2002. Made: 11.02.2002. Laid: 12.2.2002. Coming into force: 10.03.2002. Effect: S.S.I. 2001/117 revoked (with saving). Territorial extent & classification: S. General. – 12p.: 30 cm. – 0 11 061070 9 £2.50

Sea fisheries: Conservation of sea fish

The Sea Fish (Prohibited Methods of Fishing) (Firth of Clyde) Order 2002 No. 2002/58. – Enabling power: Sea Fish (Conservation) Act 1967, ss. 5 (1) (c), 15 (3), 22 (2). – Issued: 01.03.2002. Made: 13.02.2002. Laid: 13.02.2002. Coming into force: 14.02.2002. Effect: None. Territorial extent & classification: S. General. – 8p.: 30 cm. – 0 11 061051 2 £2.00

Sea fisheries: Shellfish

The Little Loch Broom Scallops Several Fishery Order 2002 No. 2002/186. – Enabling power: Sea Fisheries (Shellfish) Act 1967, ss. 1, 7 (4) (a) (iii). – Issued: 29.04.202. Made: 10.04.2002. Laid: 15.04.2002. Coming into force: 07.05.2002. Effect: None. Territorial extent & classification: S. General. – 8p.: 30 cm. – 0 11 061376 7 £2.00

The Loch Caolisport Scallops Several Fishery (Scotland) Order 2002 No. 2002/272. – Enabling power: Sea Fisheries (Shellfish) Act 1967, ss. 1, 7 (4) (a) (iii). – Issued: 20.06.2002. Made: 06.06.2002. Laid before the Scottish Parliament: 07.06.2002. Coming into force: 01.07.2002. Effect: None. Territorial extent & classification: S. General. – 4p.: 30 cm. – 0 11 061449 6 £1.75

The Loch Ewe, Isle of Ewe, Wester Ross, Scallops Several Fishery (Variation) Order 2002 No. 2002/185. – Enabling power: Sea Fisheries (Shellfish) Act 1967, ss. 1, 7 (4) (a) (iii). – Issued: 29.042002. Made: 10.04.2002. Laid: 15.04.2002. Coming into force: 07.05.2002. Effect: S.I. 1997/830 amended. Territorial extent & classification: S. General. – 8p.: 30 cm. – 0 11 061380 5 £2.00

Seeds

The Seeds (Fees) (Scotland) Regulations 2002 No. 2002/526. – Enabling power: Plant Varieties and Seeds Act 1964, ss. 16 (1) (1A) (e) (5) (a), 36. – Issued: 10.12.2002. Made: 28.11.2002. Laid before the Scottish Parliament: 02.12.2002. Coming into force: 31.12.2002. Effect: S.S.I. 2000/1 revoked. Territorial extent and classification: S. General. – 16p.: 30 cm. – 0 11 061732 0 £3.00

The Seeds (Miscellaneous Amendments) (No. 2) (Scotland) Regulations 2002 No. 2002/564. – Enabling power: Plant Varieties and Seeds Act 1964, ss. 16 (1) (1A) (2) (3), 36. – Issued: 10.01.2003. Made: 19.12.2002. Laid before the Scottish Parliament: 20.12.2002. Coming into force: 31.12.2002. for regs. 1, 2 & 01.01.2003. for regs. 3, 4, in accord. with reg. 1 (2). Effect: S.I. 1993/2005, 2009 amended in relation to Scotland & S.S.I. 2002/520 revoked (31.12.2002.). Territorial extent and classification: S. General. –With correction slip dated March 2003. – 4p.: 30 cm. – 0 11 061842 4 £1.75

The Seeds (Miscellaneous Amendments) (Scotland) Regulations 2002 No. 2002/520. – Enabling power: Plant Varieties and Seeds Act 1964, ss. 16 (1) (1A) (2) (3), 36. – Issued: 06.12.2002. Made: 26.11.2002. Laid before the Scottish Parliament: 27.11.2002. Coming into force: 01.01.2003. Effect: S.I. 1993/2005, 2009 amended in relation to Scotland. Territorial extent and classification: S. General. – 4p.: 30 cm. – 0 11 061728 2 *£1.75*

Sheriff Court

Act of Adjournal (Criminal Procedure Rules Amendment No. 2) (Anti-terrorism, Crime and Security Act 2001) 2002 No. 2002/136. – Enabling power: Criminal Procedure (Scotland) Act 1995, s. 305. – Issued: 12.04.2002. Made: 01.03.2002. Coming into force: 04.03.2002. Effect: S.I. 1996/513 amended. Territorial extent & classification: S. General. – 2p.: 30 cm. – 0 11 061317 1 *£1.50*

Act of Adjournal (Criminal Procedure Rules Amendment No. 4) (Extradition) 2002 No. 2002/517. – Enabling power: Extradition Act 1989 s. 14A (6) & Criminal Procedure (Scotland) Act 1995, s. 305. – Issued: 02.12.2002. Made: 21.11.2002. Coming into force: 01.12.2002. Effect: S.I. 1996/513 amended. Territorial extent & classification: S. General. – 4p.: 30 cm. – 0 11 061724 X *£1.75*

Act of Sederunt (Amendment of Ordinary Cause Rules and Summary Applications, Statutory Applications and Appeals etc. Rules) (Applications under the Mortgage Rights (Scotland) Act 2001) 2002 No. 2002/7. – Enabling power: Sheriff Courts (Scotland) Act 1971, s. 32. – Issued: 23.01.2002. Made: 10.01.2002. Coming into force: 17.01.2002. Effect: 1907 c. 51; S.I. 1999/929 amended. Territorial extent & classification: S. General. – 12p.: 30 cm. – 0 11 059970 5 *£2.50*

Act of Sederunt (Debt Arrangement and Attachment (Scotland) Act 2002) 2002 No. 2002/560. – Enabling power: Local Government (Scotland) Act 1947, s. 247 (2) & Taxes Management Act 1970, s. 63 (1) & Sheriff Courts (Scotland) Act 1971, s. 32, & Car Tax Act 1983, sch. 1, para. 3 (3) & Abolition of Domestic Rates Etc. (Scotland) Act 1987, sch. 2, para. 7 (2) & Court of Session Act 1988, s. 5 & Local Government Finance Act 1992, sch. 8, para. 2 (2) & Local Government etc. (Scotland) Act 1994, sch. 10, para. 2 (2) & Finance Act 1996, sch. 5, para. 13 (2) & Finance Act 1997, s. 52 & Debt Arrangement and Attachment (Scotland) Act 2002, ss. 12, 17, 18, 32, 56, 64. – Issued: 24.12.2002. Made: 19.12.2002. Coming into force: 30.12.2002. Effect: S.I. 1988/2013,. 2059; 1991/1397; 1993/1956; 1994/1443; 1996/2507; 1997/291 amended & S.I. 1996/2709 revoked. Territorial extent & classification: S. General. – 60p.: 30 cm. – 0 11 061806 8 *£7.50*

Act of Sederunt (Fees of Sheriff Officers) 2002 No. 2002/515. – Enabling power: Sheriff Courts (Scotland) Act 1907, s. 40 & Execution of Diligence (Scotland) Act 1926, s. 6. – Issued: 02.12.2002. Made: 21.11.2002. Laid before the Scottish Parliament: 25.11.2002. Coming into force: 01.01.2003. Effect: S.I. 1994/392 amended. Territorial extent & classification: S. General. – 8p.: 30 cm. – 0 11 061722 3 *£2.00*

Act of Sederunt (Fees of Sheriff Officers) (No. 2) 2002 No. 2002/567. – Enabling power: Sheriff Courts (Scotland) Act 1907, s. 40 & Execution of Diligence (Scotland) Act 1926, s. 6. – Issued: 13.01.2003. Made: 20.12.2002. Laid before the Scottish Parliament: 23.12.2002. Coming into force: 30.12.2002. Effect: S.I. 1994/392 revoked with saving and 1994/3267; 1995/3095; 1996//2858; 1997/2824; 1998/2669; 1999/150; 2000/419; 2001/439; 2002/515 revoked. Territorial extent & classification: S. General. – 12p.: 30 cm. – 0 11 061854 8 *£2.50*

Act of Sederunt (Fees of Solicitors in the Sheriff Court) (Amendment) 2002 No. 2002/235. – Enabling power: Sheriff Courts (Scotland) Act 1907, s. 40. – Issued: 10.06.2002. Made: 16.05.2002. Laid: 17.05.2002. Coming into force: 10.06.2002. Effect: S.I. 1993/3080 amended. Territorial extent & classification: S. General. – 12p.: 30 cm. – 0 11 061436 4 *£2.50*

Act of Sederunt (Fees of Solicitors in the Sheriff Court) (Amendment No. 2) 2002 No. 2002/274. – Enabling power: Sheriff Courts (Scotland) Act 1907, s. 40. – Issued: 26.06.2002. Made: 06.06.2002. Laid before the Scottish Parliament: 07.06.2002. Coming into force: 01.07.2002. Effect: S.I. 1993/3080 amended. Territorial extent & classification: S. General. – 8p.: 30 cm. – 0 11 061488 7 *£2.00*

Act of Sederunt (Fees of Solicitors in the Sheriff Court) (Amendment No. 3) 2002 No. 2002/328. – Enabling power: Sheriff Courts (Scotland) Act 1907, s. 40. – Issued: 11.07.2002. Made: 28.06.02. Laid before the Scottish Parliament: 28.06.02. Coming into force: 30.06.02. Effect: S.S.I. 2002/274 amended. Territorial extent & classification: S. General. –This Scottish Statutory Instrument has been made in consequence of a defect in S.S.I. 2002/274 and is being issued free of charge to all known recipients of that instrument. – [8]p.: 30 cm. – 0 11 061510 7 *£2.00*

Act of Sederunt (Fees of Solicitors in the Sheriff Court) (Amendment No. 4) 2002 No. 2002/568. – Enabling power: Sheriff Courts (Scotland) Act 1907, s. 40. – Issued: 10.01.2003. Made: 23.12.2002. Laid before the Scottish Parliament: 23.12.2002. Coming into force: 01.01.2003. Effect: S.I. 1993/3080 amended. Territorial extent & classification: S. General. – 8p.: 30 cm. – 0 11 061843 2 *£2.00*

Act of Sederunt (Fees of Witnesses and Shorthand Writers in the Sheriff Court) (Amendment) 2002 No. 2002/280. – Enabling power: Sheriff Courts (Scotland) Act 1907, s. 40. – Issued: 26.06.2002. Made: 07.06.2002. Laid before the Scottish Parliament: 10.06.2002. Coming into force: 01.07.2002. Effect: S.I. 1992/1878 amended. Territorial extent & classification: S. General. – 4p.: 30 cm. – 0 11 061489 5 *£1.75*

Act of Sederunt (Ordinary Cause Rules) Amendment (Applications under the Protection from Abuse (Scotland) Act 2001) 2002 No. 2002/128. – Enabling power: Sheriff Courts (Scotland) Act 1971, s. 32 & Protection from Abuse (Scotland) Act 2001, ss. 2 (1) (5) (a), 3 (1). – Issued: 08.04.2002. Made: 01.03.2002. Coming into force: 08.03.2002. Effect: 1907 c.51 amended. Territorial extent and classification: S. General. – 8p.: 30 cm. – 0 11 061281 7 £2.00

Act of Sederunt (Small Claim Rules) 2002 No. 2002/133. – Enabling power: Sheriff Courts (Scotland) Act 1971, s. 32. – Issued: 22.04.2002. Made: 01.03.2002. Coming into force: 10.06.2002. Effect: S.I. 1990/661, 2105; 199/821; 1992/249; 1993/1956 amended & S.I. 1988/1976 revoked. Territorial extent & classification: S. General. – 89p.: 30 cm. – 0 11 061354 6 £9.00

Act of Sederunt (Summary Applications, Statutory Applications and Appeals etc. Rules) Amendment (Detention and Forfeiture of Terrorist Cash) 2002 No. 2002/129. – Enabling power: Sheriff Courts (Scotland) 1971, s. 32. – Issued: 08.04.2002. Made: 01.03.2002. Coming into force: 08.03.2002. Effect: S.I. 1999/929 amended. Territorial extent & classification: S. General. – 4p.: 30 cm. – 0 11 061279 5 £1.75

Act of Sederunt (Summary Applications, Statutory Applications and Appeals etc. Rules) Amendment (No. 2) (Local Government (Scotland) Act 1973) 2002 No. 2002/130. Enabling power: Sheriff Courts (Scotland) 1971, s. 32. – Issued: 08.04.2002. Made: 01.03.2002. Coming into force: 08.03.2002. Effect: S.I. 1999/929 amended. Territorial extent & classification: S. General. – 8p.: 30 cm. – 0 11 061282 5 £2.00

Act of Sederunt (Summary Applications, Statutory Applications and Appeals etc. Rules) Amendment (No. 3) (Adults with Incapacity) 2002 No. 2002/146. – Enabling power: Sheriff Courts (Scotland) Act 1971, s. 32. – Issued: 17.04.2002. Made: 15.03.2002. Coming into force: 01.04.2002. Effect: S.I. 1999/929 amended. Territorial extent & classification: S. General. – 4p.: 30 cm. – 0 11 061344 9 £1.75

Act of Sederunt (Summary Applications, Statutory Applications and Appeals etc. Rules) Amendment (No. 5) (Proceeds of Crime Act 2002) 2002 No. 2002/563. – Enabling power: Sheriff Courts (Scotland) Act 1971, s. 32. – Issued: 09.01.2003. Made: 19.12.2002. Coming into force: 30.12.2002. Effect: S.I. 1999/929 amended. Territorial extent & classification: S. General. – 4p.: 30 cm. – 0 11 061839 4 £1.75

Act of Sederunt (Summary Cause Rules) 2002 No. 2002/132. – Enabling power: Sheriff Courts (Scotland) Act 1971, s. 32. – Issued: 22.04.2002. Made: 01.03.2002. Coming into force: 10.06.2002. Effect: S.I. 1983/747; 1986/1946, 1966; 1988/1976, 1978; 1989/436; 1990/661, 2105; 1992/249; 1993/919, 1956 amended & S.I. 1976/476; 1978/112, 1805; 1980/455; 1991/821 revoked. Territorial extent & classification: S. General. – 157p.: 30 cm. – 0 11 061355 4 £13.50

Act of Sederunt (Summary Cause Rules) (Amendment) 2002 No. 2002/516. – Enabling power: Sheriff Courts (Scotland) Act 1971, s. 32. – Issued: 02.12.2002. Made: 21.11.2002. Coming into force: 01.01.2003. Effect: S.S.I. 2002/132 amended. Territorial extent & classification: S. General. – 4p.: 30 cm. – 0 11 061723 1 £1.75

The Sheriff Court Fees Amendment Order 2002 No. 2002/269. – Enabling power: Courts of Law Fees (Scotland) Act 1895, s. 2. – Issued: 20.06.2002. Made: 05.06.2002. Laid before the Scottish Parliament: 07.06.2002. Coming into force: 01.07.2002. Effect: S.I. 1997/687 amended. Territorial extent & classification: S. General. – 12p.: 30 cm. – 0 11 061462 3 £2.50

Social care

The Community Care (Additional Payments) (Scotland) Regulations 2002 No. 2002/265. – Enabling power: Community Care and Health (Scotland) Act 2002, ss. 4, 23 (4). – Issued: 20.06.2002. Made: 05.06.2002. Laid before the Scottish Parliament: 06.06.2002. Coming into force: 01.07.2002. Effect: None. Territorial extent & classification: S. General. – 4p.: 30 cm. – 0 11 061457 7 £1.75

The Community Care and Health (Scotland) Act 2002 (Commencement No. 1) Order 2002 No. 2002/170 (C.10). – Enabling power: Community Care and Health (Scotland) Act 2002, s. 27 (2) (3). Bringing into force various provisions of the 2002 Act on 01.04.2002, 13.05.2002, 01.07.2002, 01.09.2002, 01.06.2003 in accord. with art. 2. – Issued: 24.04.2002. Made: 28.03.2002. Effect: None. Territorial extent & classification: S. General. – 4p.: 30 cm. – 0 11 061370 8 £1.75

The Community Care and Health (Scotland) Act 2002 (Consequential Amendment) Order 2002 No. 2002/233. – Enabling power: Community Care and Health (Scotland) Act 2002, s. 24. – Issued: 27.05.2002. Made: 15.05.2002. Laid: 16.05.2002. Coming into force: 07.06.2002. Effect: 2002 asp 5 amended. Territorial extent & classification: S. General. – 2p.: 30 cm. – 0 11 061425 9 £1.50

The Community Care (Assessment of Needs) (Scotland) Regulations 2002 No. 2002/304. – Enabling power: Community Care and Health (Scotland) Act 2002, s. 1 (7). – Issued: 03.07.2002. Made: 20.06.2002. Coming into force: 01.07.2002. Effect: 1968 c. 49 modified. Territorial extent & classification: S. General. – 4p.: 30 cm. – 0 11 061493 3 £1.75

The Community Care (Deferred Payment of Accommodation Costs) (Scotland) Regulations 2002 No. 2002/266. – Enabling power: Community Care and Health (Scotland) Act 2002, ss. 6 (1) (3), 23 (4). – Issued: 20.06.2002. Made: 05.06.2002. Laid before the Scottish Parliament: 06.06.2002. Coming into force: 01.07.2002. Effect: None. Territorial extent & classification: S. General. – 4p.: 30 cm. – 0 11 061460 7 £1.75

The Community Care (Disregard of Resources) (Scotland) Order 2002 No. 2002/264. – Enabling power: Social Work (Scotland) Act 1968, ss. 12 (3A) (3B), 94 (1). – Issued: 20.06.2002. Made: 05.06.2002. Laid before the Scottish Parliament: 06.06.2002. Coming into force: 01.07.2002. Effect: S.I. 1992/2977 amended. Territorial extent & classification: S. General. – 4p.: 30 cm. – 0 11 061456 9 £1.75

The Community Care (Joint Working etc.) (Scotland) Regulations 2002 No. 2002/533. – Enabling power: Community Care and Health (Scotland) Act 2002, ss. 13 (1), 14, 15 (1) (2) (4), 17 (1) (a) (i) (ii), 17 (1) (b) (ii). – Issued: 12.12.2002. Made: 29.11.2002. Coming into force: 01.01.2003. Effect: None. Territorial extent & classification: S. General. – 12p.: 30 cm. – 0 11 061750 9 £2.50

The Community Care (Personal Care and Nursing Care) (Scotland) Regulations 2002 No. 2002/303. – Enabling power: Community Care and Health (Scotland) Act 2002, ss. 1 (2) (a), 2, 23 (4). – Issued: 03.07.2002. Made: 20.06.2002. Coming into force: 01.07.2002. Effect: 1968 c.49; 1984 c.36 modified. Territorial extent & classification: S. General. – 4p.: 30 cm. – 0 11 061492 5 £1.75

The Health and Social Care Act 2001 (Commencement No. 9) (Scotland) Order 2002 No. 2002/75 (C.4). – Enabling power: Health and Social Care Act 2001, s. 70 (2) (4). Bringing into force various provisions of the 2001 Act on 01.04.2002. – Issued: 12.03.2002. Made: 27.02.2002. Effect: None. Territorial extent & classification: S. General. – 2p.: 30 cm. – 0 11 061107 1 £1.50

The Preserved Rights (Transfer to Responsible Authorities) (Scotland) Regulations 2002 No. 2002/76. – Enabling power: Health and Social Care Act 2001, s. 50 (7) (8) (9). – Issued: 12.03.2002. Made: 27.02.2002. Laid: 04.03.2002. Coming into force: 08.04.2002. Effect: None. Territorial extent and classification: S. General. – 4p.: 30 cm. – 0 11 061109 8 £1.75

The Regulation of Care (Applications and Provision of Advice) (Scotland) Order 2002 No. 2002/113. – Enabling power: Regulation of Care (Scotland) Act 2001, s. 4 (3), 7 (2) (a), 14 (3), 33 (2). – Issued: 11.04.2002. Made: 08.03.2002. Laid: 08.03.2002. Coming into force: 01.04.2002. Effect: None. Territorial extent & classification: S. General. – 8p.: 30 cm. – 0 11 061052 0 £2.00

The Regulation of Care (Excepted Services) (Scotland) Regulations 2002 No. 2002/120. – Enabling power: Regulation of Care (Scotland) Act 2001, s. 2 (2) (4) (6) (20). – Issued: 28.03.2002. Made: 11.03.2002. Laid: 11.03.2002. Coming into force: 01.04.2002. Effect: None. Territorial extent & classification: S. General. – 4p.: 30 cm. – 0 11 061198 5 £1.75

The Regulation of Care (Fees) (Scotland) Order 2002 No. 2002/112. – Enabling power: Regulation of Care (Scotland) Act 2001, s. 24 (1). – Issued: 11.04.2002. Made: 08.03.2002. Laid: 08.03.2002. Coming into force: 01.04.2002. Effect: None. Territorial extent & classification: S. General. – 4p.: 30 cm. – 0 11 060993 X £1.75

The Regulation of Care (Registration and Registers) (Scotland) Regulations 2002 No. 2002/115. – Enabling power: Regulation of Care (Scotland) Act 2001, s. 28 (1) (b) (c) (d) (2). – Issued: 11.04.2002. Made: 08.03.2002. Laid: 08.03.2002. Coming into force: 01.04.2002. Effect: None. Territorial extent & classification: S. General. – 8p.: 30 cm. – 0 11 060996 4 £2.00

The Regulation of Care (Requirements as to Care Services) (Scotland) Regulations 2002 No. 2002/114. – Enabling power: Regulation of Care (Scotland) Act 2001, s. 29. – Issued: 11.04.2002. Made: 08.03.2002. Laid: 08.03.2002. Coming into force: 01.04.2002. Effect: None. Territorial extent & classification: S. General. – 12p.: 30 cm. – 0 11 060994 8 £2.50

The Regulation of Care (Scotland) Act 2001 (Commencement No. 2 and Transitional Provisions) Order 2002 No. 2002/162 (C.8). – Enabling power: Regulation of Care (Scotland) Act 2001, s. 81 (2) (3) (4). Bringing into operation various provisions of the 2001 Act on 1 April 2002. – Issued: 17.04.2002. Made: 27.03.2002. Effect: None. Territorial extent & classification: S. General. – 12p.: 30 cm. – 0 11 061345 7 £2.50

The Scottish Commission for the Regulation of Care (Appointments and Procedure) Regulations 2002 No. 2002/106. – Enabling power: Regulation of Care (Scotland) Act 2001, sch. 1, para. 7. – Issued: 08.04.2002. Made: 06.03.2002. Laid: 08.03.2002. Coming into force: 01.04.2002. Effect: None. Territorial extent & classification: S. General. – 12p.: 30 cm. – 0 11 061262 0 £2.50

The Scottish Commission for the Regulation of Care (Consultation on Transfer of Staff) Order 2002 No. 2002/18. – Enabling power: Regulation of Care (Scotland) Act 2001, s. 30 (3). – Issued: 06.02.2002. Made: 23.01.2002. Laid: 25.01.2002. Coming into force: 15.02.2002. Effect: None. Territorial extent & classification: S. General. – 4p.: 30 cm. – 0 11 059983 7 £1.75

The Scottish Commission for the Regulation of Care (Staff Transfer Scheme) Order 2002 No. 2002/108. – Enabling power: Regulation of Care (Scotland) Act 2001, s. 30. – Issued: 08.04.2002. Made: 06.03.2002. Laid: 08.03.2002. Coming into force: 01.04.2002. Effect: None. Territorial extent & classification: S. General. – 8p.: 30 cm. – 0 11 061266 3 £2.00

The Scottish Social Services Council (Appointments, Procedure and Access to the Register) Amendment Regulations 2002 No. 2002/60. – Enabling power: Regulation of Care (Scotland) Act 2001, sch. 2, para. 7. – Issued: 01.03.2002. Made: 12.02.2002. Laid: 15.02.2002. Coming into force: 15.03.2002. Effect: S.S.I. 2001/303 amended. Territorial extent & classification: S. General. – 2p.: 30 cm. – 0 11 061057 1 £1.50

Special roads

The Glasgow-Monkland Motorway (Stage II) (Connecting Roads) Special Roads (Variation) Scheme 2002 No. 2002/363. – Enabling power: Roads (Scotland) Act 1984, ss. 7, 143 (1), 145. – Made: 31.07.2002. Coming into force: 13.08.2002. Effect: S.I. 1974/2007 varied. Territorial extent & classification: S. Local *Unpublished*

The M77 (Fenwick to Malletsheugh) Special Road Scheme 2002 No. 2002/244. – Enabling power: Roads (Scotland) Act 1984, s. 7. – Made: 13.05.2002. Coming into force: 31.05.2002. Effect: None. Territorial extent & classification: S. Local *Unpublished*

The M77 Special Road (Fenwick to Floak) Side Roads (No. 3) Order 2002 No. 2002/240. – Enabling power: Roads (Scotland) Act 1984, s. 9 (1) (c). – Made: 13.05.2002. Coming into force: 31.05.2002. Effect: S.S.I. 1999/179, 180 revoked. Territorial extent & classification: S. Local *Unpublished*

The M77 Special Road (Fenwick to Malletsheugh) Side Roads Order 2002 No. 2002/245. – Enabling power: Roads (Scotland) Act 1984, s. 9 (1) (c). – Made: 13.05.2002. Coming into force: 31.05.2002. Effect: None. Territorial extent & classification: S. Local *Unpublished*

The M77 Special Road (Floak to Malletsheugh) Side Roads (No. 2) Order 2002 No. 2002/241. – Enabling power: Roads (Scotland) Act 1984, s. 9 (1) (c). – Made: 13.05.2002. Coming into force: 31.05.2002. Effect: S.S.I. 1999/184 revoked. Territorial extent & classification: S. Local *Unpublished*

Sports grounds and sporting events

The Sports Grounds and Sporting Events (Designation) (Scotland) Amendment Order 2002 No. 2002/382. – Enabling power: Criminal Law (Consolidation) (Scotland) Act 1995, s. 18. – Issued: 28.08.2002. Made: 20.08.2002. Laid: 22.08.2002. Coming into force: 21.09.2002. Effect: S.I. 1998/2314 amended. Territorial extent & classification: S. General. 2p.: 30 cm. 0 11 061584 0 *£1.50*

Town and country planning

The Environmental Impact Assessment (Scotland) Amendment Regulations 2002 No. 2002/324. – Enabling power: European Communities Act 1972, s. 2 (2) & Town & Country Planning (Scotland) Act 1997, s. 40. – Issued: 17.07.2002. Made: 27.06.2002. Laid before the Scottish Parliament: 28.06.2002. Coming into force: 23.09.2002. Effect: S.S.I. 1999/1 amended. Territorial extent & classification: S. General. – EC note: Implement in Scotland DIR 85/337/EEC (as amended by 97/11/EEC), in relation to applications to planning authorities to determine the revised conditions to which an existing minerals planning permission should be subjected. – 8p.: 30 cm. – 0 11 061558 1 *£2.00*

The Town and Country Planning (Fees for Applications and Deemed Applications) (Scotland) Amendment Regulations 2002 No. 2002/122. – Enabling power: Town and Country Planning (Scotland) Act 1997, s. 252. – Issued: 21.03.2002. Made: 11.03.2002. Coming into force: 01.04.2002. Effect: S.I. 1997/10 amended. – 8p.: 30 cm. – 0 11 061184 5 *£2.00*

Transport

The Bus Service Operators Grant (Scotland) Regulations 2002 No. 2002/289. – Enabling power: Transport (Scotland) Act 2001, ss. 38 (5), 81 (2). – Issued: 24.06.2002. Made: 10.06.2002. Laid before the Scottish Parliament: 10.06.2002. Coming into force: 01.07.2002. Effect: None. Territorial extent & classification: S. General. – 4p.: 30 cm. – 0 11 061473 9 *£1.75*

The Bus User Complaints Tribunal Regulations 2002 No. 2002/199. – Enabling power: Transport (Scotland) Act 2001, ss. 41 (1) (2) (3), 81 (2). – Issued: 03.05.2002. Made: 22.04.2002. Coming into force: 23.04.2002. Effect: None. Territorial extent & classification: S. General. – 8p.: 30 cm. – 0 11 061397 X *£2.00*

The Home Zones (Scotland) (No. 2) Regulations 2002 No. 2002/292. – Enabling power: Transport (Scotland) Act 2001, ss. 74 (4), 81 (2). – Issued: 24.06.2002. Made: 10.06.2002. Laid before the Scottish Parliament: 10.06.2002. Coming into force: 01.07.2002. Effect: S.S.I. 2002/177 revoked. Territorial extent & classification: S. General. –The S.S.I. has been made in consequence of defects in S.S.I. 2002/177 (ISBN 0110613856) and is being issued free of charge to all known recipients of that instrument. – 12p.: 30 cm. – 0 11 061467 4 *£2.50*

The Home Zones (Scotland) Regulations 2002 No. 2002/177. – Enabling power: Transport (Scotland) Act 2001, ss. 74 (4), 81 (2). – Issued: 30.04.2002. Made: 18.04.2002. Laid: 19.04.2002. Coming into force: 20.05.2002. Effect: None. Territorial extent & classification: S. General. – 12p.: 30 cm. – 0 11 061385 6 *£2.50*

The Mobility and Access Committee for Scotland Regulations 2002 No. 2002/69. – Enabling power: Transport (Scotland) Act 2001, ss. 72, 81 (2). – Issued: 11.03.2002. Made: 25.02.2002. Laid: 26.02.2002. Coming into force: 22.03.2002. Effect: None. Territorial extent & classification: S. General. – 4p.: 30 cm. – 0 11 061094 6 *£1.75*

The Scottish Transport Group (Dissolution) Order 2002 No. 2002/263. – Enabling power: Transport (Scotland) Act 1989, s. 14 (1) (2) (3). – Issued: 20.06.2002. Made: 05.06.2002. Coming into force: 07.06.2002. Effect: 1966 c. 34; 1968 c. 73; 1975 c. 24; 1981 c. 56; 1982 c. 49; 1983 c. 29, 44 amended. Territorial extent & classification: S. General. – 8p.: 30 cm. – 0 11 061455 0 *£2.00*

The Transport (Scotland) Act 2001 (Commencement No. 3 and Transitional Provisions) Order 2002 No. 2002/291 (C.15). – Enabling power: Transport (Scotland) Act 2001, ss. 81 (2), 84 (2). Bringing into operation various provisions of the 2001 Act on 01.07.2002. – Issued: 21.06.2002. Made: 10.06.2002. Laid:-. Effect: None. Territorial extent & classification: S. General. – 4p.: 30 cm. – 0 11 061485 2 *£1.75*

The Travel Concessions (Eligible Services) (Scotland) Order 2002 No. 2002/290. – Enabling power: Transport Act 1985, s. 94 (4). – Issued: 21.06.2002. Made: 10.06.2002. Laid before the Scottish Parliament: 10.06.2002. Coming into force: 01.07.2002. Effect: None. Territorial extent & classification: S. General. – 4p.: 30 cm. – 0 11 061484 4 *£1.75*

Water

The Designation of Nitrate Vulnerable Zones (Scotland) (No. 2) Regulations 2002 No. 2002/546. – Enabling power: European Communities Act 1972, s. 2 (2). – Issued: 23.12.2002. Made: 09.12.2002. Laid before the Scottish Parliament: 11.12.2002. Coming into force: 15.01.2003. Effect: None. Territorial extent & classification: S. General. – 4p.: 30 cm. – 0 11 061794 0 *£1.75*

The Designation of Nitrate Vulnerable Zones (Scotland) Regulations 2002 No. 2002/276. – Enabling power: European Communities Act 1972, s. 2 (2). – Issued: 21.06.2002. Made: 06.06.2002. Laid before the Scottish Parliament: 07.06.2002. Coming into force: 01.07.2002. Effect: S.I. 1996/1564 amended. Territorial extent & classification: S. General. – 4p.: 30 cm. – 0 11 061486 0 *£1.75*

The New Water and Sewerage Authorities Dissolution (Scotland) Order 2002 No. 2002/277. – Enabling power: Water Industry (Scotland) Act 2002, s. 24 (1). – Issued: 20.06.2002. Made: 07.06.2002. Laid before the Scottish Parliament: 07.06.2002. Coming into force: 29.06.2002. Effect: None. Territorial extent and classification: S. General. – 2p.: 30 cm. – 0 11 061454 2 *£1.50*

The Water Industry (Scotland) Act 2002 (Commencement and Savings) Order 2002 No. 2002/118 (C.6). – Enabling power: Water Industry (Scotland) Act 2002, ss. 68(2), 72 (1). Bringing into operation various provisions of the 2002 Act on 08.03.2002, 01.04.2002. – Issued: 11.04.2002. Made: 07.03.2002 Effect: None. – 4p.: 30 cm. – 0 11 060999 9 *£1.75*

Water supply

The Domestic Water and Sewerage Charges (Reduction) (Scotland) Regulations 2002 No. 2002/47. – Enabling power: Local Government etc. (Scotland) Act 1994, s. 81. – Issued: 28.02.2002. Made: 07.02.2002. Laid: 08.02.2002. Coming into force: 01.04.2002. Effect: None. Territorial extent and classification: S. General. – 4p.: 30 cm. – 0 11 061015 6 *£1.75*

The Scottish Water (Rate of Return) (Scotland) Order 2002 No. 2002/165. – Enabling power: Water Industry (Scotland) Act 2002, s. 41 (2). – Issued: 16.04.2002. Made: 27.03.2002. Laid: 28.03.2002. Coming into force: 01.04.2002. Effect: None. Territorial extent and classification: S. Local. – 4p.: 30 cm. – 0 11 061339 2 *£1.75*

The Water and Sewerage Charges (Exemption) (Scotland) Regulations 2002 No. 2002/167. – Enabling power: Water Industry (Scotland) Act 2002, s. 40. – Issued: 16.04.2002. Made: 27.03.2002. Laid: 28.03.2002. Coming into force: 01.04.2002. Effect: None. Territorial extent and classification: S. General. – 4p.: 30 cm. – 0 11 061343 0 *£1.75*

Water Customer Consultation Panels (Scotland) Order 2002 No. 2002/473. – Enabling power: Water Industry (Scotland) Act 2002, ss. 2 (1) (2), 68 (2). – Issued: 06.11.2002. Made: 23.10.2002. Laid before the Scottish Parliament: 25.10.2002. Coming into force: 20.11.2002. Effect: None. Territorial extent and classification: S. General. – 4p.: 30 cm. – 0 11 061689 8 *£1.75*

The Water Industry (Scotland) Act 2002 (Consequential and Savings Provisions) Order 2002 No. 2002/166. – Enabling power: Water Industry (Scotland) Act 2002, ss. 24 (3), 68 (2) (3), 69. – Issued: 16.04.2002. Made: 27.03.2002. Laid: 28.03.2002. Coming into force: 01.04.2002. Effect: S.I. 1992/1332; S.S.I. 2002/33, 47 amended. – 4p.: 30 cm. – 0 11 061338 4 *£1.75*

The Water Services Charges (Billing and Collection) (Scotland) Order 2002 No. 2002/33. – Enabling power: Local Government etc. (Scotland) Act 1994, s. 79. – Issued: 21.02.2002. Made: 31.01.2002. Laid: 01.02.2002. Coming into force: 01.04.2002. Effect: None. Territorial extent & classification: S. General. – 8p.: 30 cm. – 0 11 059993 4 *£2.00*

Young offenders institutions

The Prisons and Young Offenders Institutions (Scotland) Amendment Rules 2002 No. 2002/107. – Enabling power: Prisons (Scotland) Act 1989, s. 39. – Issued: 11.04.2002. Made: 06.03.2002. Laid: 08.04.2002. Coming into force: 01.04.2002. Effect: S.I. 1994/1931 amended. – 12p.: 30 cm. – 0 11 060990 5 *£2.50*

Scottish Statutory Instruments 2002

Arranged by Number

1	Animals
2	Road traffic
3	Road traffic
4	Road traffic
5	Road traffic
6	Agriculture
7	Sheriff Court
8	Road traffic
9	Public health
10	Road traffic
11	River
12 (C.1)	Children and young persons
13	Roads and bridges
14	Road traffic
15	Local government
16	Road traffic
17	National Health Service
18	Social care
19	Public health
20	Public health
21	Animals
22	Animals
23	Police
24	Road traffic
25	Road traffic
26	Road traffic
27	Road traffic
28	Road traffic
29	Road traffic
30	Children and young persons
31	Road traffic
32	Legal services
33	Water supply
34	Animals
35	Animals
36	Food
	Agriculture
37	Legal aid and advice
38	Animals
39	Animals
40	Building and buildings
41	Road traffic
42	Road traffic
43	Agriculture
44	Agriculture
45	Housing
46	Damages
47	Water supply
48	Public health
49	Public health
50	Food
51	Sea fisheries
52	Road traffic
53	Road traffic
54	Animals
55	Local government
56	National Health Service
	Road traffic
57	Public health
58	Sea fisheries
59	Nurses, midwives and health visitors
60	Social care
61	Food
62	Race relations
63	Children and young persons
64	Food

65	Public health	101	Council tax
66	Public health	102	Council tax
67	Public health	103	National Health Service
68	Road traffic	104	Public health
69	Transport	105	National Health Service
70	Local government	106	Social care
71	Road traffic	107	Prisons
72 (C.2)	Education		Young offenders institutions
73	Road traffic	108	Social care
74 (C.3)	Education	109	Animals
75 (C.4)	Social care	110	Food
76	Social care	111	National Health Service
77	Public finance and accountability	112	Social care
78	Public finance and accountability	113	Social care
79	Road traffic	114	Social care
80	Public health	115	Social care
81	Sea fisheries	116	Police
82	Public health	117	Pesticides
83	Environmental protection	118 (C.6)	Water
84 (C.5)	Fire services	119	Criminal law
	Police	120	Social care
85	National assistance services	121	Harbours, docks, piers and ferries
86	National Health Service	122	Town and country planning
87	Food	123	Road traffic
88	Legal aid and advice	124 (C.7)	Police
89	Rating and valuation	125	Animals
90	Education	126	Public health
91	Rating and valuation	127	Public health
92	Electricity	128	Sheriff Court
93	Electricity	129	Sheriff Court
94	Electricity	130	Sheriff Court
95	Adults with incapacity	131	Adults with incapacity
96	Adults with incapacity	132	Sheriff Court
97	Adults with incapacity	133	Sheriff Court
98	Adults with incapacity	134	Public finance and accountability
99	National Health Service	135	Road traffic
100	National Health Service	136	Sheriff Court

137	High Court of Justiciary	172 (C.11)	Adults with incapacity
138	River	173	Road traffic
139	Agriculture	174	Road traffic
140	Police	175	Road traffic
141	Fire services	176	Public finance and accountability
142	Nurses, midwives and health visitors	177	Transport
143	Police	178	Roads and bridges
144	Legal aid and advice	179	Food
145	Legal aid and advice	180	Road traffic
146	Sheriff Court	181 (C.12)	Animals
147	Environmental protection		Countryside
148	Food	182	Public health
149	Food	183	Public health
150	Road traffic	184 (C.13)	Marriage
151	Road traffic	185	Sea fisheries
152	Public health	186	Sea fisheries
153	National Health Service	187	Road traffic
154	Local government	188	Road traffic
155	Local government	189 (C.14)	Adults with incapacity
156	Local government	190	Adults with incapacity
157	Local government	191	Agriculture
158	Rating and valuation	192	National Health Service
159	Rating and valuation	193	River
160	Public health	194	Road traffic
161	Licences and licensing	195	Road traffic
	Housing	196	Animals
162 (C.8)	Social care	197	Public health
163	Electricity	198	Public health
164	Plant health	199	Transport
165	Water supply	200	Road traffic
166	Water supply	201	Countryside
167	Water supply	202	Countryside
168 (C.9)	Housing	203	Road traffic
169	Food	204	Road traffic
	Animals	205	Investigatory powers
170 (C.10)	Social care	206	Investigatory powers
171	Housing	207	Investigatory powers

208	Adults with incapacity	243	Roads and bridges
209	Road traffic	244	Roads and bridges Special roads
210	Roads and bridges		
211	Road traffic	245	Roads and bridges Special roads
212	Road traffic		
213	Road traffic	246	Legal aid and advice
214	Road traffic	247	Legal aid and advice
215	Road traffic	248	Education
216	Road traffic	249	Education
217	Police	250	Road traffic
218	Public health	251	Road traffic
219	Road traffic	252	Road traffic
220	River	253	Road traffic
221	Animals	254	Legal aid and advice
222	Road traffic	255	Animals
223	Plant health	256	Road traffic
224	National Health Service	257	Road traffic
225	Road traffic	258	Road traffic
226	Road traffic	259	Road traffic
227	Road traffic	260	Marriage
228	Food	261	Road traffic
229	Road traffic	262	Rating and valuation
230	Local government	263	Transport
231	Public health	264	Social care
232	Road traffic	265	Social care
233	Social care	266	Social care
234	Food	267	Food
235	Sheriff Court	268	National Health Service
236	Road traffic	269	Sheriff Court
237	Roads and bridges	270	Court of Session
238	Animals	271	Agriculture
239	National Health Service	272	Sea fisheries
240	Roads and bridges Special roads	273	Roads and bridges
		274	Sheriff Court
241	Roads and bridges Special roads	275	Adults with incapacity
		276	Water
242	Road traffic	277	Water

278	Agriculture	314	Housing
279	Pesticides	315	Housing
280	Sheriff Court	316	Housing
281	Betting, gaming and lotteries	317	Housing
282	Education	318	Housing
283	Food	319	Housing
284	Food	320	Housing
285	Agriculture	321 (C.16)	Housing
286	Road traffic	322	Housing
287	Road traffic	323	Criminal law
288	Pensions	324	Town and country planning
289	Transport		Roads and bridges
290	Transport		Land drainage
291 (C.15)	Transport	325	Agriculture
292	Transport	326	Road traffic
293	Education	327	Road traffic
294	Harbours, docks, piers and ferries	328	Sheriff Court
295	Road traffic	329	Legal aid and advice
296	Road traffic	330	Legal aid and advice
297	Environmental protection	331	Road traffic
298	Road traffic	332	Public health
299	Road traffic	333	Public health
300	Food	334	Animals
	Agriculture	335	Contracts
301	Court of Session	336	Contracts
302	Adults with incapacity	337 (C.17)	Contracts
303	Social care	338	Road traffic
304	Social care	339	Road traffic
305	National Health Service	340	Court of Session
306	Public health	341	Road traffic
307	Public health	342	Roads and bridges
308	Road traffic	343	Road traffic
309	Road traffic	344	Road traffic
310	Harbours, docks, piers and ferries	345	Public health
311	Pensions	346	Road traffic
312	Housing	347	Roads and bridges
313	Housing	348	Roads and bridges

349	Food	384	Public health
350	Public health	385	Road traffic
351	Road traffic	386	Road traffic
352	Road traffic	387	High Court of Justiciary
353	Public health	388	Public health
354	Road traffic	389	Registration of births, deaths, marriages, etc.
355 (C.18)	Education	390	Registration of births, deaths, marriages, etc.
356	Food		Marriages
	Agriculture		
357	Public health	391	Education
358	Road traffic	392	Road traffic
359	Road traffic	393	Road traffic
360	Road traffic	394	Road traffic
361	Road traffic	395	Road traffic
362	Road traffic	396	Road traffic
363	Roads and bridges	397	Food
	Special roads	398	Road traffic
364	Road traffic	399	Road traffic
365	Road traffic	400	Road traffic
366	Road traffic	401	Public health
367 (C.19)	Education	402	Public health
368	Road traffic	403	Public health
369	Animals	404	Sea fisheries
370	Roads and bridges	405	Road traffic
371	Road traffic	406	Education
372	Road traffic	407	Electricity
373	Road traffic	408	Public health
374	Road traffic	409	Public health
375	Road traffic	410	Harbours, docks, piers and ferries
376	Road traffic	411	Housing
377	Road traffic	412	Housing
378	Road traffic	413	Housing
379	Road traffic	414	Housing
380	Road traffic	415	Housing
381	Road traffic	416	Housing
382	Sports grounds and sporting events	417	Road traffic
383	Public health	418	River

419	Roads and bridges	456	Road traffic
420 (C.20)	Police	457	Representation of the people
421	Public health	458	Police
422	Public health	459	Road traffic
423	Education	460	Roads and bridges
424	Food	461	Road traffic
425	Food	462	Road traffic
426	Roads and bridges	463	Road traffic
427	Road traffic	464	Road traffic
428	Road traffic	465	Public health
429	Road traffic	466	Road traffic
430	Public health	467 (C.25)	Scottish Public Services Ombudsman
431	Public health	468	Scottish Public Services Ombudsman
432 (C.21)	Land registration	469	Scottish Public Services Ombudsman
433 (C.22)	Housing	470	Road traffic
434	Housing	471	Road traffic
435	Road traffic	472	Prisons
436	Road traffic	473	Water supply
437 (C.23)	Freedom of information	474	Road traffic
438	National Health Service	475	Road traffic
439	Road traffic	476	Road traffic
440	Legal aid and advice	477	Road traffic
441	Legal aid and advice	478	Road traffic
442	Legal aid and advice	479	Road traffic
443 (C.24)	Criminal law	480	Road traffic
444	Housing	481	Road traffic
445	Agriculture	482	Public health
446	Road traffic	483	Plant health
447	Road traffic	484	Road traffic
448	Road traffic	485	Road traffic
449	Agriculture	486	Road traffic
450	Road traffic	487	Road traffic
451	Road traffic	488	Environmental protection
452	Road traffic	489	Agriculture
453	Road traffic		Pesticides
454	High Court of Justiciary	490	Road traffic
455	Road traffic	491	Road traffic

492	Road traffic	527	Clean air
493	Environmental protection	528	National Health Service
494	Legal aid and advice		Road traffic
495	Legal aid and advice	529	Animals
496	Legal aid and advice	530	Animals
497	Road traffic	531	Animals
498	Food	532	Legal aid and advice
499	Road traffic	533	Social care
500	Licences and licensing	534	National Health Service
501	Roads and bridges	535	National Health Service
502	Roads and bridges	536	Road traffic
503	Road traffic	537	Pesticides
504	Harbours, docks, piers and ferries	538	Road traffic
505	Road traffic	539	Road traffic
506	Road traffic	540	Animals
507	Road traffic	541	Environmental protection
508	Road traffic	542	Public finance and accountability
509	Road traffic	543	Road traffic
510	Public health	544	Public health
511	Public health	545	Public health
512 (C.26)	Consumer protection	546	Water
513	Court of Session	547	Road traffic
514	Court of Session	548	Public passenger transport
515	Sheriff Court	549	Road traffic
516	Sheriff Court	550	Public health
517	High Court of Justiciary	551	Public health
	Sheriff Court	552	Public health
518	Plant health	553	Public health
519 (C.27)	Animals	554	Road traffic
	Countryside	555	Road traffic
520	Seeds	556	Environmental protection
521	Licences and licensing	557	Harbours, docks, piers and ferries
522	Representation of the people	558	Public health
523	Food	559	Road traffic
524	Food	560	Sheriff Court
525	Road traffic	561	Representation of the people
526	Seeds	562 (C.28)	Children and young persons

563	Sheriff Court	124 (C.7)
564	Seeds	162 (C.8)
565	Agriculture	168 (C.9)
566	Court of Session	170 (C.10)
567	Sheriff Court	172 (C.11)
568	Sheriff Court	181 (C.12)
569	Proceeds of Crime	184 (C.13)
570	Court of Session	189 (C.14)
571	Road traffic	291 (C.15)
572	Road traffic	321 (C.16)
573	Road traffic	337 (C.17)
574	Road traffic	355 (C.18)
575	Road traffic	367 (C.19)

List of Scottish Commencement Orders 2002

12 (C.1)
72 (C.2)
74 (C.3)
75 (C.4)
84 (C.5)
118 (C.6)
420 (C.20)
432 (C.21)
433 (C.22)
437 (C.23)
443 (C.24)
467 (C.25)
512 (C.26)
519 (C.27)
562 (C.28)

Northern Ireland Legislation

Acts of the Northern Ireland Assembly

Acts of the Northern Ireland Assembly 2002

Budget Act (Northern Ireland) 2002: Chapter 3. – [2], 28p.: 30 cm. – Royal assent, 20th March 2002. – Explanatory notes are available to assist the reader in understanding this Act (ISBN 0105960217). – 0 10 595029 7   £5.50

Budget (No. 2) Act (Northern Ireland) 2002: Chapter 7. – [2], 16p.: 30 cm. – Royal assent, 12th August 2002. – Explanatory notes are available to assist the reader in understanding this Act (ISBN 010596025X). – 0 10 595034 3   £4.00

Carers and Direct Payments Act (Northern Ireland) 2002: Chapter 6. – [2], 13, [1]p.: 30 cm. – Royal assent, 2nd May 2002. – Note: The Personal Social Services (Amendment) Bill was introduced to the Northern Ireland Assembly on 27 November 2001. With effect from 6 March 2002 its title was changed to the Carers and Direct Payments Bill. – 0 10 595032 7   £3.00

Children (Leaving Care) Act (Northern Ireland) 2002: Chapter 11. – [2], 12, [1]p.: 30 cm. – Royal assent, 22nd November 2002. – 0 10 595038 6   £3.00

Game Preservation (Amendment) Act (Northern Ireland) 2002: Chapter 2. – [12]p.: 30 cm. – Royal assent, 13th February 2002. - Explanatory notes to this Act are published separately (ISBN 0105960195). – With binder holes. – 0 10 595028 9   £2.00

Health and Personal Social Services Act (Northern Ireland) 2002: Chapter 9. – [2], 9p.: 30 cm. – Royal assent, 4th October 2002. An Act to amend the Health and Personal Social Services (Northern Ireland) Order 1972 in relation to charges for nursing care in residential accommodation; to provide for the establishment and functions of the Northern Ireland Practice and Education Council for Nursing and Midwifery. – 0 10 595036 X   £3.00

Industrial Development Act (Northern Ireland) 2002: Chapter 1. – [2], 18p.: 30 cm. – Royal assent, 7th February 2002. - Explanatory notes to this Act are published separately (ISBN 0105960209). – 0 10 595027 0   £4.00

Limited Liability Partnerships Act (Northern Ireland) 2002: Chapter 12. – [2], 12, [1]p.: 30 cm. – Royal assent, 22nd November 2002. – 0 10 595039 4   £3.00

Local Government (Best Value) Act (Northern Ireland) 2002: Chapter 4. – [2], 3p.: 30 cm. – Royal assent, 26th March 2002. – 0 10 595030 0   £2.00

Open-ended Investment Companies Act (Northern Ireland) 2002: Chapter 13. – [8]p.: 30 cm. – Royal assent, 22nd November 2002. – 0 10 595040 8   £2.00

Personal Social Services (Preserved Rights) Act (Northern Ireland) 2002: Chapter 5. – [2], 5p.: 30 cm. – Royal assent, 26th March 2002. – Explanatory notes are available to assist the reader in understanding this Act (ISBN 0105960225). – 0 10 595031 9   £2.50

Railway Safety Act (Northern Ireland) 2002: Chapter 8. – [2], 9p.: 30 cm. – Royal assent, 13th August 2002. – Explanatory notes are available to assist the reader in understanding this Act (ISBN 0105960268). – 0 10 595035 1   £3.00

Social Security Act (Northern Ireland) 2002: Chapter 10. – [12]p.: 30 cm. – Royal assent, 17th October 2002. An Act to amend the law relating to statutory maternity pay; to amend the law relating to maternity allowance; to make provision for work-focused interviews for partners of benefit claimants; to make provision about the use of information for, or relating to, employment and training; to amend the Deregulation and Contracting Out (Northern Ireland) Order 1996. – 0 10 595037 8   £3.00

State Pension Credit Act (Northern Ireland) 2002: Chapter 14. – [2], 29, [1]p.: 30 cm. – Royal assent, 22nd November 2002. – 0 10 595041 6 *£6.00*

Acts of the Northern Ireland Assembly - Explanatory notes 2002

Budget Act (Northern Ireland) 2002: explanatory notes; Chapter 3. – [1], 4p.: 30 cm. – These Explanatory Notes refer to the Budget Act (Northern Ireland) 2002 (ISBN 0105950297) [which received Royal Assent on 20th March 2002 (c. 3)]. – 0 10 596021 7 *£2.00*

Budget Act (No. 2) (Northern Ireland) 2002: explanatory notes; Chapter 7. – [8]p.: 30 cm. – These Explanatory Notes refer to the Budget Act (No. 2) (Northern Ireland) 2002 (ISBN 0105950343) which received Royal Assent on 12th August 2002 (c. 7). – 0 10 596025 X *£2.00*

Game Preservation (Amendment) Act (Northern Ireland) 2002: explanatory notes; Chapter 2. – [8]p.: 30 cm. – These Explanatory notes refer to the Game Preservation (Amendment) Act (Northern Ireland) 2002 (ISBN 0105950289) which received royal assent on 13 February 2002. – With binder holes. – 0 10 596019 5 *£2.00*

Health and Personal Social Services Act (Northern Ireland) 2002: explanatory notes; Chapter 9. – [8]p.: 30 cm. – These Explanatory Notes refer to the Health and Personal Social Services Act (Northern Ireland) 2002 (ISBN 010595036X) which received Royal Assent on 4th October 2002 (c. 8). – 0 10 595025 4 *£2.00*

Industrial Development Act (Northern Ireland) 2002: explanatory notes; Chapter 1. – 7p.: 30 cm. – These Explanatory Notes refer to the Industrial Development Act (Northern Ireland) 2002 (ISBN 0105950270) which received royal assent on 7 February 2002. – 0 10 596020 9 *£2.50*

Personal Social Services (Preserved Rights) Act (Northern Ireland) 2002: explanatory notes; Chapter 5. – [1], 4p.: 30 cm. – These Explanatory Notes refer to the Personal Social Services (Preserved Rights) Act (Northern Ireland) 2002 (ISBN 0105950319) [which received Royal Assent on 26th March 2002 (c. 5)]. – 0 10 596022 5 *£2.00*

Railway Safety Act (Northern Ireland) 2002:chapter 8; explanatory notes. – [1], 5p.: 30 cm. – These Explanatory Notes refer to the Railway Safety Act (Northern Ireland) 2002 (ISBN 0105950351) which received Royal Assent on 13th August 2002 (c. 8). – 0 10 596026 8 *£2.00*

Statutory Rules of Northern Ireland

By Subject Heading

Adoption

The Adoption of Children from Overseas Regulations (Northern Ireland) 2002 No. 2002/144. – Enabling power: S.I. 1987/2203 (N.I. 22), arts. 10, 58ZA. – Issued: 23.04.2002. Made: 11.04.2002. Coming into force: 13.05.2002. Effect: None. – 4p.: 30 cm. – 0 337 94248 X *£1.75*

Agriculture

Agricultural Processing and Marketing Grant Regulations (Northern Ireland) 2002 No. 2002/30. – Enabling power: European Communities Act 1972, s. 2 (2). – Issued: 15.02.2002. Made: 06.02.2002 Coming into operation: 14.03.2002. Effect: S.R. 1996/196 revoked with saving. – EC note: These Regs. implement a part of the Northern Ireland Programme for Building Sustainable Prosperity (BSP) as approved by the European Commission under art. 44 of REG (EC) 1257/1999, and provide for the payment of Community support by the Department of Agriculture and Rural Development (Northern Ireland). – 12p.: 25 cm. – 0 337 94146 7 *£2.50*

Beef Special Premium (Amendment) Regulations (Northern Ireland) 2002 No. 2002/335. – Enabling power: European Communities Act 1972, s. 2 (2). – Issued: 12.11.2002. Made: 05.11.2002. Coming into operation: 01.01.2003. Effect: S.R. 2001/363 amended. – 4p.: 25 cm. – 0 337 94389 3 *£1.75*

Bovines and Bovine Products (Trade) (Amendment) Regulations (Northern Ireland) 2002 No. 2002/278. – Enabling power: European Communities Act 1972, s. 2 (2). – Issued: 14.10.2002. Made: 09.09.2002. Coming into operation: 30.09.2002. Effect: S.R. 1999/308 amended. – EC note: Gives effect (for Northern Ireland) to DEC 98/692/EC and 98/564/EC which amended 98/256/EC. It also gives effect to 2002/670/EC (which amends 98/256/EC) concerning the despatch from Northern Ireland of bovine embryos and bone in veal carcasses from calves between 6 and 9 months exported under the Date Based Export Scheme (DBES). – 12p.: 25 cm. – 0 337 94374 5 *£2.50*

Feeding Stuffs (Amendment) Regulations (Northern Ireland) 2002 No. 2002/263. – Enabling power: Agriculture Act 1970, ss. 66 (1), 68 (1) (1A), 69 (1), 74A, 75 (1), 76 (1), 77 (4), 78 (6), 79 (1), 84 & European Communities Act 1972, s. 2 (2). – Issued: 14.08.2002. Made: 05.08.2002. Coming into operation: 16.09.2002. Effect: S.R. 1999/296; 2001/47 amended & S.I. 1999/1872, 2325 amended. – 8p.: 30 cm. – 0 337 94334 6 *£2.00*

Feedingstuffs (Zootechnical Products) (Amendment) Regulations (Northern Ireland) 2002 No. 2002/162. – Enabling power: European Communities Act 1972, s. 2 (2). – Issued: 07.05.2002. Made: 23.04.2002. Coming into operation: 25.04.2002. Effect: S.I. 1999/1871 amended in relation to Northern Ireland. – 4p.: 30 cm. – 0 337 94257 9 *£1.75*

Less Favoured Area Compensatory Allowances Regulations (Northern Ireland) 2002 No. 2002/72. – Enabling power: European Communities Act 1972, s. 2 (2). – Issued: 14.03.2002. Made: 01.03.2002. Coming into operation: 06.03.2002. Effect: S.R. 2001/391 amended. – 10p.: 25 cm. – 0 337 94192 0 *£2.50*

Marketing of Quality Agricultural Products Grant Regulations (Northern Ireland) 2002 No. 2002/29. – Enabling power: European Communities Act 1972, s. 2 (2). – Issued: 14.02.2002. Made: 06.02.2002 Coming into operation: 14.03.2002. Effect: None. – 12p.: 25 cm. – 0 337 94145 9 *£2.50*

Milk Marketing Board (Residuary Functions) (Amendment) Regulations (Northern Ireland) 2002 No. 2002/151. – Enabling power: S.I. 1993/2665 (N.I. 10), arts. 17 (2) (b) (ii), 30 (b). – Issued: 26.04.2002. Made: 15.04.2002. Coming into operation: 15.05.2002. Effect: S.R. 1995/25 amended. – 4p.: 25 cm. – 0 337 94249 8 *£1.75*

Pesticides (Maximum Residue Levels in Crops, Food and Feeding Stuffs) (Amendment) (No. 2) Regulations (Northern Ireland) 2002 No. 2002/250. – Enabling power: European Communities Act 1972, s. 2 (2) & Food and Environment Protection Act 1985, s. 16 (2). – Issued: 31.07.2002. Made: 23.07.2002. Coming into operation: 01.09.2002. Effect: S.R. 2002/20 amended. – EC note: These Regs. specify maximum levels of pesticides which crops, food and feeding stuffs may contain in implementation of DIRs 2002/5/EC and 2002/23/EC. – 8p.: 30 cm. – 0 337 94319 2 *£2.00*

Pesticides (Maximum Residue Levels in Crops, Food and Feeding Stuffs) (Amendment) Regulations (Northern Ireland) 2002 No. 2002/27. – Enabling power: European Communities Act 1972, s. 2 (2) & Food and Environment Protection Act 1985, s. 16 (2). – Issued: 14.02.2002. Made: 01.02.2002. Coming into operation: 11.03.2002. Effect: S.R. 2002/20 amended. – EC note: These Regs. specify maximum levels which crops, food and feeding stuffs may contain in implementation of DIRs 2000/81/EC, 2000/82/EC, 2001/39/EC and 2001/57/EC; also 1998/82/EC (iprodione on spring onions) and 1993/58/EEC (methamidophos on cottonseed). – 24p.: 25 cm. – 0 337 94143 2 *£4.00*

Pesticides (Maximum Residue Levels in Crops, Food and Feeding Stuffs) Regulations (Northern Ireland) 2002 No. 2002/20. – Enabling power: European Communities Act 1972, s. 2 (2) & Food and Environment Protection Act 1985, s. 16 (2). – Issued: 11.02.2002. Made: 28.01.2002. Coming into operation: 04.03.2002. Effect: S.R. 1995/32, 33, 460, 461; 1996/526, 527; 1997/243, 244; 1999/114, 320, 321 revoked. – 180p.: 25 cm. – 0 337 94138 6 *£15.00*

Seed Potatoes (Crop Fees) Regulations (Northern Ireland) 2002 No. 2002/169. – Enabling power: Seeds Act (Northern Ireland) Act 1965, s. 1. – Issued: 09.05.2002. Made: 02.05.2002. Coming into operation: 30.05.2002. Effect: None. – 4p.: 30 cm. – 0 337 94259 5 *£1.75*

The Sheep Annual Premium (Amendment) Regulations (Northern Ireland) 2002 No. 2002/368. – Enabling power: European Communities Act 1972, s. 2 (2). – Issued: 16.12.2002. Made: 29.11.2002. Coming into operation: 03.12.2002. Effect: S.R. 1992/476 amended. – 4p.: 30 cm. – 0 337 94426 1 *£1.75*

Airports

The Airports Byelaws (Designation) Order (Northern Ireland) 2002 No. 2002/396. – Enabling power: S.I. 1994/426 (NI.1), art. 18 (1). – Issued: 03.01.2003. Made: 18.12.2002. Coming into operation: 03.02.2003. Effect: None. – 2p.: 30 cm. – 0 337 94434 2 *£1.50*

Animals

Animal By-products Order (Northern Ireland) 2002 No. 2002/209. – Enabling power: S.I. 1981/1115 (N.I. 22), arts. 2 (3), 5 (1), 19, 29 (1), 44, 46 (7A), 60 (1). – Issued: 07.06.2002. Made: 29.05.2002. Coming into operation: 08.07.2002. Effect: S.R. 1989/347; 1992/62; 1993/193; 2001/286 revoked. – 32p.: 30 cm. – 0 337 94279 X *£6.00*

Animal By-products (Revocation) Regulations (Northern Ireland) 2002 No. 2002/210. – Enabling power: European Communities Act 1972, s. 2 (2). – Issued: 12.06.2002. Made: 29.05.2002. Coming into operation: 08.07.2002. Effect: S.R. 1993/192; 1998/108 revoked. – 2p.: 30 cm. – 0 337 94282 X *£1.50*

Animals and Animal Products (Import and Export) (Amendment) Regulations (Northern Ireland) 2002 No. 2002/296. – Enabling power: European Communities Act 1972, s. 2 (2). – Issued: 01.10.2002. Made: 19.09.2002. Coming into operation: 21.10.2002. Effect: S.R. 2000/253 amended. – EC note: Makes provision to give effect to Commission decision 2001/327/EC concerning restrictions to the movement of animals of susceptible species with regard to foot-and-mouth disease, and introduces operational agreements for assembly centres to ensure that such centres are capable of being operated in accordance with the second indent of Article 3(2) of Council Directive 90/425/EEC. – 4p.: 30 cm. – 0 337 94361 3 *£1.75*

Foot-and-Mouth Disease (Controlled Area) Order (Northern Ireland) 2002 No. 2002/44. – Enabling power: S.I. 1981/1115 (NI. 22), arts. 5, 10 (6), 12, 14, 19, 20, 60 (1) & S.R.& O. (NI) 1962/209, art. 29 (1). – Issued: 25.02.2002. Made: 13.02.2002. Coming into operation: 15.02.2002. Effect: S.R.& O. (NI) 1962/209 amended & S.R. 2001/424 revoked. – 4p.: 25 cm. – 0 337 94161 0 *£1.75*

Products of Animal Origin (Third Country Imports) Regulations (Northern Ireland) 2002 No. 2002/340. – Enabling power: European Communities Act 1972, s. 2 (2). – Issued: 18.11.2002. Made: 07.11.2002. Coming into operation: 06.12.2002. Effect: S.R. 1991/475 revoked & S.R. 1995/201; 1997/218, 499; 1998/45; 1999/189 amended. – 56p.: 30 cm. – 0 337 94396 6 *£7.00*

Transmissible Spongiform Encephalopathy Regulations (Northern Ireland) 2002 No. 2002/225. – Enabling power: European Communities Act 1972, s. 2 (2). – Issued: 22.07.2002. Made: 24.06.2002. Coming into operation: 18.07.2002. Effect: S.I. 1981/1115 (N.I. 22); S.R. 1997/551, 552; 2001/186, 405 amended & S.R. 1998/187, 188, 365, 366, 367, 442; 1999/322, 323; 2001/292 revoked. – 84p.: 30 cm. – 0 337 94317 6 *£9.00*

Child support

The Child Support (Great Britain Reciprocal Arrangements) (Amendment) Regulations (Northern Ireland) 2002 No. 2002/121. – Enabling power: Northern Ireland Act 1998, s. 87 (5) (10). – Issued: 05.04.2002. Made: 25.03.2002. Coming into operation: 16.04.2002. Effect: S.R. 1993/117 amended. – 8p.: 25 cm. – 0 337 94228 5 *£2.00*

The Child Support (Temporary Compensation Payment Scheme) (Modification and Amendment) Regulations (Northern Ireland) 2002 No. 2002/247. – Enabling power: Child Support, Pensions and Social Security Act (Northern Ireland) 2000, s. 26 (1) (9). – Issued: 02.08.2002. Made: 19.07.2002. Coming into operation: 20.07.2002. Effect: 2000 c4 (N.I.) modified & S.R. 2001/12 amended. – Laid before the Assembly for approval. – 2p.: 30 cm. – 0 337 94326 5 *£1.50*

The Social Security and Child Support (Decisions and Appeals) (Miscellaneous Amendments) Regulations (Northern Ireland) 2002 No. 2002/189. – Enabling power: S.I. 1991/2628 (N.I. 23), arts. 22 (4) to (6), & S.I. 1995/2705 (N.I. 15), art. 32, sch. 1, para. 4 & S.I. 1997/1183 (N.I. 12), art. 13 (5) (a) (b) & S.I. 1998/1506 (N.I. 10), arts. 7 (3), 10 (1), 11A (1), 13 (2) (7), 15 (11), 16 (1), 24A (1) (2) (a), 28 (1), 74(1) (3) (5) (6), sch. 1, para. 12(1), sch. 2, para. 9, sch. 4, paras 1 to 4, 6, 7 & Child Support, Pensions and Social Security Act (Northern Ireland) 2000, sch. 7, paras. 3 (1), 6 (7) (8), 10 (1), 19 (1), 20 (1) (3)– Issued: 30.05.2002. Made: 16.05.2002. Coming into operation: 20.05.2002. Effect: S.R. 1999/162, 408; 2000/215; 2001/213 amended. – 12p.: 30 cm. – 0 337 94273 0 *£2.50*

The Social Security and Child Support (Miscellaneous Amendments) Regulations (Northern Ireland) 2002 No. 2002/164. – Enabling power: S.I. 1991/2628 (NI.23), arts. 16 (1), 18 (1) (4), 19 (5), 22 (4), 28B (2) (c), 28E (1) 28G, 43 (10) 47, 48 (4), 50, sch. 1, paras. 5, 10, 11, sch. 4B, paras. 3, 4, 5 & Child Support, Pensions and Social Security Act (Northern Ireland) 2000, s. 28. – Issued: 15.05.2002. Made: 29.04.2002. Coming into operation: In accord. with reg. 1. Effect: S.R. 1992/339, 340, 341; 1996/541; 1999/162; 2001/17, 18, 19, 20 amended. – 12p.: 30 cm. – 0 337 94263 3 *£2.50*

Coroners

Coroners (Practice and Procedure) (Amendment) Rules (Northern Ireland) 2002 No. 2002/37. – Enabling power: Coroners Act (Northern Ireland) Act 1959, s. 36 (1) (b). – Issued: 19.02.2002. Made: 08.02.2002. Coming into operation: 11.02.2002. Effect: S.R. & O. (N.I.) 1963/199 amended. – 2p.: 25 cm. – 0 337 94155 6 *£1.50*

County courts

County Court (Amendment No. 2) Rules (Northern Ireland) 2002 No. 2002/412. – Enabling power: S.I. 1980/397 (N.I. 3), art. 47. – Issued: 20.01.2003. Made: 30.12.2002. Coming into operation: 03.03.2003. Effect: S.R. 1981/225 amended. – 20p.: 30 cm. – 0 337 94591 8 *£3.50*

County Court (Amendment) Rules (Northern Ireland) 2002 No. 2002/255. – Enabling power: S.I. 1980/397 (NI. 3), art. 47. – Issued: 08.08.2002. Made: 23.07.2002. Coming into operation: 04.11.2002. Effect: S.R. 1981/225 amended. – 20p.: 25 cm. – 0 337 94330 3 *£3.00*

County Court (Blood Tests) (Amendment) Rules (Northern Ireland) 2002 No. 2002/240. – Enabling power: S.I. 1980/397 (N.I. 3), art. 47. – Issued: 23.07.2002. Made: 06.07.2002. Coming into operation: 12.08.2002. Effect: S.R. 1978/378 amended. – 4p.: 30 cm. – 0 337 94311 7 *£1.75*

The County Court Fees (Amendment) Order (Northern Ireland) 2002 No. 2002/342. – Enabling power: 1978 c. 23, s. 116 (1) (4). – Issued: 18.11.2002. Made: 05.11.2002. Coming into operation: 02.12.2002, 03.03.2003, in accord. with art. 1. Effect: S.R. 1996/103 amended. – 8p.: 25 cm. – 0 337 94393 1 *£2.00*

The Family Proceedings (Amendment) Rules (Northern Ireland) 2002 No. 2002/137. – Enabling power: S.I. 1993/1576 (NI. 6), art. 12. – Issued: 30.04.2002. Made: 25.03.2002. Coming into operation: 06.05.2002. Effect: S.R. 1996/322 amended. – EC note: Gives effect to Council regulation No. 1347/2000. – 16p.: 30 cm. – 0 337 94252 8 *£3.00*

The Family Proceedings Fees (Amendment) Order (Northern Ireland) 2002 No. 2002/344. – Enabling power: 1978 c. 23, s. 116 (1) (4). – Issued: 18.11.2002. Made: 05.11.2002. Coming into operation: 02.12.2002, 03.03.2003, in accord with art. 1. Effect: S.R. 1996/495 amended. – 8p.: 30 cm. – 0 337 94395 8 *£2.00*

Criminal injuries

Criminal Injuries Compensation (Northern Ireland) Order 2002 (Commencement No. 1) Order 2002 No. 2002/148 (C.15). – Enabling power: S.I. 2002/796 (N.I. 1), art. 1 (2). Bringing into operation various provisions of the 2002 Order on 09.04.2002, in accord. with art. 2. – Issued: 24.02.2003. Made: 31.03.2002. Effect: None. – 2p.: 30 cm. – 0 337 94870 4 *£1.50*

Criminal Injuries Compensation (Northern Ireland) Order 2002 (Commencement No. 2) Order 2002 No. 2002/205 (C.20). – Enabling power: S.I. 2002/796 (N.I. 1), art. 1 (2). Bringing into operation various provisions of the 2002 Order on 01.05.2002, in accord. with art. 2. – Issued: 24.02.2003. Made: 25.04.2002. Effect: None. – 2p.: 30 cm. – 0 337 94872 0 *£1.50*

The Northern Ireland Criminal Injuries Compensation Scheme 2002 (Commencement No. 1) Order 2002 No. 2002/204 (C.19). – Enabling power: S.I. 2002/796 (C.15), art. 3 (5). Bringing into operation various provisions of the 2002 scheme on 01.05.2002. – Issued: 26.07.2002. Made: 25.04.2002. Effect: None. – 2p.: 30 cm. – 0 337 94314 1 *£1.50*

Dangerous drugs

The Misuse of Drugs Regulations (Northern Ireland) 2002 No. 2002/1. – Enabling power: Misuse of Drugs Act 1971, ss. 7, 10, 22, 31. – Issued: 11.01.2002. Made: 02.01.2002. Coming into operation: 01.02.2002. Effect: S.I. 1987/68; 1988/206; 1989/346; 1991/1; 1995/305, 480; 1996/353; 1998/128; 1999/251 revoked & S.R. 1986/52 revoked with savings. – 36p.: 25 cm. – 0 337 94125 4 *£5.50*

Deregulation

The Deregulation (Carer's Allowance) Order (Northern Ireland) 2002 No. 2002/321. – Enabling power: S.I. 1996/1632 (NI. 11), art. 17 (1) to (3). – Issued: 25.10.2002. Made: 18.10.2002. Coming into operation: In accord. with art. 1 (1). Effect: 1992 c.7 amended. – 4p.: 30 cm. – 0 337 94381 8 *£1.75*

Diseases of fish

Diseases of Fish (Control) (Amendment) Regulations (Northern Ireland) 2002 No. 2002/53. – Enabling power: European Communities Act 1972, s. 2 (2). – Issued: 26.02.2002. Made:15.02.2002. Coming into force: 10.03.2002. Effect: S.R. 1996/16 amended. – EC note: These regulations, in addition to making a number of minor and consequential drafting amendments to the 1996 Regulations, implement, in relation to Northern Ireland, amendments to the Directive made by Council Directive 2000/27/EC. – 8p.: 25 cm. – 0 337 94163 7 *£2.00*

Education

The Education (Grants for Disabled Postgraduate Students) (Amendment) Regulations (Northern Ireland) 2002 No. 2002/272. – Enabling power: S.I. 1998/1760 (NI. 14), art. 3 (1) (2). – Issued: 24.09.2002. Made: 29.08.2002. Coming into operation: 01.09.2002. Effect: S.R. 2001/285 amended. – 2p.: 30 cm. – 0 337 94353 2 *£1.50*

The Education (Student Loans) (Amendment) Regulations (Northern Ireland) 2002 No. 2002/241. – Enabling power: S.I. 1990/1506 (N.I. 11), art. 3 (2), sch. 2, para. 1 (1). – Issued: 27.08.2002. Made: 09.07.2002. Coming into operation: 01.08.2002. Effect: S.R. 1998/58 amended. – 2p.: 30 cm. – 0 337 94320 6 *£1.50*

The Education (Student Support) (Amendment) Regulations (Northern Ireland) 2002 No. 2002/111. – Enabling power: S.I. 1998/1760 (N.I. 14), arts. 3, 8 (4). – Issued: 27.03.2002. Made: 15.03.2002. Coming into operation: 08.04.2002. Effect: S.R. 2001/277 amended. – 4p,: 25 cm. – 0 337 94221 8 *£1.75*

Education (Student Support) Regulations (Northern Ireland) 2002 No. 2002/224. – Enabling power: S.I. 1998/1760 (N.I. 14), arts. 3, 8 (4). – Issued: 04.07.2002. Made: 21.06.2002. Coming into operation: 24.07.2002. Effect: S.R. 2001/277; 2002/111 revoked (01.09.2002.). – 60p,: 25 cm. – 0 337 94299 4 *£7.00*

Students Awards (Amendment) Regulations (Northern Ireland) 2002 No. 2002/112. – Enabling power: S.I. 1986/594 (N.I. 3), arts. 50 (1) (2), 134 (1). – Issued: 27.03.2002. Made: 15.03.2002. Coming into operation: 08.04.2002. Effect: S.R. 2001/298 amended. – 4p.: 25 cm. – 0 337 94220 X *£1.75*

Students Awards Regulations (Northern Ireland) 2002 No. 2002/265. – Enabling power: S.I. 1986/594 (NI 3), arts. 50 (1) (2), 134 (1). – Issued: 24.09.2002. Made: 06.08.2002. Coming into operation: 01.09.2002. Effect: S.R. 2001/298 revoked. – 40p.: 25 cm. – 0 337 94347 8 *£6.00*

The Teachers' (Compensation for Redundancy and Premature Retirement) Regulations (Northern Ireland) 2002 No. 2002/393. – Enabling power: S.I. 1972/1073 (N.I. 10), art. 19 (1) (3) (4), sch. 3, para. 9. – Issued: 03.01.2003. Made: 18.12.2002. Coming into operation: 01.03.2003. Effect: S.R. 1991/132 amended. – 8p.: 30 cm. – 0 337 94436 9 *£2.00*

Electricity

Electricity (Applications for Consent) (Fees) (Amendment) Regulations (Northern Ireland) 2002 No. 2002/364. – Enabling power: S.I. 1992/231 (N.I. 1), art. 39 (8), sch. 8, para. 1 (3). – Issued: 06.12.2002. Made: 28.11.2002. Coming into force: 01.01.2003. Effect: S.R. 1992/178 amended. – 2p.: 30 cm. – 0 337 94408 3 *£1.50*

Employment

Employment (2002 Order) (Commencement and Transitional and Savings Provisions) Order (Northern Ireland) 2002 No. 2002/356 (C.29). – Enabling power: S.I. 2002/2836 (N.I. 2) , art. 1 (2) (3). Bringing into operation various provisions of the 2002 Order on 23.11.2002, 08.12.2002, 06.04.2003, in accord. with art. 2 (1) (2) (3). – Issued: 16.12.2002. Made: 21.11.2002. Effect: None. – 4p.: 30 cm. – 0 337 94423 7 *£1.75*

Employment Relations (1999 Order) (Commencement No. 5 and Transitional Provision) Order (Northern Ireland) 2002 No. 2002/214 (C.21). – Enabling power: S.I. 1999/2790 (N.I. 9), arts. 1 (2), 39 (3). Bringing into operation various provisions of the 1999 Order on 02.06.2002, in accord. with art. 2. Issued: 17.06.2002. Made: 31.05.2002. Effect: None. – 4p.: 30 cm. – 0 337 94287 0 £1.75

Employment Relations (1999 Order) (Commencement No. 6 and Transitional Provisions) Order (Northern Ireland) 2002 No. 2002/317 (C.26). – Enabling power: S.I. 1999/2790 (NI. 9), arts. 1 (2), 39 (3). Bringing into operation various provisions of this Order 13.10.2002. – Issued: 05.11.2002. Made: 11.10.2002. Effect: None. – 4p.: 25 cm. – 0 337 94386 9 £1.75

Employment Rights (Increase of Limits) Order (Northern Ireland) 2002 No. 2002/24. – Enabling power: S.I. 1999/2790 (NI. 9), arts.33, 39 (3). – Issued: 21.02.2002. Made: 31.01.2002. Coming into operation: 10.03.2002. Effect: S.R. 2001/54 revoked subject to art. 4. – 8p.: 25 cm. – 0 337 94156 4 £2.00

Fixed-term Employees (Prevention of Less Favourable Treatment) Regulations (Northern Ireland) 2002 No. 2002/298. – Enabling power: Employment Act 2002, s. 46. – Issued: 02.10.2002. Made: 24.09.2002. Approved by resolution of the Assembly: 23.09.2002. Coming into operation: 01.10.2002. Effect: 1992 c. 7; S.I. 1996/1919 (NI. 16), 1921 (NI. 18) amended. – EC note: Implements DIR 99/70/EC (the Fixed-term Work Directive) in Northern Ireland – 16p.: 30 cm. – 0 337 94366 4 £3.00

Maternity and Parental Leave etc. (Amendment No. 2) Regulations (Northern Ireland) 2002 No. 2002/135. – Enabling power: S.I. 1996/1919 (N.I. 16), art. 108 (1) (2) (5). – Issued: 19.04.2002. Made: 05.04.2002. Laid before the Assembly for approval by resolution. Coming into operation: 21.04.2002. Effect: S.R. 1999/471 amended & S.R. 2002/110 revoked. – 4p.: 25 cm. – 0 337 94245 5 £1.75

Maternity and Parental Leave etc. (Amendment No. 2) Regulations (Northern Ireland) 2002 No. 2002/135. – Enabling power: S.I. 1996/1919 (N.I. 16), art. 108 (1) (2) (5). – Issued: 31.05.2002. Made: 05.04.2002. Approved by resolution of the Assembly: 22.04.2002. Coming into operation: 21.04.2002. Effect: S.R. 1999/471 amended & S.R. 2002/110 revoked. – EC note: Implements for Northern Ireland DIR 96/34/EC. – This statutory rule has been made to correct an error in S.R. 2002/110 (ISBN 0337942315) which is revoked by this Statutory Rule, and is being issued free of charge to all known recipients of that statutory rule. – 4p.: 25 cm. – 0 337 94256 0 £1.75

Maternity and Parental Leave etc. (Amendment No. 3) Regulations (Northern Ireland) 2002 No. 2002/355. – Enabling power: S.I. 1996/1919 (N.I. 16), arts. 70C (2), 103 (1) to (4) (6) (7), 105 (1) (2) (4) (7), 106 (4), 107 (1), 108, 131 (1). – Issued: 16.12.2002. Made: 21.11.2002. Coming into operation: 24.11.2002. Effect: S.R. 1999/471 amended. – 8p.: 30 cm. – 0 337 94422 9 £2.00

Maternity and Parental Leave etc. (Amendment) Regulations (Northern Ireland) 2002 No. 2002/110. – Enabling power: S.I. 1996/1919 (N.I. 16), art. 108 (1) (2) (5). – Issued: 05.04.2002. Made: 14.03.2002. Approved by resolution of the Assembly. Coming into operation: 21.04.2002. Effect: S.R. 1999/471 amended. – 4p.: 25 cm. – 0 337 94231 5 £1.75

Part-time Workers (Prevention of Less Favourable Treatment) (Amendment) Regulations (Northern Ireland) 2002 No. 2002/286. – Enabling power: S.I. 1999/2790 (NI. 9), art. 21. – Issued: 02.10.2002. Made: 16.09.2002. Approved by resolution of the Assembly: 23.09.2002. Coming into operation: 01.10.2002. Effect: S.R. 2000/219 amended. – Supersedes the S.R. with the same no. and title issued 25 September 2002 (ISBN 0337943567). – 4p.: 25 cm. – 0 337 94363 X £1.75

Part-time Workers (Prevention of Less Favourable Treatment) (Amendment) Regulations (Northern Ireland) 2002 No. 2002/286. – Enabling power: S.I. 1999/2790 (NI. 9), art. 21. – Issued: 25.09.2002. Made: 16.09.2002. Laid before the Assembly for approval. Coming into operation: 01.10.2002. Effect: S.R. 2000/219 amended. – Superseded by S.I. same no. and title issued 2nd October 2002 (ISBN 033794363X). – 4p.: 25 cm. – 0 337 94356 7 £1.75

Paternity and Adoption Leave Regulations (Northern Ireland) 2002 No. 2002/377. – Enabling power: S.I. 1996/1919 (N.I. 6), arts. 70C (2), 107A (1) to (3) (6) (7), 107B (1) (2) (4) (8), 107C (1) (2), 107D (1), 112A (1) (2) (5), 112B (1) (2) (5), 112C (1) (6), 112D (1), 112E, 131 (1). – Issued: 27.01.2003. Made: 06.12.2002. Coming into operation: 08.12.2002. Effect: None. – 20p.: 30 cm. – 0 337 94712 0 £3.50

Statutory Paternity Pay and Statutory Adoption Pay (Administration) Regulations (Northern Ireland) 2002 No. 2002/379. – Enabling power: S.I. 2002/2836 (N.I. 2), arts. 8 (1) (2) (4) (5), 9 (1) (2), 11 (1) (2), 16 (1) & S.I. 1999/671, arts. 7 (1) (fa) (ga), 23. – Issued: 27.01.2003. Made: 06.12.2002. Coming into operation: 08.12.2002. Effect: None. – 8p.: 30 cm. – 0 337 94696 5 £2.00

Statutory Paternity Pay and Statutory Adoption Pay (General) Regulations (Northern Ireland) 2002 No. 2002/378. – Enabling power: Social Security Contributions and Benefits Act (Northern Ireland) 1992, ss. 167ZA (2) (a), 167ZB (2) (a), 167ZC (3) (a) (c) (d) (f) (g), 167ZD (2) (3), 167ZE (2) (a) (b) (i) (3) (7) (8), 167ZG (3), 167ZJ (1) (3) (4) (7) (8), 167ZL (8) (b) to (d) (f) (g), 167ZM (2) (3), 167ZN (2) (5) (6), 167ZP (6), 167ZS (1) (3) (4) (7) (8) & Social Security Administration (Northern Ireland) Act 1992, s. 5 (1) (g) (j) (q). – Issued: 27.01.2003. Made: 06.12.2002. Coming into operation: 08.12.2002. Effect: None. – 24p.: 30 cm. – 0 337 94704 X £4.00

Statutory Paternity Pay and Statutory Adoption Pay (Health and Personal Social Services Employees) Regulations (Northern Ireland) 2002 No. 2002/381. – Enabling power: Social Security Contributions and Benefits (Northern Ireland) Act 1992, ss. 167ZJ (9) (10), 167ZS (9) (10). – Issued: 27.01.2003. Made: 06.12.2002. Coming into operation: 08.12.2002. Effect: None. – 4p.: 30 cm. – 0 337 94688 4 £1.75

Statutory Paternity Pay and Statutory Adoption Pay (Persons Abroad and Mariners) Regulations (Northern Ireland) 2002 No. 2002/382. – Enabling power: Social Security Contributions and Benefits (Northern Ireland) Act 1992, ss. 167ZI, 167ZR. – Issued: 27.01.2003. Made: 06.12.2002. Coming into operation: 08.12.2002. Effect: 1992 c. 7 modified. – 8p.: 30 cm. – 0 337 94680 9 *£2.00*

Statutory Paternity Pay and Statutory Adoption Pay (Weekly Rates) Regulations (Northern Ireland) 2002 No. 2002/380. – Enabling power: Social Security Contributions and Benefits Act (Northern Ireland) 1992, ss. 167ZE (1), 167ZN (1) & Social Security Administration (Northern Ireland) Act 1992, s. 5 (1) (m). – Issued: 24.12.2002. Made: 06.12.2002. Coming into operation: 08.12.2002. Effect: None. – 4p.: 30 cm. – 0 337 94431 8 *£1.75*

Working Time (Amendment) Regulations (Northern Ireland) 2002 No. 2002/93. – Enabling power: European Communities Act 1972, s. 2 (2). – Issued: 19.03.2002. Made: 08.03.2002. Coming into force: 14.04.2002. Effect: S.I. 1998/386 amended. – 4p.: 25 cm. – 0 337 94197 1 *£1.75*

Energy conservation

The Domestic Energy Efficiency Grants Regulations (Northern Ireland) 2002 No. 2002/56. – Enabling power: S.I. 1990/1511 (NI. 15), art. 17 (1) (2) (3) (4) (5) (6) (7) (10). – Issued: 28.02.2002. Made: 19.02.2002. Coming into operation: 01.04.2002. Effect: S.R. 1994/306; 1996/417 revoked with savings. – 6p.: 25 cm. – 0 337 94173 4 *£2.00*

Environmental protection

The Air Quality Limit Values (Amendment) Regulations (Northern Ireland) 2002 No. 2002/357. – Enabling power: European Communities Act 1972, s. 2 (2). – Issued: 06.12.2002. Made: 21.11.2002. Coming into operation: 13.12.2002. Effect: S.R. 2002/94 amended. – 8p.: 30 cm. – 0 337 94405 9 *£2.50*

The Air Quality Limit Values Regulations (Northern Ireland) 2002 No. 2002/94. – Enabling power: European Communities Act 1972, s. 2 (2). – Issued: 22.03.2002. Made: 08.03.2002. Coming into force: 01.05.2002. Effect: S.R. 1990/145 revoked. – 24p.: 25 cm. – 0 337 94205 6 *£4.00*

The Batteries and Accumulators (Containing Dangerous Substances) (Amendment) Regulations (Northern Ireland) 2002 No. 2002/300. – Enabling power: European Communities Act 1972, s. 2 (2). – Issued: 10.10.2002. Made: 27.09.2002. Coming into force: 08.11.2002. Effect: S.R. 1995/122 amended. – EC note: Implements DIR 98/101/EC, which amends DIR 91/157/EEC. – 4p.: 30 cm. – 0 337 94369 9 *£1.75*

The Controlled Waste (Duty of Care) Regulations (Northern Ireland) 2002 No. 2002/271. – Enabling power: S.I. 1997/2778 (NI. 19), arts. 2 (3), 5 (7)– Issued: 05.09.2002. Made: 27.08.2002. Coming into operation: 01.10.2002. Effect: S.R. 2002/248 amended. – 4p.: 25 cm. – 0 337 94343 5 *£1.75*

The Controlled Waste Regulations (Northern Ireland) 2002 No. 2002/248. – Enabling power: S.I. 1994/1896 (NI. 10), art. 17 (2) & S.I. 1997/2778 (NI. 19), arts. 2 (2), 2 (3), 4 (3), 20 (3). – Issued: 30.07.2002. Made: 22.07.2002. Coming into force: 27.08.2002. Effect: S.R. 1992/254 amended. – 12p.: 25 cm. – 0 337 94318 4 *£2.50*

The Sulphur Content of Liquid Fuels Regulations (Northern Ireland) 2002 No. 2002/28. – Enabling power: European Communities Act 1972, s. 2 (2). – Issued: 13.02.2002. Made: 29.01.2002. Coming into operation: 11.03.2002. Effect: S.I. 1994/2249 revoked in relation to Northern Ireland. – EC Note: These regs. implement DIR 1999/32/EC relating to the sulphur content of certain liquid fuels. – 8p.: 25 cm. – 0 337 94144 0 *£2.00*

The Waste and Contaminated Land (1997 Order) (Commencement No. 6) Order (Northern Ireland) 2002 No. 2002/185 (C.18). – Enabling power: Northern Ireland Act 1998, sch. 1, para. 11 (2) & S.I. 1997/2778 (N.I.19), art. 1 (2). Bringing into operation certain provisions of the 1997 Order on 03.06.2002. – Issued: 21.10.2002. Made: 17.05.2002. Effect: None. – 4p.: 30 cm. – 0 337 94298 6 *£1.75*

European Communities

Animals and Animal Products (Import and Export) (Amendment) Regulations (Northern Ireland) 2002 No. 2002/296. – Enabling power: European Communities Act 1972, s. 2 (2). – Issued: 01.10.2002. Made: 19.09.2002. Coming into operation: 21.10.2002. Effect: S.R. 2000/253 amended. – EC note: Makes provision to give effect to Commission decision 2001/327/EC concerning restrictions to the movement of animals of susceptible species with regard to foot-and-mouth disease, and introduces operational agreements for assembly centres to ensure that such centres are capable of being operated in accordance with the second indent of Article 3(2) of Council Directive 90/425/EEC. – 4p.: 30 cm. – 0 337 94361 3 *£1.75*

The Batteries and Accumulators (Containing Dangerous Substances) (Amendment) Regulations (Northern Ireland) 2002 No. 2002/300. – Enabling power: European Communities Act 1972, s. 2 (2). – Issued: 10.10.2002. Made: 27.09.2002. Coming into force: 08.11.2002. Effect: S.R. 1995/122 amended. – EC note: Implements DIR 98/101/EC, which amends DIR 91/157/EEC. – 4p.: 30 cm. – 0 337 94369 9 *£1.75*

The Driving Licences (Community Driving Licence) Regulations (Northern Ireland) 2002 No. 2002/374. – Enabling power: European Communities Act 1972, s. 2 (2). – Issued: 16.12.2002. Made: 04.12.2002. Coming into operation: 20.01.2003. Effect: S.I. 1981/154 (N.I. 1) & S.R. 1996/426 amended. – 8p.: 30 cm. – 0 337 94424 5 *£2.00*

Products of Animal Origin (Third Country Imports) Regulations (Northern Ireland) 2002 No. 2002/340. – Enabling power: European Communities Act 1972, s. 2 (2). – Issued: 18.11.2002. Made: 07.11.2002. Coming into operation: 06.12.2002. Effect: S.R. 1991/475 revoked & S.R. 1995/201; 1997/218, 499; 1998/45; 1999/189 amended. – 56p.: 30 cm. – 0 337 94396 6 *£7.00*

Road Service Licensing (Community Licences) Regulations (Northern Ireland) 2002 No. 2002/116. – Enabling power: European Communities Act 1972, s. 2 (2). – Issued: 28.03.2002. Made: 19.03.2002. Coming into operation: 01.05.2002. Effect: S.I. 1981/154 (N.I.) amended. – EC note: Give effect in NI to art. 3a of REG (EEC) 684/92 on common rules for the international carriage of passengers by coach and bus, as amended by REG (EC) 11/98. – 8p.: 25 cm. – 0 337 94224 2 *£2.00*

Transmissible Spongiform Encephalopathy Regulations (Northern Ireland) 2002 No. 2002/225. – Enabling power: European Communities Act 1972, s. 2 (2). – Issued: 22.07.2002. Made: 24.06.2002. Coming into operation: 18.07.2002. Effect: S.I. 1981/1115 (N.I. 22); S.R. 1997/551, 552; 2001/186, 405 amended & S.R. 1998/187, 188, 365, 366, 367, 442; 1999/322, 323; 2001/292 revoked. – 84p.: 30 cm. – 0 337 94317 6 *£9.00*

Evidence

The Blood Tests (Evidence of Paternity) (Amendment) Regulations (Northern Ireland) 2002 No. 2002/150. – Enabling power: S.I. 1977/1250 (N.I. 17), art. 10. – Issued: 02.05.2002. Made: 15.04.2002. Coming into operation: 07.05.2002. Effect: S.R. 1978/379 amended. – 4p.: 30 cm. – 0 337 94254 4 *£1.75*

Explosives

Explosives (Fireworks) Regulations (Northern Ireland) 2002 No. 2002/147. – Enabling power: Explosives Act (Northern Ireland) 1970, s. 1 (4A), 3. – Issued: 11.06.2002. Made: 11.04.2002. Coming into operation: 06.05.2002. Effect: S.R. 1999/392 repealed. – 8p.: 25 cm. – 0 337 94275 7 *£2.00*

Fair employment

Fair Employment (Specification of Public Authorities) (Amendment) Order (Northern Ireland) 2002 No. 2002/367. – Enabling power: S.I. 1998/3162 (NI. 21), arts. 50 (1) (2), 51 (2). – Issued: 06.12.2002. Made: 29.11.2002. Coming into operation: 01.01.2003. Effect: S.R. 2000/371 amended. – 8p.: 30 cm. – 0 337 94412 1 *£2.00*

Fair Employment (Monitoring) (Amendment) Regulations (Northern Ireland) 2002 No. 2002/244. – Enabling power: S.I. 1998/3162 (N.I. 21), arts. 52 (2) to (4), 53, 54. – Issued: 07.11.2003. Made: 16.07.2002. Coming into operation: 01.01.2004. Effect: S.R. 1999/148 amended. - Supersedes draft S.R. (ISBN 0337942811) issued 31.05.2002. – 2p.: 30 cm. – 0 337 94337 0 1 *£1.50*

Family law

The Child Support Appeals (Jurisdiction of Courts) Order (Northern Ireland) 2002 No. 2002/391. – Enabling power: S.I. 1991/2628 (N.I. 23), art. 42 (1) (4). – Issued: 09.01.2003. Made: 16.12.2002. Coming into operation: 28.01.2003. subject to art. 1 (3) in accord. with art. 1 (2) (3). Effect: S.R. 1993/104 revoked. – 4p.: 30 cm. – 0 337 94455 5 *£1.75*

The Child Support (Great Britain Reciprocal Arrangements) (Amendment) Regulations (Northern Ireland) 2002 No. 2002/121. – Enabling power: Northern Ireland Act 1998, s. 87 (5) (10). – Issued: 05.04.2002. Made: 25.03.2002. Coming into operation: 16.04.2002. Effect: S.R. 1993/117 amended. – 8p.: 25 cm. – 0 337 94228 5 *£2.00*

The Child Support, Pensions and Social Security (2000 Act) (Commencement No. 8) Order (Northern Ireland) 2002 No. 2002/118 (C.8). – Enabling power: Child Support, Pensions and Social Security Act (Northern Ireland) 2000, s. 68 (2) (b). Bringing into operation various provisions of the 2000 Act on 23.03.2002, 15.04.2002, in accordance with art. 2 (1) (2). – Issued: 16.04.2002. Made: 22.03.2002. Effect: None. – 4p.: 25 cm. – 0 337 94241 2 *£1.75*

The Child Support (Temporary Compensation Payment Scheme) (Modification and Amendment) Regulations (Northern Ireland) 2002 No. 2002/247. – Enabling power: Child Support, Pensions and Social Security Act (Northern Ireland) 2000, s. 26 (1) (9). – Issued: 02.08.2002. Made: 19.07.2002. Coming into operation: 20.07.2002. Effect: 2000 c4 (N.I.) modified & S.R. 2001/12 amended. – Laid before the Assembly for approval. – 2p.: 30 cm. – 0 337 94326 5 *£1.50*

The Family Law (2001 Act) (Commencement) Order (Northern Ireland) 2002 No. 2002/138 (C.13). – Enabling power: Family Law Act (Northern Ireland) 2001, s. 4. Bringing into operation the 2001 Act on 08.04.2002 and 15.04.2002. – Issued: 26.04.2002. Made: 08.04.2002. Effect: None. – 2p.: 30 cm. – 0 337 94251 X *£1.50*

The Social Security and Child Support (Decisions and Appeals) (Miscellaneous Amendments) Regulations (Northern Ireland) 2002 No. 2002/189. – Enabling power: S.I. 1991/2628 (N.I. 23), arts. 22 (4) to (6), & S.I. 1995/2705 (N.I. 15), art. 32, sch. 1, para. 4 & S.I. 1997/1183 (N.I. 12), art. 13 (5) (a) (b) & S.I. 1998/1506 (N.I. 10), arts. 7 (3), 10 (1), 11A (1), 13 (2) (7), 15 (11), 16 (1), 24A (1) (2) (a), 28 (1), 74(1) (3) (5) (6), sch. 1, para. 12(1), sch. 2, para. 9, sch. 4, paras 1 to 4, 6, 7 & Child Support, Pensions and Social Security Act (Northern Ireland) 2000, sch. 7, paras. 3 (1), 6 (7) (8), 10 (1), 19 (1), 20 (1) (3)– Issued: 30.05.2002. Made: 16.05.2002. Coming into operation: 20.05.2002. Effect: S.R. 1999/162, 408; 2000/215; 2001/213 amended. – 12p.: 30 cm. – 0 337 94273 0 *£2.50*

The Social Security and Child Support (Miscellaneous Amendments) Regulations (Northern Ireland) 2002 No. 2002/164. – Enabling power: S.I. 1991/2628 (NI.23), arts. 16 (1), 18 (1) (4), 19 (5), 22 (4), 28B (2) (c), 28E (1) 28G, 43 (10) 47, 48 (4), 50, sch. 1, paras. 5, 10, 11, sch. 4B, paras. 3, 4, 5 & Child Support, Pensions and Social Security Act (Northern Ireland) 2000, s. 28. – Issued: 15.05.2002. Made: 29.04.2002. Coming into operation: In accord. with reg. 1. Effect: S.R. 1992/339, 340, 341; 1996/541; 1999/162; 2001/17, 18, 19, 20 amended. – 12p.: 30 cm. – 0 337 94263 3 £2.50

Family proceedings

The Children (Allocation of Proceedings) (Amendment) Order (Northern Ireland) 2002 No. 2002/350. – Enabling power: S.I. 1995/755 (N.I. 2), art. 164 (5), sch. 7. – Issued: 13.12.2002. Made: 18.11.2002. Coming into operation: 09.12.2002. Effect: S.R. 1996/300 amended. – 2p.: 30 cm. – 0 337 94399 0 £1.50

The Declarations of Parentage (Allocation of Proceedings) Order (Northern Ireland) 2002 No. 2002/119. – Enabling power: S.I. 1995/755 (NI. 2), art. 164 (5), sch. 7. – Issued: 11.04.2002. Made: 23.03.2002. Coming into operation: 15.04.2002. Effect: None. – 8p.: 25 cm. – 0 337 94237 4 £2.00

The Family Proceedings (Amendment) Rules (Northern Ireland) 2002 No. 2002/137. – Enabling power: S.I. 1993/1576 (NI. 6), art. 12. – Issued: 30.04.2002. Made: 25.03.2002. Coming into operation: 06.05.2002. Effect: S.R. 1996/322 amended. – EC note: Gives effect to Council regulation No. 1347/2000. – 16p.: 30 cm. – 0 337 94252 8 £3.00

The Family Proceedings Fees (Amendment) Order (Northern Ireland) 2002 No. 2002/344. – Enabling power: 1978 c. 23, s. 116 (1) (4). – Issued: 18.11.2002. Made: 05.11.2002. Coming into operation: 02.12.2002, 03.03.2003, in accord. with art. 1. Effect: S.R. 1996/495 amended. – 8p.: 30 cm. – 0 337 94395 8 £2.00

Fees and charges

Measuring Instruments (EEC Requirements) (Verification Fees) Regulations (Northern Ireland) 2002 No. 2002/309. – Enabling power: Finance Act 1973, s. 56 (1). – Issued: 10.10.2002. Made: 04.11.2002. Coming into force: 04.11.2002. Effect: S.R. 1993/470 revoked with saving. – 4p.: 25 cm. – 0 337 94373 7 £1.75

Fire services

Fire Services (Appointments and Promotion) (Amendment) Regulations (Northern Ireland) 2002 No. 2002/283. – Enabling power: S.I. 1984/1821 (N.I. 11), arts. 9 (5), 52 (1). – Issued: 23.09.2002. Made: 10.09.2002. Coming into operation: 01.10.2002. Effect: S.R. 1979/167 amended– 4p.: 30 cm. – 0 337 94354 0 £1.75

Fisheries

Fisheries (Amendment) Byelaws (Northern Ireland) 2002 No. 2002/11. – Enabling power: Fisheries Act (Northern Ireland) 1966, ss. 26 (1). – Issued: 31.01.2002. Made: 18.01.2002. Coming into operation: 01.03.2002. Effect: S.R. 1997/425 amended. – 4p.: 25 cm. – 0 337 94136 X £1.75

Fisheries (Amendment No. 2) Byelaws (Northern Ireland) 2002 No. 2002/274. – Enabling power: Fisheries Act (Northern Ireland) 1966, ss. 26 (1), 37 (1), 70. – Issued: 10.09.2002. Made: 02.09.2002. Coming into operation: 01.10.2002. Effect: S.R. 1997/425 amended. – 4p.: 25 cm. – 0 337 94345 1 £1.75

Fisheries (Amendment No. 3) Byelaws (Northern Ireland) 2002 No. 2002/371. – Enabling power: Fisheries Act (Northern Ireland) 1966, ss. 26 (1), 37 (1). – Issued: 10.12.2002. Made: 03.12.2002. Coming into operation: 01.01.2003. Effect: S.R. 1997/425 amended. – 4p.: 25 cm. – 0 337 94418 0 £1.75

Fisheries and Aquaculture Structures (Grants) Regulations (Northern Ireland) 2002 No. 2002/6. – Enabling power: European Communities Act 1972, s. 2 (2). – Issued: 06.02.2002. Made: 10.01.2002 Coming into force: 25.02.2002. Effect: None. – 16p.: 25 cm. – 0 337 94139 4 £3.00

Fisheries (Tagging and Logbook) (Amendment) Byelaws (Northern Ireland) 2002 No. 2002/372. – Enabling power: Fisheries Act (Northern Ireland) 1966, ss. 26 (1), 37 (1). – Issued: 10.12.2002. Made: 03.12.2003. Coming into operation: 01.01.2003. Effect: S.R. 2001/291 amended. – 4p.: 30 cm. – 0 337 94419 9 £1.75

Food

Animal By-products (Identification) (Amendment) Regulations (Northern Ireland) 2002 No. 2002/238. – Enabling power: S.I. 1991/762 (N.I. 7), arts. 15 (1) (c) (d) (f), 25 (3), 47 (2), sch. 1, para. 3. – Issued: 22.07.2002. Made: 04.07.2002. Coming into operation: 19.08.2002. Effect: S.R. 1999/418 amended. – 8p.: 30 cm. – 0 337 94307 9 £2.50

Contaminants in Food (Amendment) Regulations (Northern Ireland) 2002 No. 2002/262. – Enabling power: S.I. 1991/762 (NI. 7), arts. 15 (1) (a) (f), 16 (2), 25 (1) (a) (3), 26 (3), 47 (2). – Issued: 14.08.2002. Made: 05.08.2002. Coming into operation: 08.08.2002. Effect: S.R. 2002/219 amended. – 2p.: 30 cm. – 0 337 94333 8 £1.50

Contaminants in Food Regulations (Northern Ireland) 2002 No. 2002/219. – Enabling power: S.I. 1991/762 (NI. 7), arts. 15 (1) (a) (f), 16 (2), 25 (1) (a) (3), 26 (3), 47 (2). – Issued: 21.06.2002. Made: 12.06.2002. Coming into force: 29.07.2002. Effect: S.R. 1987/38; 1991/203, 344; 1992/416; 1996/49, 53 amended & S.R. 1979/407; 1985/163; 1997/338; 1999/302 revoked. – 6p.: 30 cm. – 0 337 94286 2 £2.50

Dairy Produce Quotas Regulations (Northern Ireland) 2002 No. 2002/88. – Enabling power: European Communities Act 1972, s 2 (2). – Issued: 28.03.2002. Made: 08.03.2002. Coming into force: 31.03.2002. Effect: SI. 1998/2880 amended in relation to Northern Ireland & S.I. 1997/733, 1093 revoked in relation to Northern Ireland & S.R. 2000/83; 2001/27 revoked. – EC note: Implement Council REG (EEC) 3950/92 establishing an additional levy in milk and milk products sector, and REG (EC) 1392/2001 laying down detailed rules for applying 3950/92. – 40p.: 25 cm. – 0 337 94219 6 £6.00

Food and Animal Feedingstuffs (Products of Animal Origin from China) (Control) Regulations (Northern Ireland) 2002 No. 2002/33. – Enabling power: European Communities Act 1972, s. 2 (2). – Issued: 18.02.2002. Made: 07.02.2002. Coming into operation: 08.02.2002. Effect: None. – EC note: Implement Commission decision 2002/69/EC concerning certain protective measures with regard to products of animal origin imported from China. – 8p,: 25 cm. – 0 337 94148 3 £2.00

Food and Animal Feedingstuffs (Products of Animal Origin from China) (Emergency Control) Regulations (Northern Ireland) 2002 No. 2002/226. – Enabling power: European Communities Act 1972, s. 2 (2). – Issued: 24.07.2002. Made: 25.06.2002. Coming into operation: 28.06.2002. Effect: S.I. 1991/762 (N.I. 7) modified & S.R. 2002/183 revoked. – EC note: Implements, for Northern Ireland, Commission Decision 2002/69/EC as amended by Decision 2002/441/EC concerning certain protective measures with regard to the products of animal origin imported from China. – 8p,: 30 cm. – 0 337 94312 5 £2.00

Food (Figs, Hazelnuts and Pistachios from Turkey) (Emergency Control No. 2) Regulations (Northern Ireland) 2002 No. 2002/307. – Enabling power: European Communities Act 1972, s. 2 (2). – Issued: 10.10.2002. Made: 02.10.2002. Coming into operation: 04.10.2002. Effect: S.R. 2002/140 revoked. – EC note: Implements EC DEC 2002/80/EC imposing special conditions on the imports of figs etc., and certain products derived thereof originating in or consigned from Turkey as amended by DEC 2002/233/EC & DEC 2002/679/EC. – 8p.: 30 cm. – 0 337 94371 0 £2.00

Food (Figs, Hazelnuts and Pistachios from Turkey) (Emergency Control) Regulations (Northern Ireland) 2002 No. 2002/140. – Enabling power: European Communities Act 1972, s. 2 (2). – Issued: 23.04.2002. Made: 09.04.2002. Coming into operation: 11.04.2002. Effect: None. – EC note: Implement EC DEC 2002/80/EC imposing special conditions on the imports of figs etc., and certain products derived thereof originating in or consigned from Turkey as amended by DEC 2002/233/EC. – 6p.: 30 cm. – 0 337 94246 3 £2.00

Food for Particular Nutritional Uses (Addition of Substances for Specific Nutritional Purposes) Regulations (Northern Ireland) 2002 No. 2002/264. – Enabling power: S.I. 1991/762 (NI.7), arts. 15 (1) (f), 16 (1), 25 (3), 26 (3), 47 (2). – Issued: 14.08.2002. Made: 05.08.2002. Coming into operation: In accord.with reg. 1 (2) (3). Effect: S.R. 1990/329 amended. – EC note: Implements Commission directive 2001/15/EC on substances that may be added for specific nutritional purposes in foods for particular nutritional uses. – 10p.: 30 cm. – 0 337 94335 4 £2.50

Food (Jelly Confectionery) (Emergency Control) Regulations (Northern Ireland) 2002 No. 2002/141. – Enabling power: European Communities Act 1972, s. 2 (2). – Issued: 23.04.2002. Made: 09.04.2002. Coming into operation: 11.04.2002. Effect: None. – EC note: Implements EC Dec 2002/247/EC suspending the placing on the market and import of jelly confectionery containing the food additive E425: Konjac. – 6p.: 30 cm. – 0 337 94247 1 £2.00

Food (Peanuts from China) (Emergency Control) (Northern Ireland) Regulations 2002 No. 2002/293. – Enabling power: European Communities Act 1972, s. 2 (2). – Issued: 27.09.2002. Made: 19.09.2002. Coming into operation: 23.09.2002. Effect: None. – EC note: Implement, for Northern Ireland, DEC 2002/79/EC imposing special conditions on the import of peanuts and certain products derived from peanuts originating in, or consigned from China as amended by EC DEC 2002/233/EC and by 2002/678/EC. – 8p,: 30 cm. – 0 337 94359 1 £2.00

Food (Star Anise from Third Countries) (Emergency Control) Order (Northern Ireland) 2002 No. 2002/82. – Enabling power: S.I. 1991/762 (N.I. 7), arts 12 (1), 26 (3), 47 (2). – Issued: 27.03.2002. Made: 06.03.2002. Coming into operation: 07.03.2002. Effect: None. – 8p.: 25 cm. – 0 337 94215 3 £2.00

Meat (Hazard Analysis and Critical Control Point) Regulations (Northern Ireland) 2002 No. 2002/217. – Enabling power: S.I. 1991/762 (N.I. 7), arts. 15 (1) (b) (f), 16 (1) & European Communities Act 1972, s. 2 (2). – Issued: 18.06.2002. Made: 10.06.2002. Coming into operation: In accord. with reg. 2, 15.07.2002, 07.06.2002. Effect: S.R. 1995/396; 1997/ 493 amended. – EC note: These regs. give effect (for Northern Ireland) to DEC 2001/471/EC laying down rules for the regular checks on the general hygiene carried out by the operators in establishments according to DIR 64/433/EC on health conditions for the production and marketing of fresh meat and DIR 71/118/EC on health problems affecting the production and placing on the market of fresh poultry meat. – 18p.: 30 cm. – 0 337 94292 7 £2.50

Notification of Marketing of Food for Particular Nutritional Uses Regulations (Northern Ireland) 2002 No. 2002/35. – Enabling power: S.I. 1991/762 (NI 7), arts. 16 (1), 25 (1) (a) (3), 26 (3), 47 (2). – Issued: 15.02.2002. Made: 08.02.2002. Coming into operation: 08.03.2002. Effect: None. – EC note: These Regs. implement art. 9 of DIR 89/398/EC on the approximation of the laws of the member states relating to foodstuffs intended for particuar nutritional uses, as amended by DIR 1999/41/EC. – 4p,: 25 cm. – 0 337 94152 1 £1.75

Plastic Materials and Articles in Contact with Food (Amendment) Regulations (Northern Ireland) 2002 No. 2002/316. – Enabling power: S.I. 1991/762 (NI. 7), arts. 15 (2), 16 (1), 25 (1) (a) (3), 32, 47 (2). – Issued: 22.10.2002. Made: 11.10.2002. Coming into operation: 30.11.2002. Effect: S.R. 1984/264 amended. – 32p.: 30 cm. – 0 337 94378 8 £5.50

Sweeteners in Food (Amendment) Regulations (Northern Ireland) 2002 No. 2002/39. – Enabling power: S.I. 1991/762 (N.I. 7), arts. 15 (1) (a), 16 (1), 25 (1) (3), 26 (3), 47 (2). – Issued: 20.02.2002. Made: 12.02.2002. Coming into operation: 0.03.2002. Effect: S.R. 1996/48 amended. – 8p.: 25 cm. – 0 337 94160 2 *£2.00*

Forestry

Environmental Impact Assessment (Forestry) (Amendment) Regulations (Northern Ireland) 2002 No. 2002/249. – Enabling power: European Communities Act 1972, s. 2 (2). – Issued: 02.08.2002. Made: 23.07.2002. Coming into operation: 27.09.2002. Effect: S.R. 2000/84 amended. – 2p.: 30 cm. – 0 337 94325 7 *£1.50*

Game

Game Preservation (Amendment) 2002 Act (Commencement) Order (Northern Ireland) 2002 No. 2002/130 (C.10). – Enabling power: Game Preservation (Amendment) Act (Northern Ireland) 2002, s. 4 (2). Bringing into operation various provisions of 2002 Act on 01.04.2002. – Issued: 22.04.2002. Made: 01.04.2002. Effect: None. – 2p.: 30 cm. – 0 337 94244 7 *£1.50*

Gas

Gas Order 1996 (Amendment) Regulations (Northern Ireland) 2002 No. 2002/291. – Enabling power: European Communities Act 1972 s. 2 (2). – Issued: 27.09.2002. Made: 18.09.2002. Coming into operation: 16.10.2002. Effect: S.I. 1996/275 (N.I. 2) amended. – 8p,: 30 cm. – 0 337 94358 3 *£2.00*

Harbours

The Belfast Harbour Order (Northern Ireland) 2002 No. 2002/40. – Enabling power: Harbours Act (Northern Ireland) 1970, s. 1 (1) (2), sch. 1 & 2, part 1. – Issued: 21.02.2002. Made: 12.02.2002. Coming into operation: In accordance with art. 1 (1). Effect: 10 & 11 Vict.c.lii; 15 & 16 Vict.c. cxxi; 17 & 18 Vict. c.xlv; 33 & 34 Vict. c.xcvii; 10 & 11 Vict.c. 27; 45 & 46 Vict. cc.lxxi; 61 & 62 Vict. c.cv; 1 Edward 7 c.cxxxiii; 8 & 9 Geo.5 c.xviii; 2 Geo. 6 c.iv; 1950 c.iv; 1956 c.iv & S.R. 1979/32 amended. – 10p.: 25 cm. – 0 337 94157 2 *£2.50*

The Belfast Harbour Order (Northern Ireland) 2002 No. 2002/40. – Enabling power: Harbours Act (Northern Ireland) 1970, s. 1 (1) (2), sch. 1, 2, part 1. – Issued: 11.06.2002. Made: 12.02.2002. Coming into operation: 21.05.2002, in accordance with art. 1 (1). Effect: 10 & 11 Vict.c.lii; 10 & 11 Vict. c. 27; 15 & 16 Vict.c. cxxi; 17 & 18 Vict. c.xlv; 45 & 46 Vict. c.clxxi; 61 & 62 Vict. c.cv; 1 Edward 7 c.xxxiii; 8 & 9 Geo.5 c.xviii; 2 Geo. 6 c.iv; 1950 c.iv; 1956 c.iv: S.R. 1979/32 amended & 33 & 34 Vict. c.xcvii repealed. – Affirmed by resolution of the Assembly, 20.05.2002. Supersedes SR, with same number and title, issued 21.02.2002. – 12p.: 25 cm. – 0 337 94276 5 *£2.50*

The Londonderry Harbour Order (Northern Ireland) 2002 No. 2002/41. – Enabling power: Harbours Act (Northern Ireland) 1970, s. 1 (1) (2), sch. 1 & 2, part 1. – Issued: 21.02.2002. Made: 12.02.2002. Coming into operation: In accordance with art. 1 (1). Effect: 17 & 18 Vict.c.clxxvii; 37 & 38 Vict. c.xlix; 45 & 46 Vict. c.cxlii; 10 & 11 Vict.c. 27; 9 & 10 Geo.5 c.lxviii; 10 & 11 Geo.5 c.lxxv & S.R. 1976/389; 1991/261 amended. – 10p.: 25 cm. – 0 337 94158 0 *£2.50*

The Londonderry Harbour Order (Northern Ireland) 2002 No. 2002/41. – Enabling power: Harbours Act (Northern Ireland) 1970, s. 1 (1) (2), sch. 1, 2, part 1. – Issued: 11.06.2002. Made: 12.02.2002. Coming into operation: 21.05.2002, in accordance with art. 1 (1). Effect: 10 & 11 Vict.c. 27; 17 & 18 Vict.c.clxxvii; 37 & 38 Vict. c.xlix; 45 & 46 Vict. c.cxlii; 9 & 10 Geo.5 c.lxviii; 10 & 11 Geo.5 c.lxxv; S.R. 1976/389; 1991/261 amended. – Affirmed by resolution of the Assembly on 20.05.2002. Supersedes SR, same number and title issued 21.02.2002. – 12p.: 30 cm. – 0 337 94277 3 *£2.50*

Londonderry Port and Harbour (Variation of Pilotage Limits) Order (Northern Ireland) 2002 No. 2002/394. – Enabling power: Harbours Act (Northern Ireland) 1970, s. 1, sch. 1. – Issued: 03.01.2003. Made: 18.12.2002. Coming into operation: 17.02.2003. Effect: None. – 4p.: 30 cm. – 0 337 94432 6 *£1.75*

The River Bann Navigation Order (Northern Ireland) 2002 No. 2002/395. – Enabling power: Harbours Act (Northern Ireland) 1970, s. 1 (1) (2), sch. 1, part I, sch. 2. – Issued: 03.01.2003. Made: 18.12.2002. Coming into operation: 17.02.2003. Effect: 10 & 11 Vict. c.16, c.27 modified & 42 & 43 Vict. c.clxxv; 17 & 18 Geo. 5; 2 Geo. 6 c.ii; S.R. & O. (N.I.) 1973/313 amended & S.R. 1988/286 revoked. – 12p.: 30 cm. – 0 337 94433 4 *£2.50*

The Warrenpoint Harbour Authority Order (Northern Ireland) 2002 No. 2002/42. – Enabling power: Harbours Act (Northern Ireland) 1970, s. 1 (1) (2), sch. 1 & 2, part 1. – Issued: 21.02.2002. Made: 12.02.2002. Coming into operation: In accordance with art. 1 (1). Effect: S.R. & O. 1971/136 amended. – 10p.: 25 cm. – 0 337 94159 9 *£2.50*

The Warrenpoint Harbour Authority Order (Northern Ireland) 2002 No. 2002/42. – Enabling power: Harbours Act (Northern Ireland) 1970, s. 1 (1) (2), sch. 1, 2, part 1. – Issued: 11.06.2002. Made: 12.02.2002. Coming into operation: 21.05.2002, in accordance with art. 1 (1). Effect: S.R. & O. (N.I.) 1971/136 amended. – Affirmed by resolution of the Assembly on 20.05.2002. Supersedes SR, same number and title issued 21.02.2002. – 12p.: 25 cm. – 0 337 94295 1 *£2.50*

Health and personal social services

The Adoption (Intercountry Aspects) Act (Northern Ireland) 2001 (Commencement No. 2) Order (Northern Ireland) 2002 No. 2002/22 (C.1). – Enabling power: Adoption (Intercountry Aspects) Act (Northern Ireland) 2001, s. 16 (2). Bringing into operation certain sections of the 2001 Act on 01.02.2002. – Issued: 14.02.2002. Made: 28.01.2002. Effect: None. – 2p.: 25 cm. – 0 337 94149 1 *£1.50*

The Adoption (Intercountry Aspects) Act (Northern Ireland) 2001 (Commencement No. 3) Order (Northern Ireland) 2002 No. 2002/45 (C.3). – Enabling power: Adoption (Intercountry Aspects) Act (Northern Ireland) 2001, s. 16 (2). Bringing into operation certain sections of the 2001 Act on 22.02.2002. – Issued: 26.02.2002. Made: 13.022002. Effect: None. – 4p.: 25 cm. – 0 337 94164 5 £1.75

Charges for Drugs and Appliances (Amendment) Regulations (Northern Ireland) 2002 No. 2002/91. – Enabling power: S.I. 1972/1265 (N.I. 14), arts. 98, 106, sch. 15. – Issued: 05.04.2002. Made: 08.03.2002. Coming into operation: 01.04.2002. Effect: S.R. 1997/382 amended. – 4p.: 25 cm. – 0 337 94226 9 £1.75

Dental Charges (Amendment) Regulations (Northern Ireland) 2002 No. 2002/84. – Enabling power: S.I. 1972/1265 (NI.14), arts. 98, 106, sch. 15. – Issued: 21.03.2002. Made: 07.03.2002. Coming into operation: 01.04.2002. Effect: S.R. 1989/111; 2001/124 amended. – 2p.: 25 cm. – 0 337 94202 1 £1.50

General Dental Services (Amendment No. 2) Regulations (Northern Ireland) 2002 No. 2002/171. – Enabling power: S.I. 1972/1265 (NI. 14), arts. 61 (1) (2) (2AA), 106, 107 (6). – Issued: 17.05.2002. Made: 07.05.2002. Coming into operation: 01.06.2002. Effect: S.R. 1993/326 amended. – 2p.: 30 cm. – 0 337 94264 1 £1.50

General Dental Services (Amendment) Regulations (Northern Ireland) 2002 No. 2002/2. – Enabling power: S.I. 1972/1265 (NI. 14), arts. 61 (1) (2) (2AA), 106, 107 (6). – Issued: 11.01.2002. Made: 03.01.2002. Coming into operation: 01.02.2002. Effect: S.R. 1993/326 amended. – 4p.: 25 cm. – 0 337 94126 2 £1.75

The General Medical Services (Amendment No. 2) Regulations (Northern Ireland) 2002 No. 2002/266. – Enabling power: S.I. 1972/1265 (N.I. 14), arts. 56, 106 (b), 107 (6). – Issued: 19.08.2002. Made: 08.08.2002. Coming into operation: 01.10.2002. Effect: S.R. 1997/380 amended. – 4p.: 30 cm. – 0 337 94340 0 £1.75

The General Medical Services (Amendment) Regulations (Northern Ireland) 2002 No. 2002/213. – Enabling power: S.I. 1972/1265 (N.I. 14), arts. 56, 106 (b), 107 (6). – Issued: 17.06.2002. Made: 30.05.2002. Coming into operation: 01.07.2002. Effect: S.R. 1997/380 amended. – 2p.: 30 cm. – 0 337 94288 9 £1.50

The Health and Personal Social Services (2002 Act) (Commencement) Order (Northern Ireland) 2002 No. 2002/311 (C.25). – Enabling power: Health and Personal Social Services (Northern Ireland) Act 2002, s. 4. Bringing into operation various provisions of the 2002 Act on 07.10.2002. – Issued: 17.10.2002. Made: 04.10.2002. Effect: None. – 2p.: 25 cm. – 0 337 94375 3 £1.50

The Health and Personal Social Services Act (Northern Ireland) 2001 (Commencement No. 3) Order (Northern Ireland) 2002 No. 2002/73 (C.6). – Enabling power: Health and Personal Social Services Act (Northern Ireland) 2001, s. 61 (2). Bringing into operation various provisions of the 2001 Act on 01.04.2002. – Issued: 13.03.2002. Made: 05.03.2002. Effect: None. – 4p.: 25 cm. – 0 337 94187 4 £1.75

The Health and Personal Social Services Act (Northern Ireland) 2001 (Commencement No. 4) Order (Northern Ireland) 2002 No. 2002/180 (C.17). – Enabling power: Health and Personal Social Services Act (Northern Ireland) 2001, s. 61 (2). Bringing into operation various provisions of the 2001 Act on 10.06.2002, in accord. with art. 2. – Issued: 20.05.2002. Made: .2002. Effect: None. – 4p.: 30 cm. – 0 337 94267 6 £1.75

The Health and Personal Social Services Act (Northern Ireland) 2001(Fund-holding Practices) (Transfer of Assets, Rights and Liabilities and Transitional Provisions) Order (Northern Ireland) 2002 No. 2002/66. – Enabling power: Health and Personal Social Services Act (Northern Ireland) 2001, s. 58. – Issued: 07.03.2002. Made: 26.02.2002. Coming into operation: 01.04.2002. Effect: None. – 10p.: 25 cm. – 0 337 94180 7 £2.50

The Health and Personal Social Services (Assessment of Resources) (Amendment) Regulations (Northern Ireland) 2002 No. 2002/113. – Enabling power: S.I. 1972/1265 (N.I. 14), arts. 36 (6), 99 (5). – Issued: 28.03.2002. Made: 15.02.2002. Coming into operation: 22.04.2002. Effect: S.R. 1993/127 amended. – 4p.: 25 cm. – 0 337 94223 4 £1.75

The Health and Personal Social Services (Penalty Charge) Regulations (Northern Ireland) 2002 No. 2002/181. – Enabling power: S.I. 1972/1073 (N.I.10), arts. 98, 106, 107 (6), sch. 15, para. 6. – Issued: 20.05.2002. Made: 10.05.2002. Coming into operation: 10.05.2002. Effect: None. – 4p.: 30 cm. – 0 337 94266 8 £1.75

The Health and Personal Social Services (Superannuation) (Additional Voluntary Contributions) Regulations (Northern Ireland) 2002 No. 2002/129. – Enabling power: S.I. 1972/1073 (N.I.10), arts. 12 (1) (2) (2A) (3), 14 (1) (2) (3) (3A), sch. 3. – Issued: 12.04.2002. Made: 28.03.2002. Coming into operation: 09.05.2002. Effect: S.R. 1999/294 amended. – 6p.: 25 cm. – 0 337 94239 0 £2.00

The Health and Personal Social Services (Superannuation) (Amendment) Regulations (Northern Ireland) 2002 No. 2002/69. – Enabling power: S.I. 1972/1073 (N.I. 10), arts. 12 (1) (2) (2A) (3), 14 (1) (2) (3) (3A), sch. 3. – Issued: 13.03.2002. Made: 28.02.2002. Coming into operation: 01.05.2002. Effect: S.R. 1995/95 amended. – 6p.: 25 cm. – 0 337 94186 6 £2.00

The Northern Ireland Practice and Education Council for Nursing and Midwifery (Appointments and Procedure) Regulations (Northern Ireland) 2002 No. 2002/386. – Enabling power: Health and Personal Social Services Act (Northern Ireland) 2002, s. 2 (5), sch., paras. 5, 22. – Issued: 09.01.2003. Made: 12.12.2002. Coming into operation: 27.01.2003. Effect: None. – 8p.: 30 cm. – 0 337 94439 3 £2.00

The Northern Ireland Social Care Council (Appointments and Procedure) (Amendment) Regulations (Northern Ireland) 2002 No. 2002/349. – Enabling power: Health and Personal Social Services Act (Northern Ireland) 2001, ss. 1 (4), 57 (3), sch. 1, para. 5. – Issued: 25.11.2002. Made: 12.11.2002. Coming into operation: 20.12.2002. Effect: S.R. 2001/313 amended. – 4p.: 25 cm. – 0 337 94398 2 £1.75

Optical Charges and Payments (Amendment No. 2) Regulations (Northern Ireland) 2002 No. 2002/221. – Enabling power: S.I. 1972/1265 (N.I. 14), arts. 62, 98, 106, 107 (6), sch. 15, para. 2A. – Issued: 26.06.2002. Made: 18.06.2002. Coming into force: 09.07.2002. Effect: S.R. 1997/191 amended. – 4p.: 30 cm. – 0 337 94296 X *£1.50*

Optical Charges and Payments (Amendment) Regulations (Northern Ireland) 2002 No. 2002/5. – Enabling power: S.I. 1972/1265 (NI. 14), arts. 62, 98, 106, 107 (6), para. 2A, sch. 15. Issued: 23.01.2002. Made: 10.01.2001. Coming into operation: 01.02.2002. Effect: S.R. 1997/191 amended. – 4p.: 25 cm. – 0 337 94129 7 *£1.75*

Optical Charges and Payments and General Ophthalmic Services (Amendment) Regulations (Northern Ireland) 2002 No. 2002/85. – Enabling power: S.I. 1972/1265 (NI. 14), arts. 62, 98, 106, 107 (6), sch. 15. – Issued: 21.03.2002. Made: 07.03.2002. Coming into operation: 01.04.2002. except for regs. 3, 6 & 09.04.2002. for regs. 3 & 6. Effect: S.R. 1986/163; 1997/191 amended. – 8p.: 25 cm. – 0 337 94203 X *£2.00*

The Personal Social Services (Preserved Rights) Regulations (Northern Ireland) 2002 No. 2002/136. – Enabling power: Personal Social Services (Preserved Rights) Act (Northern Ireland) 2002, ss. 1 (5) (6) (7), 6 (3). – Issued: 22.04.2002. Made: 29.03.2002. Coming into operation: 08.04.2002. Effect: None. – 4p.: 30 cm. – 0 337 94242 0 *£1.75*

Pharmaceutical Services and Charges for Drugs and Appliances (Amendment) Regulations (Northern Ireland) 2002 No. 2002/397. – Enabling power: S.I. 1972/1265 (N.I. 14), arts. 63 (1) (2) (2A) to (2D), 64, 98, 106, 106 (b), 107 (6), sch. 15. – Issued: 09.01.2003. Made: 18.12.2002. Coming into operation: 01.02.2003. Effect: S.R. 1997/381, 382 amended. – 4p.: 30 cm. – 0 337 94471 7 *£1.75*

Pharmaceutical Services and General Medical Services (Amendment) Regulations (Northern Ireland) 2002 No. 2002/92. – Enabling power: S.I. 1972/1265 (N.I. 14), arts. 56, 63 (1) (2) (2A) to (2D), 64, 106 (b), 107 (6). – Issued: 05.04.2002. Made: 08.03.2002. Coming into operation: 01.04.2002. Effect: S.R. 1997/380, 381 amended. – 6p.: 25 cm. – 0 337 94225 0 *£2.00*

Travelling Expenses and Remission of Charges (Amendment No. 2) Regulations (Northern Ireland) 2002 No. 2002/172. – Enabling power: S.I. 1972/1265 (N.I. 14), arts. 45, 98, 106, 107 (6), sch. 15, paras (1) (b), 1B. – Issued: 17.05.2002. Made: 07.05.2002. Coming into operation: 01.06.2002. Effect: S.R. 1989/348 amended. – 4p,: 30 cm. – 0 337 94265 X *£1.75*

Travelling Expenses and Remission of Charges (Amendment) Regulations (Northern Ireland) 2002 No. 2002/46. – Enabling power: S.I. 1972/1265 (NI. 14), arts. 45, 98, 106, 107 (6), sch. 15, para. 1B (1) (b). – Issued: 28.02.2002. Made: 15.02.2002. Coming into operation: 09.04.2002. Effect: S.R. 1989/348 amended. – 4p,: 25 cm. – 0 337 94174 2 *£1.75*

Health and safety

Biocidal Products (Amendment) Regulations (Northern Ireland) 2002 No. 2002/302. – Enabling power: European Communities Act 1972, s. 2 (2) & S.I. 1978/1039 (N.I. 9), arts. 17(1) (2) (3) (5), 40(2) (4), 55(2), sch. 3, paras 1 (1) (4) (5), 3 (1), 12 (1), 14 (1), 15. – Issued: 21.10.2002. Made: 30.09.2002. Coming into operation: 14.11.2002. Effect: S.R. 2001/422 amended. – 4p.: 30 cm. – 0 337 94377 X *£1.75*

Carriage of Dangerous Goods (Amendment) Regulations (Northern Ireland) 2002 No. 2002/34. – Enabling power: S.I. 1978/1039 (N.I. 9), arts. 17 (1) (2) (5) (6), 40 (2) to (4), 55 (2), sch. 3, paras. 1 (1) (2) (4), 25 (2), 6, 11, 13, 15. – Issued: 20.02.2002. Made: 08.02.2002. Coming into operation: 01.04.2002. Effect: S.R. 1991/471; 1997/247, 248, 249; 1998/125, 131, 132 amended. – EC note: These Regs. implement, for Northern Ireland: DIR 96/86 adapting to technical progress 94/55; and 96/87 adapting to technical progress 96/49; and 99/47 adapting to technical progress 94/55 and 96/86; and 99/48 adapting to technical progress 96/49 and 96/87. – 64p., ill.: 25 cm. – 0 337 94151 3 *£7.00*

Chemicals (Hazard Information and Packaging for Supply) Regulations (Northern Ireland) 2002 No. 2002/301. – Enabling power: European Communities Act 1972, s. 2 (2) & S.I. 1978/1039 (NI.9), arts. 17 (1) (2) (3) (5) (6), 55 (2), sch. 3, paras. 1 (1) (4) (5), 2 (2), 14 (1), 15. – Issued: 22.10.2002. Made: 30.09.2002. Coming into operation: 14.11.2002. Effect: S.R. 1997/247 amended & S.R. 1995/60; 1996/376; 1997/398; 1998/459; 1999/303; 2001/168 revoked. – EC note: Implements as respects Northern Ireland Council directive 1992/32/EEC amending for the 7th time Council directive 67/548/EEC (the substances Directive). Also Council directive 1999/45/EC (the preparations Directive) and points 29, 30 & 31 of Annex I to Council directive 76/769/EEC as amended by directive 2001/41/EC; and Commission directive 91/155/EEC (the safety data sheets Directive). It also implements 16 directives which adapt to technical progress and modify the substances Directive, the preparations Directive and the safety data sheets Directive. – 51p.: 30 cm. – 0 337 94379 6 *£6.00*

Housing

The Housing Benefit (General) (Amendment) Regulations (Northern Ireland) 2002 No. 2002/280. – Enabling power: Social Security Contributions and Benefits (Northern Ireland) Act 1992, ss. 122 (1) (d), 129 (4), 171 (1) (3) to (5). – Issued: 19.09.2002. Made: 10.09.2002 Coming into operation: 07.10.2002. Effect: S.R. 1987/461 amended. – 2p.: 25 cm. – 0 337 94350 8 *£1.50*

The Social Security and Child Support (Decisions and Appeals) (Miscellaneous Amendments) Regulations (Northern Ireland) 2002 No. 2002/189. – Enabling power: S.I. 1991/2628 (N.I. 23), arts. 22 (4) to (6), & S.I. 1995/2705 (N.I. 15), art. 32, sch. 1, para. 4 & S.I. 1997/1183 (N.I. 12), art. 13 (5) (a) (b) & S.I. 1998/1506 (N.I. 10), arts. 7 (3), 10 (1), 11A (1), 13 (2) (7), 15 (11), 16 (1), 24A (1) (2) (a), 28 (1), 74(1) (3) (5) (6), sch. 1, para. 12(1), sch. 2, para. 9, sch. 4, paras 1 to 4, 6, 7 & Child Support, Pensions and Social Security Act (Northern Ireland) 2000, sch. 7, paras. 3 (1), 6 (7) (8), 10 (1), 19 (1), 20 (1) (3)– Issued: 30.05.2002. Made: 16.05.2002. Coming into operation: 20.05.2002. Effect: S.R. 1999/162, 408; 2000/215; 2001/213 amended. – 12p.: 30 cm. – 0 337 94273 0 *£2.50*

The Social Security Benefits Up-rating Order (Northern Ireland) 2002 No. 2002/99. – Enabling power: Social Security Administration (Northern Ireland) Act 1992, ss. 132, 165 (1) (5). – Issued: 28.03.2002. Made: 13.03.2002. Coming into operation: In accord. with art. 1 (1). Effect: 1992 c. 7; S.R. 1976/223; 1987/30, 459, 461; 1992/32; 1994/461; 1995/35; 1996/73, 198 amended & S.R. 2001/41 revoked (11.04.2002.). – 60p.: 25 cm. – 0 337 94201 3 *£7.00*

The Social Security (Carer Premium Amendment) Regulations (Northern Ireland) 2002 No. 2002/322. Enabling power: Social Security Contributions and Benefits (Northern Ireland) Act 1992, ss. 122 (1) (a) (d), 131 (1), 171 (1) (3) (4) and S.I. 1995/2705 (NI. 15), arts. 6 (5), 36 (2). – Issued: 31.10.2002. Made: 21.10.2002. Coming into operation: 28.10.2002. Effect: S.R. 1987/459, 461; 1996/198 amended. – 4p.: 30 cm. – 0 337 94384 2 *£1.75*

The Social Security (Employment Programme Amendment) Regulations (Northern Ireland) 2002 No. 2002/275. – Enabling power: Social Security Contributions and Benefits (Northern Ireland) Act 2002, ss. 122 (1) (a) (d), 132 (3) (4) (b), 171 (1) (3) (4) & S.I. 1995/2705 (N.I. 15), arts. 14 (1) (4) (b), 21 (10) (c), 36 (2), sch. 1, para. 3 (b). – Issued: 16.09.2002. Made: 06.09.2002. Coming into operation: 14.10.2002. Effect: S.R. 1987/459, 461; 1996/198 amended. – 4p.: 30 cm. – 0 337 94348 6 *£1.75*

The Social Security (Intercalating Students Amendment) Regulations (Northern Ireland) 2002 No. 2002/243. – Enabling power: Social Security Contributions and Benefits (Northern Ireland) Act 1992, ss. 122 (1) (d), 133 (2) (j), 171 (1) (3) (4) & S.I. 1995/2705 (N.I. 15), art. 8 (4). – Issued: 23.07.2002. Made: 10.07.2002. Coming into operation: 01.08.2002. Effect: S.R. 1987/461; 1996/198 amended. – 4p.: 30 cm. – 0 337 94309 5 *£1.75*

The Social Security (Loss of Benefit) (Consequential Amendments) Regulations (Northern Ireland) 2002 No. 2002/80. – Enabling power: Social Security Contributions and Benefits (Northern Ireland) Act 1992, ss. 22 (5), 122 (1) (a) (d), 123 (1) (e), 131 (1), 171 (1) (3) & S.I. 1995/2705 (NI. 15), arts. 7 (3), 28 (1) (4) (d), 36 (2) & S.I. 1998/1506 (NI. 10), arts. 10 (1), 11 (3) (6), 74 (1) & Child Support, Pensions and Social Security Act (Northern Ireland) 2000, s. 60 (1) (2) (a), sch. 7, paras. 3 (1), 4 (3) (5). – Issued: 15.03.2002. Made: 06.03.2002. Coming into operation: 01.04.2002. Effect:S.R. 1975/113; 1987/459, 461; 1996/198, 519; 1999/162; 2001/213, 216 amended. – 8p.: 25 cm. – 0 337 94190 4 *£2.00*

The Social Security (Loss of Benefit) Regulations (Northern Ireland) 2002 No. 2002/79. – Enabling power: Social Security Fraud Act (Northern Ireland) 2001, ss. 6 (3) to (6), 7 (3) (4), 8 (2) to (5), 9 (1) (2) & S.I. 1998/1506 (NI. 10), art. 74 (3) to (6), sch. 2, para. 9. – Issued: 14.03.2002. Made: 06.03.2002. Coming into operation: 01.04.2002. Effect: S.R. 1999/162 amended. – 20p.: 25 cm. – 0 337 94189 0 *£3.50*

The Social Security (Miscellaneous Amendments No. 2) Regulations (Northern Ireland) 2002 No. 2002/295. – Enabling power: Social Security Contributions and Benefits (Northern Ireland) Act 1992, ss. 122 (1) (a) (d), 132 (4) (b), 171 (1) (3) (4) & S.I. 1995/2705 (N.I. 15), arts. 14 (4) (b), 36 (2). – Issued: 02.10.2002. Made: 19.09.2002. Coming into operation: 14.10.2002. Effect: S.R. 1987/459, 461; 1996/198 amended. – 4p.: 30 cm. – 0 337 94362 1 *£1.75*

The Social Security (Miscellaneous Amendments) Regulations (Northern Ireland) 2002 No. 2002/128. – Enabling power: Social Security Contributions and Benefits (Northern Ireland) Act 1992, ss. 122 (1) (a) (d), 131 (1), 132 (3) (4) (b), 171 (1) (3) (4) & S.I. 1995/2705 (N.I. 15), arts. 6 (5), 14 (1) (4) (b), 36 (2). – Issued: 12.04.2002. Made: 27.03.2002. Coming into operation: 08.04.2002. Effect: S.R. 1987/459, 461; 1996/198 amended. – 6p.: 30 cm. – 0 337 94235 8 *£2.00*

The Social Security (Paternity and Adoption Amendment) Regulations (Northern Ireland) 2002 No. 2002/363. – Enabling power: Social Security Contributions and Benefits (Northern Ireland) Act 1992, ss. 122 (1) (a) (d), 123 (1) (e), 132 (3) (4) (b), 133 (2) (d), 171 (1) (3) (4) & S.I. 1995/2705 (N.I. 15), art. 14 (1) (4) (b), 23, 36 (2), sch. 1, para. 1. – Issued: 10.12.2002. Made: 27.11.2002. Coming into operation: 08.12.2002. Effect: S.R. 1987/459, 461; 1996/198 amended. – 8p.: 30 cm. – 0 337 94413 X *£2.00*

The Social Security (Personal Allowances for Children and Young Persons Amendment) Regulations (Northern Ireland) 2002 No. 2002/267. – Enabling power: Social Security Contributions and Benefits (Northern Ireland) Act 1992, ss. 122 (1) (a) (d), 131 (1), 171 (1) (3) & S.I. 1995/2705 (N.I. 15), art. 6 (5). – Issued: 19.08.2002. Made: 08.08.2002. Coming into operation: 14.10.2002. Effect: S.R. 1987/459, 461; 1998/198 amended. – 4p.: 30 cm. – 0 337 94339 7 *£1.75*

The Social Security (Personal Injury Payments Amendment) Regulations (Northern Ireland) 2002 No. 2002/299. – Enabling power: Social Security Contributions and Benefits (Northern Ireland) Act 1992, ss. 122 (1) (a) (d), 132 (4) (b) (d), 171 (1) (3) (4) & S.I. 1995/2705 (N.I. 15), art. 14 (4) (b) (d). – Issued: 07.10.2002. Made: 26.09.2002. Coming into operation: 28.10.2002. Effect: S.R. 1987/459, 461; 1996/198 amended. – 4p.: 30 cm. – 0 337 94367 2 *£1.75*

The Social Security (Students and Income-related Benefits Amendment No. 2) Regulations (Northern Ireland) 2002 No. 2002/270. – Enabling power: Social Security Contributions and Benefits (Northern Ireland) Act 1992, ss. 122 (1) (a) (d), 132 (4) (b), 171 (1) (3) (4) & S.I. 1995/2705 (NI. 15), art. 14 (4) (b). – Issued: 05.09.2002. Made: 27.08.2002. Coming into operation: 02.09.2002. Effect: S.R. 1987/459, 461; 1996/198 amended. – 4p.: 30 cm. – 0 337 94344 3 £1.75

The Social Security (Students and Income-related Benefits Amendment) Regulations (Northern Ireland) 2002 No. 2002/222. – Enabling power: Social Security Contributions and Benefits (Northern Ireland) Act 1992, ss. 122 (1) (a) (d), 129 (2), 132 (3) (4) (b), 171 (1) (3) (4) & S.I. 1995/2705 (NI. 15), art. 14 (1) (4) (b). – Issued: 04.07.2002. Made: 18.06.2002. Coming into operation: 01.08.2002 & 26.08.2002. Effect: S.R. 1987/459, 461; 1996/198 amended. – 8p.: 30 cm. – 0 337 94300 1 £2.00

Industrial development

The Industrial Development (2002 Act) (Commencement) Order (Northern Ireland) 2002 No. 2002/134 (C.12). – Enabling power: Industrial Development Act (Northern Ireland) 2002, s. 7 (1). Bringing into operation the 2002 Act on 01.04.2002. – Issued: 14.05.2002. Made: 26.03.2002. Effect: None. – 2p.: 30 cm. – 0 337 94261 7 £1.50

Industrial relations

Code of Practice (Disciplinary and Grievance Procedures) (Appointed Day) Order (Northern Ireland) 2002 No. 2002/347. – Enabling power: S.I. 1992/807 (NI. 5), arts. 90 (7) (17), 107 (3). – Issued: 06.12.2002. Made: 08.11.2002. Coming into operation: 01.12.2002. Effect: None. – 2p.: 30 cm. – 0 337 94411 3 £1.50

Code of Practice (Industrial Action Ballots and Notice to Employers) (Appointed Day) Order (Northern Ireland) 2002 No. 2002/345. – Enabling power: S.I. 1992/807 (NI. 5), arts. 95 (5) (14), 107 (3). – Issued: 10.12.2002. Made: 07.11.2002. Coming into operation: 01.12.2002. Effect: None. – 2p.: 30 cm. – 0 337 94410 5 £1.50

Code of Practice (Redundancy Consultation and Procedures) (Appointed Day) Order (Northern Ireland) 2002 No. 2002/346. – Enabling power: S.I. 1992/807 (NI. 5) arts. 90 (7) (9) (10) (13) (17), 107 (3). – Issued: 06.12.2002. Made: 08.11.2002. Coming into operation: 01.12.2002. Effect: None. – 2p.: 30 cm. – 0 337 94409 1 £1.50

Labour Relations Agency Arbitration Scheme Order (Northern Ireland) 2002 No. 2002/120. – Enabling power: S.I. 1972/1265 (N.I. 14), art. 84A (2) (6) (7) (8)– Issued: 08.04.2002. Made: 25.03.2002. Coming into operation: 28.04.2002. Effect: 1996 c. 23 modified. – 48p.: 25 cm. – 0 337 94232 3 £6.00

Industrial training

Industrial Training Levy (Construction Industry) Order (Northern Ireland) 2002 No. 2002/245. – Enabling power: S.I. 1984/1159 (NI. 9), arts. 23 (2) (3), 24 (3) (4). – Issued: 26.07.2002. Made: 17.07.2002. Coming into operation: 31.08.2002. Effect: None. – 8p.: 30 cm. – 0 337 94313 3 £2.00

Insolvency

The Insolvency (Amendment) Rules (Northern Ireland) 2002 No. 2002/261. – Enabling power: S.I. 1989/2405 (NI.19), art. 359. – Issued: 03.09.2002. Made: 05.08.2002. Coming into operation: 05.09.2002. Effect: S.R. 1991/364 amended. – EC note: These rules amend the 1991 Rules in the light of Council REG (EC) 1346/2000 on insolvency proceedings. – 48p.: 25 cm. – 0 337 94342 7 £6.00

The Occupational and Personal Pension Schemes (Bankruptcy) Regulations (Northern Ireland) 2002 No. 2002/127. – Enabling power: S.I. 1989/2405 (NI. 19), arts, 315C (4) (a) (7) to (9), 315F (6) (a) (9) to (11) & S.I. 1999/3147 (NI. 11), arts. 12 (2) (h), 13 (1) to (3), 73 (3) (4). – Issued: 09.04.2002. Made: 27.03.2002. Coming into operation: 06.04.2002. Effect: None. – 12p.: 25 cm. – 0 337 94234 X £2.50

Insolvency: Companies and individuals

Insolvency (Northern Ireland) Order 1989 (Amendment No. 2) Regulations (Northern Ireland) 2002 No. 2002/334. – Enabling power: European Communities Act 1972, s. 2(2). – Issued: 12.11.2002. Made: 05.11.2002. Coming into operation: 05.12.2002. Effect: S.R. 1989/2405 (NI. 19) amended– 4p.: 30 cm. – 0 337 94390 7 £1.75

Insolvency (Northern Ireland) Order 1989 (Amendment) Regulations (Northern Ireland) 2002 No. 2002/223. – Enabling power: European Communities Act 1972, s. 2(2). – Issued: 18.07.2002. Made: 19.06.2002. Coming into operation: 15.07.2002. Effect: S.R. 1989/2405 (NI 19) amended– 4p.: 30 cm. – 0 337 94302 8 £1.75

Investigatory powers

Regulation of Investigatory Powers Act 2000 (Amendment) Order (Northern Ireland) 2002 No. 2002/183. – Enabling power: Regulation of Investigatory Powers Act 2000, ss. 30 (5), 31. – Issued: 17.06.2002. Made: 14.05.2002. Order laid before the Assembly for affirmation by resolution of the Assembly. Coming into operation: On the day after the day it is affirmed by resolution of the Assembly. Effect: 2000 c. 23 amended. – 4p.: 30 cm. – 0 337 94291 9 £1.75

Regulation of Investigatory Powers Act 2000 (Prescription of Offices, Ranks and Positions) Order (Northern Ireland) 2002 No. 2002/292. – Enabling power: Regulation of Investigatory Powers Act 2000, ss. 30 (1) (3), 31. – Issued: 30.09.2002. Made: 18.09.2002. Coming into operation: 24.10.2002. Effect: None. – 8p.: 30 cm. – 0 337 94360 5 *£2.00*

Justice

The Justice (Northern Ireland) Act 2002 (Amendment of section 46 (1)) Order 2002 No. 2002/414. – Enabling power: Justice (Northern Ireland) Act 2002, s. 46 (6) (a) (7). – Issued: 23.01.2003. Made: 19.12.2002. Coming into force: 20.12.2002. Effect: 1998 c. 32; 2002 c. 26 amended. – 2p.: 30 cm. – 0 337 94648 5 *£1.50*

The Justice (Northern Ireland) Act 2002 (Commencement No. 1) Order 2002 No. 2002/319 (C.27). – Enabling power: Justice (Northern Ireland) Act 2002, s. 87. Bringing into operation various provisions of the 2002 Act on 15.10.2002. – Issued: 25.10.2002. Made: 09.10.2002. Effect: None. – 4p.: 30 cm. – 0 337 94382 6 *£1.75*

The Justice (Northern Ireland) Act 2002 (Commencement No. 2) Order 2002 No. 2002/405 (C.33). – Enabling power: Justice (Northern Ireland) Act 2002, s. 87. Bringing into operation various provisions of the 2002 Act on 06.01.2003, in accord. with reg. 2. – Issued: 24.12.2002. Made: 10.12.2002. Effect: None. – 4p.: 30 cm. – 0 337 94421 0 *£1.75*

Landlord and tenant

Registered Rents (Increase) Order (Northern Ireland) 2002 No. 2002/54. – Enabling power: S.I. 1978/1050 (N.I. 20), art. 33 (2). – Issued: 27.02.2002. Made: 15.02.2002. Coming into operation: 04.03.2002. Effect: None. – 2p.: 25 cm. – 0 337 94170 X *£1.50*

Land registration

Compulsory Registration of Title (No. 2) Order (Northern Ireland) 2002 No. 2002/401. – Enabling power: Land Registration Act (Northern Ireland) 1970, s. 25 (1). – Issued: 09.01.2003. Made: 18.12.2002. Coming into operation: 01.05.2003. Effect: None. – 4p.: 30 cm. – 0 337 94479 2 *£1.75*

Compulsory Registration of Title Order (Northern Ireland) 2002 No. 2002/400. – Enabling power: Land Registration Act (Northern Ireland) 1970, s. 25 (1). – Issued: 09.01.2003. Made: 18.12.2002. Coming into operation: 01.04.2003. Effect: None. – 4p.: 30 cm. – 0 337 94487 3 *£1.75*

Land Registration (Amendment) Rules (Northern Ireland) 2002 No. 2002/229. – Enabling power: Land Registration Act (Northern Ireland) 1970, s. 81 (1) & Ground Rents Act (Northern Ireland) 2001, ss. 4 (1) to (3), 5 (2), 6 (2) to (4), 7 (3), 23 (1) 26 (2) to (5), 31 (1) & S.I. 1997/1179 (N.I.8), arts. 35, 35 (A). – Issued: 31.01.2003. Made: 26.06.2002. Coming into force: 29.07.2002. Effect: S.R. 1994/424 amended. – 16p.: 30 cm. – 0 337 94720 1 *£3.00*

Legal aid, advice and assistance

The Legal Aid in Criminal Proceedings (Costs) (Amendment) Rules (Northern Ireland) 2002 No. 2002/376. – Enabling power: S.I. 1981/228 (N.I. 8), art. 36 (3). – Issued: 03.01.2003. Made: 03.12.2002. Coming into operation: 30.12.2002. Effect: S.R. 1992/314 amended. – 2p,: 30 cm. – 0 337 94437 7 *£1.50*

Legal aid and advice

Legal Advice and Assistance (Amendment No. 2) Regulations (Northern Ireland) 2002 No. 2002/212. – Enabling power: S.I. 1981/228 (N.I. 8), arts. 5 (3) (a), 22 (1). – Issued: 25.06.2002. Made: 29.05.2002. Coming into force: 21.06.2002. Effect: S.R. 1981/366 amended. – 2p.: 30 cm. – 0 337 94297 8 *£1.50*

Legal Advice and Assistance (Amendment) Regulations (Northern Ireland) 2002 No. 2002/62. – Enabling power: S.I. 1981/228 (N.I. 8), arts. 7 (2), 22, 27. – Issued: 27.03.2002. Made: 22.02.2002. Coming into operation: 08.04.2002. Effect: S.R. 1981/228 (N.I. 8) amended & S.R. 2001/113 revoked. – 4p.: 25 cm. – 0 337 94218 8 *£1.75*

Legal Advice and Assistance (Financial Conditions) Regulations (Northern Ireland) 2002 No. 2002/61. – Enabling power: S.I. 1981/228 (N.I. 8), arts. 3 (2), 7 (3), 22, 27. – Issued: 27.03.2002. Made: 22.02.2002. Coming into operation: 08.04.2002. Effect: S.R. 1981/228 (N.I. 8) amended & S.R. 2001/112 revoked. – 2p,: 25 cm. – 0 337 94217 X *£1.50*

Legal Aid (Financial Conditions) Regulations (Northern Ireland) 2002 No. 2002/60. – Enabling power: S.I. 1981/228 (N.I. 8), arts. 9 (2), 12 (2), 22, 27. – Issued: 27.03.2002. Made: 22.02.2002. Coming into operation: 08.04.2002. Effect: S.I. 1981/228 (N.I. 8) amended & S.R. 2001/111 revoked (with saving). – 4p.: 25 cm. – 0 337 94216 1 *£1.75*

Local government

Change of District Name (Lisburn Borough) Order (Northern Ireland) 2002 No. 2002/231. – Enabling power: Local Government Act (Northern Ireland) 1972, s. 51 (1). – Issued: 05.07.2002. Made: 27.06.2002. Coming into force: 08.08.2002. Effect: None. – 2p.: 30 cm. – 0 337 94301 X *£1.50*

The Local Government (General Grant) Order (Northern Ireland) 2002 No. 2002/182. – Enabling power: S.I. 1972/1999 (N.I. 22), sch. 1, part 1, para. 3 (1). – Issued: 21.05.2002. Made: 13.05.2002. Coming into operation: In accord. with art. 1 (2). Effect: None. – Order subject to affirmative resolution of the Assembly. Superseded by approved order (same title and number, ISBN 0337943036). – 2p.: 30 cm. – 0 337 94268 4 *£1.50*

The Local Government (General Grant) Order (Northern Ireland) 2002 No. 2002/182. – Enabling power: S.I. 1972/1999 (N.I. 22), sch. 1, part 1, para. 3 (1). – Issued: 28.08.2002. Made: 13.05.2002. Coming into operation: In accord. with art. 1 (2). Effect: None. – Affirmed by resolution of the Assembly on 17th June 2002 (supersedes SR of same title and number, published 21.05.2002, ISBN 0337942684). – 2p.: 30 cm. – 0 337 94303 6 *£1.50*

Local Government Pension Scheme (Amendment No. 2 and Transitional and Provisions) Regulations (Northern Ireland) 2002 No. 2002/353. – Enabling power: S.I. 1972/1073 (N.I. 10), arts. 9, 14, sch. 3. – Issued: 10.12.2002. Made: 19.11.2002. Coming into operation: 01.02.2003. Effect: S.R. 1997/137; 2000/177; 2001/279 amended. – 24p.: 30 cm. – 0 337 94404 0 *£4.00*

Local Government Pension Scheme (Amendment) Regulations (Northern Ireland) 2002 No. 2002/115. – Enabling power: S.I. 1972/1073 (N.I. 10), arts. 9, 14, sch. 3. – Issued: 05.04.2002. Made: 20.03.2002. Coming into operation: 01.05.2002. Effect: S.R. 2000/177 amended. – 8p.: 25 cm. – 0 337 94227 7 *£2.00*

Local Government Pension Scheme Regulations (Northern Ireland) 2002 No. 2002/352. – Enabling power: S.I. 1972/1073 (N.I. 10), art. 9, sch. 3. – Issued: 10.12.2002. Made: 19.11.2002. Coming into operation: 01.02.2003. Effect: S.R. 2000/177 amended. – 100p.: 30 cm. – 0 337 94403 2 *£10.00*

Magistrates' courts

Magistrates' Courts (Blood Tests) (Amendment) Rules (Northern Ireland) 2002 No. 2002/163. – Enabling power: S.R. 1981/1675 (N.I. 26), art. 13. – Issued: 21.05.2002. Made: 25.04.2002. Coming into operation: 20.05.2002. Effect: S.R. 1978/376 amended. – 4p.: 30 cm. – 0 337 94270 6 *£1.75*

The Magistrates' Courts (Civil Jurisdiction and Judgments Act 1982) (Amendment) Rules (Northern Ireland) 2002 No. 2002/159. – Enabling power: S.R. 1981/1675 (N.I. 26), art. 13 & Civil Jurisdiction and Judgments Act 1982, s. 48. – Issued: 11.06.2002. Made: 19.04.2002. Coming into operation: 20.05.2002. Effect: S.R. 1986/3929 amended. – EC note: The amendments are needed [for Northern Ireland] in consequence of the coming into force on 1st March 2002 of Council REG (EC) 44/2001. S.I. 2001/3929, which, for the most part, will also come into force on 1st March 2002, makes the main legislative changes needed in respect of the REG. – 4p.: 30 cm. – 0 337 94269 2 *£1.75*

Magistrates' Courts (Declarations of Parentage) Rules (Northern Ireland) 2002 No. 2002/158. – Enabling power: S.R. 1981/1675 (N.I. 26), art. 13. – Issued: 21.05.2002. Made: 19.04.2002. Coming into operation: 20.05.2002. Effect: None. – 16p.: 30 cm. – 0 337 94271 4 *£3.50*

Magistrates' Courts (Detention and Forfeiture of Terrorist Cash) Rules (Northern Ireland) 2002 No. 2002/12. – Enabling power: S.R. 1981/1675 (N.I. 26), art. 13. – Issued: 20.02.2002. Made: 19.01.2002. Coming into operation: 11.02.2002. Effect: S.R. 2001/65 revoked. – 24p.: 25 cm. – 0 337 94153 X *£4.00*

The Magistrates' Courts Fees (Amendment) Order (Northern Ireland) 2002 No. 2002/343. – Enabling power: 1978 c. 23, s. 116 (1) (4). – Issued: 18.11.2002. Made: 05.11.2002. Coming into operation: 02.12.2002, 03.03.2003, in accord. with art. 1. Effect: S.R. 1996/102 amended. – 8p.: 30 cm. – 0 337 94394 X *£2.00*

Medicines

Medicated Feedingstuffs (Amendment) Regulations (Northern Ireland) 2002 No. 2002/161. – Enabling power: European Communities Act 1972, s. 2 (2). – Issued: 02.05.2002. Made: 23.04.2002. Coming into operation: 25.04.2002. Effect: S.I. 1998/1046 amended in relation to Northern Ireland. – 4p.: 30 cm. – 0 337 94258 7 *£1.75*

Northern Ireland Assembly allowances

The Allowances to Members of the Assembly (Winding Up Allowance) (Amendment) Order (Northern Ireland) 2002 No. 2002/230. – Enabling power: Allowances to Members of the Assembly Act (Northern Ireland) 2000, s. 3 (3). – Issued: 11.02.2003. Made: 25.06.2002. Coming into operation: 26.06.2002. Effect: 2000 c.3 (N.I.) amended. – 2p.: 30 cm. – 0 337 94834 8 *£1.50*

Nurses, midwives and health visitors

The Nurses, Midwives and Health Visitors (Professional Conduct) (Amendment) (No. 2) Rules 2002, Approval Order (Northern Ireland) 2002 No. 2002/117. – Enabling power: Nurses, Midwives and Health Visitors Act 1997, ss. 19 (5), 22 (3), sch. 3. – Issued: 16.04.2002. Made: 20.03.2002. Coming into operation: 31.03.2002. Effect: S.R. 1993/313 amended. – 8p.: 25 cm. – 0 337 94236 6 *£2.00*

The Nurses, Midwives and Health Visitors (Professional Conduct) (Amendment) Rules 2002, Approval Order (Northern Ireland) 2002 No. 2002/43. – Enabling power: Nurses, Midwives and Health Visitors Act 1997, ss. 19 (5), 22 (3), sch. 3. – Issued: 28.02.2002. Made: 11.02.2002. Coming into operation: 18.02.2002. Effect: S.R. 1993/313 amended in relation to Northern Ireland. – 4p.: 25 cm. – 0 337 94171 8 *£1.75*

Pensions

The Child Support, Pensions and Social Security (2000 Act) (Commencement No. 7) Order (Northern Ireland) 2002 No. 2002/68 (C.5). – Enabling power: Child Support, Pensions and Social Security Act (Northern Ireland) 2000, s. 68 (2) (a). Bringing into operation various provisions of the 2000 Act in accordance with art. 2. – Issued: 14.03.2002. Made: 28.02.2002. Effect: S.R. 2001/249 (C.12) amended. – 6p.: 25 cm. – 0 337 94184 X   £2.00

The Guaranteed Minimum Pensions Increase Order (Northern Ireland) 2002 No. 2002/98. – Enabling power: Pension Schemes (Northern Ireland) Act 1993, s. 105. – Issued: 22.03.2002. Made: 12.03.2002. Coming into operation: 06.04.2002. Effect: None. – 2p.: 25 cm. – 0 337 94199 8   £1.50

The Occupational and Personal Pension Schemes (Bankruptcy) Regulations (Northern Ireland) 2002 No. 2002/127. – Enabling power: S.I. 1989/2405 (NI. 19), arts, 315C (4) (a) (7) to (9), 315F (6) (a) (9) to (11) & S.I. 1999/3147 (NI. 11), arts. 12 (2) (h), 13 (1) to (3), 73 (3) (4). – Issued: 09.04.2002. Made: 27.03.2002. Coming into operation: 06.04.2002. Effect: None. – 12p.: 25 cm. – 0 337 94234 X   £2.50

The Occupational and Personal Pension Schemes (Contracting-out) (Miscellaneous Amendments) Regulations (Northern Ireland) 2002 No. 2002/109. – Enabling power: Pension Schemes (Northern Ireland) Act 1993, ss. 4 (3) (b), 5 (2B) (c) (3) (aa), 7 (5), 17, 24 (1A) (2) (4), 24 (A),28, 28A (2), 30 (1), 152 (2), 177 (2) to (4), 178 (1) & S.I. 1995/3213 (N.I. 22), arts. 40 (1) (2), 67 (5) (b), 89 (5), 90 (6), 166 (1) to (3). – Issued: 28.03.2002. Made: 14.03.2002. Coming into operation: 06.04.2002. Effect: S.R. 1996/493, 509, 584; 1997/56, 97, 139 amended. – 16p.: 25 cm. – 0 337 94210 2   £3.00

The Occupational and Personal Pension Schemes (Disclosure of Information) (Amendment) Regulations (Northern Ireland) 2002 No. 2002/410. – Enabling power: Pension Schemes (Northern Ireland) Act 1993, ss. 109, 177 (2) to (4), 178 (1) & S.I. 1999/3147 (N.I. 11), art. 3 (1) (b). – Issued: 13.01.2003. Made: 31.12.2002. Coming into operation: 06.04.2003. Effect: S.R. 1987/288; 1997/90; 2000/262, 335 amended. – 12p.: 30 cm. – 0 337 94527 6   £2.50

The Occupational Pension Schemes (Member-nominated Trustees and Directors) (Amendment) Regulations (Northern Ireland) 2002 No. 2002/279. – Enabling power: S.I. 1995/3213 (NI. 22), arts. 17 (1) (c), 19 (1) (c), 21 (4) (5), 166 (3). – Issued: 07.03.2002. Made: 10.09.2002. Coming into operation: 06.10.2002. Effect: S.R. 1996/431 amended. – 8p.: 30 cm. – 0 337 94351 6   £2.00

The Occupational Pension Schemes (Minimum Funding Requirement and Miscellaneous Amendments) Regulations (Northern Ireland) 2002 No. 2002/64. – Enabling power: S.I. 1995/3213 (NI. 22), arts, 56 (3), 57 (1) (b) (2) (5), 58 (2) (4) (b) (6) (a), 59 (3), 61, 73 (3), 75 (5), 122 (2), 166 (1) to (3). – Issued: 07.03.2002. Made: 25.02.2002. Coming into operation: 19.03.2002. Effect: S.I. 1995/3213 (NI. 22) & S.R. 1996/570, 585. 621 amended. – 10p.: 25 cm. – 0 337 94179 3   £2.50

The Occupational Pension Schemes (Winding Up Notices and Reports etc.) Regulations (Northern Ireland) 2002 No. 2002/74. – Enabling power: Pension Schemes (Northern Ireland) Act 1993, s. 109 (1) & S.I. 1995/3213 (NI. 22), arts, 10 (2) (b) (3), 23 (2), 26B (3) (b), 26C (2) (3), 49A (1) (2) (b) (3), 71A (4), 72A (1) (b) (2) (7)((8) (a), 72B (2) (c) (iii) (3) (5) (c) (6) (c) (8) (b), 115 (2), 121 (8), 166 (1) to (3). – Issued: 12.03.2002. Made: 05.03.2002. Coming into operation: 01.04.2002. Effect: S.R. 1997/98 amended. – 14p.: 25 cm. – 0 337 94185 8   £3.00

The Occupational Pensions (Revaluation) Order (Northern Ireland) 2002 No. 2002/369. – Enabling power: Pension Schemes (Northern Ireland) Act 1993, sch. 2, para. 2 (1). – Issued: 10.12.2002. Made: 02.12.2002. Coming into operation: 01.01.2003. Effect: None. – 2p.: 30 cm. – 0 337 94415 6   £1.50

Pensions Increase (Review) Order (Northern Ireland) 2002 No. 2002/102. – Enabling power: S.I. 1975/1503 (NI.15), art. 69 (1) (2) (5) (5ZA). – Issued: 22.03.2002. Made: 13.03.2002. Coming into force: 08.04.2002. Effect: None. – 8p.: 25 cm. – 0 337 94204 8   £2.00

The Stakeholder Pension Schemes (Amendment No. 2) Regulations (Northern Ireland) 2002 No. 2002/268. – Enabling power: S.I. 1999/3147 (N.I. 11), arts. 3 (1) (b), 73 (4). – Issued: 19.08.2002. Made: 09.08.2002. Coming into operation: 09.09.2002. Effect: S.R. 2000/262; 2001/119; 2002/216 amended. – 8p.: 30 cm. – 0 337 94338 9   £2.00

The Stakeholder Pension Schemes (Amendment) Regulations (Northern Ireland) 2002 No. 2002/216. – Enabling power: S.I. 1999/3147 (N.I. 11), arts. 3 (1) (b) (5), 73 (4) (a) – Issued: 18.06.2002. Made: 10.06.2002. Coming into operation: 04.07.2002. Effect: S.R. 2000/262 amended. – 4p.: 30 cm. – 0 337 94293 5   £1.75

Superannuation (Invest Northern Ireland) Order (Northern Ireland) 2002 No. 2002/211. – Enabling power: S.I. 1972/1073 (N.I. 10), art. 3 (4) (7). – Issued: 12.06.2002. Made: 30.05.2002. Coming into operation: 11.07.2002. Effect: None. – 2p.: 30 cm. – 0 337 94280 3   £1.50

The Welfare Reform and Pensions (1999 Order) (Commencement No. 10) Order (Northern Ireland) 2002 No. 2002/25 (C.2). – Enabling power: S.I. 1999/3147 (NI. 11), art. 1 (2). Bringing into operation various provisions of the 1999 Order on 06.04.2002. – Issued: 08.02.2002. Made: 31.01.2002. Effect: S.R. 2001/438 (C.21) amended. – 8p.: 25 cm. – 0 337 94141 6   £2.00

The Welfare Reform and Pensions (1999 Order) (Commencement No. 11) Order (Northern Ireland) 2002 No. 2002/63 (C.4). – Enabling power: S.I. 1999/3147 (NI. 11), art. 1 (2). Bringing into operation various provisions of the 1999 Order on 19.03.2002. – Issued: 06.03.2002. Made: 25.02.2002. Effect: None. – 8p.: 25 cm. – 0 337 94177 7 *£1.75*

The Welfare Reform and Pensions (1999 Order) (Commencement No. 12) Order (Northern Ireland) 2002 No. 2002/126 (C.9). – Enabling power: S.I. 1999/3147 (N.I. 11), art. 1 (2). Bringing into operation various provisions of the 1999 Order on 27.03.2002 & 06.04.2002. – Issued: 05.04.2002. Made: 26.03.2002. Effect: S.R. 2002/25 (C.2) amended. – 4p.: 25 cm. – 0 337 94229 3 *£1.75*

Pesticides

Pesticides (Maximum Residue Levels in Crops, Food and Feeding Stuffs) (Amendment) (No. 2) Regulations (Northern Ireland) 2002 No. 2002/250. – Enabling power: European Communities Act 1972, s. 2 (2) & Food and Environment Protection Act 1985, s. 16 (2). – Issued: 31.07.2002. Made: 23.07.2002. Coming into operation: 01.09.2002. Effect: S.R. 2002/20 amended. – EC note: These Regs. specify maximum levels of pesticides which crops, food and feeding stuffs may contain in implementation of DIRs 2002/5/EC and 2002/23/EC. – 8p.: 30 cm. – 0 337 94319 2 *£2.00*

Pesticides (Maximum Residue Levels in Crops, Food and Feeding Stuffs) (Amendment) Regulations (Northern Ireland) 2002 No. 2002/27. – Enabling power: European Communities Act 1972, s. 2 (2) & Food and Environment Protection Act 1985, s. 16 (2). – Issued: 14.02.2002. Made: 01.02.2002. Coming into operation: 11.03.2002. Effect: S.R. 2002/20 amended. – EC note: These Regs. specify maximum levels which crops, food and feeding stuffs may contain in implementation of DIRs 2000/81/EC, 2000/82/EC, 2001/39/EC and 2001/57/EC; also 1998/82/EC (iprodione on spring onions) and 1993/58/EEC (methamidophos on cottonseed). – 24p.: 25 cm. – 0 337 94143 2 *£4.00*

Pesticides (Maximum Residue Levels in Crops, Food and Feeding Stuffs) Regulations (Northern Ireland) 2002 No. 2002/20. – Enabling power: European Communities Act 1972, s. 2 (2) & Food and Environment Protection Act 1985, s. 16 (2). – Issued: 11.02.2002. Made: 28.01.2002. Coming into operation: 04.03.2002. Effect: S.R. 1995/32, 33, 460, 461; 1996/526, 527; 1997/243, 244; 1999/114, 320, 321 revoked. – 180p.: 25 cm. – 0 337 94138 6 *£15.00*

Plant Protection Products (Amendment) (No. 2) Regulations (Northern Ireland) 2002 No. 2002/125. – Enabling power: European Communities Act 1972, s. 2 (2). – Issued: 08.04.2002. Made: 25.03.2002. Coming into operation: 15.04.2002. Effect: S.R. 1995/371 amended & S.R. 2002/21 revoked. – 4p.: 25 cm. – 0 337 94233 1 *£1.75*

Plant Protection Products (Amendment) (No. 3) Regulations (Northern Ireland) 2002 No. 2002/289. – Enabling power: European Communities Act 1972, s. 2 (2). – Issued: 25.09.2002. Made: 17.09.2002. Coming into operation: 22.10.2002. Effect: S.R. 1995/371 amended & S.R. 2002/125 revoked. – 4p.: 25 cm. – 0 337 94355 9 *£1.75*

Plant Protection Products (Amendment) Regulations (Northern Ireland) 2002 No. 2002/21. – Enabling power: European Communities Act 1972, s. 2 (2). – Issued: 05.02.2002. Made: 28.01.2002. Coming into operation: 04.03.2002. Effect: S.R. 1995/371 amended & S.R. 2001/280 revoked. – 6p.: 25 cm. – 0 337 94137 8 *£2.00*

Pharmacy

Pharmaceutical Society of Northern Ireland (General) (Amendment) Regulations (Northern Ireland) 2002 No. 2002/206. – Enabling power: S.I. 1976/1213 (N.I. 22), art. 5. – Issued: 17.06.2002. Made: 28.05.2002. Coming into force: 01.07.2002. Effect: S.R. 1994/202 amended. – 2p.: 30 cm. – 0 337 94289 7 *£1.50*

Planning

Planning (General Development) (Amendment) Order (Northern Ireland) 2002 No. 2002/195. – Enabling power: S.I. 1991/1220 (N.I. 11), art. 13. – Issued: 30.05.2002. Made: 22.05.2002. Coming into force: 21.06.2002. Effect: S.R. 1993/278 amended. – 4p.: 30 cm. – 0 337 94278 1 *£1.75*

Plant health

The Plant Health (Amendment) Order (Northern Ireland) 2002 No. 2002/273. – Enabling power: Plant Health Act (Northern Ireland) 1967, ss. 2, 3 (1), 3A, 3B, 4 (1). – Issued: 10.09.2002. Made: 30.08.2002. Coming into operation: 23.09.2002. Effect: S.R. 1993/256 amended. – 4p.: 30 cm. – 0 337 94346 X *£1.75*

The Plant Health (Phytophthora ramorum) Order (Northern Ireland) 2002 No. 2002/269. – Enabling power: Plant Health Act (Northern Ireland) 1967, ss. 2, 3 (1) (2) (b) (4), 4 (1) (b). – Issued: 27.08.2002. Made: 15.08.2002. Coming into operation: 09.09.2002. Effect: None. – 8p.: 30 cm. – 0 337 94341 9 *£2.00*

The Plant Health (Wood and Bark) (Amendment) Order (Northern Ireland) 2002 No. 2002/285. – Enabling power: Plant Health Act (Northern Ireland) 1967, ss. 2, 3 (1), 3A, 3B, 4 (1). – Issued: 25.09.2002. Made: 16.09.2002 Coming into operation: 23.09.2002. Effect: S.R. 1993/460 amended. – EC note: Implements certain elements DIR 2002/29/EC, 2002/28/EC, also measures required by DIR 2001/32/EC & 2001/33/EC. – 4p.: 25 cm. – 0 337 94357 5 *£1.75*

The Potatoes Originating in Egypt (Amendment) Regulations (Northern Ireland) 2002 No. 2002/246. – Enabling power: European Communities Act 1972, s. 2 (2). Issued: 29.07.2002. Made: 19.07.2002. Coming into operation: 12.08.2002. Effect: S.R. 1998/107 amended. – EC note: Implements in Northern Ireland DEC 2001/664/EC, amending 96/301/EC. – 4p,: 30 cm. – 0 337 94316 8 *£1.75*

The Potatoes Originating in Germany (Notification) Order (Northern Ireland) 2002 No. 2002/7. – Enabling power: Plant Health (Northern Ireland) Act 1967, ss. 2, 3 (1), 3B (1), 4 (1). – Issued: 21.01.2002. Made: 14.01.2002. Coming into operation: 11.02.2002. Effect: None. – 4p,: 25 cm. – 0 337 94131 9 *£1.75*

Police

Police Emblems and Flags Regulations (Northern Ireland) 2002 No. 2002/23. – Enabling power: Police (Northern Ireland) Act 2000, s. 54. – Issued: 09.04.2002. Made: 24.01.2002. Coming into operation: 05.04.2002. Effect: None. – 8p.: 25 cm. – 0 337 94230 7 *£2.00*

The Police (Northern Ireland) Act 2000 (Commencement No. 4) Order 2002 No. 2002/146 (C.14). – Enabling power: Police (Northern Ireland) Act 2000, s. 79. Bringing into operation certain provisions of the 2000 Act on 15.04.2002. – Issued: 24.01.2003. Made: 28.03.2002. Effect: None. – 4p.: 30 cm. – 0 337 94656 6 *£1.50*

The Police (Northern Ireland) Act 2000 (Designated Places of Detention) Order 2002 No. 2002/179. – Enabling power: Police (Northern Ireland) Act 2000, s. 73 (10). – Issued: 24.02.2003. Made: 08.05.2002. Laid before Parliament; 10.05.2002. Coming into operation: 31.05.2002. Effect: None. – 2p.: 30 cm. – 0 337 94868 2 *£1.50*

The Police (Northern Ireland) Act 2000 (Policing Plan) Regulations 2002 No. 2002/76. – Enabling power: Police (Northern Ireland) Act 2000, s. 26 (2) (b). – Issued: 11.06.2002. Made: 05.03.2002. Coming into operation: 01.04.2002, 01.10.2002, in accord. with art. 1 (1) (2). Effect: None. – 4p.: 30 cm. – 0 337 94274 9 *£1.75*

Police (Recruitment) (Northern Ireland) (Amendment) Regulations 2002 No. 2002/385. Enabling power: Police (Northern Ireland) Act 1998, ss. 25, 26 & Police (Northern Ireland) Act 2000, ss. 41, 43, 44. – Issued: 20.12.2002. Made: 12.12.2002. Coming into operation: 17.01.2003. Effect: S.R. 2001/140 amended. – 4p.: 30 cm. – 0 337 94428 8 *£1.75*

Police Service of Northern Ireland Pensions Regulations 2002 No. 2002/100. – Enabling power: Police (Northern Ireland) Act 1998, s. 25. – Issued: 21.03.2002. Made: 07.03.2002. Coming into operation: 12.04.2002. Effect: S.R. 1988/374 amended. – 8p.: 25 cm. – 0 337 94208 0 *£2.00*

Police Service of Northern Ireland (Recruitment of Police Support Staff) Regulations 2002 No. 2002/258. – Enabling power: Police (Northern Ireland) Act 2000, ss. 43, 44. – Issued: 09.08.2002. Made: 29.07.2002. Coming into operation: 20.09.2002. Effect: None. – 4p.: 30 cm. – 0 337 94331 1 *£1.75*

Police Service of Northern Ireland Regulations 2002 No. 2002/95. – Enabling power: Police (Northern Ireland) Act 1998, s. 25. – Issued: 21.03.2002. Made: 08.03.2002. Coming into operation: In accordance with art. 1 (2). Effect: S.R. 1996/473 amended. – 16p.: 25 cm. – 0 337 94206 4 *£3.00*

Police Service of Northern Ireland Reserve (Full Time) (Appointment and Conditions of Service) Regulations 2002 No. 2002/96. – Enabling power: Police (Northern Ireland) Act 1998, s. 26. – Issued: 21.03.2002. Made: 08.03.2002. Coming into operation: In accord.with art. 1 (2). Effect: S.R. 1996/564 amended. – 8p.: 25 cm. – 0 337 94207 2 *£2.00*

Police Service of Northern Ireland Reserve (Full-time) Pensions Regulations 2002 No. 2002/101. – Enabling power: Police (Northern Ireland) Act 1998, s. 26. – Issued: 21.03.2002. Made: 08.03.2002. Coming into operation: 12.04.2002. Effect: S.R. 1994/197 amended. – 8p.: 25 cm. – 0 337 94209 9 *£2.00*

The Royal Ulster Constabulary GC Foundation Regulations 2002 No. 2002/260. – Enabling power: Police (Northern Ireland) Act 2000, s. 70. – Issued: 15.08.2002. Made: 26.07.2002. Coming into operation: 16.09.2002. Effect: None. – 4p.: 25 cm. – 0 337 94336 2 *£1.75*

Preserved rights

The Personal Social Services (Preserved Rights) (2002 Act) (Commencement) Order (Northern Ireland) 2002 No. 2002/131 (C.11). – Enabling power: Personal Social Services (Preserved Rights) Act (Northern Ireland) 2002, ss. 6, 7. Bringing into operation various provisions of the 2002 Act on 28.03.2002, 08.04.2002, in accord. with arts. 2, 3. – Issued: 22.04.2002. Made: 28.03.2002. Effect: None. – 2p.: 25 cm. – 0 337 94243 9 *£1.50*

Procedure

The Rules of the Supreme Court (Northern Ireland) (Amendment) 2002 No. 2002/15. – Enabling power: Judicature (Northern Ireland) Act 1978, s. 55. – Issued: 19.02.2002. Made: 22.01.2002. Coming into force: 15.02.2002. Effect: S.R. 1980/346 amended. – 8p.: 25 cm. – 0 337 94154 8 *£2.00*

Property

The Ground Rents (2001 Act) (Commencement No. 1) Order (Northern Ireland) 2002 No. 2002/251 (C.22). – Enabling power: Ground Rents Act (Northern Ireland) 2001, s. 32 (1). Bringing into operation certain provisions of the 2001 Act on 29.07.2002, in accord. with art. 2. – Issued: 02.08.2002. Made: 23.07.2002. Effect: None. – 2p.: 30 cm. – 0 337 94323 0 *£1.50*

Ground Rents (Multiplier) Order (Northern Ireland) 2002 No. 2002/228. – Enabling power: Ground Rents Act (Northern Ireland) 2001, s. 5 (1), sch. 1, paras. 2, 4 (3) (4). – Issued: 06.12.2002. Made: 26.06.2002. Coming into operation: 29.07.2002. Effect: None. – 2p.: 30 cm. – 0 337 94407 5 £1.50

The Property (1997 Order) (Commencement No. 3) Order (Northern Ireland) 2002 No. 2002/252 (C.23). – Enabling power: S.I. 1997/1179 (NI. 8), art. 1 (2). Bringing into operation various provisions of the 1997 Order on 29.07.2002. – Issued: 16.08.2002. Made: 23.07.2002. Effect: None. – 2p.: 25 cm. – 0 337 94322 2 £2.00

Public health

The Control of Noise (Codes of Practice for Construction and Open Sites) Order (Northern Ireland) 2002 No. 2002/303. – Enabling power: S.I. 1978/1049 (N.I. 19), arts. 51, 86. – Issued: 10.10.2002. Made: 30.09.2002. Coming into operation: 01.11.2002. Effect: S.R. 1978/349 revoked. – 4p.: 30 cm. – 0 337 94370 2 £1.75

Food Protection (Emergency Prohibitions) Order (Northern Ireland) 2002 No. 2002/339. – Enabling power: Food and Environment Protection Act 1985, ss. 1 (1) (2), 24 (3). – Issued: 12.11.2002. Made: 06.11.2002. Coming into operation: 06.11.2002. Effect: None. – 4p.: 25 cm. – 0 337 94391 5 £1.75

Food Protection (Emergency Prohibitions) (Revocation) Order (Northern Ireland) 2002 No. 2002/370. – Enabling power: Food and Environment Protection Act 1985, ss. 1 (1) (2), 24 (3). – Issued: 10.12.2002. Made: 02.12.2002. Coming into operation: 02.12.2002. Effect: S.R. 2002/339 revoked. – 4p.: 25 cm. – 0 337 94416 4 £1.75

The Producer Responsibility Obligations (Packaging Waste) (Amendment) Regulations (Northern Ireland) 2002 No. 2002/239. – Enabling power: S.I. 1998/1762 (NI. 16), arts. 3, 4 (1) (c). – Issued: 18.07.2002. Made: 08.07.2002. Coming into force: 02.09.2002. Effect: S.R. 1999/115 amended. – 4p.: 30 cm. – 0 337 94306 0 £1.75

Rates

Rates (Making and Levying of Different Rates) Regulations (Northern Ireland) 2002 No. 2002/409. – Enabling power: S.I. 1977/2157 (N.I. 28), art. 6 (3) (a). – Issued: 09.01.2003. Made: 23.12.2002. Coming into operation: 28.01.2003. Effect: S.R. 1997/50 revoked with saving. – 4p.: 25 cm. – 0 337 94495 4 £1.75

Rates (Regional Rates) Order (Northern Ireland) 2002 No. 2002/26. – Enabling power: S.I. 1977/2157 (NI. 28), arts. 2 (2), 7 (1), 27 (4). – Issued: 11.02.2002. Made: 29.01.2002. Coming into operation: 01.04.2002. Effect: None. – 2p.: 25 cm. – 0 337 94142 4 £1.50

Rates (Regional Rates) Order (Northern Ireland) 2002 No. 2002/26. – Enabling power: S.I. 1977/2157 (NI. 28), arts. 2 (2), 7 (1), 27 (4). – Issued: 12.03.2002. Made: 29.01.2002. Affirmed by resolution of the Assembly: 04.03.2002. Coming into operation: 01.04.2002. Effect: None. – 2p.: 25 cm. – 0 337 94188 2 £1.50

The Social Security and Child Support (Decisions and Appeals) (Miscellaneous Amendments) Regulations (Northern Ireland) 2002 No. 2002/189. – Enabling power: S.I. 1991/2628 (N.I. 23), arts. 22 (4) to (6), & S.I. 1995/2705 (N.I. 15), art. 32, sch. 1, para. 4 & S.I. 1997/1183 (N.I. 12), art. 13 (5) (a) (b) & S.I. 1998/1506 (N.I. 10), arts. 7 (3), 10 (1), 11A (1), 13 (2) (7), 15 (11), 16 (1), 24A (1) (2) (a), 28 (1), 74(1) (3) (5) (6), sch. 1, para. 12(1), sch. 2, para. 9, sch. 4, paras 1 to 4, 6, 7 & Child Support, Pensions and Social Security Act (Northern Ireland) 2000, sch. 7, paras. 3 (1), 6 (7) (8), 10 (1), 19 (1), 20 (1) (3)– Issued: 30.05.2002. Made: 16.05.2002. Coming into operation: 20.05.2002. Effect: S.R. 1999/162, 408; 2000/215; 2001/213 amended. – 12p.: 30 cm. – 0 337 94273 0 £2.50

The Social Security Benefits Up-rating Order (Northern Ireland) 2002 No. 2002/99. – Enabling power: Social Security Administration (Northern Ireland) Act 1992, ss. 132, 165 (1) (5). – Issued: 28.03.2002. Made: 13.03.2002. Coming into operation: In accord. with art. 1 (1). Effect: 1992 c. 7; S.R. 1976/223; 1987/30, 459, 461; 1992/32; 1994/461; 1995/35; 1996/73, 198 amended & S.R. 2001/41 revoked (11.04.2002.). – 60p.: 25 cm. – 0 337 94201 3 £7.00

The Social Security (Carer Premium Amendment) Regulations (Northern Ireland) 2002 No. 2002/322. – Enabling power: Social Security Contributions and Benefits (Northern Ireland) Act 1992, ss. 122 (1) (a) (d), 131 (1), 171 (1) (3) (4) and S.I. 1995/2705 (NI. 15), arts. 6 (5), 36 (2). – Issued: 31.10.2002. Made: 21.10.2002. Coming into operation: 28.10.2002. Effect: S.R. 1987/459, 461; 1996/198 amended. – 4p.: 30 cm. – 0 337 94384 2 £1.75

The Social Security (Employment Programme Amendment) Regulations (Northern Ireland) 2002 No. 2002/275. – Enabling power: Social Security Contributions and Benefits (Northern Ireland) Act 2002, ss. 122 (1) (a) (d), 132 (3) (4) (b), 171 (1) (3) (4) & S.I. 1995/2705 (N.I. 15), arts. 14 (1) (4) (b), 21 (10) (c), 36 (2), sch. 1, para. 3 (b). – Issued: 16.09.2002. Made: 06.09.2002. Coming into operation: 14.10.2002. Effect: S.R. 1987/459, 461; 1996/198 amended. – 4p.: 30 cm. – 0 337 94348 6 £1.75

The Social Security (Intercalating Students Amendment) Regulations (Northern Ireland) 2002 No. 2002/243. – Enabling power: Social Security Contributions and Benefits (Northern Ireland) Act 1992, ss. 122 (1) (d), 133 (2) (j), 171 (1) (3) (4) & S.I. 1995/2705 (N.I. 15), art. 8 (4). – Issued: 23.07.2002. Made: 10.07.2002. Coming into operation: 01.08.2002. Effect: S.R. 1987/461; 1996/198 amended. – 4p.: 30 cm. – 0 337 94309 5 £1.75

The Social Security (Loss of Benefit) (Consequential Amendments) Regulations (Northern Ireland) 2002 No. 2002/80. – Enabling power: Social Security Contributions and Benefits (Northern Ireland) Act 1992, ss. 22 (5), 122 (1) (a) (d), 123 (1) (e), 131 (1), 171 (1) (3) & S.I. 1995/2705 (NI. 15), arts. 7 (3), 28 (1) (4) (d), 36 (2) & S.I. 1998/1506 (NI. 10), arts. 10 (1), 11 (3) (6), 74 (1) & Child Support, Pensions and Social Security Act (Northern Ireland) 2000, s. 60 (1) (2) (a), sch. 7, paras. 3 (1), 4 (3) (5). – Issued: 15.03.2002. Made: 06.03.2002. Coming into operation: 01.04.2002. Effect:S.R. 1975/113; 1987/459, 461; 1996/198, 519; 1999/162; 2001/213, 216 amended. – 8p.: 25 cm. – 0 337 94190 4 £2.00

The Social Security (Loss of Benefit) Regulations (Northern Ireland) 2002 No. 2002/79. – Enabling power: Social Security Fraud Act (Northern Ireland) 2001, ss. 6 (3) to (6), 7 (3) (4), 8 (2) to (5), 9 (1) (2) & S.I. 1998/1506 (NI. 10), art. 74 (3) to (6), sch. 2, para. 9. – Issued: 14.03.2002. Made: 06.03.2002. Coming into operation: 01.04.2002. Effect: S.R. 1999/162 amended. – 20p.: 25 cm. – 0 337 94189 0 £3.50

The Social Security (Miscellaneous Amendments No. 2) Regulations (Northern Ireland) 2002 No. 2002/295. – Enabling power: Social Security Contributions and Benefits (Northern Ireland) Act 1992, ss. 122 (1) (a) (d), 132 (4) (b), 171 (1) (3) (4) & S.I. 1995/2705 (N.I. 15), arts. 14 (4) (b), 36 (2). – Issued: 02.10.2002. Made: 19.09.2002. Coming into operation: 14.10.2002. Effect: S.R. 1987/459, 461; 1996/198 amended. – 4p.: 30 cm. – 0 337 94362 1 £1.75

The Social Security (Miscellaneous Amendments) Regulations (Northern Ireland) 2002 No. 2002/128. – Enabling power: Social Security Contributions and Benefits (Northern Ireland) Act 1992, ss. 122 (1) (a) (d), 131 (1), 132 (3) (4) (b), 171 (1) (3) (4) & S.I. 1995/2705 (N.I. 15), arts. 6 (5), 14 (1) (4) (b), 36 (2). – Issued: 12.04.2002. Made: 27.03.2002. Coming into operation: 08.04.2002. Effect: S.R. 1987/459, 461; 1996/198 amended. – 6p.: 30 cm. – 0 337 94235 8 £2.00

The Social Security (Paternity and Adoption Amendment) Regulations (Northern Ireland) 2002 No. 2002/363. – Enabling power: Social Security Contributions and Benefits (Northern Ireland) Act 1992, ss. 122 (1) (a) (d), 123 (1) (e), 132 (3) (4) (b), 133 (2) (d), 171 (1) (3) (4) & S.I. 1995/2705 (N.I. 15), art. 14 (1) (4) (b), 23, 36 (2), sch. 1, para. 1. – Issued: 10.12.2002. Made: 27.11.2002. Coming into operation: 08.12.2002. Effect: S.R. 1987/459, 461; 1996/198 amended. – 8p.: 30 cm. – 0 337 94413 X £2.00

The Social Security (Personal Allowances for Children and Young Persons Amendment) Regulations (Northern Ireland) 2002 No. 2002/267. – Enabling power: Social Security Contributions and Benefits (Northern Ireland) Act 1992, ss. 122 (1) (a) (d), 131 (1), 171 (1) (3) & S.I. 1995/2705 (N.I. 15), art. 6 (5). – Issued: 19.08.2002. Made: 08.08.2002. Coming into operation: 14.10.2002. Effect: S.R. 1987/459, 461; 1996/198 amended. – 4p.: 30 cm. – 0 337 94339 7 £1.75

The Social Security (Personal Injury Payments Amendment) Regulations (Northern Ireland) 2002 No. 2002/299. – Enabling power: Social Security Contributions and Benefits (Northern Ireland) Act 1992, ss. 122 (1) (a) (d), 132 (4) (b) (d), 171 (1) (3) (4) & S.I. 1995/2705 (N.I. 15), art. 14 (4) (b) (d). – Issued: 07.10.2002. Made: 26.09.2002. Coming into operation: 28.10.2002. Effect: S.R. 1987/459, 461; 1996/198 amended. – 4p.: 30 cm. – 0 337 94367 2 £1.75

The Social Security (Students and Income-related Benefits Amendment No. 2) Regulations (Northern Ireland) 2002 No. 2002/270. – Enabling power: Social Security Contributions and Benefits (Northern Ireland) Act 1992, ss. 122 (1) (a) (d), 132 (4) (b), 171 (1) (3) (4) & S.I. 1995/2705 (NI. 15), art. 14 (4) (b). – Issued: 05.09.2002. Made: 27.08.2002. Coming into operation: 02.09.2002. Effect: S.R. 1987/459, 461; 1996/198 amended. – 4p.: 30 cm. – 0 337 94344 3 £1.75

The Social Security (Students and Income-related Benefits Amendment) Regulations (Northern Ireland) 2002 No. 2002/222. – Enabling power: Social Security Contributions and Benefits (Northern Ireland) Act 1992, ss. 122 (1) (a) (d), 129 (2), 132 (3) (4) (b), 171 (1) (3) (4) & S.I. 1995/2705 (NI. 15), art. 14 (1) (4) (b). – Issued: 04.07.2002. Made: 18.06.2002. Coming into operation: 01.08.2002 & 26.08.2002. Effect: S.R. 1987/459, 461; 1996/198 amended. – 8p.: 30 cm. – 0 337 94300 1 £2.00

Registration of births, deaths and marriages

Births, Deaths and Marriages (Fees) (No. 2) Order (Northern Ireland) 2002 No. 2002/242. – Enabling power: Registration of Births, Deaths and Marriages (Fees, etc.) Act (Northern Ireland) 1955, s. 1 (1) (2) & S.I. 1976/1041 (N.I. 14), art. 47 (1) (2) & 1976/1212 (N.I. 21), art. 15. – Issued: 23.07.2002. Made: 11.07.2002. Coming into operation: 01.08.2002. Effect: S.R. 1998/330 & the Births, Deaths and Marriages (Fees) Order (Northern Ireland) 2002 revoked. – 8p.: 30 cm. – 0 337 94310 9 £2.00

Roads

The Street Works (Registers, Notices, Directions and Designations) Regulations (Northern Ireland) 2002 No. 2002/10. – Enabling power: S.I. 1995/3210 (N.I. 19), arts 3 (2), 13, 14 (1) (2), 15 (1) to (3) (7), 16 (2), 17 (2) (3), 18 (1) (2) (5), 22 (1), 23 (2), 24 (1) (2), 54 (1) (2)– Issued: 28.01.2002. Made: 17.01.2002. Coming into operation: 18.03.2002. Effect: None. – 20p.: 25 cm. – 0 337 94133 5 £4.00

Road traffic

The Road Traffic (Health Services Charges) (Amendment No. 2) Regulations (Northern Ireland) 2002 No. 2002/373. – Enabling power: Health and Personal Social Services Act (Northern Ireland) 2001, ss. 25 (2) (4), 37, 57 (1) (3). – Issued: 10.12.2002. Made: 04.12.2002. Coming into operation: 01.01.2003. Effect: S.R. 2001/125 amended. – 4p.: 30 cm. – 0 337 94420 2 £1.75

The Road Traffic (Health Services Charges) (Amendment) Regulations (Northern Ireland) 2002 No. 2002/52. – Enabling power: Health and Personal Social Services Act (Northern Ireland) 2001, ss. 23 (5), 25 (2) (4), 32 (2), 37, 57 (1) (3). – Issued: 28.02.2002. Made: 15.02.2002. Coming into operation: 16.02.2002. Effect: S.R. 2001/125 amended & 2001/434 revoked. – 4p.: 25 cm. – 0 337 94172 6 £1.75

Road traffic and vehicles

The Driving Licences (Community Driving Licence) Regulations (Northern Ireland) 2002 No. 2002/374. – Enabling power: European Communities Act 1972, s. 2 (2). – Issued: 16.12.2002. Made: 04.12.2002. Coming into operation: 20.01.2003. Effect: S.I. 1981/154 (N.I. 1) & S.R. 1996/426 amended. – 8p.: 30 cm. – 0 337 94424 5 £2.00

Dundrod Circuit (Admission Charges) Regulations (Northern Ireland) 2002 No. 2002/167. – Enabling power: S.I. 1986/1887 (NI. 17), art. 3 (7A) (b). – Issued: 14.05.2002. Made: 01.05.2002. Coming into operation: 01.07.2002. Effect: S.R. 1979/196 revoked. – 2p.: 30 cm. – 0 337 94260 9 £1.50

Goods Vehicles (Testing) (Fees) (Amendment) Regulations (Northern Ireland) 2002 No. 2002/48. – Enabling power: S.I. 1995/2994 (N.I. 18), arts. 65 (1) (2), 67 (1), 110 (2). – Issued: 27.02.2002. Made: 13.02.2002. Coming into operation: 01.04.2002. Effect: S.R. 1995/450 amended & S.R. 2001/247 revoked. – 4p.: 25 cm. – 0 337 94166 1 £1.75

Motor Vehicles (Authorised Weight) (Amendment) Regulations (Northern Ireland) 2002 No. 2002/8. – Enabling power: S.I. 1995/2994 (NI. 18), arts. 55 (1) (2), 110 (2). – Issued: 25.01.2002. Made: 15.01.2002. Coming into operation: 28.02.2002. Effect: S.R. 1999/258 amended. – 8p.: 25 cm. – 0 337 94132 7 £2.00

Motor Vehicles (Construction and Use) (Amendment No. 2) Regulations (Northern Ireland) 2002 No. 2002/256. – Enabling power: S.I. 1995/2994 (N.I. 18), arts. 55 (1) (2) (6), 110 (2). – Issued: 05.08.2002. Made: 25.07.2002. Coming into operation: 01.09.2002. Effect: S.R. 1999/454 amended. – 8p.: 30 cm. – 0 337 94327 3 £2.00

Motor Vehicles (Construction and Use) (Amendment No. 3) Regulations (Northern Ireland) 2002 No. 2002/294. – Enabling power: S.I. 1995/2994 (N.I. 18), arts. 55 (1) (2), 110 (2). – Issued: 02.10.2002. Made: 19.09.2002. Coming into operation: 01.11.2002. Effect: S.R. 1999/454 amended. – 4p.: 30 cm. – 0 337 94364 8 £1.75

Motor Vehicles (Construction and Use) (Amendment No. 4) Regulations (Northern Ireland) 2002 No. 2002/375. – Enabling power: S.I. 1995/2994 (N.I. 18), arts. 55, 110 (2). – Issued: 17.12.2002. Made: 04.12.2002. Coming into operation: 28.02.2003. Effect: S.R. 1999/454 amended. – 12p.: 30 cm. – 0 337 94425 3 £2.50

Motor Vehicles (Construction and Use) (Amendment) Regulations (Northern Ireland) 2002 No. 2002/197. – Enabling power: S.I. 1995/2994 (N.I. 18), arts. 55 (1) (2) (6), 110 (2). – Issued: 12.06.2002. Made: 22.05.2002. Coming into operation: 01.09.2002. Effect: S.R. 1999/454 amended & S.R. 2002/197 revoked. – 8p.: 30 cm. – 0 337 94294 3 £2.50

Motor Vehicles (Driving Licences) (Amendment No. 2) Regulations (Northern Ireland) 2002 No. 2002/383. – Enabling power: S.I. 1981/154 (N.I. 1), arts. 5 (3) (4) (5), 19C (1) (2), 218 (1). – Issued: 20.12.2002. Made: 09.12.2002 Coming into operation: 06.01.2003. Effect: S.R. 1996/542 amended. – 4p.: 25 cm. – 0 337 94427 X £1.75

Motor Vehicles (Driving Licences) (Amendment) (Test Fees) Regulations (Northern Ireland) 2002 No. 2002/51. – Enabling power: S.I. 1981/154 (N.I. 1), arts. 5 (3) (4) (5), 218 (1). – Issued: 27.02.2002. Made: 14.02.2002 Coming into operation: 01.04.2002. Effect: S.R. 1996/542 amended & S.R. 2001/245, 310 revoked. – 4p.: 25 cm. – 0 337 94169 6 £1.75

Motor Vehicles (Exchangeable Licences) (Amendment) Order (Northern Ireland) 2002 No. 2002/328. – Enabling power: S.I. 1981/154 (N.I. 1), art 19D (2). – Issued: 07.11.2002. Made: 24.10.2002. Coming into operation: 09.12.2002. Effect: S.R. 1994/364 amended. – 2p.: 25 cm. – 0 337 94387 7 £1.50

Motor Vehicles (Third-Party Risks) (Amendment) Regulations (Northern Ireland) 2002 No. 2002/154. – Enabling power: S.I. 1981/154 (NI. 1), arts. 103 (1), 218 (1). – Issued: 30.04.2002. Made: 17.04.2002. Coming into operation: 15.07.2002. Effect: S.R. 1994/46 amended. – 4p.: 30 cm. – 0 337 94253 6 £1.75

Motor Vehicle Testing (Amendment) (Fees) Regulations (Northern Ireland) 2002 No. 2002/47. – Enabling power: S.I. 1995/2994 (NI.18), arts. 61 (6), 62, 110 (2). – Issued: 26.02.2002. Made: 13.02.2002. Coming into operation: 01.04.2002. Effect: S.R. 1995/448 amended. – 4p.: 25 cm. – 0 337 94165 3 £1.75

Passenger and Goods Vehicles (Recording Equipment) (Fees) (Amendment) Regulations (Northern Ireland) 2002 No. 2002/50. – Enabling power: Finance Act 1973, s. 56 (1) (5). – Issued: 27.02.2002. Made: 14.02.2002. Coming into operation: 01.04.2002. Effect: S.R. 1996/145 amended. – 4p.: 25 cm. – 0 337 94168 8 £1.75

Public Service Vehicles (Conditions of Fitness, Equipment and Use) (Amendment) Regulations (Northern Ireland) 2002 No. 2002/384. – Enabling power: S.I. 1981/154 (N.I. 1), arts. 66 (1), 218 (1). – Issued: 20.12.2002. Made: 09.12.2002. Coming into operation: 06.01.2003. Effect: S.R. 1995/447 amended. – 2p.: 25 cm. – 0 337 94429 6 £1.50

Public Service Vehicles (Licence Fees) (Amendment) Regulations (Northern Ireland) 2002 No. 2002/49. – Enabling power: S.I. 1981/154 (N.I. 1), arts. 61 (1), 66 (1), 218 (1). – Issued: 27.02.2002. Made: 14.02.2002. Coming into operation: 01.04.2002. Effect: S.R. 1985/123 amended & S.R. 1996/143; 2001/244 revoked. – 4p.: 25 cm. – 0 337 94167 X *£1.75*

Road Service Licensing (Community Licences) Regulations (Northern Ireland) 2002 No. 2002/116. – Enabling power: European Communities Act 1972, s. 2 (2). – Issued: 28.03.2002. Made: 19.03.2002. Coming into operation: 01.05.2002. Effect: S.I. 1981/154 (N.I.) amended. – EC note: Give effect in NI to art. 3a of REG (EEC) 684/92 on common rules for the international carriage of passengers by coach and bus, as amended by REG (EC) 11/98. – 8p.: 25 cm. – 0 337 94224 2 *£2.00*

Traffic Signs (Amendment) Regulations (Northern Ireland) 2002 No. 2002/143. – Enabling power: S.I. 1997/276 (N.I. 2), art. 28 (2). – Issued: 26.04.2002. Made: 10.04.2002. Coming into operation: 20.05.2002. Effect: S.R. 1997/386 amended. – 6p.: 25 cm. – 0 337 94250 1 *£2.00*

Salaries

Salaries (Assembly Ombudsman and Commissioner for Complaints) Order (Northern Ireland) 2002 No. 2002/320. – Enabling power: S.I. 1996/1298 (NI. 8), art. 5 (1) (2) & S.I. 1996/1297 (NI. 7), art. 4 (1) (2). Issued: 25.10.2002. Made: 17.10.2002. Coming into operation: 21.11.2002. Effect: S.R. 2001/302 revoked. – 2p.: 25 cm. – 0 337 94380 X *£1.50*

Seeds

The Forest Reproductive Material (Northern Ireland) Regulations 2002 No. 2002/404. – Enabling power: Seeds Act (Northern Ireland) 1965, ss. 1, 2 & European Communities Act 1972, s. 2 (2). – Issued: 30.01.2003. Made: 19.12.2002. Coming into operation: 01.01.2003. Effect: S.R. 1977/194; 1993/197 revoked. – 40p.: 30 cm. – 0 337 94511 X *£6.00*

Seeds (Fees) (No. 2) Regulations (Northern Ireland) 2002 No. 2002/407. – Enabling power: Seeds Act (Northern Ireland) 1965, ss. 1 (1) (2A), 2 (2) (4). – Issued: 17.01.2003. Made: 18.12.2002. Coming into operation: 29.01.2003. Effect: S.R. 2002/257 revoked. – 12p.: 30 cm. – 0 337 94447 4 *£2.50*

Seeds (Fees) Regulations (Northern Ireland) 2002 No. 2002/257. – Enabling power: Seeds Act (Northern Ireland) 1965, ss. 1 (1) (2A), 2 (2) (4). – Issued: 05.08.2002. Made: 26.07.2002. Coming into operation: 02.09.2002. Effect: S.R. 1999/379 revoked. – 15p,: 30 cm. – 0 337 94328 1 *£3.00*

Social security

The Income Support (General) and Jobseeker's Allowance (Amendment No. 2) Regulations (Northern Ireland) 2002 No. 2002/332. – Enabling power: Social Security Contributions and Benefits (Northern Ireland) Act 1992, ss. 122 (1) (a), 123 (1) (e), 171 (1) (3) (4) & S.I. 1995/2705 (N.I. 15), arts. 3 (2C), 36 (2). – Issued: 18.11.2002. Made: 04.11.2002. Coming into operation: 25.11.2002. Effect: S.R. 1987/459; 1996/198 amended. – 4p.: 30 cm. – 0 337 94397 4 *£1.75*

The Income Support (General) and Jobseeker's Allowance (Amendment) Regulations (Northern Ireland) 2002 No. 2002/203. – Enabling power: Social Security Contributions and Benefits (Northern Ireland) Act 1992, ss. 122 (1) (a), 132 (3), 171 (1) (3) to (5) & S.I. 1995/2705 (N.I. 15), arts. 14 (1), 36 (2). – Issued: 05.06.2002. Made: 24.05.2002. Coming into operation: 17.06.2002. Effect: S.R. 1987/459; 1996/198 amended. – 2p.: 25 cm. – 0 337 94283 8 *£1.50*

The Income Support (General) (Standard Interest Rate Amendment no. 2) Regulations (Northern Ireland) 2002 No. 2002/58. – Enabling power: Social Security Contributions and Benefits (Northern Ireland) Act 1992, ss. 122 (1) (a), 131 (1), 171 (1) (3) to (5). – Issued: 06.03.2002. Made: 22.02.2002. Coming into operation: 17.03.2002. Effect: S.R. 1987/459 amended & S.R. 2002/16 revoked with saving– 4p.: 25 cm. – 0 337 94178 5 *£1.75*

The Income Support (General) (Standard Interest Rate Amendment) Regulations (Northern Ireland) 2002 No. 2002/16. – Enabling power: Social Security Contributions and Benefits (Northern Ireland) Act 1992, ss. 122 (1) (a), 131 (1), 171 (1) (3) to (5). – Issued: 01.02.2002. Made: 24.01.2002. Coming into operation: 17.02.2002. Effect: S.R. 1987/459 amended & S.R. 2001/410 revoked with saving– 4p.: 25 cm. – 0 337 94135 1 *£1.75*

The Jobseeker's Allowance (Amendment) Regulations (Northern Ireland) 2002 No. 2002/388. – Enabling power: S.I. 1995/2705 (NI. 15), arts. 8 (4), 10 (1) (a) (1A) (a) (2) (d) (ii), 36 (2). – Issued: 24.12.2002. Made: 16.12.2002. Coming into operation: 17.12.2002, 01.01.2003, in accord. with reg. 1. Effect: S.R. 1996/198 amended. – 4p.: 30 cm. – 0 337 94430 X *£1.75*

Pneumoconiosis, etc., (Workers' Compensation) (Payment of Claims) (Amendment) Regulations (Northern Ireland) 2002 No. 2002/133. – Enabling power: S.I. 1979/925 (NI. 9), arts. 3 (3), 4 (3), 11 (1) (4). – Issued: 16.04.2002. Made: 03.04.2002. Coming into force: In accord. with art. 1 (1) Effect: S.R. 1988/242 amended. – 6p.: 25 cm. – 0 337 94240 4 *£2.00*

Pneumoconiosis, etc., (Workers' Compensation) (Payment of Claims) (Amendment) Regulations (Northern Ireland) 2002 No. 2002/133. – Enabling power: S.I. 1979/925 (N.I. 9), arts. 3 (3), 4 (3), 11 (1) (4)– Issued: 28.05.2002. Made: 03.04.2002. Approved by resolution of the Assembly: 22.04.2002. Coming into operation: 23.04.2002, in accord. with reg. 1 (1). Effect: S.R. 1988/242 amended. – 8p.: 30 cm. – 0 337 94272 2 *£2.00*

The Social Fund (Cold Weather Payments) (General) (Amendment) Regulations (Northern Ireland) 2002 No. 2002/315. – Enabling power: Social Security Contributions and Benefits (Northern Ireland) Act 1992, ss. 134 (2), 171 (1) (3) (4). – Issued: 18.10.2002. Made: 08.10.2002. Coming into force: 01.11.2002. Effect: S.R. 1988/368 amended. – 2p: 30 cm. – 0 337 94376 1 *£1.50*

The Social Fund (Maternity and Funeral Expenses) (General) (Amendment No. 2) Regulations (Northern Ireland) 2002 No. 2002/90. – Enabling power: Social Security Contributions and Benefits (Northern Ireland) Act 1992, ss. 134 (1) (a), 171 (1) (3) (4). – Issued: 22.03.2002. Made: 08.03.2002. Coming into operation: 30.03.2002. Effect: S.R. 2002/14 amended. – 2p.: 25 cm. – 0 337 94198 X *£1.50*

The Social Fund (Maternity and Funeral Expenses) (General) (Amendment) Regulations (Northern Ireland) 2002 No. 2002/14. – Enabling power: Social Security Contributions and Benefits (Northern Ireland) Act 1992, ss. 134 (1) (a), 171 (1) (3) (4) & S.I. 1998/1506 (NI. 10), art. 10 (1) (a). – Issued: 31.01.2002. Made: 22.01.2002. Coming into operation: 31.03.2002. Effect: S.R. 1987/150 amended. – 4p.: 25 cm. – 0 337 94134 3 *£1.75*

The Social Fund (Miscellaneous Amendments) Regulations (Northern Ireland) 2002 No. 2002/284. – Enabling power: Social Security Contributions and Benefits (Northern Ireland) 1992, ss. 134 (1) (a), 171 (3) & Social Security Administration (Northern Ireland)| Act 1992, ss. 10 (1) (2) (a) (b), 165 (4) (6). – Issued: 23.09.2002. Made: 13.09.2002. Coming into operation: 01.10.2002. Effect: S.R. 1987/150; 1988/130 amended. – 4p.: 30 cm. – 0 337 94352 4 *£1.75*

The Social Security (2002 Act) (Commencement No. 1) Order (Northern Ireland) 2002 No. 2002/351 (C.28). – Enabling power: Social Security Act (Northern Ireland) 2002, s.9 (1). Bringing into operation various provisions of the 2002 Act on 19.11.2002. – Issued: 10.12.2002. Made: 18.11.2002. Effect: None. – 4p.: 30 cm. – 0 337 94401 6 *£1.75*

The Social Security (2002 Act) (Commencement No. 2 and Transitional and Saving Provisions) Order (Northern Ireland) 2002 No. 2002/358 (C.30). – Enabling power: Social Security Act (Northern Ireland) 2002, s.9 (1) (2). Bringing into operation various provisions of the 2002 Act on 24.11.2002. & 06.04.2003. – Issued: 10.12.2002. Made: 22.11.2002. Effect: None. – 4p.: 30 cm. – 0 337 94402 4 *£1.75*

The Social Security Administration (Northern Ireland) Act 1992 (Amendment) Order (Northern Ireland) 2002 No. 2002/408. – Enabling power: Social Security Administration (Northern Ireland) Act 1992, ss. 103B (6), 165 (4) (5). – Issued: 09.012003. Made: 23.12.2002. Coming into operation: 24.02.2003. Effect: 1992 c.8 amended. – 4p.: 30 cm. – 0 337 94503 9 *£1.75*

The Social Security (Amendment) (Residential Care and Nursing Homes) Regulations (Northern Ireland) 2002 No. 2002/132. – Enabling power: Social Security Administration (Northern Ireland) Act 1992, ss. 5 (1) (q), 165 (4) & Social Security Contributions and Benefits (Northern Ireland) Act 1992, ss. 67 (2), 72 (8), 122 (1) (a), 123 (1) (e), 131 (1), 132 (2) (4) (a) (b), 133 (2) (d), 171 (1) (3) (4) & S.I. 1995/2705 (N.I. 15), arts. 6 (5), 14 (4) (a) (b), 15 (3), 23, sch. 1, para. 1 (2) (b) & S.I. 1998/1506 (N.I. 10). art. 12 (1). – Issued: 12.04.2002. Made: 29.03.2002. Coming into operation: 08.04.2002. Effect: S.R. 1987/459, 465; 1992/20, 32; 1996/198; 1999/162 amended. – 16p.: 25 cm. – 0 337 94238 2 *£3.00*

The Social Security and Child Support (Decisions and Appeals) (Miscellaneous Amendments) Regulations (Northern Ireland) 2002 No. 2002/189. – Enabling power: S.I. 1991/2628 (N.I. 23), arts. 22 (4) to (6), & S.I. 1995/2705 (N.I. 15), art. 32, sch. 1, para. 4 & S.I. 1997/1183 (N.I. 12), art. 13 (5) (a) (b) & S.I. 1998/1506 (N.I. 10), arts. 7 (3), 10 (1), 11A (1), 13 (2) (7), 15 (11), 16 (1), 24A (1) (2) (a), 28 (1), 74(1) (3) (5) (6), sch. 1, para. 12(1), sch. 2, para. 9, sch. 4, paras 1 to 4, 6, 7 & Child Support, Pensions and Social Security Act (Northern Ireland) 2000, sch. 7, paras. 3 (1), 6 (7) (8), 10 (1), 19 (1), 20 (1) (3)– Issued: 30.05.2002. Made: 16.05.2002. Coming into operation: 20.05.2002. Effect: S.R. 1999/162, 408; 2000/215; 2001/213 amended. – 12p.: 30 cm. – 0 337 94273 0 *£2.50*

The Social Security and Child Support (Miscellaneous Amendments) Regulations (Northern Ireland) 2002 No. 2002/164. – Enabling power: S.I. 1991/2628 (NI.23), arts. 16 (1), 18 (1) (4), 19 (5), 22 (4), 28B (2) (c), 28E (1) 28G, 43 (10) 47, 48 (4), 50, sch. 1, paras. 5, 10, 11, sch. 4B, paras. 3, 4, 5 & Child Support, Pensions and Social Security Act (Northern Ireland) 2000, s. 28. – Issued: 15.05.2002. Made: 29.04.2002. Coming into operation: In accord. with reg. 1. Effect: S.R. 1992/339, 340, 341; 1996/541; 1999/162; 2001/17, 18, 19, 20 amended. – 12p.: 30 cm. – 0 337 94263 3 *£2.50*

The Social Security (Attendance Allowance and Disability Living Allowance) (Amendment) Regulations (Northern Ireland) 2002 No. 2002/31. – Enabling power: Social Security Contributions and Benefits (Northern Ireland) Act 1992, ss. 67 (2), 72 (8), 171 (1) (3) (4). – Issued: 14.02.2002. Made: 06.02.2002. Coming into operation: 01.03.2002. Effect: S.R. 1992/20, 32 amended. – 4p.: 25 cm. – 0 337 94147 5 *£1.75*

The Social Security Benefits Up-rating Order (Northern Ireland) 2002 No. 2002/99. – Enabling power: Social Security Administration (Northern Ireland) Act 1992, ss. 132, 165 (1) (5). – Issued: 28.03.2002. Made: 13.03.2002. Coming into operation: In accord. with art. 1 (1). Effect: 1992 c. 7; S.R. 1976/223; 1987/30, 459, 461; 1992/32; 1994/461; 1995/35; 1996/73, 198 amended & S.R. 2001/41 revoked (11.04.2002.). – 60p.: 25 cm. – 0 337 94201 3 *£7.00*

The Social Security Benefits Up-rating Regulations (Northern Ireland) 2002 No. 2002/108. – Enabling power: Social Security Contributions and Benefits (Northern Ireland) Act 1992, ss. 90, 113 (1) (a), 171 (1) to (4) & Social Security Administration (Northern Ireland) Act 1992, ss. 135 (3), 165 (1) (3) (4). – Issued: 26.03.2002. Made: 14.03.2002. Coming into operation: 08.04.2002. Effect: S.R. 1977/74; 2001/106 amended. – 4p.: 25 cm. – 0 337 94212 9   *£1.75*

The Social Security (Carer Premium Amendment) Regulations (Northern Ireland) 2002 No. 2002/322. – Enabling power: Social Security Contributions and Benefits (Northern Ireland) Act 1992, ss. 122 (1) (a) (d), 131 (1), 171 (1) (3) (4) and S.I. 1995/2705 (NI. 15), arts. 6 (5), 36 (2). – Issued: 31.10.2002. Made: 21.10.2002. Coming into operation: 28.10.2002. Effect: S.R. 1987/459, 461; 1996/198 amended. – 4p.: 30 cm. – 0 337 94384 2   *£1.75*

The Social Security (Carer's Allowance) (Amendment) Regulations (Northern Ireland) 2002 No. 2002/323. – Enabling power: Social Security Contributions and Benefits (Northern Ireland) Act 1992, ss. 22 (5), 70, 79 (2), 90, 113, 122 (1) (d), 123 (1) (e), 131 (1), 132 (3) (4) (b), 134 (2), 171 (1) (4), sch. 3, para. 2 (8) & Social Security Administration (Northern Ireland) Act 1992, ss. 2A, 5(1), 5A, 71, 74 (2), 102 (1), 165 (1) (4) (5) & Social Security (Consequential Provisions) (Northern Ireland) Act 1992, s. 5, sch. 3, para 12 & Immigration and Asylum Act 1999, s. 115 (3) (4) & S.I. 1991/2628 (N.I. 23), sch. 1, para. 4 (1) (b) (c) (2) & S.I. 1995/2702 (N.I. 13), arts. 4, 19 (1) & S.I. 1995/2705 (N.I. 15), arts. 28 (1), 39 (1) (2) & S.I. 1999/3147 (N.I. 11), arts. 69, 73 (3) (4) (6). – Issued: 30.10.2002. Made: 21.10.2002. Coming into operation: 28.10.2002 & 01.04.2003 in accordance with regulation 1 (1). Effect: S.R. 1975/113; 1976/99; 1977/74; 1978/114; 1979/242, 243; 1987/459, 461, 465; 1988/21; 1990/375; 1992/341; 1994/370, 461; 1996/198, 518, 519, 520, 521, 622; 2000/71; 2001/18, 175, 176 amended. – 8p.: 30 cm. – 0 337 94383 4   *£2.00*

The Social Security (Claims and Payments) (Amendment No. 2) Regulations (Northern Ireland) 2002 No. 2002/254. – Enabling power: Social Security Administration (Northern Ireland) Act 1992, ss. 5 (1) (m) (q), 165 (1) (5) (6) & S.I. 1991/2628 (N.I. 23), art. 40 (2). – Issued: 02.08.2002. Made: 25.07.2002. Coming into operation: 02.09.2002 (subject to para. 1 (2)). Effect: S.R. 1987/465 amended. – 4p.: 30 cm. – 0 337 94321 4   *£1.75*

The Social Security (Claims and Payments) (Amendment No. 3) Regulations (Northern Ireland) 2002 No. 2002/297. – Enabling power: Social Security Administration (Northern Ireland) Act 1992, ss. 5 (1) (j) (q) (r), 165 (1) (4) (6). – Issued: 02.10.2002. Made: 24.09.2002. Coming into operation: in accordance with reg. 1 (1). Effect: S.R. 1987/465; 1992/7, 83; 1994/345, 484; 1996/85 amended. – 4p.: 30 cm. – 0 337 94365 6   *£1.75*

The Social Security (Claims and Payments) (Amendment) Regulations (Northern Ireland) 2002 No. 2002/59. – Enabling power: Social Security Administration (Northern Ireland) Act 1992, ss. 13A (2) (b), 165 (1). – Issued: 01.03.2002. Made: 22.02.2002. Coming into operation: 01.04.2002. Effect: S.R. 1987/465 amended & S.R. 2000/181 revoked. – 2p.: 25 cm. – 0 337 94175 0   *£1.50*

The Social Security (Claims and Payments and Miscellaneous Amendments No. 2) Regulations (Northern Ireland) 2002 No. 2002/327. – Enabling power: Social Security Contributions and Benefits (Northern Ireland) Act 1992, ss.134 (2), 171 (1) (3) and Social Security Administration (Northern Ireland) Act 1992, ss. 5 (1) (a) (q), 165 (1) (4) (5). – Issued: 31.10.2002. Made: 23.10.2002. Coming into operation: 02.11.2002 & 01.04.2003 in accordance with reg. 1 (1). Effect: S.R. 1987/465; 2000/91 amended. – 4p.: 30 cm. – 0 337 94385 0   *£1.75*

The Social Security (Claims and Payments and Miscellaneous Amendments) Regulations (Northern Ireland) 2002 No. 2002/67. – Enabling power: Social Security Administration (Northern Ireland) Act 1992, s. 5 (1) (a) (b) & S.I. 1998/1506 (NI. 10) arts. 10 (1), 11 (3) (6). – Issued: 07.03.2002. Made: 27.02.2002. Coming into operation: 02.04.2002. Effect: S.R. 1987/465; 1999/162; 2000/215 amended. – 8p.: 25 cm. – 0 337 94181 5   *£2.00*

The Social Security (Disability Living Allowance) (Amendment) Regulations (Northern Ireland) 2002 No. 2002/97. – Enabling power: Social Security Contributions and Benefits Act 1992, ss. 73 (5), 171 (3). – Issued: 25.03.2002. Made: 12.03.2002. Coming into operation: 08.04.2002. Effect: S.R. 1992/32 amended. – 4p,: 25 cm. – 0 337 94200 5   *£1.75*

The Social Security (Employment Programme Amendment) Regulations (Northern Ireland) 2002 No. 2002/275. – Enabling power: Social Security Contributions and Benefits (Northern Ireland) Act 2002, ss. 122 (1) (a) (d), 132 (3) (4) (b), 171 (1) (3) (4) & S.I. 1995/2705 (N.I. 15), arts. 14 (1) (4) (b), 21 (10) (c), 36 (2), sch. 1, para. 3 (b). – Issued: 16.09.2002. Made: 06.09.2002. Coming into operation: 14.10.2002. Effect: S.R. 1987/459, 461; 1996/198 amended. – 4p.: 30 cm. – 0 337 94348 6   *£1.75*

The Social Security Fraud (2001 Act) (Commencement No. 2) Order (Northern Ireland) 2002 No. 2002/75 (C.7). – Enabling power: Social Security Fraud Act (Northern Ireland) 2001, s. 17 (1). Bringing into operation certain provisions of the 2001 Act on 06.03.2002. & 01.04.2002. – Issued: 14.03.2002. Made: 05.03.2002. Effect: None. – 2p.: 25 cm. – 0 337 94191 2   *£1.50*

The Social Security Fraud (2001 Act) (Commencement No. 3) Order (Northern Ireland) 2002 No. 2002/165 (C.16). – Enabling power: Social Security Fraud Act (Northern Ireland) 2001, s. 17 (1). Bringing into operation certain provisions of the 2001 Act on 01.05.2002. – Issued: 12.06.2002. Made: 30.04.2002. Effect: None. – 2p.: 30 cm. – 0 337 94262 5   *£1.50*

The Social Security Fraud (2001 Act) (Commencement No. 4) Order (Northern Ireland) 2002 No. 2002/392 (C.32). – Enabling power: Social Security Fraud Act (Northern Ireland) 2001, s. 17 (1). Bringing into operation certain provisions of the 2001 Act on 19.12.2002. – Issued: 03.01.2003. Made: 18.12.2002. Effect: None. – 2p.: 30 cm. – 0 337 94435 0   *£1.50*

The Social Security Fraud (2001 Act) (Commencement No. 5) Order (Northern Ireland) 2002 No. 2002/406 (C.34). – Enabling power: Social Security Fraud Act (Northern Ireland) 2001, s. 17 (1). Bringing into operation certain provisions of the 2001 Act on 23.12.2002. & 24.02.2003. – Issued: 09.01.2003. Made: 20.12.2002. Effect: None. – 2p.: 30 cm. – 0 337 94463 6 *£1.50*

The Social Security (Guardian's Allowances) (Amendment) Regulations (Northern Ireland) 2002 No. 2002/87. – Enabling power: Social Security Contributions and Benefits (Northern Ireland) Act 1992, ss. 77 (8) (b), 171 (1) (3) (4). – Issued: 19.03.2002. Made: 07.03.2002. Coming into operation: 01.04.2002. Effect: S.R. 1975/98 amended. – 4p.: 25 cm. – 0 337 94194 7 *£1.75*

The Social Security (Hospital In-patients) (Amendment) Regulations (Northern Ireland) 2002 No. 2002/106. – Enabling power: Social Security Administration (Northern Ireland) Act 1992, ss. 71 (1) (b), 165 (1) (4). – Issued: 26.03.2002. Made: 14.03.2002. Coming into operation: 08.04.2002. Effect: S.R. 1975/109 amended & S.R. 2001/115 revoked. – 4p.: 25 cm. – 0 337 94214 5 *£1.75*

The Social Security (Incapacity) (Miscellaneous Amendments No. 2) Regulations (Northern Ireland) 2002 No. 2002/276. – Enabling power: Social Security Contributions and Benefits (Northern Ireland) Act 1992, ss. 30A (6), 30E, 167D (2), 171 (1) to (4), sch. 7, para. 2 (3). – Issued: 19.09.2002. Made: 06.09.2002. Coming into operation: 01.10.2002, 01.01.2003, in accord. with reg. 1. Effect: S.R. 1984/92; 1994/461; 1995/41; 2001/316 amended. – 4p.: 25 cm. – 0 337 94349 4 *£1.75*

The Social Security (Incapacity) (Miscellaneous Amendments) Regulations (Northern Ireland) 2002 No. 2002/86. – Enabling power: Social Security Contributions and Benefits (Northern Ireland) Act 1992, ss. 167D, 171 (1) to (4) & S.I. 1994/1898 (NI. 12), arts. 6 (1) (6) & S.I. 1999/3147 (NI. 11), art. 75 (5). – Issued: 19.03.2002. Made: 07.03.2002. Coming into operation: 05.04.2002, 08.04.2002, in accord. with reg. 1 (1). Effect: S.R. 1994/461; 1995/35, 41 amended. – 8p.: 25 cm. – 0 337 94193 9 *£2.00*

The Social Security (Industrial Injuries) (Dependency) (Permitted Earnings Limits) Order (Northern Ireland) 2002 No. 2002/107. – Enabling power: Social Security Contributions and Benefits (Northern Ireland) Act 1992, s. 171 (1), sch. 7, para. 4 (5). – Issued: 25.03.2002. Made: 14.03.2002. Coming into operation: 08.04.2002. Effect: S.R. 2001/107 amended. – 2p.: 25 cm. – 0 337 94213 7 *£1.50*

The Social Security (Industrial Injuries) (Prescribed Diseases) (Amendment) Regulations (Northern Ireland) 2002 No. 2002/237. – Enabling power: Social Security Contributions and Benefits (Northern Ireland) Act 1992, ss. 109 (2), 171 (1) (4), sch. 6, para. 1 (d). – Issued: 22.07.2002. Made: 04.07.2002. Coming into operation: 29.07.2002. Effect: S.R. 1986/179 amended– 4p.: 30 cm. – 0 337 94308 7 *£1.75*

The Social Security (Intercalating Students Amendment) Regulations (Northern Ireland) 2002 No. 2002/243. – Enabling power: Social Security Contributions and Benefits (Northern Ireland) Act 1992, ss. 122 (1) (d), 133 (2) (j), 171 (1) (3) (4) & S.I. 1995/2705 (N.I. 15), art. 8 (4). – Issued: 23.07.2002. Made: 10.07.2002. Coming into operation: 01.08.2002. Effect: S.R. 1987/461; 1996/198 amended. – 4p.: 30 cm. – 0 337 94309 5 *£1.75*

The Social Security (Loss of Benefit) (Consequential Amendments) Regulations (Northern Ireland) 2002 No. 2002/80. – Enabling power: Social Security Contributions and Benefits (Northern Ireland) Act 1992, ss. 22 (5), 122 (1) (a) (d), 123 (1) (e), 131 (1), 171 (1) (3) & S.I. 1995/2705 (NI. 15), arts. 7 (3), 28 (1) (4) (d), 36 (2) & S.I. 1998/1506 (NI. 10), arts. 10 (1), 11 (3) (6), 74 (1) & Child Support, Pensions and Social Security Act (Northern Ireland) 2000, s. 60 (1) (2) (a), sch. 7, paras. 3 (1), 4 (3) (5). – Issued: 15.03.2002. Made: 06.03.2002. Coming into operation: 01.04.2002. Effect:S.R. 1975/113; 1987/459, 461; 1996/198, 519; 1999/162; 2001/213, 216 amended. – 8p.: 25 cm. – 0 337 94190 4 *£2.00*

The Social Security (Loss of Benefit) Regulations (Northern Ireland) 2002 No. 2002/79. – Enabling power: Social Security Fraud Act (Northern Ireland) 2001, ss. 6 (3) to (6), 7 (3) (4), 8 (2) to (5), 9 (1) (2) & S.I. 1998/1506 (NI. 10), art. 74 (3) to (6), sch. 2, para. 9. – Issued: 14.03.2002. Made: 06.03.2002. Coming into operation: 01.04.2002. Effect: S.R. 1999/162 amended. – 20p.: 25 cm. – 0 337 94189 0 *£3.50*

The Social Security (Miscellaneous Amendments No. 2) Regulations (Northern Ireland) 2002 No. 2002/295. – Enabling power: Social Security Contributions and Benefits (Northern Ireland) Act 1992, ss. 122 (1) (a) (d), 132 (4) (b), 171 (1) (3) (4) & S.I. 1995/2705 (N.I. 15), arts. 14 (4) (b), 36 (2). – Issued: 02.10.2002. Made: 19.09.2002. Coming into operation: 14.10.2002. Effect: S.R. 1987/459, 461; 1996/198 amended. – 4p.: 30 cm. – 0 337 94362 1 *£1.75*

The Social Security (Miscellaneous Amendments) Regulations (Northern Ireland) 2002 No. 2002/128. – Enabling power: Social Security Contributions and Benefits (Northern Ireland) Act 1992, ss. 122 (1) (a) (d), 131 (1), 132 (3) (4) (b), 171 (1) (3) (4) & S.I. 1995/2705 (N.I. 15), arts. 6 (5), 14 (1) (4) (b), 36 (2). – Issued: 12.04.2002. Made: 27.03.2002. Coming into operation: 08.04.2002. Effect: S.R. 1987/459, 461; 1996/198 amended. – 6p.: 30 cm. – 0 337 94235 8 *£2.00*

The Social Security (Paternity and Adoption Amendment) Regulations (Northern Ireland) 2002 No. 2002/363. – Enabling power: Social Security Contributions and Benefits (Northern Ireland) Act 1992, ss. 122 (1) (a) (d), 123 (1) (e), 132 (3) (4) (b), 133 (2) (d), 171 (1) (3) (4) & S.I. 1995/2705 (N.I. 15), art. 14 (1) (4) (b), 23, 36 (2), sch. 1, para. 1. – Issued: 10.12.2002. Made: 27.11.2002. Coming into operation: 08.12.2002. Effect: S.R. 1987/459, 461; 1996/198 amended. – 8p.: 30 cm. – 0 337 94413 X *£2.00*

The Social Security Pensions (Low Earnings Threshold) Order (Northern Ireland) 2002 No. 2002/57. – Enabling power: Social Security Administration (Northern Ireland) Act 1992, s. 130A. – Issued: 01.03.2002. Made: 21.02.2002. Coming into operation: 06.04.2002. Effect: None. – 2p.: 25 cm. – 0 337 94176 9 *£1.50*

The Social Security (Personal Allowances for Children and Young Persons Amendment) Regulations (Northern Ireland) 2002 No. 2002/267. – Enabling power: Social Security Contributions and Benefits (Northern Ireland) Act 1992, ss. 122 (1) (a) (d), 131 (1), 171 (1) (3) & S.I. 1995/2705 (N.I. 15), art. 6 (5). – Issued: 19.08.2002. Made: 08.08.2002. Coming into operation: 14.10.2002. Effect: S.R. 1987/459, 461; 1996/198 amended. – 4p.: 30 cm. – 0 337 94339 7 *£1.75*

The Social Security (Personal Injury Payments Amendment) Regulations (Northern Ireland) 2002 No. 2002/299. – Enabling power: Social Security Contributions and Benefits (Northern Ireland) Act 1992, ss. 122 (1) (a) (d), 132 (4) (b) (d), 171 (1) (3) (4) & S.I. 1995/2705 (N.I. 15), art. 14 (4) (b) (d). – Issued: 07.10.2002. Made: 26.09.2002. Coming into operation: 28.10.2002. Effect: S.R. 1987/459, 461; 1996/198 amended. – 4p.: 30 cm. – 0 337 94367 2 *£1.75*

The Social Security Revaluation of Earnings Factors Order (Northern Ireland) 2002 No. 2002/89. – Enabling power: Social Security Administration (Northern Ireland) Act 1992, ss. 130, 165 (1) (3) (4) (5). – Issued: 19.03.2002. Made: 08.03.2002. Coming into force: 06.04.2002. Effect: None. – 4p.: 25 cm. – 0 337 94196 3 *£1.75*

The Social Security, Statutory Maternity Pay and Statutory Sick Pay (Miscellaneous Amendments No. 2) Regulations (Northern Ireland) 2002 No. 2002/359. – Enabling power: Social Security Contributions and Benefits (Northern Ireland) Act 1992, ss. 35A (4) (a), 159 (3), 160 (9) (c), 167 (5), 167ZP (2) (3), 171 (1) to (4), sch. 13, para. 2. – Issued: 11.12.2002. Made: 25.11.2002. Coming into operation: 08.12.2002. Effect: S.R. 1982/263; 1987/30; 1998/128; 1990/112; 1994/461; 1995/150; 2000/104 amended. – 8p.: 30 cm. – 0 337 94417 2 *£2.00*

The Social Security, Statutory Maternity Pay and Statutory Sick Pay (Miscellaneous Amendments) Regulations (Northern Ireland) 2002 No. 2002/354. – Enabling power: Social Security Contributions and Benefits (Northern Ireland) Act 1992, ss. 35 (3) 35A (4) (5) (a) (c) (i) (d), 149 (6), 160 (9) (ea), 161 (1) (3) (7), 162 (1) (b), 167 (3) (b) to (d), 171 (1) to (4), sch. 11, paras. 1, 1A & Social Security Administration (Northern Ireland) Act 1992, ss. 5 (1) (m), 124 (1) (2), 165 (1). – Issued: 06.12.2002. Made: 19.11.2002. Coming into operation: 24.11.2002, 06.04.2003, in accord. with art. 1 (1). Effect: S.R. 1982/263; 1987/30, 170; 1992/17; 1994/191; 2000/104, 324 amended. – 8p.: 30 cm. – 0 337 94400 8 *£2.50*

The Social Security (Students and Income-related Benefits Amendment No. 2) Regulations (Northern Ireland) 2002 No. 2002/270. – Enabling power: Social Security Contributions and Benefits (Northern Ireland) Act 1992, ss. 122 (1) (a) (d), 132 (4) (b), 171 (1) (3) (4) & S.I. 1995/2705 (NI. 15), art. 14 (4) (b). – Issued: 05.09.2002. Made: 27.08.2002. Coming into operation: 02.09.2002. Effect: S.R. 1987/459, 461; 1996/198 amended. – 4p.: 30 cm. – 0 337 94344 3 *£1.75*

The Social Security (Students and Income-related Benefits Amendment) Regulations (Northern Ireland) 2002 No. 2002/222. – Enabling power: Social Security Contributions and Benefits (Northern Ireland) Act 1992, ss. 122 (1) (a) (d), 129 (2), 132 (3) (4) (b), 171 (1) (3) (4) & S.I. 1995/2705 (NI. 15), art. 14 (1) (4) (b). – Issued: 04.07.2002. Made: 18.06.2002. Coming into operation: 01.08.2002 & 26.08.2002. Effect: S.R. 1987/459, 461; 1996/198 amended. – 8p.: 30 cm. – 0 337 94300 1 *£2.00*

The Social Security (Work-focused Interviews for Lone Parents Amendment) Regulations (Northern Ireland) 2002 No. 2002/105. – Enabling power: Social Security Administration (Northern Ireland) Act 1992, ss. 2A (1) (3) (c) to (f) (4) (5) (a) (b) (6) (7) (8), 165 (4) to (6). – Issued: 26.03.2002. Made: 14.03.2002. Coming into operation: 08.04.2002. Effect: S.R. 2001/152 amended. – 4p.: 25 cm. – 0 337 94211 0 *£1.75*

The State Pension Credit (2002 Act) (Commencement No. 1) Order (Northern Ireland) 2002 No. 2002/366 (C.31). – Enabling power: State Pension Credit Act (Northern Ireland) 2002, s. 21 (2). Bringing into operation various provisions of the 2002 Act on 02.12.2002 & 14.01.2003. – Issued: 10.12.2002. Made: 28.11.2002. Effect: None. – 4p.: 30 cm. – 0 337 94414 8 *£1.75*

The Tax Credits (Appeals) Regulations (Northern Ireland) 2002 No. 2002/403. – Enabling power: S.I. 1998/1506 (NI. 10), arts. 8 (6), 13 (1) (7), 15 (10) (11), 16 (1), 28 (1), 74 (1) (3) to (6), sch. 1, paras. 11, 12, sch. 4. – Issued: 08.01.2003. Made: 19.12.2002. Coming into operation: 01.01.2003. Effect: None. – 20p.: 30 cm. – 0 337 94438 5 *£3.50*

The Workmen's Compensation (Supplementation) (Amendment) Regulations (Northern Ireland) 2002 No. 2002/114. – Enabling power: Social Security Contributions and Benefits (Northern Ireland) Act 1992, s. 171 (4), sch. 8, para. 2 & Social Security Administration (Northern Ireland) Act 1992, sch. 6, para. 1. – Issued: 27.03.2002. Made: 19.03.2002. Coming into operation: 10.04.2002. Effect: S.R. 1983/101 amended & 2001/116 revoked. – 8p.: 25 cm. – 0 337 94222 6 *£2.00*

Statutory maternity pay

The Social Security Benefits Up-rating Order (Northern Ireland) 2002 No. 2002/99. – Enabling power: Social Security Administration (Northern Ireland) Act 1992, ss. 132, 165 (1) (5). – Issued: 28.03.2002. Made: 13.03.2002. Coming into operation: In accord. with art. 1 (1). Effect: 1992 c. 7; S.R. 1976/223; 1987/30, 459, 461; 1992/32; 1994/461; 1995/35; 1996/73, 198 amended & S.R. 2001/41 revoked (11.04.2002.). – 60p.: 25 cm. – 0 337 94201 3 *£7.00*

The Social Security, Statutory Maternity Pay and Statutory Sick Pay (Miscellaneous Amendments No. 2) Regulations (Northern Ireland) 2002 No. 2002/359. – Enabling power: Social Security Contributions and Benefits (Northern Ireland) Act 1992, ss. 35A (4) (a), 159 (3), 160 (9) (c), 167 (5), 167ZP (2) (3), 171 (1) to (4), sch. 13, para. 2. – Issued: 11.12.2002. Made: 25.11.2002. Coming into operation: 08.12.2002. Effect: S.R. 1982/263; 1987/30; 1998/128; 1990/112; 1994/461; 1995/150; 2000/104 amended. – 8p.: 30 cm. – 0 337 94417 2   £2.00

The Social Security, Statutory Maternity Pay and Statutory Sick Pay (Miscellaneous Amendments) Regulations (Northern Ireland) 2002 No. 2002/354. – Enabling power: Social Security Contributions and Benefits (Northern Ireland) Act 1992, ss. 35 (3) 35A (4) (5) (a) (c) (i) (d), 149 (6), 160 (9) (ea), 161 (1) (3) (7), 162 (1) (b), 167 (3) (b) to (d), 171 (1) to (4), sch. 11, paras. 1, 1A & Social Security Administration (Northern Ireland) Act 1992, ss. 5 (1) (m), 124 (1) (2), 165 (1). – Issued: 06.12.2002. Made: 19.11.2002. Coming into operation: 24.11.2002, 06.04.2003, in accord. with art. 1 (1). Effect: S.R. 1982/263; 1987/30, 170; 1992/17; 1994/191; 2000/104, 324 amended. – 8p.: 30 cm. – 0 337 94400 8   £2.50

Statutory sick pay

The Social Security Benefits Up-rating Order (Northern Ireland) 2002 No. 2002/99. – Enabling power: Social Security Administration (Northern Ireland) Act 1992, ss. 132, 165 (1) (5). – Issued: 28.03.2002. Made: 13.03.2002. Coming into operation: In accord. with art. 1 (1). Effect: 1992 c. 7; S.R. 1976/223; 1987/30, 459, 461; 1992/32; 1994/461; 1995/35; 1996/73, 198 amended & S.R. 2001/41 revoked (11.04.2002.). – 60p.: 25 cm. – 0 337 94201 3   £7.00

The Social Security, Statutory Maternity Pay and Statutory Sick Pay (Miscellaneous Amendments No. 2) Regulations (Northern Ireland) 2002 No. 2002/359. – Enabling power: Social Security Contributions and Benefits (Northern Ireland) Act 1992, ss. 35A (4) (a), 159 (3), 160 (9) (c), 167 (5), 167ZP (2) (3), 171 (1) to (4), sch. 13, para. 2. – Issued: 11.12.2002. Made: 25.11.2002. Coming into operation: 08.12.2002. Effect: S.R. 1982/263; 1987/30; 1998/128; 1990/112; 1994/461; 1995/150; 2000/104 amended. – 8p.: 30 cm. – 0 337 94417 2   £2.00

The Social Security, Statutory Maternity Pay and Statutory Sick Pay (Miscellaneous Amendments) Regulations (Northern Ireland) 2002 No. 2002/354. – Enabling power: Social Security Contributions and Benefits (Northern Ireland) Act 1992, ss. 35 (3) 35A (4) (5) (a) (c) (i) (d), 149 (6), 160 (9) (ea), 161 (1) (3) (7), 162 (1) (b), 167 (3) (b) to (d), 171 (1) to (4), sch. 11, paras. 1, 1A & Social Security Administration (Northern Ireland) Act 1992, ss. 5 (1) (m), 124 (1) (2), 165 (1). – Issued: 06.12.2002. Made: 19.11.2002. Coming into operation: 24.11.2002, 06.04.2003, in accord. with art. 1 (1). Effect: S.R. 1982/263; 1987/30, 170; 1992/17; 1994/191; 2000/104, 324 amended. – 8p.: 30 cm. – 0 337 94400 8   £2.50

Street works

The Street Works (Registers, Notices, Directions and Designations) Regulations (Northern Ireland) 2002 No. 2002/10. – Enabling power: S.I. 1995/3210 (N.I. 19), arts 3 (2), 13, 14 (1) (2), 15 (1) to (3) (7), 16 (2), 17 (2) (3), 18 (1) (2) (5), 22 (1), 23 (2), 24 (1) (2), 54 (1) (2)– Issued: 28.01.2002. Made: 17.01.2002. Coming into operation: 18.03.2002. Effect: None. – 20p.: 25 cm. – 0 337 94133 5   £4.00

Supreme Court

The Family Proceedings (Amendment) Rules (Northern Ireland) 2002 No. 2002/137. – Enabling power: S.I. 1993/1576 (NI. 6), art. 12. – Issued: 30.04.2002. Made: 25.03.2002. Coming into operation: 06.05.2002. Effect: S.R. 1996/322 amended. – EC note: Gives effect to Council regulation No. 1347/2000. – 16p.: 30 cm. – 0 337 94252 8   £3.00

The Family Proceedings Fees (Amendment) Order (Northern Ireland) 2002 No. 2002/344. – Enabling power: 1978 c. 23, s. 116 (1) (4). – Issued: 18.11.2002. Made: 05.11.2002. Coming into operation: 02.12.2002, 03.03.2003, in accord with art. 1. Effect: S.R. 1996/495 amended. – 8p.: 30 cm. – 0 337 94395 8   £2.00

The Supreme Court Fees (Amendment) Order (Northern Ireland) 2002 No. 2002/341. – Enabling power: Judicature (Northern Ireland) Act 1978, s. 116 (1) (4). – Issued: 18.11.2002. Made: 05.11.2002. Coming into operation: 02.12.2002 & 03.03.2003 in accordance with article 1. Effect: S.R. 1996/100 amended. – 16p.: 30 cm. – 0 337 94392 3   £2.50

Supreme Court, Northern Ireland

The Rules of the Supreme Court (Northern Ireland) (Amendment) 2002 No. 2002/15. – Enabling power: Judicature (Northern Ireland) Act 1978, s. 55. – Issued: 19.02.2002. Made: 22.01.2002. Coming into force: 15.02.2002. Effect: S.R. 1980/346 amended. – 8p.: 25 cm. – 0 337 94154 8   £2.00

Supreme Court, Northern Ireland: Procedure

The Rules of the Supreme Court (Northern Ireland) (Amendment No. 2) 2002 No. 2002/202. – Enabling power: Judicature (Northern Ireland) Act 1978, s. 55. – Issued: 17.06.2002. Made: 17.04.2002. Coming into operation: 21.06.2002. Effect: S.R. 1980/346 amended. – 6p.: 30 cm. – 0 337 94290 0   £2.00

Trustees

The Trustee (2001 Act) (Commencement) Order (Northern Ireland) 2002 No. 2002/253 (C.24). – Enabling power: Trustee Act (Northern Ireland) 2001, s. 45. Bringing into operation certain provisions of the 2001 Act on 29.07.2002. – Issued: 02.08.2002. Made: 23.07.2002. Effect: None. – 2p.: 30 cm. – 0 337 94324 9 £1.50

Water and sewerage

The Water Supply (Water Quality) Regulations (Northern Ireland) 2002 No. 2002/331. – Enabling power: European Communities Act 1972, s. 2 (2) & S.I. 1973/70 (NI. 2), arts. 3B, 3C. – Issued: 08.11.2002. Made: 31.10.2002. Coming into operation: In accordance with reg. 1 (2) to (5). Effect: S.I. 1994/221 amended (28.11.2002.) & S.I. 1994/221 & S.R. 1994/237 partially revoked (25.12.2003.) & S.I. 1994/221 revoked (insofar as not already revoked) (01.01.2004.) & S.R. 1996/603 partially revoked (01.01.2004.) & regs. 36, 37 and sch. 5 of these regs (S.R. 2002/331) revoked (01.01.2004.). – 48p.: 30 cm. – 0 337 94388 5 £6.00

Weights and measures

Units of Measurement Regulations (Northern Ireland) 2002 No. 2002/70. – Enabling power: European Communities Act 1972, s. 2 (2). – Issued: 08.03.2002. Made: 01.03.2002 Coming into operation: 08.04.2002. Effect: S.I. 1981/231 (N.I. 10) amended. – EC note: These Regs. implement in part the amendments made by DIR 1999/103 to DIR 80/181. – 2p.: 25 cm. – 0 337 94182 3 £1.50

Weights and Measures (Metrication Amendments) Regulations (Northern Ireland) 2002 No. 2002/71. – Enabling power: S.I. 1981/231 (N.I. 10), art. 13 (1). – Issued: 08.03.2002. Made: 01.03.2002. Coming into operation: 08.04.2002. Effect: S.R. 1984/117, 188; 1985/319; 1986/308, 311; 1991/266; 1993/441; 1998/48, 113 amended. – EC note: These Regs. implement in part the amendments made by DIR 1999/103 to DIR 80/181. – 4p.: 25 cm. – 0 337 94183 1 £1.75

Weights and Measures (Passing as Fit for Use for Trade and Adjustment Fees) Regulations (Northern Ireland) 2002 No. 2002/308. – Enabling power: S.I. 1981/231 (N.I. 10), arts. 9 (3), 43. – Issued: 10.10.2002. Made: 03.10.2002. Coming into operation: 04.11.2002. Effect: S.R. 1992/483 revoked with saving. – 8p.: 30 cm. – 0 337 94372 9 £2.00

Weights and Measures (Prescribed Stamp) (Amendment) Regulations (Northern Ireland) 2002 No. 2002/36. – Enabling power: S.I. 1981/231 (NI. 10), art. 9 (3). – Issued: 18.02.2002. Made: 08.02.2002. Coming into operation: 25.03.2002. Effect: S.R. & O. (NI) 1969/11 amended. – 4p.: 25 cm. – 0 337 94150 5 £1.75

Welfare foods

The Welfare Foods (Amendment) Regulations (Northern Ireland) 2002 No. 2002/83. – Enabling power: S.I. 1988/594 (NI. 2), art. 13 (3) (4) & Social Security Contributions and Benefits (Northern Ireland) Act 1992, s. 171 (2) to (5). – Issued: 13.03.2002. Made: 07.03.2002. Coming into operation: 01.04.2002. Effect: S.R. 1988/137 amended. – 2p.: 25 cm. – 0 337 94195 5 £1.50

Welfare of animals

Welfare of Animals (Slaughter or Killing) (Amendment) Regulations (Northern Ireland) 2002 No. 2002/304. – Enabling power: European Communities Act 1972, s. 2 (2). – Issued: 09.10.2002. Made: 01.10.2002. Coming into force: 08.11.2002. Effect: S.R. 1996/558 amended. – 4p.: 25 cm. – 0 337 94368 0 £1.75

Welfare of Farmed Animals (Amendment) Regulations (Northern Ireland) 2002 No. 2002/259. – Enabling power: Welfare of Animals Act (Northern Ireland) 1972, s. 2 (1) & European Communities Act 1972, s. 2 (2). – Issued: 07.08.2002. Made: 30.07.2002. Coming into operation: 29.08.2002, 01.01.2003, 01.01.2011, in accord. with reg. 1 (2) to (4). Effect: S.I. 1962/2557 amended in relation to Northern Ireland & S.R. 2000/270 amended. – 8p.: 30 cm. – 0 337 94329 X £2.00

Statutory Rules of Northern Ireland 2002

Arranged by Number

[* denotes SR was of a local nature and publication was not required]

1	Dangerous drugs
2	Health and personal social services
3	*
4	*
5	Health and personal social services
6	Fisheries
7	Plant health
8	Road traffic and vehicles
9	*
10	Roads
	Street works
11	Fisheries
12	Magistrates' courts
13	*
14	Social security
15	Supreme Court, Northern Ireland
	Procedure
16	Social security
17	*
18	*
19	*
20	Agriculture
	Pesticides
21	Pesticides
22 (C.1)	Health and personal social services
23	Police
24	Employment
25 (C.2)	Pensions
26	Rates
27	Agriculture
	Pesticides
28	Environmental protection
29	Agriculture
30	Agriculture
31	Social security
32	*
33	Food
34	Health and safety
35	Food
36	Weights and measures
37	Coroners
38	*
39	Food
40	Harbours
41	Harbours
42	Harbours
43	Nurses, midwives and health visitors
44	Animals
45 (C.3)	Health and personal social services
46	Health and personal social services
47	Road traffic and vehicles
48	Road traffic and vehicles
49	Road traffic and vehicles
50	Road traffic and vehicles
51	Road traffic and vehicles
52	Road traffic
53	Diseases of fish
54	Landlord and tenant
55	*
56	Energy conservation
57	Social security
58	Social security
59	Social security
60	Legal aid and advice
61	Legal aid and advice

62	Legal aid and advice	95	Police
63 (C.4)	Pensions	96	Police
64	Pensions	97	Social security
65	*	98	Pensions
66	Health and personal social services	99	Social security
67	Social security		Statutory maternity pay
68 (C.5)	Pensions		Statutory sick pay
69	Health and personal social services		Housing
70	Weights and measures		Rates
71	Weights and measures	100	Police
72	Agriculture	101	Police
73 (C.6)	Health and personal social services	102	Pensions
74	Pensions	103	*
75 (C.7)	Social security	104	*
76	Police	105	Social security
77	*	106	Social security
78	*	107	Social security
79	Social security	108	Social security
	Housing	109	Pensions
	Rates	110	Employment
80	Housing	111	Education
	Rates	112	Education
	Social security	113	Health and personal social services
81	*	114	Social security
82	Food	115	Local government
83	Welfare foods	116	European Communities
84	Health and personal social services		Road traffic and vehicles
85	Health and personal social services	117	Nurses, midwives and health visitors
86	Social security	118 (C.8)	Family law
87	Social security	119	Family proceedings
88	Food	120	Industrial relations
89	Social security	121	Family law
90	Social security		Child support
91	Health and personal social services	122	*
92	Health and personal social services	123	*
93	Employment	124	*
94	Environmental protection	125	Pesticides

126 (C.9)	Pensions	158	Magistrates' courts
127	Pensions	159	Magistrates' courts
	Insolvency	160	*
128	Housing	161	Medicines
	Rates	162	Agriculture
	Social security	163	Magistrates' courts
129	Health and personal social services	164	Family law
130 (C.10)	Game		Social security
131 (C.11)	Preserved rights		Child support
132	Social security	**165 (C.16)**	Social security
133	Social security	166	*
134 (C.12)	Industrial development	167	Road traffic and vehicles
135	Employment	168	*
136	Health and personal social services	169	Agriculture
137	Family proceedings	170	*
	Supreme Court	171	Health and personal social services
	County courts	172	Health and personal social services
138 (C.13)	Family law	173	*
139	*	174	*
140	Food	175	*
141	Food	176	*
142	*	177	*
143	Road traffic and vehicles	178	*
144	Adoption	179	Police
145	*	**180 (C.17)**	Health and personal social services
146 (C.14)	Police	181	Health and personal social services
147	Explosives	182	Local government
148 (C.15)	Criminal injuries	183	Investigatory powers
149	*	184	*
150	Evidence	**185 (C.18)**	Environmental protection
151	Agriculture	186	*
152	*	187	*
153	*	188	*
154	Road traffic and vehicles	189	Social security
155	*		Housing
156	*		Rates
157	*		Family law

	Child support	224	Education
190	*	225	European Communities
191	*		Animals
192	*	226	Food
193	*	227	*
194	*	228	Property
195	Planning	229	Land registration
196	*	230	Northern Ireland Assembly allowances
197	Road traffic and vehicles	231	Local government
198	*	232	*
199	*	233	*
200	*	234	*
201	*	235	*
202	Supreme Court, Northern Ireland	236	*
203	Social security	237	Social security
204 (C.19)	Criminal injuries	238	Food
205 (C.20)	Criminal injuries	239	Public health
206	Pharmacy	240	County courts
207	*	241	Education
208	*	242	Registration of births, deaths and marriages
209	Animals	243	Housing
210	Animals		Rates
211	Pensions		Social security
212	Legal aid and advice	244	Fair employment
213	Health and personal social services	245	Industrial training
214 (C.21)	Employment	246	Plant health
215	*	247	Family law
216	Pensions		Child support
217	Food	248	Environmental protection
218	*	249	Forestry
219	Food	250	Agriculture
220	*		Pesticides
221	Health and personal social services	251 (C.22)	Property
222	Housing	252 (C.23)	Property
	Rates	253 (C.24)	Trustees
	Social security	254	Social security
223	Insolvency		

255	County courts	286	Employment
256	Road traffic and vehicles	287	*
257	Seeds	288	*
258	Police	289	Pesticides
259	Welfare of animals	290	*
260	Police	291	Gas
261	Insolvency	292	Investigatory powers
262	Food	293	Food
263	Agriculture	294	Road traffic and vehicles
264	Food	295	Housing
265	Education		Rates
266	Health and personal social services		Social security
267	Housing	296	European Communities
	Rates		Animals
	Social security	297	Social security
268	Pensions	298	Employment
269	Plant health	299	Housing
270	Housing		Rates
	Rates		Social security
	Social security	300	European Communities
271	Environmental protection		Environmental protection
272	Education	301	Health and safety
273	Plant health	302	Health and safety
274	Fisheries	303	Public health
275	Housing	304	Welfare of animals
	Rates	305	*
	Social security	306	*
276	Social security	307	Food
277	*	308	Weights and measures
278	Agriculture	309	Fees and charges
279	Pensions	310	*
280	Housing	311 (C.25)	Health and personal social services
281	*	312	*
282	*	313	*
283	Fire services	314	*
284	Social security	315	Social security
285	Plant health	316	Food

317 (C.26)	Employment	349	Health and personal social services
318	*	350	Family proceedings
319 (C.27)	Justice	351 (C.28)	Social security
320	Salaries	352	Local government
321	Deregulation	353	Local government
322	Social security	354	Social security
	Housing		Statutory maternity pay
	Rates		Statutory sick pay
323	Social security	355	Employment
324	*	356 (C.29)	Employment
325	*	357	Environmental protection
326	*	358 (C.30)	Social security
327	Social security	359	Social security
328	Road traffic and vehicles		Statutory maternity pay
329	*		Statutory sick pay
330	*	360	*
331	Water and sewerage	361	*
332	Social security	362	*
333	*	363	Housing
334	Insolvency		Rates
335	Agriculture		Social security
336	*	364	Electricity
337	*	365	*
338	*	366 (C.31)	Social security
339	Public health	367	Fair employment
340	European Communities	368	Agriculture
	Animals	369	Pensions
341	Supreme Court	370	Public health
342	County courts	371	Fisheries
343	Magistrates' courts	372	Fisheries
344	Family proceedings	373	Road traffic
	Supreme Court	374	European Communities
	County courts		Road traffic and vehicles
345	Industrial relations	375	Road traffic and vehicles
346	Industrial relations	376	Legal aid, advice and assistance
347	Industrial relations	377	Employment
348	*	378	Employment

379	Employment
380	Employment
381	Employment
382	Employment
383	Road traffic and vehicles
384	Road traffic and vehicles
385	Police
386	Health and personal social services
387	*
388	Social security
389	*
390	*
391	Family law
392 (C.32)	Social security
393	Education
394	Harbours
395	Harbours
396	Airports
397	Health and personal social services
398	*
399	*
400	Land registration
401	Land registration
402	*
403	Social security
404	Seeds
405 (C.33)	Justice
406 (C.34)	Social security
407	Seeds
408	Social security
409	Rates
410	Pensions
411	*
412	County courts
413	*
414	Justice

List of Commencement Orders 2002

22 (C.1)
25 (C.2)
45 (C.3)
63 (C.4)
68 (C.5)
73 (C.6)
75 (C.7)
118 (C.8)
126 (C.9)
130 (C.10)
131 (C.11)
134 (C.12)
138 (C.13)
146 (C.14)
148 (C.15)
165 (C.16)
180 (C.17)
185 (C.18)
204 (C.19)
205 (C.20)
214 (C.21)
251 (C.22)
252 (C.23)
253 (C.24)
311 (C.25)
317 (C.26)
319 (C.27)
351 (C.28)
356 (C.29)
358 (C.30)
366 (C.31)
392 (C.32)
405 (C.33)
406 (C.34)

Alphabetical Index

This index is arranged alphabetically by subject terms

A

Aberdare College: Dissolution 53
Aberdeen City Council: Aberdeenshire Council: Boundaries: Blackburn: Scotland 321
Aberdeen Harbour: Constitution: Revision: Scotland 316
Abortion 101
Abortion: Wales 101
ABRO Trading Fund 70
Access to Justice Act 1999: Solicitors practising certificates 88
Accidents: Fatal: Damages: Bereavement: Variation of sum: England & Wales 38
Act of Adjournal: Criminal appeals: Scotland 317
Act of Adjournal: Criminal procedure: Rules: Anti-terrorism ... Act 2002: Scotland 344
Act of Adjournal: Criminal procedure: Rules: Convention Rights (Compliance) (Scotland) Act 2001: Scotland 317
Act of Adjournal: Criminal procedure: Rules: Extradition: Scotland 317, 344
Act of Adjournal: Criminal procedure: Rules: Sexual Offences (Procedure & Evidence) (Scotland) Act 2002: Scotland 317
Act of Sederunt: Court of Session: Personal injuries actions: Scotland 312
Act of Sederunt: Court of Session: Protection from Abuse (Scotland) Act 2001: Rules: Scotland 312
Act of Sederunt: Court of Session: Solicitors, shorthand writers & witnesses: Fees: Scotland 312
Act of Sederunt: Debt arrangement & attachment: Scotland 344
Act of Sederunt: Lands Valuation Appeal Court: Scotland 311
Act of Sederunt: Messengers-at-arms: Fees: Scotland 311
Act of Sederunt: Mortgage Rights (Scotland) Act 2001: Scotland 344
Act of Sederunt: Ordinary cause rules: Protection from Abuse (Scotland) Act 2001: Applications: Scotland 345
Act of Sederunt: Sheriff Court: Solicitors: Fees: Scotland 344
Act of Sederunt: Sheriff Court: Witnesses & shorthand writers: Fees: Scotland 344
Act of Sederunt: Sheriff officers: Fees: Scotland 344
Act of Sederunt: Small claims: Rules: Scotland 345
Act of Sederunt: Summary & statutory applications & appeals etc.: Rules: Scotland 345
Act of Sederunt: Summary cause rules: Scotland 345
Acts: Private & personal: Chronological tables 6
Additional voluntary contributions: National Health Service: Pension scheme 125
Adjacent waters: Boundaries: Northern Ireland 29, 128
Administration orders: Insurers: Financial Services & Markets Act 2000 63
Adoption & children: Acts: Explanatory notes 4
Adoption & paternity: Leave 238
Adoption & paternity: Social security 229
Adoption (Intercountry Aspects) Act (Northern Ireland) 2001: Commencement: Northern Ireland 368, 369
Adoption (Intercountry Aspects) Act 1999: Commencement: Scotland 310
Adoption pay: Administration: Northern Ireland 363
Adoption pay: General: Northern Ireland 363
Adoption pay: Health & personal social services employees: Northern Ireland 363
Adoption pay: Persons abroad & mariners: Northern Ireland 364
Adoption pay: Weekly rates: Northern Ireland 364
Adoption: Children: Overseas territories: Northern Ireland 359
Adults with Incapacity (Scotland) Act 2000: Commencement: Scotland 306
Adults with incapacity: Ethics committee: Scotland 306
Adults with incapacity: Guardians' powers: Recall: Scotland 306
Adults with incapacity: Guardianship & intervention orders: Reports: Scotland 306
Adults with incapacity: Medical treatment certificates: Scotland 306
Adults with incapacity: Public guardian: Fees: Scotland 306
Adults with incapacity: Specified medical treatments: Scotland 306, 307
Adults with incapacity: Welfare guardians: Decisions: Non-compliance: Scotland 306
Adults with incapacity: Welfare guardians: Supervision of: Scotland 307
Adur (District): Electoral changes 91

Entry	Page
Adur, Arun & Worthing: National Health Service Primary Care Trust	104
Advertising & promotion: Tobacco: Acts	4
Advertising & promotion: Tobacco: Acts: Explanatory notes	5
Advice & assistance: Assistance by way of representation: Scotland	319
Advice & assistance: Financial conditions: Scotland	319
Advice & assistance: Scotland	320
Advisory Committee for Wales (Environment Agency) : Abolition	60
Advisory Council (Scottish Qualifications Authority): Establishment: Scotland	312
Aerodromes: Designation: Facilities for consultation	23
African Development Fund: Additional subscriptions	86
Aggregates levy: Finance Act 2001: Section 16: Appointed day	7
Aggregates levy: General	7
Aggregates levy: Registration & miscellaneous provision	7
Aggregates levy: Tax credit: Northern Ireland	7
Agricultural & forestry tractors: Emission of gaseous & particulate pollutants	58
Agricultural & forestry tractors: Type approval	241
Agricultural holdings: Units of production: England	87
Agricultural marketing: Grants: Northern Ireland	359
Agricultural nitrates: Pollution: Water: Protection: Wales	247
Agricultural occupancies: Assured tenancies: Forms: England	87
Agricultural processing: Grants: Northern Ireland	359
Agricultural products grant: Marketing: Northern Ireland	360
Agriculture: Agricultural processing & marketing: Grants: Northern Ireland	359
Agriculture: Agricultural product grant: Marketing: Northern Ireland	360
Agriculture: Animals & animal products: Import & export: Wales	15
Agriculture: Beef: Labelling: Enforcement: England	8
Agriculture: Beef: Special premium: Northern Ireland	359
Agriculture: Bovines & bovine products: Trade: England	8
Agriculture: Bovines & bovine products: Trade: Northern Ireland	359
Agriculture: Bovines & bovine products: Trade: Scotland	307
Agriculture: Bovines & bovine products: Trade: Wales	10
Agriculture: Cattle: Artificial insemination: Animal health: England	9
Agriculture: Cereals marketing: Home-grown Cereals Authority: Rate of levy	8
Agriculture: Common agricultural policy: Organic products: Wales	11
Agriculture: Common agricultural policy: Support schemes: Appeals: England	8
Agriculture: Environmental impact assessment: Uncultivated land & semi-natural areas: Wales	10
Agriculture: Extensification payment: Scotland	307
Agriculture: Feedingstuffs: Amendment: England	8
Agriculture: Feedingstuffs: Amendment: Wales	10
Agriculture: Feedingstuffs: Scotland	307
Agriculture: Feedingstuffs: Food & animal: Products of animal origin: From China: Control: England	8, 9, 65
Agriculture: Feedingstuffs: Food & animal: Products of animal origin: From China: Control: Northern Ireland	367
Agriculture: Feedingstuffs: Food & animal: Products of animal origin: From China: Control: Scotland	307, 315
Agriculture: Feedingstuffs: Food & animal: Products of animal origin: From China: Control: Wales	10, 68
Agriculture: Feedingstuffs: Northern Ireland	359
Agriculture: Feedingstuffs: Zootechnical products	7
Agriculture: Feedingstuffs: Zootechnical products: Northern Ireland	360
Agriculture: Hemp: Third country imports	8
Agriculture: Hill farm: Allowance: England	9
Agriculture: Less favoured area: Compensatory allowances: Northern Ireland	360
Agriculture: Less favoured areas: Support scheme: Scotland	307
Agriculture: Livestock industries: Cattle: Artificial insemination: Animal health: Scotland	308
Agriculture: Livestock industries: Cattle: Artificial insemination: Animal health: Wales	11
Agriculture: Milk Marketing Board: Dissolution: England & Wales	10
Agriculture: Milk Marketing Board: Residuary functions: Northern Ireland	360
Agriculture: Nitrate sensitive areas: England	9
Agriculture: Nitrate vulnerable zones: Additional designations: England	9, 247
Agriculture: Olive oil: Marketing standards	8
Agriculture: Pesticides: Crops, food & feeding stuffs: Maximum residue levels: England & Wales	8, 10, 134
Agriculture: Pesticides: Crops, food & feeding stuffs: Maximum residue levels: Northern Ireland	360, 376
Agriculture: Pesticides: Crops, food & feeding stuffs: Maximum residue levels: Scotland	308, 323
Agriculture: Pig industry: Restructuring: Capital grant: Scheme: Scotland	308
Agriculture: Pig industry: Restructuring: Non-capital grant: Scheme: Scotland	308
Agriculture: Products: Animal origin: Third country imports: England	9, 67
Agriculture: Products: Animal origin: Third country imports: Scotland	308
Agriculture: Products: Animal origin: Third country imports: Wales	10, 11
Agriculture: Seed potatoes: Crop fees: Northern Ireland	360

Agriculture: Sheep: Annual premium: Northern Ireland.	360
Agriculture: Tir Mynydd: Wales	11
Agriculture: Uncultivated land & semi-natural areas: Environmental impact assessment: Scotland	307
Agriculture: Wine: Common agricultural policy: Scotland.	307
Air Force: Courts-martial.	38
Air Force: Royal: Army, Air Force & Naval Discipline Acts: Continuation	38
Air navigation	23
Air navigation: Civil aviation: Jersey	23
Air navigation: Dangerous goods	23
Air navigation: Environmental standards.	23
Air navigation: Flying restrictions: Beating retreat ceremony.	23
Air navigation: Flying restrictions: Biggin Hill.	23
Air navigation: Flying restrictions: Birmingham.	23
Air navigation: Flying restrictions: Blackpool	23
Air navigation: Flying restrictions: Bournemouth	23
Air navigation: Flying restrictions: Brands Hatch	23
Air navigation: Flying restrictions: Buckingham Palace.	23
Air navigation: Flying restrictions: Cardiff	24
Air navigation: Flying restrictions: Central London	24
Air navigation: Flying restrictions: Cranfield	24
Air navigation: Flying restrictions: Duxford.	24
Air navigation: Flying restrictions: Eastbourne	24
Air navigation: Flying restrictions: Fairford	24
Air navigation: Flying restrictions: Farnborough	24
Air navigation: Flying restrictions: Foot & mouth disease.	24
Air navigation: Flying restrictions: Foot & mouth disease: Burial sites	24
Air navigation: Flying restrictions: Glastonbury.	24
Air navigation: Flying restrictions: Golden Jubilee	24
Air navigation: Flying restrictions: Haymarket, central London	24
Air navigation: Flying restrictions: Henstridge	24
Air navigation: Flying restrictions: Hillsborough Castle	24
Air navigation: Flying restrictions: Jet formation display teams	24, 25
Air navigation: Flying restrictions: Lewknor	25
Air navigation: Flying restrictions: Manchester	25
Air navigation: Flying restrictions: Millennium Dome.	25
Air navigation: Flying restrictions: Newmarket.	25
Air navigation: Flying restrictions: North Weald	25
Air navigation: Flying restrictions: Nuclear installations	25
Air navigation: Flying restrictions: Pershore	25
Air navigation: Flying restrictions: Perth	25
Air navigation: Flying restrictions: Portadown	25
Air navigation: Flying restrictions: Portsmouth & the English Channel	25
Air navigation: Flying restrictions: Potter's Bar.	25
Air navigation: Flying restrictions: Remembrance Sunday	26
Air navigation: Flying restrictions: Rivington	26
Air navigation: Flying restrictions: Royal Air Force Leuchars	26
Air navigation: Flying restrictions: Royal Air Force Waddington	26
Air navigation: Flying restrictions: Royal Albert Hall	26
Air navigation: Flying restrictions: Security establishments in Northern Ireland	26
Air navigation: Flying restrictions: Silverstone & Turweston	26
Air navigation: Flying restrictions: Soham	26
Air navigation: Flying restrictions: Southend	26
Air navigation: Flying restrictions: Southport.	26
Air navigation: Flying restrictions: St Paul's Cathedral	26
Air navigation: Flying restrictions: State opening of Parliament	26
Air navigation: Flying restrictions: Stoke Newington	26
Air navigation: Flying restrictions: Sunbury.	26
Air navigation: Flying restrictions: Sunderland	26
Air navigation: Flying restrictions: Swindon	26
Air navigation: Flying restrictions: Trooping the Colour ceremony	26
Air navigation: Flying restrictions: Trowbridge	26
Air navigation: Flying restrictions: Wagford	27
Air navigation: Flying restrictions: Westminster	27
Air navigation: Flying restrictions: Weston Park	27
Air navigation: Flying restrictions: Whitsand Bay.	27
Air navigation: Flying restrictions: Yarlswood	27
Air quality: England	59

Entry	Page
Air quality: Limit values: England	59
Air quality: Limit values: Northern Ireland	364
Air quality: Limit values: Scotland	313
Air quality: Limit values: Wales	60
Air quality: Scotland	313
Air quality: Wales	60
Air, naval & military forces: Disablement & death: Service pensions	132
Airports: Byelaws: Designation: Northern Ireland	360
Alcoholic liquor & tobacco products: Channel Tunnel	19
Allowances: Northern Ireland Assembly: Members: Winding up allowance: Northern Ireland	374
Al-Qa'ida & Taliban: United Nations measures	245
Al-Qa'ida & Taliban: United Nations measures: Channel Islands	245
Al-Qa'ida & Taliban: United Nations measures: Isle of Man	245
Al-Qa'ida & Taliban: United Nations measures: Overseas territories	245
Amateur sports clubs: Taxation	235
Americium: Atomic energy & radioactive substances	17
Amnesic shellfish poisoning: Food protection: Orkney: Scotland	326
Amnesic shellfish poisoning: Food protection: West Coast: Scotland	326, 327, 328, 329, 330
Amnesic, paralytic & diarrhetic shellfish poisoning: Food protection: Orkney: Scotland	325
Anglia: North West Anglia Health Care: National Health Service Trust	117
Animal by-products: Identification: England	65
Animal by-products: Identification: Northern Ireland	366
Animal by-products: Identification: Scotland	314
Animal by-products: Identification: Wales	67
Animal feedingstuffs: Scotland	307
Animal feedingstuffs: Products of animal origin: From China: Emergency control: England	8, 9, 65
Animal feedingstuffs: Products of animal origin: From China: Emergency control: Northern Ireland	367
Animal feedingstuffs: Products of animal origin: From China: Emergency control: Scotland	307, 315
Animal gatherings: Interim measures: England	12
Animal gatherings: Wales	14, 15
Animal Health Act 2002: Commencement: England	12
Animal health: Acts	1
Animal health: Food & mouth disease: Declaratory: Controlled areas: England & Wales	14
Animals & animal products: Import & export: England	12
Animals & animal products: Import & export: Northern Ireland	360, 364
Animals & animal products: Import & export: Scotland	308
Animals & animal products: Import & export: Wales	15
Animals (Scientific Procedures) Act 1986: Fees	11
Animals: Animal Health Act 2002: Commencement: England	12
Animals: Animal health: Animal gatherings: Wales	14, 15
Animals: Animal health: Bovine spongiform encephalopathies: Monitoring: Scotland	308
Animals: Animal health: Cattle database: England	12
Animals: Animal health: Cattle database: Wales	15
Animals: Animal health: Cattle: Artificial insemination: England	9
Animals: Animal health: Cattle: Artificial insemination: Scotland	308
Animals: Animal health: Cattle: Artificial insemination: Wales	11
Animals: Animal health: Cattle: Movement: Notification : Scotland	309
Animals: Animal health: Cattle: Older animals: Identification: England	12
Animals: Animal health: Cattle: Older animals: Identification: Wales	15
Animals: Animal health: Disease control & animal movements: Interim measures: Scotland	309
Animals: Animal health: Disease control: Interim measures: England	12, 13
Animals: Animal health: Disease control: Interim measures: Scotland	309
Animals: Animal health: Disease control: Interim measures: Wales	15
Animals: Animal health: Foot & mouth disease: Controlled areas: Northern Ireland	360
Animals: Animal health: Foot & mouth disease: Controlled areas: Scotland	309
Animals: Animal health: Gatherings: Interim measures: England	12
Animals: Animal health: Import & export restrictions: Foot & mouth disease: England	13
Animals: Animal health: Import & export restrictions: Foot & mouth disease: Scotland	309, 316
Animals: Animal health: Import & export restrictions: Foot & mouth disease: Wales	16
Animals: Animal health: Movement: Restrictions: England	13
Animals: Animal health: Pigs: Records, identification & movement: Interim measures: England	13
Animals: Animal health: Pigs: Records, identification & movement: Scotland	309
Animals: Animal health: Pigs: Records, identification & movement: Wales	16
Animals: Animal health: Poultry breeding & animal by-products: Fees: England	13
Animals: Animal health: Products: Import & export: England	12
Animals: Animal health: Sheep & goats: Identification & movement: Interim measures: England	13, 14
Animals: Animal health: Sheep & goats: Identification: Scotland	309, 310

Animals: Animal health: Sheep & goats: Identification: Wales 16, 17
Animals: Animal health: Sheep & goats: Movements: Interim measures: Scotland 310
Animals: Animal health: Transmissible spongiform encephalopathy: England 14
Animals: Animal health: Transmissible spongiform encephalopathy: Northern Ireland 361, 365
Animals: Animal health: Transmissible spongiform encephalopathy: Scotland 310
Animals: Animal health: Transmissible spongiform encephalopathy: Wales 17
Animals: By-products: Identification: Northern Ireland 366
Animals: By-products: Northern Ireland 360
Animals: Farmed animals: Welfare: England 14
Animals: Farmed animals: Welfare: Northern Ireland 387
Animals: Farmed animals: Welfare: Scotland 310
Animals: Farmed animals: Welfare: Wales 17
Animals: Fur Farming (Prohibition) (Scotland) Act 2002: Commencement: Scotland 308, 311
Animals: Fur farming: Compensation scheme: England 11
Animals: Health: Pets: Travel scheme: Pilot arrangements: England 13
Animals: Health: Poultry breeding flocks: Hatcheries: Animal by products: Scotland 309
Animals: Movements: Interim measures: Scotland 310
Animals: Prevention of cruelty: Welfare: Slaughter or killing: Scotland 310
Animals: Products: Animal origin: Third country imports: England 9
Animals: Products: Animal origin: Third country imports: Northern Ireland 361, 364
Animals: Products: Animal origin: Third country imports: Scotland 308
Animals: Products: Animal origin: Third country imports: Wales 10, 11
Animals: Protection of: Anaesthetics: England 14
Animals: Rabies: Dogs, cats & other mammals: Importation: Wales 14
Animals: Welfare: Slaughter or killing: Northern Ireland 387
Antarctic: Regulations 17
Anti-social behaviour Orders: Magistrates' courts: England & Wales 100
Anti-Terrorism, Crime & Security Act 2001: Commencement 34, 36, 140
Anti-terrorism, crime & security: Acts: Explanatory notes 4
Anti-terrorism: Financial & other measures: Overseas territories 131
Appropriation: Acts 1
Apsley House: Functions in relation to: Contracting out 31
Aquaculture & fisheries: Structures: Grants: Wales 65, 220
Architects: Qualifications: EC recognition: European Communities 17
Ardoch Sewage Works: Argyll & Bute Council: West Dunbartonshire Council: Boundaries: Scotland 321
Argyll & Bute Council: West Dunbartonshire Council: Boundaries: Ardoch Seage Works: Scotland 321
Armed Forces Act 2001: Commencement 38
Arms & ammunition: Firearms (Amendment) Act 1988: Firearms Consultative Committee 17
Arms decommissioning: Northern Ireland: Acts 3
Arms decommissioning: Northern Ireland: Acts: Explanatory notes 5
Army, Air Force & Naval Discipline Acts: Continuation 38
Army: Courts-martial 38
Artificial insemination: Cattle: Animal health: England 9
Artificial insemination: Cattle: Animal health: Scotland 308
Artificial insemination: Cattle: Animal health: Wales 11
Arun (District): Electoral changes 91
Arun: Adur, Arun & Worthing: National Health Service Primary Care Trust 104
Asbestos: Control: At work 71
Ashford: National Health Service Primary Care Trust 104
Ashington: Education Action Zone: Extension 42
Ashworth Hospital Authority: Abolition 104
Assembly Learning Grant scheme: Education: Wales 53
Assembly Ombudsman & Commissioner for Complaints: Salaries: Northern Ireland 381
Assisted places: Education: England 45
Assisted places: Education: Incidental expenses: England 45
Assisted places: Education: Incidental expenses: Wales 54
Assisted places: Education: Wales 54
Assured tenancies: Agricultural occupancies: Forms: England 87
Asylum & immigration: Acts 3
Asylum support 80
Asylum support: Repeal 80
Asylum: Immigration & Asylum Act 1999: Commencement 80
Asylum: Immigration & asylum: Appeals: One-stop procedures 80
Asylum: Immigration & asylum: Family visitor 80
Asylum: Nationality, Immigration & Asylum Act 2002: Commencement 81
Asylum-seekers: Accommodation: Housing (Scotland) Act 2001 79
AT&T Global Network Services (UK) B.V.: Telecommunications: Public systems 236

Atomic energy & radioactive substances 17
Atomic energy & radioactive substances: Americium 17
Atomic energy & radioactive substances: Natural gas 18
Atomic energy & radioactive substances: Radioactive material: Road transport 18
Atomic Energy Authority: Special Constables 17, 136
Attendance allowance: Disability living allowance: Social security 226
Attendance allowance: Disability living allowance: Social security: Northern Ireland 382
Audit Commission: Borrowing limits 96
Aviation: Civil: Air navigation. 23
Aviation: Civil: Air navigation: Environmental standards 23
Avon & Somerset: Petty sessions areas 87
Avon, Gloucestershire & Wiltshire: Health Authority 104
Awards for All joint scheme: National Lottery: Authorisation: England 128
Awards: Students: Northern Ireland 362
Aylesbury Vale (District): Electoral changes 91
Ayr: Police cells: Legalised: Discontinuance of: Scotland 325

B

Babergh (District): Electoral changes 91
Badges: Motor vehicles: Disabled persons: Scotland. 332
Bail: Electronic monitoring: Responsible officer: England & Wales 34
Ballet, choir & music schools: Grants: Education. 46
Ballots & elections: Trade unions: Scrutineers 241
Bankers' games: Gaming clubs 18
Banking: HSBC Investment Banking Act 2002. 6
Bankruptcy: Occupational & personal pension schemes 84, 132
Banks & banking: Electronic money: Miscellaneous amendments 18, 63
Barclays Group: Reorganisation: Local acts 6
Barnet, Enfield & Haringey: Health Authority 104
Barnsley Community & Priority Services: National Health Service Trust 104
Barnstaple downstream bridge: Devon County Council: Confirmation: England 77
Barrow-in Furness: Community Learning Partnership: Education Action Zone: Extension 43
Basildon & Thurrock General Hospitals: National Health Service Trust 104
Basingstoke & Deane (Borough): Permitted & special parking area 211
Bass PLC & Interbrew SA: Mergers 29
Batteries & accumulators: Containing dangerous substances: Northern Ireland 364
Bedford: Action for Learning Partnership, Bedford: Education Action Zone: Extension. 42
Beef: Labelling: Enforcement: England 8
Beef: Special premium: Northern Ireland. 359
Beer: Excise goods, beer & tobacco products: Customs & excise 37
Beer: Excise warehousing 36
Beer: Supply: Tied estate 29
Beet seeds: England 220
Belfast Harbour: Northern Ireland 368
Bellingham: Downham & Bellingham: Education Action Zone: Extension. 44
Benefits: Loss of: Social security: Northern Ireland 371, 379, 384
Benefits: Minor: Exemption: Income tax 82
Bereavement: Damages: Variation of sum: England & Wales 38
Bereavement: Damages: Variation of sum: Northern Ireland. 38
Berkshire (East): National Health Service Trusts 109
Berkshire: West Berkshire (District): Electoral changes 93
Bermuda: Merchant shipping: Confirmation of legislation 102
Bermuda: Merchant shipping: Revocation 102
Best value performance indicators: Local government: Wales. 98
Betting, Gaming & Lotteries Act 1963: Schedule 4 18
Betting, gaming & lotteries: Gaming (Bingo) Act 1985: Fees. 18
Betting, gaming & lotteries: Gaming (Bingo) Act 1985: Monetary limit: Variation 18
Betting, gaming & lotteries: Gaming Act 1968: Fees: Variation 18
Betting, gaming & lotteries: Gaming Act 1968: Fees: Variation: England & Wales 19
Betting, gaming & lotteries: Gaming Act 1968: Fees: Variation: Scotland 310
Betting, gaming & lotteries: Gaming Act 1968: Monetary limits: Variation. 18
Betting, gaming & lotteries: Gaming Board: Fees 18
Betting, gaming & lotteries: Gaming clubs: Bankers' games 18
Betting, gaming & lotteries: Gaming clubs: Hours & charges. 18

Entry	Page
Betting, gaming & lotteries: Gaming clubs: Licensing	19
Betting, gaming & lotteries: Gaming clubs: Multiple bingo	18
Betting, gaming & lotteries: Lotteries: Monetary limits: Variation	19
Bingo & other gaming: Deregulation	39
Bingo: Gaming (Bingo) Act 1985: Fees	18
Bingo: Gaming (Bingo) Act 1985: Monetary limit: Variation	18
Bingo: Multiple: Gaming clubs	18
Bioblend & biodiesel: Customs & excise	36
Biocidal products: Northern Ireland	370
Biodiesel & bioblend: Customs & excise	36
Bird, farmed game, rabbit & poultry meat: Hygiene & inspection: Scotland	316
Birkenhead & Wallasey: National Health Service Primary Care Trust	105
Birmingham & the Black Country: Health Authority	105
Birmingham College of Food, Tourism & Creative Studies: Higher education sector: Transfer to	51
Birmingham Specialist Community: National Health Service Trust	105
Birmingham: Eastern Birmingham:;National Health Service Primary Care Trust	109
Birmingham: Heart of Birmingham Teaching: National Health Service Primary Care Trust	111
Birmingham: Health Authority	105
Birmingham: North Birmingham: National Health Service Primary Care Trust	116
Birmingham: Sandwell & West Birmingham Hospitals: National Health Service Trust	119
Birmingham: South Birmingham: National Health Service Primary Care Trust	120
Birth & death entries: Registers: Correction: De-regulation	39
Births, deaths & marriages, etc.: Registration: Fees: England & Wales	145
Births, deaths & marriages, etc.: Registration: Fees: Northern Ireland	379
Births, deaths & marriages, etc.: Registration: Fees: Scotland	321, 330
Births, deaths & marriages, etc.: Registration: Service departments registers	145
Bitton Railway	242, 243
Blaby (District): Electoral changes	91
Black Country: Birmingham & the Black Country: Health Authority	105
Blackburn with Darwen (Borough): Election years changes	89
Blackburn with Darwen (Borough): Electoral changes	89
Blackburn, Hyndburn & Ribble Valley Health Care: National Health Service Trust	110
Blackburn: Aberdeen City Council. Aberdeenshire Council. Boundaries. Scotland	321
Blackpool (Borough): Electoral changes	89
Blackpool Victoria Hospital: National Health Service Trust	105
Blackpool, Fylde & Wyre Hospitals: National Health Service Trust	105
Blackpool, Wyre & Fylde Community Health Services: National Health Service Trust	105
Blaenau Gwent & Caerphilly: Tredegar & Rhymney: Local government: Wales	96
Blood tests: County courts: Northern Ireland	361
Blood tests: Magistrates' courts: Rules: Northern Ireland	374
Boarding schools & colleges: Powers & fees: Inspection: Wales	22, 223
Bolton: Community Healthcare Bolton: National Health Service Trust	107
Bolton: Education Action Zone: Extension	43
Bonds: Personal portfolio: Taxes	235
Bootle & Litherland: National Health Service Primary Care Trust	105
Borough of Halton, Thurrock & Warrington: Election years changes	90
Bosworth & Hinckley (Borough): Electoral changes	89
Bournemouth (Borough): Electoral changes	89
Bournewood Community & Mental Health: National Health Service Trust	105
Bovine spongiform encephalopathies: Monitoring: Scotland	308
Bovines & bovine products: Trade: England	8
Bovines & bovine products: Trade: Northern Ireland	359
Bovines & bovine products: Trade: Scotland	307
Bovines & bovine products: Trade: Wales	10
Bovines: Rectal ultrasound scanning: Veterinary surgery	247
Bracknell Forest (Borough): Electoral changes	89
Bradford Community Health: National Health Service Trusts	105
Bradford District Care: National Health Service Trusts	105
Bradford, South: Community Learning Partnership: Education Action Zone: Extension	50
Bradford: Parishes: Local government	91
Braehead: Glasgow City Council: Renfrewshire Council: Boundaries: Scotland	321
Braintree: Witham, Braintree and Halstead Care: National Health Service Trusts	124
Breaking the Cycle Bridgewater: Education Action Zone: Extension	43
Breckland (District): Electoral changes	92
Brent & Harrow: Health Authority	105
Brent: National Health Service Primary Care Trust	105
Brent, Kensington, Chelsea & Westminster Mental Health: National Health Service Trusts	105

Brentwood (Borough): Permitted & special parking area 210
Brentwood: Parishes: Local government 91
Brewing: Mergers: Interbrew SA & Bass PLC: Interim provision 29
Bridgend: Electoral changes: Wales 99
Bridgewater: Breaking the Cycle: Education Action Zone: Extension 43
Bridlington: East Yorkshire College of Further Education, Bridlington: Dissolution 44
Brightlingsea Harbour: Constitution: England 71
Brighton & Hove City: National Health Service Primary Care Trust 105
Brighton & Sussex University Hospitals: National Health Service Trust 105
Brinsbury College: Dissolution 43
British nationality: British Overseas Territories Act 2002: Commencement 19
British Overseas Territories Act 2002: Commencement 19
British overseas territories: Citizenship: Acts 1
British overseas territories: Citizenship: Acts: Explanatory notes 4
Broadcasting: Communications: Regulation: Office of Communications: Acts 3
Broadcasting: Communications: Regulation: Office of Communications: Acts: Explanatory notes 5
Broadland: Parishes: Local government 91
Bromsgrove & Redditch: National Health Service Primary Care Trust 119
Broomfield Agricultural College: Dissolution 43
Broxburn (West Farm): West Lothian Council: City of Edinburgh Council: Boundaries: Scotland 321
BSE See Bovine spongiform encephalopathy
Buckinghamshire Hospitals: National Health Service Trust 106
Buckinghamshire: Health Authority 106
Buckinghamshire: South Buckinghamshire: National Health Service Trust 120
Budget (Scotland) Act 2001: Amendment: Scotland 325
Budget (Scotland) Act 2002: Amendment: Scotland 325
Budget 2003: Supporting documents 7
Budget statements: Education: England 45
Budget statements: Education: Wales 54
Budget: Acts: Explanatory notes: Northern Ireland 359
Budget: Acts: Northern Ireland 358
Budget: Acts: Scotland 304
Budget: Schools & individual schools budgets: Local Education Authorities: England 49
Building & buildings: Approved inspectors: England & Wales 19
Building & buildings: Building regulations 19
Building & buildings: Standards: Scotland 310
Building regulations 19
Building standards: Scotland 310
Building: Approved inspectors: England & Wales 19
Buildings & land: Value added tax 246
Buildings: Construction: Value added tax 246
Burnley (Borough): Electoral changes 89
Burnley Health Care: National Health Service Trust 110
Burntwood, Lichfield & Tamworth National Health Service Trust 106
Bury (Metropolitan Borough): Permitted & special parking area 211
Bury Health Care: National Health Service Trust 106, 118
Bury: National Health Service Trust 106
Bus services: Operators: Grants: England 143
Bus services: Operators: Grants: Scotland 347
Bus services: Operators: Grants: Wales 144
Buses: Community buses 143
Buses: Minibuses: Section 19 permit buses 143
Buses: User complaints: Scotland 347
Busways: Chester guided busway: 243
By-products: Animals: Identification: Northern Ireland 366
By-products: Animals: Northern Ireland 360

C

C2C Class 357/0 vehicles: Accessibility: Exemptions 41, 241
Caerleon & Malpas: Newport: Local government: Wales 99
Caerphilly: Blaenau Gwent & Caerphilly: Tredegar & Rhymney: Local government: Wales 96
Cairngorm Funicular Railway: Accessibility: Exemptions 41, 241
Calderdale: National Health Service Trust 106
Camborne, Pool & Redruth Success: Education Action Zone: Extension 43

Cambridge (City): Electoral changes 91
Cambridge: Lifespan Health Care Cambridge: National Health Service Trust 106, 113
Cambridgeshire & Peterborough Mental Health Partnership: National Health Service Trust 106
Cambridgeshire, East (District): Electoral changes 92
Cambridgeshire: Health Authority 106
Cambridgeshire: South Cambridgeshire (District): Electoral changes 93
Cambridgeshire: South Cambridgeshire: National Health Service Trust 120
Camden & Islington Mental Health: National Health Service Trust 106
Camden, London Borough: Highways: Street works: Charges 77
Camden: National Health Service Primary Care Trust 106
Cameroon & Mozambique: Admissions: Commonwealth: Acts 1
Canals & inland waterways: Wye (River): Navigation: England & Wales 19, 243
Cannock Chase: National Health Service Primary Care Trust 107
Canterbury & Coastal: National Health Service Primary Care Trust 107
Capital allowances: Energy-saving plant & machinery 81
Capital finance: Local authorities: Discount: Rate 2002/03: England 94
Capital finance: Local authorities: Discount: Rate 2002/03: Wales 97
Capital finance: Local authorities: England 94
Capital gains tax: Annual exempt amount 234
Capital gains tax: Gilt-edged securities 234
Capital grants: Education: Wales 54
Car fuel benefits: Cash equivalents: Income tax 82
Caradon (District): Electoral changes 92
Cardiff & Vale of Glamorgan: Michaelston & Grangetown: Local government: Wales 96
Care homes: Wales 21, 223
Care Standards Act 2000: Commencement: England 20, 142, 221, 222
Care Standards Act 2000: Commencement: England & Wales 21, 142, 222
Care Standards Act 2000: Commencement: Wales 21, 142, 223
Care Standards Act 2000: Establishment & agencies 20, 142, 222
Care Standards Act 2000: Miscellaneous amendments: Wales 22, 143, 223
Care Standards Act 2000: Miscellaneous regulations: Wales 21, 223
Care Standards Act 2000: Social care worker: Meaning of phrase: Extension: Wales 223
Care Standards Tribunal: Protection of children & vulnerable adults: England & Wales 21, 142, 222
Carer premium: Social security 225
Carer's allowance: Deregulation: Northern Ireland 362
Carer's allowance: Regulatory reform 145, 225
Carer's allowance: Social security 226
Carer's allowance: Social security: Northern Ireland 371, 378, 383
Carers & direct payments: Social services: Acts: Northern Ireland 358
Caribbean & North Atlantic territories: Turks & Caicos Islands: Constitution 19
Caribbean Development Bank: Further payments 86
Carmarthenshire & Pembrokeshire: Clynderwen, Cilymaenllwyd & Henllanfallteg: Local government: Wales 96
Carriage by air acts: Implementation of Montreal Convention 1999 27
Carriage of dangerous goods: Northern Ireland 370
Carrick (District): Electoral changes 92
Carriers' liability: Clandestine entrants: Level of Penalty: Code of Practice 81
Carriers' liability: Regulations 81
Cars: Value added tax 246
Cash searches: Code of practice: Proceeds of Crime Act 2002 140
Cash searches: Constables in Scotland: Proceeds of Crime Act 2002: Code of practice: Scotland 325
Cash: Detention & forfeiture: Magistrates' courts: Procedure: England & Wales 100
Castle Meads bridge: Gloucestershire Council: Confirmation: England 77
Cats, dogs & other mammals: Rabies: Importation: Wales 14
Cattle database: Wales 15
Cattle: Artificial insemination: Animal health: England 9
Cattle: Artificial insemination: Animal health: Scotland 308
Cattle: Artificial insemination: Animal health: Wales 11
Cattle: Database: England 12
Cattle: Movement: Notification: Scotland 309
Cattle: Older animals: Identification: England 12
Cattle: Older animals: Identification: Wales 15
Cells: Police: Legalised: Discontinuance of: Ayr: Scotland 325
Central Cheshire: National Health Service Primary Care Trust 107
Central Council for Education & Training in Social Work: Abolition 221
Central Derby National Health Service Trust 107
Central Police Training & Development Authority: Criminal Justice & Police Act 2001 137
Cereal seeds: England 220

Cereals marketing: Home-grown Cereals Authority: Rate of levy	8
Ceredigion & Pembrokeshire: St Dogmaels: Local government: Wales	97
Ceredigion (County): Electoral changes: Wales	97
Challenge for Corby: Education Action Zone: Extension	43
Chanctonbury: Horsham & Chanctonbury: National Health Service Primary Care Trust	111
Channel Islands: Telecommunication services	139
Channel Islands: United Nations measures: Al-Qa'ida & Taliban	245
Channel Islands: United Nations sanctions: Somalia	246
Channel Tunnel Rail Link: Thames tunnel approach	243
Channel Tunnel: Alcoholic liquor & tobacco products	19
Charging scheme: Road users: Enforcement: England & Wales	212
Charities: Exemption: England & Wales	20
Charities: Registration: Exception: England & Wales	20
Charnwood (Borough): Electoral changes	89
Chelmsford (Borough): Permitted & special parking area	210
Chelsea: Brent, Kensington, Chelsea & Westminster Mental Health: National Health Service Trust	105
Chelsea: Kensington & Chelsea: National Health Service Primary Care Trust	112
Chelsea: Kensington & Chelsea and Westminster: Health Authority	112
Chemicals: Hazard information & packaging for supply	71
Chemicals: Hazard information & packaging for supply: Health & safety: Northern Ireland	370
Cheshire & Wirral Partnership: National Health Service Trust	107
Cheshire (Central): National Health Service Primary Care Trust	107
Cheshire (Eastern): National Health Service Primary Care Trust	109
Cheshire (West): Wirral & West Cheshire Community: National Health Service Trust	107
Cheshire Community Healthcare: National Health Service Trust	107
Cheshire West: National Health Service Primary Care Trust	107
Chester & Halton Community: National Health Service Trust	107
Chester guided busway	243
Chester-le-Street & Durham: National Health Service Trust	109
Chichester (District): Electoral changes	92
Chief Inspector of Education & training: Wales	54
Child benefit tax credits: Acts	4
Child benefit tax credits: Acts: Explanatory notes	5
Child benefit: Electronic communications: Social security	228
Child care charges: Housing benefit: Council tax benefit	224
Child care: Charges: Social security: Benefits: Earnings: Computation	227
Child care: Providers: Tax credits	235
Child minding & day care: Wales	21, 223
Child support appeals: Jurisdiction of courts	62
Child Support, Pensions & Social Security Act 2000: Commencement: England, Wales & Scotland	132
Child Support, Pensions & Social Security Act 2000: Commencement: Northern Ireland	365, 375
Child support: Appeals: Jurisdiction of Courts: Northern Ireland	365
Child support: Decisions & appeals: Miscellaneous amendments: Northern Ireland	361, 365, 371, 378, 382
Child support: Miscellaneous amendments	62
Child support: Miscellaneous amendments: Northern Ireland	361, 366, 382
Child support: Northern Ireland	361, 365
Child support: Reciprocal arrangements: Northern Ireland	62
Child support: Social security & child support: Decisions & appeals: Miscellaneous amendments	62, 231, 236
Child support: Temporary compensation payment scheme: Modification & amendment	62
Child support: Temporary compensation payment scheme: Modification & amendment: Northern Ireland	361, 365
Child tax credits	233
Childcare: Education: Acts: Explanatory notes	4
Children & Family Court Advisory & Support Service: England & Wales	21
Children & young persons: Adoption (Intercountry Aspects) Act 1999: Commencement: Scotland	310
Children & young persons: Care homes: Wales	21, 223
Children & young persons: Care Standards Act 2000: Commencement: England	20, 142, 222
Children & young persons: Care Standards Act 2000: Commencement: England & Wales	21, 142, 222
Children & young persons: Care Standards Act 2000: Commencement: Wales	21, 142, 223
Children & young persons: Care Standards Act 2000: Establishment & agencies	20, 142, 222
Children & young persons: Care Standards Act 2000: Miscellaneous amendments: Wales	22, 143, 223
Children & young persons: Caring: Disqualification: Wales	22
Children & young persons: Child minding & day care: Wales	21, 223
Children & young persons: Children & Family Court Advisory & Support Service: England & Wales	21
Children & young persons: Children (Scotland) Act 1995: Commencement: Scotland	310
Children & young persons: Children Act 1989: Care Standards Act 2000: Miscellaneous regulations: Wales	21, 223
Children & young persons: Children Act 1989: Miscellaneous amendments: England	20
Children & young persons: Children Act 1989: Miscellaneous amendments: Wales	22, 143, 223

Children & young persons: Children: Disqualification from caring. 20
Children & young persons: Children: Leaving care: Wales 22
Children & young persons: Children's hearings: Legal representation: Scotland 310
Children & young persons: Children's homes: Wales. 22, 223
Children & young persons: Local authority remands: Electronic monitoring: Responsible officer: England & Wales 21
Children & young persons: National Care Standards Commission: Children's Rights Director: England 20, 222
Children & young persons: National Care Standards Commission: Inspection of schools & colleges: England 20
Children & young persons: Personal allowances: Social security 226
Children & young persons: Placement: Arrangements: Cases: Review: Wales. 21
Children & young persons: Protection of Children Act 1999: Commencement 21
Children & young persons: Protection: England & Wales 21, 142, 222
Children & young persons: Residential family centres: England. 20, 222
Children & young persons: Social care & independent healthcare: Registration: Fees: Wales. 22, 143, 223
Children & young persons: Social care & independent healthcare: Registration: Wales 22, 143, 224
Children & young persons: Social security: Allowances: Northern Ireland 371, 379, 385
Children (Scotland) Act 1995: Commencement: Scotland 310
Children Act 1989: Miscellaneous amendments: England. 20
Children Act 1989: Miscellaneous amendments: Wales 22, 143, 223
Children Act 1989: Miscellaneous regulations: Wales 21, 223
Children: Adoption: Acts: Explanatory notes 4
Children: Adoption: Overseas territories: Northern Ireland 359
Children: Allocation of proceedings: Northern Ireland 366
Children: Caring: Disqualification: Wales. 22
Children: Disqualification from caring 20
Children: Fostering services 20, 222
Children: Leaving care: Acts: Northern Ireland 358
Children: Leaving care: Wales. 22
Children: Nursery education & early years development: England 47
Children: Placement: Arrangements: Cases: Review: Wales. 21
Children: School education: Children under school age: Prescribed children: Scotland 313
Children's hearings: Legal representation: Scotland 310
Children's homes: Wales 22, 223
Chiltern (District): Electoral changes. 92
China: Food & animal feedingstuffs: Products of animal origin: Emergency control: England 9, 65
China: Food & animal feedingstuffs: Products of animal origin: Emergency control: Scotland 307, 315
China: Food & animal feedingstuffs: Products of animal origin: Emergency control: Northern Ireland. 367
China: Food & animal feedingstuffs: Products of animal origin: Emergency control: Wales. 10, 68
China: Peanuts: Emergency control: England 66
China: Peanuts: Emergency control: Northern Ireland 367
China: Peanuts: Emergency control: Scotland 315
China: Peanuts: Emergency control: Wales 68
Chiropractors Act 1994: Commencement 22
Chiropractors: Foreign qualifications: Registration: General Chiropractic Council: Rules 22
Chiropractors: General Chiropractic Council: Election of members & chairman. 22
Choir, music & ballet schools: Grants: Education. 46
Chorley & South Ribble: National Health Service Trust 112
Christchurch (Borough): Electoral changes. 89
Chronically sick & disabled persons: Health & Social Care Act 2001: Commencement 22, 221
Chronological table of local legislation 6
Chronological table of private & personal acts. 6
Chronological tables: Statutes 6
Cinemas & films: Cinematographs: Safety. 23
Cinemas & films: European Convention on Cinematographic Co-production 22, 23
Cinematographs: Safety 23
Citizenship: British overseas territories: Acts 1
Citizenship: British overseas territories: Acts: Explanatory notes 4
City colleges: Special educational needs: England. 48
City Hospital: National Health Service Trust 119
City of Edinburgh Council: West Lothian Council: Boundaries: West Farm, Broxburn: Scotland. 321
City of London: Ward elections: Local acts 6
Civic Government (Scotland) Act 1982: Houses: Multiple occupation: Licensing: Scotland 317, 321
Civil aviation: Aerodromes: Designation: Facilities for consultation 23
Civil aviation: Air navigation 23
Civil aviation: Air navigation: Dangerous goods 23
Civil aviation: Air navigation: Environmental standards. 23
Civil aviation: Air navigation: Jersey 23
Civil aviation: Carriage by air acts: Implementation of Montreal Convention 1999 27

Civil aviation: Flying restrictions	23, 24, 25, 26, 27
Civil defence: Grant: Acts	1
Civil defence: Grant: Acts: Explanatory notes	4
Civil Defence: Transfer of functions	103
Civil Jurisdiction & Judgments Act 1982: Magistrates' courts	100
Civil Jurisdiction & Judgments Act 1982: Magistrates' courts: Rules: Northern Ireland	374
Civil legal aid: Fees: Scotland	320
Civil legal aid: Financial conditions: Scotland	320
Civil legal aid: General: England & Wales	88
Civil legal aid: Scotland	320
Civil procedure: Enactments: Modification	33, 233
Civil procedure: England & Wales	33, 233
Clacton & Harwich: Education Action Zone: Extension	43
Clean air: Smoke control areas: Authorised fuels: England	27
Clean air: Smoke control areas: Authorised fuels: Scotland	310
Clean air: Smoke control areas: Authorised fuels: Wales	27
Clerk of the Crown in Chancery: Crown Office: Forms: Proclamations: Rules	27
Cleveland, East: Learning Together: Education Action Zone: Extension	49
Climate change levy: General	27
Clinical negligence & other risks indemnity scheme: National Health Service: Scotland	322
Clinical negligence scheme: National Health Service: England	114
Cloning: Human reproductive: Acts: Explanatory notes	5
Clydeport: Closure of Yorkhilll Basin: Harbours: Revision order: Scotland	316
Clynderwen, Cilymaenllwyd & Henllanfallteg: Carmarthenshire & Pembrokeshire: Local government: Wales	96
Coast protection: Notices: England	28
Code of practice: Disciplinary & grievance procedures: Appointed day: Northern Ireland	372
Code of practice: Industrial action ballots: Notice to employers: Appointed day: Northern Ireland	372
Code of practice: Redundancy consultation & procedures: Appointed day: Northern Ireland	372
Colchester (Borough): Permitted & special parking area	211
Cold weather payments: Social Fund	225
Cold weather payments: Social fund: Northern Ireland	382
Combe Down Stone Mines, Bath: Derelict land: Clearance Area	39
Combustion plants (Large): Environmental protection	60
Combustion plants (Large): National emission ceilings: Environmental protection: Pollution: Prevention & control: Scotland	314
Combustion plants (Large): Pollution: Prevention & control	60
Combustion plants (Large): Scotland	314
Comhairle nan Eilean Siar: Various harbours: Revision order: Scotland	317
Commerce: Electronic: EC directive	57
Commercial debts: Late payment:	32
Commercial debts: Late payment: Rate of interest	32
Commercial debts: Late payment: Rate of interest: Scotland	311
Commercial debts: Late payment: Scotland	311
Commercial debts: Late Payment of Commercial Debts (Interest) Act 1998: Commencement	32
Commercial debts: Late Payment of Commercial Debts (Interest) Act 1998: Commencement: Scotland	311
Commission areas: West Mercia: Justices of the peace	86
Commission for Patient & Public Involvement in Health: Functions: England	107
Commission for Patient & Public Involvement in Health: Membership & procedure: England	107
Commissioners: General & special: Jurisdiction & procedure	82, 84, 224, 234
Commissioners: Social security commissioners: Procedure: Tax credits appeals	227
Common & other land: Vehicular access: England	33
Common agricultural policy: Support schemes: Appeals: England	8
Common agricultural policy: Wine: Scotland	307
Commonhold & Leasehold Reform Act 2002: Commencement: England	78
Commonhold & Leasehold Reform Act 2002: Commencement: Wales	79
Commonhold: Acts	1
Commonhold: Acts: Explanatory notes	4
Commonwealth Institute: Cameroon & Mozambique: Admissions: Acts	1
CommuniCare: National Health Service & Community Care Trust	107
CommuniCare: National Health Service Trust	107
Communications: Interception of: Code of Practice: Regulation of investigatory powers	86
Communications: Regulation: Office of Communications: Acts	3
Communications: Regulation: Office of Communications: Acts: Explanatory notes	5
Community buses	143
Community care & health: Acts: Explanatory notes: Scotland	305
Community care & health: Acts: Scotland	304
Community Care and Health (Scotland) Act 2002: Amendments: Scotland	345
Community Care and Health (Scotland) Act 2002: Commencement: Scotland	345

Community care: Accommodation costs: Deferred payment: Scotland 345
Community care: Additional payments: Scotland. 345
Community care: Assessment of needs: Scotland 345
Community care: Disregard of resources: Scotland 346
Community care: Joint working etc.: Scotland 346
Community care: Personal & nursing care: Scotland 346
Community driving licence: Northern Ireland 364, 380
Community Health Care Service (North Derbyshire): National Health Service Trusts 121
Community Health Councils: National Health Service: England 108
Community Healthcare Bolton: National Health Service Trust 107
Community legal service: Financial: England & Wales 88
Companhia Portuguesa Radio Marconi SA: Public telecommunication systems 237
Companies: Competent authority: Fees 28
Companies: Criminal Justice & Police Act 2001: Commencement 29, 137
Companies: Directors' remuneration report 29
Companies: Disclosure of information: Designated authorities. 28
Companies: Disqualification orders 28
Companies: Fees 28
Companies: Foreign: Controlled: Excluded countries 81
Companies: Forms. 28
Companies: Insolvency Act 1986: Amendment 29, 84
Companies: Insolvency: Rules: Scotland 29, 85
Companies: Local authorities: England. 94
Companies: Open-ended investment companies: Acts: Northern Ireland. 358
Companies: Particulars of usual residential address: Confidentiality orders 28
Companies: Principal business activities 28
Companies: Summary financial statement 28
Company directors: Disqualification: Northern Ireland 128
Competition law: European Communities: Enforcement 61
Competition: Beer: Supply: Tied estate 29
Competition: Enterprise: Acts 2
Competition: Enterprise: Acts: Explanatory notes 4
Confectionery: Jelly confectionery: Food: Emergency control: Scotland 315
Connection charges: Electricity 56
Conservation: Seals: Scotland 343
Consolidated Fund: Acts 1
Constitutional law: Housing (Scotland) Act 2001: Housing support services information 29, 39, 79
Constitutional law: Northern Ireland Act 2000: Devolved government: Suspension 29, 30, 129
Constitutional law: Northern Ireland Act 2000: Modification 29, 129
Constitutional law: Scotland Act 1998: Agency arrangements: Specification 30, 40
Constitutional law: Scotland Act 1998: Cross-border public authorities 30
Constitutional law: Scottish administration: Offices 30, 40
Constitutional law: Scottish Parliament: Elections etc.. . . . . 30, 40
Constitutional law: Water Industry (Scotland) Act 2002: National security 30, 40, 247
Constitutional law: Waters: Adjacent waters: Boundaries: Northern Ireland 29, 128
Constitutional law: Welsh Administration Ombudsman: Jurisdiction: Wales. 30
Construction & open sites: Noise: Control: Codes of practice: England 142
Construction & open sites: Noise: Control: Codes of practice: Northern Ireland 378
Construction & open sites: Noise: Control: Codes of practice: Scotland 325
Construction & open sites: Noise: Control: Codes of practice: Wales. 143
Construction Board: Industrial training levy 58
Construction industry: Industrial training levy: Northern Ireland. 372
Construction industry: Sub-contractors: Income tax 83
Construction of buildings: Value added tax 246
Consular fees 40
Consular Fees Act 1980: Fees 62
Consumer protection: Dangerous substances & preparations: Safety 30
Consumer protection: Enterprise: Acts 2
Consumer protection: Enterprise: Acts: Explanatory notes 4
Consumer protection: Goods: Sale & supply: Consumers: European Communities 31
Consumer protection: Medical devices 31
Consumer protection: Personal protective equipment 31, 73
Consumer protection: Tobacco Advertising & Promotion Act 2002: Commencement: England, Wales & Northern Ireland. 31
Consumer protection: Tobacco Advertising & Promotion Act 2002: Commencement: Scotland 311
Consumer protection: Tobacco products: Manufacture, presentation & sale: Safety. 31
Contaminants: Food: England 65
Contaminants: Food: Northern Ireland 366

Contaminants: Food: Scotland	314
Contaminants: Food: Wales	67
Contaminated land & waste: Northern Ireland	364
Contracting out: Apsley House: Functions in relation to	31
Contracting out: Income-related benefits	31, 224
Contracting out: Local education authority functions	31
Contracting out: Patents	31
Contracts: Late Payment of Commercial Debts (Interest) Act 1998: Commencement	32
Contracts: Late Payment of Commercial Debts (Interest) Act 1998: Commencement: Scotland	311
Contracts: Late payment: Commercial debts	32
Contracts: Late payment: Commercial debts: Rate of interest	32
Contracts: Late payment: Commercial debts: Rate of interest: Scotland	311
Contracts: Late payment: Commercial debts: Scotland	311
Convention countries: Maintenance orders: Recovery abroad	100
Convention Rights (Compliance) (Scotland) Act 2001: Act of Adjournal: Criminal procedure: Rules: Scotland	317
Copyright, etc. & Trade Marks (Offences & Enforcement) Act 2002: Commencement	32, 34, 241
Copyright: Trade marks: Offences & enforcement: Acts: Explanatory notes	4
Copyright: Visually impaired persons: Acts	1
Corby: Challenge for Corby: Education Action Zone: Extension	43
Cornwall Healthcare National Health Service Trust	108
Cornwall, North (District): Electoral changes	93
Coroners: Practice & procedure: Northern Ireland	361
Coroners: Records: Fees for copies	32
Coroners' districts: Hertfordshire	32
Coroners' districts: Lancashire	32
Coroners' districts: Lincolnshire	32
Corporation tax: Finance leasing: Intangible assets	82
Corporation tax: Income & Corporation Taxes Act 1998: Section 349B (3)	82
COSHH: Regulations	72
Council for the Regulation of Health Care Professionals: Appointment etc.: England	73
Council tax benefit: Housing benefit: Child care charges	224
Council tax benefit: Housing benefit: Social security: Claims & information	227
Council tax: Demand notices: England	32, 144
Council tax: Dwellings & part residential subjects: Scotland	311
Council tax: Exempt dwellings: Scotland	311
Counter Fraud & Security Management Service: Establishment & constitution: National Health Service	108
Counter Fraud & Security Management Service: National Health Service	108
Countryside & Rights of Way Act 2000: Commencement: England	147
Countryside & Rights of Way Act 2000: Commencement: Wales	33
Countryside: Access: Appeals procedures: Wales	33
Countryside: Access: Maps: Provisional & conclusive maps: England	33
Countryside: Access: Provisional & conclusive maps: Wales	33
Countryside: Common & other land: Vehicular access: England	33
Countryside: Fur Farming (Prohibition) (Scotland) Act 2002: Commencement: Scotland	308, 311
Countryside: Local access forums: England	33
Countryside: Loch Lomond & the Trossachs National Park: Elections: Scotland	311
Countryside: Loch Lomond & the Trossachs National Park: Provisions: Scotland	311
Countryside: Peak District National Park Authority: Restriction of agricultural operations: England	33
Countryside: Wildlife & countryside: Sites of special scientific interest: Appeals: Wales	33
County Borough of Newport: Electoral changes: Wales	97
County Borough of The Vale of Glamorgan: Electoral changes: Wales	97
County court: Family proceedings: Fees: Northern Ireland	361, 366, 386
County courts: Blood tests: Northern Ireland	361
County Courts: Civil procedure: Enactments: Modification	33, 233
County courts: Civil procedure: Enactments: Modification: England & Wales	33, 233
County Courts: Civil procedure: England & Wales	33, 233
County courts: Family proceedings: Northern Ireland	361, 366, 386
County courts: Fees	33
County courts: Fees: Northern Ireland	361
County courts: Rules: Northern Ireland	361
County of Gwynedd: Electoral changes: Wales	97
County of Herefordshire (District): Electoral changes	91
County of Monmouthshire: Electoral changes: Wales	97
Court of Protection: Enduring powers of attorney: Rules	102, 140
Court of Protection: Enduring powers of attorney: Rules: England & Wales	102, 139
Court of Protection: Rules	102
Court of Session: Fees: Scotland	312

Entry	Page
Court of Session: Lands Valuation Appeal Court: Act of Sederunt: Scotland	311
Court of Session: Messengers-at arms: Fees: Act of Sederunt: Scotland	311
Court of Session: Personal injuries actions: Act of Sederunt: Scotland	312
Court of Session: Protection from Abuse (Scotland) Act 2001: Rules: Scotland	312
Court of Session: Solicitors, shorthand writers & witnesses: Fees: Act of Sederunt: Scotland	312
Courts: Magistrates' courts: Blood tests: Rules: Northern Ireland	374
Courts: Magistrates' courts: Civil Jurisdiction & Judgments Act 1982: Rules: Northern Ireland	374
Courts: Magistrates' courts: Declarations of parentage: Rules: Northern Ireland	374
Courts: Magistrates' courts: Fees: Northern Ireland	374
Courts: Magistrates' courts: Terrorist cash: Detention & forfeiture: Rules: Northern Ireland	374
Courts: Supreme Court of England & Wales: Fees	233
Courts-martial: Army	38
Courts-martial: Royal Air Force	38
Courts-martial: Royal Navy	38
Coventry: National Health Service Primary Care Trust	108
Coventry Millennium: Education Action Zone: Extension	43
Craven, Harrogate & Rural District: National Health Service Trust	108
Crawfish & lobsters: Fishing & landing: Prohibition: Wales	219
Crawley: National Health Service Primary Care Trust	108
Crawley (Borough): Electoral changes	89
Credit unions etc.: Financial Services & Markets Act 2000: Permission & applications	64
Credit unions: Financial Services & Markets Act 2000: Consequential amendments & transitional provisions	63
Crime: Anti-terrorism, crime & security: Acts: Explanatory notes	4
Crime: Prisoners: Short-term: Release on licence: Requisite period	140
Crime: Proceeds: Acts: Explanatory notes	5
Criminal appeals: Act of Adjournal: Scotland	317
Criminal defence service: Costs: Recovery: England & Wales	88
Criminal defence service: Funding: England & Wales	88
Criminal defence service: General: England & Wales	88
Criminal Defence Service: Representation order appeals: England & Wales	88
Criminal evidence: Police & Criminal Evidence Act 1984: Codes of practice: Statutory powers of stop & search: England & Wales	138
Criminal evidence: Police & Criminal Evidence Act 1984: Codes of practice: Visual recording of interviews	138
Criminal Injuries Compensation (Northern Ireland) Order 2002: Commencement: Northern Ireland	361, 362
Criminal injuries: Compensation scheme 2002: Commencement: Northern Ireland	362
Criminal injuries: Compensation: Northern Ireland	128
Criminal Justice & Court Services Act 2000: Commencement	34, 35
Criminal Justice & Police Act 2001: Amendment	35
Criminal Justice & Police Act 2001: Central Police Training & Development Authority	137
Criminal Justice & Police Act 2001: Commencement	29, 34, 35, 137
Criminal Justice & Police Act 2001: Commencement: England & Wales	35, 137
Criminal Justice & Public Order Act 1994: Commencement	34
Criminal Justice (International Co-operation) Act 1990: Overseas forfeiture orders: Enforcement	35, 36
Criminal Justice Act 1988: Designated countries & territories: England & Wales	34
Criminal Justice Act 1988: Offensive weapons	34, 36
Criminal Justice Act 1988: Offensive weapons: Scotland	312
Criminal law, England & Wales: Criminal Justice Act 1988: Designated countries & territories	34
Criminal law: Anti-Terrorism, Crime & Security Act 2001: Commencement	34, 36, 140
Criminal law: Bail: Electronic monitoring: Responsible officer: England & Wales	34
Criminal law: Copyright, etc. & Trade Marks (Offences & Enforcement) Act 2002: Commencement	32, 34, 241
Criminal law: Criminal Justice & Court Services Act 2000: Commencement	34, 35
Criminal law: Criminal Justice & Police Act 2001: Amendment	35
Criminal law: Criminal Justice & Police Act 2001: Commencement: England & Wales	35, 137
Criminal law: Criminal Justice & Public Order Act 1994: Commencement	34
Criminal law: Criminal Justice (International Co-operation) Act 1990: Overseas forfeiture orders: Enforcement	35, 36
Criminal law: Criminal Justice Act 1988: Offensive weapons	34, 36
Criminal law: Criminal Justice Act 1988: Offensive weapons: Scotland	312
Criminal law: Drug Trafficking Act 1994: Designated countries & territories: England & Wales	35
Criminal law: Liberty: Restriction of: Scotland	312
Criminal law: Motor salvage operators: Specified offences	35
Criminal law: Penalties for disorderly behaviour: Amount of penalty	35
Criminal law: Penalties for disorderly behaviour: Forms of penalty notice	35
Criminal law: Police & Criminal Evidence Act 1984: Department of Trade & Industry: Investigations	35
Criminal law: Police: Retention & disposal of items seized: England & Wales	35
Criminal law: Sexual Offences (Procedure & Evidence) (Scotland) Act 2002: Commencement: Scotland	312
Criminal law: Travel restriction order: Prescribed removal powers	34
Criminal law: Vehicles (Crime) Act 2001: Commencement	149
Criminal law: Vehicles (Crime) Act 2001: Commencement: England & Wales	212

Criminal law: Youth Justice & Criminal Evidence Act 1999: Commencement: England & Wales 35
Criminal law: Zimbabwe: Freezing of funds, financial assets or economic resources 34
Criminal legal aid: Fees: Scotland 320
Criminal legal aid: Fixed payments: Scotland 320
Criminal legal aid: Scotland 320
Criminal procedure: Acts: Explanatory notes: Scotland 305
Criminal procedure: Amendment: Acts: Scotland 304
Criminal procedure: Rules: Convention Rights (Compliance) (Scotland) Act 2001: Act of Adjournal: Scotland 317
Criminal proceedings: Legal aid: Costs: Northern Ireland 373
Criminal records: Enhanced certificates: Protection of vulnerable adults: Police Act 1997: England & Wales 138
Criminal records: Police Act 1997 137
Criminal records: Police Act 1997: Scotland 324
Criminal records: Registration: Police Act 1997: Scotland 324
Criminal records: Vulnerable adults: Protection: Police Act 1997: Scotland 324
Crops, food & feedingstuffs: Pesticides: Maximum residue levels: England & Wales 8, 10, 134
Crops, food & feedingstuffs: Pesticides: Maximum residue levels: Scotland 308, 323
Crops, food & feedingstuffs: Pesticides: Maximum residue levels: Northern Ireland 360, 376
Cross-border public authorities: Scotland 30
Crown Court: Rules 233
Crown Court: Special measures directions: Cross-examination: Directions prohibiting 233
Crown Office: Forms: Proclamations: Rules 27
Croydon & Surrey Downs Community: National Health Service Trust 108
Croydon: Health Authority 108
Croydon: National Health Service Primary Care Trust 108
Croydon Tramlink Class CR4000 vehicles: Accessibility: Exemptions 41, 242
Cruelty: Prevention: Animals: Protection of: Anaesthetics: England 14
Cruelty: Prevention: Farmed animals: Welfare: England 14
Cruelty: Prevention: Farmed animals: Welfare: Scotland 310
Crustaceans: Specification: Wales 220
Cumbria & Lancashire: Health Authority 108
Currency: European single: Taxes 234
Curriculum: National: Key stage 4: Exceptions: England 46
Customer consultation panels: Water: Scotland 348
Customs & excise: Beer & excise warehousing 36
Customs & excise: Biodiesel & bioblend 36
Customs & excise: Dual use items: Export control 36
Customs & excise: Equipment: Sale, supply, export & shipment: Zimbabwe 38
Customs & excise: Equipment: Supply & sale: Penalties & licences: Federal Republic of Yugoslavia 37
Customs & excise: Excise duties: Personal reliefs 36
Customs & excise: Excise goods, beer & tobacco products 37
Customs & excise: Excise goods: Accompanying documents 36
Customs & excise: Export control: Goods 37
Customs & excise: Export control: Goods: Federal Republic of Yugoslavia 37
Customs & excise: Finance Act 2002: Section 5 (6): Appointed date 37
Customs & excise: Finance Act 2002: Section 6: Appointed day 37
Customs & excise: Free zone: Port of Tilbury: Designation 38
Customs & excise: Gaming duty 37
Customs & excise: Hydrocarbon oil: Controlled oil: Registered dealers 37
Customs & excise: Hydrocarbon oil: Industrial reliefs 37
Customs & excise: Hydrocarbon oil: Marking 37
Customs & excise: Lottery duty 37
Customs & excise: Statistics of trade 232

D

Dairy produce: Quotas 65
Dairy produce: Quotas: Northern Ireland 367
Dairy produce: Quotas: Scotland 314, 315
Dairy produce: Quotas: Wales 68
Damages: Bereavement: Variation of sum: England & Wales 38
Damages: Bereavement: Variation of sum: Northern Ireland 38
Damages: Personal injury: Scotland 312
Dance & drama: Grants: Education: England 46
Dangerous drugs: Misuse of drugs: Northern Ireland 362
Dangerous goods: Air navigation 23

Dangerous goods: Carriage: Northern Ireland 370
Dangerous substances & preparations: Safety 30
Dangerous substances: Explosive atmospheres 72
Darlington: National Health Service Trust. 109
Dart Harbour & Navigation: Constitution: England 71
Darwen: Blackburn with Darwen (Borough): Election years changes 89
Data protection: Information tribunal: Enforcement appeals 38, 70
Data protection: Sensitive personal data: Processing: Elected representatives 38
Day care: Child minding: Wales 21, 223
Death: Birth & death entries: Registers: Correction: De-regulation 39
Deaths, marriages & births, etc.: Registration: Fees: England & Wales 145
Deaths, marriages & births, etc.: Registration: Fees: Northern Ireland 379
Deaths, marriages & births, etc.: Registration: Fees: Scotland 321, 330
Deaths, marriages & births, etc.: Registration: Service departments registers 145
Debt arrangement & attachment: Act of Sederunt: Scotland 344
Debt arrangement & attachment: Acts: Explanatory notes: Scotland 305
Debt arrangement & attachment: Acts: Scotland 304
Debts: Commercial debts: Late payment: 32
Debts: Commercial debts: Late payment: Rate of interest 32
Debts: Commercial debts: Late payment: Rate of interest: Scotland 311
Debts: Commercial debts: Late payment: Scotland 311
Debts: Commercial debts: Late Payment of Commercial Debts (Interest) Act 1998: Commencement 32
Debts: Commercial debts: Late Payment of Commercial Debts (Interest) Act 1998: Commencement: Scotland 311
Deceased persons: Insolvent estates: Administration of 85
Defence: Armed Forces Act 2001: Commencement 38
Defence: Army, Air Force & Naval Discipline Acts: Continuation 38
Defence: Courts-martial: Army 38
Defence: Courts-martial: Royal Air Force 38
Defence: Courts-martial: Royal Navy 38
Defence: Protection of Military Remains Act 1986: Vessels & controlled sites: Designation 38
Defence: Royal Marines: Terms of service 39
Dental charges: National Health Service: England 114, 115
Dental charges: Northern Ireland 369
Dental services & dental charges: General: National Health Service: Scotland 322
Dental services: General: National Health Service: England 114
Dental services: General: National Health Service: Scotland 322
Dental services: General: National Health Service: Wales 126, 127
Dental services: General: Northern Ireland 369
Dentists Act 1984: Dental auxiliaries 39
Dentists: Dental auxiliaries 39
Dentists: General Dental Council: Constitution 39
Dentists: General Dental Council: Election of members 39
Dentists: General Dental Council: President 39
Department of Trade & Industry: Investigations: Police & Criminal Evidence Act 1984 35
Derby (Central): National Health Service Trust 107
Derby Tertiary College, Wilmorton: Dissolution 43
Derbyshire (North): Community Health Care Service (North Derbyshire): National Health Service Trust 121
Derbyshire (Southern) Mental Health . National Health Service Trust 121
Derbyshire, North East: Coalfields: Education Action Zone: Extension 44, 49
Derbyshire: North Derbyshire Tertiary College: Designated staff 49
Derbyshire: North Derbyshire Tertiary College: Dissolution 49
Derbyshire: North Derbyshire: Community Health Care Service: National Health Service Trust 108
Derbyshire: North Derbyshire: Health Authority 116
Deregulation: Bingo & other gaming 70
Deregulation: Birth & death entries: Registers: Correction 39
Deregulation: Carer's allowance: Northern Ireland 362
Deregulation: Housing: Disposal: Local authorities: England & Wales 39
Deregulation: Local authorities: Disposal of dwelling houses: England & Wales 39
Deregulation: Restaurants: Licensing hours 39
Derelict land: Clearance Area: Combe Down Stone Mines, Bath 39
Derwentside: National Health Service Trust 109
Designs: Fees: European Communities 62
Detention: Designated places: Police (Northern Ireland) Act 2000: Northern Ireland 377
Development: International Development Act 2002: Commencement 86
Development: Procedure: Town & country planning: England 240
Devolution, Scotland: Scotland Act 1998: Agency arrangements: Specification 30, 40
Devolution, Scotland: Scotland Act 1998: Modifications: Schedule 5 . . . . 30, 40

Devolution, Scotland: Scotland Act 1998: Scottish Ministers: Transfer of functions 30, 40
Devolution, Scotland: Scottish administration: Offices 30, 40
Devolution, Scotland: Water Industry (Scotland) Act 2002: National security 30, 40, 247
Devolution, Wales: National Assembly: Representation of the people 29, 40, 146
Devolution: Housing (Scotland) Act 2001: Housing support services information 29, 39, 79
Devolution: Scotland Act 1998: Cross-border public authorities 30
Devolution: Scottish Parliament: Elections etc. 30, 40
Devon County Council: Barnstaple downstream bridge: Confirmation: England 77
Devon: North & East Devon Partnership: National Health Service Trust. 116
Devon: North & East Devon: Health Authority 116
Devon: South & West Devon: Health Authority. 120
Dewsbury: National Health Service Trust. 113
Diarrhetic shellfish poisoning: Food protection: Orkney: Scotland 330
Dingle Granby Toxteth: Education Action Zone: Extension 43
Diocese of Bradford: Educational endowments 43
Diocese of Bristol: Educational endowments 43
Diocese of Derby: Educational endowments. 43
Diocese of Lichfield: Educational endowments 43
Diocese of London: Educational endowments 43
Diocese of Newcastle: Educational endowments 43
Diocese of York: Educational endowments 44
Diplomatic service: Consular fees 40
Directors' remuneration report. 29
Disability discrimination: Code of practice: Education: Appointed day 40
Disability discrimination: Code of practice: Goods, facilities, services & premises 40
Disability discrimination: Educational institutions: Designation. 41, 42
Disability discrimination: Educational institutions: Leasehold premises: Alteration. 41, 42
Disability discrimination: Schools: Prescribed periods: England 42
Disability discrimination: Services & premises. 41
Disability living allowance: Attendance allowance: Social security 226, 228
Disability living allowance: Attendance allowance: Social security: Northern Ireland 382
Disability living allowance: Social security: Northern Ireland 383
Disability strategies: Education: Scotland 312
Disability strategies: Pupils' educational records: Education: Acts: Scotland 304
Disability strategies: Pupils' educational records: Education: Commencement: Scotland. 312
Disabled facilities: Grants: Home repair: Assistance: Maximum amounts: Wales 79
Disabled persons: Disability discrimination: Code of practice: Education: Appointed day 40
Disabled persons: Disability discrimination: Code of practice: Goods, facilities, services & premises 40
Disabled persons: Disability discrimination: Educational institutions: Designation. 41, 42
Disabled persons: Disability discrimination: Educational institutions: Leasehold premises: Alteration 41, 42
Disabled persons: Disability discrimination: Schools: Prescribed periods: England. 42
Disabled persons: Discrimination: Services & premises 41
Disabled persons: Local authorities: Traffic orders: Exemption: Scotland 332, 333
Disabled persons: Motor vehicles: Badges: Scotland. 332
Disabled persons: Public service vehicles: Accessibility 41, 241
Disabled persons: Rail vehicles: C2C Class 357/0 vehicles: Accessibility: Exemptions 41, 241
Disabled persons: Rail vehicles: Cairngorm Funicular Railway: Accessibility: Exemptions 41, 241
Disabled persons: Rail vehicles: Croydon Tramlink Class CR4000 vehicles: Accessibility: Exemptions 41, 242
Disabled persons: Rail vehicles: East Hayling Light Railway vehicles: Accessibility: Exemptions 41, 242
Disabled persons: Rail vehicles: Isle of Wight Railway LCDR no. 2515 vehicle: Accessibility: Exemptions 41, 242
Disabled persons: Rail vehicles: Middleton Railway Drewry car: Accessibility: Exemptions 41, 242
Disabled persons: Rail vehicles: South Central Class 375/3 vehicles: Accessibility: Exemptions 41, 242
Disabled persons: Rail vehicles: South West Trains Class 458 vehicles: Accessibility: Exemptions. 41, 242
Disabled persons: Rail vehicles: Summerlee Tramcar No. 392: Accessibility: Exemptions 41, 242
Disabled persons: Rail vehicles: Virgin West Coast Class 390 Vehicles: Accessibility: Exemptions. 41, 242
Disabled persons: Special Educational Needs & Disability Tribunal: General provisions & disability claims procedure 42, 53
Disabled postgraduate students: Grants: Education: England & Wales. 51
Disabled postgraduate students: Grants: Education: Northern Ireland 362
Disciplinary & grievance procedures: Code of practice: Appointed day: Northern Ireland. 372
Discrimination: Disability: Code of practice: Education: Appointed day 40
Discrimination: Disability: Code of practice: Goods, facilities, services & premises. 40
Discrimination: Disabled persons: Services & premises 41
Disease control & animal movements: Interim measures: Animal health: Scotland. 309
Disease control: Animal health: England 13
Disease control: Animal health: Wales 15
Disease control: Interim measures: Animal health: England 12, 13
Disease control: Interim measures: Animal health: Scotland 309

Disease control: Interim measures: Animal health: Wales 15
Diseases: Fish: Control: England & Wales 147, 219
Diseases: Fish: Control: Northern Ireland 362
Diseases: Prescribed: Industrial injuries: Social security 229
Disorderly behaviour: Penalties: Amount of penalty 35
Disorderly behaviour: Penalties: Forms of penalty notice 35
Disqualification orders: Companies 28
Diving safety: Merchant shipping 103
Divorces, births, deaths & marriages: Registration of: Fees: Scotland 321, 330
Docklands Light Railway: Silvertown & London City Airport extension 243
Doctors: Medical Act 1983: Amendment 73
Dogs, cats & other mammals: Rabies: Importation: Wales 14
Dogs: Fouling of land: Fixed penalties: England 59
Dogs: Guide & hearing: Carrying of: Taxi drivers' licences: Scotland 321
Domestic energy efficiency grants: Northern Ireland 364
Domestic water & sewerage: Charges: Reduction: Scotland 348
Domiciliary care agencies: England 222
Doncaster Health Authority 109
Doncaster Healthcare: National Health Service Trust 109
Dorset: East Dorset (District): Electoral changes 92
Dorset: East Dorset (District): Permitted & special parking area 210
Dorset: North Dorset (District): Electoral changes 93
Dorset: North Dorset (District): Permitted & special parking area 210
Dorset: West Dorset (District): Electoral changes 93
Dorset: West Dorset (District): Permitted & special parking area 210
Dover: HM Young Offender Institution Dover: Closure of prisons 140
Downham & Bellingham: Education Action Zone: Extension 44
Drama: Dance: Grants: Education: England 46
Driving instruction: Motor cars 147
Driving licences: Community driving licence: Northern Ireland 364, 380
Driving licences: Exchangeable licences 147
Driving licences: External law: Designation 147
Driving licences: Motor vehicles 147
Driving licences: Motor vehicles: Northern Ireland 380
Driving licences: Motor vehicles: Test fees: Northern Ireland 380
Drug Trafficking Act 1994: Designated countries & territories: England & Wales 35
Drugs & appliances: Charges: National Health Service 114
Drugs & appliances: Charges: National Health Service: Scotland 322
Drugs & appliances: Charges: Northern Ireland 369
Drugs, medicines, aids for handicapped & charities: Value added tax 246
Drugs: Misuse: Northern Ireland 362
Dual use items: Export control 36
Dudley Partnership for Achievement: Education Action Zone: Extension 44
Dunbartonshire (West) Council: Argyll & Bute Council: Boundaries: Ardoch Seage Works: Scotland 321
Dundrod Circuit: Admission charges: Northern Ireland 380
Dunham Bridge: Tolls: Revision of 77
Durham & Chester-le-Street: National Health Service Trust 109
Durham & Darlington Acute Hospitals: National Health Service Trust 108
Durham Dales: National Health Service Trust 109
Durham, County & Tees Valley: Health Authority 108
Dwellings & part residential subjects: Exempt: Council tax: Scotland 311
Dwellings: Exempt: Council tax: Scotland 311

E

Ealing, Hammersmith & Hounslow: Health Authority 109
Earnings factors: Revaluation: Social security 229
Earnings: Computation: Child care charges: Social security: Benefits 227
Earnings: Computation: Social security: Benefits 226
Earnings: Computation: Social security: Benefits: Northern Ireland 231
Earnings: Low threshold: Pensions: Social security: Northern Ireland 385
Easington & Seaham: Education Action Zone: Extension 44
Easington: National Health Service Trust 109
East Berkshire: National Health Service Trust 109
East Cambridgeshire (District): Electoral changes 92

Entry	Page
East Dorset (District): Electoral changes	92
East Dorset (District): Permitted & special parking area	210
East Elmbridge & Mid Surrey: National Health Service Primary Care Trust	109
East Gloucestershire: National Health Service Trust	110
East Hayling Light Railway vehicles: Accessibility: Exemptions	41, 242
East Kent Coastal: National Health Service Primary Care Trust	110
East Kent: Health Authority	110
East Lancashire Hospitals: National Health Service Trust	110
East Lancashire: Heywood extension: Light railways	243
East Lancashire: Health Authority	110
East Manchester: Education Action Zone: Extension	44
East Riding (District): Electoral changes	92
East Riding of Yorkshire: Parishes: Local government	94
East Staffordshire: National Health Service Primary Care Trust	110
East Staffordshire: Parishes: Local government	94
East Surrey: National Health Service Primary Care Trust	110
East Yorkshire College of Further Education, Bridlington : Dissolution	44
Eastbourne & County: National Health Service Trust	109
Eastbourne Downs: National Health Service Primary Care Trust	109
Eastern Birmingham: National Health Service Primary Care Trust	109
Eastern Cheshire: National Health Service Primary Care Trust	109
Eastleigh & Test Valley South: National Health Service Trust	110
Ecclesiastical law: Judges, legal officers & others: Fees	42
Ecclesiastical law: Legal Officers: Fees: Annual: England	42
Ecclesiastical law: Parochial fees	42
Econet Satellite Services Limited: Public telecommunication systems	237
Eden District (Cumbria): Permitted & special parking area	210
Edinburgh: Road traffic: Parking area: Scotland	333
Education & Skills: Secretary of State: Ministers of the Crown	103
Education Act 2002: Commencement: England	44
Education Act 2002: Commencement: England & Wales	51
Education Act 2002: Commencement: Wales	53
Education Act 2002: Modification of provisions: England	44
Education Act 2002: Transitional provisions: England	44
Education Act 2002: Transitional provisions: Wales	53
Education Action Forum: Proceedings	44
Education Action Zone: Ashington: Extension	42
Education Action Zone: Bedford: Action for Learning Partnership, Bedford: Extension	42
Education Action Zone: Bolton: Extension	43
Education Action Zone: Breaking the Cycle Bridgewater: Extension	43
Education Action Zone: Camborne, Pool & Redruth: Extension	43
Education Action Zone: Challenge for Corby: Extension	43
Education Action Zone: Clacton & Harwich: Extension	43
Education Action Zone: Community Learning Partnership Barrow-in-Furness: Extension	43
Education Action Zone: Coventry Millennium: Extension	43
Education Action Zone: Dingle Granby Toxteth: Extension	43
Education Action Zone: Downham & Bellingham: Extension	44
Education Action Zone: Dudley Partnership for Achievement: Extension	44
Education Action Zone: Easington & Seaham: Extension	44
Education Action Zone: East Manchester: Extension	44
Education Action Zone: Epicentre LEAP Ellesmere Port Cheshire: Extension	48
Education Action Zone: Gloucester Education Achievement: Extension	48
Education Action Zone: Greenwich-Time to Succeed: Extension	48
Education Action Zone: Hamilton Oxford schools: Partnership: Extension	49
Education Action Zone: Hastings & St Leonards: Extension	49
Education Action Zone: Heart of Slough: Extension	49
Education Action Zone: Learning Together East Cleveland: Extension	49
Education Action Zone: Leigh Park: Extension	49
Education Action Zone: London Borough of Hackney: Extension	48
Education Action Zone: New Horizons Kent-Somerset Virtual : Extension	49
Education Action Zone: North East Derbyshire coalfields: Extension	49
Education Action Zone: North Gillingham: Extension	49
Education Action Zone: Peterlee: Extension	49
Education Action Zone: Rainbow, Stoke on Trent: Extension	50
Education Action Zone: South Bradford Community Learning Partnership: Extension	50
Education Action Zone: Southend: Extension	50
Education Action Zone: Speke Garston Excellent: Extension	50

Education Action Zone: Sunderland Building Our Future: Extension 50
Education Action Zone: Telford & Wrekin: Extension 50
Education Action Zone: Wakefield Community Learning Partnership: Extension 50
Education Action Zone: Wednesbury Extension 50
Education Action Zone: Widening Horizons - North Islington: Extension 50
Education Action Zone: Withernsea & S. Holderness Rural Achievement: Extension. 50
Education Action Zone: Wolverhampton: Extension 51
Education Action Zone: Wythenshawe: Extension 51
Education development plans: Wales 54
Education: Special Educational Needs & Disability Tribunal: General provisions & disability claims procedure 42, 53
Education: Aberdare College: Dissolution 53
Education: Acts: Explanatory notes 4
Education: Admission arrangements: Co-ordination of: Primary schools: England 45
Education: Admission arrangements: Co-ordination of: Secondary schools: England 45
Education: Admission arrangements: Determination of: England 45
Education: Admission arrangements: Objection to: England 47
Education: Admission arrangements: Variation of: England 48
Education: Admission forums: England 44
Education: Admissions appeals arrangements: England 44
Education: Advisory Council (Scottish Qualifications Authority): Establishment: Scotland 312
Education: Aided places: St Mary's Music School: Scotland 313
Education: Assembly Learning Grant scheme: Wales 53
Education: Assessment arrangements: English, Welsh, Mathematics & Science: Wales 54
Education: Assisted places: England. 45
Education: Assisted places: Incidental expenses: England 45
Education: Assisted places: Incidental expenses: Wales 54
Education: Assisted places: Scotland 312
Education: Assisted places: Wales 54
Education: Birmingham College of Food, Tourism & Creative Studies: Higher education sector: Transfer to 51
Education: Boarding schools & colleges: Powers & fees: Inspection: Wales 22, 223
Education: Brinsbury College: Dissolution 43
Education: Broomfield Agricultural College: Dissolution 43
Education: Budget statements: England. 45
Education: Budget statements: Wales. 54
Education: Capital grants: Wales 54
Education: Chief Inspector of Education & training: Wales 54
Education: Derby Tertiary College, Wilmorton: Dissolution 43
Education: Development plans: England. 45
Education: Diocese of Bradford: Educational endowments 43
Education: Diocese of Bristol: Educational endowments. 43
Education: Diocese of Derby: Educational endowments 43
Education: Diocese of Lichfield: Educational endowments 43
Education: Diocese of London: Educational endowments 43
Education: Diocese of Newcastle: Educational endowments 43
Education: Diocese of York: Educational endowments. 44
Education: Disability discrimination: Educational institutions: Designation 41, 42
Education: Disability discrimination: Educational institutions: Leasehold premises: Alteration 41, 42
Education: Disability strategies: Pupils' educational records: Commencement: Scotland. 312
Education: Disability strategies: Scotland 312
Education: Disabled postgraduate students: Grants: Northern Ireland 362
Education: East Yorkshire College of Further Education, Bridlington: Dissolution 44
Education: Further: Teachers' qualifications: Wales 55
Education: General Teaching Council for Wales 55
Education: General Teaching Council for Wales: Fees 55
Education: Government of Further Education Corporations. 48
Education: Governors: Annual reports: England 46
Education: Grants: Dance & drama: England 46
Education: Grants: Disabled postgraduate students: England & Wales. 51
Education: Grants: Music, ballet, & choir schools 46
Education: Grants: Voluntary aided schools: England 46
Education: Individual pupils: Information: England 46
Education: Individual pupils' achievements: Information: Wales 54
Education: Inspectors: Education & training: Wales 54
Education: Langley Junior School: School session times: Change 49
Education: Learning & Skills Act 2000: Commencement: Savings & transitional provisions 52, 58
Education: Listed bodies: England 46
Education: Listed bodies: Scotland 312

Education: Listed bodies: Wales 54
Education: Local education authorities: Budget: Schools & individual schools budgets: England 49
Education: Local education authorities: Functions: Contracting out 31
Education: Local education authorities: Post-compulsory education awards: Wales 55
Education: London Residuary Body: Property transfer 46
Education: Longley Park Sixth Form College: Government 49
Education: Longley Park Sixth Form College: Incorporation 49
Education: Mackworth College: Dissolution 49
Education: Maintained schools: Financing: England 48
Education: Maintained schools: Pupil exclusions & appeals: England 47
Education: Maintenance allowance: Pilot areas: England 46
Education: Mandatory awards: England 51
Education: Mandatory awards: England & Wales 51
Education: National curriculum: Key stage 4: Exceptions: England 46
Education: NHS Education for Scotland: Scottish Council for Postgraduate Medical & Dental Education: Transfer of staff: Scotland . . . 323
Education: North Derbyshire Tertiary College: Designated staff 49
Education: North Derbyshire Tertiary College: Dissolution 49
Education: Nursery education & early years development: England 47
Education: Outturn statements: England 47
Education: Pupil exclusions & appeals: Pupil referral units: England 47
Education: Pupil referral units: Permanent exclusion: Appeals: England 47
Education: Pupils: Information: England 47
Education: Pupils: Permanently excluded: Amount to follow: Wales 53
Education: Pupils' educational records: Disability strategies: Acts: Explanatory notes: Scotland 305
Education: Pupils' educational records: Disability strategies: Acts: Scotland 304
Education: QCA levy 51, 53
Education: Recognised bodies: Wales 54
Education: School budget shares: Prescribed purposes: England 52
Education: School companies: England 50
Education: School companies: Private finance initiative companies: England 50
Education: School day & school year: Wales 55
Education: School day & year: Wales 54
Education: School Education (Amendment) (Scotland) Act 2002: Commencement: Scotland 313
Education: School education: Amendment: Acts: Scotland 304, 305
Education: School information: Wales 55
Education: School inspectors: England 46
Education: School organisation proposals: National Council for Education & Training for Wales 56
Education: School performance: Information: England 47
Education: School performance: Targets: England 47
Education: School teacher appraisal: Wales 56
Education: School teachers: Induction arrangements: England 46
Education: School teachers: Remuneration: England & Wales 52
Education: School teachers' pay & conditions: England & Wales 51, 52
Education: School: Children under school age: Prescribed children: Scotland 313
Education: Schools forums: England 50
Education: Schools: Chief Inspector: England 45
Education: Schools: Government: Terms of reference: Wales 55
Education: Schools: Governors: Annual reports: Wales 55
Education: Schools: Information: England 47
Education: Schools: Inspector: England 46
Education: Schools: Maintained: Financing of: Wales 55
Education: Schools: Middle schools: England 46
Education: Scottish Qualifications Authority Act 2002: Commencement: Scotland 313
Education: Scottish Qualifications Authority: Acts: Scotland 305
Education: Scottish Qualifications Authority: Acts: Explanatory notes: Scotland 306
Education: Special Educational Needs & Disability Act 2001: Commencement: England & Wales 42, 52
Education: Special Educational Needs & Disability Act 2001: Commencement: Wales 56
Education: Special Educational Needs Tribunal: Amendment: England & Wales 53
Education: Special educational needs: Approval of independent schools: England 47
Education: Special educational needs: City colleges: England 48
Education: Special educational needs: Code of practice: Appointed day: Wales 56
Education: Special educational needs: Provision of information: Local education authorities: Wales 56
Education: Special educational needs: Wales 55
Education: Special schools: Non-maintained: England 46
Education: Standards fund: England 48
Education: Standards grants: Wales 55
Education: Standards in Scotland's Schools etc. Act 2000: Commencement: Scotland 313

Education: Student allowances: Nursing & midwifery: Scotland	313
Education: Student awards: Northern Ireland	362
Education: Student loans: England & Wales	52
Education: Student loans: Northern Ireland	362
Education: Student loans: Repayment	42
Education: Student loans: Repayment: England & Wales	52
Education: Student loans: Scotland	312
Education: Student loans: Teachers: Repayments etc.: England & Wales	52
Education: Student support: England & Wales	52
Education: Student support: Northern Ireland	362
Education: Teacher qualifications & health standards: Wales	55
Education: Teacher Training Agency: Additional functions	53
Education: Teacher Training Agency: Additional functions: England	50
Education: Teacher training: Bursaries: England	45, 48
Education: Teacher training: Funding: Designation: England	45
Education: Teachers: Pensions: England & Wales	53
Education: Teachers: Qualifications & health standards: England	48
Education: Teachers: Redundancy & premature retirement: Compensation: Northern Ireland	362
Education: Teeside Tertiary College: Dissolution	50
Education: Voluntary aided schools: Liabilities & funding: Regulatory reform: England	50, 145
Educational institutions: Designation: Disability discrimination	41, 42
Educational institutions: Leasehold premises: Alteration: Disability discrimination	41, 42
Egypt: Potatoes: Originating in: England	136
Egypt: Potatoes: Originating in: Wales	136
Elected mayors: Mayor's assistants: Local authorities: England	94
Elected representatives: Data protection: Sensitive personal data: Processing	38
Elections, Councils: Local authorities: England	95
Elections: Electoral fraud: Northern Ireland: Acts	2
Elections: Electoral fraud: Northern Ireland: Acts: Explanatory notes	4
Elections: Local: Northern Ireland	129
Elections: Mayoral elections: Local authorities: England & Wales	96
Elections: Northern Ireland Assembly elections: Amendment	129
Elections: Policy development grants scheme	146
Elections: Scottish local government: Acts: Scotland	304, 305
Elections: Sex Discrimination: Election candidates: Acts	4
Elections: Sex Discrimination: Election candidates: Acts: Explanatory notes	5
Electoral changes: Adur (District)	91
Electoral changes: Arun (District)	91
Electoral changes: Aylesbury Vale (District)	91
Electoral changes: Babergh (District)	91
Electoral changes: Blaby (District)	91
Electoral changes: Blackburn with Darwen (Borough)	89
Electoral changes: Blackpool (Borough)	89
Electoral changes: Bournemouth (Borough)	89
Electoral changes: Bracknell Forest (Borough)	89
Electoral changes: Breckland (District)	92
Electoral changes: Bridgend: Wales	99
Electoral changes: Burnley (Borough)	89
Electoral changes: Cambridge (City)	91
Electoral changes: Caradon (District)	92
Electoral changes: Carrick (District)	92
Electoral changes: Charnwood (Borough)	89
Electoral changes: Chichester (District)	92
Electoral changes: Chiltern (District)	92
Electoral changes: Christchurch (Borough)	89
Electoral changes: County of Gwynedd: Wales	97
Electoral changes: County of Herefordshire (District)	91
Electoral changes: County of Monmouthshire: Wales	97
Electoral changes: Craven (District): Ribble Banks Parish Council	92
Electoral changes: Crawley (Borough)	89
Electoral changes: East Cambridgeshire (District)	92
Electoral changes: East Dorset (District)	92, 93
Electoral changes: East Riding (District)	92
Electoral changes: Epping Forest (District)	92
Electoral changes: Fenland (District)	92
Electoral changes: Forest of Dean (District)	92
Electoral changes: Great Yarmouth (Borough)	89

Electoral changes: Halton (Borough) . . . 89
Electoral changes: Harborough (District) . . . 92
Electoral changes: Hinckley & Bosworth (Borough) . . . 89
Electoral changes: Horsham (District) . . . 92
Electoral changes: Huntingdonshire (District) . . . 92
Electoral changes: Kerrier (District) . . . 92
Electoral changes: King's Lynn & West Norfolk (Borough) . . . 89
Electoral changes: Leicester (City) . . . 91
Electoral changes: Luton (Borough) . . . 89
Electoral changes: Malvern Hills (District) . . . 93
Electoral changes: Medway (Borough) . . . 89
Electoral changes: Melton (Borough) . . . 90
Electoral changes: Mid Sussex (District) . . . 93
Electoral changes: Milton Keynes (Borough) . . . 90
Electoral changes: Newport (County Borough): Wales . . . 97
Electoral changes: North Cornwall (District) . . . 93
Electoral changes: North West Leicestershire (District) . . . 93
Electoral changes: Norwich (City) . . . 91
Electoral changes: Oadby & Wigston (Borough) . . . 90
Electoral changes: Penwith (District) . . . 93
Electoral changes: Plymouth (City) . . . 91
Electoral changes: Poole (Borough) . . . 90
Electoral changes: Reading (Borough) . . . 90
Electoral changes: Redditch (Borough) . . . 90
Electoral changes: Restormel (Borough) . . . 90
Electoral changes: Slough (Borough) . . . 90
Electoral changes: South Bucks (District) . . . 93
Electoral changes: South Cambridgeshire (District) . . . 93
Electoral changes: South Norfolk (District) . . . 93
Electoral changes: South Oxfordshire (District) . . . 93
Electoral changes: South Ribble (Borough) . . . 90
Electoral changes: Telford & Wrekin (Borough) . . . 90
Electoral changes: Thurrock (Borough) . . . 90
Electoral changes: Torbay (Borough) . . . 90
Electoral changes: Vale of Glamorgan (County Borough): Wales . . . 97
Electoral changes: Warrington (Borough) . . . 90
Electoral changes: Waveney (District) . . . 93
Electoral changes: West Berkshire (District) . . . 93
Electoral changes: West Dorset (District) . . . 93
Electoral changes: West Oxfordshire (District) . . . 93
Electoral changes: Weymouth & Portland (Borough) . . . 90
Electoral changes: Windsor & Maidenhead (Royal Borough) . . . 95
Electoral changes: Wokingham (District) . . . 93
Electoral changes: Worcester (City) . . . 91
Electoral changes: Worthing (Borough) . . . 90
Electoral changes: Wychavon (District) . . . 93
Electoral changes: Wycombe (District) . . . 94
Electoral changes: Wyre Forest (District) . . . 94
Electoral Commission: Public awareness: Expenditure: Limit . . . 56
Electoral Fraud (Northern Ireland) Act 2002: Commencement . . . 146
Electoral fraud: Northern Ireland: Acts . . . 2
Electoral fraud: Northern Ireland: Acts: Explanatory notes . . . 4
Electricity & gas: Turnover: Determination for penalties . . . 56, 70
Electricity Act 1989: Offshore generating stations: Consent requirement: Scotland . . . 313
Electricity lands & generators: Rateable values: Scotland . . . 330
Electricity: Applications for consent: Fees: Northern Ireland . . . 362
Electricity: Connection charges . . . 56
Electricity: Fossil fuel levy: Scotland . . . 313
Electricity: Generation licence requirement: Exemption: England & Wales . . . 57
Electricity: Measuring instruments: EC requirements: Electrical energy meters . . . 57
Electricity: Non-fossil fuel sources: Locational flexibility: Scotland . . . 313
Electricity: Non-fossil fuel sources: Saving arrangements: Scotland . . . 313
Electricity: Pattern or construction: Installation & certification: Approval . . . 56
Electricity: Renewables: Obligations: England & Wales . . . 57
Electricity: Renewables: Obligations: Scotland . . . 313
Electricity: Standards of performance . . . 56
Electronic Commerce Directive: Financial services & markets . . . 57, 63

Electronic commerce: EC directive	57
Electronic communications: Child benefits: Social security	228
Electronic communications: Electronic Commerce EC directive	57, 63
Electronic communications: Electronic signatures	57
Electronic communications: Financial Services & Markets Act 2000: Financial promotion: Electronic Commerce Directive	57, 64
Electronic communications: Financial Services & Markets Act 2000: Regulated activities	57, 64
Electronic communications: Office of Communications Act 2002: Commencement	57
Electronic communications: Office of Communications: Membership	58
Electronic communications: Statutory payment schemes	58, 230
Electronic money: Miscellaneous amendments	18, 63
Electronic signatures	57
Ellesmere Port & Neston: National Health Service Primary Care Trust	110
Ellesmere Port: Epicentre LEAP: Education Action Zone: Extension	48
Emblems & flags: Police: Northern Ireland	377
Emission ceilings: National	59
Employee share schemes: Acts	2
Employees: Fixed-term: Less favourable treatment: Prevention	238
Employees: Fixed-term: Less favourable treatment: Prevention: Northern Ireland	363
Employment & training: Industrial training levy: Construction Board	58
Employment & training: Industrial training levy: Engineering Construction Board	58
Employment & training: Learning & Skills Act 2000: Commencement: Savings & transitional provisions	52, 58
Employment Act 2002: Commencement	224, 238
Employment programmes: Social security	226
Employment programmes: Social security: Northern Ireland	371, 378, 383
Employment relations: 1999 Order: Commencement: Northern Ireland	363
Employment rights: Increase of limits	238
Employment rights: Increase of limits: Northern Ireland	363
Employment tribunals: Enforcement of orders: Other jurisdictions: Scotland	58
Employment: 2002 Order: Commencement: Northern Ireland	362
Employment: Acts	2
Employment: Acts: Explanatory notes	4
Employment: Fair employment: Monitoring: Northern Ireland	365
Employment: Fair employment: Public authorities: Specification: Northern Ireland	365
Employment: Fixed-term employees: Less favourable treatment: Prevention: Northern Ireland	363
Employment: Maternity & parental leave: Northern Ireland	363
Employment: Northern Ireland	128
Employment: Part-time workers: Rights: Northern Ireland	363
Employment: Paternity & adoption leave: Northern Ireland	363
Employment: Statutory paternity pay & adoption pay: Administration: Northern Ireland	363
Employment: Statutory paternity pay & adoption pay: General: Northern Ireland	363
Employment: Statutory paternity pay & adoption pay: Health & personal social services employees: Northern Ireland	363
Employment: Statutory paternity pay & adoption pay: Persons abroad & mariners: Northern Ireland	364
Employment: Statutory paternity pay & adoption pay: Weekly rates: Northern Ireland	364
Employment: Terms & conditions: Employment rights: Increase of limits	238
Employment: Terms & conditions: Flexible working: Eligibility, complaints & remedies	238
Employment: Terms & conditions: Flexible working: Procedure requirements	238
Employment: Terms & conditions: Maternity & parental leave	238
Employment: Terms & conditions: Paternity & adoption: Leave	238
Employment: Terms & conditions: Redundancy payments: Local government: Continuity of employment	238
Employment: Terms & conditions: Social security: Benefits: Up-rating	227, 239
Employment: Terms & conditions: Statutory maternity pay	230, 239
Employment: Terms & conditions: Statutory paternity pay: Statutory adoption pay: Administration	230, 239
Employment: Terms & conditions: Statutory paternity pay: Statutory adoption pay: General	239
Employment: Terms & conditions: Statutory paternity pay: Statutory adoption pay: National Health Service employees	230
Employment: Terms & conditions: Statutory paternity pay: Statutory adoption pay: Persons abroad & mariners	239
Employment: Terms & conditions: Statutory paternity pay: Statutory adoption pay: Weekly rates	239
Employment: Terms & conditions: Trade unions: Recognition & derecognition ballots: Qualified persons	238
Employment: Terms & conditions: Working time	239
Employment: Terms & conditions: Working time: Northern Ireland	364
Energy conservation: Domestic energy efficiency grants: Northern Ireland	364
Energy conservation: Home energy efficiency scheme	58
Energy conservation: Warm Homes & Energy Conservation Act 2000: Commencement: Wales	58
Energy: Atomic Energy Authority: Special Constables	17, 136
Energy: Home energy efficiency scheme	58
Energy: Renewables: Electricity: Obligations: Scotland	313
Energy-saving plant & machinery: Capital allowances	81
Enfield: Barnet, Enfield & Haringey: Health Authority	104

Engineering Construction Board: Industrial training levy	58
English: Assessment arrangements: Wales	54
Enterprise: Acts	2
Enterprise: Acts: Explanatory notes	4
Environment Agency: Advisory Committee for Wales: Abolition	60
Environment: Northern Ireland	128
Environmental impact assessment: Forestry: Northern Ireland	368
Environmental impact assessment: Scotland	319, 332, 347
Environmental impact assessment: Uncultivated land & semi-natural areas: Scotland	307
Environmental impact assessment: Uncultivated land & semi-natural areas: Wales	10
Environmental protection: Advisory Committee for Wales (Environment Agency) : Abolition	60
Environmental protection: Agricultural & forestry tractors: Emission of gaseous & particulate pollutants	58
Environmental protection: Air quality: England	59
Environmental protection: Air quality: Limit values: England	59
Environmental protection: Air quality: Limit values: Northern Ireland	364
Environmental protection: Air quality: Limit values: Scotland	313
Environmental protection: Air quality: Limit values: Wales	60
Environmental protection: Air quality: Scotland	313
Environmental protection: Air quality: Wales	60
Environmental protection: Batteries & accumulators: Containing dangerous substances: Northern Ireland	364
Environmental protection: Combustion plants: Large: Scotland	314
Environmental protection: Contaminated land & waste: Northern Ireland	364
Environmental protection: Dogs: Fouling of land: Fixed penalties: England	59
Environmental protection: Financial assistance	59
Environmental protection: Financial assistance: England & Wales	59
Environmental protection: Genetically modified organisms: Deliberate release	58
Environmental protection: Genetically modified organisms: Deliberate release: Scotland	314
Environmental protection: Genetically modified organisms: Deliberate release: Wales	60
Environmental protection: Landfill: England & Wales	60
Environmental protection: Large combustion plants	60
Environmental protection: Lead shot: Use: Restriction: England	59
Environmental protection: Lead shot: Use: Restriction: Wales	60
Environmental protection: Litter: Fixed penalty: England	59
Environmental protection: Machinery: Non-road mobile: Gaseous & particulate pollutants: Emission	59
Environmental protection: National emission ceilings	59
Environmental protection: Offshore chemicals	59
Environmental protection: Offshore installations: Emergency pollution control	59
Environmental protection: Ozone-depleting substances: Controls	58
Environmental protection: Packaging waste: Producer responsibility & obligations: England	59
Environmental protection: Packaging waste: Producer responsibility & obligations: Scotland	314
Environmental protection: Packaging waste: Producer responsibility & obligations: Wales	61
Environmental protection: Pollution: Prevention & control: England & Wales	60
Environmental protection: Pollution: Prevention & control: Large combustion plants	60
Environmental protection: Pollution: Prevention & control: Large combustion plants: National emission ceilings: Scotland	314
Environmental protection: Waste incineration: England & Wales	60
Environmental protection: Waste management: Licensing: England	59
Environmental protection: Waste management: Licensing: Wales	61
Environmental protection: Waste recycling payments: England	59
Environmental protection: Waste: Controlled: Duty of care: Northern Ireland	364
Environmental protection: Waste: Controlled: Northern Ireland	364
Environmental purposes: Financial assistance: Scotland	314
Environmentally hazardous substances: Health & safety	72
Epicentre LEAP Ellesmere Port Cheshire: Education Action Zone: Extension	48
Epping Forest (District): Electoral changes	92
Epping Forest (District): Permitted & special parking area	211
Equipment: Sale, supply, export & shipment: Zimbabwe	38
Essex Rivers Healthcare: National Health Service Trusts	110
Essex: North Essex: Health Authority	117
Essex: South Essex: Health Authority	121
Essex: South Essex: Mental Health & Community Care: National Health Service Trust	121
Estates: Insolvent: Deceased persons: Administration of	85
Ethical Standards in Public Life etc. (Scotland) Act 2000: Stipulated time limits: Scotland	321
Ethics committee: Adults with incapacity: Scotland	306
Eurocall Ltd: Telecommunications: Public systems	237
Europe: Cinema: Co-production	22, 23
Europe: Economic interest grouping: Fees	63
European Communities: Amendment: Acts	2

European Communities: Amendment: Acts: Explanatory notes 4
European Communities: Animal by-products: Northern Ireland 360
European Communities: Animals & animal products: Import & export: Northern Ireland 360, 364
European Communities: Architects: Qualifications: EC recognition 17
European Communities: Batteries & accumulators: Containing dangerous substances: Northern Ireland 364
European Communities: Competition law: Enforcement 61
European Communities: Designation 61
European Communities: Designs: Fees 62
European Communities: Driving licences: Community driving licence: Northern Ireland 364, 380
European Communities: Finance: Explanatory notes 4
European Communities: Goods: Sale & supply: Consumers 31
European Communities: Products of animal origin: Third country imports: Northern Ireland 361, 364
European Communities: Professional qualifications: Recognition 141
European Communities: Professional qualifications: Recognition: Second general system 141
European Communities: Qualifications & experience: Recognition: Third general system 141
European Communities: Rights against insurers: Road traffic 147
European Communities: Transmissable spongiform encephalopathy: Northern Ireland 361, 365
European Communities: Treaties: Definition: Macedonia (Former Yugoslav Republic) 61
European Communities: Treaties: Definition: South Africa 61
European Convention on Cinematographic Co-production 22, 23
European Convention on Extradition 62
European Convention on Extradition: Armenia & Georgia 61
European Convention on Extradition: Fiscal offences 61
European economic interest grouping: Fees 63
European single currency: Taxes 234
European specialist medical qualifications 100
European Union: Extradition 61
Evidence: Northern Ireland 365
Evidence: Paternity: Blood tests: Northern Ireland 365
Exchange gains & losses: Bringing into account gains or losses 82
Exchange gains & losses: Transitional provisions & savings 82
Exchangeable licences: Driving licences 147
Excise duties: Personal reliefs 36
Excise duty: Immobilisation, removal & disposal of vehicles 148
Excise duty: Vehicle: Small islands: Designation 151
Excise goods, beer & tobacco products: Customs & excise 37
Excise goods: Accompanying documents 36
Excise warehousing: Beer 36
Excise: Duty: Rates: Fuel substitutes 37
Excluded pupils: Permanently excluded: Amount to follow: Wales 53
Explosive atmospheres: Dangerous substances 72
Explosives: Fireworks: Northern Ireland 365
Export control: Acts: Explanatory notes 4
Export control: Dual use items 36
Export control: Goods 37
Export control: Goods: Federal Republic of Yugoslavia 37
Extensification payment: Scotland 307
Extradition: European Convention 62
Extradition: European Convention: Armenia & Georgia 61
Extradition: European Convention: Fiscal offences 61
Extradition: European Union 61
Extradition: Magistrates' courts: Procedure 100
Extradition: Overseas territories 62
Extradition: Overseas territories: Hong Kong 62, 78
Extradition: Overseas territories: Hong Kong: Application 62, 78
Extradition: Terrorist bombings 62

F

Fair employment: Monitoring: Northern Ireland 365
Fair employment: Public authorities: Specification: Northern Ireland 365
Falmouth & Truro Port Health Authority 139
Family centres: Residential: England 20, 222
Family Health Services Appeal Authority: Procedure: Rules: England & Wales 125
Family Law Act (Northern Ireland) 2001: Commencement: Northern Ireland 365

Family law: Child support appeals: Jurisdiction of courts 62
Family law: Child support, pensions & social security: 2000 Act: Commencement: Northern Ireland 365
Family law: Child support: Appeals: Jurisdiction of Courts: Northern Ireland 365
Family law: Child support: Miscellaneous amendments 62
Family law: Child support: Northern Ireland 361, 365
Family law: Child support: Reciprocal arrangements: Northern Ireland 62
Family law: Child support: Temporary compensation payment scheme: Modification & amendment 62
Family law: Child support: Temporary compensation payment scheme: Modification & amendment: Northern Ireland 361, 365
Family law: Children & Family Court Advisory & Support Service: England & Wales 21
Family law: Social security & child support: Decisions & appeals: Miscellaneous amendments 62, 231, 236
Family law: Social security & child support: Decisions & appeals: Miscellaneous amendments: Northern Ireland . . . 361, 365, 371, 378, 382
Family law: Social security & child support: Miscellaneous amendments: Northern Ireland 361, 366, 382
Family proceedings: Children: Allocation of proceedings: Northern Ireland 366
Family proceedings: Fees: Northern Ireland 361, 366, 386
Family proceedings: Legal aid: Remuneration: England & Wales 88
Family proceedings: Northern Ireland 361, 366, 386
Family proceedings: Parentage: Declaration: Allocation of proceedings: Northern Ireland 366
Farmed animals: Welfare: England 14
Farmed animals: Welfare: Northern Ireland 387
Farmed animals: Welfare: Scotland 310
Farmed animals: Welfare: Wales 17
Farmed game bird meat: Hygiene & inspection: Wales 69
Farming: Fur farming: Compensation scheme: England 11
Farming: Fur farming: Prohibition: Acts: Explanatory notes: Scotland 305
Farming: Fur farming: Prohibition: Acts: Scotland 304
Fatal accidents: Damages: Bereavement: Variation of sum: England & Wales 38
Federal Republic of Yugoslavia: Equipment: Supply & sale: Penalties & licences 37
Feedingstuffs: Agriculture: Northern Ireland 359
Feedingstuffs: Amendment: England 8
Feedingstuffs: Amendment: Wales 10
Feedingstuffs: Food & animal: Products of animal origin: From China: Control: England 8, 9, 65
Feedingstuffs: Food & animal: Products of animal origin: From China: Control: Northern Ireland 367
Feedingstuffs: Food & animal: Products of animal origin: From China: Control: Scotland 307, 315
Feedingstuffs: Food & animal: Products of animal origin: From China: Control: Wales 10, 68
Feedingstuffs: Medicated 101
Feedingstuffs: Medicated: Northern Ireland 374
Feedingstuffs: Pesticides: Maximum residue levels: England & Wales 8, 10, 134
Feedingstuffs: Pesticides: Maximum residue levels: Scotland 308, 323
Feedingstuffs: Pesticides: Maximum residue levels: Northern Ireland 360, 376
Feedingstuffs: Scotland 307
Feedingstuffs: Zootechnical products 7
Feedingstuffs: Zootechnical products: Northern Ireland 360
Fees & charges: Consular Fees Act 1980: Fees 62
Fees & charges: Designs: Fees: European Communities 62
Fees & charges: European economic interest grouping 63
Fees & charges: Measuring instruments: EEC requirements: Fees 63
Fees & charges: Medicines: Human use: Medical devices 63, 101
Fees & charges: Northern Ireland 366
Fees & charges: Plant protection: Products: Fees 63, 134
Felixstowe Dock & Railway Harbour 71
Felling: Trees: Forestry: England & Wales 69
Fenland (District): Electoral changes 92
Fenland National Health Service Trust 110
Fibernet UK Ltd: Telecommunications: Public systems 237
Fibre plants: Oil & fibre plant seeds: England 220
Figs, hazelnuts & pistachios: From Turkey: Emergency control: England 66
Figs, hazelnuts & pistachios: From Turkey: Emergency control: Scotland 315
Figs, hazelnuts & pistachios: From Turkey: Emergency control: Northern Ireland 367
Figs, hazelnuts & pistachios: From Turkey: Emergency control: Wales 68
Finance Act 2001: Section 16: Appointed day 7
Finance Act 2002: Section 5 (6): Appointed date 37
Finance Act 2002: Section 6: Appointed day 37
Finance Act 2002: Section 22: Appointed day 246
Finance: Acts 2
Finance: Bills: Explanatory notes 7
Financial assistance: Environmental purposes: Scotland 314
Financial assistance: Industry: Increase of limit 83

Financial promotion & miscellaneous amendments: Financial Services & Markets Act 2000 64
Financial Services & Markets Act 2000: Consequential amendments 64
Financial Services & Markets Act 2000: Consequential amendments & transitional provisions: Credit unions 63
Financial Services & Markets Act 2000: Consequential amendments: Taxes 64
Financial Services & Markets Act 2000: Financial promotion & miscellaneous amendments 64
Financial Services & Markets Act 2000: Financial promotion: Electronic Commerce Directive 57, 64
Financial services & Markets Act 2000: Fourth motor insurance directive 64
Financial Services & Markets Act 2000: Insurers: Administration orders 63
Financial Services & Markets Act 2000: Mortgage regulation: Commencement 63
Financial Services & Markets Act 2000: Permission & applications: Credit unions etc. 64
Financial Services & Markets Act 2000: Regulated activities 57, 64
Financial services & Markets Act 2000: Variation of threshold conditions 64
Financial services & markets: Electronic Commerce Directive 57, 63
Financial services: Electronic money: Miscellaneous amendments 18, 63
Fines, forfeiture & reparation orders: Enforcement: International Criminal Court Act 2001 85
Fire services: Appointments & promotion: Northern Ireland 366
Fire services: Combined area: Administration: Scotland 314
Fire services: Police & Fire Services (Finance) (Scotland) Act 2001: Commencement: Scotland 314, 325
Firearms (Amendment) Act 1988: Firearms Consultative Committee 17
Fireworks: Explosives: Northern Ireland 365
Fish farming: Aquaculture & fisheries: Structures: Grants: Wales 65, 220
Fish farming: Registration: Businesses: Scotland 331
Fish: Conservation: Salmon: Prohibition of sale: Scotland 331
Fish: Diseases: Control: England & Wales 147, 219
Fish: Diseases: Control: Northern Ireland 362
Fisheries & aquaculture: Structures: Grants: Northern Ireland 366
Fisheries & aquaculture: Structures: Grants: Wales 65, 220
Fisheries: Byelaws: Northern Ireland 366
Fisheries: Salmon & freshwater: Mull salmon fishery district: Designation: Scotland 331
Fisheries: Salmon & freshwater: River Dee (Kirkcudbright) salmon fishery district: Baits & lures: Scotland 331
Fisheries: Sea: Northern Ireland 129, 219
Fisheries: Tagging & logbook: Byelaws: Northern Ireland 366
Fishing industry: Sea fisheries: Conservation: Shrimp fishing nets 219
Fishing vessels: 15-24 metre vessels: Safety 103
Fishing: Prohibited methods: Firth of Clyde: Scotland 343
Fixed-term employees: Less favourable treatment: Prevention 238
Fixed-term employees: Less favourable treatment: Prevention: Northern Ireland 363
Flexible working: Eligibility, complaints & remedies 238
Flexible working: Procedure requirements 238
Fodder plant seeds: England 220
Food & animal feedingstuffs: Products of animal origin: From China: Control: England 8, 9, 65
Food & animal feedingstuffs: Products of animal origin: From China: Control: Northern Ireland 367
Food & animal feedingstuffs: Products of animal origin: From China: Control: Scotland 307, 315
Food & animal feedingstuffs: Products of animal origin: From China: Control: Wales 10, 68
Food & mouth disease: Declaratory: Controlled areas: England & Wales 14
Food irradiation: Control of: Scotland 315
Food labelling: Scotland 315
Food protection: Emergency prohibitions: Amnesic shellfish poisoning: Orkney: Scotland 326
Food protection: Emergency prohibitions: Amnesic shellfish poisoning: West Coast: Scotland 326, 327, 328, 329, 330
Food protection: Emergency prohibitions: Amnesic, paralytic & diarrhetic shellfish poisoning: Orkney: Scotland 325
Food protection: Emergency prohibitions: Diarrhetic shellfish poisoning: Orkney: Scotland 330
Food protection: Emergency prohibitions: Northern Ireland 378
Food protection: Emergency prohibitions: Paralytic shellfish poisoning: Orkney: Scotland 330
Food: Additives: Wales 69
Food: Animal by-products: Identification: England 65
Food: Animal by-products: Identification: Scotland 314
Food: Animal by-products: Identification: Wales 67
Food: Contact: Plastic materials & articles: Northern Ireland 367
Food: Contaminants: England 65
Food: Contaminants: Northern Ireland 366
Food: Contaminants: Scotland 314
Food: Contaminants: Wales 67
Food: Dairy produce: Quotas 65
Food: Dairy produce: Quotas: Northern Ireland 367
Food: Dairy produce: Quotas: Scotland 314, 315
Food: Dairy produce: Quotas: Wales 68
Food: Figs, hazelnuts & pistachios: From Turkey: Emergency control: England 66

Food: Figs, hazelnuts & pistachios: From Turkey: Emergency control: Northern Ireland 367
Food: Figs, hazelnuts & pistachios: From Turkey: Emergency control: Scotland. 315
Food: Figs, hazelnuts & pistachios: From Turkey: Emergency control: Wales. 68
Food: Foot & mouth disease: Meat, meat preparations & meat products: Marking: England. 66
Food: Foot & mouth disease: Meat, meat preparations & meat products: Marking: Wales 69
Food: Import & export restrictions: Foot & mouth disease: Scotland 309, 316
Food: Irradiation: Control. 66
Food: Jelly confectionery: Emergency control: England 66
Food: Jelly confectionery: Emergency control: Northern Ireland 367
Food: Jelly confectionery: Emergency control: Scotland 315
Food: Jelly confectionery: Emergency control: Wales 68
Food: Kava-kava: England 67
Food: Kava-kava: Scotland 316
Food: Kava-kava: Wales 69
Food: Marketing: Notification of: Nutritional uses: England & Wales. 67
Food: Marketing: Notification of: Nutritional uses: Scotland 316
Food: Meat: Hazard analysis: Critical control point: England 67
Food: Meat: Hazard analysis: Critical control point: Northern Ireland 367
Food: Meat: Hazard analysis: Critical control point: Scotland. 316
Food: Nutritional uses: Addition of substances: Scotland 315
Food: Nutritional uses: Additional substances: Wales 68
Food: Nutritional uses: England 66
Food: Nutritional uses: Marketing: Northern Ireland 367
Food: Nutritional uses: Substances for specific nutritional purposes: Addition: Northern Ireland 367
Food: Peanuts: China: Emergency control: England 66
Food: Peanuts: China: Emergency control: Northern Ireland 367
Food: Peanuts: China: Emergency control: Scotland 315
Food: Peanuts: China: Emergency control: Wales 68
Food: Pesticides: Maximum residue levels: England & Wales 8, 10, 134
Food: Pesticides: Maximum residue levels: Scotland 308, 323
Food: Pesticides: Maximum residue levels: Northern Ireland 360, 376
Food: Plastic materials & articles: Contact with: England 67
Food: Plastic materials & articles: Contact with: Scotland 316
Food: Plastic materials & articles: Contact with: Wales 69
Food: Poultry, farmed game bird & rabbit meat: Hygiene & inspection: Scotland 316
Food: Products: Animal origin: Third country imports: England 9, 67
Food: Products: China: Control: Wales. 10, 68
Food: Star anise: Third countries: Emergency control: England 66
Food: Star anise: Third countries: Emergency control: Northern Ireland 367
Food: Star anise: Third countries: Emergency control: Scotland 316
Food: Star anise: Third countries: Emergency control: Wales 68
Food: Sweeteners: England 67
Food: Sweeteners: Northern Ireland 368
Food: Sweeteners: Scotland 316
Food: Sweeteners: Wales 69
Food: Welfare 65
Foot & mouth disease: Controlled areas: Northern Ireland 360
Foot & mouth disease: Controlled areas: Scotland 309
Foot & mouth disease: Import & export restrictions: England 13
Foot & mouth disease: Import & export restrictions: Scotland. 309, 316
Foot & mouth disease: Import & export restrictions: Wales 16
Foot & mouth disease: Meat, meat preparations & meat products: Marking: England 66
Foot & mouth disease: Meat, meat preparations & meat products: Marking: Wales. 69
Football (Disorder) (Amendment) Act 2002: Commencement 232
Football: Disorder: Acts 2
Football: Disorder: Acts: Explanatory notes 5
Football: Spectators: Seating: England & Wales 232
Football: Spectators: World Cup control period: England & Wales 232
Foreign companies: Controlled: Excluded countries 81
Forest of Dean (District): Electoral changes 92
Forest reproductive material: Great Britain 220
Forest reproductive material: Northern Ireland 381
Forestry: Environmental impact assessment: Northern Ireland 368
Forestry: Felling of trees: England & Wales 69
Forestry: Forest reproductive material: Northern Ireland 381
Forestry: Plant health: Great Britain. 135
Forestry: Plant health: Phytophthora ramorum: Great Britain 135

Forth Estuary Transport Authority: Scotland 332
Fossil fuel levy: Electricity: Scotland 313
Fossil fuel: Non-fossil fuel sources: Electricity: Locational flexibility: Scotland 313
Fossil fuel: Non-fossil fuel sources: Electricity: Saving arrangements: Scotland 313
Fostering services 20, 222
France Telecom Network Services-UK Ltd: Telecommunications: Public systems 237
Fraud: Social Security Fraud Act (Northern Ireland) 2001: Commencement: Northern Ireland 383, 384
Free zone: Port of Tilbury: Designation 38
Freedom of Information (Scotland) Act 2002: Commencement: Scotland 316
Freedom of Information Act 2000: Commencement 70
Freedom of information: Acts: Explanatory notes: Scotland 305
Freedom of information: Acts: Scotland 304
Freedom of information: Additional public authorities 70
Freedom of information: Excluded Welsh authorities 70
Freedom of Information: Information tribunal: Enforcement appeals 38, 70
Fuel substitutes: Excise duty: Rates 37
Fuel: Provided for private use: Consideration for: Value added tax 246
Fuels: Authorised: Smoke control areas: England 27
Fuels: Authorised: Smoke control areas: Scotland 310
Fuels: Authorised: Smoke control areas: Wales 27
Fuels: Liquid: Sulphur content: Northern Ireland 364
Fund-holding practices: Transfers: Health & Personal Social Services Act (Northern Ireland) 2001 369
Funeral & maternity expenses: Social fund 225
Funeral & maternity expenses: Social fund: Northern Ireland 382
Funeral expenses: Social fund 225
Fur Farming (Prohibition) (Scotland) Act 2002: Commencement: Scotland 308, 311
Fur farming: Compensation scheme: England 11
Fur farming: Prohibition: Acts: Explanatory notes: Scotland 305
Fur farming: Prohibition: Acts: Scotland 304
Fur farming: Prohibition: Northern Ireland 128
Further education: Teachers' qualifications: Wales 55

G

Game preservation: Acts: Explanatory notes: Northern Ireland 359
Game preservation: Acts: Northern Ireland 358
Game preservation: Commencement: Northern Ireland 368
Gaming (Bingo) Act 1985: Fees 18
Gaming (Bingo) Act 1985: Monetary limit: Variation 18
Gaming Act 1968: Fees: Variation 18
Gaming Act 1968: Fees: Variation: England & Wales 19
Gaming Act 1968: Fees: Variation: Scotland 310
Gaming Act 1968: Monetary limits: Variation 18
Gaming Board: Fees 18
Gaming clubs: Bankers' games 18
Gaming clubs: Hours & charges 18
Gaming clubs: Licensing 19
Gaming clubs: Multiple bingo 18
Gaming duty: Customs & excise 37
Gaming: Betting, Gaming & Lotteries Act 1963: Schedule 4 18
Gaming: Bingo: Deregulation 39
Gamma Telecommunications Limited: Public telecommunication systems 237
Gas & electricity: Turnover: Determination for penalties 56, 70
Gas: 1996 Order: Amendment: Northern Ireland 368
Gas: Connection charges 70
Gas: Natural: Radioactive substances 18
Gas: Standards of performance 70
Gas: Thermal energy: Calculation 70
Gateshead: National Health Service Trust 110
General & special commissioners: Jurisdiction & procedure 82, 84, 224, 234
General Chiropractic Council: Chiropractors: Foreign qualifications: Registration: Rules 22
General Chiropractic Council: Election of members & chairman: Rules 22
General Dental Council: Constitution 39
General Dental Council: Election of members 39
General dental services: National Health Service: England 114

General dental services: National Health Service: Scotland	322
General dental services: National Health Service: Wales	126, 127
General dental services: Northern Ireland	369
General medical & pharmaceutical services: National Health Service: Scotland	322
General Medical Council: Constitution	73
General Medical Council: Fitness to practice committees	100
General medical services: National Health Service: England	114, 115
General medical services: National Health Service: Scotland	322
General medical services: National Health Service: Wales	126, 127
General medical services: Northern Ireland	369
General medical services: Out of hours: National Health Service	115
General medical services: Supplementary list: National Health Service: England	114
General medical services: Supplementary list: National Health Service: Wales	127
General ophthalmic services: National Health Service: Scotland	322
General ophthalmic services: National Health Service: Wales	127
General ophthalmic services: Northern Ireland	370
General Optical Council: Registration & enrolment: Rules	130
General Osteopathic Council: Members & chairman: Election	131
General Synod measures: Tables & index	6
General Teaching Council for Wales	55
General Teaching Council for Wales: Fees	55
Genetically modified organisms: Contained use	72
Genetically modified organisms: Deliberate release	58
Genetically modified organisms: Deliberate release: Scotland	314
Genetically modified organisms: Deliberate release: Wales	60
Geneva Conventions Act: Overseas territories	70
Gillingham, North: Education Action Zone: Extension	49
Gilt-edged securities: Capital gains tax	234
Glamorgan: Vale of Glamorgan & Rhondda Cynon Taff: Llanharry, Pont-y-clun, Penllyn, Welsh St Donats & Pendoylan: Local government: Wales	99
Glasgow City Council: Renfrewshire Council: Boundaries: Braehead: Scotland	321
Glasgow: Road traffic: Parking areas: Scotland	333
Glossop: Tameside & Glossop Community & Priority Services: National Health Service Trust	123
Glossop: Tameside & Glossop National Health Service Trust	123
Gloucester Education Achievement: Education Action Zone: Extension	48
Gloucester Harbour: Constitution: England	71
Gloucestershire: Health Authority	111
Gloucestershire Council: Castle Meads bridge: Confirmation: England	77
Gloucestershire County Council: Two Mile Bend bridge: Confirmation: England	77
Gloucestershire Royal: National Health Service Trust	111
Gloucestershire: Avon, Gloucestershire & Wiltshire: Health Authority	104
Gloucestershire: East Gloucestershire: National Health Service Trust	110
Gloucestershire: Health Authority	110
Gloucestershire: South Gloucestershire: Local government	95
Goats & sheep: Identification: Scotland	309, 310
Goats & sheep: Identification: Wales	16, 17
Goats & sheep: Identification & movement: Interim measures: England	13, 14
Goats & sheep: Movements: Interim measures: Scotland	310
Golden Jubilee: Licensing: Regulatory reform: England & Wales	145
Goods & passenger vehicles: Recording equipment: Fees: Northern Ireland	380
Goods & services: Local authorities: Public bodies: England	95
Goods vehicles: Community authorisations: Road Traffic (Foreign Vehicles) Act 1972	147
Goods vehicles: Operators: Licensing: Fees	147
Goods vehicles: Plating & testing	211
Goods vehicles: Testing: Fees: Northern Ireland	380
Goods: Excise goods, beer & tobacco products	37
Goods: Excise goods: Accompanying documents	36
Goods: Export control	37
Goods: International carriage: Dangerous goods: Road: Fees	211
Goods: International transport: TIR carnets: Fees	212
Goods: Sale & supply: Consumers: European Communities	31
Government accounts: Whole of: Designation of bodies	70
Government of Further Education Corporations	48
Government resources & accounts: Whole of government accounts: Designation of bodies	70
Government stock: Irish registers: Closure & transfer	104
Government trading funds: ABRO Trading Fund	70
Government trading funds: Queen Elizabeth Conference: Trading Fund	70

Government trading funds: Royal Mint Trading Fund 70
Governors: Annual reports: Education: England 46
Grangetown & Michaelston: Cardiff & Vale of Glamorgan: Local government: Wales 96
Grants: Assembly Learning Grant scheme: Education: Wales 53
Grants: Standards: Education: Wales 55
Grants: Voluntary aided schools: England 46
Great Yarmouth (Borough): Electoral changes 89
Greater London Authority: Acceptance of office: Declaration 99
Greater London Authority: Precept Calculations: Allocation of grants 99
Greater London Magistrates' Courts Authority: Pensions 99, 134
Greater Manchester: Light rapid transit systems: Trafford depot 243, 244
Greater Manchester: Health Authority 111
Greenham & Cookham Commons: Local acts 6
Greenwich-Time to Succeed: Partnership: Education Action Zone: Extension 48
Ground Rents Act (Northern Ireland) 2001: Commencement: Northern Ireland 377
Ground rents: Multiplier: Northern Ireland 378
Guardian's allowance tax credits: Acts 4
Guardian's allowance tax credits: Acts: Explanatory notes 5
Guardian's allowances: Social security: Northern Ireland 384
Guardians' powers: Recall: Adults with incapacity: Scotland 306
Guardianship & intervention orders: Adults with incapacity: Reports: Scotland 306
Guide dogs, etc.: Private hire vehicles: Carriage: Acts 3
Guide dogs, etc.: Private hire vehicles: Carriage: Acts: Explanatory notes 5
Guildford & Waverley: National Health Service Primary Care Trust 111
Gwynedd (County): Electoral changes: Wales 97

H

Hackney, London Borough: Education Action Zone: Extension 48
Hallmarking: International Convention 71
Halstead: Witham, Braintree and Halstead Care: National Health Service Trust 124
Halton (Borough): Electoral changes 89
Halton: Borough of Halton, Thurrock & Warrington: Election years changes 90
Halton: National Health Service Trust 111
Hambleton & Richmondshire: National Health Service Trust 111
Hambleton: Parishes: Local government 94
Hamilton Oxford schools: Partnership: Education Action Zone: Extension 49
Hammersmith: Ealing, Hammersmith & Hounslow: Health Authority 109
Hampshire: Southampton & South West Hampshire: Health Authority 120
Hamptons: Teddington, Twickenham & Hamptons: National Health Service Primary Care Trust 123
Harborough (District): Electoral changes 92
Harbours, docks, piers & ferries: Aberdeen Harbour: Constitution: Revision: Scotland 316
Harbours, docks, piers & ferries: Brightlingsea Harbour: Constitution: England 71
Harbours, docks, piers & ferries: Clydeport: Closure of Yorkhilll Basin: Revision order: Scotland 316
Harbours, docks, piers & ferries: Comhairle nan Eilean Siar: Various harbours: Revision order: Scotland 317
Harbours, docks, piers & ferries: Dart Harbour & Navigation: Constitution: England 71
Harbours, docks, piers & ferries: Felixstowe Dock & Railway Harbour 71
Harbours, docks, piers & ferries: Gloucester Harbour Constitution: England 71
Harbours, docks, piers & ferries: Inverness Harbour: Constitution: Revision: Scotland 317
Harbours, docks, piers & ferries: Larne: Port: Pilotage functions 135
Harbours, docks, piers & ferries: Lymington Harbour: Constitution: England 71
Harbours, docks, piers & ferries: Mersey Docks & Harbour Company: Langton River Berth 71
Harbours, docks, piers & ferries: Peterhead Bay Authority: Constitution: Revision: Scotland 317
Harbours, docks, piers & ferries: Peterhead: Harbours: Revision: Constitution: Scotland 317
Harbours, docks, piers & ferries: Port of Ipswich Harbour: Transfer of undertaking: England 71
Harbours, docks, piers & ferries: Whitehaven Harbour Commissioners: Constitution: Harbour revision 71
Harbours, docks, piers & ferries: Yarmouth (Isle of Wight) harbour: Revision: England 71
Harbours: Belfast Harbour: Northern Ireland 368
Harbours: Londonderry Harbour: Northern Ireland 368
Harbours: Londonderry Harbour: Pilotage limits: Variations: Northern Ireland 368
Harbours: Northern Ireland 128, 368
Harbours: Warrenpoint Harbour Authority: Northern Ireland 368
Haringey: Barnet, Enfield & Haringey: Health Authority 104
Harrogate (Borough): Permitted & special parking area 211
Harrogate, Craven, & Rural District: National Health Service Trust 108

Entry	Page
Harrow & Hillingdon Healthcare: National Health Service Trust	111
Harrow: Brent & Harrow: Health Authority	105
Harrow: National Health Service Primary Care Trust	111
Hart (District): Permitted & special parking area	211
Hart: Rushmoor & Hart National Health Service Trust	119
Hart: Rushmoor & Hart: National Health Service Primary Care Trust	119
Harwich: Clacton & Harwich: Education Action Zone: Extension	43
Haslar: HM Prison Haslar: Closure of prisons	140
Hastings & St Leonards: Education Action Zone: Extension	49
Hazardous substances: Installations handling: Notification of	72
Hazelnuts & pistachios, figs: From Turkey: Emergency control: England	66
Hazelnuts & pistachios, figs: From Turkey: Emergency control: Scotland	315
Hazelnuts & pistachios, figs: From Turkey: Emergency control: Northern Ireland	367
Hazelnuts & pistachios, figs: From Turkey: Emergency control: Wales	68
Health & Personal Social Services Act (Northern Ireland) 2001: Commencement: Northern Ireland	369
Health & Personal Social Services Act (Northern Ireland) 2001: Fund-holding practices: Transfers: Northern Ireland	369
Health & Personal Social Services Act (Northern Ireland) 2002: Commencement: Northern Ireland	369
Health & personal social services employees: Statutory paternity pay & adoption pay: Northern Ireland	363
Health & personal social services: Acts: Northern Ireland	358, 359
Health & personal social services: Adoption (Intercountry Aspects) Act (Northern Ireland) 2001: Commencement: Northern Ireland	368, 369
Health & personal social services: Dental charges: Northern Ireland	369
Health & personal social services: Drugs & appliances: Charges: Northern Ireland	369
Health & personal social services: General dental services: Northern Ireland	369
Health & personal social services: General medical services: Northern Ireland	369
Health & personal social services: Medical services: Northern Ireland	370
Health & personal social services: Northern Ireland Practice & Education Council for Nursing & Midwifery: Appointments & procedure: Northern Ireland	369
Health & personal social services: Optical charges & payments: General ophthalmic services: Northern Ireland	370
Health & personal social services: Optical charges & payments: Northern Ireland	370
Health & personal social services: Penalty charges: Northern Ireland	369
Health & personal social services: Personal social services: Preserved rights: Northern Ireland	370
Health & personal social services: Pharmaceutical services: Drugs & appliances: Charges: Northern Ireland	370
Health & personal social services: Pharmaceutical services: Northern Ireland	370
Health & personal social services: Resources: Assessment: Northern Ireland	369
Health & personal social services: Social Care Council: Appointments & procedure: Northern Ireland	369
Health & personal social services: Superannuation: Additional voluntary contributions: Northern Ireland	369
Health & personal social services: Superannuation: Northern Ireland	369
Health & personal social services: Travelling expenses: Remission of charges: Northern Ireland	370
Health & safety: Asbestos: Control: At work	71
Health & safety: Chemicals: Hazard information & packaging for supply	71
Health & safety: Chemicals: Hazard information & packaging for supply: Northern Ireland	370
Health & safety: Dangerous goods: Carriage: Northern Ireland	370
Health & safety: Dangerous substances: Explosive atmospheres	72
Health & safety: Environmentally hazardous substances	72
Health & safety: Fees	72
Health & safety: Genetically modified organisms: Contained use	72
Health & safety: Hazardous substances: Installations handling: Notification of	72
Health & safety: Lead: Control: At work	72
Health & safety: Miscellaneous amendments	72
Health & safety: New substances: Notification of	72
Health & safety: Offshore safety: Miscellaneous amendments	73
Health & safety: Personal protective equipment	31, 73
Health & safety: Pressure equipment	73
Health & safety: Radioactive material: Packaging, labelling & carriage: By rail	73
Health & safety: Substances hazardous to health: Control	72
Health & Social Care Act 2001: Commencement	22, 101, 102, 104, 111, 125, 221
Health & Social Care Act 2001: Commencement: Scotland	346
Health & Social Care Act 2001: Commencement: Wales	126
Health & welfare: Value added tax	247
Health Act 1999: Commencement	73
Health authorities: Administration arrangements: Functions: National Health Service: England	114
Health authorities: National Health Service	104, 105, 106, 109, 109, 110, 111, 112, 113, 116, 117, 118, 119, 120, 121, 122, 123, 124, 125
Health authorities: National Health Service: Establishment & abolition: England	111
Health authorities: National Health Service: Membership & procedure: England	111
Health care & associated professions: Council for the Regulation of Health Care Professionals: Appointment etc.: England	73
Health care & associated professions: Doctors: General Medical Council: Constitution	73
Health care & associated professions: Doctors: Medical Act 1983: Amendment	73

Health care & associated professions: Health Act 1999: Commencement. 73
Health care & associated professions: Health professions 73, 74
Health care & associated professions: National Health Service Reform & Health Care Professions Act 2002: Commencement: England 73, 115
Health care & associated professions: Professions supplementary to medicine: Staff & property: Transfer 73
Health care professions: National Health Service: Reform: Acts 3
Health care professions: National Health Service: Reform: Acts: Explanatory notes 5
Health care: National Care Standards Commission: Director of Private & Voluntary Health Care: England 142
Health professions. 73, 74
Health Service: Health Authorities 104, 105, 106, 109, 109, 110, 111, 112, 113, 116, 117, 118, 119, 120, 121, 122, 123, 124, 125
Health Service: National Trusts . 104, 105, 106, 107, 108, 109, 110, 111, 112, 113, 116, 117, 118, 119, 120, 121, 122, 123, 124, 125, 128
Health service: National: Pilot schemes: England. 114
Health Service: Patient information: Control 125
Health services charges: Road traffic: Northern Ireland 380
Health visitors, nurses & midwives: Professional conduct: England & Wales 130
Health visitors, nurses & midwives: Professional conduct: Northern Ireland 374
Health visitors, nurses & midwives: Professional conduct: Scotland 323
Health visitors, nurses & midwives: Rules 130
Health: Community care: Acts: Explanatory notes: Scotland 305
Health: Community care: Acts: Scotland 304
Health: Plants: Potatoes: Originating in Germany: Northern Ireland. 377
Healthcare, Independent: Registration: Fees: Wales 22, 143, 223
Healthcare, Independent: Registration: Wales 22, 143, 224
Healthcare: Private & voluntary health care: Wales. 143
Heart of Birmingham Teaching: National Health Service Primary Care Trust 111
Heart of Slough: Education Action Zone: Extension 49
Heathrow Express Railway: Exemptions 244
Heathrow Express Railway: Extension 243, 244
Heathrow Terminal 5 access: Motorways: M25: Connecting roads 77
Hemp: Third country imports 8
Herefordshire (District): Electoral changes. 91
Hertfordshire: Coroners' districts 32
Hertfordshire: Health Authority 111
High Court of Justiciary: Act of Adjournal: Criminal appeals: Scotland 317
High Court of Justiciary: Act of Adjournal: Criminal procedure: Rules: Anti-terrorism ... Act 2002: Scotland 344
High Court of Justiciary: Act of Adjournal: Criminal procedure: Rules: Convention Rights (Compliance) (Scotland) Act 2001: Scotland . . 317
High Court of Justiciary: Act of Adjournal: Criminal procedure: Rules: Extradition: Scotland 317, 344
High Court of Justiciary: Act of Adjournal: Criminal procedure: Rules: Sexual Offences (Procedure & Evidence) (Scotland) Act 2002: Scotland
. . . . 317
High-speed railways: Interoperability 242
Highways: A5: Sketchley Meadow junction improvement 74
Highways: A6: Derby to Stockport: Detrunking 74
Highways: A15: North of Lincoln to North Lincolnshire: Detrunking 74
Highways: A15: South of M180: Detrunking. 74
Highways: A16: Stamford to North East Lincolnshire: Detrunking 74
Highways: A17: Newark-on-Trent to Kings Lynn: Detrunking 74
Highways: A34: Newtown, Great Wyrley, to A34/A500 Queensway roundabout: Detrunking 74
Highways: A38: Worcestershire/Gloucestershire: Detrunking 74
Highways: A45: Upton, Woodon Road to Dunchurch, M45/A45: Detrunking 75
Highways: A46: North of Lincoln: Detrunking 75
Highways: A52: Derby to Calton Moor: Detrunking 75
Highways: A57: M1 to A1: Detrunking 75
Highways: A65: Thorlby roundabout: North Yorkshire/City of Bradford boundary 76
Highways: A303: Folly Bottom junction: Detrunking 76
Highways: A303: Folly Bottom junction: Improvement slip roads 76
Highways: A449: A5 Gailey roundabout - A34 Queensway, Stafford: Detrunking 76
Highways: A452: Oglet Road, B5011 Junction/A4041 Queslett Road 76
Highways: A516: West of Derby: Detrunking 76
Highways: A523 Trunk Rd: Calton Moor to Cheshire Border 76
Highways: A523: Cheshire: Detrunking 76
Highways: A596: Calva Brow Junction, Workington 76
Highways: A606: A52 to A46: Detrunking 76
Highways: A614: Leapool to Ollerton & Blyth to Bawtry: Detrunking 76
Highways: A1041: Abbotts Rd.: Carlton New Bridge: Detrunking 77
Highways: A5011: Linley Rd.: Detrunking 77
Highways: Devon County Council: Barnstaple downstream bridge: Confirmation 77
Highways: Dunham Bridge: Tolls: Revision of 77
Highways: Gloucestershire Council: Castle Meads bridge: Confirmation. 77

Highways: Gloucestershire County Council: Two Mile Bend bridge: Confirmation: England	77
Highways: Humber Bridge: Tolls: Revision of	77
Highways: New Roads & Street Works Act 1991: Commencement: England	77
Highways: Severn Bridges: Tolls: England	77
Highways: Street works: Charges: London Borough of Camden	77
Highways: Street works: Charges: Middlesbrough Borough Council	77
Highways: Street works: Charges: Transport for London	77
Highways: Street works: Inspection fees: England	77
Highways: Street works: Inspection fees: Wales	78
Highways: Street works: Records: England	77
Highways: Street works: Recovery of costs: England	78
Highways: Street works: Reinstatement: England	78
Highways: Trent & Mersey Canal: Bridge scheme	77
Highways: Trunk roads: England & Wales	74, 75, 76, 77
Highways: Wiltshire County Council: Semington aqueduct: Confirmation: England	78
Hill farm: Allowance: England	9
Hillingdon: Harrow & Hillingdon Healthcare: National Health Service Trust	111
Hillingdon: Health Authority	111
Hinckley & Bosworth (Borough): Electoral changes	89
Historic Buildings & Monuments Commission for England: National heritage: Acts	3
Home energy efficiency scheme	58
Home zones:Transport: Scotland	347
Home-grown Cereals Authority: Rate of levy	8
Homeless persons: Advice & assistance: Scotland	317
Homeless persons: Interim accommodation: Scotland	317
Homelessness Act 2000: Commencement: Wales	79
Homelessness: Commencement: England	78
Homelessness: Local housing authorities: Acts	2
Homelessness: Local housing authorities: Acts: Explanatory notes	5
Homelessness: Priority need for accommodation: England	78
Hong Kong: Application: Overseas territories: Extradition	62, 78
Hong Kong: Overseas territories: Extradition	62, 78
Horsham & Chanctonbury: National Health Service Primary Care Trust	111
Horsham (District): Electoral changes	92
Horticultural Development Council	83
Hospital in-patients: Social security	228
Hospitals: In-patients: Social security: Northern Ireland	384
Hounslow: Ealing, Hammersmith & Hounslow: Health Authority	109
Houses: Multiple occupation: Licensing: Civic Government (Scotland) Act 1982: Scotland	317, 321
Housing (Scotland) Act 2001: Accommodation for asylum-seekers	79
Housing (Scotland) Act 2001: Appointment of arbiter: Scotland	318
Housing (Scotland) Act 2001: Commencement: Scotland	318
Housing (Scotland) Act 2001: Housing support services information	29, 39, 79
Housing (Scotland) Act 2001: Registered social landlords: Scotland	318
Housing (Scotland) Act 2001: Scottish secure tenancy etc.: Scotland	318
Housing assistance: Regulatory reform: England & Wales	79, 146
Housing benefit: Council tax benefit: Child care charges	224
Housing benefit: Council tax benefit: Social security: Claims & information	227
Housing benefit: General	224
Housing benefit: General: Northern Ireland	370
Housing renewal grants: Forms: Wales	79
Housing renewal grants: Wales	79
Housing revenue account: General fund contribution: Limits: Scotland	317
Housing support grant: Scotland	318
Housing support services: Northern Ireland	129
Housing: Allocation: England	78
Housing: Children & young persons: Social security: Allowances: Northern Ireland	371, 379, 385
Housing: Commonhold & Leasehold Reform Act 2002: Commencement: England	78
Housing: Commonhold & Leasehold Reform Act 2002: Commencement: Wales	79
Housing: Commonhold & leasehold: Acts: Explanatory notes	4
Housing: Disabled facilities: Grants: Home repair: Assistance: Wales	79
Housing: Homeless persons: Advice & assistance: Scotland	317
Housing: Homeless persons: Interim accommodation: Scotland	317
Housing: Homelessness Act 2000: Commencement: Wales	79
Housing: Homelessness: Commencement: England	78
Housing: Homelessness: Priority need for accommodation: England	78
Housing: Registration of tenant organisations: Scotland	318

Housing: Relocation grants: Forms of application: England 79
Housing: Relocation grants: Forms of application: Wales 80
Housing: Renewal grants: England. 78
Housing: Renewal grants: Prescribed form & particulars: England 78
Housing: Right to acquire: Discount: England 79
Housing: Right to buy: Designated rural areas & designated regions: England 79
Housing: Right to buy: Houses liable to demolition: Scotland. 317
Housing: Right to buy: Priority of charges: Wales 79
Housing: Right to purchase: Application form: Scotland 318
Housing: Scottish secure tenancy: Scotland 318
Housing: Social security & child support: Decisions & appeals: Miscellaneous amendments: Northern Ireland 361, 365, 371, 378, 382
Housing: Social security: Benefits: Up-rating: Northern Ireland 371, 378, 382, 385, 386
Housing: Social security: Employment programme: Northern Ireland 371, 378, 383
Housing: Social security: Intercalating students: Northern Ireland 371, 378, 384
Housing: Social security: Loss of benefit: Northern Ireland 371, 379, 384
Housing: Social security: Miscellaneous amendments: Northern Ireland 371, 379, 384
Housing: Social security: Paternity & adoption: Northern Ireland. 371, 379, 384
Housing: Social security: Personal Injury payments: Northern Ireland 371, 379, 385
Housing: Social security: Students & Income related benefits : Northern Ireland 372, 379, 385
Housing: Support services: Scotland 318
Housing: Tenancies: Scottish secure tenancies: Abandoned property: Scotland. 318
Housing: Tenancies: Scottish secure tenancies: Exceptions: Scotland 318
Housing: Tenancies: Scottish secure tenancies: Proceedings for possession: Scotland 319
Housing: Tenancies: Short Scottish secure tenancies: Notices: Scotland 319
Housing: Tenancies: Short Scottish secure tenancies: Proceedings for possession: Scotland 319
Housing: Tenants: Scottish secure tenants: Compensation for improvements: Scotland. 319
Housing: Tenants: Scottish secure tenants: Right to repair: Scotland 319
Housing: Waltham Forest Housing Action Trust: Dissolution. 79
Hove: Brighton & Hove: National Health Service Primary Care Trust 105
HSBC Investment Banking Act 2002 6
Huddersfield: National Health Service Trust 112
Huddersfield: South Huddersfield: National Health Service Trust. 121
Human intelligence sources: Covert: Regulation of investigatory powers: Codes of practice 86
Human reproductive cloning: Acts: Explanatory notes 5
Humber Bridge: Tolls: Revision of 77
Hunting: Protection of Wild Mammals (Scotland) Act 2002: Commencement: Scotland 308, 311
Huntingdonshire (District): Electoral changes 92
Hydrocarbon oil: Controlled oil: Registered dealers 37
Hydrocarbon oil: Industrial reliefs 37
Hydrocarbon oil: Marking 37

I

Immigration & Asylum Act 1999: Commencement 80
Immigration & Asylum Act 1999: Part V Exemption: Relevant employers 80
Immigration & asylum: Acts 3
Immigration & asylum: Appeals: One-stop procedures. 80
Immigration & asylum: Carriers' liability: Clandestine entrants: Level of Penalty: Code of Practice 81
Immigration & asylum: Carriers' liability: Regulations 81
Immigration & asylum: Immigration Services Tribunal 81
Immigration Services Tribunal 81
Immigration: Appeals: Notices 80
Immigration: Asylum support 80
Immigration: Asylum support: Repeal 80
Immigration: Entry otherwise than by sea or air 80
Immigration: Nationality, Immigration & Asylum Act 2002: Commencement 81
Immigration: Services Commissioner: Registration fees 81
Immigration: Short-term holding facilities 81
Immigration: Swiss free movement of persons 81
Immigration: Transit visa. 81
Immigration: Travel bans: Designation. 80
Immigration: Travel documents: Fees 81
Immigration: Withholding & withdrawal of support: Travel assistance: Temporary accommodation 81
Immunities & privileges: International Criminal Court. 86
Import & export restrictions: Foot & mouth disease: England 13

Import & export restrictions: Foot & mouth disease: Scotland	309, 316
Import & export restrictions: Foot & mouth disease: Wales	16
Incapacity: Social security	229
Incapacity: Social security: Northern Ireland	384
Income & Corporation Taxes Act 1998: Section 349B (3)	82
Income related benefits: Authorities: Subsidy	224
Income support: General: Jobseeker's allowance	224
Income support: General: Jobseekers allowance: Northern Ireland	381
Income support: General: Standard interest rate	224, 225
Income support: General: Standard interest rate: Northern Ireland	381
Income Tax (Earnings & Pensions) Act 2003: Tables, origins & destinations	6
Income tax: Benefits in kind: Employment costs resulting from disability: Exemption	82
Income tax: Capital allowances: Energy-saving plant & machinery	81
Income tax: Car fuel benefits: Cash equivalents	82
Income tax: Corporation tax: Finance leasing: Intangible assets	82
Income tax: Double taxation: Relief: Lithuania	82
Income tax: Double taxation: Relief: South Africa	82
Income tax: Double taxation: Relief: Taiwan	82
Income tax: Double taxation: Relief: United States	82
Income tax: Employments & electronic communications	82
Income tax: Exchange gains & losses: Bringing into account gains or losses	82
Income tax: Exchange gains & losses: Transitional provisions & savings	82
Income tax: Foreign companies: Excluded countries	81
Income tax: General & special commissioners: Jurisdiction & procedure	82, 84, 224, 234
Income tax: Indexation	82, 83
Income tax: Individual savings accounts	83
Income tax: Minor benefits: Exemption	82
Income tax: Open-ended investment companies: Tax	83
Income tax: Prescribed deposit-takers	83
Income tax: Retirement benefits schemes: Earnings cap: Indexation	83
Income tax: Retirement benefits schemes: Information powers	83
Income tax: Scottish Water: Transfer of functions: Tax provisions	83, 235
Income tax: Sub-contractors: Construction industry	83
Income tax: Venture capital trust: Shares & securities: Exchange of	83
Income-related benefits	224
Income-related benefits: Contracting out	31, 224
Independent healthcare: Registration: Fees: Wales	22, 143, 223
Independent healthcare: Registration: Wales	22, 143, 224
Independent schools: Approval of: Special educational needs: England	47
Individual savings accounts: Income tax	83
Industrial & provident societies: Acts	2
Industrial action ballots: Notice to employers: Code of practice: Appointed day: Northern Ireland	372
Industrial Development Act (Northern Ireland) 2002: Commencement	372
Industrial development: Acts: Explanatory notes: Northern Ireland	359
Industrial development: Acts: Northern Ireland	358
Industrial development: Financial assistance: Industry: Increase of limit	83
Industrial injuries: Dependency: Permitted earnings limits: Northern Ireland	384
Industrial injuries: Dependency: Permitted earnings limits: Social security	229
Industrial injuries: Prescribed diseases: Social security	229
Industrial injuries: Prescribed diseases: Social security: Northern Ireland	384
Industrial organisation & development: Horticultural Development Council	83
Industrial organisation & development: Potato Industry Development Council	83
Industrial relations: Disciplinary & grievance procedures: Code of practice: Appointed day: Northern Ireland	372
Industrial relations: Industrial action ballots: Notice to employers: Code of practice: Appointed day: Northern Ireland	372
Industrial relations: Labour Relations Agency: Arbitration scheme: Northern Ireland	372
Industrial relations: Redundancy consultation & procedures: Code of practice: Appointed day: Northern Ireland	372
Industrial training levy: Construction Board	58
Industrial training levy: Construction industry: Northern Ireland	372
Industrial training levy: Engineering Construction Board	58
Industry: Financial assistance: Increase of limit	83
Information tribunal: Enforcement appeals	38, 70
Information: Access: Executive arrangements: Local authorities: England	94
Information: Freedom of: Acts: Explanatory notes: Scotland	305
Information: Freedom of: Acts: Scotland	304
Inheritance tax: Accounts: Delivery: Excepted estates	84
Inheritance tax: Accounts: Delivery: Excepted settlements	84
Inheritance tax: Accounts: Delivery: Excepted transfers & terminations	84

Inheritance tax: General & special commissioners: Jurisdiction & procedure	82, 84, 224, 234
Inheritance tax: Indexation	84
Inquiries: Fees: Standard daily amount: Wales	245
Insider dealing: Securities & regulated markets	84
Insolvency Act 2000: Commencement	84
Insolvency Act 1986: Amendment	29, 84, 85
Insolvency practitioners	84, 85
Insolvency: Companies & individuals: 1989 Order: Northern Ireland	372
Insolvency: Companies & individuals: Rules: England & Wales	85
Insolvency: Deceased persons: Estates: Insolvent: Administration of	85
Insolvency: Individuals	85
Insolvency: Insolvent partnerships: England & Wales	85
Insolvency: Northern Ireland	129
Insolvency: Occupational & personal pension schemes: Bankruptcy	84, 132
Insolvency: Occupational & personal pension schemes: Bankruptcy: Northern Ireland	372, 375
Insolvency: Rules: Northern Ireland	372
Insolvency: Rules: Scotland	29, 85
Insolvent estates: Deceased persons: Administration of	85
Insolvent partnerships: England & Wales	85
Inspectors: Education & training: Wales	54
Insurers: Administration orders: Financial Services & Markets Act 2000	63
Insurers: Life assurance & other policies: Information & duties	234
Insurers: Rights against: European Communities: Road traffic	147
Interbrew SA & Bass PLC: Mergers	29
Intercalating students: Social security	226
Interception capability: Maintenance: Regulation of investigatory powers	86
International carriage: Dangerous goods: Road: Fees	211
International Court of Justice: United Nations: Immunities & privileges	86
International Criminal Court: Immunities & privileges	86
International Criminal Court Act 2001: Fines, forfeiture & reparation orders: Enforcement	85
International Development Act 2002: Commencement	86
International development Caribbean Development Bank: Further payments	86
International development: Acts	2
International development: Acts: Explanatory notes	5
International development: African Development Fund: Additional subscriptions	86
International immunities & privileges: International Court of Justice: United Nations: Immunities & privileges	86
International immunities & privileges: International Criminal Court	86
International immunities & privileges: International Maritime Organisation: Immunities & privileges	86
International Maritime Organisation: Immunities & privileges	86
Inverness Harbour: Constitution: Revision: Scotland	317
Invest Northern Ireland: Superannuation: Northern Ireland	375
Investigatory powers: Regulation: Cancellation of authorisations: Scotland	319
Investigatory powers: Regulation: Communications: Interception of: Code of Practice	86
Investigatory powers: Regulation: Covert human intelligence sources: Codes of practice	86
Investigatory powers: Regulation: Covert surveillance: Codes of practice	86
Investigatory powers: Regulation: Interception capability: Maintenance	86
Investigatory powers: Regulation: Juveniles: Scotland	319
Investigatory powers: Regulation: Northern Ireland	372
Investigatory powers: Regulation: Offices, ranks & positions: Prescription	86
Investigatory powers: Regulation: Offices, ranks & positions: Prescription: Northern Ireland	373
Investigatory powers: Regulation: Source records: Scotland	319
Investment: Open-ended investment companies: Acts: Northern Ireland	358
Invicta Community Care: Thames Gateway & Invicta Community Care: National Health Service Trust	124
Invicta Community: National Health Service Trust	112
Ipswich: Port of Ipswich Harbour: Transfer of undertaking: England	71
Irradiation: Food: Control	66
Irradiation: Food: Control: Scotland	315
Isle of Man: Trade Marks Act 1994	241
Isle of Man: United Nations measures: Al-Qa'ida & Taliban	245
Isle of Man: United Nations sanctions: Somalia	246
Isle of Wight Railway LCDR no. 2515 vehicle: Accessibility: Exemptions	41, 242
Islington: National Health Service Primary Care Trust	112
Islington: Widening Horizons - North Islington: Education Action Zone: Extension	50

J

Jelly confectionery: Food: Emergency control: England	66
Jelly confectionery: Food: Emergency control: Northern Ireland	367
Jelly confectionery: Food: Emergency control: Scotland	315
Jelly confectionery: Food: Emergency control: Wales	68
Jersey: Air navigation: Civil aviation	23
Jersey: Territorial Sea Act 1987	239
Jobcentre plus interviews: Social security	229
Jobseeker's allowance	224, 225
Jobseeker's allowance: Income support: General	224
Jobseeker's allowance: Income support: General: Northern Ireland	381
Jobseeker's allowance: Joint claims	225
Jobseeker's allowance: Northern Ireland	381
Judges, legal officers & others: Ecclesiastical law: Fees	42
Judges: Maximum number	233
Judicial Pensions & Retirement Act 1993: Qualifying judicial offices	134
Judicial pensions: Pensions appeal tribunals	132
Jurisdiction of courts: Child support appeals	62
Justice (Northern Ireland) Act 2002: Commencement: Northern Ireland	373
Justice (Northern Ireland) Act 2002: Section 46 (1): Amendment: Northern Ireland	373
Justice: Northern Ireland: Acts: Explanatory notes	5
Justices of the Peace: Bench: Size & chairmanship	87
Justices of the peace: Commission areas: West Mercia	86
Justices of the Peace: Petty sessions areas	87

K

Kava-kava: Food: England	67
Kava-kava: Food: Scotland	316
Kava-kava: Food: Wales	69
Kava-kava: Prohibition: Medicines: Human use	101, 102
Kennet & North Wiltshire: National Health Service Primary Care Trust	112
Kensington & Chelsea and Westminster: Health Authority	112
Kensington & Chelsea: National Health Service Primary Care Trust	112
Kensington: Brent, Kensington, Chelsea & Westminster Mental Health: National Health Service Trust	105
Kensington: Palace Avenue: Acquisition of freehold: Local acts	6
Kent, West: National Health Service & Community Care Trust	124
Kent: East Kent Coastal: National Health Service Primary Care Trust	110
Kent: New Horizons Kent-Somerset Virtual : Education Action Zone: Extension	49
Kent: West Kent: Health Authority	124
Kerrier (District): Electoral changes	92
King's Lynn & West Norfolk (Borough): Electoral changes	89
Kirkcudbright: River Dee: Salmon fishery district: Baits & lures: Scotland	331
Kirklees (North): National Health Service Trust	117
Knowsley: National Health Service Trust	112
Knowsley: St Helens & Knowsley Community Health: National Health Service Trust	122

L

Labour Relations Agency: Arbitration scheme: Northern Ireland	372
Lakeland: South Lakeland (District): Permitted & special parking area	210
Lambeth: National Health Service Primary Care Trust	112
Lambeth, Southwark & Lewisham Health Authority	112
Lancashire & Cumbria: Health Authority	108
Lancashire Teaching Hospitals: National Health Service Trust	112
Lancashire: Coroners' districts	32
Lancashire: East Lancashire: Health Authority	110
Lancashire: North Sefton & West Lancashire: National Health Service Trust	117
Land Registration (Scotland) Act 1979: Commencement: Scotland	319
Land registration: Rules: England & Wales	87
Land registration: Acts	2
Land registration: Acts: Explanatory notes	5

Land registration: Rules: Northern Ireland	373
Land registration: Title: Compulsory registration: Northern Ireland	373
Land: Uncultivated land & semi-natural areas: Environmental impact assessment: Scotland	307
Land: Uncultivated land & semi-natural areas: Environmental impact assessment: Wales	10
Landfill tax	87
Landfill: England & Wales	60
Landlord & tenant: Agricultural holdings: Units of production: England	87
Landlord & tenant: Assured tenancies: Agricultural occupancies: Forms: England	87
Landlord & tenant: Leasehold reform: Collective enfranchisement: Counter-notices: England	87
Landlord & tenant: Leasehold reform: Notices	87
Landlord & tenant: Leasehold reform: Notices: Wales	87
Landlord & tenant: Long residential tenancies: Principal forms	87
Landlord & tenant: Rents: Registered: Increase: Northern Ireland	373
Lands Tribunal: Fees: England & Wales	87
Lands Valuation Appeal Court: Act of Sederunt: Scotland	311
Langbaurgh National Health Service Trust	112
Langley Junior School: School session times: Change	49
Larne: Port: Pilotage functions	135
Late Payment of Commercial Debts (Interest) Act 1998: Commencement	32
Late Payment of Commercial Debts (Interest) Act 1998: Commencement: Scotland	311
Late payment: Commercial debts	32
Late payment: Commercial debts: Rate of interest	32
Late payment: Commercial debts: Rate of interest: Scotland	311
Late payment: Commercial debts: Scotland	311
Law: Constitutional: Waters: Adjacent waters: Boundaries: Northern Ireland	29, 128
Law: Constitutional: Welsh Administration Ombudsman: Jurisdiction: Wales	30
Law: Criminal: Criminal Justice & Public Order Act 1994: Commencement	34
Law: Family Law Act (Northern Ireland) 2001: Commencement: Northern Ireland	365
Law: Family law: Child Support, Pensions & Social Security Act 2000: Commencement: Northern Ireland	365
Law: Justice: Northern Ireland: Acts: Explanatory notes	5
Lead shot: Use: Restriction: Environmental protection: England	59
Lead shot: Use: Restriction: Wales	60
Lead: Control: At work: Health & safety	72
Learning & Skills Act 2000: Commencement: Savings & transitional provisions	52, 58
Leasehold reform: Collective enfranchisement: Counter-notices: England	87
Leasehold reform: Notices	87
Leasehold reform: Notices: Wales	87
Leasehold: Acts	1
Leasehold: Acts: Explanatory notes	4
Leeds Community & Mental Health Services Teaching: National Health Service Trust	112
Legal advice & assistance: Financial conditions: Northern Ireland	373
Legal advice & assistance: Northern Ireland	373
Legal aid & advice: Advice & assistance: Assistance by way of representation: Scotland	319
Legal aid & advice: Advice & assistance: Financial conditions: Northern Ireland	373
Legal aid & advice: Advice & assistance: Financial conditions: Scotland	319
Legal aid & advice: Advice & assistance: Northern Ireland	373
Legal aid & advice: Advice & assistance: Scotland	320
Legal aid & advice: Civil legal aid: Fees: Scotland	320
Legal aid & advice: Civil legal aid: Financial conditions: Scotland	320
Legal aid & advice: Civil legal aid: General: England & Wales	88
Legal aid & advice: Civil legal aid: Scotland	320
Legal aid & advice: Criminal legal aid: Fees: Scotland	320
Legal aid & advice: Criminal legal aid: Fixed payments: Scotland	320
Legal aid & advice: Criminal legal aid: Scotland	320
Legal aid & advice: Scotland	320
Legal aid, advice & assistance: Criminal proceedings: Costs: Northern Ireland	373
Legal aid: Civil: Fees: Scotland	320
Legal aid: Civil: Financial conditions: Scotland	320
Legal aid: Civil: Scotland	320
Legal aid: Criminal: Fees: Scotland	320
Legal aid: Criminal: Fixed payments: Scotland	320
Legal aid: Criminal: Scotland	320
Legal aid: Family proceedings: Remuneration: England & Wales	88
Legal aid: Scotland	320
Legal officers, judges & others: Ecclesiastical law: Fees	42
Legal Officers: Fees: Annual: Ecclesiastical law: England	42
Legal representation: Children's hearings: Scotland	310

Legal Services Commission: Community legal service: Financial: England & Wales ... 88
Legal Services Commission: Criminal Defence Service: Costs: Recovery: England & Wales ... 88
Legal Services Commission: Criminal Defence Service: Funding: England & Wales ... 88
Legal Services Commission: Criminal Defence Service: General: England & Wales ... 88
Legal Services Commission: Criminal Defence Service: Representation order appeals: England & Wales ... 88
Legal Services Ombudsman: Scottish: Compensation: Prescribed amount: Scotland ... 320
Legal services: Access to Justice Act 1999: Solicitors practising certificates ... 88
Legal services: Queen's Counsel: Fees: England & Wales ... 88
Legal services: Scottish Legal Services Ombudsman: Compensation: Prescribed amount: Scotland ... 320
Legislation: Local: Chronological tables ... 6
Leicester (City): Electoral changes ... 91
Leicestershire & Rutland Healthcare: National Health Service Trust ... 112
Leicestershire, North West (District): Electoral changes ... 93
Leicestershire, Northamptonshire & Rutland: Health Authority ... 112
Leicestershire: National Health Service Health Authorities ... 112
Leigh Park: Education Action Zone: Extension ... 49
Leigh: Wigan & Leigh: Petty sessions areas ... 87
Less favoured areas: Agriculture: Compensatory allowances: Northern Ireland ... 360
Less favoured areas: Agriculture: Support scheme: Scotland ... 307
Lewisham: National Health Service Primary Care Trust ... 113
Liberty: Restriction: Scotland ... 312
Libraries: Public lending right scheme 1982: Variation: Commencement ... 88
Licences & licensing: Houses: Multiple occupation: Licensing: Civic Government (Scotland) Act 1982: Scotland ... 317, 321
Licences & licensing: Taxi drivers' licences: Dogs: Guide & hearing: Carrying of: Scotland ... 321
Licences: Exchangeable: Motor vehicles: Northern Ireland ... 380
Licensing hours: Restaurants: Deregulation ... 39
Licensing: Compulsory: Patents & plant variety rights ... 132, 135
Licensing: Road service licensing: Community licences: Northern Ireland ... 365, 381
Licensing: Special occasions: Regulatory reform: England & Wales ... 146
Lichfield: Burntwood, Lichfield & Tamworth National Health Service Trust ... 106
Life assurance & other policies: Insurers: Information & duties ... 234
Lifeboats: Equipment: Value added tax ... 247
Lifespan Healthcare Cambridge: National Health Service Trust ... 106, 113
Light railways: Docklands: Silvertown & London City Airport extension ... 243
Light railways: East Lancashire: Heywood extension ... 243
Limited liability partnerships ... 131
Limited liability partnerships: Acts: Northern Ireland ... 358
Limited liability partnerships: Competent authority: Fees ... 131
Limited liability partnerships: Fees ... 131
Limited partnerships: Unrestricted size ... 131
Lincolnshire Healthcare: National Health Service Trust ... 113
Lincolnshire South West National Health Service Trust ... 113
Lincolnshire, North East: Parishes: Local government ... 95
Lincolnshire: Coroners' districts ... 32
Liquid fuels: Sulphur content: Northern Ireland ... 364
Lisburn: District name: Change: Northern Ireland ... 373
Listed bodies: Education: England ... 46
Lists & appeals: Alteration of: Non-domestic rating: Wales ... 144
Litherland: Bootle & Litherland: National Health Service Primary Care Trust ... 105
Lithuania: Double taxation: Relief ... 82
Litter: Fixed penalty: England ... 59
Little Loch Broom: Scallops: Several fishery: Shellfish: Scotland ... 343
Liverpool (City): Permitted & special parking area ... 209
Liverpool: Health Authority ... 113
Livestock industries: Cattle: Artificial insemination: Animal health: England ... 9
Livestock industries: Cattle: Artificial insemination: Animal health: Scotland ... 308
Lobsters & Crawfish: Fishing & landing: Prohibition: Wales ... 219
Local access forums: Countryside: England ... 33
Local authorities: Allowances: Scotland ... 321
Local authorities: Alternative arrangements: Wales ... 97
Local authorities: Calculations: Alteration: Wales ... 97
Local authorities: Capital finance & approved investments: England ... 94
Local authorities: Capital finance & approved investments: Wales ... 97
Local authorities: Capital finance: Discount rate 2002/03: England ... 94
Local authorities: Capital finance: Discount rate 2002/03: Wales ... 97
Local authorities: Capital finance: England ... 94
Local authorities: Companies: England ... 94

Local authorities: Companies: Wales 97
Local authorities: County & County Borough Councils: Members: Allowances: Wales 97
Local authorities: Discretionary expenditure limits: England 94
Local authorities: Disposal of dwelling houses: Deregulation: England & Wales 39
Local authorities: Elected mayors: Mayor's assistants: England 94
Local authorities: Elections: Councils: England 95
Local authorities: Executive & alternative arrangements: Different: Operation: Wales 98
Local authorities: Executive & alternative arrangements: Wales 98
Local authorities: Executive arrangements: Decisions, documents & meetings: Wales 98
Local authorities: Executive arrangements: Discharge of functions: Wales 98
Local authorities: Executive arrangements: Enactments: Modifications: England 94
Local authorities: Executive arrangements: Functions & responsibilities: Wales 98
Local authorities: Executive arrangements: Information: Access: England 94
Local authorities: Executive arrangements: Wales 98
Local authorities: Goods & services: Public bodies: England 95
Local authorities: Goods & services: Public bodies: Wales 98
Local authorities: Mayoral elections: England & Wales 96
Local authorities: Meetings & documents: Access: Period of notice: England 94
Local authorities: National Park Authorities: Members: Allowances: Wales 97
Local authorities: Referendums: Conduct: England 94
Local authorities: Requisite calculations: Alteration: England 96
Local authorities: Traffic orders: Disabled persons: Exemption: Scotland 332, 333
Local authorities: Traffic orders: Procedure: Scotland 333
Local authority remands: Electronic monitoring: Responsible officer: England & Wales 21
Local authority: Overview & scrutiny committees: Health scrutiny functions: England 113
Local education authorities: Budget: Schools & individual schools budgets: England 49
Local education authorities: Functions: Contracting out 31
Local education authorities: Post-compulsory education awards: Wales 55
Local elections: Northern Ireland 129
Local government Act 2000: Commencement 96
Local Government Act 2000: Commencement: Wales 98
Local Government Act 2000: Model code of conduct 96
Local Government Commission for England: Winding up 96
Local government, the regions & transport: Transfer of functions 103
Local government: Aberdeen: Boundaries: Scotland 321
Local government: Argyll & Bute: Boundaries: Scotland 321
Local government: Audit Commission: Borrowing limits 96
Local government: Best value performance indicators: Wales 98
Local government: Best value: Acts: Northern Ireland 358
Local government: Best value: Non-commercial considerations: Exclusion: Wales 98
Local government: Best value: Performance indicators: Performance standards 96
Local government: Best value: Performance plans & reviews: England & Wales 96
Local government: Cardiff & Vale of Glamorgan: Michaelston & Grangetown: Wales 96
Local government: Carmarthenshire & Pembrokeshire: Clynderwen, Cilymaenllwyd & Henllanfallteg: Wales 96
Local government: Ceredigion & Pembrokeshire: St Dogmaels: Wales 97
Local government: City of Edinburgh Council: Boundaries: Scotland 321
Local government: Early termination of employment: Discretionary compensation 134
Local government: Election years changes: Blackburn with Darwen (Borough) 89
Local government: Election years changes: Halton, Thurrock & Warrington (Borough) 90
Local government: Elections: Rules: Scotland 331
Local government: Elections: Scotland 331
Local government: Electoral changes: Adur (District) 91
Local government: Electoral changes: Arun (District) 91
Local government: Electoral changes: Aylesbury Vale (District) 91
Local government: Electoral changes: Babergh (District) 91
Local government: Electoral changes: Blaby (District) 91
Local government: Electoral changes: Blackburn with Darwen (Borough) 89
Local government: Electoral changes: Blackpool (Borough) 89
Local government: Electoral changes: Bournemouth (Borough) 89
Local government: Electoral changes: Bracknell Forest (Borough) 89
Local government: Electoral changes: Breckland (District) 92
Local government: Electoral changes: Bridgend: Cynffig, Cornelly & Pyle Communities: Wales 99
Local government: Electoral changes: Burnley (Borough) 89
Local government: Electoral changes: Cambridge (City) 91
Local government: Electoral changes: Caradon (District) 92
Local government: Electoral changes: Carrick (District) 92
Local government: Electoral changes: Ceredigion (County): Wales 97

Local government: Electoral changes: Charnwood (Borough) . . . 89
Local government: Electoral changes: Chichester (District) . . . 92
Local government: Electoral changes: Chiltern (District) . . . 92
Local government: Electoral changes: Christchurch (Borough) . . . 89
Local government: Electoral changes: Crawley (Borough) . . . 89
Local government: Electoral changes: East Cambridgeshire (District) . . . 92
Local government: Electoral changes: East Dorset (District) . . . 92
Local government: Electoral changes: East Riding (District) . . . 92
Local government: Electoral changes: Epping Forest (District) . . . 92
Local government: Electoral changes: Fenland (District) . . . 92
Local government: Electoral changes: Forest of Dean (District): . . . 92
Local government: Electoral changes: Great Yarmouth (Borough) . . . 89
Local government: Electoral changes: Gwynedd (County): Wales . . . 97
Local government: Electoral changes: Halton (Borough) . . . 89
Local government: Electoral changes: Harborough (District) . . . 92
Local government: Electoral changes: Herefordshire District Council (County) . . . 91
Local government: Electoral changes: Hinckley & Bosworth (Borough) . . . 89
Local government: Electoral changes: Horsham (District) . . . 92
Local government: Electoral changes: Huntingdonshire (District) . . . 92
Local government: Electoral changes: Kerrier (District) . . . 92
Local government: Electoral changes: King's Lynn & West Norfolk (Borough) . . . 89
Local government: Electoral changes: Leicester (City) . . . 91
Local government: Electoral changes: Luton (Borough) . . . 89
Local government: Electoral changes: Malvern Hills (District) . . . 93
Local government: Electoral changes: Medway (Borough) . . . 89
Local government: Electoral changes: Melton (Borough) . . . 90
Local government: Electoral changes: Mid Sussex (District) . . . 93
Local government: Electoral changes: Milton Keynes (Borough) . . . 90
Local government: Electoral changes: Monmouthshire (County): Wales . . . 97
Local government: Electoral changes: Newport (County Borough): Wales . . . 97
Local government: Electoral changes: North Cornwall (District) . . . 93
Local government: Electoral changes: North Dorset (District) . . . 93
Local government: Electoral changes: North West Leicestershire (District) . . . 93
Local government: Electoral changes: Norwich (City) . . . 91
Local government: Electoral changes: Oadby & Wigston (Borough) . . . 90
Local government: Electoral changes: Penwith (District) . . . 93
Local government: Electoral changes: Plymouth (City) . . . 91
Local government: Electoral changes: Poole (Borough) . . . 90
Local government: Electoral changes: Reading (Borough) . . . 90
Local government: Electoral changes: Redditch (Borough) . . . 90
Local government: Electoral changes: Restormel (Borough) . . . 90
Local government: Electoral changes: Slough (Borough) . . . 90
Local government: Electoral changes: South Bucks (District) . . . 93
Local government: Electoral changes: South Cambridgeshire (District) . . . 93
Local government: Electoral changes: South Norfolk (District) . . . 93
Local government: Electoral changes: South Oxfordshire (District) . . . 93
Local government: Electoral changes: South Ribble (Borough) . . . 90
Local government: Electoral changes: South Ribble (Borough): Ribble Banks Parish Council . . . 92
Local government: Electoral changes: Telford & Wrekin (Borough) . . . 90
Local government: Electoral changes: Thurrock (Borough) . . . 90
Local government: Electoral changes: Torbay (Borough) . . . 90
Local government: Electoral changes: Torfaen (County Borough): Wales . . . 97
Local government: Electoral changes: Vale of Glamorgan (County Borough): Wales . . . 97
Local government: Electoral changes: Warrington (Borough) . . . 90
Local government: Electoral changes: Waveney (District) . . . 93
Local government: Electoral changes: West Berkshire (District) . . . 93
Local government: Electoral changes: West Dorset (District) . . . 93
Local government: Electoral changes: West Oxfordshire (District) . . . 93
Local government: Electoral changes: Weymouth & Portland (Borough) . . . 90
Local government: Electoral changes: Windsor & Maidenhead (Royal Borough) . . . 95
Local government: Electoral changes: Wokingham (District) . . . 93
Local government: Electoral changes: Worcester (City) . . . 91
Local government: Electoral changes: Worthing (Borough) . . . 90
Local government: Electoral changes: Wychavon (District) . . . 93
Local government: Electoral changes: Wycombe (District) . . . 94
Local government: Electoral changes: Wyre Forest (District) . . . 94
Local government: Executive arrangements: Enactments: Modifications: England . . . 94

Local government: Finance: Scotland 321
Local government: General grant: Northern Ireland. 374
Local government: Glasgow City Council: Boundaries: Scotland 321
Local government: Local authorities: Allowances: Scotland 321
Local government: Local authorities: Alternative arrangements: Wales 97
Local government: Local authorities: Calculations: Alteration: Wales 97
Local government: Local authorities: Capital finance: Approved investments 94
Local government: Local authorities: Capital finance: Approved investments: Wales 97
Local government: Local authorities: Capital finance: Discount rate 2002/03: England 94
Local government: Local authorities: Capital finance: Discount rate 2002/03: Wales 97
Local government: Local authorities: Capital finance: England 94
Local government: Local authorities: Companies: England. 94
Local government: Local authorities: Companies: Wales 97
Local government: Local authorities: County & County Borough Councils: Wales 97
Local government: Local authorities: Discretionary expenditure limits: England 94
Local government: Local authorities: Elected mayors: Mayor's assistants: England 94
Local government: Local authorities: Executive & alternative arrangements: Different: Operation: Wales 98
Local government: Local authorities: Executive & alternative arrangements: Wales 98
Local government: Local authorities: Executive arrangements: Decisions, documents & meetings: Wales 98
Local government: Local authorities: Executive arrangements: Discharge of functions: Wales 98
Local government: Local authorities: Executive arrangements: Functions & responsibilities: Wales 98
Local government: Local authorities: Executive arrangements: Information: Access: England 94
Local government: Local authorities: Executive arrangements: Wales. 98
Local government: Local authorities: Goods & services: Public bodies: England 95
Local government: Local authorities: Goods & services: Public bodies: Wales 98
Local government: Local authorities: Meetings & documents: Access: Period of notice: England 94
Local government: Local authorities: National Park Authorities: Members: Allowances: Wales 97
Local government: Local authorities: Referendums: Conduct: England 94
Local government: Local authorities: Requisite calculations: Alteration: England 96
Local government: Local Government Commission for England: Winding-up 96
Local government: Newport: Caerleon & Malpas: Wales 99
Local government: Northern Ireland. 129, 373
Local government: Parishes: Bradford 91
Local government: Parishes: Brentwood. 91
Local government: Parishes: Broadland 91
Local government: Parishes: East Riding of Yorkshire 94
Local government: Parishes: East Staffordshire 94
Local government: Parishes: Hambleton. 94
Local government: Parishes: Mid Sussex 95
Local government: Parishes: Newcastle upon Tyne 95
Local government: Parishes: North East Lincolnshire 95
Local government: Parishes: North Somerset 95
Local government: Parishes: Oswestry 95
Local government: Parishes: Preston 95
Local government: Parishes: Richmondshire. 95
Local government: Parishes: Sedgefield 95
Local government: Parishes: South Gloucestershire 95
Local government: Parishes: St Albans 95
Local government: Parishes: St Edmundsbury 95
Local government: Parishes: Waverley 95
Local government: Parishes: Wear Valley 95
Local government: Pension schemes: England & Wales 134
Local government: Pension schemes: Management & investment of funds: England & Wales. 134
Local government: Pension schemes: Northern Ireland. 374
Local government: Pension schemes: Scotland 323
Local government: Peterborough (City): Election years changes. 89
Local government: Plymouth (City): Elections: Scheme 91
Local government: Police authorities: Best value: Performance indicators: England & Wales. 96, 138
Local government: Relevant authorities: Standards committee: Dispensations: England & Wales. 96
Local government: Renfrewshire Council: Boundaries: Scotland 321
Local government: West Dumbartonshire: Boundaries: Scotland. 321
Local government: West Lothian Council: Boundaries: Scotland 321
Local government: Whole authority analyses & improvement plans: Wales 99
Local housing authorities: Homelessness: Acts 2
Local housing authorities: Homelessness: Acts: Explanatory notes 5
Local pharmaceutical services: National Health Service: England 115
Loch Caolisport: Scallops: Several fishery: Shellfish: Scotland 343

Loch Ewe, Isle of Ewe, Wester Ross, Scallop Several Fishery: Shellfish: Scotland 343
Loch Lomond & the Trossachs National Park: Elections: Scotland 311
Loch Lomond & the Trossachs National Park: Provisions: Scotland 311
London government: Greater London Authority: Acceptance of office: Declaration 99
London government: Greater London Authority: Precept Calculations: Allocation of grants 99
London government: London service permits: Appeals 99, 143
London government: Transport Act 2000: Commencement 99, 242
London government: Warrant enforcement staff: Pensions 99, 133
London Residuary Body: Property transfer 46
London service permits: Appeals 99, 143
London Underground: Piccadilly Line: Heathrow T5 extension 243, 244
London, North Central: Health Authority 116
London, North West: Health Authority 118
London, South East: Health Authority 121
London: Greater London Magistrates' Courts Authority: Pensions 99, 134
London: South West London Community: National Health Service Trust 122
London: Transport for London: Highways: Street works: Charges 77
Londonderry Harbour: Northern Ireland 368
Londonderry Harbour: Pilotage limits: Variations: Northern Ireland 368
Long residential tenancies: Principal forms 87
Longley Park Sixth Form College: Government 49
Longley Park Sixth Form College: Incorporation 49
Loss of benefit: Social security: Northern Ireland 371, 379, 384
Lotteries: Betting, Gaming & Lotteries Act 1963: Schedule 4 18
Lotteries: Gaming Board: Fees 18
Lotteries: Variation of monetary limits 19
Lottery duty 37
Lottery: National: Awards for All joint scheme: Authorisation: England 128
Luton (Borough): Electoral changes 89
Lymington Harbour: Constitution: England 71

M

Macedonia (Former Yugoslav Republic): Treaties: Definition: European Communities 61
Machinery: Non-road mobile: Gaseous & particulate pollutants: Emission 59
Mackworth College: Dissolution 49
Magistrates' courts: Blood tests: Rules: Northern Ireland 374
Magistrates' courts: Civil Jurisdiction & Judgments Act 1982 100
Magistrates' courts: Civil Jurisdiction & Judgments Act 1982: Rules: Northern Ireland 374
Magistrates' courts: Declarations of parentage: Rules: Northern Ireland 374
Magistrates' courts: Fees: Northern Ireland 374
Magistrates' courts: Greater London Magistrates Courts Authority: Pensions: England & Wales 99, 134
Magistrates' courts: Maintenance orders: Reciprocal enforcement 100
Magistrates' courts: Procedure 100
Magistrates' courts: Procedure: Anti-social behaviour orders: England & Wales 100
Magistrates' courts: Procedure: Cash: Detention & forfeiture: England & Wales 100
Magistrates' courts: Procedure: Extradition 100
Magistrates' courts: Procedure: Sex offender Orders: England & Wales 100
Magistrates' courts: Special measures directions 99
Magistrates' courts: Terrorist cash: Detention & forfeiture: Rules: Northern Ireland 374
Maidstone & Malling National Health Service Trust 113
Maintenance of dependants: Convention countries: Recovery abroad 100
Maintenance of dependants: Maintenance orders: Reciprocal enforcement: Reciprocating countries: Designation 100
Maintenance of dependents: Reciprocal enforcement: Hague convention countries 100
Maintenance of dependents: Maintenance orders: Enforcement: Revocation 100
Maintenance orders: Enforcement: Revocation 100
Maintenance orders: Reciprocal enforcement: Hague convention countries 100
Maintenance orders: Reciprocal enforcement: Magistrates' courts 100
Maintenance orders: Reciprocal enforcement: Reciprocating countries: Designation 100
Maintenance orders: Recovery abroad: Convention countries 100
Major infrastructure projects: Inquiries: Procedure: Town & country planning: England 245
Malling: Maidstone & Malling National Health Service Trust 113
Malpas: Caerleon: Newport: Local government: Wales 99
Malvern Hills (District): Electoral changes 93
Mammals: Wild: Protection of Wild Mammals (Scotland) Act 2002: Commencement: Scotland 308, 311

Mammals: Wild: Protection of: Acts: Scotland	304
Manchester (Greater): Light rapid transit systems: Trafford depot	243, 244
Manchester Mental Health & Social Care Trust: National Health Service Trust	113
Manchester, East: Education Action Zone: Extension	44
Manchester, Greater: Health Authority	111
Manchester: North Manchester Healthcare: National Health Service Trust	118
Manchester: North Manchester: National Health Service Trust	117
Maps: Countryside: Access: Provisional & conclusive maps: England	33
Maps: Provisional & conclusive: Countryside access: Wales	33
Mariners: Statutory paternity pay & adoption pay: Persons abroad & mariners: Northern Ireland	364
Marketing standards: Olive oil	8
Marriage (Scotland) Act 2002: Commencement: Scotland	322
Marriage: Approval of places: Scotland	321
Marriages, births & deaths, etc.: Registration: Fees: England & Wales	145
Marriages, births & deaths, etc.: Registration: Fees: Northern Ireland	379
Marriages, births & deaths, etc.: Registration: Fees: Scotland	321, 330
Marriages, births & deaths, etc.: Registration: Service departments registers	145
Marriages: Acts: Explanatory notes: Scotland	305
Marriages: Acts: Scotland	304
Marriages: Religious marriages: Divorce: Acts	1
Maternity & funeral expenses: Social fund	225
Maternity & funeral expenses: Social fund: Northern Ireland	382
Maternity & parental leave	238
Maternity & parental leave: Northern Ireland	363
Maternity expenses: Social fund	225
Maternity pay: Sick pay: Statutory: Social security contributions	230, 239
Maternity pay: Statutory: Miscellaneous amendments: Northern Ireland	385, 386
Maternity pay: Statutory: Social security: Benefits: Up-rating: Northern Ireland	371, 378, 382, 385, 386
Mathematics: Assessment arrangements: Wales	54
Mayors: Elected: Mayor's assistants: Local authorities: England	94
Mayors: Elections: Local authorities: England & Wales	96
Measurement: Units: Weights & measures: Northern Ireland	387
Measuring instruments: EEC requirements: Electrical energy meters	57
Measuring instruments: EEC requirements: Fees	63
Measuring instruments: EEC requirements: Verification fees: Northern Ireland	366
Meat, meat preparations & meat products: Marking: Foot & mouth disease: England	66
Meat, meat preparations & meat products: Marking: Foot & mouth disease: Wales	69
Meat: Hazard analysis: Critical control point: England	67
Meat: Hazard analysis: Critical control point: Northern Ireland	367
Meat: Hazard analysis: Critical control point: Scotland	316
Meat: Hazard analysis: Critical control point: Wales	69
Meat: Hygiene & inspection: Wales	69
Meat: Poultry, farmed game bird & rabbit: Hygiene & inspection: Scotland	316
Medical & pharmaceutical services: General: National Health Service: Scotland	322
Medical Act 1983: Amendment	73
Medical degrees, postgraduate: University of St Andrews: Acts: Explanatory notes: Scotland	306
Medical degrees, postgraduate: University of St Andrews: Acts: Scotland	305
Medical devices	31
Medical devices: Medicines: Human use: Fees	63, 101
Medical examination: Merchant shipping	102
Medical profession: Abortion	101
Medical profession: General Medical Council: Fitness to practice committees	100
Medical profession: Medical qualifications: European specialist	100
Medical qualifications: European specialist	100
Medical services: General: National Health Service: England	114, 115
Medical services: General: National Health Service: Scotland	322
Medical services: General: National Health Service: Wales	126, 127
Medical services: General: Northern Ireland	369
Medical services: General: Supplementary list: National Health Service: England	114
Medical services: General: Supplementary list: National Health Service: Wales	127
Medical services: Northern Ireland	370
Medical services: Out of hours: National Health Service	115
Medical treatment certificates: Adults with incapacity: Scotland	306
Medical treatments: Specified: Adults with incapacity: Scotland	306, 307
Medicine: Professions supplementary: Staff & property: Transfer	73
Medicines: Codification amendments	101
Medicines: Feedingstuffs: Medicated	101

Entry	Page
Medicines: Feedingstuffs: Medicated: Northern Ireland	374
Medicines: Health & Social Care Act 2001: Commencement	101, 102, 104, 125
Medicines: Human use: Kava-kava: Prohibition	101, 102
Medicines: Human use: Medical devices: Fees	63, 101
Medicines: Non-veterinary products: General sale list	101
Medicines: Pharmacies: Registration & fees: Applications	102
Medicines: Prescription only: Human use	101
Medicines: Products for animal use: Fees	101
Medicines: Veterinary medicinal products: Marketing authorisations	101
Medway (Borough): Electoral changes	89
Medway: National Health Service Primary Care Trust	113
Meetings & documents: Access: Period of notice: Local authorities: England	94
Melton (Borough): Electoral changes	90
Mental health: Court of Protection: Rules	102
Mental health: Court protection: Enduring powers of attorney: Rules	102, 140
Mental health: Court protection: Enduring powers of attorney: Rules: England & Wales	102, 139
Merchant shipping: Confirmation of legislation: Bermuda	102
Merchant shipping: Diving safety	103
Merchant shipping: Fishing vessels: 15-24 metre vessels: Safety	103
Merchant shipping: Hours of work	102
Merchant shipping: Light dues	102
Merchant shipping: Medical examination	102
Merchant shipping: Revocation: Bermuda	102
Merchant shipping: Safety: Miscellaneous amendments	103
Merchant shipping: Safety: Navigation	103
Mergers: Interbrew SA & Bass PLC: Interim provision	29
Mersey Docks & Harbour Company: Langton River Berth: Harbour revision	71
Mersey: North Mersey Community: National Health Service Trust	117
Mersey: Trent & Mersey Canal: Bridge scheme	77
Merseyrail Electrics network	241
Merton, Sutton & Wandsworth: Health Authority	113
Merton: Nelson & West Merton: National Health Service Primary Care Trust	116
Messengers-at-arms: Fees: Act of Sederunt: Scotland	311
Metrication: Weights & measures: Northern Ireland	387
Metropolitan Police Authority: Civil staff pensions	134, 137
Michaelston & Grangetown: Cardiff & Vale of Glamorgan: Local government: Wales	96
Mid Sussex (District): Electoral changes	93
Mid Sussex: National Health Service Trust	105
Mid Sussex: Parishes: Local government	95
Mid Yorkshire hospitals: National Health Service Trust	113
Middle schools: England	46
Middlesbrough Borough Council: Highways: Street works: Charges	77
Middlesbrough National Health Service Trust	113
Middleton Railway Drewry car: Rail vehicles: Accessibility: Exemptions	41, 242
Mid-Sussex: Health Authority	113
Midwifery & nursing	130
Midwifery & nursing: Staff & property: Transfer	130
Midwifery: Nursing: Northern Ireland Practice & Education Council for Nursing & Midwifery: Northern Ireland	369
Midwives, health visitors & nurses: Professional conduct: England & Wales	130
Midwives, health visitors & nurses: Professional conduct: Northern Ireland	374
Midwives, health visitors & nurses: Professional conduct: Scotland	323
Midwives, health visitors & nurses: Rules	130
Milford Haven Port Authority: Local acts	6
Military, air & naval forces: Disablement & death: Service pensions	132
Milk Marketing Board: Dissolution: England & Wales	10
Milk Marketing Board: Residuary functions: Northern Ireland	360
Milton Keynes (Borough): Electoral changes	90
Milton Keynes (Borough): Permitted & special parking area	209
Minibuses: Section 19 permit buses	143
Ministers of the Crown: Civil defence: Transfer of functions	103
Ministers of the Crown: Ministry of Agriculture, Fisheries & Food: Dissolution	103
Ministers of the Crown: Secretaries of State for Education & Skills and Work & Pensions	103
Ministers of the Crown: Transport, local government & the regions: Transfer of functions	103
Ministry of Agriculture, Fisheries & Food: Dissolution	103
Misuse of drugs: Northern Ireland	362
Mobile machinery: Non-road: Gaseous & particulate pollutants: Emission	59
Mobile Telephones (Re-progamming) Act 2002: Commencement	34, 236

Mobile telephones: Re-programming: Acts	3
Mobile telephones: Re-programming: Acts: Explanatory notes	5
Mobility & Access Committee for Scotland: Scotland	347
Monmouthshire (County): Electoral changes: Wales	97
Monopolies & mergers: Interbrew SA & Bass PLC	29
Mortgage regulation: Commencement: Financial Services & Markets Act 2000	63
Mortgage Rights (Scotland) Act 2001: Act of Sederunt: Scotland	344
Motor cars: Driving instruction	147
Motor Insurance directive: Financial services & Markets Act 2000	64
Motor salvage operators	212
Motor salvage operators: Specified offences	35
Motor vehicles: Authorised weight: Northern Ireland	380
Motor vehicles: Competitions & trials: Scotland	333
Motor vehicles: Construction & use: Northern Ireland	380
Motor vehicles: Disabled persons: Badges: Scotland	332
Motor vehicles: Driving licences	147
Motor vehicles: Driving licences: Northern Ireland	380
Motor vehicles: Driving licences: Test fees: Northern Ireland	380
Motor vehicles: EC type approval	147
Motor vehicles: Exchangeable licences: Northern Ireland	380
Motor vehicles: Removal & disposal: England	209
Motor vehicles: Retention & disposal: Police: England & Wales	139
Motor vehicles: Road users: Charging: Enforcement: England & Wales	212
Motor vehicles: Testing: Northern Ireland	380
Motor vehicles: Tests	212
Motor vehicles: Third party risks: Northern Ireland	380
Motorways: A1(M)/M18: Wadworth interchange	152
Motorways: A1(M): Alconbury - Sawtry, Cambridgeshire	152
Motorways: A1(M): Allerton Park interchange	152
Motorways: A1(M): Baldersby to Blind Lane	153
Motorways: A1(M): Blind Lane interchange	152
Motorways: A1(M): Cornforth & junction 59	152
Motorways: A1(M): Hatfield tunnel	152
Motorways: A1(M): Junction 2-4	152
Motorways: A1(M): Junction 34-35	152
Motorways: A1(M): Junction 34-38	200
Motorways: A1(M): Junction 4, link & slip roads	152
Motorways: A1(M): Junction 44 & 45	152
Motorways: A1(M): Junction 6-5	152
Motorways: A1(M): Junction 6-7, Hertfordshire	153
Motorways: A1(M): Junction 6-8, Hertfordshire	153
Motorways: A1(M): Junction 8-9, Hertfordshire	153
Motorways: A1(M): Micklefield	153
Motorways: A1(M): River Don viaduct	153
Motorways: A1(M): Stevenage, Hertfordshire - Langford, Bedfordshire	152
Motorways: A14(M): Rusts Lane, Alconbury, Cambridgeshire	161
Motorways: A3(M): Junction 2, slip road	155
Motorways: A3(M): Junction 3 & 5, southbound exit slip roads	155
Motorways: A3(M): Junction 4, slip road	155
Motorways: A3(M): Junction 5	155
Motorways: A74(M): Junction 19, Ecclefechan, southbound on-slip road: Scotland	335
Motorways: A404(M): Junction 9A, southbound slip roads	182
Motorways: A404(M): Junction 9B-9A	182
Motorways: A404(M): Shoppenhanger's Rd	182
Motorways: A404(M): West of Maidenhead	182
Motorways: A48(M): Junction 29, Castleton to junction 29(A), St Mellons	214
Motorways: A48(M): Junction 29, Castleton to Junction 29(A), St Mellons	214
Motorways: A627(M)/M60/M62/M66: Maintenance	204
Motorways: A627/M60/M62/M66: Maintenance	204
Motorways: A823(M): Northbound & southbound on slip roads: Scotland	342
Motorways: A823(M): Pitreavie Spur: Scotland	339
Motorways: Glasgow-Monkland: stage II, connecting roads, special roads: Scotland	332, 347
Motorways: M1/M10: St Albans, Hertfordshire	190
Motorways: M1/M18: Junction 32, Thurcroft	191
Motorways: M1/M6/A14: M1 junction 19	190
Motorways: M1/M6: M1 junction 19	190
Motorways: M1: Catthorpe interchange, Leicestershire	190

Motorways: M1: Junction 2 & 3, slip roads	192
Motorways: M1: Junction 6, slip roads	191
Motorways: M1: Junction 6A & 8, link and slip roads	192
Motorways: M1: Junction 6A, link road	190
Motorways: M1: Junction 8-10, Hemel Hempstead	192
Motorways: M1: Junction 9, Hertsfordshire	191
Motorways: M1: Junction 10-15, Luton, Bedfordshire - Collingtree, Northamptonshire	192
Motorways: M1: Junction 11	191
Motorways: M1: Junction 14	191
Motorways: M1: Junction 15a	191
Motorways: M1: Junction 15A	191
Motorways: M1: Junction 15A, southbound entry slip road	191
Motorways: M1: Junction 19	190
Motorways: M1: Junction 21-21A, Leicestershire	192
Motorways: M1: Junction 24A, southbound exit slip road	191
Motorways: M1: Junction 27-30	192
Motorways: M1: Junction 29-30	192
Motorways: M1: Junction 33, 34 & 36	191
Motorways: M1: Junction 33, Catcliffe	191
Motorways: M1: Junction 36 to 37	191
Motorways: M1: Junction 36, Tankersley	191
Motorways: M1: Junction 41, Carr Gate	192
Motorways: M1: Junction 42, Lofthouse	191
Motorways: M1: Junction 44	191
Motorways: M1: Junction 45 to 46	192
Motorways: M1: Junction 47, Parlington	192
Motorways: M1: Kegworth - Long Eaton	192
Motorways: M1: Long Eaton, Derbyshire	192
Motorways: M1: South of junction 26	192
Motorways: M1: Tinsley Viaduct	190
Motorways: M1: Tinsley Viaduct, junction 34	192
Motorways: M2: Farthing Corner, slip road	192
Motorways: M2: Junction 1, coastbound slip road	192
Motorways: M2: Junction 1-4	193
Motorways: M2: Junction 1-4 & 3-4	193
Motorways: M2: Junction 1-4, slip roads	193
Motorways: M2: Junction 2, Londonbound exit slip road	192
Motorways: M2: Junction 3-4	193
Motorways: M2: Marker posts 51.0 - 53.5	193
Motorways: M2: Marker posts 64.0 - 84.0	193
Motorways: M2: Medway bridge	193
Motorways: M2: Medway Bridge, special track	193
Motorways: M2: Stockbury	180
Motorways: M3/A303: Popham	193
Motorways: M3: Junction 1-2	193
Motorways: M3: Junction 5, slip roads	193
Motorways: M3: Junction 6, Black Dam	193
Motorways: M3: Junction 6, westbound slip roads	193
Motorways: M3: Junction 7, slip roads	193
Motorways: M3: Junction 13, slip road	193
Motorways: M3: Junction 14, southbound carriageway	193
Motorways: M3: Marker posts 43.0 - 53.3	193
Motorways: M3: Marker posts 43.5 - 53.3	194
Motorways: M4/M25: Thorney interchange	194
Motorways: M4: Brynglas tunnels & junction 26, Malpas, Newport	217
Motorways: M4: Brynglas Tunnels, Newporet	217
Motorways: M4: Brynglas tunnels, Newport	217
Motorways: M4: Eastbound and westbound entry slip roads, junction 27, High Cross, Newport	217
Motorways: M4: Eastbound entry slip road, junction 28, Tredegar Park, Newport	217
Motorways: M4: Heathrow Spur & Concorde roundabout	194
Motorways: M4: Hillingdon & Hounslow: Speed limits	209
Motorways: M4: Junction 1-3	194
Motorways: M4: Junction 4-4B & 5-4B	194
Motorways: M4: Junction 4B - 5, slip & link roads	194
Motorways: M4: Junction 4B, westbound link roads	194
Motorways: M4: Junction 6, slip roads	194
Motorways: M4: Junction 8/9	194

Motorways: M4: Junction 8/9, 10 & 12, slip roads . . . 194
Motorways: M4: Junction 8/9, 11 & 12, slip roads . . . 194
Motorways: M4: Junction 8/9, eastbound slip road . . . 194
Motorways: M4: Junction 12 & 14, slip roads . . . 194
Motorways: M4: Junction 13 . . . 194
Motorways: M4: Junction 13 & 14, slip roads . . . 194
Motorways: M4: Junction 15 . . . 194
Motorways: M4: Junction 15-17 . . . 194, 195
Motorways: M4: Junction 20, Almondsbury interchange . . . 194, 196
Motorways: M4: Junction 24, Coldra Viaduct, Newport . . . 217
Motorways: M4: Junction 24, Coldra, Newport . . . 217
Motorways: M4: Junction 24, Coldra,, Newport . . . 217
Motorways: M4: Junction 25, Caerleon, Newport . . . 217
Motorways: M4: Junction 25, Caerleon, Newport County Borough . . . 217
Motorways: M4: Junction 25A, Grove Park, Newport County Borough . . . 217
Motorways: M4: Junction 26, Malpas, Newport . . . 217
Motorways: M4: Junction 27, Highcross & junction 28, Tredegar Park, Newport . . . 218
Motorways: M4: Junction 30, Pentwyn, Cardiff . . . 218
Motorways: M4: Junction 33, Capel Llanilltern, Cardiff . . . 218
Motorways: M4: Junction 33, Capel Llanilltern, Cardiff: A4232 . . . 217
Motorways: M4: Junction 34, Miskin interchange, Rhondda Cynon Taff . . . 218
Motorways: M4: Junction 41, Pentyla, Neath Port Talbot . . . 218
Motorways: M4: Junction 43 eastbound on-slip road, Llandarcy, Neath Port Talbot . . . 218
Motorways: M4: Junction 43, Llandarcy, Neath Port Talbot . . . 218
Motorways: M4: Junction 44, Lon-Las, Swansea city & county . . . 218
Motorways: M4: Junction 45, Swansea . . . 218
Motorways: M4: Junction 45, Ynysforgan, Swansea: Eastbound & westbound slip roads . . . 217
Motorways: M4: Junction 46, Pant Lasau Bridge, Neath Port Talbot . . . 218
Motorways: M4: London Borough of Hounslow: Bus lane . . . 209
Motorways: M4: Purley Rd. overbridge . . . 195
Motorways: M4: Westbound entry slip road, junction 28, Tredegar Park, Newport . . . 218
Motorways: M5/M42: M42 southbound link road to M5 at junction 4A . . . 202
Motorways: M5: Avonmouth Bridge, separate track & footway . . . 152
Motorways: M5: Junction 1 - M6 junction 8 . . . 195
Motorways: M5: Junction 2-5 . . . 195
Motorways: M5: Junction 4A . . . 195
Motorways: M5: Junction 5 . . . 195
Motorways: M5: Junction 5, southbound exit slip road . . . 195
Motorways: M5: Junction 6 . . . 195
Motorways: M5: Junction 6-5 . . . 195
Motorways: M5: Junction 8 . . . 195
Motorways: M5: Junction 11a . . . 195
Motorways: M5: Junction 11a-11 . . . 195
Motorways: M5: Junction 11a-12 . . . 196
Motorways: M5: Junction 12 . . . 195
Motorways: M5: Junction 12-11a . . . 196
Motorways: M5: Junction 13-14, Michaelwood services . . . 196
Motorways: M5: Junction 14-13 . . . 196
Motorways: M5: Junction 15-17, Almondsbury interchange . . . 196
Motorways: M5: Junction 17 . . . 195
Motorways: M5: Junction 18 & 18a . . . 196
Motorways: M5: Junction 18a-18 . . . 195, 196
Motorways: M5: Junction 19-20 . . . 196
Motorways: M5: Junction 20-19 . . . 196
Motorways: M5: Junction 21 . . . 195
Motorways: M5: Junction 22 . . . 195
Motorways: M5: Junction 22-23 . . . 196
Motorways: M5: Junction 25 . . . 195
Motorways: M5: Junction 27 . . . 182
Motorways: M5: Junction 27-28 . . . 196
Motorways: M5: Junction 28, 30 & 31 . . . 196
Motorways: M5: Junction 30-31 . . . 196
Motorways: M5: M5 Junction 1 - M6 Junction 8 . . . 196
Motorways: M6/A14/M1: M1 junction 19 . . . 190
Motorways: M6/M1: M1 junction 19 . . . 190
Motorways: M6: Catthorpe interchange, Leicestershire . . . 190
Motorways: M6: Croft . . . 196

Motorways: M6: Goodyers End - junction 3 197
Motorways: M6: Junction 3-4 198
Motorways: M6: Junction 4 196
Motorways: M6: Junction 4-4A & 8-9 195
Motorways: M6: Junction 4A, Warwickshire 197
Motorways: M6: Junction 8 197
Motorways: M6: Junction 8 southbound link road to M5 197
Motorways: M6: Junction 8-9 198
Motorways: M6: Junction 10A, M54 junction 3 203
Motorways: M6: Junction 11 197
Motorways: M6: Junction 15, slip roads 197
Motorways: M6: Junction 15-16 198
Motorways: M6: Junction 18, northbound exit slip road 197
Motorways: M6: Junction 19, Tabley 197
Motorways: M6: Junction 22-23, Bridges 198
Motorways: M6: Junction 24 to 25 198
Motorways: M6: Junction 25, slip roads 197
Motorways: M6: Junction 26-27, slip roads 198
Motorways: M6: Junction 27-28 198
Motorways: M6: Junction 33 197
Motorways: M6: Junction 33 to 32 198
Motorways: M6: Junction 34 197
Motorways: M6: Junction 34, slip roads 197
Motorways: M6: Junction 35 to 36 198
Motorways: M6: Junction 36-38, Killington Lake 198
Motorways: M6: Junction 37, Low Park to Low Gill 197
Motorways: M6: Junction 38, Galloper Well Bridge 197
Motorways: M6: Junction 38, northbound 197
Motorways: M6: Junction 38, Tebay 197
Motorways: M6: Junction 43, Garlands Cumwhinton Bridge 197
Motorways: M6: Junction 43, Rosehill interchange 197
Motorways: M6: Junctions 40 to 39, Trainriggs Bridge 198
Motorways: M6: Lymm 196
Motorways: M6: M1 - M42 198
Motorways: M6: Northbound exit slip road leading to Stafford service area 198
Motorways: M6: River Avon viaduct, Leicestershire 190
Motorways: M6: Thelwall Viaduct 198
Motorways: M6: West of junction 2, Coventry 198
Motorways: M6, junction 1: M69 207
Motorways: M8: Eastbound off slip road to A720 at junction 1, Hermiston interchange: Scotland 340
Motorways: M8: Eastbound on-slip road at A899, junction 3: Scotland 340
Motorways: M8: Eastbound on-slip road at junction 3: Scotland 340
Motorways: M8: Junction 6, Newhouse to junction 31, West Ferry: Scotland 334
Motorways: M8: Kingston Bridge: Scotland 340
Motorways: M8: Slip roads at junction 4: Scotland 340
Motorways: M8: Various: Scotland 342
Motorways: M8: Westbound carriageway from junction 22, Plantation to junction 26, Hillington: Scotland .. 340
Motorways: M8: Westbound off-slip road at junction 3: Scotland 340
Motorways: M8: Westerhouse Rd., eastbound slip roads at junction 10: Scotland 332
Motorways: M9: Craigforth interchange junction 10, southbound on slip: Scotland 340
Motorways: M9: Eastbound off slip at junction 2, Philipstoun: Scotland 340
Motorways: M9: Eastbound off slip at junction 4: Scotland 340
Motorways: M9: Lathallan interchange junction 4, westbound on slip: Scotland 340
Motorways: M9: Northbound on slip road at A904, West Mains 340
Motorways: M9: Northbound on slip road at junction 4, Lathallan: Scotland 340
Motorways: M9: Slip roads at junction 5: Scotland 340
Motorways: M9: Slip roads at junction 9: Scotland 340
Motorways: M9: Southbound off slip at junction 6: Scotland 341
Motorways: M10/M1: St Albans, Hertfordshire 190
Motorways: M10: Park St. 182
Motorways: M11/M25: Theydon interchange 198
Motorways: M11: Cambridgeshire 199
Motorways: M11: Junction 4, link roads 199
Motorways: M11: Junction 4, Redbridge viaduct 199
Motorways: M11: Junction 4, southbound 199
Motorways: M11: Junction 6 & 7, link & slip roads 199
Motorways: M11: Junction 6, northbound link road 199

Motorways: M11: Junction 6, Theydon interchange, M25	199
Motorways: M11: Junction 7-10, Essex	199
Motorways: M11: Junction 8, connecting roads, Essex	199
Motorways: M11: Junction 8: Speed limits	209
Motorways: M11: Junction 8-10, Essex	199
Motorways: M11: Junction 9, Great Chesterford, Essex	199
Motorways: M11: Junction 9-10	199
Motorways: M11: Junction 9-14, Cambridgeshire	199
Motorways: M11: Junction 10-11, Cambridgeshire	199
Motorways: M11: Junction 10-12, Cambridgeshire	199
Motorways: M11: Junction 12 - 11, Cambridgeshire	199
Motorways: M11: Junction 14, slip roads	199
Motorways: M18/A1(M): Wadworth interchange	152
Motorways: M18/M1: Junction 32, Thurcroft	191
Motorways: M18: Cantley Common	199
Motorways: M18: Junction 2, Wadworth	191
Motorways: M18: Junction 3 to 4	199
Motorways: M18: Junction 7	206
Motorways: M18: Thurcroft interchange & junction 2-5	200
Motorways: M20: Junction 5, Londonbound slip road	200
Motorways: M20: Junction 6, Londonbound distributor	200
Motorways: M20: Junction 9 - 11	200
Motorways: M20: Junction 9, slip roads	200
Motorways: M20: Junction 9-11	200
Motorways: M20: Junction 13 - Dover	200
Motorways: M23: Airport Way, junction 9A & 10	164
Motorways: M25/M11. Theydon interchange	198
Motorways: M25/M4: Thorney interchange	194
Motorways: M25: Bell Common tunnel	200
Motorways: M25: Holmesdale tunnel	200
Motorways: M25: Junction 2, southbound entry slip road	200
Motorways: M25: Junction 9, eastbound slip road	200
Motorways: M25: Junction 10, 12 & 14, slip roads	201
Motorways: M25: Junction 12, northbound link road	200
Motorways: M25: Junction 13, southbound carriageway	200
Motorways: M25: Junction 15, southbound carriageway	200
Motorways: M25: Junction 16	202
Motorways: M25: Junction 16 & M40, junction 1A-4	200
Motorways: M25: Junction 16, link road	200
Motorways: M25: Junction 16, southbound slip road	200
Motorways: M25: Junction 17-22	201
Motorways: M25: Junction 18, slip road	200
Motorways: M25: Junction 20-23	201
Motorways: M25: Junction 21, eastbound link road	201
Motorways: M25: Junction 22 & 23, slip roads	201
Motorways: M25: Junction 24, slip road	201
Motorways: M25: Junction 26, slip roads	201
Motorways: M25: Junction 28	201
Motorways: M25: Junction 28, slip roads	201
Motorways: M25: Junction 30-31, southbound	201
Motorways: M25: South of junction 29	201
Motorways: M26: Eastbound carriageway	201
Motorways: M27: Junction 11, slip road	201
Motorways: M27: Junction 12, eastbound slip road	201
Motorways: M27: Junction 5 - 10, slip roads	201
Motorways: M27: Junction 5, slip road	201
Motorways: M32: Junction 2	201
Motorways: M40: Eastbound junction 16-15	202
Motorways: M40: Junction 1 to 2	202
Motorways: M40: Junction 3, Buckinghamshire - junction 10, Oxfordshire	202
Motorways: M40: Junction 4-5, Buckinghamshire	202
Motorways: M40: Junction 5, Stokenchurch, Buckinghamshire	202
Motorways: M40: Junction 5-8, Buckinghamshire - Oxfordshire	202
Motorways: M40: Junction 8, Oxford Spur, northbound exit slip road	202
Motorways: M40: Junction 8-15	202
Motorways: M40: Junction 8a, northbound exit slip road	202
Motorways: M40: Junction 9	202

Entry	Page
Motorways: M40: Junction 10, Ardley interchange, Oxfordshire	202
Motorways: M40: Junction 10, northbound entry slip road	202
Motorways: M40: Junction 10, southbound exit slip road	202
Motorways: M40: Junction 12-13, northbound exit slip roads	202
Motorways: M40: Junction 16-15	202
Motorways: M42/M5: M42 southbound link road to M5 at junction 4A	202
Motorways: M42: Junction 3A	202
Motorways: M42: Junction 3A-8	195
Motorways: M42: Junction 4	203
Motorways: M42: Junction 4, Monkspath, Solihull	202
Motorways: M42: Junction 4, slip roads	203
Motorways: M42: Junction 5-6	203
Motorways: M42: Junction 7A-9	203
Motorways: M42: Junction 10	157
Motorways: M42: Junction 10-11	203
Motorways: M42: M5 Motorway, junction 4A-1	195
Motorways: M45: Dunchurch, Warwickshire	203
Motorways: M48: Junction 2	203
Motorways: M50: Junction 1-2	203
Motorways: M50: Junction 2-4	203
Motorways: M53: Junction 2 to 1	203
Motorways: M53: Junction 2 to 3	203
Motorways: M53: Junction 5	203
Motorways: M53: Junction 9	203
Motorways: M53: Junction 11 to 12	203
Motorways: M53: Junction 12, Hoole interchange	203
Motorways: M54: Junction 2 to M6 junction 10A	203
Motorways: M54: Junction 3, M6 junction 10A	203
Motorways: M56	204
Motorways: M56/M60/M61/M62/M602: Loop cutting	204
Motorways: M56/M60/M67: slip roads	203
Motorways: M56: Junction 6 to 4	204
Motorways: M56: Junction 6 to 7	204
Motorways: M56: Junction 7 to 9	204
Motorways: M56: Junction 7, eastbound entry slip road	204
Motorways: M56: Junction 10, slip roads	204
Motorways: M56: Junction 12, westbound exit slip road	204
Motorways: M56: Junction 14	204
Motorways: M56: Lymm	196
Motorways: M57	204
Motorways: M57: Junction 1 to 7	204
Motorways: M57: Junction 3 to 4	204
Motorways: M58: Junction 5, eastbound exit slip road	204
Motorways: M60/M56/M61/M62/M602: Loop cutting	204
Motorways: M60/M602: Link road	208
Motorways: M60/M61: Moss Farm footbridge & Riders Farm bridge	204
Motorways: M60/M62/M66/A627(M): Maintenance	204
Motorways: M60/M62/M66/A627: Maintenance	204
Motorways: M60/M67/M56: slip roads	203
Motorways: M60: Junction 1 to 2	205
Motorways: M60: Junction 1, clockwise exit slip road	204
Motorways: M60: Junction 1, slip roads	204, 205
Motorways: M60: Junction 3	205
Motorways: M60: Junction 4	205
Motorways: M60: Junction 5	205
Motorways: M60: Junction 6	204
Motorways: M60: Junction 8 & 7	205
Motorways: M60: Junction 10 to 8	205
Motorways: M60: Junction 10, anticlockwise exit slip road	205
Motorways: M60: Junction 12, clockwise exit link road	205
Motorways: M60: Junction 13, clockwise entry slip road	205
Motorways: M60: Junction 15	205
Motorways: M60: Junction 15, anticlockwise exit slip road	205
Motorways: M60: Junction 23, anticlockwise entry slip road	205
Motorways: M60: Junction 24, anti-clockwise exit slip road	205
Motorways: M60: Junction 25: Speed limits	209
Motorways: M61/M56/M60/M62/M602: Loop cutting	204

Motorways: M61/M60: Moss Farm footbridge & Riders Farm bridge. 204
Motorways: M61: Junction 1, Wardley Loop Bridge 205
Motorways: M61: Junction 3 205
Motorways: M61: Junction 6 to 8, Roscoe Lowe bridge 206
Motorways: M61: Junction 8 to 9 206
Motorways: M61: Junction 9 206
Motorways: M61: Kearsley Spur 206
Motorways: M61: Tramway link road 206
Motorways: M61: Wingates bridge 206
Motorways: M62/M56/M60/M61/M602: Loop cutting 204
Motorways: M62/M60/M66/A627(M): Maintenance 204
Motorways: M62/M60/M66/A627: Maintenance 204
Motorways: M62/M621: Gildersome 206
Motorways: M62: Chain Bar interchange 208
Motorways: M62: Croft 196
Motorways: M62: Junction 7, entry slip road 206
Motorways: M62: Junction 8 & 9 206
Motorways: M62: Junction 8 to 9 206
Motorways: M62: Junction 11 to 12 207
Motorways: M62: Junction 12 & 11 207
Motorways: M62: Junction 22 206
Motorways: M62: Junction 26 - 27 206
Motorways: M62: Junction 26, Chain Bar 208
Motorways: M62: Junction 29 to 30 206
Motorways: M62: Junction 29, Lofthouse 206
Motorways: M62: Junction 33, Ferrybridge 206
Motorways: M62: Junction 35 206
Motorways: M62: Junction 38, North Cave 207
Motorways: M62: River Ouse bridge 207
Motorways: M65: Junction 1 to 9 207
Motorways: M65: Junction 6, eastbound entry slip road 207
Motorways: M65: Junction 8 to 10 207
Motorways: M66/M60/M62/A627(M): Maintenance 204
Motorways: M66/M62/M60/A627: Maintenance 204
Motorways: M66: Junction 4 207
Motorways: M67/M60/M56: slip roads 203
Motorways: M67: Eastbound carriageway 207
Motorways: M67: Junction 1 207
Motorways: M67: Junction 2 to Denton roundabout 207
Motorways: M67: Junction 3 to 4, westbound carriageway 207
Motorways: M69: Junction 1 - M6 motorway junction 2 198
Motorways: M69: M6, junction 1 207
Motorways: M69: South Leicester railway bridge 207
Motorways: M69: Southbound exit slip road to M6 Motorway, junction 2 207
Motorways: M73/M74: Slip roads at Maryville interchange: Scotland 341
Motorways: M73: Baillieston roundabout: Scotland 334
Motorways: M73: Junction 2, Baillieston to junction 2A, Gartcosh: Scotland 341
Motorways: M73: Northbound off slip road to the M8 at junction 2, Baillieston: Scotland 341
Motorways: M73: Northbound on slip road & southbound off slip road at junction 2, Baillieston: Scotland . 341
Motorways: M73: Southbound on slip road at junction 2A, Gartcosh: Scotland 341
Motorways: M73: Southbound on slip road at northbound M74 at junction 1, Maryville: Scotland 341
Motorways: M74/M73: Slip roads at Maryville interchange: Scotland 341
Motorways: M74: Junction 1, Fullarton to junction 4, Maryville interchange: Scotland 341
Motorways: M74: Northbound off slip road at junction 4, Maryville: Scotland 341
Motorways: M74: Northbound off slip road at junction 8, Canderside: Scotland 341
Motorways: M74: Northbound on slip road at junction 7, Merryton: Scotland 341
Motorways: M74: Northbound on slip road at junction 8, Canderside: Scotland 341
Motorways: M74: Northbound on slip road at junction 10, Wellburn: Scotland 341
Motorways: M74: On slip roads at junction 6, Hamilton & junction 7, Merryton: Scotland 341
Motorways: M74: Slip roads at junction 8, Canderside: Scotland 341
Motorways: M74: Southbound off slip road at junction 5, Raith interchange: Scotland 341
Motorways: M74: Southbound off slip road at junction 9, Draffan: Scotland 341, 342
Motorways: M74: Southbound off slip road to Motherwell at junction 6, Hamilton interchange: Scotland . 342
Motorways: M74: Southbound on slip road at junction 4, Maryville interchange: Scotland 342
Motorways: M74: Various on slip roads at junction 6, Hamilton: Scotland 342
Motorways: M77: Northbound on slip road at junction 1, Dumbreck: Scotland 342
Motorways: M80: Northbound carriageway off & on slip roads at junction 4, Haggs: Scotland 342

Motorways: M80: Northbound carriageway slip roads at junction 4, Haggs: Scotland 342
Motorways: M90: Junction 1, Admiralty interchange, Rosyth: Scotland 340
Motorways: M90: Junction 1: Scotland 339
Motorways: M90: Junction 4, Cocklaw interchange, Kelty: Scotland 342
Motorways: M90: Junction 10, Craigend, southbound on slip road: Scotland 342
Motorways: M90: Southbound off slip road at junction 10, Craigend: Scotland 342
Motorways: M180: Junction 2 to 3 207
Motorways: M180: Junction 3, Midmoor interchange 207
Motorways: M180: Junction 4 to 5 208
Motorways: M180: Junction 4, Ermine St. 208
Motorways: M180: Junction 5, Barnetby interchange 208
Motorways: M271: Redbridge roundabout - M27 junction 3 208
Motorways: M602/M56/M60/M61/M62: Loop cutting 204
Motorways: M602/M60: Link road 208
Motorways: M602: Junction 2 to 3 208
Motorways: M606: Chain Bar 208
Motorways: M606: Chain Bar interchange 208
Motorways: M606: Junction 2, Euroway. 208
Motorways: M621/M62: Gildersome. 206
Motorways: M621: Gildersome interchange, junction 2 & junction 3 208
Motorways: M621: Junction 1 & 4 208
Motorways: M621: Junction 1 to Gildersome interchange 208
Motorways: M621: Junction 2, Elland Rd. 208
Motorways: M621: Junction 3, Holbeck & junction 7, Stourton 208
Motorways: M621: Junction 4 to 7 209
Motorways: M621: Junction 4, Hunslet 208
Motorways: M876: Off & on slip roads at junction 1, A883 interchange: Scotland 342
Motorways: M876: Westbound on slip at junction 8: Scotland 342
Mozambique & Cameroon: Admissions: Commonwealth: Acts 1
Mull salmon fishery district: Designation: Scotland. 331
Multiple bingo: Gaming clubs 18
Music, ballet & choir schools: Grants: Education. 46
Mussel fisheries: Swansea Bay Mussel Fishery: C.V. & D.M. Thomas 220

N

National Assembly for Wales: Representation of the people 29, 40, 146
National Assembly for Wales: Returning officers' charges 146
National assistance services: Personal requirements: Sums: England 103
National assistance services: Personal requirements: Sums: Scotland. 322
National assistance services: Personal requirements: Sums: Wales 104
National assistance services: Resources: Assessment: England 103
National assistance services: Resources: Assessment: Wales 104
National Care Standards Commission: Children's Rights Director: England 20, 222
National Care Standards Commission: Director of Private & Voluntary Health Care: England 142
National Care Standards Commission: Fees & frequency of inspections: England 142, 222
National Care Standards Commission: Inspection of schools & colleges: England 20
National Council for Education & Training for Wales: School organisation proposals 56
National Crime Squad: Secretary of State's objectives: England & Wales 137
National Criminal Intelligence Service: Secretary of State's objectives 137
National Curriculum: Assessment arrangements: English, Welsh, Mathematics & Science: Wales 54
National curriculum: Key stage 4: Exceptions: England 46
National debt: Government stock: Irish registers: Closure & transfer 104
National emission ceilings 59
National emission ceilings: Large combustion plants: Environmental protection: Pollution: Prevention & control: Scotland 314
National Health Service & Community Care Act 1990: Amendment: England & Wales 125
National Health Service (Primary Care) Act 1997: Commencement 115
National Health Service Act 1977: Amendment: England & Wales 125
National Health Service Health Authorities: Avon, Gloucestershire & Wiltshire 104
National Health Service Health Authorities: Ashworth Hospital 104
National Health Service Health Authorities: Barnet, Enfield & Haringey 104
National Health Service Health Authorities: Birmingham 105
National Health Service Health Authorities: Birmingham & the Black Country 105
National Health Service Health Authorities: Brent & Harrow 105
National Health Service Health Authorities: Buckinghamshire 106

National Health Service Health Authorities: Cambridgeshire 106
National Health Service Health Authorities: County Durham & Tees Valley 108
National Health Service Health Authorities: Croydon 108
National Health Service Health Authorities: Cumbria & Lancashire 108
National Health Service Health Authorities: Doncaster Health Authority 109
National Health Service Health Authorities: Ealing, Hammersmith & Hounslow 109
National Health Service Health Authorities: East Kent 110
National Health Service Health Authorities: East Lancashire 110
National Health Service Health Authorities: Gloucestershire 110, 111
National Health Service Health Authorities: Greater Manchester 111
National Health Service Health Authorities: Hertfordshire 111
National Health Service Health Authorities: Hillingdon 111
National Health Service Health Authorities: Kensington & Chelsea and Westminster 112
National Health Service Health Authorities: Lambeth, Southwark & Lewisham 112
National Health Service Health Authorities: Leicestershire 112
National Health Service Health Authorities: Leicestershire, Northamptonshire & Rutland 112
National Health Service Health Authorities: Merton, Sutton & Wandsworth 113
National Health Service Health Authorities: Mid-Sussex 113
National Health Service Health Authorities: Norfolk 116
National Health Service Health Authorities: North & East Devon 116
National Health Service Health Authorities: North Central London 116
National Health Service Health Authorities: North Cumbria 116
National Health Service Health Authorities: North Derbyshire 116
National Health Service Health Authorities: North Essex 117
National Health Service Health Authorities: North West London 118
National Health Service Health Authorities: Northumberland 117
National Health Service Health Authorities: Northumberland, Tyne & Wear 117
National Health Service Health Authorities: Oxfordshire 118
National Health Service Health Authorities: Redbridge & Waltham Forest 119
National Health Service Health Authorities: Rotherham 119
National Health Service Health Authorities: Sandwell 120
National Health Service Health Authorities: Shropshire 120
National Health Service Health Authorities: Somerset 120
National Health Service Health Authorities: South & West Devon 120
National Health Service Health Authorities: South East London 121
National Health Service Health Authorities: South Staffordshire 121
National Health Service Health Authorities: South West Peninsula 122
National Health Service Health Authorities: Southampton & South West Hampshire 120
National Health Service Health Authorities: Surrey & Sussex 122
National Health Service Health Authorities: Thames Valley 123
National Health Service Health Authorities: Trent 123
National Health Service Health Authorities: Wakefield 123
National Health Service Health Authorities: Warwickshire 124
National Health Service Health Authorities: West Kent 124
National Health Service Health Authorities: West Sussex 124
National Health Service Health Authorities: West Yorkshire 124
National Health Service Health Authorities: Worcestershire 125
National Health Service Primary Care Trusts: Adur, Arun & Worthing 104
National Health Service Primary Care Trusts: Ashford 104
National Health Service Primary Care Trusts: Birkenhead & Wallasey 105
National Health Service Primary Care Trusts: Bootle & Litherland 105
National Health Service Primary Care Trusts: Brent 105
National Health Service Primary Care Trusts: Brighton & Hove City 105
National Health Service Primary Care Trusts: Burntwood, Lichfield & Tamworth 106
National Health Service Primary Care Trusts: Camden 106
National Health Service Primary Care Trusts: Canterbury & Coastal 107
National Health Service Primary Care Trusts: Cannock Chase 107
National Health Service Primary Care Trusts: Central Cheshire 107
National Health Service Primary Care Trusts: Central Derby 107
National Health Service Primary Care Trusts: Cheshire West 107
National Health Service Primary Care Trusts: Coventry 108
National Health Service Primary Care Trusts: Crawley 108
National Health Service Primary Care Trusts: Croydon 108
National Health Service Primary Care Trusts: East Staffordshire 110
National Health Service Primary Care Trusts: East Elmbridge & Mid Surrey 109
National Health Service Primary Care Trusts: East Kent Coastal 110
National Health Service Primary Care Trusts: East Surrey 110

National Health Service Primary Care Trusts: Eastbourne Downs. 109
National Health Service Primary Care Trusts: Eastern Birmingham 109
National Health Service Primary Care Trusts: Eastern Cheshire. 109
National Health Service Primary Care Trusts: Eastleigh & Test Valley South 110
National Health Service Primary Care Trusts: Ellesmere Port & Neston. 110
National Health Service Primary Care Trusts: Fenland 110
National Health Service Primary Care Trusts: Guildford & Waverley 111
National Health Service Primary Care Trusts: Harrow 111
National Health Service Primary Care Trusts: Heart of Birmingham Teaching. 111
National Health Service Primary Care Trusts: Horsham & Chanctonbury 111
National Health Service Primary Care Trusts: Islington 112
National Health Service Primary Care Trusts: Kennet & North Wiltshire 112
National Health Service Primary Care Trusts: Kensington & Chelsea 112
National Health Service Primary Care Trusts: Lambeth 112
National Health Service Primary Care Trusts: Lewisham 113
National Health Service Primary Care Trusts: Lincolnshire South West. 113
National Health Service Primary Care Trusts: Maidstone & Malling. 113
National Health Service Primary Care Trusts: Medway 113
National Health Service Primary Care Trusts: Nelson & West Merton 116
National Health Service Primary Care Trusts: North Birmingham 116
National Health Service Primary Care Trusts: North Stoke 117
National Health Service Primary Care Trusts: North Surrey 117
National Health Service Primary Care Trusts: North Warwickshire 117
National Health Service Primary Care Trusts: Northampton 116
National Health Service Primary Care Trusts: Northamptonshire Heartlands 116
National Health Service Primary Care Trusts: Northumberland Care Trust 117
National Health Service Primary Care Trusts: Oldbury & Smethwick 118
National Health Service Primary Care Trusts: Poole 118
National Health Service Primary Care Trusts: Redditch & Bromsgrove 119
National Health Service Primary Care Trusts: Rowley Regis & Tipton 119
National Health Service Primary Care Trusts: Rugby 119
National Health Service Primary Care Trusts: Rushmoor & Hart 119
National Health Service Primary Care Trusts: Shepway 120
National Health Service Primary Care Trusts: Shropshire County 120
National Health Service Primary Care Trusts: South Birmingham 120
National Health Service Primary Care Trusts: South Stoke 121
National Health Service Primary Care Trusts: South Warwickshire 121
National Health Service Primary Care Trusts: South Western Staffordshire 121
National Health Service Primary Care Trusts: South Worcestershire 122
National Health Service Primary Care Trusts: Southampton East Healthcare 120
National Health Service Primary Care Trusts: Southwark 121
National Health Service Primary Care Trusts: Sussex Downs & Weald 122
National Health Service Primary Care Trusts: Swale 123
National Health Service Primary Care Trusts: Swindon 123
National Health Service Primary Care Trusts: Tameside & Glossop 123
National Health Service Primary Care Trusts: Teddington, Twickenham & Hamptons 123
National Health Service Primary Care Trusts: Teignbridge 123
National Health Service Primary Care Trusts: Telford & Wrekin 123
National Health Service Primary Care Trusts: Torbay 123
National Health Service Primary Care Trusts: Walsall 123
National Health Service Primary Care Trusts: Wandsworth 123
National Health Service Primary Care Trusts: Wednesbury & West Bromwich 124
National Health Service Primary Care Trusts: Western Sussex 124
National Health Service Primary Care Trusts: Westminster 124
National Health Service Primary Care Trusts: Woking Area 125
National Health Service Primary Care Trusts: Wolverhampton City 125
National Health Service Reform & Health Care Professions Act 2002: Commencement 73, 126
National Health Service Reform & Health Care Professions Act 2002: Commencement: England 73, 115
National Health Service Reform & Health Care Professions Act 2002: Commencement: England & Wales 126
National Health Service Reform & Health Care Professions Act 2002: Commencement:, Wales 128
National Health Service Reform & Health Care Professions Act 2002: Supplementary, etc. provisions 115
National Health Service Trusts: Barnsley Community & Priority Services 104
National Health Service Trusts: Basildon & Thurrock General Hospitals 104
National Health Service Trusts: Birmingham Specialist Community 105
National Health Service Trusts: Blackburn, Hyndburn & Ribble Valley 110
National Health Service Trusts: Blackpool Victoria Hospital 105
National Health Service Trusts: Blackpool, Fylde & Wyre Hospitals 105

National Health Service Trusts: Blackpool, Wyre & Fylde Community Health Services 105
National Health Service Trusts: Bournewood Community & Mental Health 105
National Health Service Trusts: Bradford Community Health 105
National Health Service Trusts: Bradford District Care 105
National Health Service Trusts: Brent, Kensington, Chelsea & Westminster Mental Health 105
National Health Service Trusts: Brighton & Sussex University Hospitals 105
National Health Service Trusts: Buckinghamshire Hospitals 106
National Health Service Trusts: Burnley Health Care 110
National Health Service Trusts: Bury 106
National Health Service Trusts: Bury Health Care 106
National Health Service Trusts: Calderdale 106
National Health Service Trusts: Cambridgeshire & Peterborough Mental Health Partnership 106
National Health Service Trusts: Camden & Islington Mental Health 106
National Health Service Trusts: Cheshire & Wirral Partnership 107
National Health Service Trusts: Cheshire Community Healthcare 107
National Health Service Trusts: Chester & Halton Community 107
National Health Service Trusts: Chorley & South Ribble 112
National Health Service Trusts: City Hospital 119
National Health Service Trusts: CommuniCare 107
National Health Service Trusts: Community Health Care Service (North Derbyshire) 121
National Health Service Trusts: Community Healthcare Bolton 107
National Health Service Trusts: Cornwall Healthcare 108
National Health Service Trusts: County Durham & Darlington Acute Hospitals 108
National Health Service Trusts: Craven, Harrogate & Rural District 108
National Health Service Trusts: Croydon & Surrey Downs Community 108
National Health Service Trusts: Darlington 109
National Health Service Trusts: Derwentside 109
National Health Service Trusts: Dewsbury 113
National Health Service Trusts: Dissolution 116
National Health Service Trusts: Dissolutions: Miscellaneous: England 116
National Health Service Trusts: Doncaster Healthcare 109
National Health Service Trusts: Durham & Chester-le-Street 109
National Health Service Trusts: Durham Dales 109
National Health Service Trusts: Easington 109
National Health Service Trusts: East Berkshire 109
National Health Service Trusts: East Gloucestershire 110
National Health Service Trusts: East Lancashire Hospitals 110
National Health Service Trusts: Eastbourne & County 109
National Health Service Trusts: Essex Rivers Healthcare 110
National Health Service Trusts: Gateshead 110
National Health Service Trusts: Gloucestershire Royal 111
National Health Service Trusts: Halton 111
National Health Service Trusts: Hambleton & Richmondshire 111
National Health Service Trusts: Harrow & Hillingdon Healthcare 111
National Health Service Trusts: Huddersfield 112
National Health Service Trusts: Invicta Community 112
National Health Service Trusts: Knowsley 112
National Health Service Trusts: Lancashire Teaching Hospitals 112
National Health Service Trusts: Langbaurgh 112
National Health Service Trusts: Leeds Community & Mental Health Services Teaching 112
National Health Service Trusts: Leicestershire & Rutland Healthcare 112
National Health Service Trusts: Lifespan Healthcare Cambridge 106, 113
National Health Service Trusts: Lincolnshire Healthcare 113
National Health Service Trusts: Liverpool Health Authority 113
National Health Service Trusts: Manchester Mental Health & Social Care 113
National Health Service Trusts: Mid Sussex 105
National Health Service Trusts: Mid Yorkshire hospitals 113
National Health Service Trusts: Middlesbrough 113
National Health Service Trusts: North & East Devon Partnership 116
National Health Service Trusts: North & South Durham 108
National Health Service Trusts: North Derbyshire Community Health Care Service 108
National Health Service Trusts: North Kirklees 117
National Health Service Trusts: North Manchester 117
National Health Service Trusts: North Mersey Community 117
National Health Service Trusts: North Sefton & West Lancashire Community 117
National Health Service Trusts: North Somerset 117
National Health Service Trusts: North Warwickshire 117

National Health Service Trusts: North West Anglia Health Care 106, 117
National Health Service Trusts: Northallerton Health Services 116
National Health Service Trusts: Oldham 118
National Health Service Trusts: Parkside 118
National Health Service Trusts: Pennine, Bury, Rochdale, Oldham, North Manchester 118
National Health Service Trusts: Pinderfields & Pontefract 113
National Health Service Trusts: Portsmouth Healthcare 118
National Health Service Trusts: Preston Acute Hospitals 112
National Health Service Trusts: Priority Healthcare Wearside 121
National Health Service Trusts: Riverside Community Health Care 119
National Health Service Trusts: Rochdale 119
National Health Service Trusts: Rochdale Healthcare 119
National Health Service Trusts: Rotherham Priority Health Services 119
National Health Service Trusts: Sandwell & West Birmingham Hospitals 119
National Health Service Trusts: Sandwell Healthcare 119
National Health Service Trusts: Scarborough, Whitby & Ryedale 120
National Health Service Trusts: Sedgefield 120
National Health Service Trusts: Sheffield Children's Hospital 120
National Health Service Trusts: Shropshire's Community & Mental Health Services 120
National Health Service Trusts: South Buckinghamshire 106, 120
National Health Service Trusts: South Cambridgeshire 120
National Health Service Trusts: South Essex Health Authority 121
National Health Service Trusts: South Essex Mental Health & Community Care 121
National Health Service Trusts: South Huddersfield 121
National Health Service Trusts: South of Tyne & Wearside 121
National Health Service Trusts: South Tees Acute Hospitals 121
National Health Service Trusts: South Tyneside 121
National Health Service Trusts: South Warwickshire Combined Care 121
National Health Service Trusts: South West London Community 122
National Health Service Trusts: South West Yorkshire Mental Health 122
National Health Service Trusts: South Yorkshire Metropolitan Ambulance & Paramedic Service 122
National Health Service Trusts: Southern Derbyshire Mental Health 121
National Health Service Trusts: Southhampton Community Health Services 120
National Health Service Trusts: St Helens 122
National Health Service Trusts: St Helens & Knowsley Community Health 122
National Health Service Trusts: Stoke Mandeville Hospital 106
National Health Service Trusts: Sunderland Health Authority 122
National Health Service Trusts: Sunderland Teaching 122
National Health Service Trusts: Surrey & Sussex Healthcare 122
National Health Service Trusts: Sussex Weald & Downs 122, 124
National Health Service Trusts: Tameside & Glossop Community & Priority Services 123
National Health Service Trusts: Taunton & Somerset 123
National Health Service Trusts: Thames Gateway 123
National Health Service Trusts: Thames Gateway & Invicta Community Care 124
National Health Service Trusts: Velindre 128
National Health Service Trusts: Walsall Community Health 123
National Health Service Trusts: Warrington 124
National Health Service Trusts: Warrington Community Healthcare 124
National Health Service Trusts: West Kent NHS and Social Care Trust 124
National Health Service Trusts: West Sussex Health & Social Care 124
National Health Service Trusts: Wiltshire & Swindon Health Care 124
National Health Service Trusts: Wirral & West Cheshire Community 107
National Health Service Trusts: Witham, Braintree and Halstead Care 124
National Health Service Trusts: Worcestershire Community & Mental Health 125
National Health Service Trusts: Worthing Priority 124
National Health Service: Clinical excellence: National institute: England & Wales 126
National Health Service: Clinical excellence: National institute: Establishment & constitution: England & Wales 126
National Health Service: Clinical negligence & other risks indemnity scheme: Scotland 322
National Health Service: Clinical negligence scheme: England 114
National Health Service: Commission for Patient & Public Involvement in Health: Functions: England 107
National Health Service: Commission for Patient & Public Involvement in Health: Membership & procedure: England 107
National Health Service: Community Health Councils: England 108
National Health Service: Counter Fraud & Security Management Service 108
National Health Service: Counter Fraud & Security Management Service: Establishment & constitution 108
National Health Service: Dental charges: England 114, 115
National Health Service: Drugs & appliances: Charges 114
National Health Service: Drugs & appliances: Charges: Scotland 322

National Health Service: England 114
National Health Service: Family Health Services Appeal Authority: Procedure: Rules: England & Wales 125
National Health Service: General Dental Council: Election of members 39
National Health Service: General dental services: England 114
National Health Service: General dental services: Scotland 322
National Health Service: General dental services: Wales 126, 127
National Health Service: General medical & pharmaceutical services: Scotland 322
National Health Service: General medical services: England 114
National Health Service: General medical services: Scotland 322
National Health Service: General medical services: Supplementary list: England 114
National Health Service: General medical services: Supplementary list: Wales 127
National Health Service: General medical services: Wales 126, 127
National Health Service: General ophthalmic services: England 114
National Health Service: General ophthalmic services: Scotland 322
National Health Service: General ophthalmic services: Wales 127
National Health Service: Health & Social Care Act 2001: Commencement 101, 102, 104, 111, 125
National Health Service: Health & Social Care Act 2001: Commencement: Wales 126
National Health Service: Health authorities: Administration arrangements: Functions: England 114
National Health Service: Health authorities: Establishment & abolition: England 111
National Health Service: Health authorities: Membership & procedure: England 111
National Health Service: Litigation Authority: Establishment & constitution: England 114
National Health Service: Local authority: Overview & scrutiny committees: Health scrutiny functions: England 113
National Health Service: Local pharmaceutical services & pharmaceutical services: England 115
National Health Service: Local pharmaceutical services: England 115
National Health Service: National insurance: Contributions: Acts 3
National Health Service: National Waiting Times Centre: Board: Scotland 323
National Health Service: NHS charges: Road traffic: Scotland 323, 333
National Health Service: NHS Education for Scotland: 323
National Health Service: NHS Education for Scotland: Transfer of staff 323
National Health Service: NHS Tribunal: Abolition: Consequential provisions: England & Wales 125
National Health Service: Optical charges & payments: England 115
National Health Service: Optical charges & payments: Scotland 322, 323
National Health Service: Optical charges & payments: Wales 127
National Health Service: Osteopaths Act 1993: Commencement 131
National Health Service: Out of hours: Medical services 115
National Health Service: Patient information: Control 125
National Health Service: Pension scheme: Additional voluntary contributions 125
National Health Service: Pension scheme: England & Wales 125
National Health Service: Pension scheme: Premature retirement: Compensation 125
National Health Service: Pharmaceutical services & general medical services: England 115
National Health Service: Pharmaceutical services & general medical services: Wales 127
National Health Service: Pilot schemes: England 114
National Health Service: Primary care trusts: Dissolution: England 118
National Health Service: Primary care trusts: Establishment: England 118
National Health Service: Primary care trusts: Functions: England 118
National Health Service: Primary care trusts: Membership, procedure & administration arrangements: England 118, 119
National Health Service: Quality improvement: Scotland 323
National Health Service: Quality improvement: Transfer of officers: Scotland 323
National Health Service: Reform: Health care professions: Acts 3
National Health Service: Reform: Health care professions: Acts: Explanatory notes 5
National Health Service: Retained Organs Commission: England 119
National Health Service: Road traffic: Charges: England & Wales 126, 212
National Health Service: Scottish Council for Postgraduate Medical & Dental Education: Transfer of staff: Scotland 323
National Health Service: Strategic health authorities & primary care trusts: Functions: England 114
National Health Service: Travelling expenses: Remission of charges: England 116
National Health Service: Trusts: Originating capital 116
National heritage: Acts 3
National heritage: Territorial waters adjacent to England 239
National Institute for Clinical Excellence: England & Wales 126
National Institute for Clinical Excellence: Establishment & constitution: England & Wales 126
National insurance: Contributions: Acts 3
National Lottery: Awards for All joint scheme: Authorisation: England 128
National Lottery: Licence fees 128
National Minimum Wage Regulations 1999: Amendment 238
National Parks: Loch Lomond & the Trossachs: Elections: Scotland 311
National Parks: Loch Lomond & the Trossachs: Provisions: Scotland 311
National Parks: Peak District National Park Authority: Agricultural operations: Restriction: England 33

National Ports Council: Pension scheme: Excess statutory surplus . . . 132
National Waiting Times Centre: Board: Scotland: Scotland . . . 323
Nationality, Immigration & Asylum Act 2002: Commencement . . . 81
Nationality: Acts . . . 3
Natural gas: Radioactive substances . . . 18
Naval, military & air forces: Disablement & death: Service pensions . . . 132
Navy: Courts-martial . . . 38
Navy: Royal: Army, Air Force & Naval Discipline Acts: Continuation . . . 38
Neath Port Talbot & Swansea: Trebanos & Clydach: Local government: Wales . . . 99
Negligence: Clinical negligence scheme: National Health Service: England . . . 114
Nelson & West Merton . . . 116
Neston & Ellesmere Port: National Health Service . . . 110
New Horizons Kent-Somerset Virtual: Education Action Zone: Extension . . . 49
New Roads & Street Works Act 1991: Commencement: England . . . 77
New substances: Notification of . . . 72
Newcastle upon Tyne: Parishes: Local government . . . 95
Newport (County Borough): Electoral changes: Wales . . . 97
Newport: Caerleon & Malpas: Local government: Wales . . . 99
NHS charges: Road traffic: Scotland . . . 323, 333
NHS Education for Scotland . . . 323
NHS Education for Scotland: Scottish Council for Postgraduate Medical & Dental Education: Transfer of staff . . . 323
NHS Tribunal: Abolition: Consequential provisions: England & Wales . . . 125
Nitrate sensitive areas: England . . . 9
Nitrate vulnerable zones: Designation: Additional: England . . . 9, 247
Nitrate vulnerable zones: Designation: Scotland . . . 348
Nitrates: Agricultural: Pollution: Water: Protection: Wales . . . 247
Noise: Control: Codes of practice: Construction & open sites: England . . . 142
Noise: Control: Codes of practice: Construction & open sites: Northern Ireland . . . 378
Noise: Control: Codes of practice: Construction & open sites: Scotland . . . 325
Noise: Control: Codes of practice: Construction & open sites: Wales . . . 143
Non-constituent & non-affiliated organisations: Registered parties . . . 145
Non-domestic rate: Scotland . . . 330
Non-domestic rates: Levying: Scotland . . . 330
Non-domestic rating: Contributions: England . . . 144
Non-domestic rating: Contributions: Wales . . . 145
Non-domestic rating: Demand notices: England . . . 32, 144
Non-domestic rating: Lists & appeals: Alteration: England . . . 144
Non-domestic rating: Lists & appeals: Alteration: Wales . . . 144
Non-domestic rating: Rural rate relief: Wales . . . 145
Non-fossil fuel sources: Electricity: Locational flexibility: Scotland . . . 313
Non-fossil fuel sources: Electricity: Saving arrangements: Scotland . . . 313
Non-maintained special schools: Education: England . . . 46
Norfolk: Health Authority . . . 116
Norfolk: King's Lynn & West Norfolk (Borough): Electoral changes . . . 89
Norfolk: Norwich (City): Permitted & special parking area . . . 211
Norfolk: South Norfolk (District): Electoral changes . . . 93
North & East Devon Partnership: National Health Service Trust . . . 116
North & East Devon: Health Authority . . . 116
North & South Durham: National Health Service Trust . . . 108
North Birmingham: National Health Service Primary Care Trust . . . 116
North Central London: Health Authority . . . 116
North Cornwall (District): Electoral changes . . . 93
North Cumbria: Health Authority . . . 116
North Derbyshire Community Health Care Service: National Health Service Trust . . . 108
North Derbyshire Tertiary College: Designated staff . . . 49
North Derbyshire Tertiary College: Dissolution . . . 49
North Derbyshire: Community Health Care Service (North Derbyshire): National Health Service Trust . . . 121
North Derbyshire: Health Authority . . . 116
North Dorset (District): Electoral changes . . . 93
North Dorset (District): Permitted & special parking area . . . 210
North East Derbyshire coalfields: Education Action Zone: Extension . . . 49
North East Lincolnshire: Parishes: Local government . . . 95
North Essex: Health Authority . . . 117
North Kirklees: National Health Service Trust . . . 117
North Manchester Healthcare National Health Service Trust . . . 118
North Manchester: National Health Service Trust . . . 117
North Mersey Community: National Health Service Trust . . . 117

North Sefton & West Lancashire Community: National Health Service Trust	117
North Somerset: National Health Service Trust	117
North Somerset: Parishes: Local government	95
North Stoke: National Health Service Primary Care Trust	117
North Stoke: National Health Service Trust	117
North Surrey: National Health Service Primary Care Trust	117
North Warwickshire: National Health Service Primary Care Trust	117
North Warwickshire: National Health Service Trust	117
North West Anglia Health Care: National Health Service Trust	106, 117
North West Leicestershire (District): Electoral changes	93
North West London: Health Authority	118
Northallerton Health Services: National Health Service Trust	116
Northampton: National Health Service Primary Care Trust	116
Northamptonshire Heartlands: National Health Service Primary Care Trust	116
Northamptonshire: Leicestershire, Northamptonshire & Rutland: Health Authority	112
Northern Ireland Act 1998: Modification	129, 225
Northern Ireland Act 2000: Devolved government: Suspension	29, 30, 129
Northern Ireland Act 2000: Modification	29, 129
Northern Ireland Act 2000: Prescribed documents	129
Northern Ireland Assembly allowances: Members: Winding up allowance: Northern Ireland	374
Northern Ireland Assembly elections: Amendment	129
Northern Ireland Practice & Education Council for Nursing & Midwifery: Appointments & procedure: Northern Ireland	369
Northern Ireland Social Care Council: Appointments & procedure: Northern Ireland	369
Northern Ireland: Aggregates levy: Northern Ireland tax credit	7
Northern Ireland: Budget: Acts	358
Northern Ireland: Budget: Acts: Explanatory notes	359
Northern Ireland: Children: Leaving care: Acts	358
Northern Ireland: Companies: Open-ended investment companies: Acts	358
Northern Ireland: Company directors: Disqualification: Northern Ireland	128
Northern Ireland: Criminal injuries: Compensation	128
Northern Ireland: Electoral Fraud (Northern Ireland) Act 2002: Commencement	146
Northern Ireland: Enactments: Modification	129
Northern Ireland: Fur farming: Prohibition	128
Northern Ireland: Harbours	128
Northern Ireland: Housing support services	129
Northern Ireland: Justice: Acts: Explanatory notes	5
Northern Ireland: Local government	129
Northern Ireland: Local government: Best value: Acts	358
Northern Ireland: Representation of the people	146
Northern Ireland: Road vehicles: Registration & licensing	212
Northern Ireland: Statutes: Binders	7
Northumberland Care Trust: National Health Service Primary care trust	117
Northumberland, Tyne & Wear: Health Authority	117
Northumberland: Health Authority	117
Norwich (City): Electoral changes	91
Norwich (City): Permitted & special parking area	211
Notice to employers: Industrial action ballots: Code of practice: Appointed day: Northern Ireland	372
Nottingham (City): Permitted & special parking area	209
Nottinghamshire: Petty sessions areas	87
Nursery education & early years development: England	47
Nurses & midwives: Nursing & midwifery	130
Nurses, midwives & health visitors: Nurses: Agencies: England	130
Nurses, midwives & health visitors: Professional conduct: England & Wales	130
Nurses, midwives & health visitors: Professional conduct: Northern Ireland	374
Nurses, midwives & health visitors: Professional conduct: Scotland	323
Nurses, midwives & health visitors: Rules	130
Nurses: Agencies: England	130
Nursing & midwifery	130
Nursing & Midwifery: Northern Ireland Practice & Education Council for Nursing & Midwifery: Appointments & procedure: Northern Ireland	369
Nursing & midwifery: Staff & property: Transfer	130
Nursing & midwifery: Student allowances: Scotland	313
Nursing homes & residential care: Social security	226
Nursing homes & residential care: Social security: Northern Ireland	382
Nursing: Personal & nursing care: Community care: Scotland	346
Nutrition: Food: Addition of substances: Nutritional purposes: Scotland	315
Nutrition: Food: Marketing: Notification of: England & Wales	67

Nutrition: Food: Marketing: Notification of: Scotland 316
Nutrition: Food: Substances for specific nutritional purposes: Addition: Northern Ireland 367
Nutrition: Marketing of food: Northern Ireland 367
Nutritional uses: Food: Additional substances: Wales 68
Nutritional uses: Food: England 66

O

Oadby & Wigston (Borough): Electoral changes 90
Occupational & personal pension schemes 132
Occupational & personal pension schemes: Bankruptcy 84, 132
Occupational & personal pension schemes: Bankruptcy: Northern Ireland 372, 375
Occupational & personal pension schemes: Contracting-out: Miscellaneous amendments: Northern Ireland 375
Occupational & personal pension schemes: Disclosure of information: Northern Ireland 375
Occupational pension schemes: Contracting-out 132
Occupational pension schemes: Member-nominated trustees & directors 132
Occupational pension schemes: Member-nominated trustees & directors: Northern Ireland 375
Occupational pension schemes: Minimum funding requirements 133
Occupational pension schemes: Minimum funding requirements: Northern Ireland 375
Occupational pension schemes: Winding up notices & reports 133
Occupational pension schemes: Winding up notices & reports: Northern Ireland 375
Occupational pensions: Revaluation 133
Occupational pensions: Revaluation: Northern Ireland 375
Offences: Sexual: Scotland 312
Offenders: Rehabilitation of Offenders Act 1974: Exceptions: England & Wales 146
Office of Communications Act 2002: Commencement 57
Office of Communications: Acts 3
Office of Communications: Acts: Explanatory notes 5
Office of Communications: Membership 58
Offshore chemicals 59
Offshore installations: Emergency pollution control 59
Offshore installations: Safety zones 130
Offshore safety: Miscellaneous amendments 73
Oil & fibre plant seeds: England 220
Oil: Hydrocarbon: Controlled oil: Registered dealers 37
Oil: Hydrocarbon: Industrial reliefs 37
Oil: Hydrocarbon: Marking 37
Oldbury & Smethwick: National Health Service Primary Care Trust 118
Oldham: National Health Service Trust 118
Olive oil: Marketing standards 8
Ombudsman: Assembly Ombudsman & Commissioner for Complaints: Salaries: Northern Ireland 381
Ombudsman: Scottish Public Services Ombudsman: Acts: Scotland 305
Ombudsman: Welsh Administration Ombudsman: Jurisdiction: Wales 30
Open-ended investment companies: Acts: Northern Ireland 358
Open-ended investment companies: Tax 83
Ophthalmic services: General: National Health Service: England 114
Ophthalmic services: General: National Health Service: Scotland 322
Ophthalmic services: General: National Health Service: Wales 127
Ophthalmic services: General: Northern Ireland 370
Optical charges & payments: National Health Service: England 115
Optical charges & payments: National Health Service: Scotland 322, 323
Optical charges & payments: National Health Service: Wales 127
Optical charges & payments: Northern Ireland 370
Opticians: General Optical Council: Registration & enrolment: Rules 130
Organic products: Wales 11
Orkney: Amnesic shellfish poisoning: Food protection: Scotland 326
Orkney: Paralytic shellfish poisoning: Food protection: Scotland 330
Osteopaths Act 1993: Commencement 131
Osteopaths: General Osteopathic Council: Members & chairman: Election 131
Oswestry: Parishes: Local government 95
Overseas insurers: Tax representatives 235
Overseas territories: Adoption: Children: Northern Ireland 359
Overseas territories: Anti-terrorism: Financial & other measures 131
Overseas territories: Extradition 62
Overseas territories: Geneva Conventions Act 70

Overseas territories: Hong Kong: Application: Extradition 62, 78
Overseas territories: Hong Kong: Extradition. 62, 78
Overseas territories: United Nations measures: Al-Qa'ida & Taliban 245
Overseas territories: United Nations sanctions: Somalia 246
Overseas territories: Zimbabwe: Restricted measures 131
Overseas territories: Zimbabwe: Restrictive measures 131
Overview & scrutiny committees: Health scrutiny functions: Local authority: England 113
Oxfordshire: Health Authority. 118
Oxfordshire: South Oxfordshire (District): Electoral changes 93
Oxfordshire: West Oxfordshire (District): Electoral changes 93
Ozone-depleting substances: Controls: Environmental protection 58

P

Packaging waste: Producer responsibility & obligations: England 59
Packaging waste: Producer responsibility & obligations: Scotland 314
Packaging waste: Producer responsibility & obligations: Northern Ireland 378
Packaging waste: Producer responsibility & obligations: Wales 61
Paralytic shellfish poisoning: Food protection: Orkney: Scotland 330
Parentage: Declaration: Allocation of proceedings: Northern Ireland 366
Parentage: Declarations: Magistrates' courts: Rules: Northern Ireland 374
Parents: Lone: Social security: Work-focused interviews. 230
Parents: Lone: Social security: Work-focused interviews: Northern Ireland. 385
Parishes: Bradford 91
Parishes: Brentwood. 91
Parishes: Broadland 91
Parishes: East Riding of Yorkshire 94
Parishes: East Staffordshire 94
Parishes: Hambleton. 94
Parishes: Mid Sussex 95
Parishes: Newcastle upon Tyne 95
Parishes: North East Lincolnshire 95
Parishes: North Somerset 95
Parishes: Oswestry 95
Parishes: Preston 95
Parishes: Richmondshire. 95
Parishes: Sedgefield 95
Parishes: South Gloucestershire 95
Parishes: St Albans 95
Parishes: St Edmundsbury 95
Parishes: Waverley 95
Parishes: Wear Valley 95
Parkside: National Health Service Trust 118
Parliament. Parliamentary pensions 131
Parliamentary pensions. 131
Parochial fees: Ecclesiastical law 42
Partnership: Limited liability 88, 89, 131
Partnership: Limited liability: Acts: Northern Ireland 358
Partnership: Limited liability: Competent authority: Fees 131
Partnership: Limited liability: Fees 131
Partnership: Limited: Unrestricted size 131
Partnership: Member limit: Removal of: Regulatory reform. 145
Part-time workers: Less favourable treatment: Prevention 238
Part-time workers: Rights: Northern Ireland 363
Passenger & goods vehicles: Recording equipment: Fees: Northern Ireland 380
Passenger & goods vehicles: Recording equipment: Fitters & workshops: Approval: Fees 212
Patents & plant variety rights: Compulsory licensing 132, 135
Patents: Contracting out 31
Patents: Rules 132
Paternity & adoption leave: Employment 238
Paternity & adoption leave: Employment: Northern Ireland 363
Paternity & adoption: Social security 229
Paternity & adoption: Social security: Northern Ireland. 371, 379, 384
Paternity & maternity leave 238
Paternity: Blood tests: Evidence: Northern Ireland 365

Entry	Page
Pathogens & toxins: Security: Dangerous substances	140
Pathogens Access Appeal Commission: Court of Appeal	233
Pathogens Access Appeal Commission: Procedure	140
Patient & Public Involvement in Health (Commission): Functions: England	107
Patient & Public Involvement in Health (Commission): Membership & procedure: England	107
Patient information: Control: National Health Service	125
Payments (direct): Carers: Social services: Acts: Northern Ireland	358
Peak District National Park Authority: Restriction of agricultural operations: England	33
Peanuts: China: Emergency control: England	66
Peanuts: China: Emergency control: Northern Ireland	367
Peanuts: China: Emergency control: Scotland	315
Peanuts: China: Emergency control: Wales	68
Pembrokeshire & Carmarthenshire: Clynderwen, Cilymaenllwyd & Henllanfallteg: Local government: Wales	96
Pembrokeshire: Ceredigion: St Dogmaels: Local government: Wales	97
Penalties for disorderly behaviour: Amount of penalty	35
Penalties for disorderly behaviour: Forms of penalty notice	35
Pendoylan, Llanharry, Pont-y-clun, Penllyn & Welsh St Donats: Rhondda Cynon Taff & Vale of Glamorgan: Local government: Wales	99
Penllyn, Llanharry & Pont-y-clun, Welsh St Donats, Pendoylan: Rhondda Cynon Taff & Vale of Glamorgan: Local government: Wales	99
Pennine Acute Hospitals: National Health Service Trust	118
Pensions: Child Support, Pensions & Social Security Act 2000: Commencement: England, Wales & Scotland	132
Pensions: Child support, pensions & social security: 2000 Act: Commencement: Northern Ireland	375
Pensions: Greater London Magistrates Courts Authority: Pensions: England & Wales	99, 134
Pensions: Guaranteed minimum pensions increase: Northern Ireland	375
Pensions: Guaranteed minimum: Increase	132
Pensions: Increase: Review	133
Pensions: Increase: Review: Northern Ireland	375
Pensions: Judicial Pensions & Retirement Act 1993: Qualifying judicial offices	134
Pensions: Judicial: Pensions appeal tribunals	132
Pensions: Local government pension scheme: England & Wales	134
Pensions: Local government pension scheme: Management & investment of funds: England & Wales	134
Pensions: Local government pension scheme: Northern Ireland	374
Pensions: Local government: Early termination of employment: Discretionary compensation	134
Pensions: Low earnings threshold: Social security	229
Pensions: Low earnings threshold: Social security: Northern Ireland	385
Pensions: Metropolitan Police Authority	134, 137
Pensions: National Health Service: Pension scheme: Additional voluntary contributions	125
Pensions: National Health Service: Pension scheme: England & Wales	125
Pensions: National Health Service: Pension scheme: Premature retirement: Compensation	125
Pensions: National Ports Council: Pension scheme: Excess statutory surplus	132
Pensions: Naval, military & air forces: Disablement & death: Service pensions	132
Pensions: Occupational & personal pension schemes	132
Pensions: Occupational & personal pension schemes: Bankruptcy	84, 132
Pensions: Occupational & personal pension schemes: Bankruptcy: Northern Ireland	372, 375
Pensions: Occupational & personal pension schemes: Contracting-out: Miscellaneous amendments: Northern Ireland	375
Pensions: Occupational & personal pension schemes: Disclosure of information: Northern Ireland	375
Pensions: Occupational pension schemes: Contracting-out	132
Pensions: Occupational pension schemes: Member-nominated trustees & directors	132
Pensions: Occupational pension schemes: Member-nominated trustees & directors: Northern Ireland	375
Pensions: Occupational pension schemes: Minimum funding requirements	133
Pensions: Occupational pension schemes: Minimum funding requirements: Northern Ireland	375
Pensions: Occupational pension schemes: Winding up notices & reports	133
Pensions: Occupational pension schemes: Winding up notices & reports: Northern Ireland	375
Pensions: Occupational pensions: Revaluation	133
Pensions: Occupational pensions: Revaluation: Northern Ireland	375
Pensions: Parliamentary	131
Pensions: Pension schemes: Local government: Scotland	323
Pensions: Personal injuries: Civilians: Second World War	133
Pensions: Personal pension schemes: Contracting-out	132
Pensions: Police Service of Northern Ireland	377
Pensions: Police Service of Northern Ireland: Reserve: Full time	377
Pensions: Polish forces: Scheme: Extension	133
Pensions: Sharing: Police: England & Wales	134, 139
Pensions: Stakeholder pension schemes	133
Pensions: Stakeholder pension schemes: Northern Ireland	375
Pensions: State pension credit: Acts	4
Pensions: State pension credit: Acts: Explanatory notes	5
Pensions: State pension credit: Acts: Northern Ireland	359

Pensions: Superannuation Act 1972: Admission to schedule 1. 133
Pensions: Superannuation: Invest Northern Ireland: Northern Ireland. 375
Pensions: Teachers: England & Wales 53
Pensions: Teachers: Superannuation: Scotland. 323
Pensions: Warrant enforcement staff 99, 133
Pensions: Welfare Reform & Pensions Act 1999: Commencement. 133
Pensions: Welfare reform & pensions:1999 Order: Commencement: Northern Ireland 375, 376
Penwith (District): Electoral changes 93
Personal & occupational pension schemes 132
Personal & occupational pension schemes: Bankruptcy 84, 132
Personal & occupational pension schemes: Disclosure of information: Northern Ireland 375
Personal allowances for children & young persons: Social security 226
Personal data: Sensitive: Processing: Data protection: Elected representatives 38
Personal injuries actions: Court of Session: Act of Sederunt: Scotland. 312
Personal injuries: Civilians: Pensions: Second World War 133
Personal injury payments: Social security 226
Personal injury: Damages: Scotland 312
Personal pension schemes: Contracting-out 132
Personal portfolio bonds: Tax. 235
Personal protective equipment 31, 73
Personal Social Services (Preserved Rights) Act (Northern Ireland) 2002: Commencement: Northern Ireland 377
Personal social services: Acts: Northern Ireland 358, 359
Personal social services: Penalty charges: Northern Ireland 369
Personal social services: Preserved rights: Acts: Explanatory notes Northern Ireland 359
Personal social services: Preserved rights: Acts: Northern Ireland 358
Personal social services: Preserved rights: Northern Ireland 370
Personal: Occupational & personal pension schemes: Contracting-out: Miscellaneous amendments: Northern Ireland 375
Perth & Kinross Council: Parking adjudicators: Scotland 333
Perth & Kinross Council: Parking area: Attendants: Uniforms: Scotland. 333
Perth & Kinross Council: Road traffic: Parking area: Scotland. 333
Pesticides: Crops, food & feeding stuffs: Maximum residue levels: England & Wales 8, 10, 134
Pesticides: Crops, food & feeding stuffs: Maximum residue levels: Northern Ireland 360, 376
Pesticides: Crops, food & feeding stuffs: Maximum residue levels: Scotland 308, 323
Pesticides: Plant protection products: England & Wales. 134, 135
Pesticides: Plant protection products: Fees 63, 134
Pesticides: Plant protection products: Northern Ireland 376
Pesticides: Plant protection products: Scotland 324
Peterborough (City): Election years changes. 89
Peterborough: Cambridgeshire & Peterborough Mental Health Partnership: National Health Service Trust 106
Peterhead: Harbours: Revision: Constitution: Scotland. 317
Peterlee: Education Action Zone: Extension 49
Petroleum: Production: Origin of goods 37
Pets: Travel scheme: Pilot arrangements: England. 13
Petty sessions areas: Avon & Somerset 87
Petty sessions areas: Nottinghamshire 87
Petty sessions areas: Wigan & Leigh 87
Pharmaceutical services: Drugs & appliances: Charges: Northern Ireland 370
Pharmaceutical services: National Health Service: England 115
Pharmaceutical services: National Health Service: Wales 127
Pharmaceutical services: Northern Ireland 370
Pharmaceutical Society of Northern Ireland 376
Pharmacies: Medicines: Registration & fees: Applications 102
Phytophthora ramorum: Plant health: England 136
Phytophthora ramorum: Plant health: Forestry 135
Phytophthora ramorum: Plant health: Northern Ireland 376
Phytophthora ramorum: Plant health: Scotland. 324
Phytophthora ramorum: Plant health: Wales 136
Piccadilly Line: Heathrow T5 extension 243, 244
Pig industry: Restructuring: Capital grant: Scheme: Scotland. 308
Pig industry: Restructuring: Non-capital grant: Scheme: Scotland. 308
Pigs: Records, identification & movement: England 13
Pigs: Records, identification & movement: Scotland 309
Pigs: Records, identification & movement: Wales 16
Pinderfields & Pontefract: National Health Service Trust 113
Pipelines: Valuation for rating: Exemption: Scotland 330
Pistachios, figs & hazelnuts: From Turkey: Emergency control: England 66
Pistachios, figs & hazelnuts: From Turkey: Emergency control: Scotland 315

Entry	Page
Pistachios, figs & hazelnuts: From Turkey: Emergency control: Northern Ireland	367
Pistachios, figs & hazelnuts: From Turkey: Emergency control: Wales	68
Pitcairn Islands	135
Pitcairn Islands: Court of Appeal	135
Planning & Compensation Act 1991: Schedule 18: Amendment	240
Planning: General development: Northern Ireland	376
Planning: Town & country: Applications & deemed applications: Fees: England	240
Planning: Town & country: Applications & deemed applications: Fees: Wales	240
Planning: Town & country: Costs of inquiries: Standard daily amount: England	240, 245
Planning: Town & country: Enforcement notices & appeals: England	240
Planning: Town & country: Enforcement: Determination by Inspectors: Inquiries procedure: England	245
Planning: Town & country: Enforcement: Hearings procedure: England	245
Planning: Town & country: Enforcement: Inquiries procedure: England	245
Planning: Town & country: Enforcement: Written representation procedure: England	240
Planning: Town & country: General development procedure: Wales	241
Planning: Town & country: General permitted development: Wales	241
Planning: Town & country: Inquiries: Costs of: Standard daily amount: Wales	240
Planning: Town & country: Use classes: Wales	241
Plant breeders: Rights: Fees	135
Plant health: England	136
Plant health: Forestry: Great Britain	135
Plant health: Northern Ireland	376
Plant health: Phytophthora ramorum: England	136
Plant health: Phytophthora ramorum: Forestry: Great Britain	135
Plant health: Phytophthora ramorum: Northern Ireland	376
Plant health: Phytophthora ramorum: Scotland	324
Plant health: Phytophthora ramorum: Wales	136
Plant health: Potatoes: Originating in Egypt: England	136
Plant health: Potatoes: Originating in Egypt: Northern Ireland	377
Plant health: Potatoes: Originating in Egypt: Scotland	324
Plant health: Potatoes: Originating in Egypt: Wales	136
Plant health: Potatoes: Originating in Germany: Northern Ireland	377
Plant health: Scotland	324
Plant health: Spruce bark: Treatment	136
Plant health: Wales	136
Plant health: Wood & bark: Northern Ireland	376
Plant protection products: England & Wales	134, 135
Plant protection products: Fees	63, 134
Plant protection products: Pesticides: Northern Ireland	376
Plant protection products: Pesticides: Scotland	324
Plant Varieties & Seeds Tribunal: England & Wales	221
Plant variety rights & patents: Compulsory licensing	132, 135
Plants: Large combustion: Scotland	314
Plastic materials & articles: Food: Contact with: England	67
Plastic materials & articles: Food: Contact with: Northern Ireland	367
Plastic materials & articles: Food: Contact with: Scotland	316
Plastic materials & articles: Food: Contact with: Wales	69
Plymouth (City): Elections: Scheme	91
Plymouth (City): Electoral changes	91
Pneumoconiosis, etc.: Workers' compensation: Claims: Payment: Northern Ireland	381
Police & Criminal Evidence Act 1984: Codes of practice: Code D: Temporary modifications	138
Police & Criminal Evidence Act 1984: Codes of practice: Modification	138
Police & Criminal Evidence Act 1984: Codes of practice: Statutory powers of stop & search: England & Wales	138
Police & Criminal Evidence Act 1984: Codes of practice: Visual recording of interviews	138
Police & Criminal Evidence Act 1984: Department of Trade & Industry: Investigations	35
Police & Criminal Evidence Act 1984: Visual recording of interviews	138
Police & Fire Services (Finance) (Scotland) Act 2001: Commencement: Scotland	314, 325
Police (Northern Ireland) Act 2000: Commencement: Northern Ireland	377
Police (Northern Ireland) Act 2000: Detention: Designated places: Northern Ireland	377
Police (Northern Ireland) Act 2000: Policing plan: Northern Ireland	377
Police Act 1997: Commencement	137
Police Act 1997: Commencement: Scotland	324
Police Act 1997: Criminal records	137
Police Act 1997: Criminal records: Enhanced certificates: Protection of vulnerable adults: England & Wales	138
Police Act 1997: Criminal records: Registration: Scotland	324
Police Act 1997: Criminal records: Scotland	324
Police Act 1997: Criminal records: Vulnerable adults: Protection: Scotland	324

Police authorities: Best value: Performance indicators: England & Wales	96, 138
Police authorities: Selection panel: England & Wales	139
Police authorities: Three year strategy	139
Police Reform Act 2002: Commencement	137
Police Reform Act 2002: Commencement: Scotland	325
Police Service of Northern Ireland	377
Police Service of Northern Ireland: Pensions	377
Police Service of Northern Ireland: Reserve: Full Time: Appointment & conditions of service	377
Police Service of Northern Ireland: Reserve: Full time: Pensions	377
Police support staff: Recruitment: Northern Ireland	377
Police: Attestation of constables: Welsh language	137
Police: Cells: Legalised: Discontinuance of: Ayr: Scotland	325
Police: Central Police Training & Development Authority: Criminal Justice & Police Act 2001	137
Police: Combined area: Amalgamation: Scotland	324
Police: Criminal Justice & Police Act 2001: Amendment	35
Police: Criminal Justice & Police Act 2001: Commencement	29, 34, 35, 137
Police: Criminal Justice & Police Act 2001: Commencement: England & Wales	35, 137
Police: Emblems & flags: Northern Ireland	377
Police: Grant: Scotland	325
Police: Motor vehicles: Retention & disposal: England & Wales	139
Police: National Crime Squad: Secretary of State's objectives: England & Wales	137
Police: National Criminal Intelligence Service: Secretary of State's objectives	137
Police: Pensions: Sharing: England & Wales	134, 139
Police: Promotion: England & Wales	139
Police: Property	139
Police: Recruitment: Northern Ireland	377
Police: Recruitment: Support staff: Northern Ireland	377
Police: Reform: Acts: Explanatory notes	5
Police: Regulations	138
Police: Retention & disposal of items seized: England & Wales	35
Police: Royal Ulster Constabulary: GC foundation: Northern Ireland	377
Police: Secretary of State's objectives	139
Police: Special constables	139
Police: Special constables: Atomic Energy Authority	17, 136
Police: Traffic wardens: Functions	137
Policing plan: Police (Northern Ireland) Act 2000	377
Policy development grants scheme: Elections	146
Polish forces: Pensions: Scheme: Extension	133
Political parties: Registration: Registered parties: Non-constituent & non-affiliated organisations	145
Pollution: Environmental protection: Air quality: England	59
Pollution: Gaseous & particulate pollutants: Emission: Non-road mobile machinery	59
Pollution: National emission ceilings	59
Pollution: Offshore installations: Emergency pollution control	59
Pollution: Prevention & control: England & Wales	60
Pollution: Prevention & control: Incineration of waste: National emission ceilings	60
Pollution: Prevention & control: Large combustion plants	60
Pollution: Prevention & control: Large combustion plants: National emission ceilings: Scotland	314
Pontefract: Wakefield & Pontefract: Community National Health Service Trust	122
Pont-y-clun, Llanharry, Penllyn, Welsh St Donats & Pendoylan, : Rhondda Cynon Taff & Vale of Glamorgan: Local government: Wales	99
Poole (Borough): Electoral changes	90
Poole (Borough): Permitted & special parking area	209
Poole: National Health Service Primary Care Trust	118
Port health authorities: Falmouth & Truro Port Health Authority: England & Wales	139
Port of Ipswich Harbour: Transfer of undertaking: England	71
Port of Tilbury: Free zone: Designation	38
Port Talbot: Neath Port Talbot & Swansea: Trebanos & Clydach: Local government: Wales	99
Portsmouth Healthcare: National Health Service Trusts	118
Post office: Telecommunication services: Channel Islands	139
Postal Services Act 2000: Section 7: Modification	139
Postal Services Act 2000: Turnover: Determination for penalties	139
Postal services: EC directive	139
Post-compulsory education awards: Local education authorities: Wales	55
Postgraduate medical degrees: University of St Andrews: Acts: Explanatory notes: Scotland	306
Postgraduate medical degrees: University of St Andrews: Acts: Scotland	305
Postgraduate students: Disabled: Grants: Education: Northern Ireland	362
Potato Industry Development Council	83
Potatoes: Originating in Egypt: England	136

Potatoes: Originating in Egypt: Northern Ireland	377
Potatoes: Originating in Egypt: Scotland	324
Potatoes: Originating in Egypt: Wales	136
Potatoes: Originating in Germany: Northern Ireland	377
Potatoes: Seed potatoes: Crop fees: Northern Ireland	360
Poultry breeding & animal by-products: Fees: Animals: Animal health: England	13
Poultry breeding flocks: Hatcheries: Animal by products: Scotland	309
Poultry meat: Hygiene & inspection: Wales	69
Poultry, farmed game bird & rabbit meat: Hygiene & inspection: Scotland	316
Powers of attorney: Court protection: Enduring powers of attorney: Rules: England & Wales	102, 139
Prescription only: Medicines: Human use	101
Preserved rights: Personal social services: Commencement: Northern Ireland	377
Preserved rights: Responsible authorities: Transfer: Scotland	346
Pressure equipment	73
Preston Acute Hospitals: National Health Service Trust	112
Preston: Parishes: Local government	95
Preston: Strand Road, Preston Railway	243, 244
Prevention & suppression of terrorism: Anti-Terrorism, Crime & Security Act 2001: Commencement	140
Prevention & suppression of terrorism: Terrorism Act 2000: Proscribed organisations	140
Prevention of cruelty: Animals: Protection: Anaesthetics: England	14
Prevention of cruelty: Farmed animals: Welfare: England	14
Prevention of cruelty: Farmed animals: Welfare: Scotland	310
Prevention of cruelty: Farmed animals: Welfare: Wales	17
Primary care trusts & strategic health authorities: Functions: National Health Service	114
Primary care trusts: Dissolution: National Health Service: England	118
Primary care trusts: Establishment: National Health Service: England	118
Primary care trusts: Functions: National Health Service: England	118
Primary care trusts: Membership, procedure & administration arrangements: England	118, 119
Primary care trusts: National Health Service 104, 105, 106, 107, 108, 109, 110, 111, 112, 113, 116, 117, 118, 119, 120, 121, 122, 123, 124, 125	
Primary schools: Education: Admission arrangements: Co-ordination of: England	45
Priority Healthcare Wearside: National Health Service Trust	121
Prisoners: Short-term: Release on licence: Requisite period	140
Prisons: Closure: HM Prison Haslar	140
Prisons: Closure: HM Young Offender Institution Dover	140
Prisons: Police cells: Ayr: Legalised: Discontinuance of: Scotland	325
Prisons: Rules: England & Wales	140
Prisons: Short-term prisoners: Release on licence: Requisite period	140
Prisons: Young offenders institutions: Scotland	325, 348
Private & personal acts: Chronological tables	6
Private & voluntary health care: Director: National Care Standards Commission: England	142
Private & voluntary health care: Wales	143
Private finance initiative companies: School companies: England	50
Private hire vehicles: Guide dogs, etc.: Carriage: Acts	3
Private hire vehicles: Guide dogs, etc.: Carriage: Acts: Explanatory notes	5
Private Security Industry Act 2001: Commencement	140
Proceeds of Crime Act 2002: Cash searches: Code of practice	140
Proceeds of Crime Act 2002: Cash searches: Constables: Code of practice : Scotland	325
Proceeds of Crime Act 2002: Commencement	141
Proceeds of Crime Act 2002: Commencement & savings	141
Proceeds of Crime Act 2002: Summary proceedings: Cash: Recovery of: Minimum amount	141
Proceeds of Crime Act 2002: United Kingdom: Enforcement	141
Proceeds of crime: Acts: Explanatory notes	5
Producer responsibility& obligations: Packaging waste: England	59
Producer responsibility& obligations: Packaging waste: Northern Ireland	378
Producer responsibility& obligations: Packaging waste: Wales	61
Products for animal use: Medicines: Fees	101
Products of animal origin: Third country imports: Northern Ireland	361, 364
Professional qualifications: Qualifications & experience: Recognition: Third general system: European Communities	141
Professional qualifications: Recognition: European Communities	141
Professional qualifications: Recognition: Second general system: European Communities	141
Professions supplementary to medicine: Staff & property: Transfer	73
Prohibited methods of fishing: Firth of Clyde: Scotland	343
Property: Commencement orders: Northern Ireland	378
Property: Commonhold & leasehold: Acts	1
Property: Commonhold & leasehold: Acts: Explanatory notes	4
Property: Ground Rents Act (Northern Ireland) 2001: Commencement: Northern Ireland	377

Entry	Page
Property: Ground rents: Multiplier: Northern Ireland	378
Protection from Abuse (Scotland) Act 2001: Applications: Act of Sederunt: Ordinary cause rules: Scotland	345
Protection of animals: Anaesthetics: England	14
Protection of Children Act 1999: Commencement	21
Protection of Military Remains Act 1986: Vessels & controlled sites: Designation	38
Protection of Wild Mammals (Scotland) Act 2002: Commencement: Scotland	308, 311
Protection of wrecks: Designation	141
Protection of wrecks: The Diamond	141
Provident societies: Acts	2
Public bodies: Local authorities: Goods & services: England	95
Public bodies: Welsh language schemes	248
Public Finance & Accountability (Scotland) Act 2000: Consequential modifications: Scotland	325
Public Finance & Accountability (Scotland) Act 2000: Documents & information: Access: Relevant persons: Scotland	325
Public Finance & Accountability (Scotland) Act 2000: Economy, efficiency & effectiveness examinations: Specified bodies: Scotland	325
Public finance & accountability: Budget (Scotland) Act 2001: Amendment: Scotland	325
Public finance & accountability: Budget (Scotland) Act 2002: Amendment: Scotland	325
Public general acts: Bound volumes	6
Public general acts: Tables & index	6
Public guardian: Fees: Adults with incapacity: Scotland	306
Public health: Care Standards Act 2000: Commencement: England	20, 142, 222
Public health: Care Standards Act 2000: Commencement: England & Wales	21, 142, 222
Public health: Care Standards Act 2000: Commencement: Wales	21, 142, 223
Public health: Care Standards Act 2000: Establishment & agencies	20, 142, 222
Public health: Care Standards Act 2000: Miscellaneous amendments: Wales	22, 143, 223
Public Health: Care Standards Tribunal: Protection of children & vulnerable adults: England & Wales	21, 142, 222
Public health: Children Act 1989: Miscellaneous amendments: Wales	22, 143, 223
Public health: Contamination of food: Scotland	325, 326, 327, 328, 329, 330
Public health: Food protection: Emergency prohibitions: Northern Ireland	378
Public health: National Care Standards Commission: Director of Private & Voluntary Health Care: England	142
Public health: National Care Standards Commission: Fees & frequency of inspections: England	142, 222
Public health: Noise: Control: Codes of practice: Construction & open sites: England	142
Public health: Noise: Control: Codes of practice: Construction & open sites: Northern Ireland	378
Public health: Noise: Control: Codes of practice: Construction & open sites: Scotland	325
Public health: Noise: Control: Codes of practice: Construction & open sites: Wales	143
Public health: Private & voluntary health care: Wales	143
Public health: Producer responsibility obligations: Packaging waste: Northern Ireland	378
Public health: Regulatory reform: Vaccine Damage Payments Act 1979	142, 145
Public health: Social care & independent healthcare: Registration: Fees: Wales	22, 143, 223
Public health: Social care & independent healthcare: Registration: Wales	22, 143, 224
Public lending right scheme 1982: Variation: Commencement	88
Public passenger transport: Bus services: Operators: Grants: Wales	144
Public passenger transport: Community buses	143
Public passenger transport: London service permits: Appeals	99, 143
Public passenger transport: Minibuses: Section 19 permit buses	143
Public passenger transport: Public service vehicles: Drivers, inspectors, conductors & passengers: Conduct	143
Public passenger transport: Public service vehicles: Operators' licences: Fees	143
Public passenger transport: Public service vehicles: Registration of local services	144
Public passenger transport: Quality partnership schemes: Existing facilities: Wales	144
Public passenger transport: Travel concessions: Eligible services: Wales	144
Public passenger transport: Vehicles: Local services: Registration: Scotland	330
Public passenger vehicles: Local services: Registration: Scotland	330
Public service vehicles: Accessibility	41, 241
Public service vehicles: Drivers, inspectors, conductors & passengers: Conduct	143
Public service vehicles: Fitness, equipment & use: Conditions of: Northern Ireland	380
Public service vehicles: Fitness, equipment, use & certification	148, 212
Public service vehicles: Licence: Fees: Northern Ireland	381
Public service vehicles: Operators' licences: Fees	143
Public service vehicles: Registration of local services	144
Public Services Ombudsman: Scottish: 2002 Act: Amendment: Scotland	343
Public Services Ombudsman: Scottish: 2002 Act: Commencement: Scotland	343
Public Services Ombudsman: Scottish: 2002 Act: Transitory & transitional provisions: Scotland	343
Public telecommunication systems: AT&T Global Network Services (UK) B.V.	236
Public telecommunication systems: Companhia Portuguesa Radio Marconi SA	237
Public telecommunication systems: Econet Satellite Services Limited	237
Public telecommunication systems: Eurocall Ltd	237
Public telecommunication systems: Fibernet UK Ltd	237
Public telecommunication systems: France Telecom Network Services-UK Ltd	237

Public telecommunication systems: Gamma Telecommunications Limited 237
Public telecommunication systems: Severn Trent Retail Services Limited 237
Public telecommunication systems: Telekom Malaysia (UK) Ltd 237
Public telecommunication systems: T-Systems Limited 237
Public telecommunication systems: Tweedwind Limited 237
Public telecommunication systems: United Networks Limited 237
Public telecommunication systems: VTL (UK) Limited 237
Public trustee: Fees: England & Wales 245
Public Trustee: Liability & Fees: Acts 3
Public Trustee: Liability & Fees: Acts: Explanatory notes 5
Pupil exclusions & appeals: Maintained schools: England 47
Pupil exclusions & appeals: Pupil referral units: England 47
Pupil referral units: Permanent exclusion: Appeals: England 47
Pupils: Individual: Achievements: Information: Education: Wales 54
Pupils: Individual: Information: Education: England 46
Pupils: Information: England 47
Pupils: Permanently excluded: Amount to follow: Wales 53
Pupils' educational records: Disability strategies: Education: Acts: Explanatory notes: Scotland 305
Pupils' educational records: Disability strategies: Education: Acts: Scotland 304
Purbeck (District): Permitted & special parking area 210

Q

QCA levy: Education 51, 53
Quality partnership schemes: Public passenger transport: Existing facilities: Wales 144
Queen Elizabeth Conference: Trading Fund 70
Queen's Counsel: Appointment: Fees: England & Wales 88

R

Rabbit meat: Hygiene & inspection: Wales 69
Rabbit, poultry & farmed game bird meat: Hygiene & inspection: Scotland 316
Rabies: Dogs, cats & other mammals: Importation: Wales 14
Race Relations Act 1976: General statutory duty: Code of practice 144
Race Relations Act 1976: General statutory duty: Code of practice: Scotland 144
Race Relations Act 1976: Statutory duties: Scotland 330
Radioactive material: Packaging, labelling & carriage: By rail 73
Radioactive material: Road transport 17, 18
Radioactive substances: Natural gas 18
Rail vehicles: C2C Class 357/0 vehicles: Accessibility: Exemptions 41, 241
Rail vehicles: Cairngorm Funicular Railway: Accessibility: Exemptions 41, 241
Rail vehicles: Croydon Tramlink Class CR4000 vehicles: Accessibility: Exemptions 41, 242
Rail vehicles: East Hayling Light Railway vehicles: Accessibility: Exemptions 41, 242
Rail vehicles: Isle of Wight Railway LCDR no. 2515 vehicle: Accessibility: Exemptions 41, 242
Rail vehicles: Middleton Railway Drewry car: Accessibility: Exemptions 41, 242
Rail vehicles: South Central Class 375/3 vehicles: Accessibility: Exemptions 41, 242
Rail vehicles: South West Trains Class 458 vehicles: Accessibility: Exemptions 41, 242
Rail vehicles: Summerlee Tramcar No. 392: Accessibility: Exemptions 41, 242
Rail vehicles: Virgin West Coast Class 390 Vehicles: Accessibility: Exemptions 41, 242
Railways: Bitton Railway 242, 243
Railways: Heathrow Express Railway: Extension 243, 244
Railways: Heathrow Express: Exemptions 244
Railways: Interoperability: High-speed 242
Railways: Light railways: Docklands: Silvertown & London City Airport extension 243
Railways: Light railways: East Lancashire: Heywood extension 243
Railways: Merseyrail Electrics network 241
Railways: Piccadilly Line: Heathrow T5 extension 243, 244
Railways: Safety: Acts: Northern Ireland 358
Railways: Safety: Acts: Explanatory notes: Northern Ireland 359
Railways: Strand Road, Preston 243, 244
Railways: Wear Valley Railway 243, 244
Rainbow, Stoke on Trent: Education Action Zone: Extension 50
Rateable values: Water undertakings: Scotland 330

Entry	Pages
Rates: Children & young persons: Social security: Allowances: Northern Ireland	371, 379, 385
Rates: Housing benefit: General: Northern Ireland	370
Rates: Making & levying: Different rates: Northern Ireland	378
Rates: Regional rates: Northern Ireland	378
Rates: Social security & child support: Decisions & appeals: Miscellaneous amendments: Northern Ireland	361, 365, 371, 378, 382
Rates: Social security: Benefits: Up-rating: Northern Ireland	371, 378, 382, 385, 386
Rates: Social security: Employment programme: Northern Ireland	371, 378, 383
Rates: Social security: Intercalating students: Northern Ireland	371, 378, 384
Rates: Social security: Loss of benefit: Northern Ireland	371, 379, 384
Rates: Social security: Miscellaneous amendments: Northern Ireland	371, 379, 384
Rates: Social security: Paternity & adoption: Northern Ireland	371, 379, 384
Rates: Social security: Personal Injury payments: Northern Ireland	371, 379, 385
Rates: Social security: Students & Income related benefits : Northern Ireland	372, 379, 385
Rating & valuation: Demand notices: England	32, 144
Rating & valuation: Electricity lands & generators: Rateable values: Scotland	330
Rating & valuation: Non-domestic rate: Scotland	330
Rating & valuation: Non-domestic rates: Levying: Scotland	330
Rating & valuation: Non-domestic rating: Contributions: England	144
Rating & valuation: Non-domestic rating: Contributions: Wales	145
Rating & valuation: Non-domestic rating: Lists & appeals: Alteration: England	144
Rating & valuation: Non-domestic rating: Lists & appeals: Alteration: Wales	144
Rating & valuation: Non-domestic rating: Rural rate relief: Wales	145
Rating & valuation: Rating lists: Valuation date: Wales	145
Rating & valuation: Valuation for rating: Exempted classes: Scotland	330
Rating & valuation: Water undertakings: Rateable values: Scotland	330
Rating lists: Valuation date: Wales	145
Rating: Non-domestic: Lists & appeals: Alteration: England	144
Reading (Borough): Electoral changes	90
Reciprocal enforcement: Maintenance orders: Hague convention countries	100
Redbridge & Waltham Forest Health Authority	119
Redditch & Bromsgrove: National Health Service Primary Care Trust	119
Redditch (Borough): Electoral changes	90
Redundancy consultation & procedures: Code of practice: Appointed day: Northern Ireland	372
Redundancy payments: Local government: Continuity of employment	238
Referendums: Conduct: Local authorities: England	94
Regions, transport & local government: Transfer of functions	103
Registered parties: Non-constituent & non-affiliated organisations	145
Registered rents: Increase: Northern Ireland	373
Registration marks: Display: Road vehicles	148
Registration of birth & death entries: Correction: De-regulation	39
Registration of births, deaths, marriages etc.: Fees: England & Wales	145
Registration of births, deaths, marriages etc.: Fees: Northern Ireland	379
Registration of births, deaths, marriages etc.: Fees: Scotland	321, 330
Registration of births, deaths, marriages etc.: Service departments registers	145
Registration of political parties: Registered parties: Non-constituent & non-affiliated organisations	145
Registration plate suppliers: Registration of: Vehicles crime: England & Wales	212
Regulation of Care (Scotland) Act 2001: Commencement: Scotland	346
Regulation of Care: Advice: Applications & provision: Scotland	346
Regulation of Care: Care services: Requirements: Scotland	346
Regulation of care: Excepted services: Scotland	346
Regulation of Care: Fees: Scotland	346
Regulation of Care: Registration & registers: Scotland	346
Regulation of investigatory powers: Cancellation of authorisations: Scotland	319
Regulation of investigatory powers: Communications: Interception of: Code of Practice	86
Regulation of investigatory powers: Covert human intelligence sources: Code of practice	86
Regulation of investigatory powers: Covert surveillance: Codes of practice	86
Regulation of investigatory powers: Interception capability: Maintenance	86
Regulation of investigatory powers: Juveniles: Scotland	319
Regulation of investigatory powers: Offices, ranks & positions: Prescription	86
Regulation of investigatory powers: Source records: Scotland	319
Regulatory reform: Carer's allowance	145, 225
Regulatory reform: Golden Jubilee: Licensing: England & Wales	145
Regulatory reform: Housing assistance: England & Wales	79, 146
Regulatory reform: Partnerships: Member limit: Removal of	145
Regulatory reform: Special occasions licensing: England & Wales	146
Regulatory reform: Vaccine Damage Payments Act 1979	142, 145
Regulatory reform: Voluntary aided schools: Liabilities & funding: England	50, 145

Rehabilitation of Offenders Act 1974: Exceptions: England & Wales 146
Relevant authorities: Standards committee: Dispensations: Local government: England & Wales 96
Relocation grants: Form of application: England 79
Renewables: Electricity: Obligations: England & Wales 57
Renfrewshire Council: Glasgow City Council: Boundaries: Braehead: Scotland 321
Rents: Registered: Increase: Northern Ireland 373
Representation of the people: Elections: Policy development grants scheme 146
Representation of the people: Electoral Fraud (Northern Ireland) Act 2002: Commencement 146
Representation of the people: England & Wales 146
Representation of the people: Local government: Elections: Rules: Scotland. 331
Representation of the people: Local government: Elections: Scotland 331
Representation of the people: National Assembly for Wales 29, 40, 146
Representation of the people: National Assembly for Wales: Returning officers' charges 146
Representation of the people: Northern Ireland 146
Representation of the people: Scotland 146
Residential care & nursing homes: Social security 226
Residential care & nursing homes: Social security: Northern Ireland 382
Residential family centres: England. 20, 222
Restaurants: Licensing hours: Deregulation 39
Restormel (Borough): Electoral changes 90
Retained Organs Commission: England. 119
Retirement benefits schemes: Earnings cap: Indexation 83
Retirement benefits schemes: Information powers 83
Rhondda Cynon Taff & Vale of Glamorgan: Llanharry, Pont-y-clun, Penllyn, Welsh St Donats & Pendoylan: Local government: Wales 99
Richmondshire: Parishes: Local government 95
Right to buy: Houses liable to demolition: Scotland 317
Right to buy: Housing: Designated rural areas & designated regions: England 79
Right to purchase: Application form: Scotland 318
Rights of way: Countryside & Rights of Way Act 2000: Commencement: England 147
River Dee (Kirkcudbright) salmon fishery district: Baits & lures: Scotland 331
River: Fish farming: Registration: Businesses: Scotland 331
River: River Bann: Navigation: Northern Ireland 368
River: Salmon & freshwater fisheries: River Dee (Kirkcudbright) salmon fishery district: Baits & lures: Scotland 331
River: Salmon & freshwater fisheries: Fish: Diseases: Control: England & Wales 147, 219
River: Salmon & freshwater fisheries: Mull salmon fishery district: Designation: Scotland 331
River: Salmon: Conservation: Prohibition of sale: Scotland 331
River: Shellfish farming: Registration: Businesses: Scotland 331
Riverside Community Health Care: National Health Service Trusts 119
Road humps: Traffic calming: Scotland. 332
Road service licensing: Community licences: Northern Ireland 365, 381
Road traffic & vehicles: Driving licences: Community driving licence: Northern Ireland 364, 380
Road traffic & vehicles: Dundrod Circuit: Admission charges: Northern Ireland. 380
Road traffic & vehicles: Goods vehicles: Testing: Fees: Northern Ireland 380
Road traffic & vehicles: Motor vehicles: Authorised weight: Northern Ireland 380
Road traffic & vehicles: Motor vehicles: Construction & use: Northern Ireland 380
Road traffic & vehicles: Motor vehicles: Driving licences: Northern Ireland 380
Road traffic & vehicles: Motor vehicles: Driving licences: Test fees: Northern Ireland 380
Road traffic & vehicles: Motor vehicles: Exchangeable licences: Northern Ireland 380
Road traffic & vehicles: Motor vehicles: Testing: Northern Ireland 380
Road traffic & vehicles: Motor vehicles: Third party risks: Northern Ireland 380
Road traffic & vehicles: Passenger & goods vehicles: Recording equipment: Fees: Northern Ireland 380
Road traffic & vehicles: Public service vehicles: Fitness, equipment & use: Conditions of: Northern Ireland. 380
Road traffic & vehicles: Public service vehicles: Licence: Fees: Northern Ireland 381
Road traffic & vehicles: Road service licensing: Community licences: Northern Ireland 365, 381
Road traffic & vehicles: Traffic signs: Northern Ireland 381
Road Traffic (Foreign Vehicles) Act 1972: Goods vehicles: Community authorisations 147
Road traffic: Disabled persons: Motor vehicles: Badges: Scotland 332
Road traffic: Driving licences: Exchangeable licences 147
Road traffic: Driving licences: External law: Designation 147
Road traffic: Edinburgh: Parking area: Scotland. 333
Road traffic: European Communities: Rights against insurers. 147
Road traffic: Glasgow: Parking area: Scotland 333
Road traffic: Goods vehicles: Community authorisations: Road Traffic (Foreign Vehicles) Act 1972 147
Road traffic: Goods vehicles: Plating & testing 211
Road traffic: Health services charges: Northern Ireland 380
Road traffic: International carriage: Dangerous goods: Road: Fees 211
Road traffic: Local authorities: Traffic orders: Disabled persons: Exemption: Scotland 332, 333

Road traffic: Local authorities: Traffic orders: Procedure: Scotland 333
Road traffic: M11: Junction 8: Speed limits 209
Road traffic: M4: Hillingdon & Hounslow: Speed limits 209
Road traffic: M4: London Borough of Hounslow: Bus lane 209
Road traffic: M60: Junction 25: Speed limits. 209
Road traffic: Minibuses: Section 19 permit buses 143
Road traffic: Motor cars: Driving instruction 147
Road traffic: Motor salvage operators 212
Road traffic: Motor vehicles: Competitions & trials: Scotland. 333
Road traffic: Motor vehicles: Driving licences 147
Road traffic: Motor vehicles: EC type approval 147
Road traffic: Motor vehicles: Tests. 212
Road traffic: NHS charges: England & Wales 126, 212
Road traffic: NHS charges: Scotland 323, 333
Road traffic: Passenger & goods vehicles: Recording equipment: Fitters & workshops: Approval: Fees. 212
Road traffic: Permitted & special parking area: Basingstoke & Deane (Borough) 211
Road traffic: Permitted & special parking area: Brentwood (Borough) 210
Road traffic: Permitted & special parking area: Bury (Metropolitan Borough) 211
Road traffic: Permitted & special parking area: Chelmsford (Borough) 210
Road traffic: Permitted & special parking area: Colchester (Borough). 211
Road traffic: Permitted & special parking area: Cumbria: Eden District 210
Road traffic: Permitted & special parking area: East Dorset (District). 210
Road traffic: Permitted & special parking area: Epping Forest (District). 211
Road traffic: Permitted & special parking area: Harrogate (Borough) 211
Road traffic: Permitted & special parking area: Hart (District). 211
Road traffic: Permitted & special parking area: Liverpool (City) 209
Road traffic: Permitted & special parking area: Milton Keynes (Borough) 211
Road traffic: Permitted & special parking area: North Dorset (District) 210
Road traffic: Permitted & special parking area: Norwich (City): Norfolk. 211
Road traffic: Permitted & special parking area: Nottingham (City) 209
Road traffic: Permitted & special parking area: Poole (Borough) 209
Road traffic: Permitted & special parking area: Purbeck (District) 210
Road traffic: Permitted & special parking area: Rushmoor (Borough) 211
Road traffic: Permitted & special parking area: South Lakeland (District) 210
Road traffic: Permitted & special parking area: Southampton (City) 210
Road traffic: Permitted & special parking area: Sunderland (City). 210
Road traffic: Permitted & special parking area: West Dorset (District) 210
Road traffic: Permitted & special parking area: Weymouth & Portland (Borough) 210
Road traffic: Permitted & special parking area: Worcester (City) 211
Road traffic: Perth & Kinross Council: Parking adjudicators: Scotland. 333
Road traffic: Perth & Kinross Council: Parking area: Attendants: Uniforms: Scotland 333
Road traffic: Perth & Kinross Council: Parking area: Scotland. 333
Road traffic: Public service vehicles: Fitness, equipment, use & certification 148, 212
Road traffic: Road users: Charging: Enforcement: England & Wales 212
Road traffic: Road vehicles: Registration & licensing: Northern Ireland 212
Road traffic: School crossing patrol sign: Scotland 333
Road traffic: School crossing patrol: England & Wales 212
Road traffic: Speed limits 149, 150, 151, 152
Road traffic: Speed limits: Scotland. 333, 334
Road traffic: Speed limits: Wales. 213
Road traffic: TIR carnets: Goods: International transport: Fees 212
Road traffic: Traffic regulation . . 152, 153, 154, 155, 156, 157, 158, 159, 160, 161, 162, 163, 164, 165, 166, 167, 168, 169, 170, 171, 172, 173, 174, 175, 176, 177, 178, 179, 180, 181, 182, 183, 184, 185, 186, 187, 188, 189, 190, 191, 192, 193, 194, 195, 196, 197, 198, 199, 200, 201, 202, 203, 204, 205, 206, 207, 208, 209
Road traffic: Traffic regulation: Scotland 332, 333, 334, 335, 336, 337, 338, 339, 340, 341, 342
Road traffic: Traffic regulation: Wales. 214, 215, 216, 217, 218
Road traffic: Traffic signs: General directions 148
Road traffic: Vehicle emissions: Fixed penalty 211
Road traffic: Vehicle excise duty: Immobilisation, removal & disposal of vehicles. 149
Road traffic: Vehicle excise duty: Small islands: Designation 148
Road traffic: Vehicles (Crime) Act 2001: Commencement: England & Wales. 212
Road traffic: Vehicles: Construction & use 148
Road traffic: Vehicles: Goods: Operators: Licensing: Fees 147
Road traffic: Vehicles: Registration & licensing 148
Road traffic: Vehicles: Removal & disposal: England 209
Road traffic: Vehicles: Removal & disposal: Scotland. 333
Road traffic: Vehicles: Testing: Disclosure of information: Great Britain 148

Road transport: Radioactive material	17, 18
Road users: Charging: Enforcement: England & Wales	212
Road vehicles: Registration & licensing: Northern Ireland	212
Road vehicles: Registration marks: Display	148
Road works: Inspection fees: Scotland	332
Roads & bridges: Forth Estuary Transport Authority: Scotland	332
Roads & bridges: Road works: Inspection fees: Scotland	332
Roads & bridges: Scotland	331, 332, 347
Roads: New Roads & Street Works Act 1991: Commencement: England	77
Roads: Street works: Registers, notices, directions & designations: Northern Ireland	379, 386
Rochdale Healthcare: National Health Service Trust	118, 119
Rochdale: National Health Service Trust	119
Rotherham Health Authority	119
Rotherham Priority Health Services: National Health Service Trust	119
Rowley Regis & Tipton: National Health Service Primary Care Trust	119
Royal Air Force: Courts-martial	38
Royal Marines: Terms of service	39
Royal Mint: Trading Fund	70
Royal Ulster Constabulary: GC foundation: Northern Ireland	377
Rugby: National Health Service Primary Care Trust	119
Rural rate relief: Non-domestic rating: Wales	145
Rushmoor & Hart: National Health Service Primary Care Trust	119
Rushmoor & Hart: National Health Service Trust	119
Rushmoor (Borough): Permitted & special parking area	211
Rutland Water: Leicestershire, Northamptonshire & Rutland: Health Authority	112
Rutland: Leicestershire & Rutland Healthcare: National Health Service Trust	112
Ryedale, Scarborough & Whitby National Health Service Trust	120

S

Safety of navigation: Merchant shipping	103
Safety: Cinematographs	23
Safety: Diving: Merchant shipping	103
Safety: Merchant shipping: Miscellaneous amendments	103
Safety: Sports grounds: Designation	232
Salaries: Assembly Ombudsman & Commissioner for Complaints: Northern Ireland	381
Salmon & freshwater fisheries: River Dee (Kirkcudbright) salmon fishery district: Baits & lures: Scotland	331
Salmon & freshwater fisheries: Fish farming: Registration: Businesses: Scotland	331
Salmon & freshwater fisheries: Mull salmon fishery district: Designation: Scotland	331
Salmon & freshwater fisheries: Salmon: Conservation: Prohibition of sale : Scotland	331
Salmon & freshwater fisheries: Shellfish farming: Registration: Businesses: Scotland	331
Salmon fishery district: Mull: Designation: Scotland	331
Salmon fishery district: River Dee (Kirkcudbright): Baits & lures: Scotland	331
Salmon: Conservation: Prohibition of sale: Scotland	331
Sandwell: Health Authority	120
Sandwell & West Birmingham Hospitals: National Health Service Trust	119
Sandwell Healthcare: National Health Service Trust	119
Savings: Individual savings accounts: Income tax	83
Scarborough, Whitby & Ryedale National Health Service Trust	120
School budget shares: Prescribed purposes: England & Wales	52
School companies: England	50
School companies: Private finance initiative companies: England	50
School crossing patrol sign: England & Wales	212
School crossing patrol sign: Scotland	333
School day & year: Education: Wales	54, 55
School Education (Amendment) (Scotland) Act 2002: Commencement: Scotland	313
School education: Amendment: Acts: Explanatory notes: Scotland	305
School education: Amendment: Acts: Scotland	304
School education: Children under school age: Prescribed children: Scotland	313
School information: Education: Wales	55
School inspectors: England	46
School organisation proposals: National Council for Education & Training for Wales	56
School performance targets: England	47
School teachers: Remuneration: England & Wales	52
School teachers' pay & conditions: England & Wales	51, 52

Schools & colleges: Boarding: Powers & fees: Inspection: Wales. 22, 223
Schools forums: England. 50
Schools: Chief Inspector: England 45
Schools: Disability discrimination: Schools: Prescribed periods: England 42
Schools: Government: Terms of reference: Wales. 55
Schools: Governors: Annual reports: Wales 55
Schools: Information: England 47
Schools: Inspector: England 46
Schools: Langley Junior School: School session times: Change 49
Schools: Maintained: Financing: England 48
Schools: Maintained: Financing: Wales 55
Schools: Maintained: Pupil exclusions & appeals: England. 47
Schools: Middle schools: England 46
Schools: Performance: Information: England. 47
Schools: Performance: Targets: England. 47
Schools: Pupil exclusions & appeals: Pupil referral units: England 47
Schools: Standards in Scotland's Schools etc. Act 2000: Commencement: Scotland 313
Schools: Teachers: Induction arrangements: Education: England 46
Schools: Voluntary aided: Grants: England. 46
Schools: Voluntary aided: Liabilities & funding: Regulatory reform: England 50, 145
Science: Assessment arrangements: Wales. 54
Scotland Act 1998: Agency arrangements: Specification 30, 40
Scotland Act 1998: Cross-border public authorities 30
Scotland Act 1998: Modifications: Schedule 5 . . . . 30, 40
Scotland Act 1998: Scottish Ministers: Transfer of functions 30, 40
Scotland: Adults with Incapacity (Scotland) Act 2000: Commencement: Scotland 306
Scotland: Budget: Acts. 304
Scotland: Electricity Act 1989: Offshore generating stations: Consent requirement: Scotland 313
Scotland: Electricity lands & generators: Rateable values: Scotland 330
Scotland: Housing (Scotland) Act 2001: Housing support services information 29, 39, 79
Scotland: Housing: Registration of tenant organisations: Scotland 318
Scotland: Housing: Scottish secure tenancy: Scotland 318
Scotland: Housing: Support services: Scotland. 318
Scotland: Peterhead Bay Authority: Constitution: Revision: Scotland. 317
Scotland: Representation of the people 146
Scotland: Scottish Parliament: Elections etc. 30, 40
Scotland: Sea fishing: Community quota & third country fishing: Enforcement: Scotland. 343
Scotland: Water Industry (Scotland) Act 2002: Commencement: Scotland 348
Scotland: Water Industry (Scotland) Act 2002: Consequential & savings provisions: Scotland. 348
Scotland: Water Industry (Scotland) Act 2002: National security 30, 40, 247
Scotland: Water undertakings: Rateable values: Scotland 330
Scottish administration: Offices 30, 40
Scottish Commission for the Regulation of Care: Appointments & procedure: Scotland 346
Scottish Commission for the Regulation of Care: Staff transfer scheme: Scotland 346
Scottish Commission for the Regulation of Care: Transfer of staff: Consultation: Scotland 346
Scottish Council for Postgraduate Medical & Dental Education: NHS Education for Scotland: Transfer of staff 323
Scottish Legal Services Ombudsman: Compensation: Prescribed amount: Scotland 320
Scottish local government: Elections: Acts: Explanatory notes 306
Scottish local government: Elections: Acts: Scotland 304
Scottish Parliament: Elections etc.: Scotland 30, 40
Scottish Parliament: Standards Commissioner: Acts. 304
Scottish Parliament: Standards Commissioner: Acts: Explanatory notes: Scotland. 305
Scottish Public Sector Ombudsman: Acts: Scotland 305
Scottish Public Services Ombudsman Act 2002: Amendment: Scotland. 343
Scottish Public Services Ombudsman Act 2002: Commencement: Scotland. 343
Scottish Public Services Ombudsman Act 2002: Transitory & transitional provisions: Scotland 343
Scottish Public Services Ombudsman: Acts: Scotland 305
Scottish Qualifications Authority Act 2002: Commencement: Scotland 313
Scottish Qualifications Authority: Acts: Explanatory notes: Scotland. 306
Scottish Qualifications Authority: Acts: Scotland. 305
Scottish Qualifications Authority: Advisory Council: Establishment: Scotland 312
Scottish secure tenancies: Abandoned property: Scotland. 318
Scottish secure tenancies: Exceptions: Scotland. 318
Scottish secure tenancies: Housing: Scotland 318
Scottish secure tenancies: Proceedings for possession: Scotland 319
Scottish secure tenancies: Short: Proceedings for possession: Scotland. 319
Scottish secure tenants: Compensation for improvements: Scotland 319

Scottish secure tenants: Right to repair: Scotland	319
Scottish Social Services Council: Appointments, procedure & access to register: Scotland	346
Scottish Transport Group: Dissolution: Scotland	347
Scottish Water: Rate of return: Scotland	348
Scottish Water: Transfer of functions: Tax provisions	83, 235
Sea fish industry: Fisheries & aquaculture: Structures: Grants: Wales	65, 220
Sea fish: Conservation: Prohibited methods of fishing: Firth of Clyde: Scotland	343
Sea fisheries: Community conservation measures: Enforcement: England & Northern Ireland	218, 219
Sea fisheries: Community conservation measures: Enforcement: Scotland	343
Sea fisheries: Community quota & third country fishing measures: Enforcement: England & Northern Ireland	218, 219
Sea fisheries: Community quota & third country fishing measures: Enforcement: Scotland	343
Sea fisheries: Community satellite monitoring measures: Wales	219
Sea fisheries: Conservation of sea fish: Lobsters & Crawfish: Fishing & landing: Prohibition: Wales	219
Sea fisheries: Conservation of sea fish: Spider Crabs: Undersized: Wales	219
Sea fisheries: Conservation of seals: Scotland	343
Sea fisheries: Conservation: Shrimp fishing nets	219
Sea fisheries: Fish: Diseases: Control: England & Wales	147, 219
Sea fisheries: Fish: Diseases: Control: Northern Ireland	362
Sea fisheries: Fisheries & aquaculture: Structures: Grants: Wales	65, 220
Sea fisheries: Little Loch Broom: Scallop several fishery: Scotland	343
Sea fisheries: Loch Caolisport: Scallop several fishery: Scotland	343
Sea fisheries: Loch Ewe, Isle of Ewe, Wester Ross, Scallop Several Fishery: Scotland	343
Sea fisheries: Northern Ireland	129, 219
Sea fisheries: Shellfish: Crustaceans: Specification: Wales	220
Sea fisheries: Shellfish: Mussels: Swansea Bay	220
Seaham: Easington & Seaham: Education Action Zone: Extension	44
Seals: Conservation: Scotland	343
Secure tenancies: Housing (Scotland) Act 2001: Scotland	318
Secure tenancies: Scottish: Abandoned property: Scotland	318
Secure tenancies: Scottish: Exceptions: Scotland	318
Secure tenancies: Scottish: Proceedings for possession: Scotland	319
Secure tenancies: Short: Scottish: Notices: Scotland	319
Secure tenancies: Short: Scottish: Proceedings for possession: Scotland	319
Secure tenants: Scottish: Compensation for improvements: Scotland	319
Secure tenants: Scottish: Right to repair: Scotland	319
Securities & regulated markets: Insider dealing	84
Sedgefield: National Health Service Trust	120
Sedgefield: Parishes: Local government	95
Seed potatoes: Crop fees: Northern Ireland	360
Seeds: Beet seeds: England	220
Seeds: Cereal seeds: England	220
Seeds: Fees: England	221
Seeds: Fees: Northern Ireland	381
Seeds: Fees: Scotland	343
Seeds: Fees: Wales	221
Seeds: Fodder plant seeds: England	220
Seeds: Forest reproductive material: Great Britain	220
Seeds: Forest reproductive material: Northern Ireland	381
Seeds: Miscellaneous amendments: Scotland	343, 344
Seeds: Oil & fibre plants: England	220
Seeds: Plant Varieties & Seeds Tribunal: England & Wales	221
Seeds: Registration, licensing & enforcement: England	221
Seeds: Vegetable seeds: England	221
Sefton: North Sefton & West Lancashire Community: National Health Service Trust	117
Semington aqueduct: Wiltshire County Council: Confirmation: England	78
Service subsidy agreements: Tendering: Transport: England	244
Service subsidy agreements: Tendering: Transport: Wales	244
Severn Bridges: Tolls	77
Severn Trent Retail Services Limited: Public telecommunication systems	237
Sewerage & water: Charges: Exemption: Scotland	348
Sewerage & water: Domestic: Charges: Reduction: Scotland	348
Sex discrimination: Election candidates: Acts	4
Sex discrimination: Election candidates: Acts Explanatory notes	5
Sex offender Orders: Magistrates' courts: England & Wales	100
Sexual Offences (Procedure & Evidence) (Scotland) Act 2002: Commencement: Scotland	312
Sexual offences: Procedure & evidence: Acts: Explanatory notes: Scotland	306
Sexual offences: Procedure & evidence: Acts: Scotland	305

Share schemes: Employees: Acts.	2
Sheep & goats: Identification & movement: Interim measures: England	13, 14
Sheep & goats: Identification: Scotland	309, 310
Sheep & goats: Identification: Wales	16, 17
Sheep & goats: Movements: Interim measures: Scotland	310
Sheep: Annual premium: Northern Ireland	360
Sheffield Children's Hospital: National Health Service Trusts	120
Shellfish farming: Registration: Businesses: Scotland	331
Shellfish: Crustaceans: Specification: Wales	220
Shellfish: Little Loch Broom: Scallop several fishery: Scotland	343
Shellfish: Loch Caolisport : Scallop several fishery: Scotland	343
Shellfish: Loch Ewe, Isle of Ewe, Wester Ross, Scallop Several Fishery: Scotland	343
Shellfish: Sea fisheries: Mussels: Swansea Bay	220
Shellfish: Swansea Bay Mussel Fishery: C.V. & D.M. Thomas	220
Shepway: National Health Service Trust Primary Care Trust	120
Sheriff Court: Act of Adjournal: Criminal procedure: Rules: Extradition: Scotland	317, 344
Sheriff Court: Act of Sederunt: Debt arrangement & attachment: Scotland.	344
Sheriff Court: Act of Sederunt: Ordinary cause rules: Protection from Abuse (Scotland) Act 2001: Applications: Scotland	345
Sheriff Court: Act of Sederunt: Small claims: Rules: Scotland	345
Sheriff Court: Act of Sederunt: Summary & statutory applications & appeals etc.: Rules: Scotland.	345
Sheriff Court: Act of Sederunt: Summary cause rules: Scotland	345
Sheriff Court: Fees: Scotland.	345
Sheriff Court: Mortgage Rights (Scotland) Act 2001: Act of Sederunt: Scotland	344
Sheriff Court: Sheriff officers: Fees: Act of Sederunt: Scotland.	344
Sheriff Court: Solicitors: Fees: Act of Sederunt: Scotland	344
Sheriff Court: Witnesses & shorthand writers: Fees: Act of Sederunt: Scotland	344
Sheriff officers: Fees: Act of Sederunt: Scotland	344
Short Scottish secure tenancies: Notices: Scotland	319
Short Scottish secure tenancies: Proceedings for possession: Scotland	319
Shorthand writers & witnesses: Sheriff Court: Fees: Act of Sederunt: Scotland	344
Shorthand writers, witnesses & solicitors: Court of Session: Fees: Act of Sederunt: Scotland	312
Shrimp: Conservation: Fishing nets.	219
Shropshire County: National Health Service Primary Care Trust	120
Shropshire: Health Authority	120
Shropshire's Community & Mental Health Services: National Health Service Trust	120
Sick pay: Maternity pay: Statutory: Social security contributions	230, 239
Sick pay: Statutory: Miscellaneous amendments: Northern Ireland.	385, 386
Sick pay: Statutory: Social security: Benefits: Up-rating: Northern Ireland	371, 378, 382, 385, 386
Signatures: Electronic	57
Sites of special scientific interest: Appeals: Wildlife & countryside: Wales	33
Slough (Borough): Electoral changes	90
Slough: Heart of Slough: Education Action Zone: Extension	49
Small claims: Rules: Act of Sederunt: Scotland	345
Smethwick: Oldbury & Smethwick: National Health Service Trust Primary Care Trust	118
Smoke control areas: Authorised fuels: England.	27
Smoke control areas: Authorised fuels: Scotland.	310
Smoke control areas: Authorised fuels: Wales.	27
Social care & independent healthcare: Registration: Fees: Wales.	22, 143, 223
Social care & independent healthcare: Registration: Wales.	22, 143, 224
Social Care Council: Appointments & procedure: Northern Ireland	369
Social care worker: Meaning of phrase: Extension: Wales	223
Social care: Care homes: Wales.	21, 223
Social care: Care Standards Act 2000: Commencement: England.	20, 142, 221, 222
Social care: Care Standards Act 2000: Commencement: England & Wales.	21, 142, 222
Social care: Care Standards Act 2000: Commencement: Wales	21, 142, 223
Social care: Care Standards Act 2000: Establishment & agencies	20, 142, 222
Social care: Care Standards Act 2000: Miscellaneous amendments: Wales	22, 143, 223
Social care: Care Standards Act 2000: Social care worker: Meaning of phrase: Extension: Wales.	223
Social Care: Care Standards Tribunal: Protection of children & vulnerable adults: England & Wales	21, 142, 222
Social care: Central Council for Education & Training in Social Work Abolition	221
Social care: Child minding & day care: Wales.	21, 223
Social care: Children Act 1989: Care Standards Act 2000: Miscellaneous regulations: Wales	21, 223
Social care: Children Act 1989: Miscellaneous amendments: Wales	22, 143, 223
Social care: Children's homes: Wales	22, 223
Social care: Community Care & Health (Scotland) Act 2002: Amendments: Scotland	345
Social care: Community Care & Health (Scotland) Act 2002: Commencement: Scotland.	345
Social care: Community care: Accommodation costs: Deferred payment: Scotland	345

Social care: Community care: Additional payments: Scotland 345
Social care: Community care: Assessment of needs: Scotland. 345
Social care: Community care: Disregard of resources: Scotland 346
Social care: Community care: Joint working etc.: Scotland 346
Social care: Community care: Personal & nursing care: Scotland. 346
Social care: Domiciliary care agencies: England 222
Social care: Fostering services 20, 222
Social care: Health & Social Care Act 2001: Commencement 22, 221
Social care: Health & Social Care Act 2001: Commencement: Scotland 346
Social care: Health & Social Care Act 2001: Commencement: Wales 126
Social care: National Care Standards Commission: Children's Rights Director: England 20, 222
Social care: National Care Standards Commission: Fees & frequency of inspections: England 142, 222
Social care: Preserved rights: Responsible authorities: Transfer: Scotland 346
Social care: Regulation of Care (Scotland) Act 2001: Commencement: Scotland 346
Social care: Regulation of Care: Advice: Applications & provision: Scotland 346
Social care: Regulation of Care: Care services: Requirements: Scotland 346
Social care: Regulation of care: Excepted services: Scotland. 346
Social care: Regulation of Care: Fees: Scotland 346
Social care: Regulation of Care: Registration & registers: Scotland 346
Social care: Residential family centres: England 20, 222
Social care: Scottish Commission for the Regulation of Care: Appointments & procedure: Scotland 346
Social care: Scottish Commission for the Regulation of Care: Staff transfer scheme: Scotland 346
Social care: Scottish Commission for the Regulation of Care: Transfer of staff: Consultation: Scotland 346
Social care: Scottish Social Services Council: Appointments, procedure & access to register: Scotland. 346
Social Fund: Cold weather payments. 225
Social fund: Cold weather payments: General: Northern Ireland 382
Social fund: Maternity & funeral expenses 225
Social fund: Maternity & funeral expenses: Northern Ireland 382
Social fund: Miscellaneous amendments. 225
Social fund: Miscellaneous amendments: Northern Ireland 382
Social landlords: Registered: Housing (Scotland) Act 2001: Scotland 318
Social security & child support: Decisions & appeals: Miscellaneous amendments 62, 231, 236
Social security & child support: Decisions & appeals: Miscellaneous amendments: Northern Ireland 361, 365, 371, 378, 382
Social security & child support: Miscellaneous amendments: Northern Ireland 361, 366, 382
Social security Act 2002: Commencement: Northern Ireland. 382
Social Security Administration (Northern Ireland) Act 1992: Amendment: Northern Ireland 382
Social Security Administration Act 1992: Amendment. 225
Social security commissioners: Procedure: Tax credits appeals 227
Social security contributions: Statutory sick pay: Statutory maternity pay 230, 239
Social Security Fraud Act (Northern Ireland) 2001: Commencement: Northern Ireland 383, 384
Social Security Fraud Act 2001: Commencement 228
Social security: Acts: Northern Ireland 358
Social security: Attendance allowance: Disability living allowance. 226
Social security: Attendance allowance: Disability living allowance: Northern Ireland. 382
Social security: Benefits: Earnings: Computation 226
Social security: Benefits: Earnings: Computation: Child care charges 227
Social security: Benefits: Earnings: Computation: Northern Ireland. 231
Social security: Benefits: Loss 229
Social security: Benefits: Loss: Northern Ireland. 371, 379, 384
Social security: Benefits: Up-rating 227, 239
Social security: Benefits: Up-rating: Northern Ireland 371, 378, 382, 383, 385, 386
Social security: Carer premium 225
Social security: Carer's allowance 226
Social security: Carer's allowance: Northern Ireland 371, 378, 383
Social security: Carer's allowance: Regulatory reform. 145, 225
Social security: Children & young persons: Allowances: Northern Ireland 371, 379, 385
Social security: Claims & payments 227
Social security: Claims & payments: Northern Ireland 383
Social security: Contracting out: Income-related benefits 31, 224
Social security: Contributions 227, 228
Social security: Contributions: Decisions & appeals. 228
Social security: Contributions: Intermediaries 228
Social security: Contributions: Intermediaries: Northern Ireland 231
Social security: Contributions: Re-rating & national insurance fund payments 228
Social security: Deregulation: Carer's allowance: Northern Ireland 362
Social security: Disability living allowance 228
Social security: Disability living allowance: Northern Ireland 383

Social security: Earnings factors: Revaluation 229
Social security: Earnings factors: Revaluation: Northern Ireland 385
Social security: Electronic communications: Child benefit 228
Social security: Employment Act 2002: Commencement 224, 238
Social security: Employment programmes 226
Social security: Employment programmes: Northern Ireland 371, 378, 383
Social security: General & special commissioners: Jurisdiction & procedure 82, 84, 224, 234
Social security: Guardian's allowances 228
Social security: Guardian's allowances: Northern Ireland 384
Social security: Hospital in-patients 228
Social security: Hospital in-patients: Northern Ireland 384
Social security: Housing benefit: Council tax benefit: Child care charges 224
Social security: Housing benefit: Council tax benefit: Claims & information 227
Social security: Housing benefit: General 224
Social security: Incapacity 229
Social security: Incapacity: Miscellaneous amendments: Northern Ireland 384
Social security: Incapacity: Northern Ireland 384
Social security: Income related benefits: Authorities: Subsidy 224
Social security: Income support: General: Jobseeker's allowance 224
Social security: Income support: General: Jobseekers allowance: Northern Ireland 381
Social security: Income support: General: Standard interest rate 224, 225
Social security: Income support: General: Standard interest rate: Northern Ireland 381
Social security: Income-related benefits & jobseeker's allowance 224
Social security: Industrial injuries: Dependency: Permitted earnings limits 229
Social security: Industrial injuries: Dependency: Permitted earnings limits: Northern Ireland 384
Social security: Industrial injuries: Prescribed diseases 229
Social security: Industrial injuries: Prescribed diseases: Northern Ireland 384
Social security: Intercalating students: Northern Ireland 371, 378, 384
Social security: Jobcentre plus interviews 229
Social security: Jobseeker's allowance 225
Social security: Jobseeker's allowance: Amendment: Northern Ireland 381
Social security: Jobseeker's allowance: Joint claims 225
Social security: Miscellaneous amendments 229
Social security: Miscellaneous amendments: Northern Ireland 371, 379, 384
Social security: Northern Ireland Act 1998: Modification 129, 225
Social security: Paternity & adoption 229
Social security: Paternity & adoption: Northern Ireland 371, 379, 384
Social security: Pensions: Low earnings threshold 229
Social security: Pensions: Low earnings threshold: Northern Ireland 385
Social security: Personal allowances for children & young persons 226
Social security: Personal injury payments 226
Social security: Personal Injury payments: Northern Ireland 371, 379, 385
Social security: Pneumoconiosis, etc.: Workers' compensation: Claims: Payment: Northern Ireland 381
Social security: Residential care & nursing homes 226
Social security: Residential care & nursing homes: Northern Ireland 382
Social security: Social fund: Cold weather payments 225
Social security: Social fund: Cold weather payments: General: Northern Ireland 382
Social security: Social fund: Maternity & funeral expenses 225
Social security: Social fund: Maternity & funeral expenses: Northern Ireland 382
Social security: Social fund: Miscellaneous amendments 225
Social security: Social fund: Miscellaneous amendments: Northern Ireland 382
Social security: State Pension Credit 230
Social security: State Pension Credit Act 2002: Commencement 230
Social security: State Pension Credit: Consequential, transitional & miscellaneous provisions 230
Social security: Statutory maternity pay 230, 239
Social security: Statutory maternity pay & sick pay: Miscellaneous amendments: Northern Ireland 385, 386
Social security: Statutory paternity pay: Statutory adoption pay: Administration 230, 239
Social security: Statutory payment schemes: Electronic communications 58, 230
Social security: Students: Income-related benefits 226
Social security: Students: Income related benefits : Northern Ireland 372, 379, 385
Social security: Students: Intercalating students 226
Social security: Tax credits 231, 232, 234, 235, 236
Social security: Tax credits up-rating 231, 235
Social security: Tax credits: Appeals 231, 234
Social security: Tax credits: Appeals: Northern Ireland 385
Social security: Tax credits: Claims & notifications 234
Social security: Tax credits: Claims & payments: Northern Ireland 232, 236

Social security: Tax credits: Decisions & appeals: Northern Ireland 232, 236
Social security: Tax credits: Northern Ireland 232, 236
Social security: Tax credits: Prescribed periods of awards 231, 235
Social security: Tax credits: Prescribed periods of awards: Northern Ireland 232, 236
Social security: Work-focused interviews: Lone parents 230
Social security: Work-focused interviews: Lone parents: Northern Ireland 385
Social security: Workmen's compensation: Northern Ireland 385
Social security: Workmen's compensation: Supplementation 231
Social services: Carers & direct payments: Acts: Northern Ireland 358
Social services: Children: Leaving care: Acts: Northern Ireland 358
Social services: Health & Personal Social Services (Northern Ireland) Act 2002: Commencement: Northern Ireland 369
Social services: Personal: Acts: Northern Ireland 358, 359
Social services: Personal: Penalty charges: Northern Ireland 369
Social services: Personal: Preserved rights: Acts: Explanatory notes 359
Social services: Personal: Preserved rights: Acts: Northern Ireland 358
Solicitors, shorthand writers & witnesses: Court of Session: Fees: Act of Sederunt: Scotland 312
Solicitors: Sheriff Court: Fees: Act of Sederunt: Scotland 344
Somalia: United Nations sanctions 246
Somalia: United Nations sanctions: Channel Islands 246
Somalia: United Nations sanctions: Isle of Man 246
Somalia: United Nations sanctions: Overseas territories 246
Somerset (North): National Health Service Trust 117
Somerset Health Authority 120
Somerset, North: Parishes: Local government 95
Somerset: Avon & Somerset: Petty sessions areas 87
Somerset: New Horizons Kent-Somerset: Education Action Zone: Extension 49
Somerset: Taunton & Somerset: National Health Service Trusts 123
South & West Devon: Health Authority 120
South Africa: Double taxation: Relief 82
South Africa: Treaties: Definition: European Communities 61
South Birmingham: National Health Service Primary Care Trust 120
South Bradford Community Learning Partnership: Education Action Zone: Extension 50
South Buckinghamshire: National Health Service Trust 106, 120
South Bucks (District): Electoral changes 93
South Cambridgeshire (District): Electoral changes 93
South Cambridgeshire: National Health Service Trust 120
South Central Class 375/3 vehicles: Accessibility: Exemptions 41, 242
South East London: Health Authority 121
South Essex: Health Authority 121
South Essex Mental Health & Community Care: National Health Service Trust 121
South Gloucestershire: Parishes: Local government 95
South Huddersfield: National Health Service Trust 121
South Norfolk (District): Electoral changes 93
South of Tyne & Wearside: National Health Service Trust 121
South Oxfordshire (District): Electoral changes 93
South Ribble (Borough): Electoral changes 90
South Ribble (Borough): Ribble Banks Parish Council: Electoral changes 92
South Staffordshire: Health Authority 121
South Stoke: National Health Service Trust 121
South Stoke: National Health Service Primary Care Trust 121
South Tees Acute Hospitals: National Health Service Trust 121
South Tyneside: National Health Service Trust 121
South Warwickshire Combined Care: National Health Service Trust 121
South Warwickshire National Health Service Primary Care Trust 121
South West London Community: National Health Service Trust 122
South West Peninsula: Health Authority 122
South West Trains Class 458 vehicles: Accessibility: Exemptions 41, 242
South West Yorkshire: Mental Health: National Health Service Trust 122
South Western Staffordshire National Health Service Primary Care Trust 121
South Worcestershire National Health Service Primary Care Trust 122
South Yorkshire Metropolitan Ambulance & Paramedic Service : National Health Service Trust 122
Southampton & South West Hampshire: Health Authority 120
Southampton (City): Permitted & special parking area 210
Southampton Community Health Services: National Health Service Trust 120
Southampton East Healthcare: National Health Service Primary Care Trust 120
Southend: Education Action Zone: Extension 50
Southern Derbyshire Mental Health: National Health Service Trust 121

Entry	Page
Southwark: National Health Service Primary Care Trust	121
Special constables: Police	139
Special Educational Needs & Disability Act 2001: Commencement: England & Wales	42, 52, 53
Special Educational Needs & Disability Act 2001: Commencement: Wales	56
Special Educational Needs & Disability Tribunal: General provisions & disability claims procedure	42, 53
Special Educational Needs Tribunal: Amendment: England & Wales	53
Special educational needs: Approval of independent schools: England	47
Special educational needs: City colleges: England	48
Special educational needs: Code of practice: Appointed day: Wales	56
Special educational needs: Education: Wales	55
Special educational needs: Provision of information: Local education authorities: Wales	56
Special occasions licensing: Regulatory reform: England & Wales	146
Special roads: Glasgow-Monkland motorway: stage II, connecting roads: Scotland	332, 347
Special roads: M77: Fenwick to Floak, side roads: Scotland	332, 347
Special roads: M77: Fenwick to Malletsheugh, side roads: Scotland	332, 347
Special roads: M77: Fenwick to Malletsheugh: Scotland	332, 347
Special roads: M77: Floak to Malletsheugh, side roads: Scotland	332, 347
Special schools: Non-maintained: England	46
Speke Garston Excellent: Education Action Zone: Extension	50
Spider Crabs: Undersized: Wales	219
Spongiform encephalopathy: Transmissible: England	14
Spongiform encephalopathy: Transmissible: Northern Ireland	361, 365
Spongiform encephalopathy: Transmissible: Scotland	310
Spongiform encephalopathy: Transmissible: Wales	17
Sports clubs, Amateur: Taxation	235
Sports grounds & sporting events: Designation: Scotland	347
Sports grounds & sporting events: Football (Disorder) (Amendment) Act 2002: Commencement	232
Sports grounds & sporting events: Football: Spectators: Seating: England & Wales	232
Sports grounds & sporting events: Football: Spectators: World Cup control period: England & Wales	232
Sports grounds & sporting events: Safety: Designation	232
Spruce bark: Treatment	136
St Albans: Parishes: Local government	95
St Andrews University: Postgraduate medical degrees: Acts: Explanatory notes: Scotland	306
St Andrews University: Postgraduate medical degrees: Acts: Scotland	305
St Dogmaels: Ceredigion & Pembrokeshire: Local government: Wales	97
St Edmundsbury: Parishes: Local government	95
St Helens & Knowsley Community Health: National Health Service Trust	122
St Helens: National Health Service Trust	122
St Leonards & Hastings: Education Action Zone: Extension	49
St Mary's Music School, Scotland: Aided places : Scotland	313
Staffordshire County: Trent & Mersey Canal: Bridge scheme	77
Staffordshire, East: Parishes: Local government	94
Staffordshire: East Staffordshire: National Health Service Primary Care Trust	110
Staffordshire: South Staffordshire: Health Authority	121
Staffordshire: South Western Staffordshire: National Health Service Primary Care Trust	121
Stakeholder pension schemes	133
Stakeholder pension schemes: Northern Ireland	375
Stamp duty & stamp duty reserve tax: Recognised exchanges: Extension of exceptions	235
Standards Commissioner: Scottish Parliament: Acts	304
Standards Commissioner: Scottish Parliament: Acts: Explanatory notes: Scotland	305
Standards committee: Relevant authorities: Dispensations: Local government: England & Wales	96
Standards in Scotland's Schools etc. Act 2000: Commencement: Scotland	313
Star anise: Third countries: Food: Emergency control: England	66
Star anise: Third countries: Food: Emergency control: Northern Ireland	367
Star anise: Third countries: Food: Emergency control: Scotland	316
Star anise: Third countries: Food: Emergency control: Wales	68
State Pension Credit	230
State Pension Credit Act 2002: Commencement	230
State Pension Credit Act 2002 (N.I.): Commencement: Northern Ireland	385
State pension credit: Acts	4
State pension credit: Acts: Explanatory notes	5
State pension credit: Acts: Northern Ireland	359
State pension credit: Consequential, transitional & miscellaneous provisions	230
Statistics of trade: Customs & excise	232
Statutes: Binders: Northern Ireland	7
Statutes: Chronological tables	6
Statutory instruments: Annual volumes	7

Statutory instruments: National Assembly for Wales: Annual volumes 7
Statutory maternity pay: Employers: Compensation. 230, 239
Statutory maternity pay: Miscellaneous amendments: Northern Ireland 385, 386
Statutory maternity pay: Social security: Benefits: Up-rating: Northern Ireland 371, 378, 382, 385, 386
Statutory maternity pay: Statutory sick pay: Social security contributions 230, 239
Statutory paternity pay: Administration: Northern Ireland 363
Statutory paternity pay: General: Northern Ireland 363
Statutory paternity pay: Health & personal social services employees: Northern Ireland 363
Statutory paternity pay: Persons abroad & mariners: Northern Ireland 364
Statutory paternity pay: Statutory adoption pay: Administration 230, 239
Statutory paternity pay: Statutory adoption pay: General. 239
Statutory paternity pay: Statutory adoption pay: National Health Service employees 239
Statutory paternity pay: Statutory adoption pay: Persons abroad & mariners 239
Statutory paternity pay: Statutory adoption pay: Weekly rates. 239
Statutory paternity pay: Statutory adoption pay: Weekly rates: Northern Ireland. 364
Statutory payment schemes: Electronic communications 58, 230
Statutory sick pay: Miscellaneous amendments: Northern Ireland 385, 386
Statutory sick pay: Social security: Benefits: Up-rating: Northern Ireland 371, 378, 382, 385, 386
Statutory sick pay: Statutory maternity pay: Social security contributions 230, 239
Stocks: Government: Irish registers: Closure & transfer 104
Stoke (North) National Health Service Trust 117
Stoke (South) National Health Service Trust 121
Stoke Mandeville Hospital: National Health Service Trust 106
Stoke on Trent: Rainbow: Education Action Zone: Extension 50
Stoke: North Stoke: National Health Service Primary Care Trust 117
Strand Road, Preston Railway. 243, 244
Strategic health authorities & primary care trusts: Functions: National Health Service 114
Street works: Inspection fees: England 77
Street works: Inspection fees: Wales 78
Street works: New Roads & Street Works Act 1991: Commencement: England 77
Street works: Records: England 77
Street works: Recovery of costs: England 78
Street works: Registers, notices, directions & designations: Northern Ireland. 379, 386
Street works: Reinstatement: England. 78
Student loans: Education: Northern Ireland. 362
Student loans: Education: Scotland 312
Student loans: England & Wales. 52
Student loans: Repayment: Education 42
Student loans: Repayment: Education: England & Wales 52
Student loans: Teachers: Repayment etc.: England & Wales 52
Student support: Education: England & Wales. 52
Student support: Education: Northern Ireland 362
Students & Income related benefits: Social security: Northern Ireland. 372, 379, 385
Students: Awards: Northern Ireland 362
Students: Disabled postgraduate: Grants: Education: Northern Ireland. 362
Students: Intercalating: Social security. 226
Students: Intercalating: Social security: Northern Ireland 371, 378, 384
Students: Nursing & midwifery: Allowances: Scotland 313
Students: Postgraduate: Disabled: Grants: Education: England & Wales. 51
Students: Social security: Income-related benefits. 226
Sub-contractors: Construction industry: Income tax 83
Substances hazardous to health: Control 72
Sulphur content: Liquid fuels: Northern Ireland 364
Summary & statutory applications & appeals etc.: Rules: Act of Sederunt: Scotland 345
Summary cause rules: Act of Sederunt: Scotland 345
Summary proceedings: Cash: Recovery of: Minimum amount: Proceeds of Crime Act 2002. 141
Summer time. 233
Summerlee Tramcar No. 392: Accessibility: Exemptions 41, 242
Sunderland (City): Permitted & special parking area 210
Sunderland Building Our Future: Education Action Zone: Extension 50
Sunderland: Health Authority. 122
Sunderland Teaching National Health Service Trust 122
Superannuation Act 1972: Admission to schedule 1 133
Superannuation: Health & personal social services: Northern Ireland 369
Superannuation: Invest Northern Ireland: Northern Ireland 375
Superannuation: Teachers: Scotland 323
Supreme Court of England & Wales: Civil procedure 33, 233

Supreme Court of England & Wales: Civil procedure: Enactments: Modification 33, 233
Supreme Court of England & Wales: Crown Court: Rules. 233
Supreme Court of England & Wales: Crown Court: Special measures directions: Cross-examination: Directions prohibiting 233
Supreme Court of England & Wales: Fees 233
Supreme Court of England & Wales: Judges: Maximum number. 233
Supreme Court of England & Wales: Pathogens Access Appeal Commission: Court of Appeal. 233
Supreme Court of England & Wales: Proscribed Organisations Appeal Commission: Appeals 233
Supreme Court: Family proceedings: Fees: Northern Ireland. 361, 366, 386
Supreme Court: Family proceedings: Northern Ireland. 361, 366, 386
Supreme Court: Fees: Northern Ireland. 386
Supreme Court: Rules: Northern Ireland 377, 386
Surrey & Sussex Healthcare: National Health Service Trust 122
Surrey & Sussex: Health Authority 122
Surrey Downs: Croydon & Surrey Downs Community: National Health Service Trust. 108
Surrey: East Surrey: National Health Service Primary Care Trust 110
Surrey: Mid Surrey: East Elmbridge & Mid Surrey: National Health Service Primary Care Trust. 109
Surrey: North Surrey: National Health Service Primary Care Trust 117
Surveillance: Covert: Regulation of investigatory powers: Codes of practice. 86
Sussex & Surrey: Health Authority 122
Sussex Downs & Weald: National Health Service Primary Care Trust 122
Sussex Weald & Downs: National Health Service Trust. 122, 124
Sussex, Mid (District): Electoral changes 93
Sussex, Mid: Parishes: Local government 95
Sussex: Brighton & Sussex University Hospitals: National Health Service Trust 105
Sussex: Mid Sussex: Health Authority 113
Sussex: Mid Sussex: National Health Service Trust 105
Sussex: Surrey & Sussex Healthcare: National Health Service Trust 122
Sussex: West Sussex Health & Social Care: National Health Service Trust. 124
Sussex: West Sussex: Health Authority 124
Sussex: Western Sussex: National Health Service Primary Care Trust 124
Sutton: Merton, Sutton & Wandsworth: Health Authority 113
Swale: National Health Service Primary Care Trust 123
Swansea Bay Mussel Fishery: C.V. & D.M. Thomas 220
Swansea Bay: Sea fisheries: Shellfish: Mussels 220
Swansea: Neath Port Talbot & Swansea: Trebanos & Clydach: Local government: Wales 99
Sweeteners: Food: England 67
Sweeteners: Food: Northern Ireland 368
Sweeteners: Food: Scotland 316
Sweeteners: Food: Wales 69
Swindon: National Health Service Primary Care Trust 123
Swindon: Wiltshire & Swindon Health Care: National Health Service Trust. 124
Swiss free movement of persons: Immigration 81
Switzerland: Immigration: Swiss free movement of persons 81

T

Tables, origins & destinations: Income Tax (Earnings & Pensions) Act 2003. 6
Taiwan: Double taxation: Relief 82
Taliban & Al-Qa'ida: United Nations measures 245
Taliban & Al-Qa'ida: United Nations measures: Isle of Man. 245
Taliban & Al-Qa'ida: United Nations measures: Overseas territories 245
Tameside & Glossop: National Health Service Trust 123
Tameside & Glossop Community & Priority Services: National Health Service Trust 123
Tamworth: Burntwood, Lichfield & Tamworth National Health Service Trust 106
Taunton & Somerset: National Health Service Trusts. 123
Tax credit: Aggregates levy: Northern Ireland tax credit 7
Tax credits 231, 232, 234, 235, 236
Tax Credits Act 2002: Commencement 233
Tax credits: Acts 4
Tax credits: Acts: Explanatory notes 5
Tax credits: Administrative arrangements 233
Tax credits: Appeals 231, 234
Tax credits: Appeals: Northern Ireland 385
Tax credits: Child tax credits 233
Tax credits: Claims & notifications 234

Tax credits: Claims & payments: Northern Ireland	232, 236
Tax credits: Decisions & appeals: Northern Ireland	232, 236
Tax credits: Income thresholds & determination of rates	234
Tax credits: Income: Definition & calculation	234
Tax credits: Northern Ireland	232, 236
Tax credits: Notice of appeal	234
Tax credits: Payments by the Board	234
Tax credits: Prescribed periods of awards	231, 235
Tax credits: Prescribed periods of awards: Northern Ireland	232, 236
Tax credits: Working tax credits: Entitlement & maximum rate	234
Tax credits: Working tax credits: Payment by employers	234
Taxes: Capital gains tax: Annual exempt amount	234
Taxes: Capital gains: Gilt-edged securities	234
Taxes: Corporation tax: Finance leasing: Intangible assets	82
Taxes: Double taxation: Relief: Lithuania	82
Taxes: Double taxation: Relief: South Africa	82
Taxes: Double taxation: Relief: Taiwan	82
Taxes: Double taxation: Relief: United States of America	82
Taxes: European single currency	234
Taxes: General & special commissioners: Jurisdiction & procedure	82, 84, 224, 234
Taxes: Income & Corporation Taxes Act 1998: Section 349B (3)	82
Taxes: Income tax: Benefits in kind: Employment costs resulting from disability: Exemption	82
Taxes: Income tax: Car fuel benefits: Cash equivalents	82
Taxes: Income tax: Employments & electronic communications	82
Taxes: Income tax: Indexation	82, 83
Taxes: Income tax: Individual savings accounts	83
Taxes: Income tax: Minor benefits: Exemption	82
Taxes: Income tax: Open-ended investment companies: Tax	83
Taxes: Income tax: Sub-contractors: Construction industry	83
Taxes: Inheritance tax: Accounts: Delivery: Excepted estates	84
Taxes: Inheritance tax: Accounts: Delivery: Excepted settlements	84
Taxes: Inheritance tax: Accounts: Delivery: Excepted transfers & terminations	84
Taxes: Inheritance tax: Indexation	84
Taxes: Landfill tax	87
Taxes: Life assurance & other policies: Insurers: Information & duties	234
Taxes: Overseas insurers: Tax representatives	235
Taxes: Personal portfolio bonds: Tax	235
Taxes: Social security & child support: Decisions & appeals: Miscellaneous amendments	62, 231, 236
Taxes: Social security commissioners: Procedure: Tax credits appeals	227
Taxes: Stamp duty & stamp duty reserve tax: Recognised exchanges: Extension of exceptions	235
Taxes: Tax credits	231, 232, 234, 235, 236
Taxes: Tax Credits Act 2002: Commencement	233
Taxes: Tax credits up-rating	231, 235
Taxes: Tax credits: Administrative arrangements	233
Taxes: Tax credits: Appeals	234
Taxes: Tax credits: Claims & notifications	234
Taxes: Tax credits: Claims & payments: Northern Ireland	232, 236
Taxes: Tax credits: Decisions & appeals: Northern Ireland	232, 236
Taxes: Tax credits: Income: Definition & calculation	234
Taxes: Tax credits: Northern Ireland	232, 236
Taxes: Tax credits: Notice of appeal	234
Taxes: Tax credits: Payments by the Board	234
Taxes: Tax credits: Prescribed periods of awards	231, 235
Taxes: Tax credits: Prescribed periods of awards: Northern Ireland	232, 236
Taxes: Taxation relief: Community amateur sports clubs	235
Taxes: Tonnage tax: Training requirements	236
Taxes: Value added tax	246
Taxes: Value added tax tribunals	247
Taxes: Value added tax: Acquisitions: Relief	246
Taxes: Value added tax: Buildings & land	246
Taxes: Value added tax: Cars	246
Taxes: Value added tax: Construction of buildings	246
Taxes: Value added tax: Drugs, medicines, aids for handicapped & charities	246
Taxes: Value added tax: Fuel: Provided for private use: Consideration for	246
Taxes: Value added tax: Health & welfare	247
Taxes: Value added tax: Lifeboats: Equipment	247
Taxes: Value added tax: Reduced rate	247

Taxes: Value added tax: Registration limits: Increase 247
Taxes: Value added tax: Special provisions. 247
Taxes: Value added tax: Special provisions: Amendment 247
Taxes: Value added tax: Transport 247
Taxi drivers' licences: Dogs: Guide & hearing: Carrying of: Scotland 321
Teacher qualifications & health standards: Wales 55
Teacher Training Agency: Additional functions. 53
Teacher Training Agency: Additional functions: England 50
Teacher training: Bursaries: England 45, 48
Teacher training: Funding: Designation: England 45
Teachers: Induction arrangements: Education: England 46
Teachers: Pensions: England & Wales 53
Teachers: Qualifications & health standards: England 48
Teachers: Redundancy & premature retirement: Compensation: Northern Ireland 362
Teachers: School: Pay & conditions: England & Wales 52
Teachers: School: Remuneration: England & Wales 52
Teachers: Schools: Appraisal: Wales 56
Teachers: Student loans: Repayment etc.: England & Wales 52
Teachers: Superannuation: Scotland 323
Teachers' qualifications: Further education: Wales 55
Teddington, Twickenham & Hamptons: National Health Service Primary Care Trust 123
Tees Valley: County Durham & Tees Valley: Health Authority 108
Teeside Tertiary College: Dissolution. 50
Teesside: South Tees Acute Hospitals: National Health Service Trust 121
Teignbridge: National Health Service Trust 123
Telecommunication services: Channel Islands 139
Telecommunications: Mobile Telephones (Re-progamming) Act 2002: Commencement 34, 236
Telecommunications: Public systems: AT&T Global Network Services (UK) B.V. 236
Telecommunications: Public systems: Companhia Portuguesa Radio Marconi SA. 237
Telecommunications: Public systems: Econet Satellite Services Limited 237
Telecommunications: Public systems: Eurocall Ltd 237
Telecommunications: Public systems: Fibernet UK Ltd 237
Telecommunications: Public systems: France Telecom Network Services-UK Ltd 237
Telecommunications: Public systems: Gamma Telecommunications Limited. 237
Telecommunications: Public systems: Severn Trent Retail Services Limited 237
Telecommunications: Public systems: Telekom Malaysia (UK) Ltd 237
Telecommunications: Public systems: T-Systems Limited 237
Telecommunications: Public systems: Tweedwind Limited. 237
Telecommunications: Public systems: United Networks Limited 237
Telecommunications: Public systems: VTL (UK) Limited 237
Telegraphs: Wireless telegraphy: Exemption 237
Telegraphs: Wireless telegraphy: Licence charges 237
Telegraphs: Wireless telegraphy: Public fixed wireless access licences 237
Telegraphs: Wireless telegraphy: Television licence: Fees 237
Telekom Malaysia (UK) Ltd: Telecommunications: Public systems 237
Telephones: Mobile Telephones (Re-progamming) Act 2002: Commencement 34, 236
Telephones: Mobile telephones: Re-programming: Acts 3
Telephones: Mobile telephones: Re-programming: Acts: Explanatory notes 5
Telford & Wrekin (Borough): Electoral changes 90
Telford & Wrekin: Education Action Zone: Extension. 50
Telford & Wrekin: National Health Service Primary Care Trust 123
Tenancies: Assured: Agricultural occupancies: Forms: England 87
Tenancies: Scottish secure tenancies: Proceedings for possession: Scotland 319
Tenancies: Scottish secure tenancies: Abandoned property: Scotland 318
Tenancies: Scottish secure tenancies: Exceptions: Scotland 318
Tenancies: Secure: Housing (Scotland) Act 2001: Scotland 318
Tenancies: Short Scottish secure tenancies: Notices: Scotland 319
Tenancies: Short Scottish secure tenancies: Proceedings for possession: Scotland 319
Tenant & landlord: Leasehold reform: Collective enfranchisement: Counter-notices: England 87
Tenant organisations: Registration: Housing: Scotland 318
Tenants: Scottish secure tenants: Compensation for improvements: Scotland. 319
Tenants: Scottish secure tenants: Right to repair: Scotland 319
Terms & conditions of employment: Employment Act 2002: Commencement 224, 238
Terms & conditions of employment: Employment rights: Increase of limits 238
Terms & conditions of employment: Fixed-term employees: Less favourable treatment: Prevention 238
Terms & conditions of employment: Flexible working: Eligibility, complaints & remedies 238
Terms & conditions of employment: Flexible working: Procedure requirements 238

Terms & conditions of employment: Maternity & parental leave 238
Terms & conditions of employment: National Minimum Wage Regulations 1999. 238
Terms & conditions of employment: Part-time workers: Less favourable treatment: Prevention 238
Terms & conditions of employment: Paternity & adoption: Leave 238
Terms & conditions of employment: Redundancy payments: Local government: Continuity of employment 238
Terms & conditions of employment: Social security: Benefits: Up-rating 227, 239
Terms & conditions of employment: Statutory maternity pay 230, 239
Terms & conditions of employment: Statutory paternity pay: Statutory adoption pay: Administration. 230, 239
Terms & conditions of employment: Statutory paternity pay: Statutory adoption pay: General 239
Terms & conditions of employment: Statutory paternity pay: Statutory adoption pay: National Health Service employees 239
Terms & conditions of employment: Statutory paternity pay: Statutory adoption pay: Persons abroad & mariners 239
Terms & conditions of employment: Statutory paternity pay: Statutory adoption pay: Weekly rates 239
Terms & conditions of employment: Statutory sick pay: Statutory maternity pay 230, 239
Terms & conditions of employment: Working time 239
Terms and conditions of employment: Trade unions: Recognition & derecognition ballots: Qualified persons 238
Territorial Sea Act 1987: Jersey 239
Terrorism Act 2000: Part VII: Continuance 240
Terrorism Act 2000: Proscribed organisations 140
Terrorism Act 2000: Schedule 7: Information 140
Terrorism Act 2000: Section 76: Cessation of effect 240
Terrorism: Anti-Terrorism, Crime & Security Act 2001: Commencement 34, 36, 140
Terrorism: Pathogens Access Appeal Commission: Court of Appeal 233
Terrorism: Prevention & suppression: Anti-Terrorism, Crime & Security Act 2001: Commencement 140
Terrorism: Prevention & suppression: Pathogens & toxins: Security: Dangerous substances 140
Terrorism: Prevention & suppression: Pathogens Access Appeal Commission: Procedure 140
Terrorism: Proscribed Organisations Appeal Commission: Appeals. 233
Terrorism: Terrorism Act 2000: Part VII: Continuance 240
Terrorism: Terrorism Act 2000: Schedule 7: Information 140
Terrorism: Terrorism Act 2000: Section 76: Cessation of effect 240
Terrorist bombings: Extradition 62
Terrorist cash: Detention & forfeiture: Magistrates' courts: Rules: Northern Ireland 374
Test Valley South: Eastleigh & Test Valley South: National Health Service Trust 110
Thames Gateway & Invicta Community Care: National Health Service Trust 124
Thames Gateway: National Health Service Trust 123
Thames Valley: Health Authority 123
Thermal energy: Gas: Calculation 70
Third country imports: Hemp 8
Third party risks: Motor vehicles: Northern Ireland 380
Thurrock (Borough): Electoral changes. 90
Thurrock: Basildon & Thurrock General Hospitals: National Health Service Trust 104
Thurrock: Borough of Halton, Thurrock & Warrington: Election years changes 90
Tipton & Rowley Regis: National Health Service Primary Care Trust 119
TIR carnets: Goods: International transport: Fees. 212
Tir Mynydd: Agriculture: Wales 11
Tobacco Advertising & Promotion Act 2002: Commencement: England, Wales & Northern Ireland 31
Tobacco Advertising & Promotion Act 2002: Commencement: Scotland. 311
Tobacco products & alcoholic liquor: Channel Tunnel 19
Tobacco products Excise goods, beer & tobacco products: Customs & excise. 37
Tobacco products: Manufacture, presentation & sale: Safety 31
Tobacco: Advertising & promotion: Acts 4
Tobacco: Advertising & promotion: Acts Explanatory notes. 5
Tonnage tax: Training requirements 236
Torbay (Borough): Electoral changes. 90
Torbay National Health Service Trust. 123
Torfaen (County Borough): Electoral changes: Local government: Wales 97
Town & country planning: Applications & deemed applications: Fees: England. 240
Town & country planning: Applications & deemed applications: Fees: Scotland 347
Town & country planning: Applications & deemed applications: Fees: Wales. 240
Town & country planning: Costs of inquiries: Standard daily amount: England 240, 245
Town & country planning: Enforcement notices & appeals: England 240
Town & country planning: Enforcement: Determination by Inspectors: Inquiries procedure: England 245
Town & country planning: Enforcement: Hearings procedure: England 245
Town & country planning: Enforcement: Inquiries procedure: England 245
Town & country planning: Enforcement: Written representation procedure: England 240
Town & country planning: General development procedure: England. 240
Town & country planning: General development procedure: Wales. 241
Town & country planning: General permitted development: Wales. 241

Town & country planning: Inquiries: Costs of: Standard daily amount: Wales. 240
Town & country planning: Major infrastructure projects: Inquiries: Procedure: England. 245
Town & country planning: Planning & Compensation Act 1991: Schedule 18: Amendment. 240
Town & country planning: Use classes: Wales 241
Toxins & pathogens: Security: Dangerous substances 140
Tractor components: Type approval 241
Tractors: Agricultural & forestry: Components: Type approval 241
Tractors: Agricultural & forestry: Emission of gaseous & particulate pollutants. 58
Trade & adjustment: Fees: Weights & measures: Northern Ireland 387
Trade Marks Act 1994: Isle of Man. 241
Trade marks: Copyright, etc. & Trade Marks (Offences & Enforcement) Act 2002: Commencement 32, 34, 241
Trade marks: Copyright: Offences & enforcement: Acts: Explanatory notes 4
Trade marks: International registration 241
Trade unions: Ballots & elections: Scrutineers 241
Trade unions: Recognition & derecognition ballots: Qualified persons 238
Trade: Statistics of: Customs & excise 232
Traffic calming: Road humps: Scotland. 332
Traffic orders: Local authorities: Disabled persons: Exemption: Scotland 332, 333
Traffic signs: General directions 148
Traffic signs: Northern Ireland 381
Traffic wardens: Functions 137
Training: Education: Acts: Explanatory notes 4
Transit visa: Immigration. 81
Transmissible spongiform encephalopathy: England 14
Transmissible spongiform encephalopathy: Northern Ireland 361, 365
Transmissible spongiform encephalopathy: Scotland. 310
Transmissible spongiform encephalopathy: Wales 17
Transport & works: Bitton Railway: England. 242, 243
Transport & works: Channel Tunnel Rail Link: Thames tunnel approach. 243
Transport & works: Chester guided busway 243
Transport & works: Docklands: Silvertown & London City Airport extension 243
Transport & works: Heathrow Express Railway: Extension 243, 244
Transport & works: Light rapid transit systems: Greater Manchester: Trafford depot 243, 244
Transport & works: Strand Road, Preston Railway: England. 243, 244
Transport & works: Wear Valley Railway: England 243, 244
Transport & works: Wye (River): Navigation: England & Wales 19, 243
Transport (Scotland) Act 2001: Commencement & transitional provisions: Scotland. 348
Transport Act 2000: Commencement 99, 143, 148, 242
Transport Act 2000: Commencement: Wales 244
Transport for London: Highways: Street works: Charges 77
Transport tribunal: Amendment 242
Transport, local government & the regions: Transfer of functions. 103
Transport: Bus services: Operators: Grants: England 143
Transport: Bus services: Operators: Grants: Scotland 347
Transport: Bus services: Operators: Grants: Wales. 144
Transport: Buses: User complaints: Scotland. 347
Transport: Channel Tunnel Rail Link: Thames tunnel approach 243
Transport: Heathrow Express: Railway: Exemptions 244
Transport: Home zones: Scotland 347
Transport: Light railways: East Lancashire: Heywood extension 243
Transport: Merseyrail Electrics network 241
Transport: Mobility & Access Committee for Scotland: Scotland 347
Transport: Piccadilly Line: Heathrow T5 extension 243, 244
Transport: Public passenger: Community buses 143
Transport: Public passenger: London service permits: Appeals. 99, 143
Transport: Public passenger: Public service vehicles: Drivers, inspectors, conductors & passengers: Conduct 143
Transport: Public passenger: Public service vehicles: Fitness, equipment, use & certification 148, 212
Transport: Public passenger: Public service vehicles: Operators' licences: Fees 143
Transport: Public passenger: Public service vehicles: Registration of local services 144
Transport: Public passenger: Quality partnership schemes: Existing facilities: Wales. 144
Transport: Public passenger: Travel concessions: Eligible services: Wales 144
Transport: Rail vehicles: C2C Class 357/0 vehicles: Accessibility: Exemptions 41, 241
Transport: Rail vehicles: Cairngorm Funicular Railway: Accessibility: Exemptions 41, 241
Transport: Rail vehicles: Croydon Tramlink Class CR4000 vehicles: Accessibility: Exemptions 41, 242
Transport: Rail vehicles: East Hayling Light Railway vehicles: Accessibility: Exemptions 41, 242
Transport: Rail vehicles: Isle of Wight Railway LCDR no. 2515 vehicle: Accessibility: Exemptions 41, 242
Transport: Rail vehicles: Middleton Railway Drewry car: Accessibility: Exemptions 41, 242

Transport: Rail vehicles: South Central Class 375/3 vehicles: Accessibility: Exemptions 41, 242
Transport: Rail vehicles: South West Trains Class 458 vehicles: Accessibility: Exemptions 41, 242
Transport: Rail vehicles: Summerlee Tramcar No. 392: Accessibility: Exemptions 41, 242
Transport: Rail vehicles: Virgin West Coast Class 390 Vehicles: Accessibility: Exemptions. 41, 242
Transport: Railways: Interoperability: High-speed 242
Transport: Scottish Transport Group: Dissolution: Scotland 347
Transport: Service subsidy agreements: Tendering: England. 244
Transport: Service subsidy agreements: Tendering: Wales. 244
Transport: Travel Concessions (Eligibility) Act 2002: Commencement: England 244
Transport: Travel Concessions (Eligibility) Act 2002: Commencement: Wales 244
Transport: Travel concessions: Eligibility: Acts 4
Transport: Travel concessions: Eligibility: Acts: Explanatory notes 5
Transport: Travel concessions: Eligible services 143
Transport: Travel concessions: Eligible services: Scotland 348
Transport: Value added tax. 247
Travel bans: Designation: Immigration 80
Travel Concessions (Eligibility) Act 2002: Commencement: England 244
Travel Concessions (Eligibility) Act 2002: Commencement: Wales. 244
Travel concessions: Eligibility: Acts 4
Travel concessions: Eligibility: Acts: Explanatory notes 5
Travel concessions: Eligible services 143
Travel concessions: Eligible services: Scotland. 348
Travel concessions: Public passenger transport: Eligible services: Wales 144
Travel documents: Fees 81
Travel restriction order: Prescribed removal powers 34
Travelling expenses: Remission of charges: Health & personal social services: Northern Ireland 370
Travelling expenses: Remission of charges: National Health Service: England 116
Treasure: Designation 244
Trees: Felling of: Forestry: England & Wales 69
Trent & Mersey Canal: Bridge scheme 77
Trent: Health Authority. 123
Tribunals & inquiries: Inquiries: Fees: Standard daily amount: Wales 245
Tribunals & inquiries: Town & country planning: Costs of inquiries: Standard daily amount: England 240, 245
Tribunals & inquiries: Town & country planning: Major infrastructure projects: Inquiries: Procedure: England 245
Trossachs: Loch Lomond & the Trossachs National Park: Elections: Scotland 311
Trossachs: Loch Lomond & the Trossachs National Park: Provisions: Scotland 311
Trunk roads: A1/A66: Holtby Grange to Leeming 154
Trunk roads: A1: Baldersby interchange 153
Trunk roads: A1: Baldersby to Blind Lane 153
Trunk roads: A1: Barnsdale Bar to Darrington 153
Trunk roads: A1: Beeston, Bedfordshire 153
Trunk roads: A1: Biggleswade North to Beeston, Bedfordshire 149
Trunk roads: A1: Biggleswade-Sandy, Bedfordshire 153
Trunk roads: A1: Black Cat roundabout, Bedfordshire 153
Trunk roads: A1: Buckden-Hail Bridge, Cambridgeshire 153
Trunk roads: A1: Catterick South to East Appleton 153
Trunk roads: A1: Consett route interchange 153
Trunk roads: A1: Dishforth interchange 153
Trunk roads: A1: Eaton Socon bypass, Cambridgeshire 153
Trunk roads: A1: Gateshead/Newcastle western bypass 153
Trunk roads: A1: Junction with A6121, Stamford, southbound entry & exit slip road 154
Trunk roads: A1: Junction with the A606 at Stamford, slip roads 154
Trunk roads: A1: Lobley Hill interchange 154
Trunk roads: A1: Long Bennington 154
Trunk roads: A1: North Brunton interchange 149, 154
Trunk roads: A1: Northbound exit slip road, Ferrybridge interchange 154
Trunk roads: A1: Oak Tree Filling Station, Burneston 154
Trunk roads: A1: Radwell, Hertfordshire 154
Trunk roads: A1: Rainton crossroads 149
Trunk roads: A1: Ranby to Markham Moor, Nottinghamshire 154
Trunk roads: A1: River Coquet bridge 154
Trunk roads: A1: Scotch Corner 154
Trunk roads: A1: Smearfield & Haggerston 154
Trunk roads: A1: Southbound exit slip road, Balderton, Nottinghamshire 154
Trunk roads: A1: Southbound exit slip road, known as Great North Rd., Balderton 154
Trunk roads: A1: Stevenage, Hertfordshire - Langford, Bedfordshire 152
Trunk roads: A1: Stibbington, Cambridgeshire 154

Entry	Page
Trunk roads: A1: Thorns Farm, Grantham bypass, Lincolnshire	155
Trunk roads: A1: Various lengths, Bedfordshire-Cambridgeshire	155
Trunk roads: A1: Warreners to Tritlington & Burgham to Bockenfield	155
Trunk roads: A2: Brenley Corner - Guston	155
Trunk roads: A2: Bridge, slip roads	155
Trunk roads: A2: Canterbury bypass	155
Trunk roads: A2: Cobham junction, slip roads	155
Trunk roads: A2: Gate services, slip roads	155
Trunk roads: A2: Horselees Rd. Bridge	155
Trunk roads: A2: Jubilee Way, Coastguard carriageway	155
Trunk roads: A2: M25 junction 2-A227 junction	155
Trunk roads: A2: Pepper Hill, Londonbound slip road	155
Trunk roads: A2: Pepper Hill, slip roads	155
Trunk roads: A2: Upper Harbledown, slip road	155
Trunk roads: A3: Copsem to Hook, Surrey	156
Trunk roads: A3: Crackenthorpe to Appleby bypass	156
Trunk roads: A3: Hindhead & Milford	156
Trunk roads: A3: Hurtmore Rd. & Milford	156
Trunk roads: A3: Hurtmore Rd. junction, slip roads	156
Trunk roads: A3: Longmoor & Weston junctions	156
Trunk roads: A3: Midleton Rd., Guildford	156
Trunk roads: A3: North of Clanfield	156
Trunk roads: A3: Ockham, southbound exit slip road	156
Trunk roads: A3: Potters Lane junction, slip road	156
Trunk roads: A3: Sheet, northbound entry slip road	156
Trunk roads: A3: South of Hindhead	156
Trunk roads: A3: University junction, Guildford	156
Trunk roads: A3: Various locations, near Guildford	156
Trunk roads: A3: Various locations, Surrey	156
Trunk roads: A3: Weston & Berelands junctions	156
Trunk roads: A4: Colnbrook bypass	156
Trunk roads: A4: Crowley Way	195
Trunk roads: A4: Crowley Way & St Brendan's roundabout	156
Trunk roads: A5/A38: Weeford Island, Staffordshire	157
Trunk roads: A5/A483: Chirk bypass, Wrexham	216
Trunk roads: A5: Berwyn Rd., Llangollen, Denbighshire	213
Trunk roads: A5: Caddington Turn & High St. North, Dunstable	157
Trunk roads: A5: Caddington Turn, Dunstable, Bedfordshire	149
Trunk roads: A5: Daventry, Northamptonshire	157
Trunk roads: A5: Dordon, Grendon & Holly Lane roundabouts, Warwickshire	157
Trunk roads: A5: Dordon, Warwickshire	157
Trunk roads: A5: Emstrey roundabout to Preston Boats roundabout	157
Trunk roads: A5: Gibbet Hill roundabout, Warwickshire	157
Trunk roads: A5: High St., Dunstable, Bedfordshire	157
Trunk roads: A5: Junction with A5127/A5148 Wall Island, Staffordshire	157
Trunk roads: A5: Junction with Leacroft Lane, Churchbridge	157
Trunk roads: A5: Junction with Norton Lane, Great Wyrley, Staffordshire	157
Trunk roads: A5: Junction with Vine Lane & Delta Way, Bridgtown	157
Trunk roads: A5: M42 junction 10	167
Trunk roads: A5: M69 junction 1, Hinckley, Leicestershire	157
Trunk roads: A5: Milton Keynes, Buckinghamshire	157
Trunk roads: A5: Newtown, Staffordshire	157
Trunk roads: A5: Old Stratford, Northamptonshire	157
Trunk roads: A5: Shawell, Warwickshire	157
Trunk roads: A5: Sheepy Rd. Bridge, Atherstone, Warwickshire	158
Trunk roads: A5: Sketchley Meadow to Nutts Lane, Hinckley	158
Trunk roads: A5: South of Gibbet Hill, Warwickshire	158
Trunk roads: A5: Tamworth, Staffordshire	158
Trunk roads: A5: Tebworth, Bedfordshire	158
Trunk roads: A5: Towcester - Weedon Bec, Northamptonshire	158
Trunk roads: A5: Vairous lengths, Flamstead - Catthorpe	158
Trunk roads: A5: Watling St., Staffordshire	158
Trunk roads: A5: Weedon Bec, Northamptonshire	158
Trunk roads: A5: Wibtoft to Smockington, Leicestershire	158
Trunk roads: A6: Blackwell to Ashford in the Water, Derbyshire	158
Trunk roads: A6: Clapham bypass & Bedford Rd., Milton Ernest, Bedfordshire	149
Trunk roads: A6: Clapham bypass, Bedford Rd., Milton Ernest, Bedfordshire	158

Trunk roads: A6: Clapham bypass, Bedfordshire 149, 158
Trunk roads: A6: Clapham bypass, C46 Highfield Rd. northbound slip road, Bedfordshire 149
Trunk roads: A6: Clapham-Milton Ernest, Bedfordshire. 158
Trunk roads: A6: Harborough Rd., Northamptonshire. 158
Trunk roads: A6: Hathern, Leicestershire 149
Trunk roads: A6: Higham Ferrers, Northamptonshire 158
Trunk roads: A6: Kibworth Harcourt to Burton Overy, Leicestershire 158
Trunk roads: A6: Loughborough town centre 158
Trunk roads: A6: Milton Rd., Clapham, Bedfordshire 149
Trunk roads: A6: Oadby to Great Glen, Leicestershire 159
Trunk roads: A6: Quorn bypass, Leicestershire 159
Trunk roads: A6: Swan St., Loughborough 159
Trunk roads: A6: Various lengths, Bedfordshire-Northamptonshire 159
Trunk roads: A7: Hoghill Farm to Kirkstile Bridge: Scotland 334
Trunk roads: A7: Longtown 149
Trunk roads: A7: West Port to Raeburn Place, Selkirk: Scotland 334
Trunk roads: A7: Westlinton Bridge 159
Trunk roads: A8: Baillieston roundabout: Scotland 334
Trunk roads: A8: Baillieston to Newhouse: Scotland 334
Trunk roads: A8: Bargeddie railway bridge: Scotland 334
Trunk roads: A8: Junction 6, Newhouse to junction 31, West Ferry: Scotland 334
Trunk roads: A8: Sinclair St. to Cartsdyke roundabout, Greenock: Scotland 334
Trunk roads: A9: Auchterarder to Blackford: Scotland 335
Trunk roads: A9: Ballinluig: Scotland 332, 333
Trunk roads: A9: Blackford: Scotland 335
Trunk roads: A9: Golspie: Scotland 333

Trunk roads: A10: Cheshunt - Thundridge, Hertfordshire 159
Trunk roads: A10: Moles interchange, Hertfordshire 159
Trunk roads: A10: Puckeridge-Colliers End, Hertfordshire 159
Trunk roads: A10: Royston to Braughing, Hertfordshire 159
Trunk roads: A10: Thunderidge, Ware, Hertfordshire 159
Trunk roads: A11/A47: Norwich, Norwich 159
Trunk roads: A11: Barton Mills - Newmarket, Suffolk 159
Trunk roads: A11: Besthorpe to Wymondham, Norfolk 159
Trunk roads: A11: Elveden, Suffolk 159
Trunk roads: A11: Six Mile Bottom, Cambridgeshire 159
Trunk roads: A11: Snetterton, Norfolk 159
Trunk roads: A11: Thetford bypass, Norfolk 159
Trunk roads: A11: Wymondham, Norfolk 159
Trunk roads: A12/A120: Colchester, Essex 160
Trunk roads: A12/A120: Crown interchange, Essex 160
Trunk roads: A12: Bascule Bridge, Lowestoft, Suffolk 160
Trunk roads: A12: Blundeston Rd. - Market Lane, Suffolk 160
Trunk roads: A12: Brentwood bypass, Essex 160
Trunk roads: A12: Breydon bridge, Great Yarmouth, Norfolk 160
Trunk roads: A12: Brook Street interchange - Trueloves interchange, Brentwood, Essex 160
Trunk roads: A12: Chelmsford bypass, Essex 160
Trunk roads: A12: Colchester, Essex 160
Trunk roads: A12: Copdock Mill interchange, Suffolk 160
Trunk roads: A12: Feering to Marks Tey, Essex 160
Trunk roads: A12: Feering, Essex 160
Trunk roads: A12: Galleywood - Margaretting, Essex 160
Trunk roads: A12: Great Yarmouth, Norfolk 160
Trunk roads: A12: Hatfield Peverel, Essex 149
Trunk roads: A12: Lowestoft, Suffolk 160
Trunk roads: A12: Marks Tey, Essex 161
Trunk roads: A12: Webbs Farm interchange, Chelmsford, Essex 161
Trunk roads: A13: M25 junction 30, slip road 161
Trunk roads: A14/A1307: Cambridgeshire 199
Trunk roads: A14/A428: Girton - Madingley, Cambridgeshire 161
Trunk roads: A14/M1/M6: M1 junction 19 190
Trunk roads: A14: B1106 western interchange, Bury St. Edmunds bypass, Suffolk 161
Trunk roads: A14: Beacon Hill interchange, Suffolk 161
Trunk roads: A14: Beacon Hill, Suffolk - Histon, Cambridgeshire 161
Trunk roads: A14: Bramford Rd. bridge, Ipswich, Suffolk 161

Trunk roads: A14: Bury St. Edmunds, slip roads, Suffolk	161
Trunk roads: A14: Claydon-Bury St. Edmunds, Suffolk	161
Trunk roads: A14: Felixstowe, Suffolk	161
Trunk roads: A14: Fen Ditton, Cambridgeshire, eastbound slip road	161
Trunk roads: A14: Fen Drayton-Swavesey, Cambridgeshire	161
Trunk roads: A14: Fenstanton interchange, westbound exit slip road	161
Trunk roads: A14: Girton interchange, Cambridgeshire, slip roads	199
Trunk roads: A14: Girton-Histon, Cambridgeshire	161
Trunk roads: A14: Godmanchester interchange, Cambridgeshire	161
Trunk roads: A14: Histon, Cambridgeshire - Whitton, Suffolk, slip roads	161
Trunk roads: A14: Huntingdon railway viaduct, Cambridgeshire	162
Trunk roads: A14: Junction 10-13, Northamptonshire	162
Trunk roads: A14: Junction 2-10, Northamptonshire	162
Trunk roads: A14: Junction 26 slip roads, Fenstanton, Cambridgeshire	162
Trunk roads: A14: Junction 9-10, Kettering, Northamptonshire	162
Trunk roads: A14: Keyston, Cambridgeshire	162
Trunk roads: A14: Levington, Seven Hills interchange, Suffolk	162
Trunk roads: A14: M1 junction 19	190
Trunk roads: A14: Milton - Histon interchanges, Cambridgeshire	162
Trunk roads: A14: Oakington/Dry Drayton interchange, Cambridgeshire	162
Trunk roads: A14: Orwell Bridge to Copdock interchange	162
Trunk roads: A14: Rothwell, Northamptonshire	162
Trunk roads: A14: Rougham, Suffolk	162
Trunk roads: A14: Rowley Mile layby, Newmarket, Suffolk	162
Trunk roads: A14: Seven Hills interchange - Stowmarket interchange, Suffolk	162
Trunk roads: A14: Spittals interchange, Cambridgeshire	162
Trunk roads: A14: Stowmarket, North interchange to Beacon Hill interchange, Stowmarket, Suffolk	162
Trunk roads: A14: Trimley St. Mary, Suffolk	162
Trunk roads: A14: Various lengths, Cambridgeshire - Northamptonshire	162
Trunk roads: A14: Westley - Moreton Hall interchanges, Bury St. Edmunds, Suffolk	163
Trunk roads: A14: Wherstead interchange - Copdock interchange, Suffolk	163
Trunk roads: A14: Woolpit interchange - Haughley Park interchange, Suffolk	163
Trunk roads: A15: Annual Lincolnshire Show	163
Trunk roads: A16: Burwell, Lincolnshire	149
Trunk roads: A16: Dalby to Ulceby Cross, Lincolnshire	163
Trunk roads: A16: Holton-le-Clay, Lincolnshire	163
Trunk roads: A16: Policemans Corner, Deeping St. Nicholas, Lincolnshire	163
Trunk roads: A17: East Heckington to Swineshead, Lincolnshire	149
Trunk roads: A17: Saracens Head, Lincolnshire	149
Trunk roads: A17: Swineshead bypass, Lincolnshire	163
Trunk roads: A17: Swineshead level crossing, Lincolnshire	163
Trunk roads: A19/A168: York Rd., interchange, Thirsk	163
Trunk roads: A19/A64: Fulford interchange	178
Trunk roads: A19/A66: Stockton Rd. interchange	163
Trunk roads: A19/A66: Tees viaduct	163
Trunk roads: A19: Barlby Rd., Selby	177
Trunk roads: A19: Catchgate Bridge	163
Trunk roads: A19: Crathorne interchange to Parkway interchange	163
Trunk roads: A19: Knayton	163
Trunk roads: A19: Riccall	163
Trunk roads: A19: Seaton to Murton	163
Trunk roads: A19: Sheraton interchange to Crathorne interchange	149
Trunk roads: A19: Sheraton interchange to Dalton Piercy junction	150
Trunk roads: A19: Sheraton to Dalton Piercy	164
Trunk roads: A19: Shipton Rd., York	150
Trunk roads: A19: South Kilvington bridge & Hag Lane bridge, Thirsk	164
Trunk roads: A19: Stockton Rd. interchange to Parkway interchange	164
Trunk roads: A19: Stockton Rd. interchange to Portrack interchange	164
Trunk roads: A19: Tontine to South Kilvington interchange	164
Trunk roads: A19: Various locations	164
Trunk roads: A19: Wolviston interchange to Stockton Ring Road interchange	164
Trunk roads: A20: Junction 13 - Dover	200
Trunk roads: A20: Limekiln roundabout & the viaduct, Dover	164
Trunk roads: A20: Roundhill Tunnels	164
Trunk roads: A20: The Viaduct & Lord Warden Square, Dover	164
Trunk roads: A20: Townwall St., Dover	164
Trunk roads: A21: Flimwell	164

Entry	Page
Trunk roads: A21: Longfield roundabout	164
Trunk roads: A21: North of Lamberhurst	164
Trunk roads: A21: Sevenoaks bypass	164
Trunk roads: A21: Tonbridge bypass, Londonbound carriageway	164
Trunk roads: A21: Various locations	164
Trunk roads: A23: Airport Way, junction 9A & 10	164
Trunk roads: A23: Hickstead and Pyecombe	165
Trunk roads: A26: Beddingham roundabout - The Lay	165
Trunk roads: A26: Newhaven Gateway	165
Trunk roads: A27: Adur interchange	165
Trunk roads: A27: Beddingham level crossing	165
Trunk roads: A27: Berwick roundabout	165
Trunk roads: A27: Broad Marsh, slip road	165
Trunk roads: A27: Brockhampton Road Bridge	165
Trunk roads: A27: Chichester bypass, eastbound carriageway	165
Trunk roads: A27: Chichester bypass, westbound carriageway	165
Trunk roads: A27: Crossbush, westbound carriageway	165
Trunk roads: A27: Hammerpot	165
Trunk roads: A27: Holmbush, eastbound exit slip road	165
Trunk roads: A27: Kingston to Hangleton	165
Trunk roads: A27: Lancing	165, 166
Trunk roads: A27: Newmarket, eastbound carriageway	166
Trunk roads: A27: Norton-Arundel	166
Trunk roads: A27: Old Shoreham Rd. & Shoreham bypass	166
Trunk roads: A27: Poling - Hammerpot	166
Trunk roads: A27: Portfield roundabout - Temple Bar interchange	166
Trunk roads: A27: Ranscombe Hill	166
Trunk roads: A27: Shoreham bypass, eastbound carriageway	166
Trunk roads: A27: Temple Bar, eastbound carriageway	166
Trunk roads: A27: University of Sussex	166
Trunk roads: A27: Westhampnett bypass	166
Trunk roads: A30/A38: M5 Motorway	196
Trunk roads: A30: Bodmin bypass	166
Trunk roads: A30: Callywith junction to Innis Downs roundabout	166
Trunk roads: A30: Helland, Nr Bodmin	166
Trunk roads: A30: Honiton bypass	166
Trunk roads: A30: Innis Downs roundabout	166, 167
Trunk roads: A30: M25 junction 13	167
Trunk roads: A30: Nr Cutteridge Lane overbridge, nr Exeter	167
Trunk roads: A30: Temple to Bolventor	167
Trunk roads: A30: Tregoss Moor	167
Trunk roads: A31: Ashley Heath, eastbound exit slip road	167
Trunk roads: A31: B3074 junction	167
Trunk roads: A31: Bere Regis - Corfe Mullen	167
Trunk roads: A31: Picket Post, slip road	167
Trunk roads: A31: Poulner & Verwood Rd., slip roads	167
Trunk roads: A31: Ringwood	167
Trunk roads: A31: Various locations, central Dorset	167
Trunk roads: A31: Various locations, East Dorset	167
Trunk roads: A31: Verwood Rd., slip road	167
Trunk roads: A34: Beedon - Chieveley	167
Trunk roads: A34: Botley & Hinksey, slip roads	167
Trunk roads: A34: Botley interchange	168
Trunk roads: A34: Botley interchange, slip road	167
Trunk roads: A34: Botley interchange, southbound carriageway	167
Trunk roads: A34: Chieveley	168
Trunk roads: A34: Drayton, southbound carriageway	168
Trunk roads: A34: Hinksey Hill interchange	168
Trunk roads: A34: Junction with Darges Lane, Great Wyrley	168
Trunk roads: A34: Kidlington/Islip, layby	168
Trunk roads: A34: Kidlington/Islip, slip road	168
Trunk roads: A34: Marcham interchange, slip roads	168
Trunk roads: A34: North of Bullington Cross	168
Trunk roads: A34: North of Whitchurch	168
Trunk roads: A34: Riverside Bridge to Gray's Bridge, Oxfordshire	168
Trunk roads: A34: South Wonston - M3 junction 9	168
Trunk roads: A34: Speed, slip road	168

Trunk roads: A34: Tot Hill & Bullington, slip roads ... 168
Trunk roads: A34: Walsall Rd., Cannock, Staffordshire ... 168
Trunk roads: A35: Charmouth to Chideock ... 168
Trunk roads: A36: Brickworth Corner to Canada Common ... 168
Trunk roads: A36: Churchill Way & Southampton Rd., Salisbury ... 150
Trunk roads: A36: Junction with A27 ... 169
Trunk roads: A36: Knook ... 150
Trunk roads: A36: Limpley Stoke ... 169
Trunk roads: A36: Plaitford, near West Wellow ... 169
Trunk roads: A36: Warminster Rd., Bath ... 150
Trunk roads: A36: West Wellow ... 150
Trunk roads: A36: Wilton Railway Bridge ... 169
Trunk roads: A36: Wiltshire ... 169
Trunk roads: A38/A30: M5 Motorway ... 196
Trunk roads: A38/A5: Weeford Island, Staffordshire ... 157
Trunk roads: A38/A61: Watchorn interchange ... 169
Trunk roads: A38: Abbey Hill, Derbyshire ... 169
Trunk roads: A38: Ashburton ... 169
Trunk roads: A38: Avon Bridge ... 169
Trunk roads: A38: Bittaford, Devon ... 169
Trunk roads: A38: Chudleigh Knighton ... 169
Trunk roads: A38: Dobwalls ... 169
Trunk roads: A38: Dobwalls Village ... 169
Trunk roads: A38: Doublebois to Turfdown ... 169
Trunk roads: A38: Droitwich Rd., Fernhill Heath ... 169
Trunk roads: A38: Drybridge interchange ... 169
Trunk roads: A38: Junction with Little Hay Lane, Weeford, Staffordshire ... 169
Trunk roads: A38: Layby south of Findern interchange, south west of Derby ... 169
Trunk roads: A38: Lee Mill to Ivybridge ... 170
Trunk roads: A38: Liskeard Bypass ... 170
Trunk roads: A38: Lower Dean interchange ... 170
Trunk roads: A38: Monks Bridge layby, near Clay Mills ... 170
Trunk roads: A38: Old Newton Rd. ... 170
Trunk roads: A38: Pottles Lane overbridge to Splatford overbridge ... 170
Trunk roads: A38: Saltash ... 170
Trunk roads: A38: Saltash Tunnel ... 170
Trunk roads: A38: South of Bassetts Pole roundabout, Warwickshire ... 170
Trunk roads: A38: Tamar Bridge to Manadon interchange ... 170
Trunk roads: A38: Watchorn interchange ... 170
Trunk roads: A38: Weeford, Staffordshire ... 170
Trunk roads: A39: Indian Queens to Blackcross ... 170
Trunk roads: A39: Knightsmill ... 170
Trunk roads: A40/A417: Gloucester Northern bypass ... 170
Trunk roads: A40/A417: Northern bypass, Gloucestershire ... 170
Trunk roads: A40/A449: Coldra to Monmouth ... 214
Trunk roads: A40/A449: Raglan interchange, Monmouthshire ... 214
Trunk roads: A40/A48: Minsterworth, Gloucestershire ... 170
Trunk roads: A40: Abergavenny - Raglan interchange, Monmouthshire ... 214
Trunk roads: A40: Bridstow Bridge, Herefordshire ... 170
Trunk roads: A40: Buckinghamshire ... 202
Trunk roads: A40: Cassington Halt bridge ... 171
Trunk roads: A40: Churcham, Gloucestershire ... 150
Trunk roads: A40: Churchdown, Gloucestershire ... 171
Trunk roads: A40: Dowdeswell layby ... 171
Trunk roads: A40: Evenlode layby ... 171
Trunk roads: A40: Gibraltar Tunnels, Monmouth, Monmouthshire ... 214
Trunk roads: A40: Glewstone to Wilton, Herefordshire ... 171
Trunk roads: A40: Hildersley, Herefordshire ... 171
Trunk roads: A40: Huntley, Gloucestershire ... 171
Trunk roads: A40: Lea Village, Herefordshire ... 171
Trunk roads: A40: Letterston, Pembrokeshire ... 213
Trunk roads: A40: Manordeilo, Carmarthenshire ... 213
Trunk roads: A40: Near Burford ... 171
Trunk roads: A40: Pencraig to Whitchurch, Herefordshire ... 171
Trunk roads: A40: Pencraig, Herefordshire ... 171
Trunk roads: A40: Ryeford, south of Ross-on-Wye ... 171
Trunk roads: A40: Square & Compass, Llangadog, Carmarthenshire ... 213

Trunk roads: A40: Travellers' Rest, Carmarthen, Carmarthenshire	214
Trunk roads: A40: Western Ave., layby	171
Trunk roads: A40: Wolvercote underbridges	172
Trunk roads: A41: Blackthorn Railway Bridge	172
Trunk roads: A41: Hartspring roundabout - Brockley Hill roundabout	172
Trunk roads: A41: New Chester Rd.	203
Trunk roads: A41: Prees Heath	172
Trunk roads: A41: Two Waters - Berkhamsted	172
Trunk roads: A42: Ashby de la Zouch, Leicestershire	172
Trunk roads: A42: Ashby-De-La-Zouch	172
Trunk roads: A42: Donington services, Leicestershire, northbound exit slip road	172
Trunk roads: A43: A413 junction, Silverstone, Northamptonshire	172
Trunk roads: A43: Abthorpe Rd. roundabout, Towcester	172
Trunk roads: A43: Juniper Hill Rd. junction, Oxfordshire	172
Trunk roads: A43: Rothersthorpe, Northamptonshire	172, 191
Trunk roads: A43: Rothersthorpe, Northhamptonshire	191
Trunk roads: A43: Silverstone Grand Prix, Northamptonshire	172
Trunk roads: A43: Towcester to M40 dualling, Northamptonshire	150, 172
Trunk roads: A43: Towcester to M40 dualling, Northamptonshire & Oxfordshire	172
Trunk roads: A43: Towcester to Whitfield Turn, Northamptonshire	172
Trunk roads: A43: Towcester, Northamptonshire	172
Trunk roads: A43: Various lengths, Northamptonshire - Oxfordshire	173
Trunk roads: A45/A508: Various lengths, Northamptonshire	173
Trunk roads: A45: Daventry Rd., Onley	150
Trunk roads: A45: Dodford, Northamptonshire	173
Trunk roads: A45: Great Billing, Northamptonshire	173
Trunk roads: A45: Wellingborough & Irthlingborough, Northamptonshire)	173
Trunk roads: A46: A50 Groby Rd. interchange, Leicestershire	173
Trunk roads: A46: Ashchurch Village	173
Trunk roads: A46: Ashton-Under-Hill, Worcestershire	173
Trunk roads: A46: Beckford, Worcestershire	173
Trunk roads: A46: Cheltenham Rd., Little Beckford	173
Trunk roads: A46: Cold Ashton roundabout to London Rd.	173
Trunk roads: A46: Dyrham Park	173
Trunk roads: A46: Halfway Houses, Lincolnshire	173
Trunk roads: A46: Junction with the M69/M6 junction 2, Warwickshire, slip road	173
Trunk roads: A46: Leicester western bypass	173
Trunk roads: A46: Lincoln Relief Road	173
Trunk roads: A46: Little Beckford, Worcestershire	173
Trunk roads: A46: Newark to Lincoln	173
Trunk roads: A46: Salford Priors roundabout, Warwickshire	174
Trunk roads: A46: Sherbourne, Warwickshire	174
Trunk roads: A46: Swinderby to Thorpe on the Hill	174
Trunk roads: A46: Swinderby, Lincolnshire	174
Trunk roads: A46: Thorpe on the Hill, Lincolnshire	174
Trunk roads: A46: Upper Swainswick to Pennsylvania	150
Trunk roads: A46: Winthorpe, Newark, Nottinghamshire	150
Trunk roads: A46: Winthorpe, Nottinghamshire to North Hykeham, Lincolnshire	174
Trunk roads: A47/A11: Norwich, Norwich	159
Trunk roads: A47: East Dereham, Norfolk	174
Trunk roads: A47: East Winch, Norfolk	174
Trunk roads: A47: Hardwick roundabout, Suffolk	174
Trunk roads: A47: Hockering, Norfolk	174
Trunk roads: A47: Markshall - Keswick, Norfolk	174
Trunk roads: A47: Narborough - Necton, Norfolk	174
Trunk roads: A47: Narborough, Norfolk	174
Trunk roads: A47: Saddlebow interchange, Kings Lynn, Norfolk	174
Trunk roads: A47: Wansford-Sutton, City of Peterborough & Guyhirn-Wisbech, Cambridgeshire	174
Trunk roads: A47: Wardley Hill, Leicestershire	174
Trunk roads: A47: Watton interchange - Postwick interchange, slip roads, Norfolk	174
Trunk roads: A47: Wireless Hill, Tixover, Leicestershire	174
Trunk roads: A48/A40: Minsterworth, Gloucestershire	170
Trunk roads: A48: Aylburton, Gloucestershire	175
Trunk roads: A48: Broadoak, Gloucestershire	175
Trunk roads: A48: Dinney Bank, Minsterworth, Gloucestershire	175
Trunk roads: A48: Minsterworth, Gloucestershire	175
Trunk roads: A49: Beeston & Tiverton	150

Trunk roads: A49: Church Stretton & Leebotwood, Shropshire	175
Trunk roads: A49: Church Stretton, Shropshire	175
Trunk roads: A49: Dinmore Hill, Herefordshire	175
Trunk roads: A49: Dorrington Railway Bridge, Shropshire	175
Trunk roads: A49: Hereford to Callow Hill	175
Trunk roads: A49: Holmer Rd., Hereford	175
Trunk roads: A49: Holmer to Hope under Dinmore	175
Trunk roads: A49: Ludlow, Shropshire	175
Trunk roads: A49: Marshbrook, Shropshire	175
Trunk roads: A49: Peterstow, Herefordshire	175
Trunk roads: A49: Prees Green	150
Trunk roads: A49: Redhill, Hertfordshire	175
Trunk roads: A49: Woofferton Railway Bridge, Shropshire	176
Trunk roads: A50: Hatton, Derbyshire	176
Trunk roads: A50: Junction with the A6, Derbyshire, slip roads	176
Trunk roads: A50: Meir tunnel, Staffordshire	176
Trunk roads: A50: Uttoxeter, Staffordshire	150, 176
Trunk roads: A50: Uttoxeter-Blythe Bridge, Staffordshire	176
Trunk roads: A50: Uttoxeter-Sudbury, Staffordshire	176
Trunk roads: A52/A453: Nottingham	176
Trunk roads: A52/A6514: Nottingham	176
Trunk roads: A52: Barrowby to Bingham	176
Trunk roads: A52: Borrowash bypass, Derby	176
Trunk roads: A52: Derby Rd.,Nottingham	176
Trunk roads: A52: Grantham Rd., Radcliffe on Trent, Nottinghamshire	150
Trunk roads: A52: Stapleford, Nottinghamshire	176
Trunk roads: A55	176
Trunk roads: A55: Bangor, Gwynedd	214
Trunk roads: A55: Bodelwyddan, Rhuddlan, Denbighshire	214
Trunk roads: A55: Broughton, Flintshire	214
Trunk roads: A55: Colwyn Bay - Llanddulas, Conwy	214
Trunk roads: A55: Conwy crossing tunnel, Conwy	214
Trunk roads: A55: Glan Conwy-Conwy Morfa, Conwy	214
Trunk roads: A55: Glan Llyn Junction, Rhuallt	214
Trunk roads: A55: Llanddulas, Conwy	214
Trunk roads: A55: Llandudno junction interchange - Conwy crossing tunnel, Conwy	214
Trunk roads: A55: Mochdre, Conwy	215
Trunk roads: A55: Northop Hall, Travellers Inn, Bodelwyddan & Mochdre, in the counties of Flintshire, Denbighshire & Conwy	215
Trunk roads: A55: Penmaenbach Tunnel & Headland, Conwy	215
Trunk roads: A55: Penmaen-bach tunnels, Conwy	215
Trunk roads: A55: Pen-y-Clip. Conwy	215
Trunk roads: A55: Ty'r Ali, Denbighshire	215
Trunk roads: A56	176
Trunk roads: A57/A628: Market St. & Mottram Moor, Hollingworth	188
Trunk roads: A57: Markham Moor to Newton on Trent, Nottinghamshire	176
Trunk roads: A57: Worksop bypass, Nottinghamshire	176
Trunk roads: A58: Chain Bar roundabout	177
Trunk roads: A59: Bale Plantation, West Marton	177
Trunk roads: A59: Preston New Rd., Salmesbury	177
Trunk roads: A59: Whalley Clitheroe bypass	177
Trunk roads: A61/A38: Watchorn interchange	169
Trunk roads: A61: Dronfield bypass	177
Trunk roads: A61: M1 junction 36	177
Trunk roads: A63: Garrison Rd.	177
Trunk roads: A63: Garrison Rd. roundabout	177
Trunk roads: A63: Hessle Rd. & Daltry St.	177
Trunk roads: A63: Hull Road	177
Trunk roads: A63: Leeds Rd., Selby	177
Trunk roads: A63: Melton	177
Trunk roads: A63: Priory Way interchange to Brighton St. interchange	177
Trunk roads: A63: Selby	150, 177
Trunk roads: A63: South Cave & Western interchanges	177
Trunk roads: A63: South Cave interchange to Welton interchange	177
Trunk roads: A63: Thorpe Park link roads	151
Trunk roads: A63: Thorpe Park link roads & roundabouts	177
Trunk roads: A63: Welton to Western interchange	178
Trunk roads: A63: Western Interchange Rd. Bridge to Cliff Mill Rail Bridge	178

Trunk roads: A64/A1079: Grimston Bar interchange	178
Trunk roads: A64/A19: Fulford interchange	178
Trunk roads: A64: Bond Hill eastbound exit slip road	178
Trunk roads: A64: East Heslerton to West Heslerton	178
Trunk roads: A64: Musley Bank interchange	178
Trunk roads: A64: Rillington	151
Trunk roads: A64: Rillington to Sherburn	178
Trunk roads: A64: Tadcaster bypass	178
Trunk roads: A65: Cleatop roundabout	178
Trunk roads: A65: Otley Rd. junction	178
Trunk roads: A65: Settle roundabout to Skirbeck	178
Trunk roads: A65: Skipton & Addingham	178
Trunk roads: A66/A1: Holtby Grange to Leeming	154
Trunk roads: A66/A19: Stockton Rd. interchange	163
Trunk roads: A66/A19: Tees viaduct	163
Trunk roads: A66: Appleby bypass	178
Trunk roads: A66: Bowes bypass	178
Trunk roads: A66: Briery interchange	178
Trunk roads: A66: Brigham & Great Broughton junctions	178
Trunk roads: A66: Brough bypass, Coltsford Bridge	178
Trunk roads: A66: Carleton Hall	179
Trunk roads: A66: Crackenthorpe to Appleby bypass	179
Trunk roads: A66: Culgaith Rd. junction	179
Trunk roads: A66: Eden bridge	179
Trunk roads: A66: Eden Bridge	179
Trunk roads: A66: Sadberge	179
Trunk roads: A66: Sadberge Village	179
Trunk roads: A66: Sedbury Lodge to Scotch Corner, Melsonby crossroads & Winston crossroads	179
Trunk roads: A66: Stainburn & Great Clifton bypass	179
Trunk roads: A66: Stockton & Darlington	179
Trunk roads: A66: Stockton Rd. interchange	164
Trunk roads: A66: Surtees bridge	179
Trunk roads: A66: Yarm Rd. interchange	179
Trunk roads: A68/A696: Various locations, Blaxter Bends to the Scottish Border	189
Trunk roads: A68: Harryburn to Newmills: Scotland	335
Trunk roads: A68: West High St., Market Place & East High St., Lauder, special event: Scotland	335
Trunk roads: A68: West High St., Market Place & East High St., Lauder: Scotland	335
Trunk roads: A69: Acomb junction	179
Trunk roads: A69: Aglionby	179
Trunk roads: A69: Brampton bypass	179
Trunk roads: A69: Constantius bridge	179
Trunk roads: A69: Haltwhistle to Melkridge	180
Trunk roads: A69: Haydon bridge	180
Trunk roads: A69: Temon bridge	180
Trunk roads: A69: West Rattenraw bridge	180
Trunk roads: A74: Floriston overbridge	180
Trunk roads: A74: Mossband viaduct	180
Trunk roads: A75: Cairntop Cottages to Barlae improvement: Scotland	331
Trunk roads: A75: Challoch Bridge at Dunragit: Scotland	335
Trunk roads: A75: College Rd. footbridge, Dumfries: Scotland	335
Trunk roads: A75: Southbound on slip road to the A74 (M) motorway at Gretna: Scotland	335
Trunk roads: A76: Carronbridge: Scotland	335
Trunk roads: A77: Dalrymple St., Girvan: Scotland	335
Trunk roads: A77: Dutchhouse roundabout to Symington: Scotland	335
Trunk roads: A77: Hansel Village, Symington: Scotland	335
Trunk roads: A77: Vicarton St., Girvan: Scotland	335
Trunk roads: A77: Whitletts roundabout to Dutch House roundabout: Scotland	336
Trunk roads: A78: Access to nos. 90, 92 & 94 Inverkip Rd., Greenock: Scotland	336
Trunk roads: A78: Ardgowan Rd. to Wemyss Bay Rd., Wemyss Bay: Scotland	336
Trunk roads: A78: Ardrossan, Saltcoats & Stevenston bypass, side roads: Scotland	331
Trunk roads: A78: Ardrossan, Saltcoats & Stevenston bypass: Scotland	331
Trunk roads: A78: Dunlop St. roundabout to South St. roundabout, Greenock: Scotland	336
Trunk roads: A78: Dutch House roundabout to Monktonhead roundabout: Scotland	336
Trunk roads: A78: Inverkip Rd., Greenock: Scotland	331, 336
Trunk roads: A78: Irvine Rd. & Main St., Largs: Scotland	336
Trunk roads: A78: Main St. & Irvine Rd., Largs: Scotland	336
Trunk roads: A80: Auchenkilns roundabout: Scotland	336

Trunk roads: A80: Moodiesburn: Scotland	336
Trunk roads: A80: Muirhead North junction: Scotland	336
Trunk roads: A80: Muirhead South junction: Scotland	336
Trunk roads: A80: Old Inns, A8011 junction: Scotland	336
Trunk roads: A80: On & off slip roads at Old Inns interchange: Scotland	336
Trunk roads: A80: Slip roads at Cumbernauld Rd.: Scotland	336
Trunk roads: A80: Woodhead Rd. junction, Muirhead: Scotland	336
Trunk roads: A82: Gavinburn to Dunglass: Scotland	337
Trunk roads: A82: Junction with Colquhoun Rd., Milton: Scotland	337
Trunk roads: A82: Loch Lomond World Invitation Golf Tournament: Scotland	334
Trunk roads: A82: Tarbet to Crianlarich: Scotland	337
Trunk roads: A83: Tarbert: Scotland	331
Trunk roads: A85: Crieff Rd., Perth: Scotland	337
Trunk roads: A85: Crieff: Scotland	334
Trunk roads: A86: Newtonmore: Scotland	334
Trunk roads: A86: Spean Bridge: Scotland	334
Trunk roads: A90: Cross St., Fraserburgh: Scotland	337
Trunk roads: A90: Dubton cottages to North Water bridge, Laurencekirk: Scotland	337
Trunk roads: A90: Glencarse village, by Perth: Scotland	337
Trunk roads: A90: Hatton Bends improvement: Scotland	331
Trunk roads: A90: Kingsway West, Dundee: Scotland	337
Trunk roads: A90: Kirriemuir junction, near Forfar: Scotland	337
Trunk roads: A90: Milton of Philorth, near Fraserburgh: Scotland	337
Trunk roads: A90: Muchalls to Westport: Scotland	337
Trunk roads: A90: Shielhill to North Powrie Farm, north of Dundee: Scotland	337
Trunk roads: A92: Balfarg junction, Glenrothes: Scotland	334
Trunk roads: A92: Forgan roundabout, near Newport-on-Tay: Scotland	337
Trunk roads: A92: Forgan roundabout, near Tayport: Scotland	337
Trunk roads: A92: Markinch junction improvement, side roads: Scotland	331
Trunk roads: A92: Preston roundabout, Glenrothes: Scotland	337
Trunk roads: A95: Auchlunkart, Near Keith: Scotland	337
Trunk roads: A95: Kinveachy junction improvement: Scotland	331
Trunk roads: A96: Alexandra Rd., Elgin: Scotland	338
Trunk roads: A96: Inveramsay Bridge, Milton of Inveramsay, near Inverurie: Scotland	338
Trunk roads: A96: South College St., Dr Gray's roundabout to River Lossie bridge & High St., Elgin: Scotland	338
Trunk roads: A120/A12: Colchester, Essex	160
Trunk roads: A120/A12: Crown interchange, Essex	160
Trunk roads: A160/A180: Brocklesby interchange	180
Trunk roads: A160: Eastfield junction	180
Trunk roads: A167: Blind Lane to Hermitage roundabout	180
Trunk roads: A168/A19: York Rd., interchange, Thirsk	163
Trunk roads: A174: Acklam	163
Trunk roads: A174: Ormesby interchange to the A1085	180
Trunk roads: A180/A160: Brocklesby interchange	180
Trunk roads: A180: Barnetby interchange	180
Trunk roads: A180: Brocklesby interchange	180
Trunk roads: A180: Great Coates interchange	180
Trunk roads: A180: Race Bridge	180
Trunk roads: A180: Stallingborough interchange	180
Trunk roads: A249: Bobbing - Stockbury	180
Trunk roads: A249: Brielle Way, Isle of Sheppey	181
Trunk roads: A249: Cowstead Corner	181
Trunk roads: A249: Cowstead Corner - Queenborough	181
Trunk roads: A249: Kingsferry roundabout - Cowstead Corner roundabout	181
Trunk roads: A249: M2 motorway, Stockbury	180
Trunk roads: A259: Barnhorn Rd.	181
Trunk roads: A259: Bexhill-Glyne Gap	181
Trunk roads: A259: Brookland level crossing	181
Trunk roads: A259: Various roads, Rye	181
Trunk roads: A282: Junction 1A-1B	181
Trunk roads: A303/M3: Popham	193
Trunk roads: A303: Cartgate roundabout to Percombe Hill junction	181
Trunk roads: A303: Folly Bottom, westbound carriageway	181
Trunk roads: A303: Marsh interchange	181
Trunk roads: A303: Near Amesbury	181
Trunk roads: A303: Pill Lane to Higher Podimore	181
Trunk roads: A303: West of Bullington Cross	181

493

Trunk roads: A339: Newbury Rd., Kingsclere	181
Trunk roads: A339: Newtown Rd. & Sandleford link	151
Trunk roads: A339: Ramsdell junction	181
Trunk roads: A339: Ringway East, Basingstoke	181
Trunk roads: A339: Swan roundabout - junction with A34	181
Trunk roads: A361: Bolham to Sampford Peverell	182
Trunk roads: A361: Junction 27	182
Trunk roads: A404: A4155 junction - Bisham roundabout	182
Trunk roads: A404: Bisham roundabout - A4155 junction	182
Trunk roads: A404: Burchett's Green - Bisham	182
Trunk roads: A404: Marlow to Handy Cross	182
Trunk roads: A405/A414: Park St.	182
Trunk roads: A405: Bucknalls Lane junction	182
Trunk roads: A405: North Orbital Rd., near Garston	182
Trunk roads: A414/A405: Park St.	182
Trunk roads: A414: Colney Heath	182
Trunk roads: A414: Near London Colney	182
Trunk roads: A414: Park St. - London Colney	182
Trunk roads: A417/A40: Gloucester Northern bypass	170
Trunk roads: A417/A40: Northern bypass, Gloucestershire	170
Trunk roads: A417/A419: Driffield junction to Daglingworth Quarry junction	182
Trunk roads: A419/A417: Driffield junction to Daglingworth Quarry junction	182
Trunk roads: A419: Blunsdon	182
Trunk roads: A419: Commonhead roundabout	182
Trunk roads: A419: Cricklade	183
Trunk roads: A419: Cricklade junction to Castle Eaton junction	183
Trunk roads: A419: M4 junction 15 to Commonhead roundabout, Swindon	183
Trunk roads: A419: Nr Cricklade	183
Trunk roads: A419: Turnpike roundabout	183
Trunk roads: A420: Shrivenham/Watchfield bypass	183
Trunk roads: A420: Tubney Woods to Bessels Leigh	183
Trunk roads: A421: Bedford bypass, Bedfordshire	183
Trunk roads: A421: Brogborough, Bedfordshire	183
Trunk roads: A421: Various lengths, Bedfordshire	183
Trunk roads: A423: Oxford southern bypass	183
Trunk roads: A428/A14: Girton - Madingley, Cambridgeshire	161
Trunk roads: A428: Cambourne, Cambridgeshire	183
Trunk roads: A428: St. Neots bypass, Bedfordshire	183
Trunk roads: A428: Various Lengths, Bedfordshire - Cambridgeshire	183
Trunk roads: A435: Gorcott Hill to Studley, Warwickshire	151
Trunk roads: A435: Washfordd to Mappleborough Green, Warwickshire	183
Trunk roads: A446: Holly Lane/Middleton Lane to Dunton Lane, Warwickshire	183
Trunk roads: A446: Lichfield Rd., Wishaw, Warwickshire	183
Trunk roads: A446: M6 junction 4	196
Trunk roads: A449: Chatley, Worcestershire	183
Trunk roads: A449: Dunsley Bank to Lawnswood, Staffordshire	184
Trunk roads: A449: Junction with Bridgnorth Rd., Stewponey, Staffordshire	184
Trunk roads: A449: Kidderminster, Worcestershire	184
Trunk roads: A449: Low Hill, Kidderminster	178, 184
Trunk roads: A449: Penkridge, Staffordshire	184
Trunk roads: A449: Stourton, Staffordshire	184
Trunk roads: A449: Waresley, Worcestershire	184
Trunk roads: A449: Worcester Rd., Kidderminster	184
Trunk roads: A449A40: Raglan interchange, Monmouthshire	214
Trunk roads: A452: Chester Rd., Walsall	184
Trunk roads: A453/A52: Nottingham	176
Trunk roads: A453: M1 junction 24 to Clifton	184
Trunk roads: A456: Hagley Causeway, Worcestershire	184
Trunk roads: A456: Hayley Green, Worcestershire	184
Trunk roads: A456: Kidderminster Rd. South & Worcester Rd., West Hagley	184
Trunk roads: A456: West Hagley, Worcestershire	184
Trunk roads: A458: Buttington Bridge & Buttington Arches near Welshpool, Powys	215
Trunk roads: A458: Cefn Railway Bridge, Tre-Wern, Powys	218
Trunk roads: A458: Llanerfyl, Powys	215
Trunk roads: A458: Middletown, Powys	215
Trunk roads: A465: Aberbaiden roundabout - Saleyard, Monmouthshire	215
Trunk roads: A465: Aberdulais interchange, Neath Port Talbot	215

Trunk roads: A465: Belmont Rd., Hereford	184
Trunk roads: A465: Belmont Rd., Herefordshire	184
Trunk roads: A465: Belmont, Herefordshire	184
Trunk roads: A465: Glynneath bypass, Rhondda Cynon Taff	215
Trunk roads: A465: Heads of the Valley trunk road: Gypsy Castle, Blaencarno, Caerphilly	215
Trunk roads: A465: Tram Inn to Didley, Herefordshire	184
Trunk roads: A465: Tredegar to Dowlais	215
Trunk roads: A470: Abercynon, Rhondda Cynon Taf-Abercanaid, Methyr Tydfil	215
Trunk roads: A470: Caersws, Powys	213
Trunk roads: A470: Llan Ffestiniog, Gwynedd	218
Trunk roads: A470: Llanrwst, Gwynedd	213
Trunk roads: A470: Lledr Valley, Conwy County Borough	215
Trunk roads: A470: Nantgarw interchange	216
Trunk roads: A470: Nantgarw to Glyntaff, Rhondda Cynon Taff	216
Trunk roads: A470: Northbound & southbound slip roads: Upper Boat interchange, Rhondda Cynon Taff	216
Trunk roads: A470: Upper Boat interchange	216
Trunk roads: A470: Upper Boat interhcange, Rhondda Cynon Taff	216
Trunk roads: A470: Upper Boat to Pontypridd, Rhondda Cynon Taff	216
Trunk roads: A477: Milton Village, Pembrokeshire	213
Trunk roads: A479: Cwm-du, Powys	213
Trunk roads: A483/A5: Chirk bypass, Wrexham	216
Trunk roads: A483: Builth Wells, Powys	216
Trunk roads: A483: Derwydd, Llandybie, Carmarthenshire	213
Trunk roads: A483: Gresford interchange, Wrexham	216
Trunk roads: A483: Llanbadarn Fynydd, Powys	213
Trunk roads: A483: Newbridge bypass, Wrexham	216
Trunk roads: A483: Rhostyllen, west of Wrexham	216
Trunk roads: A483: Southern approach to Ty-Croes, Ammanford, Carmarthenshire	213
Trunk roads: A483: Southern Approach to TyCroes, Ammanford, Carmarthenshire	213
Trunk roads: A483: Talhardd Villas, Ffairfach, Llandeilo, Carmarthenshire	213
Trunk roads: A483: Wrexham	216
Trunk roads: A487: Alexandra Rd., Aberystwyth, Ceredigion	216
Trunk roads: A487: Bridge St., Aberystwyth, Ceredigion	217
Trunk roads: A487: Llwyn Mafon, Gwynedd	216
Trunk roads: A487: Lower Town, Fishguard, Pembrokeshire	213
Trunk roads: A487: Tanygroes, Ceredigion	213
Trunk roads: A487: Various streets, Aberaeron, Ceredigion	216
Trunk roads: A494/A550: Sealand, Queensferry, Flintshire	216
Trunk roads: A500: Etruria, Stoke on Trent, slip road	185
Trunk roads: A500: M6 Junction 16 to A34 Talke interchange	185
Trunk roads: A500: Meremoor Moss roundabout	185
Trunk roads: A508/A45: Various lengths, Northamptonshire	173
Trunk roads: A516: Junction with Uttoxeter Rd., Derby, northbound exit slip road	185
Trunk roads: A523: Bosley, Cheshire	151
Trunk roads: A523: Flash Lane to Holehouse Lane, north of Macclesfield	185
Trunk roads: A523: Fools Nook to Macclesfield (South), Cheshire	151
Trunk roads: A523: Leek, Staffordshire	151
Trunk roads: A523: Macclesfield Relief Rd.	151
Trunk roads: A523: Mill St., Leek, Staffordshire	185
Trunk roads: A523: Poynton (South), Cheshire	151
Trunk roads: A523: Poynton to Hazel Grove, Cheshire & Stockport	151
Trunk roads: A523: Prestbury to Poynton, Cheshire	151
Trunk roads: A523: Prestbury, Cheshire	151
Trunk roads: A523: Rushton Spencer, Staffordshire	151
Trunk roads: A550	204
Trunk roads: A550: Welsh Rd.	185
Trunk roads: A556: Ascol Drive	185
Trunk roads: A556: Cheshire Show	185
Trunk roads: A556: Mere crossroads	185
Trunk roads: A556: Plumley Moor Rd.	185
Trunk roads: A556: Royal Horticultural Show	185
Trunk roads: A565: Formby bypass	185
Trunk roads: A565: Formby bypass, Woodvale Rally	185
Trunk roads: A565: Southport New Rd.	185
Trunk roads: A565: Southport New Rd. & Gravel Lane, Banks	185
Trunk roads: A565: Southport New Rd., Mere Brow	151
Trunk roads: A565: Southport New Rd., The Gravel	186

Trunk roads: A570/A580: Rainford bypass/East Lancashire Rd. 186
Trunk roads: A570: Mossborough roundabout 186
Trunk roads: A570: Ormskirk Rd., Bickerstaff 151
Trunk roads: A570: Rainford bypass 186
Trunk roads: A570: Southport Rd., Scarisbrick 186
Trunk roads: A580 204
Trunk roads: A580/A570: East Lancashire Rd./Rainford bypass 186
Trunk roads: A580: East Lancashire Rd. 186
Trunk roads: A580: East Lancashire Rd., Golborne Railway Bridge 186
Trunk roads: A580: East Lancashire Rd., Haydock Island 186
Trunk roads: A580: Eastbound entry slip road 186
Trunk roads: A580: Golborne Island to Church Lane 186
Trunk roads: A580: Moss Farm footbridge & Riders Farm bridge 204
Trunk roads: A585: Amounderness Way 186
Trunk roads: A585: Amounderness Way, Rossall Lane 186
Trunk roads: A585: Amounderness Way, Thornton Cleveleys 186
Trunk roads: A585: Amounderness Way, Victoria Rd. roundabout 186
Trunk roads: A585: Fleetwood Rd., Greenhalgh 187
Trunk roads: A585: Kirkham to Fleetwood 151
Trunk roads: A590: Ayside 187
Trunk roads: A590: Backbarrow 187
Trunk roads: A590: Barr End 187
Trunk roads: A590: Brettargh Holt 187
Trunk roads: A590: Cross A Moor, Puffin Crossing 187
Trunk roads: A590: Dalton roundabout 187
Trunk roads: A590: Haverthwaite junction 187
Trunk roads: A590: Lindale Hill 187
Trunk roads: A590: Oubas Hill 187
Trunk roads: A595: Bigrigg 187
Trunk roads: A595: Broad Oak, south of Ravenglass 187
Trunk roads: A595: Egremont Cemetery 187
Trunk roads: A595: Foxfield, Broughton in Furness 187
Trunk roads: A595: Hayescastle 187
Trunk roads: A595: Holme 187
Trunk roads: A595: Lillyhall, Workington 151
Trunk roads: A595: Loop Road North, Whitehaven 187
Trunk roads: A595: Thornhill 187
Trunk roads: A595: White Moss 188
Trunk roads: A596: Aspatria 188
Trunk roads: A596: Birkby 188
Trunk roads: A596: Calva Brow, Workington 188
Trunk roads: A596: Heathfield Railway bridge 188
Trunk roads: A596: Heathfield Railway Bridge 188
Trunk roads: A596: Lillyhall, Workington 151
Trunk roads: A596: Maryport New Bridge 188
Trunk roads: A596: Workington 188
Trunk roads: A596: Workington bridge 188
Trunk roads: A606: Melton Rd., Tollerton, Nottinghamshire 188
Trunk roads: A614: Bothamsall cross roads, Nottinghamshire 188
Trunk roads: A614: Howden 151, 188
Trunk roads: A616: Stocksbridge bypass 188
Trunk roads: A616: Stocksbridge bypass, South Yorkshire 188
Trunk roads: A628/A57: Market St. & Mottram Moor, Hollingworth 188
Trunk roads: A628: Salters Brook Bridge 188
Trunk roads: A629: Skipton 178
Trunk roads: A631: Tinsley viaduct 190
Trunk roads: A631: Tinsley Viaduct 190
Trunk roads: A638: Bawtry Rd. & Roman Rd. 188
Trunk roads: A638: High St., Bawtry 189
Trunk roads: A646: Burnley Rd., Hebden Bridge to Clog Works 152
Trunk roads: A650: Shipley 189
Trunk roads: A663: Broadway 189
Trunk roads: A696/A68: Various locations, Blaxter Bends to the Scottish Border 189
Trunk roads: A696: Heeston Bank 189
Trunk roads: A696: Highlander & Harnham 189
Trunk roads: A696: Otterburn 152
Trunk roads: A696: Various locations, Ponteland to Percy's Cross 189

Trunk roads: A702: Edmonston Brae, Biggar: Scotland	338
Trunk roads: A725: Eastbound & westbound slip roads from Glasgow Rd. to Douglas St., Blantyre: Scotland	338
Trunk roads: A725: Eastbound between Shawhead & Diamond interchange: Scotland	338
Trunk roads: A725: Eastbound Glasgow Rd. to Whistleberry: Scotland	338
Trunk roads: A725: Eastbound off slip road & the westbound on slip road at Bellziehill interchange, Bellshill: Scotland	338
Trunk roads: A725: Eastbound on slip road at Glasgow Rd. & eastbound off slip road at Craighead: Scotland	338
Trunk roads: A725: Eastbound on slip road from Main St., High Blantyre: Scotland	338
Trunk roads: A725: Link road between Mavor roundabout on Kingsway (A749) to junction with Hamilton Rd., (A725), East Kilbride: Scotland	338
Trunk roads: A725: Shawhead to Diamond interchange: Scotland	338
Trunk roads: A725: Slip roads at Belziehill interchange, Bellshill: Scotland	338
Trunk roads: A725: Westbound between Douglas St., Blantyre off & on slip roads: Scotland	338
Trunk roads: A725: Westbound between Shawhead & Diamond interchange: Scotland	338
Trunk roads: A725: Westbound carriageway between Shawhead & Diamond interchange: Scotland	338
Trunk roads: A725: Whirlies to Crossbaskets: Scotland	339
Trunk roads: A725: Whistleberry Rd. to Glasgow Rd., Blantyre: Scotland	339
Trunk roads: A725: Whistleberry Toll to Whistleberry Rd.: Scotland	339
Trunk roads: A725: Whitemoss roundabout to Whirlies roundabout: Scotland	339
Trunk roads: A726: BSR footbridge, East Kilbride: Scotland	339
Trunk roads: A726: Lindores Drive footbridge, East Kilbride: Scotland	339
Trunk roads: A726: Righead roundabout to Eaglesham Rd. roundabout: Scotland	339
Trunk roads: A726: West Mains roundabout to Peel Park roundabout, East Kilbride: Scotland	339
Trunk roads: A737: Dalry: Scotland	339
Trunk roads: A828: Connel Bridge, near Oban: Scotland	339
Trunk roads: A830: West of Lochailort to Kinsadel, nr Morar: Scotland	339
Trunk roads: A876: Kincardine Bridge: Scotland	334
Trunk roads: A898: Erskine bridge, southbound on slip road from the A82 eastbound: Scotland	339
Trunk roads: A898: Erskine bridge, southbound on slip road from the A82 westbound: Scotland	339
Trunk roads: A898: Off & on slip roads at Dalnottar interchange: Scotland	339
Trunk roads: A898: Slip roads at Dalnottar interchange: Scotland	340
Trunk roads: A898: Slip roads at Dalnottar: Scotland	339
Trunk roads: A898: Southbound on slip road from the A82 westbound: Scotland	340
Trunk roads: A985: Admiralty Rd., Rosyth: Scotland	340
Trunk roads: A985: Kincardine eastern link road, side roads: Scotland	332
Trunk roads: A985: Kincardine eastern link road: Scotland	332
Trunk roads: A1001: Junction 2-4	152
Trunk roads: A1033: And South Bridge Rd.: Mount Pleasant junction	189
Trunk roads: A1033: Mount Pleasant roundabout to Marfleet Ave.	189
Trunk roads: A1033: Saltend roundabout	177
Trunk roads: A1033: Somerdon Rd. to Salt End roundabout	189
Trunk roads: A1041: Bawtry Rd., Selby	177
Trunk roads: A1053: Ormesby interchange to the A1085	180
Trunk roads: A1079/A64: Grimston Bar interchange	178
Trunk roads: A1079: Barmby Moor to Canal Head	189
Trunk roads: A1079: Grimston interchange & Dunswell Lane underpass	189
Trunk roads: A1307/A14: Cambridgeshire	199
Trunk roads: A4042: Grove Park, Newport	216
Trunk roads: A4042: Llanellen, Abergavenny, Monmouthshire	213
Trunk roads: A4042: Llanellen, Monmouthshire	216
Trunk roads: A4042: Penperlleni, Monmouthshire	213
Trunk roads: A4060: Dowlais Top, Merthyr Tydfil	217
Trunk roads: A4123: Birmingham New Rd., Dudley	189
Trunk roads: A4123: Birmingham New Rd., Tipton	189
Trunk roads: A4123: Causeway Green to Warley	189
Trunk roads: A1232: M4: Junction 33, Capel Llanilltern, Cardiff	217
Trunk roads: A5092: Penny Bridge	189
Trunk roads: A5103: Princess Parkway	189
Trunk roads: A5103: slip road	203
Trunk roads: A5111: Harvey Rd., Derby	189
Trunk roads: A5111: Osmaston Park Rd., Derby	190
Trunk roads: A5111: Raynesway, Derbyshire	190
Trunk roads: A5111: Warwick Ave. & Kenilworth Ave., Derby	190
Trunk roads: A5117	204
Trunk roads: A6120: East Leeds ring road	190
Trunk roads: A6120: Moortown	152
Trunk roads: A6120: Wetherby Rd. to York Rd.	152
Trunk roads: A6514/A52: Nottingham	176

Trunk roads: A6514: Queens Medical Centre roundabout to Aspley Lane roundabout, Nottingham 190
Trunk roads: B1172: Tuttles Lane interchange, Wymondham, Norfolk 190
Trunk roads: Broadgate link road 190
Trunk roads: M898/A898: Various: Scotland 342
Trunk roads: Scotland 342
Trustee Act (Northern Ireland) 2001: Commencement: Northern Ireland 387
Trustees: Public trustee: Fees: England & Wales 245
TSE *see* Transmissible spongiform encephalopathy
T-Systems Limited: Public telecommunication systems 237
Turkey: Figs, hazelnuts & pistachios: Emergency control: England 66
Turkey: Figs, hazelnuts & pistachios: Emergency control: Scotland 315
Turkey: Figs, hazelnuts & pistachios: Emergency control: Northern Ireland 367
Turkey: Figs, hazelnuts & pistachios: Emergency control: Wales 68
Turks & Caicos Islands: Constitution 19
Tweedwind Limited Public telecommunication systems 237
Twickenham: Teddington, Twickenham & Hamptons: National Health Service Primary Care Trust 123
Two Mile Bend bridge: Gloucestershire County Council: Confirmation: England 77
Tyne & Wear: Northumberland, Tyne & Wear: Health Authority 117
Tyne & Wearside: South of Tyne and Wearside: National Health Service Trust 121
Tyneside: South Tyneside: National Health Service Trust 121

U

Uncultivated land & semi-natural areas: Environmental impact assessment: Scotland 307
United Kingdom: Enforcement: Proceeds of Crime Act 2002 141
United Nations measures: Al-Qa'ida & Taliban 245
United Nations measures: Al-Qa'ida & Taliban: Channel Islands 245
United Nations measures: Al-Qa'ida & Taliban: Isle of Man 245
United Nations measures: Al-Qa'ida & Taliban: Overseas territories 245
United Nations sanctions: Somalia 246
United Nations sanctions: Somalia: Channel Islands 246
United Nations sanctions: Somalia: Isle of Man 246
United Nations sanctions: Somalia: Overseas territories 246
United Nations: International Criminal Court: Immunities & privileges 86
United Nations: Specialized agencies: Immunities & privileges 86
United Networks Limited: Public telecommunication systems 237
United States of America: Double taxation: Relief 82
University of St Andrews: Postgraduate medical degrees: Acts: Explanatory notes: Scotland 306
University of St Andrews: Postgraduate medical degrees: Acts: Scotland 305

V

Vaccine Damage Payments Act 1979: Regulatory reform 142, 145
Vale of Glamorgan & Cardiff : Michaelston & Grangetown: Local government: Wales 96
Vale of Glamorgan & Rhondda Cynon Taff: Llanharry, Pont-y-clun, Penllyn, Welsh St Donats & Pendoylan: Local government: Wales 99
Vale of Glamorgan (County Borough): Electoral changes: Wales 97
Valuation: Valuation for rating: Exempted classes: Scotland 330
Value added tax 246
Value added tax tribunals 247
Value added tax: Acquisitions: Relief 246
Value added tax: Buildings & land 246
Value added tax: Buildings: Construction 246
Value added tax: Cars 246
Value added tax: Drugs, medicines, aids for handicapped & charities 246
Value added tax: Finance Act 2002: Section 22: Appointed day 246
Value added tax: Fuel: Provided for private use: Consideration for 246
Value added tax: Health & welfare 247
Value added tax: Lifeboats: Equipment 247
Value added tax: Reduced rate 247
Value added tax: Registration limits: Increase 247
Value added tax: Special provisions 247
Value added tax: Special provisions: Amendment 247
Value added tax: Transport 247

Vegetable seeds: England	221
Vehicle emissions: Fixed penalty	211
Vehicle excise duty: Immobilisation, removal & disposal of vehicles	149
Vehicle excise duty: Small islands: Designation	148
Vehicles (Crime) Act 2001: Commencement	149
Vehicles (Crime) Act 2001: Commencement: England & Wales	212
Vehicles crime: Registration plate suppliers: Registration of: England & Wales	212
Vehicles: Goods: Operators: Licensing: Fees	147
Vehicles: Motor vehicles: Tests	212
Vehicles: Motor: Authorised weight: Northern Ireland	380
Vehicles: Motor: Competitions & trials: Scotland	333
Vehicles: Motor: Construction & use: Northern Ireland	380
Vehicles: Motor: Driving licences: Northern Ireland	380
Vehicles: Motor: Driving licences: Test fees: Northern Ireland	380
Vehicles: Motor: EC type approval	147
Vehicles: Motor: Exchangeable licences: Northern Ireland	380
Vehicles: Motor: Testing: Northern Ireland	380
Vehicles: Motor: Third party risks: Northern Ireland	380
Vehicles: Passenger & goods: Recording equipment: Fitters & workshops: Approval: Fees	212
Vehicles: Private hire: Guide dogs, etc.: Carriage: Acts	3
Vehicles: Private hire: Guide dogs, etc.: Carriage: Acts: Explanatory notes	5
Vehicles: Public service vehicles: Operators' licences: Fees	143
Vehicles: Public service: Accessibility	41, 241
Vehicles: Public service: Fitness, equipment & use: Conditions of: Northern Ireland	380
Vehicles: Public service: Fitness, equipment, use & certification	148, 212
Vehicles: Public service: Registration of local services	144
Vehicles: Removal & disposal: England	209
Vehicles: Removal & disposal: Scotland	333
Vehicles: Road vehicles: Registration & licensing	148
Vehicles: Road: Construction & use	148
Vehicles: Road: Registration & licensing	212
Vehicles: Testing: Disclosure of information: Great Britain	148
Vehicular access: Common & other land: England	33
Velindre: National Health Service Trust	128
Venture capital trust: Shares & securities: Exchange of	83
Veterinary medicinal products: Marketing authorisations: Medicines	101
Veterinary Surgeons Act 1966: Schedule 3 amendment	247
Veterinary surgery: Bovines: Rectal ultrasound scanning	247
Virgin West Coast Class 390 Vehicles: Accessibility: Exemptions	41, 242
Visual recording of interviews: Police & Criminal Evidence Act 1984	138
Visually impaired persons: Copyright: Acts	1
Voluntary aided schools: Liabilities & funding: Regulatory reform: England	50, 145
VTL (UK) Limited: Public telecommunication systems	237
Vulnerable adults: Protection: England & Wales	21, 142, 222
Vulnerable adults: Protection: Police Act 1997: Criminal records: Scotland	324

W

Wages: National minimum wage	238
Wakefield & Pontefract Community: National Health Service Trust	122
Wakefield Community Learning Partnership: Education Action Zone: Extension	50
Wakefield: Health Authority	123
Wales: Dairy produce quotas	68
Wales: Individual pupils' achievements: Information: Education	54
Wales: Non-domestic rating: Contributions	145
Wales: Standards grants: Education	55
Wales: Statutory instruments: National Assembly for Wales: Annual volumes	7
Wallasey & Birkenhead: National Health Service Primary Care Trust	105
Walsall Community Health: National Health Service Trust	123
Walsall: National Health Service Primary Care Trust	123
Waltham Forest: Redbridge & Waltham Forest Health Authority	119
Waltham Forest Housing Action Trust: Dissolution	79
Wandsworth: National Health Service Primary Care Trust	123
Wandsworth: Merton, Sutton & Wandsworth: Health Authority	113
Warm Homes & Energy Conservation Act 2000: Commencement: Wales	58

Warrant enforcement staff: Pensions ... 99, 133
Warrenpoint Harbour Authority: Northern Ireland. ... 368
Warrington (Borough): Electoral changes ... 90
Warrington Community Healthcare: National Health Service Trusts ... 124
Warrington: Borough of Halton, Thurrock & Warrington: Election years changes. ... 90
Warrington: National Health Service Trust ... 124
Warwickshire: Health Authority ... 124
Warwickshire: North Warwickshire: National Health Service Primary Care Trust. ... 117
Warwickshire: North Warwickshire: National Health Service Trust. ... 117
Warwickshire: South Warwickshire: National Health Service Primary Care Trust. ... 121
Warwickshire: South Warwickshire Combined Care: National Health Service Trust ... 121
Waste incineration: England & Wales ... 60
Waste management: Licensing: England ... 59
Waste management: Licensing: Environmental protection: Wales ... 61
Waste recycling payments: Environmental protection: England ... 59
Waste: Controlled: Duty of care: Northern Ireland ... 364
Waste: Controlled: Regulations: Northern Ireland ... 364
Waste: Incineration: National emission ceilings: Pollution: Prevention & control ... 60
Waste: Packaging waste: Producer responsibility & obligations: England ... 59
Waste: Packaging waste: Producer responsibility & obligations: Scotland ... 314
Waste: Packaging waste: Producer responsibility & obligations: Northern Ireland ... 378
Waste: Packaging waste: Producer responsibility & obligations: Wales ... 61
Water & sewerage: Charges: Exemption: Scotland. ... 348
Water & sewerage: Domestic: Charges: Reduction: Scotland ... 348
Water & sewerage: New authorities: Dissolution: Scotland ... 348
Water & sewerage: Water supply: Water quality: Northern Ireland ... 387
Water Industry (Scotland) Act 2002: Commencement: Scotland ... 348
Water Industry (Scotland) Act 2002: Consequential & savings provisions: Scotland ... 348
Water Industry (Scotland) Act 2002: National security. ... 30, 40, 247
Water quality: Water supply: Northern Ireland ... 387
Water supply: Customer consultation panels: Scotland ... 348
Water supply: Domestic water & sewerage: Charges: Reduction: Scotland ... 348
Water supply: Scottish Water: Rate of return: Scotland ... 348
Water supply: Wafer Industry (Scotland) Act 2002: Consequential & savings provisions: Scotland ... 348
Water supply: Water & sewerage: Charges: Exemption: Scotland ... 348
Water supply: Water quality: Northern Ireland ... 387
Water undertakings: Rateable values: Scotland ... 330
Waters: Adjacent waters: Boundaries: Northern Ireland ... 29, 128
Water: Customer consultation panels: Scotland ... 348
Water: Industry: Acts: Explanatory notes: Scotland ... 306
Water: Industry: Acts: Scotland ... 305
Water: Nitrate vulnerable zones: Additional designations: England ... 9, 247
Water: Nitrate vulnerable zones: Designation: Scotland ... 348
Water: Pollution: Agricultural nitrates: Protection: Wales ... 247
Water: Water services: Charges: Billing & collection: Scotland. ... 348
Waveney (District): Electoral changes ... 93
Waverley: Guildford & Waverley: National Health Service Primary Care Trust ... 111
Waverley: Parishes: Local government ... 95
Weald: Sussex Downs & Weald: National Health Service Primary Care Trust ... 122
Wear Valley Railway ... 243, 244
Wear Valley: Parishes: Local government ... 95
Wearside: Priority Healthcare Wearside: National Health Service Trust ... 121
Wearside: South of Tyne & Wearside: National Health Service Trust. ... 121
Wednesbury & West Bromwich: National Health Service Primary Care Trust. ... 124
Wednesbury: Education Action Zone: Extension ... 50
Weights & measures: Measurement: Units: Northern Ireland ... 387
Weights & measures: Metrication : Northern Ireland. ... 387
Weights & measures: Prescribed stamp: Northern Ireland ... 387
Weights & measures: Trade & adjustment: Fees: Northern Ireland ... 387
Welfare food. ... 65
Welfare foods: Northern Ireland ... 387
Welfare guardians: Decisions: Non-compliance: Adults with incapacity: Scotland ... 306
Welfare guardians: Supervision of: Adults with incapacity: Scotland ... 307
Welfare of animals: Slaughter or killing: Northern Ireland. ... 387
Welfare of animals: Slaughter or killing: Scotland ... 310
Welfare Reform & Pensions Act 1999: Commencement ... 133
Welfare reform & pensions:1999 Order: Commencement: Northern Ireland ... 375, 376

Welfare: Animals: Farmed: Northern Ireland 387
Welsh Administration Ombudsman: Jurisdiction: Wales. 30
Welsh language schemes: Public bodies 248
Welsh language: Assessment arrangements: Wales 54
Welsh language: Police: Attestation of constables. 137
West Berkshire (District): Electoral changes. 93
West Bromwich & Wednesbury: National Health Service Primary Care Trust. 124
West Cheshire: Wirral & West Cheshire Community: National Health Service Trust 107
West Dorset (District): Electoral changes 93
West Dorset (District): Permitted & special parking area 210
West Dunbartonshire Council: Argyll & Bute Council: Boundaries: Ardoch Seage Works: Scotland. 321
West Kent: National Health Service & Community Care Trust 124
West Kent: Health Authority 124
West Lothian Council: City of Edinburgh Council: Boundaries: West Farm, Broxburn: Scotland. 321
West Mercia: Commission areas: Justices of the peace 86
West Merton: Nelson & West Merton: National Health Service Primary Care Trust 116
West Oxfordshire (District): Electoral changes. 93
Welsh St Donats, Llanharry, Pont-y-clun, Penllyn & Pendoylan: Rhondda Cynon Taff & Vale of Glamorgan: Local government: Wales 99
West Sussex Health & Social Care: National Health Service Trust 124
West Sussex: Health Authority. 124
West Yorkshire: Health Authority. 124
Western Sussex: National Health Service Primary Care Trust 124
Westminster: Brent, Kensington, Chelsea & Westminster Mental Health: National Health Service Trust. 105
Westminster: National Health Service Primary Care Trust 124
Weymouth & Portland (Borough): Electoral changes 90
Weymouth & Portland (Borough): Permitted & special parking area 210
Whitby, Scarborough & Ryedale: National Health Service Trust 120
Whitehaven Harbour Commissioners: Constitution: Harbour revision 71
Widening Horizons - North Islington: Education Action Zone: Extension 50
Wigan & Leigh: Petty sessions areas 87
Wigston & Oadby (Borough): Electoral changes 90
Wild mammals: Protection of Wild Mammals (Scotland) Act 2002: Commencement: Scotland 308, 311
Wild mammals: Protection of: Acts: Scotland 304
Wildlife & countryside: Sites of special scientific interest: Appeals: Wales 33
Wiltshire & Swindon Health Care: National Health Service Trust 124
Wiltshire County Council: Semington aqueduct: Confirmation: England 78
Wiltshire: Avon, Gloucestershire & Wiltshire: Health Authority 104
Wiltshire: Kennet & North Wiltshire: National Health Service Primary Care Trust 112
Windsor & Maidenhead (Royal Borough): Electoral changes 95
Wine: Common agricultural policy: Scotland 307
Wireless telegraphy: Exemption 237
Wireless telegraphy: Licence charges 237
Wireless telegraphy: Public fixed wireless access licences. 237
Wireless telegraphy: Television licence: Fees 237
Wirral & West Cheshire Community: National Health Service Trust 107
Wirral: Cheshire & Wirral Partnership: National Health Service Trust 107
Witham, Braintree & Halstead Care: National Health Service Trust 124
Withernsea & S. Holderness Rural Achievement: Education Action Zone: Extension. 50
Withholding & withdrawal of support: Travel assistance: Temporary accommodation 81
Witnesses & shorthand writers: Sheriff Court: Fees: Act of Sederunt: Scotland 344
Witnesses, solicitors & shorthand writers: Court of Session: Fees: Act of Sederunt: Scotland 312
Woking Area: National Health Service Primary Care Trust 125
Wokingham (District): Electoral changes 93
Wolverhampton City: National Health Service Primary Care Trust 125
Wolverhampton: Education Action Zone: Extension 51
Wood & bark: Plant health: Northern Ireland 376
Worcester (City): Electoral changes. 91
Worcester (City): Permitted & special parking area 211
Worcestershire Community & Mental Health: National Health Service Trust 125
Worcestershire: Health Authority. 125
Worcestershire: South Worcestershire: National Health Service Primary Care Trust 122
Work & Pensions: Secretary of State: Ministers of the Crown 103
Workers: Fixed-term employees: Less favourable treatment: Prevention 238
Workers: Fixed-term employees: Less favourable treatment: Prevention: Northern Ireland 363
Workers: Part-time workers: Less favourable treatment: Prevention 238
Work-focused interviews: Lone parents: Social security: Northern Ireland 385
Working tax credits: Entitlement & maximum rate 234

Working tax credits: Payment by employers 234
Working time: Amendment: Northern Ireland 364
Working time: Terms & conditions of employment 239
Workmen's compensation: Northern Ireland 385
Workmen's compensation: Supplementation 231
Worthing (Borough): Electoral changes 90
Worthing Priority: National Health Service Trust 124
Worthing: Adur, Arun & Worthing: National Health Service Primary Care Trust 104
Wrecks: Protection of wrecks: The Diamond 141
Wrecks: Protection: Designation 141
Wrekin & Telford: Education Action Zone: Extension 50
Wrekin & Telford: National Health Service Primary Care Trust 123
Wychavon (District): Electoral changes 93
Wycombe (District): Electoral changes 94
Wye (River): Navigation: England & Wales 19, 243
Wyre Forest (District): Electoral changes 94
Wythenshawe: Education Action Zone: Extension 51

Y

Yarmouth (Isle of Wight) harbour: Revision: England 71
Yorkhilll Basin: Closure: Clydeport: Harbours: Revision order: Scotland 316
Yorkshire: East Riding of Yorkshire: Parishes: Local government 94
Yorkshire: East Yorkshire College of Further Education, Bridlington : Dissolution 44
Yorkshire: South West Yorkshire: Mental Health: National Health Service Trusts 122
Yorkshire, West Yorkshire: Health Authority 124
Young offender institutions: HM Prison Haslar: Closure of prisons 140
Young offender institutions: HM Young Offender Institution Dover: Closure of prisons 140
Young offender institutions: Prisons: Scotland 325, 348
Young offender institutions: Rules: England & Wales 248
Young persons: Children: Placement: Arrangements: Cases: Review: Wales 21
Youth Justice & Criminal Evidence Act 1999: Commencement: England & Wales 35
Yugoslavia (Federal Republic): Export of goods: Control 37
Yugoslavia (Federal Republic): Equipment: Sale & supply: Penalties & licences 37

Z

Zimbabwe: Equipment: Sale, supply, export & shipment 38
Zimbabwe: Freezing of funds, financial assets or economic resources 34
Zimbabwe: Restricted measures: Overseas territories 131
Zimbabwe: Restrictive measures: Overseas territories 131
Zoo Licensing Act 1981: Amendment: England & Wales 248
Zootechnical products: Feedingstuffs 7

Stationery Office Services

Stationery Office catalogues

The Stationery Office provides a complete bibliographic service for titles published by the Stationery Office or sold on an agency basis. The services ranges from a daily listing of new publications to annual catalogues and, in collaboration with Chadwyck-Healey, a database of all UK official publications.

Bookshops

There are six Stationery Office bookshops, in London, Edinburgh, Belfast, Manchester, Birmingham and Cardiff (addresses on p. ii). In other locations the Stationery Office is represented by our network of agents (see Yellow Pages: Booksellers).

World Wide Web

The Stationery Office's Internet site contains information about publications and services, including the online bookshop an archive of Daily Lists and an ordering facility. The web site is at http://www.tso.co.uk.

TSO Select Service (formerly Selected subscription service)

The TSO Select Service is a newly-extended version of the former Selected Subscription Service. The standard modules covering Parliamentary publications and Statutory instruments remain available, but customers can now select their individual requirements from the wide range of titles published or sold by TSO. The basic benefits of the service are unchanged: single annual invoice and payment; substantial discount on cover prices; automatic supply. Further information on this improved, more flexible service is available from The Stationery Office, PO Box 29, Norwich NR3 1GN (Tel 0870 600 5522 Fax 0870 600 5533).

Standing order service

This service is open to all Stationery Office account holders, and allows customers to receive automatically all publications they require in a specified subject area. There are some 4000 categories to choose from. Further information is available from Standing Orders Department, The Stationery Office Ltd, PO Box 29, St Crispins, Duke Street, Norwich NR3 1GN (tel 0870 600 5522, fax 0870 600 5533).

Subscriptions

Annual subscriptions may be placed for all periodicals. Further information may be obtained from Subscriptions, The Stationery Office Ltd, PO Box 29, Norwich NR3 1GN (tel 0870 600 5522, fax 0870 600 5522) for Stationery Office publications, and from Agency Subscriptions for items sold but not published by the Stationery Office (tel 0870 600 5522, fax 0870 600 5533).

Statutory Instruments on CD-ROM

A comprehensive archive of Statutory Instruments is available as a CD-ROM. It contains the full text and images of SIs since 1987 and a short form of Statutory Instruments since 1980. It feature extensive keyword and index search facility with an intelligent listing of results. There is cross referencing between related Statutory Instruments and links to the related Act of Parliament.

The annual subscription costs £900 (excluding VAT) and it is updated quarterly

Terms and Conditions of Sale

DEFINITIONS

1.1 In the following and any other conditions included in the Contract, the expressions listed below shall have the meaning shown:

Expression	Meaning
The Seller (We, Us)	The Stationery Office Ltd. its staff, and authorised representatives and assignees.
The Customer (You)	whoever sends us the Order for the Goods.
Goods	the item fitting the description in your Order and as available from The Stationery Office's lists of items.
Price	that quoted in The Stationery Office's current price list plus any applicable VAT.
Force Majeure	any circumstances beyond our reasonable control, such as accidents, flood, fire or other natural disasters, and unlawful industrial disputes.
Contract	the agreement between us and you made by our acceptance of your Order.
Order	your request for the Goods.

APPLICABLE CONDITIONS

2.1 These are the only conditions which shall apply to the Contract. Any variations to them must be agreed in writing by our Head of Sales or Credit Controller.

ACCURACY OF DESCRIPTION

3.1 We shall only be liable to supply the Goods which you describe accurately in your Order.

3.2 When your Order does not accurately describe the Goods we will use our best endeavours to supply the correct Goods but you shall not rely on our skill and judgement in selecting these.

DELIVERY

4.1 You shall accept the Goods securely packaged at your address in the United Kingdom or Republic of Ireland, during normal business hours. Delivery in the United Kingdom shall be the later date of either 14 days from receiving your Order, or the publication date of the Goods.

4.2 Unless otherwise agreed we shall charge you a handling fee for delivery by mail or carrier.

4.3 We may charge you for the cost of delivery by any other method or to other countries.

4.4 Where we cannot deliver by the promised date we will promptly advise you of the reason. We may make a partial delivery of your Order where not all items are available. You have the right to return that partial delivery at our expense by the most economical method, within 5 working days of receiving it.

INABILITY TO SUPPLY

5.1 If we notify you in writing that we are unable to deliver the Goods as specified for Force Majeure or "out of stock" reasons, you shall allow us to deliver within a further reasonable time. What is a further reasonable time shall depend on the nature and duration of the force majeure or out of stock position.

5.2 You may return any Goods that are not delivered within that further reasonable time, but not within 14 days of being notified of inability to supply. On safe return of the goods in saleable condition we will cancel the invoice.

OWNERSHIP OF THE GOODS

6.1 The Goods remain our property until you pay for them, but you shall be responsible for their condition once they are delivered to your premises. You shall insure them to cover any risk this involves.

6.2 If you become insolvent we may take the Goods back at your expense and if necessary, may enter your premises to do so, or to inspect the Goods.

DAMAGE OR LOSS IN TRANSIT

7.1 We will replace at no extra cost any Goods damaged before or on delivery, if you notify us by telephone or in writing within 5 days of their receipt.

7.2 We will replace at no extra cost any Goods which have been lost in transit if you notify us by telephone or in writing within 21 days of us receiving your Order or the publication date of the Goods, whichever shall be the later.

REJECTION

8.1 We aim to take care to provide goods of a merchantable quality which are fit for their purpose and value for money. These Terms and Conditions show how we aim to do this, and do not affect your legal rights.

8.2 If you notify us by telephone within 5 working days of receipt of any Goods which are defective, and confirm this in writing at our request, and then return them at our expense stating the reason you are rejecting them, we will promptly replace them with Goods in an acceptable condition.

8.3 We will refund the price of any Goods which we are unable to replace with Goods in acceptable condition.

8.4 If you accurately described the Goods in your Order form you may within 5 days of receipt return any Goods that do not conform with your description. We will replace at no extra charge the Goods with Goods that correspond to your description.

PAYMENT

9.1 You shall pay our invoice for the Price of the Goods and any delivery charges, as defined in 4.2 and 4.3 above within days of the date of our invoice, unless our Head of Sales or Credit Controller has agreed otherwise in writing.

9.2 Your payment shall be in sterling, free from any bank or transmission charge.

INTELLECTUAL PROPERTY RIGHTS

10.1 You shall protect our copyright and all other intellectual property rights in the Goods, while they remain your property.

10.2 You shall notify any subsequent owner of such rights in the Goods.

CANCELLATION

11.1 We shall stop despatching Goods against a Standing Order within 3 working days of receiving your written request to do so. You shall pay us for any Goods despatched in that period.

11.2 You shall not cancel Orders that we have already entered into our Order processing system.

ENFORCEMENT

12.1 Our failure to enforce any of these Conditions shall not prevent us from enforcing them at a later date.

12.2 If any Condition is found to be invalid, it shall not prevent all other Conditions being enforced.

HEADINGS

13.1 The headings to each of these Conditions is for guidance only and shall not affect their interpretation.

COMMUNICATIONS

14.1 Any notification, request or other communication required under these Conditions shall be in writing, including facsimile transmission, unless specified otherwise and addressed to the Enquiries Manager.

GOVERNING LAW

15.1 Unless Goods are purchased from the Belfast or Edinburgh Bookshops, the Contract shall be in the English language, governed by English law and subject to the exclusive jurisdiction of the English courts.

15.2 Where Goods are purchased from the Belfast Bookshop, the Contract shall be in the English language, governed by Northern Ireland Law and subject to the exclusive jurisdiction of the Northern Ireland courts.

15.3 Where Goods are purchased from the Edinburgh Bookshop, the Contract shall be in the English language, governed by Scottish Law and subject to the exclusive jurisdiction of the Scottish courts.

TSO

Customer Service

We aim to provide a courteous and efficient service at all times. We have set targets for our service to our customers and monitor the performance achieved.

MAIL, TELEPHONE AND FAX ORDERS

We aim to despatch publications to customers within five days of receiving an order. Goods are despatched in accordance with our terms & conditions of sale.

STANDING ORDERS

We aim to despatch all standing order publications within two days of publication date.

SUBSCRIPTIONS

We aim to despatch all subscription publications on or before the day of publication.

PROBLEMS

If you have not received your goods and would like to ask about your order, or if you have already received your order and found it unsatisfactory in any way, please contact The Stationery Office address to which your order was sent. The addresses and telephone numbers are given on the back cover of this catalogue.

QUALITY

The Stationery Office's quality policy is to earn a reputation for excellence in satisfying customers' expectations through continual improvement and innovations

We welcome comments on our service, and any suggestions for improvement